EIGHTEENTH EDITION

KOVELS'
ANTIQUES &
COLLECTIBLES
PRICE LIST

Illustrated

**A guide to the 1985–1986 market for
professionals, dealers, and collectors**

Ralph and Terry Kovel

Crown Publishers, Inc.
New York

Books by Ralph and Terry Kovel

Dictionary of Marks—Pottery and Porcelain
A Directory of American Silver, Pewter and Silver Plate
American Country Furniture 1780–1875
Kovels' Antiques & Collectibles Price List
The Kovels' Bottle Price List
The Kovels' Collector's Guide to American Art Pottery
Kovels' Organizer for Collectors
The Kovels' Price Guide for Collector Plates, Figurines,
     Paperweights, and Other Limited Editions
The Kovels' Illustrated Price Guide to Royal Doulton
The Kovels' Illustrated Price Guide to Depression Glass and
     American Dinnerware
Kovels' Know Your Antiques
Kovels' Know Your Collectibles
The Kovels' Book of Antique Labels
The Kovels' Collectors' Source Book

Published by Crown Publishers, Inc., One Park Avenue, New York,
New York 10016, and simultaneously in Canada by General
Publishing Company Limited

Manufactured in the United States of America

CROWN is a trademark of Crown Publishers, Inc.

Library of Congress Cataloging Card Number: 83–643618

ISBN 0-517-55809-2

10   9   8   7   6   5   4   3   2   1

Dear reader,

Another year and another new edition of *Kovels' Antiques & Collectibles Price List!* This is now the eighteenth edition. That means we have recorded between 2 and 2½ million prices. Over 11,000 pictures have been used—and we took most of them! We price the ordinary and the extraordinary, whatever is reported during the year. Where else could you find the price asked for an artificial leg, a pee-pee doll, or a footed bathtub? No wonder we feel we really know the prices that are asked in the marketplace.

The book is changed slightly each year to make it easier to use. Last year we did an extensive redesigning with new type styles, new picture format, hundreds of more paragraphs and marks, hints for care and repair, and the best index possible in today's world of computers. Your comments have shown that all these changes have been a success. New features suggested by readers will be found this year. We enlarged the number of tips and changed the method of listing in a few sections.

The size of the book must remain about 800 pages because we believe the book must be small enough to go with you to the sales. To do this we edit the copy from 100,000 prices to about 45,000 prices. In the editing we consider the interests of collectors and try to have a balanced format, not too much glass, pottery, or collectibles. The prices are reported from the North American market for the North American market, and none of the prices are for items offered for sale in Europe.

Old editions of Kovels' price books should be saved for reference and tax and appraisal information. An index at the end of the book and an internal alphabetical index are always included. This year, every category is indexed as always; and every reference to the category is also indexed. For example, there is a category for "celluloid." Most items will be found there; but if there is a toy made of celluloid, it will be listed under "toy" and also indexed under "celluloid."

All pictures and all prices are new every year except for the pattern examples shown in the Depression glass and pressed glass sections. All color pictures, including those on the cover, are priced. They are not museum pieces but are items recently offered for sale.

Hints

The hints are set in easy-to-notice special type. Leaf through the book and see how to wash porcelain, store textiles, guard against theft, and much more. Most of the hints are new this year.

Record Prices

Each year we list the record prices for antiques sold at auction. In 1985 top quality antiques were still bringing top prices. They are important because they get national attention and influence other related pieces. Unfortunately, the antiques and collectibles market for the past season has been mixed. The top items have sold for record prices. Average, attractive, and even useful antiques are not selling well at auction. The large galleries report that at specialized sales many pieces are passed with no bids at all. The blockbuster sales with the great rarities generate much media attention and the publicity helps to sell some of these average pieces. Often it is the name of the collector that adds to the value. Remember a record price is influenced by how many buyers want it, as well as the trends of the time. The antiques shows and shops seem to have had a more successful year than the larger auction galleries. Sales have been steady.

$297,000 for a copy of the Emancipation Proclamation printed in 1864; $1,263 for a paperback book, *Giant* by Edna Ferber, signed by James Dean; $39,600 for a cookbook—these are some of the spectacular prices paid for paper antiques during the past 1984–1985 season.

Age is not important. Collectibles made since 1900 have set records. $14,000 for a Simon and Halbig lady doll in original gown, c. 1900, 28 inches high; $20,000 for a Wurlitzer jukebox owned by John Lennon; $77,000 for a 1930s Frank Lloyd Wright desk; $2,860 for a 1964 Noguchi cocktail table by the Herman Miller Company; $71,500 for a chair by Greene and Greene made in 1907; $93,000 for a copper urn designed by Frank Lloyd Wright in 1899; $20,900 for a 1938 Disney animation celluloid of Mickey Mouse; and $22,155 for a Royal Doulton character jug.

American furniture continued to set records: $55,000 for a paint-decorated New England cupboard; $176,000 for a tambour desk attributed to John Seymour of Boston; $165,000 for a Massachusetts Queen Anne highboy; $165,000 for a Philadelphia mahogany secretary-bookcase; and $308,000 for a Chippendale chest-on-chest attributed to Thomas Affleck. Other records were $583,000 for a Chippendale mahogany pair of drop-leaf tables, Philadelphia, 1770; $253,000 for a mahogany tray-top tea table, Boston, c. 1750; $88,000 for a Philadelphia acanthus carved wing chair; $82,000 for a mahogany sofa; and $104,500 for a pair of upholstered mahogany armchairs attributed to Duncan Phyfe.

Collectors paid high prices for "country look" antiques. Records include $15,950 for a ruddy turnstone shorebird decoy by John Dilley; $50,000 for a golden plover decoy by William Bowman of Maine; $30,800 for an American album quilt made in 1854; $69,300 for a

Boston school needlework picture of a shepherdess. Toys for the informal home included $20,750 for a four-wheeled child's riding cart with two wooden horses and $2,420 for a stuffed 23-inch mohair teddy bear.

Pottery and porcelain records included $33,000 for a Chinese export platter from the George Washington Order of Cincinnati and $29,700 for a famille rose Chinese export punch bowl; $4,895 for a baluster-shaped Rookwood Iris glaze 15-inch vase; $4,000 for a Rookwood silver overlay vase; $11,232 for a wall plaque by Clarice Cliff; and $11,600 for an Anna pottery jug.

Two lamps set records: $528,000 for a leaded glass mosaic magnolia patterned Tiffany floor lamp and $450,930 for a Galle table lamp. A record Federal mahogany lighthouse clock by Simon Willard brought $286,000 and a Biedermeier secretary brought $154,000. The only record price for glass was for a Tiffany lava Favrile vase sold at $85,800.

Some unusual items setting records include a British biscuit tin for $1,600; a patent model for brass tilters on a Shaker side chair for $17,000; a box-shaped spruce gum box for $990; a tool, a boxwood and ivory center plow plane by the Sandusky Tool Company, Sandusky, Ohio, for $8,000; and a stuffed gorilla, Gargantua II, for $18,500. A Stradivarius violin brought $457,200.

The prices in this book are reports of the general antiques market. Each year every price in the book is new. We do *not* estimate or "update" prices. The most expensive item listed is about $11,000, least expensive is 50¢. Prices represent the *actual asking price,* although the buyer may have negotiated the final price to a lower figure. *None of these prices is an estimate.* If a price range is given, it is because there were at least two identical items offered for sale at different places. The computer records the prices and prints the high and low figures. Price ranges are found only in categories such as "pressed glass," where identical items can be accurately identified. *Each price is a report of an offering in the marketplace. We* do not *ask dealers and writers who know only one area of collecting to estimate prices.* Experience has shown that a collector of one type of antique is prejudiced in favor of that item; and prices are usually high or low, but rarely a true report. Some prices in *Kovels' Antiques & Collectibles Price List* may seem high; some may seem low because of regional variations. Each price is one you could have paid for the object.

Selling Price

If you are selling your collection do *not* expect to get retail value unless you are a dealer. Wholesale prices for antiques are from 20 to 50 percent less than retail. Remember, the antiques dealer must make a profit or go out of business. For a full list of publications that have buy-sell ads, clubs, auction galleries, and other helpful information about selling antiques, see *The Kovels' Collectors' Source Book*.

How to Use This Book

There are a few rules to follow in using this book. Each listing is arranged in the following manner: CATEGORY (such as pressed glass or furniture), OBJECT (such as vase), DESCRIPTION (as much information as possible about size, age, color, and pattern). Some types of glass are the only exceptions to this rule. These are listed CATEGORY, PATTERN, OBJECT, DESCRIPTION. All items are presumed to be in good condition, undamaged, unless otherwise noted.

Several special categories were formed to make a more sensible listing possible. "Kitchen" and "tool" include special equipment. It would be unreasonable to expect the casual collector to know the proper name for an "adze" or "trephine," so we have lumped them together in special categories. Some other special categories are "commemorative," "store," and "railroad." The index can help you locate items. Several idiosyncrasies of style appear because the final prices are printed by a computer. Everything is listed according to the computer alphabetizing system. This means words such as "mt." are alphabetized as "M-T," not as "M-O-U-N-T." All numerals are before all letters, thus 2 comes before Z. A quick glance at a listing will make this clear, as it is consistent throughout the book.

We made several editorial decisions. A bowl is a "bowl" and not a dish unless it is a special dish, such as a pickle dish. A butter dish is a "butter." A salt dish is called a "salt" to differentiate it from a salt-shaker. It is always "sugar and creamer," never "creamer and sugar." Where one dimension is given, it is the height, or if the object is round, the dimension is the diameter. Height of a picture is listed before width. Glass is clear unless a color is indicated.

Every entry is listed alphabetically. The problem of language remains. Some antiques terms like "Sheffield" or "snow baby" have two meanings. Be sure to read the paragraph headings to know the meaning used. All category headings are based on language of the average person at an average show, and we use terms like "mud figures" even if that isn't technically correct.

This book does not include price listings of fine art paintings, books, comic books, stamps, coins, and a few other special categories.

All pictures in *Kovels' Antiques & Collectibles Price List* are listed with the prices asked by the seller. "Illus" (illustrated on the page), "cover" (shown on the cover), and "color" (pictured in the color section) are part of the description if a picture is shown.

There have been misinformed comments about how this book is written. We *do* use the computer. It alphabetizes, ranges prices, sets type, and does other time-consuming jobs. Because of the computer, the book can be produced quickly. The last entries are added in June; the book is available in October. This is six months faster than would be possible any other way. But it is human help that finds prices and checks accuracy. We read everything at least twice, sometimes more. We correct spelling, remove incorrect data, write category headings, and decide on new categories.

Prices are reports of sales from all parts of the United States, between June 1984 and June 1985. A few prices are from auctions, but most are from shops and shows. Every price has been checked for accuracy, but we cannot be responsible for any errors.

It is unprofessional for an appraiser to set a value for an unseen item. Because of this we cannot answer your letters asking for specific price information. We do read every letter. Please write if you have any requests for types of pieces to be included in future editions.

When you see us at the shows this year stop and say hello, but don't be surprised if we ask for your suggestions for the next edition of *Kovels' Antiques & Collectibles Price List.* Or you can write to us at P.O. Box 22200, Beachwood, Ohio 44122.

Ralph M. Kovel,
American Society of Appraisers,
Senior Member
International Society of Appraisers

Terry H. Kovel,
American Society of Appraisers,
Senior Member
International Society of Appraisers

Acknowledgments

To those in the antiques trade who knowingly or unknowingly contributed some of the prices and pictures to this book we say "Thank You!" We can't do it without you. Some of you are: William Adorjan, Becky & Bob Alexander, Jim Altman, Willie Amor, Antique Tool, The Antique Trader, Edward A. Babka, Barridoff Galleries, Birchland Antiques, Blair Museum of Lithophane & Waxes, Bornand Music Box Co., Richard A. Bourne Co., Inc., Larry Burke, Butterfield & Butterfield, Christie's, Chuck DeLuca's Maritime Auctions, Clearing House Galleries, Cola Clan, Bob & Sallie Connelly, J.D. Dalessandro, Paul Dias, William Doyle Galleries, Inc., DuMouchelles, Joseph Dziadul, Roy Ehrhardt, William Fagan, Fenner's Antiques, N. Flayderman & Co., Inc., Madeleine France, Garth's Auctions, Inc., Golden Years Glass, Goldmine, Greenwich Auction Room, Hake's Americana, Gene Harris, Leslie Hindeman Auctioneers, Hollander Gallery, Tom Horvitz, Iroquois Auctions, ITT Kruse International, James Antiques, Joseph C. Jaynes, James Julia Auctions, Lil-Bud Antiques, Ralph Losinno, Ann Gilbert McDonald, Milwaukee Auction Gallery, New Glaze, The Old House, Old Storefront Antiques, Richard Oliver, P.A.C. Palmetto Collectibles Warehouse, Paper Moon, The Paper Pile, Phillips, The Political Bandwagon, Postcard Collector, Sheldon L. Rag, Jr., Lloyd Ralston's Auctions, Bill Rogers, RSVP Antiques, Lawrence and Linda Selman, Sally Siegrist, Silver Magazine, Robert W. Skinner Gallery, C.G. Sloan & Co., Inc., Sotheby's, Ruth Spivak, Swan Galleries, Inc., Team Antiques, Tesseract, Theriault's Auctions, Tillinghast Auctioneers, Vintage Golf, Robert Wieland, Winter Associates, Richard W. Withington, Inc., Wolf's Auction Gallery, Woody Auction Co., Your Country Auctioneer.

Price Update Available

Many of you may need more current information about prices, trends, and special sales than is available in this book. We have been writing a newsletter for the serious collector and investor in collectibles and antiques for eleven years. What to buy, sell, how to refinish, reviews of price books, information about marks, fakes, and much more is included. It is a twelve-page, picture-filled newsletter about the antiques that are of interest to the average collector and investor.

If you want more information about *Kovels on Antiques & Collectibles,* send a stamped, self-addressed envelope to Kovels, P.O. Box 22200-K, Beachwood, Ohio 44122.

Almaric Walter made pate–de–verre glass under contract at the Daum glassworks from 1908 to 1914. He started his own firm in Nancy, France, in 1919. Pieces made before 1914 are signed "Daum, Nancy" with a cross. After 1919 the signature is "A. Walter Nancy."

A.WALTER, Paperweight, Bird On Waves, Blue, 6 In. 500.00
Paperweight, Leaves, 2 Entwined Salamanders, Signed, 3 1/2 In. 6050.00
Paperweight, Pate–De–Verre, Butterfly, Signed, 3 1/2 In. 200.00
Plaque, Woman, Folded Hands, Glass Insert, Signed, 8 X 6 In. 300.00

ABC plates, or children's alphabet plates, were most popular from 1780 to 1860, but are still being made. The letters on the plate were meant as teaching aids for children learning to read. The plates were made of pottery, porcelain, metal, or glass.

ABC, Book, 19th Century, Tin 50.00
Bowl, Feeding, There Was An Old Woman, Blue Rim 25.00
Chair, Doll, Litho Paper Over Wood 375.00
Cookie Jar, Truck 22.00
Creamer, Alphabet, Kittens, Lady Bug 38.00
Cup, Nursery Rhyme 35.00
Dish, Feeding, Baby Bunting & Little Dog 55.00
Dish, Feeding, Bird 28.00
Dish, Going To Market, Polychrome, Staffordshire 60.00
Dish, Ice Cream 40.00
Mug, Little Polly Flinders, Blue 15.00
Plate, 1893 Expo, Machinery Hall 85.00
Plate, 2 Children Rolling Hoops, Staffordshire, 1840s, 6 In. 35.00
Plate, Aesop's Fables Series, Brown Tones, Marked 47.50
Plate, Alphabet, Beaded Trim, Clear, Rayed Center, 7 In. 18.00
Plate, Alphabet, Boys & Girls Dancing, Verse, Staffordshire, 5 3/4 In. 75.00
Plate, Alphabet, Crusoe, Staffordshire, 8 In. 28.00
Plate, Alphabet, Mary Had A Little Lamb, Tin, 8 In. 75.00
Plate, Alphabet, Men Fighting On Donkeys, Staffordshire, 7 In. 28.00
Plate, Alphabet, Wash Day Figures, Germany 38.00
Plate, American Sports, Pitcher & Catcher 110.00
Plate, Animated Conundrums, Polychrome Transfer, Blue Rim, 5 In. 50.00
Plate, Behold Him Rising, Staffordshire, Polychrome Transfer, 5 1/2 In. 60.00
Plate, Blue Ceramic, Alphabet Outer Edge, Sign Language Inside 50.00
Plate, Boy & Girl, Campbell Kids Center, Artist, G.G.Drayton 100.00
Plate, Candle Fish, Indians & Canoe Center, Staffordshire, 7 1/2 In. 35.00
Plate, Child Fishing, 2 Line Verse, Elsmore, 5 1/2 In. 55.00
Plate, Child On Swing, Tin, 3 1/2 In. 18.00
Plate, Christmas, Snowman & Children 55.00
Plate, Clock Face, 7 In. 25.00
Plate, Cock Robin, Tin ....50.00 To 58.00
Plate, Creditors, Better Memories, Staffordshire, 5 1/8 In. 55.00
Plate, Crusoe Rescues Friday 98.00
Plate, Crusoe, 8 In. 28.00
Plate, Dog Center, Amber Glass 37.00
Plate, Elephant Fishing With 2 Girls, Staffordshire 85.00
Plate, Elephant With Howdah, 3 Figures In Howdah, Signed R.& C., 6 In. 150.00
Plate, Enameled Bird Scene, Brown, Ironstone, 7 1/4 In. 55.00
Plate, Franklin Maxim, Green & Black Transfer, 6 1/2 In. 60.00
Plate, Frosted Stork In Center, Iowa City 95.00
Plate, Garfield Center, Glass, 6 In. 65.00
Plate, Girl & Boy Rolling Hoop, Tin, 3 In. 140.00
Plate, Girl In Barn, Chickens, Pink Transfer, Staffordshire, 7 In. 75.00
Plate, Girl On Swing, Polychrome, Tin, 3 1/2 In. 30.00
Plate, Girl's Head In Center, Beaded Rim, Name Emma, Higbee Glass 85.00
Plate, Harry Baiting His Line, Polychrome Transfer, 5 1/2 In. 60.00
Plate, Hey Diddle Diddle, Tin, 8 1/2 In. 55.00
Plate, Horse Race, Red Transfer, Staffordshire 45.00
Plate, Jack & Jill Poem 38.00
Plate, Jumbo, Tin 75.00

Plate, Kate Greenaway Girl, Large Hat, Pink, Staffordshire, 7 In.	75.00
Plate, Liberty, Tin	60.00
Plate, Mary Had A Little Lamb, Tin, 8 In.	85.00
Plate, Mother & Daughter, Multicolor, Staffordshire, 7 In.	60.00
Plate, Nursery Rhyme, 1919	25.00
Plate, Nursery Rhyme, Boy Crossing Stile, Staffordshire	80.00
Plate, Nursery Rhyme, D.E.McNicol, 7 1/4 In.	24.00
Plate, Nursery Rhyme, Old Mother Hubbard, Staffordshire	58.00
Plate, Organ Grinder, Staffordshire, 8 1/4 In.	38.00
Plate, Peter Rabbit, Litho Tin, 5 1/2 In.	40.00
Plate, Stag's Head, 6 In.	25.00
Plate, Stork & Baby Center, Carnival Glass, Marigold	50.00 To 60.00
Plate, Sunbonnet Girl, Signed Roseville	67.50
Plate, Washington, Brown, Staffordshire, 7 1/4 In.	85.00
Plate, Young Artist, Baby, Palette, Brown, Ironstone, 6 1/4 In.	40.00
Plate, Zebra Hunt, Staffordshire, 8 In.	28.00
Shepherd Boy, Horn, Dog, Fence, & Goat, Polychrome, 5 1/4 In.	75.00
Table, Child's, Calumet Kid, Graniteware	150.00
Tray, Animals, Aluminum, 8 X 15 In.	18.00

Abingdon Pottery was established in 1934 by Raymond E. Bidwell as the Abingdon Sanitary Manufacturing Company. The company made art pottery and other wares. Sixteen varieties of cookie jars are known. The factory ceased production of art pottery in 1950.

ABINGDON, Bookends, Cossack	35.00
Bookends, Horse Heads, Black	75.00
Console Set, Pink Shell	20.00
Cookie Jar, Clock	29.00
Cookie Jar, Hippo, Black	75.00 To 100.00
Cookie Jar, Humpty Dumpty	50.00 To 55.00
Cookie Jar, Lady, Black	85.00
Cookie Jar, Little Bopeep	95.00 To 98.00
Cookie Jar, Little Miss Muffet	95.00
Cookie Jar, Little Old Lady	48.00
Cookie Jar, Money Bag	20.00 To 45.00
Cookie Jar, Pineapple	30.00
Cookie Jar, Rocking Horse	40.00 To 125.00
Cookie Jar, Train	49.00 To 65.00
Figurine, Donkey, No.669	10.00
Range Set, Daisy, Yellow & Brown	20.00
Vase, Cornucopia, Double, No.482	14.00
Vase, Green, No.560, 11 In.	14.00
Vase, Lilies, White, 7 1/2 In.	19.00
Vase, White, 13 1/2 In.	45.00
Wall Pocket, Double, Lilies	15.00
Wall Pocket, Humpty Dumpty, Yellow	60.00
Wall Pocket, Lily	13.00
Wall Pocket, Mammy, Chartreuse	70.00

Adams china was made by William Adams and Sons of Staffordshire, England. The firm was founded in 1769 and is still working. All types of tablewares and useful wares have been made through the years. Other pieces of Adams will be found listed under Flow Blue.

ADAMS, Bowl, Cattle Scene, Footed, 10 In.	195.00
Butter, Covered, C.1874	50.00
Celery, Vertical Pattern	25.00
Cookie Jar, Hunting Scene, Jasperware, Blue & White	118.00
Cup & Saucer, Palestine	40.00
Cup & Saucer, Rose	135.00
Plate, Palestine, Black, 8 1/2 In.	35.00
Plate, Rose, 10 1/2 In.	135.00
Plate, Spanish Convent, Light Blue, 9 1/2 In.	195/.00
Platter, Blue Feather Edge, Impressed Mark, 15 1/2 In.	55.00
Platter, Dark Blue Transfer, Sheep, Horse & Rider, Marked, 12 5/8 In.	155.00

Platter, Thistle Border, 19 3/4 In. 100.00
Tankard, Jasper, Dominion Of Canada Crest, Jasper, Marked 65.00

> *Advertising materials are listed in many sections of this book. Look in Store for most types of items. Other sections such as Doll, Knife, Card, Toy, etc., have advertising items. Some companies have made so much collectible advertising we have listed them in their own sections. Look for Coca-Cola, Planters Peanuts, etc. Look in the index for a complete listing of companies.*

> *Agata glass was made by Joseph Locke of the New England Glass Company of Cambridge, Massachusetts, after 1885. A metallic stain was applied to New England Peachblow and the mottled design characteristic of agata appeared.*

AGATA, Tumbler, Mottled, 3 3/4 In. ....600.00 To 1150.00

> *Akro agate glass was made in Clarksburg, West Virginia, from 1932 to 1951. Before that time, the firm made children's glass marbles. Most of the glass is marked with a crow flying through the letter A.*

AKRO AGATE, Ashtray, Blue & White 15.00
Bowl, Cereal, Large 10.00
Bowl, Cobalt Blue, 6 In. 10.00
Bowl, Cobalt Blue, 9 In. 15.00
Creamer, Child's, Green 8.00
Cup & Saucer, Child's, Blue, Demitasse 11.50
Cup & Saucer, Orange & White, Demitasse 11.00
Cup, Child's, Green, Rings 10.00
Cup, Child's, Stippled Band, 1 7/8 In. 4.00
Cup, Child's, Yellow & Oxblood 20.00
Figurine, Lady With Dog, 8 In. 35.00
Jar, Mexicali, Sombrero Cover, Orange & White 25.00
Jar, Powder, Scotty Dog, Blue 50.00
Pie Plate, Animals Dressed As People, Light Blue, White, Hole 12.00
Pitcher & 4 Tumblers, Child's, Green 25.00
Pitcher, Child's, Green, Clear 18.00
Pitcher, Child's, Orange 15.00
Planter, Original Dried Plant, 1 1/4 In. 12.00
Planter, Pumpkin, 6 In. 7.50
Plate, Child's, Blue, Octagonal, 4 1/4 In. 4.00
Plate, Child's, Green Stippled Band, 3 1/4 In. 2.50
Plate, Child's, Mustard, 3 1/4 In. 3.50
Plate, Child's, White, Octagonal, 3 1/2 In. 2.50
Plate, Oxblood & Lemon, Octagonal, 4 1/4 In. 13.50
Pot, Green, Scalloped, 3 1/2 In. 5.00
Powder Box, Colonial Lady, Signed 22.00
Powder Jar, Colonial Lady Cover, Opaque White ....15.00 To 37.00
Puff Box, Colonial Lady, Blue 48.50
Saucer, Azure Blue 5.00
Smoke Set, Gypsy Smoker, 5 Color, Box 45.00
Sugar & Creamer, Child's, Blue, White Lid, Octagonal, 3 In. 7.00
Tea & Water Set, Child's, Concentric Ring, 19 Piece 35.00
Tea Set, American Mail, 8 Piece, Boxed 40.00
Tea Set, Child's, Green & White 50.00
Tea Set, Child's, Playtime, Original Box, 16 Piece 95.00
Tea Set, Closed Handles, Opaque, Box, 3 Pumpkin Pieces 135.00
Tea Set, Original Box, 16 Piece 100.00
Tumbler, Child's, White, 2 In. 3.00
Water Set, Original Box, 7 Piece 65.00

> *Alabaster is a very soft form of gypsum, a stone that resembles marble. It was often carved into vases or statues in Victorian times. There are alabaster carvings being made even today. Because the alabaster is very porous, it will dissolve if kept in water, so do not use alabaster vases for flowers.*

ALABASTER, Figurine, Art Deco Fan Dancer, Italian 1200.00

> *Alexandrite is a name with many meanings. It is a form of the mineral chrysoberyl that changes from green to red under artificial light. A man-made version of this mineral is sold in Mexico today. It changes from deep purple to aquamarine blue under artificial light. The Alexandrite listed here is glass made in the late nineteenth and twentieth centuries. Thomas Webb & Sons sold their transparent glass shaded from yellow to rose to blue under the name Alexandrite. Stevens and Williams had a cased Alexandrite of yellow, rose, and blue. A. Douglas Nash Corporation made an amethyst-colored Alexandrite. Several American glass companies of the 1920s made a glass that changed color under electric lights and these were called Alexandrite too.*

ALEXANDRITE, Bowl, Ruffled Top, Honeycomb Pattern, 4 1/2 X 2 In. 750.00
Vase, Engraved Hummingbird, Initialed A.H. 165.00

Alhambra

> *Alhambra is a pattern of tableware made in Vienna, Austria, in the twentieth century. The geometric designs are in applied gold, red, and dark green. Full sets of dishes can be found in this pattern.*

ALHAMBRA, Jug, Cream & Gray Design, Gold Trim, Marked, 8 1/2 In. 135.00
Jug, Red, Green, Cream & Gray, Gold Trim, Marked, 8 1/2 In. 135.00
Mayonnaise Set, 2 Piece 41.00
Plate, 8 In. 50.00

> *Aluminum was more expensive than gold or silver until the 1850s. Chemists learned how to refine bauxite to get aluminum. Jewelry and other small objects were made of the valuable metal until 1914 when an inexpensive smelting process was invented. The aluminum collected today dates from the 1930s through 1950s. Hand-hammered pieces are the most popular.*

ALUMINUM, Bowl, Fruit, Handles, Raised Fruits & Florals, 11 In. 12.00
Bowl, W.F., Hammered, 12 In. 15.00
Bucket, Butter, Lid, Bail, 3 3/4 In. 18.00
Butter, Covered, Glass Insert, Round, 6 1/4 In. 10.00
Cake Safe, Spun, Russel Wright 40.00
Can, Malted Milk, Letters In Black, Cover, 6 In. 25.00
Chamberstick, Child's, Woodward, French Blue, 1 3/4 In., Pair 65.00
Cookie Cutter, Swansdown, Set Of 4 .... 3.00
Pitcher, Water, Club Aluminum 12.00
Stool, Art Deco 5.00
Tumbler, Kentucky Derby, 1941 .... 100.00

> *Amber glass is the name of any glassware with the proper yellow-brown shading. It was a popular color just after the Civil War and many pressed glass pieces were made of amber glass. Depression glass of the 1930s–1950s was also made in shades of amber glass. All types are being reproduced.*

AMBER GLASS, Baby Bootie 40.00
Bowl, Engraved, Inverted Chapeau Style, Grapevine, 13 In. 30.00
Cake Stand, Medallion 35.00
Candlestick, Tulip Shade, Trumpet Base, 13 3/4 In., Pair 80.00
Cruet, Enameled Lacy White Dots, Amber Handle & Stopper 118.00
Decanter, Pewter Pedestal, Spout, Handle, & Stopper, 15 In. 120.00
Dish, Daisy & Button, Square, 7 In., Pair 45.00
Mug, Dog & Tree Etching, Applied Handle, Blown 35.00
Perfume, Filigree Stopper, Panels, 9 3/8 In. 40.00
Pitcher, Daisy & Button, 8 1/2 In. 75.00
Pitcher, Water, Hobnail, Hobbs, Cased 150.00
Pitcher, Water, Thumbprint, Square Mouth, Blown, Handle 55.00
Rose Bowl, Blue Swirl Overlay, Ground Pontil 75.00
Tobacco Jar, Embossed Globe Tobacco Co., Tin Screw Cap, 7 In. 95.00
Wine, Facet Cut Stems & Upper Portion, Signed, Set Of 12 .... 900.00
AMBERETTE, see Pressed Glass, Klondike

Amberina is a two–toned glassware made from 1883 to about 1900. It was patented by Joseph Locke of the New England Glass Company. The glass shades from red to amber.

AMBERINA, see also Baccarat; Bluerina; Plated Amberina

AMBERINA, Basket, Ruffled, 7 X 4 X 3 3/4 In.	90.00
Bottle, Wine, Cranberry To Amber, Frosted Stopper, 9 In.	110.00
Bowl, 2 1/2 X 3 1/2 In.	95.00
Bowl, Cambridge, Signed, 10 In.	55.00
Bowl, Floral & Optic Pattern, 3 Legged, Red, 9 In.	175.00
Bowl, Ruffled, Shallow, 9 1/2 In.	250.00
Bowl, Scalloped Edge, Rectangular, 6 1/2 X 9 X 3 In.	175.00
Celery Dish, Blown Diamond, Square Mouth, New England, 6 1/2 In.	350.00
Celery Dish, Diamond–Quilted, C.1883, 3 1/4 X 4 3/4 In.	285.00
Celery Dish, Diamond–Quilted, Square Top, 6 1/4 In.	225.00
Celery, Inverted Thumbprint	130.00
Celery, Paneled Opalescent, 6 1/2 In.	150.00
Centerpiece, Inverted Thumbprint, Raised Floral, Footed, 10 In.	375.00
Champagne, Hollow Stem, 6 In.	200.00
Compote, Moon & Star, Covered, 6 1/4 In.	28.00
Console Set, Petaled Bowl & Candleholders, Cambridge, 5 Piece	50.00
Cruet, Baby Thumbprint, Reeded Handle	125.00
Cruet, Inverted Thumbprint	245.00
Glass, Champagne, Hollow Stem, 4 In.	200.00
Goblet, Mt.Washington	135.00
Honey Pot, 2 1/2 In.	27.00
Ivy Ball, Hobnail, 2 Bead Stem, 5 3/4 In.	42.00
Lamp, Hall, Diamond–Quilted	500.00
Mug, Baby Thumbprint, Applied Ribbed Handle, 2 1/2 In.	135.00
Mug, Barrel Shape, Enameled Flowers & Foliage, 3 5/8 In.	85.00
Mug, Barrel Shape, White Flowers, Turquoise Leaves, 4 In.	75.00
Mug, Inverted Thumbprint, 3 In.	58.00
Mug, Paneled, 2 1/4 In.	48.00
Pitcher, 6 Tumblers, 7 1/2 In.	575.00
Pitcher, Bulbous, Straight Neck, Reeded Handle, 4 1/2 In.	105.00
Pitcher, Jeweled, Reverse, Amber To Cranberry, Enameled, 7 7/8 In.	245.00
Pitcher, Thumbprint, Melon Shape, Applied Handle, Libbey, 7 1/2 In.	550.00
Pitcher, Water, Bulbous, Paneled Pattern, Enameled Bee & Foliage	295.00
Pitcher, Water, Inverted Thumbprint, Melon	250.00
Pitcher, Water, Thumbprint Pattern, New England, C.1880, 7 In.	200.00
Punch Cup, Inverted Thumbprint, Reeded Amber Handle, 2 1/2 In.	110.00
Punch Cup, New England, Reeded Handle, Optic Effect, 2 1/4 In.	88.00
Salt & Pepper, Quilt Pattern	175.00
Saltshaker, Inverted Thumbprint, Melon Ribbed, No Top	125.00
Saltshaker, Reverse, Inverted Baby Thumbprint, Pewter Top	165.00
Slipper, Cat, Hobnail	12.00
Spittoon, Hourglass Shape, Ruffled Edge	275.00
Spooner, Baby Thumbprint, 5 In.	110.00
Sugar & Creamer, Plated, New England Glass Co., Squat, 2 1/2 In.	5500.00
Syrup, Honeycomb Pattern, Covered, 8 In. ......395.00 To	550.00
Toothpick, Pink, Hobnail, Pointed, 2 7/8 In.	12.00
Tumbler, Baby Thumbprint, 3 3/4 In.	65.00
Tumbler, Diamond–Quilted, 4 1/2 In.	58.00
Tumbler, Inverted Thumbprint, 4 In. ......50.00 To	65.00
Tumbler, Ribbed, New England, 4 3/8 In.	125.00
Tumbler, Swirl Pattern, Footed, 4 In.	65.00
Vase, Art Glass, 10 In.	110.00
Vase, Bud, Dated 1893, 6 1/2 In.	290.00
Vase, Cylindrical, Wishbone Feet, Serpentine Trim, 10 1/8 In., Pair	325.00
Vase, Fan Top, Wishbone Feet, Cranberry To Amber, 8 1/8 In.	135.00
Vase, Flower Petal Shape, Applied Spiral Trim, Cranberry, 10 In.	160.00
Vase, Jack–In–The–Pulpit, Lacy Gold Design, 14 3/4 In., Pair	450.00
Vase, Lily, 15 In.	600.00
Vase, Lily, Ribbed, Fuchsia, 9 1/4 In.	425.00

Vase, Mother-Of-Pearl, Reverse, White Lining, Flowers, 9 1/4 In. 1100.00
Vase, Ruffled Top, Loop Feet, Crystal Leaves, Flower, 6 1/8 In. 395.00
Vase, Trumpet, Ruffle Top, 15 In. 65.00
Water Set, Reeded Handle, Thumbprint, Signed Libbey, 5 Piece 595.00
Wine, Fuchsia 175.00
Wine, Swirl, Short Stem 57.00

The American Art Clay Company of Indianapolis, Indiana, made a variety of art pottery wares, especially vases, from about 1930 to after World War II. The company used the mark AMACO, as well as the company name. Do not confuse this company with an earlier art pottery firm from Edgerton, Wisconsin, called the American Art Clay Works.

AMERICAN ART CLAY CO., Vase, Incised Decoration Of Lion, Green, 6 In. 75.00

The American Encaustic Tiling Company was founded in Zanesville, Ohio, in 1875. The company planned to make a variety of tiles to compete with the English tiles that were selling in the United States for use in fireplaces and other architectural needs. The first glazed tiles were made in 1880, embossed tiles were added in 1881, faience tiles in the 1920s. The firm closed in 1935 and reopened in 1937 as the Shawnee Pottery.

AMERICAN ENCAUSTIC TILING CO., Tile, Floral, High Glaze Brown, 6 X 6 In. 30.00
Tile, Garrett Hobart Portrait, Turquoise 60.00
Tile, President Harding, 3 X 3 In. 60.00
Tile, Simple Simon, 6 X 6 In. 80.00

Amethyst glass is any of the many glasswares made in the dark purple color of the gemstone called amethyst. Included in this section are many pieces made in the nineteenth and twentieth centuries. Very dark pieces are called black amethyst and are listed under that heading.

AMETHYST GLASS, Basket, White, Cranberry Lined 65.00
Berry Set, Gold Leaf, Medallion, 5 Piece 235.00
Bottle, Barber, Enamel Trim At Shoulder 68.00
Bottle, Condiment, 16 Swirled Ribs, Flared Lip, 5 3/4 In. 500.00
Bowl, Crystal Handles, Wishbone Feet, Gold Trim, 12 In. 275.00
Creamer, Dark, Sterling Silver Overlay 15.00
Cruet, Swag With Brackets, Gold Trim, Original Stopper 110.00
Cruet, Swirl Design 85.00
Figurine, Scotty, Sitting, Red Collar & Tongue, Solid, 5 In. 65.00
Hat, Button & Daisy 45.00
Jug, Wine, Flowers, Frosted, Pewter Top & Handle, 11 1/2 In. 135.00
Lemonade Set, Enameled, 13 In., 5 Piece 145.00
Luncheon Set, L.E.Smith, 24 Piece 95.00
Planter, Dancing Nudes, L.E.Smith, 7 3/4 In. 50.00
Powder Jar, Hinged Gold & Enamel Lid 185.00
Rose Bowl, Apricot, White Lining, Crimped Top 95.00
Salt, 16 Ribs In Bowl, Applied Foot, 2 3/8 In. 325.00
Tumbler, Inverted Rib, Enameled 22.00
Tumbler, White Enamel Design 20.00
Vase, Fluted, Gold Edge, Enameled Houses, 14 1/4 In., Pair 315.00
AMPHORA, see Teplitz
ANDIRON AND RELATED FIREPLACE ITEMS, see Fireplace

Stuffed animals or fish, rugs made of animal skins, and other similar collectibles are listed in this section. Collectors should be aware of the endangered species laws that make it illegal to buy and sell some of these items. Any eagle feathers, many types of cats, such as leopard, and many forms of tortoiseshell can be confiscated if discovered by the government.

ANIMAL TROPHY, Antelope, Head, Horns 750.00
Bear Head 150.00
Bear, Standing, Full Body, 6 1/2 Ft. 1450.00

Bengel Tiger, Open Mouth, Jumping Position	5000.00
Buffalo Head	750.00
Buffalo Head, Large	750.00
Cape Buffalo, Head, Curling Horns	1000.00
Elephant Foot, Made Into Ice Bucket	195.00
Owl, Great Horned	150.00
Snow Owl, Stuffed, Mounted On Perch, 100 Years Old, 21 In.	125.00
Steer Head	45.00

Animation cels are painted drawings on celluloid that are needed to make an animated cartoon. Hundreds of cels are made, then photographed in sequence to make a cartoon showing moving figures. The earliest examples were by the Walt Disney Studios; but even today, animation art continues to be made.

ANIMATION ART, Cel, Bashful, Disney, Framed & Matted, 15 X 12 In.	350.00
Cel, Dopey, Disney, Framed & Matted, 15 X 12 In.	350.00
Cel, Mickey Mouse, Hunting, Hand Painted, Disney, 18 In.	60.00

The Anna Pottery was started in Anna, Illinois, in 1859 by Cornwall and Wallace Kirkpatrick. They made many types of utilitarian wares, bricks, drain tiles and giftware. The most collectible pieces made by the pottery are the pig-shaped bottles and jugs with special inscriptions, applied animals and figures. The pottery closed in 1894.

ANNA POTTERY, Vase, Snakes, Heads, 14 1/2 In.	11660.00

APPLE PEELER, see Kitchen, Peeler, Apple

Arc-en-ciel is the correctly spelled French word for rainbow. A pottery factory named Arc-en-ceil was founded in Zanesville, Ohio, in 1903. The company made art pottery for a short time, then became the Brighton Pottery in 1905.

ARC-EN-CEIL, Vase, Eagle & Washington, Gold, 7 In.	250.00

This section includes a variety of collectibles, usually very large, that have been removed from buildings. Hardware, backbars, doors, paneling, and even old bathtubs are now wanted by collectors. Pieces of the Victorian, Art Nouveau, and Art Deco styles are in greatest demand.

ARCHITECTURAL, Altar, Hand Carved, Walnut & Butternut, Germany, 1874	2000.00
Archway, Triple, Alabaster, Middle Eastern, 20 X 18 3/8 In.	150.00
Backbar, Barbershop, Oak, Marble Counter, Mirrors, 15 Ft.6in.	10500.00
Backbar, Koken, 5 Mirrors, Columns, Marble Top, Oak, 25 Ft.	9000.00
Backbar, Marble Top, Stained Glass Doors	850.00
Ball, Carpet, Pin & White Sponging, China	95.00
Baluster, Stair, Walnut, 2 Piece, 1800s	10.00
Cabinet, Corner, Pegged Arched Doors, American, 92 1/2 In.	3250.00
Cabinet, Display, 3 Shelves, Mahogany & Marble, 73 X 41 In.	300.00
Cabinet, Display, 4 Shelves, Mahogany & Marble, 70 X 50 In.	350.00
Cabinet, Display, Oak, 49 X 23 X 36 In.	250.00
Cabinet, Wells Fargo, Original Red Paint	300.00
Caryatid, Zinc, C.1870, 6 Ft., Pair	12500.00
Ceiling, Stained & Leaded Glass, 10 X 6 Ft.	6000.00
Door Latch, Scalloped, Tree Pattern, Iron, 12 In.	100.00
Door Latch, Spear Type, Iron, 17 1/2 In.	90.00
Door Latch, Tulip Shape, Iron, 8 1/2 In.	150.00
Door Latch, Tulip Shape, Iron, 10 In.	130.00
Door, Cypress, Oval Beveled Glass, Hand Carved, 36 X 84 In.	1800.00
Door, Double, Black Walnut, Carved, 7 Ft. X 42 In.	1200.00
Door, Double, Leaded, Beveled, Oak, 94 X 46 In.	2800.00
Door, Spanish, Wrought Iron Hinges, Oak, 73 1/4 In., Pair	240.00
Door, Stained Glass, 31 1/2 X 80 In.	1000.00
Door, Stained Glass, Garden Scene, 36 X 84 In., Pair	6850.00
Doorknob, Cobalt Blue, Pair	175.00
Doorknob, White, Flower Design, Porcelain, Pair	12.50

Dumb Waiter, 3 Tier, Revolving, Walnut 2350.00
Facade, Duck & Figures 3250.00
Fence, Victorian, Cast Iron, 250 Ft. 2750.00
Finial, Roof, Urn Shape, With Flame 450.00
Fountain, Garden, Nymph Spouts Water, Cast Iron, Base 70 In. 2000.00
Front Bar, Brass Draft Beer System, Walnut, 14 Ft. 650.00
Gate Post Finial, Statue Of Liberty, Wooden & Wrought Iron 2970.00
Gate, Wrought Iron, Pair 80.00
Hardware, Tieback, Flower Pot, Painted, Wrought Iron, Pair 35.00
Hinge, Heart Top, Tulips & Scroll Below, Iron, 27 In. 325.00
Hinge, Ram's Horn, Half Circle, Wrought Iron, 8 In., Pair 130.00
Hinge, Snake Type, Curled, Iron, Pair 60.00
Lamp, Street, South Jersey 300.00
Lamppost, Street, Bronze, 3 Claw Feet, Seashells, 7 Ft. 2 In. 4500.00
Letter Slot, Copper Slot Flap, Brass, 10 X 3 In. 48.00
Newell Post, Ornate, Large 500.00
Panel, Leaded Glass, 8 X 14 In., Pair 32.50
Panel, Leaded Glass, Clear, Geometric, America, 23 X 15 In. 80.00
Panel, Leaded Glass, Opalescent, Geometric, Framed, 64 3/4 In. 500.00
Panel, Mask Of King Neptune In Wreath, Iron, 23 X 23 In. 300.00
Panel, Stained Glass, Multicolored, Framed, 36 X 36 In. 140.00
Pillar, Colonnade Of Massachusetts State House, 29 1/2 In. 4000.00
Pillar, Porch, Square Base, Ash, 8 Ft. 40.00
Post Office Front, Wooden, Brass Slot, 30 X 32 X 18 In. 295.00
Post, Newell, Walnut, Large 450.00
Sink, Pedestal, Porcelain, Round Front, 22 X 23 In. 75.00
Soap Dish, Wall Mount, Early 19th Century 20.00
Soda Fountain, Red Marble, Sink, 10 Pumps, 1920s, 8 Ft. 4500.00
Stairs, Scale Model, Walnut, C.1860 .... 1200.00
Statue, Man, Garden, 18th Century Clothes, Limestone, 42 In. 650.00
Stop Light, Chicago, Cast Aluminum, 1920s, 89 In. 850.00
Sundial, Engraved Slate Base, Iron Arm, Round, 10 In. 25.00
Toilet Tank, Pull Chain 60.00
Urn, Garden, Gadrooned, Square Plinth, Iron, C.1880, 44 In. 150.00
Urn, Garden, Iron, 12 In. 85.00
Urn, Garden, Iron, 15 In. 115.00
Valance, Federal, Gilt Tassels, Old Blue Paint, 112 Ft. 1075.00
Wall, Barbershop, 3 Stations, Beveled Mirrors, Oak, C.1890 .... 5000.00

Arequipa Pottery was produced from 1911 to 1918 by the patients of the Arequipa Sanitorium in Marin County Hills, California.

AREQUIPA, Ashtray, Brown & Mixed Colors, Marked, 4 3/4 X 2 In. 125.00
Planter, Diamond Design, Green, Marked, 3 1/4 X 3 1/4 In. 150.00
Vase, Green Matte, 4 In. 160.00
Vase, Leaf Clusters, Blue Shades, Buff Clay Body, Marked, 7 3/4 In. 308.00
Vase, Matte Green, 3 Handles 175.00
Vase, Signed F, No.110, Blue Matte, 3 1/2 In. 140.00
Vase, Square Pedestal, Tan, 4 X 4 In. 150.00
    ARGY–ROUSSEAU, see G. Argy–Rousseau

Arita is a port in Japan. Porcelain was made there from about 1616. Many types of decorations were used, including the popular Imari designs, which are listed under Imari in this book.

ARITA, Dish, Flowers, Blue And White, 8 In. 185.00
Ewer, Flowers, Polychrome, 8 In. 200.00
Vase, C.1900, 8 In. 175.00
Vase, Flowers, Foliage, Blue, Red, Turquoise, Gold, C.1890, 10 In. 500.00

Art Deco, or Art Moderne, a style started at the Paris Exposition of 1925, is characterized by linear, geometric designs. All types of furniture and decorative arts, jewelry, book bindings, and even games were designed in this style.

ART DECO, Ashtray, Club Shape, Orange Interior, 2 3/4 In. 18.00
Ashtray, Nude On Black Ceramic, Chrome 45.00

Ashtray, Onyx, Green, Bronze Lady, 8 X 6 In. 125.00
Basket, Orange Luster Interior, Green Outside, Black Design, 4 In. 35.00
Box, Cigar, Figural, Nude Woman, Lift Off Cover, 6 X 3 X 5 In. 95.00
Box, Handkerchief, Nude On Cover, Lucite 25.00
Candlestick, Silver Plate, Petal Bud Top, Tubular, 11 In., Pair 28.00
Centerpiece, Flower, 6 Petals Come Off & Are Ashtrays, Metal 37.50
Chandelier, 5 Arm, Chrome, Glass Prisms 38.00
Clock, Green Marble, Enameled Parrot, 8 1/2 In. 950.00
Cocktail Server, Glass, Chrome Pump, Revolving Tray, 6 Tumblers 55.00
Cocktail Shaker, Figural, Bell, Clapper Inside, Handle, Pat.1937 .... 20.00
Decanter, Stopper, Nude Woman In Water, Kosta, 1935, 10 3/4 In. 195.00
Desk Set, Austrian Bronze, Borzoi & Scotties, Onyx Base, 4 Piece 325.00
Dresser Set, Blue, Perfume Bottle, Powder, Tumble–Up, 6 Piece 195.00
Dresser Set, Green, Perfume Bottle, Dish, Tray, English, 10 Piece 290.00
Figurine, Dancing Girl, 2 1/2 In. 10.00
Figurine, Flapper, Seated, Marble Base, Bronze, 4 In. 225.00
Figurine, Kneeling Lady Holding Flower Basket, Porcelain, 10 In. 35.00
Figurine, Panther, Black, Ceramic, 20 In. 30.00
Fire Extinguisher, Unused, Box 10.00
Head, Lady's, Black Hair, Curl On Forehead, Ceramic, 1920s 135.00
Humidor, Figural Dog Design, Orange, Blue Luster, Porcelain, 6 In. 225.00
Incense Burner, Pagoda Shaped, Footed, Signed Vantines, 3 1/2 In. 30.00
Inkstand, Green Glass, Double Wells 125.00
Jar, Dresser, Sterling Silver Cover, Finial, Glass, 4 X 5 In. 65.00
Lamp, Hanging, Radio–Lite–Tenna, Pink Shade, Nudes, Archers, 10 In. 49.00
Lamp, Ivory, Nude, Scenic Shade 495.00
Lighter, Table, Brown & Gold 24.00
Mirror, Hand, 8 1/2 In. 15.00
Mirror, Hand, Brass, Beveled Mirror 50.00
Pitcher, Figural, Bird, Red, White, Black, 9 In. 39.00
Pitcher, Yellow, Brown & Green, Advertising, 5 In. 25.00
Salt & Pepper, Circus Elephant, Boy & Girl, Ceramic Art Studio 20.00
Saltshaker, Pyramid Glass, Cobalt, 6 In. 30.00
Sconce, Wall, White Metal, Orange Bakelite Center, 11 In., Pair 45.00
Shaker, Talcum, Lady, Blue Luster Skirt, Japan, 6 In. 48.00
Tea Set, Beige, Brown Cross Design, Suzy Cooper, 12 Piece 300.00
Tea Set, Initials MS, Jean Luce, Paris, C.1920, 30 Piece 325.00
Teapots, Set In Insulated Silver Case, 2 Of 4 .... *Illus* 220.00
Toy, Jester, Dancing, Gilt Bronze, Ivory Face, Hands, Germany, 11 In. 1250.00
Tray, Mahogany, Inlaid, Glass, Handles, 17 X 11 3/4 In. 30.00
Vase, Gray, Green, Gold, Pottery, Hyalyn, 12 In. 55.00
Vase, Green Glass, 10 In. 22.00
Vase, Ivoris, Art Deco Handles 30.00
Vase, Lady & Flowers, Square, Ceramic, 16 In. 150.00

Art Deco, Teapots, Set In Insulated Silver Case, 2 Of 4

Art Deco, Vase, Lady's Head,
White, Ceramic, 8 In.

Insects like all sorts of natural specimens. Mothballs and insect sprays will help keep stuffed animal heads free from moths or carpet beetles.

Art Glass, Bowl, Amber, Overshot Design, European, 4 X 7 1/2 In.

Vase, Lady's Head, White, Ceramic, 8 In. ....*Illus*	18.00
Vase, Lady, Standing, Green Insert, Ceramic, 11 In.	395.00

Art glass means any of the many forms of glassware made during the late nineteenth century or early twentieth century. These wares were expensive and production was limited. Art glass is not the typical commercial glass that was made in large quantities, and most of the art glass was produced by hand methods.

ART GLASS, see also separate headings such as Burmese; Cameo Glass; Tiffany; etc.

ART GLASS, Bowl, Amber, Overshot Design, European, 4 X 7 1/2 In. ....*Illus*	50.00
Bowl, White, Yellow, Gold Leaf Design, Ruffled Edge, 11 In.	100.00
Cup & Saucer, Flower Form, Pansy Design, Clear Applied Handle	75.00
Dish, Chartreuse & Blue, Octagon, Higgins, 12 In.	25.00
Inkwell, Blue Green Iridescent, Art Nouveau Brass Lid	269.00
Pitcher, Diamond–Quilted, Amber, Bulbous, Long Neck, 6 1/2 In.	186.00
Pitcher, Green Applied Pedestal Feet & Handles, 7 In., Pair	135.00
Plate, Spider Mums, 2 Glass Layers, Higgins, 1928, 8 1/2 In.	95.00
Rose Bowl, Pinched Sides, Iridescent Stripe, Amber & Purple	40.00
Rose Bowl, Rose To Pink, Satin, 4 In.	65.00
Shade, Water Lily Design, 7 1/2 In.	75.00
Spittoon, Lady's	245.00
Vase, Applied Pink Blossoms, Clear Thorn Handles, 9 In.	145.00
Vase, Art Deco, Frosted, Hunebelle, 9 1/4 In.	400.00
Vase, Cobalt, Clear Applied Handles, Pontil	35.00
Vase, Fish Among Seaweed, Clear, 7 1/2 In.	50.00
Vase, Floral, Light Blue Ground, Sterling Rim, Signed V & S, 7 In.	138.00
Vase, Paneled Domed Foot & Body, J.Hoffmann, C.1920, 4 1/2 In.	1045.00
Vase, Rainbow, Twisted Stained Glass, White Cased, 10 1/4 In.	745.00
Vase, Red Reeding, Bubble Design, Bulbous, Flared, 8 1/2 In.	45.00
Vase, Rust To Pink, Ruffled, 2 Ears, Cream Interior, 9 3/4 In.	300.00
Vase, Stick, Cut Velvet, Light & Dark Pink Ribbing, Bulbous, 5 In.	140.00
Vase, Swirl Design, 12 In.	500.00

Art Nouveau is a style of design that was at its most popular from 1895 to 1905. Famous designers, including Rene Lalique and Emile Galle, produced furniture, glass, silver, metalwork, and buildings in the new style. Ladies with long flowing hair and elongated bodies were among the more easily recognized design elements. Copies of this style are being made today. Many modern pieces of jewelry can be found.

ART NOUVEAU, see also Furniture; various glass categories; etc.

ART NOUVEAU, Bookends, Dancing Nude, 1930	40.00
Bowl, Fuchsias In Relief, Sterling Silver, Heavy, 9 1/2 In.	385.00
Box, Jewel, Silver Plated, Ornate, 5 1/2 In.	35.00
Brush, Clothes, Sterling	22.00
Desk Set, Green & Gold, Tray & 3 Open Containers	85.00
Desk Set, Sterling Silver, 2 Piece	25.00
Flask, Scent, Gold, Glass, Jewels, Hinged Cover, C.1900, 3 1/4 In.	1870.00
Flower Holder, Lady, Figural, Double, 12 In.	135.00
Holder, Bronze, Floral Petals, Woman's Head, CH Korshm, 5 In.	300.00
Jar, Cover, Lady, Molded, French, 4 1/2 In.	45.00
Paper Clip, Brass, Floral Design, Slag Glass Insert, 4 1/4 In.	50.00
Table Light, Figural, Lady In Flowing Dress	285.00
Umbrella Stand, Pottery	225.00
Vase, Chipped Ice Design, Gold Design, Honesdale Type, 12 In.	115.00
Vase, Metal, Stylized Floral Design, 15 In.	120.00
Whisk Broom, Sterling Silver	48.00

The first American art pottery was made in Cincinnati, Ohio, during the 1870s. The pieces were hand thrown and hand decorated. The art pottery tradition continued until the 1920s when studio potters began making the more artistic wares.

ART POTTERY, see also under factory name

ART POTTERY, Ashtray, Dog, California Porcelain	175.00
Base, California Faience, Pink High Glaze, Marked, 7 In.	130.00
Bowl, Burmantofts, Conch Shell & Fish, 8 In.	50.00
Bowl, Carl Walters, Black, 1923, Blue & Green Glaze, 8 1/2 In.	140.00
Bowl, Durant Kiln, Blue & Purple, Footed, 6 X 3 In.	100.00
Bowl, White Bird, Lavender, Gold, Waylande Gregory, 6 X 2 In.	165.00
Ewer, Kittens Playing With Yarn, Laughlin, 15 In.	150.00
Figurine, 3 Queens, E.Eckhardt, 6 1/2 X 5 3/4 In. ....*Illus*	300.00
Figurine, Cat, Sitting, White, Black & Gray, Blue Band, 5 5/8 In.	95.00
Figurine, Dante, Red Flambe Glaze, Austrian, C.1913	595.00
Figurine, Mad Tea Party, Eckhardt, 7 3/4 X 6 1/2 In. ......*Illus*	300.00
Figurine, Spanish Clown, Wooden Base, 25 In. ....*Illus*	2200.00
Figurine, Walrus, Carpenter, Eckhardt, 6 1/2 X 4 In. ......*Illus*	350.00
Keg, Rum, Barrel Shape, Floral Design, England, C.1835, 4 1/2 In.	300.00
Lamp, Brown, Green Matte, Bulbous, Walley, 1910, 7 1/4 In.	50.00
Lamp, Maroon, Cleftwood, Paper Label	35.00
Pitcher, Avon, Jap–Birdimal, Black, White, 1920, 5 In.	580.00
Platter, Raised Pineapple Design, Marked Cpus, 8 1/2 In.	100.00
Ramekin, Covered, Artist CAH, Dorchester, Dated 1951	55.00
Sachet Jar, Pierced Top Cover, Flowers, Pauline Pottery, C.1895	600.00
Vase, 3 Lions, Cylindrical, Gray Blue, Slate Gray, 9 1/4 In.	125.00
Vase, Art Nouveau, Flower Form, Delaherche, C.1900	1500.00

Art Pottery, Figurine

Mad Tea Party, Eckhardt,   Walrus, Carpenter,   3 Queens, E.Eckhardt,
7 3/4 X 6 1/2 In.   Eckhardt, 6 1/2 X 4 In.   6 1/2 X 5 3/4 In.

Art Pottery, Figurine

Spanish Clown,
Wooden Base, 25 In.

Art Pottery, Vase, Jasper, Blue
& White, Ecanada, 6 In.

If you are having your antiques moved in a van to a new home, watch out for damage. Check the antiques as they are unloaded. Sweep the inside of the moving van and save any small pieces of veneer or wood that might have chipped off your furniture.

Vase, California, Faience, High Glaze Blue, 4 In.	75.00
Vase, Daffodil Design, Moravian, Dark Blue, 8 In.	27.50
Vase, Green & Brown, Walley, 3 1/2 X 4 In.	195.00
Vase, Green Diamond, Red Clay, Walley, Impressed, C.1910, 6 In.	125.00
Vase, Green Glaze Flecks, Brown, Walley, C.1910, 3 1/2 In.	150.00
Vase, Green Matte, Jervis, 4 In.	55.00
Vase, Hungarian Faience, Footed, Cincinnati	210.00
Vase, Jasper, Blue & White, Ecanada, 6 In. ....*Illus*	55.00
Vase, Kezonta, Green & Blue Flowers, Gold Outlines, 16 In.	650.00
Vase, Leaves & Berries In Relief, T.J.Wheatley Co., 11 1/2 In.	525.00
Vase. Merrimac, 2 Raised Elephant Heads, 1905, Marked, 4 1/2 In.	325.00
Vase, Merrimack, Green Matte, 9 In.	110.00
Vase, Mistletoe Leaf & Berry Design, Denver Danaura, 6 In.	350.00
Vase, River Scene, Brown, M.Morgan, Limoges Style, 14 1/2 In.	5000.00
Vase, Rose & Blues, High Glaze, 2 Handles, Signed Mueller, 7 In.	35.00
Vase, Wanopee, 3 Handles, Iridescent Blue, Pinks, & Brown, 6 In.	45.00

ARTHUR OSBORNE, see Ivorex

AURENE   *Aurene glass was made by Frederick Carder of New York about 1904. It is an iridescent gold glass, usually marked "Aurene" or "Steuben."*

Aurene, Vase, Gold, Steuben,
Handles, Footed, 6 1/4 In.

Decorate with the neighborhood burglar in mind. Large windows can be made less attractive to intruders if you put plants on shelves across the window. Decorative shelves and grills are made for this. Of course, be sure you can open the windows in case of fire.

AURENE, Bowl, Peacock Blue, Signed, 5 5/8 X 3 In. 900.00
Candlestick, Gold, Steuben No.1933, C.1920, 8 1/2 In., Pair 500.00
Dish, Candy, Signed, Mirror Finish, 5 X 1 1/2 In. 250.00
Salt, Art Glass, Pair 150.00
Salt, Pedestal, Signed 165.00
Sugar & Creamer, Diamond–Quilted Pattern, Blue & Pink, Signed 685.00
Toothpick 110.00
Vase, Blue, Steuben No.2636, Signed, C.1920, 4 7/8 In. 400.00
Vase, Bud, Art Glass, 7 In. 200.00
Vase, Gold Iridescent, Scalloped, Flared, Marked, Numbered, 3 1/2 In. 185.00
Vase, Gold Iridescent, Signed & Numbered, 8 1/2 In. 325.00
Vase, Gold, Bulbous, Tapering To Base, Marked Haviland, 4 7/8 In. 350.00
Vase, Gold, Fan Shape, Steuben No.6297, C.1920, 9 In. 1550.00
Vase, Gold, Flared, Steuben No.177, 10 In. 725.00
Vase, Gold, Silver, Steuben No.131, Script Signed, 4 In. 200.00
Vase, Gold, Steuben No.7082, C.1920, 6 1/4 In. 375.00
Vase, Gold, Steuben, Handles, Footed, 6 1/4 In. ....*Illus* 375.00
Vase, Jack–In–The–Pulpit Style, Signed, Gold Iridescent, 6 In. 695.00
Vase, Ruffled, Dimpled, Marked, 3 In. 325.00
Vase, Stick, Blue, Marked, 12 In. 525.00
Vase, Swirls, Hooked Feathering On Calcite, Signed, 3 1/2 In. 875.00
Vase, Trumpet Shape, Ruffled Top, Pedestal, Signed, Blue, 9 In. 395.00
AUSTRIA, see Royal Dux; Kauffmann; Porcelain

Auto parts and accessories are collectors' items today. Gas pump globes and license plates are part of this specialty. Prices are determined by age, rarity, and condition.

AUTO, AC Spark Plug Cleaning Machine, Graphic, 1930s, 22 In. 45.00
Ashtray, Chicago Motor Club Honor Member, Brass, Enameled Center 18.00
Book, Cartoon, Ford, How To Be A Great Driver, 1949 .... 7.00
Carrier, Luggage, Running Board, Iron, Black 25.00
Clock, Dash, Waltham 85.00
Clock, Waltham, Hudson Super 6 ....5.75 To 6.50 ... 120.00
Dip Stick, Red Crown Gasoline 25.00
Emblem, AAA, For License Plate, Porcelain, Blue & White, 1920s 15.00
Fire Extinguisher, Art Deco, Chrome, Maroon Top, Unused, Box 65.00
Gas Measure, White Star Gasoline, Pat.May 18, 1909 .... 250.00
Gas Pump Globe, Aerotest Gasoline, Glass, 1930, 15 In.Diam. 85.00
Gas Pump Globe, Amico Gas 50.00
Gas Pump Globe, Apco 110.00
Gas Pump Globe, Black Mammy, Holding Spoon 1100.00
Gas Pump Globe, Bowser, Canadian 85.00
Gas Pump Globe, Clark, Glass Inserts 275.00
Gas Pump Globe, Colonial, Metal Band 35.00
Gas Pump Globe, Cosden Gasoline, Ethyl Corp.Logo 245.00
Gas Pump Globe, Crown Gasoline, Blue, Brass Collar 190.00
Gas Pump Globe, Essolene, Metal Frame 225.00
Gas Pump Globe, Fleetwing, With Bird, 3 Piece 400.00
Gas Pump Globe, Kool Motor Gas 700.00
Gas Pump Globe, Milk Glass, Eagle, Fully Feathered, 21 In. 400.00
Gas Pump Globe, Mobil Oil, Gargoyle, 1 Piece 250.00
Gas Pump Globe, Shell, Milk Glass, Red Lettering 800.00
Gas Pump Globe, Standard Oil, Crown, Box 195.00
Gas Pump Globe, Standard, Gold Crown 275.00
Gas Pump Globe, Standard, Metal Frame ....95.00 To 205.50
Gas Pump Globe, Texaco 285.00
Gas Pump Globe, Texaco, Original Paint, 1 Piece 395.00
Gas Pump Globe, White Eagle 400.00
Gas Pump, Clear Vision, 1929, 10 Gal. 550.00
Gas Pump, Milk Glass, Eagle, 21 In. 8.00
Gauge, Balloon Tire 55.00
Gauge, Buick, 1940, Pair 20.00
Gauge, Gas, Socony, 1909 .... 15.00
Gauge, Gas, Wooden, Atwater Kent, 1909 ....

Gauge, Tire, Schrader, Brass ....5.00 To 8.00
Headlight, Copper, Large 125.00
Headlight, Ford, 1905–10, Brass, Set 125.00
Heater, Diamond Hot Blast, Red Plush Cover, Charcoal Drawer 27.50
    AUTO, HOOD ORNAMENT, see also Lalique
Hood Ornament, 1942 Ford, 6 Cylinder 6.00
Hood Ornament, Art Deco, Eagle 45.00
Hood Ornament, Chrysler, 1950s 20.00
Hood Ornament, Goddess Of Speed, Packard, Wood Base, 1920s ....45.00 To 50.00
Hood Ornament, Griffin, Vauxhall, Wood Base, 1920 .... 85.00
Hood Ornament, Hand Holding Playing Cards 75.00
Hood Ornament, Indian, Pontiac, Celluloid 45.00
Hood Ornament, Jockey On Horse, Wood Base, 1920s ....65.00 To 75.00
Hood Ornament, Leaping Jaguar, Wood Base, 1920s ....75.00 To 85.00
Hood Ornament, Oldsmobile, 1950s 25.00
Hood Ornament, Pontiac 35.00
Hood Ornament, Pontiac, 1950s 20.00
Hood Ornament, Ra, Sun God, Stutz, Silvered Bronze 150.00
Hood Ornament, Ram, Dodge 45.00
Hood Ornament, Reclining Nude 12.00
Hood Ornament, Soaring Eagle, Wood Base, 1920s ....65.00 To 75.00
Hood Ornament, Spirit Of Triumph, Winged Male With Wheel, 1930s 75.00
Hood Ornament, Vauxhall Griffin 80.00
Horn, 3 Coil Bulb, Brass, Right Hand Drive 35.00
Horn, Brass 100.00
Horn, Steel, Red Paint, Hand Operated, E.A.Laboratories, No.2 .... 28.00
Jack, Car, Ford, Script, Boxed 17.00
Knob, Gearshift, Agate 14.00
Knob, Gearshift, Blue & White Marble 25.00
Lamp, Neverout, Brass 150.00
Lamp, Studebaker, 1920s, Pair 135.00
Lamp, Wheel Hub 30.00
License Plate, Arkansas, 1932, Pair 40.00
License Plate, California, 1914, Porcelain, White On Red 50.00
License Plate, Detroit, Mich., 1941, Milk Wagon 40.00
License Plate, Hawaii, 1951 .... 25.00
License Plate, Iowa, 1937 .... 3.00
License Plate, Manitoba, 1912, Porcelain, Black & White 50.00
License Plate, Manitoba, 1958, Farm, Black & Yellow 60.00
License Plate, Manitoba, 1971, Motorcycle, White & Black 3.00
License Plate, Massachusetts, 1918 .... 7.00
License Plate, Michigan, 1939, Original Wrapper, Pair 20.00
License Plate, New Hampshire, 1916, Porcelain 18.00
License Plate, New Mexico, 1937 .... 10.00
License Plate, North Dakota, 1921 .... 15.00
License Plate, Pennsylvania, 1913, Porcelain 20.00
License Plate, Pennsylvania, 1942, Motorcycle 15.00
License Plate, Prohibition, Repeal 18th Amendment 25.00
License Plate, WPA 8.50
Lock, Hudson, Brass, 6 Lever, Key 25.00
Luggage Rack, Running Board 27.50
Luggage Rack, Running Board, Folding, 1920s 18.00
Luggage Rack, Running Board, Wahl Red Cap, C.1925, Set Of 4 .... 150.00
Nozzle, Gasoline 16.00
Pump, Tire, Brass, 18 In. 24.00
Racing Car, Conical Body, Pedal Power, Miniature, Early 20th Century 550.00
Radio, Sinclair Gas Pump, Green, Dinosaur On Front, Leather Case 25.00
Sign, Chauffeur Driven Auto, Helck, Framed, 11 3/4 X 15 7/8 In. 2200.00
Sign, Dodge Motorcar, Porcelain, 1930s, 15 X 45 In. 125.00
Sign, Indian Gas, Blue & Green Logo, 12 X 4 In. 15.00
Sign, Mobil Oil, Gargoyle, Porcelain, C.1920, 24 X 19 1/2 In. 100.00
Sign, Mobil, Red, White, Blue, Porcelain, 12 X 14 In. 35.00
Sign, Oilzum Motor Oil, Tin, Blue & White, 5 X 1 In. 120.00
Sign, Oilzum, Driver In Goggles, Brass, Framed, 1910, 30 X 20 1/4 In. 425.00

Sign, Seiberling Tires, Porcelain, 2–Sided, Yellow, Brown, 36 X 18 In. 60.00
Sign, Standard Oil, Mica Axle Grease, Tin, Blue, White, 4 1/2 X 19 In. 22.00
Sign, Stanocola Gasoline, Porcelain, Round, 18 In. 65.00
Sign, Texaco, Porcelain, 1934, 15 In. 70.00
Sign, Texaco, Star, Porcelain, Round, 15 In. 35.00
Sign, Tydol Gasoline, Lady Driving, Litho On Canvas, 1920s, 55 X 36 In. 250.00
Sign, Wolf's Head Motor Oil, Oval, Double–Sided, Porcelain, 22 X 30 In. 85.00
Tire Pump, Ford, Brass 26.00
Tool Kit, Auburn, Rubber, Box 18.00
Vase, Cornucopia, Cranberry, Etched, No Bracket 35.00
Vase, Etched, Sterling Silver Rim, Clear 25.00
Water Bag, Radiator, Indian On Front 17.50
Whistle, Exhaust, Chime, Brass 90.00
Wrench, Crescent, Ford, Script, 9 In. 9.00
Wrench, Ford 2.50
Wrench, Model T 5.00
Wrench, Open End, Maxwell 4.00
Wrench, Open End, Model T, Ford Script 2.50

Autumn Leaf pattern china was made for the Jewel Tea Company from 1933. Hall China Company of East Liverpool, Ohio, Crooksville China Company of Crooksville, Ohio, Harker Potteries of Chester, West Virginia, and Paden City Pottery, Paden City, West Virginia, made dishes with this design. Autumn Leaf has remained popular and was still being made by Hall China Company until 1978. Some other pieces in the Autumn Leaf pattern are still being made.

AUTUMN LEAF, Bean Pot, Jewel Tea, 1978 .... 70.00
Berry Set, Jewel Tea, 7 Piece 70.00
Bowl, Salad, Jewel Tea 30.00
Bowl, Vegetable, Covered, Oval 15.00
Butter, Covered, Jewel Tea, 1/4 Lb. 105.00
Butter, Original Box, 1 Lb. 140.00
Cake Carrier, Handles, Metal 65.00
Cake Plate 11.00
Cake Plate, Gold Base, Jewel Tea 155.00
Cake Plate, Jewel Tea ....10.00 To 20.00
Cake Safe, With Plate 25.00
Candleholder, Golden Ray, Pair 52.00
Candy Dish, Gold Base, Jewel Tea 245.00
Canister Set, Metal, 4 Piece 29.00
Casserole, Covered, Jewel Tea 45.00
Clock, Wall, Hall, Jewel Tea 375.00
Coaster, Jewel Tea 5.00
Coffee Dispenser, Wall 57.50
Coffeepot, Drip, Jewel Tea, Ceramic 250.00
Cookie Jar 90.00
Cookie Jar, Big Ear, Jewel Tea ....85.00 To 88.00
Creamer, Jewel Tea 10.00
Cup & Saucer ....7.00 To 25.00
Custard Cup, Jewel Tea, Orange Poppy 4.00
Custard, Set Of 6 .... 30.00
Drip Jar, Covered, Jewel Tea ....9.00 To 14.00
Gravy Boat ....12.00 To 15.00
Hot Pad, Jewel Tea, Pair 30.00
Jam Jar, Covered, Jewel Tea 45.00
Mixing Bowl, 7 In. 15.00
Mixing Bowl, Set Of 3 ....22.00 To 30.00
Mug, Irish Coffee, Unused 60.00
Mustard, Covered, Jewel Tea 37.50
Percolator, Electric, Jewel Tea, 8 Cup 225.00
Pie Plate, Jewel Tea 12.50
Pitcher, Milk, Jewel Tea 20.00
Pitcher, Utility, Jewel Tea 18.00
Plate, 9 In. 5.00

Plate, Hall, 10 In.	9.00
Platter, Jewel Tea, 13 1/2 In.	14.00
Refrigerator Set, Jewel Tea	70.00
Salt & Pepper, Jewel Tea	15.00
Salt & Pepper, Jewel Tea, Small	12.50
Souffle, Jewel Tea, 2 Pt.	50.00
Teapot, Long Spout	42.00
Teapot, Strainer, Jewel Tea	38.00
Teapot, With Incisor, Jewel Tea	37.50
Tray, Jewel Tea, Oval	70.00
Tumbler, Frosted, 14 Oz., Set Of 4	40.00
Warmer, Oval	95.00 To 145.00
Water Set, Tray & 6 Tumblers, Jewel Tea	225.00

AVON, see Bottle, Avon

Baccarat glass was made in France by La Compagnie des Cristalleries de Baccarat, located 150 miles from Paris. The factory was started in 1765. The firm went bankrupt and began operating again about 1822. Cane and millefiori paperweights were made during the 1860 to 1880 period. The firm is still working near Paris making paperweights and glasswares.

BACCARAT, Atomizer, Clear Swirl & Cranberry	150.00
Bobeche, Pair	24.00
Bottle, Cologne, Cobalt Cut To Clear, Huge Stopper	125.00
Bottle, Cologne, Houbigant, Gold Trim, Stopper	65.00
Bottle, Cologne, Pinwheel Pattern, Pewter Fittings, Atomizer	65.00
Bottle, Cologne, Rose Tiente, Swirl, 7 1/2 In., Set Of 5	225.00
Bottle, Perfume, Carolina Blue	74.00
Bowl, Rose Tiente, Scalloped, Ormolu Feet, Marked, 10 3/4 In.	245.00
Bowl, Rose Tiente, Swirl, Signed, 4 1/2 In.	48.00
Butter, Covered, Signed	65.00
Candelabra, Ormolu Mounted, Early 19th Century, 16 In., Pair	1800.00
Candlestick, 6 In., Pair	100.00
Celery, Rose To Amber, Swirl, 3 1/2 X 9 1/2 In.	49.00
Celery, Signed, Cranberry, 10 In.	150.00
Goblet, Perfection, Set Of 6	150.00
Inkwell, 12 Panel, Screw-On Gold Plated Top, Cobalt, 3 3/4 In.	235.00
Jar, Amberina Swirl, Marked, 3 In.	28.00
Lamp, Sunburst Pattern, Frosted Shade, Sapphire Blue, 9 1/2 In.	175.00
Paperweight, Adlai Stevenson, Blue Starcut Back	110.00
Paperweight, Butterfly, Cobalt Ground, 1971	175.00
Paperweight, Contemporary, Blue & White Double Overlay, Gilded	200.00
Paperweight, Coronation, Clear, Fan Cut Base	200.00
Paperweight, Green & White Star Cane Carpet, Zodiac Silhouettes	250.00
Paperweight, Green Lizard, Pink Flower, Natural Ground	475.00
Paperweight, Roosevelt, Theodore, Gray Overlay, Only 22 Made	250.00
Paperweight, Sea Horse, 1975	310.00
Paperweight, Sulfide, Hoover, Herbert, Blue	75.00
Paperweight, Sulfide, Jackson, Andrew, Green	75.00 To 100.00
Paperweight, Sulfide, Kennedy, John, Blue	75.00
Paperweight, Sulfide, Kennedy, John, Green Star Cut	100.00
Paperweight, Sulfide, Kennedy, John, Green Waffle Cut	75.00
Paperweight, Sulfide, Kennedy, John, Red Star Cut	75.00
Paperweight, Sulfide, Kennedy, John, Red Waffle Cut	100.00
Paperweight, Sulfide, Lee, Robert E., Blue	100.00
Paperweight, Sulfide, Lee, Robert E., Clear, Fan Cut Base	210.00
Paperweight, Sulfide, Lincoln, Abraham, Orchid Waffle Cut	100.00
Paperweight, Sulfide, Lincoln, Purple Overlay	275.00
Paperweight, Sulfide, Luther, Martin, Blue Waffle Cut	75.00
Paperweight, Sulfide, Luther, Martin, Red Waffle Cut	75.00
Paperweight, Sulfide, Monroe, James, Lime Green Overlay	125.00
Paperweight, Sulfide, Monroe, James, Red	75.00 To 100.00
Paperweight, Sulfide, Paine, Thomas, Green Overlay	125.00
Paperweight, Sulfide, Paine, Thomas, Turquoise	100.00

Paperweight, Sulfide, Pope John, Yellow .... 75.00 To 100.00
Paperweight, Sulfide, Pope Pius XII, Overlay, White 250.00
Paperweight, Sulfide, Pope Pius, Red Star Cut .... 75.00 To 100.00
Paperweight, Sulfide, Rayburn, Sam, Blue 75.00
Paperweight, Sulfide, Rayburn, Sam, Red 100.00
Paperweight, Sulfide, Roosevelt, Eleanor, Blue 100.00
Paperweight, Sulfide, Roosevelt, Eleanor, Purple 75.00
Paperweight, Sulfide, Roosevelt, Theodore, Amethyst Star Cut Back 150.00
Paperweight, Sulfide, Roosevelt, Theodore, Blue 75.00
Paperweight, Sulfide, Stevenson, Adlai, Purple Overlay 125.00
Paperweight, Sulfide, Stevenson, Adlai, Red Star Cut .... 75.00 To 100.00
Paperweight, Sulfide, Washington, George, Blue 100.00
Paperweight, Sulfide, Wilson, Woodrow, 1972, Yellow Overlay 150.00
Paperweight, Sulfide, Wilson, Woodrow, Turquoise .... 75.00 To 100.00
Paperweight, White Dahlia, Blue Ground, Dated 1970 .... 275.00
Perfume Bottle, Guerlain .... 30.00 To 65.00
Perfume Bottle, Houbigant 35.00
Perfume Bottle, Red To Clear, Art Deco Pointed Top, 14 In. 225.00
Perfume Bottle, Swirl, Rose Tiente, 7 1/2 In. 75.00
Perfume Bottle, Swirl, Splash 65.00
Pitcher Set, Adventurine, Enameled Figures, Gold Dust Spatter 185.00
Powder Box, 3 In. 60.00
Rose Tree, Swirl, Rose Tiente 55.00
Salt, Rubina, Swirled Diamond 75.00
Torchere, Late 19th Century, Pair 48400.00
Tray, Dresser, Rose Teinte, Swirl, 8 1/2 X 12 In. 85.00
Tumble–Up, Swirl Design, Blue, 7 1/2 In. 165.00
Vase, 7 Hexagonal Cut Tiers, Etched, C.1930, Signed, 9 1/2 In. 3080.00
Vase, Crimped Ribbons Upper, 5 Feet Of Sandwich Design, 7 In. 55.00
Vase, Opaque, Painted Birds, Branch, Marked, 10 1/4 In. 185.00
Vase, Trumpet, Rose Tiente, Ormolu Base, 14 5/8 In. 225.00
Wine, Footed, Marked, Ruby 12.00
    BAG, BEADED, see Purse

Metal banks have been made since 1868. There are still banks, mechanical banks, and registering banks (those which show the total money deposited on the face of the bank). Many old banks have been reproduced since the 1950s in iron or plastic.

BANK, Abe Lincoln Bust, Banthrico, Metal 15.00
Abraham Lincoln, Bottle Shape, Glass 8.00
Acorn Shape, Advertising Acorn Stoves, Bennington Type 78.00
Alice In Wonderland, Tin, 3 1/4 In. 225.00
Apple, Cast Iron 550.00
Armored Car, 5 In. 35.00
Aunt Jemima, Cast Iron, Painted, 5 1/4 In. 60.00
Auto, Chrysler, Metal, Banthrico, 1946 .... 7.50
Auto, Ford Roadster, Banthrico, 1929 .... 15.00
Auto, Lincoln, Metal, Banthrico, 1941 .... 7.50
Auto, Touring, Banthrico, 1917 .... 15.00
Auto, Yellow Cab, Cast Iron, 6 3/4 In. 850.00
Auto, Yellow Cab, Cast Iron, Painted, 3 1/2 In. 850.00
Bank Clock, Kingsbury 62.00
Barrel, People's Saving 15.00
Baseball Player, Cast Iron .... 80.00 To 90.00
Bear, Begging, Cast Iron 45.00
Beehive, Wooden 45.00
Ben Franklin, Imperial Life Insurance Co., Asheville, N.C., Metal 32.00
Billiken, On Throne 125.00
Black Boy, Black, Cast Iron, C.1885 .... 285.00
Book, Little Bopeep, Metal 9.00
Bowling, Battery Operated 39.00
Boy On Tub, Cast Iron 45.00
Building, Cast Iron, 6 1/4 In. 125.00
Building, Finial, 4 X 2 1/2 In. 50.00

Building, Flat Iron, Cast Iron, 5 1/2 In. 75.00
Building, Iron, 3 In. 38.00
Building, Woolworth, Lead, Small 18.00
Buster Brown & Tige, Cast Iron .... 90.00 To 125.00
Camel, Cast Iron, 4 3/4 In. 50.00
Camel, Gilded, Iron, 4 1/2 In. 45.00
Campbell's Soup Vegetable Garden, Tin, Label 10.00
Cannon, Cast Iron, 4 3/4 In. 35.00
Captain Kidd, Cast Iron 195.00
Carpenter Safe, Harper, Painted Cast Iron, 4 1/2 In. 1500.00
Carpenter, Next To House, Original Paint, Cast Iron, 1907 .... 1100.00
Cash Register, Jr., Cast Iron 150.00
Cash Register, National, Brass 75.00
Cash Register, National, Figural, Metal 50.00
Cash Register, U Save A Penny, Tin, Lithograph 30.00
Cash Register, Universal 3 Coin Bank, Tin, Registers & Adds, 5 In. 55.00
Cat, Black, Shafford 35.00
Cat, Eveready Batteries, Advertising, 9 Lives 20.00
Cat, Sitting, Blue Ribbon & Bow, Original White Paint, Cast Iron, 5 In. 90.00
Cat, With Pipe, Chalkware, 10 In. ....100.00 To 195.00
Cavalier, Cast Iron, 9 In. 20.00
Chest Of Drawers, Scroddleware, Marbelized, Paw Feet, 5 1/2 In. 165.00
Cigarette Machine, Lever Dispenses Cigarettes, 6 X 3 1/2 In. 45.00
Circus Wagon, Overland, Iron, Kenton, 15 In. 170.00
City Bank, Cast Iron, 10 Lbs., 7 X 9 1/2 In. 125.00
Clown, Chein ....27.50 To 37.50
Clown, Cocked Hat, Cast Iron, Painted, 6 3/4 In. 750.00
Country Inn, Stollwerck, Tin, Litho, 3 1/4 In. 45.00
Covered Urn Form, Stoneware, Cobalt Glaze, 6 1/4 In. 125.00
Cow, Standing, Iron, Original Gilt Paint, 5 1/4 In. 95.00
Cow, Standing, Original Gilt, Cast Iron, 5 1/4 In. 90.00
Dime Register, Copper Mine, Children On Front, Tin 75.00
Dime Register, Kodak, Tin 18.00
Dime Register, Pig, Home Federal Savings & Loan, Tulsa, Pot Metal 12.00
Dime Register, Popeye 35.00
Dime Register, Prudential 125.00
Dime Register, Snow White 50.00
Dime Register, Superman 90.00
Dime Register, Trunk Shape, H & H 100.00
Dime Register, Uncle Sam, 3 Coin, Red 45.00
Dime Register, Uncle Sam, Pat.1941 .... 35.00
Dispenser, Stollwerck, Tin, Wooden, Letter Opener & Tip Tray, 6 1/4 In. 165.00
Doc Yak, Aluminum, 1930s 120.00
Dog, Black, With Pack, Iron, 8 In. 60.00
Dog, Boston Bulldog, Cast Iron, Brown, White, 5 In. 60.00
Dog, Bulldog, Georgia, Calhoun National Bank, Metal 20.00
Dog, Cocked Ear, Tan, Iron 55.00
Dog, Cocker Spaniel, Paws Apart, Beige, Iron 28.00
Dog, Labrador Retriever, Cast Iron, Painted, 4 1/2 In. 275.00
Dog, Pack On Back, Cast Iron ....75.00 To 85.00
Dog, Scotty, Lock & Key, White Metal 25.00
Dog, Scotty, Seated, Hubley, Cast Iron 75.00
Dog, Shepherd, With Pack, Iron, 5 1/4 X 8 In. ....60.00 To 75.00
Dog, Spaniel, Iron, 6 In. 95.00
Dog, St.Bernard, Cast Iron ....45.00 To 70.00
Donald Duck, In Boat, Nodder, Plaster 22.50
Donkey, Saddle, Cast Iron, 4 1/2 In. ....37.50 To 60.00
Dry Dock Savings Teller, Copper, Bank Picture, Pat Pend.1913 .... 30.00
Electrolux Refrigerator, Cast Iron 25.00
Elephant, Cast Iron ....30.00 To 195.00
Elephant, Grapette, Clear, Metal Slotted Lid 20.00
Elephant, Howdah, 4 1/2 X 3 In. 57.50
Elephant, Iron, Gilded, 3 In. 48.00
Elephant, Nixon, Agnew '68 Embossed On Side, Cast Iron 25.00

Foxy Grandpa 85.00
Fred & Wilma Flintstone 35.00
Frog, Marked Iron Art, Cast Iron, Green Paint, 8 3/8 In. 125.00
Frog, Pottery, 6 In. 28.00
Frog, Swallowing Coin, Hands On Tummy, Pottery, 6 In. ....35.00 To 45.00
Fruit Jar, Atlas, Miniature 20.00
Gas Pump, Cast Iron, Painted, 5 3/4 In. 225.00
George Washington, Bust, Painted Cast Iron, 8 In. 700.00
Globe, O'Clock, Tin & Plastic, 1950s 35.00
Globe, Round, 5 In. 50.00
Golfer, Hole In One, Battery Operated, Shields Japan Label 65.00
Graf Zeppelin, Cast Iron, Silver, A.C.Williams, 6 3/4 In. ....130.00 To 195.00
Hamm's Beer, Bear, Calendar, 16 In. 35.00
Happifats 175.00
Happy Days, Barrel Shape, Chein, Tin, 5 In. ....15.00 To 25.00
Hitler, Pig Caricature 65.00
Horse, Beauty, Old Black Paint, Cast Iron, 4 1/4 In. 30.00
Horse, Black, Iron, 4 In. 70.00
Horse, Rearing, Cast Iron, Walnut Base, 7 X 6 1/2 In. 65.00
Horse, Standing, Cast Iron, 11 X 10 In. 105.00
House, Small, Iron, 3 In. 38.00
Howdy Doody, Riding Pig 55.00
Humpty Dumpty, Advertising Philco Radios, Pottery 15.00
Humpty Dumpty, Sitting On Brick Wall, Iron 145.00
Ice Cream Freezer, Take Your Money & Freeze It, Cast Iron 185.00
Independence Hall Tower Centennial, Cast Iron, Painted ....225.00 To 325.00
Independence Hall Tower, Cast Iron 425.00
Indian Boy, Pottery, Souvenir, Biloxi, Miss., 5 In. 20.00
Indian, Cast Iron, 6 In. 65.00
Jester & Dog, Cast Iron, 11 In. 20.00
Lamp, Oil, Cast Iron, Brass, Glass Chimney, 7 1/2 X 6 1/2 In. 600.00
Laurel & Hardy, Figural, Hard Plastic, 14 In., Pair 37.50
Liberty Bell, Dated 1919, Glass 20.00
Lion, Cast Iron, 5 1/4 In. 70.00
Lion, Harris Trust & Savings, Chicago, Pot Metal 25.00
Lion, Sitting, On Tub, Gilt Paint, Cast Iron, 5 1/4 In. 95.00
Llama, Cast Iron, Original Paint, 5 In. 45.00
Locomotive, Safety, Cast Iron, Nickel Plate, 6 In. 300.00
Log Cabin Syrup, Tin, Towle, 4 X 3 In. 40.00
Log Cabin, Abe Lincoln Type, Van Dyke Tea, China 24.00
Log Cabin, Glass, Pittsburgh Paints, Smooth As Glass 20.00
Log Cabin, Tin, Litho, Chein, 3 In. 35.00

Bank, Mechanical, Indian, Bear,
C.1875, 7 5/8 X 10 9/16 In.

Bank, Mechanical, Dark Town Battery

Lucky Joe, Glass, Covered 8.00
Mailbox, Key, John Deere, International–Allis–Chalmers 6.00
Mailbox, Pot Metal 30.00
Mailbox, Tin 9.00
Mailbox, U.S.Mail, Iron 30.00
Mammy, Holding Spoon 110.00
Man From Uncle, Plastic 25.00
Man, With Hat, Watch Me Grow Tall, Tin, 6 In. 75.00
Mary With Lamb, Cast Iron ....275.00 To 375.00
Mason Jar, Zinc Top, Miniature 10.00

> *Mechanical banks were first made about 1870. Any bank with moving*
> *parts is considered mechanical. The metal banks made before World*
> *War I are the most desirable. Copies and new designs of mechanical*
> *banks have been made in metal or plastic since the 1920s.*

Mechanical, Adams Family, The Thing 15.00
Mechanical, Always Did 'Spise A Mule, Bucking Mule, C.1879, 8 In. 250.00
Mechanical, Atomic Bank, Metal, Duro 35.00
Mechanical, Barking Dog Safe 200.00
Mechanical, Black Man In Cabin, Polychrome Paint, Cast Iron, 3 5/8 In. 345.00
Mechanical, Building, Wireless, Cast Iron, Tin, Electric, 6 1/2 In. 200.00
Mechanical, Bulldog, Seated On Crate, Penny On Nose, 7 1/4 In. 225.00
Mechanical, Cabin, 1885 .... 275.00
Mechanical, Cannon & Tank, Cast Iron, Painted, 10 In. 275.00
Mechanical, Cat In Boat, Sail, Cast Iron, 11 In. 80.00
Mechanical, Chinaman, Reclining 1750.00
Mechanical, Clown On Globe, Cast Iron, Painted ....1100.00 To 1200.00
Mechanical, Creedmore, Man In Red Tunic Shoots At Tree, 1877 ....300.00 To 375.00
Mechanical, Dapper Dan Jigger 575.00
Mechanical, Dark Town Battery ....*Illus* 575.00
Mechanical, Eagle & Eaglets 325.00
Mechanical, Elephant, 3 Acrobats, Painted, Dated 450.00
Mechanical, Elephant, Jumbo, Key, England, 1940s 65.00
Mechanical, Elephant, Jumbo, Tin, Litho, 5 1/2 In. 30.00
Mechanical, Feed The Kitty 415.00
Mechanical, Football, English, Cast Iron, Painted 1100.00
Mechanical, Frankenstein's Hand, Metal, Colored 30.00
Mechanical, Frog On Bank, Drum, Polychrome Paint, Cast Iron, 4 1/4 In. 350.00
Mechanical, Fun Producing Savings Bank, Tin 275.00
Mechanical, Grenadier, Aluminum, Painted 100.00
Mechanical, Indian, Bear, C.1875, 7 5/8 X 10 9/16 In. ....*Illus* 1050.00
Mechanical, Jacob & Co.Biscuits, Lucky Money Wheel, Tin, Litho, 8 In. 100.00
Mechanical, Joe Socko, Palooka, Box 465.00
Mechanical, Jolly Nigger, Cast Iron, Painted, 6 In. 100.00
Mechanical, Jolly Nigger, Dated March 14, '82 .... 300.00
Mechanical, Kicking Donkey, Original Paint, Cast Iron, 8 1/2 In. 125.00
Mechanical, Leapfrog 675.00
Mechanical, Little Joe, Cast Iron, Painted, 5 In. 110.00
Mechanical, Magic Bank, Church, Push Button, Door Slams, Deposits Coin 375.00
Mechanical, Monkey & Parrot, Iron ....175.00 To 225.00
Mechanical, Monkey & Parrot, Tin, Litho, German, 6 In. 140.00
Mechanical, Monkey, Tips Hat, Chein, Tin ....35.00 To 45.00
Mechanical, Organ & Monkey, Seated Monkey, Atop Organ, 1882, 7 In. 300.00
Mechanical, Organ Bank, Polychrome Paint, Cast Iron, 7 1/2 In. 445.00
Mechanical, Organ, Monkey, Cat & Dog On Top, Cast Iron, Crank, Painted 275.00
Mechanical, Owl, Iron ....185.00 To 350.00
Mechanical, Pineapple, Plastic 50.00
Mechanical, Professor Pug Frogs Great Bicycle Feat, Original Paint 650.00
Mechanical, Punch & Judy, Patented 1884, 7 3/4 In. 375.00
Mechanical, Rocket Ship ....17.00 To 35.00
Mechanical, Rooster, Movable Hand, Cast Iron, Polychrome, 6 1/4 In. 190.00
Mechanical, Royal Safe Deposit, Timson & Langill, 6 In. 200.00
Mechanical, Southern Comfort, Soldier, Shoots Into Bottle 85.00
Mechanical, Sweet Thrift, Tin 135.00

Mechanical, Tammany Hall, Patent Dec. 23, 1876, Enameled Cast Iron	550.00
Mechanical, Tammany, Patented 1873, 5 3/4 In.	300.00
Mechanical, Trick Pony	350.00
Mechanical, Uncle Remus	675.00
Mechanical, Uncle Sam, Cast Iron	13.00 To 225.00
Mechanical, William Tell, Polychrome Paint, Iron, 10 1/2 In.	325.00 To 375.00
Metz Beer Barrel	15.00
Michigan Avenue National Bank Of Chicago, Metal, Bronze, Key	20.00
Middy Boy, Gold Paint	95.00 To 135.00
Milk Wagon, Horse, & Driver, Cast Iron, Large	285.00
Monkey, Long Curling Tail, Iron, 8 1/2 In.	85.00
Monkey, Tips Hat, Tin, Chein	45.00
Mother Hubbard, Harper, Painted Cast Iron, 4 1/4 In.	1900.00
Mule, With Saddle, Cast Iron	35.00
Mulligan The Cop, Figural, Cast Iron, Painted	125.00 To 200.00
Mutt & Jeff, Cast Iron	85.00
Naval Officer, Cast Iron, Old Repaint, 5 3/4 In.	105.00
Norge Refrigerator	30.00
Old Dutch Cleanser, Tin Litho	25.00
Orphan Annie & Sandy, With Horseshoe	125.00
Owl, Cast Iron, Painted, 4 1/4 In.	150.00
Owl, Glass, 6 1/2 In.	7.50
Parrot, Pot Metal, Painted, 4 3/4 In.	135.00
Pepsi–Cola, 5 Cent Vending Machine	30.00 To 60.00
Piano, Cast Iron, Nickel Plate, 5 1/2 In.	100.00
Pig, Decker's Iowana, Cast Iron	85.00
Pig, Hand Painted, 14 X 11 In.	55.00
Pig, Light Brown, Glazed, 6 In.	65.00
Pig, Lum & Abner, Souvenir Of Dick Huddleston's Store, 1940, 2 In.	32.50
Pig, Sitting, Cast Iron, 10 1/2 In.	28.00
Pig, Sponging On Cream Ground, White Clay, 6 In.	65.00
Pig, Standing, Iron, I Made Chicago Famous, Dated 1902	95.00
Political, 2 Parties, 2 Slots, Under 1 Flag, Sand Cast, 1984	45.00
Porky Pig, Hull, Yellow & Blue Rose	25.00
Progresso Tomato Sauce, Tin	5.00
Public Band Of Detroit, Banthrico, Key, Tin	35.00
Pure Premium Gasoline, Tin	17.00
Puzzle Picture Box, Tin, Litho, 2 In.	90.00
Radio, Kenton, Cast Iron	65.00
Record Player Shape, Save For Your Brunswick, Metal	60.00
Red Goose Shoes, Iron	85.00 To 90.00
Red Goose Shoes, Squat, Painted, Cast Iron	350.00
Red Goose, Chalkware, 5 In.	30.00
Red Riding Hood, Tin, 4 1/2 In.	130.00
Refrigerator, Electrolux, White, Miniature	20.00 To 32.00
Refrigerator, G.E., Motor Top, Cast Iron	50.00
Remember Pearl Harbor, Ohio Art, Tin	22.00
Rex Hot Water Heater, Tin, Green Litho, Steel, 7 1/2 In.	37.50
Rhinoceros, Iron	315.00
Rock, Prudential, Metal, 1931	55.00
Rooster, Brass	95.00
Rooster, Cast Iron	65.00
Safe, Carpenter, Cast Iron, Painted, Harper, 4 1/2 In.	1500.00
Safe, Cast Iron, Painted, 6 1/4 In.	500.00
Safe, General Lee, Harper, Painted, Cast Iron, 5 1/2 In.	1300.00
Safe, Guarded By Bulldog, Tin	45.00
Safe, House, Combination, Burglar Proof, Dated 1897	100.00
Safe, Junior Safe Deposit, Combination	30.00
Safe, Sitting Pig & Keylock, Cast Iron	35.00
Santa Claus, Candy, 6 In.	50.00
Santa Claus, On Roof, Cast Iron	175.00
Santa Claus, Papier–Mache, 1950s	20.00
Santa Claus, Sleeping In Chair, Cast Iron, 7 In.	50.00
Santa Claus, Sleeping In Chair, Die Cast, Painted, 7 In.	25.00

Santa Claus, Sleeping In Chair, Plaster, Painted, 8 In. 40.00
Santa Claus, Standing, Chalkware 48.00
Santa Claus, Standing, Pot Metal 45.00
Shelf Clock, With Candy Container, Painted 50.00
Ship, When My Fortune Ship Comes In., Iron, Red Repaint, 5 1/2 In. 375.00
Shoe Shine, Red, Amsco, Decals, Red, 8 1/2 X 7 1/2 X 6 In. 14.00
Slot Machine, 10 Cent, Tin 10.00
Snoopy, Glass 8.00
Sparkle Plenty, In High Chair, Ceramic, 1930s 275.00
Stage Coach, Horses & Driver, Cast Iron 75.00
Stan Laurel, Plastic 10.00
Statue Of Liberty, Cast Iron, 6 In. 35.00
Store, Parlor, Cast Iron, Nickel Plated, 7 In. 275.00
Sunbonnet Girl, Cast Iron 350.00
Sunoco, Blue Triangle Design, Tin 10.00
Tank Truck, Iron, 4 X 1 3/4 In. 42.00
Teddy Bear, Chalkware 12.00
Teddy Bear, Glass 10.00
Telephone, Kanter's Baby Bell, Tin, Wooden, Painted, 10 In. 40.00
Television, Emerson, Football Game On Screen, 1950 .... 10.00
Three Birds Atop Bulbous Bank, Square Base, Scroddleware, 8 1/2 In. 265.00
Thrift, Eagle Pencil Co., Holds 35 Dimes, Round, Tin 25.00
Time Around The World, Cast Iron 185.00
Top Hat, Figural, Pass Around The Hat, Iron 125.00
Train, Marked DeWitt Clinton, Original Plate & Key, 6 In. 125.00
Trolley, Cast Iron, 4 1/2 In. ....185.00 To 250.00
Trunk, Tin, Patent 1888 .... 18.00
Turk, Seated In Chair, Smoking Pipe, 9 In. 20.00
Turkey, Cast Iron 45.00
Two—Face Black Man, Cast Iron 90.00
Two—Face Black Woman, Cast Iron 50.00
Two—Face Devil, Cast Iron 220.00
U.S.Mail Box, Stoneware, 3 3/4 In. 40.00
Washington, Bust, Cast Iron, Painted, 8 In. 700.00
Watch Me Grow Tall, Man With Hat, Tin, 6 In. 75.00
Wooden, Palmer Cox Decal 55.00
World Exposition, Chicago, Pottery, Painted, 1893, 6 In. 90.00
Yank Bank, Baseball, Silhouettes Of Gehrig & Dickey, Glass 40.00

There is much confusion about the terms Banko, Korean ware, and Sumida. We are using the terms in the way most often used by antiques dealers and collectors. Korean ware is now called "Sumida" and is listed in this book under that heading. Banko is a group of rustic Japanese wares made in the nineteenth and twentieth centuries. Some pieces are made of mosaics of colored clay, some are fanciful teapots. Redware and other materials were also used.

BANKO, Bowl, Vegetable, Primitive, Set Of 7 .... 495.00
Pitcher, Old Men, 9 In. 125.00
Saki Pot, Monkeys, 8 In. 135.00
Teapot, Elephant 75.00
Teapot, Figural, Duck, Cattail Finial Lid, Dark Brown, Tan, Blue 150.00
Teapot, Figural, Wood Duck 150.00
Tobacco Jar, Old Men 135.00
Vase, Man Shooting Another From Cannon, 8 In. 125.00
Vase, Pinched Mold, 2 Applied Boars, Signed, 8 3/4 In. 165.00
Wall Pocket, Figural, Owl, Enameled, Hanging, 7 1/2 In. 70.00

Barbershop collectibles range from the popular red and white striped pole that used to be found in front of every shop to the small scissors and tools of the trade. Barber chairs are wanted, especially the older models with elaborate iron trim.

BARBER, Backbar, Koken, 2 Mirrored Sections, Beveled, Oak 2850.00
Backbar, Marble Counter, Beveled Glass, 15 Ft.6 In. X 9 Ft.3 In. 10500.00
Backbar, Oak & Marble, One Stall, 1890s 1200.00

Chair, Child's, Pedestal, White 575.00
Chair, Child's, Wooden & Porcelain 550.00
Chair, Child's, Wooden Horse's Head, Upholstered Seat, Metal Frame 190.00
Chair, Hydraulic, Koch, Brass Trim, Suede Cloth, Oak 2500.00
Chair, Koch, Carved, Oak 475.00
Chair, Koken, Child's, Porcelain, Pedestal, Upholstered 350.00
Chair, Koken, Wooden 875.00
Chair, Koken, Wooden & Porcelain 550.00
Mug Rack, Counter Model, Crystal Case Co., Dated 1897, 36 In. 1350.00
Pole, Carved Wood, Late 19th Century 165.00
Pole, Porcelain, 7 Ft.6 In. 450.00
Pole, Virginia 1250.00
Pole, Wooden, Hand Carved 250.00
Pole, Wooden, Polychrome, Turned Form, Ball Top, American, 90 In. 150.00
Pole, Wooden, Turned, Acorn Ends, Red, White, Iron Bracket, 34 1/2 In. 125.00
Pole, Yellow Acorn Finial, Black & White, 42 1/2 In., Pair 210.00
Reservoir, Hot Water, Tin & Brass, C.1880, 15 X 18 1/2 In. 370.00
Shaving Brush, Monogram, Silver Plate Handle 12.00
Shaving Kit, Eveready 15.00
Sign, Trade, Red, White, & Blue, 48 In. 80.00
Strop, Leather 8.00

Barometers are used to forecast the weather. Antique barometers with elaborate wooden cases and brass trim are the most desirable. Mercury column barometers are popular with collectors. It is difficult to find someone to repair a broken example so be sure your barometer is in working condition.

BAROMETER, Banjo, Inlaid Mahogany Veneer, Seashells, I.Tognitti, 38 In. 325.00
Banjo, Mahogany Veneer, Thermometer, Amadio & Son, 38 1/2 In. 300.00
Banjo, Mahogany, A.Moilnari Halesworth, Line Inlay, 39 In. 250.00
Cistern, C.Ciuati, Thermometer, Inlaid Stringing, Mahogany, 36 In. 1320.00
Cistern, Dollond, Thermometer, Cushion Form, Mahogany, 39 3/4 In. 2090.00
I.Vecchio, English, Thermometer, Brass Urn Finial, 38 In. 3410.00
Inlaid Shells & Flowers, C.A.Cantil, Mahogany, 38 1/2 In. 1200.00
L.C.Francis, Philadelphia, Engraved, Mahogany, C.1790, 38 In. 2310.00
Louis XIV, Boulle Marquetry, Ormolu Dial, Enameled, Brass, 45 In. 2200.00
Louis XIV, Ormolu Dial, Figure Of Vanity, Marquetry, 45 In. 2200.00
Mahogany Veneer, Thermometer, F.Salteri & Co., London, 38 1/2 In. 175.00
Mahogany, Hayden & Gibbard, Thermometer, 3 Ft.4 1/4 In. 700.00
Rosewood Veneer, T.B.Matthews, Engraved Brass Face, 38 In. 200.00
Stick, Oak, Admiral Fitzroy, Altitude Indicator, 39 1/2 X 20 In. 500.00
Surveyor, Brass Case, Adjustable Scale Magnifier, Case, 1900 .... 180.00
Thermometer, Brass Face, Broken Pediment, Inlaid Mahogany, 37 In. 660.00
Thermometer, George III, Inlaid Shells & Paterae, Mahogany 770.00
Thermometer, Leaf Inlay, Mahogany, 19th Century, 39 1/2 In. 500.00

Basalt is a special type of ceramic invented by Josiah Wedgwood in the eighteenth century. It is a fine-grained, unglazed stoneware.

BASALT, Creamer, Black, Impressed J.Glass, Hanley, 4 1/4 In. 45.00
Plaque, Mother & Child, Signed Mayer, 4 1/2 In. 290.00

Baskets of all types are popular with collectors. Indian, Japanese, African, Shaker, and many other kinds of baskets can be found. Of course, baskets are still being made; so the collector must learn to tell the age and style of the basket to determine the value.

BASKET, Apple, 14 In. 35.00
Berry, New Jersey 48.00
Braided, Round, 10 X 2 In. 22.00
Buttocks, Red & Natural Woven Design, Splint, 4 1/4 X 4 1/4 In. 85.00
Buttocks, Split Willow, Large 95.00
Buttocks, Woven Splint, Bentwood Handle, 8 X 8 X 4 1/2 In. 155.00
Buttocks, Woven Splint, Natural & Brown Design, 5 X 6 X 3 In. 145.00
Cheese, Handmade, 16 In. 35.00
Cheese, Splint, Early 19th Century, Hexagonal Base, 12 X 7 1/4 In. 200.00

Double Swing Handle, Splint, 6 X 16 X 13 1/2 In.	85.00
Egg, Nantucket, 1 Handle, C.1920	425.00
Egg, Woven Splint, 14 X 16 In.	95.00
Flower Picking, Red, Flat, 14 X 27 In.	75.00
Laundry, Splint, Woven, Bentwood Rim Handles, 20 X 33 X 13 1/2 In.	275.00
Laundry, Woven Splint, End Handles, 17 X 26 1/2 In.	60.00
Lunch, Attached Cover, Opening On Both Sides, Wicker	20.00
Market, Splint, Handle, 14 X 22 X 7 1/4 In.	50.00
Melon Rib, Woven Splint, 10 X 6 1/2 In.	150.00
Nantucket Lightship, Carved Handles, Sewing, 11 X 3 3/4 In.	450.00
Nantucket, 2 Handles, Boyer, C.1915	435.00
Nantucket, 2 Small Handles, 7 1/2 X 3 1/2 In.	650.00
Nantucket, Swing Handle, Round, 6 1/2 X 5 In.	800.00
Picnic, 4 Piece Closing Top, Handle, English, C.1910	75.00
Picnic, Tin Lined, Wicker	20.00
Picnic, Woven Wicker, Cover, Oval, Braided Handles, 18 In.	36.50
Rye Straw, 11 1/2 X 4 1/2 In.	45.00
Rye Straw, Pennsylvania, 12 X 4 In.	45.00
Rye, 13 In.	30.00
Rye, Beehive, Fitted Lid, 16 In.	85.00
Sewing, Splint, Brass Table Clamp, Round Pad At Top, 5 In.	45.00
Sewing, Wicker, 4 Leg Stool, Items Inside	39.00
Sewing, Wicker, 7 1/2 In.	12.00
Splint Melon Rib, Handle, 18 1/2 X 21 1/2 X 10 1/2 In.	160.00
Splint, Black Paint, Red & Black Design	110.00
Splint, Charcoal Carrying, 27 X 19 In.	115.00
Splint, Cheese Weave, C.1800, 8 X 15 In.	495.00
Splint, Dark Green Paint, Cover, Round, 14 1/2 X 13 In.	150.00
Splint, Handle, 8 1/2 X 9 X 4 1/2 In.	90.00
Splint, Handles, 18 X 16 In.	85.00
Splint, Melon Rib, Handle, 11 X 5 In.	105.00
Splint, Melon Rib, Handle, Gray Finish, 7 1/2 X 9 X 4 In.	165.00
Splint, Missouri, Bent Handle, 15 X 11 1/2 In.	100.00
Splint, New England, Handles, 25 X 19 In.	210.00
Splint, Primitive, Footed, 7 1/2 X 10 1/2 X 6 1/2 In.	115.00
Splint, Radiating Ribs, Bentwood Handle, 12 X 16 In.	95.00
Splint, Wall, 3 Tier, American, Open Weave, 19th Century, 22 In.	475.00
Splint, Wooden, Footed, Rectangular, 7 1/2 X 10 1/2 X 6 1/2 In.	115.00
Splint, Woven, Bentwood Swivel Handle, 10 1/2 X 5 3/4 In.	175.00
Swing Handle, Old Red, 15 In.	245.00
Tobacco, Woven Splint, Old Red Exterior, 38 X 38 In.	150.00
Twist Rope Handle, Bow At Side, Tapered Square Shape, 5 3/4 X 6 In.	70.00
Wicker, Bail Handle, Bottom 8 In.Diam.	50.00
Wicker, Lid, Cloth Handle, Round, 18 In.	45.00
Woven Splint Loom, Bentwood Hanging Loop, 13 1/2 X 15 1/2 In.	145.00
Woven Splint, 8 X 6 In.	75.00
Woven Splint, Bentwood Handle, 4 X 3 1/4 In.	85.00
Woven Splint, Bentwood Handle, 9 X 7 1/4 In.	40.00
Woven Splint, Bentwood Handle, Elongated Oval, 16 1/2 X 10 1/2 In.	130.00
Woven Splint, Bentwood Handles, Red & Blue, 9 X 13 X 4 1/2 In.	65.00
Woven Splint, Bentwood Rim & Handle, 10 1/2 X 14 1/4 X 9 1/2 In.	65.00
Woven Splint, Bentwood Sieve Handle, 6 X 3 3/4 In.	55.00
Woven Splint, Bentwood Swivel Handle On Wire Loops, 9 1/2 X 6 In.	90.00
Woven Splint, Bentwood Swivel Handle, Round, 16 X 11 In.	165.00
Woven Splint, Blue & Natural, Rewrapped Rim, 15 X 12 In.	55.00
Woven Splint, Cover, Potato Print Design & Natural, 23 X 14 1/2 In.	95.00
Woven Splint, Faded Orange & Yellow, Handle, 9 1/2 X 19 In.	45.00
Woven Splint, Lid, Blue & Yellow Watercolor Design, 16 1/2 In.	65.00
Woven Splint, Lid, Red & Blue Potato Print, 15 X 21 X 11 3/4 In.	45.00
Woven Splint, Rim Handles, 14 X 10 In.	35.00

Ernest Batchelder made ceramic and copper items in Los Angeles, California. He died in 1957.

BATCHELDER, Bowl, Blue, 6 In. 175.00
Tile, Antelope, 4 X 4 In. 50.00
Tile, Floral Relief, 4 In. 45.00
Tile, Floral, Classic, 4 X 4 In. 45.00
Tile, Heavy Border, 7 X 12 In. 95.00
Tile, Lion, 4 X 4 In. 50.00

Batman and Robin are characters from a comic strip by Bob Kane that started in 1939. In 1966, the characters became part of a popular television series. There have been radio and movie serials that featured the pair.

BATMAN, Album, Batman & Robin, 1966 .... 12.50
Bank, Figural, Ceramic, 6 In. 20.00
Bank, Figural, Robin, Ceramic, 6 In. 20.00
Bank, Robin, Ceramic, 7 In., Pair 30.00
Bookends, Batman & Robin, 1966 .... 35.00
Box, Ice Cream, Colored, 1966 .... 8.00
Cards, 1966 .... 45.00
Gum Cards, Complete Set 30.00
Hat, Dated 1966 .... 5.00
Lamp, Figural, Cape 60.00
Night–Light 35.00
Ring 10.00

Battersea enamels are enamels painted on copper and made in the Battersea district of London from about 1750 to 1756. Many similar enamels are mistakenly called "Battersea."

BATTERSEA, Box, Blue & White, Oval Quotation Top, 1800 .... 295.00
Tieback, 2 Commodore Truxton, 1 Lord Nelson, Enamel, Set Of 3 .... 495.00
Tieback, Enameled, Pair 300.00

J. A. Bauer moved his Kentucky pottery to Los Angeles, California, in 1909. The company made art pottery after 1912 and dinnerwares after 1929.

BAUER, Carafe, Yellow, Wooden Handle 18.00
Coffee Server, Orange & Red, Wooden Handle 20.00
Pitcher, Orange 29.50
Plate, Cobalt, 12 In. 20.00
Plate, Poppies, Hand Painted, Signed Louis, 1900, 7 1/2 In. 45.00

Porcelains of all types were made in the region known as Bavaria. In the nineteenth century, the mark often included the word "Bavaria." After 1871, the words "Bavaria, Germany" were used. Listed here are pieces that include the name Bavaria in some form, but major porcelain makers such as Rosenthal are listed in their own categories.

BAVARIA, Bowl, Dark Green Rim, Fruit Interior, 10 1/2 In. 16.00
Bowl, Dresser, Child's Portrait On Cover, Gold Tracery, Schumann 45.00
Bowl, Roses Pattern, 9 In. 18.00
Cake Set, Floral, 1 Large & 6 Small Plates 65.00
Chocolate Set, Blue To White Ground, Roses, Crown Mark, 13 Piece 235.00
Chocolate Set, Floral 70.00
Cup & Saucer, Demitasse, Mittertiech, Platinum Embossed, Set Of 8 .... 35.00
Cup, Saucer, & Plate, Orchids, Tirschenreuth 35.00
Fish Set, Floral, Ruffled Rim, Platter & 12 Plates, Austria 375.00
Mustache Cup, Pink & Yellow Mums, White To Pink 32.00
Pitcher, Blackberry Design, Gold Lizard Handle, D.Churchill, 9 In. 110.00
Pitcher, Pheasants, Foliage, Marigold Luster Trim 35.00
Plate, Hand Painted Leaves, Gold Rim, Marked, 10 1/2 In. 18.00
Plate, Portrait, Women Veiled With Roses, Gold Border 100.00
Syrup, Cream Roses, Pale Green, Artist Signed 35.00
Tea Set, Child's, Circus Design, Luster Trim, Marked, 15 Piece 125.00
Tea Set, Child's, Nursery Rhymes Design, 15 Piece 150.00
Tea Set, Child's, Sevres Pattern, Green Border, Gold Trim, 16 Piece 80.00
Teapot, Sugar, Creamer, Cup & Saucer, Dessert Plate, 23 Piece 75.00

Vase, Iridescent Blue, Lacy Openwork Rim, Cylindrical, 8 1/4 In. 22.00
Vase, Yellow Corn, Dragon Handle, Mug Shape, Hand Painted, 5 3/4 In. 40.00

> *Plates marked "R. K. Beck" were made by Buffalo Pottery and others. R. K. Beck was an artist who specialized in wildlife paintings. Many of his designs were reproduced on decals which were applied to plates.*

BECK, Plaque, Stag & Doe, 13 In. 68.00
Plate, Mallards, Swimming, 8 In. 20.00
Plate, Woodland Scene, 2 Deer, Buffalo Pottery, 9 1/2 In. 48.00
Platter & 4 Plates, Deer, 5 Piece 245.00

> *"Beehive, Austria," or "Beehive, Vienna," is a term used in English-speaking countries to refer to the many types of decorated porcelain bearing a mark that looks like a beehive. The mark is actually a shield, viewed upside down. It was first used in 1744 by the Royal Porcelain Manufactory of Vienna. Many factories have used it since.*

BEEHIVE, see also Royal Vienna
BEEHIVE, Basket, Ormolu Frame & Handle, Floral Spray On White, Marked, 4 In. 65.00
Basket, Reticulated, Floral, Gold Ormolu Frame, Marked Wachterbach 35.00
Cheese Dish, Autumn Flowers, Leaves, Vienna Mark, 3 In. 52.00
Cheese Dish, Floral, Vienna Mark, 3 In. 48.00
Ewer, Mythical Scenes, Handles, Stand, Marked, 23 1/4 In., Pair 1980.00
Plate, Diana, Paris & Helena, Cobalt Border, Marked, 9 7/8 In., Pair 550.00
Vase, Marie De'Medici, Charles V, Marked, C.1900, 21 5/8 In., Pair 1650.00
Vase, Oval Portrait Of 3 Women, Austrian, 11 In. 60.00

> *Beer was sold in kegs or returnable bottles until 1934. The first patent for a can was issued to the American Can Company in September of that year; and Gotfried Kruger Brewing Company, Newark, New Jersey, was the first to use the can. The cone-top can was first made in 1935, the aluminum pop-top in 1962. Collectors should look for cans in good condition, with no dents or rust. Serious collectors prefer cans that have been opened from the bottom.*

BEER CAN, Ballantine Beer 52.00
Battlin Bulldogs, Full 20.00
Buckeye Beer, Cone Top 25.00
Dow, Canadian, Cone Top 100.00
Edelbrew Brewing 30.00
Elvis Beer 3.00
F.W.Cook Brewing 35.00
Falstaff, Cone Top 16.00
Fitgers, Cone Top 27.00
Fort Pitt, Foil .... .50 To 1.00
Fort Schuyler Ale, Cone, 12 Oz. 50.00
Gold Bond, Small 4.00
Grainbelt Beer, Cone Top 25.00
Huber, Cone Top 34.00
J.R., Empty 12.00
Kuebler Cream Ale, Cone, 32 Oz. 550.00
Miller High–Life, Paper Label, 3 1/2 In. 9.00
Old Topper Ale, Crown Top 48.00
Pfiffer Brewing, Statue 30.00
Pure Spring, Gold Ground 20.00
Razorback, Set Of 6 .... 10.00
White Seal, Cone Top 45.00

> *Bells have been made of porcelain, china, or metal through the centuries. All types are collected. Favorites include glass bells, figural bells, school bells, and cowbells. Be careful not to buy a bell made from an old glass goblet.*

BELL, Art Nouveau, Graceful Lady, Hotel 19.00
Colonial Lady, Brass, England, 3 1/2 In. 65.00
Cow, Holstein Label, Leather Collar 20.00

Dated 1878, Brass	45.00
Elizabethan Lady, Brass, 5 1/8 X 2 7/8 In. ....35.00 To	85.00
Firehouse, New Haven Clock Co., 1886	350.00
French Peasant Woman, With Jug, Brass, 5 3/4 In.	85.00
Full Owl, Handle	170.00
Harness, Brass, Iron Reinforced Leather Bar, 18 In., Set Of 4	43.00
Hemony, Knight With Helmet, Figural Handle, Brass, 6 1/4 In.	75.00
Hotel, 1920s	20.00
Hotel, Desk, Brass	75.00
Indian Head, Lamasery, Brass, 7 1/4 X 3 1/4 In.	95.00
Lady In Hoopskirt, Muff & Hat, Brass, 5 3/8 X 3 1/8 In.	55.00
Lady In Hoopskirt, Powdered Wig, Fan, Brass, 5 3/4 X 3 1/2 In.	75.00
Lady, Brass, 5 In.	65.00
Lady, Colonial, Tiered Skirt, Brass, 4 In.	59.00
Lady, Southern Belle, Carrying Basket, Brass, 5 In.	65.00
Nesting Herons, 2 Fish Head Handles, Embossed, Brass, 4 1/8 In.	88.00
Nevada Silver Mine, Brass, 1870s, 12 In.	150.00
Optimist International Club, Brass	80.00
Quaker Man, Brass	28.00
Railroad, Locomotive, Brass	575.00
School Desk, Brass, Wooden Handle, Small	55.00
School, Brass, 10 In.	52.00
School, Brass, 11 In.	60.00
Schoolhouse, Cradle, Cast Iron, 21 In.	150.00
Sheep, Brass, Leather Strap ....10.00 To	40.00
Sheep, Leather & Metal Strap Mounted, Brass, Set Of 3	60.00
Ship's, Metal, Side Mounting Bracket, 6 In.	15.00
Sleigh, Acorn Shape, Riveted To Leather Belt, 1880, Set Of 27	100.00
Squirrel, Handles, Brass, 3 1/2 In.	39.00
Train, Brass, No Yoke	250.00
Trolley, Brass, Complete	85.00
Trolley, St.Louis Co., Brass	75.00
Woman, French Peasant, Jug, Brass, 6 1/4 X 3 1/4 In.	85.00

Belle Ware was made in 1903 by Carl V. Helmschmied. In 1904 he started a corporation known as the Helmschmied Manufacturing Company. His factory closed in 1908 and he worked on his own until his death in 1934.

BELLE WARE, Box, Pink, 6 In.	258.00
Jar, Dresser, Open, Violets, 4 1/4 In.	150.00

Belleek china is made in Ireland, other European countries, and the United States. The glaze is creamy yellow and appears wet. The first Belleek was made in 1857. All pieces listed are Irish Belleek. The mark changed through the years. The first mark, black, dates from 1863 to 1890. The second mark, black, dates from 1891 to 1926 and includes the words "Co. Fermanagh, Ireland." The third mark, black, dates from 1926 to 1946 and has the words "Deanta in Eirinn." The fourth mark, same as the third mark but green, dates from 1946 to 1955. The fifth mark, green, dates from 1955 to 1965 and has an R in a circle added in the upper right. The sixth mark, green, dates after 1965 and the words "Co. Fermanagh" have been omitted.

BELLEEK, see also Ceramic Art Co.; Haviland; Lenox; Ott & Brewer; Willets

BELLEEK, Basket, Bird's Nest, Flowers & Leaves On Rim, Marked, 4 X 4 In.	850.00
Basket, Floral, 4 Stand Handle, Round, Impressed Mark, 12 In.	1100.00
Basket, Heart Shape, Pearlized Braid On Top, Signed, 4 1/2 In.	190.00
Basket, Msydenham, 3 Strand, 10 In.	1850.00
Basket, Purse, Pearl, 2nd Black Mark, 6 In.	450.00
Biscuit Barrel, 2nd Black Mark, Green Trim, 8 In.	1050.00
Bowl, Candy, Double Bucket, Pearl Luster, 1st Black Mark, 12 In.	850.00
Bowl, Shell, Pink To Cream, 1st Black Mark, 5 X 6 In., Set Of 4	595.00
Bowl, Shell, Pink Trim, 1st Black Mark, 5 X 6 In.	412.00
Bread Plate, Grass, 1st Black Mark	150.00
	250.00

Bread Plate, Tridacna, Pink & Gold Trim, 1st Black Mark, 11 In. 210.00
Breakfaast Set, Echinus, Pearl, 1st Black Mark 2800.00
Breakfast Set, Neptune, Pink Trim, 2nd Black Mark 2250.00
Breakfast Set, Tridacna, Pearl, 2nd Black Mark 1850.00
Bucket, Butter, Shamrocks, Dark Green Mark 40.00
Bust, Clyte, 2nd Black Mark 1000.00
Bust, Parnell, 1st Black Mark, 11 In. 2800.00
Cake Plate, Basket Weave, 3rd Black Mark, 10 1/2 In. 55.00
Cake Plate, Neptune, Pink Trim, 2nd Black Mark 120.00
Candlestick, Allingham, Cob Luster Handle, 2nd Black Mark 375.00
Candlestick, Thorn, 2nd Black Mark, 7 In. 195.00
Centerpiece, Table, Pink, Flowered, 2nd Black Mark, 12 In. 1850.00
Centerpiece, Trumpet, 2nd Black Mark, Pink Trim, 12 1/2 In. 1750.00
Compote, Greek, Footed, Gilded, 2nd Black Mark, 10 In.Diam. 750.00
Condiment Set, Holder, Shamrock Pattern, 2nd Black Mark, 3 Piece 495.00
Cornucopia, Cherub, 1st Black Mark, 7 In. 1850.00
Creamer, Celtic, Red, Gilded, 3rd Black Mark 190.00
Creamer, Fishscale, Green Mark 38.00
Creamer, Hexagon, Pink Trim, 2nd Black Mark 125.00
Creamer, Mask, 3rd Black Mark, 5 In. 85.00
Cup & Saucer, 3rd Black Mark, Demitasse 60.00
Cup & Saucer, Artichoke, 1st Black Mark 145.00
Cup & Saucer, Basket Weave, 2nd Black Mark 45.00
Cup & Saucer, Cone, Green Trim, 2nd Black Mark 95.00
Cup & Saucer, Echinus, 1st Black Mark 120.00
Cup & Saucer, Echinus, Pink & Gilt Trim, 1st Black Mark 145.00
Cup & Saucer, Grasses, 1st Black Mark ....125.00 To 225.00
Cup & Saucer, Harp & Shamrock, 2nd Black Mark 55.00
Cup & Saucer, Institute, Pink, Gilt Trim, 1st Black Mark, Initial 150.00
Cup & Saucer, Limpet, 3rd Black Mark, Demitasse 50.00
Cup & Saucer, Limpet, Pink & Gilt Trim, 3rd Black Mark, Demitasse 85.00
Cup & Saucer, Mask, 1st Black Mark 110.00
Cup & Saucer, Mustache, Gold Trim, 1st Black Mark 195.00
Cup & Saucer, Neptune, Green Trim, 2nd Black Mark ....65.00 To 105.00
Cup & Saucer, Neptune, Green Trim, 3rd Black Mark 83.00
Cup & Saucer, Neptune, Pink To White, 2nd Black Mark ....95.00 To 125.00
Cup & Saucer, Rose & Pansy, Demitasse 35.00
Cup & Saucer, Rosebud, Demitasse 35.00
Cup & Saucer, Shamrock, 1st Black Mark, Low Shape 58.00
Cup & Saucer, Shamrock, 2nd Black Mark ....45.00 To 50.00
Cup & Saucer, Shamrock, 3rd Black Mark, Demitasse 70.00
Cup & Saucer, Shamrock, Basket Weave, 3rd Black Mark 35.00
Cup & Saucer, Shamrock, Harp Handle, 3rd Black Mark 83.00
Cup & Saucer, Shell Pattern, 2nd Black Mark 125.00
Cup & Saucer, Thistle, 1st Black Mark ....185.00 To 225.00
Cup & Saucer, Tridacna, 1st Black Mark 125.00
Cup & Saucer, Tridacna, Green Tint, 2nd Black Mark, 4 1/2 In. 115.00
Cup & Saucer, Tridacna, Green Trim, 2nd Black Mark, Demitasse 95.00
Dinner Set, Child's, Black Mark, 12 Piece 395.00
Dish, Covered, Shells, 1st Black Mark, Registry Mark, 4 1/2 In. 550.00
Dish, Muffin, Covered, Shells, 1st Black Mark, Registry, 4 1/2 In. 525.00
Dish, Shell, Pink Edge, 1st Black Mark, 5 X 6 In. 130.00
Dragon Shell, 1st Black Mark, 7 In. 1250.00
Easter Egg, Green Mark 75.00
Egg Frame, Gilt Trim, 1st Black Mark 225.00
Eggcup, Basket Weave, 1st Black Mark 95.00
Eggcup, Primrose, 1st Black Mark 95.00
Ewer, Aberdeen, 2nd Black Mark, Pair 1800.00
Figurine, Affection, 1st Black Mark, 14 In. 1800.00
Figurine, Dragon Shell, 1st Black Mark, 7 In. 1250.00
Figurine, Frog, 2nd Black Mark, 4 1/2 In. 475.00
Figurine, Meditation, 2nd Green Mark, 15 In. 525.00
Figurine, Spaniel On Pillow, 3rd Green Mark 100.00
Figurine, Swan, 1st Black Mark, 4 3/4 In. 195.00

Figurine, Swan, 2nd Black Mark, Small	85.00
Figurine, Virgin Mary, 3rd Black Mark, 12 In.	725.00
Flower Holder, Sea Horse, 3rd Black Mark	192.00
Flower Holder, Sea Horse, Cob Luster Trim, 3rd Black Mark	175.00
Flowerpot, Applied Flowers, 2nd Black Mark, 4 1/4 In.	195.00
Flowerpot, No.D222, 3rd Black Mark, 3 1/2 In.	45.00
Flowerpot, No.D51, 11 In.	695.00
Flowerpot, Shamrock, 1st Green Mark, 4 1/2 In.	35.00
Font, Angel, 2nd Black Mark	690.00
Font, Holy Water, 1st Green Mark	69.00
Frog, 2nd Black Mark, 4 1/2 In.	475.00
Honey Pot, Shamrock, 2nd Black Mark, 8 In.	535.00
Jam Jar, Ribbon, 1st Black Mark, 6 1/2 In.	265.00
Jar, Celtic Design, Gilded, Tan, 1st Black Mark, Small	225.00
Jardiniere, Floral, Coral Handles, 2nd Black Mark, 7 X 9 In.	1199.00
Jardiniere, Flowered, Footed, 2nd Black Mark, 10 1/2 In.	1750.00
Jug, Harp Handle, 1st Black Mark, Large	400.00
Jug, Snail, 1st Black Mark, 7 In.	575.00
Kettle, Echinus, Pink & Gilt Trim, 1st Black Mark, Large	585.00
Kettle, Shamrock, No.D386, 3rd Black Mark, Large	198.00
Kettle, Water, Grasses, 1st Black Mark, Large	950.00
Mug, Fruit & Reindeer Design	95.00
Mug, Shamrock, 2nd Black Mark	100.00
Mustache Cup & Saucer, Ring Handle, Gilt Trim, 1st Black Mark	195.00
Pitcher, Harp Handle, 1st Blue Mark, 5 1/2 In.	250.00
Pitcher, Harp Handle, Gold Trim, 1904, 1st Black Mark, White	295.00
Pitcher, Vines, 2nd Black Mark, Pink, 4 In.	85.00
Plaque, Commemorative, Collector's Society	75.00
Plate, 1st Black Mark, 6 1/2 In.	22.50
Plate, Celtic, 3rd Black Mark, 5 3/4 In.	75.00
Plate, Christmas, 1970, Castle Caldwell	80.00
Plate, Christmas, 1971, Celtic Cross ....45.00 To	100.00
Plate, Echinus, Pink & Gilt Trim, 1st Black Mark, 7 In.	85.00
Plate, Echinus, Pink & Gilt Trim, 1st Black Mark, 9 In.	145.00
Plate, Grasses, 1st Black Mark, 5 In.	65.00
Plate, Greek, Blue, Gilded, 2nd Black Mark, 9 1/2 In.	350.00
Plate, Institute, Pink, Gilt Trim, Monogram, 1st Black Mark, 7 In.	135.00
Plate, Lily, Green Trim, 2nd Black Mark, 6 In.	45.00
Plate, Lily, Green, 2nd Black Mark, 6 In., Set Of 4	145.00
Plate, Mask, 1st Black Mark, 6 In.	40.00
Plate, Shamrock, 1st Green Mark, 7 In., Set Of 8	75.00
Plate, Shamrock, Handles, 3rd Black Mark, 10 1/2 In.	55.00
Plate, Thorn Pattern, Pink, Gold Trim, 2nd Black Mark, 9 In.	475.00
Plate, Tridacna, 7 In.	25.00
Plate, Tridacna, No.D467, Green Tint, 8 In.	36.00
Powder Bowl, Mask, Cover, Inside Luster, 2nd Black Mark	195.00
Salt, Shamrock Shape, White & Green, 2nd Black Mark	60.00
Salt, Wink, No.D1573, Pearl Luster, Impressed Mark, Fermanagh	210.00
Shamrock, Green, 3rd Black Mark, 7 In.	225.00
Shell, Dolphin, 1st Black Mark, 5 1/2 In.	1650.00
Spill, Cleary, 1st Black Mark, 4 In.	290.00
Spill, Lily, 2nd Black Mark	125.00
Spoon Holder, Boat Shape, 1st Black Mark, 4 1/2 In.	240.00
Spoon Rest, Boat, 1st Black Mark, 4 In.	275.00
Sugar & Creamer, Cleary, 3rd Green Mark	50.00
Sugar & Creamer, Echinus Pattern, Open, Pink Trim, 2nd Black Mark	325.00
Sugar & Creamer, Gold Handle & Edges, 3rd Black Mark	150.00
Sugar & Creamer, Limpet, Gold Trim, 3rd Black Mark	125.00
Sugar & Creamer, Lotus, 3rd Black Mark ....84.00 To	162.50
Sugar & Creamer, Neptune, Green Trim, 2nd Black Mark	125.00
Sugar & Creamer, Shamrock, Basket Weave, 3rd Black Mark	75.00
Sugar & Creamer, Tridacna, 1st Black Mark	110.00
Sugar & Creamer, Tridacna, Pink Trim, 2nd Black Mark	162.00
Sugar & Creamer, Yellow Bows, Green Mark	80.00

Sugar, Ribbon, Pink Trim, 2nd Black Mark 35.00
Swan, 2nd Black Mark 85.00
Tankard, Berries, Marked, 5 In. 65.00
Tea Set, Cone, Green Trim, 2nd Black Mark, 6 Piece 435.00
Tea Set, Green Mark, 3 Piece 195.00
Tea Set, Low Lily, Green Trim, 2nd Black Mark 975.00
Tea Set, Neptune, Pink, 1st Black Mark 1900.00
Tea Set, Tray, Grasses Pattern, 1st Black Mark, 12 X 15 In. 595.00
Tea Set, Tridacna, 1st Black Mark, 8 Piece 2100.00
Teapot, Basket Weave, 2nd Black Mark 145.00
Teapot, Chinese, Dragon Spout, Footed, 1st Black Mark, 9 1/2 In. 3500.00
Teapot, Grasses Pattern, 1st Black Mark, 7 In. ....350.00 To 595.00
Teapot, Grasses, Handled, 1st Black Mark, 8 1/4 In. 750.00
Teapot, Harp & Shamrock, 2nd Black Mark 200.00
Teapot, Hexagon, Green, 2nd Black Mark 225.00
Teapot, Hexagon, Pink Trim, 2nd Black Mark 425.00
Teapot, Limpet, 3rd Black Mark 295.00
Teapot, Neptune, Green Trim, Medium, 2nd Black Mark 238.00
Teapot, Neptune, Pink Trim, 3rd Black Mark 225.00
Teapot, Pink, 2nd Black Mark 325.00
Teapot, Shamrock, Basket Weave, 2nd Black Mark, 5 1/2 In. 225.00
Teapot, Sugar, & Creamer, Shell Pattern, 2nd Black Mark 450.00
Teapot, Tridacna, D357, 1st Black Mark, Large 250.00
Teapot, Tridacna, Gilt Trim, 2nd Black Mark 295.00
Teapot, Tridacna, Green Trim, 2nd Black Mark 425.00
Teapot, Tridacna, No.D475, Gilt Trim, White, Large 295.00
Tray, Bread, Limpet, 2nd Green Mark, 11 In. 60.00
Tray, Shell, Pink, 1st Black Mark 1850.00
Tray, Tea, Echinus, No.D649, Pearl Luster Rim, Leaves, 1st Black Mark 690.00
Tray, Tea, Scalloped, 2nd Black Mark, Oval, 17 X 14 In. 250.00
Tray, Tea, Thorn, Yellow, Burnt Orange Webbing, Impressed Mark 1250.00
Tray, Tea, Tridacna, Pink, 2nd Black Mark, 16 In. 300.00
Tumbler, No.D280, 2nd Black Mark, 4 1/2 In. 98.00
Urn, Tea, Dragon, 4 Paws, Brown, Purple, 1st Black Mark, 9 X 6 In. 3800.00
Vase, Aberdeen, Applied Floral, Scroll Handle, 3rd Black Mark, 9 In. 750.00
Vase, Applied Floral, Iridescent, 2nd Black Mark, 9 X 4 1/2 In. 550.00
Vase, Applied Flowers, 2nd Black Mark, 9 In. 550.00
Vase, Bud, Shamrock, 1st Black Mark, Miniature 125.00
Vase, Cone Pattern, Green Mark, 4 X 4 In. 35.00
Vase, Fish, 1st Black Mark, 7 1/2 In. 625.00
Vase, Flying Fish, Pink Trim, 2nd Black Mark, 4 3/8 X 2 3/4 In. 495.00
Vase, Frog, 1st Black Mark, 5 1/2 In. 575.00
Vase, Grape Pattern, Yellow Trim, Green Mark, 7 In. 47.50
Vase, Honeysuckle, Pink Interior, 1st Black Mark, 7 In. 950.00
Vase, Lily Field Scene, 13 1/2 In. 200.00
Vase, Marine Center, 1st Black Mark, Large 2000.00
Vase, Molded Grape Pattern, Green Mark, 7 In. 45.00
Vase, Pedestal, Applied Flowers & Leaves, 3rd Black Mark, 8 In. 150.00
Vase, Red & White Roses, Gold Handles & Neck, 15 In. 350.00
Vase, Triple Fish, 1st Black Mark, 16 In. 2450.00
Vase, Triple, 2nd Black Mark, 8 In. 350.00
Vase, Upright Cornucopia Shape, 2nd Black Mark, 11 1/2 In. 1250.00
Wall Pocket, Swan, Gilded, 1st Black Mark, 9 In. 1450.00

Bennington ware was the product of two factories working in Bennington, Vermont. Both firms were out of business by 1896. The wares include brown and yellow mottled pottery, Parian, scroddled ware, stoneware, graniteware, yellowware, and Staffordshire–like vases.

BENNINGTON TYPE, Cuspidor 55.00
Figurine, Buffalo, 5 1/2 X 7 1/2 In. 250.00
Figurine, Pig, 5 X 2 In. 225.00
Match Holder, Dog With Hat & Pipe 25.00
Spittoon, Design 65.00
Tankard, Hand Painted Flower Design, 12 3/8 In. 400.00

BENNINGTON, Bottle, Coachman, Tassels, 1849 Mark, 11 In. 750.00
  Bottle, Pretzel, Brown, Applied Pebbles, 5 1/2 X 3 1/2 In. 48.00
  Bottle, Toby, 1840 Mark On Base, 10 3/4 In. 325.00
  Bottle, Toby, 1849 Mark, 10 1/2 In. 850.00
  Bowl, Rockingham Glaze, 10 In. 80.00
  Bowl, Rockingham, Raised Ribbed, 9 X 4 In. 120.00
  Creamer, Cow, Covered, Rockingham Glaze, 4 1/4 In. 95.00
  Creamer, Cow, Flint, 8 In. 225.00
  Cuspidor, 1849–59 Mark, 11 X 6 3/4 In. 120.00
  Dish, Soap, Feather Edge 225.00
  Figurine, Cat, Sitting, 9 1/2 In. 295.00
  Figurine, Cherub Sleeping, White, Gold, Polka Dots, Parian 60.00
  Figurine, Cherub, Hooded Cradle, Tinted Hair, Features, 4 1/2 In. 195.00
  Figurine, Poodle, With Basket Of Fruit, 1840–58, Flint, 8 1/2 In. 1300.00
  Flask, Book Form, Flint Enamel, 7 3/4 In. 140.00
  Flask, Book Shape, 4 1/8 X 5 1/2 In. 300.00
  Flask, Book Shape, Departed Spirits, 1849–58 Mark, Flint 500.00
  Flask, Book Shape, Pouring Spout, Departed Spirits, 5 1/2 In. 225.00
  Flowerpot, 9 In., 2 Piece 65.00
  Flowerpot, Embossed Cattails, Amber Glaze, 5 In. 30.00
  Flowerpot, Embossed Cattails, Amber Glaze, 6 1/2 In. 45.00
  Inkwell, Lion Head, 3 1/2 In. 225.00
  Paperweight, Spaniel, 1849 .... 550.00
  Pie Plate, Rockingham Glaze 145.00
  Pitcher, Embossed Florals, Norton & Fenton, 10 1/4 In. 120.00
  Pitcher, Hunting Scene, Applied Dog Handle 130.00
  Pitcher, Palm Tree, Glazed, Parian, Signed 135.00
  Pitcher, Paneled, 1849 Mark, 11 3/4 In. 225.00
  Pitcher, Raised Vine Pattern 250.00
  Pitcher, Wild Rose, Parian, Signed 250.00
  Poodle, Seated, 10 In. 265.00
  Salt Box, Hanging 275.00
  Snuff Jar, Cover, Toby 250.00
  Spittoon, Brown & Yellow, Raised Shell Border, Ribbed Interior 75.00
  Spittoon, Shell Design 125.00
  Syrup, Covered, Parian, 7 In. 70.00
  Tiebacks, Brilliant Blue, Petal Flower Pattern, 2 1/2 In., Pair 52.00
  Urn, Flint Enamel, 1849 Mark On Base, 13 1/2 In. 150.00
  Vaporizer, Rockingham Glaze, 6 5/8 In. 135.00
  Vase, Parian Blue & White, 8 In., Pair 150.00
  Vase, Parian Hand With Corn, Tinted Corn, 7 1/2 In. 85.00
  Vase, Pink, Blue, Yellow, Parian, 8 1/2 In. 70.00
  Vase, Portrait On Front & Back, C.1890, 8 1/2 In., Pair 375.00
  Washbowl, Impressed 1849, Fenton's Enamel, 13 1/2 X 4 3/8 In. 200.00

*Berlin, a German porcelain factory, was started in 1751 by Wilhelm
Kaspar Wegely. In 1763, the factory was taken over by Frederick the
Great and became the Royal Berlin Porcelain Manufactory. It is still
in operation today. Pieces have been marked in a variety of ways.*

BERLIN, Clock, Mantel, Maidens, Floral, Putti, Scepter Mark, 36 3/4 In. 4400.00
  Figurine, Cupid, Draped, Rose In Hand, Marked, 14 5/8 In. 605.00
  Group, Venus, 2 Putti, Shellwork Base, Orb Mark, 8 1/2 In. 522.00
  Plaque, Blossom, Profile, Maiden, 19th Century, Signed, 7 1/8 In. ....~ 1760.00
  Plaque, Gypsy Wearing Shawl, Marked, F.Tenner, 9 3/8 X 6 In. 825.00
  Plaque, Man Playing Mandolin, E.Wolff, Scepter Mark, 9 3/8 X 6 In. 605.00
  Plaque, Near Eastern Beauty, 19th Century, Marked, 9 3/8 X 6 3/8 In. 1100.00
  Plaque, Nun, In Chambers, Pensive Mood, Marked, 12 X 7 In. 1320.00
  Plaque, Princess Labelle, Wagner, Scepter Mark, 13 1/2 In. 1045.00
  Plaque, Ruth, Gray Gown, In Wheat Field, Marked, 6 3/8 X 9 1/4 In. 825.00
  Plaque, Young Girl, Brown Smock, Reading, Scepter Mark, 7 1/2 X 6 In. 1045.00

BERNARD MOORE   *Bernard Moore was an art potter working in England from about
1905 to 1915. He used his name as his mark.*

BERNARD MOORE, Bowl, Flambe & White, Motto, 11 In. 100.00
Ginger Jar, Covered, Flambe, 7 In. 175.00
Vase, Dark Baluster, 2 1/2 In. 50.00
Vase, Flambe, 9 In. 200.00
Vase, Flambe, Dragon, 1905, Blue, 3 1/2 In. 100.00
Vase, Flambe, Onion, 1 1/2 In. 40.00

Beswick *Ware.*
MADE IN
ENGLAND
John Beswick started making earthenwares in Staffordshire, England, in 1936. The company is now part of Royal Doulton Tableware, Ltd. Figurines of animals, especially dogs and horses, Beatrix Potter animals, and other wares are still being made.

BESWICK, Bottle, Liquor, Fish, Figural 12.00
Figurine, 2 Birds On Branch & Base, No.925 .... 30.00
Figurine, Appaloosa, H 1772A 75.00
Figurine, Beagle, D 1939 .... 20.00
Figurine, Cat Sitting, Black, White, Green Eyes, No.1030, 5 1/2 In. 45.00
Figurine, Clydesdale, Standing, 10 X 8 1/2 In. 48.00
Figurine, Horse & Jockey, S 1862B 100.00
Figurine, Horse Hunter, H 1484B 37.00
Figurine, Persian Cat, 5 1/2 X 5 In. 19.00
Figurine, Poodle, D 1386A 20.00
Figurine, Quarterhorse, H 2186B 40.00
Figurine, Turtle 15.00
Mug, Christmas, 1971 .... 75.00
Sugar Bowl, Tony Weller 30.00
Tankard, Scrooge & Cratchit 50.00
Teapot, Sairey Gamp, 5 In. 35.00
Toby Jug, Sam Weller, Large 55.00

Betty Boop, the cartoon figure, first appeared on the screen in 1931. Her face was modeled after the famous singer Helen Kane and her body after Mae West. In 1935 a comic strip was started. Although the Betty Boop cartoons were ended by 1938, there has been a recent revival of interest in the Betty Boop image and new pieces are being made.

BETTY BOOP, Ashtray, Lusterware, 1930s 100.00
Book, Big Little Book, Betty Boop In Snow White, 1934 .... 35.00
Buckle, Celluloid 50.00
Chalkware, 18 In. 25.00
Decal, Sheet, 1920s, Full Color 4.00
Doll, Bisque, 6 1/2 In. 75.00
Doll, Blowup, Roly Poly, Vinyl, 16 In. 20.00
Doll, Celluloid, 5 1/2 In. 10.00
Doll, Playing Violin, Celluloid, 3 In. 45.00
Doll, Wooden Jointed, 1930s, 4 1/4 In. 80.00
Figurine, Chalkware, 8 In. 45.00
Figurine, Playing Drum, Bisque, Original Paint 85.00
Figurine, Sitting, Elbows On Knees, 1921 Chicago, Chalkware 65.00
Film, Animated, Duracolor 32.00
Vase, Wall 95.00

The bicycle was invented in 1839. The first manufactured bicycle was made in 1861. Special ladies' bicycles were made after 1874. The modern safety bicycle was not produced until 1885. Collectors search for all types of bicycles and tricycles.

BICYCLE, Tricycle, 1930s, Original Red, White, & Blue Paint, 16 In. 20.00
Tricycle, C.1870, Wooden 3300.00
Tricycle, Red, White, Blue Paint, 1930s, 16 In. 27.50
Tricycle, Teddy's Cycle, Removable Celluloid Boy, Tin, Box 75.00
Velocipede, Girl's, 1865, Velvet Seat & Backrest, 20 In.Rear Wheels 495.00
Velocipede, Painted & Stenciled Wood & Cast Iron, C.1870, 40 In. 1000.00
Velocipede, White Wheels, Velvet Upholstered Seat & Back, C.1865 .... 200.00

Bing and Grondahl is a famous Danish factory making fine porcelains from 1853 to the present. Underglaze blue decoration was started in 1886. The annual Christmas plate series was introduced in 1895. Dinnerwares, stoneware, and figurines are still being made today. The firm has used the initials B & G and a stylized castle as part of the mark since 1898.

BING & GRONDAHL, Coffeepot, Blue Flowers, 10 In.	37.50
Figurine, Bird, Blue, White, Gray Bill, 4 1/4 In.	125.00
Figurine, Bird, On Branch, Pale Green, Blue Tail, 6 In.	75.00
Figurine, Boy Buttoning Blue Pants, 6 In.	125.00
Figurine, Boy, Standing, No.1617, 7 3/4 In.	110.00
Figurine, Cat, No.1553, 7 1/2 In.	65.00
Figurine, Cat, No.2256, 7 1/2 In.	100.00
Figurine, Cat, Seated, Gray & White, No.2251, 7 1/2 In.	145.00
Figurine, Else No.1574	110.00
Figurine, Girl In White, Sitting, Knitting, No.1656	125.00
Figurine, Girl Kissing Boy, No.1614	155.00
Figurine, Girl, Doll In Arms, Marked, C.1900, 7 1/2 In.	250.00
Figurine, Girl, Seated, Playing Guitar, 9 In.	295.00
Figurine, Girl, Seated, Playing Guitar, No.1684, 9 In.	295.00
Figurine, Hans Christian Andersen, No.2037	235.00
Figurine, Hunter, No.2328	212.00
Figurine, Ice Skater, No.2351	115.00
Figurine, Love Refused, No.1614	99.00
Figurine, Mother, Seated, Holding Standing Child, 6 In.	145.00
Figurine, Mouse, No.1801, Gray, 1 3/4 In.	65.00
Figurine, Old Fisherman, No.2370	190.00
Figurine, Owl, No.1899, Brown, 4 1/4 In.	47.50
Figurine, Police Officer, No.2436	160.00
Figurine, Reclining Nude, Suckling Baby, Signed, 1913, 7 In.	185.00
Figurine, Sea Gull, No.1808	50.00
Figurine, Siamese Cat, No.2308, 5 1/2 In.	65.00
Figurine, Vienna Waltz, No.2385	99.00
Frederick The Great, Commemorative, 1854–1904, 7 1/8 In.	75.00
Plaque, 12 Figure Roman Dance Scene, Signed, 5 X 9 1/2 In.	195.00
Plate, 1903, Christmas, Children	109.00
Plate, 1961, Christmas	73.00
Plate, 1969, Mother's Day, First Issue	263.00
Plate, Annual, 1904	79.00
Plate, Christmas Elf, 1963	100.00
Plate, Christmas, 1899	825.00
Plate, Christmas, 1900	625.00
Plate, Christmas, 1901	210.00
Plate, Christmas, 1902	190.00
Plate, Christmas, 1903	160.00
Plate, Christmas, 1914	75.00
Plate, Christmas, 1918	48.50 To 75.00
Plate, Christmas, 1919	75.00
Plate, Christmas, 1958	69.00
Plate, Christmas, 1960	95.00
Plate, Christmas, 1965	50.00
Plate, Christmas, 1967	20.00 To 35.00
Plate, Christmas, 1970	26.00
Plate, Christmas, 1975	25.00
Plate, Christmas, 1979	32.00
Plate, Commemorative, 1854–1904, Frederick The Great	75.00
Plate, Crystal's Joy, 1979	12.00
Plate, Mother & Child, Commemorative	20.00
Plate, Mother's Day, 1969	263.00 To 369.00
Plate, Mother's Day, 1971	25.00
Plate, Mother's Day, 1974	15.00
Plate, Olympic, 1972, Box	15.00
Tray, Copenhagen Scene, 5 X 7 1/2 In.	45.00

All types of old binoculars are wanted by collectors. Those made in the 18th and 19th centuries are favored by serious collectors. The small, attractive binoculars called opera glasses are listed in their own section.

BINOCULARS, Egyptian Figures, Occupied Japan, White Metal	32.00
English, 1837–41, A.Ross & Co., Ivory Focus Knob, Leather Case	220.00
Folding, Wenham, English, C.1863, Folding Base, Complete	795.00
High Power, Case, Small	38.00
Husbands & Clarke, Accessories, Case, C.1870	1650.00
Opera, Enameled Design, Matching Hand Holder, French	115.00
Opera, Zeiss, Gold Plated, Lady's, Alligator Skin Compact, Case	98.50
Race Track, Lady's, Mother–Of–Pearl, Gold Plated	98.50

Old birdcages are collected for use as homes for pet birds and as decorative objects of folk art. Elaborate wooden cages of the past centuries can still be found. The brass or wicker cages of the 1930s are popular with bird owners.

BIRDCAGE, Brass, 12 1/2 X 13 In.	125.00
Brass, Small	65.00
Delft, Painted Overall With Birds & Flowers, Signed	1500.00
Hendrick's, Brass	45.00
Hendrick's, Cut Glass & Brass	150.00
Painted Tole, Wire, Hip Roofed House, Dormers, Chimney, 14 1/4 In.	90.00
Painted Yellow	325.00
Victorian, Turned Finials, Old Gold Over Red, Wooden, 10 X 19 In.	95.00
Victorian, Walnut, 22 X 13 X 24 In.	200.00
Wooden Frame, Wire Bars, Bird On Cupola, 2 Doors, 27 1/2 X 36 In.	450.00

Bisque is an unglazed baked porcelain. Finished bisque has a slightly sandy texture with a dull finish. Some of it may be decorated with various colors. Bisque gained favor during the late Victorian era when thousands of bisque figurines were made. It is still being made.

BISQUE, see also named porcelain factories

BISQUE, Dish, Covered, Dog With Bone, Basket Weave, French, 5 1/2 In.	595.00
Egg, Black Baby Emerging	65.00
Figurine, 2 Dancing Pigs, German, 4 In.	65.00
Figurine, Baby Sitting, 5 1/8 X 5 In., Pair	150.00
Figurine, Billiken, Naked Baby, No.7538, 6 In.	265.00
Figurine, Black & White Children, On Chamber Pots, Kissing, 6 In.	135.00
Figurine, Boy & Girl With Cats, Pastel, 11 1/2 X 4 X 5 3/4 In.	245.00
Figurine, Boy In Lederhosen, Cigar In Hand, 12 In.	275.00
Figurine, Boy On Swing, Holds Dog, 6 In.	30.00
Figurine, Boy Urinating Into Bowl, Nightshirt, 4 In.	75.00
Figurine, Cat, Reclining, White, Black Spots, Bow, 4 1/4 X 8 3/4 In.	110.00
Figurine, Dog, Drummer's Clothes, Marked, 10 1/4 In.	195.00
Figurine, Ferdinand The Bull, 3 In.	22.00
Figurine, Girl & Animals, Multicolor, German, 12 X 4 1/2 In.	295.00
Figurine, Girl Holding Baby, Boy Holding Bowl, 14 1/2 In.	130.00
Figurine, Girl, Playing Mandolin, High Buttoned Shoes, 8 1/2 In.	65.00
Figurine, Happy Fats, Girl & Boy, German, 3/1/2 In., Pair	425.00
Figurine, Man & Woman, Winter Sled Scene, Hertwig & Co., 1900	495.00
Figurine, Monk, Basket & Lantern, German, 5 1/2 In.	35.00
Figurine, Monk, Holding Stein, German, 5 1/2 In.	35.00
Figurine, Newspaper Boy, Jockey Cap, Bundle Of Papers, White, 8 In.	49.00
Figurine, Oven Bird, Inarco, 1962	12.00
Figurine, People On Boat, Pastel, German, 12 X 6 X 13 In.	395.00
Figurine, Pig, Pink, Orange Pot, Says Boston Baked Beans, German	55.00
Figurine, Standing Wild Boar, German, 4 1/2 X 7 1/2 In.	115.00
Figurine, Teddy Bear, Dressed As Clown, German, 4 In.	32.00
Figurine, Turtle Lady, Removable Shell, 2 X 3 1/2 In.	150.00
Figurine, Whippet, Standing, Wearing Racing Coat, 5 1/2 X 6 1/4 In.	135.00
Figurine, Wolf, Standing, Red Jacket, Blue Pants, Bow Tie, 5 In.	45.00
Figurine, Young Woman, Holding Broken Jug, Anchor Mark, 37 In.	575.00

To remove the musty odor from old books, try this method. Leather-covered books should be wiped with a mixture of equal parts alcohol and water. The pages of the books should be warmed. Stand the books on edge, open them, and blow-dry them with a portable hair dryer on high heat.

Bisque, Shoe, Child's, 3 In.

Font, Holy Water, Child's Head, Porcelain, Holland	24.00
Humidor, Jolly Monk's Head, 6 X 6 In.	105.00
Night–Light, Dog Head, Glass Eyes, Brown & Tan, Candle, 3 7/8 In.	145.00
Night–Light, Owl Head, Glass Eyes, Gray, Candle, 3 1/2 In.	145.00
Nodder, Black Face & Hands, Male & Female, Candlestick, 6 In., Pair	575.00
Pin Box, Black Man On Cotton Bale	20.00
Plaque, 18th Century Couple Dancing, Gold Beading, 8 In.	65.00
Plate, Baby Angel In Relief, 6 1/4 In.	9.50
Shoe, Child's, 3 In. *Illus*	15.00
Shoe, Dutch, Dancing Pigs, Shamrocks, 3 1/2 X 6 In.	85.00
Shoe, Man's, Black, White Terrier Dog In Front, Gray Cat, 1 3/4 In.	20.00
Stopper, Bottle, Figural, Baby, Germany	20.00
Vase, Classical Profile, Matte Blue Ground, C.1880, 18 1/8 In., Pair	770.00
Wall Pocket, Boy & Girl, Sprinkling Pots, Hand Painted, Japan	42.00

Black amethyst glass appears black until it is held to the light, then a dark purple can be seen. It has been made in many factories from 1860 to the present.

BLACK AMETHYST, Basket, 11 In.	75.00
Bonbon, Small	7.00
Bowl, Art Deco, 6 1/2 X 4 In.	24.50
Bowl, Double Shield, 6 1/2 In.	18.00
Bowl, Fern, Flower Frog, Large Hobnail Pattern, 7 In.	55.00
Bowl, Ram's Head Handled, Footed, 5 1/4 X 8 1/2 In.	53.00
Candleholder, 4 1/2 In., Pair	25.00
Candleholder, Central Glass Works, 9 In., Pair	39.00
Candy Dish, Red Flowers, Gold Trim, Handle	14.00
Compote, Lace Edge, Footed, 7 1/4 In.	27.50
Compote, Sterling Overlay, 6 1/2 In.	32.00
Console Set, Candleholder, Bowl & Base, 4 Piece	78.00
Console Set, Silver Overlay, Footed Bowl, Candlestick, Pair	290.00
Dish, Square, 5 In.	20.00
Holder, Center Handle, Round, Holds 6 Tumblers	19.00
Ice Bucket	25.00
Ink Blotter, Elephant, No Blotter	35.00
Loving Cup, Etched World's Fair 1934	35.00
Loving Cup, L.E.Smith, 8 1/4 In.	23.00
Mug, Child's, Standing Dog, Sandwich	125.00
Nappy, 11 1/2 In.	25.00
Pitcher, Amethyst Picture, 2 Qt., 7 3/4 In.	28.50
Plate, Mt.Pleasant, Double Shield, 8 In., Set Of 6	58.00
Plate, Tiered, Silver Trim, 2 Piece	20.00

Powder Box, & Hatpin Holder, Enameled Bird 40.00
Powder Jar, Egyptian 50.00
Rolling Pin ....45.00 To 225.00
Salt & Pepper, Art Deco, Marked MCK 25.00
Salt & Pepper, Colonial Pattern 25.00
Salt & Pepper, Ovoid 10.00
Sugar & Creamer 10.00
Sugar & Creamer, Sterling Silver Pedestals 60.00
Sugar, Scalloped, 2 Handles, 4 In. 10.50
Tray, Center Handle, Octagon, Allover Floral Etching 24.50
Vase, 5 1/2 In. 12.00
Vase, Art Nouveau, Grecian Dancers, 2 Handles, Footed, 7 In. 35.00
Vase, Bud, U.S.Glass, 7 1/2 In. 10.00
Vase, Midnight Lace, Sandwich, C.1880, 7 In. 65.00
Vase, Pink Roses, Hand Painted, 10 In. 30.00
Vase, Ruffled, Blown, 4 1/2 In. 10.00
Vase, Scalloped, 5 In. 6.50
Vase, Sterling Silver Flowers, Ornate Mold, 6 In. 18.00

Black memorabilia has become an important area of collecting since the 1970s. Any piece that pictures a black person is included in this category and objects range from sheet music to salt and pepper shakers. The best material dates from past centuries, but many recent items are of interest even if not yet expensive.

BLACK, Album, Record, Little Black Sambo 48.00
Ashtray, Amos & Andy, I'Se Regusted, Chalk 85.00
Ashtray, Amos & Andy, Metal, 5 In. 225.00
Ashtray, Attached Boy Nodder Smoking Cigar, Austrian Bronze 95.00
Ashtray, Black Baby Boy, Nodder, Ceramic 35.00
Ashtray, Black Boy Eating Watermelon, Souvenir Of Mineola, Plaster 25.00
Ashtray, Black Boy, Bed & Pot, Says Scram Bee, This Ain'T You Hive 20.00
Ashtray, Boy Eating Levy's Jewish Rye Bread, Milk Glass 65.00
Ashtray, Coon Chicken Inn ....25.00 To 40.00
Ashtray, Man, Hatched Through Egg, Cigar Holder, Silver Plate 225.00
Ashtray, Young Girl Sitting On Wooden Bench On Rim, Metal 22.00
Book, Little Black Sambo, 1930 .... 30.00
Book, Little Black Sambo, 1959 .... 5.00
Book, Little Black Sambo, Linen, Sam Gabriel Edition, 1921, 12 X 9 In. 95.00
Bottle, Baby, Figural, Germany, 2 In. 20.00
Bottle, Perfume, Le Guilli Wogg, Black Man, Fuzzy Head 25.00
Bottle, Sprinkler, Mammy, Pfaltzgraff 95.00
Box, Alms, Boy, Mechanical, Plaster, Signed H.Lingero 1926, 12 1/2 In. 450.00
Box, Alms, Man Praying, Mechanical, Pot Metal, Wooden, Painted, 17 In. ... 300.00
Box, Candy Bar, Amos & Andy, 5 Cent Candy, Correll & Gosden 210.00
Box, Fun-To-Wash Washing Powder, Black Mammy, Unused 10.00
Broom Holder, Figural, Black Head, Cast Iron 150.00
Button, Pin Type, Aunt Jemima Breakfast Club 13.00
Candy Container, Amos & Andy, Fresh Air Taxi 300.00
Cap Pistol, Figural, Sambo, 1890 .... 125.00
Card, Birthday, Black Boy With Dog, Ah Disremembers The Date 15.00
Card, Birthday, Black Girl With Dog, Don'T Worry Bout Yo' Birfdays! 10.00
Card, Christmas, Amos & Andy, Lemme Tell Em Merry Christmas, Hall 45.00
Card, Trade, Quaker Oats, Mandy's Smile, Black Boy Eating Oatmeal 10.00
Card, Trade, The Dark Band, Photograph Of Black Traveling Band 20.00
Cigarette Holder, Boy Peeking Between Laundry, Japan 25.00
Clock, Pickaninny, Moving Eyes & Tie 275.00
Coaster, Eny, Meny, Miny, & Moe, Wooden, Set Of 4 .... 45.00
Cookie Jar, Aunt Jemima ....65.00 To 95.00
Cookie Jar, Aunt Jemima, Celluloid, Marked F & F Mold & Die Works 125.00
Cookie Jar, Signed Across Apron, Aunt Jemima's Cookie Jar 147.50
Creamer, Mammy, Figural 35.00
Creamer, Uncle Mose 25.00
Cup & Saucer, Black Waiter, China, Shoyer's Restaurant, Advertising 20.00
Dancer, Boy, Spring Connected To Clamshell, Acapulco, 5 1/2 In. 12.00

Doll, Baby, German, Celluloid, 1 In. 14.00
Doll, Black, Celluloid Head, Cloth Body, 14 In. 24.00
Doll, Girl, Cloth, Stuffed, Embroidered, Pigtails, Dress, 12 1/2 In. 45.00
Doll, Golliwog, 8 In. 75.00
Doll, Nut, Mammy, Holding Twins, Whisk Broom Body 350.00
Doll, Rag, Brother & Sister, 8 In., Pair 35.00
Doll, Rag, Handmade, 13 In. 50.00
Doll, Tod–L–Tot, Marked Sun Rubber 20.00
Doll, Walker, Mammy, Wooden, Red Print Dress, 1940s, 8 In. 25.00
Doll, Yarn Hair, Embroidered Face, Dressed, 19th Century, 18 In. 125.00
Doll, Yarn, Bell Under Skirt, Souvenir Of New Orleans, 6 In. 12.00
Figurine, Amos & Andy, Art Statuary Co., Chalkware, 7 1/2 In., Pair 175.00
Figurine, Andy, Amos & Andy, Chalkware, 11 In. 250.00
Figurine, Aunt Jemima, Cast Iron, 2 1/2 In. 75.00
Figurine, Baby, Bisque, Pigtails, 6 In. 25.00
Figurine, Black Boy Eating Watermelon, Bisque, No.3590, 4 1/2 In. 44.00
Figurine, Boy On Potty, Slice Of Watermelon, Bisque, Japan, 3 1/2 In. 20.00
Figurine, Boy Sitting On Toilet, Your Next, Niagara Falls, 8 1/2 In. 15.00
Figurine, Boy Tending Geese, Cast Iron, 1910, 2 In. 63.00
Figurine, Boy, Holding Thermometer, 1949, 3 In. 15.00
Figurine, Girl Sitting On Chamber Pot, Bisque, R Mark, 4 In. 150.00
Figurine, Man, Fishing From Stump, Chalkware, 11 In. 43.00
Figurine, Man, Log Wagon, Cast Iron, 3 1/2 In. 30.00
Figurine, Musician, Porcelain, Occupied Japan, 4 3/4 In., Pair 35.00
Flour Sack, Cake Walk, Strutting Black Couple 35.00
Foot Scraper, Aunt Jemima, Iron 125.00
Game, Board, Black Sambo, Tin 60.00
Holder, Hose, Sprinkling Sambo, Metal, 1942 .... 185.00
Hotpad Holder, Aunt Jemima, Wooden, 2 Crocheted Pads, 8 In. 18.00
Inkwell, Man's Head, Hinged Cap 145.00
Label, Black Joe Grape, Set Of 15 .... 10.00
Label, Syrup, Uncle Remus Saying Dis Sho' Am Good, Litho, Dated 1924 .... 8.00
Laundry Bag, Mammy 45.00
Lithograph, Little Black Sambo, Watering Boy, 16 In. 195.00
Match Holder, 2 Blacks In Cotton Patch, Metal, 3 1/2 In. 37.50
Match Holder, Black Boy With Watermelon 15.00
Match Holder, Boy With Geese, Bisque 49.00
Match Safe, Mammy, Wooden, Handmade 28.50
Matchbox Holder, Mammy In Pink & Green, 15 In. 12.00
Memo Minder, Mammy, Chalk, Marked Holyoke, Mass. 32.50
Memo Pad Holder, Aunt Jemima, Plaster 30.00
Mug, Mammy's Face In Relief, Japan, 5 In. 36.00
Napkin Holder, Coon Chicken Inn, Chalkware 75.00
Needle Case, Aunt Jemima, Paper 15.00
Nodder, Boy On Alligator, 7 In. 25.00
Nodder, Native Boy, Straw Hat, Legs Around Drum, 7 In. 24.00
Paddle, Cardboard, We're Clapping For Snyder's Ice Cream, Germany 55.00
Pail, Luters Lard, Mammy With Spatula & Frying Pan, 4 Lb. 45.00
Pancake Machine, Aunt Jemima, 1940s 350.00
Pen Holder, Black Metal, Boy On Knee, Arms Outstretched, 6 In. 65.00
Pencil Holder, Coon Chicken 125.00
Pie Bird 15.00
Pincushion, Mammy, Chalkware 25.00
Planter, Black Butler 65.00
Planter, Black Girl Next To Corn, 5 1/2 In. 18.00
Plaque, Mammy & Chef, Chalkware, 6 In., Pair 29.00
Plaque, Wall, Girl Holding Open Umbrella, Chalkware 10.00
Plate, Black Builders Bicentennial 1976, Martin L.King, 8 1/2 In. 18.00
Plate, Black Sambo, 9 In. 50.00
Potholder, Boy Eating Watermelon 15.00
Print, Black Boy Being Chased By White Goose, Framed, 10 X 9 In. 65.00
Print, Jockey, Laughing Horse, International Stock Food, 10 X 13 In. 40.00
Puzzle, Amos & Andy, Pepsodent Premium, Original Envelope, 8 X 10 In. 125.00
Salt & Pepper, Aunt Jemima & Mose, 5 In. 14.50

Salt & Pepper, Mammy & Chef, 8 In. 60.00
Salt & Pepper, Mother–Of–Pearl, Salty & Peppy, China, 8 In. 65.00
Salt & Pepper, White Aprons, Holding Frying Pan, Ceramic, 4 In. 12.50
Sampler, We's Free, Embroidered, 1870s, 5 X 5 In. 95.00
Shaker, Mammy, 5 1/2 In. 15.00
Sheet Music, Carolina Lullaby, Framed 28.00
Sheet Music, Shew Fly, 1869, Black Man On Cover 9.00
Sheet Music, Shortnin' Bread, Mammy Baking Bread For Children, 1939 .... 10.00
Sheet Music, Turkey In The Straw, Black Boy Climbing In House, 1904 .... 15.00
Sign, Colored Served In Rear, Tin, 1950s 17.00
Spice Set, Aunt Jemima 115.00
Spice Set, Tray, Mammy, Mississippi 125.00
Sugar & Creamer, Aunt Jemima, Celluloid, F & F Mold & Die Works 75.00
Sugar Shaker, Mammy, Marked Japan 58.00
Sugar, Chef 45.00
Syrup, Aunt Jemima, Hard Plastic 45.00
Syrup, Mammy, Weller 325.00
Tablecloth, Illustrated Man Washing Dishes, Mammy With Children 12.00
Tablecloth, Mammy Eating Chicken, Large 45.00
Tablecloth, People Eating Watermelon, Large 45.00
Teaspoon, Man's Head On Handle, Sterling Silver 45.00
Tie Rack, Hand Carved Head, Dark Wood, Red Painted Lips & Trim 45.00
Tobacco Jar, Figural, Mammy's Head, Bisque, 7 In. 125.00
Toothbrush Holder, Mammy, China 100.00
Towel, Dish, Aunt Jemima & Uncle Mose 38.00
Towel, Linen, Printed Mammy & Black Boy, Watermelon, 14 X 28 In. 30.00
Toy, 2 Musicians, Windup, Tin, Painted, Dressed, Gunthermann, 8 1/2 In. 1900.00
Toy, Alabama Coon Jigger, Windup, Tin, Lehmann, Original Box, 8 In. 300.00
Toy, Amos & Andy, Fresh Air Taxi, Iron 900.00
Toy, Amos & Andy, Walker, Marx, Moving Eyes 1100.00
Toy, Dancer, Battery Operated 125.00
Toy, Dancin' Dan, 1930s 85.00
Toy, Jazzbo Jim 185.00
Toy, Mammy, Windup, Tin, Litho, Lindstrom, 8 In. 115.00
Toy, Minstrels, Ham & Sam, Piano, Windup, Tin, Strauss, Box, 5 1/2 In. 300.00
Wrapper, Candy, Amos & Andy, Williamson Candy Co. 85.00

Blown glass was formed by forcing air through a rod into molten glass. Early glass and some forms of art glass were hand blown. Other types of glass were molded or pressed.

BLOWN GLASS, Basket, Blue Applied Handle & Edge, Pink, 6 In. 45.00
Basket, Hobnail, Applied Twisted Thorn Handle, 8 In. 175.00
Beaker, Enameled Woman, 5 In. 110.00
Bottle, Aqua Overlay, Ruffled Vaseline Edge, Square 325.00
Bottle, Red & White Looping, White Lip, Pittsburgh, 10 In. 265.00
Bowl, 16 Swirled Ribs In Bowl, Cobalt Blue Rim, 4 1/2 In. 205.00
Bowl, 19 Swirled Ribs, Flared, Cobalt Blue, 5 X 2 1/4 In. 7.50
Bowl, Folded Edge, Engraved Flowers, Swag & Dot Rim, 4 1/2 In. 30.00
Bowl, Folded Rim, Olive Green, 5 3/4 X 2 1/4 In. 275.00
Creamer, 8 Ribs, Folded Rim, Clear, 4 1/4 In. 95.00
Creamer, Molded Ribs, Folded Rim, Light Blue, 3 1/2 In. 300.00
Creamer, Simple Threading, Pale Puce, 5 In. 20.00
Egg, Easter, 5 In. 55.00
Flask, Chestnut, Light Green, 10 Diamond, Zanesville, 5 In. 800.00
Flip, Copperwheel Engraved Sprig & Lovebirds, 4 5/8 In. 95.00
Flowerpot, Attached Saucer, Folded Rims, Amethyst, 2 3/4 In. 95.00
Goblet, Enameled Crest, Prunts, Green, 5 1/2 In. 72.00
Goblet, Wafer Stem, Flared Rim, 5 1/4 In. 35.00
Inkwell, 24 Vertical Ribs, Zanesville, Amber, 1 7/8 In. 800.00
Mug, Pear Shape, Enameled Floral Design, 5 In. 165.00
Mug, Pewter Hinged Lid, Engraved Monogram & Crown, 1807, 9 In. 175.00
Pan, 20 Swirled Ribs, Folded–In Rim, Yellow, Mantua, 7 1/2 In. 700.00
Pan, Folded Rim, Clear, 7 1/4 X 2 1/4 In. 40.00
Pan, Folded Rim, Pale Aqua, 6 5/8 X 2 1/4 In. 45.00

Pan, Yellow Amber, Zanesville, 5 3/8 In. 550.00
Pitcher, Crimped Strap Handle, Ribbed Inside & Out, 6 In. 575.00
Pitcher, Pillar Mold, 8 Swirled Ribs, Hollow Handle, Pittsburgh 7200.00
Salt, Applied Cobalt Blue Ribs & Rim, Cut Panels, 1 3/4 In. 70.00
Salt, Expanded Diamond Bowl, 2 7/8 In. 65.00
Salt, Master, 24 Ribs, Flared, Amber, Zanesville, 3 3/4 In. 3900.00
Salt, Scalloped Foot, Expanded Diamond Bowl, 3 In., Pair 80.00
Shield, Hurricane, 22 In., Pair 1100.00
Sugar, Galleried Rim, Applied Finial, Lily Pad Foot, 6 3/8 In. 375.00
Toothpick, Applied Tooled Base, Cobalt Blue, 2 3/4 In. 5.00
Tumbler, 12 Swirled Ribs, 2 3/4 In. 20.00
Tumbler, 3 Mold, Ribbed Base, Copperwheel Engraved Floral Band 17.50
Whimsey, Swan On Toadstool Plinth, Amber, 4 In. 265.00
      BLUE AMBERINA, see Bluerina
      BLUE GLASS, see Cobalt Blue
      BLUE ONION, see Onion

Blue Willow pattern has been made in England since 1780. The pattern has been copied by factories in many countries, including Germany, Japan, and the United States. It is still being made. Willow was named for a pattern that pictures a bridge, birds, willow trees, and a Chinese landscape.

BLUE WILLOW, Berry Bowl, Royal 3.00
Bowl, Vegetable, Open, 7 1/2 X 6 In. 38.00
Butter 95.00
Butter Chip 10.00
Butter Chip, Allerton 18.00
Butter Chip, Buffalo 13.00
Butter, Covered, Buffalo, 1915 .... 150.00
Cake Plate, Old Lang Syne, Gold Band 95.00
Coffeepot, Demitasse 50.00
Creamer, Copeland 24.00
Cruet, Pair 25.00
Cup & Saucer .... 6.00 To 12.00
Cup & Saucer, Allerton 25.00
Cup & Saucer, Buffalo, C.1911 .... 22.00
Cup & Saucer, Burleigh Ware, Demitasse 25.00
Cup & Saucer, Child's 9.50
Cup & Saucer, Handleless 18.00
Cup & Saucer, Johnson Bros., Oversized 30.00
Cup & Saucer, Old Lang Syne, Gold Foo Dog Finials, Gold Band 65.00
Cup & Saucer, Regout 14.00
Cup, Child's 6.50
Cup, Custard, Ruffled 55.00
Cup, Marked Japan, 3 7/8 In. 15.00
Dinner Set, Royal China, 51 Piece 125.00
Dish, Cover, Oblong, Japan, 7 X 5 In. 37.50
Dish, Hot Water 95.00
Dish, Vegetable, Covered, Japan 20.00
Dish, Vegetable, Covered, Staffordshire, 9 X 9 In. 95.00
Eggcup 10.00
Eggcup, Allerton 15.00
Eggcup, Burleigh 7.50
Eggcup, Double, Alberton, England 20.00
Ginger Jar, Royal Cauldon, 5 In. 65.00
Gravy Boat, Staffordshire 20.00
Jar, Tea, Rington 110.00
Lamp Base, Kerosene, 4 1/2 In. 22.00
Lamp, Blue Willow Shade, Base, Paper Label, Japan, 10 In., Pair 95.00
Mug 18.00
Mug, Shenango Pottery 12.50
Pitcher, Allerton, 5 1/4 In. 58.00
Pitcher, Allerton, 6 In. 110.00
Plate, 6 3/4 In. 7.00

Plate, Allerton, 10 In.	12.00
Plate, Baker Ltd., 7 1/2 In.	10.00
Plate, Butterfly Border, Paden City, 7 1/2 In.	20.00
Plate, Child's, 5 In.	6.50
Plate, Divided, McNichols, 10 In.	10.00
Plate, Mason, 10 1/2 In.	55.00
Plate, Meakin, 8 3/4 In.	7.00
Plate, Regout, 8 3/4 In.	9.00
Plate, Staffordshire, 9 7/8 In.	15.00
Plate, Wedgwood, 10 In.	20.00
Platter, 13 1/2 X 10 3/4 In.	55.00
Platter, Andrew Stevenson, C.1818, 16 3/4 X 13 1/2 In.	175.00
Platter, Buffalo, C.1909, 11 X 14 In.	22.00
Platter, Buffalo, C.1914, 8 1/2 X 10 1/2 In.	22.00
Platter, English, 21 X 15 In.	65.00
Platter, Ridgway, 14 X 10 7/8 In.	35.00
Platter, Ridgway, 16 1/2 X 12 1/2 In.	65.00
Salad Bowl, 10 In.	49.00
Salt & Pepper, Tall	20.00
Salt & Pepper, Tower Shape, Japanese Mark	27.00
Sauce, Deep, Wood & Sons	6.00
Soup, Buffalo, 9 In.	9.00
Soup, Dish, Booth, Flange Rims	15.00
Sugar & Creamer, Covered, Allerton	65.00
Sugar, Child's, 2 7/8 In.	13.50
Tea Set, Copeland, Sold By Tiffany, 1880, 3 Piece	395.00
Teapot	22.50
Teapot, 2 Cup, Sadler	20.00
Teapot, Child's, Square Handles, 3 1/2 In.	45.00
Teapot, Sadler	35.00 To 51.00
Teapot, Sugar & Creamer, Child's, Square Handles, 3 Piece	45.00
Teapot, Woods	95.00
Toby Mug, 1820s	365.00
Tureen, 3 X 5 In.	35.00
Tureen, Sauce, Undertray, Covered, Staffordshire, 6 5/8 In.	135.00
Tureen, Soup, Lid, Ladle, & Underplate, Burleigh	295.00
Vegetable, Open, Old Lang Syne, Oval, Gold Band, 10 X 7 1/2 In.	65.00
Vegetable, Square, Wood & Co., 8 3/4 In.	45.00

Bluerina is a type of art glass which shades from light blue to ruby. It is often called blue amberina.

BLUERINA, Vase, Applied Flowers & Leaves, C.1880, 6 1/2 In.	125.00

The Boch Freres factory was founded in 1841 in La Louviere in eastern Belgium. The wares resemble the work of Villeroy & Boch. The factory is still in business.

BOCH FRERES, Vase, Blue Streak Glaze, Metal Mount, 12 In., Pair	125.00
Vase, Gulls Over Waves, Art Deco, Cream Glaze, 9 In.	190.00

Osso China Company was reorganized as Edward Marshall Boehm, Inc. in 1953. The company is still working in England and New Jersey. In the early days of the factory, dishes were made, but the elaborate and lifelike bird figurines are the best known ware. Edward Marshall Boehm, the founder, died in 1961; but the firm has continued to design and produce porcelain. Today, the firm makes both limited and unlimited editions of figurines and plates.

BOEHM, Ashtray, Clover Center, Glazed	50.00
Bookends, Owl, All White, 1960	450.00
Candlestick, Corinthian, Glazed	125.00
Cybis, Yellow Rose, Rosebuds	265.00
Figurine, Black Burnian Warbler	225.00
Figurine, Bluebird	200.00
Figurine, Bluejay	150.00
Figurine, Bunting, Non–Pareil	850.00

Figurine, Cat With Kittens 595.00
Figurine, Chick, Yellow 175.00
Figurine, Dachshund 400.00
Figurine, Eagle, Baby, Bicentennial, Boxed 200.00
Figurine, Fledgling Blackburnian Warbler, No.478 .... 275.00
Figurine, Fledgling Kingfisher 235.00
Figurine, Fledgling Magpie ....165.00 To 175.00
Figurine, Lion Cub 475.00
Figurine, Prairie Chicken, Pair 975.00
Figurine, Robin, With Daffodil ....3000.00 To 3500.00
Figurine, Signet 350.00
Figurine, Tree Sparrow, No.468 .... 380.00
Figurine, Warbler 150.00
Figurine, Whippet, Pair 500.00
Medallion, 25th Anniversary, Bronze, 1950–70 .... 23.00
Paperweight, Nest With Baby Bluebirds 250.00
Plate, Mute Swan 225.00

Bohemian glass is an ornate, overlay, or flashed glass made during the Victorian era. It has been reproduced in Bohemia, which is now a part of Czechoslovakia. Glass made from 1875 to 1900 is preferred by collectors.

BOHEMIAN GLASS, Banana Bowl, Brass Holder, Amber To Clear, 8 X 11 In. 375.00
Beaker, Engraved 3 Fates, Bell Shape 1320.00
Bottle, Cologne, Crystal, Rose & Gold, Stopper 85.00
Bottle, Cologne, Green, Gold Trim, Original Stopper 125.00
Bottle, Stopper, Red, 10 1/2 In. 45.00
Bottle, Wine, Red Overlay, Numbered Ground Stopper 75.00
Centerpiece, Tulip Center, Gilt, Cranberry, 21 1/2 In., Pair 770.00
Decanter Set, Vintage Pattern, Ruby Cut, Stopper, 3 Wine 90.00
Decanter, Deer & Castle, 14 1/2 In. 100.00
Decanter, Deer & Castle, Amber, 16 In. 75.00
Decanter, Etched Grapes, Cut Ruby To Clear, Stopper, 15 In. 85.00
Decanter, Ruby Stopper, White Frosted Design, 9 3/4 In. 30.00
Decanter, Ruby, Blown Stopper, Grape, Leaf Etched, 11 3/4 In. 85.00
Decanter, Vintage, Red Stained 95.00
Dish, Sweetmeat, Dove & Castle, 10 In. 65.00
Goblet, 2 Deer Feeding In Woodland, Etched, Octagonal, 7 In. 140.00
Goblet, 2 Deer, Woodland Scene, Octagon Shape, Etched, 7 In. 135.00
Goblet, Marriage Scene 1210.00
Goblet, Scene Of Boston's Quincy Market 2860.00
Lamp, Finger, Grapes, Ruby 150.00
Lamp, White To Pink, Roundels, Ovals, 22 1/2 In., Pair 495.00
Perfume Bottle, Powder Box, Amber, Clear, Etched, 3 Piece 475.00
Perfume Bottle, Vintage Pattern, 7 In. 55.00
Punch Bowl, Cover, Castles In 4 Oval Panels, 10 1/2 In. 770.00
Syrup, Three Fruits, Clear 24.00
Vase, Cranberry, 10 In. 160.00
Vase, Cut Flowers, Leaves, Flared Top, 8 In. 225.00
Vase, Deer & Trees, Frosted, Signed Pohl, 3 1/2 In., Pair 65.00
Vase, Floral, 4 1/2 In. 30.00
Vase, Foliage & Birds, Pontil, Red On Clear, 9 In. 30.00
Vase, Portrait, Overlay, Floral, Allover Vines, 13 In., Pair 550.00
Vase, Ruby Flashed, Flower Panel, Gold Enameled, 7 1/2 In. 29.00
Wine Set, Red To Clear, Decanter & 6 Wines 95.00
Wine, Vintage, Red Stained, 4 1/2 In., 4 Piece 35.00

Bone dishes were considered a necessary part of a table setting for the Victorian table. The crescent-shaped dish was kept at the edge of the dinner plate so the bones removed from the fish could be stored away from the uneaten food. Some bone dishes were made in more fanciful shapes and many resemble fish.

BONE DISH, Fish Shape, Pink, Flowers, C.1900, 5 1/2 In. 50.00
White Flowers, Fleur-De-Lis, Scalloped, Bonn Rosenguirlande 20.00

Wildrose, Royal Bonn, Blue & White 15.00

Bookends have probably been used since books became inexpensive. Early libraries kept books in cupboards, not on open shelves. By the 1870s bookends appear, especially homemade fretcarved wooden examples. Most bookends listed in this book date from the twentieth century.

BOOKENDS, Bowlers, Figural 45.00
  Boy & Dog, Frank Art 90.00
  Dog, Pottery, Cream, Black, Tan, 8 In. ....*Illus* 22.00
  End Of Trail, Marked Real Bronze 24.00
  Figurine, Lady & Man In French Clothes, Plaster, 11 In. 55.00
  Horse Head, Figural 65.00
  King Tut, Bronze 95.00
  Kneeling Nude, Full Figure, Hands Behind Head, Art Deco, Denmark 175.00
  Plane, Figural, Metal, Curtis P-40, Wooden 25.00
  Poodle, Gray, Gold Colored Base, Marked MB 30.00
  Scotty Dog, Metal, Bronze Finish, 5 1/2 In. 55.00
  Turtle, Kenton Hills 165.00

Bookmarks were originally made of parchment, cloth, or leather. Soon woven silk ribbon, thin cardboard, celluloid, wood, silver, tortoiseshell, and metals were used. Examples made before 1850 are scarce, but there are many to be found dating before 1920.

BOOKMARK, Advertising, Tootsie Roll 1.00
  Bear, Celluloid 15.00
  Bird On Rainbow, 3 1/2 X 4 In. 95.00
  Embossed Elk Head, Sterling Silver 18.00
  Portrait Of Man, Wreath Of Flowers, 3 1/2 X 4 In. 120.00
  Silk, Star Spangled Banner, Flag, Framed 38.00
  Spanish–American War, Battleship Maine, Red, White, Blue, Textile 10.00
  Statue Of Liberty, Paris Exposition, 1878, Silk 65.00
  Sterling Silver, Art Nouveau 25.00
  Ten Commandments, Woven 16.00
  Victorian, Greetings, Flowers, Celluloid 2.50
BOSTON & SANDWICH CO., see Sandwich Glass; Lutz

As soon as the commercial bottle was invented, the opener to be used with the new types of closures became a necessity. Many types of bottle openers can be found, most dating from the twentieth century. Collectors prize advertising and comic openers.

To remove the musty smell from a closed cupboard or box, try using rice. Parch several handfuls of uncooked rice in a shallow pan in the oven. Then put the pan and rice in the musty drawer. You may have to repeat the parching to keep the moisture and mildew from reappearing.

Worcestershire sauce is a good brass polish.

Bookend, Dog, Pottery, Cream, Black, Tan, 8 In.

BOTTLE OPENER, Alligator, Cast Iron ....25.00 To 40.00
Banjo Player, Wooden 10.00
Bear's Head 35.00
Bell, Pennsy Select 20.00
Black Man, Wall 50.00
Black Waiter, Holding 3 Beer Steins, Wood, Early 1900s 85.00
Bulldog, Wall Mount ....30.00 To 60.00
Canada Dry ....4.00 To 6.00
Clown 45.00
Clown, With Cigar In Mouth, Corkscrew 28.00
Cowboy Hugging Cactus Plant, Cast Metal 22.00
Cowboy, Next To Cactus 95.00
Curved Stag Horn Handle, Sterling Silver Design & Ferrule 28.00
Dog's Mouth 15.00
Dog, Setter 22.00
Donkey, Brass ....15.00 To 22.00
Dr Pepper, 10–2–4 .... 7.00
Drink Nehi 7.00
Drunk On Lamppost 20.00
Drunk On Palm Tree ....22.00 To 45.00
Drunk With Top Hat & Tails 9.00
East India Ale, Scimitar 25.00
Eldredge Brewing Co., Portsmouth, N.H., Bottle Shape 35.00
Elephant, Sitting, Pink, Iron 18.00
Fish, Brass Frame, Abalone Scales, Jointed 35.00
Fish, Cast Iron 45.00
Flamingo, Pot Metal 15.00
Foundry Man 95.00
Goat, Large Horn, Original Paint 35.00
Goat, Sitting, Backward Horns, Cast Iron 40.00
Golf Club, Can Punch, Stars & Stripes, Japan 10.00
Golfer In Knickers, Sweater, Cast Iron 19.00
Goose, Cast Iron 45.00
Goose, Original Gold Paint 40.00
Hammer, Brass 8.00
Horse's Rear End 60.00
Indian Boy, Bronze, Iroquois Beer, 5 In. 22.00
Indian Head, Molded Composition 35.00
Jayhawk, K.U.University ....14.00 To 22.00
Jumping Dolphin, Brass 60.00
Key, Corkscrew, Silver Plate, 12 In. 18.00
Lamppost, Painted, Gold Trim, Iron 20.00
Lobster, Cast Iron ....15.00 To 25.00
Maltop Malt & Hops, Buffalo, N.Y., Nude Lady 25.00
Man, 4 Eyes ....12.00 To 45.00
Man, Top Hat 25.00
Miss 4 Eyes, Wall Mount 35.00
Moxie, Slides Into Handle 9.00
Muriel Cigars, Hammer Shape 15.00
Nude Standing, Bronze, Korbel 85.00
Nude, Brass 45.00
Nude, Figural, Signed, Bronze 95.00
Old Snifter, White Metal, 6 3/4 In. 65.00
Parrot On Stand, Iron 15.00
Parrot, Cast Iron, Original Paint, 5 In. ....20.00 To 30.00
Parrot, Mother–Of–Pearl, 5 In. 25.00
Parrot, With Corkscrew 22.00
Pepsi–Cola, Bottle Shape ....10.00 To 12.00
Pig's Rear End, Tail Is Corkscrew 50.00
Ram, Horns Open Bottle, Original Paint, Cast Iron 35.00
Rooster, Cast Iron, Original Paint ....22.00 To 35.00
Shark, Aluminum 25.00
Sprite Boy, Box 15.00
Sprite Boy, Coca–Cola, Wall 23.00

Stegmaier's Gold Medal Beer, 1933	9.00
Trout	18.00
Two Nude Babies On Top, 6 In.	38.00
Wall, Sprite Boy Starr–X, Boxed	7.00
White Rock Girl	9.00
Wooden Handle, Enameled Green, Dated 1933	5.00
Yachtsman Cap	39.00

BOTTLE STOPPER, Rooster, Figural, Metal, Marked Cork–A–Bottle–Do	10.00
Swan, Figural, Ivory	10.00

Bottle collecting has become a major American hobby. There are several general categories of bottles, such as historic flasks, bitters, household, and figural. For modern bottle prices and more old bottle prices, see the book "The Kovels' Bottle Price List" by Ralph and Terry Kovel.

BOTTLE, 7–Up, Salesman Sample, Paper Label, Miniature, 1930s	15.00
Amber Brand Coffee, Glass, Label	25.00
Apothecary, Indent For Label, Hollow Ground, Cobalt Blue	68.00
Apothecary, Rexall, Porcelain, Hand Painted Latin, Set Of 5	150.00

Avon started in 1886 as the California Perfume Company. It was not until 1929 that the name Avon was used. In 1939, it became Avon Products, Inc. Each year Avon sells figural bottles filled with cosmetic products. Ceramic, plastic, and glass bottles are made in limited editions.

Avon, Cadillac, Box	5.50
Avon, Christmas Tree	2.50
Avon, Figural, Bride & Groom	15.00
Avon, M.G., 1936, Box	5.50
Avon, Santa Claus	2.50
Avon, Stein, 1979	12.00
Avon, Touring Model T, 1937, Box	5.50
Baby, Clear, Embossed Baby Picture, Happy Baby, 8 Oz.	7.50 To 15.00
Bar, Thumbprint, Applied Collar & Lip, Flint, 10 In.	55.00
Barber, Bay Rum	65.00
Barber, Blown, Opalescent, Cranberry, 7 1/4 In.	120.00
Barber, Cranberry, Seaweed Pattern	75.00
Barber, End Of Day	300.00
Barber, Fern, Square Shape, Clear Opalescent	115.00
Barber, Flowers, Urns, Bay Rum Front, 7 In.	33.00
Barber, Milk Glass, Cologne, Painted Yellow Roses	125.00
Barber, Opalescent Stars & Stripes, Blue	180.00
Barber, Opalescent Stars & Stripes, Cranberry	210.00
Barber, Polka Dot, Blue Opalescent	125.00
Barber, Polka Dot, Cranberry Opalescent	175.00
Barber, Seaweed, Cranberry, Opalescent, 7 1/4 In.	50.00
Barber, T.Noonan & Co., Barber Supplies, Boston, Dark Blue	125.00
Barber, T.Noonan & Co., Barber Supplies, Boston, Mass., Dark Amber	125.00
Barber, Witch Hazel, Camphor Glass	60.00
Bay Rum, Hand Painted Flowers, Words In Black, Milk Glass	65.00

Beam bottles are made to hold Kentucky Straight Bourbon, made by the James B. Beam Distilling Company. The Beam series of ceramic bottles began in 1953.

Beam, Convention, Mermaid	150.00
Beam, D Day	30.00
Beam, Ducks Unlimited No.1, Mallard, 1974	50.00
Beam, Elk's Centennial, 1968	8.00
Beam, Ford Paddy Wagon	64.00
Beam, Ford Pickup Truck	63.00
Beam, Ford Woodie Station Wagon	50.00
Beam, Houston Cowboys, Pair	225.00

Beam, London Bridge, 1971 .... 5.00
Beam, Oldsmobile, 75th Anniversary 50.00
Beam, Red Corvette 45.00
Beam, Telephone, Battery, 1982 .... 30.00
Beer, Biccombe's Ale, Stoneware 16.00
Beer, Coney Island, N.Y., Light Green, Embossed Top, FW VonWiegen 20.00
Beer, Groesch, Brown, Porcelain Stopper, Embossed, Label 5.00
Bitters, Abbotts, Label, Man Pouring Drink, Unopened, Dated ....25.00 To 35.00
Bitters, Brady's Family, Louisville, Ky., Amber, Square 125.00
Bitters, Brown's Celebrated Indian Herb Bitters, Amber, 12 3/8 In. 185.00
Bitters, Caroni, Emerald Green, 5 In. 30.00
Bitters, Dash Hound Bitters, Satin Glass, Dachshund On Front 75.00
Bitters, Dr.Fisch's, Figural, Fish 50.00
Bitters, Dr.Hostetter's Stomach Bitters, Amber ....12.00 To 20.00
Bitters, Grapes, Leaves, Verre De Sole Type, White, Sterling Overlay 69.00
Bitters, Hutching's Dyspepsia, N.Y., Aqua, Iron Pontil, 8 1/2 In. 235.00
Bitters, Lash's Bitters, Amber 12.00
Bitters, S.T.Drake's 1860 Plantation Bitters, Olive Yellow, 10 In. 235.00
Calabash, Flower, Soldier, Iron Pontil, Light Green, 9 3/8 In. 160.00
Calabash, Jenny Lind, Aqua, 10 In. 65.00
Calabash, Sheaf, Reverse, Tree, Light Emerald Green, 9 1/4 In. 135.00
Calabash, Sheaf, Star, Amber, Applied Handle, Iron Pontil, 9 In. 330.00
Carry Nation, Original Stopper 27.00
Catsup, Pride Of The Arm, Embossed 10.00
        BOTTLE, COCA–COLA, see Coca–Cola, Bottle
Cocoa, Wan–Eta, Boston, Amber 18.00
Cod Liver Oil, Figural, Fish, Amber, 6 1/4 In. 40.00
Decanter, Shell Ribbed, American, Stopper, C.1825, Pair 150.00
Demijohn, Olive Green, 20 In. 35.00
Detergent, Lux, Unused, 1940s 7.50
Ezra Brooks, African Lion 32.00
Figural, Barrel, Amber, 10 In. 45.00
Figural, Capital Building, Milk Glass, 8 In. 65.00
Figural, Church, Blown Glass, 4 1/2 In. 80.00
Figural, Little Scotch, Baby With Bottle, Bisque, Germany 80.00
Figural, Log Cabin, Luden's Cough Drops 160.00
Figural, Pig, Pottery, Brown Speckled, Glazed, 7 In. 250.00
Figural, World's Fair, 1939, Milk Glass ....*Color* 10.00
Flask, Chestnut, Aqua, 5 5/8 In. 75.00
Flask, Dewars, Compliments, Plated, 1897 .... 50.00
Flask, Expanded Diamond, Clear Blown, 7 1/4 In. 35.00
Flask, Horn Of Plenty, Eagle, Olive Green, 6 3/4 In. 115.00
Flask, Lady's, Enamel Design, Blue With Craquelle, Stopper, 1/2 Pt. 64.00
Flask, Lady's, Man–In–The–Moon Overlooking Farm, Sterling Cap 135.00
Flask, Leather Top, Glass Bottom, Hunter Offering Drink, Pair 75.00
Flask, Masonic, Eagle, Wreath, Aqua, Initials JP 165.00
Flask, Old Quaker Whiskey, Embossed, Paper Label, Sample, Pair 20.00
Flask, Ravenna Glass, Anchor, Eagle With Stars, Aqua 150.00
Flask, Washington & Jackson, Olive Amber, 6 3/4 In. 80.00
Flask, Washington & Taylor, Red Puce, 7 In. 445.00
Flask, Whiskey, Medicinal Embossed 10.00
Flask, Whiskey, Metal, Leather Covering, Occupied Germany 20.00
Fruit Jar, Bamberger, The Always Busy Store, Newark, Aqua, Qt. 40.00
Fruit Jar, Crowleytown, Zinc Cap, Horizontal Wrench Lugs, Aqua, Qt. 250.00
Fruit Jar, Mason, Pat.Nov.30, 1858, Aqua, Zinc Lid, 7 1/2 In. 3.00
Fruit Jar, Masons's Patent 11/30/1858, Maltese Cross 20.00
Fruit, B.B.G.M.Co., Aqua, Midget 175.00
Garnier, Spock, Bust, Dated 1979, Box 135.00
Ginger Beer, Watertown, New York 16.00
Half Post, Polychrome Enameled Floral, German, Pewter Cap, 7 1/8 In. 165.00
Hoffman, Mr.Lucky Series, 5th 22.00
Ink, Ma & Pa Carter, Germany, Pair ....100.00 To 118.00
Ink, Pauls Safety Bottle & Ink Co., Clear, Embossed 7.50
Ink, Washable, Quink, Diamond Shape 15.00

McCormick, Elvis, Forever Elvis, 1968, No.3, 7 1/2 In. 45.00
Medicine, Ayer's Cherry Pectoral, Contained Heroin, 7 In. 20.00
Medicine, Barry's Tricopherous For Skin & Hair, N.Y., Open Pontil 10.00
Medicine, Brooks Pharmacist, Baton Rouge, Cobalt, 1869, 8 1/4 In. 250.00
Medicine, Champlins Liquid Pearl, Milk Glass, Retangular, 5 In. 10.00
Medicine, Cranes Quinine & Tar Compound, Label, 5 1/2 In. 12.00
Medicine, Davis Vegetable Pain Killer, Embossed, Contained Opium 15.00
Medicine, Dr.Bell's Pine Tar Honey 7.00
Medicine, Dr.Curry's Worm Powder 20.00
Medicine, Dr.Fisch, Fish Shape, Amber 75.00
Medicine, Dr.Haynes Arabian Balsam, Embossed Words, 4 1/4 In. 15.00
Medicine, Dr.Kilmer's Swamp Root Kidney Cure, Sample, Aqua, Cork Top 20.00
Medicine, Dr.Wistar's Balsam Of Wild Cherry, Pontil, Aqua, 6 1/4 In. 30.00
Medicine, Foley Cathartic Tablet, Label, Contents, Boxed, 3 In. 15.00
Medicine, French's Witch Hazel, Rochester, N.Y., Paper Label, Cork 15.00
Medicine, Grove's Tasteless Chill Tonic, Parks Medicine Co. 10.00
Medicine, Herb, Buchu Leaves, Southern Africa 15.00
Medicine, Humphrey's Homeopathic Veterinary, Horse On Bottle 23.00
Medicine, Humphrey's No.14, Skin Disorder, Contents 15.00
Medicine, Humphrey's No.31, Painful Menstruation, Contents 20.00
Medicine, John R.Dickey's Old Reliable Eye Water, Dickey Drug Co. 10.00
Medicine, Lysol, Skull & Crossbones, 1941, Amber, Box 8.00
Medicine, Mrs.Allen's World's Hair Restorer, Amber 15.00
Medicine, One Minute Cough Cure, Labeled, Embossed Words, 4 1/2 In. 15.00
Medicine, Owl Drug Co., Blob Top, Emerald Green, 9 3/4 In. 75.00
Medicine, Paines Celery Compound, 10 In. 35.00
Medicine, Pellets, Cannabis Sativa, Label, Doses, 2 1/2 In. 125.00
Medicine, Piso's Cure For Consumption, Embossed Words, 5 In. 18.00
Medicine, United Chemists, Embossed Mortar & Pestle, 3 3/4 In. 15.00
Medicine, Veno's Lightning Cough Cure, Aqua 10.00
Milk, Cream, Restaurant, Individual, Amber 2.00
Milk, Double Baby Face, Baby Top, Brookfield 24.00
Milk, Double Baby Face, Wood's Dairy 20.00
Milk, King Brothers Dairy, Saratoga, N.Y., Dutch Girl With Pails 10.00
Milk, Sheffield Milk, 2 In. 12.00
Milk, Thatcher's Dairy, Stopper, Man Milking Cow 12.00
Milk, Turkey Hill Farm, Pictures Delivery Truck 10.00
Monarch Lion Finer Foods, 1 Gal. 12.50
Naval, S.M.S.Oldenburg, Porcelain, 1910, 13 In. 211.00
Newbro's Herbicide Kills Dandruff Germ, Embossed, Aqua, Gal. 25.00
Nurser, Acme 28.00
Nurser, Albert, Double Ender 15.00
Nurser, Crying Baby, Patented 1874, Marked 55.00
Nurser, Dimples, Double Ender 16.00
Nurser, Embossed Baby, 8 Oz. 7.00
Nurser, Embossed Cat 1.00
Nurser, Fire King, Madonna Blue, 4 Oz. 17.50
Nurser, Griptight, Double Ender 16.00
Nurser, Handy, 12 Oz. 14.00
Nurser, Submarine, Blown Glass 95.00
Nurser, Submarine, Blue & White, Staffordshire 300.00
Old Judge Coffee, 3 Lb. 26.00
    BOTTLE, PERFUME, see Perfume Bottle
Poison, Raised Beaded Sides, Amber 2.50
Sanford Paste, Bail, Weir Seal, 1 Gal. 50.00
Seltzer, Etched Letters, Germany 15.00
Shell Motor Oil, Qt. 25.00
Shoe Cleaner, Radiant Russet, Boyer Co., Paper Label 15.00
Ski Country, Bobcat 37.00
Ski Country, Redwing Blackbird 32.00
Ski Country, Wood Duck 50.00
Snuff, Agate, Scarab Sides, Green Agate Top 80.00
Snuff, Coral, Covered, Marked 42.00
Snuff, Glass, Garden Scene, 4 Adults, Playing Children 85.00

Snuff, Ivory, Covered, Carvings, 2 1/2 In. 42.00
Snuff, Jade, Dark Green, 19th Century, 4 X 2 1/2 In. 75.00
Snuff, Porcelain, Florals On Black Ground, Agate Top 36.00
Snuff, Reverse Painted Glass, Scenic, Callligraphic Poem 82.50
Soda, A.Fergason, Brandon, Manitoba 90.00
Soda, Codd's, Marble Stopper, C.1890 .... 18.00
Soda, E.P.Shaw & Co., Wakefield 20.00
Soda, Empire, Brandon, Manitoba 65.00
Soda, Graf Zep, Dirigible Raised Likeness, 9 In. 80.00
Soda, Kings Old Country, Winnipeg 40.00
Soda, Moxie, Paper Label, Boston, 7 Oz. 20.00
Soda, Palmer Cox Brownie, Embossed Figures 45.00
Soda, Regina Aereated, Regina, Saskatoon 120.00
Soda, Western Canada Soft Drink Conference, 1982 .... 10.00
Soda, Wm.Robertson 200.00
Virginia Dare Brandy Sauce, Paper Label, Embossed, Full, 4 Oz. 8.50
Whiskey, Croskey's Columbian Gin, Chicago, Amber, Square 250.00
Whiskey, Ezra Brooks, African Lion 32.00
Whiskey, Lewis & Clark Custer 50.00
Whiskey, Mt.Vernon Pure Rye, 3 In. 20.00
Whiskey, Old Cabin, Amber, Log Cabin Shape 15.00
Whiskey, Structo Toy Co., Commemorative, Unused, Box 50.00
White House Vinegar, White House Embossed, 10 In. 9.00
Wine, Grape Cluster Shape, Screw Top, Clear, France, 8 Oz. 25.00
Wine, Jamaica Spirits, Olive Green 50.00
Wine, Vin Mariani Coca, Embossed, Paris, 9 In. 85.00
Wine, Vino Castellano De Brown, Golden Amber, Iron Pontil, 12 In. 335.00
Witch Hazel, Hand Painted Flowers, Words In Black, Milk Glass 65.00

Boxes of all kinds are collected. They were made of thin strips of
inlaid wood, metal, tortoiseshell, embroidery, or other material.

BOX, see also Ivory, Box; Porcelain, Box; Shaker, Box; Store, Box; Tin,
Box; and various Porcelain categories
BOX, Air Balloon Scene, Enamel On Copper, English, 18th Century, 2 X 1 In. 250.00
Alms, Angel, Wooden, Painted, Carved, 14 1/2 In. 170.00
Alms, Man With A Banner, Mechanical, Pot Metal, 12 In. 1100.00
Alms, Man With Dog, Mechanical, Wooden, Carved, Painted, Label, 10 1/2 In. 1600.00
America, Dome Top, Iron Lock, Handles, Painted, C.1835, 26 1/3 X 10 In. 350.00
Band, Laced Seams, Stylized Painted Flowers, Oval, 9 X 15 1/2 In. 475.00
Band, Red Striping, Gold Stenciled Design, Green, Oval, 17 3/4 In. 350.00
Band, Wallpaper Covered, Harbor Scenes, 14 X 17 1/4 X 11 In. 90.00
BOX, BATTERSEA, see Battersea, Box
Bentwood, Covered, Oval, Quarter Sawed Oak, 7 X 9 X 4 In. 45.00
Bentwood, Covered, Round, 7 3/4 X 3 1/2 In. 25.00
Bentwood, Dark Gray Paint, Round, 9 1/2 X 4 1/2 In. 115.00
Bentwood, Lid, Single Finger Construction, Round, 3 X 1 1/2 In. 15.00
Bentwood, Round, 8 X 3 3/4 In. 55.00
Bentwood, Round, Brown, Paper Label, American Fig Confection, 8 3/4 In. 45.00
Bentwood, Single Finger Construction, Copper Tacks, Oval, 3 1/2 X 5 In. 35.00
Bible, 18th Century, Leather, Rose Head Nails, 6 X 9 X 14 In. 220.00
Bible, English Oak, Wrought Iron Lock, Initials & 1676, 25 1/2 In. 85.00
Bible, Original Brass H Hinges, Rose Head Nails, Pine, 10 X 17 X 18 In. 395.00
Bible, Pine, Red Paint, Back Panel Dated 1778, 9 X 24 X 14 In. 450.00
Bible, Slant Hinged Lid, Pine, Blue, 18th Century, 10 X 17 X 18 In. 395.00
Bible, Stylized Carved Foliage, Hinged Lid, Oak, 22 3/4 X 26 1/2 In. 350.00
Brass, Scenic, Hinged Lid, 5 3/4 In. 30.00
Bride's, Bentwood, Cream Paint, Striping, Polychrome Floral, 11 X 17 In. 675.00
Candle, Beveled Edge Lid, Poplar, Cherry, & Chestnut, Pebbly Finish 87.50
Candle, Chamfered Slide Cover, Square Nails, Red Paint 165.00
Candle, Pine, Sliding Lid, Fitted Interior, Molded Base, 6 X 16 1/2 In. 600.00
Candle, Red, 17 1/2 X 9 1/2 X 8 1/2 In. 98.00
Candle, Table Model, Slide Lid, Blue Green Paint, C.1820, 7 X 12 1/2 In. 130.00
Candle, Wall, Cylindrical Shape, Tinned Sheet Iron, 13 In. 325.00
Candy, Father Christmas, Figural, Cotton, Plaster Feet & Face, 12 In. 225.00

Box, Chinese, Altar, Scene Of Geishas
In Gold Leaf, Pair, 20 In.

A magnet will not be attracted to solid brass. It will cling to brass plated iron.

If you display your collection at a library, museum, or commercial store, do not let the display include your street address or city name. It is best if you don't even include your name. A display is an open invitation to a thief.

Candy, George Washington, Plaster, Paper, Painted, German, 3 3/4 In.	45.00
Candy, Wall Phone, Hello Central, Litho, Wooden, 4 1/2 In.	45.00
Cherry, Till, Pencil Drawing, Signed B.F.Kendall, 1884, 8 X 12 In.	225.00
Chinese, Altar, Scene Of Geishas In Gold Leaf, Pair, 20 In. ....*Illus*	600.00
Chip–Carved, Finger Construction, Lid Design, Old Red Finish, 5 3/4 In.	85.00
Cigar, Blue Stocking, Victorian Lady Displaying Legs & Blue Stockings	35.00
Cigar, Judge, Wooden	8.00
Cigar, King Polly, Holtzinger, Parrot Litho, 1910 Stamp	20.00
Cigar, Tango Panetela, 3 For 5 Cents, Wooden	20.00
Cigar, White Porcelain Lining, Brass Plate & Key, Mahogany, 14 X 9 In.	45.00
Cigar, Winnie Winkle	25.00
Cigarette, Mother–Of–Pearl, Covered, 10 X 4 In.	5.00
Clay, Rockingham Glaze, Foliage, Wood Lid, 12 1/2 X 15 X 15 In.	180.00
Coffer Chest, Oak, Carved Stars, Pinwheels, & Birds, 12 1/2 X 7 X 10 In.	75.00
Collar & Cuff, International, Nickel Over Brass, Wooden Base	225.00
Cutlery, 2 Section, Center Handle, Walnut, 11 1/2 X 7 1/2 In.	60.00
Decanter, Bail Handles, 4 Inserts & Tumblers, Mahogany, 14 1/2 X 9 In.	302.00
Decoupage Interior, Alligatored Red Paint, Pine, 4 3/4 X 8 X 12 In.	35.00
Delivery, Hood's Dairy, Flip Top, Wooden	22.00
Document, Leather Covered, Brass Handle, Studs, 18th Century, 5 X 8 In.	85.00
Document, Leather Covered, Hinged Lid, Tack Design, 11 X 6 X 5 1/4 In.	50.00
Document, Sailorwork, Compass Rose Inlay, 6–Pointed Star, C.1850, 14 In.	240.00
Dome Top, Beech, Wrought Iron Hinges, Lock, Floral Polychrome, 9 3/8 In.	410.00
Dome Top, Painted Polychrome Floral, Red Ground, 16 3/4 X 32 3/4 In.	175.00
Dome Top, Pine, White Paint, Houses, Trees, Wire Hinges & Hasp, 4 1/2 In.	95.00
Dome Top, Wrought Iron End Handles, Pine, 13 X 13 1/2 X 25 1/2 In.	35.00
Dome, Continental, Polished Steel, Brass Fittings, Early 19th Century	235.00
Domed Putty Top, Grained, Wooden, Ocher, C.1840, 24 X 12 X 12 1/2 In.	200.00
Dough, Pine, Varnished, Crescent Ends, 29 X 14 X 11 In.	50.00
Dough, Poplar, Dark Brown, Turned Splayed Legs, 16 X 34 X 31 In.	135.00
Dowry, Leather, Grapes, Floral Tooling, Pine, Lock, Pa., 14 X 8 In.	125.00
English, White Metal, Geo.E.Palmer, Goldington, 1767, 4 1/2 In.	60.00
Food, Staved Wood, Banded, Covered, 9 X 6 In.	98.00
Game, Lacquer, Chessboard, Carved Ivory Chessmen, China, 16 1/2 X 8 In.	575.00
Gilt Bronze & Champleve Enamel, Lid, Cushion Form, French, C.1900, 6 In.	550.00
Glove, Wooden, Dark Stain, Red Velvet Lining, 12 X 4 1/2 In.	30.00
Gum, Spruce, Slide Covered, Old Red, Pine, 3 1/2 X 5 1/2 In.	175.00
Hat, Wallpaper Covered, Philadelphia, 10 X 13 In.	40.00
Humphrey's Homeopathic Appetite, Veterinary, Original Contents	12.00
Iron, Lock, Old Paint, Key & Keeper, 5 1/4 X 9 1/4 In.	55.00
Ivory & Horn Veneer, 19th Century, Sandalwood Interior, 8 X 5 1/2 In.	200.00

Box, Knife, Federal, Mahogany Veneer,
C.1810, 14 1/4 In.

Box, Letter, Oriental, Wooden, 2 Doors,
11 X 7 X 15 In.

Jewelry Casket, Ormolut, Gilt, Hinged, Signed Moreau, French, 3 3/4 In.	275.00
Jewelry, Burl Walnut, Ormolu Mounted, Arched Lid, C.1860, 10 In.	60.00
Jewelry, Mahogany, Inlaid Top, Bun Feet, Mirror, 1830, 8 X 10 X 6 In.	150.00
Jewelry, Malachite Veneer, Footed, Satin Lined, Russia, 2 1/2 X 4 In.	200.00
Jewelry, Oak, 20 Drawer, Hinged Lid, 5 X 8 1/2 X 16 In.	250.00
Jewelry, Silver Plate, Heart Shape, Scrolls, Footed, 4 3/4 X 3 1/2 In.	18.00
Knife, Federal, Mahogany Veneer, C.1810, 14 1/4 In. ....*Illus*	1000.00
Knife, Heart Cutout, Dovetailed	195.00
Knife, Hepplewhite, Mahogany, Slant Serpentine Lid, 14 1/4 In.	150.00
Knife, Painted, Blue, Floral Border, Initialed CBC, 19th Century, 14 In.	200.00
Knife, Scalloped Divider, Trace Of Old Blue, Pine, 8 3/4 X 12 3/4 In.	40.00
Knife, Star In Lid, Silver Plated Escutcheon, Mahogany, 8 3/4 In.	200.00
Lacquer, Cylindrical, Groups Of Takamakie Shells, Japan, 4 X 4 3/8 In.	300.00
Lacquer, Gold, Geometrics, Floral, Book Design, Japan, 4 1/2 In.	1050.00
Lacquer, Leaf Shape, Chrysanthemum, Shell Accents, Tray, Japan, 9 1/2 In.	1600.00
Lap Desk, Pine, Grain Painted, American, 19th Century, 10 X 20 In.	175.00
Lap Desk, Primitive, Grain Painted, Mustard, 14 X 14 In.	70.00
Lap Desk, Roll Top, Brass Fittings, Teakwood, 25 X 11 1/2 In.	750.00
Lap Desk, Roll Top, Perpetual Calendar, Letter Slots, 14 X 14 In.	350.00
Lap Desk, Rosewood, C.1850, 15 1/2 X 6 X 10 1/2 In.	135.00

When the weather is bad, the
auction will probably be good.
Brave storms and cold and attend
the auctions in bad weather when
the crowd is small and the prices
low.

Box, Liquor Set, Napoleon III,
Brass, Mahogany Tantalus

Lap Desk, Shaker, Pine, Butternut, Yellow Stain, Drawers, 5 X 21 In. 2000.00
Lap Desk, Walnut, Opens Flat, 2 Compartments 22.00
Leather Bound Dome Top, Original Lock, Hasp, Newspaper Lined, 9 1/2 In. 60.00
Letter, Divider, Canted Sides, Walnut, 5 1/2 X 7 1/2 In. 55.00
Letter, Oriental, Wooden, 2 Doors, 11 X 7 X 15 In. .... *Illus* 140.00
Liquor Set, Napoleon III, Brass, Mahogany Tantalus .... *Illus* 1500.00
Mahogany, Satinwood Inlay, 18th Century, 15 In. 1000.00
Measure, Wooden, Round, 6 1/2 X 11 In. 35.00
Nakara, Covered, Cherub, Floral Design, Pink, 1890, 2 1/2 X 3 5/8 In. 100.00
Necktie, Victorian, French Ivory 55.00
New England, Brass Handles, Pine, Green Paint, C.1820, 24 X 9 3/4 In. 120.00
Norwegian, Gray, Laced Sides, Covered, Wooden Handle, C.1840, 18 X 14 In. 195.00
Oak, Brass Trim, Lion's Feet, 8 X 8 X 8 1/2 In. 40.00
Oak, Lion Feet, Brass Trim, 8 X 8 In. 40.00
Opium, Metal Dragon, Wooden Stand, Chinese, 9 X 9 X 3 In. 80.00
Painted Flowers, Oval Brasses, Paper Covered Pine, 5 1/2 X 9 X 15 In. 115.00
Pantry, Bentwood, Fitted Into Each Other, Covered, Set Of 5 .... 80.00
Pantry, Embossed Squirrel On Lid, 7 In. 40.00
Pantry, Wooden, Pegs, Brass Tacks, 5 1/2 In. 35.00
Pencil, Figural, Pencil 24.00
Pencil, Mother Goose, Tin 12.00
Pencil, Schoolgirl Decorated, Many Motifs, Signed By Three Names 1375.00
Pine, Book Shape, Lid, Olive Green Graining, 9 3/4 X 12 3/4 X 2 5/8 In. 70.00
Pine, Maple Veneer, Transfer Of Presidents, Brass Bail, 5 X 8 In. 40.00
Pine, Red Paint, Floral Design, 1830, Initials S.B., 17 1/4 X 10 1/2 In. 675.00
Pipe, American, Drawer, Old Red Paint, 16 1/4 In. 350.00
Pipe, Hanging, English, Leather Hinge, 19 1/4 In. 100.00
Pipe, Pine, Blue Gray Paint, 1 Drawer, Brass Pull, 13 1/4 In. 2000.00
Playing Cards, Silver Crest, Bronze, Sterling, Decorated 75.00
Polychrome Floral Design, Landscape On Lid, Poplar, 10 X 17 1/2 In. 70.00
Porcelain, Cushion Shape, Palace Garden Scene, China, 12 In.Diam. 100.00
Powder, Child's, Cobalt Blue, Gold 30.00
Powder, D'Orsay, Embossed Floral Lid, Molded Signature 150.00
Rawhide Domed Covered, Copper Tacks, Lined, Spanish, 17 1/2 In. 125.00
Salt, Hanging, Beechwood, Well Scalloped Crest, Canted Ends, 13 1/4 In. 95.00
Salt, Pine, Slanted Lid, 1 Drawer, 9 1/2 X 10 In. 280.00
Scandinavian, Pine, Anne Christi 1781 Den 24 Decenber, 9 X 22 In. 500.00
Seed, Ferry, 12 1/2 X 30 In. 20.00
Sewing, Bentwood, Cherry, 9 X 14 In. 30.00
Sewing, Wicker, Pin, Round, 9 In. 15.00
Shadow, Victorian, Lace, Thread Spools, Lace Collage, 26 X 33 1/2 In. 400.00
Singing Bird, Lid, Gilt Metal, Enameled, Lake Scenes, Austrian, 4 In. 1400.00
Singing Bird, Silver, Enameled, Scrolling, Jewels, Continental, 3 7/8 In. 715.00
Soap, Fairy, Fairbanks, Christmas, Wooden, Covered, C.1898, 16 X 9 In. 125.00
Spice, Tin Bands, 8 Wooden Canisters, 9 X 3 In. 198.00
Spice, Turned Treen, Lid Stenciled Spices, 4 Canisters, 10 In. 190.00
Storage, Bentwood, Round, 10 X 5 1/4 In. 45.00
Storage, Civil War, USN Charles B.Loring, Military Badge On Lid 550.00
Storage, Norwegian, Gray, C.1840, 18 X 14 In. 195.00
Storage, Pine, Painted Landscape Design, 6 5/8 X 13 1/4 X 8 1/2 In. 400.00
Striping & Roses On Lid, Man Ambrotype Inside Lid, Wooden, 9 3/4 In. 50.00
Stud, Hand Painted Flowers, Covered, Wooden 9.00
        BOX, TEA CADDY, see Tea Caddy
Tea, Federal, Covered, Line Inlay Edge, Mahogany, C.1800, 5 1/2 In. 325.00
Tie, Man's, Indian Design In Leather Cover 35.00
Tin, Covered, Mother & Children Scene, England, 5 1/4 X 6 In. 5.00
Tinder, Tin, Sliding Lid, Flint, Matches, Ive's Pat., Bristol, 5 In. 85.00
Tobacco, Copper, Brass, Dutch, 1800, 5 X 3 X 1 1/4 In. 190.00
Veneered Oak, Rosewood, & Patterned Inlay, C.1870, Marquetry, 12 In. 385.00
Wooden Bands, Interlaced Fingers, Old Red Paint, 12 1/2 X 6 1/4 In. 95.00
Wooden, 3 Compartment, 12 Glass Decanter, 11 X 12 X 17 1/2 In. 300.00
Wooden, Bone Shape, Brass Inlaid Scripture, 18th Century, 3 1/2 In. 75.00
Wooden, Floral Spray Painted, C.1826, 21 X 10 1/2 X 9 3/4 In. 700.00
Wooden, Hubbard's Wire Sewed Folding Box, Pat.6/28/1898 .... 32.50

Word Jewels Burned Into Cover, 5 1/2 X 3 1/2 In.	12.50
Writing, Table, Dovetailed Poplar, Fitted Interior, 21 1/2 X 18 1/2 In.	75.00
Wrought Iron End Handles, Lock & Hasp, Dome Top, Pine, 24 In.	375.00

The Boy Scout movement in the United States started in 1910. The first Jamboree was held in 1937. Collectors search for any material related to scouting, including patches, manuals, and uniforms. Girl Scouts are listed under their own heading.

BOY SCOUT, Ax, Genuine Plumb, Case	18.50
Bank, Iron	95.00
Beadcraft Outfit, Loom, Beads, & Thread, Box	42.00
Beadcraft, Original Box, Contents, 1935	25.00
Blanket, Commemorative	20.00
Book, Den, Rockwell Cover, 1954	6.00
Book, Merit Badge, Nature, 1952	7.00
Book, Scouts To The Rescue, George Durstan, 1912	15.00
Book, Year Book, 1923	35.00
Bookends, Emblem Design, Cast Iron, Large	16.00
Bookends, Figural, Scout, Cast Iron	24.00
Bugle, Brass	49.00
Button, Uniform, 1911, Set	12.50
Cup, Folding, Eagle On Top	15.00
Figurine, Cast Iron, 11 In.	60.00
First Aid Kit, Belt Mounted	25.00
First Aid Kit, Metal	10.00
Flashlight, Brass	12.50
Handbook, 1933	25.00
Handbook, Copyright 1948	4.00
Handbook, Cover By Norman Rockwell, 1933	10.00
Handbook, Norman Rockwell Cover, 1959	6.00
Hat, Wide Brim	15.00
Hatchet, Plumb, Emblem	95.00
Knife, Pocket, Cub Scout, Camillus	10.00
Knife, Pocket, Kutmaster	9.00
Knife, Pocket, Remington No.3843, Stag Handle	300.00
Knife, Remington, No.RS3333	75.00
Knife, Ulster	30.00
Manual, First Class Helps, 1931	20.00
Manual, Membership, Celluloid, 1914	10.00
Manual, Sea Explorer, 1954	12.00
Match Holder, Nickel Over Copper	25.00
Music, Sheet, Parade March	20.00
Neckerchief	10.00
Neckerchief Slide, Brass, Statue Of Liberty	15.00
Pamphlet, Pigeon Raising, Merit Badge Series, 1934	8.00
Plate, Dutch, Petrus Regout, 1937, 8 3/4 In.	35.00
Ring, Sterling Silver	5.00
Telegraph Set, Radio Blinker	20.00
Tie Rack, Wooden	28.00
Toy, Boy Scout Playing Violin, Windup, Marked Schuco, Germany	95.00
Toy, Scout Saluting, Metal, Painted Brown, 3 In.	10.00
Whistle, Brass	12.00

Bradley & Hubbard Manufacturing Company made lamps and other metalwork in Meriden, Connecticut, from the mid–nineteenth century. Their lamps are especially prized by collectors.

BRADLEY & HUBBARD, Bookends, Bronze, Woman, Columns, Label, 5 X 5 X 2 In.	50.00
Bookends, Lion & Lioness, Marked, 7 In.	120.00
Bookends, Sailing Ship, Frothy Waves	40.00
Candleholder, 7 In.	20.00
Clock, Ben Franklin, Cast Iron, Dated 1857	1495.00
Clock, Colonial Man, Clock In Stomach, Blinking Eyes	550.00
Desk Set, Art Nouveau, Marked, 3 Piece	75.00
Desk Set, Marked, Silver Plate & Brass, 5 Piece ....125.00 To 145.00

Desk Set, Milk Glass Insert, Brass & Silver Plate, 5 Pc. 145.00
Inkstand, Glass Well 10.00
Lamp Base, Metal Painted, Mottled Green, Marked, 11 In. 55.00
Lamp, 8 Panel Slag Glass Shade, White, Green, Brass Base 565.00
Lamp, 8 Petal Pink Slag Shade, Serpent Handles, 19 In. 485.00
Lamp, Banquet, Oil, 11 In. Ball Shade 300.00
Lamp, Banquet, Pierced Brass Font, Onyx, 22 1/2 In. 100.00
Lamp, Green Tapestry, Dragon Handles, Shade, Brass, 19 In. 495.00
Lamp, Hanging, Original Tin Shade, Brass 300.00
Lamp, Kerosene, Painted Shade 125.00
Lamp, Slag, Paneled 375.00
Lamp, Spelter & Bronzed Base, 4 Light, Marked, 25 In. 55.00
Lamp, Table, Cast Foot, Floral Globe, 23 In. 123.00
Lamp, Table, Green & Red Glass Shade, Overlay, 15 In. 325.00
Lamp, Table, Reverse Painted, Gilt Metal, 1910, 23 1/4 In. 300.00
Lamp, Table, Slag Glass, Marked, Dated 1915 .... 295.00
Letter Clip, Woods Scene, Brass 30.00
Match Safe, Figural, Cricket 49.00
Piano Lamp 345.00
Wall Sconces, Candle Insert, 10 In., Set Of 3 .... 95.00

> *Brass has been used for decorative pieces and useful tablewares since ancient times. It is an alloy of copper, zinc, and other metals.*

BRASS, see also Bell; Tool; Trivet; etc.

BRASS, Basin, Alms, Raised Medallion, Leaf Design, Rope Circle, 21 In. 175.00
Basin, Flat Rim, Double Dolphin Handles, Continental, 20 5/8 In. 140.00
Basin, Tinned, French, Lamb Of Gold Holding Banner, Chalice, 2 In. 250.00
Bed Warmer, Engraved Lid, Turned Handle, 43 1/2 In. 150.00
Bed Warmer, Engraved, Signed Z.P.I. 385.00
Bed Warmer, Pierced Tooled Lid, Turned Handle, 44 1/2 In. 105.00
Bed Warmer, Tooled Scroll Design Lid, 12 In. 55.00
Bed Warmer, Wrought Iron Handle 45.00
Bird In Cage, 2 Birds, Beaks Move While They Whistle, France, 20 In. 850.00
Bird In Cage, Musical, 11 In. 170.00
Bird Perched On Woven Nest, French, 2 In. 165.00
Bootblack Shoe Stand, 15 In., Pair 55.00
Bowl, Etched Scene, China, 8 In. 35.00
Bowl, Flaring, Squared Shape, Round Foot, Dick Van Erp, 3 3/4 X 11 In. 110.00
Bowl, Incised Wooden Base, Design, China, 10 In. 14.00
Box, Jade Medallion In Lid, Brass, 4 X 3 X 1 1/2 In. 55.00
Box, Tobacco, Dutch, 1830, 5 1/2 X 2 3/4 X 1 In. 180.00
Box, Wooden Pedestal, Foo Dog Handles, Jeweled Lid 55.00
Bucket, Apple Butter, 24 In. 52.50
Bucket, Forged Handle, Dated 1851 .... 50.00
Bucket, Iron Handle, Bell Brass 30.00
Bucket, Threaded, Hadley & Co., Anasonia, Ct., Dated 1851, Large 110.00
Candelabra, 7 Arm, Adjustable, Solid Brass, 17 In. 85.00
Candelabra, Baluster Form, 6 Arms, Bobeches, Carrying Rings, 22 In. 300.00
Candleholder, Bronze, Signed Carl Sorensen, Pair 47.50
Candlestand, 48 In. 98.00
Candlestick, 9 3/4 In., Pair 120.00
Candlestick, Baluster Shape, Horizontal Rib, C.1930, 8 1/2 In., Pair 48.00
Candlestick, Beehive & Diamond, 10 1/2 In., Pair 125.00
Candlestick, Beehive, Push-Up, 8 In., Pair 125.00
Candlestick, Brevets, 10 In., Pair 43.00
Candlestick, Bulbous Bobeche, Slender Stem, Disc Foot, 12 In., Pair 140.00
Candlestick, Bulbous Socket, Disc Foot, C.1910, 12 1/8 In., Pair 350.00
Candlestick, Bulbous Socket, Signed Jarvie, 11 In., Pair 150.00
Candlestick, Bulbous Stem, Screws Into Square Base, 6 1/2 In. 250.00
Candlestick, Bulbous, Disc Foot, C.1910, 12 In., Pair 750.00
Candlestick, Classical Revival, Urn Shape, Chain, 13 In., Pair 80.00
Candlestick, English, Beaded Bobeches, 18th Century, 11 In. & 8 In. 600.00
Candlestick, English, C.1880, Pair 225.00
Candlestick, Flower Form Socket, Scalloped Base, 5 In. 100.00

Candlestick, Georgian, 7 In., Pair	50.00
Candlestick, Georgian, 9 In., Pair	70.00
Candlestick, Hexagonal Base, 7 In.	150.00
Candlestick, Hogscraper, Stamped Shaw, 7 1/4 In.	125.00
Candlestick, Knob & Baluster Shape, Square Base, 1920, 17 In., Pair	135.00
Candlestick, Menorah, 17 In., Pair	125.00
Candlestick, Octagonal Standard, Domed Base, French, 9 1/2 In., Pair	600.00
Candlestick, Push Rod, Glass Globe, 11 In.	38.00
Candlestick, Push–Up, 11 In., Pair	120.00
Candlestick, Push–Up, Baluster, 9 In.	65.00
Candlestick, Push–Up, Baluster, C.1840, 8 In.	50.00
Candlestick, Push–Up, Beehive	42.50
Candlestick, Push–Up, Reverse Beehive & Diamond, 12 In., Pair	235.00
Candlestick, Push–Up, Square Base, 19th Century, 6 1/4 In., Pair	145.00
Candlestick, Push–Up, Victorian	150.00
Candlestick, Push–Up, Victorian, 10 In., Pair	130.00
Candlestick, Push–Up, Victorian, Queen Of Diamonds, 11 1/2 In., Pair	170.00
Candlestick, Rococo, Silvered, Bobeche, Urn Shape, France, 11 In., Pair	450.00
Candlestick, Rope Twist Stem, Octagonal Base, 5 3/4 In.	75.00
Candlestick, Shaped Knob & Baluster, Step–Up Base, 4 3/4 In., Pair	135.00
Candlestick, Signed Brevets, 10 In., Pair	43.00
Candlestick, Square Base, 6 In.	85.00
Chamberstick, Push–Up, 4 1/2 In.	40.00
Chamberstick, With Snuffer	100.00
Chest, Blanket, Round	425.00
Cigar Cutter, Match Holder, Collie, Austria, 2 1/4 X 1 1/2 In.	75.00
Coal Scuttle, Shovel, Liner, Late 19th Century, England, 20 In.	250.00
Coin Holder, 2 In.	14.00
Compass, Surveyor's, Leather Case, 3 In.	130.00
Compass, Surveyor's, Silver Dial, Cased, C.1840, 15 In.	325.00
Compass, Surveyor's, Wooden Box	65.00
Corkscrew, Cheshire Cat, Figural, Brass	110.00
Desk Set, Germany, Brass, 5 Piece	130.00
Dish, Alms, Adam & Eve In Garden, Foliate Border, 15 In.	300.00
Dish, Musterschutz Face, Footed	45.00
Door Knocker, Devil's Head, Serpent's Head In Ring	35.00
Door Knocker, Eagle Finial, 7 1/2 In.	35.00
Door Knocker, Lion, 3 1/2 In.	16.00
Door Knocker, Lyre Shape Striker Handles, English, C.1840, 6 1/2 In.	120.00
Door Knocker, Open Pendant Form, American, 7 In.	120.00
Door Knocker, Open Pendant, Striker Button, Stamped M.B. H5530, 7 In.	130.00
Door Porter, Swan With Ewer	80.00
Doorknob, Fancy	12.00
Dresser Set, Glass, 26 Piece	225.00
Easel, Victorian, Foliate Bulbous Design, 61 In.	250.00
Face Plate, Door Latch, Knob, Lock, Victorian	110.00
Figurine, Cat, Round Akro Agate Base, 2 1/2 In.	65.00
Figurine, Delabrierr, 2 Eaglets Fighting, Tree Branch, 13 1/2 In.	340.00
Flatware, Teak Handles, Original Case, Siam, Service For 8	95.00
Frame, Eagle, Curved Glass, Oval	125.00
Frame, Easel, 4 1/4 In.	22.00
Globe, World, Federal Style Stand, Brass Foot, 39 In.	175.00
Hairpin, Victorian, Flower, 5 1/2 In.	11.00
Head, Duck, Hanging Bill Clip, Glass Eyes, 5 In.	65.00
Hinge, Heavy, Dated 1880, Set Of 3	80.00
Holder, Bouquet, Pick For Flowers, Victorian	110.00
Horn, Coachman's, Kohler & Son, London, Leather Sheath, 27 In.	95.00
Horse Comb, Bavarian, 19th Century	170.00
Humidor, La Palina Senators, Advertising	48.00
Incense Burner, Acorn Weighted Base	45.00
Incense Burner, Animal Finial, Bulbous, Champleve, China, 9 3/8 In.	80.00
Incense Burner, Foo Dog On Top, Footed, Marked China	20.00
Incense Burner, Hanging, Church, Brass, 10 1/2 In.	110.00
Incense Burner, Monkey With Pipe In Mouth, Japanese	40.00

Incense Burner, Ogre	10.00
Incense, Turtle Shape, 5 In.	28.00
Jar, Woven Texture, Beading, Arches, Covered, 5 In.	80.00
Kettle, Copper Base, Twisted Iron Handle, Large	50.00
Kettle, Iron Bale Handle, 22 X 13 1/2 In.	55.00
Kettle, Iron Bale Handle, Spun, 15 X 7 In.	65.00
Kettle, Iron Bale, 13 X 8 1/2 In.	75.00
Kettle, Iron Handle, 10 X 5 1/4 In.	35.00
Kettle, Iron Strap Handle, John Bradley & Costol, 7 X 3 1/2 In.	37.50
Kettle, Spun, Stationary Iron Handle, 18 X 9 1/4 In.	55.00
Kettle, Wrought Iron Handle, Spun, 16 1/2 X 7 In.	45.00
Kettle, Wrought Iron, Spun, 18 1/2 X 8 1/4 In.	105.00
Key, Folding, 2 In.	6.00
Ladle, Slot Handle, 18th Century, 18 In.	100.00
Lamp, Astral, Gilt, Acid Finish Shade, C.1820, 28 In.	600.00
Lantern, Skater's	65.00
Lock, Elephant	22.00
Microscope, Drum Case, French, C.1860	75.00
Mirror, Hand, Art Nouveau	12.00
Mirror, Hand, Embossed Bulldog	25.00
Mirror, Owl Face, Glass Eyes	45.00
Mirror, Plateau, Double Beveled Edge, Filigree, 10 1/2 In.	65.00
Mold, Bullet, Colt, 28 Caliber, C.1858, Marked	75.00
Mortar & Pestle, 3 In.	75.00
Mortar & Pestle, 5 In.	55.00
Mortar & Pestle, Brass & Wood	15.00
Nozzle, Gas Pump	20.00 To 45.00
Nozzle, Hose, Fog, 2 Man Wrapped, Marked ICRR, 30 In.	60.00
Nozzle, Hose, Fog, Marked USN	50.00
Padlock, Bramah	85.00
Padlock, Embossed Cincinnati Gas & Electric	12.00
Padlock, Keen Kutter, Emblem Shape, Original Paint	110.00
Padlock, Miniature, 1700	140.00
Padlock, Scroll With Chain, 1895	85.00
Padlock, Seal Custom Excise, 1906	155.00
Padlock, World's Fair, With Chain, 1892	85.00
Pail, Iron Handle, 10 In.	75.00
Pepper Mill, Cylindrical, Jointed Crank Handle, 9 In.	85.00
Petrological, Swift, C.1900	875.00
Pig, Pen Wipe	95.00
Plaque, Transcontinental Air Transport, Santa Fe R.R., July 7, 1929	90.00
Plate, Printing, Cigar, Ornate, 3 Lb.	75.00
Plum Bob	15.00
Pot, Warming, Holding Base, Warmer, English	35.00
Powder Horn, Black Animal Horn Mouthpiece, 6 1/4 In.	35.00
Samovar, Bulbous, Footed Base, Wooden Spigot, Handles, Russian, 12 In.	100.00
Samovar, Miniature, 3 Piece	95.00
Samovar, Russian Script, 22 In.	160.00
Samovar, Turned Wooden Handles, Inscription On Lid, 25 In.	40.00
Scissors, Wick Trimmer & Tray, 9 1/2 In.	85.00
Scissors, Wick Trimmer, Stand, 19th Century, 7 1/2 In.	225.00
Sconce, Brass, Etched Spider Web Design, 2 Candle, 14 1/4 X 9 1/4 In.	55.00
Sconce, Candle, Drip Pan, 7 1/2 In., Pair	210.00
Seal, Wax, Bust, Letter G, 2 3/8 In.	45.00
Seal, Wax, Bust, Shakespeare, 2 3/8 In.	55.00
Seal, Wax, Gentleman, Bending From Waist, 2 1/8 In.	45.00
Seal, Wax, Lady's Leg, Shoe & Garter, 2 3/8 In.	155.00
Seal, Wax, Spiral Tooling, Marked Germany, 2 3/4 In.	55.00
Sextant, Rosewood Handle, Scale Marked Williams Casrdiff, C.1840	325.00
Spittoon, Dayton Mfg., Dayton, Ohio	75.00
Spittoon, Nickel Plated, Large	30.00
Spittoon, Ribbed Design, Weighted Base, 6 3/4 In.	32.00
Spurs, Don Ricardo, Leather & Silver Plate, 5 Point Rowels, Colorado	295.00
Spyglass, Collapsible, 4 Section, Extended 9 1/2 In.	75.00

Stand, Music, 48 In. 180.00
Stand, Pierced Inverted Tray, C.1800, 9 In. 250.00
Stencil Letters & Numbers, Set 25.00
Stencil, Barrel, Numbers, Letters, Rotating Placer, Dated 1868, 13 In. 90.00
Stick, Paper, Double, Hinged Flat Weights, Scroll Handles, 1912, 8 In. 110.00
Sundial, Horizontal, Engraved, German, 17th Century, 6 In. 4620.00
Sundial, Octagonal, Engraved Sun With Face, Cast 15.00
Sundial, Pocket, Universal Equatorial Dial, Silvered, German 3630.00
Swift, Table, Late 19th Century, America, 22 1/2 In. 75.00
Tamp, Pipe, Artful Dodger, 2 1/8 In. 55.00
Tamp, Pipe, Portly Man, Bent Pipe, 2 1/8 In. 55.00
Tankard, Figures & Latin Inscriptions, Hammered, 16 In. 15.00
Tape Measure, Pig Shape 45.00
Tea Strainer 22.00
Teakettle, 4 Ball Feet, Turned Wooden Handle, 7 1/2 In. 45.00
Teakettle, Bird Whistle, Mechanical 45.00
Teakettle, Fixed Handle, Brass Acorn Finial On Lid, English, 12 In. 160.00
Teakettle, Gooseneck Spout, Urn Finial, Handle, Marked H.Gordon 45.00
Teakettle, Melon Ribbed, 4 Ball Feet, Wooden Handle, 8 In. 120.00
Teakettle, Stand, Marked Brooklyn, N.Y., Dated 1892 .... 60.00
Telegraph, Marine, Double Face & Handles 775.00
Telescope, 5 Section, 3 Ft. X 2 In.Diam. 225.00
Tester, Powder, Carved Walnut Handle, 7 1/4 In. 155.00
Tray, Incised Flowers, Birds, & Animals, Raised Rim, Round, 26 1/2 In. 50.00
Tray, Inlaid Walnut, Floral Carved Handle, Scrolls, 1900, 25 In. 65.00
Tray, Pin, Art Nouveau, Lady With Flaring Skirt, 6 X 7 In. 62.00
Tray, Russian Hallmark, Handles, 8 7/8 In.Diam. 90.00
Tray, Russian, Hallmark, Handles, 19 1/2 In. 300.00
Trivet, Footman, Iron & Brass, Queen Anne Legs, 13 1/2 In. 100.00
Trolley Bar, 3 Oval Galleried Tiers, Raised On Wheels 220.00
Trolley Clanker, Push Bell 85.00
Urn, Face On Handle 15.00
Urn, Silver, Copper, Floral, Elephant Head Handles, China, 9 In., Pair 350.00
Vase, Dutch Design, People, Windmill, 7 In., Pair 45.00
Watering Can, French, Large 55.00
Watering Can, Marked H.F. & Co., Sheet, 10 In. 37.50
Wax Sealer, Wooden Handle, Civil War Era 25.00
Whistle, Air, Lukenheimer, Set Of 2 .... 340.00
Whistle, Automotive Exhaust Chime, 15 In. 65.00
Wig Stand, Cast Paw Feet, Removable Tip To Heat 45.00

BREAD PLATE, see various Pressed Glass patterns

 *Brides' baskets of glass were usually one-of-a-kind novelties made in American and European glass factories. They were especially popular about 1880 when the decorated basket was often given as a wedding gift. Cut glass baskets were popular after 1890. All brides' baskets lost favor about 1905.*

BRIDE'S BASKET, Apple Green, Raspberry Enameled Floral, Ruffled 250.00
Cranberry To Clear, Frame, C.1890, 12 1/2 In. 240.00
Cranberry To White, Cased, Ruffled, Plated Frame, 11 In. 190.00
Cranberry, Custard Overlay, Silver Plate Holder, 9 In. 150.00
Daisy & Button, World Brand Silver Plate Holder 135.00
Flowers, Leaves, Marked Silver Plate Basket, 11 1/4 In. 175.00
Opalescent Overlay, Sterling Silver Holder, Cranberry 295.00
Pink Glass Insert, Harp Frame, Paw Feet, 14 In. 100.00
Pink Insert, Enameled Flowers, Fluted, Silver Plate Holder 185.00
Pink To Rose, Ruffled, 12 X 14 In. 225.00
Raspberry Exterior, Ruffled, Silver Plate Holder 225.00
Raspberry To White Interior, Floral, Silver Plate Holder 125.00
Ruffled Edge, White To Pink Shading, Silver Plate 175.00
Ruffled, Enameled Flowers, Dots, Original Frame, 10 3/4 In. 135.00
Shaded Blue Bowl, Poole Holder, Footed 175.00
Shell Shape, Pink Satin Insert, Barbour Holder, Floral 195.00

BRIDE'S BOWL, Blue Overlay, Floral, Berries, Silver Plate Holder, 11 1/2 In. 235.00
  Cherub Compote, Silver Plated Stand, Ruffled, 11 1/8 In. 275.00
  Cranberry Bowl, Silver Plate Holder 450.00
  Cranberry, Swirl Pairpoint Pattern, Figural Birds Holder 395.00
  Floral, Rose To Pink Overlay, Ruffled, 6 5/8 X 5 In. 145.00
  Peachblow, Sunburst, Ruffled, New Martinsville, 10 3/4 In. 175.00
  Quilted White Outside, Pink Interior, Fluted, 10 X 7 1/2 In. 250.00

> *Bristol glass was made in Bristol, England, after the 1700s. The Bristol glass most often seen today is a Victorian, lightweight opaque glass that is often blue. Some of the glass was decorated with enamels.*

BRISTOL, Bottle, Cologne, Scalloped Stopper, Green Handles, Gold Trim 100.00
  Bottle, Dresser, Enameled Flowers, Ball Stopper, 9 1/2 In., Pair 65.00
  Box, Patch, Turquoise, Gold Design, Hinged, Round, 1 1/8 X 1 5/8 In. 95.00
  Cookie Jar, Coraline Floral Design, Pink Interior, White 50.00
  Dresser Set, Tray, 2 Powder Jars, Hair Receiver, Pin Dish, Ring Tree 295.00
  Easter Egg, Red Flowers, Easter Printed 30.00
  Jar, Sweetmeat, Silver Plated Top, Rim, & Handle, 5 1/2 In. 100.00
  Lamp, Fairy, Silver Plated Base, Floral Design, 13 In. 100.00
  Lamp, Floral, Brass, Oil Lamp Shaped, 12 In. 24.00
  Perfume Bottle, Matching Stopper, Enameled Flowers, Dots, 6 1/2 In. 95.00
  Planter, 4 1/2 In. 22.00
  Sweetmeat, Cow Design, Cranes & Ducks, Blue, 5 1/2 In. 295.00
  Vase, Bird On Branches, Fluted Band, Gold Beading, 11 In., Pair 87.50
  Vase, Bird, Floral, Enameled, Turquoise, Flat Oval Shape, 10 1/4 In. 175.00
  Vase, Birds, Rust To Beige, Gold Trim, Bulbous, 10 3/4 In. 95.00
  Vase, Blue Enameled Flowers, 10 1/2 In., Pair 65.00
  Vase, Blue, Copper Design, Red, White Enamel Beads, 11 In., Pair 95.00
  Vase, Bud, Gold Trim, Geometric Design, 5 In., Pair 60.00
  Vase, Bulbous Base, Petticoat Stopper, 6 In. 25.00
  Vase, Caramel, Flowers, Threaded Neck, 6 In. 75.00
  Vase, Enameled Flowers, Blue, 10 1/4 In., Pair 65.00
  Vase, Enameled Flowers, Ruffled Rim, White, 11 1/2 In., Pair 88.00
  Vase, Enameled White Flowers, Turquoise, 11 In., Pair 85.00
  Vase, Flared, Fluted, 8 In., Pair 135.00
  Vase, Floral, Green, 10 In. 40.00
  Vase, Flowers, Ferns, Light Tan Satin Ground, 12 X 7 In., Pair 150.00
  Vase, Frosted, Gold Floral, Religious, Footed, Crimped, 8 1/2 In. 18.00
  Vase, Gold & Floral, Yellow To Green, 12 1/2 In. 75.00
  Vase, Hand Painted Birds, Flowers, & Leaves, White, 11 1/2 In., Pair 150.00
  Vase, Hand Painted, Enameled Floral, Butterfly, 9 3/4 In., Pair 135.00
  Vase, Lady's Portrait, Porcelain, 12 In. 330.00
  Vase, Loop Handles, Urn Shape, Painted Courting Scene, 17 In., Pair 125.00
  Vase, Pink Casing, Hand Painted Flowers, Ruffled Crimped Rim, 9 In. 50.00
  Vase, Polychrome Enamels Of Birds & Flowers, 24 In. 450.00
  Vase, White Flowers, Green Leaves, White, 12 1/2 In., Pair 95.00
  Vase, White, Raspberries, 9 1/2 In., Pair 65.00
  BRITANNIA, see Pewter

> *Bronze is an alloy of copper, tin, and other metals. It is used to make figurines, lamps, and other decorative objects.*

BRONZE, Ashtray, Deer Stands Over Fallen Hunter 40.00
  Ashtray, Zelezny, Boy's Head, Marble, C.1911 .... 140.00
  Bell, El Camino Real, Commemorative 48.00
  Bell Push, Young Girl, Russian 150.00
  Bookends, Bust Of Warrior 35.00
  Bookends, Elephant, Trunk Raised, Signed Reed & Barton 110.00
  Bookends, End Of Trail, 5 1/2 X 5 In. ....22.00 To 35.00
  Bookends, German Shepherd 80.00
  Bookends, Indian On Horse 45.00
  Bookends, Kneeling Nude, Step Up Base, Tinos, Denmark, 7 1/2 ....155.00 To 175.00
  Bookends, Little Girls, 8 In. 55.00

Bookends, Nude Man Throwing Discus, 7 In. 65.00
Bookends, Owl On Limb 35.00
Bookends, Schnauzer, Green & Black Marble Base, German, 6 In., Pair 125.00
Bookends, Ships, 5 1/2 In. 22.00
Bookends, The Aviator, Lindbergh 55.00
Bowl, Lotus Leaf Center, Bullfrog On Lily Leaf, Chinese Markings 25.00
Bowl, Nest, 3 Birds, Austrian, Late 19th Century, 4 3/8 In. 90.00
Box, Covered, Champleve, Enameled, Arabesque, French, 1900, 6 In.Diam. 550.00
Box, Jewel, Painting On Ivory Of Girl On Lid, Signed Nica, 6 Sides 175.00
Bracket, Wall, French, Winged Cupid, Supporting Arms, 12 In., Pair 2200.00
Bust, A.Falguiere, Diana, 19th Century, Marble Socle, 24 1/2 In. 1375.00
Bust, Colombo, Napoleon, Exposition Universelle 1889, 13 In. 550.00
Bust, Colombo, Napoleon, Turned Left, Eagle Under Bust, 1885, 18 In. 1000.00
Bust, Diana, Brown Patina, Inscribed A.Falguiere, 24 1/2 In. 1375.00
Bust, Eagle Head, Green Patina, 10 In. 800.00
Bust, Francisco Goya Y Lucientes, Brown Green Patina, 24 In. 1100.00
Bust, Fromml, Shakespeare, Title Plaque, Marble Pedestal, 10 1/2 In. 270.00
Bust, G.Flamand, Ivory Face, Pedestal On Marble, Signed, 8 In. 850.00
Bust, G.Van Der Straeten, Woman, Grapes In Hair, Shawl, 9 In. 200.00
Bust, J.Laurent, Woman, Braids, Drop Necklace, Draped, Signed, 12 In. 300.00
Bust, Lacordaire, Bonnassieux, 9 1/4 In. 420.00
Bust, R.Colon Co., Portrait, Napoleon, 1885, 17 In. 650.00
Bust, Van Der Straeten, Woman, Laughing Behind Hand, C.1900, 12 In. 750.00
Button, Cameo, Marked Eingets Uster, Set Of 9, 3/4 In. 22.00
Candelabra, Napoleon Style, Pair 500.00
Candelabra, Parcel, Trefoil, 3–Light, French, 24 In., Pair 440.00
Candlestick, Figural, Dragon & Dolphin, Square Base, 11 In. 275.00
Candlestick, Herm Female, 3–Light, Electrified, 22 1/2 In., Pair 1540.00
Candlestick, Louis XV, Foliate Insert, Dore, 12 In., Pair 325.00
Candlestick, Pot Au Feu, Lion Paw Feet, 19th Century, 13 In. 100.00
Casket, Classical Figures, Caryatids, Gilt, Lebland, 1875, 12 In. 550.00
Casket, Jewel, Allover Relief Engraving, Hinged Lid, Lined, 6 1/2 In. 60.00
Censer, Dragon Handles, Monster Heads, Dragons, Japanese, 17 In. 1430.00
Censer, Duck, Wing Pierced Cover, Feathers Enameled, 16 In. 1025.00
Centerpiece, Art Nouveau, Female Nude, M.Bouval, C.1900, 6 X 7 In. 500.00
Compote, Lotus Blossom Shape, Japan, 7 1/4 X 10 In. 70.00
Cricket Cage, Pentagon Disc Design, Cicada Handle, Japan, 8 1/2 In. 225.00
Crucifix, Figure Of Christ On Cross, Medieval, 14th Century, 8 In. 1500.00
Desk, Louis XVI, 2 Drawer, Upper 2 Short Drawers, Miniature 770.00
Dispenser, Cigarette, Donkey, Pull His Ear His Tail Lifts 175.00
Door Knocker, William Wordsworth, Marked England, 1 1/4 X 3 1/4 In. 30.00
Ewer, Empire, Parcel Gilt, Bacchus Mask Spout, Handle, 24 In., Pair 1980.00

Scratches on
bronze cannot be
polished off with-
out destroying the
patina and lower-
ing the value.

Bronze, Figurine, Art Nouveau, Female, Tigers, 29 X 17 X 6 1/2 In.

Figurine, A.Grevin El Beer, Titled Ho He, 20 1/2 In. 400.00
Figurine, A.Levasseur, Dancing Lady, 25 1/2 In. 400.00
Figurine, Alex Gratcheff, Woman Pirate, Russia, C.1880, 9 1/2 In. 2500.00
Figurine, Allan Clark, Woman Walking, 1927, Art Deco, 25 1/2 In. 12100.00
Figurine, Arson, Pheasant, Walking, Oval Base, Dark Patina, 12 In. 455.00
Figurine, Art Nouveau, Female, Tigers, 29 X 17 X 6 1/2 In. ....*Illus* 900.00
Figurine, B.Boschetti, Caesar Augustus, Brown Patina, 20 1/4 In. 550.00
Figurine, B.Boschetti, Classic Female, 25 In. 375.00
Figurine, B.Moret, French, Marble Base, 19th Century, 15 In. 475.00
Figurine, B.Zach, Fencer, Cold Painted, 20th Century, 26 1/4 In. 6380.00
Figurine, Barbedienne, Mary Magdalene Contemplating, 14 In. 375.00
Figurine, Barye, Bear In A Tub 210.00
Figurine, Barye, Dromedary, Dark Brown Patina, 7 3/4 X 9 1/2 In. 475.00
Figurine, Barye, Greyhound, Seated, 1 Paw Raised, Marble Base, 6 In. 225.00
Figurine, Barye, Lion, Serpent, Green Brown Patina, Signed, 13 In. 715.00
Figurine, Barye, Reclining Cow, 9 1/4 In. 250.00
Figurine, Barye, Reclining Panther, Black Green Patina, 11 In. 715.00
Figurine, Bonheur, Horse & Jockey, Brown Patina, 24 1/2 In. 4000.00
Figurine, Bonheur, Jockey On Horse, 30 X 32 In. 5000.00
Figurine, Bound Slave, Nude Woman, French, 22 In. 900.00
Figurine, Boxer, Hole In Body, Black Base, 1 3/4 In. 90.00
Figurine, Buddha, 17th Century, 72 In. ....*Illus* 3250.00
Figurine, Buddha, 6 In. 350.00
Figurine, Bugatti, Crouching Jaguar, Marble Base, 11 3/8 In. 8800.00
Figurine, Butio, Woman With Tambourine, 16 1/2 In. 1250.00
Figurine, C.Korschann–Paris, Lady Praying, Art Nouveau, Gilt, 14 In. 525.00
Figurine, C.Masson, Mouse With Nut, Signed, 3 1/2 X 4 In. 400.00
Figurine, C.Masson, Stag & Family, 23 1/2 In. 1350.00
Figurine, C.Meunier, Man With Sledge, 21 In. 1850.00
Figurine, Cambodian, Recumbent Deer, Gilt, 20 In., Pair 300.00
Figurine, Cat, Austria, 4 3/4 X 7 In. 200.00
Figurine, Charpentier, Shepherd Boy, 16 1/2 In. 700.00
Figurine, Chiparus, Exotic Dancer, Gilt & Gold Painted, 26 7/8 In. 13200.00
Figurine, Clodion, Seated Satyr, 19th Century, Brown Patina, 25 In. 825.00
Figurine, Colin, Icarus, Rocky Base, Brown Red Patina, 1900, 28 In. 1980.00
Figurine, Confucius, Green Patina, Ming, 12 1/4 In. 395.00
Figurine, Donkey & Arab Boy, Enameled, Austrian, 5 X 5 1/4 In. 1250.00
Figurine, Drouot, Fox, Marble Plinth, 25 In. 440.00
Figurine, Dubucand, Snipe Family, Red Gold Patina, 11 X 10 1/2 In. 600.00
Figurine, E.B.Parsons, Scotty, Different Poses, 5 X 7 In., Pair 450.00
Figurine, E.Delabrierre, Retriever & 2 Pheasants, 18 In. 1045.00
Figurine, E.L.Picault, La Source Du Pactole, Signed, 20 X 30 1/2 In. 2500.00

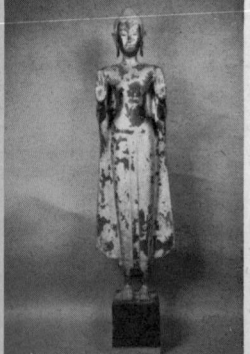

Bronze, Figurine, Buddha,
  17th Century, 72 In.

Figurine, E.Lanceray, Equestrian, Russia, Signed, Marked, 18 X 18 In. 4250.00
Figurine, E.Wante, Clown, Holding Fishing Rod, Signed, 16 In. 1750.00
Figurine, Eagle On Rock, Enamel, Japan, Late 19th Century, 14 In. 750.00
Figurine, Eagle, Wings Spread, Perched On Ball, 24 X 37 X 15 In. 600.00
Figurine, Elephant, Cambodian, Green, 16 In. 110.00
Figurine, Elephant, Running At Full Gallop, Signed 275.00
Figurine, Elk, French, C.1910 .... 7.00
Figurine, F.Preiss, Balancing, Acrobat, Bronze & Ivory, 15 1/8 In. 5500.00
Figurine, Farm Girl, Rooster, Moreau Math Hors Concours, 16 3/8 In. 605.00
Figurine, Female, Roman, Clasping Toga, 25 In. 425.00
Figurine, Freres, Dante, Copper Brown Patina, 18 3/4 In. 330.00
Figurine, Gaudez, Luli Enfant, Kitchen Worker, Tuning Violin, 20 In. 2090.00
Figurine, Girl In Buccaneer Clothes, Ivory Face, Seated, 7 1/2 In. 100.00
Figurine, Goddess Shiva, 37 1/2 In. 200.00
Figurine, Gossamer Days, No.3036, 18 1/2 In. 800.00
Figurine, Gustav Jager, Nude With Wings, Art Deco 225.00
Figurine, H.& N.Deaton, Tiger With Cub, Audubon 55.00
Figurine, H.& N.Deaton, Zebra, Audubon 75.00
Figurine, Hagenauer, African With Spear, Austrian 125.00
Figurine, Heidepriem, Hunter & Dog, Rifle, Brown Patina, 15 5/8 In. 850.00
Figurine, Humphries, Indian On Horse, Signed, 1904, 17 X 15 In. 1850.00
Figurine, Hunting Dog, Quail, Brown Patina, Susse Fres, 17 In. 2300.00
Figurine, Ibis, Oriental, Rockwork Ground, Incense Burner, 28 In. 700.00
Figurine, Indian On Horseback, 10 In. 150.00
Figurine, Indian, Hatchet Over Head, Attacked By Cougar, 24 In. 2900.00
Figurine, J.Benk, Female Nude, Dated 1907, 9 1/2 In. 580.00
Figurine, J.Cardona, Child, C.1900, 11 In. 1250.00
Figurine, J.Dubais, Lady Holding Basket & Movable Bell, 11 1/2 In. 320.00
Figurine, J.Garnier, Seal, 1895–1910, 10 In. 425.00
Figurine, J.J.Cambos, Promethee, Arms Outstretched, Arrows, 28 In. 500.00
Figurine, J.Moigniez, Ground Finch, Poised On Rock, 6 X 7 In. 275.00
Figurine, J.Moigniez, Grouse, Signed, 9 X 7 1/2 In. 350.00
Figurine, J.Moigniez, Pheasant, 1 Foot On Ground, 1 On Weasel, 19 In. 1850.00
Figurine, J.Pradier, Napoleon, Arms Back, Holds Telescope, 12 1/2 In. 450.00
Figurine, Japan, Rat, Resting On Egg 190.00
Figurine, Joan Of Arc, 15 1/2 In. 950.00
Figurine, Juan Clarra, Child, On Stool, Shoe In Hand, 12 In. 400.00
Figurine, Kauba, Indian, Signed, Pair 700.00
Figurine, Kiwi Bird, Polychrome, C.1880, Vienna 95.00
Figurine, Kruse, Marathon Man, No.3456, 19 1/2 In. 1050.00
Figurine, Lanceray, Equestrian, Russia, Signed, 16 X 19 1/2 In. 3750.00
Figurine, Laocoon, 2 Men, C.1820, 28 X 21 In. 3200.00
Figurine, LaVergne, Farmer, Rake, Signed, 19th Century, 21 1/2 In. 1395.00
Figurine, LaVergne, Young Boy, Balancing Ball, 19 In. 1495.00
Figurine, Leo Koch, Soldier, Sword & Hat In Hand, Dated 1906, 17 In. 1175.00
Figurine, Leon–Noel Delagrange, Altar Boy, Signed, 18 1/4 In. 650.00
Figurine, Lorenzl, Dancing Male, Signed 450.00
Figurine, Lowenich, Girl Dancer, Art Deco, Nude Top, 15 1/2 In. 975.00
Figurine, M.Gotze, Small Boy With Dog 500.00
Figurine, Man, Mythological, Wings Outstretched, 7 X 10 In. 340.00
Figurine, Man, Seated On Rock, Minogame Crawls On Knee, 11 1/2 In. 660.00
Figurine, Masse, Girl & Clown, Candle, Saying Good Night, 22 In. 475.00
Figurine, Mautti, Deer, Black Patina, 1874, 37 3/4 In. 1980.00
Figurine, Mercury, Poised Running, Cherub, Green Marble, 33 In. 435.00
Figurine, Mikeshin, Peter The Great, Uniform, 1909, 21 3/4 In. 3300.00
Figurine, Montagne, Mercury, Green Brown Patina, 1867, 33 In. 1650.00
Figurine, Moreau, Farm Girl, 19th Century, Revolving Base, 16 3/8 In. 605.00
Figurine, Moreau, Woman, Seated, Flowing Gown, Dark 9 1/2 In. 385.00
Figurine, Moroccan Boy, Lying Down, Austrian, 5 1/2 In. 150.00
Figurine, Mueller, Peasant Woman, Signed, 19 1/2 In. 600.00
Figurine, Nanteuil, Nude Female, Dark Brown Patina, 16 1/2 In. 700.00
Figurine, Nerim, Lioness, Signed, Green Patina, 26 In. 2400.00
Figurine, Nicolo Paganini, 11 7/8 In. 1100.00
Figurine, North African Soldier, Austria, Cold Painted, 22 1/2 In. 2200.00

Bronze, Figurine, Young Woman, Butterfly,
Gold Patina, 13 X 13 In.

Bronze, Jardiniere, Scene Of Holland,
3 Lion Head Handles, 32 In.

Figurine, Owl, Glass Eyes, Standing, 8 In.	42.00
Figurine, P.J.Mene, Caribou, Standing, Signed, Base, 7 1/2 X 5 In.	345.00
Figurine, P.J.Mene, Dog, Signed, 4 In.	225.00
Figurine, P.J.Mene, Fox, Golden Patina, 5 3/4 X 2/1 2 In.	110.00
Figurine, Pan, Fed Grapes By Female Nude, 19th Century, 3 1/4 In.	300.00
Figurine, Paul Herzel, Buccaneer, 1928, Pittsburgh & Tampa	75.00
Figurine, Philippe, Russian Dancer, Gilt Bronze, Ivory, 24 1/8 In.	4400.00
Figurine, Pierei, Garanti, Standing Woman, C.1900, 15 1/2 In.	500.00
Figurine, Robin, Life Size	175.00
Figurine, Saddlehorse, Austrian, Painted, Signed, 8 3/4 X 7 1/4 In.	350.00
Figurine, Salat, Mythological Man, Wings Out, Marble Tray, 7 1/2 In.	340.00
Figurine, Setter & Hound, Onyx Base, 4 In.	175.00
Figurine, Silvestre, Leda–Swan, Signed, Foundry Marks, 13 X 31 In.	2750.00
Figurine, Squirrel, Sitting, Eating Corn, 2 In.	65.00
Figurine, Terrier, On Hind Legs, 2 1/4 In.	135.00
Figurine, Tortoise, Crawling, Tail Curling, Wrestling Toads, 6 In.	880.00
Figurine, Two Horses Fighting, Plateau, 3 Piece	275.00
Figurine, V.Szczeblewski, Boy, Hands In Pockets, 1889, 16 1/2 In.	675.00
Figurine, Valton, Bulldog, Chained To Post, Stone Plinth, 31 1/2 In.	3025.00
Figurine, Vasili Gratchev, Romantic Couple, 1880, Signed, 15 1/2 In.	1700.00
Figurine, Venus De Milo, Patina, C.1890, 20 In.	475.00
Figurine, Vienna, Servant Boy, Carrying Waterpipe, Rug Base	295.00
Figurine, Vordermayer, Horse & Spearman, No.2710, 17 In.	1300.00
Figurine, Warner, Young Boy, Standing, Base, 9 1/2 In.	225.00
Figurine, Warrior, Sword Raised, Broken Spear, 21 In.	475.00
Figurine, Wood Duck, Polychrome, Wooden Stand, Austria, 4 In.	200.00
Figurine, Young Woman, Butterfly, Gold Patina, 13 X 13 In. ....*Illus*	600.00
Goblet, Sung Dynasty, Ku Form, Carved Stand, Chinese, 11 5/8 In.	575.00
Group, Abduction Of Hippodamia, Wooden Base, Continental, 21 In.	825.00
Group, Barbedienne Fondeur, 2 Nude Wrestlers, 13 1/2 In.	495.00
Group, Barye, Lion & Serpent, Green Brown Patina, Signed, 13 In.	715.00
Group, Barye, Theseus Slaying Centaur, Brown Black Patina, 14 In.	3575.00
Group, Bouraine, Satyr Abducting A Nymph, 20th Century, 18 5/8 In.	800.00
Group, Centaur Abducting Young Woman, 17 1/2 In.	350.00
Group, Cicion & Fondeur, Child Carrying Cock, 20 In.	1430.00
Group, Clodion, Musicians, Wearing Lion Hide, 14 1/2 In., Pair	1300.00
Group, Coustou, Rearing Horses & Trainers, Brown Patina, 15 3/4 In.	770.00
Group, Delabrierre, Retriever & 2 Pheasants, Marked, 18 In.	1045.00
Group, F.Pautrot, Robins, On Tree Trunk, Signed, 19th Century, 10 In.	425.00
Group, Lambeaux, 2 Wrestlers, Rocky Ground Base, 32 In.	4950.00
Group, Masson, Stag & Family, Leaf Molded Base, Signed, 23 1/2 In.	1320.00

Group, Max Bougeois, Roman Man & Woman, Marble Base, C.1870, 16 In. 350.00
Group, Moigniez, Ram & Reclining Ewe, Copper Patina, 1800s, 11 In. 1350.00
Group, Pautrot, Pheasants, Copper Patina, 14 1/2 In. 500.00
Group, Peyre, Two Dancing Jesters, Gilt Bronze & Ivory, 18 1/2 In. 7700.00
Group, Woman & Peacock, C.1900, 21 1/2 In. 2475.00
Holder, Book, Desk Type, Folding Ends, Minstrel & Garden Scene 75.00
Humidor, Indian Bust, Full Headdress 2625.00
Incense Burner, Foo Dog, 5 1/4 In. 25.00
Incense Burner, Phoenix, Elephant, Japan, 19th Century, 15 In. 375.00
Incense Burner, Pumpkin Shape, Teak Stand, Japan, 19th Century, 7 In. 90.00
Jardiniere, Scene Of Holland, 3 Lion Head Handles, 32 In. ....*Illus* 900.00
Jewelry Box, Allover Floral, Painting On Ivory Lid, Signed Nica 175.00
Lamp, Bell, Japanese, 17 In. 225.00
Mask, Death, Napoleon, Signed Dr.F.Antommarchi, Dated 1833, 13 In. 900.00
Mortar, Brass Pestle, 17th Century, 5 1/2 X 3 1/2 In. 350.00
Plaque, 3 Cupids, Walnut Frame, Metallic Compress Cast, Oval, 12 In. 110.00
Plaque, F.Barbedienne, Water Woman, No.157, 4 1/2 X 17 1/2 In. 140.00
Plaque, Milles, Lovers, 3/4 Relief, 16th Century Costume, 15 In. 412.00
Plaque, P.J.Mene, Dead Game Relief, 13 1/2 In. 700.00
Plaque, Roine, Paris Welcomes 10th Century, 15 X 25 1/2 In. 680.00
Plaque, Semidraped Figure, Inscription 1886–1901, 8 1/2 In. 155.00
Plaque, Whaling Boats, Harpooners, Weighted Metal Shell, 8 In.Diam. 59.00
Pot, Baluster Form, Scrolled Handles, Lion Head Feet, 6 1/8 In. 50.00
Pot, Offering, Incised Line Design, Long Tapered Handle, Egypt, 9 In. 100.00
Sconce, Neoclassical, Cold Painted Alabaster, 5–Light, 30 In., Pair 1750.00
Screen, Table, Dragons Pursuing Flaming Pearls, Ming Dynasty, 4 In. 275.00
Seal, Letter, Dog Head, Signed Fremiet 220.00
Stand, Umbrella, Cylindrical Form, Lilies, 24 In. 375.00
Statue, Troika Group, Signed Woerffel Foundry, Dated 1877, 22 In. 4400.00
Sword, Winged Shape, Comical Form, Bird Script, 19 In. 660.00
Urn, Barbedienne, Underplate, Floral, Enameled, 2 Handles, 1875, 8 In. 495.00
Urn, Louis XVI, Cover, Putto Holding Branch, Handles, 29 In., Pair 2750.00
Urn, Oriental, Silver Inlaid Cranes, Tapered Bulbous Body, 14 In. 750.00
Urn, Temple, C.1850, Japanese, 4 Ft., Pair 11000.00
Vase, Applied Sterling Silver Pussy Willows, Heintz Art, 4 1/8 In. 66.00
Vase, Art Deco, Flying Birds & Mountain, Oriental Mark 75.00
Vase, Bulbous Form, Ring Handles, Mask Panels, Chinese, 14 In. 110.00
Vase, Champleve, Chinese, 11 In. 310.00
Vase, Chinese, Birds, 15 In. ....*Illus* 175.00
Vase, Inlaid Copper, Bird On Flowering Bushes, Japanese, 9 In. 500.00
Vase, Intaglio Design Band, Twin Notched Handles, Chinese, 12 In. 60.00
Vase, Oriental, 4 Raised Owl Faces, 9 In. 325.00

To remove the remains of sticky glue and tape from antiques, try rubbing peanut butter on the sticky area until the glue is gone. Do not use this method on porous materials where the oil from the peanut butter could leave a stain.

Bronze, Vase, Chinese,
Birds, 15 In.

Vase, Reeds & Geese, Silvercrest, 14 In.	135.00
Vase, Relief Spray Of Iris, Calligraphic Signature, Japan, 18 In.	450.00
Vase, Signed Sorenson, 9 In.	45.00
Vase, Sterling Silver Overlay, Floral, Signed, Dated 1912, 11 In.	125.00
Wine, Hu Form, Incised Cicada Design, Ming, Gilded, 9 5/8 In.	90.00

Brownies were first drawn in 1883 by Palmer Cox. They are characterized by large round eyes, downturned mouths, and skinny legs. Toys, books, dinnerware, and other objects were made with the Brownies as part of the design.

BROWNIES, Book, Funny Animals, Palmer Cox	28.00
Bottle, Soda, Embossed Figures	43.00
Frame, Picture, Figural, Lithograph Of Brownies, 9 X 11 In.	275.00
Game, Horseshoe, Original Box	65.00
Game, Ring Toss	45.00
Music, Sheet, Dance Of Brownies, 1895	30.00
Music, Sheet, Frolic Of Brownies, 1896	30.00
Plate, Palmer Cox, Fisher, 5 In.	55.00
Ruler, Palmer Cox, Mrs.Windlow's Soothing Syrup Advertising	20.00
Stickpin, Palmer Cox, Uncle Sam	18.00
Tin, Brownie Peanuts, 10 Lb.	85.00

George Brush started working in 1901 in Zanesville, Ohio. He started his own pottery in 1907, but it burned to the ground and he joined McCoy in 1909. After a series of name changes, the company became The Brush Pottery in 1925. Collectors favor the figural cookie jars made by this company.

BRUSH, Cookie Jar, Cinderella, Pumpkin	34.00
Cookie Jar, Clown	40.00
Cookie Jar, Cow, Cat On Back	30.00
Cookie Jar, Davy Crockett ....40.00 To	58.00
Cookie Jar, Donkey & Cart, Brown	85.00
Cookie Jar, Elephant, Baby Bonnet	100.00
Cookie Jar, Old Shoe	35.00
Cookie Jar, Peter Pan ....55.00 To	75.00
Cookie Jar, Squirrel On Log	35.00
Cuspidor, Lady's, Brown Mottled Glaze, 3 1/2 X 6 In.	22.50
Figurine, Pig	15.00
Pot, Pale Green Jade, 1 7/8 X 4 In., Pair	75.00
BRUSH MCCOY, see McCoy	

Buck Rogers was the first American science fiction comic strip. It started in 1929 and continued until 1965. Buck has also appeared in comic books, movies, and, in the 1980s, in a television series. Any memorabilia connected with the character Buck Rogers is collectible.

BUCK ROGERS, Book, Big Little Book, Adventures Of Buck Rogers, 1934	85.00
Book, Big Little Book, Coca Malt Giveaway, 1933	30.00
Book, Comic, No.2	125.00
Book, Pop–Up, Strange Adventures In The Spider Ship	145.00
Button, Solar Scout	30.00
Dart Pistol, Daisy	15.00
Decoder Badge	42.50
Display, Water Pistol, Liquid Helium, Red & Yellow, 1936	150.00
Game, Flying Saucer, Cardboard, Tin Rim, Rocket Ships Design	95.00
Gun, Disintegrator, Pops ....45.00 To	52.00
Gun, Punch–Out, Rubber Band, 1940 ....50.00 To	60.00
Kite, Strato, 1947	20.00
Map, Solar, Mailing Tube	265.00
Patrol Ship, Shooting Rockets	595.00
Pencil Box, 1936	40.00
Pinback Button	55.00
Pistol, Atomic ....85.00 To	100.00
Pistol, Liquid Helium Water	75.00
Pistol, Ray, Sonic, Box	100.00

Pistol, Ray, Super Sonic, Box 100.00
Telescope 185.00
Toy, 6 Figures, Movable Arms, J.Dille & Co. 1600.00
Toy, Attack Ship, Tootsietoy, Box 155.00
Toy, Police Patrol Rocket Ship, 12 In. 175.00
Toy, Rocket Ship, Police Patrol 275.00
Toy, Rocket Ship, Tootsietoy, 1930s, 5 In. ....*Illus* 142.00
Toy, Rocket Ship, Windup, Marx, 12 In. 375.00
Toy, Space Ship, Morton Salt, Secret Bomb Sight, 1940s 75.00
Toy, Space Ship, Windup, Litho Tin, 1927, 12 In. ....*Illus* 430.00
Toy, Star Fighter, Fires Rockets, Corgi, No.647, Box, 6 In. 26.00
Toy, Walking Twiki, Windup, Mego, 7 In. 35.00

 *Buffalo pottery was made in Buffalo, New York, after 1902. The company was established by the Larkin Company, famous manufacturers of soap. The wares are marked with a picture of a buffalo and the date of manufacture. Deldare ware is the most famous pottery made at the factory. It is khaki-colored transfer-decorated ware.*

BUFFALO POTTERY DELDARE, Bowl, Breaking Cover, 9 In. 450.00
Bowl, Fallowfield Hunt, 9 In. 225.00
Bowl, Fruit, Village Tavern 475.00
Bowl, Ye Lion Inn, 8 X 3 3/4 In. 350.00
Candlestick, Colonial Days 575.00
Chop Plate, Evening At Ye Lion Inn, 14 In. 650.00
Creamer, Olden Days 195.00
Creamer, Village Life ....120.00 To 165.00
Cup & Saucer, Dr.Syntax Of Liverpool 375.00
Cup & Saucer, Return 200.00
Cup & Saucer, Ye Olden Days, 1924 ....150.00 To 175.00
Cup & Saucer, Ye Village Street 175.00
Fruit Bowl, Ye Village Tavern, 9 In. 600.00
Humidor, Sailor, Emerald, 8 In. 700.00
Humidor, Ye Lion Inn 475.00
Mug, Fallowfield Hunt, 2 1/2 In. 400.00
Mug, Pigeons Inn, 4 1/4 In. 145.00
Mug, Ye Lion Inn, 1909, 4 1/4 In. ....150.00 To 250.00
Pitcher, 2 Scenes, 8 In. 455.00
Pitcher, No.165, Signed & Dated, 6 In. 400.00
Pitcher, Return, 8 In. 500.00
Pitcher, To Demand My Annual Rent, 8 In. 475.00
Pitcher, With A Superior Air, 9 In. 575.00
Plaque, Breakfast At 3 Pigeons, 12 In. ....450.00 To 600.00
Plate, At Ye Lion Inn, 6 1/4 In. ....75.00 To 175.00

Buck Rogers, Toy, Space Ship, Windup,
Litho Tin, 1927, 12 In.

Buck Rogers, Toy, Rocket Ship,
Tootsietoy, 1930s, 5 In.

Plate, Breaking Cover, 10 In.	200.00
Plate, Chop, Fallowfield Hunt, 14 In.	500.00
Plate, Death, 8 1/2 In.	250.00
Plate, Hunt Scene, 9 1/2 In.	155.00
Plate, Lion Inn, 6 1/4 In., Pair	250.00
Plate, Lion Inn, Pierced, 12 In.	300.00
Plate, Start, 9 1/4 In.	180.00 To 300.00
Plate, Ye Olden Times, 9 1/4 In.	125.00 To 250.00
Plate, Ye Town Crier, 8 1/4 In.	100.00 To 225.00
Plate, Ye Village Street, 7 1/4 In.	88.00 To 175.00
Punch Bowl, Fallowfield Hunt, 14 1/2 In.	5000.00 To 6500.00
Saucer, Fallowfield Hunt	65.00
Sugar & Creamer, Village Scenes	365.00
Sugar & Creamer, Ye Olden Days	349.00
Sugar, Covered, Village Life	175.00
Sugar, Open, Ye Olden Days, 1908	235.00
Tankard, Great Controversy, 12 1/2 In.	150.00
Tankard, Hunt, 12 1/2 In.	700.00
Teapot, In Ye Olden Days, 5 3/4 In.	350.00
Teapot, Village Life	300.00 To 400.00
Teapot, Ye Olden Days, 1908	450.00
Tile, Tea, Traveling In Ye Olden Days, 6	150.00 To 275.00
Tray, Calling Card, Fallowfield Hunt	279.00
Tray, Calling Card, Return	375.00
Tray, Calling Card, Ye Lion Inn	300.00
Tray, Dancing Ye Minuet, 9 X 12 In.	525.00
Tray, Dresser, Dancing Ye Minuet	465.00 To 750.00
Tray, Heirlooms, 10 1/2 X 12 In.	535.00
Tray, Heirlooms, Artist Signed, 13 X 10 In.	600.00
Tray, Pin, Dr.Syntax, Emerald Green	535.00
Tray, Pin, Heirlooms, 3 1/2 X 6 1/4 In.	290.00
Tray, Pin, Received By Maid Instead Of Mistress	725.00
Tray, Pin, Village Scenes, 3 1/2 X 6 1/4 In.	290.00
Trivet, Traveling, Ye Olden Days, Framed, 6 1/4 In.	195.00
BUFFALO POTTERY, Ashtray, George Washington	65.00
Butter Chip, Multicolor, Art Deco Border, Dated 1927	10.00
Fish Set, Different Game Fish, Platter & 6 Plates	250.00
Mug, Advertising, Bing & Nathan, Friar, 4 1/2 In.	80.00
Pitcher, Cinderella, No.33	400.00
Pitcher, Fox Hunt, 7 In.	Color 250.00
Pitcher, George Washington	350.00 To 420.00
Pitcher, Gloriana, Blue & White	250.00
Pitcher, John Paul Jones	550.00
Pitcher, Pilgrim, No.40	500.00
Pitcher, Robin Hood, No.41	375.00
Pitcher, Roger Williams	345.00 To 385.00
Pitcher, Sailor, No.32	550.00
Plate, Christmas, 1951	42.00
Plate, Christmas, 1953	27.50
Plate, Christmas, 1954	35.00
Plate, Christmas, 1956	45.00
Plate, Christmas, 1957	42.00
Plate, Christmas, 1960	35.00
Plate, Gunner	85.00
Plate, Wild Ducks, 9 1/2 In.	45.00
Vanity Set, Roses, 6 Piece	120.00

Burmese glass was developed by Frederick Shirley at the Mt. Washington Glass Works in New Bedford, Massachusetts, in 1885. It is a two-toned glass, shading from peach to yellow. Some have a pattern mold design. A few Burmese pieces were decorated with pictures or applied glass flowers of colored Burmese glass.

BURMESE, see also Gunderson

BURMESE, Bride's Bowl, Silver Plated Holder, Large 2500.00
   Centerpiece, 4 Nosegay Vases, England, Brass Frame, 4 1/2 In. 700.00
   Condiment Set, Silver Plated Frame, 3 Piece 500.00
   Cruet, Stopper, 8 In. 395.00
   Lamp, Double Fairy, 3 Lily Epergne ....*Illus* 625.00
   Muffineer, White & Bittersweet Blossoms, Peaches & Cream Ground 585.00
   Pitcher, Water ....*Illus* 500.00
   Rose Bowl, Thistle Flower Design, 2 1/2 In. 230.00
   Shade, Lamp, Glossy, 5 X 4 1/2 In. 265.00
   Toothpick, Bulbous, Square Top, Leaves, Enameled Flowers, 3 In. 255.00
   Toothpick, Hexagonal Top, Satin Finish 350.00
   Toothpick, Rigaree Around Center, Ruffled 375.00
   Tumbler, Green, Opaque, Gold Band, 3 3/4 In. 600.00
   Vase, Flower, Leaf Design, Glossy, 4 In. 325.00
   Vase, Flowers & Leaves, 3 In., Pair 340.00
   Vase, Inverted Bell Shape, Flared, Pinched Top, Pedestal Base, 4 In. 375.00
   Vase, Red Buds, Green Leaves, 4 X 8 In. 750.00
   Vase, Ribbed Body, Flared Neck, Satin Finish, 4 In. 150.00
   Vase, Ribbed, Scalloped Top, 2 1/2 X 3 3/4 In. 175.00
   Vase, Ruffled Top, Salmon Pink To Yellow, 3 3/4 In. 165.00
   BURMESE, WEBB, see Webb Burmese

Buster Brown, the comic strip, first appeared in color in 1902. Buster and his dog Tige remained a popular comic and soon became even more famous as the emblem for a shoe company, a textile firm, and others. The strip was discontinued in 1920, but some of the advertising is still in use.

BUSTER BROWN, Bank, Buster Brown & Tige, Iron 125.00
   Bank, Horseshoe, Buster Brown & Tige, Cast Iron ....115.00 To 225.00
   Bank, With Tige, Plaster 12.00
   Billhook 10.00
   Blocks, Print, Original Box, 1910 .... 65.00
   Book, Buster Brown Abroad, R.F.Outcault, Edition Pub.Nov.1904 .... 45.00
   Book, Coloring 30.00
   Book, French 22.00
   Book, Paint, Figural, 1916, 88 Pages 50.00
   Camera, No.2 Box 22.50
   Card, Signed Outcault 5.00
   Card, Valentine, Tige, Signed Outcault, Dated 1907 .... 8.00
   Clicker ....10.00 To 12.00
   Comic Strip, 10 Segment, 1909 .... 10.00
   Creamer, Tige 40.00
   Dictionary, 1923 .... 38.00
   Dish, Child's Feeding, Tige 20.00

Burmese, Pitcher, Water

Burmese, Lamp, Double
Fairy, 3 Lily Epergne

Fan, Tige, Framed	55.00
Fork, Dog On Handle	5.00
Game, Necktie Party	135.00
Hand Mirror & Whistle	25.00
Hatchet	80.00
Mirror, Advertising, Pocket	15.00
Mirror, Hand, Silver, Small	25.00
Mug	95.00
Paper Doll, Army & Navy Suit, Other Suits, 2 Hats, 12 In.	189.50
Patch, Cloth, Pictorial, 1930s, With Tige, Set Of 3	10.00
Patch, With Tige, Square, 2 1/2 In.	5.00
Pitcher, Cream, ABC	95.00
Plate, 6 In.	50.00
Plate, Buster & Girl	47.50
Plate, Buster & Tige, Advertising, 7 In.	75.00
Plate, Buster Brown, Tige & Balloon, 8 In.	85.00
Plate, China, Germany, 7 In.	45.00
Plate, Scalloped	32.00
Postcard, Sept.& Oct.1910, Set Of 2	25.00
Ring	10.00
Sewing Box, Child's	49.00
Shoe Tree, Figural, Plastic	28.00
Sign, Display, 5 Ft.	275.00 To 295.00
Socks, 1940s	25.00
Socks, 1944	24.00
Stockings, Cotton, Black, Label, Size 7	10.00
Toy, Buster Brown In Cart, Pulled By Tige, Iron, 1900	350.00
Watch, Strap & Fob, Pocket	145.00
Whistle, Pictorial, Tin	10.00
Whistle, With Tige, 1930s	12.00
Yo–Yo, Tin Litho	20.00

Butter chips, or butter pats, were small individual dishes for butter. They were in the height of fashion from 1880 to 1910. Earlier as well as later examples are known.

BUTTER CHIP, Floral, Hand Painted, Meakin, Set Of 6	35.00
Majolica, Etruscan, Pansy	20.00
BUTTER MOLD, see Kitchen, Mold, Butter	
BUTTERMILK GLASS, see Custard Glass	

Buttons have been known throughout the centuries, and there are millions of styles. Gold, silver, and precious stones were used for the best buttons but most were made of natural materials like bone or shell, or from inexpensive metals. Only a few types are listed for comparison.

BUTTON, Brass, Military	16.00
Classical Figure, C.1850, Wedgwood	20.00
Fire Department	5.00
Flower, Paperweight, Set Of 7	75.00
Golf Sticks Over Ball, Brass, 1/2 In.	1.00
Handmade, Double Row Of Petals, Sterling Silver, 3/4 In., Set Of 6	48.00
Ivory, Carved, Ball Shape, 1/2 In.	.50
Lyre, Uniform, Original Car, 24 Piece	6.00
New York City Fire Dept., Silver, Brass, 3 Size, Set Of 6, Card, 1920	35.00
Police, Lawrence Police, Waterbury Button Co., Brass, Set Of 6	12.50
Railroad, Pennsylvania, Metal, Set Of 2	15.00
Railroad, Providence & Worcester, Dated 1872, 2 Large, 10 Small	60.00
Trojaneers, Berkeley	2.00
Trumpet Flower, Brass, 1 2/16 In.	8.50
U.S.N., C.1812	65.00
U.S.O.	2.00

Buttonhooks have been a popular collectible in England for many years but only recently have gained the attention of American collectors. The buttonhooks were made to help fasten the many buttons of the old–fashioned high–button shoes and other items of apparel.

BUTTONHOOK, Adler & Schact Clothiers	10.00
Advertising, Beck Hazzard Shoes	5.00
Advertising, Blechmans, Coatsville, Pa.	5.00
Advertising, Bond Street Spats, Metal	8.00
Advertising, Bone Handle, 8 In.	25.00
Advertising, Ivory Handle, 8 In.	25.00
Advertising, J.C.Penney	2.00
Art Nouveau, Glove, Sterling Silver	15.00
Glove, Embossed Hollow Handle, Sterling Silver, Marked	12.00
Sterling Silver, Long	25.00

The Bybee Pottery was started in 1845 and is still working. The Lexington, Kentucky, firm makes pottery that is sold at the factory. Pieces are marked with the name or with the name enclosed by the outline of the state of Kentucky.

BYBEE, Vase, Relief Grass Design, Variegated Matte Green, Marked, 11 In.	198.00

Calendars made to hang on the wall or to be displayed on a desk top have been popular since the last quarter of the nineteenth century. Many were printed with advertising as part of the artwork and were given away as premiums. Calendars with gun or gunpowder or Coca–Cola advertising are most prized.

CALENDAR PAPER, 1688, Paschal, Matted & Framed, 11 X 14 In.	75.00
1848, Slades Spice, Child	25.00
1871–1971, Harrington Richardson Centennial	15.00
1876, Centennial Home Ins.Co., 12 Pages, 7 1/2 X 5 1/2 In.	50.00
1888, Scott's Emulsion, Girl Holding Kitten & Puppy, Torn	10.00
1889, Hood's	25.00
1890, Hillman Telegraph, 3 Shoeshine Boys	85.00
1892, Phoenix Insurance	20.00
1893, Cows & Cowboy, Just Branded, Framed	15.00
1893, Hood's	32.00
1894, Card, New York Pharmacal Ass., Yonkers, N.Y., 11 In.	75.00
1894, Halfield & Kerney, Children, Folding, 7 X 12 1/2 In.	75.00
1894, Hood's Sarsaparilla, Pretty Girl	22.00
1894, Metropolitan Life Insurance Co., Knapp Lithograph	25.00
1895, Hood's, Children, Summer & Winter, Maud Humphrey	110.00
1895, New York Life Insurance, 4 Pages, Prang Floral Lithos	38.00
1895, Prang, 4 Pages	45.00
1896, Cutler & Grinder Barber Supplies, 6 X 8 1/4 In.	15.00
1896, Ida Waugh Elastic Starch, Quarterly	30.00
1897, Hood's Sarsaparilla	15.00
1897, Iroquois Brewing Co., 12 X 17 In.	250.00
1897, Louis Rhead, Publisher L.Prang, 5 Sheets, 19 X 14 In.	150.00
1898, Fairy Floral, 6 Pages, 8 1/2 X 12 In.	75.00
1898, Gems From Shakespeare, Tied With Ribbon	20.00
1899, 4 Season, Fold Up, Sayings For Each Season	25.00
1899, Beautiful Children, 3 Section, Die Cut	35.00
1899, Hood's	25.00 To 30.00
1900, Dupont Powder Co., Ram Jumping Ravine, 14 X 28 In.	250.00
1900, Hood's Sarsaparilla, Cutout Of 2 Girls	300.00
1900, Hood's, Girls	28.00
1902, Adrience Buckey Harvesting Machinery, 13 X 11 In.	35.00
1902, Favorite, Fan Shape	45.00
1902, Quaker Oats, Queens Of Home & Nation, 4 Page	40.00
1903, Cascara Quinine, Die Cut Little Girl	22.00
1903, Fairbank's Fairy Soap	145.00
1903, Prudential Insurance, Girl, Forbes Litho	10.00

1904, Christian Herald, Birds & Flowers, 29 In. 45.00
1904, Doe Wah Jack Stove Company, Round Oak 290.00
1904, Grand Union 32.00
1905, Metropolitan Insurance Co. 15.00
1905, Metropolitan Life Insurance, 4 Girls, 8 X 25 In. 38.00
1905, Youth's Companion, Girl In Bonnet, Red Carnations 40.00
1906, Fleischmann's Yeast, Horse & Wagon Scene, 10 X 14 In. 45.00
1906, Goodyear 65.00
1906, Hood's 38.00
1906, Woman In Fashion Dress, 14 X 19 In. 30.00
1907, Blacksmith Shop, Spring Blossoms, Signed Humphrey 35.00
1907, McCormick Harvesting Machines, Man, Bow, Gun, 3 Dogs 75.00
1908, Teddy Bear, Figural, Trade Card 15.00
1909, Metropolitan Life Insurance, Mother & Child 65.00
1909, T.Clark Carriage Repository, Edella, Pa., Winter Scene 10.00
1910, Head Of Buck Deer, Lavender Floral Frame, 16 X 9 In. 37.50
1911, Card, Antikamnia Tablets, Beatrice, 5 X 7 In. 50.00
1911, International Coffee 48.00
1912, Cunard Ship Docked At Boston 35.00
1912, DeLaval Cream Separator, Girl Raking Hay, 12 X 24 In. 45.00
1912, Harvesting Machinery Co. 35.00
1912, Victorian Design, Pine Frame, 16 X 20 In. 40.00
1913, Campbell Soup Girl, Friends, G.Weidersham, 7 X 10 In. 25.00
1913, Dodge 15.00
1913, Prudential Insurance, Ketterlinus Litho 5.00
1914, Dodge 15.00
1915, Putnam Dye, General Putnam Picture, Framed 25.00
1916, Pabst Malt Tonic, Beautiful Woman 85.00
1916, Twelvetrees Child, Signed, Postcard Size 27.50
1917, Pompeian Soap, Mary Pickford Picture, 7 X 28 In. 47.50
1918, Edison Mazda, Maxfield Parrish, Full Pad 110.00
1918, Fanny Farmer, Dinner, Boxed 16.00
1918, Little Girls, Signed Gregson, 6 X 32 In. 25.00
1918, Nutting, Full Pad 40.00
1918, Swift's Premium, 4 Cards, World War I, 15 In. 45.00
1920, Baldwin Locomotive Works 100.00
1920, Garage, 2 Girls In Roadster, Pad Used, 14 X 22 In. 12.00
1921, Sharples, 12 X 22 In. 100.00
1922, Hood's Sarsaparilla 15.00
1922, McCormick Deering 60.00
1923, Hunt, Lasher, Where A Hen's A Man 65.00
1923, Metropolitan Life, Pastel Of Mother & Child 22.00
1923–24, Wrigley's P.K. 12.00
1926, Parrish, Original Box, 5 X 5 In. 37.50
1927, Edison Mazda, Maxfield Parrish 60.00
1928, Chevrolet, 20 X 30 In. 27.00
1928, Fredericksburg Bakery, Fred, Pa., 2 Young Ladies 18.00
1928, Kittens 25.00
1928, Liberty 5.00
1929, Edison Mazda, Maxfield Parrish, Full Pad 90.00
1929, Engagement, Leather, Miniature 3.50
1929, Rose Marie, Armstrong, 29 X 45 In. 75.00
1930, New York Central Railroad, Full Pad 75.00
1930, Times Square, Coca–Cola, During Theater Hours 125.00
1930, Western Ammo, Hunter & Indian In Canoe, Full Pad 275.00
1932, Parrish, Original Envelope 350.00
1932, Western Cartridge, Champion Mars Guy, Osthaus 75.00
1933, There's No Place Like Home, Fox, 9 5/8 X 7 In. 65.00
1933, White Rose Gasoline 7.00
1935, Child With Teddy Bear 55.00
1935, Maxfield Parrish, Complete 35.00
1935–37, DeLaval, Poughkeepsie, N.Y., Factory, 17 X 9 In. 25.00
1936, Dr.Miles Weather 3.00
1937, Currier 15.00

1937, Ripley's Believe It Or Not 12.00
1938, Dionne Quintuplets 25.00
1938, Goodyear Tire, Sleeping Hunter With Gun & Dog 10.00
1939, Cream Top Milk Bottle 22.00
1939, John Rogers Statuaries, The Travelers 35.00
1940, Boy Scout 30.00
1940, Sunoco, Beale Patriotic Scenes 10.00
1943, Vargas 35.00
1945, Lawson Wood 18.00
1945, Our Heavyweights, Thompson Products, 26 X 16 1/2 In. 225.00
1946, Cloes Real Estate, San Diego, Girl & Dog In Car 10.00
1946, Esquire Vargas, Envelope 30.00
1946, Oer The Land Of The Free, Rockwell, 22 X 45 In. 20.00
1946, Vargas 35.00
1946, Vegas Girl 20.00
1947, Boy Scout, Dixon, Norman Rockwell 15.00
1947, Hercules Powder 28.00
1947, Squirt, Boy 24.00
1949, Boy Scout, Rockwell Illustrated, 16 X 33 In. 75.00
1949, Grapette 24.00
1951, Rockwell, 4 Seasons 35.00
1952, Silhouette, With Thermometer 9.00
1953, Ford 15th Anniversary, Norman Rockwell 15.00
1953, Parrish, Peaceful Night, Winter, Full Pad, Small 55.00
1954, Boy Scout, Norman Rockwell, 7 1/2 X 14 1/2 In. 6.50
1954, Marilyn Monroe, Original Nude 25.00
1955, Marilyn Monroe, Nude, 10 X 17 In. 22.00
1956, Hummel 30.00
1957, Travelers Insurance, Currier & Ives Illustrations 36.00
1959, Playboy, Jayne Mansfield Is Miss August 10.00
1960, Hummel 25.00
1960, Puppies Reference 20.00
1960, Texas Bar, Souvenir, Nude, 1960, 2 1/2 X 6 1/2 In. 12.00
1961, Santa Fe Railroad, Indian 25.00
1963, Hummel 35.00
1964, Hummel 35.00
1964, Maxfield Parrish, 6 Color Pictures 15.00
1965, Hummel 35.00
1966, 4 Seasons, Norman Rockwell 10.00
1967, Ridgid Tool Co. 7.50
1973, Hummel 15.00
1973, John Deere 5.00
1978, Hummel 7.00

Calendar plates were very popular in the United States from 1906 to 1929. Since then, plates have been made every year. A calendar and the name of a store, a picture of flowers, a girl, or a scene were featured on the plate.

CALENDAR PLATE, 1906, Holly & Rose, Advertising Candy Store, 9 In. 37.50
1908, J.B.Meyer, Groceries & Jewelry, Minster, Ohio, Monks 68.00
1909, Bird Center, Brownsville, Mn. 20.00
1909, Floyd Jones Sundries, Crawford, Nebraska, 8 1/2 In. 30.00
1909, Girl Center, Souvenir Of Abrams, Wisc. 37.00
1909, N.Y.State Capital Building, Green, White, 9 In. 27.50
1909, Portrait Center, Big Stone City, S.D. 35.00
1910, Cherubs, Ringing Bell, 8 In. 35.00
1910, Compliments Inglewood, Calif., Floral Garlands 25.00
1910, Fruit, Lund, Wis. 22.00
1910, Henry Jurgensen Meats, St.Paul, Mn. 21.00
1910, Hunting Scene, 7 1/2 In. 25.00
1910, Indian Chief, 8 1/2 In. 25.00
1910, Mount Vernon, Washington's Home, Circled Pink Roses 18.00
1910, Shipley, W.Va. 25.00
1910, Ships & Windmills 22.50

Candle drippings can be removed from fabric or furniture with the help of ice cubes. Rub the wax with the ice until the wax hardens. Scrape off the hard wax with a credit card or stiff cardboard. If some wax remains, put a blotter over the wax, then iron with a cool iron.

An ivory should never be washed, especially if it is painted. The best way to clean ivory is with a soft brush. If you have a friend whose hands perspire profusely, have him handle the ivory, as it will add to the patina and coloring. An ivory should be kept in high humidity, so it is always best to keep an open cup of water nearby.

Candlesticks will melt or even explode if candles burn too low. Support the arm of a candelabra when putting in the candles.

Calendar, Pompeian, Girl In Pink, Cleveland, Oh., Paper, 28 X 7 In.

1911, Flowers, Store Advertising, 7 In.	20.00
1912, Advertising, Fruit & Cherubs, Wedgwood	24.00
1912, Cherub & Fruit, Saugatuck, Michigan	25.00
1912, Floral, Champion, Mich.	22.00
1912, Indian Maiden, Wooden Frame	35.00
1914, H.B.Raezer, The Grocer, Lewisburg, Pa.	10.00
1915	10.00
1954, Fiesta	15.00
1955, Fiesta, Green	35.00
1959, Taylor Smith, Ivory & Gold	8.00
1961, Cline Mtr.Co., Pratt, Kansas	7.50
1976, 200 Anniversary Year, Eagle, Stars, & Stripes	10.00

CALENDAR, Pompeian, Girl In Pink, Cleveland, Oh., Paper, 28 X 7 In. ....*Illus*   35.00

Camark Pottery started in 1924 in Camden, Arkansas. Jack Carnes founded the firm and made many types of glazes and wares. The company was bought by Mary Daniel, who still owns the firm. Production was halted in 1983.

CAMARK, Bowl, Turquoise, Flaring Sides, Original Paper, 12 In.	30.00
Figurine, Cat, Black, 9 1/2 In.	15.00
Figurine, Cat, Black, Label, 16 In.	25.00

Vase, Aqua, 4 In. 20.00
Vase, Gold Trees, Mountains, Cream Ground, Marked, 8 1/2 In. 125.00
Vase, Matte Green Over Tan, Bulbous, Flaring, Loop Handles, 4 In. 8.00
Vase, Matte Green, Scalloped, Embossed Flowers, 7 3/4 In. 20.00

Cambridge art pottery was made in Cambridge, Ohio, from about 1895 until World War I. The factory made brown glazed decorated wares with a variety of marks including an acorn, the name "Cambridge," the name "Oakwood," or the name "Terrhea."

CAMBRIDGE

CAMBRIDGE POTTERY, Vase, Brown, Green, Oakwood, 8 In. 65.00

Cambridge Glass Company was founded in 1901 in Cambridge, Ohio. The company closed in 1954, reopened briefly, and closed again in 1958. The firm made all types of glass. Their early wares included heavy pressed glass with the mark "Near Cut." Later wares included Crown Tuscan, etched stemware, clear and colored glass. The firm used a C in a triangle mark after 1920.

CAMBRIDGE, see also Depression Glass
CAMBRIDGE, Alpine, Bowl, Crystal, Footed, 12 1/2 In. 45.00
Apple Blossom, Bowl, Light Blue, 13 In. 70.00
Apple Blossom, Bowl, Yellow, 13 In. 30.00
Apple Blossom, Cocktail, Stemmed, 3 Oz. 10.00
Apple Blossom, Cup & Saucer, Yellow 24.75
Apple Blossom, Goblet, Yellow 20.00
Apple Blossom, Relish, Amber, 5 Section 42.50
Apple Blossom, Tumbler, Juice, Yellow 15.00
Bashful Charlotte, Figurine, Clear, 11 1/2 In. 100.00
Calla Lily, Candlestick, Forest Green 18.00
Candlelight, Goblet ....15.00 To 22.00
Caprice, Bonbon, Gold Trim, Footed, 6 In. 25.00
Caprice, Bowl, 2 Handles, Footed, 6 1/4 In. 14.00
Caprice, Bowl, Blue, Footed, 12 1/2 In. 50.00
Caprice, Bowl, Crimped, 4–Footed, Yellow, 13 In. 55.00
Caprice, Bowl, Mandarin, Gold, Crimped, Oval, 13 In. 55.00
Caprice, Candelabra, 5–Light, 12 In. 70.00
Caprice, Candleholder, Blue, 3–Light Tier 45.00
Caprice, Candlestick, 2–Light, Keyhole, Blue, Pair 95.00
Caprice, Candlestick, Crystal, 2 1/2 In. 12.00
Caprice, Candy Dish, Blue, Covered 95.00
Caprice, Cocktail, 3 1/2 In. 15.00
Caprice, Compote, Moonlight Blue, Footed, Low, 7 In. 35.00
Caprice, Cordial ....32.50 To 49.00
Caprice, Creamer, Blue, Individual ....6.00 To 22.00
Caprice, Cruet, Oil, Stopper, Blue, 3 Oz. 50.00
Caprice, Cup & Saucer, Crystal ....10.00 To 15.00
Caprice, Cup, Pistachio 25.00
Caprice, Dish, Mayonnaise, Underplate, Blue, Handles, 8 1/2 In. 80.00
Caprice, Epergne, Clear 100.00
Caprice, Goblet, Blue, 10 Oz. 30.00
Caprice, Mayonnaise Set, Blue, Alpine, 3 Piece 45.00
Caprice, Pitcher, Ball, 80 Oz. 40.00
Caprice, Pitcher, Cobalt Blue, 80 Oz. 95.00
Caprice, Plate, Blue, 8 1/2 In. ....12.00 To 18.00
Caprice, Plate, Footed, Low, 8 In. 11.00
Caprice, Punch Cup, Swan Handle 24.00
Caprice, Relish, 3 Compartment, Silver Overlay, 8 1/2 In. 35.00
Caprice, Relish, Blue, 2–Part, 6 3/4 In. 40.00
Caprice, Relish, Divided, 6 1/2 In. 21.00
Caprice, Sherbet, Blue ....20.00 To 35.00
Caprice, Sugar & Creamer, Tray, Alpine 30.00
Caprice, Tumbler, Blue, Footed, 10 Oz. ....17.00 To 30.00
Caprice, Tumbler, Footed, 12 Oz. 22.00
Caprice, Vase, Blue, 8 1/2 In. 125.00
Carmen, Compote, Nude Stem, 8 In. 175.00

Cascade, Candy Dish, Crystal, Covered 40.00
Cascade, Goblet, 5 1/2 In. 8.50
Cascade, Sherbet, Crystal 9.00
Cascade, Vase, Mandarin Gold, 9 1/2 In. 46.50
Chantilly, Bowl, Footed, Fluted, 12 In. 60.00
Chantilly, Candleholder, 5 In., Pair 35.00
Chantilly, Cocktail Shaker, Sterling Silver Top & Bottom Band 30.00
Chantilly, Cup & Saucer 28.00
Chantilly, Decanter, Stopper, Footed 125.00
Chantilly, Goblet, Water, Crystal 26.00
Chantilly, Plate, Crystal, 10 1/4 In. 65.00
Chantilly, Relish, Crystal, 2 Section, 8 1/2 In. 25.00
Chantilly, Salt & Pepper, Sterling Silver Tops & Bases 35.00
Chantilly, Sugar & Creamer, Sterling Silver Base 45.00
Chantilly, Tumbler, Juice, Footed 15.00
Chantilly, Vase, Sterling Base, 12 In., Pair 42.00
Cleo, Bowl, Amber, 11 1/2 In. 22.00
Cleo, Cup & Saucer, Amber 15.00
Cleo, Plate, Blue, 8 In. 15.00
Cleo, Tray, Sandwich, Pink, Handles 35.00
Colonial, Butter, Child's, Covered 18.00
Colonial, Table Set, Cobalt Blue, 4 Piece 190.00
Crown Tuscan, Ashtray, Cobalt Blue 37.50
Crown Tuscan, Bowl, 10 In. 30.00
Crown Tuscan, Bowl, Centerpiece, Shell Shape 65.00
Crown Tuscan, Bowl, Seashell, 3-Footed, 9 In. 38.00
Crown Tuscan, Bowl, Seashell, Footed, 8 1/2 In. 48.00
Crown Tuscan, Bowl, Square, 4-Footed, 11 1/4 In. 62.00
Crown Tuscan, Box, Cigarette, Dolphin Feet, Shell, Floral, Covered 35.00
Crown Tuscan, Candy Dish, 3-Part, Painted Peacock, Covered 80.00
Crown Tuscan, Candy Dish, No.3500/57, Covered, 8 In. 95.00
Crown Tuscan, Compote, Shell, Nude Stem, 5 1/4 In. 95.00
Crown Tuscan, Plate, Seashell, 7 In. 20.00
Crown Tuscan, Vase, Bud, Rose Point Etching, 10 In. 57.00
Crown Tuscan, Vase, Cornucopia, Shell Footed, 10 In., Pair 270.00
Decagon, Bowl, Blue, 8 In. 24.00
Decagon, Bowl, Fruit, Etched, Gold Trim, Pink, 12 In. 35.00
Decagon, Dish, Mayonnaise, Underplate, Honeycomb Band, Handles 25.00
Decagon, Plate, Pink, 8 In. 6.50
Decagon, Wine, Amber 12.00
Diane, Bowl, 4-Footed, Crimped, 12 1/4 X 9 1/2 In. 40.00
Diane, Butter, Covered 100.00
Diane, Candlestick, Etched 43.00
Diane, Goblet, Water 16.00
Diane, Nut Cup Set, Footed, Set Of 8 .... 240.00
Diane, Relish, 2-Part 18.00
Diane, Salt & Pepper 30.00
Draped Lady, Console Set, Flower Frog, Amber, Frosted, 3 Piece 225.00
Draped Lady, Flower Frog, Amber Base, Rose, 8 1/2 In. 190.00
Draped Lady, Flower Frog, Scalloped Base, Ivory, 13 1/2 In. 800.00
Eagle, Relish, Crystal, 3-Part, Handles 110.00
Elaine, Goblet, 10 Oz. 15.00
Elaine, Vase, Ivy Ball, Amber 22.00
Everglade, Bowl, 4-Footed, 9 In. 25.00
Everglade, Bowl, Blue, Oval, 9 X 12 In. 55.00
Everglade, Bowl, Tulip, Moonlight Blue, 12 1/2 In. 60.00
Everglade, Centerpiece, Moonlight Blue, Oval, 12 In. 55.00
Everglade, Sugar & Creamer, Blue 65.00
Feather, Bowl, Scalloped, 4 X 9 In. 30.00
Ferlana, Creamer, Child's, Cobalt 35.00
Ferlana, Spooner, Child's, Cobalt 35.00
Flame, Candlestick, 7 In., Pair 175.00
Gadroon, Bonbon, Yellow, Square Handle 15.00
Gadroon, Compote, 8 1/2 In. 22.50

Georgian, Oyster, Carmen, Footed 10.00
Georgian, Sherbet, Mocha, Footed 10.00
Georgian, Tumbler, Cobalt, 3 1/4 In. 10.00
Georgian, Tumbler, Signed, Pink, 12 Oz. 28.00
Gloria, Relish, Amber, Divided, 12 In. 25.00
Grapevine, Creamer, Child's, Blue Ovals 50.00
Grapevine, Mug, Child's, Crystal 32.00
Gyro Optic, Tumbler, Moonlight Blue, 13 Oz. 14.00
Gyro Optic, Water Set, 7 Piece 68.00
Heirloom, Cruet, Stopper, Crystal 55.00
Heirloom, Sugar & Creamer 20.00
Heron, Flower Frog 80.00
Honeycomb, Bowl, Rubina, Flared, 10 1/2 In. 80.00
Honeycomb, Console, Amberina, 10 In. 68.00
Keyhole, Bowl, Ivy, Ruby 35.00
Keyhole, Candlestick, Clear, Label, Pair 22.00
Lady, Flower Frog, Green Frosted, 8 1/2 In. ....175.00 To 225.00
Lady, Flower Frog, Satin Crystal 150.00
Marjorie, Berry Set, 7 Piece 62.00
Marjorie, Bottle, Salad Dressing, Green 95.00
Martha, Candlestick, Crystal, Pair 39.00
Martha, Sugar & Creamer, Tray 28.00
Mt.Vernon, Candlestick, Pair 200.00
Mt.Vernon, Cordial, 1 Oz. 69.00
Mt.Vernon, Goblet 6.00
Mt.Vernon, Plate, 8 1/2 In. 4.50
Mt.Vernon, Tumbler, Footed, 3 Oz. 4.00
Nautilus, Decanter Set, Decanter 14 Oz., 6 Piece 45.00
Nude Stem, Bowl, Fluted, Royal Blue, Marked, 12 In. 95.00
Nude Stem, Candlestick, Double, Royal Blue, Pair 245.00
Nude Stem, Champagne, Optic 100.00
Nude Stem, Cocktail, Pink ....75.00 To 150.00
Nude Stem, Compote, 5 1/2 X 8 1/2 In. 65.00
Nude Stem, Compote, Crown Tuscan, Double Ball Extension 175.00
Nude Stem, Compote, Rose Design, 5 In. 110.00
Nude Stem, Goblet, Royal Blue 175.00
Nude Stem, Relish, 3–Part, Royal Blue, 12 In. 85.00
Portia, Bowl, 2 Handles 30.00
Portia, Decanter, Crystal 145.00
Portia, Ice Bucket 60.00
Portia, Relish, 3–Part 29.00
Portia, Sherbet, 6 Oz. 22.00
Portia, Sugar & Creamer, Yellow 19.00
Pouter Pigeon, Figurine, Frosted 75.00
Primrose, Bonbon, Cover, 5 In. 55.00
Primrose, Bowl, 12 X 1 3/4 In. 54.00
Primrose, Powder Box, Covered, 6 1/2 In. 35.00
Pristine, Decanter, Clear, 32 Oz. 28.00
Pristine, Sherry, 2 Oz. 15.00
Ram's Head, Console Set, Doric Candlesticks, Ivory, 3 Piece 500.00
Rose Point, Basket, 2 Handles, Crystal, 6 In. 25.00
Rose Point, Bonbon, Handles, 6 In. 20.00
Rose Point, Bottle, Oil, Stopper 120.00
Rose Point, Bowl, Footed, Handles, 10 In. 60.00
Rose Point, Box, Cigarette 75.00
Rose Point, Candleholder, Double, Pair 62.50
Rose Point, Candlestick, 2–Light, Keyhole 55.00
Rose Point, Candlestick, 3–Light, Tiered, Pair 135.00
Rose Point, Candlestick, Etched, Gold Edge, Pair 68.00
Rose Point, Candlestick, Triple 38.00
Rose Point, Candy Dish, Covered, 3–Part 55.00
Rose Point, Claret 75.00
Rose Point, Cocktail Shaker ....185.00 To 250.00
Rose Point, Cocktail, Crystal, 6 1/4 In. ....25.00 To 29.00

Rose Point, Compote, 5 1/2 In.	22.00
Rose Point, Cordial	69.00
Rose Point, Creamer, Amber	7.00
Rose Point, Decanter, Glass Stopper	170.00
Rose Point, Goblet	22.50 To 25.00
Rose Point, Holder, Cigarette, Round	110.00
Rose Point, Ice Bucket	150.00
Rose Point, Jam Jar, Sterling Silver Top	105.00
Rose Point, Jug, 76 Oz.	185.00
Rose Point, Jug, Ball, Crystal, 80 Oz.	210.00
Rose Point, Mayonnaise, Spoon, Crystal, Footed	59.00
Rose Point, Mustard, Covered	125.00
Rose Point, Pitcher, Water, Ice Lip	225.00
Rose Point, Plate, 9 1/2 In.	40.00
Rose Point, Plate, Amber, Double Scalloped, Square, 8 In.	3.00
Rose Point, Plate, Cheese & Cracker, 12 In.	35.00
Rose Point, Plate, Sandwich, Amber, Center Handle	17.00
Rose Point, Plate, Torte, 13 1/2 In.	50.00
Rose Point, Relish, Covered, 3–Part	85.00
Rose Point, Shaker, Crystal, Footed, Sterling Silver Top, Pair	40.00
Rose Point, Sherbet, High Stem	17.75
Rose Point, Sugar & Creamer, Green	15.00
Rose Point, Tray, Sandwich, Center Handle	150.00
Rose Point, Tumbler, 10 Oz.	20.00 To 50.00
Rose Point, Tumbler, Flat, 5 Oz.	57.50
Rose Point, Vase, Footed, 11 In.	70.00
Rose Point, Vase, Gold Encrusted, 6 In.	45.00
Rose Point, Wine	28.00 To 59.00
Royal, Candlestick, Blue, 7 1/2 In., Pair	78.50
Sea Gull, Flower Frog, 10 In.	40.00
Shell, Bowl, Crown Tuscan, Shallow, 13 In.	65.00
Shell, Bowl, Moontone, 13 In.	50.00
Shell, Sugar & Creamer, Crystal	35.00
Shell, Vase, Cornucopia, Footed, 9 1/2 In., Pair	165.00
Swan, Apple Green, Marked, 6 1/2 In.	75.00
Swan, Carmen, 3 1/2 In.	75.00 To 85.00
Swan, Clear, Frosted, 3 In.	36.00
Swan, Compote, Red Bowl, Clear Nude Stem, 8 1/2 In.	110.00
Swan, Crown Tuscan, 3 1/2 In.	25.00
Swan, Crystal, 3 1/2 In.	25.00
Swan, Ebony, 8 1/2 In.	115.00
Swan, Emerald, 6 1/2 In.	90.00
Swan, Figurine, Green, 7 In.	50.00
Swan, Forest Green, 8 1/2 In.	100.00
Swan, Gold, 3 1/2 In.	30.00
Swan, Saltshaker, Clear	20.00
Tally–Ho, Bowl, Ruby, 13 X 3 5/8 In.	65.00
Tally–Ho, Candleholder, Carmen, 5 In., Pair	95.00
Tally–Ho, Goblet, Hunt Scene, 18 Oz.	44.75
Tally–Ho, Ladle, Punch, Crystal, 11 In.	40.00
Tally–Ho, Plate, Handle, Carmen, 11 1/2 In.	45.00
Tally–Ho, Sauceboat, Ruby	20.00
Tally–Ho, Tumbler, Handles, Frosted, 1 1/2 Oz.	12.50
Twist, Candlestick, Jade, 8 1/2 In., Pair	50.00
Wheat, Bowl, Green, Footed, Oval, 12 3/4 In.	28.00
Wheat, Cocktail, Amber, 4 5/8 In.	6.00
Wheat, Cordial Set, Amber, Decanter & 4 Tumblers, Optic	34.00
Wheat, Pitcher, Amethyst, Moonstone Frosted Interior, 80 Oz.	52.00
Wheat, Plate, Amber, Tab Handles, 11 1/2 In.	10.00
Wheat, Tumbler, Amber, Footed, 6 In.	8.50
Wildflower, Bowl, Footed, 12 In.	30.00
Wildflower, Cake Plate, Handles	34.00
Wildflower, Candlestick, 2–Light, 6 In., Pair	55.00
Wildflower, Celery, 3–Part, Gold Etched, 10 In.	29.00

Wildflower, Dish, Mayonnaise, Footed, Pink 70.00
Windsor, Candlestick, Blue, Shell, Pair 99.00

Cameo glass was made in much the same manner as a cameo in jewelry. Parts of the top layer of glass were cut away to reveal a different colored glass beneath. The most famous cameo glass was made during the nineteenth century.

CAMEO GLASS, see also under factory names

CAMEO, Bottle, Perfume, Bamboo, Leaves, Silver Top, English, 5 1/4 In. 975.00
Bottle, Perfume, English, Lay Down, Cut Fronds, Butterfly, 9 1/2 In. 750.00
Bottle, Scent, Shape Of Swan's Head, Satin Lined Case 2090.00
Bowl, Underplate, Raspberry, Floral, Leaves, Signed Webb, 6 In. 2250.00
Mug, Carriage, Church, People, Sandwich, 4 3/4 In., Set Of 2 .... 300.00
Mug, Church & Carriage Scene, Handle, 4 3/4 In. 300.00
Rose Bowl, White Leaves Cut To Blue, Berries, Green Ground, English 1000.00
Sugar, Green, 4 1/4 In. 10.00
Tumbler, Blue, Floral, Blue, Florentine, 3 5/8 X 2 5/8 In. 95.00
Tumbler, Lemonade, Fisherman Scene, 5 1/4 In., Set Of 6 .... 355.00
Vase, Birds On Branches, Leaves, Signed Ver–Art, Black, 12 1/2 In. 295.00
Vase, Blue Ground, Floral Carving, Thomas Webb, 8 X 3 1/4 In. 2950.00
Vase, Carved White Opaque Floral, Frosted Red, 4 1/2 X 3 1/4 In. 1250.00
Vase, Castle Scene, Orange Ground, Signed Richard, 10 1/4 In. 915.00
Vase, Flowers & Scrolling Leaves, White On Red, English, 4 In. 800.00
Vase, Frosted Dragonfly, Cristallerie De Pantin, Signed, 4 1/2 In. 550.00
Vase, Green Lining, 4 Layers, Raspberries, Leaves, English, 7 In. 2450.00
Vase, Harbor Scene, Brown Cut To Yellow, De Vez, 9 3/4 In. 650.00
Vase, House & Mountain Scene, Blue Cut To Rose, De Vez, 12 In. 795.00
Vase, Iridescent, Rose & Gilt, Floral, Signed Cp, 10 1/2 In. 975.00
Vase, Mother–Of–Pearl, Vine & Butterflies, 7 1/4 X 4 1/2 In. 2750.00
Vase, Red Pekin, Carved, 8 In., Pair 150.00
Vase, Red Poppies, Butterflies, Patin, CP Signed, 10 1/2 In. 650.00
Vase, Red, White Floral, White Band, Webb, 6 1/2 X 3 1/4 In. 1395.00
Vase, Red, White Ivy Leaves, Webb, 3 5/8 In. 795.00
Vase, Sailboat Scene, Navy Blue Cut To Rose, De Vez, 12 In. 795.00
Vase, White Leaf, Cranberry, England, Late 19th Century, 12 In. 1700.00
Vase, White, Raspberries, Green Interior, 7 X 4 1/2 In. 2450.00

CAMPAIGN, see Political

The Campbell Kids were first used as part of an advertisement for the Campbell Soup Company in 1906. The kids were created by Grace Drayton, a popular illustrator of the day. The kids were used in magazine and newspaper ads until about 1951. They were presented again in 1966; and in 1983, they were redesigned with a slimmer, more contemporary appearance.

CAMPBELL KIDS, Bank, Cast Iron 165.00
Candy Container, Papier–Mache 125.00
Case, Pillow, Embroidered, Campbell Art Co., 1912 .... 100.00
Cookbook 30.00
Dish, Feeding 60.00
Dish, Feeding, Drayton, Buffalo 50.00
Doll, Boy & Girl, Movable Arms, Legs & Head 45.00
Doll, Boy, Composition, Redressed As Original, 12 In. 175.00
Doll, Cloth, Soup Girl, 22 In. 10.00
Figurine, Girl, 6 In. 20.00
Game, Puzzle, Jigsaw, Set Of 2 .... 7.00
Mug, Pair 15.00
Plaque, Potholder, 1950s, Pair 23.00
Plate, Baby, Buffalo Pottery, 7 1/2 In. 85.00
Plate, Girl Holds Doll, Boy Holds Flower, Signed Drayton 55.00
Salt & Pepper, By F & F Mold Co., Dayton, Ohio 25.00
Salt & Pepper, Figural, Plastic, 4 In. 15.00
Spoon, Figural Handle, Boy & Girl, Pair 15.00
Spoon, Souvenir, Silver Plate, Pair 20.00

Camphor glass is a cloudy white glass that has been blown or pressed. It was made by many factories in the Midwest during the mid-nineteenth century.

CAMPHOR GLASS, Bowl, Long Leaves, Scalloped, Footed, 12 3/4 X 3 3/8 In.	45.00
Box, Relief Lovebirds, Round	21.00
Dish, Raised Golfer	25.00
Figurine, Elephant, COP Molded In Glass	8.00
Lamp, Painted Violets On Shade, Miniature, 4 1/2 In.	75.00
Shaving Mug, Percival Hunt In Gold, WMH Monogram	70.00
Toothpick, Barrel Shape, Metal Rim Top & Base, Green	18.00

CANARY GLASS, see Vaseline Glass

A candlestick is designed to hold one candle; a candelabrum has more than one arm and holds many candles. The eccentricity of the English language makes the plural of candelabrum into candelabra.

CANDELABRUM, 4-Light, Empire, Ormolu Mounted, Bronze & Marble, 25 3/4 In.	2200.00
4-Socket Reeded Arms, Sterling Silver, Baluster, 16 In., Pair	275.00
Figures, Prisms, 22 In., Pair ....*Color*	550.00
French, Bronze, C.1830	225.00
Louis XV, Gilt Bronze, 5 Candle Arms, Electrified, 25 In., Pair	660.00
Louis XVI, 3-Light, Bronze, Marble, 19th Century, 20 1/2 In., Pair	1760.00

A candleholder is of course anything that holds a candle. This would include candelabra, candlesticks, and other lighting devices but these are listed in other places in this book.

CANDLEHOLDER, see also Brass and various Porcelain categories

CANDLEHOLDER, Hand Held, Tin, Pair	25.00
Iron, Venetian Gothic, 3 Curved Legs, 66 1/2 In., Pair	700.00
Pleated Reflector, Back Handle, Tin	95.00
Sticking Tommy, Iron, 9 3/4 In.	65.00
Toggle Arm, Wrought Iron, 18th Century	450.00

Candlesticks were made of brass, pewter, Sandwich glass, sterling silver, plated silver, and all types of pottery and porcelain. The earliest candlesticks, dating from the sixteenth century, held the candle on a pricket (sharp pointed spike). These lost favor because in times of strife the large church candlesticks with prickets became formidable weapons, so the socket was mandated. Candlesticks changed in style through the centuries and designs range from classic to rococo to Art Nouveau to Art Deco.

CANDLESTICK, Beehive, 11 In., Pair	120.00
Brass, Beaded Bobeche Rim, Twisted Baluster, 11 In., Pair	425.00
Brass, Push-Up, Square Weighted Base, 5 5/8 In.	55.00
Brass, Victorian, Push-Up, 9 In., Pair	150.00
Bulbous Stem, Octagonal Base, Brass, 5 3/4 In.	160.00
Bulbous Stem, Square Base, Scrolled Feet, Brass, 7 In.	100.00
Dolphin Base, Vaseline Glass, Pair	775.00
Dore Bronze & Marble, French, C.1870, Pair	4500.00
Ecclesiastical, Glass Pieces, Brass, Pair	40.00
Empire Style, Female Herm, 2 Arm, French, 22 1/2 In., Pair	1540.00
Enameled Blue Floral, Copper, Footed, Art Crafts, 15 In., Pair	176.00
Hanging, Owl, Open Lace Body, Solid Head, Iron, 11 In.	45.00
Hog Scraper, Early 19th Century, 7 In.	80.00
Hog Scraper, Iron, Pair	110.00
Push-Up, Beehive, Diamond-Quilted, England, 8 3/4 In., Pair	75.00
Push-Up, Brass, Marked B, 7 3/8 In., Pair	285.00
Push-Up, Victorian, Brass, 11 1/2 In., Pair	90.00
Queen Anne, Brass, Scalloped Base & Lip, 7 5/8 In.	315.00
Queen Anne, Brass, Scalloped, Bulbous Ornament, 8 3/4in., Pair	760.00
Queen Anne, Push-Up, Brass, 8 1/2 In., Pair	625.00
Queen Anne, Quatrefoil Base, Petal Lip, Brass, 8 3/8 In.	225.00
Queen Anne, Scalloped Base, 8 3/4 In., Pair	980.00

Queen Anne, Scalloped Base, Brass, 6 3/4 In.	300.00
Rectangular Pan & Push–Up, Conical Snuffer, Brass, 5 In.	85.00
Scalloped Base & Lip, Stamped Geo.Grove, Brass, 8 In., Pair	1640.00
Spiral Twist, Round Wooden Base, Iron, 18th Century, 8 In.	130.00
Spirally Turned Stem, Adjustable, Lignum Vitae, 9 3/4 In., Pair	605.00
Stem Screws Into Domed Foot, Brass, 6 1/2 In.	55.00
Tin, Push–Up, 4 In.	45.00
Twisted Iron Stem, Oak Base, 17 In.	33.00
Victorian, Brass, 4 In., Pair	60.00
Victorian, Push–Up, Brass, 10 5/8 In., Pair	95.00
Wrought Iron, Spiral, Turned Wooden Base, 7 1/2 In.	55.00
Yellow Glass, Etched Grapes & Leaves, 16 In., Set Of 4	605.00

CANDLEWICK, see Imperial; Pressed Glass

> *Candy containers have been popular since the late Victorian era. Collectors have long favored the glass containers; but now all types, including tin and papier–mache, are collected. Probably the earliest glass container sold commercially was the Liberty Bell made in 1876 for sale at the Centennial Exposition. Thousands of designs were made until the cost became too high in the 1960s. By the late 1970s, reproductions were being made and sold without the candy.*

CANDY CONTAINER, Airplane, Bomber, Army	27.50
Airplane, Spirit Of Goodwill, Full Paint, Closure, Prop	95.00
Airplane, Spirit Of Goodwill, Original Propeller & Paint	47.00
Army Hat, Crystal	18.00
Automobile	12.00
Automobile, Early, No Closure	45.00
Barney Google	220.00 To 325.00
Baseball Player	195.00
Baseball Player, Next To Barrel	160.00
Basket, Hanging, No Chain	12.50
Bathtub, Cobalt Blue	30.00
Battleship	20.00
Bird, Wing Lifts	22.00
Black Cat, Sitting, Papier–Mache, Metal Closure, 7 In.	60.00
Black Child, Loft Candy	35.00
Bookends, Rooster	75.00
Boot, 3 1/4 In.	7.00
Bulldog, Seated, Glass	30.00
Bulldog, Sitting, Black Paint, Tin Closure, 4 1/4 In.	75.00
Bulldog, Tout Co., Jeanette, Pa.	45.00
Bunny Coming Out Of Egg, Papier–Mache, German	95.00
Bunny With Carrot, Papier–Mache, German	75.00
Bunny With Nodding Head, Cardboard	9.00
Bunny, Papier–Mache, Glass Eyes	14.00
Bureau, Advertising, Roberts Furniture Store	175.00
Calf Truck, Wooden, Red Wagon, Stencil	30.00
Camera	175.00
Candlestick Phone, Glass Receiver, Tin Closure	85.00
Candlestick, 2 Handles, Souvenir	250.00
Car, 5 In.	20.00
Cash Register	100.00
Cat, Black Spring Head, Orange Body, German	40.00
Charlie Chaplin	25.00
Chicken By Hatched Egg, Papier–Mache	20.00
Chicken In Eggshell Auto	125.00
Chicken On Drum, Reading Book	26.00
Chicken On Nest, Glass	20.00
Chicken On Oblong Basket	75.00
Christmas Tree	40.00
Clock, Mantel, Octagonal	140.00
Clock, Painted, Milk Glass, Oval	75.00
Clown On Horse	125.00 To 150.00
Colt Pistol, Glass	40.00

Dog On Barrel	125.00
Dog, Chain Around Neck	20.00
Dog, Shoe In Mouth, Composition, Original Paint, 4 In.	50.00
Dog, Sitting, Glass, 3 1/4 In.	9.00
Dog, With Candy, Small	8.00
Dog, With Hat, 2 1/2 In.	7.00
Dolly's Milk	35.00
Don't Park Here	125.00
Donkey, With Cart, 4 1/2 In.	10.00
Duck	45.00 To 55.00
Duck, Rectangular Basket	30.00
Duck, Sailor, Head Wobbles On Spring, Germany	18.00
Dwarf, Papier–Mache	25.00
Easter Egg, Tin, Chein	15.00
Egg, Picture Of Rabbit	9.00
Electric Iron	26.00
Elephant, Clear, 4 1/2 X 7 In.	25.00
Engine, Tin Closure, Interior Scene	35.00
Father Christmas, Marked Germany, 4 1/2 In.	95.00
Father Christmas, White Coat, 9 In.	350.00
Felix The Cat, Unmarked	52.00
Felix, Germany, 5 In.	125.00
Fire Engine, 5 In.	20.00 To 40.00
Fire Engine, Original Closure	15.00
G.O.P.Elephant	100.00
Glass, Pink, Signed Marly, 10 In.	85.00
Gun	18.00
Happifats, Full Paint & Closure	250.00
Happifats, On Drum	165.00
Hat, Homburg	15.00
Hearse, Tassels At Windows, Tin Closure, Clear, 4 1/2 In.	200.00
Hen On Nest	18.00
Hen On Nest, Papier–Mache	30.00
Horse Pulling Cart	22.00
Hotdog, Painted Glass, 5 1/4 In.	450.00
Jack–O'–Lantern	125.00
Jeep, Glass	25.00
Kewpie	10.00
Lamp	18.00
Lantern, Bail	9.00
Lantern, Beaded Trim	20.00
Lantern, Original Cover, 3 1/2 In.	15.00
Lantern, Red & Gold Beaded Sections, Original Cover	24.00
Lantern, Red Metal Top, Wire Handle, Candy & Sticker	30.00
Lantern, Stough Co.	20.00
Lighthouse	12.00
Limousine, West Bros., 350	140.00
Locomotive, No.999, Screw On Metal Cap	42.50
Locomotive, Red Wheels	25.00
Mandolin, Little Girl	67.00
Musical Clarinet, Original Label, Candy	32.00
Opera Glasses	65.00
Owl	80.00
Phonograph	175.00
Pig	65.00
Pumpkin Head Kid, 4 In.	20.00
Pumpkin Head Kid, In Tuxedo On Box, 5 In.	50.00
Rabbit Pushing Chick In Cart, Full Paint	250.00
Rabbit Pushing Wheelbarrow	125.00
Rabbit Running On Log, Painted, Original Closure	125.00
Rabbit, 6 In.	14.00
Rabbit, Musical, Nodder, Germany, Papier–Mache	250.00
Rabbit, Pulling Egg, Pastel Colors	24.00
Rabbit, Pushing Chicken Shell Cart, Painted Glass	300.00

Rabbit, Santa Claus, German 295.00
Rabbit, Sitting, 3 1/2 X 4 3/4 In. 22.00
Rabbit, Sitting, 6 1/2 In. 20.00
Rabbit, Sitting, Carrot, Early 1900s 25.00
Revolver, Metal Screw Top, 5 In. 13.50
Revolver, Tin Cap 20.00
Rocking Horse, Clown Rider 165.00
Rooster, Crowing 149.00
Santa Claus, 7 In. ....175.00 To 200.00
Santa Claus, Chimney 60.00
Santa Claus, Climbing Down Chimney, Tin Closure 85.00
Santa Claus, Cotton, On Chimney, Paper, 2 1/2 X 3 In. 48.00
Santa Claus, Head, Celluloid 52.00
Santa Claus, Nodder, Papier–Mache 25.00
Santa Claus, Paint & Closure 67.00
Santa Claus, Papier–Mache 32.00
Santa Claus, Plastic Head 50.00
Santa's Boot 12.00
Santa, Leaving Chimney 75.00
Santa, With Double Cuff 75.00
Scotty ....5.00 To 22.50
Scotty, Hound Pup With Chain Collar 15.00
Shoe, High Button, Ladies, Glass 40.00
Skeleton, Pulling Pumpkin, Cardboard 16.00
Skookum 165.00
Snow White, Glitter, Papier–Mache, 1938, 5 1/2 In. 85.00
Spark Plug ....35.00 To 40.00
Speedboat 27.50
St.Nick, Papier–Mache 300.00
Station Wagon, Woodie, 4 1/2 In. ....18.00 To 20.00
Stork, Wire Legs, Wooden Beak, Cardboard, 9 3/4 In. 40.00
Stump, Papier–Mache, Ax In Stump 32.00
Submarine, 6 In. 48.00
Suitcase ....35.00 To 40.00
Tank, World War II 20.00
Taxi, 12 Vent, Long's 125.00
Telephone, 9 3/8 In. 200.00
Telephone, Original Closure & Candy 30.00
Train 25.00
Train Engine 15.00
Trumpet 35.00
Turkey, 2 In. 15.00
Ugly Duckling 45.00
Uncle Sam, On Firecracker, Papier–Mache, C.1920, 4 1/2 In. 130.00
Wagon, Glass 75.00
Witch On Broom, Pulling Cart 35.00
Witch On Pumpkin, Papier–Mache, 6 In. 35.00
Witch, Pulling Pumpkin Cart, Wooden Wheels 48.00
Zeppelin, Full Paint, Closure, Contents 250.00
Zeppelin, Side Embossed Los Angeles, Glass, 1925, 5 3/4 In. 180.00

Canes and walking sticks were used by every well–dressed man in the nineteenth century, but by World War I the style had changed. Today canes are used by few but the infirm. Collectors prize old canes made with special features such as hidden swords, whiskey flasks, or risque pictures seen through peepholes. Examples with solid gold heads or made from exotic materials like walrus vertebrae are among the higher priced canes.

CANE, Alligator Handle, Sterling Silver Ferrule, Bamboo, 34 In. 85.00
American Legion, Signed Paris 1927 .... 35.00
Animal Carving, Glass Eyes 35.00
Art Nouveau, Figural Lady Handle, Metal 5.00

Automatic, Fireless Torpedo, Cap Gun, Kotz Mfg. Co., Pat.1911	60.00
Bamboo, Curved Root End Handle, 35 3/4 In.	50.00
Celluloid Handle, Dog Head, Glass Eyes	28.00
Civil War Characters, Crowned With Eagle Head, Hand Carved	375.00
Crouching Lion Handle, Horn Top, Ebony, 36 In.	350.00
Curly Maple, Custom Made	125.00
Duck Head Handle From Cap Bomb, Carved	95.00
Figures, Symbols, Silver Ferrule, 34 1/2 In.	250.00
Folds Into Chair, Souvenir, Kentucky Derby, Marked 3 Places	65.00
Glass, Spatter Glass, Aqua With Spiral Twist, 30 1/2 In.	70.00
Gold Handle, Dog's Head, Inscribed 1901, 34 In.	600.00
Hand Carved Snake Head	18.00
Head, Ivory, Carved, British Officer Bust, 19th Century, 3 1/8 In.	80.00
Hickory, Silver Boar's Head, Glass Eyes, Acorns, Oak Leaves, 35 In.	95.00
Horn Shoe, Toes Sticking Out, English, 32 1/2 In.	300.00
Horse's Head Handle, Silver Ferrule, Ebony Shaft, 35 In.	325.00
Hound Dog Handle, Ebony Stick, Horn Top, 36 1/2 In.	200.00
Ivory & Wood, Captain's Going Ashore Stick	19800.00
Ivory, Greyhound, Glass Eyes	45.00
Ivory, Inlaid, Geometric Pieces, Metal Tip, 33 1/2 In.	150.00
Ivory, Inlaid, Nantucket, Octagonal Ivory Knob, C.1845	24200.00
Mahogany, Band Of Ebony Inlay, 36 In.	70.00
Masonic, Carved, Mid–19th Century	85.00
Mermaid With Arched Back, Arms Outstretched, 38 In.	440.00
Porcelain Handle, Repousse Brass Ferrule, Germany, 34 In.	150.00
Postage Stamp, Made In Prison, Silver Tip, Silver Ferrule, 34 1/2 In.	190.00
Rattlesnake Skin Covered, 33 1/2 In.	130.00
Rhinoceros Hide, Bent Handle, Solid Hide, 34 3/4 In.	35.00
Spanish Niello Silver, Vine Pattern, Burl Walnut, 34 1/2 In.	210.00
Swagger Stick, Kenya Prison	65.00
Swirled White Interior, Blown Glass, Clear, Framed, 26 1/2 In.	85.00
Sword, Hickory, Dark Finish, 10 Blade, 34 In.	95.00
Sword, Walking Stick, Rosewood, Carvings, Pewter Bands, 17 In.	85.00
Thornwood, Root Handle, Figures Of Reclining Hounds, 36 In.	140.00
Thornwood, Thorns Removed, 43 1/2 In.	20.00
Walking Stick, Agate Handled, Gold Ferrule, Ebony Shaft, 34 In.	200.00
Walking Stick, Amber Blown, Twisted, Massillon, Ohio, 36 1/4 In.	50.00
Walking Stick, Aqua Blown, Twisted Handle & Top, 54 In.	45.00
Walking Stick, Bamboo, 35 In.	50.00
Walking Stick, Bone & Horn, Steel Core, Braided Leather Top, 34 In.	105.00
Walking Stick, Cactus Heart, Copper Band, Matrix Turquoise, 35 1/2 In.	150.00
Walking Stick, Canon City Prison, Cattle Horns	29.50
Walking Stick, Carved, Polychrome, Eagle With Snake, Turtle, 36 In.	60.00
Walking Stick, Cork, Head Of Bacchus, Grapes, Leaves, 36 In.	230.00
Walking Stick, Eagle Claw, Pine, Rope Design, Alaska, 36 1/2 In.	50.00
Walking Stick, Ebony, Ivory Carved Form Of Sphinx, 37 1/2 In.	370.00
Walking Stick, Ebony, Ivory Handle, Seated Woman With Scarf, 39 In.	350.00
Walking Stick, Giraffe Head, African Wood, 36 In.	250.00
Walking Stick, Glass, Ribbed, Twisted Top & Handle, Aqua, 51 1/2 In.	85.00
Walking Stick, Glass, Threaded, Black Spiral, Mushroom Knob, 40 In.	560.00
Walking Stick, Gold Filled Handle, Leaf Pattern, C.1880, 35 In.	310.00
Walking Stick, Gorilla, Glass Eyes, Man's Head, Skull, 37 In.	520.00
Walking Stick, Green Jadeite Handle, Crystal Bands, Rosewood, 39 In.	400.00
Walking Stick, Greyhound's Head, Ivory, Glass Eyes	550.00
Walking Stick, Hickory, Carved Snake Coiled Around, Pearl Eyes, 35 In.	105.00
Walking Stick, Horn, Variegated Colors, Silver Top, Brass Tip, 35 In.	80.00
Walking Stick, Ivory Face & Hand, Horn Top, French, 36 In.	200.00
Walking Stick, Ivory Handle, 36 1/2 In.	160.00
Walking Stick, Ivory Skull Handle, Small Frog, Malacca Shaft, 35 In.	530.00
Walking Stick, Japanese, Bamboo, Animals, Dragon Top, 35 In.	85.00
Walking Stick, Japanese, Bamboo, Carved Rats & Fruit, Root End, 36 In.	95.00
Walking Stick, Japanese, Ivory Handle, Head Of Smiling Man, 36 In.	525.00
Walking Stick, Labrador's Head, Ivory, Glass Eyes, 34 1/2 In.	500.00
Walking Stick, Lady's, Double Loop End, Twisted Two Thirds Down	55.00

Walking Stick, Lady's, Ivory Hand Clenching Stick, 34 3/4 In. 250.00
Walking Stick, Lady's, Monkey Head, Glass Eye, Hinged Mouth, 32 In. 300.00
Walking Stick, Malacca, Handle Of Woman's Leg, 35 In. 85.00
Walking Stick, Man's Clenched Fist On Top, Wooden, Metal Band, 37 In. 250.00
Walking Stick, Natural Piercing, Chola Cactus, Root End, 36 In. 45.00
Walking Stick, Northwest Indian, Carved, Pine, Totem Of Figures, 32 In. 200.00
Walking Stick, Oriental, Bamboo, Opens To German Steel Skewer 160.00
Walking Stick, Painted, Faces, King & Queen, Crowns, 36 In. 175.00
Walking Stick, Parrot Head, Glass Eyes, Braided Leather Band, 39 In. 155.00
Walking Stick, Pearl Inlaid, Hearts, Triangles, Brass Tip, 36 1/4 In. 175.00
Walking Stick, Pitcairn Island, Fish Holding Ball, 36 1/2 In. 35.00
Walking Stick, Pony, Fish, Snake, Shield, 34 1/2 In. 150.00
Walking Stick, Pussy Willow, Black, Solid Silver Top, 33 1/2 In. 70.00
Walking Stick, Pussy Willow, Gall Growths, Mississippi River, 39 In. 35.00
Walking Stick, Rhinoceros Horn, 34 In. 345.00
Walking Stick, Simon Bros.& Co., Ebony, Gold Head, Dated 1890 .... 120.00
Walking Stick, Snake, Burned Pattern Of Snake, 35 In. 125.00
Walking Stick, Squared, Snake Eating Frog, Bird, Fish, Lizard, 42 In. 230.00
Walking Stick, Squared, Twisted Tip & Handle, Blown, Aqua, 38 3/4 In. 85.00
Walking Stick, Swirled, Amber Blown Glass, 36 1/4 In. 85.00
Walking Stick, Tigerwood, Bark End Handle, Natural Stripes, 36 In. 30.00

Canton china is blue–and–white ware made near Canton, China, from about 1785 to 1895. It is hand decorated with Chinese scenes.

CANTON, Basket With Undertray, Blue & White, Reticulated, 9 1/2 X 3 3/4 In. 600.00
Bowl, Salad, Shaped Rim, Blue & White, 19th Century, 9 1/2 In. 400.00
Candlestick, C.1830, 11 1/2 In. 1350.00
Coffeepot, 6 In. 195.00
Creamer, Blue & White 45.00
Creamer, Fish Shape 45.00
Dish, Enameled Birds, Insects, Canton, 1825, 8 In. 30.00
Dish, Leaf Shape ....75.00 To 95.00
Dish, Vegetable, Covered, Fruit Finial, Lemon Peel Glaze, 9 1/2 In. 195.00
Fruit Basket & Underplate, C.1810, Pierced 950.00
Ginger Jar, Floral, Large 58.00
Pitcher, Mountain & Tree Scenes 375.00
Planter, Blue & White, Large 350.00
Platter & Sugar Bowl, Late 19th Century, Platter 13 1/4 In. 150.00
Platter, 19th Century, Oval, 12 3/4 X 10 1/2 In. 275.00
Platter, Octagonal, 15 In. 500.00
Platter, Well & Tree, 18 In. 250.00
Sauce, Handle 125.00
Sugar 260.00
Teapot, Blue & White, 5 1/2 In. 275.00
Tray, 11 In. 125.00
Tureen, Covered, Attached Underplate, Figural Handles 435.00
Vase, Blue & White, 10 In. 125.00

Capo–di–Monte porcelain was first made in Naples, Italy, from 1743 to 1759. The factory moved near Madrid, Spain, and reopened in 1771 and worked to 1834. Since that time the Doccia factory of Italy acquired the molds and is using the N and crown mark. Societe Richard Ceramica is a modern–day firm often referred to as Ginori or Capo–di–Monte. This company uses the crown and N mark.

CAPO–DI–MONTE, Bell, Christmas, 1973, Limited Edition, Crown Mark 49.00
Bust, Woman, Marked, 6 In. 475.00
Cask, Corn N Mark, C.1870, 8 X 8 X 12 In. 750.00
Compote, Covered, Blue Crown Mark, 8 1/2 X 7 In. 150.00
Compote, Covered, Hand Painted Cupids, Cherub Finial, 8 In. 65.00
Cup & Saucer, Cherubs In Relief, Oversize 60.00
Cup & Saucer, Classical Figures, Heraldic Crest, Marked 500.00
Cup & Saucer, Cupids & Flower Garlands, Blue Crown N Mark 55.00
Cup & Saucer, Ducks, Herons, Demitasse, Footed, Crown Over N 68.00
Cup & Saucer, Ducks, Herons, Marked, Demitasse 69.00

Cup & Saucer, Maidens, Dogs, Tree, Mountains	65.00
Cup & Saucer, Phaeton, 1860	65.00
Cup & Saucer, Relief Figures	110.00
Dish, Children In Relief, Triangle Shape, Footed, 7 In.	50.00
Figurine, Cavalier, C.1880, 9 In.	325.00
Figurine, Dwarf Musicians & Conductor, 1860, 3 1/2 In.	275.00
Figurine, Fat Man, Playing Trumpet, Marked, 6 In.	125.00
Figurine, Flamingo Dancers, Girl's Arms Away, Marked, 8 In.	125.00
Figurine, Flower Girl, C.1880, 9 In.	325.00
Figurine, Horse & Rider, Dated 1840	225.00
Figurine, Hunchback Dwarf Musicians, 1860, 3 1/2 In.	265.00
Figurine, Lady & Harp, Man & Viola, 9 In., Pair	125.00
Figurine, Lady, Feathered Hat, Signed, 20 In.	575.00
Figurine, Madonna & Child, Crown Over N Mark, 15 In.	125.00
Figurine, Man & Woman, Pair	85.00
Figurine, Man, Playing Trumpet, Marked, 6 In.	125.00
Figurine, Napoleon, Rearing Horse, 12 X 9 X 5 In.	475.00
Figurine, Nude Child Sitting, With Book, Crown N, 3 1/2 In.	45.00
Group, Nativity Scene, Marked, Bronze Base, 11 X 7 1/2 In.	1650.00
Lamp, Perfume, Owl With Glass Eyes	85.00
Mustache Cup, Saucer, Nude Children, Garlands, Left Handed	165.00
Perfume Bottle, Cherub In Garden, Crown Mark, 3 In.	62.00
Plate, Floral Center, Blue, Ginori, 7 1/2 In.	42.00
Plate, Floral Center, Pink, Ginori, 7 1/2 In.	42.00
Stein, 100 Years War, Lion Lid, 3/10 Liter	210.00
Urn, Crown Mark, C.1800, 12 In.	250.00
Vase, High Relief, C.1900, Gold Crown N Mark, 16 In., Pair	575.00
Vase, Mantel, Cherubs, Pedestal Base, 11 In., Pair	125.00

Captain Marvel was introduced in February 1940 in Whiz comic books. An orphan named Billy Batson met the wizard Shazam and whenever he said the magic word he was transformed into a superhero. A movie serial was released in 1940. The comic was discontinued in 1954. A second Captain Marvel appeared in 1966, a third in 1967. Only the original was transformed by shouting "Shazam."

CAPTAIN MARVEL, Bank, Dime	45.00
Button, 1941	10.00
Paper Doll, Punch Out, 1945	7.50
Pencil, Flying With Giant Pencil, Brass Printer Plate, 1948	25.00
Toy, Racer, Keywind	35.00
Wristwatch, Box	150.00

Captain Midnight began as a radio show in September 1940. The first comic book appeared in July 1941. Captain Midnight was really the aviator Captain Albright, who was to defeat the Nazis. A movie serial was made in 1942 and a comic strip was published for a short time. The comic book Captain Midnight ended his career in 1948. The radio premiums are the prized collector memorabilia today.

CAPTAIN MIDNIGHT, Album, Stamp	10.00
Badge, Decoder, Brass	18.00
Book, Trick & Riddle Book, 1939	22.50
Cloth Patch, 1950s	20.00
Cup, Ovaltine, Capped	15.00
Decoder Whistle, 1947	25.00
Decoder, C351	25.00
Decoder, C441	25.00
Decoder, C460	35.00
Decoder, C471	20.00
Decoder, Original Manual & Mailing Envelope, 1945	110.00
Decoder, ROA, 1938	40.00
Manual, Secret Squadron, 1948, 16 Page	50.00
Medal, Flight Patrol, 1940	35.00
Medal, Membership	20.00

Mirro–Flash Code–O–Graph, 1946 .... 25.00
Mug, Shake–Up, 15th Anniversary 60.00
Ring, Sliding Secret Compartment 37.50
Spinner, 1940 .... 10.00
Wings 8.00

CARAMEL SLAG, see Chocolate Glass

> *The cards listed here include advertising cards, greeting cards, baseball cards, playing cards, valentines, and others. Color pictures were rare in the nineteenth century, so companies gave away colorful cards with pictures of children, flowers, products, or related scenes that promoted the company name. These were often collected and stored in albums. Greeting cards are also a nineteenth–century idea that has remained popular. Baseball cards also date from the nineteenth century when they were used by tobacco companies as give-aways. The gum cards were started in 1933, but it was not until after World War II that the bubble gum cards favored today were produced. Today over 1,000 cards are issued each year by the gum companies.*

CARD, see also Postcard

CARD, Advertising, Arm & Hammer, Birds, Set Of 60 .... 50.00
Advertising, Ayer's Cherry Pectoral, Heroin & Oil Of Almonds 5.00
Advertising, Coffee Company, 1880s, 20 Assorted 22.00
Advertising, Color, Rice Krispies, Set, 1933 .... 6.00
Advertising, John Primble Razor Blades, 20 Attached Packages 20.00
Advertising, McLaughlins Coffee, Army, Navy, White House Reception 15.00
Advertising, McLaughlins Coffee, Inauguration, President Lincoln 15.00
Advertising, McLaughlins Coffee, Signing Declaration Of Independence 15.00
Advertising, Peruvian Syrup, Contained Cocaine 7.00
Advertising, Piedmont Cigarettes, 38 Baseball Players, Ames, Birdwell 549.00
Advertising, Quaker Bitters 4.00
Advertising, Straight Arrow Injun–City, Nabisco 12.00
Advertising, Sweet Caporal Cigarettes, 18 Baseball Players 100.00
Advertising, Trade, American Machine Co., Fluting Machine 4.00
Advertising, Trolley, Claussen's Bread, Football Scene 20.00
Advertising, Trolley, Wrigley's Gum, Elf Scene, John Bliss, 1900s 55.00
Baseball, Babe Ruth, Goudey No.149, 1933 .... 350.00
Baseball, Bucky Dent, 1974 .... 1.00
Baseball, Juan Marichal, 1974 .... 1.00
Baseball, Stargell, 1974 .... 2.00
Baseball, Steve Stone, 1974 .... 2.50
Christmas, 16th Medical Regiment 14.00
Christmas, Fringe & Tassel, 5 1/2 X 8 In. 35.00
Christmas, House Scene, Silent Night, Parrish, 7 1/4 X 5 7/8 In. 15.00
Christmas, Village Scene, Christmas Morn, Parrish, 7 1/4 X 5 3/4 In. 15.00
Greeting, Christmas, Victorian, Satin, Cardboard Easel, 9 In. 34.00
Gum, Kennedy, Set 25.00
Lobby, 7th Heaven 18.00
Lobby, Beyond Victory, RKO Film 20.00
Lobby, Gun Fury, Rock Hudson, 3–D 40.00
Lobby, Saps At Sea, Laurel & Hardy 60.00
Playing, 52 American Beauties, Gil Elvgren Pinup Girls, Unused, 1949 .... 35.00
Playing, Braille 4.00
Playing, California Attractions, 1898 .... 9.50
Playing, Golden Dreams, Marilyn Monroe 40.00
Playing, Lady Holding Daisies, 1800 Clothes, Leather Case 14.00
Playing, Lamplighter Of Venice, Parrish 125.00
Playing, Marilyn Monroe, Boxed, 1956 .... 15.00
Playing, Mash, Unused 2.00
Playing, Miniature, German, Framed, C.1925 .... 75.00
Playing, Monkees, Educational 50.00
Playing, Washington D.C., Faces 20.00
Trolley, Advertising Hotels, 10 X 20 In., Set Of 9 .... 250.00
Valentine, Changing Faces 20.00

Valentine, Charlie Chaplin, 1916, German 35.00
Valentine, Figural, Opens Like Straight Razor, I'M Keen About You 15.00
Valentine, Foil, White Lace, Pink & Green Shades, 33 1/2 X 44 1/2 In. 275.00
Valentine, Folded, Inscription, Heart Design Inside 55.00
Valentine, Foldout, 1920s 7.50
Valentine, German, Foldout, Double, 17 In. 65.00
Valentine, Girl & Dog, Standing 18.00
Valentine, Heart Shape, Victorian Girl Center, Celluloid Ruffle Trim 25.00
Valentine, Hendrich Longstreet, C.1804, Hearts, Snowflakes, 16 X 16 In. 1100.00
Valentine, St.Patrick, Set Of 15 .... 4.50
Valentine, Twelvetrees, Signed 5.00
Valentine, Wizard Of Oz, Official 10.00
   CARDER, see Aurene; Steuben

Carlsbad, Germany, is a mark found on china made by several factories in Germany. Most of the pieces available today were made after 1891.

CARLSBAD, Berry Bowl, Pink, Scalloped Border, Signed 95.00
   Berry Bowl, Scalloped Border, Signed Kauffmann 95.00
   Bowl, Flower Blossom Shape, Iridescent Blue & Purple, 7 1/4 In. 85.00
   Chocolate Pot, Blue, Portrait, Victoria 110.00
   Coffee & Tea Set, Wedding Band, 11 Cup & Saucer 175.00
   Cup & Saucer, Handleless, Mulberry Vincennes Pattern 40.00
   Cup, Mustache, Pond With Duck 25.00
   Cup, Mustache, Think Of Me 25.00
   Dinner Set, Purple Violet, 70 Piece 450.00
   Dish, Flower Shape, Blossom, Blue & Purple, 7 In. 65.00
   Ewer, Pansy Design, Light Green, Gold Trim, Handles, 14 In. 70.00
   Ewer, Victoria Handle, Green, Gold, Florals, 14 In. 60.00
   Match Striker, Devil 35.00
   Plate, Cherubs, Rust Border, Gold Lace Border, 8 In. 20.00
   Plate, Portrait, Young Woman, C.1900 .... 85.00
   Plate, Roses & Violets, Gold Rim, 8 1/2 In. 20.00
   Plate, White, Reticulated Border, C.1860, Marked, 7 In. 15.00
   Vase, Louis XIV & Louis XVI Portrait, Hand Painted, 11 In., Pair 425.00

Carlton ware was made at the Carlton Works of Stoke-on-Trent, England, about 1890. The firm traded as Wiltshaw & Robinson until 1957. It was renamed Carlton Ware Ltd. in 1958.

CARLTON WARE, Dish, Red Lobster, Oval, Green 9.00
   Sugar Shaker, Tree Shape, Beige Ground, Marked, 4 1/2 In. 45.00
   Vase, Chinoiserie, Flambe, Black Medallions, 1900, 10 1/2 In. 245.00
   Vase, Cobalt, Stylized Trees, Spotted Ground, 5 1/2 In. 95.00
   Vase, Enameled, 9 In. 110.00
   Vase, Helmet, Rouge Royale, 7 In. 69.00
   Vase, Oriental Design, Blue, 6 In. 65.00
   Vase, Oriental Design, Enameled Picture, Neck Band, 8 1/2 In. 50.00
   Vase, Oriental, Pagodas, Man In Boat, Marked, 10 1/4 In. 245.00

Carnival, or taffeta, glass was an inexpensive, pressed, iridescent glass made from about 1907 to about 1925. Over 1,000 different patterns are known. Carnival glass is currently being reproduced. If the letter N for Northwood is included in the description, it appears on the piece of glass.

   CARNIVAL GLASS, see also Northwood
CARNIVAL GLASS, Acanthus, Bowl, Smoke, 8 In. 45.00
   Acanthus, Plate, Scalloped Rim, Smoke, 10 1/4 In. 135.00
   ACORN BURRS & BARK, see Acorn Burrs
   Acorn Burrs, Berry Set, Green, 5 Piece 265.00
   Acorn Burrs, Creamer, Marigold 80.00
   Acorn Burrs, Tumbler, Marigold 50.00
   AMARYLLIS, see Tiger Lily
   AMERICAN BEAUTY ROSES, see Wreath of Roses
   APPLE BLOSSOM BORDER, see Blossoms & Band

Arcs, Bowl, Amethyst, 5 In. 47.50
    ARGONAUT SHELL, see Nautilus
    AURORA, see Flowers
Australian Swan, Bowl, Amethyst, Large 85.00
    AUTUMN, see Wild Berry
Autumn Acorns, Bowl, Green, Ruffled, 9 In. 55.00
Banded Grape, Mug, Marigold 23.00
    BANDED MEDALLION & TEARDROP, see Beaded Bull's Eye
    BATTENBURG LACE NO.1, see Hearts & Flowers
    BATTENBURG LACE NO.2, see Captive Rose
    BATTENBURG LACE NO.3, see Fanciful
Beaded Bull's Eye, Vase, Amber, 11 In. 45.00
Beaded Bull's Eye, Vase, Green, 13 In. 35.00
Beaded Cable, Rose Bowl, Blue 75.00
Beaded Cable, Rose Bowl, Marigold 55.00
Beaded Cable, Rose Bowl, Purple 70.00
Beaded Shell, Mug, Amethyst ....75.00 To 85.00
Beaded Shell, Spooner, Marigold 40.00
    BLACKBERRY B., see Blackberry Spray
Blackberry Bramble, Compote, Amethyst, 5 In. 38.00
Blackberry Bramble, Compote, Purple 40.00
Blackberry Spray, Compote, Green 42.00
Blackberry Spray, Dish, Marigold, Jack-In-The-Pulpit Shape 22.00
Blackberry Spray, Hat, Marigold On Clear, Fenton, 6 In. 35.00
Blackberry Wreath, Bowl, Marigold, Millersburg, 10 In. 45.00
Blackberry, Compote, Marigold, Miniature 50.00
Blackberry, Hat, Red ....265.00 To 275.00
Bouquet, Water Set, Marigold, 5 Piece 535.00
Broken Arches, Punch Cup, Marigold 18.00
Brooklyn Bridge, Bowl, Marigold, Fluted, 8 1/2 X 2 1/2 In. 265.00
Butterfly & Berry, Berry Bowl, Red, Master 130.00
Butterfly & Berry, Berry Set, Marigold, 6 Piece 130.00
Butterfly & Berry, Bonbon, Marigold, Footed, 4 3/4 In. 35.00
Butterfly & Berry, Butter, Marigold, Covered 90.00
Butterfly & Berry, Tumbler, Marigold ....12.00 To 28.00
    BUTTERFLY & CABLE, see Springtime
Butterfly & Fern, Bowl, Marigold, Footed, 4 7/8 In. 35.00
Butterfly & Fern, Butter, Green, Covered 27.00
Butterfly & Fern, Pitcher, Green 350.00
Butterfly & Fern, Tumbler, Marigold 40.00
    BUTTERFLY & GRAPE, see Butterfly & Berry
    BUTTERFLY & PLUME, see Butterfly & Fern
Butterfly, Bonbon, Marigold, 2 Handles 22.00
Butterfly, Bonbon, Purple, Ruffled Edge, Handles, 5 In. 45.00
Butterfly, Candy Dish, Purple, Horlacker Advertising 125.00
    CABBAGE ROSE & GRAPE, see Wine & Roses
    CACTUS LEAF RAYS, see Leaf Rays
Captive Rose, Bowl, Cobalt Blue, Fluted, 9 1/8 X 3 In. 48.00
Caroline, Bowl, Marigold, Crimped, 7 In. 24.00
    CATTAILS & FISH, see Fisherman's Mug
    CATTAILS & WATER LILY, see Waterlily & Cattails
    CHERRIES & MUMS, see Mikado
Cherry Chain, Bowl, Blue, 5 1/2 In. 60.00
Cherry Chain, Plate, Marigold, Small 65.00
    CHERRY WREATHED, see Wreathed Cherry
    CHRISTMAS CACTUS, see Thistle
    CHRISTMAS PLATE, see Poinsettia
    CHRISTMAS ROSE & POPPY, see Six-Petals
Christmas, Compote, Marigold 1500.00
Chrysanthemum, Bowl, Marigold, 9 In. 38.00
Coin Dot, Bowl, Green, Ribbon Candy Edge, 8 1/2 In. 34.00
Coin Dot, Bowl, Marigold, 7 In. 35.00
    COLONIAL, see Colonial Carnival
Colonial Carnival, Candlestick, Amber, 10 1/2 In. 195.00

Concave Diamonds, Tumbler, Ice Blue 30.00
Concave Diamonds, Water Set, Ice Blue, 7 Piece 375.00
    CONSTITUTION, see God & Home
Corinth, Vase, Green, 8 1/4 In. 34.00
Corn, Bottle, Marigold, 5 In. 225.00
Cosmos & Cane, Bowl, Marigold, 8 1/2 In. 50.00
Cosmos & Cane, Compote, White, Ruffled 135.00
Cosmos, Bowl, Marigold, 10 In. 45.00
Cosmos, Sauce, Green, Polished Base, 5 In. 25.00
Crackle, Candy Jar, Marigold, Covered 28.00
Dahlia, Creamer, White, Gold Design 145.00
Dahlia, Pitcher, Purple 775.00
    DAISY & LATTICE & BAND, see Lattice & Daisy
Daisy & Plume, Rose Bowl, Purple, 3-Footed 125.00
Daisy Squares, Compote, Amber 325.00
    DANDELION VARIANT, see Paneled Dandelion
Dandelion, Mug, Purple, Northwood ....235.00 To 250.00
Dandelion, Tumbler, Green, Northwood 90.00
Dandelion, Water Set, Purple, Northwood, 5 Piece 975.00
Dandelion, Water Set, Red, 7 Piece 275.00
Diamond & File, Banana Boat, Marigold, 9 1/4 In. 40.00
Diamond & File, Banana, Marigold, 9 1/2 In. 23.00
Diamond Lace, Bowl, Fruit, Amethyst, 10 In. 65.00
Diamond Lace, Water Set, Amethyst, 7 Piece 395.00
    DIAMOND POINT & DAISY, see Cosmos & Cane
Diamond Point, Vase, Bud, Amethyst, 10 In. 28.00
Diamond Point, Vase, Purple, 10 In. 20.00
Diamond Ring, Bowl, Marigold, 9 In. 35.00
Diamond Ring, Bowl, Smoky, 8 1/2 In. 29.00
Diamond, Tumbler, Green, Millersburg 40.00
    DOGWOOD & MARSH LILY, see Two Flowers
Double Scroll, Candlestick, Cobalt Blue, Pair 165.00
Double-Stem Rose, Bowl, Peach, Dome Footed, 9 In. 40.00
Dragon & Lotus, Bowl, Blue, Scalloped, 8 3/4 In. 60.00
Dragon & Lotus, Bowl, Marigold, Fluted, 8 1/2 In. ....38.00 To 45.00
Dragon & Lotus, Bowl, Peach, Ruffled, 9 In. 450.00
    DRAPE & TIE, see Rosalind
Eastern Star, Bowl, Purple, Deep Ruffled, 8 In. 40.00
    EGYPTIAN BAND, see Round-Up
    EMALINE, see Zippered Loop, Lamp
Embroidered Mums, Bowl, Marigold, 9 In. 48.00
Emu, Bowl, Marigold, 5 In. 75.00
    FAN & ARCH, see Persian Garden
Fanciful, Bowl, White, 9 In. 110.00
    FANTASY, see Question Marks
Fashion, Bowl, Ice Cream, Clambroth, 9 In. 25.00
Fashion, Pitcher, Water, Purple 895.00
Fashion, Punch Cup, Marigold ....10.00 To 60.00
Fashion, Rose Bowl, Marigold 75.00
Fashion, Water Set, Marigold, 6 Piece 210.00
    FEATHER & HOBSTAR, see Inverted Feather
    FENTON'S BUTTERFLY, see Butterfly
    FIELD ROSE, see Rambler Rose
Fieldflower, Water Set, Marigold, 6 Piece 215.00
Fine Cut & Roses, Candy Dish, Purple, Footed 45.00
Fine Cut & Roses, Rose Bowl, Green 150.00
Fine Cut & Roses, Rose Bowl, Purple ....65.00 To 150.00
Fine Rib, Vase, Amethyst, 13 In. 50.00
Fine Rib, Vase, Red, 10 In. 250.00
Fisherman's Mug, Mug, Amethyst ....90.00 To 125.00
    FISHERMAN'S NET, see Treebark
Fishscale & Beads, Candy Dish, Peach, 7 In. 52.00
    FLORAL & DIAMOND POINT, see Fine Cut & Roses
Floral & Grape, Pitcher, Marigold, Handles, 9 In. 90.00

Floral & Grape, Water Set, Marigold, 7 Piece ....200.00 To 245.00
Floral & Grape, Water Set, Purple, 6 Piece 295.00
    FLORAL & GRAPEVINE, see Floral & Grape
    FLOWERING ALMONDS, see Peacock Tail
Flowers, Bowl, Green, 10 In. 75.00
Flute, Berry Set, Purple, 7 Piece 245.00
Flute, Cruet, Marigold, Clear Stopper 75.00
Four Flowers, Bowl, Peach, 6 In. 35.00
    FOUR FRUIT & HOBSTAR, see Hobstar & Fruit
Frosted Block, Plate, Clambroth, 9 In. 20.00
Fruit Salad, Punch Cup, Purple 25.00
Fruits & Flowers, Berry Bowl, Purple, Master 85.00
Fruits & Flowers, Bonbon, Blue, Footed ....65.00 To 85.00
Garden Path, Bowl, Marigold, Fluted, 9 In. 75.00
Garden Path, Bowl, White, 10 In. 135.00
Garland, Rose Bowl, Marigold 45.00
God & Home, Water Set, Ice Green, 7 Piece 125.00
Golden Honeycomb, Plate, Marigold, 6 In. 22.00
Good Luck, Bowl, Marigold, Candy Ribbon Edge 85.00
Good Luck, Bowl, Purple, 8 1/2 In. 55.00
Good Luck, Bowl, Purple, Ruffled, 9 In. 100.00
Grape & Cable, Banana Boat, Marigold ....100.00 To 175.00
Grape & Cable, Berry Bowl, Purple, Master 85.00
Grape & Cable, Bottle, Cologne, Marigold ....125.00 To 135.00
Grape & Cable, Bottle, Perfume, Purple 650.00
Grape & Cable, Bowl, Amethyst, Northwood, 10 In. 185.00
Grape & Cable, Bowl, Blue, Crimped, 7 1/2 In. 35.00
Grape & Cable, Bowl, Green, Footed, 8 In. 60.00
Grape & Cable, Bowl, Marigold, Footed, Northwood, 8 In. 75.00
Grape & Cable, Bowl, Purple, Fluted, 9 In. 150.00
Grape & Cable, Butter, Amethyst, Covered 185.00
Grape & Cable, Butter, Green, Covered 175.00
Grape & Cable, Butter, Purple, Covered ....185.00 To 200.00
Grape & Cable, Creamer, Purple ....100.00 To 125.00
Grape & Cable, Dish, Purple, Northwood, 7 In. 58.00
Grape & Cable, Dish, Sweetmeat, Purple ....210.00 To 225.00
Grape & Cable, Hatpin Holder, Green ....75.00 To 150.00
Grape & Cable, Hatpin Holder, Purple 175.00
Grape & Cable, Humidor, Cobalt Blue, Stippled, Covered 750.00
Grape & Cable, Ice Cream Set, Amethyst, 7 Piece 530.00
Grape & Cable, Pitcher, Water, Green ....160.00 To 235.00
Grape & Cable, Powder Jar, Purple 110.00
Grape & Cable, Punch Cup, White ....50.00 To 65.00
Grape & Cable, Shot Glass, Marigold, Northwood 185.00
Grape & Cable, Spooner, Purple 100.00
Grape & Cable, Sugar, Marigold, Covered ....75.00 To 85.00
Grape & Cable, Sugar, Purple, Covered ....110.00 To 120.00
Grape & Cable, Table Set, Red 450.00
Grape & Cable, Tankard, Amethyst 42.00
Grape & Cable, Tray, Dresser, Green 245.00
Grape & Cable, Water Set, Marigold, 7 Piece ....325.00 To 350.00
Grape & Cable, Water Set, Purple, 7 Piece ....375.00 To 550.00
Grape & Gothic Arches, Butter, Green, Covered 250.00
Grape & Lattice, Plate, Marigold, 7 1/2 In. 35.00
Grape Arbor, Pitcher, Marigold ....160.00 To 225.00
Grape Arbor, Tumbler, Blue 100.00
Grape Arbor, Tumbler, Purple 40.00
    GRAPE DELIGHT, see Vintage
Grape, Bowl, Marigold, 8 In. 39.00
Grape, Bowl, Purple, Fluted, Northwood, 9 In. 65.00
Grape, Carafe, Water, Purple 120.00
Grape, Chop Plate, Purple 265.00
Grape, Humidor, Blue, Stippled, Northwood 950.00
Grape, Plate, Amber, 8 In. 75.00

Grape, Plate, Marigold, Imperial, 9 In. 65.00
Grape, Punch Bowl, Marigold, Imperial 250.00
Grape, Rose Bowl, Purple, 6 Short Square Feet, 4 In. 75.00
Grape, Water Set, Marigold, Engraved, 7 Piece 175.00
Grape, Wine, Green, Imperial 25.00
Greek Key, Bowl, Marigold, 8 1/2 In. 75.00
Heart & Vine, Bowl, Green, Scalloped, 9 In. 95.00
Heart & Vine, Candy Dish, Amethyst, Ribbon Edge, 9 In. 50.00
Hearts & Flowers, Bowl, Ice Blue, 8 1/2 In. 225.00
Hearts & Flowers, Compote, White ....85.00 To 125.00
Heavy Grape, Bowl, Purple, Fluted, 7 In. 37.50
Heavy Grape, Chop Plate, Green 150.00
Heavy Grape, Chop Plate, Purple 375.00
Heavy Grape, Plate, Green, 8 In. 45.00
          HERON & RUSHES, see Stork & Rushes
Hobnail, Banana Boat, Blue, 12 In. 22.00
Hobnail, Butter, Marigold, Covered 400.00
Hobnail, Punch Set, Aqua, Fenton, 10 Piece 75.00
Hobnail, Rose Bowl, Vaseline, 4 1/2 In. 12.00
Hobnail, Tumbler, Blue 795.00
Hobstar & Arches, Bowl, Marigold, 9 In. 40.00
Hobstar & Feathers, Punch Cup, Purple 15.00
Hobstar Flower, Compote, Marigold, Gold Trim, Northwood 45.00
Hobstar, Compote, Green, Small 35.00
Hobstar, Spooner, Marigold 35.00
          HOLLY SPRAY, see Holly Sprig
Holly Sprig, Bowl, Amethyst, 8 1/2 In. ....55.00 To 65.00
Holly Sprig, Sauce, Peach 55.00
Holly Whirl, Bowl, Amethyst, 10 In. 48.00
Holly, Bowl, Green, Handles, 6 1/2 In. 45.00
Holly, Bowl, Red, 9 In. 595.00
Holly, Goblet, Marigold 17.00
          HONEYCOMB COLLAR, see Fishscale & Beads
Honeycomb, Rose Bowl, Purple 200.00
          HORSE MEDALLIONS, see Horses' Heads
Horses' Heads, Bowl, Amethyst, 8 1/2 In. 135.00
Horses' Heads, Bowl, Purple, Fluted, 8 3/8 X 3 In. 125.00
Imperial Grape, Bowl, Marigold, 10 In. 40.00
Imperial Grape, Carafe, Water, Green 139.00
Imperial Grape, Compote, Marigold, 4 1/2 X 5 1/2 In. 65.00
Imperial Grape, Cup, Green, 3 1/8 X 2 1/2 In. 50.00
Imperial Grape, Decanter, Purple, Stopper 75.00
Imperial Grape, Pitcher, Marigold 75.00
Imperial Grape, Plate, Green, 9 In. 115.00
Imperial Grape, Punch Set, Amethyst, 16 Piece 185.00
Imperial Grape, Punch Set, Green, 8 Piece 180.00
Imperial Grape, Saucer, Green, 5 7/8 In. 50.00
Imperial Grape, Tray, Smoke, Center Handle 58.00
Imperial Grape, Tumbler, Marigold 18.00
Imperial Grape, Wine, Green 30.00
Inverted Feather, Cracker Jar, Green, Covered ....165.00 To 190.00
Inverted Strawberry, Candlestick, Green 125.00
Inverted Strawberry, Spittoon, Marigold 425.00
Inverted Strawberry, Water Set, Amethyst, 7 Piece 225.00
Iris, Compote, Amethyst 65.00
Iris, Goblet, Buttermilk, Amethyst 28.00
Iris, Tankard, Marigold 425.00
Iris, Tumbler, White 150.00
Iris, Water Set, Marigold, 5 Piece 635.00
          KIMBERLY, see Concave Diamonds
Kittens, Bowl, Marigold, Small 90.00
Kittens, Cup & Saucer, Marigold ....165.00 To 250.00
Kittens, Spooner, Marigold 125.00
Kittens, Toothpick, Marigold 105.00

Kookaburra, Bowl, Purple, 5 In. 45.00
Kookaburra, Bowl, Purple, 10 In. 100.00
  LABELLE ELAINE, see Primrose
Lattice & Daisy, Tumbler, Marigold ....15.00 To 18.00
Lattice & Grape, Tumbler, Marigold ....20.00 To 32.00
  LATTICE & GRAPEVINE, see Lattice & Grape
Leaf & Beads, Candy Dish, Green, Footed 40.00
Leaf & Beads, Nappy, Green 70.00
Leaf Chain, Bowl, Aqua, Ruffled, 7 In. 95.00
Leaf Chain, Bowl, Blue, 9 In. 45.00
Leaf Chain, Plate, Marigold, 9 In. 105.00
  LEAF MEDALLION, see Leaf Chain
Leaf Rays, Nappy, Marigold 25.00
Leaf Rays, Nappy, White, Handles ....37.00 To 40.00
Leaf Swirl, Compote, Amber, 6 In. 39.00
Little Fishes, Bowl, Marigold, Footed, 8 1/2 In. 95.00
Little Flowers, Bowl, Blue, 5 In. 30.00
Little Flowers, Bowl, Purple, 11 In. 95.00
Little Flowers, Rose Bowl, Ice Green, Fenton 775.00
Little Stars, Bowl, Amethyst, 7 In. 75.00
Loganberry, Vase, Marigold, 10 1/2 In. 145.00
  LOOPED PETALS, see Scales
Lustre Flute, Sugar, Green 15.00
Lustre Rose, Bowl, Marigold, Footed, 8 In. 45.00
Lustre Rose, Butter, Marigold, Covered 55.00
Lustre Rose, Creamer, Marigold 40.00
Lustre Rose, Tumbler, Marigold 15.00
Lustre Rose, Water Set, Marigold, 7 Piece 225.00
Magpie, Bowl, Purple, 10 In. 100.00
Many Fruits, Punch Cup, Amethyst, Set Of 6 .... 100.00
Maple Leaf, Tumbler, Blue 45.00
Maple Leaf, Tumbler, Marigold 15.00
Maple Leaf, Tumbler, Purple 45.00
Maple Leaf, Water Set, Amethyst, 7 Piece 325.00
Marilyn, Mug, Green 125.00
  MARYLAND, see Rustic
  MELINDA, see Wishbone
Memphis, Punch Bowl Set, Marigold, 7 Piece 235.00
Memphis, Punch Cup, Marigold 15.00
Memphis, Punch Cup, Purple 25.00
Mikado, Compote, Blue 95.00
Mikado, Compote, Marigold 125.00
Milady, Tumbler, Marigold 75.00
Morning Glory, Tumbler, Green 1150.00
  MULTI FRUIT & FLOWERS, see Many Fruits
  MUMS & GREEK KEY, see Embroidered Mums
Nautilus, Pitcher, Purple, Northwood 190.00
Northern Star, Bowl, Marigold, 5 1/4 In. 15.00
Octagon, Bowl, Marigold, 9 In. 36.00
Octagon, Decanter, Marigold, Stopper ....85.00 To 95.00
  OLD FASHION FLAG, see Iris
  OLE CORN, see Corn, Bottle
Open Rose, Bowl, 9 In. 35.00
Open Rose, Plate, Green, Stippled, 9 In. 95.00
Open Rose, Plate, Marigold, 9 In. 68.00
Orange Tree Orchard, Tumbler, White 50.00
Orange Tree, Bowl, Marigold, Footed, 10 In. 65.00
Orange Tree, Bowl, Marigold, Footed, Northwood, 9 1/2 In. 85.00
Orange Tree, Butter, Marigold, Footed 110.00
Orange Tree, Creamer, White 175.00
Orange Tree, Hatpin Holder, Marigold 50.00
Orange Tree, Loving Cup, Marigold ....95.00 To 125.00
Orange Tree, Mug, Marigold ....28.00 To 30.00
Orange Tree, Mug, Vaseline 150.00

Orange Tree, Punch Bowl, Marigold ....190.00 To 200.00
Orange Tree, Rose Bowl, Marigold 40.00
Orange Tree, Rose Bowl, Red, Footed 495.00
Orange Tree, Sauce, Marigold, Footed 15.00
Orange Tree, Shaving Mug, Marigold, Fenton 42.00
Orange Tree, Sugar, White 80.00
Oriental Poppy, Pitcher, Marigold 350.00
Oriental Poppy, Tumbler, Amethyst ....35.00 To 45.00
Palm Beach, Butter, White, Covered 95.00
Palm Beach, Creamer, White 80.00
Palm Beach, Spooner, White 250.00
    PANELED BACHELOR BUTTONS, see Milady
Paneled Dandelion, Tumbler, Purple 35.00
Pansy, Bowl, Marigold, Ruffled, 9 In. 85.00
Pansy, Creamer, Amethyst 30.00
Pansy, Dish, Pickle, Purple, Imperial 35.00
Pansy, Relish, Marigold, Oval, 9 In. 40.00
Panther, Berry Bowl, Blue 145.00
Panther, Bowl, Nut, Marigold, Footed, 5 In. 60.00
    PARROT TULIP SWIRL, see Acanthus
Pastel Panels, Tumbler, Ice Green 65.00
Peach, Berry Set, White, Northwood, 5 Piece 350.00
Peach, Butter, White, Covered 425.00
Peach, Tumbler, Cobalt Blue 75.00
Peacock & Grape, Bowl, Green, 9 In. 90.00
Peacock & Grape, Bowl, Green, Ruffled, 8 1/2 In. 40.00
Peacock & Grape, Bowl, Marigold, 8 1/2 In. 39.50
Peacock & Urn, Berry Bowl, Marigold, Master, 10 In. 160.00
Peacock & Urn, Bowl, Ice Cream, Amethyst, 10 In. 350.00
Peacock & Urn, Bowl, Ice Cream, Marigold 175.00
Peacock & Urn, Bowl, Ice Cream, Purple, 10 In. 285.00
Peacock & Urn, Bowl, Marigold, Ruffled, 10 In. 125.00
Peacock & Urn, Bowl, Purple, Fluted, 8 3/4 X 2 In. 70.00
Peacock & Urn, Bowl, Purple, Scalloped, 8 X 2 1/2 In. 65.00
Peacock At The Fountain, Berry Set, White, 5 Piece 175.00
Peacock At The Fountain, Bowl, Fruit, Amethyst, 10 In. 235.00
Peacock At The Fountain, Bowl, Fruit, Marigold, Northwood 160.00
Peacock At The Fountain, Bowl, Ice Blue, 5 In. 75.00
Peacock At The Fountain, Butter, Marigold, Covered 150.00
Peacock At The Fountain, Butter, Purple, Covered ....195.00 To 325.00
Peacock At The Fountain, Cup, White 50.00
Peacock At The Fountain, Orange Bowl, Cobalt Blue 250.00
Peacock At The Fountain, Punch Bowl, Amethyst 100.00
Peacock At The Fountain, Punch Cup, Purple 25.00
Peacock At The Fountain, Table Set, Marigold ....365.00 To 395.00
Peacock At The Fountain, Tumbler, Cobalt Blue 60.00
Peacock At The Fountain, Tumbler, Marigold 35.00
Peacock At The Fountain, Tumbler, Purple ....40.00 To 45.00
Peacock At The Fountain, Water Set, Purple, 7 Piece 450.00
    PEACOCK EYE, see Eastern Star
    PEACOCK EYE & GRAPE, see Vineyard
    PEACOCK ON FENCE, see Peacock
Peacock Tail, Bowl, Marigold, 10 In. 18.00
Peacock Tail, Compote, Green, 5 In. 29.00
Persian Garden, Bowl, Ice Cream, White, Master 295.00
Persian Garden, Bowl, White, 5 In. ....40.00 To 60.00
Persian Garden, Plate, Purple, 6 In. 175.00
Persian Medallion, Bowl, Green, 7 In. 65.00
Persian Medallion, Bowl, Ice Cream, Amethyst 30.00
Persian Medallion, Bowl, Marigold, 8 In. 40.00
Persian Medallion, Bowl, Purple, Ruffled, 7 5/8 In. 22.00
Persian Medallion, Compote, Green 48.00
Persian Medallion, Compote, Marigold, Candy Ribbon Edge 39.00
Petals & Fan, Bowl, Peach, Ruffled, 6 In. 35.00

PINE CONE WREATH, see Pine Cone

Pine Cone, Bowl, Ice Cream, Amethyst, 6 In.	35.00
Pine Cone, Bowl, Marigold, Ruffled, 6 In.	25.00
Pineapple, Compote, Marigold	45.00
Plume Panels, Vase, Red, 11 In.	485.00

PONY ROSETTE, see Pony

Pony, Bowl, Marigold, 8 1/2 In.	45.00
Primrose, Bowl, Marigold, 10 In.	79.00

PRINCESS LACE, see Octagon

Puzzle, Bonbon, White, Footed, Handles	50.00
Puzzle, Compote, White, Floral & Wheat Exterior, Handles	80.00
Question Marks, Bonbon, Marigold, 2 Handles	19.00
Question Marks, Compote, Marigold	28.00
Raindrops, Bowl, Peach, Dome, Footed, 9 In.	60.00 To 68.00
Rambler Rose, Tumbler, Marigold	25.00
Raspberry, Pitcher, Milk, Green	190.00
Raspberry, Pitcher, Milk, Marigold	125.00
Raspberry, Pitcher, Water, Green	250.00
Raspberry, Tumbler, Amethyst	30.00 To 36.00
Raspberry, Tumbler, Green	38.00
Raspberry, Water Set, Marigold, 7 Piece	210.00
Ripple, Dish, Purple, 7 In.	65.00
Ripple, Vase, Bud, Marigold, 9 5/8 In.	22.00
Ripple, Vase, Purple, 11 1/2 In.	40.00

ROBIN RED BREAST, see Robin

Robin, Mug, Marigold	39.00
Robin, Pitcher, Cobalt Blue	50.00
Robin, Water Set, Green, 7 Piece	125.00
Robin, Water Set, Marigold, 5 Piece	350.00
Robin, Water Set, Red, 7 Piece	195.00
Robin, Water Set, White, 7 Piece	125.00
Rosalind, Dish, Jelly, Amethyst, 6 In.	495.00

ROSE & RUFFLES, see Open Rose

Rose, Tumbler, Marigold	12.00
Roses & Fruit, Compote, Marigold	385.00

ROSES & LOOPS, see Double–Stem Rose

Rosette, Bowl, Amethyst, Footed	88.00
Rosette, Bowl, Marigold, Footed, 8 3/4 In.	45.00
Rustic, Vase, Bud, Marigold, 16 In.	35.00

SAILBOAT & WINDMILL, see Sailboats

Sailboats, Sauce, Marigold	25.00
Sailboats, Wine, Marigold	32.00 To 35.00
Scales, Banana Boat, Peach, 6 3/4 In.	32.50
Scales, Bowl, Peach, 7 In.	55.00
Scales, Plate, Amethyst, 6 In.	30.00
Scales, Shade, Nu Art, Marigold	25.00
Scotch Thistle, Compote, Amethyst	48.00

SCROLL EMBOSSED, see Eastern Star
SEA LANES, see Little Fishes

Shell, Carnival, Bowl, Marigold, 8 In.	25.00
Singing Birds, Butter, Green, Covered	45.00
Singing Birds, Mug, Amethyst	70.00
Singing Birds, Mug, Aqua	1100.00
Singing Birds, Mug, Green	150.00
Singing Birds, Mug, Marigold	125.00
Singing Birds, Mug, Purple	55.00 To 90.00
Singing Birds, Tumbler, Purple	45.00 To 49.00
Singing Birds, Water Set, Marigold, 7 Piece	560.00
Six–Petals, Bowl, Peach, 7 3/4 In.	65.00
Six–Petals, Bowl, White, 7 1/2 In.	68.00
Ski Star, Bowl, Peach, 10 1/2 In.	75.00
Ski Star, Bowl, Purple, Ruffled, 7 In.	75.00
Soda Gold, Water Set, Marigold, 7 Piece	235.00

SPIDER WEB, see Soda Gold

Split Diamond, Creamer, Marigold	35.00
SPRING FLOWERS, see Bouquet	
Springtime, Butter, Red, Covered	275.00
Springtime, Creamer, Amethyst	100.00
Springtime, Creamer, Purple	90.00
Springtime, Pitcher, Purple	600.00
Springtime, Spooner, Green	85.00 To 90.00
Springtime, Sugar, Purple	100.00
Stag & Holly, Bowl, Marigold, Ruffled, 10 1/2 In.	110.00
Stag & Holly, Orange Bowl, Marigold, 8 1/2 In.	110.00
Star Medallion, Bowl, Smoke, 7 In.	25.00
Star Medallion, Pitcher, Milk, Marigold	25.00
Star Medallion, Tumbler, Marigold	18.00 To 42.00
Star Of David & Bows, Bowl, Amethyst, 8 1/2 In.	70.00
STAR OF DAVID MEDALLION, see Star of David & Bows	
Star Of David, Bowl, Purple, Fluted, 9 X 2 1/4 In.	58.00
STIPPLED CLEMATIS, see Little Stars	
STIPPLED DIAMOND & FLOWER, see Little Flowers	
STIPPLED LEAF & BEADS, see Leaf & Beads	
Stippled Petals, Bowl, Fruit, Peach	45.00
Stippled Petals, Bowl, Peach, Dome, Footed, 9 In.	55.00
STIPPLED POSY & PODS, see Four Flowers	
Stippled Rays, Bowl, Amethyst, 9 3/4 In.	60.00
Stippled Rays, Bowl, Marigold, Candy Edge, 8 3/4 In.	36.00
Stippled Rays, Bowl, Purple, 9 In.	95.00
Stippled Rays, Compote, Green, 4 1/2 In.	30.00
Stork & Rushes, Berry Bowl, Amethyst, 4 1/2 In.	34.00
Stork & Rushes, Cup, Punch, Marigold	12.50
Stork & Rushes, Punch Cup, Purple	22.00
Stork & Rushes, Punch Set, Marigold, 7 Piece	185.00
Stork & Rushes, Tumbler, Marigold	28.00 To 30.00
STRAWBERRY, see Wild Strawberry	
Strutting Peacock, Creamer, Amethyst, Covered	48.00 To 55.00
SUNFLOWER, see Dandelion	
SUNFLOWER & WHEAT, see Fieldflower	
Swan, Carnival, Bowl, Amethyst, 10 In.	195.00
Swan, Carnival, Bowl, Marigold, Ruffled, 9 In.	185.00
Swirl Hobnail, Rose Bowl, Marigold	185.00
Swirl Hobnail, Spittoon, Amethyst	495.00
Target, Vase, White, 6 In.	48.00 To 50.00
TEARDROPS, see Raindrops	
Thin Rib Swirled, Vase, Marigold, 10 In.	18.00
Thistle & Thorn, Creamer, Marigold	36.00 To 40.00
Thistle & Thorn, Plate, Marigold, Footed, 8 1/2 In.	90.00
Thistle, Bowl, Amethyst, 8 In.	40.00
Thistle, Bowl, Green, 9 In.	35.00
Thistle, Bowl, Green, Candy Ribbon Edge, 7 3/4 In.	70.00
Three Fruits, Bonbon, Cobalt Blue, 8 X 3 7/8 In.	50.00
Three Fruits, Bowl, Amethyst, 5 In.	47.50
Three Fruits, Bowl, Aqua, Fluted, 8 In.	165.00
Three Fruits, Plate, Marigold, 9 In.	70.00
Thunderbird, Bowl, Purple, 5 In.	45.00
Tiger Lily, Pitcher, Water, Green	175.00
Tiger Lily, Tumbler, Green	25.00
Tree Of Life, Bowl, Marigold, 5 In.	20.00
Tree Trunk, Vase, White, 7 In.	50.00
Treebark, Pitcher, Marigold	28.00
Treebark, Tumbler, Marigold	14.00
Treebark, Vase, Marigold, 7 1/2 In.	24.00
Tulip Scroll, Vase, Amethyst, 7 In.	150.00
Two Flowers, Bowl, Amber, Spatula-Footed, 7 In.	45.00
Two Flowers, Bowl, Ice Cream, Marigold, Spatula-Footed	68.00
Two Flowers, Bowl, Marigold, Footed, 5 5/8 In.	26.00
Vineyard, Tumbler, Amethyst	45.00

Vineyard, Water Set, Marigold, 5 Piece	150.00
Vineyard, Water Set, Purple, 5 Piece	525.00
Vintage, Berry Set, 6 Piece, Green	135.00
Vintage, Compote, Purple	45.00
Vintage, Fernery, Purple	48.00
Vintage, Lemonade Set, Marigold, C.1920, 7 Piece	140.00
Vintage, Mug, Marigold	35.00
Vintage, Plate, Purple, 7 1/2 In.	125.00
Vintage, Rose Bowl, White ....95.00 To 115.00
Vintage, Wine, Marigold ....15.00 To 20.00

WAFFLE BAND, see Lustre Flute

Waffle Block, Basket, Marigold, Handles	45.00
Water Lily & Cattails, Tumbler, Marigold ....35.00 To 90.00
Wide Panel, Pitcher, Lemonade, White	65.00
Wild Blackberry, Bowl, Marigold, 9 In.	85.00
Wild Strawberry, Bowl, Marigold, 10 In.	85.00
Wild Strawberry, Plate, Purple, 9 In.	90.00

WINDMILL MEDALLION, see Windmill

Windmill, Bowl, Marigold, Footed, 9 In.	95.00
Windmill, Bowl, Vaseline, Ruffled, 7 3/4 In.	95.00
Windmill, Pitcher, Water, Orange	85.00
Wishbone, Epergne, Amethyst	325.00
Wreath Of Roses, Rose Bowl, Marigold	35.00
Wreathed Cherry, Bowl, White, Oval, 10 1/2 In.	210.00
Wreathed Cherry, Spooner, White, Red Design	110.00
Wreathed Cherry, Tumbler, Amethyst	45.00
Wreathed Cherry, Tumbler, Marigold	45.00
Zig-Zag, Bowl, Marigold, 9 In.	100.00
Zippered Loop, Lamp, Marigold, 8 1/2 In.	295.00

The first carousel or merry-go-round figures carved in the United States were made in 1867 by Gustav Dentzel. Collectors discovered the charm of the hand-carved figures in the 1970s and they were soon classed as folk art. Most desirable are the figures other than horses, such as pigs, camels, lions, or dogs. A jumper is a figure that was made to move up and down on a pole, a stander was placed in a stationary position.

CAROUSEL, Attack Cat, Dentzel, C.1905	13000.00
Camel, Outside Figure, Jeweled, Looff, 78 X 66 In.	6900.00
Camel, Outside, Jeweled, 78 X 66 In.	12500.00
Deer, Dentzel, Park Paint, Real Antlers, C.1900	5000.00
Deer, Rifle Trappings, Dentzel, 1906	9500.00

Carousel, Horse, Jumper,
Herschell-Spillman, Partial Paint

Carousel, Horse, C.W.Parker,
Old Paint, 65 X 60 In.

Dog 24000.00
Elephant Chariot, Heyn, Wooden 10000.00
Elephant, Clown On Top Of Head, Heyn, Wooden 12500.00
Giraffe, Child's Carousel 1000.00
Head, Carved, Wooden, Late 19th Century, 14 In. 225.00
Horse, A.Herschel, Jewels & Gold Leaf, 1930s 2500.00
Horse, Blue & Red Saddle Blanket, Red Brown, 50 X 40 In. 1250.00
Horse, C.W.Parker, Old Paint, 65 X 60 In. ....*Illus* 2100.00
Horse, Carved Mane & Saddle, Horsehair Tail, Painted, 53 X 52 In. 300.00
Horse, Cast Iron 165.00
Horse, Charles Dare, Tonawanda, N.Y. 875.00
Horse, F.Heyns, Prancer, Jewels, Park Paint 3300.00
Horse, Fiberglass, C.W.Parker, C.1960 .... 1195.00
Horse, Glass Eyes, Laminated & Carved Wood, 48 X 50 1/2 In. 1100.00
Horse, Jumper, Glass Eyes, Hair Tail, Heyn, 6 X 4 Ft. 3500.00
Horse, Jumper, Herschell–Spillman, Partial Paint ....*Illus* 2750.00
Horse, Jumper, Spillman, Wooden 3500.00
Horse, Jumping, Spillman, Original Paint, Rocking Mechanism, 1930 ...... 3200.00
Horse, Kiddie, Herschell, Metal 300.00
Horse, Kiddie, Mangel, Metal 400.00
Horse, On Wheels 900.00
Horse, Parker, 1923, Metal 650.00
Horse, Prancer, Glass Eyes, Hair Tail, Heyn 5000.00
Horse, Traveling, Carved, English, Late 19th Century, 40 X 26 In. 1500.00
Indian Head, Ornament, Painted, Cast Metal, 12 X 20 In. 100.00
Lion, Jumper, Heyn, Wooden 5000.00
Mighty Mouse, Wooden 450.00
Motorcycle, Child's, Wooden, Hand Painted, 1930s 400.00
Pig, Dark Paint, French, 62 In. 4500.00
Pig, Dentzel, C.1912 .... 8500.00
Pig, Heyn, Wooden 5000.00
Pole, Brass 50.00
Rooster, Wooden, C.1900, European 1980.00
Sea Lion, German, Wooden 7200.00
Seat, Rocketship, Kiddie Ride, Late 1950s 225.00
Swan, Wooden, Painted 13500.00
Tiger, Jumper, 4 Legs Down, Heyn 5000.00
Warhorse, Jumper, Stein & Goldstein, Coney Island Style 14000.00
Zebra, Jumping, Philadelphia Toboggan Co. 5000.00

The word "carriage" has several meanings, so this section lists baby carriages, buggies for adults, horse–drawn sleighs, and even strollers. Doll–sized carriages are listed under "toy."

CARRIAGE, Baby Buggy, Attached Parasol, Wicker 600.00
Baby Buggy, Wicker, C.1900 .... 200.00
Baby Buggy, Wicker, 1800s, Large 795.00
Baby Buggy, Wicker, Round Window In Hood, 1900 .... 200.00
Baby Buggy, Windows, Wicker 325.00
Buggy, Heywood, Wicker, Convertible Hood 150.00
Buggy, Wood Spoke Wheels, Original Paint, 48 X 44 In. 500.00
Hearse, Horse Drawn, Side Lamps, Hand Carved 5500.00
Oil Tanker, Studebaker, Horse Drawn, 1892 .... 3800.00
Popcorn Machine, Model C 2900.00
Stroller, 1890s, Natural Wicker 575.00
Stroller, Child's, Wicker Basket, Reined Horse, C.1860 .... 4500.00
Stroller, Doll, High Wheels, Original Paint & Upholstery, Wicker 495.00
Stroller, Natural, Wicker, Needs Parasol, 1890s 575.00
Walker, Windsor, Bentwood Legs, Original Paint & Stencils 225.00

Cased glass is made with one thin layer of glass over another layer or layers of colored glass. Many types of art glass were cased. Cased glass is usually a well–made piece by a reputable factory.

CASED GLASS, Vase, Blue, Ruffled Edge, 9 In. 95.00
Vase, Yellow, White, 10 In. 125.00

An eye on the cash was a necessity in stores of the nineteenth century, too. The cash register was invented in 1884. John and James Ritty invented a large clocklike model that kept a record of the dollars and cents exchanged in the store. John Patterson improved the cash register with a paper roll to record the money. By the early 1900s, elaborate brass registers were made. About World War I, the fancy case was exchanged for the more modern types.

CASH REGISTER, Dodge, Compartment For Coins, 1 Drawer, Note Pad, 10 X 16 In.	595.00
National, 1950, 8 Drawer, Electric	1350.00
National, 2 Drawer, Counter Top	2000.00
National, 6 Drawer, Model S/N 333317, Quarter Sawed Oak	1295.00
National, Autographic Ticket, Fleur–De–Lis Design	800.00
National, Bronze, Pat.1915, 21 X 13 3/4 X 15 1/2 In.	325.00
National, Floor Model, Register Reel, Oak Base, Brass	1800.00
National, Model 30, Brass, Autographic Register	850.00
National, Model 50, Clock	1200.00
National, Model 128, Brass, Milk Glass Shelf	395.00
National, Model 130, Brass Base	725.00 To 750.00
National, Model 310, Candy Store	825.00 To 900.00
National, Model 313, Nickel Over Brass	650.00
National, Model 317, Brass, Plated	975.00
National, Model 324, 12 In.	300.00
National, Model 336, Brass	2250.00
National, Model 349, Brass	325.00 To 375.00
National, Model 356, Brass, 1 Cent To $20	250.00
National, Model 442, Brass, Crank, Oak Base	400.00
National, Model 552, Floor, 5 Drawer, Purchase Sign	1350.00
National, Nickeled Brass	795.00
Oak & Brass Trim, 3 1/2 Ft.	390.00

Castor sets holding just salt and pepper castors were used in the seventeenth century. The sugar castor, mustard pot, spice dredger, bottles for vinegar and oil, and other spice holders became popular by the eighteenth century. These sets were usually made of sterling silver. The American Victorian castor set, the type most collected today, was made of silver plated Britannia metal. Colored glass bottles were introduced after the Civil War. The sets were out of fashion by World War I. Be careful when buying sets with colored bottles; many are reproductions.

CASTOR SET, see also various Porcelain and Glass categories

CASTOR SET, 3–Bottle, Burmese, Silver Plate Holder, 7 In.	325.00
3–Bottle, Rubena Cut Panels, Silver Plated Holder, 5 3/4 In.	150.00
4–Bottle, 2 Open Salts, 19th Century, Silver Plate, 9 1/4 In.	45.00
4–Bottle, Pedestal Base, Beverly, Mass.	350.00
4–Bottle, Pewter Frame, Miniature	95.00
4–Bottle, Silver, Meriden	135.00
5–Bottle, Blown 3 Mold, Pewter Holder, Signed E.Smith	95.00
5–Bottle, Coin Spot, Silver Plate, Bowl Frame, 14 In.	100.00
5–Bottle, Etched, Silver Plated Holder	195.00
5–Bottle, Gothic Arch, Bell, Pewter Frame, Dated 1858	135.00
5–Bottle, Quadruple Silver Plate	235.00
5–Bottle, Simpson Hall Miller, Sterling Silver Tops	200.00
5–Bottle, Staffordshire Bottles, Silver Plate Holder, Davenport	375.00
6–Bottle, Vaseline, Diamond & Button, Engraved, 18 In.	450.00

The pickle castor was a glass jar about six inches in height, held in a special metal holder. It became a popular dinner table accessory about 1890. The jar had a top that was usually silver or silver plate. The frame, also of a silver metal, had a handle that arched above the jar and a hook that held a pair of tongs. By 1900, the pickle castor was out of fashion. Many examples found today have reproduced glass jars in old holders.

CASTOR, PICKLE, see also various Glass categories

CASTOR, Pickle, Amber Glass Insert, Footed, Footed, Meriden 225.00
Pickle, Amber Inset, 4 Foot Silver Frame, Tongs 150.00
Pickle, Amethyst & Clear Insert, James Tufts Quadruple Stand 225.00
Pickle, Broken Column, Cover, Tongs 125.00
Pickle, Cased Rainbow, Royal Ivy, Silver Frame, Footed, Tongs 350.00
Pickle, Clear Block Insert, Reed & Barton Cover, Fork 75.00
Pickle, Clear Embossed Insert, Tongs 115.00
Pickle, Cobalt, Moon & Star, Rayed Round Base, Silver Plate Holder 225.00
Pickle, Cranberry Opalescent Coin Dot Insert, Forbes, Footed 150.00
Pickle, Cranberry, Enameled Blues, Greens, Silver Plate Frame, Tongs 245.00
Pickle, Cranberry, Floral Enameled Insert, Footed, Holder 285.00
Pickle, Cranberry, Inverted Thumbprint Insert, Hartford 110.00
Pickle, Cranberry, Pairpoint Frame 200.00
Pickle, Cut Class Jar, Pierced Silver Plate Holder, Tongs, 11 In. 120.00
Pickle, Daisy & Button, Hartford Silver Co., Lid & Castor, Amber 275.00
Pickle, Diamond & Button, Apple Green 185.00
Pickle, Dog Finial 68.00
Pickle, Double, Floral, Diamond, Footed, Tongs, Fork, Meriden, 1896 .... 225.00
Pickle, Double, Silver Plated Frame, Racine Silver Plate Co. 500.00
Pickle, Double, Twin Pattern, Glass, Silver Plate, Tongs 125.00
Pickle, Egyptian Figures, Sterling Silver Fork, Christmas 1872 .... 225.00
Pickle, Enameled Floral, Cranberry, Silver Plate Lid 110.00
Pickle, Frosted Stork, Silver Plated Holder 78.00
Pickle, Grape & Vine, Milk Glass Insert, Pairpoint Frame, Footed 185.00
Pickle, Inverted Thumbprint Blue Jar, Tongs, Signed 295.00
Pickle, Inverted Thumbprint Insert, Hartford Silver Plate Frame 150.00
Pickle, Inverted Thumbprint, Cranberry, Reed Barton Holder, Tongs 215.00
Pickle, Near Cut Jar, Silver Plate Holder & Tongs, Meriden 85.00
Pickle, Paneled Zipper Insert, Meriden, Footed Stand, Fork & Tongs 85.00
Pickle, Pewter, Victorian, Tongs 45.00
Pickle, Pomona, Cornflower 400.00
Pickle, Pressed Glass Jar, Silver Plate, Tongs 77.50
Pickle, Square Glass Insert, Webster & Son Quadruple Plate, Flowers 250.00
Pickle, Stork In Rushes, Webster, Tongs 85.00
Pickle, Sunken Daisy, Silver Plate Frame 78.50
Pickle, Topaz, Daisy & Button Jar, Silver Plate Holder 150.00
Pickle, Vaseline Glass Insert, Tongs 65.00
CATALOG, see Paper, Catalog
CAUGHLEY, see Salopian

The firm Cauldon Limited worked in Staffordshire, Great Britain, and went through many name changes. John Ridgway made porcelain at Cauldon Place, Hanley, until 1855. The firm of John Ridgway, Bates and Co. of Cauldon Place worked from 1856 to 1859. It became Bates, Brown–Westhead, Moore and Co. from 1859 to 1862. Brown–Westhead, Moore and Co. worked from 1862 to 1904. About 1890, this firm started using the words "Cauldon" or "Cauldon ware" as part of the mark. Cauldon Ltd. worked from 1905 to 1920. Cauldon Potteries from 1920 to 1962.

CAULDON, see also Indian Tree
CAULDON, Plate, Butterflies Of The World, 9 In. 25.00
Plate, Roses, Allover Gold, Turquoise Enameled, Signed Hillman 450.00
Teapot, Sugar, & Creamer, Gold Trim, Marked 110.00
Wash Set, Rust & Black, 4 Piece 150.00

Celadon is a Chinese porcelain having a velvet–textured green–gray glaze. Japanese, Korean, and other factories also made a celadon–colored glaze.

CELADON, Bench, Garden, Prunis Blossoms, Chinese, 19th Century 450.00
Bowl, 3 In. 6.00
Bowl, Carved, Geometric, Green Glaze, Koryo, Imperial Mark, 6 1/2 In. 495.00
Bowl, Linear Interior Design, 10 1/2 In. 80.00
Charger, Village & Lake Scene, Blue & White, Chinese, 15 7/8 In. 80.00
Cup Stand, Green Glaze, Conical Shape, Saucer, Koryo, 11th Century 550.00

Dish, Birds, Butterflies, Floral, Scalloped, 5 3/4 In. 30.00
Dish, Carved, Foliate Medallion, Gray Olive Green Glaze, 14 1/2 In. 190.00
Dish, Fish, Impressed Fish On Base, Gold, 6 In. 45.00
Dish, Shrimp, Bird & Butterfly, C.1790, 10 X 9 In. 275.00
Dish, Shrimp, Peonies, Birds & Butterflies, 10 1/4 In., Pair 400.00
Eggcup, Victorian 18.00
Jar, Foo Dog Finial, Covered, Raised Enamel Bird & Floral, 15 In. 175.00
Plate, Fuji, 9 In. 15.00
Saki Pot, Green Foliage, Ribbed, Domed Cover, 5 1/4 In. 75.00
Teapot, Domed Cover, Globular Form, Jade, China, 4 In. 400.00
Teapot, Seiji 41.50
Tureen, Cover, Peonies, Birds, & Butterflies, 10 1/2 In. 2600.00
Vase, Wall, 12 In. 65.00

> *Celluloid is a trademark for a plastic developed in 1868 by John W.
> Hyatt. Celluloid Manufacturing Company, the Celluloid Novelty
> Company, Celluloid Fancy Goods Company, and American Xylonite
> Company all used Celluloid to make jewelry, games, sewing
> equipment, false teeth, and piano keys. Eventually, the Hyatt
> Company became the American Celluloid and Chemical
> Manufacturing Company—the Celanese Corporation. The name
> "Celluloid" was often used to identify any similar plastic. Celluloid
> toys are listed under toys.*

CELLULOID, Ball, Baby's, C.1880 .... 85.00
Box, Necktie, French Ivory 55.00
Box, Tie, Indian Chief On Cover, 14 In. 37.50
Cane, Carnival, Girl With Feather, Hat, 1940s, 10 In. 16.00
Clown, Movable Arm, 4 In. 35.00
Comb & Brush Set, Baby, Rattle, Pink & Blue Floral 15.00
Doll, Carnival, 12 In. 35.00
Dresser Set, 6 Piece 20.00
Dresser Set, With Clock, 12 Piece 125.00
Dresser Set, Yellow, 6 Piece 30.00
Engraving, 3 Wood Scenes, Louis K.Harlow, 5 X 9 In. 25.00
Fan, Child's, Lacy 22.00
Figurine, Bride & Groom, Dressed, 1940s, 3 In. 20.00
Figurine, Felix 15.00
Hair Receiver Set, Mirror 18.00
Hair Receiver, Ivory .... 5.00 To 10.00
Holder, String, Ball 10.00
Manicure Set, Elephant Skin Case, 15 Piece 55.00
Pin Tray & Comb, Ivory 10.00
Pin, Art Deco, Flapper Girl's Head 15.00
Powder Dish, Ivory 10.00
Rattle, Baby, Sad Dog Face, Wooden 12.00
Rattle, Bird 15.00
Rattle, Peacock, C.1900 .... 16.00
Rattle, Pheasant, C.1900 .... 14.00
Rattle, Rhino & Bear, C.1900 .... 10.00
Rattle, Roly Poly Face 18.00
Rattle, Twisted Handle, C.1903 .... 9.50
Sharpener, Pencil, Airplane 35.00
Tape Measure, Celluloid Pig 22.00
Toaster Cover, Mammy's Head 16.00

> *The Ceramic Art Company of Trenton, New Jersey, was established in
> 1889 by J. Coxon and W. Lenox and was an early producer of
> American Belleek porcelain.*

CERAMIC ART CO., Figurine, Elephant, Small 15.00
Figurine, Man, With Harem 55.00
Salt & Pepper, Figural, Pig, Marked 12.50
Vase, Bud, 7 In., Pair 45.00
Vase, Comedy/Tragedy, 3 In. 12.00

Chalkware is really plaster of Paris decorated with watercolors. The pieces were molded from known Staffordshire and other porcelain models and painted and sold as inexpensive decorations.

CHALKWARE, Bank, Frosty The Snowman, Hall, 12 In. 13.00
Bank, Santa Claus, Asleep In Chair 50.00
Bank, Winston Churchill 24.00
Bust, Indian 85.00

CHALKWARE, FIGURINE, see also Kewpie

Figurine, 3 Baby Pigs In Bonnets, Pink, 2 In. 29.00
Figurine, Boy Carrying Dog, Roger Type, 12 In. 39.00
Figurine, Bugs Bunny, Carrot In Hand, Mexico, 19 In. 25.00
Figurine, Bulldog, Sitting, With Bow, 4 X 5 In. 10.00
Figurine, Cat, Seated, Spotted, Painted, 10 1/2 In. 400.00
Figurine, Cat, Seated, White Eyes, Black Repaint, 16 In. 385.00
Figurine, Charlie McCarthy 20.00
Figurine, Child & Dog, Can't You Talk 18.50
Figurine, Dog, Red, Black & Yellow, Oval Base, 4 3/4 In. 70.00
Figurine, Dog, Seated, 8 1/2 In. 55.00
Figurine, Dog, Seated, Traces Of Old Paint, 5 5/8 In. 55.00
Figurine, Dog, Yellow, Blue, Green; 7 In., Pair ....*Illus* 250.00
Figurine, Easter Rabbit, Coming Out Of Egg, Red Paint, 6 1/2 In. 35.00
Figurine, Ewe & Lamb, Red, Black & Yellow, Green Gold Base, 6 In. 320.00
Figurine, Girl Holding Flowers, 9 In. 10.00
Figurine, Hank Aaron, Atlanta Uniform, Bronze Color, 12 X 9 In. 35.00
Figurine, Laurel & Hardy, 20 In., Pair 75.00
Figurine, Lion, 20 In. 30.00
Figurine, Man, Red Cap, Chasing Pink Pig, 4 In. 55.00
Figurine, Marine Saluting, 15 In. 13.50
Figurine, Oriental Holy Man, Brown Robe, 8 In. 20.00
Figurine, Pigs, Baby, Pink, Wearing Diapers, Blue Bonnets 29.00
Figurine, Rabbit With Carrot, Dark Colors, 10 In. 12.00
Figurine, Red Goose, 5 In. 35.00
Figurine, Shepherd Boy & Lamb, 11 X 9 1/2 In. 75.00
Figurine, Spaniel, Beige & Black, 9 In. 75.00
Figurine, Tappan Chef 20.00
Floral & Fruit Arrangement 175.00
Holder, Sucker, Statue Of Liberty 200.00
Man Chasing Pink Pig, Green Trim, China, 3 1/4 In. 55.00
Nodder, Cat, Red & Black, 6 In. 325.00
Nodder, Yellow Kid, Wooden Base, Marked Christmas 1912, 4 3/4 In. 12.50
Pen & Pen Holder, Dutch Boy, Hanging, 10 3/4 In. 18.00
Pitcher, Art Nouveau, Lady, Flowing Hair, High Relief, 15 X 9 In. 125.00
Salt & Pepper, Maggie & Jiggs 25.00

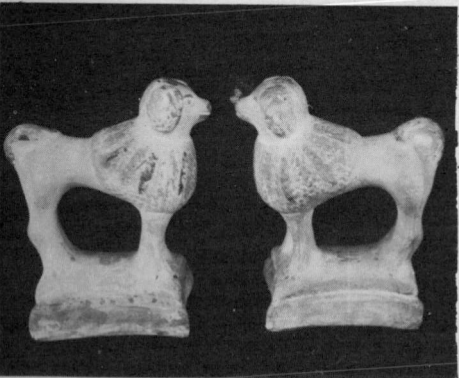

If you discover a cache of very dirty antiques and you are not dressed in work clothes, make a temporary cover up from a plastic garbage bag.

Chalkware, Figurine, Dog, Yellow, Blue, Green, 7 In., Pair

String Holder, Boy In Top Hat 25.00
String Holder, Cat 22.00
String Holder, Dutch Girl ....10.00 To 15.00
String Holder, Figural, Kitten 20.00
String Holder, French Chef 20.00
String Holder, Kitty With Twine Ball 20.00
String Holder, Man In Sombrero 12.50

Charlie Chaplin, the famous comic and actor, lived from 1889 to 1977. He made his first movie in 1913. He did the movie "The Tramp" in 1915. The character of the Tramp has remained famous and is in use today in a series of television commercials for computers. Dolls, candy containers, and all sorts of memorabilia picture Charlie Chaplin. Pieces are being made even today.

CHARLIE CHAPLIN, Book, Comic, In The Army, 1917 .... 35.00
  Candy Container & Bank 45.00
  Candy Container, Original Paint 110.00
  Cup 18.00
  Doll, Composition Head, Hands, Feet, Ball Jointed, Dressed 225.00
  Doll, Original Label & Clothes 195.00
  Figure, Dances On Box, Negro Scene, Flat Tin, 1920s 650.00
  Figure, Jointed, Dances From String, 1930s, Celluloid, 6 In. 75.00
  Figure, Mechanical, Plastic, Italy, 1950s 95.00
  Figurine, Bisque, Germany 65.00
  Figurine, Chalkware, Statue Arts, 11 In. 50.00
  Jug, 1920, Stoneware, 9 In. 130.00
  Lamp, Chalkware, Black, Drunk Leaning On Pole, 1920s, 23 In. 75.00
  Pencil Box, Tin ....20.00 To 26.00
  Pencil Case, Signed Clive, Orange 22.00
  Postcard 15.00
  Poster, Gold Rush, 20 X 54 In. 275.00
  Poster, Gold Rush, United Artists, 38 X 30 In. 75.00
  Poster, Great Dictator, United Artists, 38 X 30 In. 75.00
  Poster, Kid, German Issue, 27 X 50 In. 500.00
  Poster, Modern Times, United Artists, 38 X 30 In. 95.00
  Poster, The Gold Rush, United Artists Re–Release, 1941 .... 200.00
  Spoon, Figural, Plated 10.00
  Stickpin, 1920s 35.00
  Toothpick 25.00
  Toothpick, Coral 25.00
  Toy, Figure Dances On Front Of Tin Box, Black Scene, 1920s 650.00
  Toy, Jointed, Dances From String, Celluloid, 1930s, 6 In. 77.00
  Toy, On Bicycle 215.00
  Toy, Squeeze, Composition Head, 1920s, Japanese 225.00
  Toy, Windup, Tin, Litho, Iron Feet, 8 1/2 In. 700.00

Charlie McCarthy was the ventriloquist's dummy used by Edgar Bergen from the 1930s. He was famous for his work in radio, movies, and television. The act was retired in the 1970s.

CHARLIE MCCARTHY, Book, Big Little Book, Charlie McCarthy & Edgar ....7.00 To 35.00
  Book, Coloring 14.00
  Bust, Charlie, Movable Eyes & Mouth, Cardboard 12.00
  Doll, Composition, Excelsior Stuffed Body 85.00
  Figurine, Charlie, Chalkware, Blue, 14 1/2 In. 35.00
  Game, Hats 15.00
  Game, Question & Answer, 1938, Complete 25.00
  Game, Radio Party 25.00
  Game, Rummy, 1938 .... 25.00
  Game, Topper, Original Box, 1938 .... 25.00
  Knife, Cowboy 18.00
  Pencil Sharpener, Figural, 1930 .... 25.00
  Print Block, Chase & Sanborn 25.00
  Puppet, Hand, Composition Head 45.00
  Puppet, Radio Premium, 21 In. 35.00

Spoon, Figural, Silver Plated	4.50 To 17.50
Toy, Car, Windup, Tin, Litho, Marx, 7 In.	275.00
Toy, Crazy Car, Windup	250.00 To 325.00
Toy, Dancing, Jointed, Marks, Original Label, 11 In.	145.00
Toy, Dipsy Car, Box	385.00
Toy, Private Car, Windup, With Mortimer Snerd	225.00 To 300.00

Chelsea grape pattern was made before 1840. A small bunch of grapes in a raised design, colored with purple or blue luster, is on the border of the white plate. Most of the pieces are unmarked. The pattern is sometimes called "Aynsley" or "Grandmother." Chelsea sprig is similar but has a sprig of flowers instead of the bunch of grapes.

CHELSEA GRAPE, Cup & Saucer, Bouillon	10.00
Mug, Shaving, Large	38.00
Ramekin, Underplate	12.00
Shaving Mug, Purple Grapes, Large	45.00
Tea Set, 3 Piece	175.00

CHELSEA KERAMIC ART WORKS, see Dedham

CHELSEA SPRIG, Plate, Handles, Lyre & Wreath, 9 1/2 In.	20.00
Plate, Lavender Thistles, 9 In., Pair	45.00

Chelsea porcelain was made in the Chelsea area of London from about 1745 to 1784. Recent copies of this work have been made from the original molds.

CHELSEA, Bowl, Covered, Stand, Sunflower, Marked, C.1755, 9 & 5 In.	6325.00
Figurine, Child, With Goats, C.1880, Gold Anchor Mark, 3 In., Pair	260.00
Figurine, Colonial Man & Woman, Gold Anchor Mark, 7 1/2 In., Pair	215.00
Figurine, Man & Woman, Tree Stump, Lamb At Feet, Marked, 11 In., Pair	710.00
Flask, Brown, Green, Marked, 5 1/4 In.	275.00
Pitcher, Green Brown, Handle, Late 19th Century, 7 1/2 In.	300.00
Pitcher, Pink Lilies, Multicolored Leaves, Cream, 8 In.	87.00
Plate, Lyre & Wreath, Shells, 10 In.	10.00
Tile, Lady's Head, Bonnet, Gray Blue, C.1886, 4 1/4 In.	90.00
Vase, Bird, Tooled Gilt Panels, Handles, 1760–65, Marked, 10 In., Pr.	1430.00

Chinese export porcelain is all the many kinds of porcelain made in China for export to America and Europe in the eighteenth and nineteenth centuries.

CHINESE EXPORT, see also Canton; Celadon; Nanking

CHINESE EXPORT, Basin, Famille Verte, Scholar Scene, Kangxi, 13 1/2 In.	825.00
Basket, Underplate, Reticulated Chestnut, Blue & White	450.00
Bottle, Blue Fitzhugh, Pinecone, Breast Medallion, 9 3/4 In.	650.00
Bough Pot, Oriental Men, Strap Handles, C.1780, 7 In., Pair	925.00
Bowl, Famille Rose, Gilt Bronze, Blossoms, Handle, 20 In.	440.00
Bowl, Famille Rose, Phoenix Bird, Gilt, Guangxu, 8 1/8 In.	522.00
Bowl, Hunting, Full Cry, Treeing The Fox, C.1785, 11 5/8 In.	825.00
Bowl, Landscape Scene, Blue & White, Lobed	375.00
Bowl, Mandarin Figures, Reserve, Polychrome, 10 1/4 In.	850.00
Bowl, Polychrome Enameled Florals, Blue Rim, Gilt, 8 5/8 In.	65.00
Bowl, Porcelain, Mountain Scene, Copper Rim, 3 7/8 X 8 In.	400.00
Bowl, Vegetable, Cover, Polychrome & Gilt Design, 9 1/2 In.	120.00
Box, Cushion, Cover, Famille Rose, 10 1/2 In.	110.00
Charger, Porcelain, Blue Waves, Dragons, Chin'Lung, 21 In.	875.00
Charger, Tobacco Leaf, Underglaze, 1760–80, 13 1/2 In.	1850.00
Creamer, Helmet, Polychrome Floral, 4 7/8 In.	55.00
Creamer, Polychrome Floral, Monk With Banner, 4 In., Pair	145.00
Cup & Saucer, Arms Of New York State	230.00
Cup & Saucer, Deep, C.1850	85.00
Cup & Saucer, Handleless	75.00
Cup & Saucer, Handleless, Polychrome Floral Design	50.00
Cup & Saucer, Handleless, Purple & Red Enameled Flowers	50.00
Dish, Lettuce Leaf, Green Enamel Fluted, C.1770, 14 In., Pair	2650.00
Dish, Serving, Covered, Thousand Butterflies, 9 1/4 In.	375.00

Chinese Export, Tureen, Flower,
Pig's Head Handles, Covered, C.1770

If you want to use a valuable Chinese export punch bowl at a party, try this: Buy a piece of light-weight clear plastic hose at a hardware store. Slit the hose and use it to protect the rim of the bowl from the punch ladle.

Dresser Set, Enameled, Blue, Aqua, Green, Floral, 4 Piece		125.00
Figurine, Boy On Water Buffalo, Crystal, Stand, 3 5/8 In.		175.00
Figurine, Dog, Standing, White, Collar, Bell, 4 1/2 In., Pair		450.00
Figurine, Foo Dog, Agate, Carved, 20th Century, 5 3/8 In.		650.00
Figurine, Hotei, Famille Rose, C.1900, 12 In.		85.00
Figurine, Hotei, Fat, Jolly, Famille Rose, 1890, 12 In.		59.00
Figurine, Hotei, Jolly, Famille Rose, 1890, 12 In.	65.00 To	80.00
Figurine, Kuan Ti, Carved, C.1820, 9 In.		275.00
Figurine, Phoenix Bird, On Rock, Enameled, 9 1/4 In., Pr.		925.00
Figurine, Quanyin & Bird, Carved Amethyst, Base, 5 7/8 In.		100.00
Gravy Boat, Foliated Handle, Fitzhugh		380.00
Jar, Ginger, Kimona Girl Raised, 4 Sided, 3 X 3 X 5 1/2 In.		95.00
Jar, Storage, Cover, Blue, White, Bulbous, Cracked, 10 1/2 In.		175.00
Jar, Temple, Rose Mandarin, Gilt Foo Dogs, Lizard, 24 1/2 In.		700.00
Jug, Cider, Domed Cover, Foo Dog Finial, C.1800, 8 1/2 In.		300.00
Lamp, Candle, Vertical Piercing, Blue & White, 8 1/2 X 6 In.		650.00
Mug, Floral Bud Bands, Painted Genre & Panels, 5 1/8 In.		175.00
Mug, Floral, Woven Strap Handle, Cylindrical, 4 3/8 In.		150.00
Mug, Porcelain, Stalk Handle, Floral, Monogram, 6 In.		450.00
Plate, Coats Of Arms, Link Border, C.1770, 10 In., Pair		225.00
Plate, Polychrome Floral, Pink & Orange Borders, 9 1/4 In.		25.00
Plate, Rockefeller, Sampan Scenes, 1795–1810, 9 3/4 In., Pair		1100.00
Platter, Blue Fitzhugh, Medallion, 20 In.		925.00
Platter, Famille Rose, Gilt Border, 1775, 11 1/2 In., Pair		900.00
Punch Bowl, Floral Interior & Exterior, 15 1/2 In.		625.00
Punch Bowl, Genre Scenes, Birds, Geometric Interior, 4 In.		350.00
Punch Bowl, Gilt Polychrome Figural Reserves, 11 1/8 In.		275.00
Salt Cellar, Griffin Crest, Chamfered, C.1731, 3 In., Pair		950.00
Snuff Bottle, Copper, Lion's Mask, Spoon, 5 1/4 In.		175.00
Snuff Bottle, Lid, Floral, Yellow, Jade, 2 1/2 In.		125.00
Snuff Box, Gold, Lace Agate, Chased Scenes, Marked, 2 1/2 In.		6800.00
Soup, Dish, Famille Rose, Celadon, Pheasant, 14 Piece		1050.00
Tea & Coffee Service, Armorial, C.1760, 18 Piece		250.00
Tea Caddy, Covered, Eagle In Medallion Each Side, Gilt		50.00
Tea Caddy, Landscape Scene, Blue & White		250.00
Tea Set, Heraldic Shield, Monogram, Cobalt Bands, 1800, 4 Pc.		850.00
Teabowl, American Marine Design, C.1795, 3 1/2 In.		500.00
Teapot, Earthenware, Twig Handle & Spout, Incised Signed		45.00
Teapot, Polychrome Floral Enameling, 5 1/8 In.		85.00
Teapot, Polychrome Floral Enameling, 7 1/4 In.		195.00
Teapot, Polychrome Floral, Gilded Fruit Finial, 6 1/4 In.		115.00
Tureen, Covered, Stand, Animals, Flowers, C.1770, 14 In.		2200.00

Tureen, Floral Finial, Covered, Rope Handles, 9 1/4 In.	825.00
Tureen, Flower, Pig's Head Handles, Covered, C.1770 ....*Illus*	2200.00
Tureen, Underplate, Covered, Foo Dog Finial, 15 In.	850.00
Vase, Chinese Famille, Jaune, Table Lamp Mounted	110.00
Vase, Famille Rose, Lion Handles, Electrified, 17 1/2 In.	620.00
Vase, Famille Rose, Ovoid, 19th Century, 14 In.	250.00
Vase, Famille Rose, Turquoise, Quail Scene, 13 1/2 In.	7700.00
Vase, Gilt Bronze Mount, Turquoise, 16 1/4 In., Pair	2200.00
Vase, Landscape Scene, Famille Verte, Lamp Mounted, 21 In.	60.00
Vase, Polychrome Blossoms, Baluster, Silver Mount, 7 In.	200.00
Vase, Silver, Shield, Peonies, Stippled Ground, 5 3/4 In.	140.00
Wine Cup, Famille Rose, Lotus Shape, Guangxu, 7 1/2 In.	825.00
Wash Bowl, Birds, Rose, & Butterfly, Fitzhugh, 16 In.	750.00

Chocolate glass, sometimes mistakenly called caramel slag, was made by the Indiana Tumbler and Goblet Company of Greentown, Indiana, from 1900 to 1903.

CHOCOLATE GLASS, Berry Bowl, 4 In., Set Of 6	120.00
Berry Bowl, Cactus, Small	45.00
Berry Bowl, Leaf Bracket, 4 3/4 In.	35.00
Bowl, Geneva, 8 1/4 X 5 1/4 In.	65.00
Bowl, Leaf Bracket, Footed, 4 1/2 In.	23.00
Bowl, Vintage Pattern, 3 Feet, 6 In.	95.00
Butter, Button & Arches, Covered	55.00
Butter, Covered, Cactus	150.00
Butter, Covered, Dewey, Individual	135.00
Butter, Covered, Leaf Bracket	125.00
Butter, Leaf Bracket	85.00
Celery, Leaf Bracket	110.00
Celery, Shell & Leaf	85.00
Compote, Cactus, 5 1/2 In.	65.00
Compote, Cactus, Red Agate, 8 X 8 In.	200.00
Compote, Covered, Rose In Snow	55.00
Creamer, Leaf Bracket	65.00
Creamer, Shuttle	95.00
Cruet, Dewey, Original Stopper, Amber	135.00
Cruet, Leaf Bracket, Original Stopper	150.00
Dish, Dolphin, Beaded Rim	165.00
Dish, Hen, Covered ....*Illus*	160.00
Fernery, Vintage Pattern, 6 In.	145.00
Figurine, Dog, Imperial	25.00

Chocolate Glass, Dish, Hen, Covered

Chocolate Glass, Lamp

Figurine, Dolphin 85.00
Figurine, Swan 20.00
Lamp .... *Illus* 425.00
Mug, Herringbone 62.00
Mug, Herringbone Buttress ....30.00 To 65.00
Nappy, Leaf Bracket 75.00
Nappy, Leaf Bracket, Handle, Triangular ....45.00 To 65.00
Pitcher, Lemonade, Cactus 65.00
Pitcher, Water, Heron Pattern 425.00
Plate, Cactus, 7 1/2 In. 110.00
Plate, Serenade, Greentown, Large 165.00
Relish, Leaf Bracket, Oval ....45.00 To 65.00
Salt & Pepper, No Lid 105.00
Salt Dip, Wheelbarrow 10.00
Sauce, Cactus 40.00
Saucer, Cactus 35.00
Spooner, Cactus 50.00
Spooner, Leaf Bracket 65.00
Spooner, Wildrose & Bowknot 125.00
Stein, Indoor Drinking Scene 115.00
Stein, Outdoor Drinking Scene, Pouring Spout 125.00
Sugar, Covered, Cactus ....95.00 To 125.00
Sugar, Covered, Scroll & Acanthus, Footed 40.00
Syrup, Cactus 90.00
Syrup, Cord Drapery 165.00
Table Set, Leaf Bracket, 4 Piece 375.00
Toothpick, Cactus ....55.00 To 125.00
Toothpick, Cactus, Double 65.00
Tumbler, Cactus ....35.00 To 55.00
Tumbler, Leaf Bracket 50.00
Tumbler, Sawtooth 70.00
Tumbler, Shuttle ....50.00 To 85.00
Tumbler, Shuttle Pattern, Greentown, 3 3/4 In. 75.00

CHRISTMAS PLATE, see Collector Plate

The first decorated Christmas tree in America is claimed by many states, including Pennsylvania (1747), Massachusetts (1832), Illinois (1833), Ohio (1838), and Iowa (1845). The first glass ornaments were imported from Germany about 1860. Manufacturers in the United States were making ornaments in the early 1870s. Electric lights were first used on a Christmas tree in 1882. Character light bulbs became popular in the 1920s, bubble lights in the 1940s, twinkle bulbs in the 1950s, plastic bulbs by 1955.

CHRISTMAS TREE, Candleholder, Tin, Clip–On, Germany, 12 Piece 28.00
Candleholder, Tin, Red, Blue, Green, Silver, 1900, Set Of 7 .... 25.00
Carpet, Santa Claus, Sleigh, Reindeer, Holly, 5 X 6 Ft. 110.00
Creche, Mother–Of–Pearl, Carved, Framed, 2 X 8 X 10 In. 50.00
Fence, Folding, 108 In. 8.00
Fence, Wooden, Folding, Red & Natural 27.00
Holder, Stars & Stripes, Cast Iron, Original Paint 22.50
Light Bulb, Angel, Brown Hair, 4 In. 27.00
Light Bulb, Betty Boop, Magenta Dress, 3 1/4 In. 50.00
Light Bulb, Bird, Figural, Blue 10.00
Light Bulb, Bird, Germany, Clear Glass 25.00
Light Bulb, Bird, Set Of 4 .... 70.00
Light Bulb, Boy Blue 25.00
Light Bulb, Boy, Holding Airplane 38.00
Light Bulb, Candy Cane, Set Of 4 ....60.00 To 75.00
Light Bulb, Cat In Boot 32.00
Light Bulb, Cat, Sitting 40.00
Light Bulb, Chinese Lantern, 2 1/2 In. 5.00
Light Bulb, Cross 13.00
Light Bulb, Diamond–Quilted, Rose, 3 1/2 In. 90.00
Light Bulb, Dick Tracy 45.00

Light Bulb, Dog, In Basket 24.00
Light Bulb, Dog, In Hunting Outfit 25.00
Light Bulb, Dog, With Bandage 42.00
Light Bulb, Donald Duck 15.00
Light Bulb, Duckling 22.00
Light Bulb, Dunce Head 37.00
Light Bulb, Elephant, 4 In. 25.00
Light Bulb, Father Christmas, 1930s 71.50
Light Bulb, Girl Head, Glass Eyes, Figural 95.00
Light Bulb, House, 2 1/2 In. 6.00
Light Bulb, Humpty Dumpty, Red, Black, Milk Glass, 3 1/8 In. 20.00
Light Bulb, Japanese Lantern, Hand Painted 15.00
Light Bulb, Jiminy Cricket 15.00
Light Bulb, Kitten 25.00
Light Bulb, Lantern ....3.00 To 6.00
Light Bulb, Lantern, Noma, String Of 20, 1950, Japan 5.00
Light Bulb, Little Red Riding Hood ....30.00 To 52.00
Light Bulb, Mazda, String, Box 7.50
Light Bulb, Mickey Mouse, Noma, Box 100.00
Light Bulb, Minnie Mouse ....15.00 To 35.00
Light Bulb, Monkey, Germany, Clear Glass 125.00
Light Bulb, Mother Goose 35.00
Light Bulb, Parakeet, Plastic, 1940s 8.00
Light Bulb, Parrot 18.00
Light Bulb, Pig 25.00
Light Bulb, Pinocchio 15.00
Light Bulb, Pluto 15.00
Light Bulb, Sandy 45.00
Light Bulb, Santa Claus, Double Faced 16.00
Light Bulb, Santa Claus, Full Length, Milk Glass, 4 1/4 In. 20.00
Light Bulb, Santa, Plastic 12.00
Light Bulb, Smitty 35.00
Light Bulb, Snowman ....10.00 To 25.00
Light Bulb, Star, 5 Pointed 16.00
Light Bulb, Star, With Face 26.00
Light Bulb, Street Lamp 11.00
Light Bulb, Teddy Bear 40.00
Light Bulb, Umbrella, 4 1/4 In. 30.00
Light, 16 Ribs, Broken Swirl, Folded Rim, Amethyst, 3 In. 115.00
Light, Blown Sapphire Blue Bowl, 4 1/2 In. 55.00
Light, Expanded Diamond, Folded Rim, Amber, 3 3/8 In. 65.00
Light, Expanded Diamond, Folded Rim, Amethyst, 3 1/8 In. 65.00
Light, Star, Tin 14.00
Ornament, Air Balloon, Crinkle Wire 15.00
Ornament, Angel & Lute, Sepia & Red, Papier–Mache 17.50
Ornament, Angel, Bow & Arrow, C.1880, Papier–Mache, 1 1/2 In. .. 17.50
Ornament, Angel, Horn & Flowers, C.1880, Papier–Mache 17.50
Ornament, Angel, Tree Top, Die Cut 25.00
Ornament, Angel, Wax ....95.00 To 110.00
Ornament, Apple 65.00
Ornament, Baby Bunting, Glass, Large 85.00
Ornament, Ball, Hand Painted, Dressed Rabbits, Polish 1.00
Ornament, Ball, Occupied Japan, Box 10.00
Ornament, Balloon, Tinsel Wrapped, Scrap Art 7.50
Ornament, Banana, Yellow, 4 1/2 In. 80.00
Ornament, Basket, Paper Flowers, Wire 25.00
Ornament, Bear, With Muff, Glass 75.00
Ornament, Bell, With Crown 20.00
Ornament, Bird, Angel Hair Tail, Flip Feet 17.00
Ornament, Bird, Blue, Chenille Wings & Tail, 2 X 3 In. 14.00
Ornament, Bird, On Metal Perch, Bisque 36.00
Ornament, Box, Children Design, Papier–Mache, C.1910, 3 In. 38.00
Ornament, Box, Hangs On Tree, Papier–Mache, Children, 1910 ..... 38.00
Ornament, Boy, Green & Pink, Painted Face, C.1910, 3 3/4 In. 50.00

Ornament, Bugle, Silver, 3 7/8 In.	16.00
Ornament, Butterfly, Gold, Dresden	75.00
Ornament, Candle Lantern, 8 Panel, German	22.50
Ornament, Cat's Head, Lauschan	67.50
Ornament, Children & Snowball, Santa, Bisque, Germany	30.00
Ornament, Christmas Stocking, Victorian	65.00
Ornament, Clown Head, Celluloid	6.00
Ornament, Clown Head, Glass, Large	58.00
Ornament, Clown, Glass, 3 In.	20.00
Ornament, Coffeepot	48.00
Ornament, Crown, Glass	65.00
Ornament, Cuckoo Clock, Glass, German	35.00
Ornament, Dog, On Ball, Glass	58.00
Ornament, Doll's Head, Blown Glass	45.00
Ornament, Duck, Glass	30.00
Ornament, Eagle, Glass Eyes, Dresden	250.00
Ornament, Ear Of Corn	30.00 To 55.00
Ornament, Elephant, Glass, German	90.00
Ornament, Elephant, On Wheels, 1918, German	235.00
Ornament, Fairy Boat	15.00
Ornament, Father Christmas, White, Papier–Mache	475.00
Ornament, Fish	25.00 To 35.00
Ornament, Foxy Grandpa	180.00
Ornament, Ginger Bread Man, Extended Arms & Legs, Glass	24.50
Ornament, Girl In Rose, Glass, 3 In.	80.00
Ornament, Girl, In Beehive, Glass	62.00
Ornament, Gnome, On Stump, Glass	145.00
Ornament, Grape, Magenta, 2 1/4 In.	22.00
Ornament, Grapes, Silver, Kugels	125.00
Ornament, Happy Hooligan, Glass	150.00
Ornament, Head, Bow In Hair, Glass	80.00
Ornament, Horn, Blown Glass	5.00
Ornament, Horse, Dresden	165.00
Ornament, Horse, Silver, Blown Glass	35.00
Ornament, House With Bay Windows, Evergreens	25.00
Ornament, Insect, On Flower, Glass	65.00
Ornament, Keystone Cop	190.00
Ornament, Lamb, Woolly, Black	45.00
Ornament, Los Angeles Zeppelin, American Flag	200.00
Ornament, Lyre, Gold, Lyre	20.00
Ornament, Man In Moon, Blown Glass	40.00
Ornament, Man, Devil Looking, Glass, 3 In.	105.00
Ornament, Monkey, With Stick, Silver With Red, Black, & Gold	45.00
Ornament, Moose, Dresden	145.00
Ornament, Mushroom With Baby Mushroom, 2 3/4 In.	17.50
Ornament, Peach, On Metal Clip, Glass Coating, 4 1/4 In.	22.50
Ornament, Peacock	37.50
Ornament, Pear, Cotton Batting	10.00
Ornament, Pear, Face Of Old Man, Leaves For Hair, 3 1/4 In.	60.00
Ornament, Pickle, Mottled Bluish Green On Silver, 4 3/4 In.	60.00
Ornament, Pinocchio Head, Glass, 5 In.	24.50
Ornament, Pipe	10.00
Ornament, Plum	30.00
Ornament, Pocket Watch, Blown Glass	55.00
Ornament, Revolver, Pink & Blue	110.00
Ornament, Sailboat, Gold Mesh & Braid	150.00
Ornament, Santa Claus, Candy Container, German, 5 In.	75.00
Ornament, Santa Claus, Full Figure, Blown, 5 In.	45.00
Ornament, Santa Claus, Hard Plastic	10.00
Ornament, Santa Claus, Head, Blown Glass	40.00
Ornament, Santa Claus, In Balloon, Glass, Litho, 5 1/2 In.	50.00
Ornament, Santa Claus, In Mica Sleigh, German	60.00
Ornament, Santa Claus, In Sleigh, German, 12 In.	265.00
Ornament, Santa Claus, Pulling Sleigh, Bisque	35.00

Ornament, Santa Claus, Sack, Coming Out Of Chimney 55.00
Ornament, Santa Claus, With Bag, Blown Glass 20.00
Ornament, Shoe, Paper Face 69.00
Ornament, Snowman Holding Broom 20.00
Ornament, Snowman Twirler, Hallmark, 1977, Box 22.00
Ornament, Snowman, Colored Bag, Milk Glass, 3 In. 7.50
Ornament, Squirrel With Nut, Glass, German 75.00
Ornament, Stag, Leaping, Blue, Blown Glass 40.00
Ornament, Star, Clip-On 45.00
Ornament, Stork 5.00
Ornament, Stork, Dresden 200.00
Ornament, Strawberry 35.00
Ornament, Swanboat 30.00
Ornament, Teapot 20.00
Ornament, Teddy Bear ....19.00 To 20.00
Ornament, Tree Top, Princess, Composition 30.00
Ornament, Tree Top, Red 1.00
Ornament, Trumpet, Gold, 3 7/8 In. 23.00
Ornament, Turnip, Glass, 7 In. 60.00
Ornament, Turnip, Pink, White, & Blue On Silver, 6 In. 37.50
Ornament, Umbrella, Tinsel Wire, Paper Flower, 5 In. 30.00
Stand, Clockwork, Tin, Wooden, German, 11 In.Diam. 150.00

CHRISTMAS, Book, Santa Claus Toy, Florence Notter, Illustrated, 1913 .... 28.00
Book, Song, Coloring, Unused, 34 Songs, 1938 .... 10.00
Book, When Santa Claus Was Lost, Leather Bound, 1914 .... 16.00
Button, Santa Claus Face, Merry Christmas, 1920s 15.00
Cake Mold, Santa Claus, Aluminum 24.00
Charm, Santa Claus, Top Opens, Santa Claus Pops Up, 14K Gold 125.00
Cup, Santa Claus, Holly, Cherub & Merry Christmas, Porcelain 25.00
Doll, Father Christmas, Papier-Mache, White, Glitter, 7 In. 225.00
Doll, Santa Claus, Composition, Felt Suit, 6 In. 45.00
Doll, Santa Claus, Felt Clothes, U.S.Zone, Germany, 10 In. 95.00
Doll, Santa Claus, Stuffed, Fat, 24 In. 45.00
Fence, Tin Posts, Wood Knobbed, C.1915, 45 X 30 In. 148.00
Mask, Father Christmas, 1930s 15.00
Mold, Chocolate, 4 Santa Claus, Tin, Dresden, 4 1/2 X 9 1/4 In. 65.00
Mug, Child's, Santa Claus, Examining His Record, 3 1/2 In. 60.00
Music, Sheet, All I Want For Christmas Is My 2 Front Teeth 8.00
Music, Sheet, Santa Claus Is Comin' To Town 5.00
Nativity Set, Joseph, Mary, & Infant, Crib, Anri, 6 X 8 In. 850.00
Paperweight, Santa, North Pole, Snow 15.00
Pillow, Santa Claus, Figural 10.00
Plaque, Santa Claus Face, Plaster, Cotton Beard, Eyebrows, 24 In. 50.00
Rug, Hooked, Santa Claus, Sleigh, C.1920, Round, 13 In. 95.00
Rug, Santa Claus & Deer On Roof Top, 22 X 34 In. 40.00
Santa Claus, Blue, Plaster, Painted, 2 1/2 In. 125.00
Santa Claus, Cardboard Hands & Feet, Folding Crepe Paper, 20 In. 15.00
Santa Claus, Celluloid, Pointy Cap, Bag, U.S.A.Mark, 4 In. 22.00
Santa Claus, Cloth Dressed, Plastic Face & Boots, 14 In. 175.00
Santa Claus, Embossed Paper, Glitter, Germany, 10 In. 15.00
Santa Claus, Leaving North Pole, Elves & Sleigh, 10 X 28 In. 20.00
Santa Claus, Mechanical, Batteries, 1940s 85.00
Santa Claus, Riding Sleigh, Christmas Toys, Celluloid, 3 1/4 In. 35.00
Santa Claus, With Pack, Holding Tree, Composition, 1910 .... 95.00
Santa Claus, Wooden, Carved & Painted, 19th Century, 17 In. 700.00
Santa, Folding, Accordion Type, Open To 18 In. 15.00
Toy, Santa Claus, Crepe Paper, Stuffed, Batting Beard, 24 In. 75.00
Toy, Santa Claus, Sawdust Stuffed, Felt Suit, Beard, 28 In. 160.00
Toy, Santa Claus, Sleigh, Deer, Mechanical, Deer, Pat.1923, Strauss 377.50
Toy, Santa Claus, Tricycle, Windup, Japan 10.00
Tree Holder, Art Deco 95.00
Tree Holder, Dark Green, Gold Embossed Geometrics, Germany 45.00
Tree Holder, Tin, Green, Decals 55.00

Tumbler, 12 Days Of Christmas, Set Of 12 .... 48.00

Art Deco chrome items became popular in the 1930s. Collectors are most interested in pieces made by the Chase Brass and Copper Company of Waterbury, Connecticut.

CHROME, Bowl, Stemmed Nude, Cambridge Insert, Farber Ware, 7 1/2 In. 100.00
  Box, Glass Lined, Chase Brass, 8 In. 35.00
  Caddy, Shot Glasses, Art Deco 10.00
  Chase, Jar, Syrup 14.00
  Cocktail Set, Tray, 6 Chrome Stems, Signed Farber Bros. 125.00
  Cocktail Shaker, Art Deco, Century NYC 35.00
  Cocktail Shaker, Black Rings, Chase No.90034 .... 20.00
  Cocktail Shaker, Zeppelin Shape, Cups, Spoons, Squeezer, Sugar Holder 1300.00
  Coffeepot, Gooseneck, Wooden Handle, Farber Ware 30.00
  Coffeepot, Sugar & Creamer, Continental, Black Knobs, Chase 45.00
  Figurine, Archer, French 55.00
  Food Warmer, Beveled Edges, 4 Compartment, Porcelain Inserts, 21 In. 80.00
  Lamp, Black Base, Art Deco Chrome Shade, Chase, 9 In. 85.00
  Lamp, Desk, Chase 90.00
  Samovar & Tray, Art Deco, Russian, 8 In. 78.00
  Samovar, Child's, Russian 37.00
  Snack Tray, Chase, Set Of 6 .... 42.00
  Sugar & Creamer, Cover, Ivory Knob & Handles, Chase 15.00
  Tea Set, Tray, Art Deco, French Ivory Handles, Chase, 4 Piece 125.00

Carved wooden or cast–iron figures were used as advertisements in front of the Victorian cigar store. The carved figures are now collected as folk art. They range in size from counter type, about three feet, to over eight feet high.

CIGAR STORE FIGURE, Englishman, Hand On Breast, 22 In. 550.00
  Indian Scout, Wooden, Polychrome, 69 1/2 In. 325.00
  Indian, Feathered Headdress, Dagger In Hand, 65 In. 2400.00
  Indian, Plaster Head & Hands, Life–Size ....*Illus* 175.00
  Indian, Princess, Holding Rose & Cigars, 1880, 61 In. 4950.00
  Princess, Zinc, Base Inscription Smoke Shop, 65 In. 5000.00

Cinnabar is a vermilion or red lacquer. Some pieces are made with hundreds of thicknesses of the lacquer that is later carved.

CINNABAR, Bowl, Covered, Cinnabar, Round, Carved, 4 X 7 In. 425.00
  Box, Carved, Jade Medallion In Lid, 5 1/2 X 3 1/2 X 1 5/8 In. 125.00
  Box, Covered, Scenic, Square, 3 1/2 In. 35.00

Cigar Store Figure, Indian,
Plaster Head & Hands, Life Size

If you are a collector of old Christmas tree ornaments or Christmas lights, use these on the tree. Do not use burning candles. It is too dangerous.

Box, Lid, Reserve Of Birds & Florals, Greek Key Border, 5 3/4 In. 65.00
Box, Scholars & Greek Key Pattern Border, 5 1/2 X 3 1/2 In. 45.00
Tureen, Ram Form, 13 In. 250.00
Vase, 3 1/2 In., Pair 55.00
Vase, Key Design, Rope Border, Baluster Shape, 19th Century, 6 In. 225.00

*Civil War mementos are important collectors' items. Most of the
pieces are military items used from 1861 to 1865.*

CIVIL WAR, Album, Albert Pike, Indian Confederate Leader 745.00
American Flag, 34 Stars, Roses, Framed, Round, Crewel Work, 18 In. 95.00
Box, Ammunition, Buckle, Shells, Loading Equipment 75.00
Box, McKeever, Brass Plate On Front, 1st Model 37.00
Buckle, Belt, Washington Greys 85.00
Buckle, Naval Officer's, Original Belt & Frogs 95.00
Cup, Tin Case 45.00
Dagger, Slater Bros., Sheath, Sheffield Handle, 5 3/4 In.Blade 150.00
Discharge & Pay Voucher, Medical, Private M.Cuddleback, 1862 .... 32.50
Discharge Papers, Sergeant Major ....40.00 To 55.00
Drum, Commemorative, 12 Figures Of Soldiers In Battle Poses 400.00
Fife, Rosewood 135.00
Flag, Confederate, Captured, 11 Stars 1650.00
Gauntlets, Cavalry 55.00
Hat, Campaign, Snowflake Vent, Tan 100.00
Hat, Campaign, Star Vent, Tan 90.00
Holster, For Colt Dragon, Quick Draw Style 90.00
Horse Bit, Brass, U.S., Pair 5.00
Kepi, Confederate Veteran's, Gray 125.00
Letter, Chas. Magnus Pictorial Stationery 35.00
Match Holder, Embossed Train 38.00
Medical Kit, Amputation, U.S.N., Mahogany 1200.00
Photograph, Soldier, On Tin Plaque 22.00
Poster, Cavalry Recruiting, Dated June 22, 1863, 17 X 23 In. 495.00
Print, Mother & Daughter Fishing, No.1527, 25 1/2 X 21 1/2 In. 60.00
Shaving Kit, Fitted, Tin 225.00
Shaving Mug, Brush Pocket, Handle, Tin 40.00
Shaving Mug, Double Compartment, Copper 125.00
Snuff Box, Signed Col.Frank Jones, Dec.25, 1866, Sterling Silver 125.00
Song Sheet, By Magnus, Civil War Lithograph 30.00
Spurs, Officer's 85.00
Sword, Inscription On Scabbard, Used At Gettysburg 525.00
Sword, Scabbard, Foot Officer's, 1850, Ames 350.00
Sword, U.S., Signed W. Rose 300.00
Tumbler, Liquor, North & South, Hands, Constitution, 35 Star Flag 145.00
Uniform, Cavalry Officer's, Frock Coat, Trousers, Blue Wool Serge 695.00
Wax Sealer, Wooden Handle, Brass 22.50
      CKAW, see Dedham

*Clambroth glass, popular in the Victorian era, is a grayish color and
is semiopaque like clambroth.*

CLAMBROTH, Bottle, Barber, Cork & Porcelain Stopper, Water 34.00
Candlestick, Hexagonal, 6 7/8 In., Pair 75.00
Candlestick, Petal Top, Hexagonal Stepped Stem, Jade 750.00
Candlestick, Teardrop Stem, 7 1/4 In., Pair 100.00
Creamer, Heron 40.00
Creamer, Swan 45.00
Finger Bowl 40.00
Jigger, 10 Panels, Handle, 1 7/8 In. 40.00
Lamp, Fluted Stem, Petal Font, Square Foot, 12 3/4 In. 200.00
Mug, Stork & Peacock 40.00
Punch Bowl, Waffle Block Pattern, Base 165.00
Shaker, Talcum 20.00
Syrup, Paneled, Pewter Top, Flint 225.00
Tumbler, Sterilizer, 5 In. 18.00
Vase, Embossed Roses, 8 In. 22.00

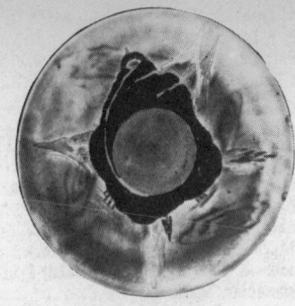

Clarice Cliff, Vase, Lotus,
Persian Pattern,
Marked, 12 In.

Clarice Cliff, Bowl,
Persian Pattern,
Marked, 7 1/2 In.

Clarice Cliff, Plaque,
Blue Pines,
Stylized Trees, 13 In.

Vase, Hand, Ruffled Top, Hand Painted Design, 6 1/2 In. 125.00
Vase, Spill, Vintage Pattern, Apple Green, Flint 330.00

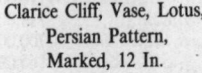 *Clarice Cliff was a designer who began working at several English factories in the 1920s. Her original designs and shapes were in the Art Deco style. She died in 1972.*

CLARICE CLIFF, Ashtray, Tonquin 16.00
Basket, Celtic Harvest, Art Deco, Marked, 12 3/4 X 9 1/4 In. 225.00
Berry Bowl, Gay Day, Bizarre, 3 1/2 In. 45.00
Biscuit Barrel 475.00
Bowl, Bizarre, Cottage & Hills, 8 In. ....125.00 To 140.00
Bowl, Crocus Acorn, 8 In. ....35.00 To 50.00
Bowl, Design Of 2 Parakeets 143.00
Bowl, Fantastique, 8 In. 140.00
Bowl, Inspiration, 8 In. 880.00
Bowl, Persian Pattern, Marked, 7 1/2 In. ....*Illus* 880.00
Candleholder, Bizarre, Signed, 3 1/2 X 2 1/4 In. 85.00
Coffee Set, Chintz, Bizarre, 15 Piece 150.00
Coffeepot, Bizarre, Art Deco, Marked, Green On Cream, 7 In. 145.00
Cup Plate, Bizarre, Signed, 3 In. 37.50
Dinner Set, Blue Flowers, Vanessa Bell Design, 104 Piece 2200.00
Figure, Centerpiece, Age Of Jazz, 7 In., Set Of 4 .... 3300.00
Gravy Boat, Canterbury Bells 100.00
Gravy Boat, Platter, Tonquin, Black 23.00
Jardiniere, Inspiration, Landscape 220.00
Jug, Art Deco, Celtic Harvest, Marked, 11 1/4 In. 165.00
Jug, Art Deco, Embossed Flowers, Marked, 8 5/8 In. 75.00
Jug, Bizarre, Art Deco, Orange, Blue, & Cream, Marked, 5 3/4 In. 175.00
Jug, Embossed Flowers, Gray, Branch Handle, Marked, 8 1/4 In. 70.00
Jug, Wisteria, Lotus, Flowers, 8 In. 165.00
Pitcher, Bizarre Ware, Landscape, Pagoda, Signed, 5 In. 100.00
Pitcher, Milk, Tonquin, Brown 48.00
Pitcher, Newport Pottery 150.00
Pitcher, Pineapple Pattern, 7 X 8 In. 65.00
Pitcher, Tonquin, Brown & White, 11 1/2 In. 14.00
Pitcher, Water, Autumn Crocus, 7 3/4 In. 450.00
Plaque, Blue Pines, Stylized Trees, 13 In. ....*Illus* 2420.00
Plaque, Blue, Green, & Pink, Blue Bands, 10 1/4 In. 495.00
Plaque, Cottage Garden, 18 In. 2090.00
Plaque, Inspiration, 13 In. Diam. 2420.00
Plaque, Masque Form 1100.00
Plate, Bizarre, 9 In. 39.00
Plate, Crocus, Square, 6 In. ....10.00 To 12.00
Plate, Viscaria, Rectangular, 9 In. 35.00

Shoe, Dutch, Leaves, Gray, Gold, & Brown, Marked, 5 3/8 In. 88.00
Sugar Shaker, My Garden, 6 In. 50.00
Tea Set, Bizarre, Crocus Pattern, 15 Pieces 800.00
Tea Set, Fantastique, Blue Bands, Service For 2 .... 1320.00
Tea Set, Stylized Flowers, 5 Piece 150.00
Tray, Geometric, 11 In. 180.00
Tureen, Canterbury Bells 150.00
Tureen, Islands Moderne .... 80.00 To 115.00
Vase, Art Deco, Hand Painted Leaf Design, Marked, 9 1/4 In. 85.00
Vase, Blue Pines Design, Blue & Mauve Trees 820.00
Vase, Branch Handle, Parakeet 715.00
Vase, Embossed Flowers, Marked, Gray Ground, 7 1/4 In. 75.00
Vase, Embossed Tree Branches & Flowers, Gray, Marked, 8 In. 110.00
Vase, Floral, Art Deco, Triangular, Marked, 3 In. 45.00
Vase, Hanging, Lady, Ball Gown, Gray, Marked, 10 1/2 X 5 In. 110.00
Vase, Lotus, Handle, 12 In. 715.00
Vase, Lotus, Persian Pattern, Marked, 12 In. ....*Illus* 7700.00
Vase, Protruding Parakeets, 12 1/2 In. 165.00
Vase, Willow Tree Lotus, 8 In. .... 45.00 To 80.00
Vase, Yo–Yo, 2–Cone Shape, Streaked Turquoise, 9 In. 935.00
Vegetable Dish, Charlotte, Blue, Round 18.00
Wall Pocket, Mask Of Woman 350.00

Clewell ware was made in limited quantities by Charles Walter Clewell of Canton, Ohio, from 1902 to 1955. Pottery was covered with a thin coating of bronze, then treated to make the bronze turn different colors. Pieces covered with copper, brass, or silver were also made. Mr. Clewell's secret formula for blue patina bronze was burned when he died in 1965.

CLEWELL, Bowl, Copper With Green Patina, Marked, 8 In. 320.00
Box, Covered, Hammered Copper, Cream Interior, 4 3/4 X 6 1/2 In. 132.00
Ewer, Paneled, Bronze Clad, 5 3/4 In. 95.00
Vase, Bud, 6 1/2 In. 80.00
Vase, Bud, Copper Overlay, Dark Patina, 6 3/4 In. 200.00
Vase, Bud, Copper Overlay, Rough To Smooth Surface, 10 In. 200.00
Vase, Copper Overlay, 8 1/2 In. 140.00
Vase, Copper, Allover Green Copper Patina, Marked, 8 3/4 In. 176.00
Vase, Copper, Green Patina, Marked, 4 3/4 In. 198.00
Vase, Orange & Green Patina, Signed 3–25, 3 1/2 X 6 In. 375.00

Clews pottery was made by George Clews & Co. of Brownhill Pottery, Tunstall, England, from 1806 to 1861.

CLEWS, see also Flow Blue
CLEWS, Cup Plate, Landing Of Lafayette, 3 1/2 In. 360.00
Cup Plate, Landing Of Lafayette, 4 3/8 In. 350.00
Cup Plate, Landing Of Lafayette, Oval, 3 1/2 In. 480.00
Plate, Knighthood Conferred On Don Quixote, Dark Blue, Signed, 10 In. 145.00
Plate, Landing Of Lafayette, Blue, 7 3/4 In. 140.00
Plate, Landing Of Lafayette, Blue, 9 In. 90.00
Plate, Landing Of Lafayette, Dark Blue, Signed, 9 In. 175.00
Plate, States, Dark Blue, Signed, 10 5/8 In. 220.00
Plate, Toddy, America & Independence, Blue States Transfer, 4 3/4 In. 200.00
Platter, Landing Of Lafayette, 19 In. 675.00
Platter, Landing Of Lafayette, Blue, 17 In. 625.00
Vase, Gouda Style, 6 In. 20.00

Clifton Pottery was founded by William Long in Clifton, New Jersey, in 1905. He worked there until 1908 making a line called "Crystal Patina." Clifton Pottery made art pottery. Another firm, Chesapeake Pottery, sold majolica marked "Clifton ware."

CLIFTON, Bottle, Water, Redware, Black Indian Design, Ark., 8 1/2 X 6 1/2 In. 99.00
Bowl, Indian Ware, 8 In. 85.00
Bowl, Redware, Black Indian Design, Marked Florida & 184, 1 3/4 In. 22.00
Coffeepot, Indian Design, Glossy White 50.00

Dish, Leaf Shape, Standing Squirrel, Marked, 10 X 9 In. 130.00
Humidor, Indian Ware, 6 X 6 In. 60.00
Plate, Strawbery, Ribbed Ground, 10 3/4 In. 105.00
Teapot, Dark Brown Design, Deep Red Clay, No Lid, 10 X 3 1/2 In. 15.00
Teapot, Indian, Small 55.00
Vase, Green Drip, 1903, 4 1/2 In. 50.00
Vase, Indian Ware, Redware With Black Indian Design, Marked, 3 In. 27.00
Vase, Redware, Black Indian Design, 4 Mile/Arizona, 2 3/4 In. 27.00
Vase, Straight Neck, Bulbous, Crystalline Glaze, 1905, 8 1/2 In. 275.00
Vase, Streaked Greens, Handles, Dated 1906, 6 In. 275.00
Waste Bowl, Blackberry 85.00

Clocks of all types have always been popular with collectors. The eighteenth–century tall case, or grandfather's clock, was designed to house a works with a long pendulum. In 1816, Eli Terry patented a new, smaller works for a clock; and the case became smaller. The clock could be kept on a shelf instead of the floor. By 1840, coiled springs were used and even smaller clocks were made. Battery– powered electric clocks were made in the 1870s.

CLOCK, 30–Hour, Swan Neck Pediment, Easton, C.1800 .... 4620.00
A.Stowell, Lyre, Reverse Glass, Brass Eagle On Top 2000.00
A.Whitcomb, Federal, Shelf, Kidney Dial, C.1790 .... 19800.00
Abel Hutchins, Tall Case, Inlaid Mahogany, Cherrywood, 7 Ft. 8 In. 4950.00
Abiel Chandler, Banjo, Brass Trim, & Works, Metal Face, Signed, 33 In. 550.00
Abner Rogers, Grandfather, 8–Day, Time & Strike, 88 In. 11350.00
Act Of Parliament, Wall 3000.00
Advertising, 7–UP, You Like It, It Likes You, Wood Frame ....65.00 To 75.00
Advertising, AC Spark Plugs, 16 X 16 In. 75.00
Advertising, Alarm, Goodyear Tire 25.00
Advertising, Alarm, Star Brand Shoes, Iron 25.00
Advertising, B.L.Johnson Confectioner, Sessions 1300.00
Advertising, Baird, Moliscorium 725.00
Advertising, Bath Hotel, Meal Times, Messages Change Every 5 Minutes 1760.00
Advertising, Benrus Watches, Table 50.00
Advertising, Blank Roasted Coffee, Ingraham 1700.00
Advertising, Blatz, Mantel, Ceramic Figure Drinking Beer 50.00
Advertising, Bull Durham Cigars, Copper, C.1900, 12 In. 450.00
Advertising, Calumet Baking Powder, Sessions, Closed Lettering 1000.00
Advertising, Calumet Baking Powder, Sessions, Open Lettering 1300.00
Advertising, Canada Dry, Metal Frame, Lighted, Electric 65.00
Advertising, Carstairs Seal, Electric 42.00
Advertising, Cat's Paw, Electric, Heels & Soles 45.00
Advertising, Cholat Geurin–Boutron, Pendulette, 1910, 19 In. 150.00
Advertising, Chrysler Motors, Deco Face, Indian Symbol, Square, 7 In. 95.00
Advertising, Dayton Tires, Electric, Lighted, Round 48.00
Advertising, Deer Run Whiskey, Ingraham 1700.00
Advertising, Dowagic Drills & Seeders, Large Watch, 10 3/4 In. 275.00
Advertising, Dr Pepper, Cap Form 35.00
Advertising, Dr Pepper, Wall, Good For Life, Electric 165.00
Advertising, Duffy Malt Liquor 2000.00
Advertising, Ever–Ready Safety Razor, 8–Day, Pendulum, 1910, 28 In. 1700.00
Advertising, Farmers Exchange, On Glass GRO 350.00
Advertising, G.W.Bishop Drugs & Jewelry, Sessions 1300.00
Advertising, Garfield Tea & Syrup, Figural 1000.00
Advertising, General Electric Refrigerator, Coil Top ....90.00 To 150.00
Advertising, Gilbert, Peters Shoes 45.00
Advertising, Golden Girl Cola, Bottle, Girl, Cup Of Coffee 75.00
Advertising, Goulding's Manures, Best, All Crops, Baird, Wooden, 31 In. 1400.00
Advertising, Gulf Gasoline 125.00
Advertising, Gulf Group Insurance, Curved Glass, Lighted 30.00
Advertising, Hoffman Old Time Coffee, Ingraham 1700.00
Advertising, Hostetter's Stomach Bitters, Ingraham 1700.00
Advertising, Hovis Bread, Wall, Mahogany, Brass Bezel, 1910, 16 In. 150.00
Advertising, International Time Recording Co., Iron Wheel, 34 In. 275.00

Cuckoo clocks sometimes need minor first aid or major repair. First try home remedies. If the clock stops, it may be because it is not level. Try shifting the clock a bit. The clock will not run correctly in a draft. Hang the clock so it is flat against the wall. Have the clock oiled every two years, cleaned every four years. Major repairs should be done by a professional.

Clock, Ansonia, Glass Panels, Footed

Advertising, John Deere, 14 In.	60.00
Advertising, Jolly Tar, Baird Clock, 8–Day, Pendulum, 1892, 30 1/2 In.	1150.00
Advertising, Keebler, Bluebird, Box	55.00
Advertising, Kleenatub & Wrigley Scouring Soap, Sessions	1500.00
Advertising, Kleenatub & Wrigleys Soap, Time To Buy, Regulator, 1903	885.00
Advertising, Koldraft, Lighted Reverse Painted, Metal Sign	65.00
Advertising, Lewis & Pe–Ko	950.00
Advertising, Liberty Flour, Tin Face, Electric, 1935, 15 1/2 In.	100.00
Advertising, Lucky Strike Cigarettes, School	1200.00
Advertising, Lucky Strike, R.A.Patterson	700.00
Advertising, Merrick's Spool Cotton, School, Short Drop	950.00
Advertising, Milk Maid Milk, 8–Day, Brass Movement, 17 1/2 In.Diam.	225.00
Advertising, Old Charter Whiskey	55.00
Advertising, Old Milwaukee Beer	27.50
Advertising, Old Mr.Boston, Gilbert, Bottle Shape, 8–Day, 21 5/8 In.	100.00
Advertising, Olympia Beer	30.00
Advertising, Orange Crush, Plastic, Electric, 16 In.	100.00
Advertising, Pabst Blue Ribbon, Wood, Lamp On Top, 11 X 23 In.	45.00
Advertising, Parker Duofold, Second Hand Is Pen	150.00
Advertising, Parry Buggies, School	1200.00
Advertising, Pepsi–Cola, Talking	160.00
Advertising, Phelps Mfg.Co., Whistle, Litho, Pressed Wood, 24 In.	130.00
Advertising, Pierce's Lignite Floor Varnish, Sessions	1500.00
Advertising, Reed's Gilt Edge Tonic, Tall, Hubbell, Ebonized, 24 In.	1100.00
Advertising, Refrigerator, General Electric, Figural	200.00
Advertising, Regal Beer	65.00
Advertising, Seidlitz Paints, Curved Glass, Lighted	30.00
Advertising, Shell Gasoline, All Wood	3000.00
Advertising, Sleepy Eye Flour & Cereal, Sessions	2500.00
Advertising, Smith Brothers, Jewelers, Round	20.00
Advertising, Spalding Co., Wooden	385.00
Advertising, St.Charles Evaporated Milk	200.00
Advertising, Star Brand Shoes Are Better, Ansonia	55.00
Advertising, Stegmaier Gold Medal Beer	38.00
Advertising, Tappan, Curved Glass, Lighted	30.00
Advertising, Time To Save, Parkville Bank, Reverse Glass, Neon, 23 In.	175.00
Advertising, Tuxedo Brand Cheese	48.00

Advertising, Use Menu Baking Powder, Sessions 1200.00
Advertising, Vanner & Prest's Moliscorium, Baird, 31 In. 475.00
Advertising, Vantage Cigarettes, Battery Operated 20.00
Advertising, Vernor's Bottle Cap 30.00
Advertising, Victor, Looks Like Record 700.00
Advertising, Wilson Whiskey, Electric 75.00
Advertising, Wise Potato Chip, Figural, Electric 70.00
Alarm, Big Ben, Lowe Bros., Jewelers & Opticians, Pat.1902 .... 35.00
Alarm, Canada, Bird Pulling Worm Scene, Green 60.00
Alarm, Music Box, Kaiser Waltz, Tole, Brass, German, 4 In. 150.00
Alarm, Musical, Hymne, De La Bolivia, Sheet Metal, Germany, C.1920 .... 80.00
Animated, Alarm, Bugs Bunny, Ingraham 125.00
Animated, Big Bad Wolf, Ingersoll 195.00
Animated, Bulldog, Eyes Revolve To Show Time, Carved Wood 475.00
Animated, Early Bird, Alarm 125.00
Animated, Football, Wall 385.00
Animated, Spinning Wheel 75.00
Animated, Steersman Of USA, Drummer Playing On Dial 145.00
Ansonia, Bobbing Doll, Round Clock, Cast Metal Above, Swing, C.1890 .... 775.00
Ansonia, Choctaw Model, Floral & Butterfly Design, 1/2 Hour Strike 235.00
Ansonia, Crystal Regulator, Royal Bonn China Case 2300.00
Ansonia, Dakia Model, China, Porcelain Dial, Visible Escapement 325.00
Ansonia, Glass Panels, Footed ....*Illus*   500.00
Ansonia, La Chapelle, Outside Escapement, Porcelain 525.00
Ansonia, La Charney, Outside Escapement, Porcelain 500.00
Ansonia, La Rata, Outside Escapement, Porcelain 475.00
Ansonia, Mantel, 2 Lions' Heads, Iron 140.00
Ansonia, Mantel, 8–Day, Time & Strike, Walnut 300.00
Ansonia, Mantel, Brass, Gallery Frame, 8–Day, Pendulum, 11 1/2 In. 175.00
Ansonia, Mantel, Bronze, Trilby 350.00
Ansonia, Mantel, Green Onyx Glass & Brass, 8–Day, Strike, 11 In. 300.00
Ansonia, Porcelain, Royal Bonn 350.00
Ansonia, Regulator A, Calendar 425.00
Ansonia, Regulator, Bagdad Model, Oak 1275.00
Ansonia, Regulator, Capitol Model, 2 Weight, Walnut 1050.00
Ansonia, Regulator, Crystal, Marchioness 550.00
Ansonia, Regulator, Crystal, Marquis 400.00
Ansonia, Regulator, Long Drop, 8–Day, Walnut 320.00
Ansonia, Regulator, Outside Escapement, Mercury Pendulum, 8–Day 850.00
Ansonia, Regulator, Queen Mary, Strike 675.00
Ansonia, School, Octagonal Face, Pointed Drop, Oak, 25 In. 175.00
Ansonia, Swinger, Fisherman 1500.00

Clock, Chinese, 8–Day,
Porcelain Dial, C.1820, 17 1/2 In.

Ansonia, Swinger, Huntress 1500.00
Ansonia, Swinging Doll, Tree, Round Brass Clock, C.1890, 8 In. 500.00
Ansonia, Tuxedo, Rose China 195.00
Atkins, Shelf, Rosewood, Gilt Eglomise Tablet, 30–Day, 1855 .... 1300.00
Automata, 14 Figurines, Moving Arms, Hands, & Dancing, 8–Tune, 31 In. .. 6500.00
Bailey, Banks & Biddle, Grandfather, Moon Dial, 8 Ft. 5500.00
Banjo, Brass Motor, Reverse Painted Naval Battle, 34 In. 900.00
Banjo, Federal, Mahogany, Eglomise, Floral Arrays, C.1820, 35 In. 880.00
Banjo, Mercury Barometer, Thermometer, Mahogany Case, Mid–1800s 375.00
Barns, Bartholomew & Co., Shelf, Triple Decker, 8–Day, Mahogany 425.00
Big Ben, Alarm, Nickel Case, Black Face, Repeat Alarm, Pat.1919 .... 30.00
Birge & Fuller, Empire, 8–Day, Time & Strike, 33 In. 295.00
Birge & Fuller, Steeple, Mahogany, Wagon Spring, Reverse Paint, 26 In. .. 1400.00
Brewster & Ingraham, Steeple, 8–Day, Time & Strike 185.00
Brewster, Mantel, Rosewood, Beehive, 8–Day, Time & Strike, 1840, 19 In. .. 375.00
C.D.Hostetter, Tall Case, Moon Phase Dial, Ship Flying Flag, C.1830 ..... 9800.00
C.Grottendieck, Bracket, Mahogany, 8–Day, Bells, Pendulum, 18 1/2 In. .. 375.00
Carriage, Beveled Glass Panels, Brass, French, 4 In. 325.00
Carriage, Double Train Movement, Push Repeat Top, French, Case, 6 In. ... 950.00
Carriage, French Gilt Bronze, Enameled, Limoges 3410.00
Cartel, Bronze Bow, Foliate Dial, Time, Strike Movement, 1900, 16 In. 400.00
Chelsea, Pillar & Scroll, Reverse Glass, Gold Leaf, 30 In. 500.00
Chinese, 8–Day, Porcelain Dial, C.1820, 17 1/2 In. ....*Illus* 900.00
Columbus, Wooden Works, 1892 Columbian Exposition Souvenir 275.00
Cuckoo, Black Forest, Hand Carved, German, C.1930 .... 120.00
Cuckoo, Musical, Wood Cutter, Animated 125.00
DeLamache, Mantel, Black Marble Case, 8–Day, Time & Strike, 15 1/2 In. .. 120.00
Desk, Alarm, Silver–Gilt, Enameled, Bun Feet, Swiss, C.1900, 2 1/8 In. 770.00
Desk, Cloisonne, Mountain Scene Face, Chinese Symbols, 4 X 3 In. 925.00
Desk, Gilt Metal, Baroque Scroll, 2 Putto, Porcelain Dial, 1900, 10 In. 95.00
Desk, Nickel Plated, 8–Day, Contemporary Lucite Base, 3 1/2 In. 70.00
Dutch Rococo, Walnut, Marquetry, Signed
    Gerardus Pousset, C.1740, 123 In. ....*Illus* 14000.00
E.Howard, Regulator, Wall, Walnut, Reverse Painted Door, 1875, 43 In. 3400.00
E.Hubert, Tall Case, Signed, Dutch Rococo Burl Walnut, Bronze Finials 6600.00
E.Sanford, Grandfather, Plymouth, Connecticut, Painted Old Red 5775.00
Eli Terry, Shelf, Pillar & Scroll, Mahogany Veneer On Pine, 31 In. 2050.00
Eli Terry, Shelf, Wooden Works, Label, Mahogany On Pine, 31 5/8 In. 1250.00
Elite, Grandfather, 5 Tubular Chimes, Moon Dial, 8 Ft. 6 In. 7000.00
Elmer Stennis, Grandfather, Handmade, Inlaid, Roxbury Style 1760.00
English, Bracket, 8 Bells & A Gong, Fusee Movement, Mahogany, 26 In. 2250.00
English, Grandfather, 8–Day, Time & Strike, Walnut Inlay, Oak, 77 In. 850.00
English, Grandfather, Bell Striker, 12 In.Dial 900.00
English, Skeleton, Fusee Movement, Brass, 16 In. 650.00
F.Kroeber, Mirror Side, Arctic Model, Indicator Pendulum, Walnut 350.00
F.W.Burnham, Pillar & Scroll, Mantel 5200.00
Figural, Lady Of Liberty, Cast Iron 85.00
French, 15–Jewel, Paperweight, Glass & Brass Case, 7 In. 400.00
French, Carriage, Repeating, 19th Century, Glass & Brass, 6 1/4 In. 275.00
French, Carriage, Strike, Original Case, Brass, 5 X 3 1/2 In. 650.00
French, Crystal Regulator, Mercury Pendulum, Blue Numerals 350.00
French, Egyptian Revival, Garniture, Gilt Bronze, Cloisonne, 3 Piece 5500.00
French, Elephant, Bronze Boulle, C.1850 .... 8500.00
French, Horses & Jockey On Top, Bronze & Brass, C.1850 .... 650.00
French, Louis XV, 2 Candelabra, Cloisonne & Bronze, 22 1/2'In., 3 Pc. 1540.00
French, Louis XVI, 2 Vases, Gilt Bronze & Marble, Sevres, 29 In., 3 Pc. 1320.00
French, Mantel, 19th Century, Gilt Bronze & Cloisonne, Marked, 17 In. 1100.00
French, Mantel, Bronze, Circular Dial, Cartouche Case, 26 1/2 In. 1430.00
French, Mantel, Bronze, Silvered, Architectural Case, Key, 16 1/2 In. 660.00
French, Mantel, Egyptian Design, Basalt, Bronze Sphinx Mount 375.00
French, Mantel, Empire, Ormolu, Columns, 8–Day, Time, Strike, 21 1/2 In. .. 500.00
French, Mantel, Female Hermes, Lion On Base, Bronze, Gilt, 26 1/2 In. 1430.00
French, Mantel, Louis XVI, Cupid, Draped Plinth, Bronze, Marble, 22 In. .. 2750.00
French, Mantel, Steel Dial, Rosettes, Brass Works, Mahogany, 13 1/2 In. ... 60.00
French, Open Umbrella, Gold Leaf Numerals, Enameled, C.1900, 3 1/2 In. .. 450.00
French, Ormolu Mounted Porcelain Case, Scroll Feet, 15 X 11 3/4 In. 325.00

Think about security when you landscape your house. Cut bushes low under windows. Don't plant trees or bushes near doors where prowlers could hide. Place decorative lights in the yard to illuminate windows and doors. You might try the early 19th-century style of landscaping in Midwest farm areas—no shrubbery plantings, but flowers were always near the house.

Be careful about displaying paperweights or other heavy objects on glass shelves. With each new purchase you add more weight to the display shelf, until one day there is a crash and the shelf and weights are damaged. It may seem safe for years, but a slight jar from a slamming door may be enough to cause the glass to crack. We also add a word of warning about wall hung shelves on metal strips. These develop "creep" and after several years may pull loose at the top and eventually collapse.

Clock, Dutch Rococo, Walnut,
Marquetry, Signed Gerardus
Pousset, C.1740, 123 In.

French, Regulator, Gilt Bronze, Boulle Marquetry, 7 Ft.10 In.	5500.00
French, Seated Woman, Twisted Ribbon Panels, Signed, 21 1/2 In.	880.00
French, Shield Clock, Bronze Dore, Time, Balance Wheel, C.1875, 18 In.	1275.00
Friesland Style, Grandfather, Floral Frame, 19th Century, 52 1/2 In.	150.00
Friesland, Wall, Father Time Figures, Cornice, Genre Scene, 45 In.	700.00
G.Williams, Grandfather, Mahogany, Axbridge, Pendulum, Weight, 83 In.	500.00
Gabs Patent Welch Spring, Astronomical, Calendar, 1880, 30 1/2 In.	3400.00
Gale, Calendar, Drop	2950.00
Gawen Brown, Grandfather, Tombstone Arched Door, Maple, C.1770, 86 In.	4300.00
General Electric, Cased, Bundled Columns, Mahogany, C.1930, 19 In.	75.00
George Haprer, Tall Case, English	1100.00
George III, Painted Dial, Moon Phases, Inlaid Mahogany, 7 Ft. 8 In.	4400.00
George Mitchell, Split–Column, Miniature	1175.00
German, Carriage, Cylindrical Music Box, C.1890	80.00
German, Gothic, 8–Day, Brass Movement, Chime, Inlaid Mahogany, 18 In.	160.00
German, Key Wind, Triple Bim Bam, 39 In.	325.00
German, Kundo, 400–Day, Glass Dome, Brass Pendulum, 9 In.	150.00
German, Wall, Broken Crest, 8–Day, Gilt Metal Mounted, C.1920, 33 In.	425.00
Gilbert, Cabinet, 8–Day, Time & Strike, Golden Oak	150.00
Gilbert, Hanging, Weight Driven, Rosewood, Brass Heads, C.1870	1400.00
Gilbert, Mantel, Liberty Bell, 8–Day, Time & Strike	150.00
Gilbert, Mantel, Round Top, Bim Bam Chime, 1920s	75.00

Gilbert, Mantel, Wooden, Black, Columns, Footed, 8–Day, Time & Strike	95.00
Gilbert, Maranville, 30–Day, Large	1250.00
Gilbert, Regulator, 3 Weights, Rosewood, C.1871	1400.00
Gilbert, Regulator, Crystal, Tuscan	650.00
Gilbert, Regulator, No.10, Oak	1400.00
Gilbert, Regulator, No.11, Striking, Oak	1400.00
Gilbert, Stella Model, Mantel, 8–Day	110.00
Goliath, 8–Day, 1/4 Hour Repeater, Swiss, 4 Ft.	650.00
Gothic, Silver, Enameled, Kaiser Inscription, Austria, 1898, 18 In.	1800.00
Grande Sommerie, Music Box, Gilt, Ebonized Case, 8–Day, 19 1/2 In.	300.00
Grandfather, Chippendale, Ship On Dial, Bracket Base, 6 Ft. 9 In.	1900.00
Grandfather, Edwardian, Oak, Arts & Crafts, Mullioned Door, 82 In.	300.00
Grandfather, Gargoyles, Ram's Head, Devils, & Symbols, Austria	3850.00
Grandfather, Gothic Revival, 8–Day, Walnut & Mahogany, 90 In.	600.00
Grandfather, Mahogany, Inlaid Swans, Reeded Columns, 1810, 94 In.	6200.00
Grandfather, Mission, Oak, Brass Numerals, 3 Shelves, American, C.1912	45.00
Grandfather, Quarter Columns, Brass Works, Moon Dial, Mahogany, 99 In.	7750.00
Henry Smith, Banjo, Cherry Valley, C.1820	2200.00
Hotchkiss & Benedict, Empire, Shelf, Mahogany, Label, 1830, 38 In.	1000.00
Howard & Davis, Banjo, Square Bottom	1800.00
Howard, Banjo, No.5, Late 19th Century, 29 1/2 In.	800.00
Howard, Watchman's, No.26, Walnut	1400.00
Hunghans, Swing Arm, Diana	385.00
Hutchins, Tall Case, Federal, Inlaid Mahogany, C.1805, 7 Ft.8 In.	5775.00
Ingersoll, Alarm, Bakelite	15.00
Ingraham, Art Deco, Figural, Lady With Urn Leaf Branch, Windup	95.00
Ingraham, Banjo, Nyanza	300.00
Ingraham, Banjo, Treasure Island, 8–Day, Time & Strike	475.00
Ingraham, Calendar, Rosewood, Grain Painted, 8–Day, 24 In.	225.00
Ingraham, Dew Drop, 8–Day, Time & Strike	300.00
Ingraham, Dew Drop, Time & Calendar	285.00
Ingraham, Gingerbread, 8–Day, Time & Strike, Oak	120.00
Ingraham, Ionic, 8–Day, Label, Rosewood	315.00
Ingraham, Ionic, Time Only, 8–Day, Rosewood Case, Dial 9 In.	300.00
Ingraham, Kitchen, 8–Day, Time & Strike, Golden Oak	125.00
Ingraham, Regulator, Simple Calendar, Store, Oak	385.00
Ingraham, School, Drop Octagon, 8–Day, Pressed Oak	225.00
Ingraham, School, Time & Calendar, Oak, Long Drop	325.00
Ingraham, Urania, Kitchen, Alarm	175.00
Ingraham, Wall, 8–Day, Time & Strike	350.00
Ithaca, Calendar, Double Dial, Original Works	780.00
Ithaca, Calendar, Mahogany, Double Dial, C.1866, 29 X 12 In.	850.00
Ithaca, Library, Double Dial, Calendar	650.00
Ithaca, Shelf, Calendar, Double Dial, All Original	975.00
J.Bowen, Mantel, Ebonized & Brass Mounted, Key, 14 1/2 In.	605.00
J.C.Brown, Ripple Front, Mantel, C.1850	985.00
J.E.Caldwell, Carriage, Glass, Brass, Blue Enameled Dial, 5 1/4 In.	375.00
J.J.Moto, Grandfather, Mahogany, Scroll Top, Illuminated Dial	1200.00
J.Pradier, Sleeping Woman Bronze, 8–Day, Time & Strike, 14 1/2 In.	800.00
Jacob Heggans, Grandfather, Walnut, Star & Shield Finial, 30–Hour	2700.00
Jacob Massy, Tall Case, Faux Tortoiseshell Lacquer, C.1720	9500.00
James C.Cole, Banjo, Tapered Eglomise, Gilt Molding, C.1830, 35 In.	1100.00
Japy Freres, Mantel, Sterling Silver, Sold By Shreve, Crump, Low, 1905	1450.00
Jerome, Shelf, Ogee, Brass Works, Mahogany Veneer, 25 5/8 In.	135.00
Jeromes & Darrow, 8–Day, Wooden Works, Carved Pillars, Glass Tablets	500.00
John Fisher, Grandfather, Calendar, Cherry, C.1750, 8 Ft. 6 In.	8000.00
John Harbud, Shelf, Brass Side Handle, Brass Works, Mahogany Veneer	175.00
John Jackson, Grandfather, English, Lacquered, C.1790, 97 In.	7500.00
John Wood, Grandfather, Swan's Neck Crest, C.1780, 8 Ft. 4 In.	2530.00
Joseph Ives, Federal, Mirror, Mahogany	2500.00
Junghans, Mantel, Mahogany, Chime, Silent & Rectangular Dial, 14 In.	450.00
Junghans, Swinger, Statue Of Liberty	475.00
Kitchen, Kentucky Strike, Oak & Rosewood	199.00
L.Marcrisen, Grandfather, Pewter Face, Animated Tick & Strike, 1822	2750.00

L.Marti, Mantel, Marble, Black Onyx, 8–Day, French Brass, 14 In. 75.00
Leroy, Louis XVI, Garniture, Gilt Bronze, Scroll, Winged Term, 3 Piece 1540.00
Longines, 8–Day, Up & Down Indicator 350.00
Lux, Animated, Bird In Nest, No Key 40.00
Lux, Mother Feeding Baby Birds 14.00
Lux, Scotty, Wagging Tongue 48.00
Mantel, Art Deco, Marble, Glass, 8–Day, Pendulum, France, 11 X 9 In. 310.00
Mantel, Beehive, Dome, Maidens, Cupids, Clouds, Marked, C.1900, 15 In. 715.00
Mantel, Bronze, Gargoyles, Cupids, 8–Day, Strike, 2 X 1 1/2 Ft. 1950.00
Mantel, Cast Iron, G.Washington & Mt.Vernon Portrait, 30–Hour, 16 In. 250.00
Mantel, Champleve, Brass, Octagonal Dial, Medallions, 4 Lions, 8 In. 750.00
Mantel, Champleve, Enamel, Onyx, Portrait Pendulum, LeRoy, 16 In. 1320.00
Mantel, Eastlake, Walnut, Glass Door, Painted Stencil Design, 23 In. 100.00
Mantel, French, Rococo, Striking, Roman Numerals, Scroll Base, 16 In. 450.00
Mantel, Iron, Fruit & Flowers, 8–Day, Time & Strike, C.1860, 20 In. 275.00
Mantel, Marble, Foliate Carved Wreath, Gilt Dial, C.1900, 35 In. 1540.00
Mantel, Polychrome Fruit & Flowers, Cast Iron, C.1860 .... 302.50
Mantel, Porcelain, Robin Egg Blue, Polychrome Floral, 1900, 14 In. 75.00
Mantel, Porcelain, White Enamel Face, Roman Numerals, Floral Design 150.00
Mark Leavenworth & Son, Shelf, 30–Hour, Carved Case 1650.00
Marlowe, Desk, 8–Day, Gold Plate, Penholder Sides, Signed, 8 X 5 In. 85.00
Marsh & Gilbert, Mantel, Eagle, Glazed Door, Wooden Movement, C.1825 .... 750.00
Marsh & Gilbert, Motor Gearing, 8–Day, Wooden Works, 39 In. 875.00
Morbier, Grandfather, Alarm, Repeater, Lyon Style, French 900.00
Morbier, Lyre Pendulum 475.00
Morbier, Wall, Brass Frame, Porcelain Dial, Weight Driven, 53 In. 350.00
Munger & Benedict, Wall, Eagle Pendulum Bob, Pewter Pulley Wheels 1650.00
New Haven, Banjo, Porcelain Dial, 8–Day, Miniature 95.00
New Haven, Banjo, Walnut, Eglomise, Federal, Railroad Scene, 40 In. 175.00
New Haven, Boudoir, Pink Roses, Pink & Blue Ground, Gold Coin, Limoges 45.00
New Haven, Calendar, Walnut, 8–Day, Painted Dial, C.1900, 32 In. 450.00
New Haven, Columbia 475.00
New Haven, Elbe, 8–Day, Time & Strike, Walnut 230.00
New Haven, Elfrida Model, Oak 1100.00
New Haven, Figural, Lily Pad With Frog, Porcelain Face 165.00
New Haven, Gingerbread, 8–Day, Time & Strike, Oak 125.00
New Haven, Mantel, Calendar, Pressed Oak, 8–Day, Time & Strike, 23 In. 150.00
New Haven, Mantel, Lohengrin Model, Music Box, C.1890 .... 275.00
New Haven, Regulator Calendar, Oak, 3 1/2 Ft. 495.00
New Haven, Regulator, Crystal, Thoreau 385.00
New Haven, Regulator, Maywood Model, All Original 450.00
New Haven, Regulator, Store, Golden Oak 300.00
New Haven, School, Long Drop, Time & Calendar, Oak 250.00
New Haven, Statue, Carthage, Black Base, Ormolu Mounts 350.00

Clock, Paperweight,   Clock, Plato, Metal,
Nickel Plated,   Art Nouveau,
19th Century, 7 1/2 In.   C.1903, 6 In.

Clock, Shelf, Double Dial, Calendar, Oak, 19th Century, 29 In.   Clock, Waterbury, Calendar, Double Dial, Oak, 24 In.   Clock, Shelf, Double Dial, Calendar, Walnut, 32 In.

Occupied Japan, Owl, Eyes Roll Back & Forth, Box, 11 In. 350.00
Paperweight, Nickel Plated, 19th Century, 7 1/2 In. ....*Illus* 275.00
Plato, Brass, Glass, Bail Handle, Cylindrical Glass, C.1903, 6 In. 80.00
Plato, Metal, Art Nouveau, C.1903, 6 In. ....*Illus* 120.00
R.Brackett, Unity, Pillar & Scroll Case, Original Works & Dial 850.00
R.Whiting, Grandfather, Wooden Works, Second Hand, Grained, 84 In. 550.00
R.Wilson, Grandfather, Original Grain & Finish, Pine, C.1830 .... 3750.00
Raingo Frs., Mantel, Louis XVI, Gilt Bronze, Figures & Putti, 26 In. 1650.00
Read & Watson, Grandfather, Burl Veneer Rosettes, Cherry, 93 1/2 In. 1750.00
Regulator, 1 Weight, Ogee Pendant, Austria, 37 1/2 In. 250.00
Regulator, Calendar, Scrolled Fretwork, Walnut, 29 1/4 In. 200.00
Regulator, Russian, Napoleon III, Boulle Marquetry, 7 Ft.10 In. 5500.00
Rogers, Grandfather, Chippendale, Carved, C.1770, 7 Ft. 11 In. 6600.00
Roosevelt, Man Of The Hour, Electric 95.00
Roxbury, Grandfather, Hepplewhite, Massachusetts, Cherry, 7 Ft. 3 In. 6500.00
S.Hoadley, Grandfather, Brass Finials, Grain Painted, C.1830, 86 In. 13000.00
S.Hoadley, Shelf, Masonic Design Dial 1900.00
Sailboat, Wooden, Chrome Sail, China 46.00
Sam Rogers, Grandfather, Brass Ball Finial, Painted Dial, Mahogany 10000.00
Sambo, Blinking Eyes, Hat, Striped Pants, Iron, 1860, 16 In. 1200.00
Sangamo, Banjo, Electric, Raised Flowers, 1930s 59.00
School, Ansonia, Brass & Copper, C.1850 .... 300.00
School, Battery Operated, Bell Ringer, 1915 .... 550.00
Sessions, Banjo, 8–Day, Time & Strike, Bim Bam Movement 125.00
Sessions, Bucking Horse, Brass Works 45.00
Sessions, Calendar, Regulator, Oak, 8–Day, Time & Strike, 33 In. 300.00
Sessions, Coin–Operated, 10 Cent, Alarm, Wall 45.00
Sessions, Mantel, Gold Dial, Lion's Feet 85.00
Sessions, Regulator, No.5, Walnut 1050.00
Sessions, Regulator, Store, Time & Calendar, Oak 250.00
Seth Thomas, Alarm, 8–Day, Rosewood 95.00
Seth Thomas, Art Deco, Blue Mirror Glass Front 110.00
Seth Thomas, Artist Signed Dorrot, Bronze 600.00
Seth Thomas, Banjo, Dover, 8–Day, Miniature 85.00
Seth Thomas, Banjo, Jeweled, 8–Day, Brass Sidearms, Miniature 95.00
Seth Thomas, Calendar, No.1, Office, Burl Walnut Case 2250.00
Seth Thomas, Calendar, No.4, Rosewood, 8–Day, Weight Driven, 42 3/4 In. 900.00

Seth Thomas, Calendar, Office, Weight Driven, Walnut, 50 In. 4500.00
Seth Thomas, Carved Columns, Wooden Works, Paw Feet 1175.00
Seth Thomas, Chime, Sonora 265.00
Seth Thomas, Lincoln, Walnut 850.00
Seth Thomas, Lincoln, Weight Driven, Oak Case 925.00
Seth Thomas, Mantel, Brass, Porcelain Dial, 8–Day, 11 X 6 3/4 X 5 In. 175.00
Seth Thomas, Mantel, Gothic, Beehive, Convex Glass, Walnut, 9 1/2 In. 35.00
Seth Thomas, Mantel, Rosewood, 8–Day, Zinc Dial, Pendulum, 14 In. 140.00
Seth Thomas, Master, 8–Day, Westminster Chime, Double Spring, 38 In. 900.00
Seth Thomas, Regulator, 2 Weight, Original Label 875.00
Seth Thomas, Regulator, Crystal 350.00
Seth Thomas, Regulator, Double Dial Calendar, Bank 2250.00
Seth Thomas, Regulator, No.11 .... 1250.00
Seth Thomas, Regulator, No.31, Oak 2600.00
Seth Thomas, Regulator, Rosewood, Weight Driven, 8–Day, C.1860, 31 In. 550.00
Seth Thomas, Shelf, Alarm, Second Hand, Roman Numerals, 7 X 9 In. 75.00
Seth Thomas, Shelf, Empire, 8–Day, Time & Strike, Bull's–Eye 150.00
Seth Thomas, Ship's Bell, Exposed Bell ....395.00 To 550.00
Seth Thomas, Ship's, Brass, 8–Day 300.00
Seth Thomas, Sonora, 5 Bells ....285.00 To 350.00
Seth Thomas, Watchman's, Oak, C.1900, 5 Ft. 1200.00
Shelf, Double Dial, Calendar, Oak, 19th Century, 29 In. ....*Illus* 500.00
Shelf, Double Dial, Calendar, Walnut, 32 In. ....*Illus* 1500.00
Shelf, Federal, Eglomise Panel, 2 Columns, Mahogany, C.1820, 18 In. 750.00
Shelf, Federal, Mahogany & Eglomise, Hinged Door, C.1835, 28 In. 385.00
Shelf, Federal, Mahogony, Eglomise Panel House Scene, C.1820, 29 In. 750.00
Shelf, Iron Front, Mother–Of–Pearl Inlay 200.00
Shelf, Ogee Case, Reverse Painting On Glass Door 175.00
Sohm, Office Regulator, Electric, C.1890 .... 750.00
Standard Clock Co., School, Pendulum, Golden Oak Case, 5 Ft. 550.00
Standard Electric Co., Master, 1930 ....550.00 To 650.00
Standard Electric Time Clock Co., Pendulum Movement, Oak 450.00
Standard Toulet, Pigeon Racing Recorder, Oak, Paper Mechanism, 8 In. 85.00
Teddy Bear, Illuminated, 1960s 39.00
Terry & Andrews, Shelf, Mother–Of–Pearl, Iron, Strike Lyre, 15 3/4 In. 160.00
Thomas Bean, Tall Case, Chippendale, Japanned, C.1770, 83 In. 4500.00
   CLOCK, TIFFANY, see Tiffany, Clock
U.Nardin, Box Chronometer 900.00
United Clock, Bowler's, Bowling Alley, Pins, Gold Metal 35.00
Vaillant A Paris, Mantel, Gilt Bronze, Chariot, Figure, 17 In. 935.00
Vienna, Wall, 2 Brass Weights, Carved Walnut Case 550.00
Viennese, Desk, Firescreen Form, Man, Woman, Gilt Metal, Enamel, 6 In. 715.00
Vor Singery, Mantel, Figural, Signed, French 475.00
W.Bird, Bracket, Brass Dial, 5 Posted Movement, Ebonized, 18 1/4 In. 2750.00
W.Johnson, Four Pillar, Reverse Glass 220.00
Wadsworth, Lounsbury & Turner, Mantel, Mahogany, C.1830, 29 In. 575.00
Wag–On–Wall, Painted Wooden Face, 2 Spandrels, 11 1/2 X 16 1/2 In. 225.00
Waltham, Auto Dashboard, Second Hand, 8–Day 110.00
Warren Telechron, Art Deco, Blue Mirror, Chrome Base 45.00
Waterbury, 8–Day, Time & Strike, China 300.00
Waterbury, Art Nouveau, 1890 Mark, 3 X 4 In. 165.00
Waterbury, Calendar, Double Dial, Oak, 24 In. ....*Illus* 550.00
Waterbury, Calendar, Double Dial, Oak, 8–Day, Time, Strike, 1900, 29 In. 1100.00
Waterbury, Calendar, Paperweight Pendulum 350.00
Waterbury, Cambridge Model, Time & Strike, Wall, Oak 695.00
Waterbury, Cottage, Gothic Style, 8–Day, Rosewood 110.00
Waterbury, Floral Design, Time & Strike, 8–Day, Porcelain 310.00
Waterbury, Jeweler Regulator, No.41, Walnut, Wall Case 3950.00
Waterbury, Regulator, Jeweler's, Porcelain Dial, Second Hand, Walnut 3950.00
Waterbury, Regulator, No.3, Oak 1300.00
Waterbury, Regulator, Wall, 2 Weights, Dead Beat Escapement, 50 In. 975.00
Waterbury, School, 8–Day, Pendulum Movement, Miniature 125.00
Waterbury, Shelf, Calendar, No.40, Oak, 8–Day, Time & Strike, 24 In. 550.00
Waterbury, Shelf, Calendar, No.43, Oak, 8–Day, Time & Strike, 29 In. 500.00

Waterbury, Steeple, Mahogany, 30–Hour, Painted Panel, C.1860, 20 In. 110.00
Welch, Mantel, Iron, Side Urns & Statue, 8–Day, Time & Strike 235.00
Welch, Regulator, Arditi Model, Double Dial 1000.00
Welch, Regulator, No.11, Oak 995.00
Welch, Regulator, Sembrich Model, 8–Day, Time & Strike, Walnut 625.00
Welch, Wall, Rosewood, Chamfered Square Pendulum Box, 8–Day, 24 In. 375.00
Westclox, Alarm, Big Ben, Pat.1906–19 .... 30.00
Western Union, Regulator 350.00
Willard, Banjo, Mahogany, Reverse Paintings, Brass Works, 33 1/2 In. 1250.00
Willard, Banjo, Reverse Glass Of Eagle, Mahogany, C.1825, 32 In. 5225.00
Willard, Grandfather, Drawer, Line & Fan Inlay, Mahogany, C.1810 .... 6325.00
Willard, Grandfather, Mahogany, Pendulum, 1800–30, 90 3/4 In. 3200.00
Willard, Lyre–Form, Wall, Scroll & Acanthus, Mahogany, C.1830, 40 In. 3190.00
Willard, Shelf, Mahogany, Eglomise, C.1820, 36 1/2 In. 7700.00
William Smith, English, Verge Escapement, Gilt & Red Lacquer, 19 In. 3080.00
Wingate, Tall Case, Federal, Carved Maple, C.1810, 7 Ft.10 1/2 In. 2850.00
Wm.Young, Grandfather, Dundee, Painted 4 Seasons Dial, Oak, 72 In. 2800.00
Yaeger, Hunting, Walnut, Carved Deer Crest, Oak Leaf Design, 30 In. 425.00

Cloisonne enamel was developed during the tenth century. A glass enamel was applied between small ribbonlike pieces of metal on a metal base. Most cloisonne is Chinese or Japanese. Pieces marked "China" are twentieth–century examples.

CLOISONNE, Bowl, Cherry Blossom & Chinese Peach Design, Turquoise, 9 In. 250.00
Bowl, Covered, Multicolored Florals, Black Ground, 5 X 7 In. 125.00
Bowl, Multicolored, Blue, Green, Red, Floral, 4 In. 75.00
Box, 3 Teal Panels, Characters, Footed, Black, 3 1/2 X 3 In. 85.00
Box, Floral, Black Matte, 2 3/4 X 2 X 1 1/4 In. 110.00
Box, Red, White Flowers, 2 1/2 X 3 In. 25.00
Buckle, Abstract Floral Design 65.00
Candlestick, Pricket, 18th Century, 16 1/2 In., Pair 3850.00
Case, Cigarette, 3 Dragons, Green Ground, Chinese Red, Green 125.00
Case, Cigarette, Cobalt, Chinese Red, White, Gold, Pink, Dragon 125.00
Charger, Hawk Attacking Egret, Japan, 14 In. 335.00
Charger, Imperial Dragon, Indian Red Field, 15 In.Dia. ....*Illus* 225.00
Flowers, Red, Yellow, White, & Turquoise, 8 In. 150.00
Jar, Covered, Flowers, Butterflies, Footed, Goldstone, C.1890, 4 In. 225.00
Jar, Covered, Red, Blue, Yellow Flowers, 11 1/2 In. 350.00
Jar, Covered, Rose Petal, White Ground, 6 1/2 In., Pair 135.00
Jar, Temple, Chinese Openwork, Chrysanthemums, Leaves, 11 In. 500.00
Jardiniere, Bronze, 8 X 7 In. 550.00
Lamp, Green, Harp & Finial, Prunus Blossoms, 9 X 23 In., Pair 395.00
Lamp, Teakwood Base, Pair 110.00
Pedestal, Marble, Onyx, Foliate Cartouches, Arabesques, 43 1/4 In. 1650.00

Cloisonne, Charger, Imperial Dragon, Indian Red Field, 15 In.Dia.

Cloisonne, Vase, Hummingbirds, Spray Of Flowers, 6 In., Pair

Some repairs make the sale of an antique very difficult, if not impossible. Don't buff pewter. Don't wash ivory. Don't repaint old toys. Don't tape old paper. Don't wash oil paintings.

Cloisonne, Vase, Dragon, White Waves, Black Field, 7 In.

Cloisonne, Vase, Japanese, Enamel, Emerald Green, 7 1/4 In.

Plaque, Ocean Scene, Turtles & Crabs, Blues, Round, 12 In.	350.00
Plate, Butterflies & Birds, Goldstone Border, 7 In.	67.00
Plate, Copper, 2 Finches, Floral Border, Japan, 12 In.	150.00
Plate, Cranes, Scenic Terrain, Peonies, Marine Blue, 9 3/4 In.	295.00
Plate, Jade Carved Insert, 4 1/2 In.	40.00
Plate, Mountains, River, & Flowers, Goldstone, Pink Edge, 8 1/4 In.	425.00
Plate, Snowflake Floral, Blue Ground, Scalloped Edge, 9 In.	120.00
Sugar, Yellow Dragons, Black Ground, Handle, 4 1/2 In.	85.00
Teapot, Cobalt, Floral, Miniature	125.00
Tray, Brass Sides & Feet, 8 In.	100.00
Tray, Footed, 19th Century, 9 X 6 In.	95.00
Vase, Allover Engraved Branches, Florals, & Birds, Red, 11 3/4 In.	1100.00
Vase, Alternating Goldstone & Blue Panels, C.1890, 5 In.	195.00
Vase, Bird & Butterflies, Blue, Top Border, Japanese, 7 1/2 In.	225.00
Vase, Bird In Cherry Tree, Pink Ground, 7 1/2 X 18 1/2 In.	1600.00
Vase, Black, 7 Flowers, 7 In.	99.50
Vase, Black, Raspberry Flowers, Base, 7 In., Pair	90.00
Vase, Blossoms, Gray Green Ground, Light Crazing, C.1900, 12 In.	375.00
Vase, Blue & Black Foil, Carp, Japanese, 5 1/2 In.	600.00
Vase, Blue & Green Alternating Foil Panels, Japanese, 5 1/4 In.	165.00
Vase, Blue Floral & Leaves, White Ground, China, 4 In.	55.00
Vase, Canary Foil, Pink Floral, Japanese, 4 7/8 In.	600.00
Vase, Classic Shape, Opaque Chrysanthemums, Salmon, 4 In.	160.00
Vase, Copper, Floral Bands, Polychrome, Squat, Japanese, 9 1/2 In.	200.00
Vase, Dragon & Birds, Multicolored, Blue Ground, Chinese, 12 In.	340.00
Vase, Dragon, White Waves, Black Field, 7 In. ....*Illus*	130.00
Vase, Egyptian Design, Blue Mottled Ground, Japanese, 1900, 9 In.	495.00
Vase, Flattened Baluster, Birds, Floral Sprays, Signed, 3 1/2 In.	3800.00
Vase, Floral, Gray Ground, Japanese, 6 1/8 In.	225.00
Vase, Florals, Cloud Cloisons, Blue, Marked, 4 In.	45.00
Vase, Flowers & Woman, Deep Red, 5 In.	150.00
Vase, Flowers, Black, 10 In., Pair	225.00
Vase, Foil Ground, Pink & Silver Flowers, 1 1/2 X 2 1/2 In.	70.00
Vase, Foil Panels, Butterflies, Abstract Design, 5 1/2 In.	170.00
Vase, Goldstone, Floral, Scrolled Leaf, Butterflies, 3 3/4 In.	110.00
Vase, Gourd, Chinese, Black, 1880, 9 In., Pair	150.00
Vase, Gray, Brown, Lavender, Silver Wire, Japanese, 7 In., Pair	990.00
Vase, Green, Pink, Transparent, Japanese, 5 In.	1250.00
Vase, Hummingbirds, Spray Of Flowers, 6 In., Pair ....*Illus*	320.00
Vase, Iris, Cobalt, Floral Rim, Kinkozan, Japanese, 8 1/2 In.	175.00
Vase, Irises, Kingfisher, Silver, Red Foil, 7 In.	225.00
Vase, Japanese, Enamel, Emerald Green, 7 1/4 In. ....*Illus*	60.00

Vase, Multicolored Flowers, Bush, Blue Ground, 5 In.	105.00
Vase, Multicolored, Goldstone, 5 In.	100.00
Vase, Opaque Chrysanthemums, Tendrils, Salmon, 4 In.	160.00
Vase, Pigeon Blood, Bamboo Design, Pink Peony, 8 1/2 In.	135.00
Vase, Pink, White, Red Flowers On Black Ground, Pair	52.00
Vase, Spring Coil Cloisons, Floral Reserves, Blue, 3 X 5 In.	100.00
Vase, Spring Scroll, Black, Goldstone, Bulbous, 4 1/2 In., Pair	165.00
Vase, Spring Scroll, Multicolored, Cobalt Floral, Bulbous, 5 In.	70.00
Vase, White & Blue Birds, Green Collar, Japanese, 9 7/8 In.	660.00
Vase, White & Pale Blue, 4 1/2 In.	65.00
Vase, White Bird, Plum Branches, Midnight Ground, Japanese, 9 In.	660.00
Vase, White Flowers, Branches, Red Ground, 6 In.	115.00
Vase, White Roses, Ruby, 7 1/2 In.	375.00
Vase, Wiseman, Colored Robes, Flasks, Dragon, Japanese, 9 In., Pair	880.00
Vase, Yellow, Blue, Green, Lilac, 6 In.	260.00

CLOTHING, see Textile

Cluthra glass is a two–layered glass with small air pockets that form white spots. The Steuben Glass Works of Corning, New York, made it after 1903. Kimball Glass Company of Vineland, New Jersey, made Cluthra from about 1925.

CLUTHRA, see also Steuben

CLUTHRA, Rose Bowl, Internal Bubble, Rigaree Protrusions, Mottled, 8 In.	150.00
Vase, 3–Part, Pink To White, Signed, 10 In.	850.00
Vase, Amethyst, Signed, Steuben, 11 X 10 In.	1400.00
Vase, Amethyst, Steuben, 8 1/2 In.	625.00
Vase, Lavender, Steuben, 4 1/2 In.	65.00
Vase, Pink, Steuben, C.1920, 10 1/2 In. ....*Illus*	900.00
Vase, Rippled Surface, Gold Trim, 6 In.	185.00
Vase, Rose, Signed, Steuben, 11 In.	1450.00
Vase, Shaded Green, Steuben, 12 In.	850.00
Vase, White To Green, Signed, Steuben, 6 3/4 In.	275.00
Vase, White, Steuben, 9 1/2 X 10 In.	550.00

Coalport ware has been made by the Coalport Porcelain Works of England from 1795 to the present time. Early pieces were unmarked. About 1810–1825 the pieces were marked with the name "Coalport" in various forms. Later pieces also had the name "John Rose" in the mark. The crown mark has been used with variations since 1881.

COALPORT, Bowl, Grape, Floral, Cobalt Blue, Gold, Footed, 10 In.	65.00
Box, Enameled, Green Trim, Gilded, Lid, Signed, 5 1/2 In.	150.00
Cup & Saucer, Demitasse, Gold Enameled Design, Signed, C.1891	135.00

Cluthra, Vase, Pink, Steuben,
C.1920, 10 1/2 In.

If you use plate hangers to display your plates, be sure they are not too tight. The clips should be covered with a soft material. The end clips may scratch or chip the plate.

Coalport, Dinner Set, Canton Pattern, Stylized Floral, 379 Piece

Cup & Saucer, Harebell Pattern, Oversize	25.00
Cup & Saucer, Rose Red Floral Border, Swirl Shape, 1883	39.00
Cup & Saucer, Tree, Gold Key Border, C.1890	40.00
Dinner Set, Canton Pattern, Stylized Floral, 379 Piece ....*Illus*	3500.00
Flower Arrangement, Miniature	12.00
Pitcher, Blue & White, Marked, Pre–1891, 6 In.	58.00
Plate, Fluted, Blue Flowers, Gold Ground, 8 In.	65.00
Plate, Gold Trim, Cobalt Blue, 8 In.	45.00
Plate, Hand Painted, Gold & Pastels, Numbered, C.1900, 9 3/4 In.	110.00
Plate, Japan Pattern, Marked, C.1805, 8 3/8 In., 8 Piece	1320.00
Plate, Signed & Numbered, C.1900, 6 In., Set Of 6	95.00
Saucer, Blue & Pastels, C.1900, 6 In.	110.00
Sweetmeat, Floral Center, Border, Apricot, Brown, Square, 9 In.	150.00
Tumbler, Dawn	35.00
Urn, Covered, Reserve Of Loch Achray, Roman Ruins, Ivory, 11 In.	285.00
Vase, Gold Outlining, Cobalt Blue, 8 In.	45.00

Cobalt blue glass was made using oxide of cobalt. The characteristic bright dark blue identifies it for the collector. Most cobalt glass found today was made after the Civil War.

COBALT BLUE, Bank, Piggy	25.00
Bottle, Toilet, Drop Nipple Stopper, Blown	350.00
Box, Lid, Hand Painted Design, 3 In.Diam.	35.00
Box, Patch, Lacy Foliage, Cream Enameled, Round, 1 1/4 In.	95.00
Candlestick, Ribbed Pattern, 4 7/8 In., Pair	100.00
Cordial, Crystal Stem	8.00
Creamer, Applied Handle, 4 In.	525.00
Creamer, Applied Handle, Threading At Neck, 5 In.	1350.00
Creamer, New England, Crimped Handle, C.1835, 3 3/4 In.	395.00
Cruet, 5–Footed, S Handle, Applied Design	295.00
Cruet, Amber Handle & Stopper, 7 3/4 In.	65.00
Goblet, Crystal Pattern, Crystal Ball Stem ....18.00 To 24.00	
Holder, Thimble, With Original Sterling Silver Thimble	95.00
Inkwell, Colorado	45.00
Mug, Applied Foot, Handle, Gilded Wreath, Violet Base	20.00
Mustard, Covered, Sterling Silver Holder	75.00
Pin Dish, White Lace Trim, 4 In.Diam.	30.00
Pitcher Set, Ruffled, Enameled, 4 Tumblers	85.00
Pitcher Set, White Ship, 8 Tumblers, 3 3/4 In.	85.00
Pitcher, Ball, Ribbed, Small	25.00
Pitcher, Blown, Applied Foot & Handle, 4 1/4 In.	115.00
Pitcher, Enameled, 3 1/2 In.	34.00
Pitcher, Enameled, Victorian, 8 In.	65.00
Pitcher, Harpo Pattern, Louie Glass Co., Clear Handle, 8 In.	40.00

Pitcher, Melon Rib, Applied Handle, 4 Tumblers 245.00
Pitcher, Tilt, Ribbed, 46 Oz. 45.00
Plate, Dessert, Blown, Polished Pontil, 8 1/2 In., Set Of 11 .... 150.00
Plate, Dinner, Ground Bottom, 10 3/4 In. 25.00
Plate, Luncheon, 8 1/4 In. 12.00
Plate, Silver Floral Design, 12 In. 65.00
Salt, Boat Shape, 3 5/8 In. 100.00
Salt, Christmas, Patent Date, Agitator 95.00
Sugar & Creamer, Farber Ware Floral Holder, Dated 1932 .... 60.00
Sugar, Flared Foot, Folded Rim, Expanded Diamond, 4 1/2 In. 600.00
Toothpick, Hat Shape 15.00
Urn, Figural & Wreath Design, Faceted Body, 11 In., Pair 95.00
Vase, 4 1/4 In. 25.00
Vase, Bulbous, 10 In. 45.00
Vase, Enameled, 2 3/4 In. 22.00
Vase, New England Glass Co., Pair 395.00
Vase, Ruffled, 6 In. ....Color 85.00
Vase, Silver Mount, Swags, Pendants, Merrill Shops, 9 In., Pair 225.00
Vase, White Enamel, 2 Masted Ship, Scrolls, Bulbous, 10 1/4 In. 48.00
Wine, Crystal Pattern, Crystal Ball Stem 35.00

Coca–Cola was first served in 1886 in Atlanta, Georgia. It was advertised through signs, newspaper ads, coupons, bottles, trays, calendars, and even lamps and clocks. Collectors want anything with the word "Coca–Cola," including a few rare products like gum wrappers and cigar bands. The famous trademark was patented in 1893, the "Coke" mark in 1945. Many modern items and reproductions are being made.

COCA–COLA, Apron, Tan, Green Stripes, Coke Patch, Knee Length 35.00
Ashtray, Around The World, Metal 35.00
Ashtray, Carnival Glass, Marigold, 1930 .... 300.00
Ashtray, Coke Adds Life, Glass 1.50
Bag, Vinyl, Red, Coca–Cola In Bottles 65.00
Bank, Dispensing, Linemar, Tin, 1960 .... 200.00
Bank, Old–Fashioned Pop Machine Picture, Tin, 4 In. 17.50
Bank, Plastic, Insert Nickel & Bottle Pops Out 8.00
Banner, Santa Claus, Children At Christmas Tree, 1950, 22 1/2 In. 5.00
Bell, Red Art Glass 49.00
Billfold, Pigskin, 1940s, Box 15.00
Blotter, 1904 .... 175.00
Blotter, 3 Ladies Pictured, How About A Coke, 8 X 2 In. 5.00
Book, Case Shape, Coke Bottling Co. 6.00
Bottle Opener & Ice Pick, 1930s 15.00
Bottle, 75th Anniversary, Beaumont, Tx., Hutchinson, 1982 .... 35.00
Bottle, Aqua, Straight Sided 8.00
Bottle, Baltimore Orioles 8.00
Bottle, Bear Bryant, Full 4.00
Bottle, Cola Clan 3rd Convention, Amber, 1977 .... 20.00
Bottle, Dizzy Dean World Series Graduate League, 1982 .... 35.00
Bottle, Georgia Bulldog, Full 4.00
Bottle, Light Green, Straight Sided 12.00
Bottle, Seltzer 35.00
Bottle, Soda Water, Marshalltown, Iowa, Square, 6 Stars 18.00
Bottle, St.Louis Cards, Full 6.00
Bottle, St.Wall–Emp., Biedenharn, Paper Label ....Color 125.00
Bottle, Washington, D.C., 9th Convention, 1983 .... 20.00
Bottle, Yugoslavia, 1982 .... 12.50
Bowl, Popcorn, 1935 .... 65.00
Box, Pencils, Pen, Ruler, Eraser, Blotters, 1937 .... 58.00
Box, Steel, Beaverboard, 13 X 8 X 16 In. 40.00
Calendar, 1914, Betty, Framed 475.00
Calendar, 1929, Full Pad 265.00
Calendar, 1935, 50th Anniversary, Framed 185.00
Calendar, 1943, Women In World War II Defense Work, 6 Pages 55.00

Calendar, 1948	50.00 To 75.00
Calendar, 1957, Flower Prints, 14 X 6 In.	4.00
Calendar, 1960, Puppies, Lougheed	10.00
Canister, Syrup, Embossed Coca–Cola, 1950s	65.00
Card, Window, Young Lady Holding Coke Glass, 1915	375.00
Cards, Nature Study	25.00
Cards, Playing, Better With Coke	35.00
Cards, Playing, Girl & Snowman, Cellophane Wrapped, 1959	50.00
Cards, Playing, Girl In Pool, Cellophane Wrapped, 1959	50.00
Cards, Playing, Girl With Bowling Ball, 1961	20.00
Cards, Playing, Welcome Friends, 1958	25.00
Carrier, Metal, Large	50.00
Carrier, Slat Side, 6 Bottles	47.50
Case, Plastic, Holds 24 Bottles	20.00
Chair, Stadium	175.00
Clock, Counter, With Sign, 1950s	200.00
Clock, Drink Coca–Cola In Bottles, Square, Electric	215.00
Clock, Electric, 18 In.	65.00
Clock, Fintail, Drink Coca–Cola, 1950s	45.00
Clock, Gilbert, Regulator, Walnut, Door, 5 Cent, 30 In.	325.00
Clock, Plastic, 21 X 12 In.	20.00
Clock, Round, 1951	135.00
Clock, Wooden Frame, Square, 1939, 16 In.	125.00
Coaster, 50th Anniversary, Solid Brass, 1936	20.00
Coke Machine, Table Top, Coin–Operated	295.00
Cooler, Aluminum	125.00
Cooler, Red, Tin, 24 X 24 In.	35.00
Cooler, Salesman's Sample, Open Bottom, Books, Metal	550.00
Cooler, Salesman's Sample, Plastic	100.00
Crate, Shipping, Wooden, Drink Coca–Cola In Bottles On Sides	65.00
Dinner Set, 1930, 5 Piece	650.00
Dish, Pretzel, 1936	65.00
Dispenser, Plastic, 1950s	15.00
Display, Bottle, Original Cap, 20 In.	100.00
Display, Bottle, White Rubber, 42 In.	350.00
Door Pull, Bottle, Figural	120.00
Door Push, Ice Cold In Bottles, Porcelain, 4 X 30 In.	75.00
Drink Rack, Red & Yellow, 4 Top Hooks	95.00
Game, Checkers, Compliments Of Coca–Cola Bottling Co., 1931	40.00
Gum Jar, Marked Franklin Careo Co.	95.00
Holder, For 2 Bottles, 1950s	20.00
Ice Pick With Opener	15.00
Jersey, Mean Joe Green, Large	15.00
Key Chain, Bottle	5.50
Key Chain, Brass Medallion, 50th Anniversary	3.00
Kick Plate, White & Yellow, Red Back, 12 X 29 In.	55.00
Knife, 75th Anniversary, Jackson, Tn., Case	35.00
Knife, Pocket, 1933	27.00
Knife, Pocket, Bone	78.00
Lamp, Coke Cup, Plastic, 20 In.	70.00
Lighter, Bottle Shape, 1950	8.50
Lighter, Cigarette, Coke Can Shape	15.00
Lighter, Cigarette, Figural	29.00
Lighter, Coke Can, Miniature, 1950	20.00
Match Striker, Black, Red Back, Canadian, Porcelain, 4 1/4 In.	80.00
Match Striker, Wall, 1930s	75.00
Mirror, Pocket, 1910	185.00
Mirror, Pocket, 1911	150.00
Mirror, Pocket, 1916	195.00
Mirror, Pocket, Boy Fishing, 3 In.	2.00
Mirror, Pocket, Hamilton King, 1912	200.00
Mug, Cowboy, Green	10.50
Needle Case, Cardboard, 1925	26.00
Ornament, Christmas, Santa Claus, Various Poses, 1980, Set Of 4	12.00

Panda, Holding Coke, Battery Operated	58.00
Paperweight, 1948	20.00
Paperweight, 1980 Winter Olympics, Lake Placid, Marble	15.00
Pencil Box, 1930s	35.00
Pencil Sharpener, Bottle Shape, Metal, 1953	12.50
Pencil, Mechanical, Bottle Floating In Liquid In Top, 1950s	12.50
Ping–Pong Set, 1940s	65.00
Plate, China, 1924	125.00
Plate, China, 1930, 7 In.	175.00
Plate, Christmas, Santa Claus With Children & Dog, 1981	3.00
Popgun, Clown, 1950s, 7 In.	15.00
Poster, Girl Holding Bottle, Wooden Frame, 1942, 32 X 60 In.	150.00
Push Plate, Porcelain, Red, White, & Yellow, 17 X 54 In.	160.00
Rack, Bag, Hanging	95.00
Radio, AM, Bottle Shape	7.50
Ring, In Ring Box, Size 9	12.50
Ruler, Golden Rule	35.00
Salt & Pepper, Cans, Miniature	8.00
Shade, Leaded Glass, 18 In.	3995.00
Sign, Bottle & 5 Cent, Metal, 1933, 18 X 54 In.	175.00
Sign, Bottle In Circle, Tin, 1948, 18 X 54 In.	90.00
Sign, Cardboard, Drink Coca–Cola, 10 In.Diam.	12.00
Sign, Christmas Bottle, Tin, 36 X 54 In.	125.00
Sign, Christmas, Tin, 1923, 6 X 13 In.	75.00
Sign, Coke Bottle, Red, White, Button, 12 In.	35.00
Sign, Coke Bottle, Red, White, Button, 36 In.	85.00
Sign, Counter, Clock, Please Pay When Served, 1950s	145.00
Sign, Desk, Plastic, Wooden Base	65.00
Sign, Drink Coca–Cola Ice Cold, Metal, Embossed, 20 X 28 In.	35.00
Sign, Flange, Porcelain, 1938, 16 X 16 In.	90.00
Sign, Metal, Red, White Script, 1960, 3 Ft. 4 In.	65.00
Sign, Plastic Face, Metal, Work Safely, Electric, 16 X 16 In.	82.00
Sign, Plastic, 16 In.Diam.	25.00
Sign, Porcelain, Red, Round, 26 In.	75.00
Sign, Porcelain, Syrup Dispenser, Late 1930s	110.00
Sign, Reverse Glass, Drink Coca–Cola, Picture, 6 X 1 X 1/4 In.	65.00
Sign, Sign Of Good Taste, Fishtail Design, Tin, 53 X 18 In.	125.00
Thermometer, Bottle Shape, 1958	20.00
Thermometer, Bottle Shape, 29 In.	10.00
Thermometer, Bottle Shape, Patent Dec.25, 1923, 16 In.	55.00 To 85.00
Thermometer, Enjoy Coca–Cola, Round, 1960s	40.00
Thermometer, Fishtail, Glass, 1957	95.00
Thermometer, Girl Silhouette, Canadian, Yellow, 1942	220.00
Thermos, Masonite, 1944	100.00
Toy, Gun, Pop, Paper, 1954	3.00
Toy, Gun, Pop, Santa Claus, 1950s, 7 In.	15.00
Toy, Trailer, Buddy L, Tractor Trunk, 10 1/2 In.	15.00
Toy, Truck, Musical, Wooden, 1960s	30.00
Toy, Truck, Smith–Miller, Early 1950s, Box	600.00
Tray, 1909, Hamilton King Coca–Cola Girl, 16 1/2 X 13 1/2 In.	700.00
Tray, 1914, Betty, Oval	285.00
Tray, 1917, Elaine	160.00 To 175.00
Tray, 1921, Summer Girl	170.00
Tray, 1923, Flapper Girl	85.00 To 145.00
Tray, 1925, Girl At Party	85.00 To 135.00
Tray, 1930, Bathing Beauty	145.00
Tray, 1931, Boy With Dog, Norman Rockwell	325.00
Tray, 1932, Girl In Yellow Bathing Suit	150.00 To 275.00
Tray, 1933, Frances Dee	40.00 To 185.00
Tray, 1934, Johnny Weissmuller & Maureen O'Sullivan	150.00 To 375.00
Tray, 1935, Madge Evans	135.00
Tray, 1936, Hostess	60.00
Tray, 1937, Running Girl	75.00 To 110.00
Tray, 1938, Girl In Large Hat, Yellow Dress	55.00 To 85.00

Tray, 1939, Springboard Girl	50.00
Tray, 1940, Sailor Girl	45.00
Tray, 1941, Skater	65.00
Tray, 1943, Girl With Wind In Her Hair	32.50 To 45.00
Tray, 1950, Girl With Menu	20.00 To 35.00
Tray, 1978, Capt.Cook, Bicentennial, Vancouver, 1778–1978, 13 In.	9.00
Tray, 1981, Calendar Girl From 1927	15.00
Tray, 1981, Red River Co–Op, Red, Cars, People, Limited Edition	7.00
Tray, 1982, Brandon 100th Anniversary, Steamboat Scene	7.00
Tray, Tip, 1905, Juanita, Woman Drinking, Round	200.00
Tray, Tip, 1906, Drink Coca–Cola, Relieve Fatigue, 5 Cents, Oval	200.00
Tray, Tip, 1909, Coca–Cola Girl, Flowered Hat, Oval	130.00
Tray, Tip, 1912, Hamilton King Girl	185.00
Tray, Tip, 1914, Betty	75.00 To 135.00
Tray, Tip, 1917, Elaine	100.00 To 150.00
Tray, Tip, 1920, Garden Girl	135.00
Tray, Tip, 1923, Flapper	85.00
Tray, Tip, 1941, Ice Skater	35.00
Tray, Tip, 1950, Girl With Menu	35.00
Tray, Tip, 1961, Thanksgiving	25.00
Tray, Tip, Girl With Coca–Cola, 1982, 4 1/2 X 6 1/2 In.	2.50
Tray, TV, 1956	15.00
Tray, Wire Wrap, Silver 6 Oz. Bottle	95.00
Truck, Buddy L, Cast Iron, 10 1/2 In.	50.00 To 55.00
Tumbler, Santa, Set Of 9	35.00
Tumbler, Trademark Under Logo, 1940s	5.00
Vending Machine, 10 Cent	300.00
Wallet, Man's, Pigskin, Embossed Gold Coke Bottle & Ad	15.00
Watch Fob, Gibson Girl, Celluloid, 1910	375.00
Watch Fob, Girl With Glass In Hand	250.00
Watch, Pocket	80.00
Whistle, Bottle Cap	6.00
Wine Set, Carafe & 4 Wines	22.50
Wristwatch, 75th Anniversary, Jackson, Tn., Hand Is Bottle, 1980	85.00

Coffee grinders of home size were first made about 1894. They lost favor by the 1930s. Large floor–standing or counter model coffee grinders were used in the nineteenth–century country store. The renewed interest in fresh–ground coffee has produced many modern electric and hand grinders; and reproductions of the old styles are being made.

COFFEE GRINDER, Arcade Crystal, Wall Mount, Glass, Iron, No Lid	60.00
Arcade Crystal, Wall, Iron & Glass	70.00
Arcade, Brass Tone, Wall	100.00
Arcade, Dated 1890	65.00
Arcade, Imperial, Lap Style, Iron Top	60.00
Arcade, Wall, Crystal, No.3, Glass, Painted	115.00
Brass Hopper, Iron Crank, Marked Adams, Poplar, 6 X 6 In.	50.00
Cast Iron, Old Red Paint, 2 3/4 In.	22.50
Cast Iron, Painted, National, 14 X 24 X 16 In.	400.00
Child's, Lap, Cast Iron, Wooden, 2 1/2 X 4 In.	75.00
Child's, Pride Label, 3 1/2 In.Square	85.00
Crescent, 31 In.Wheels, Rutland, Vermont, 5 Ft.	1200.00
Double Wheel, Crescent 7, Rutland, Vt., Cast Iron, 24 1/2 In.	95.00
Double Wheel, Parker, 9 In.	395.00
Elgin National Coffee Mills, Eagle Finial, Floor Model	825.00
Elgin, Eagle Finial, Original Paint	350.00
Embossed, National Specialty, Philadelphia, No.5, Cast Iron	475.00
Enterprise No.2, Wheel, Counter Top	126.50
Enterprise, Iron Handle, Pat.1873, Wood Base, 11 In.	125.00
Enterprise, No.2, Wheel, Dated 1870, Original Paint, 25 In.	600.00
Enterprise, No.7, Painted, Decals	450.00
Enterprise, Wall, Open Hopper	52.00
Golden Rule Coffee, Wall, Advertising, Cast Iron	175.00

Golden Rule, Wall Hanging	180.00
Kitchen Aid, Electric	25.00
Landers, Frary, Clark, 1901, 12 In.	425.00
Lap, Brass Cup, Cherry	110.00
Lap, Dovetailed Box, Mechanical Meshed Gear, Iron	95.00
Lap, Pine, Cast Iron Fittings	80.00
Lap, Signed Adams, Maple Box & Drawer, Iron Cup	110.00
Lap, Strobridge	80.00
Lap, Universal 109, Tin, Patent 1905	55.00
Red, Salesman's Sample, 4 In.	95.00
Table Model, Cast Iron, Wooden Drawer, 12 × 6 In. .... *Illus*	390.00
Wall, Arcade, Brass Tone	100.00
Wall, Regal, Tin & Wooden	48.00
Wooden, Iron, Drawer Front	85.00
Wooden, Tin Hopper, Inscription, 1860, 6 X 9 1/2 In.	65.00

Coin spot is a glass pattern that was named by the collectors. It, of course, features coinlike spots as part of the glass. Colored, clear, and opalescent glass was made with the spots. Many companies used the design in the 1870–90 period. It is so popular that reproductions are still being made.

COIN SPOT, Cruet, White Spots, Original Stopper, Opalescent Blue	60.00
Lamp, Kerosene, Blue Base	150.00
Lamp, Oil, Black Glass Base, White, Pair	595.00
Pitcher, 3 Tumblers, White	165.00
Pitcher, Cranberry, Applied Handle, 6 3/4 In.	100.00
Pitcher, Crimped Edge, Blue Handle, Opalescent Blue, 8 In.	120.00
Syrup	75.00
Tumbler, Fine Ribbed, Opalescent Cranberry	85.00
Tumbler, Opalescent Clear	15.00
Vase, Ruffled Top, Pink & White, 6 In.	65.00
Water Set, Shaped Tumblers, Clear To Opalescent, 7 Piece	275.00

The vending machine is an ancient invention dating back to 200 B.C. when holy water was dispensed in a coin-operated vase. Smokers in seventeenth-century England could buy tobacco from a coin-operated box. It was not until after the Civil War that the technology made modern coin-operated games and vending machines plentiful. Slot machines, arcade games, and dispensers are all collected.

COIN–OPERATED MACHINE, Baseball Game, Paupa & Hochreim, C.1918, 1 Cent	950.00
Career Pilot, Mutoscope	775.00
Championship Duck Shoot	135.00
Claw Digger, Steam Shovel, 25 Cent	1390.00
Dispensing, Cards, Grandma, Genco	1500.00
Football Game, Chester Pollard	825.00
Football, Baker Novelty, 1933, 17 1/2 X 14 In.	200.00
Gum Ball, Ad–Lee E–Z Choose	450.00
Gum Ball, Atlas Master, 1 Cent	29.50
Gum Ball, Baker Boy	400.00
Gum Ball, Bink's Whiz Bowler, 1 Cent	125.00
Gum Ball, Dandy Vendor	325.00
Gum Ball, Hit The Target, 1 Cent	100.00
Gum Ball, Lindy Takes Off, Statue Of Liberty, C.1929	475.00
Gum Ball, Masters, 1 Cent	150.00
Gum, Mills, Hit The Target, 1 Cent	100.00
Gum, Pulver, Porcelain, Red, Clown Dispensing	275.00
Gum, Pulver, Yellow Kid, Red Porcelain Case	95.00
Gum, Rockola, 4 Aces Payoff, Metal	1300.00
Gum, Silver Queen, 1 Cent	140.00
Gum, Volkmann Stollwerck & Co., 4 Column, 1892	750.00
Gum, Zeno, Last Patent 1902	100.00
Horoscope, Solar, Astrological Globe, 6 Ft.	275.00
Jennings, Golf Ball	1800.00
Lifter Machine, Rosenfield	750.00
Lighter Fluid, Van Lansing, 1 Cent	500.00

Nickel Flip, Cigar Advertising, Oak, C.1900 .... 300.00
Nut, Asco, With Cup Dispenser, Light & Key, 5 Cent 90.00
Peanut, Advance, C.1920 .... 100.00
Peanut, Cadillac, Junior, 5 Cent 65.00
Peanut, Sel–Mor, Cast Iron, Decal, Paint, 1 Cent 135.00
Peanut, Victor, Art Deco, 1940, 5 Cent 47.50
Peep Show, Cail–O–Scope 875.00
Peep Show, Mills, 1905 .... 750.00
Perfume Dispenser, Choice Of 4, Key, Marque, 10 Cent 115.00
Perfume Dispenser, Oval Mirror, Brass Mechanism 150.00
Pinball, Gottlieb, Hi–Diver 150.00
Pinball, Jungle, 4 Player, Painted, Glass, Early 1960s 125.00
Pinball, Williams, Golden Gloves Boxers 150.00
Pop–N–Hot Popcorn, Hume–Hagenson, 10 Cent 500.00
Popcorn, Holcomb & Hoke, Counter, 1920s 1250.00
Popcorn, Starr, Scoop, Sacks, 1930, 27 In. X 6 Ft. 750.00
Rocketship, Kiddie Ride, Late 1950s 225.00
Shooting Gallery, U.S.Marshal, 10 Shots, C.1950 .... 300.00
Slot, Advance, Climax, 1 Cent 550.00
Slot, Bally, Double Bell 3000.00
Slot, Bally, Joker Poker With Hi–Lo Payout 2195.00
Slot, Buckley, Point Maker 600.00
Slot, Caille, Black Cat, Upright Case 850.00
Slot, Caille, Double, Carved Oak, C.1890 .... 2100.00
Slot, Caille, Nude Center Pull, 25 Cent 7500.00
Slot, Caille, Nude Front, 5 Cent 2000.00
Slot, Caille, Superior, Dancing Girl Front, 10 Cent 1850.00
Slot, Double Pace, Stand, 5 Cent 1800.00
Slot, Jennings, Chief, Bronze, 25 Cent 1475.00
Slot, Jennings, Chief, Tic–Tac–Toe, 1 Dollar 3500.00
Slot, Jennings, Club Chief, 50 Cent 1500.00
Slot, Jennings, Club Special Sportsman, 10 Cent 1175.00
Slot, Jennings, Hand Carved Indian, Bursting Cherry 2800.00
Slot, Jennings, Hunting Scene, Chief 1200.00
Slot, Jennings, Peacock, Front Vendor 2000.00
Slot, Jennings, Standard Chief, 35 Cent 1350.00
Slot, Jennings, Standard Chief, 5 Cent 850.00
Slot, Jennings, Sun Chief 700.00
Slot, Jennings, Wild Indian, Standard Chief, 1 Dollar 2000.00
Slot, Mills, Bull's–Eye, English 695.00
Slot, Mills, Bursting Cherry, Hand Carved Indian 2800.00
Slot, Mills, Double Dewey, Upright 6800.00
Slot, Mills, Hi–Top Bonus, 25 Cent 1500.00
Slot, Mills, Hi–Top, 10 Cent 875.00
Slot, Mills, Horse Head Bonus, 1937 .... 1750.00
Slot, Mills, Lion Front, 5 Cent 1200.00
Slot, Mills, Little Duke, 1 Cent 1350.00
Slot, Mills, Poinsettia, Fortune Reels, 25 Cent 1450.00
Slot, Mills, Single Dewey 8495.00
Slot, Mills, Vest Pocket, 5 Cent 495.00
Slot, Mills, Wise Cracker, 4 Column, 5 Cent 1900.00
Slot, Pace, All–Star Comet Bell, 1936 .... 1200.00
Slot, Pok–O–Reel, Penny, 8 1/2 X 11 X 10 In. 55.00
Slot, Rol–A–Top, Bird & Fruit Front, 5 Cent 2450.00
Slot, Watling, Operators Bell, Cast Iron, Oak Sides 1300.00
Stamp, Uncle Sam, Porcelain Front 100.00
Stimulator, Park Novelty, Redbird, Trade, C.1904 .... 725.00
Strength Machine, Gottlieb, 1930s, 5 Cent 125.00
Strength Tester, Barbell, Floor, Exhibit Supply 400.00
Target Practice, Mills, 1 Cent 75.00
Trade Stimulator, 2–Wheel Bicycle, C.1893 .... 1900.00
Trade Stimulator, American Eagle, Daval, 1 Cent 185.00
Trade Stimulator, Shocker, A.B.T. 125.00
Trade Stimulator, Sparks, Champion, 1 Cent 175.00

Trade Stimulator, Spiral, Cigar Store	1800.00
Trade Stimulator, Steven's, Beer Barrel	275.00

> *Collector plates are modern plates produced in limited editions. Some will be found listed under the factory name, such as Bing & Grondahl, Royal Copenhagen, Royal Doulton, and Wedgwood. Pictures and more price information can be found in "Kovels' Price Guide for Collector Plates, Figurines, Paperweights and Other Limited Editions."*

COLLECTOR PLATE, Anri, A Time For Secrets	95.00
Anri, Christmas, 1971	100.00
Anri, Christmas, 1979	100.00
Anri, Christmas, Wooden, 1971	110.00
Avondale, First Born	40.00
Bareuther, Christmas, 1976	25.00
DeGrazia, Flower Girl, 1978	475.00
DeGrazia, Little Cocopah, 1980	475.00
DeGrazia, Pima Drummer Boy, 1980	495.00
Franklin Mint, Bald Eagle	100.00
Franklin Mint, Christmas, 1977	30.00
Gorham, Kennedy, 1976	50.00
Gorham, Winter Trails, No.2	49.00
Haviland, Landy & Unicorn, Parlon, 1977	27.00
Haviland, Unicorn, Sight, Parlon, 1978	13.00
Haviland–Parlon, Amy & Snoopy	35.00
Haviland–Parlon, Christmas, 1977	50.00
Hibel, King David	250.00
Masseria, Juliana, 1983	70.00
Pickard, Little Foxes, 1979	120.00
Pickard, Panther, Lockhart, 1978	175.00
Pickard, Statue Of Liberty	150.00
Poole, Christmas, Magi, 1973	125.00
Rockwell, Christmas Trio, 1976	14.00
Rockwell, First Smoke, 1977	13.00
Rockwell, Heritage, Cobbler, Knowles, 1978	135.00
Rockwell, Heritage, Toy Maker, Knowles, 1977	180.00
Rockwell, Lost In Cave, 1978	11.00

> *Comic art, or cartoon art, is a relatively new field of collecting. Original comic strips, magazine covers, and even printed strips are collected. The first daily comic strip was printed in 1907. The paintings on celluloid used for movie cartoons are listed in this book under Animation Art.*

COMIC ART, Aces & Kings War Cartoons, Ding Darling, Copyright 1917	15.00
Book, Barkers Komic Picture Souvenir, Black Cartoons	35.00
Book, Crackajack Funnies, No.17, 1939	27.00
Book, Famous Funnies, No.17, 1935	35.00
Bringing Up Father, Framed, Full Page, Color, Chicago Herald, 1923	10.00
Krug, I Call It Urban Renewal, Framed, 1969, 15 X 18 1/2 In.	65.00
Pad, Sketch, Dumbo, Ink Drawings, Stamped Disney, 1940, 13 X 17 In.	300.00
Print, Judge, 1899	15.00
Print, Ten Little Niggers German	85.00
Sections From New York Herald, 1900–17, Bound	1600.00
Uncle Wiggily, Framed, Full Page, Color, Chicago Herald, 1920	10.00

> *Commemorative items have been made to honor members of royalty and those of great national fame. World's fairs and important historical events are also remembered with commemorative pieces. The date and the name of the event are usually part of the design.*

COMMEMORATIVE, see also Coronation; World's Fair

COMMEMORATIVE, Ashtray, Churchill, White, This Was Their Finest Hour	30.00
Coffee Mug, Queen Elizabeth Trip To U.S., May, 1939	25.00
Creamer, World War I, Liberty China	50.00
Cup & Saucer, George VI, Visit To Canada 1939	49.00

Jug, Queen Victoria, Silver Lip, Doulton, 1897, 8 In. 320.00
Jug, Victoria Jubilee, Stoneware, 1887, 6 In. 135.00
Loving Cup, Queen Elizabeth II, Papers 400.00
Mug, Queen Victoria Jubilee, Dated 1897 .... 48.00
Picture, Thos.Hunter Dela.Bldg., Framed, 1876, 10 1/2 In. 20.00
Pin, George Washington Bicentennial, 1732–1932 .... 8.00
Pin, Spirit Of St.Louis, Brass, 1927 .... 17.00
Pitcher, Commodore Dewey, 1899 .... 45.00
Plaque, Royal Couple, Flags, Messages, 1901, 12 X 11 In. 160.00
Plate, Dominion Of Canada, Royal Winton, C.1900, Square, 9 In. 45.00
Plate, Lind 1927, Limoges 15.00
Plate, Nouveau Head, McCall's Centennial, 1896–1976, 10 In. 90.00
Platter, Martyr's, Lincoln, Garfield Portrait, Christ Handles 350.00
Spill Holder, Man & Woman, C.1840, 5 In. 55.00
Spoon, 350th Anniversary, Mayflower 5.00
Statue, Prince Albert Of England, Naval Uniform, 11 3/4 In. 55.00
Tobacco Jar, Victoria & Albert Wedding, 1840, Stoneware 150.00

The term "contemporary glass" refers to art glass made since 1950.
Some contemporary glass factories, such as Orrefors or Baccarat, are
listed under their own categories.

CONTEMPORARY GLASS, Vase, Lundberg, Fish, Air Bubbles, Blue, 1982, 5 1/4 In. ... 360.00
Vase, Moss & Metallic Green, Orange, Ovoid, 8 1/2 In. 300.00

Cookbooks are collected for various reasons. Some are wanted for the
recipes, some for investment, and some as examples of advertising.
Cookbooks and recipe pamphlets are included in this section.

COOKBOOK, American Everyday, 1955, Large 7.50
Boston School Kitchen Text Book, 1887 .... 12.00
Calumet, Kewpie Cover 20.00
Ceresota 15.00
Czechoslovakian Pastries, 1957, 106 Pages 4.00
Fanny Farmer, 1906 .... 15.00
Frugal Housewife Cookbook, 1833 .... 35.00
Granite Iron Ware, Copyright 1887 .... 85.00
Jack & Mary Jell-O, 1937 .... 10.00
Jewel Stove, Soft Covered 3.00
Keen Kutter ....10.00 To 15.00
Knox Gelatine, Dainty Desserts For Dainty People, 1924 .... 4.00
Majestic Stoves, C.1900 .... 12.00
Memtha–Col, Mammy On Cover 6.50
Miss Parlo's, 1881 .... 15.00
Moxie 18.00
Naturopathic, Vegetarian, 72 Pages, Advertising 24.00
New Dr.Price 3.00
New Perfection, 1916 .... 5.00
Pillsbury, 1941 .... 6.00
Rumford, Wheat Girl Cover, 1909 .... 8.00
White House, 1912 .... 49.50
White House, Ziemann & Gillette, Copyright 1887–1915 .... 25.00

Cookie jars with brightly painted designs or amusing figural shapes
became popular in the mid-1930s. Many companies made them and
collectors search for cookie jars either by design or by maker's name.
Listed here are examples by the less common makers. Major factories
are listed under their own names in other sections of the book.

COOKIE JAR, ABC, Cookie Truck 22.00
ABC, Donkey & Cart 33.00
Alice In Wonderland 55.00
Aunt Jemima ....100.00 To 150.00
Baby Elephant With Sailor Hat, Marked San Juan, 12 In. 20.00
Bear, Beer 55.00
Bear, Hamm's 45.00
Bear, Kraft, Regal China 69.00

Bear, Turnabout .... 28.00 To 50.00
Birdhouse 60.00
Black Amethyst, Covered, Hand Painted Flowers 48.50
Black Chef, Pearl China 125.00
Bobwhite, Red & White, Lid .... 15.00 To 45.00
Bunny, Pink Flower 17.00
Cat, American Bisque 22.50
Cat, Black, Siamese 35.00
Cat, Gold & Floral Design 35.00
Chef, National Silver .... 50.00 To 55.00
Chef, Red Hat, Mustache, Maurice Of Cal., 1976, Large 20.00
Chick With Tam 30.00
Chinese Man, Long Coat, Yellow 30.00
Churn Boy 30.00
Cinderella's Pumpkin 36.00
Clown, Metlox 20.00
Clown, Shawnee 50.00
Clown, USA 15.00
Coffeepot 14.00
Cookstove, Black 25.00
Cow, Twin Winton 25.00
Crocodile 40.00
Dad's Cookies, Glass 65.00
Davy Crockett, Brush 65.00
Dog, In Basket 25.00
Dutch Boy, American Bisque 15.00
Dutch Boy, Striped Pants 38.00
Dutch Girl, Great Northern 50.00
Ear Of Corn, Stanfordware 25.00
Elephant With Baby Bonnet 35.00
Elephant, Bisque, American 15.00
Elf, Advertising, Keebler 42.00
Elsie The Cow, Bordens 65.00
Floral, Brown, Stoneware, Marcrest 10.00
Goldilocks, White 70.00
Happy Face 16.00
Hippopotamus Fishing 20.00
Hollow Tree, Keebler 52.00
Horse, Circus, Black 50.00
Horse, Circus, Dog On Back, 10 In. 35.00
House, Dark 32.50
Howdy Doody 150.00
Joe And Donald, Turnabout 45.00
Kitten On Beehive 30.00
Kittens, Green Basket Weave Base 20.00
Lamb On Basket 15.00
Little Red Riding Hood, Napco 50.00
Locomotive, Gold 55.00
Majorette Head 50.00
Mammy & Chef, Brown Face, Green Apron, Blue Pants, Pair 175.00
Mammy, Braxton 68.00
Mammy, Lid In Belly 40.00
Mesie, Metlox 40.00
Mickey And Minnie, Turnabout 50.00
Mickey Mouse, With Birthday Cake 56.00
Monk, Thou Shalt Not Steal, Crystal .... 20.00 To 33.00
Muffets, Ernie 22.00
Mugsy 50.00
Old King Cole 95.00
Old Shoe, Brush 35.00
Oscar The Grouch 35.00
Peek-A-Boo, Vantellingen .... 250.00 To 350.00
Peter Pan, Brush 75.00
Pinocchio 55.00

Pluto And Dumbo, Turnabout ....25.00 To 50.00
Popeye 225.00
Poppy, Red Glass 30.00
Pumpkin, W24, Brush 35.00
Pup, Advertising, KenL Ration 38.00
Puppy, American Bisque 12.00
Quaker Oats, Regal China ....49.00 To 75.00
Rabbit In Hat 12.00
Rabbit With Carrot 40.00
Raggedy Ann & Andy, Tin 15.00
Raised Cookies On Jar 15.00
Red Apple, Large 17.50
Ring For Cookies, American Bisque 40.00
Santa Claus 65.00
Squirrel, Twin Winton 19.00
Strawberry, Holiday Art 45.00
Sylvester Chasing Tweety, Orange Top, 5 In. 25.00
Tea Kettle, Black, Wire Bail, Japan 9.50
Teddy Bear, Holding Pink Flower, Yellow Bow On Back ....20.00 To 35.00
Teddy Bear, Red Bow At Neck, Marked Wetlex USA 15.00
Teddy Bear, Red Bow At Neck, Metlox USA 20.00
Thumper 40.00
Toastem Bear, Kraft 60.00
Topo Gigio 45.00
Truck, American, Bisque 25.00
Turtle, Butterfly On Lid ....20.00 To 21.00
Tweetie Bird 30.00
W.C.Fields ....50.00 To 75.00
Windmill 42.00
Winnie The Pig, USA 30.00
Yogi Bear 55.00

COORS
U.S.A.

Coors ware was made by a pottery in Golden, Colorado, owned by the Coors Beverage Company. It was produced from the turn of the century until the pottery was destroyed by fire in the 1930s. The name "Coors" is marked on the back.

COORS, Bowl, Rosebud, Ivory, Small 8.50
Bowl, Rosebud, White, 6 In. 20.00
Bowl, Rosebud, Yellow, 6 In. 10.00
Casserole, Bean Pot, Covered, Burgundy 20.00
Coffeepot 45.00
Cookie Jar, Green, Covered 25.00
Cookie Jar, Rosebud, Tab Handles, Covered 35.00
Custard Cup 5.00
Mortar & Pestle 12.00
Mug, Advertising, Miniature, 1 1/2 In. 6.00
Pie Holder 12.50
Pitcher, Batter, Rosebud 25.00
Plate, Rosebud, Orange, 9 In. 15.00
Salt & Pepper, Yellow 23.00
Teapot, Rosebud 75.00
Vase, Colorado, 6 In., Pair 35.00
Vase, Greek Key, Blue, 5 In. 28.00
Vase, Monk, Laugh/Cry, Orange, 5 In., Pair 50.00
Vase, Orange, Lined In Turquoise, Top Handle, Marked 1939, 5 In. 35.00
Vase, White, Lined In Green, Ring Handles, Marked, 8 In. 35.00

Don't wash ivory. The yellow color is preferred and white ivory has a much lower value.

COPELAND SPODE ENGLAND

Josiah Spode established a pottery at Stoke–on–Trent, England, in 1770. In 1833, the firm was purchased by William Copeland and Thomas Garrett and the firm mark was changed. In 1847, Copeland became the sole owner and the mark changed again. W. T. Copeland & Sons continued until a 1976 merger when it became Royal Worcester Spode. Pieces are listed in this book under the name that appears in the mark. Copeland Spode, Copeland, and Royal Worcester have separate listings.

COPELAND SPODE, Coffeepot, Jasperware, Blue, White, Hunting Scene, 10 1/2 In. ...	135.00
Coffeepot, Jasperware, Dancing Maiden, 8 1/2 In.	85.00
Holder, Toast, With Underplate	35.00
Pitcher, Jasperware, Drinking Scene, Grapes & Vines	45.00
Pitcher, Jasperware, Football Scene, Blue & White	38.00
Plate, Dinner, Magenta, Bird Design, Gold Border	40.00
Teapot, Raised Dancing Hours Figures, Marked, 4 1/2 In.	89.00
COPELAND, Candleholder, Dancing Lady, Garret, 8 In.	295.00
Figurine, Spring, Parian, 1850, 10 In.	115.00 To 125.00
Pitcher, Churchill, Commemorative, 6 3/4 In.	150.00
Plate, Turkey, 10 1/2 In.	80.00

COPPER LUSTER, see Luster, Copper

Utilitarian items, such as teakettles and cooking pans, have been handcrafted from copper in America since the days of the early colonists. Copper became a popular metal with the Arts and Crafts makers of the early 1900s and decorative pieces such as bookends and desk sets were made.

COPPER, Ashtray, Gustav Stickley, Signed, 6 3/4 In.	160.00
Basin, Side Handle, Tin Lined, 13 X 5 In.	72.00
Bed Warmer, 18th Century, Pierced Lid With Shield, Star, 54 In.	125.00
Bed Warmer, Brass, Maple Handle	240.00
Bed Warmer, Tong Handle	295.00
Boiler, 1 In.Lip At Bottom To Fit Wooden Stove, Polished & Coated	75.00
Bowl, Dated 1832, Cyrillic Inscription, Russian, 9 1/4 In.	65.00
Bowl, Hammered, Wooden Stand, Dark Patina, Preston, 3 X 5 In.	11.00
Bowl, Nut, 3 Applied Knob Feet, 3 1/2 X 7 In.	225.00
Box, Stamp, Hammered, Signed Gustav Stickley	210.00
Box, Tobacco, Dutch, Oval, 1880, 3 1/2 X 2 X 1 1/2 In.	85.00
Bucket, Handle, Keswick, England, 1800, 15 In.	85.00
Candlestick, Applied Wire Scrolls, Disc Base, 14 1/2 In.	125.00
Chamberstick, Gustav Stickley, Removable Bobeche, 1905, 9 In.	425.00
Chamberstick, Hammered, Gustav Stickley, Logo, Signed, C.1910, 9 In.	250.00
Chamberstick, Russian, Hallmark, 4 1/4 In.	125.00
Coffee Set, Heinrichs, Paris, 4 Piece	55.00
Coffeepot, Warmer, Porcelain Base, Tilting, Copper	225.00
Crumber, Incised Flower, Riveted Handle, Scraper, 8 X 9 In.	125.00
Dish, Chafing, Terra Cotta, Wooden Knob, Covered, 15 1/2 In.	250.00
Flask, Powder Flask, Mass.Arms Co., Chicopee Falls, Embossed, 4 In.	95.00
Funnel, Strainer, Mechanical	42.50
Jar, Dovetailed, Handle, Old Patina, 7 1/8 In.	40.00
Jardiniere, Russian, Dovetailed	65.00
Jug, Milking, Hold Flowers	90.00
Kettle, 25 In.Diam.	90.00
Kettle, Candy Maker's, Double Handle	150.00
Lantern, Gustav Stickley, Tinted Amber Glass, 1912, 22 X 12 In.	1700.00
Mailbox, Hammered, Hinged, Covered, 13 X 9 1/4 X 3 1/4 In.	49.50

COPPER, MOLD, see also Kitchen, Mold

Mold, Food, Fruit, Tin	90.00
Mold, Swirl	110.00
Mug, Zinc Lining, Double Handle, 1800s	50.00
Pan, Child's, Brass Handle	25.00
Pitcher, Hammered, Avon, 3 1/2 In.	16.50
Pitcher, Hammered, Snake Handle, 19th Century, Turkish, 16 In.	65.00

Coralene, Pitcher, Water,
Blue Satin, Wheeling

Pitcher, J.S.& S., 12 1/2 In.	20.00
Plaque, Cocker Spaniel, Square, 3 3/4 In.	22.00
Plaque, Gustav Stickley, 4 Raised Buttons, Signed, 14 In.	625.00
Plaque, Seahorses & Waves, Stone Eyes, Storer, Dated 1909, 14 In.	1500.00
Plaque, Wall, Gustav Stickley, 4 Stylized Floral Buds, 1905, 20 In.	3100.00
Pot, 3 Legs, 4 1/4 X 4 In.	13.00
Pot, Ring Handle On Lid, Handmade, European, 9 X 8 1/2 In.	145.00
Sconce, Brass, 2 Candles, Bobeches, Stickley Bros., 15 X 10 In.	412.50
Sconce, Hammered, 10 X 2 7/8 In., Pair	38.50
Sconce, Wall, Gustav Stickley, Oval Form, 14 X 6 1/2 In.	800.00
Shade, Hanging, Stylized Cutout Design, Screening, 9 1/2 X 7 In.	88.00
Spatula, 1 Piece, Hold For Hanging, 10 1/2 In.	95.00
Spittoon, Lady's, Bees In Relief On Top, Signed Edward Hueck	75.00
Still, Handmade, 18 X 9 In.	75.00
Sugar & Creamer, Hallmark	45.00
Sugar Shaker, Pierced Brass Top, 9 In.	44.00
Sugar Shaker, Slant Sided, Pierced Brass Screw Top, 9 In.	44.00
Teakettle, American, Gooseneck Spout, Dovetailed Rim	135.00
Teakettle, Brass Finial On Lid, Dovetailed, 11 1/2 In.	180.00
Teakettle, Flat Bail, Brass Finial, 4 Qt.	175.00
Teakettle, Gooseneck Spout, Brass Handle & Finial, 11 1/2 In.	55.00
Teakettle, Gooseneck Spout, Hand Stamped G.T.Rissler, 6 3/4 In.	245.00
Teakettle, Gooseneck Spout, Hinged Flap, 11 1/4 In.	95.00
Teakettle, Gooseneck Spout, Marked J.Kidd, Swivel Handle, 12 In.	385.00
Teakettle, Gooseneck, Flap, Konrad Jonsson, Strengnas, 8 1/4 In.	65.00
Teakettle, Hand Seamed, Dovetailed Joints, Acorn Finial, Signed	155.00
Teakettle, Lid, Gooseneck Spout, Flap, Dovetailed, 6 1/2 In.	100.00
Teakettle, Turned Wooden Swing Handle, C.1850, 3 X 3 In.	125.00
Tray, Eagle Design, Round, 22 In.	135.00
Tray, Enameled Stylized Floral Design, Art Crafts Shop, 6 In.Diam.	88.00
Tray, Hammered, Brass Handles, Gustav Stickley, 1910, 17 3/4 X 12 In.	200.00
Tray, Hammered, Craftsmen, Laguna Beach, 14 In.	110.00
Tray, Pen, Hammered, Hubbard	25.00
Tray, Russian, Hallmark, Handles, 16 In.	125.00
Trivet, Hammered, Blue Glass Band, Signed J.Burdick 1908, 5 3/4 In.	210.00
Urn, Brass Stylized Bird Finial, Ring Handles, Covered, 25 In.	80.00
Vase, Bud, Hanging, Incised Design, Coil Holder, 2 In.	50.00
Vase, Bud, Triangular, Scalloped Edge, Riveted, 6 1/2 In.	50.00
Vase, Enameled Girl, French, C.1900, 6 In.	350.00
Vase, Figural, 4 Petal Flower, Hammered, 5 In.	25.00
Vase, Gustav Stickley, 2 Strap Handles, Wide Mouth, 1912, 5 X 8 In.	70.00
Vase, Hammered, Russian, 17 In.	85.00

Vat, Cheese Maker's, Wisconsin, 54 X 30 In. 350.00
Warmer, 3–Part, Bakelite Handles, Chase 48.00

Coralene glass was made by firing many small colored beads on the
outside of glassware. It was made in many patterns in the United
States and Europe in the 1880s. Reproductions are made today.

CORALENE, Bowl, Yellow Beads, Magenta To White Ground, Crimped Edge 895.00
Ewer, 5 1/2 In. 150.00
CORALENE, JAPANESE, see Japanese Coralene
Lamp, Fairy, Brass Stand, Yellow Tulip Shade, 7 1/4 In. 60.00
Pitcher, Tankard Shape, Gold Beading, Blue Iris, Marked, 4 In. 200.00
Pitcher, Water, Blue Satin, Wheeling ....*Illus* 600.00
Tankard, 4 3/4 In. 150.00
Vase, Beading In Design Of Star & Flowers Overall, 11 In. 650.00
Vase, Branches & Flowers, Patent Mark, Ovoid, 10 In. 275.00
Vase, Brown, Floral, Ruffled, Gold Handles, Patent Mark, 5 1/2 In. 195.00
Vase, Cocoa Ground, Yellow Green Beading, Jap.Pat.Mark, 5 In. 189.00
Vase, Fisherwomen At Seaside, Ribbon Handles, 12 1/2 In. 250.00
Vase, Gold Beading, Handles, 8 1/2 In. 245.00
Vase, Green Ground, Cobalt & Gold Trim, Flowers, 8 1/2 In. 310.00
Vase, Pale Yellow, Greens, Pat.Mark, 6 1/2 In. 165.00
Vase, Peachblow, 5 In. 250.00
Vase, Pink Roses, Gold & Caramel Ground, 5 In. 120.00
Vase, Pink Shaded To White, Art Glass, Bulbous, Square Rim, 5 In. 125.00
Vase, Seaweed Pattern, High Satin, 7 1/2 In. 130.00
Vase, Star Pattern, Enameled Dot Top Rim, 2 5/8 X 5 1/2 In. 425.00
Vase, Wheat Pattern, White Lining, 3 1/8 X 6 1/4 In. 450.00
Vase, Wisteria, Beaded, Signed, 8 3/4 In. 110.00

X   *The Cordey China Company was founded in 1942 by Boleslaw Cybis*
in Trenton, New Jersey. The firm produced gift shop items.
Production stopped in 1950 and Cybis Porcelains was founded.

CORDEY, Ashtray, Signed 45.00
Bottle, Cologne, No.7024 ....50.00 To 60.00
Box, Bluebirds & Pink Flowers, Round, 9 In. 125.00
Box, Curved Lid With Oriental Lady In Relief, 4 In. 38.00
Bust, Man & Lady, No.5034 & No.5029, Pair 85.00
Bust, Russian Peasant, No.103, 15 1/4 In. 195.00
Cornucopia, Applied Leaves & Roses, Gold Trim, 6 In., Pair 45.00
Figurine, Ballerina, No.4101, 10 In. 175.00
Figurine, Colonial Dandy & His Lady, Lace Trim, 10 1/2 In., Pair 150.00
Figurine, Colonial Girl & Boy, 16 In., Pair 125.00
Figurine, Dancing Ballerina, No.4101, Signed, 10 3/4 In. 225.00
Figurine, Gentleman, Aristocratic, No.4153, Lace, Signed, 13 1/2 In. 155.00
Figurine, Girl, With Basket, Gathering Fruit In Skirt, No.304, 16 In. 75.00
Figurine, Grape Harvester, Marked No.305, 16 1/4 In. 85.00
Figurine, Lady, Basket Of Grapes, 16 In. 195.00
Figurine, Lady, No.5054, 9 1/2 In. 50.00
Figurine, Lamb, Base, No.6025 ....117.00 To 125.00
Figurine, Lamb, With Flowers, 8 In. 125.00
Figurine, Man & Lady, Green & Pink Clothing, No.301, 16 In., Pair 150.00
Figurine, Man, Frock Coat, Lady, Fancy Dress, Upswept Hair, 8 In., Pair 150.00
Figurine, Peasant, Russian, 15 In. 195.00
Figurine, Victorian Man & Woman, 15 1/2 In., Pair 185.00
Lamp, Figural, Junior Prom Girl, No.5001, Shade 37.00
Lamp, Figural, Man, No.5041, Base, Electric, 11 In. 90.00
Shelf, Wall, Yellow Flowers, Pair 115.00
Torso, Woman's, Lace, Signed, 6 3/4 In. 75.00

There has been a need for a corkscrew since the first bottle was sealed
with a cork, probably in the seventeenth century. Today collectors
search for the early, unusual patented examples or the figural
corkscrews of recent years.

CORKSCREW, Alligator Shape, Horn, Carved 175.00

American Tucker Patent 715.00
Anheuser – Busch, In Bottle, Williamson, Newark, N.J., Dated 1897 .... 25.00
Brown & White Legs 245.00
Bull's Head 33.00
C.Birkhofer Brewing Co., Minneapolis, Minn., Wooden Handle 38.00
Cheshire Cat Handle, Iron, C.1870, 5 In. 110.00
Daisy, Burley & Co., Bar Mount, Chicago 1895 .... 195.00
Erotic Male & Female 165.00
Horn Handle 12.00
Ivory & Sterling Silver, American 365.00
Kissing Doves, Metal 15.00
Legs, German 50.00
Lemp Beer, Bullet 23.00
Old Snifter, With Removable Hat 55.00
Saratoga Victoria Natural Water, Wall Mount 165.00
Schlitz 5.00
Scrimshaw Handle, American 240.00
Spider Eating A Fly 77.00
Sterling Silver Roundlet, Tiffany 195.00
Stockings, Blue & White 285.00
T–Screw, With Pipe Tamper Ends, 18th Century 465.00
Waiter 28.00
Waiter, Head With Attached Corkscrew, Pulls Out Of Body, Wooden 55.00
Wine Taster's, French 155.00
With Can Opener, King, Iron, 1892 .... 10.00

*Coronation cups have been made since the 1800s. Pottery or glass with
a picture of the monarch and date have been souvenirs for many
coronations. The pieces that mention King Edward VIII, the king who
was never crowned, are not rare; and collectors should be sure to
check values before buying.*

CORONATION, see also Commemorative
CORONATION, Ashtray, Elizabeth II, Royal Blue Jasper, 1953 .... 50.00
Badge, Edward VIII, Enameled, 1937 .... 6.00
Book, Coloring, 18 Pages, 1953, 11 X 14 In. 18.00
Button, Elizabeth, 1953 .... 9.00
Card, Playing, King George V, Dated 1911, Box 18.00
Creamer, Edward VII & Alexandra, 1902, Porcelain, 4 1/2 In. 65.00
Cup & Saucer, George V, Mary 65.00
Cup, Elizabeth II, Paneled Foot, 1953 .... 45.00
Dish, Edward VIII, Square, 4 In. 45.00
Mug, Edward VIII 32.00
Mug, Elizabeth, 4 In. 20.00
Mug, King George & Queen Elizabeth, 1937, 3 In. 20.00
Mug, King George, Queen Mary, 1911 .... 55.00
Paperweight, Queen Elizabeth II 325.00
Plate, Edward VIII, 6 In. 18.00
Plate, Edward VIII, 1937 .... 22.00
Plate, Elizabeth II, 9 In. 15.00
Plate, Elizabeth II, Coat Of Arms, 10 In. 25.00
Plate, Elizabeth, Burleigh, Gold Border, 1953, 10 1/2 In. 25.00
Spoon, Edward VII, 1902 .... 20.00
Sugar, Edward VIII, Blue & White Jasper, Dipped, 1937 .... 85.00
Tray, King George, Torquay Incised, 1937, 5 In. 25.00
Trivet, Elizabeth II, Phoenix 18.00

*Cosmos is a pressed milk glass pattern with colored flowers made
from 1894 to 1915 by the Consolidated Lamp and Glass Company.
Tablewares and lamps were made. A few pieces were also made of
clear glass with painted decorations.*

COSMOS, Bottle, Cologne, Original Stopper 135.00
Butter, Covered 65.00
Butter, Covered, Pink Band ....130.00 To 225.00

Decanter, Stopper, 9 1/2 In., Pair 200.00
Pitcher & 4 Tumblers 268.50
Pitcher, Water, Pink Band, 8 1/2 X 7 In. 165.00
Salt & Pepper, Pink Band, Original Tops 140.00
Spooner, Pink Band 200.00
Sugar & Creamer, Covered, & Spooner, 3 Piece 85.00
Sugar, Covered, Pink Band 200.00
Tumbler, Pink Band ....45.00 To 75.00
Water Set, Pitcher & 4 Tumblers ....*Illus* 275.00
Water Set, Pitcher & 6 Tumblers, Pink Band, 7 Piece 600.00
    COUNTRY STORE, see Store

Linen or wool coverlets were made during the nineteenth century.
Most of the coverlets date from 1800 to 1850. Four types were made:
the double woven, jacquard, summer and winter, and overshot.

COVERLET, Birds In Design, Blue & White, 64 X 84 In. 185.00
Blue & White, 2 Piece Overshot, 70 X 80 In. 90.00
Blue, Gold, & Natural White, 68 X 87 In., 2 Piece 175.00
Boutonne Style, Blue Medallions, Wool, Cotton, 77 X 95 In. 125.00
Double Weave, Blue, White, & Brick Red Design, 70 X 80 In. 235.00
Double Weave, Geometric Design, 72 X 84 In. 300.00
Eagles, American Flag, Washington Scene, Ohio Maker, 1850 .... 400.00
Geometric Pattern, Homespun, 1840, 64 X 83 In. 220.00
Homespun, Fringed, C.1840, 94 X 94 In. 335.00
Jacquard, 2 Piece, Double Weave, Liberty Border, S.Latourette, 1833 .... 475.00
Jacquard, 4 Rose Medallions & Stars, Peace & Plenty, 60 X 88 In. 295.00
Jacquard, Bird Border & Corners, J.& S.Slaybaugh, 66 X 80 In. 425.00
Jacquard, Birds, Roses, Sidewheel Ship Border, C.1845, 74 X 88 In. 1550.00
Jacquard, Birds, Signed, Columbia, N.A., 1838, 88 X 61 In. 750.00
Jacquard, Blue, Red, & White, 74 X 82 In. 495.00
Jacquard, Blue, White Design, Marked W & LUN, 68 X 71 In. 95.00
Jacquard, Central Birds Feeding Young, 76 X 88 In. 325.00
Jacquard, Central Medallion, Eagles In Spandrels, 82 X 86 In. 350.00
Jacquard, David Brown, C.Smellser 1844, 76 X 96 In. 400.00
Jacquard, Double Weave, Central Floral Medallion, 78 X 82 In. 200.00
Jacquard, Double Weave, Floral Design, Blue & Red, 78 X 89 In. 100.00
Jacquard, Floral Center, CH.S.Meily, 1848, 76 X 82 In. 400.00
Jacquard, Floral Medallions, P.N.Chambersburch, 1861, 79 X 80 In. ... 225.00
Jacquard, Foliage Scrolls, Building In Border, 72 X 84 In. 310.00
Jacquard, Medallion Center, Foliage & Lyre Border, 84 X 98 In. 400.00
Jacquard, Medallions, Eagle Border, Emily Covert, 1837, 70 X 96 In. ... 300.00
Jacquard, Medallions, G.Heilfbonn, Lancaster, O.1852, 68 X 94 In. 175.00
Jacquard, Medallions, Yearous, Loudonville, O., 1859, 2 Piece 100.00
Jacquard, New York, 1836, J.C.Knowles, 6 Ft. 10 In. X 7 Ft. 750.00
Jacquard, Peacocks Feeding Young, Christian Border, 80 X 94 In. 425.00
Jacquard, Red, Navy, Signed P.H.Anshutz, 84 X 84 In., 2 Piece 350.00
Jacquard, Rose Medallions, Wm.H.VanGordon, 1852, 72 X 82 In. 200.00
Jacquard, Snowflakes, Tulips, Blue, White, 1841, 100 X 80 In. 660.00
Jacquard, Star Medallions, W.Fasig, Richland Co., 70 X 90 In. 200.00
Linsey-Woolsey, Floral, Indigo, Natural, 88 X 100 In. 800.00
Lions Corners, Blue, White, Reversible, E.Wilson, 1836, 80 X 94 In. ... 800.00
Optical Pattern, 3 Piece Overshot, Indigo Blue, Brown, 88 X 98 In. 275.00
Optical Pattern, Applied Fringe, 72 X 90 In., 2 Piece 175.00
Overshot, Blue & White, 76 X 100 In. 85.00
Overshot, Blue & White, 84 X 86 In. 385.00
Overshot, Unusual Woven Border With Fringe, 100 X 100 In. 325.00
Plaid Pattern, Fringe, 72 X 84 In. 295.00
Quilted, America, C.1800, Linsey-Woolsey, 88 X 82 In. 150.00
Rooster Corners, Red, Green, Henry Oberly, Womelsdorf, 90 X 74 In. ... 600.00
Rose Design, Turkey Red, Natural, C.1849, 7 X 6 Ft. 295.00
S-Scrolls, Peacocks, Urns, Stars, Leaves, 1822, 83 X 72 In. 1430.00
Summer, Winter, American, Lydia Mullener, 1840, 80 X 98 In. 550.00
Tobacco Rust, Homespun & Wool, Full Fringe, 100 X 90 In. 650.00
White Ground, Red Bands, Star In Square, C.1885, 90 X 74 In. 425.00

Windowpane Design, Blue & White, 72 X 88 In., 2 Piece	190.00
Woven Overshot, Optical Pattern, 84 X 100 In.	125.00
Woven, Red, Green, & 2 Shades Of Blue, 78 X 86 In.	270.00

Guy Cowan made pottery in Rocky River, Ohio, a suburb of Cleveland, from 1913 to 1931. The Cowan Pottery made art pottery and wares for florists. A stylized mark with the word "Cowan" was used on most pieces. A commercial, mass–produced line was marked "Lakeware." Collectors today search for the Art Deco pieces by Guy Cowan, Viktor Schreckengost, Waylande Gregory, or Thelma Frazier Winter.

COWAN, Bowl & Figurine, Fluted, Sinz, 10 In.	150.00
Bowl, Blue Luster, Pedestal, Hexagonal, 10 1/2 In.	25.00
Bowl, Center, Blue Inside, Kneeling Nude	245.00
Bowl, Jazz, Viktor Schreckengost, C.1931, 8 X 14 In.	2550.00
Candleholder, Blue Luster, 3 In., Pair	15.00
Candleholder, Branched, Art Nouveau, Cream Glaze, Marked, 3 Candle	65.00
Candleholder, Triple, Ivory, 8 In., Pair	60.00
Candlestick, Green Matte, 4 X 4 In.	25.00
Candlestick, Seahorse	25.00
Charger, Bottle Green Glaze, Hand Turned, Pierced Back, Marked, 11 In.	33.00
Compote, Fruit, Cobalt	22.00
Console Set, Triple Candlesticks, 3 Piece	45.00
Figurine, Cockatoo, Art Deco, Aqua, 14 1/2 In., Pair ....*Illus*	450.00
Flower Frog, Nude, 6 1/2 In.	135.00
Holder, Flower, Nude, 6 In.	14.00
Lamp, Art Deco, Mottled Glaze, 8 1/2 In.	135.00
Lamp, Floor, Wrought Iron, Marble Base, Candle Socket, 62 In., Pair	120.00
Lamp, Table, 23 In.	65.00
Match Holder, Seahorse Design, Green	17.50
Sugar, Creamer, & Tray, Art Deco	28.00
Vase, Bluish Green High Glaze, 12 1/2 In.	20.00
Vase, Bulbous, Matte Green To Rose, 5 In.	50.00
Vase, Bulbous, Orange Metallic Glaze, Small	28.00
Vase, Medium Blue Shades, Over Lime, Marked, 8 1/4 In.	55.00
Vase, Orange Luster, 5 In.	20.00
Vase, Orange Metallic Glaze, 4 In.	28.00

Cracker Jack, the molasses–flavored popcorn mixture, was first made in 1896 in Chicago, Illinois. A prize was added to each box in 1912. Collectors search for the old boxes and toys and advertising materials. Many of the toys are unmarked.

CRACKER JACK, Baseball Card, 1914	20.00
Book, Paint, 1912	15.00
Book, Paint, 1917	20.00
Book, Riddle	29.00

Cosmos, Water Set,
Pitcher & 4 Tumblers

Cowan, Figurine, Cockatoo,
Art Deco, Aqua, 14 1/2 In., Pair

Cranberry Glass, Butter, Silver Plate, Cow On Lid

Cranberry Glass, Lamp, Hanging,
Hobnail, Brass Ring, 13 1/2 In.

Book, Uncle Sam's Songs	30.00
Bookmark, Bulldog	3.00
Bookmark, Dog, Tin	8.00
Bookmark, Spaniel	12.00
Candy Container, Hand Painted, Ceramic, 1948, 7 In.	65.00
Catalog, Premium	75.00
Catalog, Premium, 24 Page, Rueckhum Bros.& Ekstein	35.00
Chester, Stand Up, Tin	55.00
Doll, Sailor Outfit, 13 In.	10.00
Figurine, Smitty, Stand Up, Tin	20.00
Game, No.12	20.00
Jockey On Horse	8.50
Mystery Coin	28.00
Pencil, Wooden	15.00
Rainbow Spinner, Marked, C.1940	6.50
Roulette Wheel, Tin	25.00
Sailing Ship	8.50
Sign, Dated 1943, Paper, 27 X 60 In.	125.00
Top, Tin	20.00
Train Set, 2 Piece	25.00
Tray, Tin, Miniature, 1901	28.00
Watch, Pocket, Tin	30.00
Wheelbarrow, Tin, Litho	12.00
Whistle, Blue, Marked	15.00
Whistle, Dated 1917	7.50
Whistle, Dog, Tin, Marked	17.50
Whistle, Double, Tin	12.00

Crackle glass was originally made by the Venetians, but most of the ware found today dates from the 1800s. The glass was heated, cooled, and refired so that many small lines appeared inside the glass. It was made in many factories in the United States and Europe.

CRACKLE GLASS, Decanter, Enameled, 11 1/2 In.	35.00
Dish, Candy, Blue Lid, Yellow Base, Floral Handle, 5 In.	95.00
Pitcher, 8 3/4 In.	18.00
Pitcher, 9 In.	18.00
Vase, Blue & White, Gold Aurene Interior, 9 1/2 In.	395.00

Cranberry glass is an almost transparent yellow–red glass. It resembles the color of cranberry juice. The glass has been made in Europe and America since the Civil War. It is still being made and reproductions can fool the unwary.

CRANBERRY GLASS, see also Northwood; Rubena Verde; etc.

CRANBERRY GLASS, Basket, Clear Applied Handles, 10 In.	135.00
Basket, Clear Twisted Handle, Ruffled Rim	135.00
Basket, Crimped, Twisted Thorn Handle, Triangular, 6 In.	65.00
Basket, Vaseline Rim, Crystal Twisted Rope Handle, 6 In.	69.00
Bottle, Barber, Daisy & Fern, Opalescent	95.00
Bottle, Barber, Hobnail	155.00
Bottle, Barber, Inverted Diamond, Paneled Diamond Swirl	125.00
Bottle, Barber, Inverted Thumbprint, Ring Neck	125.00
Bowl, Bubble Lattice, 7 In.	75.00
Bowl, Enamel Design, C.1875, 10 1/2 In.	300.00
Bowl, Hobnail, White Ruffled Rim	150.00
Bucket, Whipped Cream, Crackled, Silver Plated Handle	150.00
Butter, Cover, Royal Oak	110.00
Butter, Silver Plate, Cow On Lid ....*Illus*	275.00
Celery, Swirl, Satin Finish	90.00
Centerpiece, Tulip Vase, Bowl, Bohemian, 21 1/2 In., 2 Piece	770.00
Compote, Clear Knobbed Stem, Red Foot, Polished Pontil	95.00
Compote, Melon Sectioned, 5 3/4 X 3 3/4 In.	98.00
Cruet, Clear Handle, Faceted Stopper, 5 3/4 In.	97.00
Cruet, Faceted Stopper, Craquelle, Clear Handle	155.00
Cruet, Inverted Thumbprint, Fluted Lip, Ball Stopper, 6 In.	65.00
Cruet, Wine, Optic Rib, Clear Stopper, 11 In.	150.00
Decanter, Enamel Floral, Amber Berry Prunt, Footed, 10 In.	180.00
Decanter, Stopper, Grapes, Hobstars, Fans, Clear, 15 In.	135.00
Epergne, 19th Century, Central Lily, Trumpet Base, 20 In.	275.00
Epergne, Applied Art Glass Design, 2 Side Trumpeters	350.00
Epergne, Lily, Teardop Shape, Crimped, 5 1/4 In.	18.00
Epergne, Single, Crystal Rigaree, 12 In.	135.00
Ewer, Floral, Clear Handle, 8 1/2 X 4 1/4 In.	165.00
Finger Bowl, Paneled, Square Top	98.00
Finger Bowl, Polished Pontil	58.00
Flagon, Enameled Cavalier, Clear Base, Pewter Lid, 16 In.	230.00
Glass, Liqueur, Cranberry Bowl, Gold Panels, 4 In.	40.00
Holder, Cigarette, Sterling Silver Overlay, Signed, 6 In.	95.00
Jam, Silver Lid, Threaded	100.00
Jar, Pickle, Opalene Floral, Silver Plate Stand, Fork, 9 In.	100.00
Jar, Wheeling Drape, Covered, Finial	125.00
Lamp, Finger, Seaweed, Clear Grip, Opalescent Cranberry	275.00
Lamp, Hanging, Hall, Swirl	75.00
Lamp, Hanging, Hobnail, Brass Ring, 13 1/2 In. ....*Illus*	425.00
Lamp, Hanging, Prisms, 13 In.	800.00
Lamp, Miniature	400.00
Muffineer, Drape Pattern, Hallmarked Top, 6 1/2 In.	78.00
Pickle Castor, Cone, Pairpoint Silver Frame, Footed, Tongs	285.00
Pitcher, Bulbous, Clear Applied Handle, Gold Trim, 6 In.	98.00
Pitcher, Bulbous, Reeded Handle, Enamel Flowers, Gold Band	115.00
Pitcher, Bull's-Eye, Square Top	245.00
Pitcher, Clear Handle, Inverted Thumbprint, 5 In.	120.00
Pitcher, Diamond–Quilted, Figure Of Girl, 9 In.	295.00
Pitcher, Enameled Floral, Clear Handle, 9 In.	110.00
Pitcher, Enameled Forget–Me–Nots, Swirl, 9 In.	175.00
Pitcher, Fluted, Enameled Dot Band, 7 In.	85.00
Pitcher, Hobnail, Clear Applied Handle, 5 1/4 In.	65.00
Pitcher, Inverted Thumbprint, Square Top, Handle, 5 7/8 In.	98.00
Pitcher, Melon Ribbed, Diamond Design, Squat, 5 X 5 In.	85.00
Pitcher, Opalescent Swirl, 10 In.	275.00
Pitcher, Reverse Swirl, Square Mouth, 6 1/2 In.	65.00
Pitcher, Tankard, Inverted Thumbprint, Handle, 8 1/2 In.	295.00
Pitcher, Water, Chrysanthemum Base, Swirl	500.00
Pitcher, Water, Coin Spot Pattern, Ruffled, Clear Handle	175.00
Pitcher, Water, Leaf, Umbrella, Yellow Cased	360.00
Pitcher, Water, Optic Effect, Clear Handle, 12 3/4 In.	285.00
Plate, 8 In.	28.00

Rose Bowl, Polka Dot 85.00
Salt, Blue & White Flowers, Green Leaves, Gold, 1 3/4 In. 65.00
Salt, Clear & Vaseline, Silver Plate Holder, 3 X 2 In. 100.00
Salt, Hallmarked Holder, Clear Rigaree, 4 1/2 In. 85.00
Salt, Master, White Threading, Scalloped, 2 3/4 In. 58.00
Salt, Rib, 2 Rows Clear Rigaree, Footed Holder, 1 1/2 In. 98.00
Salt, Scalloped, Ribbed, 2 3/4 In. 38.00
Salt, Silver Plate Holder, 3 X 2 1/2 In. 88.00
Shade, Diamond–Quilted 155.00
Shade, Hall, Hobnail, Late 19th Century, 6 1/2 X 13 In. 90.00
Shade, Swirled Opalescent Stripes 60.00
Shade, Swirled Windows, Opalescent Stripes, 2 X 5 1/2 In. 60.00
Sugar & Creamer, Floral, Silver Plate Holder 185.00
Sugar & Creamer, Reverse 44, Open, Flashed 55.00
Sugar Shaker, Cut Panels, Silver Plate Top, 5 1/4 In. 50.00
Sugar Shaker, Ribbed Opalescent Lattice 90.00
Sugar, Covered, Guttate 125.00
Syrup, 19th Century, Silver Plate Spout, Handle, 6 3/4 In. 250.00
Tray, Dresser, Violets & Ribbons 30.00
Tumble–Up, Inverted Thumbprint, Blown 105.00
Tumbler, Allover Enameled Floral, Miniature, 2 In. 25.00
Tumbler, Allover Enameled, Multicolor, Gold, 3 3/4 In. 55.00
Tumbler, Coin Spot, Set Of 5 .... 100.00
Tumbler, Floral, Gold, 4 In. 38.00
Tumbler, Inverted Thumbprint 30.00
Tumbler, Leaf, Umbrella 50.00
Tumbler, Thumbprint 35.00
Vase, Enameled Flowers, Gold, C.1890, 8 1/2 In., Pair 195.00
Vase, Enameled Flowers, Shoulder & Base, Gold Trim, 11 In. 145.00
Vase, Enameled Lilies–Of–The–Valley, Gold Leaves, 8 In. 70.00
Vase, Enameled, Gilt, Silver Scrolls, Bulbous, C.1890, 8 In. 100.00
Vase, Fan Top, Clear Ruffle, Wishbone Feet, 10 3/4 In. 198.00
Vase, Fan Top, Footed, Gold Panel, Enameled, 10 3/4 In. 198.00
Vase, Flowers, Gold Band & Trim, Footed, 8 3/4 In., Pair 345.00
Vase, Gold Bands, White Outlined Gold Leaves, 9 In., Pair 350.00
Vase, Gold Design, Forget–Me–Nots, Gold Scroll Band, 11 In. 145.00
Vase, Gold Sanded Floral, White Enameled, 10 In., Pair 295.00
Vase, Gold Scrolls, Bands, 2 5/8 In., Pair 60.00
Vase, Pedestal Foot, Gold Leaves, Enameled Dot, 5 In. 55.00
Vase, Portrait, Woman, Art Nouveau, Gold, Bouck, 6 In. 195.00
Vase, Rigaree Rim, Enameled Flowers, 12 1/2 In., Pair 595.00
Vase, Roses With Buds, Enameled Design, 8 3/8 In., Pair 275.00
Vase, Ruffled Top, Optic Design, 5 1/4 In., Pair 145.00
Vase, Trough, Crystal Thorn Feet, 2 3/4 X 2 1/4 X 7 In. 175.00
Vase, White & Lavender Flower, 11 1/4 In. 195.00
Vase, White Overlay, Floriform Mouth, C.1880, 16 In., Pair 935.00
Water Set, Daisy & Fern, 7 Piece 550.00
Water Set, Floral Enamel Design, 19th Century, 6 Piece 290.00
Water Set, Hobnail, 7 Piece 250.00
Water Set, Inverted Thumbprint, Bulbous, 5 Piece 195.00
Wine, Swirl, Clear Footed, Stemmed 25.00
Wine, Threaded Rim, Cut Ovals, Clear Stem, Set Of 12 .... 400.00

Creamware, or queensware, was developed by Josiah Wedgwood about 1765. It is a cream–colored earthenware that has been copied by many factories.

CREAMWARE, see also Wedgwood
CREAMWARE, Bowl, Mixing, White Banded, Round, 6 X 13 In. 60.00
Bowl, White Center Band, Graduated, Set Of 4 .... 160.00
Cup Plate, Purple Luster Floral Design, 3 1/4 In. 45.00
Inkstand, Seated Spaniel, Pounce Box, Paw Feet, 7 1/2 X 8 1/2 In. 225.00
Mug, Blue Sponging, Gilt Rim, 3 5/8 In. 85.00
Pitcher, Floral, Blue, Brown, Green & Tan, 4 1/2 In. 15.00
Pitcher, Red Transfer, Ladies All Saying, Pink Luster, 3 1/8 In. 95.00

Pitcher, Vintage Design, Pink & Purple Luster, Enameling, 8 In.	40.00
Planter, Cameo, 8 In.Diam.	75.00
Plate, Embossed Feather Rim, Brown Sponging, Green Dots, 9 In.	60.00
Tumbler, Gaudy Floral Enameling, Purple Luster Rim, 2 5/8 In.	35.00

Crown Derby is the nickname given to the works of the Royal Crown Derby factory, which began working in England in 1859. An earlier and more famous English Derby factory existed from 1750 to 1848. The two factories were not related. Most of the porcelain found today with the Derby mark is the work of the later Derby factory.

CROWN DERBY, see also Derby; Royal Crown Derby

CROWN DERBY, Canister, Coffee, Gold Trim, 1800–30	100.00
Cup & Saucer, Gold Trim, 1800–30	150.00
Dish, Leaf Shape, Interior Cornflower, 1785–80, 3 1/2 In., Pair	70.00
Figurine, 4 Seasons, Putto, C.1775, 6 To 6 3/8 In., Set Of 4	522.00
Figurine, Falstaff, C.1820, Crossed Batons, 13 1/4 In.	275.00
Figurine, Leopard, Seated, Salmon Coat, Tree, C.1760, 4 In.	660.00
Figurine, Mansion House Dwarf, 1875, Marked, 7 & 6 1/2 In., Pair	1760.00
Fork, Porcelain Handle, Blue, White Oriental Scene, Box, 6	65.00
Group, Mythological, Incised Mark, 1775–80, 7 5/8 In.	440.00
Plate, Dinner, King's Pattern, C.1825, Marked, 10 1/8 In., 18 Pc.	440.00
Plate, Ivory With Brown Roses, 6 In.	12.50
Plate, Persian Design, Gold On Pink	250.00
Tazza, New Imari, Knopped Stem, Petal Base, 5 X 9 1/2 In., Pair	500.00
Tureen, Sauce, Covered, Stand, Japan, Quatrefoil, C.1815, 2 Piece	495.00

Crown Milano glass was made by Frederick Shirley about 1890. It had a plain biscuit color with a satin finish. It was decorated with flowers and often had large gold scrolls.

CROWN MILANO, Box, Jewel, Cream To Brown, Glass, Gold Floral, Mark, 7 1/2 In.	425.00
Carafe, Roses, Blue Flowers Allover, Stopper, Marked, 10 In.	300.00
Cracker Jar, Silver Plate Bail, Lid, Signed, Nasturtium, 8 In.	545.00
Cup & Saucer, Handleless, Burmese, Gold Floral, Mt.Washington	1200.00
Decanter, Enameled Roses, Gold Scrolled Neck, Stopper, 10 In.	1250.00
Ewer, Geometric Patterns, Enameled, Multicolor, 13 In.	1750.00
Ewer, Shepherd Tending Flock, Brook, Country Church	2450.00
Jam Jar, Forget–Me–Nots, Silver Plate Lid, Bail, Signed, 7 In.	385.00
Jar, Holly Pattern, Enameled, Cream, Mt.Washington, 3 3/4 In.	375.00
Jar, Sweetmeat	675.00
Urn, Old Blossoms, Foliage, Crown Lid, Signed, 16 1/2 In.	2950.00
Vase, Applied Scroll Handles, Gold Enamel Acorns, 8 1/4 In.	1150.00
Vase, Canada Geese, Cream, Handles, Mt.Washington, 11 1/2 In.	3025.00
Vase, Colonial Children Scene, Rococo, Marked, 13 3/4 In.	1100.00
Vase, Ducks On Front & Reverse, Frank Guba, 10 1/2 In.	2250.00
Vase, Earth Tone Enameled, Geometric Pattern, Handles, 8 In.	745.00
Vase, Mallards Flying, Signed Frank Guba, 17 In.	3750.00
Vase, Scroll Handles, Gold Border, Acorns, Label, 8 1/4 In.	1150.00
Vase, Square, Scroll Handles, Gold Acorn, 8 1/4 In.	985.00

CROWN TUSCAN, see Cambridge

Cruets of glass or porcelain were made to hold vinegar, oil, and other condiments. They were especially popular during Victorian times but have been made in a variety of styles since the eighteenth century.

CRUET, Chintz, Fostoria, Stopper	32.00 To 57.50
Chocolate Glass, Leaf Bracket, Stopper, Greentown	165.00
Colony, Fostoria, Stopper	25.00
Cord Drapery, Glass	11.00
Custard Glass, Georgia Gem, Orange Stopper, Green	225.00
Hanover, Glass	20.00
Harvard, Glass	18.00
Heart With Thumbprint, Glass	65.00
Intaglio, Glass, Blue	90.00
Jeweled Heart, Glass, Green	75.00
Plain Scalloped Panel, Green	*Color* 85.00

Pressed Optic, Vaseline ....*Color*   85.00
Royal Ivy, Rubena 275.00

There are many marks that include the words "CT Germany." The first mark with those words was used by a company in Altwasser, Germany, in 1845. The initials stand for C. Thielsch, a partner in the firm. The Hutschenreuther firm took over the company in 1918 and continued to use the "CT."

C.T.

CT GERMANY, Chocolate Set, Brown To White, Pink Roses, Hand Painted, 1855 ......   450.00
Plate, Portrait, Woman, Signed, 7 In. 35.00

Cup plates are small glass or china plates that held the cup while a gentleman of the mid–nineteenth century drank his coffee or tea from the saucer. The most famous cup plates were made of glass at the Boston and Sandwich factory located in Sandwich, Massachusetts. There have been many new glass cup plates made in recent years for sale to the gift shops or the limited edition collectors. These are similar to the old plates but can be identified. The numbers refer to "American Glass Cup Plates" by Ruth Webb Lee and James H. Rose.

CUP PLATE, Adams, Men In Boat, Pink, 4 In. 30.00
  Benjamin Franklin, Sandwich Glass 25.00
  Black Transfer, Vincenne, Staffordshire, 4 1/4 In. 17.50
  Blue Transfer, Country Estate, Cows, Staffordshire, 3 5/8 In. 30.00
  Cadmus 50.00
  Gaudy Dutch, Grape, 3 1/2 In. ....160.00 To 425.00
  George Washington, Sandwich Glass 25.00
  Ironstone, Jenny Lind, Signed J.T.Close, 4 1/8 In. 85.00
  Lacy, 3 7/16 In. 75.00
  Lacy, Cobalt Blue, 3 5/16 In. 75.00
  Lacy, Flint, Sandwich Glass 35.00
  Lafayette & Washington, Wood, 3 3/4 In. 320.00
  Landing Of Lafayette, Staffordshire, Clews, 4 3/8 In. 350.00
  Landing Of Lafayette, Staffordshire, Clews, Oval, 3 1/2 In. 480.00
  Orange Spray Of Tulips, Blue Border, Leeds, 4 1/2 In. 440.00
  Roman Rosette, 3 9/16 In. 6.00
  Sweetheart, Cobalt 175.00
  Three Weeks After The Wedding Day, Sandwich Glass 25.00
  Valentine 35.00
  Victoria, Lacy, Fire Polished, 3 1/2 In. 40.00
  Washington, Star Border, Sandwich Glass, Clear 35.00

Currier & Ives made the famous American lithographs marked with their name from 1857 to 1907. The mark used on the print included the street address in New York City, and it is possible to date the year of the original issue from this information. Earlier prints were made by N. Currier and use that name from 1835 to 1847. Many reprints of the Currier or Currier & Ives prints have been made and it is the undamaged, untrimmed originals that are priced here unless otherwise noted. Many collectors also buy the insurance calendars that were based on the old prints. The words large, small, or medium folio refer to size.

CURRIER & IVES, American Farmyard Evening 695.00
  American Fruit Piece, 1850, 20 X 27 In. 1495.00
  American Homestead, 8 X 12 1/2 In., Set Of 4 ....   1300.00
  American Homestead, Autumn, Framed, 12 1/4 X 16 1/4 In. 225.00
  Assassination Of President Lincoln, 7 X 12 In. 60.00
  Bower Of Roses, Young Lady Reclining, 12 X 20 In. 170.00
  Brook Trout, Just Caught, 11 X 16 In. 330.00
  Celebrated Trotting Mares Maud S., Aldine, 20 3/4 X 33 In. 1050.00
  City Of New York & Environs, Framed, 8 X 13 In. 250.00
  Comical Picnic, Black, 1881, 12 X 13 1/4 In. 155.00
  Day Before Marriage, Mahogany Frame, 12 5/8 X 16 5/8 In. 40.00
  Death Of General Lyon, 8 X 12 In. 60.00

Death Of Lt.Col.Henry Clay, Jr., 8 X 12 In. 35.00
Dr.Franklin's Experiment, June 1752, 8 X 12 In. 625.00
Drive Through The Highlands, 10 X 14 In. 495.00
Farmer's Friends, 8 X 12 In. 150.00
Fruits, Summer Varieties, Cross Corner Frame, 14 X 16 In. 75.00
General Franz Sigel, Civil War, 1862, Framed, 11 X 8 In. 50.00
General John C.Breckenridge, Black & White, 8 X 12 In. 30.00
General Sheraton, 16 X 18 In. 50.00
General Shields, Battle Of Winchester, Va., 1862, 7 X 12 In. 160.00
George Washington, Uniform, Mahogany Frame, 18 X 20 In. 125.00
Great Fire At Boston, Nov.9th & 10th, 1872, 8 X 12 In. 219.00
Grottoes Of The Sea, 7 X 12 In. 80.00
Henry Clay, Matted & Framed, 16 1/2 X 20 3/4 In. 55.00
Home In The Country, 12 X 17 In. 295.00
Home In The Wilderness, 8 X 12 In. 595.00
Home On The Mississippi, 8 X 12 In. 295.00
John J.Dwyer, Champion Of America, Medium 265.00
Life In The Woods, Framed, 26 3/4 X 54 1/2 In. 2100.00
Life On Prairie, Trapper's Defense, 1862, 18 1/2 X 27 In. 3100.00
Lightning Express Leaving Junction, Framed, 20 X 17 In. 600.00
Little Cherubs, Framed, 11 X 8 In. 75.00
Mammoth Iron Steamship, Great Eastern, 10 X 14 1/2 In. 30.00
Maple Sugaring, 8 X 12 In. 550.00
Mountain Spring, West Point, Cozzen's Dock, 11 X 15 In. 445.00
My Little Playfellow, 11 X 8 In. 35.00
Pair Of Children, 16 X 20 In. 300.00
Penobscot, 20 X 34 In. 630.00
Print, Group Of Wild Flowers, Walnut Frame, 10 X 14 In. 52.00
Print, Little Brother, 11 X 8 In. 28.00
Print, Little Jennie, 3/4 Length 28.00
Print, Little Sister, 11 X 8 In. 28.00
Queen Of The Turf, Maud S., Large Folio, 18 X 28 In. 675.00
Rarus, Horse & Sulky, Rosewood Frame, 13 7/8 X 17 7/8 In. 165.00
Rival Roses, Small 85.00
Rush For The Heat, Winter Sleigh Race, 3/4 View 470.00
Scene Of The City Of Chicago, 20 X 32 In. 1250.00
Scenery Of The Upper Mississippi, Framed, 8 X 12 In. 135.00
Sports' Who Lost Their 'Tin, 16 X 20 In. 100.00
Storming Of Fort Donelson, Tenn., 12 X 8 In. 170.00
The Happy Home, Framed, 11 X 8 In. 45.00
Two Little Fraid Cats, 15 X 11 In. 75.00
Western Farmer's Home, 8 X 12 In. 250.00
Who Will Love Me?, Bust View, Small 50.00
Woodlands In Winter, Small 395.00

Custard glass is an opaque glass sometimes called "buttermilk glass."
It was first made in the United States after 1886 at La Belle
Glass Works, Bridgeport, Ohio. It is being reproduced.

CUSTARD GLASS, see also Maize
CUSTARD GLASS, Adonis, Berry Bowl, Master, Canary 12.00
Alaska, Spooner, Blue Opalescent 40.00
Argonaut Shell, Banana Boat 190.00
Argonaut Shell, Bowl, Signed, 3 X 5 In. 65.00
Argonaut Shell, Creamer, Gold & Enamel 125.00
Argonaut Shell, Cruet, Stopper, Gold 325.00
Argonaut Shell, Pitcher, Water, Gold 325.00
Argonaut Shell, Sugar & Creamer, Covered 40.00
Argonaut Shell, Tumbler 25.00
Argonaut Shell, Water Set, 6 Piece 675.00
Beaded Swag, Goblet, Souvenir, Dow City, Iowa, Heisey 75.00
Chrysanthemum Sprig, Berry Bowl, Master, Gold 175.00
Chrysanthemum Sprig, Butter, Covered ....175.00 To 210.00
Chrysanthemum Sprig, Celery ....595.00 To 650.00
Chrysanthemum Sprig, Compote, Jelly, Gold, Enameled 95.00

Chrysanthemum Sprig, Creamer, Gold & Enamel 110.00
Chrysanthemum Sprig, Cruet, Original Stopper ....275.00 To 295.00
Chrysanthemum Sprig, Salt & Pepper 185.00
Chrysanthemum Sprig, Spooner, Blue, Northwood 225.00
Chrysanthemum Sprig, Spooner, Green, Pink, Gold, Northwood 140.00
Chrysanthemum Sprig, Sugar, Creamer, Spooner, Blue, Northwood 1000.00
Chrysanthemum Sprig, Table Set, 4 Piece 595.00
Chrysanthemum Sprig, Toothpick, Blue ....300.00 To 340.00
Chrysanthemum Sprig, Tumbler ....40.00 To 49.00
Croesus, Cruet, Green, Small 100.00
Diamond With Peg, Napkin Ring 150.00
Diamond With Peg, Shot Glass, Pink Rose, Souvenir 40.00
Diamond With Peg, Tumbler ....40.00 To 48.00
Geneva, Banana Boat, Green, Red Paint, Footed, 11 X 7 1/2 In. 150.00
Geneva, Berry Bowl, Master, Red & Green 125.00
Geneva, Spooner ....45.00 To 65.00
Geneva, Syrup 250.00
Georgia Gem, Berry Bowl, Master ....65.00 To 75.00
Georgia Gem, Berry Bowl, Small ....25.00 To 28.00
Georgia Gem, Butter, Enameled Flowers 250.00
Georgia Gem, Pitcher & 4 Tumblers, Enameled Leaves 435.00
Grape & Cable, Bowl, Deep Orange, Nutmeg 195.00
Grape & Cable, Cookie Jar 495.00
Grape & Cable, Sugar & Creamer, Breakfast, Nutmeg 125.00
Grape & Cable, Tray, Dresser, Nutmeg 145.00
Grape & Cable, Tumbler, Nutmeg Stain, Northwood 65.00
Grape & Gothic Arches, Creamer, Pearlized 90.00
Grape & Gothic Arches, Spooner 85.00
Grape Arbor, Vase, Nutmeg, 5 In. 40.00
Heart & Thumbprint, Sugar 780.00
Honeycomb, Wine 55.00
Intaglio, Berry Set, Gold Trim, Blue, 6 Piece 395.00
Intaglio, Butter, Blue Design, Covered 245.00
Intaglio, Cruet, Crystal Stopper 145.00
Intaglio, Salt & Pepper 140.00
Intaglio, Table Set, 4 Piece ....450.00 To 490.00
Intaglio, Tumbler, Green & Gold 55.00
Inverted Fan & Feather, Saltshaker, Original Top, Gold Trim 175.00
Inverted Fan & Feather, Table Set 800.00
    IVORINA VERDE, see Winged Scroll
Jackson, Berry Bowl, Master 325.00
Jackson, Salt & Pepper, Enameled 125.00
Jackson, Water Set, Goofus Gold, 7 Piece 335.00
    LITTLE GEM, see also Georgia Gem
Little Gem, Table Set, Enameled Flowers, 4 Piece ....375.00 To 425.00
Little Gem, Toothpick 35.00
Lotus & Grape, Nappy, Handles, 6 1/2 In. 35.00
Louis XV, Berry Bowl, Master, Northwood 140.00
Louis XV, Butter, Covered ....110.00 To 170.00
Louis XV, Creamer, Gold ....55.00 To 75.00
Louis XV, Cruet, Clear Stopper ....65.00 To 105.00
Louis XV, Salt & Pepper, Gold Trim 155.00
Louis XV, Sauce, Gold Trim, Oval, Set Of 4 .... 80.00
Louis XV, Spooner ....45.00 To 65.00
Louis XV, Sugar ....85.00 To 95.00
Louis XV, Tumbler, Gold 50.00
Louis XV, Water Set, 4 Piece 285.00
    MAIZE, see Maize category
Maple Leaf, Creamer ....60.00 To 85.00
Maple Leaf, Salt & Pepper 425.00
Maple Leaf, Sugar, Covered 110.00
Maple Leaf, Table Set, Original Paint, 4 Piece 465.00
Maple Leaf, Tumbler, Pair 150.00
Northwood Fan, Creamer 75.00

Never put anything hot in a cut-glass bowl. It was not made to withstand heat and will crack.

Early plates often have no rim on the bottom.

Cut Glass, Basket, Hobstar & Cane

Northwood Fan, Spooner	75.00
Peacock At Urn, Dish, Ice Cream	55.00 To 65.00
Pineapple & Fan, Tankard, Pink, Heisey	125.00
Poppy, Dish, Pickle, Nutmeg	47.50
Ring & Beads, Mug, Souvenir, Sedgwick, Maine, 3 In.	28.00
Ring Band, Butter, Roses, Gold Trim, Covered, Heisey	220.00
Ring Band, Creamer, Gold Trim, Heisey	80.00
Singing Bird, Berry Bowl, Dome Footed	75.00
Vermont, Celery, Design	165.00
Vermont, Spooner	65.00
Vermont, Toothpick	65.00
Wild Bouquet, Cruet, Orange Stopper, Gold & Enamel	510.00
Winged Scroll, Butter, Covered	70.00 To 135.00
Winged Scroll, Toothpick, Heisey	105.00 To 140.00

Cut glass has been made since ancient times, but the large majority of the pieces now for sale date from the brilliant period of glass design, 1880 to 1905. These pieces have elaborate geometric designs with a deep miter cut.

CUT GLASS, see also listings under factory name

CUT GLASS, Basket, Hobstar & Cane ......*Illus*	975.00
Basket, Queen's Lace Pattern, 9 1/2 X 9 1/2 In.	175.00
Bell, Deep Cut, Pinwheel, Notched Handle, 5 In.	295.00
Bottle Condiment, Cut Finial Stopper, Comet & Caning, 4 1/2 In.	95.00
Bottle, Cologne, Green To Crystal, Dated 1905, London, 8 3/8 In.	165.00
Bottle, Cologne, Green To Crystal, Silver Top Dated 1905, England	175.00
Bottle, Cologne, Lavender To Crystal, Cut Stopper, 9 In.	125.00
Bottle, Water, Fluted Neck, Bull's–Eyes, Ovals, Star Bottom	34.00
Bowl, Brilliant Cut, Nassau Pattern, J.Hoare & Co., 8 In.	250.00
Bowl, Expanding Star Pattern, Flat Bottom, 8 In.	200.00
Bowl, Flat Star Variations, Central Hobstar, C.1900, 8 3/4 In.	100.00
Bowl, Harvard & Devonshire, 10 X 5 In.	290.00
Bowl, Hobnail Heart, Sawtooth Scalloped Rim, T.B.Clark, 7 X 8 In.	175.00
Bowl, Nassau Pattern, Signed J.Hoare & Co., 8 In.	200.00
Bowl, Notched Cane, Button, Hobstar, 10 X 6 1/2 X 4 In.	120.00
Bowl, Overall Cutting, Fans, & Cane, Hobstar Base, 9 X 3 3/4 In.	140.00
Bowl, Pinwheel, Pineapple, Hobstar Bottom, 8 X 3 1/2 In.	130.00
Bowl, Sawtooth Rim, Pinwheels, Pineapple, Fan, 9 X 4 In.	150.00
Bowl, Scalloped Rim, Hobstar Base, Cane Pattern & Fans, 9 In.	145.00
Box, Dresser, Covered, Intaglio, Engraved Florals, Birds, 6 In.	125.00
Box, Geometric Design, Hobstars & Diamonds At Sides, 5 1/2 In.	250.00
Box, Handkerchief, Hinged Lid, Intaglio Flowers, Square, 7 In.	325.00
Butter Tub, Crosscut, Buttons, Sunflower, Tab Handles, 4 1/2 In.	165.00
Candlestick, Faceted Knop, Baluster Shape, Sinclaire, 14 1/8 In.	550.00

Candlestick, Notched Prism, Flute, Teardrop Stem, 9 1/4 In., Pair	310.00
Candy Dish, Divided, Handles, Bevel, Prisms, & Hobstars, 9 1/2 In.	135.00
Candy, Covered, Stars, Thumbprint Fluting, Star Bottom	85.00
Celery, Allover Cut, Hobstar, Diamond & Prism, 10 X 4 1/2 In.	125.00
Celery, Boat Shape, Cut To Cane Pattern, Hobs, Flowers, 10 X 3 In.	70.00
Celery, Cane Pattern, Boat Shape, Scalloped, 13 1/2 X 4 1/2 In.	125.00
Celery, Cane Pattern, Intaglio Flowers, 10 1/2 In.	70.00
Centerpiece, Boat Shape, Handles, Waterford Type, 4 X 8 3/4 In.	200.00
Champagne, Allover Cut, Monarch Pattern, Signed Hoare, Set Of 4	395.00
Chandelier, Empire, Chains, Graduated Tiers, Electrified, 40 In.	1210.00
Chandelier, Gas, Rock Crystal, Teardrop, Florets, French, 32 In.	1320.00
Charger, Scalloped, Alternating Hobstar, Pinwheel, C.1880, 12 In.	200.00
Compote, Brilliant, Bull's–Eye, Rayed Base, Pedestal, 6 X 9 In.	185.00
Compote, Bull's–Eye, Star Center, Rayed, Footed, 6 X 3 1/2 In.	60.00
Compote, English Georgian, C.1830, 9 1/2 In.	290.00
Compote, Fruit, Stem, Hobstars, Fans, Caning, & Strawberry, 13 In.	395.00
Compote, Hobstar & Sawtooth, Rayed Base, Clarke, 7 3/4 X 6 In.	300.00
Compote, Hobstars, Diamond, Teardrop In Stem, 12 In.	250.00
Compote, Pedestal, Bevel & Prism Stem, 7 3/4 In.	150.00
Compote, Sawtooth Scalloped Rim, Hobstars, Notched Prisms, 9 In.	275.00
Compote, Sawtooth, Starburst, Scalloped, 11 1/2 X 7 In.	175.00
Compote, Scalloped Rim, Flared Base, Hobstars, 9 In.	375.00
Cruet, Diamonds, Fan, & Crosshatch, Trefoil Spout, 7 In.	65.00
Cruet, Notched Handle, Intaglio Floral, Rayed Base, 11 1/4 In.	155.00
Cruet, Pinwheel Design, Stopper, 7 In.	55.00
Cruet, Pyramid, 24 Star Base, 7 1/2 In.	40.00
Cruet, Tankard, Lapidary Cut Stopper, 12 In.	145.00
Cruet, Whiskey Jug, Applied Facet Hobstar & Fan, Stopper, 5 In.	100.00
Decanter, Bowling Pin Shape, Harvard & Cosmos Pattern, Stopper	375.00
Decanter, Double Row Of Harvard Cut, Rayed Base, 11 1/4 In.	225.00
Decanter, Green Cut To Clear, Owl, Sterling Silver Mounted, 9 In.	750.00
Decanter, Hobstars, Fans, Hobstar Stopper, 12 In.	195.00
Decanter, Pineapple & Fan, Notched Stem, Stopper, 10 1/2 In.	50.00
Decanter, Silver Frame & Handle, German, Crown Mark, 12 In.	325.00
Decanter, Stopper, Rayed Base, Cranberry Stained, 12 3/4 In., Pr.	325.00
Decanter, Wine, Harvard & Floral, Handle, Rayed Base, 11 1/2 In.	195.00
Dish, Cheese & Cracker, 2 Tier, Elevated Center, 9 1/2 In.	140.00
Dish, Hobstar, Triangular, Salesman Sample, Miniature	85.00
Dish, Shell, Palm Leaf Fan Pattern, 6 In.	275.00
Dresser Jar, Sterling Silver Top, 14 Panels, Gorham, 2 3/4 In.	85.00
Ewer, Footed, Silver Plate Hinged Top, Hobnails, 1900, 12 1/2 In.	190.00
Flask, Lady's, Panel Cutting, Notched Prism Between, Silver Top	100.00
Flask, Lady's, Repousse Sterling Silver Top, Geometric Cutting	95.00
Flower Center, Brilliant Cut, Signed Strauss, 10 X 7 1/2 In.	575.00
Girondoles, 4 Column, Scroll Arms, Regency Brass, 1820, 19 In., Pr.	475.00
Goblet, Dorflinger, Allover Cut, 6 1/2 In., Set Of 5	750.00
Goblet, Wine, Star & Pineapple Design, Scottish, Set Of 12	90.00
Holder, String, Notched Prism, Gorham Sterling Silver Top	185.00
Humidor, Vertical Hobstars, Zipper Pattern, 4 1/2 X 9 In.	475.00
Inkwell, Beveled, Waffle Base, Dominick & Haff, Square, 2 In.	85.00
Inkwell, Domed Repousse Sterling Silver Lid, Rayed Base, 2 In.	100.00
Inkwell, Step Cut, Hinged Lid, Clear, 3 7/8 X 3 3/8 In.	150.00
Inkwell, Strawberry & Fan, Dome Shape, Floral Sterling Lid	95.00
Inkwell, Waffle Cut Base, Sterling Silver Lid, Square, 2 In.	80.00
Jar, Dresser, Allover Intaglio Grapes & Leaves, Sterling Lid	135.00
Jug, Whiskey, Cranberry To Clear, Matching Stopper, American	485.00
Knife Rest, Notched Panel Stem, Faceted Ball Ends, 5 1/2 In.	40.00
Knife Rest, Notched Prism, Star Ends, 1 3/4 X 5 1/4 In.	35.00
Lamp, Green, Crystal Prisms, 10 1/2 In., Pair	275.00
Lamp, Rose Pattern, Mushroom Shade, Etched, 17 1/2 In.	1150.00
Lamp, Stags & Castles, Marble & Brass Stand, Signed, Ruby, Pair	635.00
Mayonnaise, Underplate, Butterfly Pattern, Crescent Cut Rims	125.00
Muffineer, Allover Brilliant Cut, Sterling Silver Top	190.00
Muffineer, Geometric Cutting, Rayed Bottom	110.00

Nappy, Cane & Fan Cuttings, Star Design, Hawkes, 5 1/8 In. 140.00
Orange Bowl, Corinthian Pattern, Pedestal, Oval, 10 X 7 In. 750.00
Paste Pot, Sterling Silver Cover 48.00
Perfume Bottle, Chatelaine, Hinged Sterling Top, 2 1/2 In. 55.00
Perfume Bottle, Cylindrical, Notched Ribbing, Brass Top 68.00
Perfume Bottle, Green To Clear, 3 In. 165.00
Perfume Bottle, Lay Down, Cane, Silver Cap, Blue, 7 1/2 In. 325.00
Pitcher, Champagne, Hobstar Base, Cut Flowers, 13 1/2 In. 325.00
Pitcher, Champagne, Hobstar Base, Flower, Leaves, 13 In. 175.00
Pitcher, Champagne, Starburst, Notched Prisms, C.1900, 11 1/4 In. 160.00
Pitcher, Claret, Silver Plated Top & Handle, England, 11 3/4 In. 100.00
Pitcher, Floral Cutting, Notched Handle & Spout, 9 In. 75.00
Pitcher, Hobstar & Hobstar With Fan, American, 8 1/4 In. 140.00
Pitcher, Hobstar Bottom, Brilliant, Bulbous, 10 X 9 1/2 In. 600.00
Pitcher, Pinwheel & Starburst Design, 10 In. 135.00
Pitcher, Pinwheel Pattern, Triple Notched Handle, 13 In. 495.00
Pitcher, Pinwheels, Hobstar, & Diamond, Star Base, 9 In. 130.00
Pitcher, Step Cut Spout, Double Notched, 9 In. 250.00
Pitcher, Strawberry Diamond Band, Sterling Silver, Frosted, 7 In. 42.00
Pitcher, Tankard, Rayed Base, Hobstar, Notched Handle, 9 In. 95.00
Pitcher, Water, Blue, Ruffled, Enameled, 8 Tumblers 185.00
Pitcher, Water, Hobstar Alternating With Cane, American, 8 In. 275.00
Pitcher, Water, Step Cut Spout, Brilliant, Rayed Base, 8 1/2 In 95.00
Pitcher, Wine, Silver Plate Collar, Panel Cut, 12 1/2 In. 235.00
Plate, Cheese, Dome Cover, Comet, Hobstar, & Zipper, Sawtooth Edge 475.00
Plate, Empress Eugenie Pattern, 6 1/4 In. 225.00
Plate, Heart Shape, Hobstar & Fan Design, 7 X 6 In. ....315.00 To 325.00
Plate, Pinwheels, Crosshatch, Star Bottom, 6 1/2 In. 10.00
Platter, Ice Cream, Hobstars, Blown Blank, Marked, 17 1/2 X 10 In. 675.00
Pokal, Lid, Red, White Candy Stripe Stem, Swags, Bubbles, 17 In. 300.00
Powder Jar, Embossed Sterling Silver Cover, Pineapple & Fan 145.00
Powder Jar, Nouveau Sterling Silver Top, Hobstars 125.00
Powder Jar, Russian & Crosshatch Buttons, Footed 250.00
Powder Jar, Sterling Silver Lid, Alvin, Monogram 75.00
Powder Jar, Sterling Silver Top, Name Cora 55.00
Powder Jar, Sterling Silver Top, Pineapple & Fan, 4 1/2 In. 135.00
Puff Box, Hinged, Overall Intaglio Flowers & Leaves, 5 1/4 In. 135.00
Punch Bowl, Hobstar & Sawtooth, 13 3/4 In. ....*Illus* 575.00
Punch Bowl, Hobstar, Notched Prism, C.1880, 14 In., 1 Piece 850.00
Punch Bowl, Pedestal, Lobed Rim, Pinwheel & Hobstars, 12 In. 400.00
Punch Bowl, Sawtooth, Diamond Crosshatched, 1880–1920, 13 1/4 In. 825.00
Punch Bowl, Scalloped, Hobstars Within Miters, 12 In. 300.00

Never put hot glass in cold water or cold glass in hot water. The temperature change can crack the glass.

Cut Glass, Punch Bowl, Hobstar
& Sawtooth, 13 3/4 In.

Relish, Hobstars, Vertical Notched Prism Middle, 8 X 4 3/4 In. 110.00
Relish, Triple Square Pattern, Signed Clarke 55.00
Rose Bowl, Floral & Cane, 3 Footed, Large 50.00
Rose Bowl, Hobstars, Diamond Banding, 6 In. 140.00
Rose Bowl, Pedestal, Hobstar, Crosshatch, & Fan, 8 1/4 In. 675.00
Sachet Jar, Sterling Hinged Lid, Beading, Stopper, 3 3/8 In. 90.00
Salt & Pepper, Faceted, Amber, 4 3/4 In., Pair 67.50
Salt & Pepper, Harvard Pattern, Cornflower 22.50
Salt & Pepper, Paneled, Cobalt, Glass Top, 2 1/2 In. 35.00
Salt, Ruffled Sterling Silver Rim 45.00
Sconce, Rococo, Gilt Bronze, Prism Tiers, Electrified, 27 In., Pair 2090.00
Shade, Mushroom Dome, Hobstars, Signed Hoare, 7 1/2 In. 150.00
Shade, Mushroom, Hobstars In Diamonds, Signed Hoare, 7 1/2 In. 225.00
Spittoon, Lady's, Hobnail, Strawberry Diamond, Sterling Rim 395.00
Spooner, Cut To Pieces, Hobstars, Fan, 4 1/2 In. 85.00
Sugar & Creamer, Allover Hobstars, Notched Handle 425.00
Sugar & Creamer, Allover Notched Prism, Embossed Sterling Rim 195.00
Sugar & Creamer, Gravy Boat Shape, Allover Cut, Notched Handles 135.00
Sugar & Creamer, Harvard & Floral, Notched Handle, Brilliant 75.00
Sugar & Creamer, Hobstars, Fan, Hobstar Bottom, Cut Handles 125.00
Sugar Shaker, Sterling Silver Top, Initialed, 1900, 5 1/2 In. 50.00
Syrup, Brilliant Cut, Sterling Silver Top 125.00
Syrup, Hobstars, Beaded Silver Plate Handle & Top 165.00
Syrup, Notched Prisms, Ornate Lid & Handle 110.00
Syrup, Thumbprint & Fans, Silver Plate Top, 7 1/4 In. 145.00
Tankard, Harvard Cut, Brilliant, 1880-90, 12 In. 675.00
Toothpick, Diamond Fan, Crosscut Hatching, Rayed Base 95.00
Toothpick, Faceted Base, Strawberry & Fan Top 18.00
Tray, Deep Brilliant Hobstar Cut, 5 1/2 In. 39.00
Tray, Dresser, Russian & Crosshatch Buttons, 11 1/4 X 6 1/4 In. 295.00
Tray, Ice Cream, Brilliant, 14 In. 235.00
Tray, Ice Cream, Hobstars, Strawberry, Hobnail Diamond, 12 X 8 In. 95.00
Tray, Iris, Signed Hawkes Graphic, 1904, 6 1/2 In. 165.00
Tray, Russian Pattern, Handles, Cut Buttons, 15 In. 575.00
Tray, Serving, Checkered Diamonds & Fans, 9 1/2 X 6 1/2 In. 155.00
Tumbler, Etched, Wheeling Glass, Dated 1804 .... 75.00
Tumbler, Hobstar Center, Diamond Fan, Rayed Bottom, Set Of 6 .... 150.00
Tumbler, Old Colony, Dorflinger, 3 3/4 In. 125.00
Tumbler, Pinwheel & Hobstars, Set Of 6 .... 140.00
Tumbler, Pinwheels, Diamond, & Fan, Star Base, Set Of 6 .... 170.00
Tumbler, Sterling Silver Mount, Diamond, Motto, Russia, 4 In., Pair 300.00
Tumbler, Water, Hobstars, Fans 25.00
Vase, American, Footed, 15 In. 395.00
Vase, Chalice, Tazza Cut, Flowers, Leaves, Hobstar Foot, 8 In. 175.00
Vase, Corset Shape, Colonna Pattern, Libbey, 7 1/2 In. 125.00
Vase, Corset Shape, Cosmos & Caning, Cut Edge, 12 In. 80.00
Vase, Corset Shape, Strawberry & Honeycomb, Gorham Rim, 5 1/2 In. 65.00
Vase, Corset Shape, Zipper, Fan, Strawberry Diamond, 9 In. 260.00
Vase, Cut Prisms, Herringbone, Hobstars, Rayed Base, 15 In. 280.00
Vase, Etched, Dorflinger, Signed Kalana Art 425.00
Vase, Geometric Cutting, Teardrop In Stem, Hobstar Foot, 12 In. 375.00
Vase, Hobstar Foot, Bull's-Eye, Eye Stopper, Signed Clarke, 14 In. 375.00
Vase, Hobstar Foot, Fan Shape, Hobstars & Diamonds, 9 X 9 In. 325.00
Vase, Red Cut To Apple Green, 8 In. 450.00
Vase, Sawtooth Edge, Tulip Shape, Notched Cutting, C.1890, 18 In. 850.00
Vase, Scalloped Notched Rim, Wheel Cut Scrolling, 7 1/4 In. 98.00
Vase, Swag & Diamond Rim, Etched, Stem, Bohemian, 16 In., Pair 325.00
Vase, Thistle & Bull's-Eye, Fan & Diamond, 16 In. 250.00
Vase, Trumpet, Footed, Lattice, Fans, Star Bottom, 12 1/2 In. 98.00
Vase, Trumpet, Hobstar Flanked By Crosshatch, American, 15 In. 130.00
Vase, Trumpet, Hobstars, Notched Flutes, Faceted Knob, Base, 14 In. 185.00
Vase, Trumpet, Ray Starred Base, Amber, 12 In. 75.00
Vase, Trumpet, Scalloped Foot, Step Cutting, Hobstars, 10 1/4 In. 325.00
Vase, White To Cranberry, Gold Design, 16 In. 575.00

Vase, Zipper Pattern, 15 In. 200.00
Water Set, Honeycomb Handle, C.1920, Pitcher 7 In., 7 Piece 325.00
Water Set, Sunburst & Fan, Ruby To Clear, 7 Piece 149.00
Whiskey Set, Fluted Ovals, Handle, Neck Ring, Teardrop, Set Of 4 .... 375.00
Wine, Duchess, Green To Clear, Marked Sinclaire, 6 Piece 270.00
Wine, Flute, Knob Stem, Flashed Fan Base, Set Of 4 .... 80.00
Wine, Waffle, Diamonds, & Fans, Notched Stem, Rayed Base 15.00

Cut velvet is a special type of art glass, made with two layers of blown glass, which shows a raised pattern. It usually had an acid finish or velvetlike texture. It was made by many glass factories during the late Victorian years.

CUT VELVET, Punch Cup, Pink 85.00
Vase, Diamond–Quilted, Brass Arranger Top, Iridescent, 5 In. 145.00

CYBIS

Boleslaw Cybis came to the United States from Poland in 1939. He started making porcelains on Long Island, New York, in 1940. He moved to Trenton, New Jersey, in 1942 to work for Cordey and started his own Cybis Porcelains in 1950. The firm is still working.

CYBIS, Bust, Eros, 9 1/2 In. 175.00
Bust, Eros, Wooden Base, 6 1/2 In. 295.00
Bust, Funny Face Boy Clown 325.00
Figurine, Alexander The Elephant, Pink Saddle 275.00
Figurine, Baby Owl 50.00
Figurine, Carousel Ticonderoga Horse 875.00
Figurine, Cat, With Blue Ribbon 350.00
Figurine, Chantilly Kitten 135.00
Figurine, Cybele 575.00
Figurine, Desdemona, No.90 .... 1575.00
Figurine, Elizabeth Anne 200.00
Figurine, Funny Face Clown 250.00
Figurine, Little Princess 450.00
Figurine, Madonna Queen Of Angels, White 175.00
Figurine, Melissa 450.00
Figurine, Owl 55.00
Figurine, Peter Pan, 1958 .... 350.00
Figurine, Pollyanna 225.00
Figurine, Priscilla 950.00
Figurine, Snail 255.00
Figurine, Springtime 450.00
Figurine, Tinkerbell, 1959 .... 750.00
Figurine, Turtle, With Frog On Back 95.00
Figurine, Wendy ....140.00 To 215.00
Figurine, Windflower 250.00
Plaque, Indian, Framed, Dated 50.00

There are some collectibles that are identified by the name of the country, not a factory mark. Anything marked "Czechoslovakia" is popular today. The name, first used as a mark after the country was formed in 1918, appears on glass and porcelain and other decorative items. The name is still used in some trademarks.

CZECHOSLOVAKIA, Basket, Art Deco, Red, White, & Blue, Pottery, 4 X 5 1/2 In. 45.00
Bottle, Oil & Vinegar, Luster, Gold Design, Pair 35.00
Box, Cigarette, Floral, 2 Ashtrays 30.00
Candy Dish, Covered, Amethyst, Grapes, 10 In. 65.00
Cigarette Holder, Nude, Opalescent, Yellow 21.00
Creamer, Character, Parrot, Color 35.00
Creamer, Chicken 15.00
Creamer, Figural, Parrot 35.00
Decanter Set, Clear To Cranberry, Gold Overlay, 9 In., Pair 750.00
Decanter Set, Cranberry To Clear, Gold, 5 Tumblers, 7 Piece 750.00
Dish, Animal, Stylized Flowers, Yellow Chick, Covered 25.00
Dish, Frosted Glass, Cameo Inset, Filigree, Footed 45.00
Egg, Easter, Sugar, Paper Scene Inside, 4 In. 7.00

Daum Nancy, Vase,   Daum Nancy, Bowl, Yellow To Green Shading, Signed, 11 3/8 In.
Floral, Multicolored,
  Signed, 11 In.

Figurine, Girl Smoking A Cigar, Evening Gown, 5 In. 35.00
Lamp, Silhouette Lady & Man, Mushroom Shade, Frosted Glass 350.00
Liqueur Set, Gold Overlay Rim & Body, Hand Painted, Set 750.00
Perfume Bottle, Purple, Atomizer, Rose & Pearl Top 150.00
Perfume Bottle, Tall Stopper, Cut 75.00
Powder Jar, Cut Glass, Amber 70.00
Stemware Service, Etched Animal & Birds Scenes, 148 Piece 2200.00
Vase, Amphora, 6 3/4 In. 40.00
Vase, Crane, Leaves, Orange, Silver Design, 9 3/4 In., Pair 35.00
Vase, Glass, Cobalt, Silver Rose Design, Ruffled Lip, 8 In. 40.00
Vase, Silver Bird, Black Amethyst, 10 1/2 In. 55.00

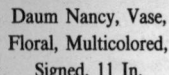

D'Argental is a mark used by the St. Louis, France, glassworks. The firm made multilayered, acid-cut cameo glass in the late nineteenth and twentieth centuries. D'Argental is the French name for the city of Munzthal, home of the glassworks. Later they made enameled etched glass. Compagnie des Cristalleries de St. Louis is still working.

D'ARGENTAL, Lamp, Sealing Wax, Signed, 7 1/4 In. 750.00
Vase, Scene Of Forest Landscape, Lake, Deer, Signed, 8 5/8 In. 975.00
Vase, Thistles & Leaves, Bulbous, Signed, 3 1/2 In. 348.00

Jean Daum started a glassworks in Nancy, France, in 1875. The company, now called "Cristalleries de Nancy," is still working. The "Daum Nancy" mark has been used in many variations. The name of the city and the artist are usually both included.

DAUM NANCY, Ashtray, Mortar & Pestle Shape, Marked 85.00
Bottle, Spirit, Strawberry Design, Metal Cup At Base, 5 3/4 In. 495.00
Bowl, 4 Sided, Folds Inward, Gold Ground, Signed, 6 X 2 1/4 In. 700.00
Bowl, Crows Flying, Purple Over White, Yellow, Marked, 7 1/2 In. 1150.00
Bowl, Summer Scene, Mountains, Blue Ground, Signed, 6 X 2 1/2 In. 875.00
Bowl, Thistle Pattern, Amber, Rim, Pinched 4 Lobes, Signed, 5 In. 350.00
Bowl, Trees, 3 Applied Feet, Signed, 6 In. 975.00
Bowl, Trefoil Top, Ferns On Bottom, 3 Curled Feet, Signed, 6 In. 650.00
Bowl, Yellow To Green Shading, Signed, 11 3/8 In. ....*Illus* 650.00
Chandelier, 4 Hanging Lights, Orange, Patina Bronze, Marked 2200.00
Cordial Set, Ribbed, Gold Trim, Signed, Round Tray, 7 Piece 250.00
Creamer, Thistles, Signed 300.00
Decanter, Cross Of Lorraine Stopper, Gold Enamel, Signed, 13 In. 2250.00
Decanter, Signed, 10 1/2 In. 225.00
Flower Holder, Spatter, Blues, Greens, Opaque, Marked, 5 X 7 In. 175.00
Lamp, Table, Green Brown, Trumpet Shape, Signed, 14 X 5 In. 3650.00
Perfume Bottle, Atomizer, Shades Of Blue, No Bulb, Marked 325.00
Perfume Bottle, Yellow Green, No Stopper, C.1900, 4 1/2 In. 300.00
Salt, Mottled Gold Ground, Flowers, Leaves, Signed, 1 1/4 X 2 In. 295.00

Lamp, Hand, Flat, Brass
Collar, Applied Handle, Blue,
4 In.

Soft Paste, Pitcher, 5 In.

Majolica, Pitcher, Made In
Japan, 5½ In.

Souvenir, Creamer, Individual,
Green, 1917, 2½ In.

Lefton, Pitcher, Lincoln, 5 In.

Fairing, Man, Lady, Checker Game, 4 × 5 In.

Political, Poster,
Coolidge, Economy,
21 × 30 In.

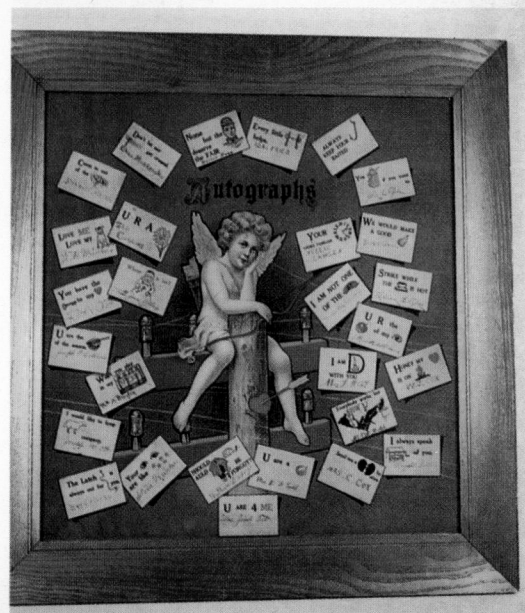

Textile, Printed Fabric,
Cupid, 26 × 26 In.

Tobacco Jar, Manila Bay & Dewey, Ohio

Buffalo Pottery,
Pitcher, Fox
Hunt, 7 In.

Furniture, Table,
Galle, 18 In.
Diameter

Candelabrum, Figures, Prisms, 22 In., Pair

Cobalt Blue, Vase, Ruffled, 6 In.

Nippon, Salt & Pepper, 2 In.

Opalescent, Shaker, Swirl,
C. 1890, Blue, 4 In.

Toy, Cow, Moos, Moves, 8 × 7 In.

Coca-Cola, Bottle, St.
Wall-Emp., Biedenharn,
Paper Label

Bottle, Figural, World's Fair, 1939,
Milk Glass

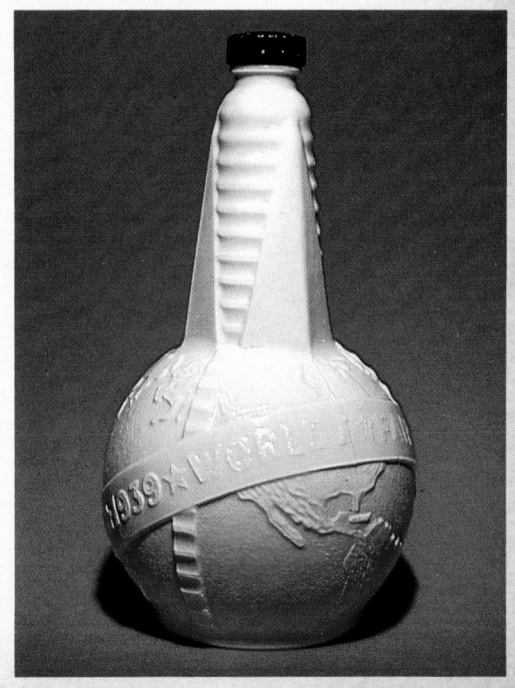

Window, Stained Glass, Boy
Leaning Over Balcony, 85 × 73 In.

Pottery, Pitcher, Parrot,
Wade-Heath, English, 1930s

Salt, Red Crocus On Green Ground, Signed, Oval 425.00
Salt, Tab Handles, Rain Scene, Pink To Green Ground, Signed 650.00
Salt, Winter Scene, Snow On Branches, Enameled Poplars, Signed 550.00
Shade, Mottled, Bronze Base, Rose Finial, Signed, 8 In. 495.00
Toothpick, Winter Scene, Marked, 2 In. 495.00
Tumbler, Blue Sky Summer Scene, Barrel Shape, 4 3/4 In. 650.00
Tumbler, Boats Scene, Barrel Shape, Signed, 4 7/8 In. 650.00
Tumbler, Late Summer Scene, Barrel Shape, Signed, 5 In. 650.00
Tumbler, Violets, Barrel Shape, Signed, 5 In. 650.00
Tumbler, Water, Barrel Shape, Landscape, Marked, Frosted White 650.00
Tumbler, White Bowl, Lilac Stem, 3 In., Set Of 4 .... 300.00
Vase, Branches On Rim, Spherical, Late 19th Century, 5 1/4 In. 225.00
Vase, Bud, Enameled Thistle Sprig, Amber, Signed, Label, 4 1/2 In. 225.00
Vase, Bud, Lily-Of-The-Valley, Sterling Silver Foot, 4 3/8 In. 150.00
Vase, Double Overlay, Iris & Leaves, Marked, 22 In. 1800.00
Vase, Dove Wing, Turquoise, Yellow, 8 In., Pair 300.00
Vase, Egg Shape, Flowers, Broken Egg Rim, Signed, 3 1/2 In. 425.00
Vase, Floral, Multicolored, Signed, 11 In. ....*Illus* 800.00
Vase, Iris, Green, Sterling Silver Scroll, XII Mark, 8 1/2 In. 825.00
Vase, Lime Green, Bubbles, Bulbous, Applied Handles, 10 X 10 In. 350.00
Vase, Lobed Base, Trapped Bubble, Deco, Signed, 6 1/4 In. 325.00
Vase, Overlay Etched, Purple Speckled Ground, Signed, 8 In. 1045.00
Vase, Scene, Signed, 12 In. 800.00
Vase, Scene, Springtime, 6 In. 485.00
Vase, Summer Scene, Blue Sky, Signed, 11 1/2 In. 1100.00
Vase, Tree Landscape, Pink Ground & Foot, Signed, 11 1/2 In. 1100.00
Vase, Winter Scene, Diamond Shape, 4 1/2 In. 475.00
Vase, Winter Scene, Oval, Gold To Yellow, 2 1/2 X 4 In. 750.00
Vase, Yellow & White, Cylindrical, Footed, Signed, 8 1/4 In. 575.00

Davenport pottery and porcelain were made at the Davenport factory in Longport, Staffordshire, England, from 1793 to 1887. Earthenwares, creamwares, porcelains, ironstone, and other ceramics were made. Most of the pieces are marked with a form of the word "Davenport."

DAVENPORT
LONGPORT
STAFFORDSHRE

DAVENPORT, Dish Set, Erica Pattern, Green Transfer, 19 Piece 375.00
Eggcup, C.1820, Pair 3600.00
Pitcher, Rural Scene, Blue & White, 6 X 7 1/2 In. 95.00

Davy Crockett, the American frontiersman, was born in 1786 and died in 1836. He became popular again in 1954 with the introduction of a television series about his life. Coonskin caps and buckskins became popular and hundreds of different Davy Crockett items were made.

DAVY CROCKETT, Belt, Leather 4.00
Bowl 10.00
Bowl, 4 3/4 In. 10.00
Bowl, Cereal ....8.00 To 9.50
Cap 7.00
Clock, Pendulum 75.00
Clock, Wall, Davy On Face & Pendulum 100.00
Cookie Jar 65.00
Cookie Jar, Full Figure 65.00
Glass, Juice, Set Of 7 .... 14.00
Hat, Coonskin 9.00
Lamp, Original Shade 35.00
Lunch Box 20.00
Medal, Sharpshooter 12.00
Mug ....5.00 To 12.50
Mug & Cereal Bowl 14.50
Mug, Fire King 12.50
Mug, Milk Glass 12.50
Night-Light 14.00
Pencil Case 18.00

Pinback	3.00 To 5.50
Pistol, Flintlock, Model Kit, Box	16.00
Pitcher, Water, 1955	35.00
Ring, Compass	8.00
Ring, Figural Head	20.00
Rule	5.00
Tray, Tin, Walt Disney, 14 1/2 X 10 1/2 In.	28.00
Tumbler	4.00 To 10.00
Wallet	8.00 To 25.00
Wristwatch	42.00

De Vez is a name found on special pieces of French cameo glass made by the Cristallerie de Pantin about 1890. Monsieur de Varreaux was the art director of the glassworks and he signed pieces "de Vez."

DE VEZ, Atomizer, Mountains, Lake, Cottage, Boat, 2 Cuttings, 8 In.	425.00
Mountain Scene, Opalescent, Signed, 10 1/2 In.	525.00
Vase, 3 Acid Cuttings, Mountain Lake, Foliage, Signed, Pink, 6 1/2 In.	595.00
Vase, Boats In Harbor Scene, Yellow To Off–White, Signed, 9 3/4 In.	650.00
Vase, Dog With Bird In Mouth, Swimming, Gold Ground, Signed, 6 In.	750.00
Vase, Frosted Gold Ground, Trees, Mountains, Signed, 9 3/4 In.	695.00
Vase, Inlet With House On Shore, Gold Ground, Signed, 12 In.	795.00
Vase, Landscape Scene Of River, 3 Cuttings, Frosted Gold, 9 3/8 In.	595.00
Vase, Sailboat, Pink Ground, Blue To Yellow Scene, Signed, 8 1/8 In.	695.00
Vase, Sailboats, Scene, Drop Down Neck, Signed, 9 5/8 In.	795.00
Vase, Scene Of Venice, Blue Cut To Yellow, Cameo, Signed, 11 3/4 In.	700.00
Vase, Stylized Birds, Tail Feathers Form Pattern, Signed, 7 1/2 In.	675.00
Vase, Swan On Lake & Background, Signed, Framed By Vine, 9 5/8 In.	850.00
Vase, Towers On Island, Branches Frame Scene, Signed, 8 1/4 In.	595.00

Decoys are carved or turned wooden copies of birds or fish. The decoy was placed in the water or propped on the shore to lure flying birds to the pond for hunters. Some decoys are handmade, some are commercial products. Today there is a group of artists making modern decoys for display, not for use in a pond.

DECOY, American Merganser Hen, Marked C.F.Spear, Wooden	6400.00
Bass, Large	230.00
Black Duck, Albert Laing	5830.00
Black Duck, C.1950, Ken Harris	175.00
Black Duck, Cork Body, Shang Wheeler	2200.00
Black Duck, Cork Body, Turned Wooden Head, Shang Wheeler	5775.00
Black Duck, Elmer Corweel, East Harwich, Mass.	3300.00
Black Duck, Harry V.Shourds, Tuckerton, New Jersey	440.00
Black Duck, Preening, Original Paint, Shang Wheeler	3300.00
Black Duck, Primitive, Tack Eyes, Repaint, Turned Head, 20 In.	55.00
Black–Bellied Plover, Chief Cuffee Of Shinnecock Reservation	440.00
Black–Bellied Plover, George Boyd	2860.00
Blue Winged Teal, Mason	3850.00
Bluebill Drake, Glass Eyes, Jasper N.Dodge 1883–94 Label, 15 1/2 In.	75.00
Bluebill Drake, Glass Eyes, Victor Animal Trap Co., 14 In., Pair	60.00
Bluebill Drake, Lead Weight & Line, Initialed T.F., 13 1/2 In.	75.00
Bluebill Drake, Stylized Carving, Glass Eyes, Old Paint, 14 1/4 In.	55.00
Bluebill Drake, Tom Schroeder, Glass Eyes, Repaint, 15 In.	175.00
Bluebill Hen, Sleep, Glass Eyes, Old Repaint, 10 1/4 In.	40.00
Bluebill, Hampbank Style, Capt.John Cook, Original Paint	110.00
Bluebill, Low Head, Downward Slanting Body, Repaint, 15 In.	35.00
Bluebill, Primitive, Wooden, Old Paint, Tack Eyes, 12 In.	40.00
Bluebill, Wisconsin, 1930s	75.00
Brant Goose, Greenbackville, Va., 1925	125.00
Bufflehead Drake, Gus Wilson	4250.00
Bufflehead Drake, Old Paint, Primitive, Doug Jester, Va., 10 1/4 In.	55.00
Bufflehead Hen, Mason	750.00
Bufflehead, Standard Grade, Bourne, Pair	3500.00
Bufflehead, Standard, Mason, Pair	3500.00
Canada Goose, 2 Piece Head & Neck, Pine, 23 3/4 In.	145.00

Canada Goose, 2 Piece Head & Neck, Tack Eyes, 28 X 15 1/2 In.	305.00
Canada Goose, Balsa Body, Carved Wooden Head, Glass Eyes, 22 In.	115.00
Canada Goose, Hollow Carved, Original But Worn Paint	5500.00
Canada Goose, Joe Lincoln, 1859–1938	8800.00
Canada Goose, Old Black & White Paint, Traces Of Brown, 22 1/2 In.	245.00
Canada Goose, Original Paint, Weight, 17 In.	200.00
Canada Goose, Primitive, Old Paint, 23 1/2 In.	275.00
Canada Goose, Smith Clinton Verity, Long Island	7300.00
Canadian Goose, Solid, Original Paint, 17 In.	200.00
Canvasback Drake, Evans Ammoth, Original Paint	195.00
Canvasback Drake, Glass Eyes, 14 1/4 In.	60.00
Canvasback Drake, Lem Dudley, Knot Island, Va.	4800.00
Canvasback Drake, Moodly Linn, Wisconsin, Original Paint, 1940s	50.00
Canvasback, Glass Eyes, 17 1/2 In.	30.00
Canvasback, Hand Carved, Perdew	3250.00
Canvasback, High Turned Head, Glass Eyes, 15 In.	75.00
Canvasback, John Schweikart, Michigan, Pair	9900.00
Canvasback, Original Paint, Toby Sherburne, 1930s	85.00
Canvasback, Repaint, Lead Weight Marked, Bartlett & Capd., 14 3/4 In.	60.00
Canvasback, Signed Capt.Harry R.Jobes	75.00
Carrylite, Salesman Sample, 1940, 5 In.	20.00
Coot, Primitive, Black Paint, 11 3/4 In.	25.00
Curlew, Chief Cuffee Of Shinnecock Reservation	330.00
Curlew, Nathan Cobb, Old Paint	3300.00
Duck, Pre–1926, Mason, Original Paint	225.00
Duck, Tack Eyes, Primitive, 13 1/2 In.	105.00
Duck, Wooden, Handmade, 1885	75.00
Duck, Wooden, Red Head, Weight & Sinker	25.00
Eider, Gus Wilson, 1932, Pair	5400.00
Eider, Gus Wilson, Pair	6325.00
Fish Spearing, Wooden, Handmade	24.00
Fish, Pike, Small	125.00
Fish, Wood, Weighted, 8 In.	45.00
Flying Shorebird, Removable Wings, Painted, Sheet Metal, 9 In.	35.00
Folding, Tin, Plover	68.00
Golden Plover, John Dilly, Shot Scars On Side, Replaced Bill	2200.00
Goldeneye Drake, Wooden, Turned Head	82.00
Goldeneye, John Schweikart, Michigan, Pair	10175.00
Goose, Canvas, Carved Head, 23 In.	155.00
Goose, Flying, Maine, Tin Wings	175.00
Goose, Hand Carved, Wooden, Large	65.00
Goose, Tack Eyes, C.1915, W.H.Hocker	210.00
Goose, Wire & Frame Canvas Cover, C.1930, Dick Higgins	95.00
Greenwing Teal Drake, Mason, Worn Paint, 12 In.	100.00
Hen, Seneca Lake, Mason	350.00
Lead, Miniature, 3 In.	10.00
Mallard Drake, A.Elmer Crowell, Half Size	1430.00
Mallard Drake, Marked D.W.S, Snow Of Michigan, 17 1/4 In.	22.50
Mallard Hen, A.Elmer Crowell, Half Size	1210.00
Mallard Hen, Glass Eyes, Branded Clare, 17 3/4 In.	60.00
Mallard Hen, Original Paint, Illinois, 18 In.	135.00
Mallard, A.Elmer Crowell, East Harwich, Mass., Original Paint	2200.00
Mallard, Charles Perdew, Pair	5500.00
Mallard, Original Paint, Glass Eyes	75.00
Mallard, Papier–Mache	25.00
Merganser Drake, Solid, Original Paint, 18 In.	250.00
Merganser Hen, Solid, Original Paint, 17 In.	300.00
Merganser, George Huey	3000.00
Merganser, Maine	550.00
Merganser, Red–Breasted, Mason Premier	1100.00
Merganser, W.E.Howard, Falmouth, Mass., Pair	385.00
Owl, Papier–Mache, Painted Eyes	24.50
Pintail Duck, California, Dick Jansen, Pair	350.00
Pintail, 1800s	250.00

Dedham, Pitcher, Night & Morning,   Dedham, Plate, Horse Chestnut,   Dedham, Plate, Cosmos,
Crackleware, 4 1/2 In.   Crackleware, 8 1/2 In.   Crackleware, 6 In.

Red–Breasted Merganser, A.Elmer Crowell 13000.00
Red–Breasted Merganser, Ira Hudson 7700.00
Redhead Drake, Bobtail Repaint, 15 In. 35.00
Redhead, Mason, Pair 2000.00
Ringbill, Ward Bros., Pair 3250.00
Robin Snipe, Mason 3025.00
Ruddy Turnstone, Bill Bowman 10000.00
Ruddy, Alvirah Wright, C.1860 .... 6600.00
Scoter, Old Monhegan 95.00
Scoter, White–Winged, Gus Wilson 1650.00
Swan, Hollow Cedar, Original Paint, New Jersey 1045.00
Swan, Tack Eye, Original Paint 275.00
Willet, William Bowman, Lawrence, N.Y., C.1880 .... 7750.00
Wood Duck, Preening, Conklin 700.00
Yellowlegs, Original Paint 605.00

Chelsea Keramic Art Works was established in 1872 in Chelsea, Massachusetts, by members of the Robertson family. The factory closed in 1889 and was reorganized as the Chelsea Pottery U.S. in 1891. It became the Dedham Pottery of Dedham, Massachusetts, in 1895. The factory closed in 1943. It was famous for its crackleware dishes, which picture blue outlines of animals, flowers, and other natural motifs.

DEDHAM, Bowl, Crackleware Glaze, Rabbits, Marked, 8 1/2 In. 150.00
Bowl, Rabbits, 5 In. 60.00
Bowl, Serving, Rabbits, Marked, 8 In. 150.00
Bowl, Swan, C.1920, Stamped, 5 1/4 In. 225.00
Bowl, Turtle, C.1929, Marked, 6 In. 700.00
Bread Plate, Mushroom Pattern, Blue Mark, 6 In. 75.00
Centerpiece, Lily Pad, Mustard, Green, Incised CKAW, 3 1/2 & 5 In. 1600.00
Charger, Elephant, C.1929, Marked, 12 In. 900.00
Charger, Rabbits, C.1929, Stamped, 12 In. 225.00
Creamer, Rabbits 150.00
Cup & Saucer, Butterfly, C.1929, Stamped, 4 In. 475.00
Cup & Saucer, Polar Bear, C.1929, Stamped, 4 In. 325.00
Cup & Saucer, Rabbits 68.00
Cup & Saucer, Rabbits, Miss Oshe, 3 In. 125.00
Dish, Vegetable, Rabbits 30.00
Dish, Vegetable, Rabbits, Covered, Marked, 9 1/2 In. 250.00
Ewer, Keramic, Applied Flowering Vines, AHK, Chelsea, Dated 1881 .... 467.00
Figurine, Rabbit, 2 3/4 In. 250.00
Mug, Rabbits 125.00
Paperweight, Rabbit 250.00
Pitcher, Azalea 425.00

Pitcher, Grape Pattern, Marked, 4 1/2 In. 700.00
Pitcher, Night & Morning, Crackleware, 4 1/2 In. ....*Illus*   300.00
Pitcher, Oak Block, Marked, 5 3/4 In. 900.00
Pitcher, Rabbits, Bulbous, C.1929, Stamped, 4 3/4 In. 100.00
Planter, Blocked Mirror Pattern, Ruffled, Marked, 8 3/4 X 3 3/4 In. 350.00
Planter, Circular Mirror Design, Marked, 6 X 3 1/4 In. 200.00
Planter, Leaf Design, Pedestal, Ruffled, Marked, 8 11/16 X 4 1/2 In. 300.00
Plate, Bird In Potted Orange Tree, Crackleware, 8 In. 195.00
Plate, Butter, Crab, C.1929, Marked Registered, 6 1/4 In. 500.00
Plate, Butter, Elephant, Marked, 6 1/4 In. 300.00
Plate, Butter, Turtle, C.1910, Marked, 6 In. 125.00
Plate, Coat Of Arms, Rabbit Border, Marked, 8 3/4 In. 1600.00
Plate, Cosmos, Crackleware, 6 In. ....*Illus*   175.00
Plate, Crab & Waves, Crackled Ground, Blue Design, Marked, 6 In. 308.00
Plate, Crab, Crackleware, 7 3/4 In. ....*Illus*   375.00
Plate, Crab, Incised, C.1920, 8 1/2 In. 250.00
Plate, Dolphin Pattern, Marked, 8 1/2 In. 325.00
Plate, Dolphin, Blue Stamp, 8 1/2 In. ....*Illus*   325.00
Plate, Elephant, Crackleware, 7 1/4 In. ....*Illus*   300.00
Plate, Fairbank's House, Rabbit Border, Marked, 8 1/2 In. 2200.00
Plate, Fish, Blue Waves, Crackleware, Pre-1929 Mark, 8 1/2 In. 1100.00
Plate, Flower Pattern, 5 Petals, Blue Mark, 8 1/2 In. 125.00
Plate, Grape Design Rim, Rabbit Center, Dark Blue, Marked, 6 1/8 In. 200.00
Plate, Horse Chestnut, Crackleware, 8 1/2 In. ....*Illus*   140.00
Plate, Iris Pattern, Crackleware, 8 1/2 In. ....70.00 To 145.00
Plate, Lily, C.1910, Marked, 6 In. 550.00
Plate, Lobster, 2 Marks, 6 1/2 In. 185.00
Plate, Lobster, Crackleware, 7 1/2 In. ....*Illus*   400.00
Plate, Magnolia, Blue Stamp, 8 1/2 In. ....*Illus*   150.00
Plate, Owl Border, Incised, C.1920, 8 1/2 In. 700.00
Plate, Pond Lily Pattern, Crackleware, 8 1/2 In. 125.00
Plate, Poppy & Leaves Center, Poppy Pods Border, Rabbit, 8 1/2 In. 380.00
Plate, Poppy, 8 1/2 In. 385.00
Plate, Poppy, Blue Border, Crackleware, Pre-1929 Mark, 8 1/2 In. 495.00
Plate, Rabbits, 2 Ear, 10 In. 85.00
Plate, Rabbits, 6 1/2 In. ....70.00 To 75.00
Plate, Rabbits, 6 In. 85.00
Plate, Rabbits, 8 1/2 In. 90.00
Plate, Rabbits, 9 1/2 In. 95.00
Plate, Rabbits, Commemorative Tercentenary 1636-1936, 8 1/2 In. 220.00
Plate, Rabbits, Marked, 8 In. 88.00
Plate, Serving, Rabbit Pattern, Crackleware, Marked, 12 In. 150.00
Plate, Snowtree Border, Stamped & Impressed 10 In. 150.00
Plate, Swan, C.1929, Stamped Registered, 8 1/4 In. 100.00

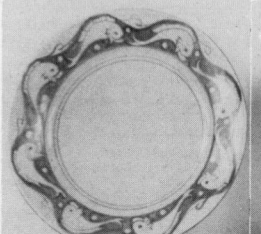

Dedham, Plate, Dolphin,
Blue Stamp, 8 1/2 In.

Dedham, Plate, Magnolia,
Blue Stamp, 8 1/2 In.

Don't brag about the value of your collection to strangers. It might lead to extra interest by the local burglary groups.

Dedham, Plate, Crab,
Crackleware, 7 3/4 In.

Dedham, Plate, Lobster,
Crackleware, 7 1/2 In.

Dedham, Plate, Turkey,
Crackleware, 8 1/4 In.

Dedham, Plate, Elephant,
Crackleware, 7 1/4 In.

Plate, Tulip, 6 1/2 In.	120.00
Plate, Turkey, 8 1/2 In.	135.00
Plate, Turkey, Crackleware, 8 1/4 In. ....*Illus*	150.00
Plate, Water Lily Border, Blue Mark, 8 1/2 In.	130.00
Plate, Woodcock In Flight, Blue, White Ground, Marked, 8 In.	1430.00
Platter, Dolphin Border, C.1929, Marked, 13 X 8 In.	1200.00
Soup, Dish, Rabbit, Wide Flat Rim, Initialed NG, 5/4/10, 9 1/8 In.	70.00
Sugar, Covered, Magnolia, Bulbous, Handles, C.1929, Marked, 4 1/4 In. ...	200.00
Tray, Lobster, C.1929, Marked, 9 1/2 X 5 3/4 In.	575.00
Trivet, Turkey, Circular Design, Square Ground, Marked, 6 In.	400.00
Vase, Chocolate, Dark Brown, Taupe, Tan, Volcanic, Robertson, 9 In.	385.00
Vase, Deep Rose, Experimental, Hugh Robertson, C.1890, 2 3/4 In.	300.00
Vase, Dogwood, Crackle & Spongeware, Marked, Blue, Oval	450.00
Vase, Green, Slate & Gray, C.1900, Marked, 9 In.	550.00
Vase, Hand Thrown, Signed H.R., Green Glaze, 5 3/4 In.	275.00
Vase, Lime To Dark Moss Green, Marked, 8 In.	220.00
Vase, Mottled Black & Brown Glaze, Cylindrical, Marked, 9 1/4 In.	500.00
Vase, Overall Green Glaze, Artist Signed, 6 In.	200.00
Vase, Oxblood Glaze, Marked, 6 1/2 In.	1200.00
Vase, Volcanic, Chocolate, Dark Brown, Taupe, Tan, Marked, 8 In.	385.00
Vase, Volcanic, Gray & Black, Green & Blue Runs, Robertson, 8 In.	285.00
Vase, Volcanic, Orange Peel, Red Glaze Runs, White, Robertson, 7 In.	770.00

Vase, Volcanic, Red, Orange, & Black, Marked, 8 In. 1000.00

> *John and Elizabeth Degenhart started the Crystal Art Glass of Cambridge, Ohio, in 1947. Quality paperweights and other glass objects were made. John died in 1964 and his wife took over management and production ideas. Over 145 colors of glass were made. In 1978, after the death of Mrs. Degenhart, the molds were sold. The D in a heart trademark was removed so collectors can easily recognize the true Degenhart pieces.*

DEGENHART, Cookie Jar, Robin, Covered, Opaline 60.00
   Dish, Bird With Berry Cover, Marked, Vaseline 57.00
   Dish, Turkey Cover, Marked, Amber 50.00
   Figurine, Owl, Cobalt Blue, Carnival Glass, Marked 118.00
   Saltshaker, Bird, Pink 30.00
   Toothpick, Sky Blue, Heart Shape 19.00

> *Degue is a signature found acid–etched on pieces of French glass made in the early 1900s. Cameo, mold blown, and smooth glass with contrasting colored rims are the types most often found.*

DEGUE, Vase, Cameo Flowers, Gilded Enamel Trim, Signed St.Denis, 7 3/4 In. 200.00

> *Delatte glass is a French cameo glass made by Andre Delatte. It was first made in Nancy, France, in 1921. Lighting fixtures and opaque glassware in imitation of Bohemian opaline were made. There were many French cameo glass makers, so be sure to look in other appropriate sections.*

DELATTE, Vase, Gold Ground, Peacock, Signed, 8 3/4 In. 850.00
   Vase, Pedestal Foot, Carved To Blue Flowers, 7 In. 750.00
      DELAWARE, see Custard Glass; Pressed Glass
      DELDARE, see Buffalo Pottery Deldare

> *Delft is a tin–glazed pottery that has been made since the seventeenth century. It is decorated with blue on white or with colored decorations. Most of the pieces sold today were made after 1891, and the name "Holland" appears with the Delft factory marks.*

DELFT, Biscuit Jar 45.00
   Bowl, Covered, 18th Century, Chinese Figures, Loop Handles, 7 1/4 In. 935.00
   Bowl, Windmill & Sailboat Scene, 3 1/2 X 6 In. 24.00
   Canister Set, Dutch Scene, Windmill, Czechoslovakia, 12 Piece 225.00
   Charger, Dutch Countryside Scene, 12 In. 65.00
   Charger, Floral Bouquets, Center Sunburst, 18th Century, 13 3/4 In. 275.00
   Charger, Floral Trees & Balustrade, Blue, White, 13 1/4 In. 175.00
   Charger, Floral, Blue & White, Signed P, 13 1/2 In. 250.00
   Charger, Flowering Tree Center, Floral Border, 13 3/4 In. 220.00
   Charger, Geometric Design, 2 Color, 18th Century, 14 In. 175.00
   Charger, Polychrome, Blue Underglaze, 18th Century, 13 In. 300.00
   Charger, Stylized Floral, Late 18th Century, 14 In. 400.00
   Charger, Tavern Scene, Dutch, Signed, 24 In. 750.00
   Coffee Grinder, Wall, Windmill Design 110.00
   Creamer, Cow, Blue & White, Sailboats 68.00
   Dutch, Plate, Bird Center, Yellow & Red Border, C.1670, 8 1/2 In. 325.00
   English, Plate, Blue & White, Floral Design Center, C.1740, 10 In. 285.00
   Figurine, Lion, Seated, Polychrome, 18th Century, Signed AK, 3 5/8 In. 150.00
   Funnel, Blue & White Sailboats 68.00
   Jar, Dome Covered, Foo Dog Finial, Ovoid, 18th Century, 13 1/4 In., Pr. 700.00
   Lamp, Blue & White, Signed Holland, 8 In. 25.00
   Measuring Cup, Blue And White, Set 95.00
   Mug, Floral, Windmill Scene, House, 4 3/4 In. 15.00
   Pitcher, 3 Sizes, 1/4, 1/2, 1 Cup, Set 95.00
   Pitcher, Blue & Green, Thoovt & La Bouchere, 1898, 6 1/2 In. 85.00
   Plaque, Farm Scene, Windmills, Floral & Scroll, Boch, 15 1/4 In. 68.00
   Plaque, Peace, World War II 125.00
   Plaque, Rembrandt's Portrait, 13 1/4 In. 100.00
   Plate, Annual, 1970, Moederdag 20.00

Plate, Bianca Sopra, Bianca Rim, Blue Oriental Design, 8 7/8 In.	230.00
Plate, Central Blue Floral Design, Blue, White, 9 1/8 In., Pair	150.00
Plate, Floral Design, Polychrome, 18th Century, 8 3/4 In.	100.00
Plate, Stylized Cobalt Blue Floral, Rolled Rim, 9 In.	100.00
Platter, Scene, 11 3/4 In.	100.00
Puzzle Jug, Motto, Squirrels, 13 In. ....*Illus*	225.00
Tea Caddy, Polychrome, Rectangular, Marked, C.1700, 5 In.	412.00
Tile, Animals, Birds, Trees, & Flowers, 5 1/2 X 11 In., Pair	50.00
Tile, Christmas, 1951, Multicolor Faience, 8 X 5 3/4 In.	75.00
Tile, Fireplace, Man, Polychrome	25.00
Tile, Hares & Stylized Plants, 5 1/2 X 11 In.	32.50
Tile, Scenic, Windmill & Boat, Multicolor Faience, Square, 4 1/2 In.	40.00
Tray, Center Blue & White Grape Design, Pewter Framed	68.00
Urn, Metal, Covered, Seated Dog Knop, 18th Century, 17 In., Pair	750.00
Vase, Floral Design, Blue & White, Bulbous, Signed DP, 8 In.	95.00

Dental cabinets, chairs, equipment, and other related items are listed here. Other objects may be found listed under Medical.

DENTAL, Cabinet, 1919	420.00
Cabinet, Backboard With Mirror, Oak, C.1880	1200.00
Cabinet, Floor Model, Oak, C.1895	850.00
Cabinet, Harvard Co., Painted Interior, Natural Oak Exterior, 70 In.	1450.00
Cabinet, Oak, Harvard Dental Cab., 19th Century, 60 1/2 X 28 1/2 In.	275.00
Cabinet, Oak, Portable	50.00
Drill, Hand Crank	125.00
Sign, Plate Glass, Dr.Grant	45.00
Tool Set, Forceps, Plugger, Prober, Drills, Syringe, Wooden Box	85.00
Tooth Extractor, 18th Century, Ring Turned Iron Tool, Swivel Hook	64.50
Tooth Extractor, Iron	85.00
Toothkey, 5 Interchangeable Claws, C.1830	200.00
Toothkey, Iron, Hardwood Handle, 6 In.	135.00
Toothkey, Ivory Handle, Swivel Claw, C.1800	285.00
Toothkey, Rosewood Handle, Locking Swivel Claw, C.1800	275.00

DENVER
C T L
P Co

William Long of Steubenville, Ohio, founded the Lonhuda Pottery Company in 1892. In 1900 he moved to Denver, Colorado, and organized the Denver China and Pottery Company. This pottery worked until 1905 when Long moved to New Jersey and founded the Clifton Pottery. Long also worked for Weller Pottery, Roseville Pottery, and American Encaustic Tiling Company.

DENVER, Vase, Leaves & Berries, Medium To Dark Green, Marked, 6 X 4 In.	350.00

Delft, Puzzle Jug,
Motto, Squirrels, 13 In.

American Sweetheart

Bubble

Depression glass was an inexpensive glass manufactured in large quantities during the 1920s and early 1930s. It was made in many colors and patterns by dozens of factories in the United States. The name "Depression glass" is a modern one. For more descriptions, history, pictures, and prices of Depression glass, see the book "The Kovels' Illustrated Price Guide to Depression Glass and American Dinnerware."

DEPRESSION GLASS, Adam, Ashtray, Pink	19.50
Adam, Bowl, Pink, 7 3/4 In.	9.00
Adam, Butter, Pink, Covered	70.00
Adam, Cake Plate, Pink, Footed	12.00
Adam, Candlestick, Pink, Pair	55.00
Adam, Candy Dish, Pink, Covered	52.50
Adam, Coaster, Pink	10.00
Adam, Cup & Saucer, Green	14.00
Adam, Goblet, Iced Tea, Pink	40.00
Adam, Pitcher, Green, 8 In.	30.00
Adam, Plate, Green, 10 In.	12.50
Adam, Plate, Pink, 7 1/2 In.	6.50
Adam, Salt & Pepper, Pink, Footed, 4 In.	48.00
Adam, Sherbet, Pink	15.50
Adam, Sugar & Creamer, Pink, Covered	35.00
Adam, Tumbler, Green, Footed, 4 1/2 In.	14.00
ALPINE CAPRICE, see also Caprice	
AMERICAN BEAUTY, see English Hobnail	
American Pioneer, Lamp, Electric, Pink, 8 1/2 In.	50.00
American Sweetheart, Bowl, Cereal, Pink	8.50 To 9.00
American Sweetheart, Bowl, Monax, 9 In.	34.50
American Sweetheart, Bowl, Pink, 6 In.	8.00
American Sweetheart, Creamer, Monax	7.00
American Sweetheart, Cup & Saucer, Monax	9.00 To 30.00
American Sweetheart, Pitcher, Pink, 8 In.	350.00
American Sweetheart, Plate, Monax, 9 In.	5.50 To 7.50
American Sweetheart, Platter, Oval, Pink, 13 In.	12.50
American Sweetheart, Salver, Monax, 10 1/2 In.	11.00 To 13.50
American Sweetheart, Soup, Dish, Monax	38.00 To 39.00
American Sweetheart, Sugar & Creamer, Monax	13.00
American Sweetheart, Tumbler, Pink, 4 In.	28.00
APPLE BLOSSOM, see Dogwood	
Aunt Polly, Bowl, Blue, 8 In.	25.00
Aunt Polly, Butter, Blue, Covered	95.00 To 100.00

Aunt Polly, Sherbet, Blue 9.00
Aunt Polly, Sugar, Blue 21.00
Aunt Polly, Water Set, Blue, 8 Tumblers 175.00
Avocado, Bowl, Crystal, 7 1/2 In. 6.00
Avocado, Cup, Green ....19.00 To 26.00
    B PATTERN, see Dogwood
    BALLERINA, see Cameo
    BANDED CHERRY, see Cherry Blossom
    BANDED FINE RIB, see Coronation
    BANDED RIBBON, see New Century
Banded Ring, Decanter, Stopper, 5 Shot 25.00
    BANDED RINGS, see Ring
    BASKET, see No. 615
Beaded Block, Pitcher, Crystal, 5 3/4 In. 65.00
Beaded Block, Sugar, Green 20.00
    BEVERAGE WITH SAILBOAT, see White Ship
    BIG RIB, see Manhattan
    BLOCK, see Block Optic
Block Optic, Candy Dish, Green, Covered ....21.00 To 28.00
Block Optic, Candy Dish, Yellow, Covered 38.00
Block Optic, Cup & Saucer, Pink 6.00
Block Optic, Goblet, Pink, 4 Oz. 9.00
Block Optic, Goblet, Yellow, 7 1/2 In. 20.00
Block Optic, Mug, Coffee, Green 23.00
Block Optic, Pitcher, Green, 54 Oz. ....25.00 To 29.00
Block Optic, Plate, Green, 8 In. 2.75
Block Optic, Plate, Pink, 8 In. 3.00
Block Optic, Plate, Yellow, 8 In. ....4.50 To 13.00
Block Optic, Salt & Pepper, Green, Squat 37.00
Block Optic, Sherbet, Pink 2.50
Block Optic, Sherbet, Yellow, Square 5.00
Block Optic, Sugar & Creamer, Green, 4 In. 8.00
Block Optic, Tumble-Up, Green 45.00
Block Optic, Tumbler, Green, 5 In. ....*Color* 10.00
    BOUQUET & LATTICE, see Normandie
Bowknot, Tumbler, Green, Footed ....8.00 To 8.50
    BRIDAL BOUQUET, see No. 615
Bubble, Bowl, Blue, 5 1/4 In. 5.50
Bubble, Creamer, Blue 8.00
Bubble, Cup & Saucer, Blue ....3.50 To 4.00
Bubble, Grill Plate, Blue 8.00
Bubble, Plate, Crystal, 9 1/4 In. 3.00

Cameo

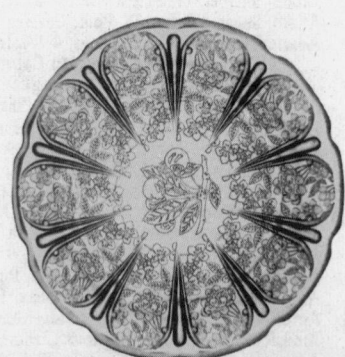

Cherry Blossom

Bubble, Soup, Dish, Blue ....4.50 To 5.00
Bubble, Sugar & Creamer, Blue 20.00
Bubble, Sugar & Creamer, Green 7.00
Bubble, Tumbler, Red, 9 Oz. 8.00
    BULLSEYE, see Bubble
    BUTTONS & BOWS, see Holiday
    CABBAGE ROSE, see Sharon
    CABBAGE ROSE WITH SINGLE ARCH, see Rosemary
Cameo, Bowl, Cereal, Yellow 18.00
Cameo, Bowl, Green, 5 3/8 In. 25.00
Cameo, Bowl, Pink, 3–Footed, 11 In. 25.00
Cameo, Bowl, Vegetable, Yellow, Oval 33.00
Cameo, Butter, Green 115.00
Cameo, Cake Plate, Green, 3–Footed 13.00
Cameo, Cookie Jar, Green, Covered 35.00
Cameo, Creamer, Green, 3 1/4 In. 15.00
Cameo, Cup & Saucer, Green 10.00
Cameo, Decanter, Green Frosted, Stopper 95.00
Cameo, Dish, Mayonnaise, Green 15.00
Cameo, Grill Plate, Green 7.50
Cameo, Pitcher, Green, 5 3/4 In. 130.00
Cameo, Plate, Green, 9 1/2 In. 9.00
Cameo, Plate, Green, Square, 8 In. 28.00
Cameo, Platter, Green 12.00
Cameo, Salt & Pepper, Green ....32.00 To 52.00
Cameo, Sherbet, Green, Footed 10.00
Cameo, Soup, Dish, Green, 9 In. ....24.00 To 27.00
Cameo, Tray, Green, 10 1/2 In. 6.00
Cameo, Tumbler, Green, 5 Oz. 16.00
Cameo, Vase, Green, 8 In. 22.50
Candlewick, Cup & Saucer 10.00
Candlewick, Dish, Jelly 7.00
Candlewick, Mayonnaise Set, 3 Piece 24.00
Candlewick, Plate, 6 In. 9.00
Candlewick, Sugar & Creamer 28.00
Cape Cod, Cake Stand, Crystal, Footed 32.00
Caprice, Candy Dish, Blue, 3–Footed, Covered 59.50
Caprice, Cordial, Crystal 32.00
Caprice, Mayonnaise Set, Blue, 3 Piece 55.00
    CHAIN DAISY, see Adam
    CHERRY, see Cherry Blossom
Cherry Blossom, Berry Bowl, Green 13.00
Cherry Blossom, Bowl, Pink, 4 1/2 In. 7.50
Cherry Blossom, Bowl, Vegetable, Green, Oval 32.00
Cherry Blossom, Butter, Pink, Covered 65.00
Cherry Blossom, Creamer, Delphite ....10.00 To 13.00
Cherry Blossom, Cup & Saucer, Child's, Blue 18.00
Cherry Blossom, Cup & Saucer, Green 23.00
Cherry Blossom, Pitcher, Pink, 8 In. 30.00
Cherry Blossom, Plate, Green, 9 In. 12.00
Cherry Blossom, Relish, Pink, Divided, 13 In. 26.00
Cherry Blossom, Sherbet, Pink ....8.00 To 10.00
Cherry Blossom, Sugar & Creamer, Pink, Covered ....23.50 To 29.00
Cherry Blossom, Tea Set, Delphite 110.00
Cherry Blossom, Tray, Sandwich, Green 18.50
Cherry Blossom, Tumbler, Delphite, Footed, 4 1/2 In. 13.00
    CHERRY–BERRY, see Strawberry
Chesterfield, Pitcher, Amber, Covered 95.00
Circle, Bowl, Green, 4 1/2 In. 2.75
Circle, Goblet, Wine, Green 4.00
Circle, Sherbet, Green 3.00
    CIRCULAR RIBS, see Circle
Cloverleaf, Ashtray, Black, 4 In. ....31.00 To 35.00
Cloverleaf, Bowl, Green, 7 In. ....22.50 To 29.00

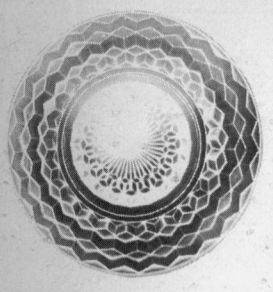

Cubist

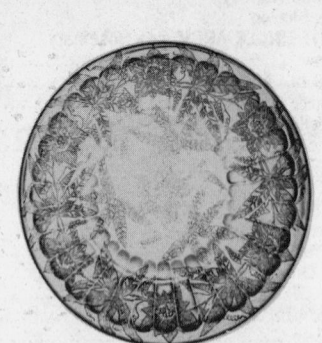

Floral

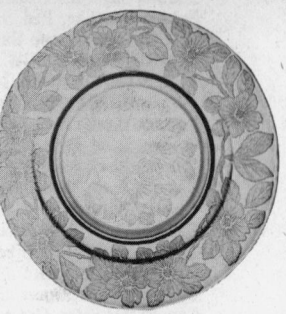

Dogwood

Cloverleaf, Candy Dish, Green, Covered ....25.00 To 32.00
Cloverleaf, Creamer, Black ....6.50 To 8.50
Cloverleaf, Cup & Saucer, Black ....7.00 To 12.00
Cloverleaf, Cup & Saucer, Green 42.00
Cloverleaf, Plate, Green, 6 In. ....2.50 To 5.00
Cloverleaf, Plate, Green, 8 In. ....4.75 To 5.00
Cloverleaf, Salt & Pepper, Green 25.00
Cloverleaf, Sherbet, Green 4.75
Cloverleaf, Sugar & Creamer, Topaz 18.00
Colonial, Cup & Saucer, Green, Rope, Fluted 5.00
Colonial, Cup, White 40.00
Colonial, Pitcher, Green, 8 In. 45.00
Colonial, Plate, Green, Rope, Fluted, 8 1/2 In. 3.00
Colonial, Saltshaker, Crystal, Pair 45.00
Colonial, Soup, Dish, Green 37.50
Colonial, Sugar & Creamer, Green, Covered 40.00
Colony, Compote, Crystal, 6 1/2 In. 40.00
Columbia, Butter, Crystal, Covered 13.00
Columbia, Cup & Saucer, Crystal 5.00
Columbia, Plate, Crystal, 9 1/2 In. 3.75
Coronation, Berry Bowl, Pink 2.75
Coronation, Bowl, Pink, 4 1/4 In. 3.00
Coronation, Sherbet, Pink 2.00
    CRISS CROSS, see X Design
    CUBE, see Cubist
Cubist, Bowl, Green, 6 1/2 In. 9.00
Cubist, Candy Dish, Green, Covered ....14.00 To 20.00
Cubist, Coaster, Green 2.95
Cubist, Plate, Green, 8 In. 3.50
Cubist, Powder Jar, Pink, Covered 8.50
Cubist, Salt & Pepper, Green 27.00
Cubist, Sugar, Pink 6.00
    DANCING GIRL, see Cameo
    DIAMOND, see Windsor
    DIAMOND PATTERN, see Miss America
Diamond Quilted, Bowl, Blue, 7 In. 16.00
Diamond Quilted, Creamer, Pink 5.00

Diamond Quilted, Plate, Green, 6 In. 2.00
Diamond Quilted, Sherbet, Green 3.00
Diana, Creamer, Pink, Oval 3.00
Diana, Saltshaker, Pink 15.00
Diana, Saucer, Pink 2.00
Dogwood, Bowl, Pink, 5 1/2 In. 14.00
Dogwood, Cake Plate, Pink, 13 In. 80.00
Dogwood, Cup & Saucer, Pink 11.00
Dogwood, Plate, Pink, 9 1/4 In. 15.00
Dogwood, Soup, Cream, Yellow 39.00
Doric & Pansy, Teapot, Pink, Covered 75.00
Doric & Pansy, Tray, Ultramarine, Round, 10 In. 20.00
Doric, Berry Bowl, Green, 4 1/2 In. 5.50
Doric, Bowl, Pink, 8 1/4 In. 10.00
Doric, Butter, Pink, Covered 55.00
Doric, Coaster, Green ....6.00 To 10.00
Doric, Creamer, Green 13.00
Doric, Plate, Green, 10 In. 8.00
Doric, Plate, Pink, 9 In. 7.50
Doric, Salt & Pepper, Green 20.00
    DOUBLE SWIRL, see Swirl
    DRAPE & TASSEL, see Princess
    DUTCH, see Windmill
    DUTCH ROSE, see Rosemary
    EARLY AMERICAN HOBNAIL, see Hobnail
    EARLY AMERICAN ROCK CRYSTAL, see Rock Crystal
    ELONGATED HONEYCOMB, see Colony
    ENGLISH HOBNAIL, see also Miss America
English Hobnail, Bowl, Amber, 5 In. 9.00
English Hobnail, Lamp, Turquoise, 9 1/4 In. 130.00
English Hobnail, Tumbler, Crystal, Square Footed, 4 Oz. 5.00
    FAN & FEATHER, see Adam
    FINE RIB, see Homespun
Fire–King, Custard, Crystal 2.00
    FLAT DIAMOND, see Diamond Quilted
Floragold, Candy Dish, Crystal, Covered 30.00
Floragold, Platter, Iridescent, 11 1/2 In. 12.50
Floragold, Sugar & Creamer, Iridescent, Covered 17.50
    FLORAL RIM, see Vitrock
Floral, Bowl, Pink, Covered, 4 In. 10.00
Floral, Bowl, Vegetable, Pink, Oval 9.00
Floral, Butter, Green, Covered 30.00
Floral, Creamer, Pink ....6.00 To 7.00
Floral, Pitcher, Lemonade, Pink, 10 1/4 In. ....140.00 To 160.00

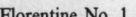

Florentine No. 1

Florentine No. 2

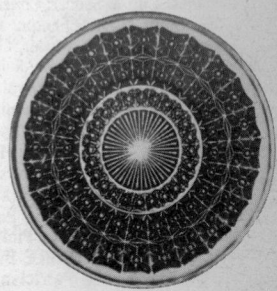

Holiday

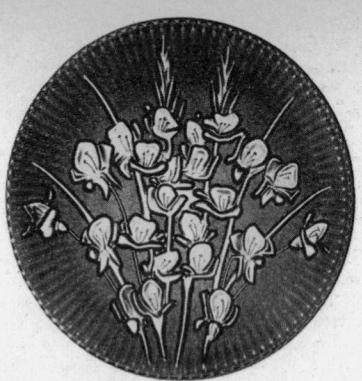

Iris, Beaded Edge

Floral, Plate, Pink, 6 In. ....2.75 To 3.75
Floral, Plate, Pink, 9 In. ....10.00 To 11.00
Floral, Salt & Pepper, Pink, 6 In. 30.00
Floral, Sherbet, Pink 7.00
Floral, Sugar, Green, Covered ....17.50 To 23.00
Floral, Sugar, Pink, Covered 15.00
Florentine No.1, Cup & Saucer, Pink 8.75
Florentine No.1, Salt & Pepper, Green 20.00
Florentine No.1, Saltshaker, Green 12.50
Florentine No.2, Berry Bowl, Yellow, 4 1/2 In. 9.50
Florentine No.2, Candlestick, Green, Pair 32.00
Florentine No.2, Candlestick, Yellow 15.00
Florentine No.2, Candy Dish, Green 60.00
Florentine No.2, Condiment Set, Yellow, 5 Piece 105.00
Florentine No.2, Cup & Saucer, Yellow 10.00
Florentine No.2, Gravy Bowl, Platter, Yellow 75.00
Florentine No.2, Pitcher, Yellow, 8 In. 120.00
Florentine No.2, Plate, Green, 10 In. 8.00
Florentine No.2, Salt & Pepper, Green 20.00
Florentine No.2, Sherbet, Green ....5.00 To 6.00
    FLOWER BASKET, see No. 615
    FLOWER RIM, see Vitrock
    FROSTED BLOCK, see Beaded Block
Fruits, Cup & Saucer, Green 5.00
Georgian, Basket, Fenton, Blue, 7 In. 55.00
Georgian, Cup & Saucer, Green 9.00
Georgian, Plate, Green, 8 1/2 In. 6.00
    GLADIOLI, see Royal Lace
    HAIRPIN, see Newport
    HANGING BASKET, see No. 615
Harp, Cake Plate, Crystal, Footed 15.00
Heritage, Bowl, Fruit, Crystal, 10 1/2 In. 6.00
    HEX OPTIC, see Hexagon Optic
Hexagon Optic, Pitcher, Pink, Green Applied Handle 35.00
Hexagon Optic, Plate, Pink, 8 In. 3.00
    HEXAGON TRIPLE BAND, see Colony
    HINGE, see Patrician
Hobnail, Sherbet, Pink 3.00
Hobnail, Vase, Pink, 7 In. 12.00
Holiday, Butter, Pink, Covered ....14.00 To 28.00
Holiday, Creamer, Pink 4.00
Holiday, Cup & Saucer, Pink ....8.00 To 15.00

Holiday, Sherbet, Pink 5.00
Holiday, Sugar & Creamer, Pink 12.00
Homespun, Tumbler, Juice, Pink, Footed 5.00
    HONEYCOMB, see Hexagon Optic
    HORIZONTAL FINE RIB, see Manhattan
    HORIZONTAL RIBBED, see Manhattan
    HORIZONTAL ROUNDED BIG RIB, see Manhattan
    HORIZONTAL SHARP BIG RIB, see Manhattan
    HORSESHOE, see No. 612
    IRIS & HERRINGBONE, see Iris
Iris, Berry Bowl, Iridescent, Beaded 4.50
Iris, Bowl, Crystal, Scalloped, 5 1/2 In. 5.25
Iris, Butter, Iridescent, Covered ....30.00 To 34.00
Iris, Coaster, Crystal ....25.00 To 28.00
Iris, Goblet, Crystal, 5 3/4 In. 9.50
Iris, Goblet, Wine, Iridescent 14.50
Iris, Plate, Crystal, 9 In. ....28.00 To 30.00
Iris, Plate, Iridescent, 9 In. 17.50
Iris, Sherbet, Iridescent 7.50
Iris, Soup, Dish, Crystal 65.00
Iris, Soup, Dish, Iridescent 20.00
Jadite, Bowl, Mixing, 9 In. 7.50
Jadite, Eggcup 5.00
Jubilee, Cup & Saucer, Yellow 13.50
Jubilee, Plate, Yellow, 7 In. 5.50
Jubilee, Sugar & Creamer, Yellow ....27.00 To 35.00
June, Plate, Topaz, 10 1/4 In. 48.00
    KNIFE & FORK, see Colonial
    LACE EDGE, see also Coronation
Lace Edge, Bowl, Cereal, Pink, 6 In. 8.00
Lace Edge, Bowl, Pink, Footed, 10 1/2 In. 90.00
Lace Edge, Bowl, Pink, Ribbed, 9 1/2 In. 17.00
Lace Edge, Cookie Jar, Pink 39.50
Lace Edge, Cup & Saucer, Pink 22.00
Lace Edge, Goblet, Pink, 5 In. 40.00
Lace Edge, Grill Plate, Pink ....10.00 To 11.00
Lace Edge, Plate, Pink, 7 1/4 In. 12.50
Lace Edge, Rose Bowl, Pink 12.00
Laurel, Compote, Jade 185.00
Laurel, Creamer, Child's, Ivory 19.00
    LILY MEDALLION, see American Sweetheart
    LINCOLN DRAPE, see Princess
    LOOP, see Lace Edge
    LORAIN, see No. 615
    LOUISA, see Floragold
    LOVEBIRDS, see Georgian

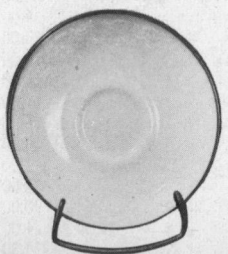

Laurel   Madrid   Mayfair Open Rose

LYDIA RAY, see New Century

Madrid, Bowl, Amber, 5 In.	4.00
Madrid, Bowl, Amber, 7 In.	6.50
Madrid, Bowl, Vegetable, Amber, Oval	7.00
Madrid, Butter, Amber, Covered	55.00 To '52.00
Madrid, Cake Plate, Amber	10.00
Madrid, Console, Amber, 11 In.	6.50
Madrid, Cookie Jar, Amber, Covered	25.00 To 30.00
Madrid, Cookie Jar, Pink, Covered	17.50 To 32.00
Madrid, Cup, Amber	3.00 To 6.00
Madrid, Grill Plate, Amber	5.00 To 7.00
Madrid, Pitcher, Amber, Square, 8 In.	35.00
Madrid, Pitcher, Green, Square, 8 In.	110.00
Madrid, Pitcher, Ice Lip, Amber, 8 1/2 In.	50.00
Madrid, Plate, Amber, 9 In.	3.00
Madrid, Relish, Amber	8.00
Madrid, Salt & Pepper, Amber, Original Top	77.50
Madrid, Salt & Pepper, Pink	40.00
Madrid, Saltshaker, Blue, Footed	32.00
Madrid, Sugar & Creamer, Amber, Covered	28.00
Madrid, Tumbler, Amber, 4 1/2 In.	7.00
Madrid, Tumbler, Juice, Amber, Footed, 4 In.	12.00

MAGNOLIA, see Dogwood

Manhattan, Ashtray, Crystal, 4 In.	4.00
Manhattan, Compote, Pink, 5 3/4 In.	8.00
Manhattan, Cup & Saucer, Crystal	12.00
Manhattan, Goblet, Wine, Crystal, 3 1/2 In.	6.25
Manhattan, Pitcher, Juice, Crystal, 42 Oz.	13.00 To 15.00
Manhattan, Sherbet, Pink	5.00
Manhattan, Soup, Cream, Crystal, 4 1/2 In.	5.00
Manhattan, Sugar & Creamer, Crystal, Gold Trim	19.00
Manhattan, Tray, Crystal, 14 In.	6.00

MANY WINDOWS, see Roulette

MAYFAIR, see Rosemary

Mayfair Open Rose, Berry Bowl, Blue	25.00
Mayfair Open Rose, Bowl, Vegetable, Pink, Covered, 10 In.	68.00
Mayfair Open Rose, Butter, Blue, Covered	225.00
Mayfair Open Rose, Cookie Jar, Pink, Covered	35.00
Mayfair Open Rose, Cup & Saucer, Pink	22.50
Mayfair Open Rose, Decanter, Pink, Stopper	45.00
Mayfair Open Rose, Grill Plate, Pink	22.50
Mayfair Open Rose, Pitcher, Pink, 8 In.	35.00
Mayfair Open Rose, Plate, Pink, 8 In.	18.00
Mayfair Open Rose, Sugar & Creamer, Pink	30.00

MEADOW FLOWER, see No. 618

MEANDERING VINE, see Madrid

MISS AMERICA, see also English Hobnail

Miss America, Bowl, Cereal, Green	12.00
Miss America, Bowl, Crystal, 6 1/4 In.	6.00
Miss America, Bowl, Green, 6 In.	9.00
Miss America, Bowl, Vegetable, Pink, Oval	12.00
Miss America, Candy Dish, Pink, Covered	77.00 To 80.00
Miss America, Celery Dish, Pink	10.00 To 14.00
Miss America, Compote, Pink, 5 In.	17.00
Miss America, Condiment, Pink, Metal Top, 5 In.	18.00
Miss America, Cup, Green	7.50 To 8.00
Miss America, Goblet, Pink, 5 1/2 In.	32.00
Miss America, Grill Plate, Pink, 10 In.	12.00
Miss America, Pitcher, Pink, Ice Lip	90.00
Miss America, Plate, Pink, 8 1/2 In.	11.00 To 14.00
Miss America, Relish, Crystal, 11 1/2 In.	12.50
Miss America, Salt & Pepper, Pink	40.00
Miss America, Sherbet, Pink	10.00
Miss America, Sugar & Creamer, Crystal	9.00

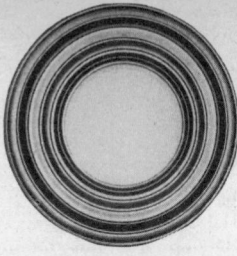

Miss America   Moderntone   Mt. Pleasant

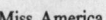

Miss America, Tumbler, Pink, 4 In.	35.00 To 40.00
Miss America, Tumbler, Water, Pink, 10 Oz.	19.00 To 28.00
MODERNE ART, see Tea Room	
Moderntone, Cup & Saucer, Cobalt Blue	9.50
Moderntone, Plate, Amethyst, 10 1/2 In.	13.00
Moderntone, Salt & Pepper, Cobalt Blue	22.50
Moderntone, Sugar & Creamer, Cobalt Blue	12.00
Moondrops, Cocktail Shaker, Green	25.00 To 29.50
Moondrops, Cup & Saucer, Green	6.00
Moondrops, Sugar & Creamer, Crystal, Covered	18.00
Moondrops, Vase, Green, Ruffled, Flat, 7 3/4 In.	32.50
Moondrops, Vase, Pink, 7 1/2 In.	32.00
Moonstone, Bowl, Covered, 6 1/2 In.	12.00
Moonstone, Goblet, Crystal, 10 Oz.	12.50
Moonstone, Perfume Bottle, Crystal, Stopper	10.00
Moonstone, Plate, Crystal, 8 In.	7.50 To 8.50
Moonstone, Powder Jar, Opalescent	12.00
Moonstone, Sugar & Creamer, Crystal	11.50
Mt.Pleasant, Creamer, Black Amethyst, Scalloped Edge	7.50
Mt.Pleasant, Salt & Pepper, Cobalt Blue	25.00
New Century, Pitcher, Green	23.00
New Century, Saltshaker, Green	10.00
New Century, Tumbler, Green, 8 Oz.	7.50
Newport, Creamer, Cobalt Blue	9.00
Newport, Cup & Saucer, Cobalt Blue	9.00
Newport, Sherbet, White, Set Of 6	25.00
Newport, Soup, Cream, Cobalt Blue	9.50
Newport, Sugar, Cobalt Blue	9.00
NO. 601, see Avocado	

No. 612   Normandie   Patrician

No.610, Dish, Pickle, Pink 22.50
No.610, Ice Bucket, Pink 57.50
No.612, Cup & Saucer, Green 8.50
No.612, Plate, Green, 11 In. 9.00
No.612, Sugar & Creamer, Green 16.00
No.615, Plate, Yellow, 7 1/2 In. 9.00
No.615, Relish, Green, 4–Part 15.00
No.615, Tumbler, Green, Footed, 4 3/4 In. 15.75
No.618, Bowl, Crystal, 7 In. 4.00
No.618, Plate, Crystal, 11 1/2 In. 10.00
No.618, Relish, Crystal, Oval, 11 1/2 In. 10.00
Normandie, Bowl, Iridescent, 5 In. 4.00
Normandie, Pitcher, Amber 45.00
Old Cafe, Plate, Pink, 6 1/2 In. 4.00
Old Cafe, Sherbet, Pink 4.00
    OLD FLORENTINE, see Florentine No.1
    OPALESCENT HOBNAIL, see Moonstone
    OPEN LACE, see Lace Edge
    OPEN ROSE, see Mayfair Open Rose
    OPEN SCALLOP, see Lace Edge
    OPTIC RIB, see Imperial Optic Rib
Orange Blossom, Bowl, White, 5 1/2 In. 2.50
    ORIENTAL POPPY, see Florentine No. 2
Oyster & Pearl, Bowl, Ruby, 10 In. 28.00
    PANELED ASTER, see Madrid
    PANELED CHERRY BLOSSOM, see Cherry Blossom
    PANSY & DORIC, see Doric & Pansy
    PARROT, see Sylvan
Patrician, Berry Bowl, Amber, Large 22.00
Patrician, Bowl, Vegetable, Amber, Oval 15.00
Patrician, Butter, Amber, Covered 65.00
Patrician, Cup & Saucer, Amber 11.00
Patrician, Grill Plate, Crystal 5.00
Patrician, Pitcher, Crystal, 8 1/4 In. 55.00
Patrician, Pitcher, Water, Green, 8 In. 80.00
Patrician, Plate, Crystal, 10 1/2 In. 4.00
Patrician, Saltshaker, Green 20.00
Patrician, Tumbler, Amber, Footed, 5 1/4 In. 27.50
Patrician, Tumbler, Crystal, 4 1/2 In. 11.00
    PETAL SWIRL, see Swirl
    PINEAPPLE & FLORAL, see No. 618
    PINWHEEL, see Sierra
    POINSETTIA, see Floral
    POPPY NO. 1, see Florentine No. 1
    POPPY NO. 2, see Florentine No. 2
    PRIMUS, see Madrid
Princess, Ashtray, Green ....60.00 To 65.00
Princess, Bowl, Green, Octagonal, 9 In. 23.00
Princess, Cake Plate, Green 14.00
Princess, Candy Jar, Pink, Covered 34.00
Princess, Cookie Jar, Green, Covered 35.00
Princess, Creamer, Topaz, Oval 12.00
Princess, Cup & Saucer, Topaz 10.00
Princess, Grill Plate, Green, 9 1/2 In. 8.50
Princess, Grill Plate, Topaz, 10 1/2 In. 9.00
Princess, Pitcher, Green, 6 In. ....34.00 To 35.00
Princess, Pitcher, Green, 8 In. ....20.00 To 29.00
Princess, Pitcher, Pink, 8 In. 28.00
Princess, Plate, Amber, 8 1/4 In. 6.50
Princess, Plate, Pink, 8 1/2 In. 4.50
Princess, Plate, Topaz, 8 In. 4.50
Princess, Platter, Green, 12 In. 14.00
Princess, Relish, Green 10.00
Princess, Salt & Pepper, Green 32.00

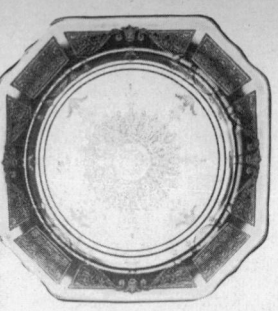

Princess

Sharon

Royal Lace

Princess, Salt & Pepper, Topaz ....35.00 To 36.50
Princess, Sugar & Creamer, Green, Covered 23.00
Princess, Sugar & Creamer, Topaz, Covered 25.00
Princess, Tumbler, Green, Footed, 10 Oz. 17.00
Princess, Tumbler, Topaz, Footed, 5 1/2 In. 15.00
    PRISMATIC LINE, see Queen Mary
    PROVINCIAL, see Bubble
    PYRAMID, see No. 610
Queen Mary, Creamer, Pink 4.00
Queen Mary, Cup & Saucer, Pink 10.00
Queen Mary, Sherbet, Pink 4.00
Queen Mary, Sugar, Pink, Oval 4.00
Radiance, Bonbon, Red, Footed, 6 In. 9.00
    RASPBERRY BAND, see Laurel
    REX, see No. 610
    RIBBED, see Manhattan
Ribbon, Bowl, Green, 8 In. 7.00
Ribbon, Candy Dish, Green, Covered ....21.00 To 22.00
Ribbon, Cup & Saucer, Green 13.00
Ribbon, Plate, Green, 8 In. 2.50
Ribbon, Tumbler, Green, 9 1/2 In. 4.25
Ring, Decanter, Stopper, Cobalt 20.00
Ring, Tumbler, Cobalt, 6 1/2 Oz. 4.00
Rock Crystal, Pitcher, Pink, 1/2 Gal. 65.00
Rock Crystal, Vase, Green, Rolled Top, 12 In. 55.00
    ROSE LACE, see Royal Lace
Rosemary, Creamer, Pink 7.50
Roulette, Cup & Saucer, Green ....5.00 To 8.95
Roulette, Plate, Green, 6 In. 2.00
Roulette, Plate, Green, 8 In. 2.75
Roulette, Sherbet, Green 3.00
Royal Lace, Bowl, Pink, Footed, 10 In. 22.00
Royal Lace, Butter, Cobalt Blue, Covered 295.00
Royal Lace, Butter, Crystal, Covered 42.00
Royal Lace, Butter, Pink, Covered 70.00
Royal Lace, Candleholder, Cobalt Blue, Pair 67.50
Royal Lace, Cookie Jar, Cobalt Blue, Covered 175.00
Royal Lace, Cookie Jar, Crystal, Covered 22.00
Royal Lace, Cookie Jar, Green, Covered 52.50
Royal Lace, Cookie Jar, Pink, Covered ....22.00 To 24.00
Royal Lace, Creamer, Green 15.00
Royal Lace, Cup & Saucer, Cobalt Blue 21.00
Royal Lace, Cup & Saucer, Green 15.00
Royal Lace, Pitcher, Cobalt Blue, 8 1/2 In. 140.00

Royal Lace, Plate, Cobalt Blue, 8 1/2 In. ....15.00 To 20.00
Royal Lace, Plate, Crystal, 9 In. 5.00
Royal Lace, Salt & Pepper, Pink, Tall 25.00
Royal Lace, Sherbet, Cobalt Blue, Metal Holder 17.00
Royal Lace, Sherbet, Green 12.00
Royal Lace, Tumbler, Cobalt Blue, 4 1/4 In. 18.00
Royal Ruby, Goblet, Crystal Ball, Bubble Stem & Foot 6.00
Royal Ruby, Salad Bowl, Large 15.00
Royal Ruby, Salt & Pepper, Honeycomb Inside 60.00
Royal Ruby, Tumbler, Wine, 2 1/2 Oz. ....5.75 To 7.00
    RUSSIAN, see Holiday
    SAIL BOAT, see White Ship
    SAILING SHIP, see White Ship
Sandwich Anchor Hocking, Cup & Saucer, Crystal 3.00
Sandwich Anchor Hocking, Nappy, Crystal, Ruffled 3.00
Sandwich Anchor Hocking, Punch Bowl Set, 12 Cup, Crystal 55.00
Sandwich Anchor Hocking, Tumbler, Crystal, 4 In. 6.00
    SAWTOOTH, see English Hobnail
    SAXON, see Coronation
    SHAMROCK, see Cloverleaf
Sharon, Berry Bowl, Pink, 5 In. 8.00
Sharon, Bowl, Amber, 8 1/2 In. 4.00
Sharon, Bowl, Fruit, Pink, 10 1/2 In. 24.00
Sharon, Bowl, Pink, 5 In. ....6.00 To 7.00
Sharon, Bowl, Pink, 8 3/8 In. 12.00
Sharon, Bowl, Vegetable, Pink, Oval, 9 1/2 In. 14.00
Sharon, Butter, Amber, Covered ....35.00 To 37.00
Sharon, Butter, Green, Covered ....43.00 To 65.00
Sharon, Butter, Pink, Covered ....30.00 To 40.00
Sharon, Cake Plate, Amber ....10.00 To 20.00
Sharon, Cake Plate, Crystal 14.00
Sharon, Cake Plate, Pink 23.00
Sharon, Candy Jar, Amber, Covered ....29.00 To 35.00
Sharon, Candy Jar, Pink, Covered ....30.00 To 37.00
Sharon, Creamer, Amber 8.50
Sharon, Cup & Saucer, Pink ....13.00 To 14.00
Sharon, Dish, Jelly, Amber, 7 1/2 In. 25.00
Sharon, Pitcher, Amber, Ice Lip 95.00
Sharon, Pitcher, Pink, Ice Lip .... 87.00 To 105.00
Sharon, Pitcher, Water, Amber, Ice Lip 80.00
Sharon, Pitcher, Water, Pink, Ice Lip 95.00
Sharon, Plate, Pink, 9 1/2 In. ....9.00 To 10.00
Sharon, Platter, Green, Oval, 12 1/2 In. 11.50
Sharon, Platter, Pink, Oval, 12 1/2 In. 11.00
Sharon, Salt & Pepper, Amber 25.00
Sharon, Salt & Pepper, Green ....28.00 To 42.00
Sharon, Salt & Pepper, Pink 32.00
Sharon, Sherbet, Pink 9.00
Sharon, Soup, Cream, Green, 5 In. 18.00
Sharon, Soup, Cream, Pink, 5 In. ....24.00 To 30.00
Sharon, Sugar & Creamer, Green, Covered 35.00
Sharon, Sugar & Creamer, Pink, Covered ....24.00 To 25.00
Sharon, Tumbler, Pink, 4 1/8 In. 15.00
Sierra, Bowl, Pink, 8 1/2 In. 5.50
Sierra, Bowl, Vegetable, Pink, Oval 19.00
Sierra, Butter, Pink, Covered 40.00
Sierra, Plate, Pink, 9 In. 8.00
Sierra, Platter, Pink, Oval, 11 In. 11.00
Sierra, Salt & Pepper, Pink 22.00
Sierra, Sugar & Creamer, Pink, Covered 20.00
Sierra, Tray, Pink 7.50
    SMOCKING, see Windsor
    SNOWFLAKE, see Doric
    SPIRAL OPTIC, see Spiral

Spiral, Cake Plate, Footed 19.00
Spiral, Ice Tub 11.50
Spiral, Sherbet, Green 3.50
    SPOKE, see Patrician
Starlight, Cup & Saucer, Crystal 4.25
Strawberry, Butter, Green, Covered 85.00
Sunflower, Cake Plate, Pink 15.00
    SWEET PEAR, see Avocado
Swirl, Candy Dish, Ultramarine, Covered, Round 75.00
Swirl, Coaster, Ultramarine, 3 1/4 In. 6.00
Swirl, Salt & Pepper, Ultramarine 25.00
    SWIRLED BIG RIB, see Spiral
    SWIRLED SHARP RIB, see Diana
Sylvan, Bowl, Vegetable, Green, Oval 30.00
Sylvan, Cup & Saucer, Green 32.00
Sylvan, Saltshaker, Green 65.00
Sylvan, Sherbet, Amber .... 9.00 To 15.00
Sylvan, Sugar & Creamer, Green 100.00
    TASSELL, see Princess
Tea Room, Cake Plate, Green, Handles 18.00
Tea Room, Relish, Green 12.00
Tea Room, Sugar & Creamer, Pink, Footed 24.00
Tea Room, Tumbler, Pink, 6 Oz. 15.00
Tea Room, Vase, Pink, 11 In. 70.00
Thistle, Bowl, Cereal, Pink 12.00
    THREE PARROT, see Sylvan
Twisted Optic, Plate, Green, 6 In. 1.00
    VERTICLE RIBBED, see Queen Mary
Vitrock, Plate, White, 8 1/2 In. 4.00
Waterford, Platter, Pink, 13 1/2 In. 7.00
    WEDDING BAND, see Moderntone
    WHITE SAIL, see White Ship
White Ship, Cocktail Shaker, Stirrer 12.00
White Ship, Pitcher, Water 25.00
White Ship, Plate, 6 In. 7.00
    WILD ROSE, see Dogwood
Windmill, Cocktail Shaker, Blue 14.00
Windmill, Ice Bucket 9.00
Windmill, Tumbler, Blue, 9 Oz. 10.00
    WINDSOR DIAMOND, see Windsor
Windsor, Ashtray, Pink, 5 3/4 In. 21.00
Windsor, Bowl, Crystal, 8 1/2 In. 12.00
Windsor, Pitcher, Green, 6 3/4 In. .... 42.50 To 45.00
Windsor, Pitcher, Pink, 6 3/4 In. .... 15.00 To 28.00

Swirl

Sylvan

Windsor

Derby, Figurine, Shepherd & Shepherdess,
    6 5/8 In., Pair

Windsor, Platter, Green, 13 5/8 In.	15.00
Windsor, Relish, 11 1/2 In.	5.00
Windsor, Sugar & Creamer, Green	8.50 To 9.00
Windsor, Tumbler, Pink, 4 In.	7.00
WINGED MEDALLION, see Madrid	
X Design, Butter, Pink, Covered, 1/4 Lb.	25.00

Derby porcelain was made in Derby, England, from 1756 to the present. The factory changed names and marks several times. Chelsea Derby (1770–1784), Crown Derby (1784–1811), and the modern Royal Crown Derby are some of the most famous periods of the factory.

DERBY, see also Chelsea; Crown Derby; Royal Crown Derby

DERBY, Cup & Saucer, Japan Pattern, Red Underglaze Mark, C.1800–25	75.00
Figurine, Shepherd & Shepherdess, 6 5/8 In., Pair ....*Illus*	100.00
Figurine, Shepherd & Shepherdess, Bloor, 18th Century, 6 5/8 In., Pair	100.00
Group, Music, Bisque, 10 In.	350.00
Ornament, House, Porcelain	1250.00
Vase, Design In Japanese Palette, Stylized Flowers, C.1884	280.00

The DeVilbiss Company has made atomizers of all types since 1888 but no longer makes the perfume bottle tops so popular with collectors. These were made from 1920 to 1968. The glass bottle may be by any of many manufacturers even if the atomizer says DeVilbiss.

DEVILBISS, Atomizer & Serving Tray, Oriental Lady, 13 1/2 X 10 1/2 In.	25.00
Atomizer, Amber Glass Base, Medical, Box, Instructions	15.00
Atomizer, Amber Lace	50.00
Atomizer, Blue Glass, Black Design	55.00
Atomizer, Blue, Black Butterflies, 7 In.	47.50
Atomizer, Blue, Black Design On Base	38.00
Atomizer, Gold & Black Enamel, Signed	65.00
Atomizer, Orange, Gold, & Black, Art Nouveau, 10 In.	115.00
Atomizer, Vaseline, Quilted Pattern	50.00
Dresser Set, Enameled Flowers, Gold Trim, Signed, 7 Piece	650.00
Perfume Bottle Atomizer, Blue, 22K Gold, Stopper	45.00
Perfume Bottle Atomizer, Crystal Top, Gold Crackle Bottom	25.00
Perfume Bottle Atomizer, Cut Crystal, Gold Bulb	75.00
Perfume Bottle Atomizer, Gold & Black Enameled, Marked	65.00
Perfume Bottle Atomizer, Red & Black, Art Glass	150.00
Perfume Bottle Atomizer, Silver, Bulb	70.00
Perfume Bottle, Black Art Deco Trim, Gold Crackle, Signed, 7 In.	55.00

The comic strip "Dick Tracy" started in 1931. He was the hero of movies from 1937 to 1947, starred in a radio series in the 1940s and a television series in the 1950s. Memorabilia from all these activities is collected.

DICK TRACY, Badge, Girls Division 35.00
  Badge, Lieutenant 65.00
  Badge, Sergeant 50.00
  Book, Big Little Book, The Hotel Murders 7.00
  Book, Cutout, Bonnie Braids, 1951 .... 50.00
  Book, Dick Tracy & Blackmailers, C.Gould, 1939 .... 30.00
  Book, Secret Code 55.00
  Book, Secret Service Patrol, Illustrations, 1938 .... 45.00
  Book, Tracy & Mad Killer, Better Little Book, No.14346, H.Berke 15.00
  Booklet, Vault Of Death, Big Thrill Chewing Gum, 1934 .... 20.00
  Bulb, Christmas 39.00
  Button, Pinback, Secret Service Patrol Member 25.00
  Camera, Case ....15.00 To 40.00
  Car, Police 45.00
  Comic, Popped Wheat, 1940 .... 10.00
  Dart Board, Box 32.50
  Doll, Little Honeymoon, Ideal, Boxed 50.00
  Game, Card, Box, 1934 .... 35.00
  Game, Detective, 1937 .... 19.00
  Game, Target, Box 35.00
  Glass, Drinking, Satin 22.50
  Gun, Pot Metal, Plastic Holster 20.50
  Handcuffs 15.00
  Hypnotic Eyes, 1940s 20.00
  Mask & Vest, Paper 12.00
  Pep Button 8.50
  Picture, Pop–Up, Capture Of Boris Arson, 1930s 45.00
  Pin, Detective 15.00
  Pin, Member 14.00
  Pistol, Pop, Tin 45.00
  Pistol, Pop, Tin, 1930s 20.00
  Pistol, Tin, 1940s 30.00
  Target, Boxed 35.00
  Thermos 6.00
  Tie Clasp, Dick Tracy Jr. 15.00
  Toy, Car, Windup, 12 In. 85.00
  Toy, Flagship, Wooden, Original Box, Pair 50.00
  Toy, Police Car & Station, Marx, Tin Litho, Box 165.00
  Toy, Police Car, Windup 59.00
  Toy, Squad Car, Box 150.00
  Toy, Squad Car, Dick Tracy & Sam Catchum, Windup, Tin, 11 In. 250.00
  Toy, Squad Car, Windup, Battery For Lights, Green 70.00
  Wrist Radio, 1961, Box 25.00
  Wristwatch, Boxed 150.00
  Wristwatch, Metal Band 75.00
  Wristwatch, New Haven, Oblong Face, Original Box, 1937 .... 200.00
  Wristwatch, New Haven, Round, Box ....65.00 To 100.00
  DICKENS WARE, see Royal Doulton; Weller

The Dionne quintuplets were born in Canada on May 28, 1934. The publicity about their birth and their special status as wards of the Canadian government made them famous throughout the world. Visitors could watch the girls play, reporters interviewed the girls and the staff, and thousands of special dolls and souvenirs were made picturing the quints at different ages. Emilie died in 1954, Marie in 1970. Yvonne, Annette, and Cecile still live in Canada.

DIONNE QUINTUPLETS, Book, We're Two Years Old & Soon We'll Be Three, Pair   21.00
  Box, Cookie, Sunshine, Advertising 45.00
  Calendar, 1936, Advertising, Borden's 10.00

Camera, Original Box 5.00
Card, 1935, 1936, 6 X 10 In., Pair 20.00
Doll, Jointed, 1936, Madame Alexander, 7 In. 225.00
Fan, Dated 1936 ....19.00 To 20.00
Paper Doll, Cut 35.00
Picture, Dressed As Nursery Rhyme Characters, Framed 45.00
Print Set, Colored, Dated 1935 .... 45.00
Print Set, Quaker Oats Premium, Each Print 5 X 7 In. 135.00
Print, Framed, 1935, 5 3/4 X 7 3/4 In. 16.50
Scrapbook, 70 Pages, 1930s 35.00
Spoon, Set Of 5 ....80.00 To 95.00

Walt Disney and his company introduced many comic characters to the world. Collectors search for examples of the work of the Disney Studios and the many commercial products modeled after his characters. These collectibles are called "Disneyana."

DISNEYANA, Acrobat, Mickey Mouse, Squeeze, Wood, 1930s 35.00
Bank, Bambi 20.00
Bank, Dime, Mickey Mouse, 1939 .... 68.00
Bank, Donald Duck, 2nd National, Chein, Mechanical 150.00
Bank, Mickey Mouse, Jam Jar, Tin Lid, 1935 .... 100.00
Bank, Mickey Mouse, Treasure Chest, Papier–Mache, Painted, 6 In. 50.00
Bell, Bicycle, Mickey Mouse ....20.00 To 25.00
Book, Cinderella, Fold Away, 1917 .... 45.00
Book, Coloring, Mickey Mouse Presents Disney Silly Symphony 15.00
Book, Comic, Mickey Mouse, Hard Cover, 1937 .... 150.00
Book, Comic, Uncle Scrooge, No.386 .... 125.00
Book, Fantasia, 1940 .... 40.00
Book, First, Donald Duck, 1935 .... 200.00
Book, Guide To Disneyland, Full Color, 1959 .... 22.50
Book, Mickey Mouse & His Friends, Linen 115.00
Book, Mickey Mouse Presents Walt Disney Nursery Stories, 1937 .... 135.00
Book, Mickey Mouse Stories No.2, D.McKay Co., 1934 .... 40.00
Book, Mickey Mouse, Hard Cover, 1937 .... 125.00
Book, Mickey Mouse, Linen, 1930s 40.00
Book, Mickey, Never Fails 55.00
Book, Pop–Up, Mickey Mouse, Blue Ribbon Books, 3 Pop–Ups, 1933 .... 150.00
Book, Program, Fantasia, Full Color, 1940 .... 25.00
Book, Punch Out, Sword In Stone, 1956 .... 10.00
Book, Song, Snow White, Disney Enterprises, 1938 .... 50.00
Book, Song, Snow White, Songs From Movie, 50 Pages, 1938 .... 50.00
Bottle Opener, Mickey Mouse, 1950s 6.00
Bowl, Cereal, Minnie Mouse, Salem China Co., 1934 .... 37.00
Bowl, Mickey Mouse, Beetleware ....7.00 To 13.00
Bracelet, 5 Signed Charms 6.00
Bracelet, Ferdinand The Bull, Box 40.00
Brooch, Mickey Mouse, Composition, Brier Mfg. Co., ... 50.00
Brush Set, Mickey Mouse, Pie–Eyed Mickey On Brush, 1936 .... 75.00
Camera, Mickey Mouse 16.00
Candy Jar, Mickey, Donald, Lollypops For Good Boys & Girls, 7 In. 35.00
Car, Donald Duck & Pluto, 1940s 25.00
Car, Donald Duck, Windup, 1930s 35.00
Card, Lobby, Snow White, Full Color, 1938, 11 X 14 In. 200.00
Card, Playing, Miniature, Original Box, 1 3/4 X 2 1/2 In. 35.00
Cards, Mickey Mouse, Old Maid 75.00
Catalog, Mickey Mouse, War Bond Advertising, 1944 .... 18.50
    DISNEYANA, CEL, see Animation Art
Chair, Director's, Mickey Mouse 50.00
Charm, Mickey Mouse, Celluloid 5.00
Chest, Toy, Mickey Mouse, Padded Seat Top, Litho, 1930s 145.00
Circus Train, Lionel, Mickey Mouse Waving, Circus Tent 1300.00
Clock Radio, Mickey Mouse, General Electric 40.00
Clock, Alarm, Mickey Mouse, U.S.Time 185.00
Clock, Mickey, Alarm, Animated, Head Moves, Ingersoll 290.00

Clock, Wall, Pluto, Eyes Roll, Tongue Moves 75.00
Cookie Jar, Donkey, Eeyore, Disney Prod. 60.00
Cookie Jar, Dumbo, Turnabout ....25.00 To 48.00
Cookie Jar, Mickey & Minnie Mouse, Turnabout ....38.00 To 40.00
Cookie Jar, Mickey Mouse With Birthday Cake 55.00
Cookie Jar, Thumper 55.00
Cup & Saucer, Beswick China 50.00
Cup, Drinking, Single Plate, Mickey With Teeth Playing Banjo 115.00
Doll, Ferdinand The Bull, Composition, Ideal, 1940s 110.00
Doll, Ferdinand, Knickerbocker, Jointed, Composition 115.00
Doll, Goofy, Walt Disney Products, Label, 1974 .... 8.00
Doll, Grumpy, Cloth, Ideal 30.00
Doll, Mickey Mouse, Cloth, Laws Of Italy, 14 In. 275.00
Doll, Mickey Mouse, Felt, Steiff, 6 In. 245.00
Doll, Mickey Mouse, Pie Eyes, Tooth, 11 In. 65.00
Doll, Mickey Mouse, Seiberling, Latex, 6 1/2 In. 125.00
Doll, Mickey Mouse, Steiff, 1930s, 9 In. 350.00
Doll, Mickey Mouse, Steiff, Paper Label, 4 1/2 In. ....275.00 To 325.00
Doll, Mickey Mouse, Stuffed, Steiff, 11 In. 375.00
Doll, Mickey Mouse, Wooden, Marked, 7 In. 275.00
Doll, Minnie Mouse, English, Deans Rag Book Co., 7 In. 295.00
Doll, Pinocchio, Jointed, Ideal, 8 In. 85.00
Ears, Slip On, Mickey Mouse, 1950s 7.50
Figurine, Bashful, Ceramic, Evan Shaw, 6 1/4 In. 75.00
Figurine, Donald Duck, Bisque, 1 3/4 In. 25.00
Figurine, Donald Duck, Bisque, Trumpet, 1930s, 3 1/2 In. 35.00
Figurine, Donald Duck, Carnival, Chalkware, 13 In. 35.00
Figurine, Elephant, Vernon Kilns No.41 .... 100.00
Figurine, Fiddler Pig, Bisque, Walt Disney, 1934, 3 1/2 In. 35.00
Figurine, Jiminy Cricket, Hard Rubber, Marx, 6 1/2 In. 10.00
Figurine, Mickey & Minnie Mouse, Celluloid, 3 1/2 In. 95.00
Figurine, Mickey Mouse, Bisque, 4 1/2 In. 75.00
Figurine, Mickey Mouse, Fun Flex, Part Label, 3 1/2 In. 55.00
Figurine, Mickey Mouse, With Cane, Bisque, 4 1/2 In. 75.00
Figurine, Minnie Mouse, Bisque, 4 In. 40.00
Figurine, Minnie Mouse, Solid Rubber 15.00
Figurine, Pinocchio, Bisque, 3 In. 28.00
Figurine, Seven Dwarfs, Seiberling, Hard Rubber 225.00
Figurine, Snow White, Soap, Lightfoot Schultz Co., 1938 .... 125.00
Figurine, Thumper, American Pottery, 5 In. ....18.00 To 35.00
Game, Bean Bag, Mickey Mouse 75.00
Game, Canasta, Mickey Mouse, 1950 .... 7.50
Game, Parade, Walt Disney, 1939 .... 100.00
Game, Pin The Tail On Mickey, Walt Disney Ent. 55.00
Game, Snow White & Seven Dwarfs, 1937 ....75.00 To 120.00
Handkerchief, Mickey Mouse ....10.00 To 12.00
Handkerchief, Mickey Mouse, Days Of Week, Set Of 7, 1930 .... 175.00
Holder, Pencil, Figural, Mickey Mouse, Dixon, 1925 .... 125.00
Horn, Party, Mickey Mouse, Walt E.Disney, 1930s ....45.00 To 50.00
House, Mickey Mouse, Cardboard, 1930s, 2 1/2 Ft. 250.00
Lamp, Dopey, 1930s 65.00
Lamp, Mickey Mouse, Plaster, Painted, 7 In. 500.00
Luncheon Set, Mickey Mouse, Tin, Litho, Ohio Art Co., 3 Piece 75.00
Map, Mickey Mouse, Globe Trotters 115.00
Marionette, Minnie Mouse, High–Heeled Shoes, 13 In. 125.00
Mask, Party, Snow White & Seven Dwarfs, Paper, 1930 .... 125.00
Movie, Mickey Mouse's Monkey Shine, 1930 .... 15.00
Movie, Safety, Donald Duck Teaches A Lesson, 1949 .... 3.00
Mug, Mickey Mouse Club, 1955 .... 12.00
Music Box, Mickey Mouse, Donald & Goofy, Bicentennial 45.00
Napkin Ring, Figural, Mickey Mouse, Plastic, Green 17.50
Nodder, Donald Duck, Papier–Mache 15.00
Pail, Sand, Donald Duck, Tin, 3 1/2 In. 25.00
Pail, Sand, Mickey & Pluto Selling Cold Drinks, Signed 55.00

Pail, Sand, Mickey Mouse, Minnie Mouse, Other Characters, C.1934 .... 225.00
Pail, Sand, Mickey Mouse, Tin, Litho, 8 In. 12.00
Paper Doll, Mickey Mouse, Uncut, Hinges, 1944 .... 35.00
Pencil Box, Ludwig Von Drake, Our Teacher 18.00
Pencil Case, Donald Duck, Mickey Mouse, Hassenfeld Bros., Inc. 20.00
Pencil Sharpener, Figural, Donald Duck, 1 1/4 In. 8.00
Phone, Mickey Mouse, 1964 .... 45.00
Pin, Globe Trotter's Club, I Eat N.B.C. Bread, 1938, 1 1/4 In. 35.00
Pin, Tinkerbell, Rhinestone 12.00
Pitcher, Dumbo, 6 In. 22.00
Pitcher, Milk, Donald Duck ....35.00 To 38.00
Planter, Donald Duck As Cowboy, Ceramic ....25.00 To 35.00
Planter, Snow White 20.00
Porringer, Mickey Mouse, Sterling Silver 120.00
Poster, Donald & Horace Eat A Good Breakfast, War 70.00
Poster, Victory Through Air Power, 1943, 1/2 Sheet 145.00
Projector, Movie, Mickey Mouse, Original Box, 1950s 25.00
Puppet, Hand, Mickey & Minnie, 1950s, Pair 30.00
Puppet, Hand, Mickey Mouse, 1931 .... 125.00
Puzzle, Bambi, W.D.Jaymar 10.00
Puzzle, Pinocchio, Set Of 5, Original Box 85.00
Radio, Mickey Mouse, General Electric 48.00
Radio, Mickey Mouse, Wood, Mickey On Front, Emerson, 1933 .... 675.00
Rattle, Mickey Mouse, Celluloid, 1930s 100.00
Ring, Mickey Mouse Club 8.00
Ring, Minnie Mouse, Sterling Silver 35.00
Roller Skates, Donald Duck, Kuson 10.00
Rug, Characters On Flying Carpet, 4 X 5 Ft. ....150.00 To 175.00
Rug, Train Scene, Labels, 1 Ft. 10 In. X 3 Ft. 2 In. 75.00
Salt & Pepper, Alice In Wonderland 48.00
Salt & Pepper, Donald Duck ....15.00 To 22.00
Salt & Pepper, Donald Duck, Flower On Head 12.00
Salt & Pepper, Mickey & Minnie, Ceramic 15.00
Shade, Reverse Painted, Mickey Mouse & Donald Duck 25.00
Sheet Music, Snow White, One Song, Dated 1937 .... 14.00
Sheet Music, When You Wish Upon A Star, Pinocchio, 1939 .... 18.00
Sheet Music, Who's Afraid Of The Big Bad Wolf, 1933 .... 45.00
Soap, Donald Duck & Mickey Mouse, Figural, Pair 150.00
Soap, Ferdinand The Bull, Figural, Original Box 22.00
Spoon, Mickey Mouse, 5 1/2 In. ....15.00 To 20.00
Spoon, Snow White, Silver Plated 10.00
Sprinkling Can, Donald Duck 55.00
Tile, Goofy, Gardener, 4 X 4 In. 8.00
Toothbrush Holder, Mickey Mouse & Minnie, Bisque, Dated 1930 .... 115.00
Toothbrush Holder, Three Little Pigs, Bisque ....65.00 To 69.00
Toy, Acrobat, Pinocchio, Windup, Marx, 1940 .... 125.00
Toy, Carpet Sweeper, Donald Duck, Tin Litho 50.00
Toy, Donald Duck, Drummer, Linemar 150.00
Toy, Donald Duck, Duet, Windup, Boxed 485.00
Toy, Donald Duck, On Skis, Windup, Marx, Box 175.00
Toy, Donald Duck, On Tricycle, Metal, Windup, Celluloid, British 475.00
Toy, Donald Duck, Pull, Fisher Price, Walt Disney Prod. 20.00
Toy, Donald Duck, Squeeze Action, Tin, Litho, Marx, 6 In. 80.00
Toy, Donald Duck, Standing By Whirligig, Celluloid, Windup Cart 450.00
Toy, Donald Duck, Windup, Tin, Litho, Marx, Original Box, 10 1/2 In. 350.00
Toy, Dopey, Windup, Tin, Litho, Marx, 8 In. 150.00
Toy, Express, Mickey Mouse 395.00
Toy, Ferdinand The Bull, Windup, Tin, Marx, Original Box, 6 In. 100.00
Toy, Ferris Wheel, Disneyland, Windup, Tin, Chein ....175.00 To 200.00
Toy, Goofy, Rides Unicycle, Tin, Windup, Linemar, 1950s 450.00
Toy, Handcar, Mickey & Minnie Mouse, Track, Box ....400.00 To 800.00
Toy, Mickey Mouse In Fire Engine, Rubber, Donald Duck, 6 X 4 In. 30.00
Toy, Mickey Mouse, Drummer, Battery Operated, Walt Disney, Linemar 195.00
Toy, Mickey Mouse, Ferris Wheel, Windup, Tin, Chein, 17 In. 170.00

Having trouble with stains in a glass bottle or vase? Sometimes this type of stain can be removed. Fill the bottle with water, drop in an Alka-Seltzer, and let it soak for about 24 hours. Then rub the ring with a brush or a cloth. If the deposit is a chemical deposit, this treatment should remove it. If the ring is caused by etching of the glass, it cannot be removed unless the bottle is polished.

Doll, Mutt & Jeff, Stuffed, Profile,
10 1/2 X 14 1/2 In.

Toy, Mickey Mouse, Magician, Battery Operated, Linemar, Box	750.00
Toy, Mickey Mouse, On Unicycle, Windup, Linemar	425.00
Toy, Mickey Mouse, On Wood Rocking Horse, Windup, Celluloid	900.00
Toy, Mickey Mouse, On Wooden Rocking Horse, Mechanical, Celluloid	350.00
Toy, Mickey Mouse, Playing Xylophone, Windup, Tin, Marx, 7 In.	225.00
Toy, Mickey Mouse, Steiff, 12 In.	450.00
Toy, Mickey Mouse, Tractor, Sun Rubber	35.00
Toy, Mickey Mouse, Twirling Tail, Linemar	150.00
Toy, Mickey Mouse, Twirling Tail, Marx	100.00
Toy, Minnie Mouse, Wooden, Fun–O–Flex	88.00
Toy, Pinocchio, Windup, Composition, Painted, 7 1/2 In.	50.00
Toy, Pinocchio, Windup, Tin, Litho, Marx, 9 In.	110.00
Toy, Pinocchio, Xylophone, Battery Operated	40.00
Toy, Plane, Mickey's Air Mail, Blue & Silver, Rubber	175.00
Toy, Pluto, Friction, Marked Walt Disney Productions, Linemar	20.00
Toy, Pluto, Pulls Cart, Friction, Linemar, 1950s	115.00
Toy, Pluto, Roll Over, Windup, 1939	95.00
Toy, Prince Charming & Cinderella, Dancing, Windup, Plastic	25.00
Toy, Roadster, Disney Parade, Windup, Tin, Marx, Box, 11 In.	175.00
Toy, Roller Coaster, Mickey, Windup, 1950s	225.00
Toy, Tractor, Mickey Mouse Driving, Vicero Sunoco, Canada	60.00
Toy, Train, Windup, Casey Jr.	68.00
Toy, Trolley, Mickey Mouse, Battery Operated, 1960s	64.50
Toy, Washing Machine, Mickey Mouse, Litho, Ohio Art Co.	55.00
Tumbler, Snow White, Welch Giveaway	9.00
Viewer & 4 Filmstrips, Chicken Little, 1933–43	45.00
Viewer, Mickey Mouse, 4 Short Filmstrips, 1939	45.00
Wallpaper, Mickey Mouse, Donald Duck, Friends, 1930s, 19 In.	50.00
Watch Fob, Mickey Mouse	35.00
Watch, Pocket, Mickey Mouse	90.00
Watch, Pocket, Mickey Mouse, Series No.1	295.00
Weather House, Mickey Mouse, Forecaster, 1940s	45.00 To 50.00
Wristwatch, Donald Duck, Ingersoll, U.S.Time, 1948	125.00
Wristwatch, Jiminy Cricket, U.S.Time, Original Band, 1948	85.00
Wristwatch, Mickey Mouse, Ingersoll, Leather Strap, 1930s	145.00
Wristwatch, Mickey Mouse, Ingersoll, Metal Band, Box, 1930s	150.00
Wristwatch, Mickey Mouse, Ingersoll, Oblong, 1938	250.00
Wristwatch, Mickey Mouse, Ingersoll, U.S.Time, 1948	125.00
Wristwatch, Porky Pig, 1949, Original Box	175.00
Wristwatch, Snow White Kissing Dopey	40.00

DOCTOR, see Medical; Dental

Doll entries are listed by marks printed or incised on the doll, if possible. If there are no marks, the doll is listed by the name of the subject or country.

DOLL, A.B.G., Character, Flirty Eyes, Open Mouth, Composition, Marked, 29 In. 895.00
A.M. 3/0, Floradora, Composition, Original Clothes, 14 In. 175.00
A.M. 33, Googly, Painted Eyes, 7 In. 285.00
A.M. 99, Kiddie Joy, Kid Body, 25 In. 350.00
A.M. 300, Lady, Closed Mouth, Brown Hair, Black Dress, 8½ In. 575.00
A.M. 324, Googly Boy, Bent Limb Body, Intaglio Eyes, Bunting, 6 In. ... 250.00
A.M. 341, Dream Baby, Bisque Head & Hands, Cloth Body, 5½ In. 95.00
A.M. 341, Dream Baby, Closed Mouth, 18 In. 385.00
A.M. 351, Baby, Black, Brown Eyes, 25 In. 700.00
A.M. 351, Baby, Boy, 5 Piece, 20 In. 445.00
A.M. 351, Baby, Open Mouth, 2 Lower Teeth, Composition, Marked, 22 In. 650.00
A.M. 351, Black, 10 In. 225.00
A.M. 351, Black, 23 In. 475.00
A.M. 351, Character Baby, 8 In. 295.00
A.M. 351, Dream Baby, 22 In. 350.00
A.M. 351/3K, Black, 14 In. 295.00
A.M. 351/3K, Black, Earthenware, 16 In. 250.00
A.M. 362, Black, 13 In. 325.00
A.M. 390, Little Aristocrat, Kiss Throwing Walker, 23 In. 1025.00
A.M. 390, Twins, 17 In. 265.00
A.M. 500, Baby Berry, Toddler, Closed Mouth, 8 In. 400.00
A.M. 971, Baby, Bisque Head, Sleep Eyes, Bent Limb Body, 14½ In. 245.00
A.M. 985, Baby, Sleep Eyes, Bent Limb Body, Blue Baby Dress, 19½ In. . 350.00
A.M., Bisque, Ball Jointed, Sleep Eyes, Dressed, 18 In. 200.00
A.M., Dream Baby, Bisque, Cloth Body, 8 1/2 In. 225.00
A.M., Dream Baby, Composition Hands, Original Chemise, 16 In. 450.00
A.M., Floradora, Kid Body, Fur Eyebrows, Redressed Old Clothes, 20 In. 275.00
A.M., Girl, Owl Look, Dressed, 1894, 24 In. 275.00
A.M., Infant, Bisque Head, Cloth Body, Closed Mouth, 14 In. 485.00
A.M., Nobbi Kid, Formal Dressed, 7 1/2 In. 495.00
A.M., Open Mouth, Glass Eyes, Ball Jointed, Dressed, Marked, 25 In. 795.00
A.M., Queen Louise, Bisque, Original Dress & Hat, Sleep Eyes, 25 In. 475.00
A.M., Rockabye Baby, Black, Bent Limb Body, Sweater, 10 1/2 In. 350.00
Advertising, Bob's Big Boy 7.00
Advertising, Ceresota Flour Boy, Rag 150.00
Advertising, Cracker Jack Sailor Boy, Rag, 15 In. 106.00
Advertising, Curad 12.50
Advertising, Jolly Green Giant, Rag, Lithograph, 1960, 16 In. 25.00

Doll, Bisque Head, Germany, Sleeping Glass Eyes, 16 1/2 In.
Doll, Bisque Head, Girl, Stationary Glass Eyes, C.1890, 9 In.
Doll, Heubach, Bisque, German, Intaglio Eyes, 11 3/4 In.

Doll, French, Bisque,
Fashion Dome Head,
Kid, Glass Eyes, 17 In.

Advertising, Phillips 66	65.00
Advertising, Pillsbury Doughboy	7.00
Advertising, Poll Parrot Shoes, Bisque, 3 1/2 In.	35.00
Advertising, Pop'N Fresh, 13 In.	7.00
Advertising, Smile Soda, Composition, Orange Head, Smile Bowtie, 12 In.	200.00

DOLL, ALEXANDER, see also Doll, Madame Alexander

Alexander, Marie, Dionne Quintuplets, Sleep Eyes, Hair, Tag, 11 1/2 In.	375.00
Amah, Door Of Hope Mission, Cloth Body, Wood Head, Bun, Slippers, 10 In.	100.00
American Character, Sweet Sue, White Dress, Pink Shoes, 1955, 25 In.	60.00
American Character, Sweet Suzanne, Brown Wig, Sleep Eyes, 1956, 14 In.	65.00

DOLL, ARMAND MARSEILLE, see Doll, A. M.

Artist Model, Jointed, Cherry & Birch, Carved, 19th Century, 16 In.	175.00
Baby, Cloth Body, Excelsior, Composition, 14 In.	20.00
Baby, Composition, Painted Face, Molded Hair, Cotton Romper, 1925, 9 In.	30.00
Belton Type, Closed Mouth, Repainted Body, Marked 3–France, 11 In.	500.00
Belton, Closed Mouth, Paperweight Eyes, Original Nun Outfit, 12 In.	275.00
Belton, Girl, Threaded Eyes, Closed Mouth, Antique Dress, 14 1/2 In.	1500.00
Belton, Jumeau, Bisque, Closed Mouth, Wood Torso, 17 In.	1850.00

DOLL, BERGMANN, see also Doll, S & H; Simon & Halbig

Bergmann, Bisque Head, Ball Jointed Body, Auburn Curls, Dressed, 29 In.	725.00
Bergmann, Child, Dress, 33 In.	1150.00
Bergmann, Girl, Long Auburn Curls, Brown Eyes, Real Hair Lashes, 29 In.	775.00
Bergmann, Googly, 32 1/2 In.	825.00
Bisque Head, Germany, Sleeping Glass Eyes, 16 1/2 In. ....*Illus*	250.00
Bisque Head, Girl, Stationary Glass Eyes, C.1890, 9 In. ....*Illus*	600.00
Bisque Shoulder Head, Impressed F Germany, 19 In. ....*Illus*	300.00
Bisque Shoulder Head, Kid Body, Bisque Hands, Paperweight Eyes, 17 In.	375.00
Bisque, Bald Shoulder Head, Blue Glass Eyes, Cloth Body, 23 In.	675.00
Bisque, Blue Glass Eyes, Closed Mouth, Cloth Body, GK, 15 1/2 In.	575.00
Bisque, Blue Glass Eyes, Pierced Ears, Swivel Neck, Kid Body, 13 In.	725.00
Bisque, Boy, Chinese, Jointed, 4 In.	39.00
Bisque, Boy, Googly, Molded Hair, Jointed At Shoulder, 3 1/2 In.	35.00
Bisque, Dollhouse, Lady, Painted, 7 1/2 In.	120.00
Bisque, German, Painted Features, Painted Shoes & Socks, Jointed, 5 In.	100.00
Bisque, Googly, Swivel Waist, Sitting, 6 1/2 In.	1400.00
Bisque, Jointed Shoulders, Blue Hat, 4 1/2 In.	30.00
Bisque, Man, Black Suit, Belgian, Incised D.F.B., 12 In.	850.00
Bisque, Molded Open–Close Mouth, Glass Eye, Jointed, Marked 1, 15 In.	475.00
Bisque, Musical, Mechanical, Brown Glass Eyes, GK 34–23, 17 1/2 In.	2200.00
Bisque, Petite Francaise France J, Anchor V, 7 Liane, Blue Eyes, 19 In.	450.00
Bisque, Pin Jointed, Blond Braid, Painted Face, German, 5 1/2 In.	65.00
Borgfeld, Little Annie Rooney, Kallus, 1926	375.00
Boy, That Kid, Red Hair, Freckles, Smile, Buck Teeth, Hasbro, 9 In.	125.00
Bru, Brevette, Bisque, Paperweight Eyes, Wedding Dress, 22 In.	3200.00
Bye–Lo, Baby, 17 In.Head, Copyright 1923	1250.00
Bye–Lo, Baby, Marked, Original Outfit, Fully Jointed, 4 In.	450.00
Bye–Lo, Baby, Signed, Original Chemise, 16 In.	750.00
Bye–Lo, Brown Eyes, 13 In.	150.00
Cabbage Patch, Black Girl, 16 In.	60.00
Cabbage Patch, Cloth Face, Trunk With 3 Changes Of Clothes, 22 In.	1250.00
Cabbage Patch, Koosas Pig, 16 In.	60.00
Celluloid Head, Cloth Body, Dressed, Germany, 1900s, 8 In.	45.00
Character, Toodles, Jointed Elbows, 1955, 19 In.	42.00
China Head, Blue Glass Eyes, Curly Hair, Cloth Body, 14 1/2 In.	1425.00
Chinese Boy Warrior, Papier–Mache, Original Clothes, 12 In.	95.00
Cloth, Girl, Printed, Art Fabric, 8 In.	55.00
Cloth, Painted, Molded Hair, Features, 20 1/2 In.	700.00
Cloth, Stuffed, Printed Face, Green & White Dress, Apron, 13 1/4 In.	145.00
Clown, Molded Rubber Face, Joker Type, Stuffed, 19 In.	20.00
Connie Lynn, Baby, Fur Wig, 22 In.	225.00
Demalcol, Googly, Bisque Head, Composition Body, Dressed, 9 In.	795.00
Denamaur, French, Open Mouth, Blue Glass Eyes, Marked, 21 In.	1505.00
Dresser, Holding 10 In.Mirror, Starched Evening Gown, 1920s, 7 In.Base	95.00
Dressmaker, Bisque Shoulder, Wooden, Movable Arms, Legs, 10 1/2 In.	15.00

Dutch, Wooden, Hand Carved, Pegged, Painted, Primitive, 11 1/2 In. 35.00
E.Denamaur, Bisque Head, Pierced Ears, Paperweight Eyes, Marked, 17 In. 1950.00
Eden Bebe, Anile Perroit, 23 In. 190.00
Eden Bebe, Fashion, Bisque Hands, Legs, & Feet Knees Down, 16 1/2 In. 2800.00
Eden Bebe, Open Mouth, Bisque Head, Paperweight Eyes, Signed, 22 In. 995.00
Eegee, Hard Plastic, Boxed, 25 In. 30.00
Eegee, Lester, Tan Corduroy Jacket, Brown Denim Pants, 1973, 24 In. 15.00
Effanbee, American Children, Ice Queen, 21 In. 350.00
Effanbee, Anne Shirley, Original Formal Dress, 20 In. 150.00
Effanbee, Anne Shirley, Original Formal Dress, 27 In. 250.00
Effanbee, Baby Tinyette, Composition, Painted Face, Bonnet, 1935, 8 In. 350.00
Effanbee, Becky Thatcher 49.00
Effanbee, Betsy Ross ....40.00 To 55.00
Effanbee, Candy Kid, 12 In. 110.00
Effanbee, Candy Kid, Composition, Redressed, 13 1/2 In. 185.00
Effanbee, Champagne Lady, Black, 18 In. 65.00
Effanbee, Charlie McCarthy, Composition, Excelsior Body, 19 In. 125.00
Effanbee, Chipper Face Girl, Happy Mother's Day Tag, 14 In. 50.00
Effanbee, Cinderella, Special Faces Made For Disneyland, 14 In. 95.00
Effanbee, Googly, Reverse U Mouth, Composition, Twelvetrees, 10 In. 360.00
Effanbee, Grande Dames, Hester, 1982, 15 In. 70.00
Effanbee, Little Lady, Evening Dress, 18 In. 85.00
Effanbee, Nutcracker, Pink Tulle, Ballerina Series, 15 In. 40.00
Effanbee, Patsy Ann, No Clothing, Marked, 19 In. 200.00
Effanbee, Patsy Joan, Composition, Brown Bobbed Molded Hair, 15 In. 375.00
Effanbee, Red Shoes, Ballerina Series, Red Trim On White, 11 In. 30.00
Effanbee, Rose Marie, Composition, Wig, Cloth Body, 24 In. 80.00
Effanbee, Shirley Temple, 36 In. 195.00
Effanbee, Snow White, Special Faces Made For Disneyland, 14 In. 95.00
Effanbee, Suzanne, 14 In. 50.00
Effanbee, Swan Lake, Ballerina Series, White Tulle, 13 In. 35.00
Emmett Kelly, 14 In. 125.00
English, Black Girl, Plaster Type, 17 In. 195.00
Eskimo, Regal Canada, Original Clothes, Wicker Sled, 10 In. 40.00
F S & Co., Character Baby, Sleep Eyes, Treble Tongue, 15 1/2 In. 375.00
F.G., Child, Bisque Arms & Head, Paperweight Eyes, Dressed, 14 1/2 In. 4500.00
Fashion, Bisque Arms, Paperweight Eyes, Kid Body, 17 In. 1995.00
Fashion, Limoges, Kid Body, 19 In. 450.00
Fashion, Tricolor Eyes, Kid Body, Old Clothes, Smiling, 20 1/2 In. 995.00
Felix The Cat, Stuffed, 1930s, English Version, 12 In. 95.00
Flapper, Boudoir, Composition, Black Hair, Shadow Eyes, 1920, 23 1/2 In. 215.00
Flapper, Little Girl, Bisque, Movable Arms & Legs, 3 In. 35.00
French, Bisque Head, Paperweight Eyes, Pierced Ears, Dressed, 23 In. 650.00
French, Bisque, Fashion Dome Head, Kid, Glass Eyes, 17 In. ....*Illus* 1000.00
French, Black Glass Eyes, Bamboo Teeth, Papier–Mache, 20 In. 700.00
French, Brown Bisque, Body Marked, Fancy Costume, 16 In. 1275.00
French, Closed Mouth, Human Hair, Straight Wrist, 17 In. 950.00
French, Fashion, Slight Smile, 15 In. 1300.00
French, Fashion, Tricolor Eyes, Smiling Face, Dressed, 20 1/2 In. 995.00
French, Mon Cheri, Pierced Ears, Bulging Eyes, 16 In. 350.00
Frozen Charlie, 1850, Original Clothes & Paper Drum, 3 1/2 In. 125.00
Frozen Charlotte, China, 1 In. 14.00
Frozen Charlotte, Outstretched Arms, German, 2 In. 29.00
 DOLL, FULPER, see Doll, Horsman
Gaultier, French, Bisque Head, Closed Mouth, Bonnet, Marked, 11 In. 995.00
Gebruder Heubach 7602, Pouty, 12 In. 495.00
Gebruder Heubach 7622, Boy, Composition, Jointed, Marked, 16 1/2 In. 1500.00
Gebruder Heubach, Googly, All Original, 7 In. 600.00
Georgene Novelty, Beloved Belindy, Black, 1928, 18 In. 95.00
German, Bisque, Black, 10 In. 350.00
German, Bisque, Lady, Upswept Hair, 1890, 22 In. 650.00
German, Fashion, 21 In. 695.00
German, Flapper, 14 In. 175.00
German, Ginny, Bisque, 8 In. 10.00

German, Girl, Composition & Papier-Mache, Dressel Type, 18 In. 375.00
German, Mabel, Bisque Head & Arms, Straw Body, Blue Sleep Eyes, 17 In. 250.00
German, Mohair Wig, Jointed Arms, Painted Shoes, Socks, Victorian, 5 In. 125.00
German, No.6764, Half, Arms Away, China, 3 In. 35.00
Gesland, Fashion, Stockinette Body, Bisque Hands, Lower Legs, 16 In. 2000.00
Ginny, Wee Imp, Box, 8 In. 185.00
Girl, Black, Hard Plastic, 1940s, 4 In. 22.50
Goebel, Character Baby, Blue Eyes, Old Baby Clothes, 28 In. 1800.00
Googly Girl, Swivel Head, Painted Eyes, 5 In. 200.00
Handwerck & Halbig, Blue Sleep Eyes, Ball Jointed Body, 30 In. 895.00
Handwerck 11-5, Bisque, Dressed, 14 In. 300.00
Handwerck, Bisque, Sleep Eyes, 21 In. 295.00
Handwerck, Girl, Jointed Body, Blue Stationary Eyes, 43 In. 2200.00
Handwerck, Pink Cloth Stuffed Sateen, Mohair Wig, 21 In. 375.00
Handwerck, Semihard Head, Pierced Ears, Feathered Brows, 30 In. 895.00
Hasbro, Atomic G.I.Joe, 12 In. 22.50
Heineken Beer, Ribbon Winner, 17 In.Pottery Head 75.00
Heubach 250/6, 25 In. 375.00
Heubach 6896, Somber Face, Intaglio Eyes, All Original, 10 In. 450.00
Heubach Koppelsdorf 300, Toddler Body, Blue Sleep Eyes, 19 In. 530.00
Heubach Koppelsdorf 300-1, Character Baby, 15 In. 350.00
Heubach Koppelsdorf 301, Unis France, Ball Jointed Body, 24 In. 700.00
Heubach Koppelsdorf 342, Baby, Bisque, Bent Limb, 25 In. 675.00
Heubach Koppelsdorf 399, Baby, Black, Bisque Head, Marked, 15 In. 275.00
Heubach Koppelsdorf, Bisque, Dressed, 10 1/2 In. 150.00
Heubach, Baby Stuart, Bellows Type Voice Box, Dressed, 11 In. 875.00
Heubach, Bisque, German, Intaglio Eyes, 11 3/4 In. ....*Illus* 150.00
Heubach, Character, Pouty, Closed Mouth, Papier-Mache Body, 12 In. 600.00
Heubach, Girl, Bisque, 9 In. 525.00
Heubach, Googly, Painted Eyes, Composition Body, 7 In. 335.00
Heubach, Pouty, Ball Jointed, 15 In. 795.00
Hollywood, Plastic, Sleep Eyes, Jointed, Original Clothing, 1940s, 5 In. 22.50
Horsman, Baby, Bent Leg, 17 In. 25.00
Horsman, Baby, Can'T Break 'Em Head, Dressed, Early 1900s, 16 In. 95.00
Horsman, Campbell Kid, 1910, 12 In. 155.00
Horsman, Mama, Composition Head & Limbs, Sleep Eyes, Dressed, 19 In. 75.00
Horsman, Rosebud, 19 In. 85.00
Horsman, Toddler, Precious, Composition, Original Wig & Clothes, 12 In. 50.00
Howdy Doody, Plastic, 3 1/2 In. 30.00
Ideal, Andy Gibb, Box, 6 In. 8.50
Ideal, Deanna Durbin, 16 In. 375.00
Ideal, Deanna Durbin, 19 In. 250.00
Ideal, Howdy Doody, Cloth Body, Rubber Hands, Plastic Head, 18 1/2 In. 85.00
Ideal, Miss Ideal, Original Clothes, 25 In. 75.00
Ideal, Saucy Walker, 32 In. 105.00
Ideal, Saucy Walker, Box, 22 In. 80.00
DOLL, J.D.K., see also Doll, Kestner
J.D.K. 11, Kid Body, Marked, 21 1/2 In. 125.00
J.D.K., Kid Body, 23 In. 250.00
J.D.K.129, Character, 25 In. 475.00
J.D.K.211, Character, 10 In. 400.00
J.D.K.257, Character Baby, Bisque Head, 5 Piece Bent Limb Body, 31 In. 2400.00
Jeri, Hilda, Human Hair, Glass Eyes, 20 In. 200.00
Jerri Lee, Original Clothes, 16 In. 175.00
Jumeau, Bisque Head, Open Mouth, Teeth, Ball Jointed, Dressed, 22 In. 995.00
Jumeau, Bisque Head, Paperweight Eyes, Marked, Dressed, 29 1/2 In. 1800.00
Jumeau, Bisque Head, Paperweight Inset Eyes, Closed Mouth, 1880, 13 In. 1800.00
Jumeau, Bisque, Closed Mouth, Long Curls, Jointed Body, Dressed, 13 In. 295.00
Jumeau, Brown Eyes, Open Mouth, Incised 1907 No.14, 29 In. 2600.00
Jumeau, Depose Tete, Paperweight Eyes, Closed Mouth, Marked, 15 In. 1550.00
Jumeau, Fashion, Kid Body, Original Clothes, 17 In. 1900.00
Jumeau, Glass Eyes, Pierced Ears, Composition, Silk Dress, 24 1/2 In. 149.00
Jumeau, Open Mouth, Glass Eyes, Ball Jointed, Teeth, Clothes, 22 In. 1350.00
Jumeau, Open Mouth, Glass Eyes, Human Hair, Bisque Head, Dressed, 17 In. 1050.00

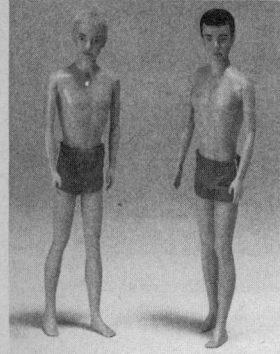

Doll, Mattel, Ken, Blond Flocked Hair,
   Red Swimsuit, Box, 1961

Doll, Mattel, Ken, Brunette Flocked Hair,
   Red Swimsuit, 1961

Jumeau, Paperweight Glass Eyes, Pierced Ears, Marked, 34 In.	3500.00
Jutta, Toddler, 1914, 18 In.	400.00
K * R 22, Baby, 24 In.	625.00
K * R 100, Kaiser Baby, Dressed, 20 In.	875.00
K * R 101, Brown Eyes, Hairline On Forehead, Redressed, New Wig, 19 In.	2295.00
K * R 107, Boy, Carl, Sandy Hair, Dark Suit, 12 1/2 In.	5900.00
K * R 114, Boy, Human Hair Wig, Clothes, 19 In.	3595.00
K * R 126, Baby, Flirty Eyes, 26 In.	850.00
K * R 126, Baby, Gray Sleep Eyes, Bisque Head, Tremble Tongue, 24 In.	525.00
K * R, Hilda, Solid Dome, 14 In.	2195.00
Kaiser, Boy, Look–Alike, Marked Einco, 12 In.	425.00
Kallus, Pinky, Composition Head, Jointed Arms & Legs, 10 In.	125.00
Kammer & Reinhardt, Baby, Bisque, 2 Teeth, Tongue, Limb Body, 14 In.	425.00
Kammer & Reinhardt, Character Boy, Carl, Intaglio Eyes, 12 In.	3630.00
Kathe Kruse, Boy, Signed On Foot & Head, 17 In.	450.00
Kathe Kruse, Boy, 20 In.	465.00
Kathe Kruse, Girl, Cloth, U.S.Zone, Germany, Signed, Wrist Tag, 14 In.	550.00
Kathe Kruse, Girl, Dated & Signed Foot, Original Dress, 1957, 14 In.	525.00
Kathe Kruse, Girl, Human Hair, 13 In.	340.00
Kay–Sam, Little Girl With Freckles, 16 In.	25.00
DOLL, KESTNER, see also Doll, J.D.K.	
Kestner 3–2, Baby, Parted Teeth, 11 In.	295.00
Kestner 13, Open Mouth, Brown Sleep Eyes, Ball Jointed, 20 1/2 In.	400.00
Kestner 14 171, Child, Bisque, Open Mouth, Sleep Eyes, 1900, 26 In.	600.00
Kestner 136, Baby, Blue Eyes, Human Hair Wig, Original Dress, 32 In.	850.00
Kestner 143, Character, Mohair Wig, Buster Brown Suit, 12 In.	600.00
Kestner 143, Girl, Bisque, Antique Clothes, 21 In.	1200.00
Kestner 146, Girl, Mohair Long Curls, Brown Stationary Eyes, 30 In.	850.00
Kestner 148, Kid Body, Redressed, 18 In.	310.00
Kestner 150, Bisque, Sleep Eyes, Open Mouth, 4 Teeth, Dressed, 7 1/2 In.	350.00
Kestner 151, Baby, Gray Sleep Eyes, Bald Dome, Original Clothes, 23 In.	500.00
Kestner 152, Baby, Velvet Suit, 13 1/2 In.	275.00
Kestner 154, Brown Eyes, Original Antique White Dress, 30 In.	750.00
Kestner 154, Girl, 17 In.	375.00
Kestner 154, Kid Body, Dressed As Baby, 28 In.	325.00
Kestner 154, Nurse Outfit, 17 In.	285.00
Kestner 156, Mama, Papa Pull String, Sleep Eyes, Ball Jointed, 25 In.	650.00
Kestner 164, Baby, 30 In.	750.00
Kestner 164, Ball Jointed Body, 29 In.	395.00
Kestner 164, Bisque Head, Glass Sleep Eyes, 26 In. ....*Illus*	250.00
Kestner 167, Bisque, Schmitt Type Body, Dressed, 16 In.	650.00
Kestner 171, Sleep Brown Eyes, Ball Jointed, White Dress, 25 In.	450.00

Kestner 171, Sleep Eyes, Original Human Hair Wig, Ball Jointed, 25 In. 595.00
Kestner 172, Gibson Girl, Hat & Parasol, 20 In. 3200.00
Kestner 182, Character Girl, Brown Hair, Closed Mouth, Dressed, 15 In. 2400.00
Kestner 192, Straight Wrists, Ball Jointed, Pierced Ears, 23 In. 695.00
Kestner 220, Oriental, Closed Mouth, All Original, 16 In. 3350.00
Kestner 245, Hilda, 18 In. 1500.00
Kestner 247, Boy, 15 In. 650.00
Kestner, Bisque Head, Closed Mouth, Leather Body, 20 In. 850.00
Kestner, Century Baby, 11 In. 400.00
Kestner, Dark Eyes, 4 Teeth, Bisque, Wool & Velvet Costume, 32 In. 1100.00
Kestner, Pouty, 16 In. 950.00
Kestner, Saucy Walker, Wrist Tag, Box, 16 In. 95.00
Kestner, Turned Head, Marked 0, 28 In. 750.00
Kestner, Turned Shoulder Head, Open Mouth, Kid Body, Dressed, 19 In. 450.00
    DOLL, KEWPIE, see Kewpie Doll
Kley & Hahn 520, Girl, Dressed, All Original, 13 In. 2600.00
Knickerbocker, Annie, Original Box, 10 In. 25.00
Knickerbocker, Kirk, Star Trek, Soft Poseable, 12 1/2 In. 5.00
Knickerbocker, Raggedy Ann & Andy, 20 In., Pair 30.00
Knickerbocker, Raggedy Ann, Box, 12 In. 15.00
Koestner, Bisque, Original Body, Dressed, 24 In. 400.00
Konig & Warnecke, Baby, Bisque, Sleep Eyes, 2 Teeth, Limb Body, 15 In. 400.00
Laurel & Hardy, Vinyl, Cloth Suit, 14 In., Pair 50.00
Lenci, Boy, Dutch, Italy, 1930, Tags & Labels, 9 In. 150.00
Lenci, Character, Cloth, Felt Swivel Head, Closed Mouth, Jointed, 22 In. 900.00
Lenci, Character, Cloth, O Shape Mouth & Eyes, Ringlet Curls, 20 In. 1000.00
Lenci, Child, 1930s, 28 In. 825.00
Lenci, Loretta, 12 In. 130.00
Lenci, Nun, Rosary Beads, 14 In. 550.00
Lenci, Peasant Girl, All Original, 14 In. 495.00
Lenci, Peasant Lady, Original Tag, 8 1/2 In. 100.00
Lenci, Portrait, Painted Face, Organdy Gown, Hooped Petticoat, 19 In. 725.00
Lenox, Abigail, Nectar Color Lawn Dress, 20 In. 425.00
Lenox, Amanda, Pink & Green Plaid Dress, 16 In. 385.00
Lenox, Jessica, Gray Irish Linen Outfit, 20 In. 450.00
Lenox, Maggie, Pink Dress, White Lace Overlay, 16 In. 375.00
Lenox, Mary Anne, White Cotton Dress, Lace Trimmed, 20 In. 425.00
Lenox, Rebecca, Gauzy White Dress, 16 In. 375.00
Little Lulu, Rag, 21 In. 42.50
Little Max, Joe Palooka, Original Clothes, 19 In. 55.00
Little Red Riding Hood, Rag, 15 In. 38.00
Loni, Dressd In Red Jumper, Green Blouse, Felt Shoes, Steiff, 16 In. 150.00
M.Mossor, French Twerp, 21 In. 265.00
Madame Alexander, Agatha, Box, 21 In. 325.00
Madame Alexander, Amy, 12 In. 50.00
Madame Alexander, Baby Victoria, Blue Gown & Hat, Box, 18 In. 175.00
Madame Alexander, Baby, Black, 25 In. 625.00
Madame Alexander, Baby, Black, Sweet Tears, 14 In. 150.00
Madame Alexander, Baby, Rock-A-Bye, Black, 12 In. 500.00
Madame Alexander, Ballerina, Box, 14 In. 295.00
Madame Alexander, Beth, 12 In. 50.00
Madame Alexander, Betty Big Girl, 30 In. 55.00
Madame Alexander, Binny Walker, Hard Plastic, 15 In. 145.00
Madame Alexander, Black Girl, Rubber, 10 In. 45.00
Madame Alexander, Black, Celluloid, Jointed, 4 In. 27.00
Madame Alexander, Bride, 1975, 17 In. 110.00
Madame Alexander, Bride, 1980, 17 In. 100.00
Madame Alexander, Bridesmaid, 1975, 17 In. 110.00
Madame Alexander, Butch, Composition, Cloth, Repaired Crown, 22 In. 155.00
Madame Alexander, Carmen Miranda, Composition, 1942, 15 In. 195.00
Madame Alexander, Cinderella, Box, 14 In. 80.00
Madame Alexander, Cissette, Southern Belle, 1968, 11 In. ....475.00 To 525.00
Madame Alexander, Colonial Girl, 8 In. 500.00
Madame Alexander, Cornelia, Box, 21 In. 325.00

Madame Alexander, Dionne Quints, Toddlers, Dressed, 11 1/2 In., Set 1250.00
Madame Alexander, Dionne Quints, White Organdy Dresses, 7 1/2 In., Set 750.00
Madame Alexander, Edith The Lonely, 8 In. 1489.00
Madame Alexander, Elise Ballerina, Pink, Box, 17 In. 80.00
Madame Alexander, Elise, Ballerina, Silver, 21 In. 75.00
Madame Alexander, Elvis Presley, No.1, 14 In. 95.00
Madame Alexander, Goya, 21 In., Boxed 240.00
Madame Alexander, Heidi, Box, 14 In. 80.00
Madame Alexander, Indian Girl, 8 In. 550.00
Madame Alexander, Jane Withers, 14 In. 450.00
Madame Alexander, Jane Withers, 21 In. 700.00
Madame Alexander, Jeannie Walker, Brown Sleep Eyes, Cloth Tag, 13 In. 325.00
Madame Alexander, Jo, Red Dress, Box, 12 In. 110.00
Madame Alexander, Joanie, 1959, 36 In. 255.00
Madame Alexander, Laurie, 12 In. 65.00
Madame Alexander, Leslie Uggums, Bride, Wrist Tag, Box, 17 In. 325.00
Madame Alexander, Little Lady, Original Shoes, Redressed, 18 In. 185.00
Madame Alexander, Little Red Riding Hood, 8 In. 35.00
Madame Alexander, Little Shaver, 12 In. 150.00
Madame Alexander, Little Women, Amy, 12 In. 300.00
Madame Alexander, Little Women, Amy, Separated Fingers, 14 In. 400.00
Madame Alexander, Little Women, Beth, 12 In. 300.00
Madame Alexander, Little Women, Including Laurie, 8 In., Set 360.00
Madame Alexander, Little Women, Jo, 12 In. 300.00
Madame Alexander, Little Women, Meg, 12 In. 300.00
Madame Alexander, Lucinda, Box, 14 In. 80.00
Madame Alexander, Maggie Walker, Hand Painted, 15 In. 95.00
Madame Alexander, Manet, 21 In., Boxed 250.00
Madame Alexander, Margaret O'Brien, Original Clothes, 21 In. 650.00
Madame Alexander, Mary Ellen, Hand Painted, Walker, Tagged, 31 In. 395.00
Madame Alexander, Mary Mine, 8 In. 85.00
Madame Alexander, McGuffey Ana, 14 In. 65.00
Madame Alexander, McGuffey Ana, With Poke Bonnet, 11 In. 175.00
Madame Alexander, Melanie, 1981, 21 In. 335.00
Madame Alexander, Miss Muffet, 8 In. 35.00
Madame Alexander, Mommy's Pet, Pink & Blue Check Outfit, Box, 21 In. 200.00
Madame Alexander, Nina Ballerina, Red Hair, Tagged, 15 In. 250.00
Madame Alexander, Pinky, Composition, Cloth, Crazing, 19 In. 165.00
Madame Alexander, Pocahontas, With Papoose, Wrist Booklet, Box, 8 In. 550.00
Madame Alexander, Poor Cinderella, 12 In. 50.00
Madame Alexander, Puttin', Box, 14 In. 50.00
Madame Alexander, Rebecca, Box, 14 In. 80.00
Madame Alexander, Renoir Rebecca, 14 In. 65.00
Madame Alexander, Romeo, 12 In. ....42.00 To 50.00
Madame Alexander, Scarlett, 14 In. 90.00
Madame Alexander, Scarlett, 1976, Box, 21 In. 375.00
Madame Alexander, Scarlett, 8 In. 42.00
Madame Alexander, Scarlett, Box, 21 In. 315.00
Madame Alexander, Scarlett, Green Dress, 12 In. 115.00
Madame Alexander, Scarlett, Portrait, Floral Print Outfit, Box, 21 In. 750.00
Madame Alexander, Scarlett, Portrait, Taffeta Outfit, 1977, Box, 21 In. 450.00
Madame Alexander, Shari Lewis, No.1432, 1959, Wrist Tag, Box, 21 In. 450.00
Madame Alexander, Sleeping Beauty, Box, 14 In. 90.00
Madame Alexander, Sleeping Beauty, Unused, Box, Dated 1965, 14 In. 125.00
Madame Alexander, Tinkerbell, Box, 11 In. 550.00
Madame Alexander, Tyrolean Boy & Girl, 8 In., Pair 250.00
Madame Alexander, Wendy Ann, Painted Eyes, Tagged Clothes, 9 1/2 In. 95.00
Mae West, Boudoir, Satin Lace Gown, Hat, C.1920, 30 In. 215.00
Mama Katzenjammer, Composition, Mouth Opens, 1920s, 9 In. 225.00
Marin, Boy, Flamenco, Label, 13 1/2 In. 22.00
Martha Chase, Boy, 16 In. 250.00
Mattel, Barbie, Airline Hostess 125.00
Mattel, Ken, Blond Flocked Hair, Red Swimsuit, Box, 1961 ....*Illus* 65.00
Mattel, Ken, Brunette Flocked Hair, Red Swimsuit, 1961 ....*Illus* 65.00

MIJ, Bisque, 7 1/4 In. 45.00
MIJ, Bisque, Ribbon In Hair, 4 In. 25.00
Morimura Bros., Toddler, Bisque, Jointed, Original Wig, Clothes, 21 In. 235.00
Morimura, Character Baby, Bisque Head, Jointed, Period Clothes, 8 In. 175.00
Mortimer Snerd, Clown Outfit, 13 In. 95.00
Motschmann Type, Baby, China, Squeaker, Swivel Neck, 11 In. 1650.00
Mutt & Jeff, Stuffed, Profile, 10 1/2 X 14 1/2 In. ....*Illus* 225.00
Nancy Ann, Auburn Wig, Dress, Hand Painted, 11 In. 30.00
Nancy Ann, November Girl, Jointed, Bisque 35.00
Nippon, Lord Nelson, Bisque Head, Ball Jointed, Admiral Suit, 22 In. 325.00
Norah Wellings, Island, Black, 14 In. 62.00
Norah Wellings, Sailor, 8 In. ....25.00 To 35.00
Norah Wellings, Scotsman, 8 In. 39.00
Nun, Hand Painted Head, Latex Body, Stuffed, Arms Outstretched, 26 In. 52.00
O.I.C.255, Baby, Long Screamer, Germany, 15 In. 1650.00
Opal Butler, Baby Stuart, 11 In. 100.00
Otto Reinecke, PM 914, Toddler Body, 12 In. 295.00
Otto–Curo, Character Girl, Cream Silk Antique Dress, Hat, Coat, 34 In. 1250.00
    DOLL, PAPER, see Paper Doll
Papier–Mache, Boy, Glass Eyes, Original Wig, Straw Filled Body, 18 In. 200.00
Papier–Mache, Girl, Jointed Arms, Legs, Sleep Eyes, Closed Mouth, 22 In. 125.00
Papier–Mache, Girl, Waxed Body, Glass Eyes, 19 In. 325.00
Parian, Boy, Molded Blouse, Original Wardrobe & Trunk, 17 In. 950.00
Parian, Man, Blond Molded Hair, 23 In. 500.00
Parian, Tinted, Seated In 1800s Parian Bathtub, Marked, 2 1/2 X 1 In. 65.00
Parrish, Selling Fool, RCA Radiotrons 750.00
Parrish, Wooden Soldier, Movable Joints, 1 1/2 Ft. 900.00
    DOLL, PINCUSHION, see Pincushion Doll
PM 23, Baby, Original Layette, 10 In. 175.00
Poor Pitiful Pearl, Vinyl Body, 17 In. 35.00
Porzellanfabrig, 162 2/0, Toddler Body, 15 In. 370.00
Pouty Face, Tearful, Stuffed, 14 In. 8.00
Queen Louise, Bisque Head, Ball Jointed, Dressed, 24 1/2 In. 295.00
R & A, Baby, Molded Bonnet, Redress In Romper, 9 In. 425.00
R & B, Nancy Lee, Composition, Gloves, Wrist Tag, 21 In. 175.00
R & B, Sonja Henie, Original Clothes, No Skates, 14 In. 80.00
R.D., French, Closed Mouth, Blue Glass Eyes, Long Curls, Marked, 19 In. 1995.00
Recknagel, Bisque Head, Composition Body, C.1890, 20 In. 350.00
Revalo, Toddler, 11 In. 250.00
Revlon, Swivel Waist, Hose, Shoes & Panties, 1956, 17 In. 40.00
Rose O'Neill, Composition, Signed, 11 In. 110.00
    DOLL, S & H, see also Doll, Bergmann; Doll, Simon & Halbig

Doll, Simon & Halbig 1042, Bisque Head, Jointed, Marked, 21 In.
Doll, Kestner 164, Bisque Head, Glass Sleep Eyes, 26 In.
Doll, S & H 1079, Bisque Head, Open Mouth, Marked, 25 1/2 In.
Doll, Bisque Shoulder Head, Impressed F Germany, 19 In.

Doll, S.F.B.J. 13, Paris,
Bisque, 28 In.

Doll, S.F.B.J.251, Paris, Bisque, 23 In.

Save your doll's packaging, tags, and inserts. These can triple the price when the doll is sold.

S & H 201/2, Blachette, 10 In.	295.00
S & H 919, Character Girl, Open–Close Mouth, Ball Jointed, 8 In.	2090.00
S & H 1039, Walking & Talking, Mechanical, Flirty Eyes, 20 In.	995.00
S & H 1079, Bisque Head, Open Mouth, Marked, 25 1/2 In. ....*Illus*	500.00
S & H 1079, Bisque Swivel Head, Kid Body, 26 In.	365.00
S & H 1079, Sleep Eyes, Auburn Hair, Pierced Ears, Ball Jointed, 20 In.	395.00
S & H 1249, Child, Sleep Eyes, 4 Teeth, Blond, Costume, 1900, 25 In.	700.00
S & H 1249, Santa Claus, 35 1/2 In.	1950.00
S & H 1249, Santa Claus, Ball Jointed, 22 In.	595.00
S & H 1349, Blond, Sleep Eyes, Ball Jointed, With Wardrobe, 20 In.	350.00
S & H 1385, Fashion, Lady, Marked, All Original, Box, 14 In.	1800.00
S & H 1906, Boy, Mohair Wig, Pique Suit, Matching Hat, 34 In.	995.00
S & H, Boy, Mohair Wig, White Pique Suit & Hat, 34 In.	900.00
S & H, Brown Sleep Eyes, Original Mohair Wig, 24 In.	595.00
S & H, Fashion Dome Head, Completely Dressed, 15 In.	800.00
S & H, Girl, Open Mouth, Brown Eyes, Gibson Girl Outfit, 20 In.	350.00
S.F.B.J. 13, Paris, Bisque, 28 In. ....*Illus*	800.00
S.F.B.J. 60, Bisque Head, Adult Body, Curls, Gray Coat Dress, 20 In.	895.00
S.F.B.J. 60, Bisque Head, Open–Close Eyes, Upper Teeth, Dressed, 25 In.	798.00
S.F.B.J. 60, Bisque Head, Sleep Eyes, Original Clothes, 11 In.	285.00
S.F.B.J. 60, Open Mouth, Brown Hair, Dressed, Marked, 21 In.	795.00
S.F.B.J. 60, Open Mouth, Open–Close Eyes, Blond, Dressed, Marked, 22 In.	875.00
S.F.B.J., Black, Open Mouth, Braids, Incised 34–29, 20 In.	4250.00
S.F.B.J., Character, Baby Twerp, 7 In.	750.00
S.F.B.J., Child, Bisque, Gray Sleep Eyes, Wooden Jointed, 1900, 23 In.	650.00
S.F.B.J., Laughing Jumeau, 26 In.	250.00
S.F.B.J.236, Baby, Velvet Suit, 26 IN.	1500.00
S.F.B.J.236, Open Mouth, Brown Hair, Paper Label, 20 In.	1750.00
S.F.B.J.236, Toddler, Laughing, Sailor Suit, 15 In.	1200.00
S.F.B.J.247, Character, Twerp Toddler, Original Clothes, 9 In.	975.00
S.F.B.J.251, Paris, Bisque, 23 In. ....*Illus*	1500.00
S.F.B.J.251, Toddler Body, Blue Glass Eyes, 20 In.	1500.00
S.F.B.J.301, Bisque Head, Open Mouth, Open–Close Eyes, Dressed, 29 In.	1050.00
S.F.B.J.301, Bisque, Composition, Paperweight Eyes, Cropped Wig, 7 In.	150.00
Sailor, Glass Eyes, Composition, Hand Painted, Late 1800s, 10 1/2 In.	75.00
Santa Claus, Composition, Jointed, Oil Cloth Boots, Sack, 19 In.	185.00
Santa Claus, Composition, Molded Beard & Hat, Original Outfit, 18 In.	175.00
Saucy Walker, All Hard Plastic, Braided Wig, Original Clothes, 22 In.	47.00
Schmitt, Girl, Blond, Closed Mouth, Marked, 15 1/2 In.	5950.00
Schoenau & Hoffmeister, Ball Jointed Body, 33 In.	595.00
Schoenau & Hoffmeister, Child, 4 Teeth, Ball Jointed, Star, 17 In.	225.00
Schoenau & Hoffmeister, Princess Elizabeth, Toddler Body, 23 In.	2800.00

Schoenau, German Girl, Sleep Eyes, Ball Jointed, My Cherub, 25 In. 325.00
Schoenhut, Baby, With Wardrobe, 14 In. 400.00
Schoenhut, Girl, Bisque Head, Ball Jointed, Dimple In Chin, 23 1/2 In. 295.00
Schoenhut, Girl, Dolly Face, Redressed, 19 In. 390.00
Schoenhut, Girl, Painted Eyes & Mouth, Blond Hair, 1911, 21 In. 475.00
Schoenhut, Pout, Closed Mouth, Original Clothes, 16 In. 695.00
Schoenhut, Pouty Face, Original Blue Collar Middy Dress, 16 In. 425.00
Schoenhut, Spring Jointed, Open–Close Mouth, Dated 1911, 14 1/2 In. 350.00
Schoenhut, Toddler, Baby Face, 12 In. 400.00
Schoenhut, Walker, Baby Face, Original Clothes, C.1911, 11 In. 450.00
Schutz, Boy, Paperweight Eyes, Jointed Kid, Molded Hair, Marked, 16 In. 95.00
Scootles, Composition, 12 In. 245.00
Shaker, Woman, Black Cape, Cloth, Handmade, Embroidered Face, 13 1/2 In. 65.00
    DOLL, SHIRLEY TEMPLE, see Shirley Temple
    DOLL, SIMON & HALBIG; see also Doll, Bergmann; Doll, S & H
Simon & Halbig 1042, Bisque Head, Jointed, Marked, 21 In. ....*Illus* 450.00
Simon & Halbig 1078, Sleep Eyes, 8 In. 235.00
Simon & Halbig 1249, Santa Claus, Ball Jointed, 22 In. 595.00
Simon & Halbig 126/26, Character, 10 In. 275.00
Simon & Halbig 949, Lady, Bisque Head, Arms, Kid Jointed Body, 17 In. 600.00
Simon & Halbig, Bisque, Ball Jointed Body, Sleep Eyes, Dressed, 24 In. 375.00
Simon & Halbig, Bisque, Ball Jointed, Composition, Brown Eyes, 29 In. 950.00
Simon & Halbig, Character Child, 20 In. 1050.00
Steiff, Man, Sitting, Stick In Mouth, Stuffed, Cloth, Dressed, 12 In. 75.00
Steiff, Mickey Mouse, 1930s, 9 In. 250.00
Steiff, Puppet, Owl, Glowing Eyes, 8 1/2 In. 30.00
Steiff, Santa Claus, C.1960, Tagged, 14 In. 250.00
Steiner A–11, Le Parisien, Straight Wrist, Closed Mouth, 18 1/2 In. 3150.00
Steiner Bourgoin, Wire Eyed, Closed Mouth, Composition, Marked, 29 In. 5800.00
Steiner, Bisque Head, Pierced Ears, Open Mouth, Dressed, 25 In. 1050.00
Steiner, Windup, Was Over Papier–Mache, Dated 1867, 20 In. 1400.00
Stockinette, Black Chenille, Button Eyes, Pinafore, Brewer, Ma., 18 In. 225.00
Stocking, Painted Face, Bonnet & Dress, 1 Leg Very Large, 24 In. 49.00
Sun Rubber, Babe, 9 In. 7.00
Terri Lee, Original Clothes, 16 In. 175.00
Tete Jumeau, Blue Eyes, Closed Mouth, 12 In. 2750.00
Tete Jumeau, Brown Eyes, Closed Mouth, 14 1/2 In. 3150.00
Tete Jumeau, Closed Mouth, Blue Paperweight Eyes, Cork Pate, 32 In. 4600.00
Tete Jumeau, Closed Mouth, Paperweight Eyes, White Dress, 24 In. 2995.00
Tete Jumeau, Red Cheeks, Original Paper Label, 22 In. 3150.00
Toddler, Magic Skin, Hard Plastic Head, Yellow Pigtails, 24 In. 25.00
Topsy–Turvy, Black & White, 17 In. 48.00
Topsy–Turvy, Red Riding Hood, Wolf, & Grandmother, Stuffed, 17 In. 65.00
Troll, Dam, Girl, Box, 9 In. 25.00
Uncle Sam, Papier–Mache, Cloth Standing Figure, 11 3/4 In. 100.00
Uncle Sam, Papier–Mache, Molded Shoulder, Clothed, 1910, 20 In. 120.00
Uncle Sam, Papier–Mache, Molded Shoulder, Clothed, 1930, 22 In. 145.00
Ventriloquist, Black Boy, Wood Head, Lever Operated Mouth, 33 In. 700.00
Ventriloquist, Wood, Carved, Stuffed Cloth Body, Wig, 28 In. 210.00
Vogue, Baby Dear, Painted Eyes, Original Trunk & Wardrobe, 17 In. 225.00
Vogue, Bobby Dear & Baby Dear One, E.Wilkens, 2 Teeth, Pair 400.00
Vogue, Jeff, Pajama Outfit, Box 70.00
Vogue, Jill, No.7409, Red Hair, Blue Dress, Boxed, 1957 .... 65.00
Vogue, Sailor Boy, Cracker Jack, Original, 13 In. 10.00
Vogue, Star Bright, 17 In. 75.00
Vogue, Top–Knot Baby Dear, Trunk & Wardrobe 225.00
Walk–A–Way Baby, Marx, Original Box 35.00
Walker, Brushed Hair, Fringed Costume, Painted Boots, 1873, 17 In. 5500.00
Wizard Of Oz, Wizard, Mego, 1974, Box, Set Of 4, 12 In. 90.00
Wooden, Glass Eyes, Bonnet, Queen Anne Type, C.1800, 14 In. 3250.00
    DONALD DUCK, see Disneyana

Iron doorstops have been made in all types of designs. The vast majority of the doorstops sold today are cast iron and were made from about 1890 to 1930. Most of them are shaped like people, animals, flowers, or ships.

DOORSTOP, Alligator, Original Green, Mouth Open, Iron, 8 1/2 In.	125.00
Basket Of Apple Blossoms	40.00
Basket Of Fruit, Flat & Hollowed Back, Original Paint, 10 1/2 In.	70.00
Basket Of Tulips, Iron, Painted, Albany Foundry, C.1870, 7 1/2 In.	110.00
Bird, Drinking From Urn, Brass, Flatback, 10 In.	125.00
Bird, Red, What Cheer, Iowa Pottery	35.00
Bowl Of Violets	75.00
Bowl, Yellow & Green Daisies, Iron, 6 3/4 In.	45.00
Bulldog, Chalkware	12.50
Bulldog, Iron, Brown & White Paint	60.00 To 65.00
Bulldog, Two, Iron	75.00
Cat, Angora, Signed Hubley	95.00
Cat, Arched Back, Green Eyes	135.00
Cat, Black, Art Deco, Full Figure	55.00
Cat, Full Figure, Art Deco, Iron	68.00
Cat, Seated, Hubley	95.00 To 130.00
Coach & Horses, Iron, Colored, 12 In.	75.00
Cockatoo, 11 In.	45.00
Conestoga Wagon & Oxen	130.00
Cornucopia Of Flowers	95.00
Cottage, Cape Cod	90.00
Cottage, Shrubbery, Flowers, Original Paint, 8 3/4 X 6 In.	70.00
Covered Wagon, 1930	115.00
Dancer, Spanish, Holding Fan	105.00
Dog, Boston Bull, Hubley	65.00
Dog, Boston Terrier, Facing Left	75.00
Dog, English Pointer, Cast Iron, 13 In.	55.00
Dog, Fox Terrier, Iron, Original Paint	70.00
Dog, German Shepherd, Black, Hubley	110.00
Dog, German Shepherd, Bronzed, World Radio	40.00
Dog, Pointer, Bronze Finish, Wooden Base, 15 In.	95.00
Dog, Springer Spaniel	48.00
Dog, Terrier, Hubley	65.00
Dutch Boy & Girl, Standing, Original Paint, 4 X 5 3/4 In.	70.00
Dwarf, Full Figure, Hands In Pocket, Iron, 10 1/2 X 6 In.	215.00
Dwarf, With Beard, Red Hat, Black Shoes, Iron, 11 In.	130.00
Dwarf, With Lantern & Keys, 10 In.	135.00
Elf, Original Paint, 11 In.	125.00
Fireman, Gloucester, Yellow Slicker, Painted, Iron, 6 1/2 In.	65.00
Fisherman, Small	40.00
Flowerpot, Iron	35.00
Fox, Sleeping, Gray, Iron, 7 1/2 In.	65.00
Frog, Cast Iron, Original Paint	55.00
Fruit Boy, Top Hat	150.00
George Washington On Horse, Pot Metal	40.00
Golfer	185.00 To 195.00
Gothic Gate, Cast Iron	55.00
Horse & Chariot, Cast Iron, Original Paint, 19 In.	135.00
Horse, Prancing, White, Iron, 12 X 12 In.	135.00
Horse, Standing, Hunter, Artist Initials, Metal Crafters, 12 In.	65.00
Humpty–Dumpty, Cast Iron, Painted White, 5 In.	75.00
Jockey, Black, Ring In Hand	65.00 To 115.00
Kittens, Drayton	135.00
Lady, Colonial, Iron, 10 1/2 In.	65.00
Lady, On Sofa, Iron	110.00
Lady, Standing, Holding Basket, Original Paint, Cast Iron, 8 In.	60.00
Lion, 8 3/4 In.	175.00
Lion, 9 1/2 In.	100.00
London Royal Coach	85.00

Old Man Of The Sea	70.00
Owl, Flat Back, Original Paint, 6 3/4 In.	60.00
Parrot, Iron, 7 In.	75.00
Parrot, On Hoop	90.00
Peacock	95.00
Pony, Western, With Saddle, Cast Iron	85.00
Rabbit, Cast Iron, White, Pink Ears	125.00
Rabbit, Full Figure, Sitting On Basket, Black, Iron, 5 3/8 In.	85.00
Raggedy Ann	14.00
Sailing Ship, Iron, 10 1/2 In.	24.00
Scotty, 9 Lb., 10 X 8 In.	95.00
Seal, Balancing Ball, Chalkware	15.00
Soldier, Colonial, 7 1/2 In.	55.00
Squirrel, Eating Nut, Sitting On Log, Original Paint	135.00
Squirrel, Sitting Holding Acorn, Bronze, 10 In.	245.00
Stage Coach, 1930	90.00
Turtle, Full Figure, Shades Of Brown, Iron, 9 X 7 In.	80.00
Windmill, Cast Iron, Original Paint, 7 X 7 In.	89.00
Witch On Broomstick, Cast Iron	125.00
Witch, Salem, Brass	125.00

Doulton pottery and porcelain were made by Doulton and Co. of Burslem, England, after 1882. The name "Royal Doulton" appeared on their wares after 1902. Other pottery by Doulton is listed under Royal Doulton.

DOULTON, Ashtray, Stoneware, Funny Bird On Rim, Marked, 4 1/4 X 4 1/8 In.	225.00
Beaker, Lambeth, Tan, Brown, & Blue, Signed, 4 1/2 In.	65.00
Berry Bowl, Willow, 7 In.Diam.	75.00
Bottle, Whiskey, Chivas, Embossed Man On Horse, Chivas Emblem, 8 In.	95.00
Bowl, Fruit, Burslem, Willow, 1891–1902, 8 In. Diam.	85.00
Bowl, Salt, 2 Cupid, Tinworth, 4 In.	275.00
Celery, Burslem, Blue Floral & Border, Gold, 13 In.	55.00
Coffee Set, Belmont Pattern, Coffeepot, 12 Cup & Saucer, Demitasse	250.00
Cup & Saucer, English Flower Pattern, Cobalt Border	36.00
Cuspidor, Lambeth, Foliage Pattern, All Around Marijuana Leaves	350.00
Decanter, Lambeth, Pair	375.00
Dish, Soap, Wright's Coaltar Dragonfly, Stoneware	55.00
Ewer, Burslem, Flow Blue Flowers, Gold Trim, Handle, 6 1/2 In.	95.00
Ewer, Lambeth, Rosettes, Ribbed Handle	85.00
Foot Warmer, Lambeth	65.00
Jar, Covered, Lambeth, Dated 1876, 5 1/2 In.	90.00
Jug, Geese In Grass, Lambeth, Marked, 16 1/4 In. ....*Illus*	650.00

Doulton, Jug, Geese In Grass,
Lambeth, Marked, 16 1/4 In.

If you spill nail polish on furniture, try this cure. Rub the spot with 0000 steel wool dipped in liquid wax polish. Wipe, then rewax with your usual furniture polish.

Jug, Lambeth, America, Commemorative, Utah As A State 177.00
Jug, Lambeth, Embossed Flowers All Around, Brown Handle & Rim 90.00
Jug, Lambeth, Stoneware, Queen Victoria 1897, Tan, Olive, 5 1/2 In. 195.00
Jug, Stoneware, Geese, Gray & Green, Lambeth, C.1895, 16 1/4 In. 650.00
Loving Cup, Lambeth, Green, White Design, Motto, Brown, Handles, 7 In. 195.00
Mug, Lambeth, Those Who Have Money, Tan, Brown, 5 1/4 In. 55.00
Mug, Lambeth, Writing On Front, Tan & Brown, 5 1/4 In. 75.00
Pitcher, Burslem, Jacobean 115.00
Pitcher, Burslem, Landscape, Houses, Windmills Both Sides, Blue 70.00
Pitcher, Cow Scene, Tan Ground, Artist Hannah Barlow, 9 1/4 In. 695.00
Pitcher, Embossed Flowers, Gold & Aqua Trim, Marked, 7 7/8 In. 165.00
Pitcher, Lambeth, Disdain Me Not, Brown, 4 X 5 1/2 In. 75.00
Pitcher, Lambeth, Natural Foliage Ware, 9 In. 75.00
Pitcher, Lambeth, Tan, Brown, Green, & White, Signed, 7 In. 125.00
Pitcher, Morrison Ware, Blue, 9 1/2 In. 175.00
Plaque, Burslem, Girl In Snow, Basket, Blue, White, 7 1/2 X 9 1/2 In. 395.00
Plate, Scenic, Mottled Border, Lacy Gold Design, Marked, 10 1/8 In. 145.00
Stand, Umbrella, Lambeth, 10 X 24 In. 385.00
Tankard, Bear Handle, Bear, Geese, Hannah Barlow, Dated 1878 .... 950.00
Vase, Burslem, Beige, Floral, Footed, 2 Handles, 1890s 195.00
Vase, Burslem, Blue & Beige Flowers, Serpent Handles 150.00
Vase, Burslem, Floral, Cream Ground, Foot Ring, Black Mark, 5 1/2 In. 60.00
Vase, Burslem, Florals Both Sides, C.1880, Gold Handles, 10 1/2 In. 165.00
Vase, Burslem, Gold Scrolls, Marked, 3 1/2 X 4 1/8 In. 95.00
Vase, Burslem, Lilies, Banded In Gold, A3596, 11 In. 150.00
Vase, Burslem, Pitcher, White, Gold Leaves, Spout, Handle, 1890s 195.00
Vase, Burslem, Spittoon Shape, Paisley Pattern, Reserves, 7 In. 150.00
Vase, Cattle & Sheep, Hannah Barlow, Stoneware, 16 In. 750.00
Vase, Faience, Flowers, Mary Butterton, 11 X 9 In. 190.00
Vase, Handles, Tinworth, 8 In. 140.00
Vase, Homeless, Mouse, Tinworth, 8 In. 275.00
Vase, Horses, Donkeys, & Sheep, Hannah Barlow, 6 In. 550.00
Vase, Horses, Hannah Barlow, Stoneware, 12 In. 425.00
Vase, Impasto, 8 In. ....20.00 To 30.00
Vase, Scrolling Plants, Frank Butler, 11 In. 115.00
Wash Set, Burslem, Scalloped Bowl, Blue Flowers, 6 Piece 695.00
   DR. SYNTAX, see Adams; Staffordshire

Moriage is a type of decoration on Japanese pottery. Raised white designs are applied to the ware. Dragonware is a form of moriage pottery. White dragons are the major raised decorations. The background color is gray and white, orange and lavender, or orange and brown. It is a twentieth-century ware.

DRAGONWARE, Box, Blue Jewel Eyes, Scrolled Feet, 4 3/4 X 2 1/4 In. 35.00
Cup, Demitasse 12.00
Tea Set, Gray, Moriage, 17 Piece 30.00
Tea Set, Noritake, Service For 6 .... 135.00
Tea Set, Raised Star, Moriage, No.34 .... 95.00
Wall Pocket, Gray, Coiling, Hand Painted, Nippon, 6 3/4 In. 65.00

Dresden china is any china made in the town of Dresden, Germany. The most famous factory in Dresden is the Meissen factory. Figurines of eighteenth-century ladies and gentlemen, animal groups or cherubs, and other mythological subjects were popular. One special type of figurine was made with skirts of porcelain-dipped lace. Do not make the mistake of thinking that all pieces marked "Dresden" are from the Meissen factory. The Meissen pieces usually have a crossed swords mark, and are listed under Meissen.

DRESDEN, Candelabra, 3 Arm, Applied Roses, Pair 195.00
Card Holder, Pink 15.00
Card Holder, Yellow 15.00
Clock-On-Stand, Mantel, Vines On Sides, Scroll Feet, C.1900, 16 In. 715.00
Console Set, Seated Putti Arms, Standing Putti Supports, 3 Piece 675.00
Cup & Saucer, Oval Medallions, Gold, Green 55.00

Dish, 3 Section, Floral Design, Gold Trim, Marked 50.00
Dish, Cheese, Painted Flowers Allover, Oval, 6 1/2 X 4 1/2 In. 25.00
Figurine, Angel Band, White, C.1910, 6 In., 8 Piece 150.00
Figurine, Ballerina, 9 In. 72.00
Figurine, Ballerina, Lace On Skirt, 7 In. 175.00
Figurine, Ballerina, Popplesdorf Mark, 7 In. 150.00
Figurine, Boy On Sled, Girl Standing, Marked, 5 X 3 1/8 X 4 In. 145.00
Figurine, Child In Lace Dress, 2 1/2 In. 65.00
Figurine, Farm Girl Feeding Chickens, 7 1/2 In. 125.00
Figurine, Lady & 2 Children, With Lamb, 9 In. 500.00
Figurine, Lady In 18th Century Clothes, Fan, 4 1/2 In. 42.00
Figurine, Lady, Playing Harp, Popplesdorf Mark, 4 In. 85.00
Figurine, Man & Woman With Cupids, 14 In. 850.00
Figurine, Matron, Ermine Wrap, Flowers On Dress, Marked, 9 X 9 In. 400.00
Figurine, Monkey Band, C.1890, 5 In., 8 Piece 1100.00
Figurine, Nude Sitting, 8 In. 150.00
Figurine, Young Gentleman, With Flowers, Leaning Against Pedestal 325.00
Fish Set, C.1875, Platter 15 In., 7 Piece ....160.00 To 195.00
Group, Allegorical With Dolphins & Cupid, 17 In. 750.00
Group, Musicians, 19 In. 775.00
Inkwell, Pot Attached To Saucer Base, Flowers, Gold Trim, Small 62.50
Lamp, Floral Design, Polychrome, Miniature, 8 In. 435.00
Lamp, Mandarin, C.1860, Shade, 15 In. 250.00
Mustache Cup & Saucer, Floral 37.00
Plate, Florals, Water Scene, 10 1/2 In. 16.00
Plate, Flowers, Gold Edge, Signed, 6 In., Set Of 6 .... 130.00
Plate, Molded Scrolled Border, Flowers, Marked, 8 1/2 In. 40.00
Tray, Pin, Yellow Flowers, Gold Trim 18.00
Vase, Classical Portrait, Cobalt, 6 In. 135.00
Vase, Lady Oval Portrait, Olive Green, C.1910, Marked, 10 In. 302.00
Vase, Portrait, 3 In. 65.00
Vase, Portrait, Artist Signed, 19 In. 700.00
Vase, Shield Painted Cover, Lover Panel, Stand, Marked, 41 In., Pair 6325.00

Duncan & Miller is a term used by collectors when referring to glass made by the George A. Duncan and Sons Company or the Duncan and Miller Glass Company. These companies worked from 1893 to 1955, when the use of the name "Duncan" was discontinued and the firm became part of the United States Glass Company.

DUNCAN & MILLER, Adoration, Goblet 25.00
Adoration, Ice Bucket, With Tongs 65.00
Arliss, Whiskey, Ruby 20.00
Ashtray, Duck, 5 In. 14.00
Ashtray, Duck, 8 In. 28.00
Astaire, Tumbler, Whiskey, 2 Oz. 8.00
Canterbury, Ashtray, 3 In. 6.00
Canterbury, Basket, Etched Flower, 8 In. 45.00
Canterbury, Basket, Green, 3 1/2 In. 25.00
Canterbury, Bowl, Amber, Ruffled, 8 In. 65.00
Canterbury, Bowl, Chartreuse, 5 1/2 In. 10.00
Canterbury, Bowl, Pink, Ruffled, 9 In. 35.00
Canterbury, Bowl, Ruby, 10 In. 24.00
Canterbury, Candleholder, 2 In., Pair 22.50
Canterbury, Candy Dish, Crystal, Covered 15.00
Canterbury, Champagne 7.00
Canterbury, Condiment Set, Labels, Crystal, 3 Piece 75.00
Canterbury, Goblet, Marigold, 8 Oz. 18.00
Canterbury, Mayonnaise Set, Chartreuse, 3 Piece 47.50
Canterbury, Plate, 8 In. ....5.00 To 8.00
Canterbury, Relish, Floral Etched, 3 Handles, 8 In. 20.00
Canterbury, Rose Bowl, 5 1/2 In. 9.00
Canterbury, Sherbet, 5 1/2 In. 6.00
Canterbury, Smoke Set, Box & 2 Ashtrays, Chartreuse 25.00
Canterbury, Sugar & Creamer, Individual ....14.00 To 16.00

Canterbury, Sugar & Creamer, Tea Size	10.00
Canterbury, Table Set, Condiment, 4 Piece	12.00
Canterbury, Tray, Condiment, Metal Mounted	15.00
Canterbury, Tumbler, Blue Opalescent, 8 Oz.	32.00
Canterbury, Tumbler, Juice, Chartreuse, 4 Oz.	5.00
Canterbury, Vase, Crimped, Chartreuse, 4 1/2 In.	18.00
Canterbury, Vase, Crimped, Pink Opalescent, 5 In.	22.50
Canterbury, Vase, Flower Arranger, Silver Overlay, 7 In.	67.50
Canterbury, Vase, Hat Shape, Clear, 4 In.	10.00
Canterbury, Vase, Hat Shape, Pink Opalescent, 4 In.	19.00
Canterbury, Wine	7.00
Caribbean, Candelabrum, Italian Blue, 8 In., Pair	165.00
Caribbean, Mustard, Blue	75.00
Caribbean, Punch Bowl Set, Amber, 16 Piece	190.00
Chanticleer, Cocktail Shaker, Ruby	247.50
Chanticleer, Tumbler, Frosted, 3 Oz.	10.00
Chanticleer, Vase, Blue Satin, 3 1/2 In.	95.00
Chantilly, Goblet	23.00
Cornucopia, Vase, Cranberry, Pink, 8 In.	75.00
Diamond Ridge, Bottle, Water, Blown	95.00
Diamond Ridge, Pitcher, Water	65.00
Diamond Ridge, Punch Cup	7.00
Diamond Ridge, Sugar, Covered, 4 3/4 In.	35.00
Diamond Ridge, Vase, Blown, 10 In.	87.00
Duck, Ashtray, Crystal, Covered	44.00
First Love, Banana Boat	82.00
First Love, Candleholder, 2–Light, Pair	65.00
First Love, Candlestick, 3–Light, No.41, Etch, 5 In.	48.00
First Love, Console Set, 2–Light Candlesticks, 3 Piece	95.00
First Love, Goblet, Blue, 10 Oz.	25.00
First Love, Goblet, Champagne	14.00
First Love, Relish, 2–Part, 6 In.	25.00
First Love, Stack Set, Sugar, Creamer, & Butter Chip	45.00
First Love, Vase, 5 In.	20.00
Georgian, Ice Bucket, Silver Plate Overlay, Green	38.00
Georgian, Salt & Pepper, Cobalt Blue	52.00
Heron, Tumbler, Crystal	88.00
Hobnail, Bowl, Royal Blue, Crimped, 9 In.	50.00
Hobnail, Candy Jar, Covered, Footed	40.00
Hobnail, Cocktail, 3 1/2 In.	15.00
Hobnail, Cruet Set, 2 Bottles, Tray, Crystal	50.00
Hobnail, Cruet, Oil, Stopper, Cranberry, 5 Oz.	40.00
Hobnail, Dish, Mayonnaise, Handles, 5 In.	8.00
Hobnail, Goblet, Footed, 9 Oz., Set Of 8	45.00
Hobnail, Goblet, Pink Opalescent	30.00
Hobnail, Hat, Pink, 2 1/2 In.	27.00
Hobnail, Jug, Flip, Amber, 5 10 Oz.Tumblers	100.00
Hobnail, Plate, 8 1/4 In.	8.00
Hobnail, Plate, 11 In.	12.00
Hobnail, Tumbler, Footed, Pink, 13 Oz.	30.00
Indian Tree, Goblet	14.00
Indian Tree, Plate, Etched, 6 1/8 In.	7.00
Indian Tree, Sugar & Creamer, Tray	30.00
Lily Of The Valley, Goblet	30.00
Lily Of The Valley, Tumbler, Juice, Footed	27.00
Mardi Gras, Carafe, Water	35.00
Mardi Gras, Champagne	24.00
Mardi Gras, Compote, 5 In.	20.00
Mardi Gras, Pitcher, Water	85.00
Mardi Gras, Toothpick	25.00
Mardi Gras, Wine, Crystal, 4 1/4 In.	8.00
Pall Mall, Swan, Ruby, 12 In.	65.00
Passion Flower, Vase, Etched, 5 1/8 In.	12.00
Radiance, Tumbler, Ruby, 12 Oz.	12.00

Sandwich, Ashtray 5.00
Sandwich, Basket, Handle, 8 1/2 In. 110.00
Sandwich, Box, Cigarette, Covered 20.00
Sandwich, Cake Plate, Footed 55.00
Sandwich, Celery, Crystal, 3–Part, 10 1/2 In. 22.00
Sandwich, Champagne, Saucer, 5 1/4 In. 8.00
Sandwich, Coaster .... 5.50 To 6.00
Sandwich, Cracker Plate, 13 In. 22.00
Sandwich, Creamer, Teardop Bead Handle 5.00
Sandwich, Cruet, Oil, 3 Oz. 22.00
Sandwich, Cup & Saucer .... 10.50 To 12.00
Sandwich, Dish, Deviled Egg, Ground Bottom 49.50
Sandwich, Goblet, Water .... 6.00 To 14.00
Sandwich, Jug, Water .... 60.00 To 75.00
Sandwich, Juice, Footed, 5 Oz. 8.00
Sandwich, Mayonnaise, 2 Piece 15.00
Sandwich, Nappy, Heart Shape, Applied Handle, 5 1/4 In. 16.00
Sandwich, Pitcher, 64 Oz. 45.00
Sandwich, Pitcher, Ice Lip, 1/2 Gal. 70.00
Sandwich, Plate, 7 In. .... 5.50 To 8.00
Sandwich, Plate, 8 1/4 In. 8.00
Sandwich, Platter, 16 In. 58.00
Sandwich, Relish, 2–Part, 7 In. 12.00
Sandwich, Relish, Rectangular, 10 X 6 In. 22.00
Sandwich, Rose Bowl, Crimped, 11 1/2 In. 20.00
Sandwich, Salt & Pepper, Tray 80.00
Sandwich, Sherbet, Green, 5 Oz. 10.00
Sandwich, Sugar, Creamer, & Tray, 5 Oz. 22.00
Sandwich, Sugar, Open 5.00
Sandwich, Tumbler, 13 Oz. 8.00
Sandwich, Tumbler, Footed, 10 Oz. 10.00
Sandwich, Wine .... 6.00 To 8.00
Sanibel, Candy Dish, Pink 25.00
Sanibel, Plate, 8 1/2 In. 22.00
Sanibel, Relish, 2–Part, 8 1/2 In. 25.00
Spiral Flutes, Bowl, Green, Flanged, 6 3/4 In. 5.00
Spiral Flutes, Candlestick, Blue Opalescent, Pair 120.00
Spiral Flutes, Cigarette Holder, Saucer Base, Crystal 10.00
Spiral Flutes, Cup & Saucer, Amber 9.00
Spiral Flutes, Ice Tub, Green 30.00
Spiral Flutes, Sugar, Green, Covered 9.00
Swan, Chartreuse, 7 In. .... 22.00 To 35.00
Swan, Emerald Green, Clear Head & Neck, 13 In. 48.00
Swan, Green Body, 10 1/2 In. 30.00
Swan, Green, Crystal Neck, 12 In. 75.00
Swan, Milk Glass, 7 1/2 In. 300.00
Swan, Ruby Neck, 5 1/2 In. 22.00
Swan, Ruby, 6 In. 25.00
Swan, Ruby, 7 In. 65.00
Swan, Ruby, 10 In. 45.00
Swan, Ruby, 12 In. 38.00
Swan, Ruby, Crystal Neck, 8 In. 60.00
Swan, Sanibel, Blue Opalescent, 6 In. 48.00
Swan, Solid, 7 In. 60.00
Swan, Sylvan, 7 1/2 In. 23.00
Swan, Sylvan, Pink Opalescent, 8 In. 75.00
Swan, Vaseline Opalescent 65.00
Swirl, Table Set, 4 Piece 175.00
Swirl, Vase, Cornucopia, 11 In. 35.00
Teardrop, Bowl, Handles, 5 In. 5.00
Teardrop, Champagne, Set Of 4 .... 30.00
Teardrop, Compote, Clear 45.00
Teardrop, Cordial 16.00
Teardrop, Cruet, Stopper, 3 Oz. 20.00

Durand, Vase, Iridescent Blue, Silver
Thread Design, 6 1/2 In.

Fairing, Trinket Box,
Dresser, Clock, 5 In.

Fairing, Trinket Box, Dresser,
With Books, 5 1/2 In.

Teardrop, Dish, Ice Cream, 5 Oz.	6.00
Teardrop, Dish, Oval, Crystal, 7 1/2 X 3 In.	9.50
Teardrop, Goblet, Footed, 7 In.	8.00
Teardrop, Goblet, Luncheon, 9 Oz.	10.00
Teardrop, Goblet, Water	9.00
Teardrop, Nut Dish, Divided, 6 In.	6.00
Teardrop, Pitcher, Lemonade, 4 Handles, 7 In.	7.00
Teardrop, Plate, 7 In.	8.00
Teardrop, Plate, 14 In.	20.00
Teardrop, Plate, 8 1/2 In.	10.00
Teardrop, Plate, Handle, 6 In.	6.00
Teardrop, Relish, 2–Part, 6 In.	4.00
Teardrop, Salt & Pepper, Original Lids	8.00
Teardrop, Sugar & Creamer, Open Handles	16.00
Teardrop, Sugar, Large	8.00
Teardrop, Sugar, Open, 3 1/4 In.	5.00
Teardrop, Tumbler, 12 Oz.	12.50
Teardrop, Wine, 3 Oz.	12.00
Tepee, Punch Cup	8.00
Terrace, Relish, 4–Part, Gold Trim, Engraved	17.50
Three Feathers, Cornucopia, Paper Label, Cranberry, 8 In.	75.00
Viking, Boat	185.00

*Durand glass was made by Victor Durand from 1879 to 1935 at
several factories. Most of the iridescent Durand glass was made by
Victor Durand, Jr., from 1912 to 1924 at the Durand Art Glass
Works in Vineland, New Jersey.*

DURAND, Bowl, Chinese Shape, Blue Glaze, 6 In.	125.00
Bowl, Fruit, Blue Iridescent, Wide Flat Rim, Marked, 14 1/2 In.	800.00
Candlestick, Flower Finial, Pink Tulip Cup, Bobeches, 7 1/2 In., Pair	125.00
Compote, Gold Iridescent, Signed & Numbered, 7 X 6 3/4 In.	350.00
Lamp Base, White Metal, Swirled Glass Center Vase, 21 In.	100.00
Lamp, Floor, Bronze, Claw Feet, Crackled Multicolored Shade, 63 In.	300.00
Lamp, Gold Loop On Calcite, Signed, Electric, 7 1/2 In.	625.00
Lamp, Ribbed Art Glass Shade, 12 In.	425.00
Night–Light, Silver Plated, Blue & White Shade	250.00
Plate, Flashed Ruby, Bridgeton Rose, Charles Link, 8 In.	300.00
Plate, White Pulled Feathers, Pink Concentric Circles, Ruby, 8 In.	300.00
Relish, Bridgeton Rose, Footed, 6 In.	225.00
Relish, Bridgeton Rose, Pair	295.00
Shade, Gas, White, Blue, Gold Leaves, Gold Lining, Scalloped, 5 1/2 In.	120.00
Shade, Gold Lined, Ribbed, Bulbous, 9 1/2 In.	625.00
Shade, Red, Art Glass, Ribbed, 12 In.	425.00
Sherbet, Pulled Feather, Blue & White, Set Of 6	695.00

Vase, Butterfly, Blue Threaded, Signed, 6 1/2 In.	750.00
Vase, Feather Pull Design, Applied Handles, Stringing, Signed, 8 In.	850.00
Vase, Green King Tut Swirl, White Ground, Gold Interior, 9 In.	155.00
Vase, Intaglio Cut, Signed V.Durand, 7 3/4 In.	1350.00
Vase, Iridescent Blue, Silver Thread Design, 6 1/2 In. ....*Illus*	190.00
Vase, Translucent Green & Brown, Signed, 5 1/2 In.	425.00
Wine, Dark Raspberry, Ribbed, Pale Vaseline Stem	100.00

Elfinware was made from about 1918 to 1940. It is a Dresden–like porcelain that was sold in dime stores and gift shops. Many pieces were decorated with raised flowers. The small pieces are marked with the name "Elfinware" or with a crown and M mark. The words "Germany" or "Made in Germany" also appear on some pieces.

ELFINWARE, Ashtray, Blue, Marked Germany	12.00
Basket, Blue Luster, Marked Germany, Miniature	25.00
Box, Oval, 1 3/4 X 2 3/4 In.	35.00
Box, Painted Applied Flowers, Lid, Signed, 2 1/2 X 3 1/2 In.	45.00
Shoe, Pink, Applied Flowers	18.00

Elvis Presley, the famous singer, lived from 1935 to 1977. He became famous by 1956. Elvis appeared on television, starred in 27 movies, and performed in Las Vegas. Memorabilia from any of the Presley shows, his records, and even memorials made after his death are collected.

ELVIS PRESLEY, Album, 25th Anniversary Limited Edition, 8 Record, Unused	300.00
Bracelet, Dog Tag, Original Card, Dated 1956	15.00
Bracelet, Lady's	8.00
Card, Gum, Set, 1956	325.00
Earrings, Pierced	30.00
Poster, Live A Little, Love A Little, 1968, 18 1/2 X 28 In.	100.00
Puzzle, Jigsaw, 1977	12.50
Record Album, Blue Hawaii	75.00
Record Album, Elvis–A Canadian Tribute, Gold Vinyl	10.00
Record Album, Spinout	50.00
Record, L.P., Golden Hits, 1958	10.00
Record, Love Me Tender, 78	50.00
Sheet Music, Blue Christmas, Photograph Of Elvis	10.00
Sheet Music, You Don't Have To Say You Love Me	15.00
Stirrer, Guitar, Figural, King Of Rock & Roll	10.00

Russian, French, and English workmen of the eighteenth and nineteenth centuries made small boxes and table pieces of enamel on metal. One form of English enamel is called "Battersea" and is listed under that name.

ENAMEL, Dish, Garden Scene, Woman In Window, Qianlong, 6 1/4 In.	75.00
Humidor, Designs, Wheel Etched, Maroon, Blue, Green, Russia, 8 1/4 In.	140.00
Picture Frame, Silver, Blue Velvet, Russian, 5 1/2 X 4 3/4 In., Pair	450.00
Plaque, Admiral Nelson, Carved Frame, 6 1/2 X 5 1/2 In.	480.00
Plate, Nursery Rhyme, Border, 6 In.	7.50
Russian, Snuffbox, Eagle, Lid Design, Applied Beading, Gold Inside	1200.00
Russian, Spoon, Demitasse, Cloisonne Dots, 3 Color Handle, Set Of 12	200.00
Russian, Spoon, Sazikov	250.00
Russian, Teaspoon, 1881, 5 1/2 In.	150.00
Stemware Service, Blue, Charioteer Scenes, Baluster Stem, 120 Piece	1540.00

ES Germany porcelain was made at the factory of Erdmann Schlegelmilch from 1861 to 1925 in Suhl, Germany. The porcelain was sold decorated or undecorated. Other pieces were made at the factory in Saxony, Prussia, and are marked "ES Prussia." Reinhold Schlegelmilch, a brother, made the famous wares marked "RS Germany."

ES GERMANY, Bowl, Floral, 10 In.	23.00
Bowl, Portrait, 11 1/4 In.	100.00
Creamer, Footed	38.00

Jar, Portrait, Woman, Rose, Iridescent, Covered, Saxe, 7 1/2 In. 155.00
Lamp, Aladdin, Floral & Leaf, Raised Gold Tracery, Prov. Saxe 110.00
Plate, Blue, Portrait 75.00
Plate, Transfer Print Of Roses, Scalloped, Gold Rim, 9 1/2 In. 22.00
Relish, Hand Painted, Orchids 12.00
Sugar & Creamer, Floral Design, Covered, Gold Trim, Green Mark 45.00
Vase, Aladdin Lamp, Floral, Gold Tracery, 4 1/4 X 9 1/4 In. 145.00
Vase, Floral, Provincial Saxe, Hand Painted, 9 In. 115.00
Vase, Green & Gold, 4 Portraits, 4 3/4 X 4 In. 175.00
Vase, Portrait, Iridescent, Blue Neck & Base, Signed, 11 1/4 In. 255.00
Vase, Portrait, Turquoise, Jeweling, Double Handles, 11 1/4 In. 245.00

All types of Eskimo artifacts are collected. Carvings of whale or walrus teeth are listed under Scrimshaw. Baskets are in the Basket category. All other types of Eskimo art are listed here.

ESKIMO, Doll, Hand Carved, Primitive, American, 12 In. 150.00
Figurine, Otter, Fish, Greenstone, Initials G.W.103, 11 5/8 In. 100.00
Figurine, Seals Playing, Walrus Ivory, Colored Features, 2 In., Pair 290.00
Net Toggle, Walrus Ivory, Seal Shape, 2 In. 25.00

ETLING FRANCE *Etling glass is very similar in design to Lalique and Phoenix glass. It was made in France for Etling, a retail shop. It dates from the 1920s and 1930s.*

ETLING, Bowl, Shells, 10 In. 100.00

ФАБЕРЖЕ *Faberge was a firm of jewelers and goldsmiths founded in St. Petersburg, Russia, in 1842, by Gustav Faberge. Peter Carl Faberge, his son, was jeweler to the Russian Imperial Court from about 1870 to 1914.*

КФ

FABERGE, Chalk Holder, Silver Gilt, Cylindrical Shape, C.1900, 8 In. 1650.00
Cigarette Case, St.George Medallion, Royal Blue, C.1900, 3 3/4 In. 3850.00
Clock, Desk, Nephrite Body, Seed Pearls, Silver Gilt, C.1910, 4 In. 8525.00
Compact, Powder Blue, Silver Gilt, Cabochon Thumbpiece, 2 1/1 In. 2400.00
Flowerpot, Stand, Terra–Cotta, Silver Mounted, Greek Key, 1 3/4 In. 1980.00
Punch Bowl, Silver, Ball Feet, Ring Handles, Russian Style, C.1910 .... 6600.00
Salad Server, Silver, Shell, Scroll, C.1910, 11 1/2 In., Pair 715.00

Definitions of the words differentiating the types of pottery and porcelain are difficult because there is so much overlapping of meaning. Faience is tin–glazed earthenware, especially the wares made in France, Germany, and Scandinavia. It is also correct to say that faience is the same as majolica or Delft, although usually the term refers only to the tin–glazed pottery of the three regions mentioned.

FAIENCE, Charger, Brown, Medallion, Floral, 19th Century, 17 In. 100.00
Inkwell, Master, Animals & Peasant 95.00
Plate, Art Nouveau, 5 1/2 In. 65.00
Stein, Bird & Florals, Pear Shape, 1 Liter 121.00
Tile, Floral Basket, Butterflies, Multicolor, Rookwood, Framed, 6 In. 175.00
Tile, Pig In Sailboat, Franklin Pottery, 6 X 6 In. 45.00
Toby Jug, Polychrome Glaze, Marked France, 7 1/4 In. 55.00
Urn, German, Gold Edge Flowers, Leaves, Crown Mark, 9 X 11 In., Pair 750.00
Vase, Matte Yellow, Cylinder Shape, 4 X 2 In. 135.00

Fairings are small souvenir china boxes and figurines that were sold at country fairs during the nineteenth century. Most were made in Germany. Reproductions of fairings are being made, especially of the famous "twelve months of marriage" series.

FAIRING, Box, Trinket, Baby Sitting In Basket, Horn & Punch Doll, 6 X 5 In. 250.00
Box, Trinket, Baby, In High Chair, Rattle In Hand 85.00
Box, Trinket, Blond Child, Holding Book, Dog, Blue Ottoman 85.00
Box, Trinket, Girl Playing With Umbrella, Marked, 4 3/4 In. 65.00
Box, Trinket, Pedestal, Scenic 30.00
Box, Trinket, Porcelain, 2 Men Playing Billiards, 3 1/2 X 2 In. 85.00
Figurine, Returning At One O'clock In Morning 65.00

Man, Lady, Checker Game, 4 X 5 In. ....*Color* 85.00
Trinket Box, Dresser, Clock, 5 In. ....*Illus* 50.00
Trinket Box, Dresser, With Books, 5 1/2 In. ....*Illus* 55.00
    FAMILLE ROSE, see Chinese Export

Fans have been used for cooling since the days of the ancients. By the eighteenth century, the fan was an accessory for the lady of fashion and very elaborate and expensive fans were made. Sticks were made of ivory or wood, set with jewels or carved. The fans were made of painted silk or paper. Inexpensive paper fans printed with advertising were giveaways in the late nineteenth and early twentieth centuries.

FAN, Advertising, 666 Medicines, Wooden Handle, Color 7.50
  Advertising, Hamburg Amerika Shipping Lines ....55.00 To 65.00
  Advertising, Hires Root Beer, Chinese 165.00
  Advertising, Hires Root Beer, Dutch Girl 100.00
  Advertising, Hoffman Willis Ice Cream Co., Girl Eating Ice Cream 15.00
  Advertising, Kewpie Ice Cream, Signed O'Neill 38.00
  Advertising, Moxie, Cutout Of Each Leaf, Celluloid 50.00
  Advertising, Moxie, Girl Holding Tumbler, Cardboard, 1924 .... 25.00
  Advertising, Moxie, Girl, Flowing Hair, Muriez Ostriche, Cardboard, 1916 .... 25.00
  Advertising, Moxie, Moxie On Each Blade, Celluloid 95.00
  Advertising, Moxie, Picture Of Lady 35.00
  Advertising, Putnam Dyes, The Charm Of Color 8.00
  Advertising, Singer Sewing Machine 26.00
  Advertising, Tip Top Bread, Die Cut Litho, Baker Boy 22.00
  Advertising, Zulu Kenyon 6.00
  Black Silk, Carved Outside Sticks, Mourning 20.00
  Cardboard, Woman's Portrait, Olivia, Dated 1911 .... 7.50
  Celluloid, Original Box With Glass Lid 20.00
  Celluloid, Ornate, Ribbons, 15 Section 20.00
  Dayton, Electric, 6 Brass Blades & Cage, 12 In. 45.00
  Electric, Luminaire, Motor, 6 Blades 300.00
  Electric, Westinghouse, Table Model, Brass 110.00
  Fly, Clock Mechanism, Patent 1874 .... 425.00
  G.E., Brass, 1901 .... 55.00
  Gouache On Paper, 4 People, Sheep Nearby, Pearl Sticks, 10 In. 125.00
  Gouache On Skin, Piaza Navona Scene, Watercolor, Italy, C.1780 .... 575.00
  Gouache On Vellum, Folding, Scenes, Europe, 18th Century, 11 1/8 In. 160.00
  Ivory, Brise, Harbor, Forest Scenes, Tortoise Guard, 18th Century, 8 In. 575.00
  Ivory, Folding, Conversion Of St.Paul Scene, England, C.1780, 10 3/4 In. 110.00
  Lace, Painted Ivory Sticks, 19th Century, 10 1/2 In. 180.00
  Mandarin, 50 Faces Per Side, Chinese Export, Fitted Box, 11 In. 60.00
  Mandarin, 75 Faces Per Side, Chinese, Black Lacquer Box, C.1860, 11 In. 85.00
  Mother-Of-Pearl, Hand Painted Lace Inserts, Enamel Flowers, French 85.00
  Oscillating, G.E., Brass Blades, 13 In. 15.00
  Ostrich Feather, Celluloid Sticks 45.00
  Ostrich Feather, Plastic Handle, Pink, Original Box 25.00
  Ostrich Feather, Silver Filigree, 19th Century, Florals, 13 1/4 In. 175.00
  Printed Fabric, Red Velvet Handle, Victorian 28.00
  Ribbon, Celluloid 15.00
  Robbins Meyers, Electric, 6 Brass Blades, Steel Cage, 16 In. 45.00
  Satin, White, Hand Painted 12.00
  Silk & Ivory, Painted Flowers 24.00
  Silk, Gauze, Venus & Cherubs, Pearl, France, 1890s, 12 3/4 In. 120.00
  Silk, Painted Florals, Large 18.00
  Silk, White, Pierced Ivory Sticks, C.1890 .... 28.00
  Silk, White, Wedding, Trimmed In Lace, Hand Painted Flowers, Sequins 45.00
  Silver, Filigree, Floral, Ostrich Feathers, 1890s, 13 3/4 In. 175.00
  Vellum, Painted, Nymph & Cupid Scene, Ivory, Gold Frame, 20 In. 750.00
  Vellum, Watercolor, Folding, Lovers, Carved Ivory, Europe, C.1770, 11 In. 125.00
  Voile & Lace, White, Flowers & Butterflies, Wood Frame, Opens To 25 In. 50.00

Federzeichnung is the very strange German name for a pattern of mother-of-pearl satin glass. The pattern had irregularly shaped sections of brown glass covered with a pattern of gold squiggle lines. It was first made in the late nineteenth century.

FEDERZEICHNUNG, Vase, Brown, Mother-Of-Pearl, White Interior, 6 X 5 In. 1650.00
Vase, Butterscotch, Mother-Of-Pearl, Signed, 10 3/4 In. 1750.00

Fenton Art Glass Company, founded in Martins Ferry, Ohio, by Frank L. Fenton, is now located in Williamstown, West Virginia. It is noted for early carnival glass produced between 1907 and 1920. Many other types of glass were also made.

FENTON, Acanthus, Plate, Amber, 7 1/4 In. 6.00
Apple Tree, Vase, Milk Glass, Blue 110.00
Aqua Crest, Bonbon, 6 In. 12.00
Aqua Crest, Bowl, 4 1/2 In. 20.00
Aqua Crest, Candleholder 20.00
Aqua Crest, Server, 3-Tier, Metal Handle, 10 In. 50.00
Aqua Crest, Vase, 10 In. 75.00
Aqua Crest, Vase, Ruffled, 4 In. 22.00
Beaded Melon, Candy Dish, Green, Covered 50.00
Beaded Melon, Vase, Gold Overlay, 4 3/4 In. 18.00
Beaded Melon, Vase, Green, 4 In. 40.00
Beaded Melon, Vase, Yellow Inside, White, 5 1/2 In. 20.00
Blackberry, Compote, Blue, Miniature 110.00
Block & Star, Salt & Pepper, Milk Glass, White, 3 1/4 In. 16.00
Buttons & Braids, Pitcher, Water, Green Opalescent 95.00
Cactus, Compote, Milk Glass, White, 5 1/2 In. 10.00
Cherry & Scale, Water Set, 6 Tumblers 600.00
Coin Dot, Lamp, French, Opalescent, Squatty, Shade, Pair 120.00
Coin Dot, Pitcher, Cranberry Opalescent, 9 1/2 In. 90.00
Coin Dot, Pitcher, Lime Opalescent, 4 In. 65.00
Coinspot, Lamp, 23 In., Pair 150.00
Coinspot, Pitcher, Water, Ice Lip, Opalescent 85.00
Creamer, Beaded Melon, Ivy Color, Milk Glass, 4 In. 30.00
Crystal Crest, Top Hat, Crimped 45.00
Daisy & Button, Bell, Apple Green, Metal Clapper, 5 5/8 In. 14.00
Dancing Ladies, Vase, Mongolian Green, Flared, 8 3/4 In. 225.00
Dancing Ladies, Vase, Periwinkle Blue, 9 In. ....*Illus* 190.00
Diamond Optic, Hat, Ruby, 4 In. 55.00
Diamond Optic, Pitcher, Cranberry, 6 In. 75.00
Diamond Optic, Pitcher, Water, Ruby Overlay 75.00

Fenton, Dancing Ladies, Vase,
   Periwinkle Blue, 9 In.

Diamond Optic, Salt & Pepper, Amber 40.00
Diamond Optic, Tumbler 28.00
Diamond Optic, Vase, Ruby, Flared, 6 In. 75.00
Diamond Optic, Vase, Tulip, Mulberry, Melon Rib, 5 1/4 In. 45.00
Dolphin, Compote, Florentine Green, 10 In. 95.00
Dolphin, Server, Sandwich, Center Handle 35.00
Dot Optic, Basket, Cranberry, 7 In. 85.00
Dot Optic, Hat, French Opalescent, 4 1/2 In. 65.00
Dot Optic, Pitcher, Lemonade, Blue 30.00
Dot Optic, Vase, Cranberry Opalescent, 3 3/4 In. 22.00
Dot Optic, Vase, Cranberry, 8 In. 85.00
Emerald Crest, Bowl, 5 1/2 In. 20.00
Emerald Crest, Dish, Ruffled, Gold & Green Design, 6 1/2 In. 25.00
Flower Frog, Figural, September Morn, Green 135.00
Flower Frog, Light Green Transfer, Star Base 120.00
Flower Frog, Opaque Black 170.00
Flower Frog, Opaque Jade 120.00
Flower Frog, Opaque Yellow, Jade Base 275.00
Flower Frog, Pink Transfer, Star Base 87.75
Georgian, Cup & Saucer, Red 16.00
Georgian, Plate, Ruby, 8 In. 4.00
Georgian, Salt & Pepper, Amber 45.00
Georgian, Salt & Pepper, Cobalt Blue 65.00
Georgian, Sherbet, Ruby 12.00
Gold Crest, Candleholder, Cornucopia, Pair 30.00
Gold Crest, Vase, 3 Sided, Original Label, 8 In. 50.00
Gold Crest, Vase, Ruffled, 4 1/4 In. 22.00
Hanging Heart, Vase, Oriental Ivory, 9 In. 175.00
Hobnail, Basket, Blue, 5 In. 22.00
Hobnail, Basket, Cranberry, 7 1/2 In. 70.00
Hobnail, Basket, Cranberry, 10 1/2 In. 100.00
Hobnail, Basket, Lily-Of-The-Valley, Blue 50.00
Hobnail, Basket, Plum Opalescent, 4 1/2 In. 65.00
Hobnail, Bonbon, Blue, Square, 6 In. 16.00
Hobnail, Bonbon, Topaz Opalescent, 3 Sided, 5 1/2 In. 15.00
Hobnail, Bottle, Cologne, Ocean Green, Original Stopper 20.00
Hobnail, Bowl, Cranberry, 10 In. 70.00
Hobnail, Bowl, Crimped, Opaque Blue, 9 1/2 In. 36.00
Hobnail, Bowl, Opalescent, Crystal, Ruffled, 5 In. 13.00
Hobnail, Candleholder, Marigold, 6 In., Pair 15.00
Hobnail, Compote, Ruffled, Plum, 5 In. 65.00
Hobnail, Console Set, Ruffled Top, Blue, 3 Piece 65.00
Hobnail, Cruet, Oil, Cranberry 25.00
Hobnail, Cruet, Stopper, Cranberry 65.00
Hobnail, Epergne, 3 Lily, Blue, 8 X 6 1/2 In. 50.00
Hobnail, Hat, Top, 2 1/2 In. 14.00
Hobnail, Iced Tea, Cranberry 30.00
Hobnail, Iced Tea, Yellow 26.00
Hobnail, Lamp Base, Cranberry, Opalescent, 12 In. 30.00
Hobnail, Nappy, Blue, 6 In. 12.00
Hobnail, Pitcher, Milk Glass, Original Label, 80 Oz. 20.00
Hobnail, Pitcher, Water, Cranberry, Large 165.00
Hobnail, Salt & Pepper, Cranberry 47.00
Hobnail, Shade, Cranberry, Fluted Top 125.00
Hobnail, Shoe With Kitten, Vaseline Opalescent 25.00
Hobnail, Sugar & Creamer, Individual, Blue 20.00
Hobnail, Sugar & Creamer, White 16.00
Hobnail, Vase, 10 1/2 In. 90.00
Hobnail, Vase, Bud, Blue Opalescent, 10 In. 30.00
Hobnail, Vase, Cone Shape, Footed, Ruffled Top, Blue, 8 In. 47.50
Hobnail, Vase, Cranberry, 4 1/2 In. 17.50
Hobnail, Vase, Cranberry, 8 In., Pair 150.00
Hobnail, Vase, Fan, French Opalescent, 8 In. 30.00
Hobnail, Vase, Footed, Crimped, Topaz, 5 1/2 In. 24.00

Hobnail, Vase, Opalescent Green, 11 1/2 In.	57.00
Hobnail, Vase, Ruffled Top, Blue, 5 In.	47.50
Hobnail, Vase, Ruffled Top, Cranberry, 8 In.	62.50
Hobnail, Water Set, Blue, 5 Piece	195.00
Hobnail, Water Set, Opalescent Blue, 7 Piece	225.00
Ivory Crest, Vase, Ruffled Top, 7 1/2 In.	45.00
Lincoln Inn, Cup & Saucer, Cobalt	16.00
Lincoln Inn, Tumbler, Juice, Footed, Red	10.00
Mikado, Compote, Ebony	110.00
Milady, Vase, Ming Crystal, 11 In.	135.00
Ming, Jar, Macaroon, Reed Handle, Green	125.00
Ming, Vase, Crystal, 8 In.	20.00
Mosaic Inlaid, Vase, C.1926, Red & Yellow Spots On Blue, 10 In.	250.00
Northern Star, Bowl, Marigold, 4 In.	15.00
Peach Crest, Bowl, Shell, 10 1/4 In.	40.00
Peach Crest, Candlesticks	25.00
Peach Crest, Hat, Top, Ruffled Edge, 4 In.	32.00
Peacock, Vase, Mongolian Green, 8 In.	145.00
Persian Medallion, Vase, Tulip, Flowering Dill	25.00
Pineapple, Bowl, Fruit, Ruby, Footed, 11 In.	65.00
Rib Optic, Bottle, Wine, Cranberry Opalescent	75.00
Rib Optic, Guest Set, Celeste Blue Stretch, Royal Blue Handles	100.00
Rib Optic, Ivy Ball, Green Opalescent	45.00
Rosaline, Bonbon, Butterfly	27.00
Rosaline, Box, Chessie	200.00
Rosaline, Candy Dish, Handles	30.00
Scroll, Vase, Mosaic, Dated 1852	200.00
Silver Crest, Basket, Hand Painted Violets	16.00
Silver Crest, Compote, Footed, 8 X 6 1/2 In.	14.00
Silver Crest, Compote, Low, 8 1/2 In.	8.00
Silver Crest, Compote, Ruffled Edge, 5 In.	12.00
Silver Crest, Epergne, 3 Lily, 11 In.	30.00
Silver Crest, Plate, 7 1/2 In.	9.50
Silver Crest, Server, Chrome Center Handle, 8 1/2 In.	8.00
Snow Crest, Vase, Amber, Ruffled Top, 9 1/2 In.	32.00
Snow Crest, Vase, Emerald Green, Squat, 4 In.	25.00
Thumbprint, Basket, Black, Crimped, Ruffled, Sticker, 8 X 8 In.	38.00
Thumbprint, Sherbet, Label, Amber	4.00
Vase, White, Yellow Interior, 6 1/2 In.	65.00

Fiesta, the colorful dinnerware, was introduced in 1936 by the Homer Laughlin China Co., redesigned in 1969, and withdrawn in 1973. The simple design was characterized by a band of concentric circles, beginning at the rim. Cups had full-circle handles until 1969, when partial-circle handles were made. Harlequin and Riviera were related wares. For more information and prices of American dinnerware, see the book "The Kovels' Illustrated Price Guide to Depression Glass and American Dinnerware."

FIESTA, Ashtray, Cobalt Blue	24.00
Ashtray, Gray	28.00
Ashtray, Green	20.00
Ashtray, Ivory	22.00
Ashtray, Red	39.00
Ashtray, Turquoise	20.00
Ashtray, Yellow	24.00 To 35.00
Bowl, Blue, 11 3/4 In.	48.00
Bowl, Cobalt Blue, 4 3/4 In.	8.25
Bowl, Cobalt Blue, 5 1/2 In.	8.50
Bowl, Cobalt Blue, 8 1/2 In.	18.00
Bowl, Dark Blue, 4 3/4 In.	9.50
Bowl, Green, 4 3/4 In.	6.00 To 6.50
Bowl, Ivory, 4 3/4 In.	6.50

Bowl, Light Green, 5 1/2 In.	8.50
Bowl, Mixing, Green, Kitchen Kraft, 10 In.	60.00
Bowl, Mixing, Red, 6 In.	33.00
Bowl, Nesting, Red No.1	85.00
Bowl, Nesting, Red No.2	195.00
Bowl, Nesting, Red No.3	30.00
Bowl, Nesting, Yellow, Set Of 3	65.00
Bowl, Old Ivory, 4 3/4 In.	7.25
Bowl, Old Ivory, 8 1/2 In.	14.25
Bowl, Red, 4 1/4 In.	9.00
Bowl, Red, 8 1/2 In.	20.00 To 25.00
Bowl, Rose, 8 1/2 In.	14.00
Bowl, Salad, Green, 9 1/2 In.	35.00
Bowl, Salad, Yellow, 9 1/2 In.	35.00
Bowl, Stack, Kitchen Kraft, Yellow	18.00
Bowl, Turquoise, 4 3/4 In.	9.50
Bowl, Turquoise, 5 1/2 In.	9.50
Bowl, Turquoise, 8 1/2 In.	14.25
Bowl, Turquoise, 9 1/2 In.	21.50
Bowl, Yellow, 4 3/4 In.	6.50 To 7.25
Bowl, Yellow, 5 1/2 In.	7.50 To 9.50
Bowl, Yellow, 8 1/2 In.	14.50
Bowl, Yellow, 9 In.	14.00
Cake Plate, Cobalt Blue	25.00
Cake Plate, Green, Kitchen Kraft, 11 In.	30.00
Cake Plate, Yellow	22.00
Candleholder, Bulb, Yellow	18.00
Candleholder, Stick, Old Ivory, Pair	95.00
Canister, Cobalt Blue, Kitchen Kraft, Covered, Original Stickers	175.00
Carafe, Green	65.00
Carafe, Red	90.00 To 125.00
Carafe, Turquoise	75.00
Carafe, Yellow	65.00 To 85.00
Casserole, Cobalt Blue, Covered, 7 1/2 In.	28.00
Casserole, Green, Covered	45.00
Casserole, Green, Kitchen Kraft	85.00
Casserole, Light Green	23.00
Casserole, Red, Individual	35.00
Casserole, Red, Kitchen Kraft	85.00
Casserole, Turquoise, Covered	30.00
Chop Plate, Red	12.00
Chop Plate, Red, 13 In.	23.00
Coffeepot, Gray, Covered	95.00
Coffeepot, Light Green	43.00
Coffeepot, Red	60.00 To 95.00
Coffeepot, Red, Covered	110.00
Coffeepot, Yellow	75.00
Compote, Green, 12 In.	38.00
Compote, Turquoise	30.00
Compote, White, 3 1/2 X 5 In.	16.00
Compote, Yellow, 12 In.	50.00
Cookie Jar, Old Ivory, Indian Decals, Large	125.00
Creamer, Chartreuse	9.00 To 9.50
Creamer, Red	9.50
Creamer, Red, No.5	20.00
Creamer, Stick Handle, Old Ivory	17.00
Creamer, Yellow	9.00
Cup & Saucer, Cobalt Blue	15.00 To 17.50
Cup & Saucer, Dark Green	16.00 To 18.00
Cup & Saucer, Gray	18.00 To 23.00
Cup & Saucer, Green	14.00
Cup & Saucer, Medium Green	23.00
Cup & Saucer, Old Ivory	14.75
Cup & Saucer, Old Ivory, Demitasse	20.00

Cup & Saucer, Red ....17.00 To 25.00
Cup & Saucer, Rose ....16.00 To 18.00
Cup & Saucer, Turquoise ....12.00 To 16.00
Cup & Saucer, Yellow ....11.00 To 16.00
Cup & Saucer, Yellow, Stick Handle, Demitasse 8.50
Cup, Green 30.00
Cup, Rose 1.00
Cup, Rose, Demitasse 75.00
Cup, Turquoise 10.00
Egg Cooker, Red, 4 Poacher Cups 75.00
Egg Cooker, Red, Hankscraft 22.50
Eggcup, Chartreuse 42.00
Eggcup, Cobalt Blue 26.00
Eggcup, Dark Green 49.50
Eggcup, Gray 40.00
Eggcup, Green 18.00
Eggcup, Red 42.00
Eggcup, Turquoise ....18.00 To 32.00
Eggcup, Yellow ....18.00 To 45.00
Fork, Cobalt Blue, Kitchen Kraft 48.00
Fork, Green, Kitchen Kraft ....30.00 To 40.00
Gravy Boat, Chartreuse 22.00
Gravy Boat, Gray 25.00
Gravy Boat, Green 20.00
Gravy Boat, Red 25.00
Gravy Boat, Yellow, Luray 20.00
Grill Plate, Rose 20.00
Juice, Red 25.00
Marmalade, Ivory 85.00
Mug, Chartreuse 39.00
Mug, Cobalt Blue 35.00
Mug, Green 25.00
Mug, Medium Green 35.00
Mug, Old Ivory 32.00
Mug, Red ....32.00 To 46.00
Mug, Tom & Jerry, Cobalt Blue 35.00
Mug, Tom & Jerry, Red 40.00
Mug, Turquoise ....22.00 To 26.00
Mustard, Cobalt Blue 75.00
Mustard, Green 35.00
Mustard, Red, Covered 65.00
Mustard, Turquoise, Covered 50.00
Nappy, Gray, 8 1/2 In. 12.00
Nappy, Green, 8 1/2 In. 13.00
Nappy, Light Green, 8 1/2 In. 10.50
Nappy, Old Ivory, 5 1/2 In. 5.00
Nappy, Turquoise, 8 1/2 In. 19.00
Pie Plate, Green 6.50
Pie Plate, Green, Kitchen Kraft, 10 In. 35.00
Pie Plate, Red 6.50
Pie Plate, Yellow, Kitchen Kraft, 10 In. 33.00
Pitcher, Disc, Amberstone 22.00
Pitcher, Disc, Cobalt Blue 28.00
Pitcher, Green, Ice Lip 30.00
Pitcher, Juice, Yellow ....10.75 To 15.75
Pitcher, Turquoise 25.00
Pitcher, Water, Chartreuse 40.00
Pitcher, Water, Green 30.00
Pitcher, Water, Old Ivory 35.00
Pitcher, Yellow, Disc 35.00
Pitcher, Yellow, Ice Lip ....29.00 To 32.00
Pitcher, Yellow, Small 25.00
Plate, Calendar, 1955, Green, 10 In. 30.00
Plate, Chartreuse, 10 In. 14.00

Plate, Cobalt Blue, 6 In.	3.50
Plate, Cobalt Blue, 9 In.	9.00
Plate, Cobalt Blue, 9 1/2 In.	6.50
Plate, Cobalt Blue, 10 In.	18.00
Plate, Cobalt Blue, 14 3/8 In.	16.50
Plate, Dark Blue, 10 In.	8.00
Plate, Dark Green, 9 In.	6.00
Plate, Dark Green, Deep	18.00
Plate, Gray, 7 In.	6.00
Plate, Green, 7 In.	3.00
Plate, Green, 9 1/2 In.	5.25
Plate, Green, 10 In.	12.00
Plate, Medium Green, 10 In.	20.00
Plate, Old Ivory	15.00
Plate, Old Ivory, 6 In.	1.75
Plate, Old Ivory, 7 In.	4.25 To 5.00
Plate, Old Ivory, 9 In.	9.00
Plate, Old Ivory, 10 In.	8.00 To 12.00
Plate, Red, 6 In.	6.00
Plate, Red, 7 In.	4.50
Plate, Red, 9 In.	12.00
Plate, Red, 10 In.	12.00 To 20.00
Plate, Red, 13 In.	19.00
Plate, Rose	23.00
Plate, Rose, 7 In.	7.50
Plate, Rose, 9 In.	6.00 To 10.00
Plate, Rose, 10 In.	17.50 To 23.00
Plate, Turquoise, 6 In.	2.50
Plate, Turquoise, 7 1/4 In.	6.00
Plate, Turquoise, 9 1/2 In.	5.00 To 5.25
Plate, Yellow, 6 In.	2.50
Plate, Yellow, 7 In.	3.00
Plate, Yellow, 9 In.	4.50 To 9.00
Plate, Yellow, 9 1/2 In.	5.25
Platter, Green, 14 In.	20.00
Platter, Turquoise, 12 In.	15.00
Platter, Yellow, Kitchen Kraft, 13 In.	45.00
Relish, Cobalt Blue	75.00
Salad, Yellow, 10 In.	55.00
Salt & Pepper, Green	8.00 To 20.00
Salt & Pepper, Red	8.00 To 18.00
Salt & Pepper, Turquoise	8.00
Salt & Pepper, Yellow	8.00
Saltshaker, Red, Kitchen Kraft	22.00
Sauce, Turquoise	17.00
Saucer, Green	5.00
Saucer, Turquoise	2.50
Saucer, Yellow	2.50
Shaker, Red, Ball	7.00
Soup Plate, Cobalt Blue	15.00
Soup Plate, Gray, 8 In.	25.00
Soup Plate, Medium Green	20.00
Soup Plate, Red	20.00
Soup Plate, Rose	16.00
Soup Plate, Turquoise, 8 In.	22.00
Soup Plate, Yellow, 8 In.	10.00 To 22.00
Soup, Cream, Green	15.00 To 25.00
Soup, Cream, Ivory	25.00
Soup, Cream, Rose	20.00
Soup, Cream, Turquoise	20.00 To 25.00
Soup, Cream, Yellow	12.00 To 25.00
Soup, Plate, Cobalt Blue	10.00
Spoon, Red, Kitchen Kraft	45.00
Sugar & Creamer, Cobalt Blue	15.00

Sugar, Cobalt Blue, Covered 14.00
Sugar, Gray, 6 In. 3.00
Sugar, Old Ivory, Covered 15.00
Sugar, Red ....5.00 To 9.00
Sugar, Red, Covered 25.00
Sugar, Red, No.5 .... 25.00
Sugar, Rose, Covered 14.00
Sugar, Yellow, Covered 12.00
Syrup, Cobalt Blue 60.00
Syrup, Green ....90.00 To 110.00
Syrup, Yellow, Covered 75.00
Teapot, Green 15.00
Teapot, Green, Large 54.00
Teapot, Light Green, Medium 32.00
Teapot, Red 80.00
Teapot, Turquoise 50.00
Teapot, Yellow ....50.00 To 55.00
Tray, Utility, Green, 10 1/2 In. 30.00
Tray, Utility, Yellow 12.00
Tumbler, Cobalt Blue, 10 Oz. 20.00
Tumbler, Green, 10 Oz. 19.00
Tumbler, Juice, Red ....15.00 To 16.00
Tumbler, Juice, Turquoise 15.00
Tumbler, Old Ivory, 10 Oz. 21.00
Tumbler, Red, 10 Oz. 24.00
Tumbler, Turquoise, 10 Oz. 19.00
Tumbler, Yellow, 10 Oz. ....19.00 To 23.00
Vase, Bud, Yellow 30.00
Vase, Green, 10 In. 225.00
Vase, Old Ivory, 8 In. 145.00
Vase, Red, 10 In. 200.00
Vase, Yellow, 10 In. 225.00

Findlay, or onyx, glass was made using three layers of glass. It was manufactured by the Dalzell Gilmore Leighton Company about 1889 in Findlay, Ohio. The silver, ruby, or black pattern was molded into the glass. The glass came in several colors, but was usually white or ruby.

FINDLAY ONYX, Bowl, Cream Color, 8 In. 575.00
Celery, Ivory With Silver 365.00
Celery, Platinum 650.00
Pitcher, Water, Platinum Luster On Cream, Fluted Top 800.00
Saltshaker, Bluish Green Tinge, Gold Tracery, 2 3/4 In. 650.00
Spooner, Platinum, 6 In. 395.00
Spooner, White Design, Raspberry, Bulbous, 4 X 4 1/2 In. 785.00
Sugar Shaker 375.00
Sugar, Lid, Cream, Platinum Floral, 6 X 4 1/2 In. 485.00
Table Set, Priscilla, 4 Piece 225.00
Vase, White, Silver Inlay, 4 In. 225.00

It is said that every little boy wanted to be a fireman or a train engineer 75 years ago and the collectors today reflect this interest. All types of firefighting equipment are wanted, from fire marks to uniforms to toy fire trucks.

FIREFIGHTING, Alarm Box, Chicago, Cast Iron Stand, Clock Drive, C.1920 .... 275.00
Alarm Box, Gamewell, Cast Iron, 17 In. 140.00
Alarm Box, Street, Early 20th Century 95.00
Alarm, Fyr–Cry, Original Decals, 8 In. 35.00
Ashtray, Figural, Extinguisher, 1930s 38.00
Ashtray, Figural, Sprinkler, Grinnel, Advertising, 1930s 45.00
Ax, Fireman, Warren Axe Co., Warren, Pa. 25.00
Ax, Parade 250.00
Badge, For Cap 6.00
Bell, Brass 150.00

Bell, Fire Department, Vanduzen, Wall, Brass, 12 In. 135.00
Bell, Fire Engine, Bronze Nickel 125.00
Bell, Firehouse 42.00
Belt, Black Patent Leather, Nickle Plated Buckle, 57 In. 35.00
Book, San Francisco 1906 Earthquake, Fire Illustrations 25.00
Box, Alarm, Fluted Cast Iron Pedestal, Original Paint, C.1920 .... 275.00
Box, Alarm, With Fluted Post, Cast Iron, Dated 1924 .... 275.00
Box, Fire Alarm, Complete 100.00
Bucket, Alert Eagle Fire Society, American Burning Ship, Date 2250.00
Bucket, Leather, Polychrome Transfer, England, 15 1/2 In. 100.00
Bucket, Water, Leather 110.00
Cap, Black Patent Leather Bill, Gold Braid, Gold Initial M 65.00
Coat, Dress, Double Breasted Wool, Gilded Buttons, C.1900 .... 150.00
Constitution, Warren, Mass., Fire Station, 1885 .... 4.00
Emblem, 4th Annual Convention, Alexandria Bay, N.Y., 1898 .... 20.00
Extinguisher, Blue Fish, Glass 15.00
Extinguisher, C.& N.W. R.R., Blue 85.00
Extinguisher, Grenade Type, Hanging, Ivory & Plastic Holder 20.00
Extinguisher, Phoenix, Contents, Pat.1893 .... 28.50
Helmet, Chief, Aluminum, Marked Chief E.C.F.D., H.Ak.Pat.1897 .... 65.00
Helmet, French, Brass 175.00
Helmet, Gold Eagle, Gilded Brass Trim, Montgomery, '82 .... 150.00
Helmet, Large Eagle 225.00
Helmet, Leather & Steel, American Eagle On Crown 100.00
Helmet, Leather, Eagle 145.00
Helmet, Leather, White Chief 100.00
Helmet, New Jersey, Trumpet, Dated 1871 .... 145.00
Helmet, Phoenix Steam Fire Co., Painted 750.00
Holder, Flag, Graveyard, Firehat, Horn, Pennsylvania, Iron 75.00
Horn, Engraved Floral, Silver Plated Brass, 20 3/4 In. 525.00
Horn, Engraved Hatchets, Brass, 14 3/4 In. 275.00
Horse Collar, Horse Pump Wagon, Red Paint, Carved Wood 130.00
Hose Tip, Brass, Seward, Ill., First Fire Truck 50.00
Lantern, Brass, Marked Boston Wovenhose & Rubber Co. 95.00
Nozzle, Brass, 13 In. 30.00
Nozzle, Brass, 2 Handles, 24 In. 75.00
Nozzle, Cord Wrapped, 30 In. 50.00
Nozzle, Marked Elkhart, Brass, 10 In. 40.00
Pump, Fire Engine, Cast Iron, 2 Horse 150.00
Trumpet, Engraved Figures, Eagle's Head Cord Ring, 23 In. 750.00
Trumpet, Engraved Tempest Engine Co. No.1, Brass 550.00
Wagon, Horse Drawn 500.00

The fireplace was used to cook and to heat the American home in past centuries. Many types of tools and equipment were used. Andirons held the logs in place, firebacks reflected the heat into the room, and tongs were used to move either fuel or food. Many types of spits and roasting jacks were made and are listed under Kitchen.

FIREPLACE, Andirons, Ball Finial, 18th Century, 17 1/2 In. 450.00
Andirons, Ball Finial, Arched Legs, Penny Feet, Iron, 17 In. 350.00
Andirons, Ball Finial, Scroll Feet, Bradley & Hubbard, Brass 150.00
Andirons, Ball Finial, Turned Standard, Iron, 14 In. 40.00
Andirons, Brass & Iron, Ball & Acorn Design, Penny Feet, 29 In. 275.00
Andirons, Brass, Ball & Claw Feet, Federal, 24 In. 175.00
Andirons, Brass, Claw Foot, Cannonball Steeple Finial, 27 In. 190.00
Andirons, Brass, Fluted, Ball Columns, 20 1/2 In. 80.00
Andirons, Brass, Louis XV, Scroll, Fruit & Leaf Strands, 23 In. 225.00
Andirons, Brass, Pierced Scroll Work, Ball Feet, Federal, 22 In. 100.00
Andirons, Brass, Scrolled Supports, Ball Feet, 1820, 22 In. 425.00
Andirons, Brass, Stylized Curtain Swags, Pair 20.00
Andirons, Chippendale, Brass, 18 3/4 In. 25.00
Andirons, Empire, Gilt, Bronze, Urn, Sphinxes, France, 18 In. 850.00
Andirons, Federal, Ball Feet, Brass, C.1820, 22 In. 425.00
Andirons, Federal, Ball Feet, Brass, Scrolled Supports, 21 In. 100.00

Andirons, Federal, Urn Shape, Snake Feet, Brass, C.1920, 24 In. 50.00
Andirons, Figural, Black Man & Woman, Cast Iron, C.1910, 16 In. 150.00
Andirons, Figural, Hessian Soldier, Drawn Saber, Iron, 17 In. 225.00
Andirons, Form Of Griffins, Brass, C.1875 .... 385.00
Andirons, Gooseneck, Handwrought 650.00
Andirons, Gooseneck, Penny Feet, Faceted Balls, Wrought Iron 85.00
Andirons, Hessian Soldier, Figural, Iron, American, 18 1/2 In. 165.00
Andirons, Iron, Ball Finial, Straight Legs & Standard, 13 In. 40.00
Andirons, Iron, Hammered, Brown, 18 X 25 In. 308.00
Andirons, Knife Blade, Brass Finials, 14 1/2 In. 350.00
Andirons, Knife Blade, Ring Tops, Wrought Iron, 18 3/4 In. 50.00
Andirons, Knife Blade, Urn Finials, Penny Feet, Brass, 18 3/4 In. 250.00
Andirons, Lemon Top, Boston, Bell Metal, C.1790, 13 In. 325.00
Andirons, Marked Davis, Boston, Brass & Wrought Iron, C.1800 .... 1100.00
Andirons, Scrolled Legs, Brass, American, C.1830, 20 In. 225.00
Andirons, Silvered Brass, Ball Top, Baluster Support, 25 In. 500.00
Andirons, Tool Set, Stand, Bronze, Lion's Head, C.1900, 8 Piece 1430.00
Andirons, Wrought Steel, Brass Finials, 17 3/4 In. 175.00
Bellows, Brass Nozzle, Original Design, 17 3/4 In. 30.00
Bellows, Brass On Polished Pine, 19th Century 570.00
Bellows, Bronze Powder, Stencil, Floral, Brass Nozzle, 17 1/2 In. 40.00
Bellows, Carved Foliage Wreath, Walnut, 17 1/2 In. 25.00
Bellows, Original Smoke Graining & Leaf Decoration 130.00
Bellows, Yellow, Red Fruit Design, 18 1/4 In. 60.00
Box, Tinder, Asbestos Lined, Handles, Brass 75.00
Broiler, Rectangular Wrought Iron Frame, 21 1/2 In. 80.00
Broiler, Spit, Wooden Handles, 4 Hooks, 20 In. 195.00
Broom, Hearth, Birch Splint, 36 In. 95.00
Bucket, Coal, Brass Rod Spindles, Removable Bucket, 14 1/2 In. 4400.00
Bucket, Peat, Late 18th Century, Brass Bound Mahogany, 15 1/2 In. 935.00
Chenet, Bronze, Baroque Form, Paw Feet, Lion Mask, 19 In., Pair 495.00
Chenet, Bronze, Louis XVI, Acanthus Leaves Urn, Putti, 19 In., Pair 770.00
Chenet, Louis XV, Bronze, Harlequin, Lattice Base, 16 In., Pair 1045.00
Coal Hog, Pedestal Base, Brass Bail & Handle, Tin, 6 In. 75.00
Coal Scuttle, Bale, Helmet Style, Brass 220.00
Crane, Georgian Brass & Bell Metal 380.00
Crane, Hearth, Cast Iron, Rack & Peg Adjustment 150.00
Crane, Wrought Iron, 14 3/4 X 34 In. 45.00
Crane, Wrought Iron, Stamped Crawford 30.00
Ember Holder, Art Nouveau Top, Cast Iron 100.00
Fender, Iron Frame, Brass Rail, Wire Grill, 49 1/2 X 12 In. 45.00
Fender, Pierced Brass, Leaves, Paw Feet, 19th Century, 51 In. 250.00
Fender, Serpentine, Iron, Brass Trim, 36 X 14 X 15 In. 300.00
Fender, Victorian, Brass, Paw Feet, Reticulated Grill, 47 X 10 In. 170.00
Fireback, Crest Dragon & Horse, Inscription, England, 24 X 32 In. 300.00
Fireback, Iron, Angel & Child, Punched Design, 30 X 29 In. 30.00
Fireboard, Federal, Louvered Design, Gilded Medallions In Corner 1000.00
Fireboard, Fruits & Leaves, Oil On Canvas, C.1835, 43 X 38 In. 1300.00
Firedog, Lion's Head Mask, Paw Feet, Tools, C.1900, 38 In., 8 Pc. 1430.00
Firedog, Turks' Heads, 5 1/2 In., Pair 35.00
Fork, 2 Tine, Early 19th Century, Forged Iron, American 95.00
Grate, Coal, Brass, Iron, Man On Backplate, English, 31 X 31 In. 550.00
Griddle, Pivot Hanging Ring, 1 Arm, 18th Century, 11 In. 195.00
Griddle, With Drip Tray, Iron 175.00
Holder, Kettle, Wrought Iron, Pump Handle For Tilting Kettle 320.00
Iron, Waffle, Cast Iron 45.00
Log Holder, Wooden, Open Sides, Bun Feet, 18 X 24 In. 160.00
Mantel & Mirror, Floral Inlaid, Pilasters, C.1900, 64 X 40 In. 300.00
Mantel, Carved Flowers & Shells, White Marble 2700.00
Mantel, Eagle, Banner, Mariner's Compass, Pine 800.00
Mantel, Federal, Molded Cornice, Glyph Transverse, 62 X 90 In. 800.00
Mantel, Poplar, Wide Top Shelf, Refinished, 86 X 54 1/2 In. 65.00
Mantel, Victorian, Beveled Mirror, White, Walnut, 2 Piece 550.00
Mantel, Wooden, 56 X 55 In. 200.00

Panel, From Fender, Brass Serpentine, 5 1/4 X 54 In. 50.00
Peel, Hand Forged Iron, Open Oval Handle, 54 In. 260.00
Peel, Ram's Horn Finial, Wrought Iron, 39 In. 105.00
Peel, Wrought Iron, 48 1/4 In. 50.00
Roaster, Chestnut, Wrought Iron, Copper, Brass, 20 1/4 In. 150.00
Roaster, Reflector Bird, Tin, 4 Hanging Hooks, 10 X 10 In. 145.00
Roaster, Wrought Iron, Adjustable Circle, Game Forks, 29 1/2 In. 500.00
Screen, Carved Walnut, Signed Luigi Frutini, Firenze, Large 1155.00
Screen, Leaded Glass, Geometric, Brass Framed, 29 1/2 In. 200.00
Screen, Louis XV, Gilt Bronze, Cartouche, Tapestry, 33 X 37 In. 935.00
Screen, Mirrored, Cutwork Metal Frame 225.00
Screen, Victorian, Carved, Tripod Base, Needlepoint 250.00
Sifter, Ember, Ram's Head Handle, 44 In. 55.00
Skimmer, Wrought Iron, 10 X 17 In. 65.00
Spider, Wrought Iron, Rattail Handle, Bowl, 3 Feet, 17 X 6 In. 135.00
Spit, Penny Feet, Wrought Iron, 14 X 6 In. 1200.00
Spit, Roasting, Reflecting Clock, Tin, Meat Ring, 19 X 50 In. 425.00
Spit, Wrought Iron, 2 Arms, 2 Hooks, 14 X 19 3/4 In. 90.00
Tilter, Holds & Tilts Hanging Teakettle In Fireplace, 18 In. 325.00
Toaster, Hearth, Ram's Horn Design At End 575.00
Toaster, Revolving, Iron, Initialed ST, Dated 1802, 19 In. 235.00
Toaster, Wooden Handle 135.00
Tongs, Brass Handle, Iron, 28 1/2 In. 20.00
Tongs, Ember, Iron, 20 In. 55.00
Tongs, Ember, Rattail Curls On Handles, Iron, 18th Century 85.00
Tongs, Iron Pipe 175.00
Tongs, Wrought Iron, Brass Handle, 21 In. 25.00
Trammel, Twisted Detail, 3 Adjustable Hooks, Wrought Iron, 64 In. 85.00
Trammel, Wrought Iron, 22 In. 45.00
Tray, Mitt Drying, Clamps On Stove Pipe, Tin, 1870, 13 X 20 In. 55.00
Waffle Iron, Cast Iron 45.00
Waffle Iron, Long Handle ....45.00 To 60.00
Waffle Iron, No.5, Long Handle 65.00
Wood Box, Hinged Top, Embossed Figures Of Brass, 15 1/2 X 19 In. 175.00

MF *Fischer porcelain was made in Herend, Hungary. The factory was founded in 1839 and has continued working into the twentieth century. The wares are sometimes referred to as "Herend" porcelain.*

FISCHER, Ewer, Cerise, Burnt Orange, Gold, Cobalt Handle, Footed, 10 1/2 In. 150.00
Figurine, Peasant, Dancing 300.00
Jug, Decorated, 10 In. 325.00
Urn, Gold Trim, Wings, Signed, 11 In. 195.00
Vase, Near East Huntsman Scene, Gilt Border, 18 7/8 In., Pair 935.00
Vase, Pilgrim, Chinese Bouquet, Enameled, Signed & Numbered, 13 In. 165.00

Fishing reels of brass or nickel were made in the United States by 1810. Bamboo fly rods were sold by 1860, often marked with the maker's name. Metal lures, then wooden and metal lures were made in the nineteenth century. Plastic lures were made by the 1930s. All fishing material is collected today and even equipment of the past thirty years is of interest if in good condition with original box.

FISHING, Anchor, For Wooden Duck Decoys, Bell Type, Set Of 5 .... 35.00
Box, Bait, Wooden, 20 In. 60.00
Box, H.T.Tindall, Hinged Cover, Tin 310.00
Box, Minnow, Dowagiac, Dovetailed, Wooden 12.00
Box, Tackle, Horrocks, Tin Litho, Fish 30.00
Bucket, Minnow, Polished Copper 167.00
Creel, Tole, Green Paint, Gold Stenciled Fish, Leurre, 3 X 3 3/4 In. 40.00
Creel, Wicker ....30.00 To 35.00
Creel, Woven Reeds, Leather Trim 15.00
Decoy, Ice, Bear Creek Bait Co., 6 In. 12.00
Fly Rod, Bamboo 49.00

Fly Rod, Montague, Sunbeam, Split Bamboo ....75.00 To 95.00
Fly Rod, Renfrows Grand Mesan 125.00
License, Nebraska, In Display Pin, 1936, 1 1/2 X 2 1/4 In. 7.50
Lure, Blatz Beer, Bottle Shape, Labels 10.00
Lure, Flat Fish 10.00
Lure, Hagen Spinner, 3–D Metal, Fish Shape, 1952 .... 7.00
Lure, Oriental Wiggler No.4, Al Foss, Tin Box, Pat.May 14, 1918 .... 36.00
Lure, River Runt, Pocket Catalog, Original Box 15.00
Net Frame, Folding, Metal, C.1900 .... 15.00
Plug, Wooden, 11 In. 145.00
Pole, Split Bamboo, Windsor 85.00
Reel, Brass, Ivory Handle With Scrolling, Foliage, London, Cog Wind 2550.00
Reel, Chief 7.00
Reel, Eclipse 8.00
Reel, Heddon No.108F, 1929 .... 45.00
Reel, Meisselbach 25.00
Reel, Penn, No.85 .... 10.00
Reel, Pflueger Rocket No.1345, Bait Casting, Thumb Guard 35.00
Reel, Pflueger, Progress, Box 23.00
Reel, Shakespeare Silent Tru–Art, For Trout 40.00
Reel, Shakespeare, Criterion, No.1960 .... 8.00
Reel, Tripart, Meisselback 580 .... 35.00
Reel, Trout, Brass Handle & Mount, Wooden, C.1840 .... 43.00
Reel, Winchester 60.00
Rod & Reel, Stubby, 1921 .... 12.00
Rod, Casting, Richardson, Steel, Cloth Case, 4 Piece 15.00
Rod, Casting, Winchester, No.6390, 2 Piece 85.00
Rod, Casting, Winchester, Steel, 4 Piece 65.00
Rod, Fly, Cloth Case, Steel, 4 Piece 12.00
Rod, Fly, Heddon, Bamboo 45.00
Trap, Minnow, Wire Holder, Glass, G.F.Orvis Maker, Manchester, Vt. 40.00
FLAG, see Textile, Flag

Flash Gordon appeared in the Sunday comics in 1934. The daily strip started in 1940. The hero was also in comic books from 1930 to 1970, in books from 1936, in movies from 1938, on the radio in the 1930s and 1940s, and on television from 1953 to 1954. All sorts of memorabilia are collected, but the ray guns and rocket ships are the most popular.

FLASH GORDON, Figurine, Syrocco, Original Box, 1944 .... 225.00
Game, Boxed, 1965 .... 10.00
Kite ....12.00 To 30.00
Pistol, Clicker, Tin, Litho, Original Box 125.00
Pistol, Space ....45.00 To 65.00
Poster, Movie, Conquers The Universe, 1940 .... 45.00
Puzzle, Boxed 30.00
Ray Gun, Air Blaster, Red Aluminum 55.00
Record, Picture, 1948 .... 25.00
Rocketship, Marx 250.00
Telephone, 2–Way, Comic Display Package, Marx 45.00
Toy, Rocket Fighter, Windup, Tin, 12 In. 185.00

Flow blue, or flo blue, was made in England about 1830 to 1900. The plates were printed with designs using a cobalt blue coloring. The color flowed from the design to the white plate so the finished plate has a smeared blue design. The plates were usually made of ironstone china.

FLOW BLUE, Basin & Ewer Set, Abbey, George Jones 495.00
Basin, Coburg, 13 In. 75.00
Berry Bowl, Genevese, Meakin 19.00
Biscuit Jar, Gold Trim, Marked Sampson Hancock 135.00
Biscuit Jar, La Belle, Burgess & Leigh 185.00
Bone Dish, Celtic, Grindley 45.00
Bone Dish, Clarissa, Johnson Bros. 45.00

Bone Dish, Gironde ....25.00 To 30.00
Bone Dish, Holland, Meakin 36.00
Bone Dish, Osborne, Ridgway 30.00
Bone Dish, Persian, Johnson Bros. 35.00
Bowl, Alaska, 10 In. 50.00
Bowl, Daisy Seven Petals, Brush Stroke Design Interior, 5 In. 25.00
Bowl, Duchess, Scalloped, 9 1/2 In. 60.00
Bowl, Fairy Villas, 10 In. 75.00
Bowl, Fruit, Abbey, 13 In. 175.00
Bowl, Fruit, Melbourne, 12 In. 145.00
Bowl, Ivy, 11 In. 50.00
Bowl, Kelvin, 7 In. 48.00
Bowl, Lotus, 10 1/2 In. 160.00
Bowl, Lusitania, 8 In. 59.00
Bowl, Madras, Doulton, 8 1/4 X 3 In. 55.00
Bowl, Melbourne, Keeling & Co., 5 1/4 In., Pair 18.00
Bowl, Pansy, 10 In. 45.00
Bowl, Paris, New Wharf Pottery, 9 In. 35.00
Bowl, Persian, Oval, Handles, Footed, 11 1/2 In. 75.00
Bowl, Spinach With Circled Flower, 8 In. 40.00
Bowl, Splendid, 9 In. 40.00
Bowl, Togo, 10 In. 35.00
Bowl, Trent, 7 In. 30.00
Bowl, Vegetable, Chatsworth, Covered, 12 In. 48.00
Bowl, Vegetable, Conway, Open, 9 In. 45.00
Bowl, Vegetable, Indian, Covered ....95.00 To 125.00
Bowl, Vegetable, Lorne, Covered 150.00
Bowl, Vegetable, Melbourne, Oval, 9 In. 60.00
Bowl, Vegetable, Milford, Finial On Cover, Underplate, 10 3/4 In. 145.00
Bowl, Vegetable, Rhine, 9 X 6 1/2 In. 98.00
Bowl, Vegetable, Rose, Grindley, Oval, Covered 100.00
Bowl, Vegetable, Scinde, Alcock, Open 225.00
Bowl, Vegetable, Touraine, Covered, 11 3/4 In. 185.00
Bowl, Vegetable, Touraine, Oval, Small 95.00
Bowl, Vegetable, Troy, Covered, C.1840 .... 325.00
Bowl, Vegetable, Victoria, 10 In. 65.00
Bowl, Vegetable, Watteau, Ashworth, Handles, Covered, 10 1/4 In. 95.00
Bowl, Vegetable, Watteau, New Wharf Pottery, 9 In. 70.00
Bowl, Waldorf, New Wharf, 9 In. 70.00
Butter Chip, Clarissa 18.00
Butter Chip, Dresden, Set Of 6 ....60.00 To 75.00
Butter Chip, Gironde 18.00
Butter Chip, Hofburg 16.00
Butter Chip, Melbourne 30.00
Butter Chip, Ophir 15.00
Butter Chip, Touraine 35.00
Butter Chip, Venice 16.00
Butter Chip, Watteau 15.00
Butter, Drainer, Colonial, Meakin 90.00
Butter, Touraine, Covered 60.00
Cake Plate, Abbey, 9 1/2 In. 48.00
Cake Plate, Arcadia 150.00
Cake Plate, Grosvenor 45.00
Cake Plate, Indian 175.00
Cake Plate, Nonpareil, Burgess & Leigh 85.00
Celery, La Belle 70.00
Chamber Pot, Verona 82.00
Chocolate Pot, Abbey, 6 In. 85.00
Chop Plate, La Belle, 12 3/4 In. 95.00
Compote, Oriental, Ridgway, Handles, 10 X 5 1/2 In. 225.00
Creamer, Abbey, G.Jones, 3 In. 47.50
Creamer, Bouquet, Alcock, 5 In. 75.00
Creamer, Cashmere 195.00
Creamer, Ebor, Ridgway, Large 145.00

Creamer, Fairy Villas 75.00
Creamer, La Belle ....85.00 To 135.00
Creamer, Madras, Doulton, 5 1/2 In. 79.00
Creamer, Manhattan, Alcock 145.00
Creamer, Oriental 45.00
Creamer, Sabraon 195.00
Creamer, Spinach, Crow's Foot 45.00
Creamer, Sydney, New Wharf Pottery 40.00
Creamer, Touraine 150.00
Creamer, Versailles ....40.00 To 47.00
Cup & Saucer, & Luncheon Plate, Argyle, Grindley 75.00
Cup & Saucer, Abbey 40.00
Cup & Saucer, Alaska, Grindley 60.00
Cup & Saucer, Ashburton, Demitasse 45.00
Cup & Saucer, Byzantium, Child's 45.00
Cup & Saucer, Canton 115.00
Cup & Saucer, Chapoo, Wedgwood, Handleless 130.00
Cup & Saucer, Cheswick, Ridgway 45.00
Cup & Saucer, Daisy, Burgess & Leigh 42.00
Cup & Saucer, Damascus 30.00
Cup & Saucer, Dundee, Ridgway, Demitasse 65.00
Cup & Saucer, Geisha 38.00
Cup & Saucer, Hong Kong, Handleless 65.00
Cup & Saucer, Jewel, Johnson 45.00
Cup & Saucer, Kremlin 75.00
Cup & Saucer, Madras, Doulton 79.00
Cup & Saucer, Maling, Newcastle 67.00
Cup & Saucer, Melbourne 32.00
Cup & Saucer, Morning Glory, Gaudy Ironstone, Handleless .. 90.00
Cup & Saucer, Normandy 65.00
Cup & Saucer, Poppy 45.00
Cup & Saucer, Regent, Meakin 75.00
Cup & Saucer, Scinde, Alcock 115.00
Cup & Saucer, Scinde, Handleless 110.00
Cup & Saucer, Shanghai, W.C.Corn, C.1900 .... 32.00
Cup & Saucer, Spinach 45.00
Cup & Saucer, Spinach, Incised Mark 95.00
Cup & Saucer, Tonquin, Handleless 95.00
Cup & Saucer, Touraine, Large 275.00
Cup & Saucer, Touraine, Small ....38.00 To 65.00
Cup & Saucer, Verona, Ridgway 55.00
Cup & Saucer, Versailles, Furnival 79.00
Cup & Saucer, Waldorf 55.00
Dish, Soap, Harvest, 3 Piece 85.00
Dish, Soup, Amoy, 10 1/2 In. 120.00
Eggcup, Delft, Minton 40.00
Eggcup, Lorne, Grindley 34.00
Eggcup, Osborne 85.00
Gravy Boat, Andorra 75.00
Gravy Boat, Carlton 150.00
Gravy Boat, Celtic, Grindley 42.00
Gravy Boat, Cheswick, Ridgway, Underplate 100.00
Gravy Boat, Delft, Minton 75.00
Gravy Boat, Diana 40.00
Gravy Boat, Duchess, Underplate 100.00
Gravy Boat, Florence, Underplate 105.00
Gravy Boat, Holland 95.00
Gravy Boat, Ovando 50.00
Gravy Boat, Oxford, Ford & Son 59.00
Gravy Boat, Pekin, Underplate 75.00
Gravy Boat, Sabraon 185.00
Gravy Boat, Scinde, Covered 175.00
Gravy Boat, Touraine ....95.00 To 105.00
Gravy Boat, Venice 65.00

Bugs, unfortunately, also like collections! Flies stain paper; cockroaches eat paper and books; silverfish and firebrat damage paper, leather, and fabrics; moths and earpot beetles eat upholstery, stuffed animals, furs, and fabrics; termites eat wood, paper, and parts of rugs; powder post beetles and dry wood termites eat wood. Use proper sprays, check often for damage, and hire profes-sional exterminators if you have a serious problem.

Infrequent waxing of furniture is best. Once a year is enough. Go heavy on elbow grease; light on wax. We always knew that lazy housekeeping with antiques is the best. Do as little as possible to clean and shine pieces and avoid creating problems.

Gravy Boat, Verona, Underplate	95.00
Gravy Boat, Watteau, Doulton, 1896	57.50
Holder, Toothbrush, Eastern Flowers, Covered	185.00
Holder, Toothbrush, Indian, Covered	135.00
Jam Jar, Abbey, Covered, 4 1/2 In.	75.00
Ladle, Delft, 10 In.	65.00
Ladle, Sauce, Formosa	200.00
Loving Cup, Watteau, Doulton	150.00
Mug, Fleur–De–Lis, Puzzle, Sailboat & Water Design, Base Chain	60.00
Mug, Whampoa	75.00
Nappy, Clayton, Johnson, Oval	40.00
Nappy, Duchess, Oval	38.00
Pie Plate, Albany, Grindley	12.00
Pitcher & Bowl, Glendwood, 13 In.Pitcher, 18 In.Bowl	295.00
Pitcher, Acantha	100.00
Pitcher, Cashmere, Stained, 2 1/2 Qt.	225.00
Pitcher, Chrysanthemum, 7 In.	135.00
Pitcher, Hofberg, Grindley, 6 In.	55.00
Pitcher, Ivy, 10 In.	35.00
Pitcher, La Belle, 2 1/2 Qt.	185.00
Pitcher, Ladas, Ridgway, 6 In.	125.00
Pitcher, Madras, Doulton, 8 1/2 In.	125.00
Pitcher, Manhattan, Alcock, Embossed Grape Clusters, Vine, Handles	165.00
Pitcher, Milk, Alaska	78.00
Pitcher, Milk, Cashmere, 2 1/2 Qt.	225.00
Pitcher, Milk, Clematis	85.00
Pitcher, Rose, 8 In.	80.00
Pitcher, Tulips, 7 1/2 In.	95.00
Pitcher, Water, Madras, Doulton, 8 In.	200.00
Pitcher, Water, Oregon, 13 In.	395.00
Pitcher, Water, Scinde, Walker	325.00
Pitcher, Water, Touraine	400.00
Planter, La Francais, Windmill Transfer Center	65.00
Plate, Alaska, 9 In.	40.00
Plate, Albany, 9 In.	47.00 To 48.00
Plate, Albany, Johnson, 9 In.	47.00
Plate, Amoy, 8 5/16 In.	75.00
Plate, Amoy, Davenport, 10 1/2 In.	88.00 To 95.00
Plate, Anemone, 10 1/4 In.	55.00
Plate, Arabesque, Mayer, 9 1/2 In.	45.00 To 55.00
Plate, Arcadia, 10 In.	35.00
Plate, Argyle, Grindley, 10 In.	48.00
Plate, Ashburton, Grindley, 6 3/4 In.	20.00 To 27.00
Plate, Athens, 7 In.	35.00
Plate, Baltic, 10 In.	40.00
Plate, Beaufort, 10 In.	50.00 To 55.00

Plate, Blue Rose, 7 In.	18.00
Plate, Brazil, Grindley, 9 In.	29.00
Plate, Brunswick, 9 In.	42.00
Plate, Camellia, Wedgwood, 10 1/4 In.	65.00
Plate, Carlton, 9 1/2 In.	60.00
Plate, Chapoo, 10 In.	75.00 To 95.00
Plate, Chen–Si, 9 In.	85.00
Plate, Chinese Ching, Adams, 9 In.	60.00
Plate, Chiswick, 7 In.	18.00
Plate, Chusan, Clementson, 9 1/4 In.	90.00
Plate, Claremont, Clementson, Dated June 30, 1856, 8 1/2 In.	52.00
Plate, Clarence, Grindley, 6 In.	26.00
Plate, Clover, 10 In.	20.00
Plate, Clytie, 9 In.	75.00
Plate, Coburg, Edwards, 9 In.	45.00
Plate, Colonial, 9 In.	30.00
Plate, Conway, 10 In.	50.00
Plate, Corinthia, Wedgwood	35.00
Plate, Countess, 8 In.	32.00
Plate, Dover, 5 7/8 In.	20.00
Plate, Fairy Villas, 9 In.	30.00 To 40.00
Plate, Fairy Villas, 10 In.	40.00 To 43.00
Plate, Formosa, 10 1/2 In.	45.00
Plate, Formosa, 9 In.	55.00
Plate, Geisha, Ford & Sons, 7 In.	15.00
Plate, Georgia, Johnson Bros., 7 In.	32.00
Plate, Holland, Johnson Bros., 10 In.	40.00 To 55.00
Plate, Indian, 8 In.	45.00
Plate, Iris, Pearl Pottery, 10 In.	19.00
Plate, Ivanhoe, 10 In.	75.00
Plate, Janette, Grindley, 8 1/2 In.	23.00
Plate, Kelvin, Meakin, 9 1/2 In.	40.00
Plate, Kyber, Adams, 10 In.	58.00 To 65.00
Plate, La Belle, 9 1/2 In.	50.00 To 60.00
Plate, Lancaster, 9 In.	35.00
Plate, Leicester, 7 3/4 In.	42.00 To 48.00
Plate, Linda, Maddock, 9 In.	38.00
Plate, Madras, 7 In.	35.00
Plate, Mandarin, Blue, Bristol, 10 In.	65.00
Plate, Manhattan, 8 In.	18.00
Plate, Manilla, Walker, 9 In.	75.00
Plate, Martha Washington, States, 9 In.	65.00
Plate, Melbourne, Grindley, 9 In.	18.00
Plate, Melrose, Doulton, 10 1/4 In.	40.00
Plate, Nonpareil, Burgess & Leigh, 1891, 8 3/4 In.	45.00
Plate, Olympia, Grindley, 10 In., Set Of 8	125.00
Plate, Ophir, 10 In.	28.00
Plate, Oregon, 9 5/8 In.	90.00
Plate, Oriental, Timor, 9 In.	30.00
Plate, Osborne, 10 In.	34.00
Plate, Peach Royal, 11 In.	48.00
Plate, Pelew, 9 1/4 In.	20.00
Plate, Penang, Ridgway, 7 In.	35.00
Plate, Persian, 9 In.	25.00
Plate, Progress, 10 In.	38.00
Plate, Rhine, Dimmock, 10 In.	75.00
Plate, Rose, Grindley, 9 In.	19.00 To 40.00
Plate, Roseville, Maddock, 9 In.	40.00
Plate, Scinde, 8 1/4 In.	75.00
Plate, Scinde, 10 1/2 In.	110.00
Plate, Scinde, Alcock, 9 1/2 In.	40.00 To 80.00
Plate, Shanghai, 10 In.	50.00
Plate, Shell, 5 In.	75.00
Plate, Spinach, 7 In.	40.00

Plate, Sydenham, Morley, 10 In. 45.00
Plate, Temple, 9 7/8 In. 100.00
Plate, Tokio, Johnson, 10 In. 75.00
Plate, Tonquin, Heath, 9 1/2 In. 65.00
Plate, Touraine, Alcock, 8 1/2 In. 47.00
Plate, Tyrolean, 12 In. 95.00
Plate, Verona, Wood & Son, 8 In. 58.00
Plate, Vincennes, Alcock, 10 1/2 In. 62.00
Plate, Virginia, Maddock, 5 In. 35.00
Plate, Waldorf, Wood & Sons, 10 In. 53.00
Plate, Watteau, 10 In. 50.00
Plate, Yedo, 9 1/2 In. 28.00
Platter, Albany, 12 In. 55.00
Platter, Amoy, Floral, 12 X 15 In. 145.00
Platter, Andorra, 11 In. 20.00
Platter, Argyle, Grindley, 15 1/2 X 11 In. ....66.00 To 95.00
Platter, Baltic, Grindley, 16 X 12 In. 135.00
Platter, Beaufort 120.00
Platter, Berwick 100.00
Platter, Cashmere, 17 In. 350.00
Platter, Celtic, 19 In. 135.00
Platter, Colonial, Fairies At Sunrise, 12 X 9 1/2 In. 85.00
Platter, Conway, New Wharf Pottery, 10 1/2 X 7 7/8 In. 84.00
Platter, Coral, Johnson Bros. 45.00
Platter, Corean, 15 3/4 In. 55.00
Platter, Cows, Wedgwood, 17 In. 235.00
Platter, Delft, Minton, 13 1/2 X 10 1/4 In. 75.00
Platter, Dudley, 12 In. 55.00
Platter, Eclipse, 14 In. 95.00
Platter, Fairy Villas, 8 1/2 In. 48.00
Platter, Gironde, 19 X 13 1/2 In. 150.00
Platter, Gladys, 11 In. 60.00
Platter, Hindustan, C.1850, 12 X 16 In. 220.00
Platter, Indian, 13 1/2 X 10 1/2 In. 185.00
Platter, Indiana, Wedgwood, Oval, 18 X 14 1/2 In. 195.00
Platter, Janette, Grindley, 15 In. 75.00
Platter, Jewel, 14 In. 85.00
Platter, Kirkee, 12 X 15 1/2 In. 200.00
Platter, Kyber, Adams, 17 In. 295.00
Platter, La Belle, Burgess & Leigh, 12 1/2 X 17 In. 140.00
Platter, Landscape, 14 X 10 1/2 In. 125.00
Platter, Linda, Nest Of 4 .... 295.00
Platter, Melrose, Doulton, 11 In. 50.00
Platter, Melrose, Doulton, 18 In. 100.00
Platter, Normandy, Johnson Bros., 14 1/2 X 10 1/4 In. 125.00
Platter, Oriental, Oval, 10 In. 90.00
Platter, Oxford, Ford & Sons, 14 X 11 In. 125.00
Platter, Pelew, 13 1/4 X 10 1/4 In. 190.00
Platter, Savoy, Johnson Bros., 14 1/4 X 10 1/2 In. 115.00
Platter, Scinde, 20 1/4 In. 250.00
Platter, Tonquin, Heath 345.00
Platter, Touraine, 15 In. 125.00
Platter, Touraine, Oval, 10 1/2 In. 75.00
Platter, Trent, Ford & Sons, Burste, 18 In. 40.00
Platter, Vermont, 12 In. 75.00
Platter, Verona, 17 In. 150.00
Relish, Geisha 42.00
Relish, Kenworth, Johnson Bros., 8 In. 50.00
Relish, La Belle 65.00
Relish, Lorne 75.00
Relish, Melbourne 75.00
Sauce, Argyle, Johnson Bros. 25.00
Sauce, Clayton, Johnson Bros., Set Of 6 .... 96.00
Sauce, Ebor 15.00

Sauce, Florida, Johnson Bros. 28.00
Sauce, Indian Jar, 5 In. 13.00
Sauce, Knox, New Wharf Pottery ....20.00 To 60.00
Sauce, Kyber, Meir & Son, 7 In. 38.00
Sauce, Ladle, Clarence, New Wharf Pottery 285.00
Sauce, Manhattan, Large, Set Of 12 .... 195.00
Sauce, Marguerite, Grindley 16.00
Sauce, Pelew ....36.00 To 38.00
Sauce, Princeton, Johnson Bros. 28.00
Sauce, Sydney, Pair 24.00
Sauce, Touraine 27.00
Sauce, Waldorf 30.00
Sauce, Warwick, Pour Spout Either End 75.00
Soap Dish, Athens 115.00
Soup, Cream, Madras, 9 In. 40.00
Soup, Dish, Arcadia 35.00
Soup, Dish, Brazil 40.00
Soup, Dish, Brazil, Grindley 44.00
Soup, Dish, Duchess, Grindley, Flange, 9 In. 45.00
Soup, Dish, Dumbarton, New Wharf Pottery 20.00
Soup, Dish, Fairy Villas 52.00
Soup, Dish, Heron, Charles Meigh, Rim, C.1840 .... 75.00
Soup, Dish, Melbourne, Grindley 20.00
Soup, Dish, Melrose, 10 In. 47.50
Soup, Dish, Navy, Till & Son 27.00
Soup, Dish, Nonpareil, Burgess & Leigh 52.00
Soup, Dish, Rose, Grindley 35.00
Soup, Dish, Scinde, Alcock, 10 1/2 In. 90.00
Soup, Dish, Waldorf, New Wharf Pottery, 9 In. 45.00
Soup, Dish, Watteau 45.00
Soup, Nonpareil, Burgess & Leigh 52.00
Sugar & Creamer, Daisy, Covered 190.00
Sugar & Creamer, La Belle ....190.00 To 225.00
Sugar & Creamer, Mongolia, Johnson Bros. ....45.00 To 175.00
Sugar & Creamer, Plymouth, New Wharf Pottery 135.00
Sugar & Creamer, Touraine 250.00
Sugar, Amoy, Covered 110.00
Sugar, Cashmere, Covered 295.00
Sugar, Chen–Si, Covered, 8 In. 200.00
Sugar, Colonial, Meakin, Covered, 6 In. 75.00
Sugar, Daisy, Burgess & Leigh, Covered 190.00
Sugar, Holland 115.00
Sugar, La Belle, Covered 120.00
Sugar, Marechal Niel 95.00
Sugar, Marguerite, Covered 95.00
Sugar, Touraine, Covered 150.00
Syrup, La Belle 125.00
Teapot, Argyle, Tea Ball, Buffalo Pottery, 1914 .... 150.00
Teapot, Indian ....195.00 To 275.00
Teapot, Manila 165.00
Teapot, Oregon, Mayer 250.00
Teapot, Scinde, Alcock 275.00
Teapot, Venice, Upper Hanley Pottery 150.00
Teapot, Vermont 210.00
Tray, Chusan, Clementson, C.1875, Open Handles, Pedestal 150.00
Trivet, Abbey, 5 In. 45.00
Tureen, Ashburton, Covered 195.00
Tureen, Chapoo, Small 165.00
Tureen, Haddon, Covered 365.00
Tureen, Kyber, Adams, Handles, Footed 275.00
Tureen, Sauce, Indiana, Wedgwood, Tray, Covered 75.00
Tureen, Sauce, Melrose, Doulton, Covered, Base 100.00
Tureen, Soup, Marguerite, Grindley 295.00
Tureen, Soup, Oriental, Ridgway, 8 1/2 X 12 In. 295.00

Tureen, Togo, Underplate, 12 In.	300.00
Vase, La Belle, Roses On Pink Ground, 9 1/2 In.	125.00
Vase, Lily	125.00
Washbowl, Syrian	110.00
Waste Bowl, Argyle, Grindley	45.00
Waste Bowl, Gainsborough, Ridgway	59.00
Waste Bowl, Kyber	65.00
Waste Bowl, Morning Glory	125.00
Waste Bowl, Nonpareil, Burgess & Leigh	60.00
Waste Bowl, Spinach	35.00
Waste Bowl, Victoria, Wood & Sons, 10 In.	75.00

FLYING PHOENIX, see Phoenix Bird

Folk art is listed in many sections of the book under the actual name of the object. See categories such as Box; Cigar Store Figure; Weather Vane; Wooden; etc.

FOLK ART, Basket, Made Entirely Of Bottle Caps, Handle, Early 1900s	110.00
Basket, Wooden, 12 X 13 In.	25.00
Bird, Carved, Hanging Branch, Bead Eyes, Original Paint, 7 In.	55.00
Bird, Parrot, In Iron Hoop, Full–Bodied, Green, Yellow, 14 In.	715.00
Black Man, Full Length, Music Box, Holds Ashtray, 35 In.	2000.00
Bottle, From Gourd, Pinwheel Design, Pennsylvania Dutch	30.00
Bracelet, Made From Human Hair, C.1845, Mounted On Paper & Framed	25.00
Bride's Box, Pennsylvania, Painted Couple Inside Top Lid	265.00
Bulto, Blessed Virgin, Glass Eyes, Base, Mexican, 20 In.	375.00
Bulto, Christo, Carved, Base Dated 1897, 25 1/2 In.	600.00
Bulto, St.Michael, Carved, Glass Eyes, Mexican, 18 1/2 In.	380.00
Cab, Carved Of Log, Shoe Leather Roof, 13 In.	150.00
Carving, 2 Birds, Basket Of Apples, Painted, 5 1/2 X 7 In.	2400.00
Dinosaur, Gray & White Stripes, E.Pierce, 2–14–76, 8 In.	160.00
Dog's Head, Shield Shape Back, 9 3/4 X 9 3/4 In.	25.00
Dog, Standing, Bared Teeth, E.Pierce, 8–4–76, 10 In.	325.00
Drawing, White Stag On Black Paper, M.H.Elliott, 25 1/2 X 33 In.	295.00
Eagle, Carved Wood, Gessoed, Gilded, Orb Perched, C.1880, 23 1/2 In.	600.00
Eagle, Carved, Painted, American, 42 In.	220.00
Eagle, Old Gold, Wooden, 9 In.	110.00
Eagle, On Perch, 8 5/8 In.	75.00
Eagle, Pine, Lineal Carved, 19 X 8 In.	120.00
Footstool, Turtle Shape, Yellow Edge Stripe, Upholstered, 17 In.	150.00
George Washington, Standing, Lead, 19th Century, 58 In.	1500.00
Head, Boar, Carved, Black Paint, Pink & Blue Accent, 15 In.	55.00
Hitler & Liberty Bell, Hand Carved	50.00
Horse & Rider, Hair Tail, Carved Wood, Jointed Rider	85.00
Horse, Laminated Wood, Marble Eyes, Brown Paint, Base, 36 X 37 In.	2650.00
Horse, On Wheels, Wooden Base, Marked Germany, 12 X 12 In.	225.00
Horse, Signed & Dated 6–15–76, Elijah Pierce, 5 1/2 In.	225.00
Horse, Whittled, Movable Legs, Leather Ears & Tail, 11 In.	30.00
Indian Chief, Crossed Arms, Chair, Octagonal Base, 6 In.	150.00
Indian Maiden, Sandstone, Carved, Primitive, 11 1/2 In.	35.00
Jumping Jack, Hand Carved, 19th Century, 15 In.	225.00
Knitty Knotty Pinwheels, Diamonds, Chip Carved	55.00
Lady, Peaked Cap, Red Dress, Shop Display, Iron, 12 In.	1045.00
Lion, Standing, Teeth Bared, 6 1/2 In.	385.00
Log Cabin, Shoe Leather Roof, 13 In.	150.00
Marionette, Man, Carved, Fabric Jointed, Wood Base, 30 In.	500.00
Model, Side Wheeler, Lewiston, Rowboats, Flag, Burgee, 14 X 35 In.	1760.00
Monk, Baby On Back, Erotic, Carved From Horn	165.00
Monkey, Carved From Peach Pit	6.00
Monkey, Pyramid, Soapstone, 4 1/2 In.	45.00
Owl, Maine, Pine & Old Gilt, 8 3/4 In.	625.00
Painting, On Wood, Diamond Shape Checkerboard, Pa., Dutch, 26 In.	150.00
Peacock, Silhouette, Sheet Metal, 12 X 14 In.	825.00
Picture, Woman, Human Hair, Satin Dress, Art Nouveau, 8 X 10 In.	20.00
Pioneer Woman, On Log, Apron Up, Sandstone, 12 1/2 In.	275.00

Pipe Tamp, Whale Bone, Lady's Leg, Incised Design, 2 1/2 In.	135.00
Planter, Crowing Rooster, Old White & Red Paint, 23 In.	75.00
Plaque, 2 Soldiers, Wearing Blue, Gray, Carrying Flag, Round, 19 In.	95.00
Plaque, Eagle, Gilded Pine, Wings Spread, 13 X 29 In.	770.00
Preacher, Black, Seated, Pulpit, Wood, 10 In.	3080.00
Puzzle Box, Recumbent Hound As Removable Lock, C.1890, 10 3/4 In.	285.00
Rooster, Hen, Hand Carved, Wooden, Signed, 1900s, 3 1/2 In.	125.00
Rooster, Silhouette, Galvanized Sheet Metal, Wooden Base, 27 In.	105.00
Sailor's Valentine, Double Sided, C.1850, Shells, Seeds, 20 1/4 In.	650.00
Sailor's Valentine, Heart, Folding, 1839, Abalone Frame, 8 X 10 In.	605.00
Santos, St.Christopher, Wooden Base, 28 In.	100.00
Santos, Virgin, Wooden Base, 16 In.	70.00
Sculpture, Exotic Nude, Stone, S.Moselsio, 1890, 24 3/4 In.	675.00
Sculpture, Seated Nude, Stone, C.Heintzelman, 23 In.	400.00
Shoe Horn, Carved Horn Duck Head Handle, 19th Century, 7 1/2 In.	39.00
Statue Of Liberty, Gate Post Finial, 1900, 20 In.	2970.00
Stork, Standing In Foliage, C.1910, 20 In.	412.00
Totem Pole, Ebony, Carved, Boma, Canada, 6 1/2 In.	35.00
Toy, Hound, Black & White, Jointed Legs, Tail & Ears	25.00
Uncle Sam, Carved, Painted, American, 6 1/4 In.	50.00
Uncle Sam, Profile, Flat, Polychrome, Wooden, C.2900, 93 In.	1250.00
Walking Stick, Snake, Turtle, & Man's Head, 36 In.	255.00
Wax Seal, Whale Bone, Turned, Brass Tip, 2 7/8 In.	95.00
Wheelbarrow, Wooden, Red, Green, 11 In.	27.00
Whirligig, Black Man, Yellow Hat, Red Pants, 19 1/4 In.	4180.00
Whirligig, Black Painted Hair, Shoes, Metal Base, 13 In.	990.00
Whirligig, Chicken, Polychrome Paint, Wooden, 22 1/2 In.	150.00
Whirligig, Dewey Boy, Wooden, Swivel Arms & Paddles, 12 1/2 In.	250.00
Whirligig, Duck, Martin Yanovic, Ontario, 1936	750.00
Whirligig, Dutch Pair Churning, Polychrome Repaint, 16 X 19 In.	30.00
Whirligig, Fish & Chips, Carver Zenas Publicover	475.00
Whirligig, Indian, Chief, Headdress, Seated In Canoe, 12 In.	1760.00
Whirligig, Man In Top Hat, Tie, Black Coat, New England, 15 In.	675.00
Whirligig, Man, Facial Features, Baffles For Arms, 17 In.	550.00
Whirligig, Man, Milking Cow	115.00
Whirligig, Mountain Man Sawing Wood, Metal	150.00
Whirligig, Sailor In Whites, Semaphore Flags, 16 X 6 1/4 In.	240.00
Whirligig, Sailor, Boat Dated 1936, Carved, 16 5/8 In.	400.00
Whirligig, Soldier, Carved Features, Hat, Pine, 14 3/4 In.	775.00
Whirligig, Traffic Cop, Arms, Zenas Publicover, Nova Scotia, 1930	900.00
Whirligig, Uncle Sam, Hand Car, Turns Windmill, Paint, 1900, 34 In.	350.00
Whirligig, Windmill, Wooden	798.00
Whirligig, Windmill, Wooden, Painted Red, White, & Blue, 21 1/2 In.	225.00
Whirligig, Wooden Indian In Canoe, Polychrome Paint, 10 1/2 In.	260.00
Whistle, Figural, Owl, Carved From Coal, 4 In.	150.00
Yard Ornament, 2 White Horses, Red & Green Wagon	85.00

Cold feet have been a problem for generations. Our ancestors had many ingenious ways to warm feet with portable foot warmers. Some warmers held charcoal, others held hot water. Pottery, tin, and soapstone were the favored materials to conduct the heat. The warmer was kept under the feet, then the legs and feet were tucked into a blanket, providing welcome warmth in a cold carriage or church.

FOOT WARMER, Brass, Victorian	340.00
Buggy, Coal Tray, Fabric Covered	15.00
Carpet Cover, Brass Ends, Marked Lehmans, 8 X 14 In.	40.00
Carpet Cover, Charcoal Drawer	50.00
Carriage, Carpet Cover	18.00
Clark Heater, No.2, Carpet Covered	17.50
Doulton	30.00
Hand Punched, Tin	65.00
Henderson, Stoneware	50.00
Original Stencil, Tin	75.00
Pewter, Brass, Oval Shape, Ring Finial, English	30.00

Pierced Design, Sliding Lid, Wire Bale, 8 1/4 X 11 1/4 X 7 In. 75.00
Punched Tin Top, Turned Corner Posts, 7 1/2 X 9 1/4 X 6 In. 110.00
Punched Tin, Butternut Frame, Hearts, Circles, 6 X 7 1/2 In. 85.00
Punched Tin, Mortised Butternut Frame, Black Paint, 8 X 9 In. 55.00
Punched Tin, Wooden Frame, 8 X 6 In. 95.00
Punched Tin, Wooden Frame, Turned Corner Posts, 7 3/4 X 9 In. 35.00
Vent Hole & Ring Top, Albany, Signed C.Jager Co., 7 X 9 In. 220.00
Wire Carrier, Wood Handle, Tin Lined, Wood Top, 10 1/2 X 7 In. 80.00

Fostoria glass was made in Fostoria, Ohio, from 1887 to 1891. The factory was moved to Moundsville, West Virginia, and most of the glass seen in shops today is a twentieth-century product. The company was sold in 1983; and new items will be easily identifiable, according to the new owners, Lancaster Colony Corporation.

FOSTORIA, see also Milk Glass
FOSTORIA, Acanthus, Plate, Amber, Etching, 7 1/4 In. 6.00
Acanthus, Plate, Green, 9 1/2 In. 17.00
Acanthus, Relish, Green, 2 Section 22.50
Acanthus, Sugar, Green 24.00
Alexis, Saltshaker 9.00
American Lady, Champagne, Amethyst 24.00
American Lady, Tumbler, Amethyst, Footed, 10 Oz. 20.00
American, Ashtray, 2 3/4 In., Set Of 12 .... 50.00
American, Basket, Reeded Handle 100.00
American, Bonbon, 3 Toes, 7 In. 10.00
American, Bonbon, Ruby 50.00
American, Bowl & Mug, Child's 38.50
American, Bowl, 4 1/2 In. 3.00
American, Bowl, 7 In. 22.50
American, Bowl, Boat Shape, 8 1/2 In. 10.00
American, Bowl, Divided, Oval, 10 In. 18.00
American, Bowl, Footed, 8 In. 10.00
American, Bowl, Fruit, 20 In. 28.00
American, Bowl, Fruit, Footed, 16 In. ....109.00 To 115.00
American, Bowl, Salad, 10 In. ....25.00 To 30.00
American, Bowl, Vegetable, 2 Section, 10 In. 32.50
American, Box, Cigarette, Covered 30.00
American, Box, Covered, 5 X 3 1/2 In. 47.00
American, Butter, 1 Lb. ....95.00 To 127.50
American, Butter, Dome Lid 58.00
American, Cake Plate, Pedestal, Round ....48.00 To 59.00
American, Cake Salver, Round 45.00
American, Candleholder, 3 In., Pair 18.00
American, Candlestick, 2–Light, 4 3/8 In., Pair 40.00
American, Candy Dish, Covered, Triangular, 3–Part 38.00
American, Celery, 6 In. 29.00
American, Coaster, Set Of 4 .... 17.00
American, Cocktail, Cone, 2 7/8 In. 12.00
American, Compote, Cheese 18.50
American, Compote, Covered, 9 In. 25.00
American, Condiment Set, 6 Piece 200.00
American, Creamer 5.00
American, Cruet, 7 Oz. ....24.00 To 30.00
American, Cup & Saucer ....8.75 To 12.00
American, Decanter, Stopper, 9 1/4 In. 60.00
American, Dish, Jelly, Covered 38.00
American, Dish, Olive, 6 In. ....8.00 To 10.00
American, Dish, Shrimp 155.00
American, Goblet, Footed, 9 Oz. 12.00
American, Goblet, Footed, Hexagon, 10 Oz. 13.00
American, Goblet, Low, 5 1/2 In. 7.00
American, Goblet, Rose Etching, 7 In. 10.00
American, Gravy Boat, Underplate 49.00
American, Hat, 3 In. ....18.00 To 22.50

American, Iced Tea, Footed, 5 3/4 In.	16.00
American, Jam Pot, Covered	95.00
American, Lamp, Hurricane	65.00
American, Loving Cup, Footed	75.00
American, Mayonnaise Set, 3 Piece	28.00 To 30.00
American, Mug, 12 Oz.	40.00
American, Mustard, Covered	18.00 To 32.50
American, Napkin Ring, Set Of 8	36.00
American, Oyster Cocktail, 4 1/2 Oz.	8.00
American, Pitcher, Water, 2 Qt.	70.00
American, Plate, 6 In.	4.00
American, Plate, 12 In.	18.00 To 24.00
American, Plate, Sandwich, Center Handle, 12 In.	25.00
American, Plate, Torte, 14 In.	22.00 To 39.00
American, Plate, Torte, 20 In.	65.00
American, Plate, Torte, Ruby, 14 In.	39.00 To 50.00
American, Platter, 12 In.	45.00 To 55.00
American, Punch Bowl, 14 In.	88.00
American, Punch Cup, Straight Sided	6.00
American, Relish, 2 Section	22.00
American, Relish, 4 Section, Square, 11 In.	50.00
American, Rose Bowl, 5 In.	15.00 To 25.00
American, Salt Dip	4.50
American, Saltshaker, 3 1/2 In., Pair	16.00
American, Salver, Square Pedestal, 10 In.	75.00
American, Sauce Boat	70.00
American, Sherbet, Flared, Stemmed	7.00 To 8.50
American, Sherbet, Footed, Low, 5 Oz., 3 1/4 In.	3.00 To 13.25
American, Soup, Cream	37.50
American, Sugar & Creamer, Large	12.50 To 20.00
American, Sugar & Creamer, Small	10.00 To 15.00
American, Sugar Shaker	35.00 To 40.00
American, Syrup	25.00 To 45.00
American, Syrup, Ivory, Handle	85.00
American, Tankard, Beer	40.00
American, Toothpick	15.00 To 18.50
American, Tray, Lunch, Handle, 12 In.	40.00
American, Tumbler, Footed, 4 3/8 In.	7.00
American, Vase, Flared, 6 In.	22.50 To 26.00
American, Vase, Straight Sided, 10 In.	30.00
American, Whiskey, 2 Oz.	8.50
Arcadia, Cup & Saucer	18.50
Baroque, Bowl, Flared, Topaz, 12 In.	25.00
Baroque, Bowl, Handles, 10 X 10 1/2 In.	24.00
Baroque, Bowl, Topaz, Handles, 8 1/2 In.	18.00
Baroque, Candleholder, 3–Light, Pair	30.00 To 35.00
Baroque, Candlestick, 2–Light, Pair	22.00 To 25.00
Baroque, Candlestick, Topaz, 5 1/2 In., Pair	34.00
Baroque, Candy Dish, Covered, Yellow, 9 In.	45.00
Baroque, Celery, Oval, 11 In.	14.50
Baroque, Compote, 5 1/2 In.	12.00 To 14.50
Baroque, Cruet, Yellow, Stopper	350.00
Baroque, Cup & Saucer	12.00 To 15.00
Baroque, Cup & Saucer, Blue	29.50
Baroque, Goblet, Water, 9 Oz.	14.50
Baroque, Ice Bucket, Blue	95.00
Baroque, Ice Bucket, Topaz	58.00
Baroque, Ice Bucket, Yellow	45.00
Baroque, Jelly, Blue, Footed	60.00
Baroque, Plate, 9 1/2 In.	16.00
Baroque, Plate, Blue, 7 In.	9.00 To 13.00
Baroque, Relish, 3 Section	15.00
Baroque, Sherbet	8.00 To 9.50
Baroque, Sherbet, Topaz	16.50

Baroque, Sugar & Creamer	12.00
Baroque, Sugar, Topaz	15.00
Baroque, Tray, Handles, 10 1/4 In.	17.50
Baroque, Tumbler, Topaz, Footed, 9 Oz.	20.00
Beacon, Champagne	30.00
Beacon, Sherbet	27.00
Beverly, Cake Plate, Center Handle, Fleur-De-Lis, 11 3/4 In.	20.00
Beverly, Compote, Green, Low, 8 1/2 In.	14.50
Beverly, Creamer, Amber	20.00
Beverly, Cup & Saucer, Amber	16.00
Beverly, Pitcher, Water, Green	225.00
Beverly, Plate, Amber, 8 3/4 In.	4.75
Beverly, Platter, Amber, 15 In.	24.00
Beverly, Tumbler, Amber, Iced Tea, 6 In.	18.00
Bookends, Horse, Rearing	42.00
Brighton, Cocktail	28.00
Brighton, Wine	30.00
Brunswick, Sherbet, Amber	14.00
Buttercup, Creamer	17.50
Buttercup, Cup & Saucer	25.00
Buttercup, Plate, 9 1/2 In.	35.00
Buttercup, Sugar	17.50
Cameo, Goblet, Water	19.00
Cameo, Wine	19.00
Carmen, Sugar, Covered, 1896	25.00
Century, Basket, Reeded Handles, 10 1/2 In., Pair	88.00
Century, Bowl, Flared, Footed, 11 In.	35.00
Century, Butter, Covered, 1/4 Lb.	32.00
Century, Cocktail, Oyster	11.00
Century, Compote, 4 3/8 In.	8.00
Century, Cruet	45.00
Century, Dish, Mayonnaise	20.00
Century, Pitcher, 3 Pt., 7 1/8 In.	75.00
Century, Plate, 7 In.	5.00
Century, Relish, 3-Part, 11 1/8 In.	25.00
Century, Salt & Pepper, Individual	10.00
Century, Sherbet, 4 1/2 In.	15.00
Century, Sugar & Creamer, Covered	17.50 To 25.00
Century, Tray, Muffin	27.50
Century, Tumbler, Footed, 12 Oz.	15.00
Chintz, Bowl, 12 In.	30.00
Chintz, Bowl, Divided, Square, 6 In.	25.00
Chintz, Bowl, Topaz, Oval, 9 1/2 In.	30.00
Chintz, Candleholder, Topaz, Double, Pair	47.00
Chintz, Compote, 5 1/2 In.	18.00
Chintz, Creamer, Individual	9.00
Chintz, Creamer, Large	17.50
Chintz, Cup & Saucer	22.50
Chintz, Goblet, 9 Oz.	13.00 To 15.00
Chintz, Plate, 7 1/2 In.	7.50
Chintz, Plate, Topaz, 7 1/2 In.	9.00
Chintz, Sherbet, Topaz, 4 3/8 In.	19.00
Chintz, Soup, Cream, Topaz, 7 1/4 In.	7.00
Chintz, Sugar, Large	17.50
Chintz, Tray, Tidbit, Footed	27.50
Chintz, Tumbler, Topaz, Footed, 6 In.	22.75
Christiana, Wine	38.00
Circlet, Tumbler, Juice, 5 Oz.	28.00
Colonial Dame, Goblet, Green, 11 Oz.	8.00 To 20.00
Colony, Bowl, Flared, 11 In.	12.00
Colony, Bowl, Footed, Low, 10 In.	40.00
Colony, Candleholder, 3 In., Pair	19.00
Colony, Candlestick, 8 3/4 In., Pair	35.00
Colony, Candlestick, Prisms, 14 1/2 In., Pair	150.00

Colony, Celery, 11 1/2 In.	12.00
Colony, Cocktail	12.00
Colony, Compote, Covered, Label, 6 In.	32.00
Colony, Cup & Saucer	7.75 To 9.00
Colony, Dish, Mayonnaise, 3 Piece	28.50
Colony, Goblet, Footed, 9 Oz.	12.00
Colony, Pitcher, 6 In.	12.00
Colony, Plate, 8 1/2 In.	3.50
Colony, Plate, Torte, Center Feather Handle, 13 In.	22.50
Colony, Relish, 2 Section	14.50
Colony, Salver, Footed, 12 In.	29.00
Colony, Sherbet, Flared, 5 Oz.	5.00
Colony, Sugar & Creamer, Individual	18.00
Colony, Tray, Muffin	22.00
Colony, Urn, Covered, Footed	65.00
Coronet, Candlestick, Double	27.50
Coronet, Plate, 9 1/2 In.	125.00
Coronet, Relish, 3 Section	12.00
Corsage, Celery, 11 1/2 In.	25.00
Corsage, Cocktail, Oyster	17.50
Corsage, Sugar & Creamer	25.00 To 28.00
Corsage, Wine, Plum	9.00
Cupid, Console, Ebony, Footed, 12 In.	65.00
Czarina, Toothpick, Pedestal, Footed	28.50
Daisy, Wine, 5 1/2 In.	22.50
Dolly Madison, Cordial	44.00
Doncaster, Champagne	24.00
Edgewood, Carafe, 6 Tumbler	90.00
Fairfax, Bonbon, Blue	17.50
Fairfax, Bowl, Topaz, Oval, 12 1/2 In.	22.00
Fairfax, Butter, Green, Covered	65.00 To 68.00
Fairfax, Butter, Pink, Covered	65.00 To 85.00
Fairfax, Butter, Yellow, Covered	79.00
Fairfax, Candleholder, Scroll, Black, 5 In.	15.00
Fairfax, Champagne, Green	16.00
Fairfax, Cheese & Cracker Set, Green	22.00
Fairfax, Coaster, Topaz	3.75
Fairfax, Cocktail, Oyster, Pink	18.00
Fairfax, Compote, Green, 7 In.	16.00
Fairfax, Creamer, Footed, Amethyst	9.00
Fairfax, Cruet	79.00
Fairfax, Cup & Saucer	9.00 To 10.00
Fairfax, Cup & Saucer, Amber	5.00 To 7.50
Fairfax, Cup & Saucer, Green	5.00 To 7.00
Fairfax, Cup & Saucer, Orchid	20.00
Fairfax, Cup & Saucer, Pink	5.00 To 7.00
Fairfax, Finger Bowl, Topaz, Blown	10.00
Fairfax, Parfait, Blue	32.50
Fairfax, Pitcher, Blue, 7 3/8 In.	6.00
Fairfax, Plate, 7 1/2 In.	6.00
Fairfax, Plate, Amber, 8 3/4 In.	6.00
Fairfax, Plate, Blue, 6 In.	4.00
Fairfax, Plate, Green, 8 3/4 In.	6.00
Fairfax, Plate, Orchid, 8 3/4 In.	12.00
Fairfax, Plate, Pink, 6 In.	4.00
Fairfax, Relish, Green, 8 1/2 In.	8.50
Fairfax, Salt & Pepper, Green	29.00
Fairfax, Soup, Bouillon, Saucer, Green	8.50
Fairfax, Soup, Cream, Amber	10.00
Fairfax, Sugar & Creamer, Amber, Individual	15.00
Fairfax, Tray, Cheese & Cracker, Amber	22.00
Fairfax, Tray, Server, Green, Center Handle	12.00
Fairfax, Tumbler, Water, Footed	14.00
Glacier, Compote	6.00

Grape, Console Bowl, Rolled Rim, Brocade Blue, 10 In. 48.00
Heather, Cruet, Stopper 47.50
Heirloom, Bowl, Blue, 10 In. ....22.00 To 22.50
Heirloom, Candleholder, Floral Design, Green 32.00
Heirloom, Console Set, Sea Green, Flared Bowl, 3 Piece 70.00
Hermitage, Cup & Saucer, Wisteria 30.00
Hermitage, Dish, Ice Cream, Green 6.00
Hermitage, Sherbet, Topaz, Low 12.00
Hermitage, Sugar & Creamer, Footed 20.00
Holly, Oyster Cocktail 30.00
Holly, Sherbet ....20.00 To 27.00
Ivy, Oyster Cocktail 28.00
Jamestown, Goblet, Amber, Stem, 5 3/4 In. 7.00
Jamestown, Goblet, Water, Ruby 10.00
Jamestown, Sherbet, Amber 8.00
Jenny Lind, Box, Pink, Oval, Covered, Milk Glass 30.00
Jenny Lind, Decanter, Milk Glass, 11 In. 48.00
Jenny Lind, Tray, Oval, Milk Glass, Brush & Comb, 12 In. 35.00
Juliet, Cocktail 30.00
June, Bonbon, Yellow 16.00
June, Candy Dish, Topaz, Covered, Footed 280.00
June, Celery, Yellow, 11 1/2 In. 32.00
June, Champagne 10.00
June, Champagne, Blue, 6 Oz. 30.00
June, Cocktail, 5 1/4 In. 27.00
June, Compote, Blue, 7 In. 68.00
June, Cruet, Yellow, Footed 225.00
June, Cup & Saucer, Blue 30.00
June, Cup & Saucer, Pink 35.00
June, Cup & Saucer, Yellow 32.50
June, Cup, Footed, Blue 39.00
June, Goblet, 10 Oz. ....14.00 To 16.00
June, Goblet, Blue, 10 Oz. 38.00
June, Parfait, Blue 60.00
June, Parfait, Topaz 18.00
June, Plate, Blue, 7 1/2 In. ....8.50 To 12.50
June, Plate, Blue, 10 1/4 In. 48.00
June, Plate, Yellow, 10 1/4 In. 47.50
June, Sugar & Creamer, Topaz 49.50
June, Tray, Sandwich, Pink, Center Handle 62.50
June, Tumbler, Footed, 9 Oz. 25.00
June, Tumbler, Footed, Blue, 9 Oz. 23.00
June, Tumbler, Iced Tea, Footed, 12 Oz. 36.00
June, Wine, 5 1/2 In. 21.75
Lafayette, Bowl, 12 In. 16.00
Laurel, Champagne 24.00
Laurel, Cocktail, Oyster 10.00
Laurel, Plate, 8 In. 5.00
Laurel, Tumbler, Juice, 5 Oz. 28.00
Lenox, Champagne 24.00
Lily-Of-The-Valley, Iced Tea, Handle, Set Of 7 .... 110.00
Lyre, Candlestick, Double, Pair 88.00
Manhattan, Candy Jar, Covered 12.00
Manhattan, Pitcher, 42 Oz. 7.50
Manor, Sugar & Creamer, Individual, Green 23.00
Mayfair, Cup & Saucer, Topaz, Footed 5.00
Mayfair, Grill Plate, Pink, 9 1/2 In. 23.00
Mayfair, Pitcher, Pink, 60 Oz. 33.00
Mayfair, Plate, Ebony, 6 1/2 In. 5.00
Mayfair, Plate, Pink, 5 1/2 In. 3.00
Mayfair, Plate, Topaz, 9 In. ....7.00 To 8.00
Mayfair, Soup, Dish, Amber, 7 In. 7.00
Mayfair, Tray, Sandwich, Amber, Center Handle 18.00
Mayflower, Console Set, 3-Light Candleholder 55.00

Mayflower, Goblet, Water, Footed	12.00
Meadow Rose, Candlestick, Single, Pair	20.00
Meadow Rose, Candlestick, Triple, Pair	35.00
Meadow Rose, Champagne, Blue	25.50
Meadow Rose, Cocktail	20.00
Meadow Rose, Cup & Saucer	25.00
Meadow Rose, Dish, 3 Section, Round, 7 In.	30.00
Meadow Rose, Goblet, 10 Oz.	18.00
Meadow Rose, Mayonnaise Set, 3 Piece	28.00
Meadow Rose, Relish, 3 Section, 10 1/2 In.	27.50
Melrose, Tumbler, Water, 4 3/4 In.	9.50
Millefleur, Tumbler, 10 Oz. ....4.00 To	6.00
Minuet, Bowl, Cereal, Yellow, 6 In.	15.00
Minuet, Sherbet, Green Base	17.00
Minuet, Soup, Cream, Footed, Yellow	13.00
Mulberry, Goblet, 10 Oz.	8.00
Mulberry, Wine, 4 1/2 Oz.	32.00
Navarre, Bowl, Footed, Royal Blue, 9 In.	65.00
Navarre, Bowl, Gold, 9 In.	40.00
Navarre, Cake Plate, Handle, 10 In.	26.00
Navarre, Candlestick, Triple	24.00
Navarre, Candy Dish, Covered	50.00
Navarre, Champagne, Blue	19.50
Navarre, Champagne, Footed, 5 1/2 Oz.	16.00
Navarre, Claret, Pink	27.50
Navarre, Cocktail, Footed, 3 1/2 Oz.	14.00
Navarre, Cordial	49.99
Navarre, Cup & Saucer	24.50
Navarre, Goblet, 10 Oz.	19.00
Navarre, Iced Tea, Footed, 13 Oz.	16.00
Navarre, Mayonnaise Set, 3 Piece	22.00
Navarre, Pitcher	90.00
Navarre, Plate, 9 1/2 In.	39.50
Navarre, Relish, 2 Section, 6 In.	15.00
Navarre, Shaker, Footed, Pair	75.00
Navarre, Sherbet, Low	18.00
Navarre, Sherbet, Tall	17.00
Navarre, Sugar & Creamer	24.75
Navarre, Tumbler, Blue, Footed, 10 Oz.	20.00
Navarre, Tumbler, Water, Footed, 9 Oz.	16.00
Navarre, Wine, Footed, 3 Oz.	18.00
New Garland, Cruet, Topaz, Clear Stopper	95.00
Nosegay, Sherbet	24.00
Oak Leaf, Ice Bucket	37.50
Oak Leaf, Tray, Green, Footed, 12 In.	60.00
Pilgrim, Sugar & Creamer	45.00
Pioneer, Bouillon, Amber, Flat, Handles	5.00
Pioneer, Bowl, Fruit, Blue	6.00
Pioneer, Bowl, Green, 5 1/2 In.	5.50
Pioneer, Cup & Saucer	5.00
Pioneer, Cup & Saucer, Blue	8.00
Pioneer, Cup & Saucer, Green ....4.00 To	6.00
Pioneer, Eggcup, Green, Set Of 6	40.00
Pioneer, Plate, Green, 9 1/2 In.	18.00
Priscilla, Butter, Green, Gold, Covered	45.00
Priscilla, Pitcher, Amber, Footed, 10 In.	55.00
Priscilla, Saltshaker, Green, Original Lid	45.00
Priscilla, Soup, Bouillon, Green	8.00
Priscilla, Sugar & Creamer, Tray, Green	22.00
Priscilla, Water Set, Regal Blue, 7 Piece	250.00
Puritan, Iced Tea, Footed	4.00
Raleigh, Nappy, Green, 7 In.	6.50
Regent, Sherbet, Encrusted Gold Optic, Footed	15.00
Revere, Cordial	25.00

Rheims, Oyster Cocktail 24.00
Richmond, Wine 24.50
Rogene, Compote, 5 In. 16.00
Romance, Bowl, 13 In. 28.00
Romance, Cocktail, 3 1/2 Oz. 17.50
Romance, Creamer ....10.00 To 17.50
Romance, Cup & Saucer 17.50
Romance, Goblet, Water 18.00
Romance, Plate, 7 1/2 In. 6.00
Romance, Relish, Divided, Etched, 10 In. 40.00
Romance, Server, Center Handle 20.00
Romance, Sugar & Creamer ....26.00 To 47.00
Romance, Tumbler, Water 24.00
Romance, Wine, Etched 25.00
Rondeau, Champagne 23.00
Rose, Champagne 23.00
Royal, Bowl, Amber, 9 In. 32.00
Royal, Cocktail, Amber 24.00
Royal, Compote, Blue, 6 In. 30.00
Royal, Creamer, Footed, Amber 17.50
Royal, Cup & Saucer, Amber, Flat 20.00
Royal, Cup & Saucer, Blue 16.00
Royal, Cup & Saucer, Green 22.50
Royal, Dish, Pickle, Green, 8 In. 18.00
Royal, Plate, Green, 10 1/2 In. 25.00
Seascape, Sugar & Creamer, Pink 20.00
Seville, Candy Dish, Amber, Covered 95.00
Seville, Plate, Amber, 8 1/2 In. 6.50
Seville, Soup, Cream, Flat, Amber 12.50
Seville, Tumbler, Green, Footed, 12 Oz. 20.00
Shirley, Candleholder, 3 1/2 In., Pair 35.00
Shirley, Celery, 11 In. 35.00
Silver Flutes, Goblet, 10 Oz. 16.50
Silver Flutes, Sherbet 15.00
Silver Flutes, Tumbler, Footed, 5 Oz. 15.00
Spinet, Parfait 36.00
Spinet, Plate, 7 1/2 In. 22.00
Spire, Cocktail 28.00
Sprite, Cocktail 28.00
Stardust, Wine 28.00
Sunray, Bowl, Crystal, Footed, 11 1/2 In. 12.00
Sunray, Jam Jar, Covered, 7 In. 25.00
Sunray, Sugar & Creamer, 4 In. 18.00
Swirl, Ice Bucket, Blue 28.00
Trojan, Bowl, Console, Topaz, Swirl Handles, 9 3/4 In. 65.00
Trojan, Cruet, Stopper, Pink 350.00
Trojan, Cup & Saucer, Yellow 20.00
Trojan, Goblet, Water, Yellow, 8 1/4 In. 26.00
Trojan, Plate, Torte, Yellow, 13 In. 55.00
Trojan, Plate, Yellow, 6 In. 6.00
Trojan, Relish, 2 Section, Topaz, 8 1/2 In. 12.00
Trojan, Sherbet, Low, Topaz, Set Of 6 .... 75.00
Trojan, Tumbler, Footed, Yellow, 10 Oz. 20.00
Trojan, Tumbler, Topaz, Footed, 5/3/4 In. 18.00
Trojan, Vase, Blue, Footed, Flared, 7 In. 42.00
Vernon, Cup & Saucer, Orchid 29.50
Vernon, Pitcher, 7 1/2 In. 8.00
Vernon, Plate, Orchid, 9 1/2 In. 19.50
Vernon, Sherbet, Stem, Blue 17.00
Versailles, Baker, Blue, Oval, 9 In. 40.00
Versailles, Bowl, Cereal, Blue, 6 In. 34.00
Versailles, Bowl, Yellow, 2 Handles, 10 In. 29.00
Versailles, Cake Plate, Pink, Handles, 10 In. 29.95
Versailles, Candleholder, Scroll, Yellow, 5 In., Pair 55.00

Versailles, Cocktail, Green	18.00
Versailles, Cordial, Green, Set Of 2	40.00
Versailles, Creamer, Yellow	27.50
Versailles, Cruet, Stopper, Pink	325.00
Versailles, Cup & Saucer	27.00
Versailles, Cup & Saucer, Blue	35.00
Versailles, Cup & Saucer, Green	20.00
Versailles, Cup & Saucer, Pink	29.00 To 30.00
Versailles, Goblet, Water	25.00 To 32.00
Versailles, Ice Bucket, Green, Tongs	95.00
Versailles, Iced Tea, Green	20.00
Versailles, Pitcher, Blue, 8 3/4 In.	13.00
Versailles, Pitcher, Yellow	295.00
Versailles, Plate, 8 3/4 In.	8.00
Versailles, Plate, Blue, 9 1/2 In.	27.00
Versailles, Plate, Green, 7 1/2 In.	6.00
Versailles, Plate, Topaz, 8 3/4 In.	8.00
Versailles, Relish, Green	15.00
Versailles, Server, Green, Center Handle	38.00
Versailles, Sherbet, 4 1/4 In.	21.50
Versailles, Soup, Cream, Green, 7 In.	42.50
Versailles, Sugar & Creamer, Pink	30.00
Versailles, Sugar & Creamer, Yellow	25.00
Versailles, Sugar, Pail Shape, Pink	150.00
Versailles, Sugar, Yellow	27.50
Versailles, Tumbler, Blue, Footed, 9 Oz.	27.50
Versailles, Tumbler, Green, Footed, 5 1/4 In.	20.00
Vesper, Bowl, Amber, Centerpiece, 11 In.	25.00
Vesper, Bowl, Amber, Cereal, 6 1/2 In.	15.00 To 24.00
Vesper, Bowl, Green, 10 1/2 In.	35.00
Vesper, Creamer, Amber, Footed	20.00
Vesper, Ice Bucket, Amber	55.00 To 75.00
Vesper, Plate, 10 1/2 In.	29.00
Vesper, Plate, Amber, 8 1/2 In.	5.00 To 9.50
Vesper, Server, Green, Center Handle, 11 In.	35.00
Vesper, Sugar, Amber	20.00 To 30.00
Vesper, Tumbler, Amber, 9 Oz.	17.50
Vesper, Vase, 8 1/2 In.	35.00
Victoria, Celery, Frosted & Clear	35.00
Victoria, Nappy, Clear, Applied Handles, Triangular, Frosted	15.00
Wakefield, Champagne	30.00
Washington, Pitcher, Water, Lid, Etched	59.50
Watercress, Champagne	13.50
Willowmere, Champagne, 5 3/4 In.	16.00
Willowmere, Cocktail	14.00 To 22.50

       FOVAL, see Fry Foval
       FRAME, see Furniture, Frame

Francisware is a named glassware made by Hobbs, Brockunier and Company of Wheeling, West Virginia, in the 1880s. It is a clear or frosted hobnail or swirl pattern glass with amber-stained rim. Some pieces were made by a pressed glass method, others were mold blown.

FRANCISWARE, Dish, Ice Cream, Hobnail, Frosted, 14 3/8 X 9 1/2 In.	135.00
Finger Bowl, Swirl, Amber Rim, Frosted	25.00
Pitcher, 5 Tumblers	160.00
Pitcher, Water, Hobnail, Frosted, Amber Rim, Hobbs, Brockunier	185.00
Sugar, Frosted Hobnail, Covered, Amber Rim On Bowl	55.00
Table Set, Hobnail, Frosted, Amber Rim, 4 Piece	285.00
Toothpick, Amber Rim, Frosted	85.00
Toothpick, Frosted, Amber	95.00
Toothpick, Hobnail, Amber Rim, Frosted	45.00
Tumbler, Hobnail, Clear	35.00
Tumbler, Hobnail, Frosted	40.00
Tumbler, Hobnail, Vaseline, Hobbs, Brockunier & Co.	25.00

Water Set, Amber Rims, Frosted, 7 Piece	375.00
Water Set, Hobnail, Clear, 5 Piece	295.00

Frankart, Inc., New York, New York, mass–produced nude "dancing-lady" lamps, ashtrays, and other decorative Art Deco items in the 1920s and 1930s. They were made of white lead composition and spray–painted. "Frankart Inc." and the patent number and year were stamped on the base.

FRANKART, Ashtray, Holder, Nude, Standing, Arms Outstretched, Green	210.00
Ashtray, Monkey	47.00
Bookends, Bronze Finish	18.00
Bookends, Dutch Boy & Girl, Bronzed	45.00
Bookends, Female Head, Bronze ....115.00 To	150.00
Bookends, Sitting Lions	58.00
Bookends, Spaniel	75.00
Box, Cigarette, Held By 2 Nudes	450.00
Figurine, Flapper, Marked, 7 1/2 In.	195.00
Lamp, 2 Horse Heads, Brass Wash, Art Deco, Signed, 24 X 11 In.	65.00
Lamp, Desk, Scotty Figure	45.00
Lamp, Elephant, Hand Painted, Elephants On Paper Shade, 13 In.	150.00
Lamp, Female Nude Kneeling, Globe	450.00
Lamp, Ivory, Nude, On Stair Step, 10 X 5 In.	550.00
Lamp, Kneeling Nude, Turned, Holding Tray, Black	185.00
Lamp, Lady's Head	85.00
Lamp, Sailor Boy, 11 In.	225.00
Plaque, Nude, Standing	165.00
Smoking Stand, Nude, 25 In. ....430.00 To	450.00

Frankoma Pottery was originally known as The Frank Potteries when John F. Frank opened shop in 1933. The factory is now working in Sapulpa, Oklahoma. Early wares were made from a light cream-colored clay, but in 1956 the company switched to a red burning clay. The firm makes dinnerwares, utilitarian and decorative kitchen wares, figurines, flowerpots, and limited edition and commemorative pieces.

FRANKOMA, Ashtray, Arrowhead, Turquoise & Brown, 4 X 2 1/2 In.	3.00
Bookends, Dog Head, 6 1/2 In.	65.00
Boot, Cowboy, Red	10.00
Bowl, Cactus, Carved, Red Bud, No.207	50.00
Candleholder, Oral Roberts, Tulsa, 1971	10.00
Casserole, Browns	12.00
Ewer, Wagon Wheel, Green, Handle, 8 In.	10.00
Figurine, Elephant, White Sand, 1968	115.00
Figurine, Peter Pan	45.00
Honey Jar, Bee Finial, Green	10.00
Mug, Donkey, 1975	10.00
Mug, Donkey, 1976	14.50
Mug, Donkey, 1980	8.00
Mug, Elephant, 1968 ....45.00 To	50.00
Mug, Elephant, 1969	80.00
Mug, Elephant, 1975	10.00
Mug, Elephant, 1983	12.50
Mug, Elephant, Nixon–Agnew, 1973	25.00
Mug, Uncle Sam, White, 1976 Centennial	8.00
Mug, Wagon Wheel, Green	3.50
Planter, Figural, Duck, 12 In.	22.00
Plate, 1965, Christmas	150.00
Plate, 1968, Flight Into Egypt ....10.00 To	17.50
Plate, 1969, Christmas, Laid In Manger, Marked, 8 1/2 In.	5.50
Plate, 1970, Christmas, King Of Kings ....17.50 To	22.00
Plate, 1971, Christmas, No Room At The Inn	18.00
Plate, 1972, Easter ....12.00 To	13.00
Plate, 1973, Patriots	10.00
Plate, 1974, David Musicians	10.00
Plate, 1975, Victories	10.00

Plate, 1976, Freedom	18.00
Plate, 1977, Christmas	15.00
Plate, 1978, Martha	10.00
Plate, 1981, Joseph	10.00
Plate, Wildlife, Deer	35.00
Plate, Wildlife, Turkey	23.00
Shaker, Green, 2 1/2 In., Pair	6.00
Shaker, Wagon Wheel, Gold, 2 1/2 In., Pair	6.00
Sugar & Creamer, Wagon Wheel, Gold, 4 In.	8.00
Sugar & Creamer, Wagon Wheel, Green, 4 In.	8.00
Teapot, Individual, Wagon Wheel, 4 3/4 In.	12.00
Toby Jug, Uncle Sam, 1976	18.50
Toothpick, Wagon Wheel, Green, 2 1/2 In.	4.00
Trivet, Alphabet, Cherokee	15.00
Trivet, Cattlebrand, Green	10.00
Trivet, Cattlebrand, Yellow	18.00
Vase, Blue, John Frank, 12 In.	45.00
Vase, Bottle Shape, No.210	100.00
Vase, Brown & Black, John Frank, 11 3/4 In.	50.00
Vase, Cactus, Prairie Green, ADA, No.4	15.00
Vase, Green & Brown, John Frank, 16 In.	60.00
Vase, Painted Girl, No.701	46.00
Vase, Thunderbird Canteen, Prairie Green, ADA, No.59	12.00
Vase, Turquoise, Brown Clay, Lavender, Marked, 12 1/2 In.	22.00
Vase, Turquoise, Brown Shading Trim, Signed JNF No.1405, 12 In.	25.00
Wall Pocket, Acorn	9.00

Fry glass was made by the H. C. Fry Glass Company of Rochester, Pennsylvania. The company, founded in 1901, first made cut glass and other types of fine glasswares. In 1922, they patented a heat-resistant glass called "Pearl Oven glass." For two years, 1926–27, the company made Fry Foval, an opal ware decorated with colored trim. Reproductions of this glass have been made. The company also made Depression glass.

FRY FOVAL, Basket, Cobalt Blue Handle, 7 1/4 X 7 1/2 In.	285.00
Cruet, Opalescent White, Cobalt Stopper & Handle	285.00
Cup & Saucer, Blue Handle	65.00
Cup & Saucer, Cobalt Handle, Ground Pontil	55.00
Cup & Saucer, Green	85.00
Cup & Saucer, Opalescent	20.00
Perfume Bottle, Jade Foot & Stopper, Etched, 7 1/2 In.	125.00
Plate, Opaque White, French Blue Trim, 8 1/2 In.	40.00
Vase, 3 Applied Leaves, Blown, 10 In.	130.00
Vase, Black Amethyst Stem & Foot, Ovoid Bowl, 11 1/2 In.	250.00
Vase, Opalescent, Teal, Silver Deposit Design, 5 X 7 1/2 In.	250.00

FRY, see also Cut Glass

FRY, Bottle, Barber, Stopper, Pair	150.00
Butter, Finial Cover, Dome	12.00
Casserole, Covered, Oval, 8 In.	15.00
Casserole, Holder, Dated	25.00
Custard, Glass, Set Of 4	19.00
Juicer, Heat Resisting, 6 1/2 In.	15.00
Reamer, Opalescent	10.00
Trivet, Round, 8 In.	15.00
Tumbler, Floral Engraved, Crystal, Black Foot, Scalloped, Small, 4 Piece	15.00
Vase, 3 Applied Aqua Leaves, 6 1/2 X 10 In.	95.00
Vase, Crackle Glass, Applied Blue Rosettes, Flared Top, 10 X 8 1/2 In.	135.00
Vase, Crackle, Clear, Green Pedestal, Bell Shape, 8 In.	35.00

Fulper, Flower Frog, Lily Pad, Blue, 4 In.Diam.

Furniture, Armchair, Oriental,
Carved, Rosewood

F
U
L
P
E
R

Fulper is the mark used by the American Pottery Company of Flemington, New Jersey. The art pottery was made from 1910 to 1929. The firm had been making bottles, jugs, and housewares from 1805. Doll heads were made abut 1928. The firm became Stangl Pottery in 1929. Fulper art pottery is admired for its attractive glazes and simple shapes.

FULPER, Bottle, Deep Blue & Gray Flambe, 3–Sided Pinch, Marked, 7 3/4 In.	66.00
Bowl, Blue Ground, Cream & Brown, 10 In.	35.00
Bowl, Bulb, Brown Glaze, 8 1/2 In.	85.00
Bowl, Covered, Flower Basket	65.00
Bowl, Early Ink Stamp, Blue Crystal, 11 X 8 In.	375.00
Bowl, Effigy Pattern, Chocolate Gloss With Blue, 8 In.	350.00
Bowl, Green, 9 In.	65.00
Bowl, Lily Pad Frog, Aqua, Paper Label, 9 In.	80.00
Bowl, Metallic Green Over Cream, Fluted, 8 X 5 In.	150.00
Bowl, Mustard, Green, Blue, & Yellow Crystalline, Ink Mark, 10 X 3 In.	225.00
Bowl, Olive Green Crystalline, 16 In.	115.00
Bowl, Variegated Cobalt Blue, 9 1/2 X 3 1/2 In.	75.00
Box, Art Deco, Standing Woman, Covered, Signed	95.00
Candleholder, Cobalt Flambe, 6 In.	40.00
Candleholder, High Gloss, 3 1/2 In., Pair	60.00
Chamberstick, Handle On Back, Pink Matte, 7 1/2 In.	60.00
Decanter, Round Body, Thin Neck, Black To Green Flambe, 10 In.	145.00
Decanter, Whiskey, Green, Pinched	75.00
Flower Frog, Aqua & Rose Semigloss, 5 In.	35.00
Flower Frog, Lily Pad, Blue, 4 In.Diam. ....*Illus*	12.00
Flower Frog, Mushroom, Signed, Brown Glaze	22.00
Flower Frog, Nude ....100.00 To 110.00	
Jar, Crystal Flower, Olive Green, 3 1/2 In.	40.00
Jug, Musical, Metallic Glaze	150.00
Jug, Musical, Stopper, Blue, Silver Deposit, Grapevine, 15 1/2 In.	176.00
Lamp, Ballerina, Pink	120.00
Lamp, Blue Flambe Over Mustard, Bulbous, Painted Shade, 1920, 12 In.	525.00
Lamp, Perfume, Ballerina	145.00
Lamp, Perfume, Parrot, Blue	700.00
Lamp, Table, Earthenware, Leaded Shade, C.1915	7150.00
Mug, Mustard Matte, 45 In.	45.00
Pitcher, Curled Handle, Bulbous	75.00
Pitcher, Green Coils, 6 1/2 In.	45.00
Powder Jar, Figural, Lady With Fan, Lavender	185.00
Sugar & Creamer, Black Drip Over Green	295.00

Vase, 7 Sided, Brown Drip, Vertical Mark, Yellow, 9 In. 180.00
Vase, Black & Brown Drip, Green Shiny Glaze, 9 1/2 In. 90.00
Vase, Black Glaze, Chinese Shape, Incised Mark, 9 1/2 X 6 1/2 In. 400.00
Vase, Blue & Green Crystalline, Art Nouveau Design, Ink Mark, 8 In. 225.00
Vase, Blue Crystalline, 3 In. 60.00
Vase, Blue Drip Over Mustard, 3 3/4 In. 75.00
Vase, Blue Drip, Gray Ground, 31 1/4 In. 350.00
Vase, Blue Flambe Over Green, C.1915, 10 1/2 In. 150.00
Vase, Blue Flambe, Cobalt Crystals, Marked, 6 1/2 In. 110.00
Vase, Blue Multicolor, 5 Free Ring Handles, Ball Shape, 10 In. 395.00
Vase, Blue Wisteria Glaze, 2 Handles, Marked, 8 In. 50.00
Vase, Blue, 2 3/4 In. 25.00
Vase, Bud, Brown Drip On Blue, 8 In. 48.00
Vase, Bulbous, 3 Handles, Purple, 9 X 6 In. 95.00
Vase, Caramel Gloss, Crystalline Glaze, Chipped Ice, Marked, 3 In. 66.00
Vase, Chinese Shape, Mirrored Black Glaze, 9 1/2 In. 400.00
Vase, Copper Dust, 10 In. 275.00
Vase, Crystalline Buttress, Green, 8 1/2 In. 95.00
Vase, Crystalline, 8 In. 75.00
Vase, Cucumber Glaze, Loop Handles, Squat, Stamped, C.1915, 9 1/4 In. 350.00
Vase, Fan, Butterscotch Mirror Glaze, Black Crystalline, Marked 175.00
Vase, Green & Blue Flambe, Crystalline Glaze, Ink Mark, 7 1/2 In. 395.00
Vase, Green & Brown, Handles, 5 In. 60.00
Vase, Green Crystalline Glaze, 6 In. 100.00
Vase, Green, Black, Brown Glaze, 9 1/2 In. 120.00
Vase, Green, Crystalline Buttress, 8 1/2 In. 95.00
Vase, Handles, Blue, Cream, & Brown, 9 In. 95.00
Vase, Handles, Green To Rose, 12 In. 95.00
Vase, Honeycomb Shape, Handles, Copper Dust Glaze, 6 1/2 In. 265.00
Vase, Light & Dark Blue, Cream, Brown, Handles, Impressed Mark, 7 In. 225.00
Vase, Maroon, 3 Handles, Spiral Shape, Foot Ring, Marked, 6 X 8 In. 65.00
Vase, Matte Green, Gunmetal Spots, Marked, 9 1/2 In. 154.00
Vase, Medium Blue Flambe, Cobalt Crystals, 6 1/2 In. 110.00
Vase, Mottled Black Over Green Glaze, Wheel Thrown, 8 3/4 In. 50.00
Vase, Mottled Green, 8 1/2 In. 65.00
Vase, Orchid, 12 1/2 In. 75.00
Vase, Pale Matte Pink, Raised Mark, 5 1/2 X 5 1/2 In. 75.00
Vase, Rose & Green, 8 1/4 In. 125.00
Vase, Rose Crystalline Glaze, 3 Handles, Ink Mark, 6 3/4 In. 175.00
Vase, Rose Glaze, 9 1/2 In. 80.00
Vase, Speckles, Iridescent Smoky Black, 12 In. 145.00
Vase, White, 3 Handles, 7 In. 45.00
Vase, White, Green Ground, Rings, Crystalline Glaze, Marked, 8 3/4 In. 225.00
Wall Pocket, Geometric 125.00
Wall Pocket, Pipes Of Pan, Blue On Blue, Marked 165.00

All types of furniture are listed in this section. Examples dating from the seventeenth century to the 1950s are included. Prices for furniture vary in different parts of the country. Oak furniture is most expensive in the West; large pieces over eight feet high are sold for the most money in the South where high ceilings are found in the old homes. Condition is very important when determining prices. These are NOT average prices but rather reports of unique sales.

FURNITURE, Armchair, see also Furniture, Chair
FURNITURE, Armchair, Adjustable Arms & Back, Hunzinger, Dated 1866 .... 100.00
Armchair, Adjustable, Decal, Gustav Stickley, 1912, 38 X 30 In. 500.00
Armchair, Arts & Crafts, Curved Crest Rail, Oak 660.00
Armchair, Cartouche Crest, Leather Upholstered, Walnut 300.00
Armchair, Cast Iron, U Shape Trellis Back, Scroll Arms, Pair 90.00
Armchair, Cherry, Spanish Feet, Shaped Crest, Vase Splat, 1780 .... 1900.00
Armchair, Child's, Back Rabbit Ear, Plank Seat, Red, 22 1/4 In. 20.00
Armchair, Child's, Fumed Oak, Velvet Seat, Gustav Stickley, 26 In. 357.50
Armchair, Corner, George III, Arched Yoke Back, Mahogany 605.00
Armchair, English Tudor, Wainscot, Oak 1925.00

Furniture, Armchair, Wingback, Upholstered, Pair, 43 In.

Furniture, Armchair, Welsh,
Folk Carving, 17th Century, 52 In.

Armchair, English, Acanthus Leaf Carving At Top, Mahogany	180.00
Armchair, George III, Acanthus & Spray Splat, Mahogany, Set Of 8	6050.00
Armchair, George III, Mahogany, Upholstered	247.00
Armchair, Gustav Stickley, Adjustable, C.1907, 39 X 31 3/4 In.	1100.00
Armchair, Horn	440.00
Armchair, Hudson Valley, Rush Seat, Maple, Ash, & Cherry, 1690–1710	4800.00
Armchair, Ladder Back, 4 Graduated Slats, Rush Seat, Maple	175.00
Armchair, Ladder Back, 5 Graduated Slats, Canadian, Chestnut	225.00
Armchair, Ladder Back, Child's, Splint Seat, 25 1/2 In.	50.00
Armchair, Ladder Back, Massachusetts, Ash & Maple, C.1750, 41 In.	1300.00
Armchair, Ladder Back, Pennsylvania, Shaped Arms, Splint Seat	200.00
Armchair, Ladder Back, Scrolled Arms, Finials, 4 Slats, Rush Seat	300.00
Armchair, Library, Overstuffed Backrest, Mahogany, C.1790	1870.00
Armchair, Library, Upholstered Backrest, Walnut, C.1775, Pair	4290.00
Armchair, Lloyd Manufacturing Co., Upholstered, C.1930, Pair	209.00
Armchair, Louis XIV, Upholstered Back, Scroll Arms, Walnut, C.1900	125.00
Armchair, Louis XV, Bergere, Walnut, Bow Front, Signed D.Jullienne	3200.00
Armchair, Louis XVI, Original Tapestry Cover, Carved Walnut	475.00
Armchair, Louis XVI, Walnut, Rectangular Upholstered Back, Pair	2000.00
Armchair, Maple, Ash, Rush Seat, Reel & Lemon Finial, 1670	660.00
Armchair, Neoclassical, Striped, Upholstered Seat, Pair ....*Illus*	1300.00
Armchair, Open Oak Arms, Leather Back & Seat, C.1928, 32 In., Pair	5500.00
Armchair, Oriental, Carved, Rosewood ....*Illus*	600.00
Armchair, Oriental, Carved, Scrolling Foliate, Marble Seat, Pair	700.00
Armchair, Pierced Leaf Carved Backrest, Mahogany, C.1790, Pair	3200.00

Furniture, Armchair, Neoclassical,
Striped, Upholstered Seat, Pair

Spool-turned furniture or
Jenny Lind pieces with
sharp corners are older
than those with rounded
corners.

Armchair, Provincial, Wingback, Upholstered, 34 In., Pair	30.00
Armchair, Quarter Sawn Oak, Inset Seat	50.00
Armchair, Renaissance Style, Walnut, Open, Upholstered, Pair	225.00
Armchair, Slat Back, Maple, 4 Slat, Sausage, Ring Stiles, Rush Seat	900.00
Armchair, Slat Back, New England, Ash & Maple, C.1750, 35 3/4 In.	400.00
Armchair, Slat Back, Open Arms, Cushion Seat, C.1910, 38 1/2 In.	125.00
Armchair, Slip Seat Covering Commode Insert, Walnut	6600.00
Armchair, Stickley, Back Slat, Open Arm, C.1912, Pair	1200.00
Armchair, Victorian, Mahogany, Rose Carving, Tufted Upholstery	180.00
Armchair, Victorian, Upholstered Seat & Back, Carved Crest	475.00
Armchair, Welsh, Folk Carving, 17th Century, 52 In. ....*Illus*	950.00
Armchair, Wicker And Cane ....*Illus*	300.00
Armchair, Wicker, Rocker ....*Illus*	225.00
Armchair, Wing, Federal, Arched Cresting, Loose Cushion, C.1810	1100.00
Armchair, Wing, Federal, Cherrywood, Upholstered, Casters, C.1800	1540.00
Armchair, Wing, Queen Anne, Mahogany, Blue Damask Upholstered	300.00
Armchair, Wing, Upholstered, Arched Cresting Rail, Walnut, C.1780	1650.00
Armchair, Wingback, Upholstered, Pair, 43 In. ....*Illus*	250.00
Armchair, Writing, Shepherd's Crook, Plum Pudding Mahogany	8800.00
Armoire, French Provincial, Oak, 1 Door, 82 X 30 X 18 In.	600.00
Armoire, Louis XVI, Pine, Paneled Doors, Painted Interior, 7 Ft.	3100.00
Armoire, Mahogany, Mirror, Floral Inlaid Panels, 4 X 7 Ft.	550.00
Armoire, Napoleon III, Rosewood, Ormolu, Bronze Finial, 84 In.	2200.00
Armoire, Pine, Double Panel Doors, Wide Stripped, 2-Drawer, 58 In.	875.00
Armoire, Spanish, Walnut, 62 X 85 In.	3850.00
Bar & Stools, Kidney Shape, Jazz Pattern, Back Mirror, Shelves	715.00
Bed Steps, Regency, Mahogany, Circular, Commode, England, 20 In.	100.00
Bed, Arched Headboard, Square Stiles, Brass, 74 X 54 X 60 In.	210.00
Bed, Bamboo, Maple & Bird's-Eye Maple, C.1880, 78 X 55 X 38 In.	200.00
Bed, Campaign, Victorian, Iron, American, C.1870, 44 X 50 X 12 In.	175.00
Bed, Cannonball, Curly Maple, Scrolled, Rope Frame, 44 X 52 In.	450.00
Bed, Cannonball, Male & Figured Maple, C.1830	696.00
Bed, Cannonball, Scalloped Head & Footboard, Pine, 69 1/2 In.	650.00
Bed, Canopy, Victorian, Mahogany, Carved Foliate, 92 X 68 In.	3700.00
Bed, Cherry, Rope, Turned Posts, Ball Finial, 52 In.	75.00
Bed, Child's, Turned Posts, Rails, Dark Red Paint, 25 1/2 X 55 In.	250.00
Bed, Day, Louis XVI, Double Cane Back, Reeded Legs	400.00
Bed, Empire, Mahogany Veneer, Crest, Paw Feet, America, 46 X 63 In.	700.00
Bed, Empire, Mahogany, Paneled Ends, Ormolu, 6 Ft. 6 In.	2500.00
Bed, Folding, Cherry & Maple, C.1780, 3/4 Size	7500.00
Bed, Four-Poster, American Empire, Mahogany, Twist Baluster Post	320.00
Bed, Four-Poster, Federal, Curly Maple, 1815, 6 Ft. 8 In. X 55 In.	2900.00
Bed, Four-Poster, Federal, Maple, Baluster Turned Supports, Canopy	500.00
Bed, Inlaid Geometric Panel Back, Cornice, Oak, 6 Ft. 10 In.	9350.00

Furniture, Chair, Wicker,	Furniture, Armchair,	Furniture, Armchair,
Asymmetrical Back	Wicker, Rocker	Wicker And Cane

Bed, Iron, White, Double 385.00
Bed, Murphy, Oak 475.00
Bed, Opium, Ivory Inlay, Silk Spread, Early 19th Century 7500.00
Bed, Rope, Acorn Finials, Paneled Headboard, 52 1/4 X 69 1/4 In. 550.00
Bed, Rope, Ball Finials, Shaped Headboard, Cherry, 52 In. 75.00
Bed, Rope, Chamfered Posts, Pine Headboard, Birch, 51 1/2 X 37 In. 150.00
Bed, Rope, Curly Maple Posts, Poplar Head, Footboard, 76 X 54 In. 900.00
Bed, Rope, Poplar, Turned Post, Brass Casters, 55 X 76 X 64 In. 600.00
Bed, Rope, Youth, Maine, Old Red Paint, C.1820, 40 X 50 In. 550.00
Bed, Rosewood, New Orleans, C.Lee, Oversize, 8 Ft. 2 In.Tall 3500.00
Bed, Semicircular Headboard, J.Leleu, Mahogany, 58 1/2 X 50 In. 4400.00
Bed, Settle, Shaped Arms, Box Seat Folds Down, Pine, 72 X 50 In. 600.00
Bed, Shaker, Infant's, Pine, Blue, Mauve, Tapered Leg, 27 X 48 In. 400.00
Bed, Shaker, Sister's, Mt.Lebanon, N.Y., Iron Wheels, Pine, Pair 2200.00
Bed, Sheraton, Pencil Post 2500.00
Bed, Sleigh, Empire, Inlaid Rosewood, French, 40 X 48 X 54 In. 1600.00
Bed, Spanish Renaissance, Carved 1400.00
Bed, Tall Post, Federal, Tiger Maple, C.1830, 62 In. 1600.00
Bed, Tester, Brass, Crown Top, 19th Century, 9 Ft. 1300.00
Bed, Tester, Carved Maple, Turned Post, Red, 67 X 54 X 76 In. 2200.00
Bed, Tester, New Orleans Style, C.1850, 9 Ft.Tall 3500.00
Bed, Tester, Rope, Rolling Pin Headboard, Maple & Poplar 1250.00
Bed, Trundle, Cannonball Post, Wooden Wheels, Rope, 43 X 67 In. 300.00
Bed, Victorian, Black Walnut, Oval Headboard, C.1870 .... 850.00
Bedroom Set, Bed, Commode, & Dresser, Walnut 3500.00
Bedroom Set, Empire, Carved, Twin Canopied Beds, 6 Piece 2350.00
Bedroom Set, Framed Mirror, Solid Birch, 3 Piece 1000.00
Bedroom Set, Grape Cluster At Top, Marble Tops, Walnut, 3 Piece 2500.00
Bedroom Set, Louis XV, Walnut, C.1880, 5 Piece 7750.00
Bedroom Set, Norman Bel Geddes Design, C.1937, Label, 7 Piece 1500.00
Bedroom Set, Renaissance Revival, Burl Walnut, Marble, 1875, 2 Pc. 2300.00
Bedroom Set, Renaissance Revival, Walnut, 4 Piece 1155.00
Bedroom Set, Renaissance, Bird's-Eye Maple, Putti Masks, 7 Piece 3575.00
Bench, Beaded Edge, 3 Plank, Painted Pine & Chestnut, 142 In. 200.00
Bench, Butcher, 4 Legs, 18 In. 65.00
Bench, Child's, Queen Anne Style, Walnut, 26 3/4 X 32 1/2 In. 950.00
Bench, Cobbler's, 2 Drawers, Leather Seat, Cherry & Pine, 38 In. 75.00
Bench, Cobbler's, Original Leather Seat, Old Blue Paint 850.00
Bench, Cutout Ends, Mortised, Old Brown Finish, Pine, 103 X 18 In. 85.00
Bench, Cutout Ends, Square Nails, Poplar, 43 X 16 1/2 In. 110.00
Bench, Feet Mortised Through Top, Yellow, Cherry, 11 1/2 In. 170.00
Bench, Fern Leaf, Scroll, American, Iron, Late 19th Century, Pair 9100.00
Bench, Fern Pattern, American, Cast Iron, 19th Century, Pair 9075.00
Bench, Fireside, Walnut, 2 Hinged Lids 1100.00
Bench, Hall, Tudor, Carved Oak, Crest Over 7 Panels, 1722, 45 In. 400.00
Bench, Mammy's, Rocking, Grain Painted, 19th Century 400.00
Bench, Mammy's, Turned Spindle, Painted, Scroll Arms, 19th Century 300.00
Bench, Mortised, Rake Legs, New York State, C.1820, 9 1/2 X 43 In. 150.00
Bench, Piano, Cast Iron, Victorian, Ornate 75.00
Bench, Piano, Oak, Gustav Stickley, 21 X 36 In. 1100.00
Bench, Primitive, Cutout Feet, Walnut, 14 3/4 X 30 1/4 In. 65.00
Bench, Primitive, Foot Rail, Bootjack Cutout Ends 95.00
Bench, Queen Anne, Slip Seat, English, Mahogany, 65 X 15 1/2 In. 750.00
Bench, Rake Legs, Pennsylvania, Pine, C.1820, 16 X 12 X 48 In. 325.00
Bench, Shoe, Star Brand, Wooden, 6 Ft. 375.00
Bench, Spindle Back, Mortise, Tenon, & Pegged Construction, Pine 850.00
Bench, Trolley, Wooden Seat & Back, Cast Iron Arms & Legs 300.00
Bench, Walnut, Primitive, Cane Seat, 71 X 18 X 10 In. 270.00
Bench, Water, Blue, Slant Apron, Bootjack End, 12 X 15 X 33 In. 75.00
Bench, Water, Bootjack End, 2 Shelves, Poplar, 36 X 33 1/2 In. 310.00
Bench, Water, Shaker, Pine, Hancock, Ma., C.1840, 22 X 48 1/2 In. 400.00
Bench, Windsor, 1 Board Seat, Birdcage Spindles, Bamboo, 76 In. 1550.00
Bench, Windsor, Bamboo Turnings, Spindle Back, 85 1/4 In. 1600.00
Bench, Windsor, Bamboo, Removable Baby Guard, Graining, 34 1/4 In. ... 1600.00

Bench, Windsor, Plank Bottom, Upholstered Cushion, 44 X 28 In. 500.00
Bidet, Walnut, 19th Century, 32 1/2 X 30 3/4 X 12 1/2 In. 25.00
Billiard Table, Brunswick, 6 Legs, Mahogany & Rosewood 600.00
Bin, Flour, Original Mustard Graining, 43 In. 450.00
Bookcase, 2 Door, Mullioned Windows, Label, 56 X 42 X 13 In. 2000.00
Bookcase, 2 Glass Doors, 2 Drawers, American, Walnut, 53 X 60 In. 475.00
Bookcase, 5 Stacks, 1 Drawer, Oak, 6 Ft. 50.00
Bookcase, Chippendale, Mahogany, 2 Glazed Doors, Slant Front 500.00
Bookcase, Country, Cherry, New Hampshire, Red Paint, 5 Ft.10 In. 2300.00
Bookcase, Double Glass Doors, Marquetry Inlaid 1550.00
Bookcase, Empire, Mahogany, 2 Door Top, 4 Drawer Bottom, 87 In. 750.00
Bookcase, Federal, Mahogany, 6 Movable Tiers, 1805, 8 Ft. 5 In. 13750.00
Bookcase, Glass Enclosed, Walnut, 5 X 8 Ft. 1500.00
Bookcase, Globe Warnicke, Oak, 3 Stack 200.00
Bookcase, Golden Quarter Sawn Oak, 3 Stack 375.00
Bookcase, Gustav Stickley, Double Door, C.1912, 55 1/2 X 48 In. 1800.00
Bookcase, Louis XVI, Inlaid Tulipwood, 2 Doors, 1910, 4 Ft. 10 In. 770.00
Bookcase, Mahogany, Swell–Front Base, 9 1/2 X 8 1/2 Ft. 475.00
Bookcase, Oak, 1 Glass Door, Ball Feet, 51 X 31 X 14 1/2 In. 110.00
Bookcase, Oak, Gustav Stickley, 2 Door, C.1904, 56 X 48 In. 4400.00
Bookcase, Oak, Metal Shelves, Sliding Doors, 38 1/4 X 41 1/2 In. 100.00
Bookcase, Oak, Stickley, 4 Shelves, Label, C.1910, 55 X 30 X 12 In. 725.00
Bookcase, Renaissance Revival, American, Flora Crest, 43 X 67 In. 375.00
Bookcase, Revolving, Danner, Cherry, 1876 .... 1500.00
Bookcase, Secretary, Chippendale, Mahogany, 78 X 29 X 15 In. 300.00
Bookcase, Secretary, Federal, Inlaid Mahogany, 6 Ft. 3200.00
Bookcase, Secretary, Mahogany, 9 1/2 X 8 1/2 Ft. 475.00
Bookcase, Sectional, Victorian, Walnut, Carved, 1870, 101 X 47 In. 1100.00
Bookcase, Sliding Door, L.&J.G.Stickley, 54 X 36 X 13 1/2 In. 1100.00
Bookcase, Victorian, 2 Glass Doors, Mahogany, 48 X 55 In. 130.00
Box, Blanket, New England, Grain Painted Pine, C.1830, 22 X 19 In. 350.00
Box, Blanket, New England, Grain Painted Pine, C.1830, 37 X 23 In. 850.00
Box, Blanket, Snipe Hinges, Walnut, 18th Century, 17 1/2 X 12 In. 335.00
Box, Dough, Early 19th Century, 44 X 22 X 30 In. 295.00
Box, Pine, Painted, Dome Lift Top, Canted Sides, 17 X 26 In. 150.00
Breakfront Bookcase, Cornice, 13 Paned Doors, Mahogany, 6 1/2 Ft. 4675.00
Breakfront, Chippendale Style, Mahogany Mullioned Doors, 77 In. 550.00
Breakfront, Dutch Marquetry, Walnut, Fruitwood, 84 X 59 X 13 In. 1800.00
Bureau Bookcase, George III, Slant Front, Mahogany, 7 Ft. 4 In. 1750.00
Bureau Bookcase, Upper Mirrored Doors, Burr Walnut, 6 Ft. 10 In. 3300.00
Bureau Cabinet, George II, Parcel Gilt, Mahogany, 7 Ft. 11 In. 7700.00
Bureau, Bow Front, England, 4 Drawers, Mahogany, C.1800, 36 1/2 In. 1700.00
Bureau, Bow Front, Rhode Island, Mahogany, C.1780, 37 1/2 X 32 In. 6000.00
Bureau, Chippendale, Serpentine Front, 4 Drawer, Mahogany, C.1770 .... 3250.00
Bureau, Chippendale, Serpentine, 4 Drawer, Maple, 1780, 33 In. 3600.00
Bureau, Classical Revival, Mahogany, C.1825, 37 X 65 In. 1700.00
Bureau, Connecticut, Graduated Drawers, Cherry, C.1780, 33 1/2 In. 6500.00
Bureau, Cylinder, George III, Mahogany, C.1800, 46 In. 2600.00
Bureau, Empire, Stencil & Freehand Design, Mahogany 1870.00
Bureau, Federal, 4 Drawers, Mahogany, C.1810, 12 1/2 X 13 In. 1100.00
Bureau, Federal, Drop Panel, Bird's–Eye Maple 3500.00
Bureau, Federal, Inlaid, New Hampshire, Cherry, C.1815, 39 In. 2000.00
Bureau, Federal, Mahogany, Bow Front, Graduated Drawers, 36 In. 2200.00
Bureau, Federal, Maple & Birch, C.1790, 38 In. 850.00
Bureau, Federal, Pine, Grain Painted, 4 Drawers, 1815, 40 X 37 In. 3000.00
Bureau, French, Serpentine Front, Carved Drawer Fronts, Walnut 2200.00
Bureau, Leather Surface, 3 Frieze Drawers, Tulipwood, 31 1/2 In. 3850.00
Bureau, Marble Top, Arched Mirror, 4 Drawers, 54 1/2 X 82 1/2 In. 1100.00
Bureau, New England, 4 Drawers, Maple, C.1770, 35 3/4 In. 5250.00
Bureau, Renaissance Revival, Drop Well, Walnut, Mirror, 93 In. 350.00
Bureau, Rococo Revival, Rosewood, C.1860, 44 1/2 X 82 In. 700.00
Bureau, Sheraton, Cherry & Maple, Country 935.00
Bureau, Slant Front, 4 Drawers, Burl Walnut, 39 In. 880.00
Bureau, Slant Front, Fret Carved Cornice, Mahogany, 2–Part, C.1775 .... 4400.00

Furniture, Cabinet, Chinese,
2 Shelves Below, 70 X 34 X 15 In.

Furniture, Cabinet, Corner,
2 Pegged Arched Doors, 92 1/2 In.

Bureau, Slant Front, George II, Mahogany, 33 1/2 X 40 3/4 In. 3575.00
Cabinet On Chest, Bombe, Walnut Marquetry, Glazed Door, Dutch 3850.00
Cabinet On Chest, Chippendale, Mahogany, Cornice, 1770, 87 In. 1800.00
Cabinet, 8 Drawers, Recessed Panels, Ivory Molding, 10 X 15 In. 200.00
Cabinet, Allover Floral & Landscape, Red Lacquer, 34 X 53 In. 100.00
Cabinet, American Renaissance, Gilt Bronze, Porcelain, 4 Ft. 825.00
Cabinet, Carved, Gilt, 3–Tier, Marble Columns, Plaques, 33 X 16 In. 1000.00
Cabinet, Chinese, 2 Shelves Below, 70 X 34 X 15 In. ....*Illus* 1700.00
Cabinet, Corner, 2 Pegged Arched Doors, 92 1/2 In. ....*Illus* 3250.00
Cabinet, Corner, Camphored Panel Doors, Drawers, Kentucky, Walnut 995.00
Cabinet, Corner, Cherry, Blind Doors, 82 1/2 In. ....*Illus* 700.00
Cabinet, Corner, Cherry, Blue Green Paint, 4 Blind Doors, 82 In. 700.00
Cabinet, Corner, George III, Frieze Cornice, Mahogany, 43 1/2 In. 550.00
Cabinet, Corner, Hanging, Pendant, Mahogany, 1880s, 44 1/2 In. 550.00
Cabinet, Corner, Walnut, 9–Pane Glass Door, Drawer, 77 In. 450.00
Cabinet, Curio, Mahogany, 79 X 33 X 17 In. ....*Illus* 1900.00
Cabinet, Display, Cornice, 2 Arched Doors, Walnut, 72 In. 200.00
Cabinet, Doctor's, Glass Sides, Milk Glass Shelves, C.1895 .... 1000.00
Cabinet, Dressing, Art Deco, Blue Lacquered, Red & Chrome 10500.00
Cabinet, Edwardian, Inlaid Satinwood, C.1900, 4 Ft. 5 In. 1100.00

Furniture, Cabinet, Corner,
Cherry, Blind Doors, 82 1/2 In.

Furniture, Cabinet, Curio,
Mahogany, 79 X 33 X 17 In.

Cabinet, Edwardian, Inlaid Satinwood, C.1900, 4 Ft.5 In.	1100.00
Cabinet, Fall Front, Ivory, Tortoiseshell Inlay, Stand, 40 1/2 In.	900.00
Cabinet, Floor, Tudor Style, 2–Door, Fitted For Bar, Oak, 90 In.	160.00
Cabinet, French, 16 Drawers, Walnut, 18th Century, 25 X 45 In.	700.00
Cabinet, Gilt Mounted, Black Lacquer, 17th Century, 28 1/2 In.	2475.00
Cabinet, Gothic, Rosewood, 2 Arched Glazed Doors, 6 Ft. 7 In.	2000.00
Cabinet, Hanging, Glass Door, Oak, 29 X 34 In.	50.00
Cabinet, Italian Renaissance, 2 Doors, Carved Cherubs, 61 In.	1100.00
Cabinet, Louis XVI, Gilt Bronze Mounted, Ebonized, 6 Ft.	9075.00
Cabinet, Mahogany, Carved, 2 Drawers Above 2 Doors, 43 1/2 In.	260.00
Cabinet, Mirror, Marble Top, 3 Drawers, Mahogany, 19th Century	2000.00
Cabinet, Music, Victorian, Carved Oak, Cabriole Legs, 54 X 16 In.	90.00
Cabinet, Napoleon III, Ebonized Wood, 3 Doors, 47 In. X 7 Ft.	3850.00
Cabinet, Napoleon III, Gilt Bronze, Marquetry, C.1870, 41 In.	1900.00
Cabinet, Napoleon III, Marquetry, 5 Ft. 5 In. X 41 In.	1875.00
Cabinet, Oak, Arts & Crafts, 4 Paneled Doors, Pilaster, 30 In.	100.00
Cabinet, Painted & Ebonized, C.1870, 6 Ft. 2 In.	4200.00
Cabinet, Regency, 3–Part, Glazed Doors, Mahogany, 7 Ft. 6 In.	2850.00
Cabinet, Serpentine Front, 2 Doors, 5 Sliding Shelves, Mahogany	2000.00
Cabinet, Serpentine Front, 4 Drawers, Painted, 7 Ft. 3 In.	3575.00
Cabinet, Sewing, Shaker, Birch, Cherry & Pine, 6 Drawers, 27 In.	9000.00
Cabinet, Spice, Pine, 5 Drawers, Scalloped Top Shelf, 43 In.	150.00
Cabinet, Tambour, Walnut, Drawer, Shelf, 29 3/4 X 15 1/2 X 12 In.	300.00
Cabinet, Traveling, Marquetry, 17th Century, 19 X 16 1/2 In.	1400.00
Cabinet, Y Support, Metal Foliate Design, Oak, Fruitwood, 36 In.	1750.00
Canape, George I, Mahogany, Upholstered Serpentine Back, 83 In.	1500.00
Candlestand, 1 Board Cherry Top, Rounded Corners, 16 X 28 In.	875.00
Candlestand, 1 Board Top, Banded Ash Inlay, 17 3/4 In	325.00
Candlestand, 2 Board Top, Gallery, Drawer, Cherry, 26 1/2 In.	1300.00
Candlestand, Adjustable, American, 18th Century, 24 In.	400.00
Candlestand, Adjustable, Curly Maple Top, 22 X 28 In.	425.00
Candlestand, Chippendale, Walnut, New England, C.1780, 28 In.	750.00
Candlestand, Cut Corners, Trace Of Old Red, Cherry, 25 In.	150.00
Candlestand, Egyptian Revival, Marble, C.1865, 28 X 17 1/2 In.	150.00
Candlestand, Federal, Country, Rounded, Spade Feet, C.1810	275.00
Candlestand, Federal, Inlaid Birchwood, C.1805, 28 1/2 X 21 In.	3400.00
Candlestand, Federal, Snake Feet, Painted & Grained, 26 In.	1320.00
Candlestand, Federal, String Inlay Edges, Mahogany, 28 1/2 In.	650.00
Candlestand, Federal, Tilt Top, Mahogany, C.1800, 28 In.	825.00
Candlestand, George II, Serpentine Outline, Mahogany, 21 In.	880.00
Candlestand, George III, Carved Foliage Stem, Mahogany, 20 In.	9900.00
Candlestand, George III, Mahogany, Tripod Legs, Spiral Shaft, 1800	160.00
Candlestand, Hepplewhite, Mahogany, Tripod, Octagonal Top, 19 In.	175.00
Candlestand, Maple Dish Top, Splayed Legs, 15 X 26 3/4 In.	150.00
Candlestand, New England, Oval Top, Brown, C.1810, 27 1/2 In.	1750.00
Candlestand, Pedestal, 3 Foot, Square Top, Cherry, 1760, 16 In.	275.00
Candlestand, Queen Anne, Connecticut, Original Finish	795.00
Candlestand, Queen Anne, Snake Foot, Round Molded Top, Maple	350.00
Candlestand, Screw Type, Tripod Base, New England	2850.00
Candlestand, Snake Feet, 2 Board Top, Cherry, 15 3/4 X 26 1/2 In.	425.00
Candlestand, Table, Adjustable, American, 2 Sockets, Tin, 38 In.	750.00
Candlestand, Tilt Top, Hepplewhite, Birch, Mahogany, 28 3/4 In.	275.00
Candlestand, Tilt Top, Mahogany, Bird's–Eye Maple, 19th Century	1500.00
Candlestand, Tilt Top, New England, Mahogany, C.1780, 27 3/4 In.	425.00
Candlestand, Tripod, Molded Rim, Mahogany, C.1755, 27 3/4 In.	660.00
Candlestand, William & Mary, Tripod, Octagonal Top, Walnut, 34 In.	275.00
Canterbury, 4 Open Compartments, Drawer In Base, Rosewood	800.00
Canterbury, 5 Section Upper, Drawer, Mahogany, 27 X 22 1/2 In.	1100.00
Canterbury, Mahogany, 1860, 17 X 14 X 24 In.	600.00
Card Table, Regency, Mahogany, England, 30 1/2 X 35 1/2 X 18 In.	350.00
Carrier, Baby, Converts To Stroller, Retractable Wheels, Wicker	225.00
Cassone, Italian Baroque, Oak, Walnut, Gadroon Lid, 69 1/2 In.	375.00
Cellarette, Brass Loop Lifting Handles, Inlaid Mahogany, 27 In.	880.00
Cellarette, George III, Mahogany, Lead Lined, C.1800, 28 X 24 In.	1700.00

Cellarette, Regency, Brass, Ram's Mask Handles, 34 X 29 In. 1650.00
Chair Table, Bold Turning, Black, 19th Century, 28 X 41 1/2 In. 3500.00
Chair Table, New England, 2 Board Round Top, Pine, C.1750, 27 In. 3500.00
Chair Table, New Hampshire, 18th Century, Top 52 In. 3200.00
Chair Table, Painted Pine & Maple, C.1780, 54 X 26 In. 1600.00
Chair Table, Red & Brown Graining, Birch & Pine 4674.00
Chair, 7 Spindle Bow Back, Saddle Seat, Old Red Paint, 16 1/2 In. 425.00
Chair, Adjustable Back, Gustav Stickley, Leather Cushions, 37 In. 2900.00
Chair, Adjustable, Open, Limbert, C.1910, 39 1/2 In. 575.00
Chair, Balloon Back, Design, Brown, 6 Chair & Rocker 1500.00
Chair, Bamboo, Oriental Hardwood, 19th Century ....*Illus* 330.00
Chair, Bamboo, Tub Shape, Gray Loose Cushion Seat, Pair 280.00
Chair, Banister Back, Shaped Crest, Black Paint, Rush Seat 175.00
Chair, Barrel, Seat Storage, 3 Lap Wooden Hoops, 14 X 28 In. 225.00
Chair, Belter, Pierce Carved Laminated Rosewood, Pair 4700.00
Chair, Bergen County, Turned Feet, Black, Yellow Seat, Pair 575.00
Chair, Bow Back, Arms, Grain Painted Design Over Original Green 1050.00
Chair, Bow Back, Arms, New England, 7 Spindle, C.1780, 36 In. 1000.00
Chair, Bow Back, Brace Back, William Seaver, C.1790, 37 In., Pr. 2200.00
Chair, Bow Back, Rhode Island, Arms, Ash & Maple, C.1795, 37 In. 650.00
Chair, Child's, Bentwood, Cane Seat, Refinished, Thonet, 25 In. 85.00
Chair, Child's, Music Box In Seat, Switzerland, 26 In. 90.00
Chair, Child's, Red Paint, Splint Seat, 18th Century 625.00
Chair, Child's, Slatted Bow Back, Plank Seat, 19th Century 85.00
Chair, Child's, Thumb Back, Plank Seat, Gloucester, C.1830 .... 110.00
Chair, Child's, Turned Maple, Rush Seat, Delaware River, 1780–1800 .... 220.00
Chair, Chinese, Pierced Carved, Serpent Design 250.00
Chair, Chippendale, Ball & Claw Foot, New York 1500.00
Chair, Chippendale, Carved Crest, American, 41 1/2 In., Pair 1100.00
Chair, Chippendale, Chestnut, Birch Ribbon Back, Rush Seat 95.00
Chair, Chippendale, Country, Cherry, Dark, Rush Seat, Pair 550.00
Chair, Chippendale, Mahogany, Joseph Short, Serpentine Arms, 1780 .... 7000.00
Chair, Chippendale, Mahogany, Needlepoint Seat, Ladder Back 380.00
Chair, Chippendale, Philadelphia Style, Carved Back, C.1900 .... 425.00
Chair, Chippendale, Rush Slip Seat, Maple 175.00
Chair, Chippendale, Rustic, Cupid Crest Rail, Rush Seat, Pair 650.00
Chair, Chippendale, Shell Crest, Carved Ears, Mahogany, 41 In., Pr. 550.00
Chair, Corner, Ball & Claw Feet, Inlaid Marquetry 725.00
Chair, Corner, English, Crest, Scrolled Arms, Walnut, 32 In., Pair 750.00
Chair, Corner, George II, Mahogany, Double Pierced Splat Back 650.00
Chair, Corner, Pierced & Carved Slats, Upholstered Seat, Cherry 700.00
Chair, Corner, Queen Anne, Needlepoint Seat, C.1750 ....*Illus* 1000.00

To cover a scratch in a piece of furniture made of dark wood, rub a walnut, Brazil nut, or butternut into the scratch. Eyebrow pencil or shoe polish in a matching shade will also work.

Furniture, Chair, Bamboo,
Oriental Hardwood, 19th Century

Furniture, Chair, Corner, Queen Anne,
Needlepoint Seat, C.1750

Furniture, Chair, Porter's, Leather,
English, 19th Century, 65 In.

Chair, Corner, Rhode Island, Vase Splats, Upholstered Seat, Cherry 1300.00
Chair, Cromwellian, Cherry, C.1650 .... 6000.00
Chair, Demi-Arm, Rococo, Rosewood, Circular Pierced Back, Pair 950.00
Chair, Desk, George II, Walnut U Crest Rail, 2 Vase Splat, C.1750 .... 1500.00
Chair, Dining, George II, Carved Parcel Gilt, Mahogany, C.1850 .... 1600.00
Chair, Dining, Shaker, Hancock, Mass., Dark Brown, Pair 2475.00
Chair, Dutch Marquetry, Mid-18th Century 225.00
Chair, Elizabethan Revival, Rosewood, 19th Century, 40 In. 125.00
Chair, Elizabethan Revival, Walnut, Pierced Back, C.1845, Pair 500.00
Chair, Fanback, Wallace Nutting, 8 Spindles, 37 1/2 In., Pair 500.00
Chair, Federal, Inlaid Mahogany, Upholstered, H Stretcher, C.1790 .... 19800.00
Chair, Flemish Baroque, Oak, Pierced Splat Crest, H Stretcher 280.00
Chair, French Provincial, Fruitwood, C.1880, Pair 400.00
Chair, French Provincial, Walnut, Open Arm, Pierced Vase Splat 50.00
Chair, Gentleman's, Carved Walnut, Cushion Seat, Upholstered Back 275.00
Chair, George I, Open Backrest, Vase Shaped Splat, Walnut, C.1725 .... 6400.00
Chair, George II, Walnut, Upholstered Seat, England, C.1750 .... 550.00
Chair, George III, Open Backrest, Overstuffed Seat, Mahogany, Pr. 600.00
Chair, George III, Solid Cartouche Shaped Backrest, Yew Wood, Pr. 8500.00
Chair, Gustav Stickley, Slat Sided, Chamfered Arms, C.1912, 32 In. 1000.00
Chair, Hepplewhite, Martha Washington, Mahogany, Upholstered 450.00
Chair, Hepplewhite, Urn Splats, Mahogany, Silk Damask Seat, Pair 1200.00
Chair, Hitchcock, Rush Seat, Fruit Stenciled, Dark Color 40.00
Chair, Ice Cream, Thonet Bentwood, Signed, C.1889 .... 100.00
Chair, Italian Rococo, Reduced Back, 2 Crossbars, C.1760, Pair 300.00
Chair, Italian, Neoclassical, Brass Inlaid, Walnut 775.00
Chair, Ladder Back, Bulbous Turnings, Rush Seat 825.00
Chair, Ladder Back, Canadian, Homespun Upholstered, Blue Paint 125.00
Chair, Ladder Back, Child's, Rush Seat 160.00
Chair, Ladder Back, Country, Splint Seat 200.00
Chair, Ladder Back, Gustav Stickley, C.1907, 36 In. 200.00
Chair, Ladder Back, Mushroom Arms, Mustard Over Orange Paint 595.00
Chair, Ladder Back, Sausage Turnings, 4 Slats, Woven Splint Seat 160.00
Chair, Ladder Back, Shaker, Rush Seat, Enfield 875.00
Chair, Ladder Back, Turned Legs, Mushroom Arms, Woven Splint Seat 700.00
Chair, Ladder Back, Varnish Stain, Rush Seat, 3 Graduated Slats 35.00
Chair, Lady's, Louis XV, Balloon Back, Rosewood, Finger Carving 125.00
Chair, Lloyd Manufacturing Co., Tubular Chrome, C.1930 .... 85.00
Chair, Lolling, Federal, Mahogany, Needlepoint Serpentine Crest 1800.00
Chair, Louis XV, Cane Seat & Back, Painted Frames, Pair 110.00
Chair, Louis XV, Caned, Cartouche Shape, 18th Century 1200.00
Chair, Lounge, Child's, Foliate Carving, Pawed Feet, C.1830 .... 625.00

Chair, Morris, Cane Seat, Wicker, Traces Of Original Paint 495.00
Chair, Office, Stickley, Oak, Leather Back, Seat, No.361, C.1907 .... 1500.00
Chair, Open Backrest, Vase Shaped Splat, Upholstered, Walnut, Pair 1650.00
Chair, Oriental, Lacquered, Upholstered Seat, 19th Century, Pair 325.00
Chair, Parlor, Rococo Revival, Walnut, Round Seat, C.1865, Pair 325.00
Chair, Pennsylvania Balloon, Fruit Painted Crest, Yellow 35.00
Chair, Pierced Splat, Maple, Rush, Mass., C.1780, 38 In. 625.00
Chair, Plank Seat, Half Spindle Back, Brown Foliage 25.00
Chair, Plank Seat, L.N.Howe Of Montpelier, Vermont 65.00
Chair, Porter's, Leather, English, 19th Century, 65 In. ....*Illus* 2600.00
Chair, Queen Anne, Balloon Seat, Stretcher Base, Walnut, C.1760 .... 2250.00
Chair, Queen Anne, Duck Feet, Slip Upholstered Seat, Walnut 800.00
Chair, Queen Anne, Duck Feet, Vase Splat, Crest, Rush Seat 50.00
Chair, Queen Anne, Mahogany, Balloon Seat, Cabriole, C.1760 .... 4000.00
Chair, Queen Anne, Maple, Molded Crest, Upholstered Seat, C.1750 .... 2420.00
Chair, Queen Anne, Maple, Yoke Crest, Vase Splat, Rush Seat 425.00
Chair, Queen Anne, New England, Spanish Feet, Maple, C.1730, 39 In. 500.00
Chair, Queen Anne, Open Backrest, Vase Shaped Splat, Walnut, Pair 5500.00
Chair, Queen Anne, Scrolled Wings, Trapezoidal Seat, 45 In. 500.00
Chair, Queen Anne, Spanish Feet, Vase Splat, Rush Seat, Cherry 150.00
Chair, Queen Anne, Vase Splat & Crest, Carved Ears, Rush Seat 425.00
Chair, Queen Anne, Vase Splat, Rush Seat, Maple, C.1770, 41 In. 2600.00
Chair, Queen Anne, Walnut, Molded Crest, Vase Form Splat, C.1740 .... 1300.00
Chair, Queen Anne, Walnut, Shell Carved Top Rail, Upholstered 175.00
Chair, Renaissance Revival, Walnut, Burl Panel, C.1865, 56 In. 110.00
Chair, Set, Carved Saber Legs, Boston, C.1825, 4 .... 9000.00
Chair, Set, Chippendale Style, 4, 38 1/2 In. ....*Illus* 1550.00
Chair, Set, Dining, 3 Transverse Splats, Upholstered Seat, 8 .... 6350.00
Chair, Set, Dining, Acanthus Splats, Mahogany, C.1785, 4 .... 2200.00
Chair, Set, Dining, Chippendale, Mahogany, Upholstered Seat, 10 .... 3500.00
Chair, Set, Dining, Empire, Bleached Mahogany, Upholstered, 6 .... 3200.00
Chair, Set, Dining, English Oak, 18th Century, 6 ....*Illus* 2000.00
Chair, Set, Dining, Federal, Mahogany, Shield Shaped Back, 8 .... 1800.00
Chair, Set, Dining, George III, Mahogany, Ladder Back, 6 .... 850.00
Chair, Set, Dining, George III, Upholstered Seat, Mahogany, 12 .... 7975.00
Chair, Set, Dining, Griffins, Leather Front, Back, & Seat, Oak, 6 .... 6000.00
Chair, Set, Dining, Hepplewhite, English, 2 Armchairs, 4 Side 4100.00
Chair, Set, Dining, Italian Provincial, Caned Seats, Walnut, 6 .... 750.00
Chair, Set, Dining, Italian Rococo, Painted, Upholstered Seat, 6 .... 4100.00
Chair, Set, Dining, Oak, 2 Slat Back, H.C.Dexter, C.1915, 6 .... 175.00
Chair, Set, Dining, Open Backrest, Leaves On Splat, Mahogany, 8 .... 2900.00
Chair, Set, Dining, Open Backrest, Splayed Seat, Oak, C.1825, 8 .... 1100.00

Furniture, Chair, Set, Chippendale
Style, 4, 38 1/2 In.

Furniture, Chair, Set, Dining,
English Oak, 18th Century, 6

Chair, Set, Dining, Pierced Splat, Carved Scrolls, Mahogany, 6	8250.00
Chair, Set, Dining, Queen Anne, Bow Front, Cabriole Legs, 10	4250.00
Chair, Set, Dining, Queen Anne, Mahogany, Upholstered Set, 12	2000.00
Chair, Set, Dining, Regency, Mahogany, Upholstered Seat, C.1815, 12	4500.00
Chair, Set, Dining, Regency, Open Backrest, Mahogany, 8	2000.00
Chair, Set, Dining, Regency, Parcel Gilt, Ebonized, Caned, 6	2200.00
Chair, Set, Dining, Stickley, Leather Seat, Ladder Back, C.1904, 10	700.00
Chair, Set, Dining, Thomas Nisbet, New Brunswick, Tiger Maple, 6	3650.00
Chair, Set, Dining, Transitional Country, Upholstered Seat, 6	3000.00
Chair, Set, Dining, Voluted Frame, Mahogany, 19th Century, 6	2200.00
Chair, Set, Dining, William IV, Open Backrest, Mahogany, C.1825, 4	715.00
Chair, Set, Eagle & Vine Design, Cream Color, 4	3200.00
Chair, Set, Empire, Crotch Mahogany Veneer, Slip Seat, 5	325.00
Chair, Set, England, Flame Grain Paneled, C.1810, 33 1/2 In., 6	750.00
Chair, Set, Federal, Cane Seat, Tiger Maple, C.1820, 8	5500.00
Chair, Set, Federal, Carved Curly Maple, Cane Seat, C.1820, 8	2750.00
Chair, Set, George II, Bowed Rails, V Shaped Splats, Walnut, 4	2090.00
Chair, Set, George III, Beechwood, Medallion Back, 8	6750.00
Chair, Set, George III, Prince Of Wales Plume, Mahogany, 6	750.00
Chair, Set, Half Spindle, Plank Seat, Morning Glories, 4	750.00
Chair, Set, Hitchcock, Plank Seat, Gold Design, 5	225.00
Chair, Set, Larkin, No.1, 1 Master, 5 High Backs, Golden Oak	2100.00
Chair, Set, Larkin, No.1, Spoon Carved Fringe, Golden Oak, 6	2100.00
Chair, Set, Plank Seat, Half Spindle Back, Rabbit Ear Posts, 8	500.00
Chair, Set, Pressback, Rope Twist Spindles, 4	600.00
Chair, Set, Provincial, Oak, Leather Seat, 18th Century, 6	2000.00
Chair, Set, Regency, Black, Gold, Upholstered Seat, 5 & 1 Armchair	1200.00
Chair, Set, Saber Back, Dolphin Back, Cane Seat, Rosewood, 6	600.00
Chair, Set, Shaw Furn., Oriental Lacquered, 2 Armchairs, 1 Side	575.00
Chair, Set, Spindle Back, Plank Seat, Old Paint, Striping, 4	180.00
Chair, Set, Square Legs, Upholstered Slip Seat, 5	750.00
Chair, Set, Stacking, Gilbert Rhode Design, Tubular Chrome, 6	305.00
Chair, Set, Stenciled, Rush Seat, 17 3/4 In., 6	1200.00
Chair, Set, Thumb Back, Gilt Stenciled, Painted, C.1830, 6	2000.00
Chair, Set, Windsor, Birdcage, 6	1600.00
Chair, Set, Windsor, Fanback, Pennsylvania, Early 20th Century, 6	650.00
Chair, Set, Windsor, Rhode Island, Brace Back, 5	3250.00
Chair, Set, Winged Portrait Over Splat, Ivory Inlay, 38 In., 4	2400.00
Chair, Shaker, Arms, Maple & Tiger Maple, Rush Seat, 37 In.	300.00
Chair, Shaker, Birch, Taped Seat, 40 In.	1500.00
Chair, Shaker, Ladder Back, New Lebanon	1000.00
Chair, Shaker, Maple, Dark Stain, Shawl Bar, 33 In.	375.00

Furniture, Chair, Wicker, Heart–Shaped Back

To get rid of the musty smell in an old chest of drawers, just line the drawers with fresh grass clippings. Be sure they are not damp. Stir every so often, so they dry, not rot.

A fresh ink stain on wood can be removed by washing with water and then applying lemon juice.

Furniture, Chair, Windsor, Hoop Back,
Jos.Ward, Pair

Furniture, Chest, 4 Drawers, Continental, C.1790,
26 1/2 X 57 In.

Chair, Shaker, Maple, Dark Varnish, Taped Seat, 38 1/2 In. 525.00
Chair, Shaker, Maple, Original Finish, Taped Seat, 36 In. 650.00
Chair, Shaker, Revolving, Black Paint, 9 Metal Spindles, C.1830 .... 6000.00
Chair, Shaker, Tilter, Maple & Cherry, 42 1/2 In. 300.00
Chair, Shaker, Tilter, Mt.Lebanon, 14 In. 525.00
Chair, Slat Back, Painted, Woven Splint Seat, Delaware River 550.00
Chair, Slipper, Connecticut Form, Duck Feet, Double Bearing Arms 2200.00
Chair, Slipper, Louis XV, Painted Frame, Upholstered In Silk, Pair 220.00
Chair, Slipper, Rococo, Rosewood, Leaf Carved Back, Pair 1200.00
Chair, Spindle Back, Plank Seat, Original Red & Black Graining 45.00
Chair, Spindle Back, Writing Arm, Tall, Drawer 1200.00
Chair, Square Legs, Pierced Splat, Rush Seat, Birch, Brown Paint 350.00
Chair, Teak, Oriental, Bird Back, Shaped Seat, Beasts, 34 In. 275.00
Chair, Transitional, Spanish Feet, Maple, Cherry Finish, Rush Seat 975.00
Chair, Vase Finials, Upholstered Back & Seat, Painted Red Maple 650.00
Chair, Vase Splat, Shaped Crest, Spanish Feet, Rush Seat, Cherry 675.00
Chair, Wainscot, Paneled Oak 130.00
Chair, Wallace Nutting, Brewster 1950.00
Chair, Wicker, Asymmetrical Back ....*Illus* 300.00
Chair, Wicker, Curlicues, Beadwork & Ram's Horn, C.1880 .... 365.00
Chair, Wicker, Heart–Shaped Back ....*Illus* 400.00
Chair, William & Mary, Banister Back, Rush, Double Arch Crest 150.00
Chair, William & Mary, Caned Back & Seat, England, 47 In. 150.00
Chair, William & Mary, New England, Maple & Ash, C.1750, 42 In. 600.00
Chair, Windsor, Arched Cresting Rail, Arms, Dipped Seat, Yew & Elm 660.00
Chair, Windsor, Arms, Branded Cole, Nova Scotia, C.1815 .... 1200.00
Chair, Windsor, Arms, Comb Back, S.Paine, Painted Brown, C.1770 .... 4400.00
Chair, Windsor, Bamboo Turnings, Arms, 18th Century, 35 In. 550.00
Chair, Windsor, Bamboo, Plank Seat, Black Repaint, Striping 100.00
Chair, Windsor, Bamboo, Shaped Seat, 17 1/2 In. 200.00
Chair, Windsor, Birdcage, Painted, Penn., C.1800, 32 In., Pair 425.00
Chair, Windsor, Bow Back, 7 Spindles, Plank Seat, C.1780, Pair 4300.00
Chair, Windsor, Bow Back, 7 Spindles, Rhode Island, C.1790, Pair 2000.00
Chair, Windsor, Bow Back, 7 Spindles, Saddle Seat, Black 600.00
Chair, Windsor, Bow Back, 9 Spindles, 16 1/2 In. 150.00
Chair, Windsor, Bow Back, 9 Spindles, Fluted Bow, 17 1/2 In. 500.00
Chair, Windsor, Bow Back, 9 Spindles, Saddle Seat, 16 3/8 In. 150.00
Chair, Windsor, Bow Back, 9 Spindles, Signed S.J.Tucke, C.1790 .... 695.00
Chair, Windsor, Bow Back, Arms, Oval Saddle Seat, 18 In. 825.00
Chair, Windsor, Bow Back, Splayed Legs, Saddle, Red, Pair 570.00
Chair, Windsor, Bow Back, Wallace Nutting, Saddle Seat, 37 In., Pr. 550.00

Chair, Windsor, Comb Back, Arms, Original Paint, Penna., 1740–70 .... 950.00
Chair, Windsor, Comb Back, English, Late 18th Century, 37 In. 225.00
Chair, Windsor, Continuous Arm, Rhode Island 725.00
Chair, Windsor, English, Arms, Dark Finish 375.00
Chair, Windsor, Fanback, 7 Spindles, H Stretcher 210.00
Chair, Windsor, Fanback, 7 Spindles, Seat Height 17 1/2 In. 200.00
Chair, Windsor, Fanback, 9 Spindles, Serpentine Crest, Green 467.00
Chair, Windsor, Fanback, New England, 5 Spindles, C.1770, 43 In. 1700.00
Chair, Windsor, Fanback, New England, Green Paint, C.1760, 35 In. 2900.00
Chair, Windsor, Fanback, Shaped Seat, Potty Seat Cutout, Bamboo 85.00
Chair, Windsor, Gragg Boston, Original Finish, C.1810 .... 385.00
Chair, Windsor, Hoop Back, Branded E.B.Tracy, Red Over Gren 500.00
Chair, Windsor, Hoop Back, Jos.Ward, Pair ....*Illus* 1100.00
Chair, Windsor, Low Back, Arms, Painted Brown, Arrow Feet, 1760 .... 4125.00
Chair, Windsor, Sack Back, Arms, Black, 19th Century 475.00
Chair, Windsor, Sack Back, Arms, Painted & Turned, 7 Spindles 2300.00
Chair, Windsor, Sack Back, Elm Spindles, Arms, English 300.00
Chair, Windsor, Scrolled Arms, Bamboo, Red Graining, 17 3/4 In. 1175.00
Chair, Windsor, Splayed Feet, Carved Comb, Arms, Black & Red Paint 9500.00
Chair, Wing, Federal, Mahogany, Arched Back, Flaring Arms, C.1810 .... 1550.00
Chair, Wing, Queen Anne, Scrolled Ears Form Arms, Mahogany, 46 In. 200.00
Chair, Wing, Queen Anne, Walnut, Claw & Ball Feet, 52 In. 2500.00
Chair, Wing, William & Mary, Shaped Crest, Scrolled Wings & Arms 450.00
Chair, Writing Arm, Original Paint, Drawer, C.1810, Oversized 1600.00
Chaise, Louis XVI, Painted, Balloon Shaped Upholstered Seat 1750.00
Cheese Press, Mesquite Wood Butterfly Turnbuckles, Dated 1850 .... 1250.00
Chest, 2 Drawers, Italian Rococo, Painted, Marble Top, 34 1/2 In. 6000.00
Chest, 2 Drawers, Mule, Pine, Tapered Legs, 43 X 42 3/4 In. 500.00
Chest, 2 Drawers, Quilt, Mahogany, Tilt Top, Lock, 42 X 38 In. 450.00
Chest, 3 Drawers, Cherry, 2 Glove Boxes, Carved Leaf Pulls, 40 In. 200.00
Chest, 3 Drawers, Crest, Birch & Curly Maple, 18 1/2 X 18 1/4 In. 540.00
Chest, 3 Drawers, Graduated, Pine, W.E.Whiting 1882, 29 1/2 In. 3750.00
Chest, 3 Drawers, Hepplewhite, Mahogany, 8 X 4 1/2 X 9 1/2 In. 245.00
Chest, 3 Drawers, Hinged Top, English, Oak, C.1790, 61 1/2 X 35 In. 1200.00
Chest, 4 Dovetailed Drawers, Birch, 20 3/4 X 42 1/2 In. 1000.00
Chest, 4 Drawers, American Empire, Mahogany, 40 X 43 1/2 In. 160.00
Chest, 4 Drawers, Applied Beading, Walnut, 39 1/2 X 40 3/4 In. 1050.00
Chest, 4 Drawers, Banded, Gentleman's, Mahogany, Bow Front, 20 In. 550.00
Chest, 4 Drawers, Bat Wing Brasses, Cherry, 38 1/4 X 41 1/4 In. 1525.00
Chest, 4 Drawers, Brown Finish, Poplar, 23 3/4 X 25 3/4 In. 375.00
Chest, 4 Drawers, Chippendale, Penn., Ogee Feet, Cherry, C.1790 .... 3400.00
Chest, 4 Drawers, Cock–Beaded, Graduated, Federal, Mahogany, 37 In. 600.00
Chest, 4 Drawers, Cock–Beaded, Hepplewhite, Veneer, 37 3/4 In. 550.00
Chest, 4 Drawers, Cock–Beaded, Sheraton, Cherry, 40 3/4 X 40 In. 700.00
Chest, 4 Drawers, Continental, C.1790, 26 1/2 X 57 In. ....*Illus* 1700.00
Chest, 4 Drawers, Country, Beaded Frame, Pine, 41 3/8 In. 1250.00
Chest, 4 Drawers, Dovetailed, Chippendale, Pine, Signed Beck 1150.00
Chest, 4 Drawers, Federal, Mahogany, White Marble Top 400.00
Chest, 4 Drawers, French Feet, Line Inlay, Walnut 38 X 38 1/4 In. 600.00
Chest, 4 Drawers, Graduated, Chippendale, C.1780, 37 X 36 In. 300.00
Chest, 4 Drawers, Graduated, George III, Mahogany, 33 1/2 In. 2750.00
Chest, 4 Drawers, Graduated, Hepplewhite, Cock–Beaded, 1780, 44 In. 850.00
Chest, 4 Drawers, Graduated, Sheraton, Cherry, 36 In. 750.00
Chest, 4 Drawers, Hepplewhite, Curly Maple, 38 3/4 X 38 1/4 In. 800.00
Chest, 4 Drawers, Hepplewhite, Scalloped Top, French Foot, Cherry 1600.00
Chest, 4 Drawers, Mother–Of–Pearl Center Knobs, Maine, Grained 6600.00
Chest, 4 Drawers, Oxbow Shaped, Bracket Base, Cherry 5500.00
Chest, 4 Drawers, Pine, Rectangular Top, 35 X 38 X 17 In. 110.00
Chest, 4 Drawers, Reeded Corner Columns, Tiger Maple 550.00
Chest, 4 Drawers, Serpentine Front, Inlaid Mahogany, 32 1/2 In. 4400.00
Chest, 4 Drawers, Serpentine Front, Mahogany, 40 X 35 1/2 In. 3850.00
Chest, 4 Drawers, Sheraton, Cherry, C.1850, Miniature 475.00
Chest, 4 Drawers, Swell Front, Bird's–Eye Maple 3200.00
Chest, 4 Drawers, Swept Foot, Hepplewhite, Mahogany, C.1820 .... 525.00

Chest, 4 Drawers, Windsor, Keyhole, Tiger Maple 950.00
Chest, 5 Drawers, Burled Maple, Colonial Hardware, 51 X 36 In. 365.00
Chest, 5 Drawers, Cherry, Chippendale, 38 1/2 X 35 1/4 In. 2800.00
Chest, 5 Drawers, Eastlake, Walnut, Burl Walnut, 76 X 42 In. 600.00
Chest, 5 Drawers, George III, Applewood, 31 1/2 X 29 In. 2640.00
Chest, 5 Drawers, Graduated, Bracket Base, Old Finish 3100.00
Chest, 5 Drawers, Graduated, Chippendale, Maple, 1770, 50 X 36 In. 2800.00
Chest, 5 Drawers, Porcelain Pulls, Dark Red, Pine, Miniature 150.00
Chest, 5 Drawers, Queen Anne, Cherry, C.1750, 35 1/2 X 42 1/4 In. 1850.00
Chest, 5 Drawers, Queen Anne, Maine, All Original, Maple, C.1790 .... 1800.00
Chest, 5 Drawers, Scalloped Apron, Red Flame Grained, Pine, 37 In. 525.00
Chest, 5 Drawers, Sheraton, Beading, Walnut, 41 X 41 3/4 In. 850.00
Chest, 5 Drawers, Victorian, French Style, Marble Top, American 300.00
Chest, 5 Drawers, Wide Dovetailing, Maple, 20 1/4 X 37 1/2 In. 875.00
Chest, 6 Drawers, Cherry & Curly Maple, 43 1/2 X 51 1/2 In. 600.00
Chest, 6 Drawers, Chippendale, Connecticut, Tiger Maple, C.1790 .... 4000.00
Chest, 6 Drawers, Molded Fronts, Original Brasses, Tiger Maple 3750.00
Chest, 6 Drawers, New England, Old Red Paint, C.1780, 55 1/2 In. 4500.00
Chest, 6 Drawers, New Hampshire, Tray Top, Painted, C.1790, 60 In. 3600.00
Chest, 6 Drawers, Rhode Island, Maple, C.1790, 35 1/4 X 50 1/4 In. 3450.00
Chest, 6 Drawers, Thumb Graduated, Chippendale, 1780, 53 In. 3500.00
Chest, 7 Drawers, Curly Maple Facade Top & Sides, 47 1/2 In. 650.00
Chest, 7 Drawers, Graduated, George III, Mahogany, 1800, 72 In. 3400.00
Chest, 8 Drawers, Pennsylvania, Walnut, 23 1/2 X 41 X 67 3/4 In. 5000.00
Chest, 8 Drawers, Queen Anne, Walnut, Cabriole Legs, C.1760, 69 In. 7700.00
Chest, 8 Drawers, Spice, Glass Panel Door, Curly Maple, 18 1/2 In. 750.00
Chest, 9 Drawers, On Frame, Walnut, 40 X 20 X 69 1/2 In. 3000.00
Chest, 9 Drawers, Pennsylvania Country, Cherry, 39 X 66 7/8 In. 2700.00
Chest, Apothecary, 24 Drawers, American, Painted Gray, 1830, 24 In. 725.00
Chest, Apothecary, 64 Drawers, 2 Parts 715.00
Chest, Apothecary, Rosehead Nails, C.1800 .... 3500.00
Chest, Asymmetrical Drawers, Japanese, Kiri Wood, 35 1/2 In. 950.00
Chest, Bedside, Hinged Top, Fall Front, Inlaid Mahogany, 31 In. 950.00
Chest, Bedside, Hinged Top, Inside Well, Inlaid Mahogany, 27 In. 675.00
Chest, Blanket, 2 Drawers & Till, Pine, 52 3/4 X 27 1/2 In. 450.00
Chest, Blanket, 6–Board, Old Red Paint, Pine, 43 X 18 1/2 In. 175.00
Chest, Blanket, Base Molding, Till, Grain Painted, Poplar, 41 In. 35.00
Chest, Blanket, Bracket Base, Apple Green, 42 In. 195.00
Chest, Blanket, Brown Grain Painted, 1820, 41 1/2 X 20 In. 600.00
Chest, Blanket, Brown Graining, Poplar, 39 3/4 X 23 3/8 In. 300.00
Chest, Blanket, Butt Hinges, Rose Head Nails, Green Paint 325.00
Chest, Blanket, Cherry, 25 X 12 1/4 X 14 1/2 In. 200.00
Chest, Blanket, Child's, Cherry, Drawer, C.1860, 15 1/2 X 10 In. 295.00
Chest, Blanket, Child's, Painted Brown, C.1730, 27 X 30 1/2 In. 2200.00
Chest, Blanket, Chippendale, 2 Drawers, Tiger Maple 950.00
Chest, Blanket, Chippendale, 2 False Drawers Over 2 Drawers 800.00
Chest, Blanket, Chippendale, Pine, Lift Top, Floral Design 1200.00
Chest, Blanket, Chippendale, Walnut, Hinged, Pa., 1770, 9 X 12 In. 700.00
Chest, Blanket, Dovetailed, Secret Compartment, Old Mustard 595.00
Chest, Blanket, Drawer, Molding Around Top, Red Paint 750.00
Chest, Blanket, Drawer, Original Red Paint, New England 175.00
Chest, Blanket, Drawers, Paneled, English, Iron Hinges, 40 3/4 In. 170.00
Chest, Blanket, English, Oak, Carved, 17th Century, 21 X 43 1/2 In. 225.00
Chest, Blanket, Grained, Inside Tilt, 31 X 15 X 18 In. 120.00
Chest, Blanket, Green Paint, Poplar & Pine, 19 1/2 X 12 1/2 In. 355.00
Chest, Blanket, Gustav Stickley Label, Red Decal, Oak 3100.00
Chest, Blanket, Iron Hinges, M.Heller, 1804, 50 1/2 X 18 1/2 In. 325.00
Chest, Blanket, Mustard Grain, Zigzag Striping, Tilt Inside 300.00
Chest, Blanket, Nantucket, Original Green Paint, 19th Century 900.00
Chest, Blanket, New England, 2 Drawers, Painted, C.1700, 41 In. 600.00
Chest, Blanket, Oak, Triparite Front, Foliate Design, 28 In. 225.00
Chest, Blanket, Ohio, Grained Design, Poplar, 45 3/4 X 24 3/4 In. 3100.00
Chest, Blanket, Original Flame Graining, 37 1/4 X 21 3/4 In. 225.00
Chest, Blanket, Original Sponging, Pine, 48 3/4 X 24 3/4 In. 800.00

Chest, Blanket, Paneled Pine, Grain Painted, Till, C.1850, 42 In. 400.00
Chest, Blanket, Pennsylvania Dutch, 40 X 16 X 40 In. ....*Illus* 2750.00
Chest, Blanket, Pennsylvania, 3 Drawers, Pine, 53 X 28 3/4 In. 3700.00
Chest, Blanket, Pennsylvania, Anna Barbara Schendelin, Pine, 1767 .... 1200.00
Chest, Blanket, Pennsylvania, Iron Hinges, Poplar, 51 X 23 3/4 In. 350.00
Chest, Blanket, Pennsylvania, Painted Designs, C.1800, 36 3/4 In. 5500.00
Chest, Blanket, Pennsylvania, Pine Till, Poplar, 51 X 23 1/2 In. 300.00
Chest, Blanket, Pennsylvania, Walnut, C.1820, 13 3/4 X 8 1/4 In. 325.00
Chest, Blanket, Pilgrim, Oak, Painted, 1670–90, 26 X 50 1/2 In. 3025.00
Chest, Blanket, Pine, 2 Full Drawers, Black Graining, 43 In. 425.00
Chest, Blanket, Pine, Grained, Dovetailed, 37 X 19 In. 170.00
Chest, Blanket, Pine, Grained, Tilt Interior, Bracket Feet, 37 In. 190.00
Chest, Blanket, Pine, Lift Top, 2 Drawers, Bracket Feet, 36 1/4 In. 5000.00
Chest, Blanket, Pine, Painted Tulips, Dated 1783, 22 1/2 In. 9700.00
Chest, Blanket, Pine, Painted, Tulips & Urns, Dated 1789, 20 In. 2750.00
Chest, Blanket, Pine, Red Painted Designs, 1820, 35 X 40 X 19 In. 1300.00
Chest, Blanket, Poplar, Panels, 3 Drawers, Red Graining, 48 In. 1050.00
Chest, Blanket, Queen Anne, Painted Red, C.1750, 37 X 42 In. 660.00
Chest, Blanket, Shaker, Sabbath Day Lake, Original Green 15400.00
Chest, Blanket, Straight 6 Board, End Cleat Hinges 450.00
Chest, Blanket, Strap Hinges, Red Flame Graining, Pine 145.00
Chest, Blanket, Striped Graining, Poplar, 50 1/2 X 28 In. 250.00
Chest, Blanket, Till, Bear Trap Lock, European, 50 X 20 In. 800.00
Chest, Blanket, Turned Feet, Old Red Paint 250.00
Chest, Blanket, Virginia, Lift Top, Abraham Golladay, Painted, 1822 .... 1500.00
Chest, Blanket, William & Mary, 2 Drawers, Pine, C.1740, 46 1/2 In. 1300.00
Chest, Bookcase Top, 4 Drawers, Cherry, 40 3/4 X 72 3/4 In. 4000.00
Chest, Bow Front, Bellflower Inlay, Claw Feet, Enamel Pulls 5500.00
Chest, Bow Front, New England, Tiger Maple, C.1800, 40 X 38 In. 1750.00
Chest, Brass, 5 Drawers, C.1860, 38 X 17 X 12 In. ....*Illus* 700.00
Chest, Burled Panels, Original Hardware 125.00
Chest, Chippendale, Cherry, C.1780, 36 In. 1900.00
Chest, Chippendale, Cherry, Ogee Feet, C.1780, 36 X 37 In. 1900.00
Chest, Chippendale, Curly Maple, Bracket Feet, C.1790, 47 1/2 In. 2750.00
Chest, Chippendale, Curly Maple, Tag, C.E.Dawes, 1770–90, 40 In. 900.00
Chest, Chippendale, Walnut, Graduated Drawers, 1765, 35 1/2 In. 11000.00
Chest, Dovetailed Case, Brown Paint, Pine, Miniature 90.00
Chest, Dower, 2 Deer Inside Till, Painted, Miniature 975.00
Chest, Dower, 3 Drawers, Painted, Penna., C.1790, 30 X 50 X 21 In. 1200.00
Chest, Dower, Pennsylvania, Design, Painted 1995.00
Chest, Dower, Pennsylvania, Original Brasses, Dated 1794 .... 2850.00
Chest, Dutch Armada, Polychrome Design, Ironwork 2500.00

Furniture, Chest, Blanket, Pennsylvania Dutch,
40 X 16 X 40 In.

Furniture, Chest, Brass,
5 Drawers, C.1860,
38 X 17 X 12 In.

Furniture, Chest, English, Mahogany,
31 1/2 X 38 X 18 1/4 In.

Furniture, Chest, Lift Top, Chippendale,
Oak, 20 1/2 X 43 X 27 In.

Chest, Empire, Walnut, Curly Pilasters, Pittsburgh Pulls, 44 In.	195.00
Chest, English, Mahogany, 31 1/2 X 38 X 18 1/4 In. ....*Illus*	625.00
Chest, Fall Front, Leather Lined Surface, Mulberry, 5 Ft. 7 In.	2475.00
Chest, Federal, Mahogany, Maple, Inlaid, 1795, 41 X 40 X 20 In.	3200.00
Chest, Flour, Cutting Board & Dough Trough, Mustard Grain Paint	465.00
Chest, Gentleman, Mahogany, Brass Pulls, 18th Century, 31 1/2 In.	625.00
Chest, George III, Mahogany, Writing Shelf, England, 31 X 30 In.	475.00
Chest, Green & Gold Backsplash, Maine, Grain Painted	1450.00
Chest, Hepplewhite, Cherry, Cock-Beaded Drawers, 42 In.	2000.00
Chest, Hepplewhite, Cherry, Inlaid Escutcheons, 38 X 36 In.	650.00
Chest, Immigrant's, Dome Top, Till, Bear Trap Lock, 48 X 24 In.	150.00
Chest, Immigrant, Dome, Walnut, Iron Strap Hinges, 18 1/2 X 41 In.	100.00
Chest, Lift Top, Chippendale, Oak, 20 1/2 X 43 X 27 In. ....*Illus*	300.00
Chest, Mahogany, Carved Skirt, Miniature, 15 In. ....*Illus*	325.00
Chest, Mahogany, Miniature, C.1840, 13 X 7 X 12 In. ....*Color*	275.00
Chest, Marriage, Chinese, Leather & Lacquerware, 32 1/2 X 21 In.	3000.00
Chest, Mule, Dovetailed, Poplar, Drawer, Turned Feet, Flared Taper	500.00
Chest, Oak, Brass Mounts, Hinged Top, Drawer, 23 1/2 X 35 X 22 In.	155.00
Chest, On Frame, Queen Anne, Grained Dark Oak, 38 X 60 In.	2600.00
Chest, Oriental, Carved Teak, Inlay, C.1900, 39 1/4 X 21 1/4 In.	375.00

Furniture, Chest, Wellington, Walnut,
C.1850, 59 X 19 X 29 In.

Furniture, Chest, Mahogany, Carved Skirt,
Miniature, 15 In.

Furniture, Chiffonier, Bamboo,   Furniture, Commode, Regency, Walnut, French,
Oriental, Hand Decorated, 59 In.   35 X 54 X 26 In.

Chest, Penn., Fluted Quarter Columns, Walnut, C.1790, 65 X 41 In.	6800.00
Chest, Pharmacy, 20 Labeled Drawers, English, Mahogany	900.00
Chest, Pin, Dovetailed Drawers, Pugwash, Nova Scotia, C.1870	395.00
Chest, Pine, Dark Brown Fan Graining, 43 X 22 X 27 In.	150.00
Chest, Queen Anne, Tray Top, Carved Candle Drawer, Cherry & Pine	8500.00
Chest, Shaker, Signed William Ezra Whiting–1882, Pine & Poplar	4125.00
Chest, Sheraton, Bow Front, Curly Maple Facade, 37 1/2 In.	1250.00
Chest, Spanish, Walnut, Lid, Carved Birds, Cartouche, 13 In.	320.00
Chest, Split Drawers, Bronze Mounted, Tansu, 46 X 37 1/2 In.	1300.00
Chest, Walnut, Fruitwood Veneer, Marquetry, Dutch, 59 X 40 3/4 In.	1250.00
Chest, Walnut, S.German, Serpentine, String Inlay, 30 X 45 X 26in.	2600.00
Chest, Watchmaker, Oak, 23 Drawers, Hamilton Mfg.Co., 43 X 70 In.	275.00
Chest, Wellington, Walnut, C.1850, 59 X 19 X 29 In. ....*Illus*	950.00
Chest–On–Chest, 5 Drawers, Molded Frieze, Stringing, Mahogany	2400.00
Chest–On–Chest, George III, Early 19th Century	2500.00
Chest–On–Chest, Queen Anne, New England, Maple, C.1760, 74 In.	5775.00
Chiffonier, Bamboo, Oriental, Hand Decorated, 59 In. ....*Illus*	550.00
China Cabinet, Bow Front, American, Oak, 20th Century	440.00
China Cabinet, Curved Glass, Claw Feet	995.00
China Cabinet, Mahogany, Ogee Pediment, 4 Drawers, 71 X 35 In.	160.00
China Closet, Mission Oak, Glass Doors, 59 X 47 X 15 In.	450.00
China Closet, Oak, Veneer, Curved Glass Sides, Mirror Back, 70 In.	800.00
China Closet, Serpentine, Oak, Gadrooned, Mirror, 62 X 39 X 19 In.	900.00
Clothes Closet, Pennsylvania Dutch, Grain Painted	4800.00
Coffer, Italian Renaissance, Walnut, Lid, Panel Front, 62 In.	950.00
Commode, French, Bronze Mounts, Marble Top, 36 X 42 X 18 In.	1050.00
Commode, French, Sculptural Ormolu Mounts, 19th Century	8250.00
Commode, Genoese Kingwood & Pallisonder Marquetry, 35 In., Pair	5225.00
Commode, German Rococo, Tulipwood, Parquetry, Marble, 4 Ft. 9 In.	6310.00
Commode, Inlaid Marquetry & Parcel Gilt Front, 4 Ft.6 In.	6600.00
Commode, Lift Top, Pine, Deep Well, 2 Doors, 21 1/2 X 30 X 29 In.	75.00
Commode, Lift Top, Pine, Nova Scotia, C.1860	395.00
Commode, Louis XV, 3 Drawers, Cabriole Legs, 28 X 31 In.	80.00
Commode, Louis XV, Gilt Bronze Mounted, Black Lacquer, 39 In.	2200.00
Commode, Louis XV, Gilt Bronze Mounted, Kingwood, 4 X 3 Ft.	1750.00
Commode, Louis XV, Kingwood, Burl Walnut, 2 Crossbanded Drawers	4000.00
Commode, Regency, Ormolu, Kingwood, Marble Top, 41 In.	3600.00
Commode, Regency, Walnut, French, 35 X 54 X 26 In. ....*Illus*	9500.00
Commode, Serpentine Front, Carving, Marble Top, Rosewood, Pair	2500.00
Commode, Victorian, Marble Top, 1 Drawer, Walnut, 17 X 29 1/2 In.	325.00
Commode, Walnut, White Marble, 1 Long Drawer, 2 Doors, 30 X 33 In.	250.00
Console, Charles X, Mahogany, Walnut, Marble, Paw Feet, 36 3/4 In.	825.00
Couch, Fainting, Blue Velvet Cover, Oak, 1880–1900	500.00
Cradle, Bentwood Frame, Wooden Slat, Oval, 45 In.	195.00

Cradle, Hooded, New England, Painted Red Wash Inside, C.1820 .... 500.00
Cradle, Mahogany, Turned Posts, Dark Finish, 24 X 41 In. 230.00
Cradle, New England, Old Blue Paint Over Original Red, C.1800 .... 575.00
Cradle, Pine, Pennsylvania, Tombstone Headboard, 35 In 345.00
Cradle, Scalloped End, Cutout Rockers, Red Paint, 16 1/4 In. 500.00
Cradle, Turned Spindle, Pennsylvania, Pine, 18th Century 385.00
Cradle, Yellow & White Design, Original Brown Paint, Poplar 90.00
Credenza, Sheaves Of Wheat, Rosewood, 19th Century, 56 X 44 In. 1200.00
Cupboard, 2 Doors, 1 Long Drawer, Shaped Legs, Gray Paint 850.00
Cupboard, 2 Drawers, 2 Piece, Maple Front, Walnut 650.00
Cupboard, 5 Shelves, 3 Drawers, Butternut, 7 X 10 1/2 Ft. 1500.00
Cupboard, Butterfly Shelves, Original Glasses, Cherry, C.1750 .... 4500.00
Cupboard, Butternut, Cutout Feet, Door, Thumb Latch, 33 1/2 In. 470.00
Cupboard, Child's, Step Back, Blind Doors, Primitive 95.00
Cupboard, Chippendale, Step Back, Pine, C.1760, 6 Ft. 11 In. 2400.00
Cupboard, Corner, 2 Piece, Cherry, Poplar, 44 3/4 X 86 3/4 In. 1300.00
Cupboard, Corner, American, Raised Panel Door, Pine, C.1760, 80 In. 1600.00
Cupboard, Corner, Ball & Stick ....*Illus* 600.00
Cupboard, Corner, Barrel Back, Pine, C.1730, 46 X 86 In. 3200.00
Cupboard, Corner, Canadian, Ball Drop Cornice, Pine, 85 3/4 In. 1200.00
Cupboard, Corner, Cherry & Poplar, Paneled Doors, Reeded 1300.00
Cupboard, Corner, Connecticut, 4 Doors, Pine, C.1815, 78 1/2 In. 2300.00
Cupboard, Corner, Dutch Walnut, Marquetry, Arched Door, 26 1/2 In. 700.00
Cupboard, Corner, Hanging, Alligatored Finish, Oak, 14 X 19 In. 375.00
Cupboard, Corner, Hanging, Curved Door, Dated 1732, 36 X 20 In. 225.00
Cupboard, Corner, Hanging, Georgian, Oak & Walnut, 41 3/4 X 35 In. 400.00
Cupboard, Corner, Lancaster County, Paint Decorated 5200.00
Cupboard, Corner, Open Top, 1 Bottom Door, Old Red 1800.00
Cupboard, Corner, Paneled Doors, Cherry, 47 1/2 X 81 3/4 In. 1700.00
Cupboard, Corner, Paneled Doors, Pine, English, 32 X 69 In. 600.00
Cupboard, Corner, Pegs & Square Nails, Pine, 1800s 2600.00
Cupboard, Corner, Pennsylvania, Blind Doors, C.1880, 7 1/2 Ft. 1300.00
Cupboard, Corner, Pine, Fluted Pilasters, Paneled Doors, 17 In. 325.00
Cupboard, Corner, Pine, Mustard, Red Paint, Shelves, 1880, 83 In. 2900.00
Cupboard, Corner, Urn Finial, Cherrywood, C.1790, 7 Ft. 6 In. 5500.00
Cupboard, Country, Curly Maple Drawer, Refinished, 77 1/2 In. 600.00
Cupboard, Country, Pine, Paneled Doors, 3 Shelves, 59 X 84 In. 1000.00
Cupboard, Court, Jacobean, Carved Cornice, Lozenge Inlay, 64 In. 250.00
Cupboard, Court, Wallace Nutting 3500.00
Cupboard, Dutch, New York State, Walnut, Early 18th Century 5600.00
Cupboard, Dutch, Pine, Overhang Molding, Spoon Rack, 47 X 53 In. 925.00
Cupboard, French Gothic, Oak, 48 X 48 In. 1650.00
Cupboard, Frieze Top, Inlaid Door, Oak Marquetry, 4 1/2 Ft. 2400.00
Cupboard, Hanging, 2 Doors, Recessed, 18th Century, 39 In. 200.00
Cupboard, Hanging, 4 Bottom Drawers, Panel Doors, Pine, C.1790 .... 875.00
Cupboard, Hanging, Shaker, Cherry & Pine, Natural, 1 Door, 24 In. 1000.00
Cupboard, Hanging, Shaker, Pine, Original Mustard, 24 X 12 In. 1000.00
Cupboard, James II, Oak, Ball Feet, England, 65 X 59 X 21 1/2 In. 650.00
Cupboard, Jelly, Dovetailed, Friendsville, Pa., Red, 41 X 42 In. 825.00
Cupboard, Jelly, Grained, 2 Doors, 2 Drawers, 48 X 21 X 49 In. 350.00
Cupboard, Jelly, Inch Thick Boards Throughout, Original Paint 710.00
Cupboard, Jelly, Original Muted Salmon, 34 1/2 X 58 1/2 In. 990.00
Cupboard, Jelly, Shaker, Enfield, Conn., 3 Shelves, 41 X 49 In. 675.00
Cupboard, Jelly, Single Board Doors, Old Brown Paint, 42 X 43 In. 235.00
Cupboard, Livery, Hanging, Jacobean Oak, 24 1/2 X 27 3/4 In. 440.00
Cupboard, Mercer County, Ohio, Blue, Dated 1865 .... 2375.00
Cupboard, Open, Maine, 1 Butterfly Shelf, Red, Blue, Dated 1804 .... 4750.00
Cupboard, Overhanging Cornice, Carved Frieze, Carved Oak, 5 Ft. 1300.00
Cupboard, Paneled Doors, 2 Drawers, Cornice, Cherry, 85 1/4 In. 1100.00
Cupboard, Pennsylvania Dutch, Grain Painted 4500.00
Cupboard, Pennsylvania, Dovetailed, Shoe Feet, Pine 2200.00
Cupboard, Pennsylvania, Original Glass, Painted Finish, Walnut 2600.00
Cupboard, Pennsylvania, Saffron Yellow, Spoon Slots, Dated 1810 .... 4800.00
Cupboard, Pewter, 1 Board Door, Pine & Poplar, 31 X 59 1/2 In. 650.00

Cupboard, Pewter, Paneled Doors, Red Interior, Pine, 73 1/2 In. 1250.00
Cupboard, Pine, Blue Paint, Beaded Door, 7 Shelves, 85 In., Pair 3250.00
Cupboard, Pine, Paneled Doors, 1 Piece, Reconstructed, 70 3/4 In. 350.00
Cupboard, Pine, Paneled Doors, Cornice, Refinished, 79 1/2 In. 1000.00
Cupboard, Pine, Possum Belly, Tin Lined Drawers 300.00
Cupboard, Pine, Shelves, 5 Drawers, 29 1/2 X 16 In. ....*Illus* 200.00
Cupboard, Seed, 24 Drawers, Original Graining, Painted Labels 1695.00
Cupboard, Shaker, Flat Front, 4 Batten Doors, Blue, 70 X 49 In. 875.00
Cupboard, Slant Back, 5 Shelves, Beaded Edge, Pine, C.1800, 74 In. 4600.00
Cupboard, Spice, Hanging, Lock, Key, Oak, 19th Century, 16 X 16 In. 975.00
Cupboard, Stenciled Name Of Henry W.Jacobs, Guilford, Vermont 225.00
Cupboard, Step Back, 2 Upper Doors, 1 Lower, C.1800, 41 X 78 In. 1500.00
Cupboard, Step Back, 7 Drawers, Wooden Pulls, Pine, 16 X 24 In. 300.00
Cupboard, Step Back, Blue Over Old Red, 42 1/2 X 21 X 75 In. 1000.00
Cupboard, Step Back, Cherry, 2 Drawers, 4 Doors, 45 X 84 In. 500.00
Cupboard, Step Back, Chippendale, Walnut, Cornice, 1785, 7 Ft.4 In. 4125.00
Cupboard, Step Back, Pine, Bracket Base, 3 Drawers, Dough Tray 1700.00
Cupboard, Tudor, Carved Oak, 2 Doors, Inlaid Arched Panels, 66 In. 1750.00
Cupboard, Wall, 2 Piece, Scalloped Base, Paneled Door, 3 Drawers 850.00
Cupboard, Wall, Dutch, Marquetry, Walnut, 19th Century, 37 3/4 In. 650.00
Cupboard, Wall, Ohio, Curly Maple Pilasters, Cherry, 2 Piece 3600.00
Cupboard, Wall, Ohio, Double Doors, Pie Shelf, Cherry, 84 3/4 In. 3600.00
Daybed, Grain Painted Pine, C.1830, 27 1/2 X 24 In. 475.00
Daybed, New England, 5 Stiles, Cushion, Painted Black, 1730–50 .... 3300.00
Daybed, Rush Covered, Wooden Posts & Headboard, Pennsylvania 1050.00
Daybed, Stickley, Slat, Cushions, Label, C.1907, 29 3/4 X 79 In. 850.00
Daybed, Victorian, Spool Turned, 27 X 74 X 31 In. 40.00
Desk Bookcase, Pennsylvania, 4 Drawers, Walnut, C.1790, 90 1/2 In. 5000.00
Desk, American, Cherry, Weller, Brown & Mesmer, 31 X 27 X 14 In. 1800.00
Desk, Biedermeier, Crotch Mahogany, 1840, 37 X 25 In. 425.00
Desk, Bonheur Du Jour, Hinged Writing Flap, Satinwood, 37 1/2 In. 6600.00
Desk, Bookcase, Victorian, Walnut, Drop Front, Glass Doors, 86 In. 450.00
Desk, Carlton House, Satinwood, 40 X 60 X 26 In. ....*Illus* 3750.00
Desk, Chippendale, 2 Pedestals, Walnut, Leather Inset, 25 X 45 In. 130.00
Desk, Chippendale, Country, Slant Lid, 4 Drawers, 37 1/2 X 44 In. 1600.00
Desk, Chippendale, Slant Top, Tiger Maple, Bracket Feet, C.1780 .... 3250.00
Desk, Clerk's, Lift Slant Lid, Blue Paint, C.1820, 32 1/2 X 42 In. 1300.00
Desk, Counter, Slant Lid, Drawer, Pine, C.1820, 12 1/2 X 24 In. 135.00
Desk, Countertop, Storekeeper's, Rose Head Nails, Pine 495.00
Desk, Cylinder Roll Top, Fitted Interior, Cherry 450.00
Desk, Davenport, China, Carved, Lacquered & Gilt, 28 3/4 X 36 In. 1600.00
Desk, Double Pedestal, Walnut, Leather Top, England, 54 X 32 In. 1500.00

Furniture, Cupboard, Corner,
Ball & Stick

Furniture, Cupboard, Pine, Shelves,
5 Drawers, 29 1/2 X 16 In.

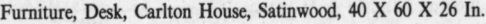

Furniture, Desk, Carlton House, Satinwood, 40 X 60 X 26 In.

Furniture, Desk, Lady's, Continental, 30 1/4 X 34 3/4 In.

Desk, Drop Front, Hepplewhite, Inlaid, All Original, Walnut	6500.00
Desk, Drop Front, Oak, Gustav Stickley, C.1912, 44 X 32 X 14 In.	900.00
Desk, Drop Front, Tudor Style, Oak, 38 X 45 In.	170.00
Desk, Executive, 6 Drawers, Oak, 5 X 4 Ft.	800.00
Desk, Federal, Mahogany Veneer, Tambour, 46 In.	1500.00
Desk, Flat Top, Oak, Inlaid, Floral Panels, Drawer, 29 X 27 In.	350.00
Desk, G.Eidlitz Designer, American, Cherry, C.1879, 27 X 31 In.	1800.00
Desk, George III, Satinwood, Painted, 6 Drawers, 40 X 60 X 26 In.	3750.00
Desk, Gustav Stickley No.708, 2 Drawers, 1904, 36 X 40 X 22 In.	400.00
Desk, Gustav Stickley, Flat Top, C.1912, 36 X 34 X 20 In.	375.00
Desk, Kneehole, England, 2 Upper Banks Of Drawers, Walnut, C.1900	450.00
Desk, Kneehole, England, Walnut Veneer, C.1740, 28 1/2 In.	675.00
Desk, Kneehole, George III, Mahogany, Molded Top, 31 X 29 1/2 In.	350.00
Desk, Kneehole, Louis XV, Provincial Paint, 2 Drawers, 4 Ft. 3 In.	3500.00
Desk, Kneehole, Mahogany, Leather, Brass Bail Pulls, 1900, 60 In.	800.00
Desk, Kneehole, Mahogany, Leather, Brass Pulls, 55 X 31 1/2 In.	575.00
Desk, Kneehole, Mahogany, Stringed Flame Panels, 50 X 34 In.	700.00
Desk, Kneehole, Mission Oak, 3 Drawers, 36 X 54 X 29 1/2 In.	275.00
Desk, Kneehole, Walnut, Leather Top, Brass Trim, 50 1/2 X 27 In.	700.00
Desk, Lady's, Continental, 30 1/4 X 34 3/4 In. _Illus_	225.00
Desk, Lady's, Flat Top, Gustav Stickley, 36 X 38 In.	650.00
Desk, Lady's, Fluted Posts, 3 Drawers, Pine, 37 1/2 X 46 1/2 In.	950.00
Desk, Lady's, Renaissance Revival, Cylinder Front, Gallery, 54 In.	500.00
Desk, Lecturn, Fitted Interior, Pine & Walnut, 19 X 13 In.	125.00
Desk, Lift Top, Rosewood, 18th Century, Restored, 37 X 24 1/2 In.	1300.00
Desk, Lift Top, Vermont, Sponge Painted Pine, C.1800, 33 In.	1200.00
Desk, Oak, Limbert, Drop Front, 1 Drawer, 2 Doors, 46 X 36 In.	550.00
Desk, Oxbow, 4 Drawers, Slant Top, Mahogany, 40 X 44 In.	2100.00
Desk, Partner's, American Empire, Mahogany, 10 Drawers, Scroll	450.00
Desk, Partner's, Pedestal, Leather Top, Mahogany, C.1890, 6 Ft.	6000.00
Desk, Partner's, Raised Panels, Carved Handles, Oak, 53 X 66 In.	2500.00
Desk, Partner's, Tooled Leather Top, Knop Pulls, Mahogany, 5 Ft.	4400.00
Desk, Pedestal, Burl Walnut, 6 Drawers, 43 In. X 4 Ft.	2475.00
Desk, Queen Anne, Slant Front, New England, Pine, C.1730	900.00
Desk, Regency, Brass Gallery, Leather Top, 25 X 30 In.	270.00
Desk, Roll Top, C Curve, Mahogany, 50 In.	475.00
Desk, Roll Top, Cherry, 4 Drawers, Cherry, American, 45 In.	725.00
Desk, Roll Top, Drop Down, Child's, Blackboard, Oak, C.1923	55.00
Desk, Roll Top, Golden Oak, 21 Drawers, 2 Cabinets	4950.00
Desk, Roll Top, Oak, 21 Small Drawers, 1900, 66 X 37 X 50 In.	1800.00
Desk, Roll Top, Paneled Sides, American, 50 X 49 X 34 In.	850.00
Desk, Roll Top, Quartered Oak, Privacy Panel, 20 Inside Drawers	2500.00

Desk, Roll Top, Quartered Oak, Raised Panel, 54 In. 1900.00
Desk, Roll Top, Regency, Cylinder, Brass Bindings & Moldings 1300.00
Desk, Roll Top, S Curve, English, Oak, C.1880, 4 Ft. 6 In. 1500.00
Desk, Rosewood, C.1850, 23 In. X 3 Ft. 2 In. 525.00
Desk, School, Hepplewhite, For 4 Pupils, Red, 8 Ft. 650.00
Desk, School, Prince Edward Island, Pine, Square Nails, C.1860 .... 325.00
Desk, Schoolmaster's, Country, Dark Finish, 36 X 31 1/2 X 37 In. 175.00
Desk, Schoolmaster's, Country, Walnut, Lift Top, 34 X 29 X 41 In. 500.00
Desk, Schoolmaster's, Graduated Drawers, Onioned Feet, Red Paint 280.00
Desk, Schoolmaster's, Grain Painted, American, C.1800, 50 1/2 In. 350.00
Desk, Schoolmaster's, Marlborough Legs, Blue Green Paint, C.1800 .... 2500.00
Desk, Schoolmaster's, Old Blue–Gray Paint 815.00
Desk, Secretary, Serpentine Drawers, Mahogany, 3 Ft.3 In. 1800.00
Desk, Shaker, Cherry, Tilt Top, Tiger Maple Front, 2 Piece, 65 In. 800.00
Desk, Shaker, Deaconess, Maple, Slant Lid, 3 Feet, 29 X 21 X 17 In. 5000.00
Desk, Shaker, School, Enfield, N.H., Old Blue 2200.00
Desk, Shaker, School, Pine, Original Blue Paint, 31 In. 2000.00
Desk, Shaker, Table, Cherry, 6 Drawer Interior, 1850, 13 X 27 In. 575.00
Desk, Slant Front, 4 Dovetailed Drawers, Maple, 38 X 41 In. 2500.00
Desk, Slant Front, 4 Drawers, Fitted, Birch, 38 1/2 X 40 In. 900.00
Desk, Slant Front, 4 Drawers, Fitted, Walnut, 39 1/2 X 40 In. 2300.00
Desk, Slant Front, 4 Drawers, Fitted, Walnut, 41 3/4 X 44 1/2 In. 5000.00
Desk, Slant Front, 4 Drawers, French Feet, Tiger Maple 1900.00
Desk, Slant Front, Child's, New England, 28 In. 2750.00
Desk, Slant Front, Child's, William & Mary, Walnut, 1710–40, 24 In. 6900.00
Desk, Slant Front, Chippendale, Cherry, 4 Drawers, 1770, 41 In. 2600.00
Desk, Slant Front, Chippendale, Cherry, Bracket Feet, C.1790 .... 3500.00
Desk, Slant Front, Chippendale, Cherry, Ogee Feet, 43 In. 1300.00
Desk, Slant Front, Chippendale, Mahogany, C.1785, 43 1/2 In. 2750.00
Desk, Slant Front, Chippendale, Original Red, Tiger Maple, 36 In. 3800.00
Desk, Slant Front, Connecticut, Graduated Drawers, Cherry 3900.00
Desk, Slant Front, Connecticut, Serpentine Feet, Cherry, C.1780 .... 4500.00
Desk, Slant Front, Curly Maple, New England, 1720–40, 40 X 37 In. 1200.00
Desk, Slant Front, Fan Carved Drawers, Walnut, C.1770, 40 X 42 In. 2650.00
Desk, Slant Front, George III, 3 Drawers, Mahogany, 40 X 42 In. 1100.00
Desk, Slant Front, Italian Rococo, 3 Drawers, Walnut, 42 In. 5500.00
Desk, Slant Front, Louis XV, Fruitwood, Cabriole Legs, 21 X 43 In. 5225.00
Desk, Slant Front, New England, Tiger Maple, C.1800, 42 1/2 In. 3850.00
Desk, Slant Front, Queen Anne, Stand, Cabriole Legs, C.1735, 43 In. 5500.00
Desk, Slant Front, Spooled Corner Columns, 4 Drawers 3600.00
Desk, Slant Front, Tiger Maple, Chippendale, C.1780, 39 In. 3250.00
Desk, Slant Front, Walnut, Bracket Feet, Inlay, Invected Corner 850.00

White rings on furniture can sometimes be removed with liquid metal polish or auto paint cleaner. Apply the cleaner to a soft cloth and rub until the ring is gone. Then repolish the surface.

Furniture, Dresser, Queen Anne,
Mirror, C.1750, 26 X 6 X 14 In.

Desk, Table Top, Slant Top, Compartments, Red Paint, 25 X 10 In. 165.00
Desk, Travel, Camphorwood, Brass Bound, Cylinder Top, 19 1/2 In. 1300.00
Desk, William & Mary, On Stand, 18th Century, Oak, 31 X 39 1/2 In. 300.00
Desk, Wooton, Rotary, Walnut, 2–Pier, Leather Top, 32 In. X 5 Ft. 1650.00
Desk, Wooton, Walnut, 3/4 Gallery, 2 Convex Doors, 6 Ft.4 In. 6700.00
Dining Set, Charles Eames, Plastic, Red Vinyl, C.1955, 5 Piece 400.00
Dining Set, Gothic Renaissance, Mahogany, C.1890, 12 Piece 4500.00
Dining Set, Heywood Wakefield, Solid Birch, 6 Chairs, 8 Ft. 1100.00
Dining Set, Jacobean Style, Paine, Table, 6 Chairs, Buffet, C.1930 .... 2500.00
Dining Set, Maple, Modified Windsor Style, Table, Hutch, 6 Chairs 795.00
Dining Set, Oak, Gustav Stickley, Sideboard, Server, 1907, 9 Piece 4000.00
Dining Set, Round Oak Table, Claw Feet, 4 Oak Caned Seat Chairs 800.00
Dining Set, Signed Stickley Bros., Oak, 10 Piece 7500.00
Dining Set, Walnut, Berkey & Gay, Grand Rapids, 1920s, 10 Piece 5000.00
Dresser, Child's, Oak, Mirror, 7 X 15 X 21 In. 145.00
Dresser, Cornice & Frieze, 3 Shelves, Clock, Oak, 7 Ft. 3 In. 6600.00
Dresser, Mirror Built Into Base, Columned Front, Top Mirror 210.00
Dresser, Queen Anne, Mirror, C.1750, 26 X 6 X 14 In. ....*Illus* 450.00
Dresser, Welsh, 3 Drawers, Brass Handles, Oak, 36 X 39 In. 880.00
Dresser, Welsh, 3 Drawers, Brass Loop Handles, Oak, 32 In. 1750.00
Dresser, Welsh, 3 Open Shelves, 2 Top Drawers, Oak, 6 Ft. 2 In. 2400.00
Dresser, Welsh, 5 Drawers, Columns, Veneer Walnut, 21 X 54 In. 595.00
Dresser, Welsh, Bleached Pine, C.1820 .... 2650.00
Dresser, Welsh, Open Shelves, Cupboard Doors, Oak, 6 Ft. 11 In. 2000.00
Dresser, Welsh, Pine, Mahogany, C.1880 .... 1295.00
Dry Sink, 2 Doors, 2 Small Drawers At Side, Original Red Paint 750.00
Etagere, American, Walnut, C.1870, Base 40 In. X 64 In. 850.00
Etagere, Burl Walnut, Turned Columns, 43 X 24 X 16 In. 750.00
Etagere, Center Gallery, Curved & Beveled Glass, Mahogany, C.1900 .... 850.00
Etagere, Empire, Walnut, Carved Pineapple 875.00
Etagere, English, Bronze Gallery, Rosewood, C.1850, 24 X 41 In. 1100.00
Etagere, Mirrors, Bowed Lower Shelf, Rosewood & Walnut, 93 In. 600.00
Etagere, Rosewood, Bronze Filigree Gallery, C.1850, 41 X 24 In. 1100.00
Fauteuil, Louis XV, Upholstered, Cabriole Legs, Serpentine Front 2300.00
Fauteuil, Louis XVI, Green Floral Brocade Upholstered 60.00
Footstool, American Renaissance Revival, Upholstered, 1870 .... 150.00
Footstool, Bamboo Turnings, Octagonal Top, 8 X 14 X 6 In. 225.00
Footstool, Cherry, Bootjack Ends, Hand Grip, 5 1/2 X 8 X 14 In. 175.00
Footstool, Chinese Padouk, Caned Top, Cabriole Legs, 5 1/2 In. 275.00
Footstool, Chippendale, Mahogany, Needlework, England, 24 X 28 In. 425.00
Footstool, Cricket, Button Feet, C.1820, 7 1/2 X 7 1/2 X 12 In. 130.00
Footstool, Cutout Legs, Scrolled Apron, Brown Graining, 7 1/2 In. 155.00
Footstool, French Provincial, Walnut, Petit Point, C.1800, 8 In. 300.00
Footstool, George III, Velvet Upholstered, 25 X 18 1/2 In., Pair 225.00
Footstool, Gustav Stickley, Leather, C.1907, 4 1/2 X 12 In. 350.00
Footstool, Leather Top, Gustav Stickley, Marked, 20 1/2 In. 750.00
Footstool, Leather, Limbert, Branded, 15 1/2 X 18 In. 110.00
Footstool, Lunenburg County, Nova Scotia, Pine 225.00
Footstool, Mahogany, Bone Inlay, Bootjack Ends, 16 X 7 In. 120.00
Footstool, Mustard Paint, Splayed Bootjack Ends, 7 X 8 X 14 In. 45.00
Footstool, Plush Upholstery, Rose, Mahogany, 8 3/4 X 13 3/4 In. 50.00
Footstool, Red Paint, White Striping, Pine, 20th Century, 6 In. 35.00
Footstool, Renaissance Revival, Walnut Base, Burl Apron, Round 105.00
Footstool, Shaker, Mt.Lebanon, Slanted Top, Bulbous Legs, C.1900 .... 300.00
Footstool, Traces Of Green, Pine, 6 1/4 X 13 1/2 In. 45.00
Footstool, Windsor, Country, Splayed Legs, Black Paint, 8 1/2 In. 90.00
Frame, Easel, Fretwork, Doors, Walnut, 10 X 6 1/2 In. 45.00
Frame, Floral, Calligraphic Design, Chinese, Painted, 16 1/4 In. 200.00
Frame, Gilded Vining Oak Leaf & Acorn, Pine, 12 5/8 X 15 In. 35.00
Frame, Mortised Corners, Old Glass, Cherry, 13 1/2 X 17 1/2 In. 85.00
Frame, Original Red Flame Graining, Poplar, 14 1/2 X 16 1/2 In. 120.00
Garden Seat, Chinese, Blue & White Porcelain, 19 In. 550.00
Garden Seat, England, 19th Century, Porcelain, 18 3/4 In. 200.00
Garden Seat, Green Paint, Wrought Iron & Steel, 4 Ft. 1875.00

Furniture, Lowboy, Queen Anne, Walnut, C.1710, 29 In.

Furniture, Highboy, George III, Mahogany, C.1780, 6 X 22 X 43 In.

Garden Seat, Oriental, Barrel Shape, Porcelain, 19 In.	1550.00
Hall Seat, 2 Carved Lion Panels, Lift Seat, Oak, C.1900, 42 In.	350.00
Hall Tree, Gnarled Sapling, Carved, Foliage, 5 Brass Hooks, 64 In.	115.00
Hall Tree, Mirror, Cast Iron	1500.00
Hall Tree, Paneled Beveled Mirror, 41 In. X 7 Ft.	675.00
Hall Tree, Renaissance Revival, Walnut, C.1865, 33 X 85 In.	350.00
Hall Tree, Umbrella Holder Each Side, Drip Pans, Walnut	550.00
Highboy, George III, Mahogany, C.1780, 6 X 22 X 43 In. ....*Illus*	1600.00
Highboy, Queen Anne, 7 Drawers, Cherry, 35 1/2 X 69 1/2 In.	2650.00
Highboy, Queen Anne, Cherrywood, 8 Drawers, 1750–56, 6 Ft.	6600.00
Highboy, Queen Anne, Green & Orange Lacquer, C.1850, 8 Ft.	7000.00
Highboy, Queen Anne, Maple, Flat Top, 3 Drawers, 61 In.	2000.00
Highboy, William & Mary, 5 Drawers, Walnut, C.1750, 67 1/2 In.	1400.00
Highboy, William & Mary, Herringbone Inlay, 5 Ft. 3 1/2 In.	9500.00
Highchair, Bow Back, Bamboo Turnings, Saddle Seat, Footrest	375.00
Highchair, Country, Black Repaint, 33 1/2 In.	85.00
Highchair, Ladder Back, 3 Back Slats, Woven Splint Seat, 37 In.	550.00
Highchair, Oak, Turns Into Stroller, Cane Bottom	245.00
Highchair, Victorian, Oak, 40 In.	120.00
Highchair, William & Mary, Open Back, Removable Guard, Walnut	1750.00
Highchair, Windsor, Bow Back, Plank Seat, Painted Green, C.1800	1900.00
Highchair, Windsor, Footrest, Yellow Striping, Bamboo, 35 1/2 In.	200.00
Huntboard, Pennsylvania, Tiger Maple & Walnut	3200.00
Huntboard, Queen Anne, Mahogany, Cabriole Legs, 68 X 20 In.	175.00
Hutch Table, Tilt Top, Pegged, Traces Of Red Paint, Early 1800s	2500.00
Hutch, Butternut, Pie Shelf, Scalloped, 19 1/2 X 49 X 6 Ft.7 In.	2250.00
Hutch, Pine, 3/4 Gallery Top, American, 2 Paneled Doors, 60 In.	650.00
Jardiniere, Louis XVI, Mahogany, 1 Drawer, 20 X 12 In.Diam.	1100.00
Jardiniere, Sarcophagus Form, Lined, Mahogany, C.1850, 24 In.	1900.00
Kas, 2 Piece, Removable Door, Floral Design, Scandinavia	850.00
Kas, Arched Panel Doors, Scrolled Apron, Poplar, 85 3/4 In.	725.00
Kas, Raised Panel Doors, Shelves & Open Space, Pine, 69 3/4 In.	750.00
Kas, Zoar, Ohio, Varnish Finish, Walnut, 51 1/2 X 76 In.	675.00
Keyholder, Renaissance Style, Oak, Ormolu Masks Door, 16 X 13 In.	300.00
Lectern, Louis XV, Walnut, Serpentine, 37 X 19 In.	350.00
Library Steps, Oak, Painted, 67 X 23 In.	320.00
Light Stand, Inlaid Silhouette, Hepplewhite	900.00
Linen Press, Carved In Salem Style, Mahogany, 54 X 93 In.	3300.00
Linen Press, Chippendale, Maple & Chestnut, C.1780, 6 Ft. 7 In.	8500.00
Linen Press, Hepplewhite, Applewood, Paneled Doors, 78 In., 2 Pc.	1900.00
Love Seat, Camelback, Rose Carved Crests, Walnut, 19th Century	275.00
Love Seat, Chippendale, Arched Upholstered Back, England, 35 In.	850.00

Love Seat, Finger Carved Serpentine Top, Walnut	400.00
Love Seat, George II, Upholstered In Gold Damask, Cabriole Legs	1250.00
Love Seat, Reed, Cane Set, Serpentine Roll On Back & Arms, C.1895	950.00
Lowboy, Chippendale, Mahogany, Acanthus, 3 Drawers, C.1770, 29 In.	2750.00
Lowboy, English, 1 Long, 3 Small Beaded Drawers, Oak, 18 1/2 In.	900.00
Lowboy, Pennsylvania, Mahogany, 28 In.	6300.00
Lowboy, Queen Anne, 3 Drawers, Walnut, 35 3/4 X 40 1/2 In.	1600.00
Lowboy, Queen Anne, Maple & Cherry, Connecticut, 18th Century	6875.00
Lowboy, Queen Anne, Massachusetts, Mahogany, C.1760, 34 X 30 In.	8250.00
Lowboy, Queen Anne, Walnut, C.1710, 29 In. ....*Illus*	4800.00
Magazine Rack, Carved & Cutout Welcome On Front	135.00
Mirror, 3 Inlaid Panels, Oyster Veneered Walnut, 24 1/2 X 41 In.	1750.00
Mirror, American Empire, Convex Girandole, 1820, 45 X 37 In.	4500.00
Mirror, American Empire, Gilded, C.1830, 54 X 27 In.	150.00
Mirror, Beveled, Oak Frame Panel, Peg Feet, 10 1/4 X 8 1/4 In.	60.00
Mirror, Bird's-Eye Maple, Parcel Gilt, 23 X 20 In.	150.00
Mirror, Bull's-Eye, Eagle On Top, C.1930, 19 1/2 X 19 1/2 In.	250.00
Mirror, Canted Molded Frame, Inlaid, Walnut Parquetry, 37 1/2 In.	1540.00
Mirror, Carved & Gilt Eagle On Crossed Cannons, 43 X 33 In.	1100.00
Mirror, Carved Leaf Tips, Pierced Cornice, Walnut, 38 In.	605.00
Mirror, Cheval, American, Cartouche Shaped, 19th Century, 76 In.	675.00
Mirror, Cheval, Classical, Mahogany, Crest, C.1815, 6 Ft. 10 In.	2550.00
Mirror, Cheval, England, Brass Arms, Candle Sockets, Walnut	850.00
Mirror, Cheval, Lion's Paw Casters, Mahogany, 5 Ft. 9 1/2 In.	660.00
Mirror, Cheval, Victorian, Rosewood, C.1850, 5 Ft. 10 In.	880.00
Mirror, Cheval, Victorian, Rosewood, Rococo, C.1850, 5 Ft.10 In.	880.00
Mirror, Chip Carved Maple Frame, 5 3/8 X 6 3/4 In.	215.00
Mirror, Chippendale, Jigsaw, Gilt Interior Edge, 41 X 20 In.	200.00
Mirror, Chippendale, Mahogany, Gesso, Crest, 43 X 23 In.	425.00
Mirror, Chippendale, Philadelphia, Mahogany & Gilt, C.1755, 56 In.	4000.00
Mirror, Chippendale, Scroll Top, Mahogany, Pine, 12 1/4 X 20 In.	200.00
Mirror, Chippendale, Scroll, Foliate Crest, C.1790, 33 In.	450.00
Mirror, Chippendale, Scroll, Old Glass, Cherry, 10 X 19 1/2 In.	250.00
Mirror, Courting, Black & Gold Paint, Pine Frame, 12 X 17 In.	200.00
Mirror, Dressing, Irish, Reverse Gilt Glass Studs, Oval, 32 In.	4700.00
Mirror, Dressing, Queen Anne, Gilt, Easel Back, Label, 13 1/2 In.	600.00
Mirror, Eagle Top, Chain Swag To Top Side Ornaments, 1807	3050.00
Mirror, Easel, Victorian, Nickel Plate, Ornate, 18 X 8 In.	95.00
Mirror, Egyptian Revival, Parcel Gilt, Fruitwood, 5 Ft.7 In.	1210.00
Mirror, Empire, Corner Blocks, Black & Gold, 10 5/8 X 12 3/4 In.	95.00
Mirror, Empire, Gilded Gesso Frame, Reverse Glass, 22 X 32 In.	90.00
Mirror, Empire, Reverse Paint Fruit Basket, 2-Part, 12 X 24 In.	225.00
Mirror, Empire, Split Turnings, Gilded & Black, 15 1/2 X 34 In.	385.00
Mirror, Federal, A.Kimbel & J.Cabus, Reverse Painted Ship	385.00
Mirror, Federal, Bird's-Eye Maple Pilasters, Acorn Drops, 35 In.	355.00
Mirror, Federal, Convex, Carved, Gessoed Floral, Eagle Top, 57 In.	850.00
Mirror, Federal, Inlaid Mahogany, Medallion, Swans, C.1800, 48 In.	700.00
Mirror, Federal, Reverse Glass, Cromwell's Bridge, 17 X 38 In.	225.00
Mirror, Floral Encrusted, Enameled, Sitzendorf, 22 5/8 In.	725.00
Mirror, George I, Carved Ground, England, C.1710, 21 3/4 X 40 In.	9800.00
Mirror, George I, Parcel Gilt Mahogany, 41 In.	150.00
Mirror, George II, Carved Scroll, Gilt Wood, Candle Arms, 39 In.	6700.00
Mirror, George II, Double Rectangular Plate, Mahogany, 5 Ft.	3100.00
Mirror, George II, Swan's Neck Cresting, Side Vines, Walnut, 5 Ft.	6100.00
Mirror, George III, Mahogany, Gilt Carved, Eagle, 47 X 28 In.	525.00
Mirror, Gesso & Grisaille Design, 18th Century, 20 X 62 In.	950.00
Mirror, Gilt & Gessoed, Foliate Crest, Sconce, Oval Plate, 59 In.	650.00
Mirror, Gilt Mahogany, John Elliott, Philadelphia, 1760, 46 In.	2550.00
Mirror, Gilt Phoenix, Carved & Gilt Sides, Mahogany, 42 X 23 In.	1200.00
Mirror, Green Tinted Glass, Abstract, French, C.1930, 11 In.	900.00
Mirror, Hall, Beveled Glass, Cameo Type Insert, Oak	95.00
Mirror, Italian Rococo, Arched, Floral Sprays, Frame, 5 Ft. 5 In.	2900.00
Mirror, Mahogany & Eglomise, C.1815, 41 X 22 In.	385.00
Mirror, Mahogany On Pine Frame, Cornice, 2-Part, 14 X 26 3/4 In.	70.00

Never store textiles on or in paper, cardboard, or unsealed wood. Store in unbleached muslin.

If you own a wicker chair that makes small popping noises when you sit in it, dampen it with water. It is too dry and can crack if not kept moist.

Furniture, Plant Stand,
Birdcage Holder, Wicker

Mirror, Mantel, Reverse Painted Glass, 52 1/2 X 41 In. 2800.00
Mirror, Neoclassical, Flowering Vines, Swag Draped, 3 Ft. 1325.00
Mirror, Neoclassical, Inlaid Mahogany, Bronze Holders, 34 In. 665.00
Mirror, Oak, Spindle Sided, C.1916, 33 1/2 X 40 1/2 In. 110.00
Mirror, Painted & Parcel Gilt, Vines, Draped Urn, 5 Ft. 3 In. 1300.00
Mirror, Pier, 3 Sizes, Frame, French, C.1925, 36 1/4 X 81 1/2 In. 2400.00
Mirror, Pier, German, Inlaid Mahogany, Sprays & Urns, 5 Ft. 4 In. 7000.00
Mirror, Pier, Marble Base, Carved Crest, Walnut, C.1850, 4 X 9 Ft. 4000.00
Mirror, Pier, Pierced & Scrolled Crest, 19th Century, 88 In. 100.00
Mirror, Pier, Renaissance Revival, Marble Shelf 400.00
Mirror, Pier, Revival, Matching Marble Top Base 800.00
Mirror, Pier, Verre Eglomise, Gilt Wood, Lozenge Edge, 7 Ft. 1 In. 4950.00
Mirror, Pine, Carved, Crest With Hole, Painted Black, 19 In. 1200.00
Mirror, Portrait Medallion, 18th Century, 4 Ft. 3 In. 990.00
Mirror, Queen Anne, Continental 450.00
Mirror, Queen Anne, Ogee Frame, Mahogany On Pine, 9 3/4 X 16 In. 175.00
Mirror, Queen Anne, Scalloped Top Crest, Pine, 14 X 24 1/2 In. 250.00
Mirror, Regency, Irish, Cut Glass Studs, 23 1/2 X 29 1/2 In. 3300.00
Mirror, Reverse Glass Painting, Houses, Yellow Edge, 21 3/4 In. 250.00
Mirror, Rococo, Gilt, Shell, Foliage, C.1880, 38 X 33 In. 90.00
Mirror, Scroll, Original Glass, C.1880, 13 3/4 X 22 1/2 In. 230.00
Mirror, Shaving, Bow Front, 3 Drawers, Urn Finials, Mahogany 85.00
Mirror, Shaving, Bow Front, Ebony Line Inlay, English, Mahogany 175.00
Mirror, Shaving, Federal, Curly Maple, Carved, 2 Drawers, 23 In. 1450.00
Mirror, Shaving, Hepplewhite, Mahogany, 5 Drawers, 26 X 30 In. 250.00
Mirror, Shaving, Victorian, Domed, Marble & Walnut Base, 28 In. 160.00
Mirror, Silver, Arched Crest, Allover Repousse, S.A., 35 X 24 In. 500.00
Mirror, Stripe Graining, Reverse Glass, 9 1/2 X 16 1/2 In. 160.00
Mirror, Table, Folding, Cast Brass, Rococo, 3-Part, 14 X 30 In. 75.00
Mirror, Table, French, Adjustable, Sockets, Malachite, 27 In. 1300.00
Mirror, Traveling, Scalloped Top, 5 X 10 In. 100.00
Mirror, William & Mary, England, Walnut, 1680, 14 X 16 In., Pair 300.00
Parlor Set, Continental, Ivory, Leather Upholstered, 3 Piece 4950.00
Parlor Set, Eastlake, Gilt Incised, Walnut, C.1880, 3 Piece 1550.00
Parlor Set, Eastlake, Walnut, 4 Piece 600.00
Parlor Set, Eastlake, Walnut, Carved, Gilt, C.1880, 3 Piece 1550.00
Parlor Set, Ivory & Quill, Late 19th Century, 3 Piece 4950.00
Parlor Set, Louis XIV, Shaw Furniture Co., Upholstered, 5 Piece 1400.00
Parlor Set, Renaissance Revival, Ebony, Sofa, 4 Chairs, C.1865 .... 875.00
Parlor Set, Rococo, Settee, 4 Armchairs, Upholstered Seat, Maple 600.00
Parlor Set, Victorian Renaissance, Upholstered, 3 Piece 425.00
Pastry Rack, French, Grilled Open Shelves, Brass & Iron, 84 In. 650.00

Pedestal, Baroque, Gilt Bronze Mounted, Wooden, 4 Ft.1 In., Pair 3300.00
Pedestal, Eastlake, Ebonized & Incised Painted, Oval Top, 40 In. 1550.00
Pedestal, Georgian, Mahogany, Reeded, Square Base, 70 In., Pair 400.00
Pedestal, German Renaissance, Walnut, C.1870, 23 X 46 1/2 In. 2400.00
Pedestal, Gothic, Oak, Fluted Frieze, Arched Columns, 47 1/2 In. 1300.00
Pedestal, Louis XVI, Henry Dasson, Mahogany, 1890, 42 1/4 In. 2750.00
Pedestal, Prunus Border, Marble Top, Teak, C.1900, 32 1/2 In. 400.00
Pedestal, Storage, Keyhole, Painted Top & Base, Walnut, 49 In., Pr. 1450.00
Pedestal, Victorian, Marble, Round Top, Column Support, 32 In. 200.00
Pew, Walnut, Portable, Horsehair, 19th Century, 11 1/2 In. 125.00
Piano Bench, Victorian, Ornate, Iron 75.00
Pie Safe, 2 Drawers, 2 Doors, 6 Pierced Tins, Gallery, 55 In. 235.00
Pie Safe, Original Pierced Tin, Walnut, 45 X 57 In. 650.00
Pie Safe, Pine, Door, Cream Over Blue Paint, 11 X 26 X 44 In. 150.00
Pie Safe, Poplar, 12 Punched Tin Panels, White Paint, 40 X 17 In. 350.00
Pie Safe, Poplar, Punched Tin Panels, Old Paint, 46 X 65 In. 650.00
Pie Safe, Star & Hearts Pattern, Walnut, C.1820, 43 X 57 In. 975.00
Plant Stand, Birdcage Holder, Wicker ....*Illus* 175.00
Planter, Reticulated Checkerboard Basket, Kohn, Mahogany, 34 In. 1540.00
Planter, Shaw Furniture Co., Rectangular, Lacquered, 48 X 37 In. 175.00
Plat Bureau, Louis XV, Tulipwood, Kingwood, 31 In. X 4 Ft. 9 In. 3300.00
Plat Bureau, Louis XV, Tulipwood, Parquetry, 30 In. X 5 Ft. 3100.00
Plate Rack, Gustav Stickley, C.1904, 28 X 48 In. 1700.00
Pole Screen, Florals, Federal 225.00
Pole Screen, Needlework Called Hatchment 6050.00
Pool Table, Brunswick, Balke, Baby Grand, 1914, 4 X 7 Ft. 4000.00
Pool Table, Brunswick, Balke, Inlaid Rosewood, 1880, 9 Ft. 2 In. 2500.00
Pool Table, Brunswick, Carved, Walnut, 1905, 4 1/2 X 9 Ft. 6500.00
Pool Table, Brunswick, Inlaid Bird's-Eye Maple, 1880s, 4 X 8 Ft. 7500.00
Pool Table, Brunswick, Inlaid, Rosewood, 1880s, 4 X 8 Ft. 5500.00
Pool Table, Brunswick, Walnut Inlay, Iron, C.1845, 4 X 8 Ft. 16500.00
Porch Set, Rattan, 2 Chairs, 2 End Tables, Couch, Plant Stand 600.00
Porch Set, Rattan, Settee, Chairs, Table, Lamp, Philippine, 7 Piece 950.00
Porch Set, Wicker, White Paint, Armchair, Rocker & Center Table 200.00
Porch Swing, Oak, Gustav Stickley, C.1906 .... 18000.00
Potty Chair, Pine, Teddy Bear Decals 30.00
Potty Chair, Scalloped Back, Mortised Seat, Walnut, 15 1/2 In. 95.00
Potty Chair, Windsor, Spindle Back, Design 50.00
Rack, Cup, Hooks, Slot, Grape Design, Woodburned, 1912, 20 In. 30.00
Rack, Hanging, Hand Carved Griffin, Walnut, 12 1/2 X 21 In. 85.00
Rack, Shaving Mug, Walnut, Holds 50 Mugs 1750.00
Rack, Spoon, Primitive, Scalloped On Ends, 43 1/2 X 6 1/4 In. 150.00
Rack, Towel, 5 Bars, Folds Down, Walnut, Extends 39 In. 45.00
Rack, Wall, Magazine, Bent Twigs & Limbs 45.00
Rocker, Child's, Arms, Spindle Back, Plank Seat, 20 1/4 In. 40.00
Rocker, Child's, Ladder Back, Rush Seat 160.00
Rocker, Child's, Painted Design 395.00
Rocker, Child's, Painted, Crest, Spindle Back, Bamboo Turned Legs 50.00
Rocker, Child's, Shaker, Original Finish & Seat 1400.00
Rocker, Child's, Shoe-Fly, Oak, 1900s 65.00
Rocker, Child's, Thonet, Bentwood, C.1910 .... 125.00
Rocker, Child's, Thumb Back, Windsor 120.00
Rocker, Comb Back, Arms, Conch Shell Design 525.00
Rocker, Ladder Back, Arms, Rush Seat, 5 Graduated Slats 175.00
Rocker, Ladder Back, Arms, Splint Seat, Traces Of Old Paint 55.00
Rocker, Ladder Back, Arms, Woven Splint Seat 65.00
Rocker, Ladder Back, Finials, Black Paint Over Red Wash, 47 In. 275.00
Rocker, Limbert, Arms, Back Slat, Curved Arms, Cushion Seat, 34 In. 400.00
Rocker, Limbert, Slat Sided, C.1912, 41 In. 300.00
Rocker, Lincoln, Mahogany, Upholstered Back & Arms, 1850-70 .... 150.00
Rocker, Mission, Oak, Slat Back, Cushion, C.1910, 35 X 25 In. 150.00
Rocker, Oak, Barrel Shaped, Cushion Seat, C.1915, 31 1/2 X 24 In. 350.00
Rocker, Oak, Tall Back, 5 Vertical Slats, Open Arms, 40 In. 125.00
Rocker, Platform, Huntzinger, Turned, Upholstered, 43 1/2 In. 300.00

Furniture, Screen, 2–Panel, Pewter,
Embossed, Art Nouveau, Floral

Furniture, Secretary Bookcase,
Mahogany, 88 X 37 X 19 In.

Rocker, Platform, Leather Seat & Armrest, Mission Oak 625.00
Rocker, Quadruple Tiered Comb Back, John Saxton 1100.00
Rocker, Red, Black Grain, Yellow Striping, Crest, Rush Seat, Small 25.00
Rocker, Rush Slip Seat, Refinished, Light, Gustav Stickley, 34 In. 155.00
Rocker, Shaker, 3 Slats, Stamped F.W., Watervliet 1550.00
Rocker, Shaker, 4 Slats, Shawl Bar, Mt.Lebanon 1595.00
Rocker, Shaker, Arm Rope Twist Turnings, Plush Seat, Cloth Back 250.00
Rocker, Shaker, Bird's–Eye Maple, Old Finish 5500.00
Rocker, Shaker, Elder's, Maple, Ash Splint Seat, C.1815, 46 In. 4000.00
Rocker, Shaker, Eldress's, Sabbathday Lake, 4 Slats 3500.00
Rocker, Shaker, Ladder Back, 3–Slat, Turned Finial, Dark, Reed Seat 300.00
Rocker, Shaker, Maple, Chrome Yellow Paint, Taped Seat, 1850 .... 1400.00
Rocker, Shaker, Maple, Original Dark Finish, Taped Seat, 16 In. 750.00
Rocker, Shaker, Mt.Lebanon, Bentwood 150.00
Rocker, Shaker, Sister's, 3 Slats, Maple, C.1820, 15 1/2 In. 325.00
Rocker, Tall Back, Slat Sided, Gustav Stickley, 41 In. 550.00
Rocker, Wicker, Rolled Crest, Arms, Scrolls, American, 39 1/2 In. 250.00
Rocker, Windsor, John Saxton, Shelburne, Vermont 1100.00
Rocker, Windsor, Plank Seat, Medallion In Cage Back, Bamboo 200.00
Salon Set, Louis XVI, Needlepoint Upholstered, 3 Piece 1100.00
Screen, 2–Panel, Cherry Tree Painted, Gold Japan, 64 X 70 In. 400.00
Screen, 2–Panel, Pewter, Embossed, Art Nouveau, Floral ....*Illus* 400.00
Screen, 2–Panel, Table, Lacquered, Ivory Frame, Japan, 19th Century 475.00
Screen, 3–Panel, George II, Mirrors, Fretwork, 72 In. 500.00
Screen, 3–Panel, Gustav Stickley, Oak, C.1913, 66 In. 6000.00
Screen, 4–Panel, Coromandel, Lacquer, Courtier, Scene, 94 In. 5500.00
Screen, 4–Panel, Louis XV, Beveled Glass Lattice, Cream Paint 400.00
Screen, 4–Panel, Mahogany Frame, Pleated Damask, 69 In. 180.00
Screen, 4–Panel, Near Eastern, Carved Floral, 18 1/2 X 74 In. 425.00
Screen, 5–Panel, Hunt Scene, Wallpaper, 72 X 22 In.Panel 475.00
Screen, 6–Panel, Japanese, Silver Squares, Silk Border, 65 In. 3500.00
Screen, 6–Panel, Japanese, Trees, Floral, Late 17th Century, 65 In. 2400.00
Screen, 8–Panel, Chinese, Gilt, Black Lacquer, 6 Ft.3 1/2 In. 11500.00
Screen, Beveled Glass Panels, Glazed, Giltwood, C.1900, 65 In. 500.00
Screen, Pole, Mahogany, Tripod Base, Needlepoint, 64 1/2 In. 100.00
Screen, Pole, Tapered Form, Oval Painted Panel, Mahogany, Pair 990.00
Seat, Windsor, Bow Back, Upholstered, Rhode Island, C.1780, 36 In. 600.00
Secretary Bookcase, 13–Pane Doors, Pollard Oak, 7 Ft.1 In. 3000.00
Secretary Bookcase, Adjustable Shelves, Mahogany, 7 Ft. 8 In. 6600.00
Secretary Bookcase, Federal, Mahogany, Maple, C.1810, 6 Ft.4 In. 2300.00
Secretary Bookcase, Mahogany, 88 X 37 X 19 In. ....*Illus* 4250.00
Secretary Bookcase, New York, Carved Mahogany, C.1790, 7 Ft. 3500.00
Secretary Cabinet, 12–Pane Doors, Arched Cornice, Mahogany, 7 Ft. 3100.00
Secretary Cabinet, 13–Pane Doors, Mahogany, 7 Ft. 4950.00

Secretary Cabinet, Beveled Glass Mirror, 3 Drawers 300.00
Secretary Cabinet, Brass Rim, Cupboard Doors, Rosewood, 44 In. 6600.00
Secretary, Bonnet Top, 2 Doors, Gothic Arch Windows, Mahogany 2100.00
Secretary, Bow Front, Slant Lid, American 4200.00
Secretary, Child's, Cubbyholes, Grained Drawers, 27 3/4 In. 950.00
Secretary, Country, Cherry, Cock–Beaded, Pencil Date 1784, 43 In. 2300.00
Secretary, Country, Slant Lid, Poplar, Red Paint, 43 X 85 In. 1400.00
Secretary, Cylinder, Eastlake, Walnut, 44 1/2 X 92 1/2 In. 1100.00
Secretary, Federal, Mahogany, Tracery, String Inlay, 2–Part, 81 In. 1300.00
Secretary, Federal, New England, Mahogany, C.1820, 13 X 29 1/2 In. 1700.00
Secretary, Glazed Doors, 3 Upper Shelves, Walnut, 44 1/2 X 89 In. 2500.00
Secretary, Louis XVI, Fruitwood Parquetry, Kingwood, 18th Century 2600.00
Secretary, Marquetry, Continental, 2 Glass Doors, Inlaid, 63 In. 750.00
Secretary, Oriental, Fall Front, Landscape Scene, Lacquer, 57 In. 250.00
Secretary, Ormolu, Ebony, Boullework, France, 67 1/2 X 43 X 19 In. 1900.00
Secretary, Pine, Country, Inscribed 30 June, 1864, 66 1/2 In. 350.00
Secretary, Queen Anne, Chinoiserie Design, England, C.1750 .... 2500.00
Secretary, School Master's, Grain Painted, Pine, C.1800, 61 In. 1200.00
Secretary, Sheraton, Blind Door, Satinwood Panels 2250.00
Secretary, Stepback, Freight Office, Old Green Paint, Dated 1860 .... 2500.00
Secretary, Traveling, Slant Front, Ivory Trim, 20 1/2 X 12 In. 4950.00
Secretary, Victorian, Walnut, Cutout Base, 9 Pigeon Holes 2495.00
Server, Brass Gallery, 2 Drawers, Mahogany, Kittinger 450.00
Server, Marble Top, Molded Mirror, Walnut, English, 1800x, 66 In. 700.00
Server, Mirror, Cock–Beaded Drawers, 20th Century, 30 1/2 In. 275.00
Server, Sheraton, Curly Maple, Bow Front, 1 Drawer, 41 1/2 In. 375.00
Server, Victorian, Carved Oak, Marble, 2 Drawers, Paw Feet, 46 In. 500.00
Serving Stand, Hepplewhite, Grain Painted Design, 19th Century 1400.00
Settee, 3 Arched Crests, Vase Form Splat, Pa., C.1845, 23 In. 2000.00
Settee, Arched Upholstered Backrest, Carved Mahogany, 5 1/2 Ft. 2750.00
Settee, Empire, Mahogany, Serpent Legs, Claw Feet, C.1830 .... 450.00
Settee, Empire, Paw Feet, Velvet Upholstery, Cherry, 57 1/2 In. 550.00
Settee, Federal, Mahogany, Upholstered, Turned Legs, 1815, 60 In. 8250.00
Settee, Foliate Carved Crest, Serpentine Apron, Walnut, 59 In. 300.00
Settee, Four Chairback, Regency, Mahogany, 68 In. ....*Illus* 2000.00
Settee, French Style, Victorian, Upholstered, C.1880, 42 X 67 In. 300.00
Settee, Garden, Cast Iron, Bent Branch Form, 33 X 35 X 20 In. 550.00
Settee, George III, Green Upholstery, Shell Cabriole Legs, Pair 1400.00
Settee, George III, Mahogany, 3–Arched Crest, Upholstered 4500.00
Settee, George III, Mahogany, Upholstered Backrest, 5 Ft. 2000.00
Settee, Italian Rococo, Upholstered Back, Seat, Painted, 5 Ft. 715.00
Settee, Mahogany, Stickley, Slat Back, Leather Seat, 46 X 24 In. 525.00
Settee, Neoclassical, Mahogany, Ormolu, Caryatid Arm Support 2500.00
Settee, New England, Rolled Arms, Red Paint Traces, C.1800, 81 In. 800.00

Furniture, Settee, Four Chairback, Regency, Mahogany, 68 In.

Furniture, Settee, Porch Set, Rattan,
7 Piece Set, 56 X 32 1/2 In.

Settee, Original Leather Cushion Seat, Stickley, Brown Patina 1950.00
Settee, Pine, Provincial, Rounded Back, Scrolled Holds, 62 In. 1800.00
Settee, Porch Set, Rattan, 7 Piece Set, 56 X 32 1/2 In. ....*Illus* 950.00
Settee, Queen Anne, Backrest, Upholstered, Walnut, 46 In. 1100.00
Settee, Renaissance Revival, Medallion Back, Tufted, 63 In. 275.00
Settee, Rococo Revival, Mahogany, Carved Rose Crest, Cabriole Leg 300.00
Settee, Round Arch Crest, Pine, Maple, Blue Paint, C.1820, 50 In. 550.00
Settee, Sheraton, Carved Cornucopia, Claw Feet 1320.00
Settee, Walnut, Spool Legs, Cushion Seat, 6 Ft. 295.00
Settee, Wicker, Arched Crest, Caned Back, Cushions, 39 X 73 In. 300.00
Settee, Windsor, Scroll Knuckle Hold, Plank Seat, 7 Ft. 6600.00
Settle, Concave Form, Paneled Back, Walnut, Pine, 5 Ft.10 In. 1000.00
Settle, Empire, Arrow Back, Bulbous Arm, Black Repaint, 75 1/2 In. 375.00
Settle, Gustav Stickley, Paneled, C.1912, 84 X 29 X 36 In. 9000.00
Settle, Hall, Gustav Stickley, Oak, Vertical Slats, 30 X 56 In. 2100.00
Settle, Lift Top, Carved, English, 47 1/2 X 36 X 17 3/4 In. 375.00
Settle, Mission, Oak, Back Slats, Cushion Seat, C.1910, 30 X 67 In. 800.00
Settle, Oak, Gustav Stickley, C.1907, 36 X 79 In. 6700.00
Settle, Plank Seat, Scrolled Arms, Vase Splats, 82 In. 400.00
Settle, Provincial, Painted Oak, Plank Seat, 65 X 73 1/2 In. 1900.00
Settle, Sheraton, Acorn Finials, Rush Seat, 79 In. 550.00
Sewing Stand, Drop Leaf, 2 Drawers, Mahogany 250.00
Shaving Stand, Drawer, Circular Cutout For Bowl, Finial Legs 245.00
Shaving Stand, Victorian, Walnut & Rosewood 675.00
Shelf, 4 Open Shelves, Walnut, Fruitwood, Hanging, 4 Ft.5 In. 715.00
Shelf, Brown Sponge Design On Ocher, Hanging, C.1840, 28 In. 750.00
Shelf, Central Bull's-Eye Mirror, Parasol Rack, Hanging, C.1800 .... 425.00
Shelf, Pine, Mahogany Graining, Hanging, English, 57 X 62 In. 230.00
Shelf, Pine, Painted, Spindle Frame, Hanging, 30 X 8 X 40 In. 250.00
Shelf, Shaker, Cherry, 4 Tenoned Shelves, 30 X 24 X 6 3/4 In. 750.00
Sideboard, American, Marble Top, Ebonized, C.1865, K19 X 43 In. 350.00
Sideboard, Bow Front, 1 Center Drawer, Inlaid Mahogany, 7 Ft. 5225.00
Sideboard, Bow Front, 1 Drawer, Cellaret, Mahogany, 6 Ft. X 35 In. 1450.00
Sideboard, Bow Front, Acanthus Inlay, Cellaret Drawer, C.1790 .... 8800.00
Sideboard, Bow Front, George III, Medallions, Mahogany, 33 In. 8250.00
Sideboard, Demilune, 3 Drawers, Paine Furniture, 42 In. 75.00
Sideboard, Eastlake, 2 Shelves Above 2 Drawers, Oak 350.00
Sideboard, Eastlake, Center Mirror, Side Shelves, Walnut, C.1880 .... 160.00
Sideboard, Federal, Acanthus Carved Columns, 1820–40, 6 Ft.2 In. 2425.00
Sideboard, Federal, Mahogany, 2 Wine Wells, Beading, 41 X 67 In. 575.00
Sideboard, Federal, Mahogany, Veneer, Reeded Columns, 42 X 73 In. 4000.00
Sideboard, Federal, Splashback Bow Front, Mahogany, 79 In. 400.00
Sideboard, Federal, Stringed Outline, Mahogany, 66 X 40 1/2 In. 375.00
Sideboard, George III, Mahogany, Concave Front, 35 3/4 X 109 In. 1000.00
Sideboard, George III, Serpentine Front, Frieze Drawer, Mahogany 8250.00
Sideboard, George III, Serpentine Front, Mahogany, 4 Ft. 8 In. 6600.00
Sideboard, George III, Side Door, Inlaid Mahogany, 36 3/4 In. 2875.00
Sideboard, Gustav Stickley, Oak, 3 Small Drawers, Long Drawer 550.00
Sideboard, Gustav Stickley, Oak, C.1902, 44 X 60 X 24 In. 1900.00
Sideboard, Hepplewhite, D Shape, 3 Drawers, Side Doors, 5 1/2 Ft. 3000.00
Sideboard, Limbert, Oak, Mirror, 2 Drawers, No.1456, 52 1/2 In. 700.00
Sideboard, Limbert, Oak, Mirror, 4 Drawers, C.1905, 47 1/2 X 60 In. 1650.00
Sideboard, Mahogany, Bow Front, 3 Drawers, 3 Carved Doors, 38 In. 200.00
Sideboard, Mirror, 3 Drawers, Angular Cornice, 59 X 69 X 22 In. 500.00
Sideboard, Oak, Gustav Stickley, Arched Apron, 1910, 48 X 54 In. 500.00
Sideboard, Regency, 3–Tiered Mirror, England, 19th Century 1500.00
Sideboard, Serpentine Front, Inlay, Mahogany, 27 1/2 X 42 In. 5400.00
Sideboard, Stickley Bros., Oak, 2 Doors, C.1912, 46 X 54 In. 375.00
Sideboard, Stickley, Oak, 3 Drawers, C.1907, 49 X 66 X 24 In. 850.00
Sofa, American, Horsehair Upholstery, Mahogany, C.1830, 14 1/2 In. 650.00
Sofa, Belter, Recamier, Laminated Rosewood, C.1855 .... 2200.00
Sofa, Carved Camelback, Down Cushion, Brocade Cover 1900.00
Sofa, Chinese, Ivory & Wood Inlay, Camphor, Sandalwood, C.1830 .... 7500.00
Sofa, Classical, Mahogany, Bird's–Eye Maple, C.1825, 6 Ft. 3100.00

Sofa, Country, Turned Leg, Rolled Arm, 19th Century	550.00
Sofa, Empire, Carved Full–Bodied Swans On Each End	1200.00
Sofa, Federal, Inlaid Mahogany, Curving Arms, 51 In.	715.00
Sofa, Federal, Mahogany Inlaid, Arched, C.1810, 74 In.	2400.00
Sofa, Federal, Mahogany, Scrolled Arms, Pineapple Supports, 75 In.	500.00
Sofa, Federal, Mahogany, Square, Upholstered, C.1815, 33 X 78 In.	1850.00
Sofa, Flame Birch Panels, Upholstered, C.1810, 6 Ft. 3 In.	3850.00
Sofa, Hepplewhite Style, 1950s, 31 X 72 X 31 In. ....*Illus*	275.00
Sofa, Hepplewhite, Kittinger, 31 X 72 X 31 In.	300.00
Sofa, Hepplewhite, Mahogany, Satinwood, C.1790, 26 1/2 X 69 In.	2600.00
Sofa, Medallion Back, American, Serpentine Seat, Walnut, 62 In.	300.00
Sofa, Oval Medallion Back, Scroll Arm, American, Walnut, 61 In.	425.00
Sofa, Queen Anne, Double Arched Upholstered Back, 45 In.	600.00
Sofa, Recamier, Belter, Rosewood, Rococo, Upholstered, C.1855	2200.00
Sofa, Recamier, Classical, Mahogany, Brass, 1825, 6 Ft. 7 In.	5500.00
Sofa, Rococo Revival, Walnut, Carved Crest,, 39 1/4 X 71 1/2 In.	225.00
Sofa, Serpentine Upholstered Back, Seat & Arms, Mahogany, C.1810	2475.00
Stand, 1 Drawer, 1–Board Top, Walnut, 17 1/4 X 28 1/4 In.	160.00
Stand, 1 Drawer, Cock–Beaded, Hepplewhite, Cherry, 27 3/4 In.	350.00
Stand, 1 Drawer, Curly Cherry, Pennsylvania, 22 1/4 X 31 In.	95.00
Stand, 1 Drawer, Dovetailed, 2–Board Top, Cherry, 17 X 29 In.	200.00
Stand, 1 Drawer, Dovetailed, Black Over Red, Cherry, 29 1/2 In.	175.00
Stand, 1 Drawer, Dovetailed, Curly Maple, 28 1/2 In.	320.00
Stand, 1 Drawer, Dovetailed, Maple Legs, Cherry, 19 X 20 X 29 In.	250.00
Stand, 1 Drawer, Empire, Curly Maple, 2–Board Top, 20 In.	170.00
Stand, 1 Drawer, Hepplewhite, Black & Red Graining, 29 In.	395.00
Stand, 1 Drawer, Nail Construction, Brown Over Green, Pine, 29 In.	200.00
Stand, 1 Drawer, Ogee Front, Cherry, 19 X 19 X 29 In.	250.00
Stand, 1 Drawer, Open Shelf, Polychrome & Gilt, 23 In.	85.00
Stand, 1 Drawer, Walnut, Turned Legs, Yellow Paint, 21 X 27 In.	25.00
Stand, 2 Drawers Rounded, Swirled Pulls, Curly Maple, 28 1/2 In.	500.00
Stand, 2 Drawers, Cock–Beaded, 1–Board Mahogany Top, 29 3/4 In.	250.00
Stand, 2 Drawers, Dovetailed, Cherry, Beading, 18 X 18 3/4 In.	250.00
Stand, 2 Drawers, Drop Leaf, Flame Mahogany Veneer, 29 1/2 In.	175.00
Stand, 2 Drawers, Drop Leaf, Massachusetts, Mahogany, C.1810	950.00
Stand, 2 Drawers, Hepplewhite, Original Brasses, Birch, 31 1/2 In.	700.00
Stand, 3 Drawers, Empire, Carved Feet, Mahogany	250.00
Stand, 3 Drawers, Gustav Stickley, Drop Leaf, C.1904, 28 X 16 In.	700.00
Stand, 3 Drawers, Turned Legs, Cutout Corners, Curly Maple	825.00
Stand, Adirondack, Hearts, Black & Gold Paint, Cloth, 32 X 13 In.	90.00
Stand, Banded Inlay At Apron, Drawer, Walnut, 22 3/4 X 29 In.	285.00
Stand, Cherry, Turned Legs, Drawer, Board Top, Red, 20 3/4 In.	200.00
Stand, Chinese, Huang–Huali, Carved, Marble, Beaded Border, 17 In.	425.00
Stand, Curly Maple Apron & Drawer, Old Red, Maple, 30 In.	375.00

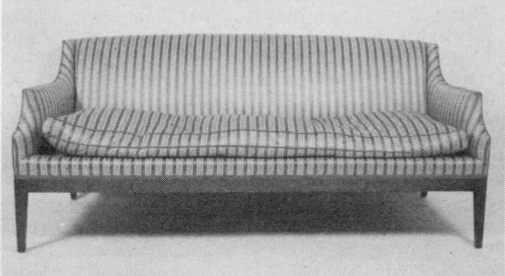

Furniture, Sofa, Hepplewhite Style, 1950s, 31 X 72 X 31 In.

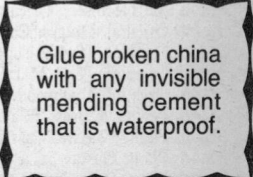

Glue broken china with any invisible mending cement that is waterproof.

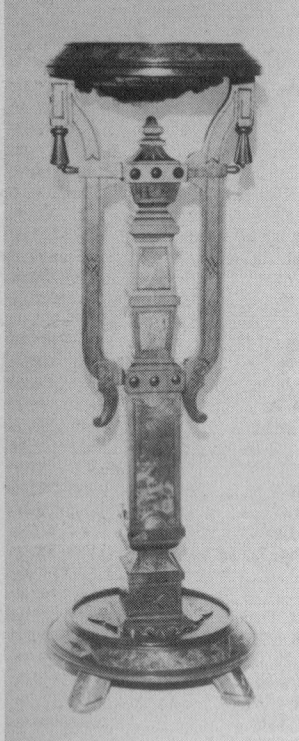

Furniture, Stand, Fern, Walnut, C.1880

Cigarette burns on wooden furniture are difficult to conceal. Rub the burn with scratch-cover polish. If that does not help, rub the burn with a paste of rottenstone (found in most hardware stores) and linseed oil.

If the name "England" (or that of some other country) appears, the dish was made after 1891, but it may have been made as early as 1887. The words "made in England" (or some other country) indicate the piece was made after 1914.

If you want to remove a grease stain from silk, wool, or paper, cover it with grated chalk. Cover the chalk with a piece of a brown paper bag. Use a warm iron on the paper. Repeat if necessary. Be sure the iron is not too hot to scorch the paper.

Stand, Curly Maple Drawer, Rope Carved Legs, Cherry, 27 1/2 In.	200.00
Stand, Empire, Ovolo Corners, Fluted Columns, Mahogany, C.1840	650.00
Stand, Empire, Rope Legs, Burl Inlay, Bird's-Eye Veneer, 28 In.	450.00
Stand, Fern, Walnut, C.1880 ....*Illus*	600.00
Stand, Hepplewhite, Drawer, Original Black & Red Graining, 29 In.	395.00
Stand, Inlay Stringing, Randolph, Vermont, Cherry, 18 1/2 X 28 In.	525.00
Stand, Knitting, Country, Maple, Basket, Spool Turned, 26 In.	50.00
Stand, L Drawer, Cock-Beaded, Hepplewhite, Walnut, 20 1/2 In.	175.00
Stand, Magazine, Limbert, Oak, 4 Shelves, Branded, 1912, 37 X 16 In.	350.00
Stand, Marble Insert, Oriental, Fretwork Apron, Teakwood, 19 In.	150.00
Stand, Oriental, Dragon Carved Apron, 30 1/4 In.	150.00
Stand, Oriental, Marble Top, Sunflower Apron, 19 In.	175.00
Stand, Oriental, Teak, Marble Top, Paw Feet	350.00
Stand, Oriental, Teakwood, Marble, Carved, China, 32 X 21 1/2 In.	400.00
Stand, Pewter & Brass Inlay, England, Mahogany, C.1900, 38 In.	95.00
Stand, Plant, 12 Arm, Cast Iron, 19th Century, 34 In.	5500.00
Stand, Plant, Gustav Stickley, Grueby Tile, C.1902	7800.00
Stand, Plant, Oak, Gustav Stickley, C.1912, Logo, 16 X 12 X 12 In.	150.00
Stand, Plant, Round, Stickley Bros., 30 X 14 In.Diam.Top	90.00
Stand, Plant, Victorian, 12 Arms, 34 In.	550.00
Stand, Poplar Top, Cherry, Signed, 19 X 21 1/2 X 28 3/4 In.	275.00
Stand, Sewing, 2-Tier Top, Finial For Pincushion, Mahogany, 14 In.	95.00

Stand, Sewing, Cloth Pouch, Sheraton	5800.00
Stand, Sewing, George III, Mahogany, Schmieg & Kotzian, 29 In.	375.00
Stand, Shaker, Pine & Poplar, Natural, Tapered Leg, 30 X 21 In.	350.00
Stand, Smoking, Art Deco, Chrome & Slag Glass	125.00
Stand, Square Top, Rounded Corners, Reeded Legs, Golden Mahogany	1100.00
Stand, Teakwood, Marble, Carved, Pierced Apron, China, 14 X 33 In.	275.00
Stand, Telephone, Oak, Stool, Swing Phone Rest, 18 X 30 In.	280.00
Stool, Bench, Floral Needlepoint Seat Cover, 1930s	18.00
Stool, Bleach Board Top, Natural, 4 Legs, 10 X 20 X 10 In.	75.00
Stool, Cherry, Classical, Upholstered, C.1820, 19 In., Pair	2100.00
Stool, George I, Upholstered, Serpentine Rails, Walnut, C.1725	1550.00
Stool, Gilded Ball & Claw Footed, French Style, Pair	2100.00
Stool, Joint, Stretcher Base, Flamestitch Cover	375.00
Stool, Joint, William & Mary, England, 17th Century, 20 1/4 In.	375.00
Stool, Milking, Shaker, Hancock, Mass., 12 In.	1100.00
Stool, Milking, Shaker, Maple, Natural, Handle, 13 X 16 X 11 In.	250.00
Stool, Piano, Brass Ring, Brass Inlay, Tripod	150.00
Stool, Piano, Empire, Heavily Carved	1210.00
Stool, Piano, Iron Legs With Lady's Head On Each	85.00
Stool, Piano, Italian Rococo, Walnut, Revolving, Shell Seat, C.1890	1300.00
Stool, Poplar, Brown Paint, Bootjack Ends, 16 In.	200.00
Stool, Queen Anne, Walnut, Upholstered Seat, 18 X 22 X 16 In.	300.00
Stool, Shaker, Maple, Turned Seat, 3 Legs, 12 X 8 1/2 In.	1000.00
Stool, Shoeshine, Leather Covered, Double Seat, Drawers	2500.00
Stool, Soda Fountain, Porcelain, White, Revolving Seat, Brass Foot	65.00
Stool, Tavern, English Oak, Mark Rowe & Son, 30 In., Set Of 4	160.00
Stool, Tudor Style, Lift Top, Carved Oak, 24 X 20 In.	20.00
Stool, Turned & Carved Stretchers, Mahogany, 22 X 15 X 17 In.	800.00
Stool, Victorian, 5 Carved Cabriole Legs	45.00
Stool, Windsor, Saddle Seat, 3 Legs, Tulip Design, W.Steeley	160.00
Table & Chair, Child's, Gustav Stickely, Leather Seat	550.00
Table & Desk, Dressing, Inlaid Rosewood, Hinged Spring Activated	9900.00
Table, 2 Drawers In Apron, Leaves, Walnut, 37 3/4 X 45 3/4 In.	775.00
Table, 3 Leaves, Spoon Carved Fringe, Pedestal, Gold Oak, 72 In.	5800.00
Table, Adjustable, Shaker, Tilt Top, Spider Legs, 36 X 24 In.	3300.00
Table, Architect's, Louis XVI, Mahogany, Brass, Hinged Top, 26 In.	2200.00
Table, Architect's, T.Wilson, London, Mahogany, C.1830, 34 1/2 In.	1300.00
Table, Architect's, Triple Top, Red Walnut, 33 X 29 1/2 In.	4700.00
Table, Art Deco, Walnut, Chrome & Glass Base, 1930, 49 X 27 In.	650.00
Table, Banquet, 3 Pedestals, 2 Inlaid Leaves, C.1790, Open 14 Ft.	16000.00
Table, Banquet, 3-Part, Engish D End, Georgian Style, Mahogany	3750.00
Table, Banquet, Hepplewhite, Mahogany, Opens To 44 3/4 X 83 In.	800.00
Table, Banquet, Louis XV, Walnut, Gilt, 3-Part, 156 X 39 1/2 In.	900.00
Table, Bedside, Italian, Walnut, 1 Drawer, 1780, 15 In.	450.00
Table, Bedside, Pierced Gallery, Lift Handles, Mahogany, 32 In.	1210.00
Table, Bombe, Bronze Dore Mounts, Marquetry, Rosewood, C.1880	9000.00
Table, Bow Front, Shell Inlaid, Mahogany, C.1790, 29 1/2 In.	775.00
Table, Breakfast, Bombay Ebony Crossbanded, Mahogany, C.1775	9500.00
Table, Breakfast, Drop Leaf, Empire, Mahogany, 1825, 38 X 25 In.	350.00
Table, Breakfast, Duncan Phyfe Style, End Drawer, Brass	375.00
Table, Breakfast, Federal, Cherry, Drop Ends, American, 1830, 29 In.	475.00
Table, Breakfast, George III, Mahogany, C.1820, 28 X 60 X 43 In.	1300.00
Table, Breakfast, Inlaid Satinwood, Mahogany, C.1810, 4 1/2 Ft.	4125.00
Table, Breakfast, Mother-Of-Pearl Inlay, Black Lacquer, Round	2200.00
Table, Breakfast, Reeded Edge, 4 Tapering Legs, Mahogany, C.1800	880.00
Table, Breakfast, Regency, Baluster Stem, Mahogany, 4 Ft. 3 In.	2550.00
Table, Breakfast, Round Top, Inlaid Mahogany, C.1800, 28 In.	1200.00
Table, Breakfast, Tilt Top, Brass Casters, C.1790, 54 X 38 In.	2995.00
Table, Butterfly Leaf Corners, Pedestal Base, Marble Top, C.1870	150.00
Table, Card, American, Curved Sides, Mahogany, 1795, 30 1/2 In.	1100.00
Table, Card, Banding, Serpentine Apron, Mahogany, 35 X 38 In.	625.00
Table, Card, Bowed Apron, Beaded Drawer, Cherry, 36 X 29 1/2 In.	930.00
Table, Card, Chippendale, Pine, Birch, Natural, Traces Of Red Paint	795.00
Table, Card, David Webb, Mass., Mahogany & Satinwood, C.1800	6600.00

Table, Card, Duncan Phyfe, Mahogany, Brass Paw Caps, 36 1/4 18 In. 150.00
Table, Card, Empire, Mahogany, Spandrels, Brass Paw Feet, 36 In. 200.00
Table, Card, Empire, Serpentine Apron, Swing Top, 33 1/2 X 29 In. 625.00
Table, Card, Federal, Inlaid Edge, Mahogany, 36 1/4 X 29 1/2 In. 350.00
Table, Card, Federal, Inlaid Mahogany & Cherrywood, C.1800, 30 In. 1320.00
Table, Card, Federal, Mahogany Inlay, Curved Top, 1790, 35 In. 2500.00
Table, Card, Federal, Mahogany, Demilune, Peck & Hills, 36 X 18 In. 300.00
Table, Card, Federal, Mahogany, Flip Top, Brass Paw Feet, 36 In. 150.00
Table, Card, Federal, North Shore, Mass., Mahogany, C.1815 .... 950.00
Table, Card, Federal, Shaped Top, American, Mahogany, 35 3/4 In. 225.00
Table, Card, Federal, String Inlay, Mahogany, C.1795, 29 1/4 In. 1000.00
Table, Card, Flame Birch Veneer Panels, Cuffed Feet 2200.00
Table, Card, Georgian, Walnut, 18th Century, 32 3/4 X 16 1/2 In. 800.00
Table, Card, Hepplewhite, Country, Bellflower Inlay 5500.00
Table, Card, Mahogany, Sheraton Style, C.1850 .... 400.00
Table, Card, Maryland, Inlaid Edges, Mahogany, C.1790, 28 1/2 In. 2400.00
Table, Card, Massachusetts, Carved Mahogany, C.1815, 29 1/2 In. 600.00
Table, Card, Nehemiah Adams, Inlaid Mahogany, C.1800, 29 1/4 In. 2500.00
Table, Card, Philadelphia, Line & Diamond Inlay, Mahogany, C.1805 .... 5775.00
Table, Card, Queen Anne, Walnut, Drawers, C.1770, 34 X 27 In. 2910.00
Table, Card, Rhode Island, Drawer, Mahogany, C.1780, Pair 4800.00
Table, Card, Sheraton, Banded Inlay, Cherry, 18 1/2 X 28 In. 325.00
Table, Card, Sheraton, Fluted Legs, Inlay 1500.00
Table, Card, Sheraton, Mahogany, Biscuit Corners, 36 X 17 In. 700.00
Table, Card, Sheraton, Satinwood Inlay, New Hampshire, 1790–1810 .... 3500.00
Table, Carved, Square Marble Top, Mahogany, Victorian 100.00
Table, Center, American, Turtle Shaped, Rosewood, C.1855, 44 In. 2000.00
Table, Center, Dresden, 7 Porcelain Panels, 28 5/8 In. 2100.00
Table, Center, Eastlake, Walnut, Marble, 30 X 37 X 28 In. 375.00
Table, Center, Empire, Mahogany, Black Marble Top, 29 X 41 In. 935.00
Table, Center, Empire, Mahogany, Paw Feet, C.1830, 31 In. 550.00
Table, Center, Frieze, Fluted Legs, Carolean Oak, 27 1/2 In. 1000.00
Table, Center, Gilt Incised, Ebony Inlay, American, 4 Ft. X 30 In. 3850.00
Table, Center, Gothic, Oak, Pedestal, 1 Drawer, Arched Door, 36 In. 500.00
Table, Center, Louis XV, Carved, Marble Top, Walnut, 4 Ft. 10 In. 2300.00
Table, Center, Louis XV, Ebonized, Brass, 1 Drawer, 31 In. X 5 Ft. 3400.00
Table, Center, Louis XV, Tulipwood, Kingwood, Marble, 36 X 45 In. 9350.00
Table, Center, Marquetry, Walnut, Burl, Apron, Shelf, 24 X 46 In. 550.00
Table, Center, Renaissance, Ebony, Inlaid, C.1865, 30 In. X 4 Ft. 3850.00
Table, Center, Rococo Revival, Rosewood, C.1860, 30 1/2 X 41 In. 650.00
Table, Center, Rococo, Rosewood, Turtle Shape, 1855, 31 X 44 In. 1980.00
Table, Center, Tilt Top, Octagonal Pedestal, Mahogany, 40 1/2 In. 880.00
Table, Center, Walnut, Victorian, Square, Carved, C.1880 .... 400.00
Table, Center, William IV, Gadrooned Rim, Rosewood, 1890s, 28 In. 1400.00
Table, Chamber, Federal, Mahogany, Brass Pulls, 34 X 32 X 18 In. 1500.00
Table, Child's, Graniteware Top, Scene On Top 90.00
Table, Chinese, Carved Scene Of Trees, People, Lacquer, 12 1/2 In. 495.00
Table, Chinese, Chou, Rosewood, Reticulated Carved Apron, 60 In. 300.00
Table, Chinese, Teak & Mahogany, 4 Ft. X 1 Ft. 8 In. 1000.00
Table, Chinoiserie Design, Red Lacquer, Gilt Figures, 20 In. 45.00
Table, Chinoiserie Lacquer, Sutherland, Gilt, 33 X 27 In. 9350.00
Table, Chippendale, Birdcage, Mahogany, Spindles, 34 In.Diam. 150.00
Table, Chippendale, Chinese, Walnut, Burl Paneled Top, 60 X 30 In. 650.00
Table, Circular Tilt Top, Fluted Stem, Tripod, Mahogany, 29 In. 2200.00
Table, Claw Feet, Lion's Head, 1 Leaf, Oak, Round, 54 In. 2000.00
Table, Coffee, Louis XV, Variegated Marble Top 80.00
Table, Conference, Twin Pedestals, Golden Oak, Oval, C.1920, 10 Ft. 3950.00
Table, Console, George III, Mahogany, D Shape Top, Gallery, 28 In. 250.00
Table, Continental, Triangular, 18th Century, 28 X 24 In., Pair 550.00
Table, Corner, Queen Anne, Walnut, Leaf, 1750–70, 43 X 29 In. 7450.00
Table, Country, Pine, French, Pullout Board, Drawer, 74 X 30 In. 1200.00
Table, Crap, Victorian, Walnut, 1880s, 60 X 42 In. 1500.00
Table, Cricket, Circular Top, Fruitwood & Elmwood, 28 1/2 In. 715.00
Table, Curio, Louis XVI, Gilt Bronze Mounted, Mahogany, 27 1/2 In. 880.00

Table, Dining, 2 Pedestals, Brass Casters, Mahogany, 11 Ft.1/2 In. 8010.00
Table, Dining, Carved Walnut, Oval, Putti Legs, C.1900, 29 In. 1000.00
Table, Dining, Chinese Chippendale, Apron, Double Legs, 73 In. 900.00
Table, Dining, Chippendale Style, Walnut, 68 X 42 In. 725.00
Table, Dining, Chippendale, Walnut, 2–Part, C.1775, 8 Ft. 5 In. 2450.00
Table, Dining, Double Pedestal, 1 Leaf, Mahogany, 6 Federal Chairs 1450.00
Table, Dining, Drop Leaf, Mahogany, Circular, Casters, 6 Ft. 8 In. 7000.00
Table, Dining, Extension, 4 Leaves, Turned Legs, Oval, Cherry 450.00
Table, Dining, Federal, Mahogany, Drop Leaf, 1795, 46 X 69 In. 2000.00
Table, Dining, George III, Stringing, Mahogany, C.1800, 7 Ft. 2 In. 1550.00
Table, Dining, Gustav Stickley, C.1907, Set Of 6 V–Back Chairs 2800.00
Table, Dining, Hastings, 7 Leaves, Quarter Sawn Oak, 60 In. 4000.00
Table, Dining, Hepplewhite, 3 Sections, Ribbon Back 3600.00
Table, Dining, Limbert, Pedestal, Round, C.1910, 30 X 48 In.Diam. 500.00
Table, Dining, New England, Drop Leaf, Maple, C.1760, 41 1/2 In. 3800.00
Table, Dining, Oak, 5 Leaves, Square, Extend To 8 Ft. 825.00
Table, Dining, Pedestal, George III, 2 Leaves, Mahogany, 9 1/4 Ft. 5500.00
Table, Dining, Queen Anne, Swing Leg, Drawer, Mahogany 1750.00
Table, Dining, Regency, Mahogany, 1840, 59 1/4 X 53 X 28 In. 4000.00
Table, Dining, Regency, Mahogany, Brass Feet, Leaves, 59 X 45 In. 250.00
Table, Dining, Regency, Mahogany, Splay Tripod Base, 72 X 42 In. 950.00
Table, Dining, Rhode Island, Drop Leaf, Mahogany, C.1770, 48 In. 1500.00
Table, Dining, Shaker, Pine, Ash, Maple, C.1820, 26 1/2 In. 450.00
Table, Dining, Shaker, Pine, Butternut, Breadboard Top, 82 X 30 In. 7000.00
Table, Dining, Sheraton, Double Pedestal, 2 Leaves, Mahogany 1000.00
Table, Dining, Swing Leg, Chippendale, Cherry, C.1775, 48 X 48 In. 1850.00
Table, Dining, Swing Leg, Connecticut, Cherry, C.1775, 46 X 48 In. 850.00
Table, Dining, Troy Sunshade, G.Rohde, Chrome, 1934, 48 X 21 In. 120.00
Table, Dining, Tudor Style, Draw Ends, Oak, 56 1/4 X 30 In. 150.00
Table, Dining, Tudor Style, Oak, 56 X 28 X 32 In. 250.00
Table, Dining, Waterfall Legs, Oval, Oak, 11 X 5 Ft. 4200.00
Table, Director's, Oak, Gustav Stickley, 29 X 96 In. 11000.00
Table, Double Pedestal, Baker, Banded, Mahogany, 3 Leaves 1600.00
Table, Dough, Massachusetts, Painted Red, C.1800, 36 X 29 In. 1600.00
Table, Dressing, 3 Drawers, England, Oak, 19th Century, 28 3/4 In. 500.00
Table, Dressing, Beidermier, Walnut, Fruitwood, Mirror, 48 In. 425.00
Table, Dressing, Blue, Cabriole Legs, Serpentine, 43 X 35 In. 1200.00
Table, Dressing, Divided Center, 3 Wells, Mahogany, C.1780, 29 In. 495.00
Table, Dressing, Empire, Crotch Grain Mahogany, Large 125.00
Table, Dressing, Feather Banded, 2 Frieze Drawers, Walnut, 32 In. 2300.00
Table, Dressing, Federal, Inlaid Mahogany, 1810–20, 65 X 37 In. 375.00
Table, Dressing, Federal, Inlaid Mahogany, Swivel Mirror, 1810–20 .... 375.00
Table, Dressing, Flame Veneer Drawer Fronts, Mahogany, 57 In. 300.00
Table, Dressing, Mirror, Mahogany, C.1815, 38 In. X 5 Ft. 6 In. 3300.00
Table, Dressing, Mirrored, Gustav Stickley, Circle Pulls 1400.00
Table, Dressing, Painted White, Green & Gold Design 2950.00
Table, Dressing, Provincial, Oak, Tassel Pulls, 29 1/2 X 35 In. 400.00
Table, Dressing, Regency, Mahogany, Inlay, England, 1880, 28 1/2 In. 450.00
Table, Dressing, Victorian, Mahogany, Drawers, Curved Mirror 250.00
Table, Dressing, William & Mary, Inlaid Walnut, 28 In. 750.00
Table, Dressing, William & Mary, Inlaid Walnut, Rope Twist Legs 700.00
Table, Drop Leaf, 8 Legs, Carved Rope Trim, Mahogany, 24 X 52 In. 450.00
Table, Drop Leaf, Bird's–Eye Maple Top & Skirt, Cherry, C.1820 .... 1275.00
Table, Drop Leaf, Curly Maple, 2 Leaves, 17 X 39 1/2 In. 825.00
Table, Drop Leaf, Divided Top, Gateleg, Fruitwood, 19th Century 450.00
Table, Drop Leaf, Empire, Mahogany, Pedestal, C.1850, 30 In. 175.00
Table, Drop Leaf, Federal, Mahogany, False Drawer, 1810, 23 3/4 In. 800.00
Table, Drop Leaf, George III, Mahogany, 24 X 28 In. 175.00
Table, Drop Leaf, Greco–Roman, Revival, Mahogany, C.1825, 29 In. 350.00
Table, Drop Leaf, Hepplewhite, Cherry, Wooden Hinges, 1810, 48 In. 300.00
Table, Drop Leaf, Inlaid Satinwood, 2 Drawers, 27 1/2 In. 1875.00
Table, Drop Leaf, Mahogany, Swing Leg, Restored, 27 X 32 In. 750.00
Table, Drop Leaf, Maple, Spool Turned Legs, Natural, 41 In. 175.00
Table, Drop Leaf, New England, Painted & Grained, 1800–20, 27 In. 1450.00

Table, Drop Leaf, Oak, Canted Corners, Trestle Base, 44 X 45 In.	200.00
Table, Drop Leaf, Queen Anne, Cabriole Legs	1400.00
Table, Drop Leaf, Queen Anne, Mahogany, Pad Feet, 48 X 16 1/2 In.	275.00
Table, Drop Leaf, Queen Anne, Tapered Swing Leg, Duck Feet	900.00
Table, Drop Leaf, Sheraton, Cherry & Birch, 42 1/4 X 27 In.	175.00
Table, Drop Leaf, Swing Leg, Chippendale, Mahogany, 48 X 27 In.	2800.00
Table, Drop Leaf, Swing Leg, Mahogany, 19th Century, 28 In.	525.00
Table, Drop Leaf, Tapered Legs, Pine, C.1880	345.00
Table, Drum, Regency, England, Marquetry & Mahogany, 29 3/4 In.	100.00
Table, Eagle Pedestal, Octagonal, 23 X 30 In. ....*Illus*	425.00
Table, Elizabethan, Carved Oak, Leaf Tip Border, 1 Drawer, 43 In.	180.00
Table, End, Louis XV, Walnut & Fruitwood Veneer, 28 In., Pair	225.00
Table, End, Square Top, 1 Drawer, Mahogany, 25 In., Pair	325.00
Table, Farm, Divided Dovetailed Drawer, Pine, Large	850.00
Table, Farm, Poplar, Drop Leaf, 4 Legs, 60 X 37 X 28 In.	450.00
Table, Federal, Cherry Inlaid Stringing, Pembroke, 36 X 20 In.	2200.00
Table, French, Animal Paw Feet, Cloisonne Mounted Onyx, 30 In.	3300.00
Table, Frieze Carved Fretwork, George III, Mahogany, 36 In., Pair	10000.00
Table, Game, Checkerboard Top, Tapered Legs, Grained Paint	1000.00
Table, Game, English, 26 X 35 1/2 X 17 1/2 In. ....*Illus*	1600.00
Table, Game, Federal, Mahogany, Satinwood, Inlaid, 1810, 38 X 19 In.	3000.00
Table, Game, Foldover, Queen Anne, Mahogany, C.1800	650.00
Table, Game, George II, Pierced Carved Apron, H.Tibits, Mahogany	3575.00
Table, Game, George III, Inlaid Satinwood, Mahogany, C.1790, 30 In.	2875.00
Table, Game, Hepplewhite, Serpentine, Mahogany	1150.00
Table, Game, Hinged Oblong Top Over Frieze, 30 X 13 1/2 X 27 In.	150.00
Table, Game, Louis XVI, Ormolu, Mahogany, Inlay Frieze, 34 X 18 In.	1400.00
Table, Game, Mahogany, Upholstered Inset, 1 Drawer, 34 1/2 In.	1000.00
Table, Game, New Hampshire, Scrubbed Top, Grained Base	3200.00
Table, Game, Oak, Gustav Stickley, C.1904, 42 X 29 In.	800.00
Table, Game, Rococo Revival, American, 19th Century, 35 X 30 In.	200.00
Table, Game, Serpentine Rail, Carved, Mahogany, 35 1/2 In.	7700.00
Table, Game, Sheraton, Lift Top, Legs Doweled To Skirt	3500.00
Table, Game, Square Legs, Bowed Apron, Maple, 35 1/4 X 27 1/4 In.	625.00
Table, Game, Trestle, Sliding Panel, Reverse Chess Board, 27 In.	5500.00
Table, Game, Triangular, Dished For Chips, Mahogany, C.1740	7450.00
Table, Garden, Painted Metal, Leaf Design Legs	280.00
Table, Gateleg, Charles II, Oak, 58 In.	3850.00
Table, Gateleg, Drawer Each End, Ball Feet, Oval, Walnut, 31 In.	900.00
Table, Gateleg, Drop Leaf, Double, Cherry, C.1820, 44 In. X 28 In.	350.00
Table, Gateleg, Frieze Drawer, Oak, C.1700, 5 1/2 Ft. X 28 In.	1000.00
Table, Gateleg, Hepplewhite, C.1850	1500.00

Furniture, Table, Eagle Pedestal, Octagonal, 23 X 30 In.

Furniture, Table, Game, English, 26 X 35 1/2 X 17 1/2 In.

Furniture, Table, Italy, Carved,

32 1/2 X 51 1/2 X 22 1/2 In.

Furniture, Table, Library, Drop Leaf,

2 Drawers, 24 X 47 In.

Table, Gateleg, Hinged Oval Top, Frieze Drawer, Oak, 4 Ft. 9 In.	3650.00
Table, Gateleg, Mortised & Pinned Frame, Drawers, Oak, 29 In.	300.00
Table, Gateleg, William & Mary, Walnut & Maple, 1720–60, 41 In.	4600.00
Table, George III, Mahogany, Pembroke, 1 Drawer, 29 X 32 In.	1800.00
Table, George III, Mahogany, Pembroke, Drop Ends, 1790, 28 X 42 In.	1400.00
Table, George III, Tripod, Mahogany, Serpentine, 15 In.Diam., Pr.	350.00
Table, German, Mahogany, Brass, Oval Top, C.1790, 26 In.	800.00
Table, Gold Design, Black Lacquer, Chinese, 28 In., Nest Of 4	550.00
Table, Gustav Stickley, Round, Oak, C.1904, 30 X 48 In.	900.00
Table, Gustav Stickley, Spindle Sided, C.1904, 48 X 29 In.	2200.00
Table, Gustav Stickley, Spindle Sided, C.1905, 36 X 24 X 29 In.	3400.00
Table, Hepplewhite, Band Inlay, Stringing, Walnut, 44 1/4 X 29 In.	250.00
Table, Hepplewhite, Walnut, Drawer, Square Legs, 36 X 21 In.	300.00
Table, Hunt, George III, Mahogany, Satinwood, Oxbow, 42 X 32 In.	1100.00
Table, Hunt, Scrolled Steel Base, Plate Glass, 88 X 29 1/2 In.	350.00
Table, Hutch, 4–Board Top, Lift Lid In Base, Poplar, 47 3/4 In.	375.00
Table, Hutch, Maple & Pine, Red Wash, C.1780, 25 1/2 In.	850.00
Table, Hutch, New York, Trestle Feet, Round Top, Cherry, C.1750	2750.00
Table, Hutch, Random Board Top, Original Red, 6 Ft. X 36 In.	2675.00
Table, Hutch, Square Posts, Pine Seat, Round Top, 43 X 30 1/2 In.	425.00
Table, Ice Cream, Glass Top, Wooden Trestle, 30 X 36 X 20 In.	50.00
Table, Italy, Carved, 32 1/2 X 51 1/2 X 22 1/2 In. ....*Illus*	150.00
Table, Leather Worker, Tray, Vise, Pedal, 1820, 11 X 22 1/2 In.	260.00
Table, Library, Dark, Gustav Stickley, Red Decal, 36 X 30 In.	475.00
Table, Library, Drawer, Copper Pulls, 29 1/2 X 44 X 28 In.	125.00
Table, Library, Drop Leaf, 2 Drawers, 24 X 47 In. ....*Illus*	1000.00
Table, Library, Leather Top, Gustav Stickley, 66 X 30 In.	1500.00
Table, Library, Oak, Stickley Bros., Round, 46 In.	425.00
Table, Library, Oak, Stickley, C.1912, 29 X 42 X 28 In.	600.00
Table, Library, Regency, Mahogany, Baluster Gallery, 1820, 20 In.	400.00
Table, Library, Regency, Thomas Nisbet, New Brunswick	795.00
Table, Library, Revival, Walnut, Trumpet Legs, C.1865, 30 In.	250.00
Table, Library, Victorian, Walnut, Burl Veneer, Marble, 45 X 29 In.	200.00
Table, Lift Lid Dough Box, Pennsylvania, Old Red Paint	1050.00
Table, Limbert, Medial Shelf, Cutout Sides, C.1910, 29 3/4 X 44 In	600.00
Table, Louis XV, Marble, Fruitwood Veneer, 21 1/4 X 30 1/4 In.	200.00
Table, Louis XV, Red Lacquer, Dish Top, 1 Drawer, 29 X 34 X 22 In.	1200.00
Table, Louis XVI Revival, Walnut, Marble, C.1870, 33 X 17 1/2 In.	300.00
Table, Louis XVI, Gilt Bronze Mounted, Mahogany, 26 1/2 X 19 In.	880.00
Table, Louis XVI, Green Marble Top, Frieze Drawer, 31 1/2 In.	2200.00
Table, Lyre Base, Mahogany, C.1815, 18 X 16 X 28 In.	875.00

Table, Mahogany, Victorian, Ivory Ball Feet, 34 X 15 1/2 In.	275.00
Table, Mission, Legs Extended In Top, C.1906, 28 1/4 X 28 3/4 In.	375.00
Table, Mortised & Pinned Construction, Drawer, 15 1/2 X 25 In.	225.00
Table, Neoclassical, Mahogany, Gallery Top, Tambour Door, 19 In.	300.00
Table, Onyx, Cloisonne, Enameled, Paw Feet, French, 30 X 18 1/2 In.	3300.00
Table, Oriental, Carved, Rosewood, C.1800, 30 In.	550.00
Table, Oriental, Mother-Of-Pearl, Rosewood, 19th Century, 34 In.	200.00
Table, Parlor, Oak, Rectangular, Lower Shelf	70.00
Table, Parquetry, Walnut, Fruitwood Veneer, Chevron Inlay, 29 In.	175.00
Table, Pegged Construction, Swedish, Original Blue Paint, C.1860	550.00
Table, Pembroke, Beacon Hill	195.00
Table, Pembroke, Brass Castors, Mahogany, 18 1/4 X 28 1/2 In.	850.00
Table, Pembroke, Drawer, Leaves, Cherry, 36 X 27 1/2 In.	1050.00
Table, Pembroke, Duncan Phyfe, Inlaid Mahogany, C.1795, 29 In.	1600.00
Table, Pembroke, Federal, Curly Maple, Serpentine, 1800, 28 3/4 In.	4125.00
Table, Pembroke, Federal, Inlaid Mahogany, Leaves, 1790, 29 1/2 In.	3000.00
Table, Pembroke, Holly Drawer & Legs, Mahogany Veneer, 38 3/4 In.	6950.00
Table, Pembroke, Mahogany, 19th Century, 20 1/4 X 31 X 27 1/2 In.	750.00
Table, Pembroke, Pierced Stretchers, Cherry	1700.00
Table, Pembroke, Reeded Edge Top, Mahogany, 17 X 33 X 28 3/4 In.	310.00
Table, Pembroke, Square Tapered Legs, Cherry, 21 X 41 X 41 In.	200.00
Table, Pier, Meissen, Marble, Demilune, Cabriole Legs, 32 X 36 In.	4400.00
Table, Pier, Mirrored Base, Giltwood, Rosewood, C.1830, 39 1/2 In.	1650.00
Table, Pier, Victorian, Carved, C.1900, 33 1/4 X 42 X 21 3/4 In.	425.00
Table, Pine & Maple, Stretcher Base, C.1880, 5 Ft. X 28 In.	1200.00
Table, Pine Oval Top, Figured Maple Base, 25 1/2 In.	1500.00
Table, Queen Anne, Drop Leaf, Swing Leg, Tiger Maple Top	7500.00
Table, Queen Anne, Swing Leg, Tiger Maple, C.1740	4500.00
Table, Refectory, Elizabethan, Oak & Elm, 34 X 106 In.	4950.00
Table, Refectory, English, Oak, 17th Century, 121 1/2 X 33 1/2 In.	800.00
Table, Refectory, Spanish, Walnut, 16th Century	4950.00
Table, Refectory, Walnut, 17th Century, 31 X 60 X 29 1/4 In.	750.00
Table, Regency, Drawers, Cusped Legs, Inlaid Mahogany, 4 Ft. 4 In.	2475.00
Table, Regency, Egyptian, Slate Top, Falcon Legs, 29 X 28 In.Diam.	4000.00
Table, Renaissance, Walnut, Round, 50 In., Pair	2750.00
Table, Repousse, Iron, Tripod, Glass Top, 3 Supports, Plant Holder	100.00
Table, Round, Pine & Butternut	355.00
Table, Satinwood Marquetry, Portrait Medallions, Gilt, 35 In.	9900.00
Table, Sawbuck, 36 In. X 9 Ft. 5 In.	5500.00
Table, Sawbuck, Wrought Iron Braces, Pine Top, 66 X 28 1/2 In.	350.00
Table, Serpentine Front, Inlaid Marquetry, Mahogany, 33 1/4 In.	8800.00
Table, Serving, Drop Leaf, Mahogany, Spindles, 34 X 36 In.	375.00
Table, Serving, Tudor Style, 1 Drawer, Oak, 36 X 32 In.	60.00
Table, Sevres Plaque Insets, Gilt Bronze Mounted	11500.00
Table, Sewing, 3 Drawers, Old Varnish, 16 X 21 1/2 X 28 In.	260.00
Table, Sewing, Empire, 2 Drawers, Turned Legs	770.00
Table, Sewing, Empire, Cloth Bag, Ormolu Mount	3650.00
Table, Sewing, Empire, Sewing Bag, Mahogany	1200.00
Table, Sewing, Federal, Mahogany, Basket, C.1805, 29 3/4 In.	2200.00
Table, Sewing, Felt Top, Bag Slide, Trestle Base, Walnut, 29 In.	290.00
Table, Sewing, Folds, Salesman's Sample, 21 X 13 In.	45.00
Table, Sewing, Lacquered, Paw Feet, China, 1850, 27 X 24 X 16 In.	200.00
Table, Sewing, Wicker, Lift Top, Bamboo Legs, C.1885	125.00
Table, Shaker, Harvest, Pine, Red, Sabbathday Lake, 60 X 27 In.	550.00
Table, Shaker, Maple, Pine Top, Natural Finish, 25 X 38 In.	900.00
Table, Shaw Furniture, Triangular, Drop Leaf, Lacquered, 29 In.	175.00
Table, Sheraton Pembroke, Curly Maple, Reeded Legs, Shaped Leaves	375.00
Table, Sheraton, Drop Leaf, Swing Leg, Cherry	550.00
Table, Sheraton, Swing Leg, Mahogany, Reeded Legs, 18 In.Leaves	795.00
Table, Side, Boston, Tiger Grain Painted Base, Marbelized Top	485.00
Table, Side, Cast Iron, Inlaid Marble Top, Rococo, Base, 31 In., Pr.	3025.00
Table, Side, Louis XV, Fruitwood, White Marble, 18 X 28 3/4 In.	1900.00
Table, Side, Louis XVI, Gilt Bronze Mounted, Mahogany, 30 1/2 In.	550.00
Table, Side, Wrought Iron, Parcel Gilt, Marble Top, D Shape, 5 Ft.	4125.00

Table, Silver, Serpentine Pierced Gallery, Mahogany, 29 1/2 In. 7150.00
Table, Sofa, Regency, Rosewood, 2 Drop Ends, 2 Drawers, 39 X 28 In. 4250.00
Table, Sorting, Shaker, Bird's-Eye Maple, Cherry, Red, 29 X 18 In. 2000.00
Table, Spanish Baroque, Shaped Trestle Supports, Iron, 19 1/2 In. 280.00
Table, Spanish, Colonial, Sabina Wood, Dated Between 1820 & 1840 .... 1600.00
Table, Spoon Carved Fringe, Pedestal, Paw Feet, Golden Oak, 72 In. 5800.00
Table, Sweetmeat, 3 Tiers, Castors Implanted In Legs 400.00
Table, Tavern, Connecticut, Old Gray Paint Over Red, 18th Century 1000.00
Table, Tavern, Double Vase & Ring Turned, 32 X 22 In. 1300.00
Table, Tavern, Drawer, 2-Board Removable Top, Pine, 28 1/4 In. 1050.00
Table, Tavern, Maple & Pine, C.1780, 48 X 27 1/2 In. 2400.00
Table, Tavern, Maple Base, Pine 1-Board Top, C.1760 .... 1000.00
Table, Tavern, Massachusetts, Pine Top, Drawer, Oak, 17th Century 1000.00
Table, Tavern, New England, Red Paint, Maple, C.1750, 27 1/2 In. 2750.00
Table, Tavern, Pine, Provincial, Door, 29 1/2 X 64 X 25 In. 425.00
Table, Tavern, Queen Anne, Country, Breadboard Ends, 18th Century 1450.00
Table, Tavern, Queen Anne, Drawer, Pine Breadboard Top 700.00
Table, Tavern, Queen Anne, Maple Base, 1 Drawer, 28 1/2 X 26 In. 1250.00
Table, Tavern, Queen Anne, Red Paint, 18th Century 1300.00
Table, Tavern, Sheraton, Grain Painted 1050.00
Table, Tavern, Turned Legs, Mahogany, 18th Century, 28 1/2 In. 715.00
Table, Tavern, William & Mary, New England, Maple & Pine, C.1730 .... 1000.00
Table, Tavern, William & Mary, New England, Maple, C.1750, 24 In. 850.00
Table, Tavern, Wrought Iron Mug Holders At Each Leg, Oak, 42 In. 850.00
Table, Tea, Cabriole Leg, Swing Leg, Round Top, 35 In. 6000.00
Table, Tea, Chippendale, Mahogany, Birdcage, 3 Cabriole Legs, 1760 .... 3000.00
Table, Tea, Drop Leaf, Pad Foot, Cabriole Leg 6000.00
Table, Tea, George III, Canted Corners, Mahogany, 35 1/2 X 29 In. 1300.00
Table, Tea, Gustav Stickley, Finial, C.1904, 28 X 24 In. 500.00
Table, Tea, Gustav Stickley, Shelf, C.1907, 29 X 24 In.Diam. 350.00
Table, Tea, New England, Gray Green Paint, Marked, C.1780, 26 In. 1600.00
Table, Tea, New England, Tilt Top, Mahogany, C.1780, 26 In. 900.00
Table, Tea, Queen Anne, Maple, Cyma Skirt, Cabriole Legs, 1770-90 .... 8250.00
Table, Tea, Queen Anne, Painted & Grained, C.1790, 22 X 27 In. 1775.00
Table, Tea, Queen Anne, Tiger Maple, Splayed Legs, 1760, 26 In. 3100.00
Table, Tea, Round, Gustav Stickley, 1907, 29 X 24 In. 750.00
Table, Tea, Sheraton, Mahogany, C.1795 .... 750.00
Table, Tea, Tilt Top, Cherry, 18th Century 975.00
Table, Tea, Tilt Top, Dished Revolving Top, Walnut, C.1770, 28 In. 3300.00
Table, Tea, Tilt Top, Empire, Rosewood 880.00
Table, Tea, Tilt Top, New England, Birchwood, C.1810, 39 X 30 In. 880.00
Table, Tea, Tilt Top, Salem, Mass., Mahogany, C.1795, 34 X 29 In. 1350.00
Table, Tea, Tilt Top, Snake Feet, 1-Board Top, Mahogany, 29 1/2 In. 1550.00
Table, Tea, Tilt Top, Snake Feet, Cherry, 35 X 28 1/2 In. 1875.00

Furniture, Table, Teakwood,
Carved Skirt, 33 X 36 X 36 In.

Furniture, Table, Wicker,   Furniture, Table, Wicker,
Round Shelf   Scrolled Apron

> The general rule about dovetailing is: the fewer number of joints, the older the piece. An early eighteenth-century drawer was joined with one huge dovetail or was pegged together.

Furniture, Table, Work, Veneer,
Mahogany, C.1815, 29 X 22 X 17 In.

Item	Price
Table, Tea, Tilt Top, Snake Feet, Mahogany, 30 1/2 X 28 1/4 In.	500.00
Table, Tea, Walnut Tilt Top, English, Mahogany, 36 3/4 X 29 In.	285.00
Table, Teakwood, Carved Skirt, 33 X 36 X 36 In. ....*Illus*	800.00
Table, Tilt Top, Branded S.Eliot, Walnut, 30 X 31 In.	850.00
Table, Tilt Top, Carved, George III, Tripod, Mahogany, 28 In.	6050.00
Table, Tilt Top, Mahogany, Bird Cage, Oval, 28 In.Closed	275.00
Table, Tilt Top, Oval, Inlaid Mahogany, C.1810, 28 X 41 1/2 In.	2750.00
Table, Tilt Top, Ovoid	125.00
Table, Tilt Top, Queen Anne, Tripod Base, Walnut, 34 1/2 Diam.	500.00
Table, Tilt Top, Serpentine Top	385.00
Table, Tilt Top, Tripod, George III, Carved, Mahogany, 30 1/4 In.	2200.00
Table, Tip, Federal, Red, Black Painted Checkerboard, 1820, 19 In.	1000.00
Table, Trestle, 2–Board Top, Breadboard Ends, 8 1/2 Ft.	5250.00
Table, Trestle, Maine, Red Washed Base, 19th Century, 9 Ft. 4 In.	3500.00
Table, Trestle, Provincial, Scandinavian, Pine, 69 X 28 1/2 In.	1500.00
Table, Trestle, Spanish Renaissance, Walnut, 52 1/2 X 29 In.	1925.00
Table, Tripod, Cabriole Legs, Paw Feet, Elmwood, 30 1/2 In.	550.00
Table, Tudor Style, Butterfly Joints, Oak, 20 In.	50.00
Table, Turtle Shape Top, Flame Grain Veneer, 19th Century, 29 In.	425.00
Table, Victorian, Walnut, Marble Top, C.1870, 44 X 28 In. ....*Illus*	850.00
Table, Vitrine, Louis XV, Heart Shape Top Lifts, 29 X 14 1/2 In.	2475.00
Table, Wicker, Round Shelf ....*Illus*	500.00
Table, Wicker, Scrolled Apron ....*Illus*	350.00
Table, William & Mary, Trestle Foot, Wallace Nutting, 60 X 30 In.	800.00
Table, Work & Game, Drop Leaf, Drawer, Inlaid Rosewood, 28 1/2 In.	1800.00
Table, Work, 2 Drawers, Removable 2–Board Top, Walnut, 66 1/2 In.	180.00
Table, Work, Cherry Legs, Drawer, Butternut, 40 1/2 X 29 X 29 In.	220.00
Table, Work, Drawer, Lift Top, Fitted Interior, Mahogany, 30 In.	300.00
Table, Work, Empire, Double Drawer, C.A.Greger, Delta, Ohio, C.1840	450.00
Table, Work, Empire, Mahogany, Acanthus, Paw Feet, 22 X 18 In.	125.00
Table, Work, English, Boy, Horse, Papier–Mache, C.1850, 29 In.	500.00
Table, Work, Federal, Drop Leaves, Drawer, Mahogany, C.1815, 29 In.	575.00
Table, Work, Federal, Mahogany, 2 Drawers, C.1810, 27 1/2 In.	1650.00
Table, Work, Floral Inlay, Geometric Edge, Ivory Corners, Mahogany	180.00
Table, Work, George III, Hinged Lid, Block Toes, Mahogany, 30 In.	1050.00
Table, Work, Hepplewhite, Pine, 1 Drawer, Leaves, 24 X 47 3/4 In.	225.00
Table, Work, Hepplewhite, Pine, Tapered Legs, Dark Finish, 73 In.	150.00
Table, Work, Hepplewhite, Walnut, False Drawer, 44 X 59 In.	225.00
Table, Work, Hinged Leaves, Leather Top, Mahogany, C.1820, 33 In.	3950.00
Table, Work, Inlaid Satinwood, 19 1/2 X 30 In.	1750.00
Table, Work, Louis XV, Kingwood, Cabriole Legs, 29 X 27 In.	800.00
Table, Work, Oval, Satinwood Crossbanded, C.1780, 27 3/4 In.	6250.00

Table, Work, Queen Anne, Cherry, 2 Drawers, C.1740, 51 X 29 In. 950.00
Table, Work, Queen Anne, Cherry, 2 Drawers, Virginia, 1740, 51 In. 950.00
Table, Work, Regency, Penwork & Inlaid, Sycamore, 19 1/4 X 37 In. 5775.00
Table, Work, Rococo Revival, Mahogany, Hinged Lid, C.1840, 21 In. 350.00
Table, Work, Shaker, Pine & Birch, Taped Leg, 26 X 43 In. 1100.00
Table, Work, Shaker, Pine, Figured Birch, Red, 1 Drawer, 26 In. 850.00
Table, Work, Shaker, Tapered Legs, Old Red Paint 4300.00
Table, Work, Square Legs, Butternut Top, Poplar, 43 X 28 1/2 In. 70.00
Table, Work, Tray Top, Regency, Rosewood, 32 In. 600.00
Table, Work, Veneer, Mahogany, C.1815, 29 X 22 X 17 In. ....*Illus* 3300.00
Table, Writing, 1 Drawer, Dovetailed, Old Blue Paint 250.00
Table, Writing, Austrian, Neoclassical, Parcel Gilt, Ebonized, 1830 .... 825.00
Table, Writing, Chippendale, Pine, Bayberry & Red Paint 325.00
Table, Writing, Empire, Mahogany, Leather Top, 4 Ft.3 1/2 In. 2300.00
Table, Writing, Gilt Tooled Surface, 3 Drawers, Mahogany, 1780s 3300.00
Table, Writing, Inlaid, Foliate Scrolls, Italian, Kingwood, 30 In. 3100.00
Table, Writing, Leather, 4 Opposing Drawers, Mahogany, 29 In. 2300.00
Table, Writing, Louis XV, Gilt Bronze Mount, Kingwood, 30 1/2 In. 5400.00
Table, Writing, Parcel Gilt & Painted, Austria, C.1830, 28 1/2 In. 825.00
Table, Writing, Regency, Japanned, Late 19th Century, 30 1/2 In. 5775.00
Table, Writing, Regency, Leather Surface, Rosewood, 4 Ft. 4 In. 1550.00
Table, Writing, Tooled Leather Surface, Paneled Frieze, Mahogany 2100.00
Tabourette, Gustav Stickley, Octagonal, C.1912, 16 1/4 X 18 In. 425.00
Tabourette, Limbert, Oak, Octagon, Cutout Base, 1910, 24 X 17 In. 1700.00
Tea Caddy, Georgian, Mahogany, Rococo Post, England, 5 1/2 X 9 In. 225.00
Tea Caddy, Mahogany, Mother–Of–Pearl Inlay, English 275.00
Tea Cart, 4 Glass Shelves, Pierced Galleries, Brass, 27 1/2 In. 180.00
Tea Cart, Oak, Stickley Bros., Glass Tray, 1914, 29 X 16 X 30 In. 475.00
Telephone Stand, Mahogany, Seat, 1930s 45.00
Tender, Child's, Original Stenciling, Old Paint, C.1810, 30 In. 6750.00
Towel Rack, Turned Feet & Posts, Painted Black, 33 3/4 In. 85.00
Urn, Knife, Acorn Finial, Square Base, Mahogany, 24 1/2 In., Pair 3400.00
Vanity & Bench, Mirrored, Chrome & Lucite Pull, America 325.00
Vargueno, Geometric, Wrought Iron Locks, Spanish, 24 X 38 In. 2000.00
Vitrine, Breakfront, William & Mary, Oak, Cornice, 3 Panels, 81 In. 800.00
Vitrine, Corner, Empire, Mahogany, 2 Doors, Mirror Interior, 71 In. 400.00
Vitrine, Ebonized, Porcelain Crest, Finials, & Feet, 1 Door, 7 Ft. 6500.00
Vitrine, French Style, Brass Mountings, Mirrored Back, Mahogany 750.00
Vitrine, Louis XV, Gilt Bronze, Marble, 1 Glazed Door, 5 Ft.5 In. 3575.00
Vitrine, Louis XV, Mahogany, Oval, Bronze Lion Mask, 4 Ft.11 In. 1100.00
Vitrine, Louis XV, V.Martin, Marble, Carbriole Legs, 4 Ft. 7 In. 1775.00
Vitrine, Louis XVI, Ebonized, Recessed Top, Glazed, Brass, 6 Ft. 2000.00
Vitrine, Mahogany, Ormolu, Mirror, Cabriole Legs, 55 X 29 X 14 In. 750.00
Wall Shelf, Pine, Smoke Finish, Sculpted Birds, 19th Century 450.00
Wardrobe, Burled Wood, 3 Doors, 3 Drawers, 74 X 70 1/2 X 21 In. 550.00
Wardrobe, Grained, 7 Ft.9 In. 950.00
Washstand, 1 Drawer, Corner, Pine, Brown Graining, 26 X 32 In. 215.00
Washstand, 3 Drawers, Corner, Federal, Mahogany, C.1790, 37 In. 550.00
Washstand, Backboard, Elm, C.1890 .... 265.00
Washstand, Corner, Inlaid, Splashboard, New England, C.1800, 44 In. 300.00
Washstand, Marble Top, Tiles By Lester Durant, Walnut, C.1855 .... 350.00
Washstand, Mirror & Marble Top, China Basin & Reservoir, 6 Ft. 385.00
Washstand, Rockingham Glazed Knobs, Blue & Red Paint 3800.00
Washstand, Shaker, 1 Drawer, Pine, Red Stain, 1850, 36 1/2 X 32 In. 2250.00
Washstand, Still Life Of Fruit On Each Shelf, Yellow 1850.00
Washstand, Victorian, Marble Top, Drawer, Door In Base 95.00
Washstand, Victorian, Walnut, 3 Drawers 160.00
Whatnot, Victorian, American, 59 1/2 X 35 1/2 X 13 In. 90.00
Window Bench, Moorish, Mahogany, Straight Back, 27 X 33 In. 225.00
Window Seat, Chippendale, Mahogany, Upholstered, 30 1/2 In. 750.00
Window Seat, Louis XV, Beechwood, Cabriole Legs, 6 Ft.5 In. 1980.00
Window Seat, Louis XV, Beechwood, Signed Chevigny, 6 Ft. 2000.00
Window Seat, Oak, Spindle Sided, C.1912, 30 X 14 X 16 1/2 In. 400.00
Window Seat, Yellow Painted Rush Seat, Red & Black 1800.00

Workstand, American, 1 Drawer, Walnut, 1830–60, 29 In.	80.00
Workstand, Empire, American, Drawer, Painted, C.1820, 29 In.	160.00

A porcelain works was started in Furstenberg, Germany, in 1747. It is still working. Many of the modern products are made in the old molds.

FURSTENBURG, Figurine, Allegorical, Seated Poseidon, Sea Nymphs, C.1890, 7 In.	575.00
Figurine, Lady, On Couch, Pink & White Lace, 8 In.	275.00
Figurine, Lady, With Fan, Pink Lace, Mark, 8 X 6 1/2 In.	425.00
Figurine, Spring, Lady, Holds Bouquet, Footed Brass Base, 9 In.	400.00
Plate, Fruit, Inlaid Gold Leaf Edge, Underglazed Crown F, 9 In.	75.00
Plate, Inlaid Mold, Gold Leaf Border, Fruit Center, 10 In.	55.00

G-ARGY-ROUSSEAU   *Gabriel Argy–Rousseau, born in 1885, was a French glass artist who produced a variety of objects in the Art Deco style. His mark, "G. Argy–Rousseau," was usually impressed.*

G.ARGY–ROUSSEAU, Bowl, Foliage And Fruit, Red, Green, Brown, 5 1/2 In.	895.00
Lamp, Green, Blue Shade With Geometrics, Metal Base, 8 In.	3000.00
Pendant, Purple Berries, Leaves, Pate–De–Verre, 2 5/8 In.	750.00
Vase, Gray, Green, Blue, Branches, 6 In.	850.00
Vase, Pate–De–Verre, Blue, Purple, & Black, 3 In.	675.00

Galle was a designer who made glass, furniture, and other Art Nouveau items, including pottery. Emile Galle founded his factory in France in 1874. After Galle's death in 1904, the firm continued to make glass and furniture until 1931. The name "Galle" was used as a mark, but it was often hidden in the design of the object.

GALLE FURNITURE, Chair, Carved Art Nouveau Tendrils And Leaves	650.00
Desk, Shelves, Art Nouveau Design, 5 Ft. High	1500.00
Table, 18 In.Diam. ....*Color*	695.00

GALLE POTTERY, Ewer, Lotus And Insect, 8 In.	600.00
Ewer, Man On Barrel, 8 In.	595.00
Figurine, Duck, Imari Colors, Signed, 15 1/2 X 7 In., Pair	1450.00

GALLE, Bonbon, Underplate, Bugs, Bows, Enameled, C.1880, Covered, Signed	950.00
Bowl, Pink, Acid Cut Green Foliage, Signed, 2 1/2 In.	300.00
Chandelier, Flowering Dogwood Boughs, Signed, 15 3/4 In.	4180.00
Compote, Patriotic Design, Reticulated Faience, Blue	325.00
Decanter Set, Enameled Cornflowers, Rope Handles, Pale Blue, 5 Piece	825.00
Lamp, Blue, Shade, Marked, 16 In.	2100.00

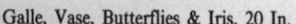

Galle, Vase, Butterflies & Iris, 20 In.

Galle, Vase, Teardrop, Amethyst
Tree & Landscape, Signed, 7 In.

Lamp, Coprin Et Pappillons, Mushroom–Shaped Shade, C.1900, 4 1/2 In.	1700.00
Lamp, Green Butterflies, Yellow Ground, Signed, 2 7/8 X 6 1/4 In.	1850.00
Perfume Bottle, Teardrop Stopper, Red & Gold, Signed	850.00
Pitcher, Thistle, Original Stopper, Signed, 9 1/2 In.	1050.00
Shot Glass, Pink Orchid Floral Cameo, Signed, 2 1/4 In.	275.00
Tray, Thistle Spray, Leaves, Inlaid Woods, Signed, 24 X 16 In.	550.00
Urn, Mushrooms All Around, Brown, 3 1/4 X 2 1/4 In.	550.00
Vase, 3 Fish, Seaweed & Coral, Green Ground, Signed, 9 1/2 In.	575.00
Vase, Acorns & Leaves, Gold Ground, Bronze Base, Signed, 4 3/5 In.	2300.00
Vase, Allover Orange Floral, Signed, 3 In.	385.00
Vase, Arabesque, Ruffled Base, Applied Cabochons, 6 1/2 In.	800.00
Vase, Banjo, Red Leaves Carved In 2 Layers, Signed, 7 In.	695.00
Vase, Blown–Out Hyacinth, Purple & Lavender, 12 1/2 In.	5250.00
Vase, Blue Leaves & Flowers, Frosted Ground, Bulbous, Signed, 8 In.	475.00
Vase, Box Elder Branches, Squat Bulbous Base, Signed, 17 1/4 In.	700.00
Vase, Branches, Signed, 17 1/4 In.	700.00
Vase, Butterflies & Iris, 20 In. ....*Illus*	1100.00
Vase, Double Overlay, Etched Phlox, Tapered, Signed, 11 1/2 In.	1210.00
Vase, Floral, Bulbous, Frosted Ground, Signed, 8 1/4 In.	475.00
Vase, Floral, Red, Yellow, White, 3 In.	450.00
Vase, Gourd Shape, Etched Interior, Oak Leaves, Acorns, Signed, 9 In.	2250.00
Vase, Green Leaves On Frosted Ground, Signed, 3 X 2 1/2 In.	400.00
Vase, Hanging Wisteria, Signed, 6 In.	795.00
Vase, Hollyhocks, Frosted Blue To Green, 23 In.	3500.00
Vase, Lake Como, Triple Overlay, Peacock & Trees, Signed, 13 1/2 In.	6050.00
Vase, Lavender Clematis, Frosted Ground, Signed, 30 In.	2600.00
Vase, Lavender, Signed, 10 In.	550.00
Vase, Lavender, White, Marked, 3 X 3 In.	250.00
Vase, Layers Of Blue Flowers, Gold Ground, Bulbous, Signed, 7 1/2 In.	2250.00
Vase, Leaves & Berries, Orange To Brown, Cameo, 6 1/2 In.	475.00
Vase, Leaves, Berries, Red Base, Signed, 5 1/4 In.	795.00
Vase, Purple Crocus, Frosted Ground, Signed, 3 1/2 In.	325.00
Vase, Purple Flowers, Pale Pink Ground, Signed, 4 In.	250.00
Vase, Purple Violets, White Opaque Ground, Signed, 6 In.	200.00
Vase, Red & Orange Floral, Teal Ground, Signed, 7 1/2 In.	900.00
Vase, Stick, Grape Vine On Frosted Peach, Signed, 30 In.	2600.00
Vase, Teardrop, Amethyst Tree & Landscape, Signed, 7 In. ....*Illus*	375.00
Vase, Thistle, Yellow–Green On Frosted White To Pink Ground, 8 In.	660.00
Vase, Tree, Amethyst, Teardrop Shape, Signed, 7 In.	375.00
Vase, Wisteria, Acid Etched Yellow Ground, Signed, 8 1/4 In.	350.00
Wall Pocket, Butterflies & Bows, Fan Shape, Signed, 14 In.	950.00

Game plates are any make of plate decorated with pictures of birds, animals, or fish. The game plates usually came in sets consisting of twelve dishes and a serving platter. These sets were most popular during the 1880s.

GAME PLATE, Bird, Coronet Pattern, Gold Trim, Limoges, 10 In.	85.00
Deer, Z.S.& Co., Bavaria, 9 In.	45.00
Gold Rococo Border, Artist Signed, Limoges, 13 1/2 In.	269.00
Gold Trim, Signed L.Couderl, Limoges, 11 In.	115.00
Herring Gull, Buffalo Pottery, 1907	35.00
Pheasants In Field, Haviland, Artist Signed	95.00
Rococo Gold Border, Fruit & Flowers, Limoges, 13 1/4 In., Pair	575.00
Rococo Gold Scalloped Border, Signed, Limoges, 13 1/2 In.	225.00
Sandpipers, Artist Signed, Limoges	85.00

Children's games of all sorts are collected. Of special interest are any board games or card games. Other games may be found listed under Toy, Card, or the name of the character or celebrity featured in the game.

GAME, Above The Clouds, Zeppelin Cover, Milton Bradley	8.00
Addams Family, Milton Bradley	20.00
Airplane Express, Milton Bradley	25.00
Airways, Lindstrom, 14 Airplanes Of 1930s On Base, 1934, 24 X 14 In.	75.00

Ally Sloper, Clown Toss, 1900, Box	35.00
Alphabet, Cards, Stick Figures, Verses, 1930	15.00
Authors, Box, Parker Bros.	10.00
Authors, McLoughlin	22.00
Barney Google, Milton Bradley, 1923 ....85.00 To 95.00	
Baron Munchausen, Parker Bros.C.1933	18.00
Baseball, Parker Brothers, 1902	22.00
Baseball, Wilder Mfg.Co., 1930s	35.00
Basketball, Springboard, Litho, Crowd & Flag Backdrop, 1930s	25.00
Beany & Cecil	8.00
Bird Wonderland, Educational, Original Box	25.00
Black Joe's Trip, Paper	6.00
Blondie & Dagwood, Westinghouse, King Features, 1940 Premium	30.00
Bonzo, With Balls, 1930s, 4 In.	75.00
Bowling, Athol, Mass.	17.00
Bowling, Lucky Strike, Linstrom, Tin Litho, 1933 ....20.00 To 45.00	
Calling Superman Spin Cycle	25.00
Card, Playing, Actor & Actresses, Charlie Chaplin, Tom Mix, Etc.	10.00
Card, Playing, Camel Cigarettes	8.50
Card, Playing, Coldspot Refrigerator, 1935	12.00
Card, Playing, Indian Maid Portrait, Burntwood Box, 1908	20.00
Card, Playing, Panama Canal, Oval Scenes, Original Box	12.00
Card, Playing, Pornographic, 1950s	10.00
Carou, Gambling, 1920	22.00
Carpet Bowl, English, Original Box	22.00
Checkerboard, C.1870, Salmon & Black	195.00
Checkerboard, Holden, Mass., Inlaid Walnut, 1892	195.00
Checkerboard, Inlaid, Walnut & Maple, 22 In.	105.00
Checkerboard, Reverse On Glass, Framed, 1880s, 22 In.	465.00
Chick In The Coop, 1930s	20.00
Christmas Tree, Litho Paper On Wood, Parker Bros., 20 X 24 In.	200.00
Chuck–A–Luck, Ivory Dice, Numbered Felt, 17 1/2 In.	150.00
Circination Or Swinging 'Round The Circle, McLoughlin, Box	185.00
Cole's Bread, Tin, White Balls For Black Woman's Teeth, Round	45.00
Consul The Educated Monkey, Tin, Instructions, Complete	85.00
Croquet, Table, 1890 ....45.00 To 60.00	
Dart Board, Super Target, Outerspace	40.00
Dart, Sambo, Black Boy With Big Eyes, Tooth Missing, 14 X 23 In.	65.00
Dart, Suction, Wooden Paddles, Box, 1920s	10.00
Dice, Dr.Daniels	35.00
Dodging Donkey, Parker Bros.	55.00
Dominoes, Advertising, Sapolio Soap	20.00
Dominoes, Dr.Daniels	40.00
Dominoes, Shrewsbury Tomato Ketchup, Dovetailed Box, 1930s	22.00
Dominoes, Victorian Animals, England, Box, 1940s	20.00
Dominoes, White, Celluloid, Wooden Box, Set	50.00
Eddie Cantor, Parker Brothers, C.1938	20.00
Ella Cinders, Milton Bradley, 1944	20.00
Felix The Cat, Target, Tin	9.00
Fibber McGee, 1936	10.00
Fish Pond, Milton Bradley	65.00
Five Wise Birds, Complete With Gun & Box	16.00
Flip Your Wig, Beatles	40.00
Football, Electric, Jim Prentice	32.00
Football, Tom Hamilton, Parker Bros., 1946	20.00
Fortune Wheel, Honeycomb Trim	30.00
Foxy Grandpa Hat Party, Box, Selchow–Righter	20.00
Gang Busters, Radio, 1939	25.00
Goldie Locks & Three Bears, McLoughlin, 1890	110.00
Good Time Charlie, Battery Operated	48.00
Hockey, Katzenjammer Kids, Box	18.00
India, McLoughlin Bros.	50.00
Jack Straw, Depicts Brownies, Box, Instructions	11.00
Junior Combination, Plays 12 Games, Milton Bradley, 1905	25.00

Komical Konversation Kards, Parker Bros., 1893 ....12.50 To 15.00
License Plate Bingo, Dave Garroway, Cards, 1958 .... 35.00
Little Black Sambo, 1945 .... 22.50
Little Bopeep, 1930 .... 22.00
Mah–Jongg, Bone & Bamboo Tiles, 4 Racks, Carved Box 750.00
Monopoly, 1935 .... 40.00
Mysto Magic, Gilbert 35.00
Nancy & Sluggo, 1944 .... 55.00
Old Maid, McLoughlin, 1898 .... 15.00
Ouija Board, Wooden 10.00
Party, Donkey, All Cloth, Box, Milton Bradley, 1932 .... 10.00
Pinball, Poosh–M–Up, Northwestern Products, 23 X 13 In. 45.00
Play Ball, Baseball Game, Wooden Bats, Rosebud Art Co., Box 22.00
Pollyanna, The Glad Game, Board, Oct.19, 1915 .... 40.00
Pretty Little Village, Box, Milton Bradley 95.00
Prince Valiant, Game Of Valor, Transogram, Box ....30.00 To 35.00
Pumpkin Face Ring Game, Box, 1927 .... 20.00
Puss In Boots, Box, Milton Bradley 15.00
Puzzle, Blocks, Aunt Louisa's, Lithographed, Original Wood Box 396.00
Puzzle, Blocks, Wooden, Westinghouse Electric, Dated 1926, Boxed 15.00
Puzzle, Cubes, Robinson Crusoe, McLoughlin 195.00
Puzzle, Indian Camp Scroll, Box, McLoughlin 190.00
Puzzle, Jigsaw, Aeroplane & Dirigible, Milton Bradley 18.00
Puzzle, Jigsaw, American Steel, Farm Scene, 1933 .... 18.00
Puzzle, Jigsaw, Amos & Andy, Pepsodent, Envelope 45.00
Puzzle, Jigsaw, Andy Gump, Box, 1933 .... 10.00
Puzzle, Jigsaw, Animal, Set Of 4, Box, 1940 .... 10.00
Puzzle, Jigsaw, Barker's Almanac, 1902 .... 9.00
Puzzle, Jigsaw, Brownie Town, Clean Up Campaign, Wooden, 1920s 20.00
Puzzle, Jigsaw, Chase & Sanborn, Girl Picking Tea, Ceylon Tea 20.00
Puzzle, Jigsaw, Continental Autos, Beacon, Flyer, Reversible, 1930s 30.00
Puzzle, Jigsaw, Dennis The Menace, Framed Tray, Whitman 15.00
Puzzle, Jigsaw, Dr.Seuss, Essolube Advertising 20.00
Puzzle, Jigsaw, Flying A Production, Buffalo Bill Jr., 1956 .... 12.00
Puzzle, Jigsaw, Humpty–Dumpty, Wooden, Color 18.00
Puzzle, Jigsaw, Jiggs & Maggie, 1932 .... 10.00
Puzzle, Jigsaw, McKesson Drugs, Our Gang, Mounted, 1932 .... 60.00
Puzzle, Jigsaw, North Atlantic Squadron, Box, McLoughlin, 8 X 20 In. 275.00
Puzzle, Jigsaw, Patriotic, West Point, Original Envelope, C.1942 .... 5.50
Puzzle, Jigsaw, Pretty Good, Eh, Mrs.Holstein, Cows & Horses, 250 Pieces ... 10.00
Puzzle, Jigsaw, Rough Riders, Teddy Roosevelt, Box 125.00
Puzzle, Jigsaw, Sohio Radio, 1933 .... 45.00
Puzzle, Jigsaw, Victor Talking Machine, Record Shape, 45 Artists, 1908 .... 65.00
Puzzle, Jigsaw, White Sewing Machine & Bicycle 125.00
Puzzle, Victor Talking Machine Co., 45 Recording Artists, Dated 1908 .... 55.00
Ring Toss, Box, 1912 .... 10.00
Rockets Away, Launcher, Futuristic Space City, 1950s 80.00
Roulette Wheel, Claw Foot Table, Mason 2750.00
Roulette Wheel, Wooden Case, Chips, Cards, 1940s 125.00
Royal Jack Straws, 1906 .... 6.00
Santa Claus Ring Toss 3.00
Shoot A Loop, Tin, Marble, Wolverine ....20.00 To 22.50
Shooting Gallery, Wyandotte, Unused 75.00
Skittles & Cakes, 1946 .... 45.00
Skittles, Wooden, Penguins In Boat, French 145.00
Snake Eyes, Black Man & Woman On Front, 1930s 35.00
Sound–O Radio 43.00
Star Trek, 1979, Milton Bradley 18.00
Steeple Chase, Tin, Box 25.00
Tiddly Winks, Milton Bradley 10.00
Topsy Turvy, Comic Characters, 1908 .... 45.00
Touring Card, 1926 .... 10.00
Untouchables 35.00
Wheel Of Fortune, Bronze, Cast Iron Base, 19th Century, 11 1/2 In. 300.00

Wheel Of Fortune, Paper Under Glass Design, Case, 1895, 2 Ft.	650.00
Whippet Race, Pressman & Co., 1930	20.00
White Rose Curling, Box	20.00
Wild Bill Hickok	10.00
Wings, 1928	25.00
Wonder Speller, Educational, Box	25.00
Yacht Race, Clark & Snowdon, 1890	120.00

Gaudy Dutch pottery was made in England for America from about 1810 to 1820. It is a white earthenware with Imari–style decorations of red, blue, green, yellow, and black. Only sixteen patterns of Gaudy Dutch were made: Butterfly, Carnation, Dahlia, Double Rose, Dove, Grape, Leaf, Oyster, Primrose, Single Rose, Strawflower, Sunflower, Urn, War Bonnet, Zinnia, and No Name. Other similar wares are called "Gaudy Ironstone" and "Gaudy Welsh."

GAUDY DUTCH, Bowl, Butterfly, 11 In.	3900.00
Bowl, Waste, Dove	575.00
Coffeepot, War Bonnet	3900.00
Creamer, Double Rose	400.00
Cup & Saucer, Butterfly	195.00
Cup & Saucer, Double Rose	90.00
Cup & Saucer, Oyster	65.00
Cup Plate, Grape, 3 1/2 In.	425.00
Plate, Butterfly, 6 1/2 In.	300.00
Plate, Butterfly, 7 1/4 In.	275.00
Plate, Double Rose, 6 1/2 In.	110.00
Plate, Double Rose, 7 1/2 In.	105.00
Plate, Double Rose, 9 In.	135.00
Plate, Double Rose, 10 In.	370.00
Plate, Grape, 8 1/2 In.	400.00
Plate, Single Rose, 7 In.	45.00
Plate, Toddy, Double Rose, 4 1/2 In.	150.00
Plate, War Bonnet, 8 In.	170.00
Plate, Zinnia, Marked Riley, 5 3/4 In.	175.00
Sugar, Single Rose, Covered	675.00
Tea Bowl & Saucer, Carnation	495.00
Tea Bowl & Saucer, Double Rose	395.00
Tea Bowl & Saucer, Dove	75.00
Tea Bowl & Saucer, Oyster	395.00
Tea Bowl & Saucer, Sunflower	775.00
Teapot, War Bonnet, 6 1/2 In.	225.00

Some collectors have named the ironstone wares with the bright Gaudy Dutchlike patterns "Gaudy Ironstone." There may be other examples found in the listing for Ironstone or under the name of the ceramics factory.

GAUDY IRONSTONE, Bowl, Waste, Floral Design, 6 1/2 X 3 1/8 In.	35.00
Bowl, Waste, Strawberry, 5 1/4 X 3 1/2 In.	115.00
Bowl, Waste, Urn, 5 5/8 X 3 1/2 In.	65.00
Cup Plate, Floral Border, 3 3/4 In.	15.00
Mug, Morning Glory, Blue & Copper Luster, 3 3/8 In.	18.00
Pitcher, Red, Blue, & Green Luster, 6 1/4 In.	47.50
Plate, Floral In Underglaze Blue, 10 1/8 In.	85.00
Plate, Poppies & Cornflowers, 9 3/4 In.	28.00
Plate, Red Rose, 8 7/8 In.	50.00
Plate, Toddy, Sleeping Eye, 5 In.	225.00
Plate, Urn, 7 In.	10.00
Platter, Morning Glory, Copper Luster, 14 1/2 In.	135.00
Sauce Boat, Strawberry, Enameling, 5 1/8 In.	150.00
Sugar, Urn, Covered	259.00
Tea Bowl & Saucer, Floral	50.00
Teapot, Morning Glory, Blue, Red, Green & Black, 9 3/4 In.	25.00

Gaudy Welsh is an Imari-decorated earthenware with red, blue, green, and gold decorations. It was made after 1820.

GAUDY WELSH, Bowl, 4 3/4 X 2 5/8 In.	40.00
Creamer, Oyster	65.00
Creamer, Tulip	50.00
Cup & Saucer, Oyster	35.00
Cup & Saucer, Seeing Eye	100.00
Cup & Saucer, Tulip	30.00 To 47.00
Cup, Wagon Wheel	50.00
Jar, Biscuit, Silver Plated Lid, Rim & Handle	50.00
Mug, Tulip	10.00
Pitcher, Milk, Wagon Wheel, 8 1/2 In.	175.00
Pitcher, Oyster, 4 1/2 X 4 1/2 In.	50.00
Pitcher, Oyster, 5 1/2 In.	75.00
Pitcher, Pagoda, 5 5/8 In.	15.00
Plate, Dessert, Oyster, 6 In.	19.00
Plate, Wagon Wheel, 8 3/4 In.	75.00

In the late nineteenth century Geisha Girl porcelain was made in Japan for export. It was an inexpensive porcelain often sold in dime stores or used as free premiums. Pieces are sometimes marked with the name of a store. Japanese ladies in kimonos are pictured on the dishes. Borders of red, blue, green, gold, brown, or several of these colors were used. Modern reproductions are being made.

GEISHA GIRL, Berry Set, 5 Piece	75.00
Bowl, Petal Rim, Gold Trim, Orange, 10 In.	60.00
Bowl, Red, 4 1/2 In.	13.50
Chamberstick	28.00
Chocolate Set, Red Trim, 9 Piece	100.00 To 110.00
Cookie Jar	65.00
Creamer	12.00
Cup & Saucer, Green Trim	8.00
Cup & Saucer, Orange	6.50
Cup & Saucer, Red	6.50 To 9.50
Cup, Demitasse	6.00
Dish, Mayonnaise, Red	8.50
Dresser Set, Signed, 10 Piece	195.00
Hatpin Holder, 4 In.	25.00
Match Holder, Hanging, Orange, 3 1/4 In.	17.00
Nut Set, Red, 7 Piece	30.00
Pitcher, 4 In.	35.00
Plate, 7 1/4 In.	6.00
Plate, Green, 6 In.	4.50 To 6.00
Plate, Green, 7 In.	5.00 To 6.00
Salt & Pepper, Floral, 3 1/2 In.	12.00
Sugar & Creamer, Cobalt Blue Trim, Gold Leaf, Covered	35.00
Sugar, Orange Border, Covered, 5 In.	12.00
Tea Cup	5.00
Tea Set, 15 Piece	125.00
Tea Set, Orange, 11 Piece	100.00
Teapot, 3 In.	15.00
Toothpick	20.00

Gene Autry was born in 1907. He began his career as the "Singing Cowboy" in 1928. His first movie appearance was in 1934, his last in 1958.

GENE AUTRY, Book, Better Little Book, Autry & Bandit Of Silver Tip	12.00
Book, Big Little Book, Riders Of Range	12.00
Book, Boston Garden Rodeo, 1948	5.00
Book, Ghost Riders, Hardcover	8.00
Book, Song	14.00
Boots, 4 Buckle	65.00
Comic Book	10.00

Guitar, Made By Harmony, Wooden, Case, 1940s 165.00
Gun & Holster Set, Double 75.00
Gun, Cap ....20.00 To 40.00
Gun, Cap, Belt, & Holster 55.00
Horn, Bicycle, Boxed 55.00
Lunch Box, Melody Ranch, Tin, Bullet Shape Thermos, Box 55.00
Paper Tablet 10.00
Pennant, With Champ, Back In The Saddle Again Written 25.00
Photograph, The Phantom Empire, Black & White 8.00
Pinback, Champ 8.00
Pistol, 50 Shot, Repeater, Puffs Smoke, Box 50.00
Puzzle, Cardboard, Tray 6.00
Ranch Set, Figures, Chuck Wagon, 38 Piece 32.00
Record, Rudolph, 78 RPM 12.00
Reel, Viewmaster, Box, 1950 .... 12.00
Ring, Portrait 40.00
Sheet Music, Cowboy's Heaven, 1934 .... 6.00
Spurs, Official, Box 20.00
Thermos 19.00
Wristwatch 20.00

Black and blue decorated Gibson Girl plates were made in the early 1900s. Twenty-four different 10 1/2-inch plates were made by the Royal Doulton Pottery at Lambeth, England. These pictured scenes from the book "A Widow and Her Friends" by Charles Dana Gibson. Another set of twelve 9-inch plates featuring pictures of the heads of Gibson Girls had all-blue decoration. Many other items also pictured the famous Gibson Girl.

GIBSON GIRL, Art Book, Charles Dana Gibson, Americans 1902 .... 90.00
Frame, Brass 65.00
Pitcher, Water ....285.00 To 350.00
Plaque, Playing Golf, Burnt Outlining, 14 X 10 In. 10.00
Plate, A Quiet Dinner With Dr.Bottles 80.00
Plate, Calendar, 1909 .... 38.00
Plate, Failing To Find Rest & Quiet In Country 65.00
Plate, Girl On Pier, Souvenir, Centerville, Michigan, 7 1/2 In. 20.00
Plate, Hostile Criticism 65.00
Plate, Message From Outside World 65.00
Plate, Mr.Diggs Is Alarmed, Royal Doulton 65.00
Plate, She Becomes A Trained Nurse 85.00
Plate, She Contemplates The Cloister ....80.00 To 85.00
Plate, She Decides To Die In Spite Of Dr.Bottles, 10 In. 65.00
Plate, She Finds Exercise Does Not Improve Her Spirits 65.00
Plate, She Goes Into Colors 65.00
Plate, She Looks For Relief Among The Old Ones 65.00
Plate, They All Go Skating 65.00
Plate, They Go Fishing 65.00
Plate, They Take A Morning Run 65.00

GILLINDER *Gillinder pressed glass was first made by William T. Gillinder of Philadelphia in 1863. The company had a working factory on the grounds at the Centennial and made small, marked pieces of glass for sale as souvenirs. They made a variety of decorative glass pieces and tablewares.*

GILLINDER, Paperweight, Ruth The Gleaner, Clear, Centennial Souvenir 85.00
Shoe, Crystal, 1876 Centennial, Signed 45.00
Sugar Shaker, 6 Lobe 142.00

The Girl Scout movement started in 1912, two years after the Boy Scouts. It began under Juliette Gordon Low of Savannah, Georgia. The first Girl Scout cookies were sold in 1928. Collectors search for anything pertaining to the Girl Scouts, including uniforms, publications, and old cookie boxes.

GIRL SCOUT, Book Of Games, 1929 ....10.00 To 15.00

Camera, Official, Telescopic Sight, Box 55.00
Canteen, Box, 1940s 8.00
Knife, Pocketkut, Master 9.00
Mug, USA 10.00
Sewing Kit, Leatherette Case 17.50
Uniform, 1930s 18.00

GLASS, CONTEMPORARY, see Contemporary Glass

Eyeglasses, or spectacles, were mentioned in a manuscript in 1289 and have been used ever since. The first glasses with rigid side pieces were made in London in 1727. Bifocals were invented by Benjamin Franklin in 1785. Lorgnettes were popular in late Victorian times.

GLASSES, Ben Franklin Style, 14K Gold 30.00
Ben Franklin Style, Aqua 16.00
Granny, Victorian, Sterling Silver, Chain, C.1860 .... 35.00
Lorgnette, Art Nouveau, Fold Into Handled Case, Sterling Silver 75.00
Lorgnette, Art Nouveau, Sterling Silver, Gold Wash 75.00
Lorgnette, Chain, Sterling Silver 34.00
Lorgnette, Folding, White Gold, Sterling Silver Chain 50.00
Lorgnette, Gold Covered, Engraved 725.00
Lorgnette, Marcasite Clip Handle 130.00
Lorgnette, Tortoiseshell 45.00
Magnifying, Ivory Handle, Inlaid Stones, C.1920, Japanese 225.00
Pince Nez, Sterling Silver, Chain 45.00

W. Goebel Porzellanfabrik of Oeslau, Germany, now Rodental, West Germany, has made many types of figurines and dishes. The firm is still working. The pieces marked "Goebel Hummel" are listed under Hummel in this book.

GOEBEL, Ashtray, Thumper, Full Bee 125.00
Bank, No.29/0, Boy Blowing Horn, Crown Mark 65.00
Condiment Set, Friar Tuck 20.00
Condiment Set, Monk, Full Bee ....55.00 To 65.00
Cookie Jar, Cardinal, Red Robe 125.00
Creamer, Friar Tuck, 2 1/2 In. 15.00
Creamer, Monk, Full Bee, 5 1/2 In. 48.00
Figurine, Flamenco Woman Dancer, Art Deco, 10 In. 150.00
Half–Doll, Plumed Hat, Long Gray Hair, Crown Mark, 4 1/2 In. 235.00
Jar, Monks, Covered, 4 1/2 In. 30.00
Night–Light, Figural, Dog, Crown Mark 60.00
Pitcher, Friar Tuck, 5 In. 40.00
Pitcher, Friar Tuck, No.747 2/0, Full Bee 14.00
Plaque, Angel, Hanging, Stylized Bee, 5 X 5 In. 38.00
Plaque, Jasperware, Girl With Jars, Fisherman, High Relief 225.00
Plate, Annual, 1971 .... 600.00
Plate, Annual, 1975 .... 47.00
Plate, Annual, 1980 .... 36.00
Salt & Pepper, Egghead 28.00
Salt & Pepper, Pup, Crown Mark 15.00
Sugar & Creamer, Friar Tuck 25.00
Toby Jug, Mrs.Gamp, Full Bee 39.00

Porcelain has been made by three branches of the Goldscheider family. The family left Vienna during World War II and started factories in England and in Trenton, New Jersey.

GOLDSCHEIDER, Bust, Chinese Boy & Girl, 8 In., Pair 145.00
Cigarette Holder & Ashtray, Dutch Girl At Well 45.00
Figurine, Bachelor Carnation & Lady Violet, 7 In., Pair 97.00
Figurine, German Shepherd, Lying Down, 8 In. 65.00
Figurine, Girl, Short Flowered Dress, 8 In. 175.00
Figurine, Lady Caller, 6 In. 50.00
Figurine, Lady, Green Ruffled Dress, Yellow Hat, Marked, 8 In. 62.00
Figurine, Lady, Hooped Skirt, 8 In. 49.00
Figurine, Madonna, Signed, 5 In. 22.00

Figurine, Man, Holding Cape & Bouquet, 9 1/2 In. 75.00
Figurine, Oriental Actor, Turquoise Base, 12 In. 95.00
Figurine, Renaissance Madonna, P.Finns, Gold Crest, 12 In. 50.00
Figurine, Southern Belle & Man, P.Porcher, Gold Crest, Pair 95.00
Figurine, Southern Belle, 11 In. 55.00
Figurine, Wolfhound, 11 In. ....155.00 To 168.00

Lawton Gonder opened Gonder Ceramic Arts, Inc. in 1941. He worked in the old Peters and Reed pottery in Zanesville, Ohio. Gonder pieces include lamp bases marked "Eglee" and many wares with Oriental-type glazes.

GONDER, Figurine, Mandarin Lady, Jade Green, 12 In. 12.00
Figurine, South Seas Island Girl, Lime Green, Marked, 14 In. 30.00
Jar, Temple, Yellow, Covered, 9 1/2 In. 18.00

Goofus glass was made from about 1900 to 1920 by many American factories. It was originally painted gold, red, green, bronze, pink, purple, or other bright colors. Many pieces are found today with flaking paint and this lowers the value.

GOOFUS GLASS, Bowl, Pears & Apples, 10 In. 28.00
Bowl, Pedestal, Crimped, Fluted, Greek Key, Northwood, 9 1/2 In. 30.00
Bowl, Red Cherries, Gold Trim, 9 In. 20.00
Bowl, Red Raspberry, 9 In. 21.00
Bowl, Red Roses On Gold, 9 1/2 In. 12.00
Bowl, Ruffled, Strawberries, 10 In. 23.00
Bowl, Silver & Red, Blooms & Blossoms, Tricornered, 7 In. 25.00
Bread Tray, Last Supper 30.00
Cake Plate, Grape, Lavender & Pink Rim, 11 In. 45.00
Compote, Cherries & Leaves, 6 1/2 In. 17.50
Compote, Strawberry, 10 X 9 In. 45.00
Cruet, Wild Rose & Bowknot, Frosted, Original Stopper 65.00
Jar, Black, Bird & Grapes, Pair 35.00
Jar, Pickle, Painted Ship In Full Sail, Seagulls, 9 1/2 In. 25.00
Jar, Powder, Gibson Cameo Top, Clear 25.00
Jar, Powder, Red & Gold Roses, Covered 30.00
Lamp, Red Roses, Leaves, Gold Ground, Milk Glass Chimney 75.00
Plate, Apple, 8 1/2 In. 25.00
Plate, Carnation, 6 In. 15.00
Plate, Gold, Ruby Flowers, 11 In. 20.00
Plate, Roses & Gold, 10 1/2 In. 30.00
Plate, Scalloped, Red Iris, Gold Trim, 10 1/2 In. 15.00
Plate, World's Fair, St.Louis, 1904 .... 18.00
Vase, Bird On Vine, 9 1/2 In. 15.00
Vase, Cabbage Rose, 6 In. 40.00
Vase, Red & Gold, Flowers, Birds, 9 1/2 In., Pair 45.00
Vase, White, Puffed Out Roses, Bulbous, 5 1/2 In. 22.00

Goss china has been made since 1858. English potter William Henry Goss first made it at the Falcon Pottery in Stoke-on-Trent. The factory name was changed to Goss China Company in 1934 when it was taken over by Cauldon Potteries. Production ceased in 1940. Goss china resembles Irish Belleek in both body and glaze. The company also made popular souvenir china, usually marked with local crests and names.

W.H.COSS

GOSS, Bust, Dickens, 8 In. ....45.00 To 75.00
Bust, Lord Byron, 8 In. ....45.00 To 75.00
Bust, Shakespeare 25.00
Bust, Sir Walter Scott, 5 In. ....30.00 To 45.00
Creamer, Victoria Jubilee, 1887 .... 55.00
Cup, Elgin Crest 22.00
Figurine, Annette 100.00
Figurine, Daisy 90.00
Figurine, Peggy ....65.00 To 90.00
Pitcher, Milk, Jubilee Of Queen Victoria, 1887 .... 55.00

Planter, Posy Duck	30.00
Skull, Alas Poor Yorick	95.00
Vase, Floral, Green, Beaded Enamel, Blown Bottom, 12 1/2 In.	75.00
Vase, Model Of Leather Bottle, Crest Of Worthing, Marked, Miniature	10.00
Vase, Tyg, Crest Of Bedford, Marked, Miniature	10.00

Pottery has been made in Gouda, Holland, since the seventeenth century. Two firms, the Zenith pottery, established in the eighteenth century, and the Zuid–Hollandsche pottery, made the brightly colored wares marked "Gouda" from 1880 to about 1940. Many pieces featured Art Nouveau or Art Deco designs.

GOUDA, Ashtray, Blue Green Matte, Cobalt Blue On Rim, Marked, 4 1/4 In.	48.00
Bowl, Floral, Covered, 6 In.	60.00
Bowl, Peacock Design, 18 X 5 In.	300.00
Candlestick, Gold Panels, Colored Flowers, Marked, 5 3/8 X 3 In., Pair	75.00
Candlestick, Orange, Blue, & Green, 4 1/2 X 4 1/2 In.	69.00
Candlestick, Saucer, Handle, 6 1/2 In.	60.00
Compote, Design Inside Bowl, Burnt Orange, House Mark, 6 1/2 In., Pair	60.00
Compote, Footed, 5 1/2 In.	355.00
Creamer, Burnt Orange & Brown, 2 1/2 In.	38.00
Cup & Saucer, Windmill Scene, Royal	49.00
Dish, Art Nouveau, Green, Bronze, Covered, Marked, 6 X 4 In.	110.00
Figurine, Plazuid Girl, 11 In.	155.00 To 165.00
Humidor, House, Tan, Blue, & Green, Matte, Signed, Large	145.00
Jar, Gray, Tulip Band, Covered, Signed DAM Holland, 16 3/4 In.	100.00
Lamp, Abstract Floral Design, Ivora Mark, 11 1/2 In.	120.00
Match Holder, Ivora, 2 3/4 In.	39.00
Pitcher, Black & Glazed Purple, 7 In.	75.00
Pitcher, Gold Design, Black, 5 In.	55.00
Pitcher, Peacock Eyes, Gold Trim, Black Matte, Marked, 2 5/8 In.	30.00
Powder Box, High Glaze, Regina 85, Round, 5 X 2 In.	110.00
Tobacco Jar, Melon Ribbed, Signed, 5 1/2 X 6 1/2 In.	130.00
Vase, Art Deco Design, House Mark, 8 1/8 In.	88.00
Vase, Art Nouveau, Artist Signed, 5 3/4 In.	95.00
Vase, Brown, Gold, & Green Design, Schoolhouse Mark, 2 X 2 In.	45.00
Vase, Bulbous, Cobalt Bands, Floral, Black Matte, House Mark, 5 1/4 In.	55.00
Vase, Floral Design, Marked, 6 1/4 In.	50.00
Vase, Flower & Thorns In Deco Design, Marked, 8 1/4 In.	110.00
Vase, Flowers, Green, White, Marked 1041, 5 1/4 In.	60.00
Vase, Flowers, Squat, 3 In.	35.00
Vase, High Glaze, Handles, Zuid, Holland, 10 1/2 In.	275.00
Vase, Stylized Florals, Marked Regina Bochara, 10 1/2 In.	125.00
Warmer, Food, Pierced, Yellow, House Mark	22.00

Graniteware is an enameled tinware that has been used in the kitchen from the late nineteenth century to the present. Earlier graniteware was green or turquoise blue, with white spatters. The later ware was gray with white spatters. Reproductions are being made in all colors.

GRANITEWARE, Ashtray, Gray	12.00
Basin, Blue, White Interior, 10 In.	22.00
Basin, Emerald & White	40.00
Basket, Berry, Dark Blue & White Swirl, 6 In.	43.00
Bathtub, Baby's, Gray	140.00
Bedpan, Blue, Covered	15.00
Bedpan, Gray, Meinecke	10.00
Bedpan, White, Covered	7.00 To 10.00
Bedpan, With Urinal, Covered, Gray	22.00
Boiler, Coffee, Gray, 3 Gal.	45.00
Bowl, Blue Swirl, 9 In.	35.00
Bowl, Child's, Light Blue, White, 4 In.	32.00
Bowl, Gray, 11 X 2 1/2 In.	12.50
Bowl, Gray, 5 In.	50.00
Bowl, Mixing, Yellow & White Swirl	45.00
Bowl, Soup, Gray	15.00

Cake Pan, Blue & White Swirl, 9 X 13 In. 52.00
Candleholder, White, Plate Style, Handle, 7 In. 22.00
Candlestick, Beehive, Gray 95.00
Canner, Green 15.00
Chamber Pot, Blue, Covered 65.00
Chamber Pot, Gray & White, Covered 22.00
Chamberstick, Blue & White 22.00
Coffeepot, Blue & White Swirl, 7 1/2 In. 40.00
Coffeepot, Blue & White Swirl, 10 In. 37.50
Coffeepot, Blue & White Swirl, Gooseneck ....60.00 To 65.00
Coffeepot, Blue & White, 12 In. 35.00
Coffeepot, Blue, Domed Lid 35.00
Coffeepot, Child's, Blue ....42.00 To 45.00
Coffeepot, Child's, Tin Lid, Gray 37.50
Coffeepot, Gray & Black, Bail Handle, 11 1/2 In. 50.00
Coffeepot, Gray, 8 1/2 In. ....14.00 To 22.00
Coffeepot, Gray, 10 In. 12.00
Coffeepot, Gray, Commercial 165.00
Coffeepot, Green Trim, Glass Top, Yellow 25.00
Coffeepot, Powder Blue & White Swirl, Gooseneck 50.00
Coffeepot, Red, 6 Cup 27.00
Coffeepot, White, Birds & Flowers 168.00
Colander, Blue 12.00
Colander, Diffused, Brown & White Swirl 35.00
Colander, Gray, Attached Drip Tray, Footed 75.00
Colander, Gray, Straight Sides 15.00
Colander, Robin's Egg Blue & White, Long Handle 42.00
Colander, Speckled Black & White, Footed 17.00
Cup & Saucer, Child's, Blue & Multicolor 18.00
Cup, Blue 12.00
Cup, Gray ....8.50 To 12.50
Dish, Soup, Gray, Liner 22.00
Dishpan, Cobalt Swirl 45.00
Dishpan, Gray, Oval 21.00
Double Boiler, Blue Swirl 55.00
Double Boiler, Speckled Blue, Covered 42.00
Dustpan, Child's, Black 20.00
Dutch Oven, Red Porcelain Lid, Farmer's Premium, 1940s, Gray 10.00
Eggcup, Pale Blue 14.00
Eggcup, Rose & White 8.50
Feeder, Invalid, White 9.00
Funnel, Blue 7.00
Funnel, Brown 16.00
Funnel, Gray, Handle, 3 1/2 In. 15.00
Funnel, White, Black Trim, 4 In. 13.00
Grinder, White, Marked Harras 45.00
Heater, Bath, Blue & White 12.00
Hot Plate, Electric, Green Speckle 45.00
Kettle, Berlin, Covered 58.00
Kettle, Gooseneck Spout, Gray 37.50
Kettle, Preserving, Child's, Gray, Bail Handle 10.00
Kettle, Preserving, Original Label, Cobalt Blue & Red 25.00
Kettle, Preserving, Signed L&G, Gray, 22 In. 38.00
Ladle, Black & White Mottled 9.00
Ladle, Blue & White Swirl 12.00
Ladle, Cobalt Blue, 12 In. 10.00
Ladle, Gray 20.00
Ladle, Mottled Blue 50.00
Ladle, Oyster, Gray 15.00
Loaf Pan, Bread, Gray 9.00
Measure, Cobalt Blue & White, 1 Pt. 45.00
Measure, Gray, 1 Qt. 20.00
Measure, Gray, 1 Cup ....30.00 To 65.00
Mixing Bowl, Red, 9 1/2 In. 12.00

Mold, Food, Scalloped, Gray 20.00
Mold, Pudding, Gray 65.00
Mold, Ring 85.00
Muffin Pan, Gray, 6 Hole 25.00
Muffin Pan, Gray, 8 Hole 26.00
Mug, Blue Swirl 20.00
Mug, Cobalt Blue & White ....14.00 To 22.00
Mug, Crystolite With White Swirl 25.00
Mug, Farmer's, Blue & White 38.00
Pail, Bail Handle, Gray, Covered, 6 1/2 X 5 In. 22.00
Pail, Berry, Blue & White, Covered, Medium 48.00
Pail, Berry, Blue & White, Covered, Miniature 130.00
Pail, Berry, Gray Mottled, Bail, Covered, 1/2 Gal. 39.00
Pail, Berry, Gray, Bail, Covered, 6 1/2 In. 42.00
Pail, Cream, Gray, Qt. 25.00
Pail, Lunch, Gray, 3 Piece 75.00
Pail, Lunch, Gray, Round, Bail Handle, Tin Cover, 7 1/2 In. 35.00
Pail, Lunch, Miner's, Gray ....65.00 To 95.00
Pail, Milk, Gray, 7 In. 35.00
Pail, Water, Blue & White Swirl 50.00
Pail, Water, Gray & Brown 35.00
Pan, Angel Food Cake, Robin's Egg Blue & White Swirl 135.00
Pan, Bread, Gray 18.00
Pan, Cake, Tube, Blue 16.00
Pan, Frying, Gray, Pouring Spout, 7 In. 18.00
Pan, Gray On Gray, 10 X 6 In. 12.00
Pan, Light Blue, White Specks, Handle, 13 X 3 In. 25.00
Pan, Loaf, Gray 10.00
Pan, Pudding, Crystolite With White Swirl 55.00
Pan, Sauce, Long Curving Handle 25.00
Pan, Strainer, Brown & White 16.00
Pan, Tart, 4 Cup 55.00
Pan, Utility, Gray, 12 1/2 X 2 1/2 In. 15.00
Pan, Utility, Powder Blue & White Swirl 18.00
Pan, White, Blue Trim, 6 X 9 In. 10.00
Percolator, Turquoise 25.00
Picnic Set, Cream, Green Border, 1930s, 18 Piece 55.00
Pie Pan, Brown & White Swirl 38.00
Pie Pan, Gray On Gray, 9 In. 8.00
Pie Pan, White Swirl, Turquoise 15.00
Pie Peeler, Long Iron Handle, Gray, Hand Crafted 18.00
Pie Plate, Blue & White ....8.00 To 14.00
Pitcher & Bowl, Blue Diffused 75.00
Pitcher, Gray, 8 In. 85.00
Pitcher, Molasses, Gray 52.00
Pitcher, Syrup, Aqua & White Swirl 75.00
Pitcher, Syrup, Figure Of Head On Top, Pewter Trim 195.00
Pitcher, Syrup, Floral, Blue 58.00
Pitcher, Turquoise, White Mottled, 11 In. 75.00
Pitcher, Water, Light Gray 26.00
Pitcher, White, Black Trim, 2 Qt. 13.00
Platter, Turkey, Mottled Blue & White 70.00
Potty, Child's, Blue 15.00
Potty, Child's, Cream, Green 12.00
Potty, Child's, Gray 12.00
Rack, Utensil, White 75.00
Rice Ball, Gray 165.00
Roaster, 3 Piece 125.00
Roaster, Blue 12.00
Roaster, Brown & White Swirl 38.00
Roaster, Cobalt Blue & White Swirl 38.00
Roaster, Gray 23.00
Roaster, Jade Green, Republic Metalware, Covered, 1909 .... 39.00
Roaster, Savory, Speckled Gray 10.00

Roaster, White Spatter, Green, Covered	35.00
Salt Box, Wall, White	39.50
Saucepan, Blue & White Swirl, Large	40.00
Saucepan, Blue & White, Shamrock, Covered	38.00
Saucepan, Mottled Blue & White, Tubular Handle	36.00
Saucepan, Red & White Swirl	45.00
Scoop, Grocer's, Gray, Manufacturer's Mark	78.00
Scoop, Thumb, Gray, Dull Handle	35.00
Sieve, Gray, Pan Shape, Handle, 7 In.	12.50
Skillet, Aqua & White Swirl	75.00
Skillet, Black, Side Pour	15.00
Skillet, Rolled Handle, Gray, 9 In.	25.00
Skimmer, Gray	25.00
Slop Jar, Blue & White Swirl, Covered	90.00
Soap Dish, Gray, Wall	27.50
Soap Dish, Insert, Blue & White Swirl	45.00
Soap Holder, Over Tub, White	50.00
Spittoon, Blue & White Swirl	65.00
Spoon, Basting, Green, Cream	9.00
Spoon, Basting, White, Black	7.00
Spoon, Floral, Pewter Trim	100.00
Stove, Wood, Home Comfort, Towel Bars, Water Reservoir, Gray	1800.00
Strainer, Blue & White Swirl, Round	35.00
Strainer, Brown & White Swirl	20.00
Strainer, Soup, Blue Outside, White Inside, Elliptical	48.00
Strainer, Tea, Gray	38.00
Sugar Shaker, White & Blue	75.00
Sugar, Gray, Covered	100.00
Table, Child's, Scene In Middle, Trimmed In Blue, White	60.00
Tea Set, Child's, White, Blue Band, 12 Piece	85.00
Teakettle, Gray, Over Iron, Dated 1889	48.00
Teakettle, Tulip Design, Green	14.00
Teapot, Blue & Cream Mottled, Gooseneck, English	50.00
Teapot, Blue & White, Gold Stripe, Gooseneck, Bulbous, 6 In.	57.00
Teapot, Child's, Dark Blue	16.00
Teapot, Child's, Green	15.00
Teapot, Dark Gray, Pewter Trim, 11 In.	300.00
Teapot, Shamrock, White Swirl	130.00
Teapot, Speckled Blue, Hinged Cover, Manning–Bowman Co.	150.00
Teapot, Violets, Pink, Gooseneck	65.00
Teapot, White, Pewter Cover, Handle	85.00
Tray, Tip, Blue & White Swirl	25.00
Tray, White, Blue Trim, Rayed, Handles, 18 X 13 In.	22.00
Trivet, Portland Stove Foundry, Yellow	35.00
Tumbler, White, Dark Blue Trim, L & G Mfg.Co., 16 Oz.	4.50
Warmer, Baby Bottle, Gray & White	65.00
Washboard, Blue	45.00 To 65.00

Greentown glass was made by the Indiana Tumbler and Goblet Company of Greentown, Indiana, from 1894 to 1903. In 1899, the factory name was changed to National Glass Company. A variety of pressed, milk, and chocolate glass was made.

GREENTOWN, see also Chocolate Glass; Custard Glass; Holly Amber; Milk Glass; Pressed Glass

GREENTOWN, Berry Bowl, Brazen Shield, Blue, Small	30.00
Butter, Cactus	125.00
Butter, Teardrop & Tassel, Covered	30.00
Cake Plate, Cord Drapery	30.00
Compote, Austrian, 7 7/8 X 8 1/4 In.	40.00
Compote, Teardrop & Tassel, Nile Green	250.00
Creamer, Austrian	28.00 To 30.00
Cruet, Dewey	55.00
Dish, Hen Cover, Basket Weave Base, Opaque White, 5 3/8 In.	75.00
Goblet, Shuttle	45.00

Graniteware and other enameled kitchenware should be cleaned with water and baking soda. If necessary, use chlorine bleach.

Grueby, Vase, Lotus
Foliage, Green Glaze,
A.Lingley, 8 In.

Grueby, Vase, Molded
Foliage, Green Glaze,
Impressed Mark, 6 In.

Mug, Dewey, Blue	95.00
Mug, Holly	65.00
Pitcher, Water, Melrose	35.00
Punch Cup, Austrian, Gold Trim	18.00
Relish, Teardrop & Tassel, Oval, Green	40.00
Salt & Pepper, Cactus, Vaseline, Opalescent	45.00
Salt & Pepper, Shuttle	40.00
Spooner, Austrian, Large	28.00
Stein, Buttermilk, Serenade, Green Paint	25.00
Stein, Serenade	35.00
Sugar, Dolphin, Footed, Covered	175.00
Tankard Set, Brazen Shield, Blue, 7 Piece	425.00
Tray, Dewey, Serpentine, Amber, 10 In.	32.50
Tumbler, Austrian, Green	125.00
Tumbler, Brazen Shield, Cobalt Blue	40.00
Tumbler, Cord Drapery	45.00
Wine, Austrian, Canary	110.00
Wine, Austrian, Vaseline	95.00 To 110.00
Wine, Herringbone Buttress, Deep Green	160.00
Wine, Shuttle	12.00

Grueby Faience Company of Boston, Massachusetts, was incorporated in 1897 by William H. Grueby. Garden statuary, art pottery, and architectural tiles were made until 1920. The company developed a matte green glaze that was so popular it was copied by many other factories making a less expensive type of pottery. This eventually led to the financial problems of the pottery.

GRUEBY, Bowl, Matte Green, Blue, Lime Interior, Marked, 4 In.	140.00
Bowl, White, Green Interior, Low, 5 In.	100.00
Bowl, Yellow, Rolled Rim, C.1905, 9 1/2 In.	75.00
Tile, Sailing Ship, Blue, Cream, Tan & Brown, Initials Painted, 6 In.	495.00
Tile, Turtle & Leaves, C.1905, 6 In.	175.00
Vase, 2 Color, Buds Against Spiked Leaves, Dated & Marked, 7 In.	1400.00
Vase, 3 Tab Handles, Rolled Rim, C.1905, 9 1/4 In.	325.00
Vase, Blue, Bulbous, Vertical Details, C.1905, Signed, 4 In.	225.00
Vase, Carved Out Leaves Encircle Cucumber, Green, 6 In.	430.00
Vase, Cylindrical, Green Mottled, C.1905, 9 In.	250.00
Vase, Dark Blue, Bulbous, Rolled Rim, C.1910, Marked, 3 X 6 In.	275.00
Vase, Foliage, Green Glaze, 1894, Marked, 7 In.	250.00
Vase, Foliage, Green Glaze, Lotus, Ovoid, 1894, Marked, 5 In.	195.00
Vase, Green Glaze, 5 Recessed Panels, Marked, 7 1/2 In.	275.00
Vase, Green Glaze, Melon Form, 8 1/2 In.	395.00
Vase, Green Glaze, Scalloped, Leaves, Artist Signed, C.1910, 7 3/4 In.	175.00
Vase, Green, Tricorner Top, Buds, 7 1/2 In.	125.00

Vase, Lotus Foliage, Green Glaze, A.Lingley, 8 In. ....*Illus*   450.00
Vase, Matte Green, 5 1/2 In. ....*Color*   600.00
Vase, Matte Green, Leaves, Bulbous, 1900, Artist Initialed, 11 In. 800.00
Vase, Molded Foliage, Green Glaze, Impressed Mark, 6 In. ....*Illus*   225.00
Vase, Yellow Buds, Green Glaze, C.1910, Stamped, 5 3/8 In. 700.00

 *Included in this category are shotguns, pistols, and other antique firearms. Rifles are listed in their own section. Be very careful when buying or selling guns because there are special laws governing the sale and ownership. A collector's gun should be displayed in a safe manner, probably with the barrel filled or a part missing to be sure it cannot be accidentally fired.*

GUN, BB, Daisy 104, Double Barrel, Box 400.00
BB, Daisy, No.25, Wooden Handle, 50 Shot Pump, Early 1930s 48.00
BB, King 500, Pat.1917 ....   40.00
BB, Red Ryder 45.00
Cannon, Carriage, Cast Iron, 23 1/2 In. 200.00
Carbine, Cartridge, Sharp 850.00
Derringer, Double Barrel, Remington, 41 Cal. 350.00
Musket, Flintlock, 1892 Springfield, 69 Caliber 925.00
Muzzle Loader, 58 Caliber Smooth Bore, Capped Lock, 1865–70 ....   250.00
Pistol, 5 1/4 Barrel, Rejector On Side, 7 1/2 In. 80.00
Pistol, Bedford County, Percussion, Signed Amos Border 650.00
Pistol, Civil War Officer's, Manhattan Fire Arms Co., Newark, N.J. 75.00
Pistol, Colt 45, 13 3/4 In. 250.00
Pistol, Colt 51, Navy, Ivory Handle, Matching Numbers 475.00
Pistol, Colt, Centennial, Gold Work, Case, Pair 180.00
Pistol, Colt, Russell Waddell & Majors, Dated 1849, Holster 650.00
Pistol, Colt, U.S.Army, Ivory Grips, Nickel Plated, Backward Stamp 2450.00
Pistol, Derringer, Silver Trim, Marked, 6 3/4 In. 270.00
Pistol, Dueling, Gold Inlay, Damascus Finish, Fluted Handle, Cased, Pair 4450.00
Pistol, Flintlock, 50 Caliber, English, Marked George I, 18th Century 395.00
Pistol, Flintlock, 50 Caliber, French, C.1750, 6 1/4 In. 300.00
Pistol, Flintlock, 6 In.Barrel, Brass Mountings 135.00
Pistol, Flintlock, Checkered Walnut Stock, 11 1/2 In. 250.00
Pistol, Flintlock, Curly Maple Stock, Handmade, H.White, 14 3/4 In. 190.00
Pistol, Flintlock, Curly Walnut Stock, Initialed I.C., 12 3/8 In. 240.00
Pistol, Flintlock, Em.W.Bond, English, 9 In.Barrel 175.00
Pistol, Flintlock, Royal Highland Regiment, American Revolution, Scotch 825.00
Pistol, Greatcoat, English, Double Sidelocks, C.1690, Matched Pair 5500.00
Pistol, I.Johnson, Pocket, 22 Caliber, Sold By Lovel Arms, 1875–95 ....   100.00
Pistol, Knife, Percussion, Sterling Silver Barrel 350.00
Pistol, Muff, Percussion, Burled Grips 70.00
Pistol, Officer's, Silver Mounted, Ketland & Co., C.1770 ....   775.00

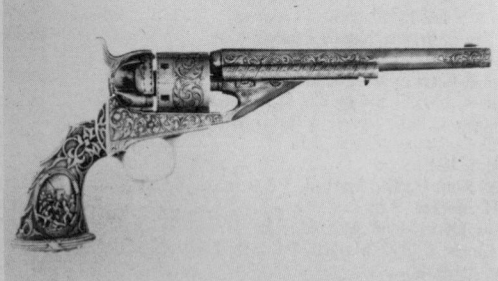

Small nicks and scratches in iron can be covered with black crayon. Wipe off the excess with paper.

Gun, Revolver, Colt, Navy Model, Tiffany Grips, 1861

Pistol, Pepperbox, Dragoon Size, Allen & Thurber, C.1850, 6 In. 300.00
Pistol, Percussion Cap, Barrel, 8 In. 130.00
Pistol, Percussion, Checkered Grip, 8 1/2 In., Pair 300.00
Pistol, Percussion, Derringer, 41 Caliber, Walnut, Inlaid German Silver 185.00
Pistol, Sharps, 4 Barrel, Brass Mounted, 6 1/2 In. 260.00
Pistol, Smith & Wesson, 22 Caliber 49.00
Pistol, Starr, Percussion, Civil War Soldier's Name & Regiment 385.00
Pistol, Williams, Pocket, London, 1770, Pair 800.00
Revolver, Adams, Tranter Double Action, 30 Caliber, Box, England, C.1853 .... 550.00
Revolver, Colt Model 1862 Police, 36 Caliber, C.1865 .... 190.00
Revolver, Colt, Model 1849, 5 In.Barrel, Pocket 350.00
Revolver, Colt, Model 1862, Police, 36 Caliber, C.1865 .... 190.00
Revolver, Colt, Navy Model, Tiffany Grips, 1861 ....*Illus* 5500.00
Revolver, Colt, Open Top, 22 Caliber, Brass Frame, Walnut Grips 175.00
Revolver, European, 6 In.Octagon Barrel, 1870s 45.00
Revolver, Front Loading, Pocket, Slocum, Sliding Chamber, C.1863 .... 270.00
Revolver, Merwin & Hulbert, 44/40 Caliber, With Constable Badge 225.00
Revolver, Percussion, Cooper, 1863 .... 275.00
Revolver, Smith & Wesson, 22 Caliber, Civil War Era, 1859 .... 95.00
Revolver, Smith & Wesson, 2nd Issue, 22 Caliber, Rosewood Handle 117.50
Revolver, Smith & Wesson, No.1, 22 Caliber, Rosewood, Nickel Plated 200.00
Revolver, Smith & Wesson, No.1, 3rd Issue, 22 Caliber, Rosewood Grips 135.00
Revolver, Smith & Wesson, No.2, 32 Caliber 160.00
Revolver, Star, Civil War, Cap & Ball 200.00
Revolver, Whitney, No.1, 22 Caliber, Narrow Cylinder, Brass Frame 175.00
Shotgun, Double Barrel Percussion, Marked Ondon, C.1850 .... 75.00
Shotgun, Hammer, Colt, Double Barrel, 10 Gauge 350.00
Shotgun, Percussion, Hand Whittled Wood Ramrod, 37 In. 275.00
Shotgun, Percussion, Marked New York, Cherry, 53 In. 135.00
Shotgun, Winchester, 12 Gauge, Featherweight 395.00
Shotgun, Winchester, Model 12, 16 Gauge, 6 Digit Serial No. 350.00

Gunderson glass was made at the Gunderson-Pairpoint Glass Works of New Bedford, Massachusetts, from 1952 to 1957. Gunderson Peachblow is especially famous.

GUNDERSON, Ewer, Peachblow, 6 In. 135.00
Rose Bowl, Tightly Crimped, Applied Leaves, 3 1/2 In. 50.00

Gutta-percha was one of the first plastic materials. It was made from a mixture of resins from Malaysian trees. It was molded and used for daguerreotype cases, toilet articles, and picture frames in the nineteenth century.

GUTTA-PERCHA, Case, Brown, Foliage, 2 Tintypes, Man, Woman, 3 1/4 X 3 3/4 In. 50.00
Case, Children Playing, Dark Brown, 2 Tintypes, 3 X 4 5/8 In. 35.00
Case, Columbia Seated, Label, 3 1/4 X 3 3/4 In. 40.00
Case, Compote Of Fruit, 2 Tintypes, Women, 3 3/4 X 3 1/4 In. 15.00
Case, Deer, Black, Tintype, Child, Long Dress, 3 1/2 X 3 7/8 In. 35.00
Case, Floral, Brown, Tintype, Child, 3 1/4 X 3 3/4 In. 25.00
Case, Fruit & Flowers, Tintype Of Young Woman, 2 5/8 X 3 In. 35.00
Hand Mirror, Floral, Dragon, Black, Diatite Pat.1866, 8 3/4 In. 20.00
Match Safe, Arm & Hammer Soda 42.00
Match Safe, Roseberry Cigars 34.00

Haeger Potteries, Inc., Dundee, Illinois, started making commercial art wares in 1914. Early pieces were marked with the name "Haeger" written over an "H." About 1938, the mark "Royal Haeger" was used. The firm is still making florist wares and lamp bases.

HAEGER, Bowl, Crackled Glaze, 10 1/2 In. 45.00
Cookie Jar, Nummy Cookies Frog 26.00
Figurine, Dutch Girl & Boy, Matte Green, 9 In., Pair 50.00
Head, Man & Woman, Art Deco, 8 In., Pair 55.00
Planter, Blue, Lady Pushing Baby Buggy, Toddler 8.00
Planter, Victorian Lady, Blue, Wicker Baby Buggy, Sticker 10.00
Vase, Aztec Gold, Bulbous, Twin Spout, Haeger USA 4001, 8 In. 18.00

Vase, Bulbous, Green Drip Glaze, Green, 8 In. 18.00
Vase, Original Label, Blue, 8 In. 35.00
Vase, Pedestal, Marbelized Brown & Cream, Ribbed, Marked, 6 1/2 In. 22.00
Vase, Pillow, Ivory, Oval Base, Baby Rabbit, Sticker 15.00

Hall China Company started in East Liverpool, Ohio, in 1903. The firm made all types of wares. Collectors search for the Hall teapots made from the 1920s to the 1950s. The dinnerwares of the same period, especially Autumn Leaf pattern, are also popular. The Hall China Company is still working. Autumn Leaf pattern dishes are listed in their own category in this book.

HALL, Baker, Blue Bouquet, Black, Fluted, 7 3/4 In. 12.00
Baker, French, Orange Poppy, 8 In. 8.00
Baker, Pie, Crocus 25.00
Bean Pot, Chinese Red, Handles 15.00
Berry Bowl, Wildfire 4.75
Bowl, Blue Bouquet, Handles, Eva Ziesel, 11 3/4 In. 12.00
Bowl, Mixing, Orange Poppy, 6 In. 6.50
Bowl, Mixing, Orange Poppy, 9 In. 15.00
Bowl, Mixing, Red Poppy, No.5 .... 10.00
Bowl, Mixing, Wildfire, 9 In. 12.00
Bowl, Salad, Orange Poppy 10.00
Bowl, Salad, Red Poppy 10.00
Bowl, Vegetable, Red Poppy, 9 In. 9.00
Box, Westinghouse, Green, Oblong, Covered 16.00
Box, Westinghouse, Orange, Oblong, Covered 16.00
Cake Plate, Red Poppy 12.00
Cake Plate, Springtime 12.00
Canister Set, Salt & Pepper, Red, Sunshine 175.00
Casserole, Rose Parade Pattern, Covered, 7 1/2 In. 20.00
Coffeepot, E–Line, Cameo Rose, Electric 60.00
Coffeepot, Irish, Occidental Ins.Co., Advertising 20.00
Coffeepot, Orange Poppy, Covered 40.00
Coffeepot, Wildfire 30.00
Cookie Jar, Cactus, Banded 75.00
Cookie Jar, Crocus 45.00
Cookie Jar, Orange Poppy, Pretzel 40.00
Cookie Jar, Pig, Basket, Medallion, Gold Trim 22.00
Cookie Jar, Taverne 55.00
Creamer, Cameo Rose 10.00
Creamer, Chinese Red 5.00
Creamer, Red Poppy 10.00
Cup & Saucer, Wildfire 6.50
Cup, Red Poppy 5.50
Dish, Refrigerator, Tea, Covered, 4 X 6 In. 10.00
Drip Jar, Red Poppy, Covered 20.00
Jug, Aladdin, Canary & Gold 13.00
Jug, Orange Poppy 15.00
Jug, Red Poppy, 6 1/4 In. 14.00
Jug, Sani–Grid, Chinese Red, Small 15.00
Mug, Beverage, Taverne 25.00
Mug, White, Pedestal, Black Base 3.00
Mustard, Orange Poppy 45.00
Pitcher, Green, Made For Westinghouse, 8 In. 17.00
Pitcher, Milk, Wildfire, 6 1/2 In. 30.00
Pitcher, Water, Rose Parade, Ovoid 25.00
Platter, Red Poppy, 11 1/4 In. 18.50
Platter, Wildfire, 13 1/2 In. ....14.00 To 18.00
Punch Set, Tom & Jerry, Black With Gold, 7 Piece ....88.00 To 98.00
Range Set, Red Poppy, Handled Salt & Pepper 35.00
Salt & Pepper, Red Poppy, Handles 20.00
Salt & Pepper, Rose White 12.00
Salt & Pepper, Sani–Grid, Rose White 15.00
Salt & Pepper, Wildfire 8.50

Saucer, Red Poppy	4.00
Soup, Coupe, Red Poppy	12.00
Soup, Dish, Flat, Wildfire	9.00
Sugar & Creamer, Cameo Rose	25.00
Sugar & Creamer, Rose Parade	16.00
Teapot, Airflow, Chinese Red	50.00
Teapot, Airflow, Gold Floral	45.00
Teapot, Aladdin, Black	30.00
Teapot, Aladdin, Cobalt Blue & Gold	23.00
Teapot, Aladdin, Marine	20.00
Teapot, Aladdin, Yellow	18.00
Teapot, Art Deco, Squat	24.00
Teapot, Baltimore, Marine	22.50
Teapot, Basket, Canary	75.00
Teapot, Cameo Rose	45.00
Teapot, Crest	18.00
Teapot, Football, Chinese Red	325.00
Teapot, Globe, Emerald	52.00
Teapot, Hollywood, Black	22.00
Teapot, Hollywood, Chartreuse, Plain	20.00
Teapot, Lipton, Gold Flowers, White	15.00
Teapot, Lipton, Maroon	18.00
Teapot, Los Angeles, Celadon	20.00
Teapot, McCormick Co., Baltimore, Green, Silver Trim, 7 In.	35.00
Teapot, McCormick, Blue & Gray	20.00
Teapot, Melody, Orange Poppy	80.00
Teapot, Mustard Yellow, Boston, Gold Trim	20.00
Teapot, Nautilus, Turquoise	80.00
Teapot, New York, Red Poppy	36.00
Teapot, Parade, Canary	30.00
Teapot, Philadelphia, Turquoise	20.00
Teapot, Red Poppy, New York	39.95 To 40.00
Teapot, Red, Airflow	25.00
Teapot, Ronald Reagan, Marked	40.00 To 45.00
Teapot, Sani–Grid, Red	25.00
Teapot, Streamline, Green, Covered	30.00
Teapot, Sugar, & Creamer, Embossed Lipton's Tea, Blue	70.00
Teapot, Surfside, Canary, Gold	65.00
Teapot, Surfside, Green	65.00
Teapot, Windshield, Ivory, Gold Dots, 6 Cup	22.50
Teapot, Yellow & Gold Acorns, Hook Cover	27.50

Halloween is an ancient holiday that has been changed in the last 200 years. The jack–o'–lantern, witches on broomsticks, and orange decorations seem to be a twentieth–century creation. Collectors started to become serious about collecting Halloween–related items in the late 1970s. The papier–mache decorations, now replaced by plastic, and old costumes are in demand.

HALLOWEEN, Box, Candy, Black Cat On Pumpkin, Papier–Mache, 2 1/2 In.	60.00
Box, Candy, Pugs, 5 Blacks Riding On Jelly Bean Airship	125.00
Candleholder, Skull, Bisque, Painted, Movable Jaw, 3 1/4 In.	100.00
Cat, Black, Applied Ears, 2 1/2 In.	85.00
Cat, Black, Wood Hanging Match	27.00
Cat, Black, Yard Ornament	30.00
Clicker, Pumpkin, Wooden	35.00
Costume, Chinaman, Halco Brand, Complete	55.00
Costume, Chock Full Of Nuts Peanut Jar, Strap, 22 X 46 In.	200.00
Costume, Clown	35.00
Costume, Devil, Tail & All	15.00
Costume, Ghost, Hooded, Girl's	28.00
Costume, Hippie, 1960s, Box	15.00
Costume, Rin Tin Tin's Rusty, Original Box	25.00
Costume, Snoopy, 1960s, Box	10.00
Costume, WAC, 1940s, 5 Piece	42.00

Costume, Winky Dink	55.00
Devil, Pitch Fork, 15 1/2 In.	15.00
Hat, Cone Type, Halloween Scenes, Germany	1.60
Horn, Black Cat, Litho, 7 In.	75.00
Horn, Graphic, Dated 1921, Marx, 15 In.	16.00
Jack-O'-Lantern, Black, White Face, 2 1/2 In.	85.00
Jack-O'-Lantern, Paper Eyes & Teeth, Papier-Mache	10.00
Jack-O'-Lantern, Papier-Mache, Cat	22.00
Jack-O'-Lantern, Papier-Mache, Painted, On Wire, 2 1/4 In.	70.00
Jack-O'-Lantern, Smiling, 3 1/2 In.	50.00
Jack-O'-Lantern, Swivels Open For Candle, Wire Base, 6 In.	300.00
Jack-O'-Lantern, Tin, 6 In.	160.00
Lantern, Owl, Papier-Mache, 10 1/2 In.	185.00
Lantern, Paper Cut, Black	17.00
Lantern, Skeleton Faces On Each Side	10.00
Lantern, Witch, Owl, Black Cat	5.00
Mask, Batman, Glasses	6.00
Mask, Face, Cisco Kid & Pancho, Pair	25.00
Mask, Pie-Eyed Mickey Mouse, Par-T-Mask, Paper, 10 In.	18.00
Mask, Red Devil, Kresge's 10 Cent Tag, Stiffened Net	6.00
Mask, Western Bandana, Steer Head On Leather Slide	20.00
Mask, Witch, Attached Black Hood, 1940s	6.50
Pumpkin On Leaves, Painted Plaster & Cloth, 1 1/4 In.	55.00
Pumpkin, Witch & Fire	12.00
Skeleton Dancer, 1930s, 18 1/2 In.	25.00
Skeleton, Folding Arms & Legs, Creases, German, 26 In.	22.00
Tambourine, Black & Orange Pumpkin	14.00
Tambourine, Jack-O'-Lantern Face, Tin, 1930s	17.50
Witch, Jack-O'-Lantern, Cardboard, Original Candle, 1930s	17.50
Witch, Papier-Mache, Japan, 3 In.	40.00

Hampshire pottery was made in Keene, New Hampshire, between 1871 and 1923. Hampshire developed a line of colored glazed wares as early as 1883, including a Royal Worcester-type pink, olive green, blue, and mahogany. Pieces are marked with the printed mark or the impressed name "Hampshire Pottery" or "J.S.T. & Co., Keene, N.H."

HAMPSHIRE, Bowl, Molded With Trees, 5 X 3 In.	45.00
Chocolate Pot, Clinton, Massachusetts, Library	55.00
Chocolate Pot, Matte Cobalt Blue Glaze, Covered, Marked, 11 In.	110.00
Clock, Matte Blue	200.00
Coffee Set, Ivory & Green, Gold Trim, Signed, 13 Piece	175.00
Inkwell, Green, 4 In.	85.00
Jug, Peanut, Green	38.00
Lamp, Oil, Monumental, Footed, Green, Embossed Tulips, 15 In.	195.00
Pitcher, Raised Leaves, Green Glaze, 8 In.	85.00
Stein, State Capitol, Albany, N.Y., Decal, Marked, 6 In.	38.50
Stein, Windmill Scene, 6 In.	40.00
Teapot, Butterfly Finial	65.00
Vase, Cylindrical, Matte Green, Marked, 5 In.	275.00
Vase, Embossed Vertical Design, Matte Green, Marked, 7 In.	75.00
Vase, High Relief Panel Design, Matte Green, Marked, 14 3/4 In.	198.00
Vase, Relief Crocus Design, Matte Green, Marked, 8 1/2 In.	154.00
Vase, Stylized Design, Leaves, Handles, Matte Green, 8 X 6 In.	110.00
Vase, Volcanic Blue Glaze, 6 In.	60.00

Philip Handel worked in Meriden, Connecticut, about 1885 and in New York City from about 1900 to the 1930s. His firm made art glass and other types of lamps. Handel shades were made not only of leaded glass in a style reminiscent of Tiffany but also of reverse painted glass.

HANDEL, Humidor, Copper Ring & Hinge, Green, Gold Interior, 7 1/2 In.	350.00
Lamp, 4-Branch, Pond Lily, Bent Glass Shades, Bronze, Signed, 16 In.	1900.00
Lamp, 12 Glass Panels, Stamped Base	300.00
Lamp, Birds Of Paradise, Red, Blue, Orange, Yellow, 12 In.	1195.00

Lamp, Boudoir, No.6649	400.00
Lamp, Boudoir, Roses, Gray, Signed	450.00
Lamp, Bronze, Forest Design, Marked, 13 1/2 In.	145.00
Lamp, Caramel Glass Panels, Signed Shade & Base, 18 X 26 In.	2800.00
Lamp, Chipped Ice Shade, Reverse Painted, Florals, Bronze, 24 In.	1900.00
Lamp, Desk, Brass, Hubbel Socket With Acorn Pull	175.00
Lamp, Filagree, Caramel Glass Panels, Signed, 18 X 26 In.	2800.00
Lamp, Floor, Lyre Frame, Cylindrical, Round Copper Foot, 57 In.	275.00
Lamp, Gooseneck, Chipped Ice Cylinder Shade, Moonlight Scene	425.00
Lamp, Organ, Floor	1500.00
Lamp, Piano, Poppy Blossom, Rose Leaded Shade, Bronze Base, 14 In.	750.00
Lamp, Satin Glass Shade, Bronze, 14 In.	175.00
Lamp, Table, Leaded, Carmel, Amber, Green, Signed, 19 In.	700.00
Lamp, Table, Palm Tree, Red Sunset	1500.00
Lamp, Table, Reverse Painted, Bronze, Domed Shade, 24 X 18 In.	2300.00
Lamp, Top Of Jewel Colors, Polychrome Base, Signed, 18 In.	850.00
Lamp, Torchere, Art Deco Reverse Painted Shade, 14 In., Pair	800.00
Light, Wall, Bronze Holder, Frosted Glass, Pair	265.00
Vase, Teroma, Woodland Scene, Signed Bedigie, 10 In.	1450.00

HARDWARE, see Architectural

Harlequin dinnerware was produced by the Homer Laughlin Company from 1938 to 1964, and sold without trademark by the F.W. Woolworth Co. It has a concentric ring design like Fiesta, but the rings are separated from the rim by a plain margin. Cup handles are triangular in shape.

HARLEQUIN, Ashtray, Basketweave, Dark Green, Set Of 3	20.00
Ashtray, Rose	20.00
Bowl, Salad, Gray, Individual	15.00
Butter, Red, Covered	50.00
Creamer, Red	4.00
Dish, Nut, Yellow	5.00
Eggcup, Red	8.50
Jug, Water, Green	25.00
Pitcher, Water, Yellow, 5 Tumblers	135.00
Plate, Red, 7 In.	2.00
Platter, Blue, 11 In.	5.00
Salt & Pepper, Red	2.50
Saucer, Yellow	1.00
Teapot, Green	22.00
Teapot, Yellow	25.00

Hatpins were fashionable from 1860 to 1920 when the large, heavy hat required special long–shanked pins to hold the hat in place. Naturally, hatpin holders were made during the same years. The hatpin holder resembles a large saltshaker, but it often has no opening at the bottom as a shaker does. Hatpin holders were made of all types of ceramics and metal. Look for other prices under the name of specific manufacturers.

HATPIN HOLDER, Blue Design, Violets, Raised Beaded Edge, Porcelain	55.00
Brass, Egyptian Design	35.00
Desert Scene, Japan	35.00
Porcelain, Violets, Raised White Beading, Saucer Type	55.00
Pottery, Purple Floral, 4 3/4 In.	29.00
Pottery, Roses, 4 3/4 In.	29.00

Hatpins were popular from 1860 to 1920. The long pin, often over four inches long, was used to hold the hat in place on the hair. The tops of the pins were made of all materials from solid gold and real gemstones to ceramics and glass. Be careful to buy original hatpins and not recent pieces made by altering old buttons.

HATPIN, 14K Gold Head	30.00
Art Nouveau Woman's Head, Sterling Silver	35.00
Black Balls On End, White Paper, 12 In., Set Of 6	20.00

Haviland, Gravy Boat, Butterflies,
Attached Saucer, H & Co.

Haviland, Sugar, Creamer, Tray,
Blue, Green, C.1890

Butterfly, Carnival Glass	20.00
Cameo	45.00
Filigree Setting, Pink Stone, 8 In.	12.50
Love Knot, Sterling Silver	22.00
Sunflower, Brass	14.00
Turtle, Blue Stone, 9 In.	27.50

HAVILAND & CO. *Haviland china has been made in Limoges, France, since 1842. The factory was started by the Haviland Brothers of New York City. Other factories worked in the town of Limoges making a similar chinaware. It is possible to match existing sets of dishes through dealers who specialize in Haviland china. Listings of these china matching services can be found in "The Kovels' Collectors' Source Book." Porcelains made by other factories in Limoges, France, are listed in this book under "Limoges."*

HAVILAND TYPE, Vase, Raised Flowers, 12 In.	*Color*	200.00
HAVILAND, Bowl, Vegetable, Newark, Covered, 10 1/2 In.		45.00
Bowl, Vegetable, Princess, Oval		35.00
Charger, Princess, Green 1893 Mark, 12 1/2 In.	67.50 To	75.00
Chocolate Pot, Blue Floral & Gold Gilt Design, 8 3/4 In.		95.00
Chocolate Set, Pink Flowers, 9 Piece		140.00
Clam Plate, Green & Gold		15.00
Cup & Saucer, Apple Blossom		25.00
Cup & Saucer, Demitasse, Theodore Haviland	*Color*	10.00
Cup & Saucer, Drop Rose, Demitasse		39.00
Cup & Saucer, Pink Roses		25.00
Cuspidor, Pink, White, & Gold		140.00
Dessert Set, Moss Rose, 28 Piece		250.00
Dome, Cheese, Blue Chrysanthemum, Fancy Finial		35.00
Dresser Set, Floral & Gold, 6 Piece		65.00
Eggcup, Denver Dry Goods		38.00
Fish Set, Deep Sea Life, Red & Purple Coral, 13 Piece		350.00
Game Set, Birds & Florals, Pre–1891, Platter 14 X 8 In., 15 Piece		350.00
Gravy Boat, Butterflies, Attached Saucer, H & Co.	*Illus*	25.00
Oyster Plate, Seaweed Design, Set Of 12		450.00
Pitcher, Floral, Pink, Green Ground, Handle, Artist Mark, 8 1/4 In.		110.00
Plate, Blue Chrysanthemum, 10 In.		18.00
Plate, Field Flowers, C.1880, 8 In.		40.00
Plate, Floral, Center Monogram, Hand Painted, Marked, 8 1/2 In.		35.00
Plate, Martha Washington, States, 1890s, Marked		75.00
Plate, Moss Rose, Pink Edge, 8 1/2 In.		22.50
Plate, Pink Floral, 10 In.		15.00
Plate, Ranson, 8 In., 6 Piece		35.00
Platter, Princess, 12 In.		35.00
Platter, Turkey, Pink Flowers, 20 In.		75.00

Soup, Cream, Underplate, Frontenac, Handle 18.00
Sugar, Creamer, Tray, Blue, Green, C.1890 ....*Illus* 85.00
Tea Set, Moss Rose, Butter Tub, 16 Piece 58.00
Tray, Dresser, Baltimore Rose, 12 In. 55.00
Tray, Pen, Pink Edge, Roses 19.00
Vase, Hand Painted Scenic Cartouche Front, Marked, 4 In. 45.00
Vase, Raised Flowers, Dark Green, 12 In. 200.00
Vase, Roses, Ovoid, Signed M.J.Towner, 1910, 11 1/2 In. 600.00

T. G. Hawkes & Company of Corning, New York, was founded in 1880. The firm cut glass blanks made at other glassworks until 1962. Many pieces are marked with the trademark, a trefoil ring enclosing a fleur-de-lis and two hawks. Cut glass by other manufacturers is listed either under the factory name or the general category "Cut Glass."

HAWKES, see also Cut Glass
HAWKES, Bottle, Cologne, Cut, Polish Intaglio, 14K Gold Stopper, Marked 495.00
Bowl, Engraved Masted Sailing Vessel, Cornucopia, Signed, 10 1/2 In. 95.00
Carafe, Water, Venetian 175.00
Cocktail Shaker, Block & Thumbprint, Strainer, Cap 150.00
Compote, Iris, Ball Stem, Signed 250.00
Compote, Trapped Bubble Stem, Wheel Spokes From Top, Covered, 8 In. ... 95.00
Cordial, Rock Crystal, Engraved 37.00
Cruet, Oil & Vinegar, Hobstars, Bubble Cut, 8 In. 250.00
Decanter, Allover Enameled Bluebirds & Lattice, Ball Type, Handle 72.00
Decanter, Panels, Teardrop Stopper, Signed, 13 1/2 In. 195.00
Dish, Blown-Out, Signed, 6 In. 285.00
Finger Bowl, Chrysanthemum 125.00
Flower Frog, Floral, Engraved, Marked, 7 X 12 In. 265.00
Goblet, Intaglio, Iris, Knobbed Stem, Engraved Foot, Marked 45.00
Ice Bucket, Engraved Log Cabin Scene, Signed 375.00
Lamp, 3 Fish, Engraved, Signed, 12 In. 395.00
Pitcher, Double Notched Handle, Step Cut Spout, 9 3/4 In. 250.00
Plate, Russian, 12 In. 260.00
Punch Bowl, Albion, Signed, 14 In. 1600.00
Punch Bowl, Base, Hobstar & Fan, Swirled, Signed, 15 X 13 1/2 In. 3950.00
Rose Bowl, Apple Green, Intaglio Cut, 5 3/4 In. 100.00
Tray, Center Medallion Of Bird In Flight, Signed, 8 1/2 X 12 In. 245.00
Tumbler, Diamond & Fan Cut, 6 Oz., 5 Piece 150.00
Vase, Albion, Signed, 14 In. 900.00
Vase, Bud, Etched Garlands, Green & Gilt, 10 In. 95.00
Vase, Concave Sides, Hobstar & Notched Prism, Signed, 14 In. 500.00
Vase, Floral Swags & Ribbons, Green, Gold Trim, Marked, 8 1/4 In. 115.00
Vase, Floral Swags & Ribbons, Green, Gold Trim, Signed, 8 1/2 In. 125.00
Vase, Garlands, Geometric Design, Sterling Silver Rim, 6 1/4 In. 275.00
Vase, Gravic Tulip, Sterling Silver Rim, 10 In. .... 285.00 To 310.00
Vase, Green, Etched Garlands, Gilt, 10 In. 128.00
Vase, Stars & Stripes, Signed, 3 3/4 X 10 In. 95.00
Vase, Trumpet, Clover Mark, 14 In. 175.00
Vase, Trumpet, Navarre, Signed, 16 1/2 In. 1000.00
Vase, Trumpet, Queens, Signed, 16 In. 1250.00
Whipped Cream Set, Signed, 2 Piece 375.00
Wine, Aquilla, Set Of 6 .... 60.00
Wine, Hobnail, Green To Clear, Rayed Base, Signed, 6 1/2 In., Set Of 4 .... 150.00
Wine, Rock Crystal, Engraved 37.00

Heintz Art Metal shop made jewelry, copper, silver, and brass in Buffalo, New York, from 1915 to about 1935. It became Heintz Brothers Manufacturers about 1935. The most popular items with collectors today are the copper desk sets and vases made with silver overlay designs.

HEINTZ ART, Ashtray, Sterling Silver Golfer In Knickers, 3 1/2 X 5 1/2 In. 45.00
Vase, Bulbous, Sterling Silver Rose, Bronze, 5 In. 95.00
Vase, Sterling Silver Florals, Bronze, 12 In. 135.00

Vase, Sterling Silver On Bronze, Signed, 8 In. 90.00

 *Heisey glass was made from 1896 to 1957 in Newark, Ohio, by A. H. Heisey and Co., Inc. The Imperial Glass Company of Bellaire, Ohio, bought some of the molds and the rights to the trademark. Some Heisey patterns have been made by Imperial since 1960. After 1968, they stopped using the "H" trademark.*

HEISEY, see also Custard Glass

HEISEY, Alexandrite, Champagne 65.00
   Alexandrite, Cocktail 65.00
   Alexandrite, Console Set, Empress Bowl, 10 In., 3 Piece 800.00
   Alexandrite, Cordial 175.00
   Alexandrite, Goblet, 10 Oz. 85.00
   Alexandrite, Vase, Dolphin Foot, Signed, 9 1/2 In. 500.00
   Augusta, Goblet, Wide Optic, 11 Oz. 15.00
   Banded Flute, Champagne, Crystal 15.00
   Banded Flute, Oyster Cocktail, 5 1/2 In. 12.00
   Banded Flute, Punch Cup 10.00
   Barcelona, Goblet 22.00
   Basket, Crystal, Handle, Signed, 16 In. 425.00
   Beaded Panels & Sunburst, Celery 45.00
   Beaded Swag, Sugar & Creamer, Covered, Opalescent 185.00
   Beaded Swag, Toothpick, Opalescent 63.00
   Beaded Swag, Toothpick, White Opalescent, Hand Painted Flowers 85.00
   Beau Knot, Cruet, Stopper, Handle 175.00
   Beau Knot, Dish, Mayonaisse, Footed, Ladle 40.00
   Beau Knot, Vase, Fan .... '95.00
   Belvedere, Plate, Torte, Fern Shape, 14 1/2 In. 55.00
   Bookends, Fish .... 55.00 To 135.00
   Bookends, Horse, Rearing 1400.00
   Bookends, Pony, Sitting 105.00
   Bookends, Scotty 175.00
   Botanical, Cigarette Box, Covered, Crystal 80.00
   Cabochon, Goblet, Southwind Cutting 17.00
   Cabochon, Wine, Paper Label 12.00
   Candlestick, Clear, Round Base, 9 1/2 In, Pair 100.00
   Caprice, Candy Dish, Blue, Covered 80.00
   Carcassone, Cigarette Holder, Cobalt 75.00
   Carcassone, Goblet, Short Stem 15.00
   Carcassone, Pitcher, Etched Houston Post, American Legion 145.00
   Carcassone, Sherbet, Low 12.00
   Cascade, Candlestick 48.00
   Cherub, Candlestick, Flamingo 375.00
   Chintz, Plate, 7 In. 6.50
   Coarse Rib, Plate, 8 In. 19.00
   Coarse Rib, Sugar & Creamer, Flamingo 50.00
   Coarse Rib, Sugar & Creamer, Orchid Etch 45.00
   Cocktail Shaker, Moon Glow 40.00
   Colonial, Boat, French Dressing, Crystal 14.00
   Colonial, Bowl, Signed, 4 In. 50.00
   Colonial, Candlestick, 2–Light, Prism Bobeche, 1930s, Pair 68.00
   Colonial, Celery 15.00
   Colonial, Cocktail Shaker, Fisherman Deep Plate, Etched 135.00
   Colonial, Creamer 30.00
   Colonial, Cruet, Catsup, Stopper, 13 Oz. 70.00
   Colonial, Cruet, Stopper 25.00
   Colonial, Dish, Cheese & Cracker 35.00
   Colonial, Goblet, 10 Oz. 7.00
   Colonial, Nappy, Scalloped, 4 1/2 In. 6.00
   Colonial, Oyster Cocktail, 5 Oz. 6.00
   Colonial, Punch Cup, Set Of 12 .... 75.00
   Colonial, Punch Cup, Starred Bottom, Marked 10.00
   Colonial, Sherbet, Stemmed, Footed, 4 Oz. 15.00

Colonial, Sherry, 1 1/2 Oz. 18.00
Colonial, Tumbler, Star Bottom, 3 3/4 In. 12.00
Colonial, Wine, 3 1/2 Oz. 15.00
Colt, Standing 110.00
Course Rib, Celery, Amber Flash, 12 In. 28.00
Course Rib, Nappy, 5 In. 6.00
Crystolite, Ashtray ....4.00 To 6.00
Crystolite, Basket, Handle, 6 In. 300.00
Crystolite, Bonbon, 2 Handles, 7 In. 28.00
Crystolite, Bottle, Cologne, Drip Stopper 135.00
Crystolite, Bowl, Console, Marked, 12 1/2 In. 26.00
Crystolite, Box, Cigarette, Covered ....18.00 To 38.00
Crystolite, Box, Cigarette, Footed 20.00
Crystolite, Candlestick, 4 In. 8.50
Crystolite, Card Case, Monogram 30.00
Crystolite, Champagne 8.00
Crystolite, Cigarette Holder 14.00
Crystolite, Coaster, Round 6.00
Crystolite, Cordial 58.00
Crystolite, Cruet, Oil, Stopper 22.50
Crystolite, Goblet, Marked, 10 Oz. 14.00
Crystolite, Mustard, Covered, Crystal 25.00
Crystolite, Perfume, Stopper 79.00
Crystolite, Pitcher, Water 115.00
Crystolite, Plate, 7 1/2 In. 6.50
Crystolite, Plate, 8 In. 15.00
Crystolite, Puff Box, 4 3/4 In. 42.50
Crystolite, Punch Cup .... 5.00 To 12.00
Crystolite, Sugar & Creamer, Individual, Marked 15.00
Crystolite, Sugar & Creamer, Large 40.00
Crystolite, Tray, 13 In. 28.00
Crystolite, Tray, Round, 13 In. 22.00
Crystolite, Tumbler, Flat, Marked 12.00
Daisy & Leaves, Vase, Signed, 21 In. 125.00
Danish Princess, Champagne 14.00
Danish Princess, Wine 16.00
Diamond Optic, Plate, Green, 6 In. 4.00
Diamond Optic, Platter, Topaz, 12 In. 23.00
Diamond Point, Dish, Jelly, Crystal 4.00
Dolphin, Box, Covered, Floral, Finial, Marked 50.00
Dolphin, Candlestick, 10 In., Pair 195.00
Dolphin, Candlestick, Cobalt, 10 In., Pair 3000.00
Dolphin, Candlestick, Crystal, 10 In., Pair 550.00
Dolphin, Candlestick, Moongleam, 10 In., Pair 1200.00
Dolphin, Dish, Mayonnaise, Moongleam, Footed 30.00
Double Rib & Panel, Mustard, Covered 42.50
Elephant, Baby 140.00
Empress, Bowl, Crystal, Lion Head, 11 In. 275.00
Empress, Bowl, Sahara, 4 1/2 In. 9.50
Empress, Bowl, Serving, Green, Handles 45.00
Empress, Candleholder, 2–Light, Flamingo, Pair 170.00
Empress, Candleholder, Dolphin Foot, Sahara, Pair 165.00
Empress, Candlestick, Dolphin Footed, Pair 185.00
Empress, Candlestick, Dolphin Footed, Sahara, 6 In., Pair 170.00
Empress, Candlestick, Sahara, 7 In., Pair 95.00
Empress, Cocktail Shaker 30.00
Empress, Cornucopia, 7 1/2 In. 36.00
Empress, Cruet 79.00
Empress, Cup & Saucer, Etched 23.00
Empress, Cup & Saucer, Sahara ....27.50 To 33.50
Empress, Cup, Sahara 10.00
Empress, Dish, Mayonnaise, Dolphin Footed 15.00
Empress, Ice Bucket 89.00
Empress, Nut Cup, Dolphin Footed, Marked, Pink 12.00

Empress, Plate, 10 1/2 In.	45.00
Empress, Plate, Pink, 4 1/2 In.	3.50
Empress, Plate, Sahara, Square, 8 In.	17.50
Empress, Plate, Serving, Handles, Sahara, 12 In.	60.00
Empress, Plate, Tangerine, Square, 8 In.	85.00
Empress, Powder Jar, Covered, Sahara	20.00
Empress, Punch Cup, Clear	10.00
Empress, Salt & Pepper, Silver Floral Overlay	39.50
Empress, Sugar & Creamer, Dolphin Footed	55.00
Empress, Sugar & Creamer, Flamingo, Individual	55.00
Empress, Vase, Sahara, Footed, 9 In.	85.00
Fancy Loop, Toothpick	37.00
Fandango, Creamer	40.00
Fandango, Salt	14.00
Fern, Dish, Mayonnaise, 2 Sections, Tab Handles	45.00
Fern, Relish, 4-Part, 9 In.	22.50
Figurine, Asiatic Pheasant	175.00
Figurine, Bull, Marked	1150.00
Figurine, Colt, Marked, Pair	75.00
Figurine, Colt, Standing	95.00
Figurine, Donkey	210.00 To 295.00
Figurine, Elephant, Amber, Marked, Small	2500.00
Figurine, Elephant, Marked, Medium	750.00
Figurine, Elephant, Marked, Small	250.00
Figurine, Geese, Set Of 3	395.00
Figurine, Geese, Wings Half Up, Marked, Pair	125.00
Figurine, Giraffe, Head Back	145.00
Figurine, Goose, Wings Down	200.00
Figurine, Goose, Wings Up	105.00
Figurine, Hen	350.00
Figurine, Horse, Show, Marked	700.00
Figurine, Madonna	65.00
Figurine, Mallard, Wings Halfway	20.00
Figurine, Mare, Lying	2500.00
Figurine, Pig, Mother, Marked	450.00
Figurine, Piglets, Sitting, Marked	70.00
Figurine, Piglets, Standing, Marked	70.00
Figurine, Plug Horse	85.00
Figurine, Pony, Cobalt, Kicking	2400.00
Figurine, Pony, Cobalt, Standing	2400.00
Figurine, Pony, Kicking	125.00
Figurine, Pony, Standing	60.00
Figurine, Rooster	375.00
Figurine, Scotty	80.00 To 125.00
Figurine, Sitting Duck, Chocolate Glass	25.00
Figurine, Sparky	65.00
Figurine, Sparrow	70.00
Figurine, Tropical Fish, Purple	325.00
Figurine, Wood Duck, Floating, Heisey Label	150.00
Flamingo, Basket	175.00
Flamingo, Candleholder, 3-Light, Pink, Marked, Pair	175.00
Flamingo, Candlestick, Triplex	55.00
Flamingo, Console Set, Silver Overlay Trim, Marked, 3 Piece	245.00
Flamingo, Mustard, Covered	60.00
Flat Panel, Sugar & Creamer, Floral Cutting, Crystal	35.00
Flat Panel, Tray, 5-Part, Floral, 10 1/2 In.	26.00
Giraffe, Head Back	165.00
Greek Key, Bread Plate, Oval, 12 X 7 1/2 In.	33.00
Greek Key, Butter, Covered	125.00
Greek Key, Humidor	225.00
Greek Key, Ice Tub, With Underplate	75.00
Greek Key, Jelly, Handles, 5 In.	25.00
Greek Key, Nappy, 5 1/2 In.	80.00
Greek Key, Punch Bowl, Pedestal	125.00

Greek Key, Punch Cup, Pink 20.00
Greek Key, Sherbet, Low, Footed 18.00
Greek Key, Straw Holder 128.00
Greek Key, Sugar & Creamer, Individual, Oval 100.00
Greek Key, Tray, French Bread, 12 1/2 In. 150.00
Greek Key, Tumbler, Water, 5 1/2 Oz. 50.00
Horsehead, Ashtray 49.50
Impromptu, Goblet, 10 Oz. 15.00
Impromptu, Pitcher, Ball, 47 Oz. 120.00
Ipswich, Bowl, Floral, Footed, 11 In. 45.00
Ipswich, Candy Dish, Amethyst, Covered, Imperial 65.00
Ipswich, Champagne ....9.00 To 11.25
Ipswich, Cruet, Sahara 65.00
Ipswich, Goblet ....12.00 To 25.00
Ipswich, Goblet, Green, Stemmed 42.00
Ipswich, Perfume Bottle, Long Applicator, 6 1/4 In. 150.00
Ipswich, Plate, 8 In. 20.00
Ipswich, Rose Bowl, Footed, 11 In. 45.00
Ipswich, Sherbet ....9.00 To 18.00
Ipswich, Sherbet, Green 29.00
Ipswich, Soda, Footed 9.00
Ipswich, Tumbler, Footed, 10 Oz. 12.50
Jamestown, Cocktail 20.00
Kenilworth, Cordial, Cobalt 150.00
Kohinoor, Vase, Ball, 6 In. 30.00
Lamp, Hula Girl 95.00
Lariat, Basket, Footed, Round, 8 1/2 In. 100.00
Lariat, Bowl, Etched, 12 In. 20.00
Lariat, Candleholder, 2–Light 30.00
Lariat, Candlestick, 3–Light, 7 In. ....28.00 To 35.00
Lariat, Cocktail 6.00
Lariat, Compote, Clear, Rolled Edge, 4 1/2 X 6 In. 18.00
Lariat, Cup & Saucer ....17.00 To 20.00
Lariat, Dish, Mayonnaise Set, 3 Piece 45.00
Lariat, Goblet, Cobalt, Spanish Stem 105.00
Lariat, Goblet, Cocktail 6.00
Lariat, Goblet, Moonglow 25.00
Lariat, Punch Bowl, Ladle, 12 Cups 325.00
Lariat, Punch Cup, Crystal 6.00
Lariat, Punch Set, Bowl, Ladle, Underplate, & 12 Cups 325.00
Lariat, Relish, 3–Part, 12 X 8 In. 16.00
Lariat, Relish, 4–Part 18.00
Lariat, Sherbet, Blue 16.00
Lariat, Sugar & Creamer 30.00
Lariat, Sugar, Silver Deposit Flowers, Scrolls, Covered 12.00
Lariat, Tumbler, Iced Tea 85.00
Locket On Chain, Bowl, Footed, 8 In. 155.00
Locket On Chain, Butter, Covered 175.00
Maple Leaf, Bowl, Fruit, Gold Trim, Green 60.00
Mayflower, Goblet 14.00
Minuet, Champagne, Tall 25.00
Minuet, Goblet 35.00
Minuet, Plate, 8 In. 25.00
Moongleam, Banana Boat, 7 1/2 X 3 In. 35.00
Moongleam, Basket 135.00
Moongleam, Bonbon, 2 Handles, 5 In. 17.50
Moongleam, Candlestick, 3–Light 82.50
Moongleam, Decanter, Crystal Stopper 150.00
Moongleam, Flower Frog, Duck, 2 Piece 225.00
Moongleam, Ice Bucket, Marked 90.00
Moongleam, Mustard, Double Rib & Panel 65.00
Moongleam, Plate, 4 1/2 In. 12.50
Moongleam, Plate, Green, 4 1/2 In. 15.00
Moongleam, Tray, 3–Part, Center Handle 38.00

Narrow Flute, Bowl	33.00
Narrow Flute, Celery, 9 In.	19.00
Narrow Flute, Custard, Footed, 4 Oz., Set Of 6	65.00
Narrow Flute, Plate, 5 In.	2.50
Narrow Flute, Plate, 6 In.	2.50
Narrow Flute, Sugar & Creamer, Footed	60.00
Narrow Flute, Tankard, 3 Pt.	65.00
Narrow Flute, Tumbler, 10 Oz.	25.00
New Era, Bowl, Pedestal, Partly Frosted, 9 3/4 X 11 X 4 In.	28.00
New Era, Cordial	10.00
New Era, Plate, 7 X 9 In.	9.00
New Era, Sherbet, Stemmed, 4 1/2 In.	10.00
New Era, Wine, Marked, 3 Oz.	12.00
Oceanic, Bowl, 12 X 2 In.	16.00
Octagon, Creamer, Moongleam	12.00
Old Colony, Plate, Square, 8 In.	16.00
Old Dominion, Goblet, Sahara	18.00
Old Dominion, Wine, Sahara, 2 1/2 In.	40.00
Old Sandwich, Tumbler, 8 Oz.	11.00
Old Sandwich, Water Set, Sahara, 7 Piece	325.00
Old Williamsburg, Butter, Covered	67.50
Old Williamsburg, Goblet, Water	20.00
Old Williamsburg, Sherbet	20.00
Orchid Etch, Ashtray	32.50
Orchid Etch, Bowl, Ruffled, Large	62.50
Orchid Etch, Butter, Covered	135.00
Orchid Etch, Candleholder, 2 1/2 In., Pair	49.75
Orchid Etch, Candy Dish, Dolphin Handles, Clear	110.00
Orchid Etch, Compote, 6 1/2 In.	39.50
Orchid Etch, Honey, Footed, 7 In.	35.00
Orchid Etch, Plate, 8 1/2 In.	15.75
Orchid Etch, Plate, 14 1/2 In.	46.00
Orchid Etch, Plate, Sandwich, Flat, 15 In.	95.00
Orchid Etch, Relish, 3–Part	40.00
Orchid Etch, Sugar & Creamer	50.00
Orchid Etch, Tumbler, Iced Tea, 12 Oz.	29.75
Oxford, Champagne, Crystal, Saucer Shape, 6 1/2 Oz.	10.00
Oxford, Goblet	12.00
Paneled Cane, Butter, Covered	28.50
Paperweight, Rabbit	110.00
Peerless, Cordial, 4 1/2 In.	12.00
Peerless, Dish, Handles, Triangular, 6 X 2 1/4 In.	17.50
Peerless, Punch Bowl	130.00
Peerless, Spooner	30.00
Pied Piper, Champagne, Marked	16.00
Pied Piper, Claret, 4 Oz.	22.50
Pied Piper, Goblet	25.00
Pied Piper, Iced Tea, Handle	50.00
Pied Piper, Plate, 8 1/4 In.	15.00
Pied Piper, Shot Glass, Etched, 2 Oz.	29.00
Pineapple & Fan, Berry Bowl, 8 In.	45.00
Pineapple & Fan, Cruet	135.00
Pineapple & Fan, Pitcher, Water, Clear To Gold	65.00
Pineapple & Fan, Salt & Pepper	55.00
Pineapple & Fan, Sugar, Emerald, Gold	65.00
Pineapple & Fan, Table Set, Gold Trim	400.00
Pineapple & Fan, Tankard, Pink	125.00
Pineapple & Fan, Toothpick, Emerald Green, Gold	185.00
Pineapple & Fan, Tumbler	40.00
Pineapple & Fan, Tumbler, Emerald	80.00
Pinwheel & Fan, Punch Bowl, High Base, 14 In.	225.00
Plain Panel, Eggcup	17.00
Plantation Ivy, Cocktail, Etched, 3 1/2 Oz.	20.00
Plantation Ivy, Goblet, 10 Oz.	20.00

Plantation Ivy, Plate, Etched, 8 1/2 In.	20.00
Plantation, Candleholder, 2–Light Branch, Bobeche & Prisms	45.00
Plantation, Candleholder, 5 In., Pair	55.00
Plantation, Candy Dish, Covered, 8 In.	65.00
Plantation, Cocktail, Fruit, Stem	14.00
Plantation, Compote	35.00
Plantation, Cruet, Original Stopper ....58.00 To 125.00
Plantation, Goblet, Stem, 10 Oz.	15.00
Plantation, Iced Tea, Footed	25.00
Plantation, Jam Jar, Pineapple Shape	70.00
Plantation, Parfait	23.00
Plantation, Relish, 3–Part, 11 1/2 In.	24.00
Plantation, Relish, Divided, Sterling Silver Foot, 4 In.	56.00
Plantation, Sherbet	12.00
Plantation, Sugar, Footed	22.50
Plantation, Syrup ....60.00 To 75.00
Pleat & Panel, Compote, Handles, Moongleam	26.00
Pleat & Panel, Compote, Jelly	10.00
Pleat & Panel, Cup & Saucer, Flamingo	80.00
Pleat & Panel, Dish, Lemon, No Cover	15.00
Pleat & Panel, Goblet, Flamingo, 8 Oz.	27.50
Pleat & Panel, Pitcher, Flamingo, Ice Lip	68.00
Pleat & Panel, Plate, 10 3/4 In.	15.00
Pleat & Panel, Plate, Flamingo, 7 In.	10.00
Pleat & Panel, Plate, Green, 14 In.	30.00
Pleat & Panel, Sherbet, Flamingo, Footed, 3 1/2 In.	15.00
Pleat & Panel, Soup, Cream	10.00
Pleat & Panel, Sugar, Covered, Footed, Flamingo	20.00
Pleat & Panel, Tray, 5–Part, 10 In.	28.00
Pleat & Panel, Tumbler, Iced Tea, Flamingo, 5 1/2 In.	20.00
Prince Of Wales Plumes, Punch Set, Bowl & 8 Cups	325.00
Priscilla, Custard, Handles, 5 Oz.	7.00
Priscilla, Jelly, Footed, Handle, 6 In.	18.00
Priscilla, Pitcher, Water	125.00
Provincial, Goblet, Amethyst, 10 Oz.	15.00
Provincial, Plate, 11 In.	18.00
Provincial, Plate, Dessert, Amethyst	10.00
Provincial, Sugar & Creamer, Amethyst	65.00
Provincial, Tumbler, Imperial, Ruby	18.00
Punty & Diamond Point, Punch Cup	12.00
Puritan, Bowl, Footed, 8 X 8 1/2 In.	28.00
Puritan, Box, Cigarette, Horsehead Finial Cover ....55.00 To 65.00
Puritan, Cocktail, 3 Oz.	12.50
Puritan, Goblet, 6 In.	12.00
Puritan, Jar, Pickle, Covered	40.00
Puritan, Jelly, Crimped, Handle, 5 In.	12.50
Puritan, Jug, Squatty, 3 Qt.	125.00
Puritan, Nut Dish, Footed, Clear, 4 3/4 X 2 3/4 In.	17.00
Puritan, Toothpick	65.00
Queen Ann, Berry Set, Flamingo, 5 Piece	65.00
Queen Ann, Bowl, Everglade Cutting, 12 In.	38.00
Queen Ann, Compote, Jelly, Footed, Handle, 6 In.	33.00
Queen Ann, Compote, Nut, Footed, Oval, Orchid Etch, 7 In.	68.00
Queen Ann, Cup & Saucer, Orchid Etch	85.00
Queen Ann, Dish, Footed, 6 In.	72.00
Queen Ann, Ice Tub, Silver Overlay	85.00
Queen Ann, Plate, 12 In.	26.00
Queen Ann, Plate, Orchid Etch, 10 1/2 In.	125.00
Queen Ann, Plate, Sahara, Square, 8 In.	12.00
Queen Ann, Punch Bowl, Footed	175.00
Queen Ann, Sugar, Minuet Etch	35.00
Raleigh, Cigarette Set, 5 Piece	35.00
Recessed Panel, Candy Jar	25.00
Revere, Cake Plate	40.00

Revere, Coaster, 4 1/2 In.	4.00
Revere, Plate, Cobalt, 8 In.	30.00
Rib & Panel, Compote, Covered, Silver Plate Overlay, Flamingo, 8 In.	125.00
Rib & Panel, Cruet	28.00
Rib & Panel, Pitcher, Water	75.00
Rib & Panel, Plate, 5 In.	2.50
Rib & Panel, Plate, 8 In.	5.00
Ridgeleigh, Ashtray, Square, Individual	5.00
Ridgeleigh, Candelabra, Bobeche, Prisms, 7 In.	75.00
Ridgeleigh, Cigarette Urn, 3 In.	16.50
Ridgeleigh, Compote, Covered, Footed, Low, 6 In.	25.00
Ridgeleigh, Goblet	25.00
Ridgeleigh, Jar, Cigar, Round	10.00
Ridgeleigh, Mustard, Covered, Crystal	35.00
Ridgeleigh, Plate, 13 1/2 In.	16.00
Ridgeleigh, Plate, Flamingo, 7 1/2 In.	8.00
Ridgeleigh, Plate, Silver Deposit, Square, 8 In.	16.00
Ridgeleigh, Plate, Wide Foot, Pink, 6 In., Set Of 12	100.00
Ridgeleigh, Relish, 2–Part, Handles	16.00
Ridgeleigh, Relish, 3–Part, Crystolite	25.00
Ridgeleigh, Shaker, Rooster Top	135.00
Ridgeleigh, Sugar & Creamer, Individual, Amethyst	30.00
Rooster, Bowl, Console, Pink, 14 X 7 1/2 In.	60.00
Rooster, Cocktail Set, 4 Stems & Shaker, Frosted Stems	325.00
Rooster, Cocktail Shaker	45.00
Rooster, Head, Cock	65.00
Rosalie, Bowl, Dressing, Divided	24.75
Rosalie, Candlestick, Empress, Bowl, Footed, 11 In.	145.00
Rosalie, Champagne	18.00
Rosalie, Console Set	145.00
Rosalie, Sugar & Creamer, Dolphin Footed	35.00
Rose Etch, Bowl, Flared, Low, Marked, 9 3/4 In.	40.00
Rose Etch, Cruet, Stopper	50.00
Rose Etch, Goblet	35.00
Rose Etch, Plate, Luncheon	23.00
Rose Etch, Tumbler, Iced Tea, Footed	28.00
Rose Etch, Tumbler, Juice, Footed	26.00
Rose Etch, Tumbler, Water, Footed	26.00
Rose, Butter, Covered, 6 In.	150.00
Rose, Champagne	27.50
Rose, Compote, Footed, Low, 6 1/2 In.	60.00
Rose, Compote, Honey	35.00
Rose, Sugar & Creamer	50.00
Saturn, Fingerbowl, 4 In.	10.00
Saturn, Parfait, 5 Oz.	15.00
Saturn, Salt & Pepper, Metal Lid	45.00
Seahorse, Cocktail, Stemmed	245.00
Spanish, Champagne, Cobalt Bue	125.00
Spanish, Cocktail, Cobalt Blue	135.00
Spanish, Goblet, Cobalt Blue	105.00
Spanish, Iced Tea, Cobalt Blue	85.00
Spanish, Tumbler, Juice, Cobalt Blue	85.00
Sparta, Sherbet, 3 1/2 In.	9.00
Sunburst, Jar, Tobacco	125.00
Sunburst, Punch Cup, Set Of 12	145.00
Sunflower, Bowl, Console, 13 In.	35.00
Sussex, Sherbet, Cobalt	35.00
Swan, Nut Dish, Master	45.00
Swingtime, Creamer	15.00
Swirl, Vase, Ultramarine, 8 1/2 In.	16.00
Symphony, Champagne, 6 Oz.	36.00
Symphony, Cocktail, 3 1/2 In.	62.00
Symphony, Goblet, 9 Oz.	38.00
Symphony, Tumbler, Footed, 8 Oz.	48.00

Symphony, Tumbler, Iced Tea, 12 Oz.	58.00
Tally Ho, Cocktail, Cone	29.75
Tally Ho, Goblet, Etched	65.00
Thumbprint & Panel, Candleholder, 2–Light	25.00
Trojan, Goblet, 8 Oz.	35.00
Twist, Bonbon, 2 Handles, 6 In.	15.00
Twist, Bowl, Flamingo, 12 In.	55.00
Twist, Celery, Flamingo, 13 In.	25.00
Twist, Celery, Moongleam, 13 In.	20.00
Twist, Compote, Pink, 7 In.	28.00
Twist, Cruet, Crystal, Pair	25.00
Twist, Cup & Saucer, Moongleam, Handleless	30.00
Twist, Nappy, Moongleam, 4 1/4 In.	14.50
Twist, Plate, Moongleam Green, 4 1/2 In.	14.00
Twist, Relish, Flamingo, Divided, 13 In.	30.00
Tyrolean, Champagne	28.00
Tyrolean, Cocktail	35.00
Tyrolean, Goblet, Tall	35.00
Tyrolean, Tumbler, Iced Tea, Orchid Etch	22.00
Tyrolean, Tumbler, Juice, Footed, 5 Oz.	35.00
Tyrolean, Wine, Etch	55.00
Victorian, Bowl, Floral, 10 1/2 In.	45.00
Victorian, Box, Cigarette, Covered, Crystal, Marked	45.00
Victorian, Goblet, Footed, Clear	15.00
Victorian, Pitcher, Water, Clear	150.00
Victorian, Wine, 2 1/2 Oz.	18.00
Warwick, Bowl, Horn Of Plenty, Sahara, 11 In.	105.00
Warwick, Candleholder, 2–Light, Marked	15.00
Warwick, Plate, Crystal, 7 In.	7.00
Warwick, Vase, Crystal, 7 In.	7.00
Waterford, Cake Plate, Crystal	5.00
Waterford, Sugar, Crystal	3.00
Waverly, Bowl, Orchid Etch, Crimped, 12 In.	65.00
Waverly, Bowl, Rose Etch, 10 In.	80.00
Waverly, Bowl, Seahorse Handle, 6 1/2 In.	45.00
Waverly, Butter, Covered, Square	130.00
Waverly, Champagne	12.50
Waverly, Cigarette Holder, Orchid Etch	110.00
Waverly, Cigarette Holder, Rose	105.00
Waverly, Compote, Footed, 6 In.	35.00
Waverly, Compote, Stemmed, Oval	135.00
Waverly, Cruet	50.00
Waverly, Cup & Saucer, Rose	85.00
Waverly, Plate, 7 In.	7.50
Waverly, Plate, Center Handle, 14 In.	55.00
Waverly, Plate, Orchid Etch, 7 1/4 In.	28.00
Waverly, Plate, Rose, 8 1/2 In.	24.00
Waverly, Relish, 3–Part, 12 In.	25.00
Waverly, Relish, Marked, Oval, 11 In.	30.00
Waverly, Relish, Marked, Round, 7 In.	25.00
Waverly, Salt & Pepper, Orchid Etch	87.50
Waverly, Sugar & Creamer, Footed	52.50
Whirlpool, Goblet	17.50
Whirlpool, Sherbet	12.00 To 15.00
Whirlpool, Sugar & Creamer, Footed	23.00
Whirlpool, Tumbler	35.00
Winged Scroll, Box, Trinket, Gold Trim, Green	35.00
Winged Scroll, Butter, Covered, Custard Glass	150.00
Winged Scroll, Cruet	225.00
Winged Scroll, Spooner	75.00
Winged Scroll, Sugar & Creamer, Covered	125.00
Winged Scroll, Toothpick	140.00
Winged Scroll, Tumbler, Green	55.00
Yeoman, Bowl, Green, Footed, Scalloped, 11 1/2 In.	30.00

Yeoman, Butter Chip, Marked	7.50
Yeoman, Creamer, Oval	12.00
Yeoman, Cup, Moongleam	13.00
Yeoman, Dish, Rose Engraved, Handles, 6 In.	10.00
Yeoman, Gravy Boat	12.00
Yeoman, Sugar, Silver Deposit, 2 In.	12.00
Zodiac, Goblet, Clear	35.00
Zodiac, Relish, 4–Part, 7 1/2 In.	27.50

HEREND, see Fischer

Gebruder Heubach, a German firm working from 1820 to 1925, is best known for bisque dolls and doll heads, their principal products. They also manufactured bisque figurines, including piano babies, beginning in the 1880s, and glazed figurines in the 1900s.

HEUBACH, Box, Pheasants, Cover, Grassy Ground, Marked, 5 3/4 X 2 1/2 In.	125.00
Bust, Boy & Girl, Holding Hands To Cheeks, 4 1/2 In., Pair	325.00
Dish, Jasperware, Full Figure Indian, Hatched, Wheat Rim, 4 1/4 In.	58.00
Figurine, Baby, Standing Before Chair, Signed, 14 In.	450.00
Figurine, Boy, Blue Eyes, Closed Mouth, Bisque, 12 In.	600.00
Figurine, Boy, Dutch, 6 1/2 In.	225.00
Figurine, Boy, Girl Playing Musical Instrument, Marked, 10 In., Pr.	225.00
Figurine, Boy, Girl, Old Style Dress, Sailor Suit, Signed, 13 In., Pr.	400.00
Figurine, Children, Intaglio Eyes, Pair	165.00
Figurine, Court Lady & Man, Pastel Clothing, Marked, 15 In.	300.00
Figurine, Dancing Girl, Aqua Dress, White Trim, Marked, 11 1/2 In.	235.00
Figurine, Dancing Girl, Bisque, 16 In.	300.00
Figurine, Dancing Girl, Blond Hair, 11 In.	325.00
Figurine, Dancing Girl, Green Dress, Blond Hair, Marked, 6 1/2 In.	65.00
Figurine, Dog, Intaglio Eyes, Rust Collar, Marked, 5 X 9 In.	150.00
Figurine, Dog, White, Brown Intaglio Eyes, Marked, 9 X 3 3/4 In.	150.00
Figurine, Duck, 6 1/2 In.	150.00
Figurine, Dutch Boy & Girl, Sitting, Sunburst Mark, 8 1/2 In.	385.00
Figurine, Dutch Boy, Bisque, 3 3/4 In.	45.00
Figurine, Dutch Boy, Seated, Blond, Dutch Hat, Marked, 4 3/8 In.	65.00
Figurine, Dutch Boy, Sitting, All In Blues, Marked, 4 3/8 In.	65.00
Figurine, Dutch Girl, Red Skirt, Green Top, Cap, Marked, 4 1/4 In.	65.00
Figurine, Fan Tailed Dove, Bisque, White, 4 1/8 X 3 3/4 In.	85.00
Figurine, Girl, Boy, Playing Tambourine & Mandolin, 9 1/4 In., Pr.	225.00
Figurine, Girl, In Nightie, Bisque, Impressed Mark, 5 1/2 In.	330.00
Figurine, Girl, Leaning On Basket, C.1900, 12 3/4 In.	495.00
Figurine, Girl, Seated, Cobalt, Pinafore, Greenaway Bonnet, 4 In.	90.00
Figurine, Girl, With Parrot, Blue Skirt, Pink Vest, Marked, 13 In.	295.00
Figurine, Girl, With Tambourine, 2 1/2 X 3 3/4 In.	75.00
Figurine, Little Girl, Ruffled Nightie, Floppy Hat, Marked, 5 In.	310.00
Figurine, Monkey, Holding Top Hat In Lap, Bowtie, 9 1/2 In.	375.00
Figurine, Peasant Girl, Peanut Basket, Apron, Headdress, 8 1/2 In.	195.00
Figurine, Sunbonnet Girl, 2 1/2 X 3 3/4 In.	75.00
Figurine, Woman Standing Behind Ship's Wheel, Marked, 11 1/4 In.	285.00
Figurine, Young Boy, Dressed As Clown, C.1900, 13 In.	495.00
Holder, Card, 3 X 4 In.	35.00
Toothpick, Crawling Baby, Holder On Back, Rising Sun Mark	95.00
Vase, Dutch Boy Standing At Side, Blue Shirt, Marked, 6 3/8 In.	110.00

Higbee glass was made by the J. B. Higbee Company of Bridgeville, Pennsylvania, about 1900. Tablewares were made and it is possible to assemble a full set of dishes and goblets in some Higbee patterns. Most of the glass was clear, not colored.

HIGBEE, see also Pressed Glass

HIGBEE, Bowl, Pineapple & Fan, Sawtooth Rim, Small	50.00
Butter, Covered, Paneled Thistle, Bee Mark	40.00
Compote, Arrowhead In Oval	35.00

HISTORIC BLUE, see Adams; Clews; Ridgway; Staffordshire

Holly Amber, Compote   Holly Amber, Dish

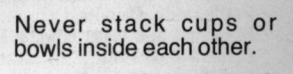

Never stack cups or bowls inside each other.

Hobnail glass is a pattern of glass with bumps in an allover pattern. Dozens of hobnail patterns and variants have been made. Clear, colored, and opalescent hobnail have been made and are being reproduced.

HOBNAIL, see also Fenton; Francisware

HOBNAIL, Bowl, Blue, Elm Enterprises, 9 In.	42.50
Bowl, Blue, Ruffled Edge, Elm Enterprises, 10 In.	45.00
Butter, Covered, Blue, Frosted, Footed, Pyramid Shape	85.00
Butter, Covered, Child's, Thumbprint Base, Amber	85.00
Cruet, Stopper, Crystal, 2 In.	12.00
Mustard, Covered, Blue, Glass Spreader, 3 In.	12.50
Mustard, Moonstone	4.00
Pitcher, Cranberry, Elm Interprises, 5 1/2 In.	52.50
Pitcher, Water	30.00
Plate, English, Square, 7 1/2 In.	4.00
Toothpick, Vaseline	10.50
Vase, Cranberry, Round, Elm Enterprises	35.00
Vase, Green Opaline, French, C.1900, 3 In.	95.00
Vase, Mother–Of–Pearl, Shaded To Gold At Square Top, 6 X 4 1/2 In.	600.00
Vase, Opalescent, Deep Cranberry, Fenton, 5 1/2 In.	75.00
Vase, Opalescent, Green, Crimped, 4 1/2 In.	19.00
Vase, Opalescent, Ruffled, Blue, 5 1/2 In.	35.00
Vase, Opalescent, Yellow, Imperial, 8 In.	45.00

Holly amber, or golden agate, glass was made by the Indiana Tumbler and Goblet Company from January 1, 1903, to June 13, 1903. It is a pressed glass pattern featuring holly leaves in the amber–shaded glass. The glass was made with shadings that range from creamy opalescent to brown–amber.

HOLLY AMBER, Compote	*Illus*	1100.00
Dish	*Illus*	175.00
Mug, 4 1/2 In.		475.00
Relish, Oval, 4 1/2 X 1 7/8 In.		350.00
Toothpick, 2 1/2 In.	150.00 To	300.00
Wine, Air Twist Stem, Flint, C.1750		220.00

Hopalong Cassidy was named William Lawrence Boyd when he was born in Cambridge, Ohio, in 1895. His first movie appearance was in 1919, but the first Hopalong Cassidy film was not until 1934. Sixty-six films were made. In 1948, William Boyd purchased the television rights to the movies, then later made 52 new programs. In the 1950s, Hopalong Cassidy was seen in comics, records, toys, and other products. Boyd died in 1972.

HOPALONG CASSIDY, Bank ....10.00 To 28.00
 Bedspread, Bar 20 .... 65.00
 Bedspread, Chenille, Blue 100.00
 Billfold 12.00
 Book, Dell, 1950 .... 22.00
 Book, Pop–Up ....10.00 To 30.00
 Bottle, Milk, Dairylea, Qt. 35.00
 Breakfast Set, Plate, Bowl, & Mug, Milk Glass 85.00
 Camera Box, 1940 .... 125.00
 Can, Popcorn 22.00
 Card, Trade, 1950, Set Of 48 .... 35.00
 Clip, Money 39.00
 Clothes, Blouse, Pants, Sanforized, Hoppy Youngster, 1950 ..... 145.00
 Dental Kit, Toothpaste, Brush, & Mirror 55.00
 Flashlight 15.00
 Fork 10.00
 Game, Canasta Set, Box 60.00
 Game, Card, Boxed 18.00
 Game, Chinese Checkers, Badge Forms Board, Bradley 65.00
 Game, Milton Bradley, 1950s 45.00
 Game, Target, Marx, 27 X 16 In. 100.00
 Gun & Holster Set, Double Gun 125.00
 Gun, Cap, Wyandotte 55.00
 Gun, Zoomerrang, Shoots Paper Roll 24.00
 Hair Barrette, On Card 18.00
 Horseshoe, Good Luck, Bar 20 Ranch, Plastic, Dated 1950 ..... 10.00
 Horseshoe, Plastic 12.50
 Knife, Picture, Pocket ....26.00 To 30.00
 Knife, Sheath, Miniature 28.00
 Lamp, Aladdin, Gun & Holster 85.00
 Lunch Box & Thermos 25.00
 Mug, Black & White 9.00
 Napkins, Package ....10.00 To 20.00
 Plaque, Wall, Holstered Gun, Milk Glass, 9 1/2 In. 125.00
 Plate & Mug, W.S.George 25.00
 Plate, 9 In. 25.00
 Portrait, Metal Frame Mirror, 4 X 6 In. 50.00
 Poster, Bond Bread, Hoppy, 21 X 27 In. 45.00
 Puzzle, Milton Bradley, Set Of 3 .... 35.00
 Rack, Clothes, Bunkhouse, Wood, 24 In. 85.00
 Radio, Arvin, Red Metal 150.00
 Radio, Arvin, Red Plastic Case 125.00
 Ring, Signet, Adjustable Metal, Hoppy's Head In Center 15.00
 Savings Club Kit, Original Mailing Envelope, 1950 .... 75.00
 Tablet, Writing, Pictured On Cover, Unused 10.00
 Tumbler, Black & White, 4 In. ....10.00 To 16.00
 Wallet, Leather, Signed 15.00
 Watch, Engraved Good Luck From Hoppy On Back 45.00
 Wristwatch, Boy's, Original Strap 40.00
 Wristwatch, Girl's, On Saddle, Box 125.00

Howdy Doody and Buffalo Bob were the main characters in a children's series televised from 1947 to 1960. Howdy was a redheaded puppet. The series became popular with college students in the late 1970s when Buffalo Bob began to lecture on the campuses.

HOWDY DOODY, Album, Double Record, Original Jacket 20.00
 Book, Little Golden, 1954 .... 7.00
 Buffalo Bob, Piano, Windup 150.00
 Child's Set, 3 Piece 45.00
 Climber, Mailer 27.50
 Clockadoodle, Box 300.00
 Cookie Jar, Abingdon 55.00
 Doll, Composition Face & Hands, Cloth Body, Sleep Eyes, 19 In. 65.00
 Doll, Ventriloquist, Vinyl, 30 In. 28.00

Feeding Set, Child's, Taylor Smith Taylor, Box	150.00
Game, Box	22.50
Game, Carnival, Electric	54.50
Game, T.V.	20.00
Key Chain, Flasher	14.00
Lunch Box, Tin	25.00
Mixer, Ovaltine	20.00
Mug, Shake–Up, Ovaltine, Letter To Mom, Instructions	60.00
Night–Light, Figural	45.00 To 50.00
Pencil, Figural Head	15.00
Photograph, Clarabell, 3 7/8 X 5 1/2 In.	10.00
Puppet Show, Original Card	49.00
Puppet, 20 In.	70.00
Puppet, Moving Mouth, Box, 12 In.	22.00
Puzzle, Complete	15.00
Record, With Jacket	7.00
Rocker, Musical	85.00
Straw Holder, Box	35.00
T-Shirt, With Friends, National Broadcasting Co.	20.00
Thermos	3.50
Toy, Band, Windup, Box	450.00
Toy, Figure, Dilly Dalli, Plastic, Mouth Opens, 3 In.	15.00
Toy, Puppet, 20 In.	70.00
Toy, Squeeze, Full Figure	15.00
Tumbler, Welch's Grape Juice, Howdy & Friends On Picnic, 1953	20.00
Wristwatch, Animated	85.00

Hull pottery was made in Crooksville, Ohio, from 1905. Addis E. Hull bought the Acme Pottery Company and started making ceramic wares. In 1917, A. E. Hull Pottery began making art pottery as well as the commercial wares. For a short time, 1921 to 1929, the firm also sold pottery imported from Europe. The dinnerwares of the 1940s, including the Little Red Riding Hood line, the high gloss artwares of the 1950s, and the matte wares of the 1940s, are all popular with collectors. The firm is still in business.

Hull
U.S.A

HULL, Ashtray, Mermaid	20.00
Bank, Little Red Riding Hood	200.00 To 275.00
Basket, Blossom Flite, 11 1/2 In.	35.00 To 45.00
Basket, Bow Knot, 10 1/2 In.	130.00
Basket, Bow Knot, 25 In.	60.00
Basket, Dogwood, 7 1/2 In.	65.00 To 85.00
Basket, Parchment & Pine, 9 X 16 In.	65.00
Basket, Serenade, 5 In.	20.00
Basket, Sunglow, Pink, 6 1/2 In.	12.00
Basket, Tokay, Mask Sprayed, 1958	45.00
Basket, Water Lily, 14 In.	80.00
Basket, Wild Flower, 10 1/2 In.	77.00 To 95.00
Basket, Wild Flower, 16 In.	80.00
Basket, Woodland, Turquoise, 10 1/2 In.	30.00
Biscuit Jar, Little Red Riding Hood	165.00
Butter, Little Red Riding Hood, Covered	100.00 To 140.00
Candleholder, Blossom Flite, Pair	15.00
Candleholder, Bow Knot, Blue, Pair	55.00
Candleholder, Calla Lily, Handles, Pair	30.00
Candleholder, Parchment & Pine, 2 1/2 In.	5.00
Candlestick, Bow Knot, Pair	35.00
Candlestick, Butterfly, Ivory, Pair	25.00
Candlestick, Pine, Parchment, Pair	18.00
Candlestick, Woodland, Green To Cream, Pair	26.00
Casserole, Debonair, Divided, Black Accents, Pink & Gray, 8 1/2 In.	13.00
Console Bowl, Bow Knot	60.00
Console Bowl, Butterfly, Ivory, Turquoise Interior, Footed	40.00
Console Bowl, Magnolia, Matte Pink & Blue, 12 In.	40.00
Console Bowl, Parchment & Pine	15.00 To 27.00

Console Bowl, Pink Spatter 15.00
Console Bowl, Serenade, Blue, 12 In. 15.00
Console Bowl, Wild Flower, 12 In. 42.00
Console Set, Blossom Flite, 3 Piece 29.00
Console Set, Open Rose, Doves, 3 Piece 90.00
Console Set, Parchment & Pine, 3 Piece ....25.00 To 65.00
Console Set, Water Lily, 3 Piece 65.00
Console Set, Wild Flower, 3 Piece 70.00
Cookie Jar, Aunt Jemima 82.00
Cookie Jar, Cinderella's Pumpkin 52.00
Cookie Jar, Happy Squirrel 75.00
Cookie Jar, Little Red Riding Hood, Green Basket 130.00
Cornucopia, Bow Knot, Double ....25.00 To 75.00
Cornucopia, Magnolia, 9 In., Pair 25.00
Cornucopia, Magnolia, Double, Pink & Blue 25.00
Cornucopia, Magnolia, Glossy, 8 1/2 In. 13.00
Cornucopia, Magnolia, Yellow Top, Beige Base, 8 1/2 In. 30.00
Cornucopia, Open Rose, 8 1/2 In. ....18.00 To 38.00
Cornucopia, Parchment & Pine, 7 3/4 In. 75.00
Cornucopia, Parchment & Pine, 12 In., Pair 55.00
Cornucopia, Water Lily, Brown, 6 1/2 In. ....15.00 To 25.00
Cornucopia, Wild Flower, Paper Label, 8 1/2 In. 18.00
Cracker Jar, Little Red Riding Hood 125.00
Creamer, Little Red Riding Hood, 5 In. ....35.00 To 75.00
Dish, Little Red Riding Hood & Wolf 400.00
Dish, Tokay, Green Grapes, Leaf Shape, White, 14 In. 12.00
Ewer, Blossom Flite, 13 1/2 In. 65.00
Ewer, Bow Knot, 5 1/2 In. 35.00
Ewer, Cornucopia, 7 1/2 In. 40.00
Ewer, Ebb Tide, Aqua & Peach, 14 In. 45.00
Ewer, Magnolia, Blue Glaze 22.00
Ewer, Magnolia, Matte, 13 1/2 In. 65.00
Ewer, Mardi Gras, 10 In. 22.00
Ewer, Rosella, Pink, 7 In. 23.00
Ewer, Tulip, 13 In. 85.00
Ewer, Wild Flower, 8 1/2 In. 55.00
Ewer, Wild Flower, 13 1/2 In. 100.00
Ewer, Woodland, 13 1/2 In. 65.00
Ewer, Woodland, Gloss, Pink To Green, 5 1/4 In. 20.00
Ewer, Woodland, Speckled Pink, Brown Trim, 13 1/2 In. 40.00
Flowerpot, Tulip, Attached Saucer, Paper Label 35.00
Flowerpot, Woodland, 10 In. 18.00
Jar, Little Red Riding Hood, Basket At Feet, Covered 120.00
Jardiniere, Bow Knot, 5 3/4 In. ....30.00 To 55.00
Jardiniere, Poppy, 4 1/2 In. 30.00
Lamp, Little Red Riding Hood ....550.00 To 650.00
Lamp, Poppy 75.00
Match Holder, Little Red Riding Hood ....295.00 To 395.00
Mustard, Little Red Riding Hood, Spoon ....130.00 To 150.00
Pitcher, Ebb Tide 20.00
Pitcher, Little Red Riding Hood, Side Pour 150.00
Pitcher, Little Red Riding Hood, Top Pour 150.00
Pitcher, Open Rose, 4 3/4 In. 15.00
Pitcher, Sunglow, 5 1/2 In. 14.00
Pitcher, Woodland, 6 1/2 In. 15.00
Planter, 2 White Swans, 10 3/4 X 9 In. 35.00
Planter, Baby With Rattle 15.00
Planter, Bandana Duck, 5 X 7 In. 35.00
Planter, Hanging, Iris, 4 In. 40.00
Planter, Lovebirds, Aqua 10.00
Planter, Rooster, Pink & Green 12.00
Planter, Southern Belle, Pair 25.00
Planter, Swan 10.00
Planter, Telephone, 9 In. 125.00

Planter, Woodland, 7 1/2 In.	15.00
Rose Bowl, Iris, 7 In.	35.00
Salt & Pepper, Little Red Riding Hood, Large	30.00 To 38.00
Salt & Pepper, Little Red Riding Hood, Small	14.00 To 18.00
Salt Box, Little Red Riding Hood	225.00
Sugar & Creamer, Butterfly	40.00
Sugar & Creamer, Little Red Riding Hood	75.00 To 85.00
Sugar, Woodland, Open, Matte	10.00
Swan, Yellow, Green, No.69	30.00
Tea Set, Blossom Flite, Set	85.00
Tea Set, Bow Knot, 3 Piece	60.00
Tea Set, Ebb Tide	55.00
Tea Set, Little Red Riding Hood	275.00
Tea Set, Magnolia	75.00 To 110.00
Teapot & Sugar, Bow Knot, 2 Piece	95.00
Teapot, Bow Knot	85.00 To 125.00
Teapot, Parchment & Pine, 12 In.	45.00
Teapot, Serenade, Yellow	75.00
Teapot, Sugar, & Creamer, Butterfly	60.00
Toothpick, Little Red Riding Hood	36.00
Vase, Bow Knot, 5 In.	25.00
Vase, Bow Knot, 8 1/2 In.	48.00
Vase, Bow Knot, 10 1/2 In.	38.00 To 85.00
Vase, Bud, Tulip, 6 In.	25.00
Vase, Calla Lily, 6 In.	30.00
Vase, Calla Lily, 10 In.	65.00
Vase, Cornucopia, Parchment & Pine, 12 In., Pair	55.00
Vase, Dogwood, 4 3/4 In.	15.00
Vase, Ebb Tide, 11 3/4 In.	15.00
Vase, Fan, Sunglow, 6 1/4 In.	13.00
Vase, Iris, 7 In.	25.00
Vase, Magnolia, Matte, 15 1/2 In.	125.00
Vase, Magnolia, Matte, Handle, Blue To Pink, 6 1/2 In.	17.00
Vase, Magnolia, Tab Handle, Blue & Pink, 12 1/2 In.	40.00
Vase, Open Rose, 8 1/2 In.	39.00 To 46.00
Vase, Open Rose, Oil Lamp Shape, 10 1/2 In.	75.00
Vase, Parchment & Pine, 7 In.	10.00
Vase, Poppy, Matte Pastels, 7 In.	35.00 To 40.00
Vase, Rose, Matte, 8 1/2 In.	22.50
Vase, Rosella, 8 1/2 In.	12.00
Vase, Thistle, 6 1/2 In.	20.00
Vase, Tokay, Handles, 6 In.	10.00
Vase, Tulip, 6 1/2 In.	25.00
Vase, Tulip, 10 In.	38.00
Vase, Tulip, Yellow Top, Blue Base, 10 In.	40.00
Vase, Water Lily, 6 1/2 In.	20.00
Vase, Water Lily, 9 In.	28.00
Vase, Wild Flower, 7 1/2 In.	15.00
Vase, Wild Flower, 10 1/2 In.	50.00
Vase, Wild Flower, 12 1/2 In.	55.00
Vase, Wild Flower, Matte Blue To Pink, 8 1/2 In.	25.00
Vase, Wild Flower, Pink & Blue, 15 1/2 In.	185.00
Vase, Woodland, 15 1/2 In.	65.00
Wall Pocket, Bow Knot	45.00
Wall Pocket, Bow Knot, Cup & Saucer Shape	42.00 To 45.00
Wall Pocket, Bow Knot, Flat Iron	55.00
Wall Pocket, Cup	42.00
Wall Pocket, Little Red Riding Hood	115.00 To 225.00
Wall Pocket, Saucer	42.00
Wall Pocket, Sunglow, Flatiron	15.00 To 22.50
Wall Pocket, Woodland, Glossy, 7 1/2 In.	22.50

Hummel figurines, based on the drawings of Berta Hummel, are made by the W. Goebel Porzellanfabrik of Oeslau, Germany, now Rodenthal, West Germany. They were first made in 1934. The mark has changed through the years. The following are the approximate dates for each of the marks: "Crown" mark, 1935 to 1949; "U. S. Zone, Germany," 1946 to 1948; "West Germany," after 1949; "full bee," with variations, 1950 to 1959; "stylized bee," 1960 to 1972; "three line mark," 1968 to 1979; "vee over gee," 1972 to 1979; "new mark," 1979 to present.

HUMMEL, Bell, 1978 .... 59.00
Bell, 1979 .... 21.00
Bookends, No. 60A&B, Goose Girl, Farm Boy, Stylized Bee 200.00
Candleholder, No. 38, Angel With Lute, Full Bee, 2 In. 60.00
Candleholder, No. 192, Candlelight, Vee Over Gee 60.00
Candy Box, No. 53, Joyful, Full Bee 115.00
Figurine, No. 5, Strolling Along, Stylized Bee 89.00
Figurine, No. 6/O, Sensitive Hunter, Full Bee 215.00
Figurine, No. 7, Merry Wanderer, Full Bee 280.00
Figurine, No. 10/I, Flower Madonna, Blue, Three Line Mark 135.00
Figurine, No. 10/I, Flower Madonna, White, Full Bee 100.00
Figurine, No. 12, Chimney Sweep, Three Line Mark 85.00
Figurine, No. 13/V, Meditation, New Mark 560.00
Figurine, No. 15/0, Hear Ye, Hear Ye, Full Bee 235.00
Figurine, No. 21/II, Heavenly Angel, Vee Over Gee 123.00
Figurine, No. 21/O, Heavenly Angel, Full Bee 110.00
Figurine, No. 23/I, Adoration, Stylized Bee 153.00
Figurine, No. 23/III, Adoration, Vee Over Gee 162.00
Figurine, No. 47/II, Goose Girl, Crown Mark 644.00
Figurine, No. 47/O, Goose Girl, Crown Mark 275.00
Figurine, No. 49/O, To Market, Crown Mark 250.00
Figurine, No. 56A, Culprits, Full Bee ....150.00 To 200.00
Figurine, No. 57/0, Chick Girl, Crown Mark 215.00
Figurine, No. 57/0, Chick Girl, Full Bee 120.00
Figurine, No. 63, Singing Lesson, Stylized Bee 60.00
Figurine, No. 66, Farm Boy, Stylized Bee 88.00
Figurine, No. 68, Lost Sheep, Full Bee 200.00
Figurine, No. 71, Stormy Weather, Full Bee 385.00
Figurine, No. 71, Stormy Weather, New Mark 149.00
Figurine, No. 71, Stormy Weather, Stylized Bee 225.00
Figurine, No. 71, Stormy Weather, Vee Over Gee 163.00
Figurine, No. 72, Spring Cheer, Full Bee 205.00
Figurine, No. 73, Little Helper, Stylized Bee 95.00
Figurine, No. 84/V, Worship, New Mark ....425.00 To 448.00
Figurine, No. 88, Heavenly Protection, Full Bee 98.00
Figurine, No. 94/3/O, Surprise, Full Bee 145.00
Figurine, No. 96, Little Shopper, Crown Mark 145.00
Figurine, No. 110/0, Let's Sing, Full Bee 115.00
Figurine, No. 111/I, Wayside Harmony, Full Bee ....125.00 To 130.00
Figurine, No. 111/I, Wayside Harmony, Stylized Bee 100.00
Figurine, No. 112/I, Just Resting, Vee Over Gee 65.00
Figurine, No. 124/0, Hello, New Mark 59.00
Figurine, No. 124/I, Hello, Green Pants, Full Bee, 7 In. 225.00
Figurine, No. 127, Doctor, Full Bee 125.00
Figurine, No. 133, Mothers Helper, Full Bee 160.00
Figurine, No. 135, Soloist, Stylized Bee 89.00
Figurine, No. 136/I, Friends, Stylized Bee 100.00
Figurine, No. 142/I, Apple Tree Boy, Stylized Bee 109.00
Figurine, No. 143, Boots, Full Bee 495.00
Figurine, No. 143/0, Boots, Full Bee ....135.00 To 140.00
Figurine, No. 143/0, Boots, New Mark 59.00
Figurine, No. 143/O, Boots, Full Bee 165.00
Figurine, No. 144, Angelic Song, Full Bee 133.00
Figurine, No. 152/A, Umbrella Girl, Full Bee 700.00

Figurine, No. 152/B/II, Umbrella Girl, Vee Over Gee 412.00
Figurine, No. 153/0, Auf Wiedersehen, With Hat, Full Bee ....1500.00 To 1600.00
Figurine, No. 154, Waiter, Crown Mark 825.00
Figurine, No. 154/0, Waiter, Full Bee 135.00
Figurine, No. 163, Whitsuntide, Full Bee 575.00
Figurine, No. 169, Bird Duet, Full Bee 128.00
Figurine, No. 169, Bird Duet, Vee Over Gee 115.00
Figurine, No. 170, School Boys, New Mark 825.00
Figurine, No. 170, School Boys, Stylized Bee 1300.00
Figurine, No. 170/I, School Boys, Three Line Mark 424.00
Figurine, No. 170/III, School Boys, Vee Over Gee 875.00
Figurine, No. 171, Little Sweeper, Full Bee 115.00
Figurine, No. 174, She Loves Me, She Loves Me Not, Crown Mark 250.00
Figurine, No. 175, Mother's Darling, Stylized Bee 140.00
Figurine, No. 176/I, Happy Birthday, New Mark 99.00
Figurine, No. 177, School Girls, New Mark 800.00
Figurine, No. 177, School Girls, Stylized Bee 1300.00
Figurine, No. 177/III, School Girls, Vee Over Gee 875.00
Figurine, No. 179, Coquettes, Full Bee 200.00
Figurine, No. 184, Latest News, New Mark 89.00
Figurine, No. 187, Display Plaque, Full Bee 445.00
Figurine, No. 188, Celestial Musician, New Mark 89.00
Figurine, No. 197, Be Patient, Full Bee 375.00
Figurine, No. 199/I, Feeding Time, Full Bee 285.00
Figurine, No. 200/0, Little Goat Herder, Three Line Mark 95.00
Figurine, No. 203/2/0, Signs Of Spring, Stylized Bee 80.00
Figurine, No. 217, Boy With Toothache, Full Bee 150.00
Figurine, No. 220, We Congratulate, New Mark 59.00
Figurine, No. 226, Mail Coach, New Mark 208.00
Figurine, No. 226, The Mail Is Here, Three Line Mark 239.00
Figurine, No. 262, Heavenly Lullaby, Three Line Mark 282.00
Figurine, No. 304, Artist, New Mark 79.00
Figurine, No. 309, With Loving Greetings, New Mark 65.00
Figurine, No. 311, Kiss Me, New Mark 75.00
Figurine, No. 317, Not For You, Three Line Mark ....85.00 To 95.00
Figurine, No. 327, The Run–A–Way, Stylized Bee 750.00
Figurine, No. 328, Carnival, Three Line Mark 117.00
Figurine, No. 333, Blessed Event, Vee Over Gee 165.00
Figurine, No. 347, Adventure Bound, Three Line Mark 1648.00
Figurine, No. 347, Adventure Bound, Vee Over Gee 1100.00
Figurine, No. 353/0, Spring Dance, New Mark 103.00
Figurine, No. 353/I, Spring Dance, Three Line Mark 275.00
Figurine, No. 369, Follow The Leader, Vee Over Gee 341.00
Figurine, No. 392, Little Band, On Base, New Mark 95.00
Figurine, No. 396, Ride Into Christmas, Three Line Mark 1660.00
Figurine, No. 396, Ride Into Christmas, Vee Over Gee 184.00
Sign, Dealer, Merry Wanderer, Stylized Bee, Oval 55.00

LORENZ
HUTSCHEN REUTER   *Hutschenreuther Porcelain Company of Selb, Germany, was
                     established in 1814 and is still working. The company makes fine
                     quality porcelain dinnerwares and figurines. The mark has changed
                     through the years, but the name and the lion insignia appear in most
GERMANY   versions.*

HUTSCHENREUTHER, Centerpiece Set, Bowl, Cherub Candlesticks, 3 Piece 70.00
Dinner Set, White, Gold Border, C.1890, Setting For 12 .... 500.00
Figurine, Ballerina & Male Dance, Kissing, 9 1/4 In. 260.00
Figurine, Bird Group, Mother Feeding Babies, 6 In. 75.00
Figurine, Boston Bulldog 125.00
Figurine, Child With Fawn 45.00
Figurine, Colt, Marked, 5 In. 65.00
Figurine, Dancing Girls, White, C.Werner, 9 In. 130.00
Figurine, Horses & Colts, Standing, Marked, Pair 185.00
Figurine, King Arthur, Full Regal Robe, Kneeling, 5 1/4 In. 95.00
Figurine, Mouse, Sitting On Haunches, White, 2 1/2 In. 70.00

Figurine, Nude, Art Deco, 9 In.	75.00
Figurine, Panda, Blue Eyes, Artist Signed, 3 1/2 In.	75.00
Figurine, Peasant Girl, Sheaf Of Wheat, Marked, 4 X 6 In.	235.00
Figurine, Seated Nude, C.Werner, 11 X 9 In.	295.00
Plate, Dice Throwers, 11 3/4 In.	85.00
Plate, Jaffrey, Bavaria, 8 1/2 In.	45.00
Plate, Polychrome Transfer, Gold Rim, 10 3/4 In., Set Of 8	110.00
Plate, Portrait, Maiden & 4 Cherubs, Pulling Cart, 10 In.	115.00
Plate, Unicorn, Hallett, Set Of 5	160.00
Platter, Floral, Cream Ground, 15 In.	15.00

An icon is a special, revered picture of Jesus, Mary, or a saint. These are usually Russian or Byzantine. The small icons collected today are made of wood and tin or precious metals. Many modern copies have been made in the old style and are being sold to unsuspecting tourists in Russia and Europe.

ICON, Eucharist With 2 Priests, Head Of Christ Center, Painted, Miniature	175.00
Joseph In Prayer, Landscape, Late 19th Century, 17 X 10 In.	160.00
Mother Of God, Reverse, Cross On Mountain, Brass, C.1750, 5 X 3 1/2 In.	385.00
Mother Of God, Silver Plated Riza	200.00
Okhlad, Silver, Gild & Enamel, Border, Alekseev, 1900, 12 X 10 1/2 In.	3025.00
Our Lady Of Joy To Those Who Suffer, Russian, 17 3/4 X 15 In.	660.00
Resurrection, 13 Scenes, Faux Enamel Border, Russia, 14 X 12 1/8 In.	500.00
Russian, Baptism Of Christ, 18th Century, 21 1/2 X 15 1/4 In.	990.00
St.Elijah, Hagiographical, Russian, 19th Century, 12 X 10 1/2 In.	1045.00
St.Nicholas, Miracle Worker, 19th Century, Russian, Marked, 12 1/2 In.	300.00

Imari patterns are named for the Japanese ware decorated with orange and blue stylized flowers. The design on the Japanese ware became so characteristic that the name "Imari" has come to mean any pattern of this type. It was copied by the European factories of the eighteenth and early nineteenth centuries.

IMARI, Bowl, 6 Lobed, Brocaded Panels, Gold Trim, C.1860, 6 1/4 In.	65.00
Bowl, Allover Designs, 6 In.	27.50
Bowl, Barber's, Iron Red, Green Chrysanthemums, Grapes, 9 1/2 In.	440.00
Bowl, Bridge, Landscape, C.1700, 11 In.	150.00
Bowl, Butterflies, Floral, Scalloped, 7 X 3 In.	95.00
Bowl, Design Of People, C.1900, 9 3/4 X 4 3/4 In.	675.00
Bowl, Floral Panels, C.1890, 11 In.	90.00
Bowl, Landscape, Bridge, C.1700, 11 In.	140.00
Bowl, Scalloped Rim, 6 Panels, Center Flower, 9 1/2 In.	40.00
Candelabra, Louis XV, Gilt Bronze Mount, Electrified, 6 Ft.20 In., Pr.	52250.00
Charger, 13 1/2 In.	75.00
Charger, Bird & Floral, Dark Blue, 19th Century, 17 In.	495.00
Charger, Child Scene, Blue & White, 19th Century, Signed, 20 1/2 In.	190.00
Charger, Flowers, Blue Center, Lotus Design, Meiji Period, 24 In.	660.00
Charger, Foo Dogs & Scenes, Scalloped, Blue & White, 15 1/2 In.	90.00
Charger, Geisha Design, Other, Bird & Fish, 14 3/4 In., Set Of 2	350.00
Charger, Large Eagle On Mountain, Blue & White, 18 1/2 In.	375.00
Charger, People Scene, White Ground, Gold Tracery, Marked, 16 In.Diam.	985.00
Charger, Phoenix, Fans, Landscape, Meiji Period, 24 In.	825.00
Dish, Fluted, 1850, 12 In.	85.00
Dish, Fluted, 1860, 9 In.	60.00
Dish, Polychrome Enameling, Underglaze Blue, Triangular, 6 1/2 In.	50.00
Dish, Soup, C.1860, Mason's Ironstone	95.00
Jardiniere, Floral, Dragon, Orange, Blue, Green, 16 In.	2700.00
Plate, Scalloped, C.1860, White Dragon Center, 8 1/2 In.	185.00
Platter, Fish Shape, 19th Century	235.00
Punch Bowl, 19th Century, 13 1/4 X 5 1/4 In.	825.00
Punch Bowl, Blue, White, Chrysanthemum, Scalloped, 6 1/4 X 15 1/2 In.	300.00
Punch Bowl, Fluted Rim, 12 1/4 In.	225.00
Tea Set, Arita Island, Teapot, 4 Cups & Saucers, C.1890	295.00
Umbrella Stand, Orange, Blue, Gold Floral, Cylindrical, 24 X 9 1/2 In.	625.00
Vase, Blossoms, Birds, Bronze Mount, Leaf Molded Handles, 17 In., Pair	1540.00

Vase, Flared Rim, Swollen Form, Late 19th Century, 12 In. 200.00
Vase, Floral, Lions, Bronze, Handles, Rosewood Base, C.1850, 30 In. 4400.00
Vase, Landscape, Ruyi Collar, Chrysanthemums, Meiji Period, 23 In. 1760.00
Vase, Orange, Blue, Green, Gilt Design, 24 In. 550.00
Vase, Panels Of Bird, Bird On Handles, Gilt Bronze, C.1850, 30 In. 4400.00

Imperial Glass Corporation was founded in Bellaire, Ohio, in 1901. It became a division of Lenox, Inc., in 1977 and was sold to Arthur R. Lorch in 1981. It was sold again in 1982. It went bankrupt in 1982 and some of the molds and assets have been offered to other companies. The Imperial glass preferred by the collector is stretch glass, art glass, carnival glass, and the top-quality tablewares.

IMPERIAL, Candlewick, Ashtray, 4 In. ....8.00 To 10.00
Candlewick, Ashtray, Chrome Handles, Clear, Round 15.00
Candlewick, Ashtray, Pink, Gold, & Blue, Nested, Set Of 3 ....21.00 To 30.00
Candlewick, Basket, 6 1/2 In. 20.00
Candlewick, Bell, 5 In. 25.00
Candlewick, Bonbon, Crystal, Handles, 5 1/2 In. 15.00
Candlewick, Bookends, Crystal, Eagle Adapter 200.00
Candlewick, Bowl, 3-Footed, 6 In. 22.00
Candlewick, Bowl, Crystal, 2-Part, 6 1/2 In. 12.00
Candlewick, Bowl, Crystal, Handle, 7 In. 12.75
Candlewick, Bowl, Float, 10 In. ....15.00 To 20.00
Candlewick, Bowl, Heart, 4 1/2 In. 10.00
Candlewick, Butter, Covered, Round, 1/4 Lb. ....20.00 To 37.00
Candlewick, Cake Plate, Pedestal 35.00
Candlewick, Cake Stand, 10 In. 40.00
Candlewick, Candleholder, Beaded 18.00
Candlewick, Candleholder, Eagle Peg 150.00
Candlewick, Candleholder, Etched, Pair 20.00
Candlewick, Candlestick, 3-Light, Pair 50.00
Candlewick, Candy Dish, Covered, 6 1/2 In. 30.00
Candlewick, Celery, 13 1/2 In. 20.00
Candlewick, Cheese & Cracker Set, 2 Piece 55.00
Candlewick, Cigarette Set, 6 Piece 65.00
Candlewick, Coaster 6.00
Candlewick, Compote, 4-Ball Stem, 5 1/2 In. 28.00
Candlewick, Condiment Set, 4 Piece 30.00
Candlewick, Console Set, Bowl & 2-Light Candlesticks, Etched 150.00
Candlewick, Creamer, Crystal 10.50
Candlewick, Cruet Set, 3 Piece 70.00
Candlewick, Cruet, Handle, 7 In. 14.00
Candlewick, Cup & Saucer ....7.00 To 48.00
Candlewick, Dish, Covered, Tall Finial, 6 In. 24.00
Candlewick, Dish, Jelly, Crystal, 4 In. 10.00
Candlewick, Dish, Pickle, Open Handle, 10 In. 20.00
Candlewick, Goblet, 4-Ball Stem, 9 Oz. 16.00
Candlewick, Goblet, 5 Oz. 16.00
Candlewick, Goblet, Dubarry Etched, 9 Oz. 35.00
Candlewick, Goblet, Etched Rose Of Sharon, 12 Oz. 35.00
Candlewick, Ladle 10.00
Candlewick, Marmalade Set, 4 Piece 28.00
Candlewick, Mayonnaise Set, 4 Piece 25.00
Candlewick, Mustard, Covered 22.00
Candlewick, Nappy, Heart Shape, Handles, 6 In. 13.00
Candlewick, Pitcher, 20 Oz. 28.00
Candlewick, Plate, 4 1/2 In. 5.50
Candlewick, Plate, 8 In. ....5.00 To 10.00
Candlewick, Plate, 9 In. ....7.50 To 11.00
Candlewick, Plate, Butter, Etched Starlight, 4 1/2 In. 11.00
Candlewick, Plate, Canape, Round, Glass, 6 In. 30.50
Candlewick, Plate, Crystal, 2 Handles, 10 In. 18.75
Candlewick, Plate, Deviled Egg 50.00
Candlewick, Plate, Gold Balls, Floral Cutting, Handles, 10 In. 40.00

Candlewick, Powder Jar	20.00
Candlewick, Punch Bowl, Underplate, 12 Cup	195.00
Candlewick, Relish, 2–Part, Oval, 8 In.	16.00
Candlewick, Relish, 3–Part, Crystal, Oblong, 13 In.	25.00 To 30.00
Candlewick, Relish, 4–Part, 4 Handles, 8 1/2 In.	20.00
Candlewick, Salad Set, 3 Piece	28.00
Candlewick, Salt & Pepper, Chrome Top	12.00
Candlewick, Salt & Pepper, Sterling Top	20.00
Candlewick, Salt Dip, 2 In.	6.00 To 10.00
Candlewick, Saucer	2.00
Candlewick, Shaker, Crystal, Pair	4.00
Candlewick, Soup, Cream, 5 In.	12.00
Candlewick, Spoon & Fork, Salad, 11 1/2 In.	27.50 To 32.00
Candlewick, Sugar & Creamer	10.00
Candlewick, Sugar & Creamer, Etched Floral	45.00
Candlewick, Sugar & Creamer, Individual, Tray, 2 1/2 In.	21.00
Candlewick, Tidbit Set, Heart Shape, 3 Piece	30.00
Candlewick, Tray, 4–Part, Handles, 12 In.	25.00
Candlewick, Tray, Center Handle, 8 1/2 In.	17.50
Candlewick, Tray, Dresser, Mirror Bottom, 10 1/2 In.	20.00
Candlewick, Tray, Pale Blue, 12 In.	50.00
Candlewick, Tray, Wafer, Center Handle, 11 1/2 In.	40.00
Candlewick, Tumbler, Crystal, Footed, 12 Oz.	11.50
Candlewick, Vase, Crimped Top, 8 In.	20.00 To 37.00
Candlewick, Vase, Fan, Crystal, 8 1/2 In.	17.00 To 21.00
Cape Cod, Bowl, Salad, Fluted, 11 1/2 In.	30.00
Cape Cod, Butter, Covered, Handles, 5 In.	30.00
Cape Cod, Cruet, Pointed Stopper, Crystal	35.00
Cape Cod, Cruet, Yellow, 4 Oz.	45.00
Cape Cod, Decanter	28.00
Cape Cod, Decanter, Cobalt Blue	140.00
Cape Cod, Goblet, 8 Oz.	18.00
Cape Cod, Parfait	6.50 To 40.00
Cape Cod, Pitcher, Flat, Large	47.00
Cape Cod, Pitcher, Ice Lip, Crystal, 48 Oz.	75.00
Cape Cod, Plate, Cupped, 16 In.	30.00
Cape Cod, Sherbet	5.00
Cape Cod, Tumbler	5.00
Cape Cod, Whiskey, Cobalt Blue	18.00 To 22.00
Cape Cod, Wine, 3 Oz.	20.00
Figurine, Donkey, Chocolate Glass, Large	25.00
Freehand, Vase, Gold & White Loopings, Lustered Throat, 9 3/4 In.	135.00
Freehand, Vase, Imbedded Vines & Leaves, Cobalt Blue, 4 1/2 In.	150.00
Freehand, Vase, Iridescent Marigold Throat, Cobalt Blue, 7 In.	90.00
Freehand, Vase, Lustered Throat, Yellow, 10 In.	65.00
Freehand, Vase, Sky Blue & Cobalt Blue Loopings, 8 1/2 In.	175.00
Hobnail, Vase, Royal Blue Opalescent, 8 In.	75.00
Nucut, Bell, Clear, Glass Clapper, 6 3/4 In.	22.00
Tradition, Goblet, Water	5.00
Tradition, Sherbet	3.50

Indian Tree is a china pattern that was popular during the last half of the nineteenth century. It was copied from earlier Indian textile patterns that were very similar. The pattern includes the crooked branch of a tree and a partial landscape with exotic flowers and leaves. Green, blue, pink, and orange were the favored colors used in the design.

INDIAN TREE, Bowl, Maddox, 5 1/2 In.	7.00
Butter Chip, Maddox	12.50
Cup & Saucer, Knowles	14.00
Dessert Set, Hand Painted, Octagonal, 5 Piece	95.00
Plate, 4 3/4 In.	8.00
Plate, Gold Etched Band, Pickard, 7 3/4 In.	70.00
Plate, Johnson Bros., 10 In.	21.00

Plate, Maddox, 8 In.	9.00
Platter, Oval, Maddox, 19 In.	85.00
Soup, Maddox, 8 In.	14.50

Indian art from North America has attracted the collector for many years. Each tribe has its own distinctive designs and techniques. Baskets, jewelry, pottery, and leatherwork are of greatest collector interest. Eskimo art is listed in another section in this book.

INDIAN, Bag, Bandleer, Great Lakes, Beaded, Geometric Designs, 34 In.	325.00
Bag, Beaded, Iroquois, Floral, C.1800	150.00
Bag, Beaded, Nez Perce, Geometric, White, Early 1900s, 12 3/4 X 16 In.	75.00
Bag, Beaded, Seneca, Floral, C.1800	110.00
Bag, Game Carrier, Sioux, Leather	90.00
Bag, Plains, Hide, Yellow & Green Bead, Fringed, Drawstring, 13 In.	90.00
Bag, Plateau, Elk, Floral, Polychrome, Metal Beading, 1900s, 10 3/4 In.	45.00
Bag, Sinew Sewn, Twisted Leather Carrying Strap, 5 1/2 X 4 1/2 In.	65.00
Bag, Sioux, Geometric Design, Red Horsehair Dangles, 1895, 12 1/2 In.	375.00
Bag, Strike–A–Light, Sioux, Quilled, Orange, Blue Design, 8 In.	65.00
Basket, California Shalishan, Coil Design, Quill, 4 1/2 X 2 3/4 In.	150.00
Basket, California, Geometric Design, Shades Of Brown, 25 X 13 In.	350.00
Basket, Cherokee, Melon Rib, Andrews, N.C., Splint, 11 3/4 In.	25.00
Basket, Hat, Hoopa, 6 1/2 X 3 In.	200.00
Basket, Klamath, Burden, Quill Decoration, Miniature	42.00
Basket, Lid, Aleut, Twined, Embroidered Flowers, Cylindrical, 3 In.	975.00
Basket, Lid, Hupa, Twined, Geometric Design, Yellow, 4 1/2 In.	90.00
Basket, Macah, Blues & Natural, Striped, Dark Bottom, 8 X 5 In.	185.00
Basket, Maidu, Coiled, Bowl Shape, Geometric Design, 7 X 4 1/4 In.	275.00
Basket, Ottowa, Splint Ash, Open Hand Holds In Rim, 14 X 19 In.	45.00
Basket, Pima, Colored Pattern, Miniature	235.00
Basket, Santa Clara Pueblo, Pottery, 1940s	45.00
Basket, Shuswap, Birch Bark, 10 X 10 X 14 In.	90.00
Basket, Tlingit, Rattle Lid, Brown Zigzag Designs, 5 1/4 X 3 In.	255.00
Basket, Trinket, Makah, Lid, Ships & Birds, 4 1/2 X 3 1/2 In.	85.00
Basket, Woodland, 2 Swivel Handles, Splint, 11 1/2 X 9 X 5 3/4 In.	90.00
Belt Pouch, Cheyenne, Beaded Dogs, White Ground, Fringed, 4 1/2 In.	100.00
Belt, Beaded, Sioux, White, Blue & White Tipi, Metal Buckle, 40 In.	60.00
Belt, Cheyenne, Fully Beaded, Sinew Sewn, 2 1/2 X 28 In.	265.00
Belt, Silver, 8 Oval Conchos, Corn Leaf Design, Buckle	375.00
Blanket, Chamoya, Gray, White & Black, Wool, 48 X84 In.	250.00
Blanket, Chimayo, Woven, Red, Arrows, Stripes, Diamonds, 40 X 72 In.	90.00
Blanket, Navajo, Saddle Design, 6 X 3 1/2 Ft.	145.00
Blanket, Navajo, Storm Design, Natural, White, Black, 19 X 42 In.	65.00
Blanket, Northwest Plains, Strip, Beaded, Stars, White, C.1890, 64 In.	400.00
Bow, Plains, Wooden, Senew, Plaited Quill Wrapping, Arrows, 42 In.	400.00
Bowl, Aleut, Basketry, Sweet Grass, Red & Blue Embroidered, 9 In.	200.00
Bowl, Cherokee, Raised Squaw Heads, Signed L.B.Maney, Large	150.00
Bowl, Navajo, Silver, Indian Bird Hallmark, 4 1/4 X 1 1/2 In.	110.00
Bowl, Olla, Acoma, Deer Design, Signed Leno, Large	250.00
Bowl, San Ildefonso, Black On Black, Signed Marie, 5 1/2 In.	785.00
Bowl, Woodlands, Carved Human Head Handle, Burl, 22 In.	9625.00
Bowl, Woodlands, Wooden, Head Handle, Other End Terraced, 13 X 10 In.	7100.00
Box, Birchbark, Micmac, Dyed Quill Top, Chevron Design, 2 3/4 In.	225.00
Box, Feather, Maori, Wooden, Carved, Tiki Figures, Abalone, 15 In.	600.00
Box, Micmac, Pine, Domed Bark Lid, Dyed Quill Covered, 1850, 8 In.	135.00
Bracelet, Zuni, Inlaid Turquoise & Coral, 1 1/2 In.	120.00
Breastplate, Plains, Bone, Leather Strips, 9 1/2 X 8 1/2 In.	275.00
Buckle, Solid Nickel Silver, Geometric Design, 1921 Silver Dollar	25.00
Button, Navajo, Silver, Stamp & Repousse Design, Turquoise, 16 Piece	110.00
Cane, Sioux, Catlinite, Wooden, Corkscrew Body, Floral Incised, 37 In.	500.00
Cane, Sioux, Corkscrew Form, Painted Design, Wooden	500.00
Canoe, Birchbark, 1920s, 14 Ft.	500.00
Canoe, Northwest, Wooden, Model, Totemic Design, 26 In.	1750.00
Cap, Iroquois, Glengarry, Beaded Floral, Black Velvet, Stand, 10 In.	90.00
Carving, Soapstone, Eskimo, Waterfowl, Mother & Brood, Set Of 8	175.00

Case, Awl, Covered, Outline Beading, Tin Cone Dangles, 10 1/2 In.	15.00
Choker, Zuni, Silver, Inlaid, Bowl, Ears Of Corn, 18 1/4 In.	120.00
Container, Birchbark, Geometric Designs, Moose, Indians, 15 In.	550.00
Cribbage Board, Eskimo, Ivory, Incised Animals, Black Pigment, 17 In.	250.00
Cribbage Board, Eskimo, Ivory, Seals, Bear, & Walruses	1700.00
Cuff, Woodland, Floral Beading, Black Velvet, 1880, 7 1/2 In., Pair	85.00
Cup & Saucer, Cochita Pueblo, Red Clay, White Slip, Rain God Designs	32.50
Dish, Navajo, Silver, Hand Raised, C.1910, 5 In.	175.00
Doll, Hand Carved, Greenland Costume, 8 1/2 In.	100.00
Doll, Northern Plains, Dress, High Top Beaded Moccasins, Belt, 13 In.	425.00
Doll, Plains, Beaded Buckskin Dress, Human Hair Braids, 1900s, 13 In.	425.00
Doll, Santa Fe, Cloth Armature Body, Goods & Tray, 1914, 9 1/2 In.	75.00
Doll, Sioux, Fringed & Beaded Skirt & Moccasins, 13 In.	45.00
Doll, Skookum, C.1920, 12 1/2 X 13 1/2 In., Pair	55.00
Doll, Yankton Sioux, Beaded Eyes, Mouth, Horsehair Braids, 12 1/2 In.	200.00
Dress, Plains, Leather, Long Beaded Fringe, Tooled Panels, 49 In.	310.00
Drum, Blackfoot, Rawhide Over Hollow Cottonwood Tree, 8 1/2 In.	135.00
Figurine, Bear, Eskimo, Grooved Paws, Eyes Baleen Inlaid, 3 3/4 In.	125.00
Fish Hook, Northwest Coast, Primitive Carved, 9 1/4 In.	185.00
Garters, Chippewa, Loom Beaded, Yarn Fringe, 36 In., Pair	40.00
Gauntlet, Shoshone, Hide, Beaded, Floral, Fringed Cuffs, 13 In.	60.00
Gloves, Flathead, Ellen Big Sam, Beaded Cuffs, C.1890	200.00
Guantlets, Blackfoot, Fringed Hide, Beaded, Horsetrack Design, 15 In.	100.00
Hat, Apache, Scout, Horsehair Band, Feathers	165.00
Headdress, Roach, Porcupine & Deer Hair	140.00
Hide, Shoshoni, Painted, Geometric, 12 X 17 In.	70.00
Jar, Effigy, Cochiti, Red Clay, Black Designs, Effigy Handle, 5 In.	55.00
Jar, Tacoma, Black Geometric, Red, Yellow On Varnish, 1920, 2 1/2 In.	35.00
Jar, Zia Olla, White Slipped, Triangle Pattern, 7 1/2 X 10 1/2 In.	175.00
Jar, Zia, Red & Brown Bird, White Slip, Reyes Pinto, 5 3/4 In.	85.00
Jar, Zuni, Red, White Slip, Gray Dear, 7 1/4 X 6 In.	205.00
Jug, Water, Zuni, Polychrome, C.1890, 6 3/4 X 8 1/2 In.	950.00
Kachina, Hopi, Cottonwood, Carved, Painted, Feather, 8 1/4 In.	400.00
Knife, Eastern Woodlands, Crooked, Carved Handle, 10 1/4 In.	45.00
Knife, Leg, Apache, Handmade, Diamond Back Design Sheath, Leather	100.00
Ladle, Northeast, Wooden, Tapering Handle, Flared Hook	210.00
Leggings, Cheyenne, Strips Of Geometric Beading, White, Yellow Ochre	105.00
Leggings, Sioux, Woman, Geometric Beading, White, 17 In.	395.00
Manta, Jemez, Loom Woven, Embroidered, Cotton, Fringe, 45 X 52 In.	425.00
Mask, Iroquois, Wood, Tin Eyes, Black Horsehair, Painted, 11 In.	20.00
Mask, Northwest, Kwakiutl, Black, Red, White, Movable Eyes, 13 1/2 In.	1250.00
Moccasins, Canadian Cree, Embroidered, 10 In.	85.00
Moccasins, Central Plains, Beaded, Blue, Divided Toe Flap, 10 1/2 In.	225.00
Moccasins, Cheyenne, Rain Dance Ceremonial, Elk Hide, Pair	175.00
Moccasins, Child's, Cheyenne, Intricate Beaded Pattern	40.00
Moccasins, Infant, American Plains, Partially Beaded	20.00
Moccasins, Northern Plains, Beaded Stripes, Blue Ground, 1900, 11 In.	100.00
Moccasins, Plains, Beaded, Opalescent Ground, 9 In.	45.00
Moccasins, Sioux, Beaded, White, Green Leather Stained, 10 1/2 In.	275.00
Moccasins, Sioux, Child's, Red & Blue Beaded, White Ground, 6 1/2 In.	95.00
Moccasins, Sioux, Hide, Beaded, Triangles, 10 1/2 In., Pair	120.00
Necklace & Earrings, Nuni, Signed E.Etsate	150.00
Necklace, Colored Burnt Wooden Beads, On Cord	95.00
Necklace, Pipe Bone, South Plains, 1895	90.00
Necklace, Pueblo, He–Shi, Cut Rolled Turquoise, Branch Coral, 1940	85.00
Necklace, Santo Domingo, He–Shi, Jet, Coral, Spondulus, Turquoise	310.00
Necklace, Woodland, Bear Claw, Horn, Bead Spacers, Fur Band	45.00
Olla, Zia, Polychromed, Painted, White, Black & Red, Scroll Design	800.00
Paddle, Ceremonial, Austral Islands, Carved Handle, 32 1/2 In.	250.00
Pants, Sioux, Buckskin, Beaded, Floral & Flag On Back Pocket, 40 In.	450.00
Papoose Basket, Karok, Sun Shade, C.1880, Doll Size	250.00
Pendant, Maori, Nephrite, Hands On Hips, Incised Face, 4 In.	225.00
Pincushion, Iroquois, Beads, Lady's High Button Shoe Shape, 9 In.	15.00
Pipe Bag, Cree, Beaded, Fringed, Blue, Geometric Designs, 28 In.	80.00

Pipe Bag, Northern Plains, Hide, Yellow Paint, Blue Beads, 32 In.	150.00
Pipe Bag, Sioux, Yellow Ocher Paint, Geomtric Beading, 18 In.	200.00
Pipe Bowl, Chippewa, Black Pipe Stone, Lead Inlay, 4 1/2 In.	60.00
Pipe, Plains, Catlinite, Wooden Stem, Red Quill Wrapped, 34 In.	25.00
Pipe, Woodlands, Catlinite Bowl, Wooden Stem, 21 1/2 In.	30.00
Plate, Blackware, Feather Design, Signed Maria/Papoui, 5 1/4 In.	400.00
Pot, Hopi, Signed, 8 X 6 In.	205.00
Powder Horn, American, Scrimshaw, Brass Tacks	185.00
Purse, Hupa, Elkhorn, For Dentalia Shell Money, Zigzag, 6 1/4 In.	650.00
Quirt, Cheyenne, Horse, Wooden Rod, Old Patina & Leather, 17 1/4 In.	25.00
Quiver, Arrow, Cheyenne, C.1870, 14 X 24 In.	195.00
Rattle, Northwest, Carved, Eagle Shape, Abalone Eyes, Painted, 14 In.	260.00
Rattle, Southern Plains, Leather, Wooden Handle, Elk Hide, 12 In.	25.00
Ring, Turquoise, Silver, Signed, 1 3/8 In.	45.00
Rug, Navajo, Brown, Gray, Red, Hand Spun Wool, 1910, 30 X 41 1/2 In.	150.00
Rug, Navajo, Diamond Design, C.1930, 29 X 56 In.	75.00
Rug, Navajo, Gray Ground, Diamonds, Columns, Black Border, 38 X 51 In.	200.00
Rug, Navajo, Hand Woven, Black & White, 31 X 49 In.	225.00
Rug, Navajo, Lines, C.1910, 4 1/2 X 3 1/2 Ft.	245.00
Rug, Navajo, Rattlesnake Pattern, Tan, Black, White, 62 X 30 In.	125.00
Rug, Navajo, Red, Brown, Gray, & Natural, 21 X 42 In.	65.00
Rug, Navajo, Red, Gray, White, Black, C.1930, 41 X 59 In.	175.00
Rug, Navajo, Wool, Serrated, Natural, Brown, Red, 1920, 38 X 70 In.	125.00
Rug, Stripes & Diamonds, Gray Ground, 45 X 63 In.	395.00
Sash, Assumption, Woodland, Zigzag, Red Field, Fringe, 88 X 9 In.	1100.00
Sash, Iroquois, Beaded, C.1850, Purple	100.00
Serape, Saltillo, Woven, Red, Diamond, Concentric Bands, 71 X 42 In.	35.00
Sheath, Knife, Sioux, Buckskin, Beads, Diamond Design, Red Paint, 8 In.	80.00
Sheath, Knife, Sioux, Hide, Hourglass Beaded, Turquoise, 5 1/2 In.	210.00
Shirt, Assiniboine, Ft.Belknap, Beaded Buckskin, C.1900, Large	500.00
Shirt, Woodlands, Man's, Maroon, Ribbon Applique	42.50
Spoon, Goat Horn, Openwork Handle, Abalone Shell, Label 1905, 7 In.	425.00
Spoon, Haida, Horn, Carved Openwork Handle	700.00
Spoon, Northwest, Horn, Sheep, No.8, Incised Los Angeles 1896, 8 In.	90.00
Spoon, Plains, Horn, Quill Handle, Tin Cones, Purple Horsehair	310.00
Spoon, Sioux, Horn, Bird Head Handle, Artist Chief Mato, 10 1/2 In.	475.00
Totem Pole, Haida Argillite, Carved, Bear, Wolf, 4 1/4 In.	50.00
Totem Pole, Haida, Eagle, Raven, Bear, Sacred Frog, Cedar, 1890, 17 In.	75.00
Totem Pole, Northwest, Wooden, 3 Bears, Eagle, Abalone Eyes, 27 In.	1300.00
Tray, Basket, Apache, Woven, Terrace & Linear Design, 10 1/2 In.	90.00
Tray, Basket, Pima, Polychrome, Dark Brown, Red Lines, 8 1/2 In.	75.00
Vase, Sioux, Step Design, Artist V.Pawnee Legging, 4 In.	25.00
Wedding Band, Zuni, Silver & Turquoise Inlay	45.00

An inkstand was made to be placed on a desk. It held some type of container for ink, and possibly a sander, a pen tray, a pen, a holder for pounce, and even a candle to melt the sealing wax. Inkstands date to the eighteenth century and have been made of silver, copper, ceramics, and glass.

INKSTAND, Brass, Art Deco Design, Crystal Cut Wells, Hinged, 6 X 8 1/2 In.	85.00
Brass, Boat Shape, Center Quill Holder Base, 4 Ball Feet	55.00
Brass, Crystal Cut Well, Hinged, Paw Feet, 5 X 4 X 5 1/2 In.	85.00
Bronze, Egyptian Revival, 2 Wells, Sphinx On Cover, 6 X 12 1/4 In.	220.00
Double, Cherubs & Devils, Marble Insert, Bronze	175.00
Figural, Brass Plated Iron, Mailbox Well, Dogs, 7 1/4 X 7 1/4 In.	95.00
Leaf Sprig Shape, Lidded Walnut Inkwell, Stamp Box, Bronze, 9 In.	110.00
Oval Acanthus Cover, 3 Wells, Pomegranate Finial, Brass, 5 1/4 In.	150.00
Silver Plate, 2 Cut Glass Bottles, Sheffield, 1839, 13 1/2 In.	275.00
Silver Plate, 2 Horns, Spherical Glass Inkwell, Whiting, 9 1/2 In.	500.00
Silver Plate, 3 Acanthus Feet, Branches, Copenhagen, 19th Century	310.00
Silver Plate, Tortoiseshell, 2 Bottles, Mappin & Webb, 12 In.	375.00

Inkwells, of course, held ink. Ready–made ink was first made about 1836 and was sold in bottles. The desk inkwell had a narrow hole so the pen would not slip inside. Pottery, glass, pewter, silver, and other materials were used to make inkwells. Look in other sections for more listings of inkwells.

INKWELL, Art Deco, 2 Crystal Wells, Hinged Covers, Brass Pen Holder, 8 In.	85.00
Art Deco, 2 Elephant Head Sides, Insert In Middle, Bronzed Metal	225.00
Art Nouveau Tray, Lady's Head On Sterling Silver Lid	50.00
Art Nouveau, Brass, Marked Germany, Glass Insert	150.00
Barrel Shape, Hinged Brass Fitting, Cobalt Blue	27.50
Bear, Seated, Wearing Necktie, Hinged Head, Metal, 4 In.	65.00
Beer Bottle, Brass, Johann Hoff., Berlin Logo, 2 7/8 In.	55.00
Black Man Form, Ebonized Wood, Glass Eyes, Ivory Teeth, 5 1/2 In.	250.00
Black Porcelain Round Base, Glass Top, Fount–O–Ink Co.	35.00
Blown Glass, 3–Mold, Olive Amber, 2 5/8 In.	95.00
Blown Glass, 3–Mold, Olive Amber, 2 X 1 3/4 In.	85.00
Blown Glass, 3–Mold, Olive Green, 2 1/4 In.	90.00
Blown Glass, 3–Mold, Olive Green, 2 5/8 X 2 In.	65.00
Bonzo, Hinged Lid, Glass, 3 1/2 In.	35.00
Boxer's Head, Cherry Carved, Glass Eyes, Hinged Top, C.1840, 4 In.	260.00
Brass, Bear, Glass Eyes	40.00
Brass, Gallery Tray, French, C.1880	350.00
Bronze, Octopus & Art Nouveau Girl, 8 1/2 X 9 In.	140.00 To 400.00
Bulldog Pup, Porcelain, Red & Orange	85.00
Camel, Saddle Lifts For Well, Brass	75.00
Candleholder, Bronze, Tipping Pheasant Well, 19th Century	265.00
Champleve, Enameled, 2 Dome Covered Pots Within Border, Soapstone	90.00
Chinese Famille Noire, Domed Top, Porcelain & Ormolu, 5 1/8 In.	175.00
Colonial Man, Playing Bass Fiddle, 2 Wells, 7 1/2 In.	150.00
Copper, Hinged Cover, Strapwork Corners, Curled Feet, 3 1/2 X 5 In.	110.00
Crab, Figural	44.00
Crystal Cut Well, Hinged Top, Pen Rest, Paw Feet, Brass, 4 X 5 In.	85.00
Cut Block, Azure Blue, 2 1/2 In.	95.00
Diagonal Rib Cutting, Crystal Well, Sterling Silver Top, 2 In.	68.00
Dog, Glass, Head Lifts Off, Signed Bonzo	125.00
Dog, Hinged Cover, Enameled, 3 3/4 In.	120.00
Donkey Standing, Metal, Hinged Saddle, Natural Colors, 3 1/2 In.	65.00
Double Glass Wells, Copper Lids, Tray	67.50
Drum Shape, Center Hole, Holes For Quills, Stoneware, 1 5/8 In.	17.50
Elephant, Hindu Riding On Head, Howda Lifts For Well, 7 1/2 In.	85.00
English Bull, With Top Hat, Metal	125.00
English Bulldog, Top Hat, Metal	125.00
Esterbrook, Dripless, Boxed	7.00
Flow Blue, Floral, Brass Stand, Hinged, Tray, 5 3/4 X 6 In.	195.00
Frog Holding Water Lily, Hinged Top, Metal, 3 In.	65.00
Frog, Hinged Lily Pad On Back, Baby Frog On Pad, Metal, 4 In.	95.00
Glass Insert, Turned Wood, Yellow & Black Paint, 3 1/4 X 1 7/8 In.	35.00
Glass, Cobalt, Block Etched, Hinged Top, Tray	275.00
Hammered Copper, Gustav Stickley, Hinged Cover, Riveted, 2 1/2 In.	132.00
Hand Painted Scenes, Gold, Hinged, Angelica Kauffmann, 3 1/2 In.	95.00
Hercules, Fighting Snake, Marble Base, Brass, 7 1/2 In.	300.00
Majolica, Lily Pad, Pink, Green, & Brown, 4 In.	85.00
Maple Cover, Painesville, Ohio, On Stand, Penholder	150.00
Monkey, Seated, Robed, Brush Wiper, Bronze	300.00
Moose Head, Hinged Top, Metal, 4 1/2 In.	65.00
Mushroom Paperweight Base, Hat Shaped Cover, Emerald Green, Blown	135.00
Orange Dog, Seated, 4 In.	45.00
Owl, Hinged Head, Glass Eyes, Glass Insert, Carved, 5 In.	60.00
Painted Flowers, Side Opening For Pen, Porcelain	30.00
Pear Shape Base, Black Amethyst, Art Deco, Turns In All Directions	75.00
Pelican, Bronze, 2 X 2 In.	85.00
Pewter Neck, Sterling Silver Monogrammed Dome Lid, Cut Crystal	30.00
Porcelain, Hand Painted, Floral, Lines, Side Open For Pen	30.00

Raised Flowers & Beading, Pagoda Shape, Porcelain, Blue & White 38.00
Reindeer, Brass & Copper 85.00
Stacked Cookies, Bisque, Top Cookie Marked Beurre, Nantes 75.00
Sterling Silver, Double, Square Hinged Top, LAC, 1860, 8 1/2 In. 275.00
Teakettle, Original Hinged Brass Cover On Spout, 8 Panels 235.00
Travel, Brass, 2 Lb.Weight Shape, Brass 125.00
Wide Flat Base, Ceramic Insert, Pewter, Round, 7 In. 65.00
Wooden, Black Paint, Gilt Stenciled Eagles, 2 Glass Inserts, 5 In. 45.00

Insulators of glass or pottery have been made for use on telegraph or telephone poles since 1844. Thousands of different styles of insulators have been made. Most common are those of clear or aqua glass, most desirable are the threadless types made from 1850 to 1870.

INSULATOR, American Tel.& Tel., Rose 20.00
BTC Montreal, Purple 8.00
California, Burgundy 20.00
Canadian Pacific Ry.Co. 18.00
Castle, Blue, Round Turrents 175.00
Chambers, Companion, Light Aqua 165.00
G.N.W.Tel.Co., Steel 14.00
H.G.Co., Yellow Green, White Smoke Swirls, Pat.May 2, 1893 .... 40.00
Hawley, Aqua 5.00
Hemingray, No.4, Aqua 8.00
Hemingray, No.9, Light Seven–Up Green 5.00
Hemingray, No.D510, Carnival 25.00
Jumbo, Brown, Porcelain 85.00
Lynchburg, No.1, Light Aqua 20.00
Manhattan, Blue, Dated 20.00
Maywell, No.19 B, USA, Pink Cast 8.00
McMicking, Blue Aqua 65.00
NEGM, Light Aqua 20.00
Prism, Triple Petticoat, Blue 50.00
Pyrex, No.171, Carnival 25.00
W.Brookfield, Deep Yellow Green 40.00
Whitall, Tatum, No.14, Straw 5.00
IRISH BELLEEK, see Belleek

Iron is a metal that has been used by man since prehistoric times. It is a popular metal for tools and decorative items like doorstops that need as much weight as possible. Items are listed here or under other appropriate headings such as Doorstop, Kitchen, or Tool. The tool that is used for ironing clothes, an iron, is listed under Kitchen, Iron or Kitchen, Sadiron.

IRON, Anvil, Stake, 40 Lbs. 70.00
Ashtray, Drunk & Lamppost 7.50
Ashtray, Figural, Lady's Hands, Leaf & Grape 45.00
Bell, Swivel Mount, America, 12 In. 45.00
Betty Lamp, Brass Hinged Whale Oil Cover, Dated 1855 .... 825.00
Bookends, Art Nouveau, Dancing Nudes 37.50
Bookends, Embossed Great Books 58.00
Bookends, End Of The Trail, 4 In. 16.00
Bookends, Flower Basket 55.00
Bookends, Girl At Fountain 20.00
Bookends, Lion On Rocks, Original Paint 19.00
Bookends, Man In Knickers, Gold Tone Finish 36.00
Bookends, Pointer, Aluminum Repaint, 7 3/4 In. 25.00
Bookends, Rabbit, Leading Parade With Baton, White 22.00
Bookends, Scotty Dog 45.00
Bookends, Sphinx 13.00
Bootjack, Cricket 24.00
Bootjack, Naughty Nellie ....28.00 To 65.00
Bootjack, Try Me, Embossed 18.00
Broom Holder, Figural, Lady 140.00
Buddha, Forge Welded, Sino–Nepalese, Palm Upraised, 13 In. 98.00

Cookware, Child's, Greycraft, Box, 5 Piece 70.00
Curling, Mustache, Shaving 18.00
Curtain Weight, Theater, Figural, Tassel, 10 1/2 In., Pair 195.00
Door Knocker, Empire, Seashells, Brass Name Plate, 1830–40, 7 3/4 In. 375.00
Door Knocker, Lady's Head, C.1870 .... 75.00
Door Knocker, Woodpecker, Original Paint, 3 1/2 In. 36.50
    IRON, DOORSTOP, see Doorstop
Dough Scraper, Incised Stars, Dated 1848, 3 X 3 In. 210.00
Eagle, 19th Century, 33 In. 2000.00
Eagle, Old Gold Paint, Wing Span 31 In. 100.00
Eagle, Wing Span 15 In. 55.00
Figurine, Baby Crawling, Brass Chick Hatching From Egg, Italy 130.00
Figurine, Colonial Man Sitting On Rum Barrel, 2 1/2 X 1 3/4 In. 165.00
Figurine, Eagle, Outstretched Wings, 36 In. 575.00
Figurine, Reclining Woman, Advertising, Ballibzin Coke 75.00
Foot Scraper, Brushes At Side 34.00
Foot Scraper, Dachshund 75.00
Foot Scraper, Scotty 65.00
Foot Scraper, Scroll Design 7.00
Fork & Spatula, Fork On One End, Spatula On Other, 15 In. 60.00
Grave Marker, Fire Department, Dated 1897 .... 90.00
Heater, Hot Water, Lion's Head On Door 65.00
Hitching Post, Form Of An Eagle's Head 175.00
Hitching Post, Horse, Late 19th Century, 4 Ft.2 In. 250.00
Hook, Boot, Whalebone Handle 155.00
Key Drop, Watchman's, Newman's Patrol Station, Pat.1900–1907 .... 18.00
Lock, Elbow, Brass Knobs, 4 3/8 X 5 5/8 In. 75.00
Mailbox, Door, 1909 .... · 20.00
    IRON, MATCH HOLDER, see Match Holder
Mortar & Pestle, Leather Flange, Wooden Lid, Hole For Pestle, 7 In. 40.00
Mortar & Pestle, Old Black Paint, 5 3/4 In. 22.50
Pipe Holder, Scotty Dog 12.00
Porringer, Kendrick, 1/2 Pt. 75.00
Pump, Water, Iowa Pump Co., Name & Design On Front 264.00
Rattle, Baby, 8 Jingle Bells, Black Wooden Handle, 6 In. 67.00
Rush Light, Primitive, Candle Socket, Twisted Stem, Tripod Base, 15 In. 85.00
Safe, Meillink, Stenciling, Small 150.00
Scale, National Specialty Store, 2 Lb. 300.00
Scissors, Frogged, 18th Century, 6 1/2 In. 155.00
Scraper, Dough, Incised Pot Of Tulips, Horse On Base, A.L., Dated 1830 .... 800.00
Service Bell, 2 3/4 In. 10.00
Smoking Stand, Dragon ....25.00 To 70.00
Spittoon, Turtle, Hinged Brass Lid, Step On To Open Head, 10 X 14 In. 195.00
Spittoon, Turtle, Mechanical, Tin Insert, Signed, 14 In. 165.00
Spool Holder, Grapevine Pattern, Victorian 75.00
Spur, Sunburst Rowel, Straight Shank 235.00
Teapot, Bamboo Relief Design, Japanese, 9 In. 50.00
Tie Backs, Curtain, Figural Basket Of Flowers, Original Paint, Pair 22.00
Tractor Seat, Deering 30.00
Tractor, Arcade Oliver, Original Red Paint, Rubber 110.00
Whip, Buggy, Salesman's Sample 175.00
Windmill Weight, Bobtailed Horse 200.00
Windmill Weight, Chicken ....180.00 To 375.00
Windmill Weight, Crescent Moon, Wooden Base 95.00
Windmill Weight, Dempster Horse, Long Tail 135.00
Windmill Weight, Dempster Horse, Short Tail 135.00
Windmill Weight, Eclipse 375.00
Windmill Weight, Elipse, Crescent Shape 75.00
Windmill Weight, Horse With Bobbed Tail, 16 3/4 In. 225.00
Windmill Weight, Rooster, Marked Hummer E 184, Large 400.00
Windmill Weight, Rooster, Marked Hummer E 184, Small 150.00
Windmill Weight, Short Tailed Horse 110.00

Ironstone china was first made in 1813. It gained its greatest popularity during the mid-nineteenth century. The heavy, durable, off-white pottery was made in white or was decorated with any of hundreds of patterns. Much flow blue pottery was made of ironstone. Some of the decorations were raised. Many pieces of ironstone are unmarked but some English and American factories included the word "Ironstone" in their marks.

IRONSTONE, see also Chelsea Grape; Gaudy Ironstone; Moss Rose; Staffordshire

IRONSTONE, Bedpan, Child's	25.00
Bedpan, Meinecke, 1900	18.00
Bowl & Pitcher, Blue, Roses, Scalloped, C.1908, Homer McLaughlin	145.00
Bowl, Fruit, Bell Flower, Edwards	12.00
Bowl, Oriental Scene, C.1860, Mason, English, 8 In.	160.00
Bowl, Syllabub, White, Meakin, 9 X 6 In.	145.00
Bowl, Vegetable, Covered, Blue Floral, Red & Gilt Rim, 12 1/2 In.	95.00
Bowl, Vegetable, Covered, Wheat & Blackberry, Meakin	80.00
Bowl, Vegetable, Wheat & Blackberry, Turner Goddard, 9 In.	80.00
Bowl, White, Low Pedestal, Deep, Burgess	55.00
Bowl, White, Meakin, 10 In.	15.00
Butter Chip, Tea Leaf, Meakin, Set Of 4	32.00
Butter Chip, White, Meakin	5.00
Chamber Pot, Covered, Ornate Pattern, White, Johnson Bros.	30.00
Chop Plate, Blue Bonnet	12.00
Coffee Server, Figural Goose Spout, Acorn Finial	45.00
Coffeepot, Baltimore Shoe, Brougham & Mayer, 1850s	115.00
Coffeepot, Gothic, Edwards	165.00
Coffeepot, Wild Rose	45.00
Compote, Pink Flowers, Pedestal, Johnson Bros., 4 1/2 X 8 In.	65.00
Compote, Scalloped Rim & Base, T.& R.Boote & Co., 10 5/8 In.	80.00
Crock, Cover, Sanford's Inks & Pastes, Handle, Cobalt	75.00
Cup & Saucer, Child's, Aqua Monochrome Floral	35.00
Cup & Saucer, Corn & Oats, Davenport	25.00
Dinner Set, Child's, Miniature, 27 Piece	88.00
Gravy Boat, Pankhurst	32.00
Gravy Boat, Underplate, Wedgwood	22.00
Jug & Bowl, Multicolor, Mason, C.1840	590.00
Jug, Black Transfer, Handle, Elsmore & Roster, Dated 1859, 9 In.	605.00
Ladle, White, 12 1/2 In.	35.00
Mold, Food, Crown Design	54.00
Mold, Food, Fish	40.00
Mold, Food, Grape	40.00
Mold, Food, Leaf, Jones	54.00
Mold, Food, Shell	40.00
Mold, Pineapple Bottom, Fluted Interior, 8 1/2 X 6 3/4 In.	50.00
Mold, Pudding, Asparagus Design	42.00
Pitcher & Bowl, Sprig Pattern, Small	85.00
Pitcher & Bowl, Tracery Pattern, White, Johnson Bros.	100.00
Pitcher & Bowl, White, Green Design	90.00
Pitcher, Brown, White, Ships, Flowers, C.1845	38.00
Pitcher, Hot Water, Moss Rose, Embossed, Meakin	365.00
Pitcher, Hyacinth, Wedgwood, 9 1/4 In.	40.00
Pitcher, Milk, Lily Shape, Burgess	95.00
Plate, Abbey, Set Of 6, 1840s	75.00
Plate, Aurora Pattern, Pink, Maroon, 9 In.	12.50
Plate, Blue Feather Edge, 10 7/8 In.	12.50
Plate, Cobalt Blue Ground, Enameled, 8 1/2 In.	35.00
Plate, Columbia Pattern, Edwards, 8 1/2 In.	25.00
Plate, Excelsior Pattern, Mulberry Polychrome, 8 1/2 In.	25.00
Plate, Japan Pattern, Mason, Pair	425.00
Plate, Machu Pattern, Mason, 8 In.	8.00
Plate, Persian, Brown Transfer, Meakin, 9 3/4 In.	10.00
Plate, Tillenburg, Dark Blue, 12 Sides, Clemenson	45.00

Platter, Ashworth Hanley, 13 X 10 In. 25.00
Platter, Blue Feather Edge, Octagonal, 12 1/4 In. 35.00
Platter, Blue Feather, Impressed Best Goods, 14 1/4 In. 35.00
Platter, Blue Willow Design, 15 1/2 In. 75.00
Platter, Hanley Pattern, Ashworth Bros., 13 X 10 1/2 In. 40.00
Platter, Hanley Pattern, Ashworth Bros., 19 X 15 In. ....40.00 To 75.00
Platter, Pastoral Scene, Adams, Blue & White, 15 In. 150.00
Platter, Spring, 14 In. 28.00
Platter, Turkey, White, Meakin, 16 1/2 X 11 1/2 In. 125.00
Platter, Well & Tree, C.1830, Oriental Scene, 20 1/2 In. 150.00
Potlid, Man Shaving, R.B.Ede & Co., London, Shaving Cream, 3 In. 35.00
Potlid, Purple Transfer, Washington Crossing Delaware, 4 In. 55.00
Potty, Covered, Gothic, Meigh 88.00
Sauce, Covered, Ribbed, Raspberry, Meakin 53.00
Slop Pail, Covered, Iron Bail Handle, Embossed, 9 In. 35.00
Soup Tureen, White, Penman–Brown 195.00
Spooner, White, Marked Buffalo China 1921 .... 28.00
Sugar, Covered, Corn, White, Wedgwood 50.00
Sugar, Covered, Gothic, Ridgway 60.00
Sugar, Excelsior Pattern, Mulberry Polychrome 25.00
Syrup, Swan Finial, Pewter Top 55.00
IRONSTONE, TEA LEAF, see Tea Leaf Ironstone
Teapot, Cable & Ring Pattern, J.&G. Meakin, 8 1/2 In. 60.00
Teapot, Gooseneck Spout, Wheat In Relief, Pierced Handle, Ribbed 75.00
Teapot, St.Louis, Edwards 95.00
Teapot, Wheat Design, White, Adams 65.00
Toothbrush Holder, Johnson Bros. 15.00
Tureen, Covered, Red Transfer, Boat Scene, Turner & Son, 9 1/4 In. 85.00
Tureen, Covered, White, C.1869, Meakin, Oval 145.00
Tureen, Covered, Wild Rose, Tray & Ladle, Meakin 95.00
Tureen, Registration 1855, Acorn Finial On Grape Leaves, White 85.00
Tureen, Soup, Ladle, Twin Leaves, 4 Piece 270.00
Tureen, Vegetable, Covered, Brown, Rosalind, Meakin, 11 X 5 1/2 In. 165.00
Tureen, White, Wedgwood 80.00
Umbrella Holder, White, Bulbous, Hall, 10 In. 85.00
Vase, Birds & Floral, Cylinder Shape, Mason, 10 In. 250.00
Vegetable, Covered, White, Atlantic Shape, Round 85.00

Laszlo Ispanky began his American career as a designer for Cybis Porcelains. In 1966, he established his own studio in Pennington, New Jersey; and, since 1976, he has worked for Goebel of North America. He works in stone, wood, or metal, as well as porcelain. The first limited edition figurines were issued in 1966.

ISPANKY, Figurine, Cleopatra 2000.00
Figurine, Dawn, 1970, 14 1/2 In. 625.00
Figurine, Lorelei, 1973 .... 550.00
Figurine, Peace, 13 In. 250.00
Pitcher, Romeo & Juliet 150.00

"IVOREX"
OSBORNE—(COPYRIGHT:
MADE IN ENGLAND.

Arthur Osborne made Ivorex plaques in England in the beginning of the 1900s. The plaques, made of a material he called "sterine wax," pictured buildings or room interiors modeled in three dimensions. After Osborne's death his daughter Blanche ran the company. It was closed in 1965, then purchased by W. H. Bossons Ltd. in 1971. Production of the plaques started again in 1980.

IVOREX, Plaque, A Friendly Call, A.Osborne, 9 X 6 In. 15.00
Plaque, Burns & Highland Mary 25.00

The tusk of an elephant is ivory; and to many, that is the only true ivory. To most collectors, the term "ivory" also includes such natural materials as walrus, hippopotamus, or whale teeth or tusks, and some of the vegetable materials that are of similar texture and density. Other ivory items are listed under Scrimshaw or Netsuke.

IVORY, Ball, Mystery, 3 Elephants Hold Ball, Trunk, 4 X 6 In. 80.00

Ivory, Okimono, Laughing
Chinese Boy, Japan,
C.1900, 6 In.

Ivory, Bottle, Snuff, Relief
Garden Scene,
Painted, 8 In.

Ivory, Figurine, Elephant With Howda,
19th Century, 6 In.

Beads, Graduated Sizes, Ivory Clasp, American, 24 In.	100.00
Book, Memorandum, Front Shield, Gold Letters, Days, 2 1/2 X 1 1/4 In.	50.00
Bookmark, Oriental	20.00
Bottle, Snuff, Bell Shape	65.00
Bottle, Snuff, Boy & Girl Either Side, Gourd Shape, 2 X 3 In.	150.00
Bottle, Snuff, Figural, Elephant & Man	295.00
Bottle, Snuff, Garden Scene, 2 1/2 In.	58.00
Bottle, Snuff, Paneled Dome Cover, Rose & Ring Handles, Signed, 8 In.	200.00
Bottle, Snuff, Relief Garden Scene, Painted, 8 In. ....*Illus*	200.00
Canape Picks, Carved Elephant Tops, Fitted Box, 3 3/4 In., Set Of 6	50.00
Candlestick, Young Boys Huddled Together, Renaissance, 9 In., Pair	825.00
Card Case, 19th Century, Chinese	225.00
Card Case, Carved Scene, C.1880, French	225.00
Card Case, Scene, Of Tale Of William Tell, German	185.00
Clothespin, Whalebone, Drawstring Calico Bag, Set Of 4	495.00
Comb, Mantilla	12.00
Corset Stay, Whalebone, Engraved Views Of New Bedford Harbor	8800.00
Cue Ball	18.00
Cutlery Set, Will & Finck	225.00
Doctor's Lady, Moveable Bracelet, 4 In.	65.00
Doctor's Lady, Reclining On Wooden Couch, 4 In.	75.00
Etching, Nude, Sheaves Of Wheat, Boilly, Framed, 19th Century, 8 3/8 In.	60.00
Figure, Flower Vendor, 2 Children, Baskets, Meiji Period, 4 In.	1430.00
Figurine, 5 Mice Pushing Egg, Mahogany Base, 5 In.	475.00
Figurine, Boat With Family, Japanese, 8 1/2 In.	2000.00
Figurine, Chinese Boy, Laughing, With Pomegranate, Japan, 1900, 6 In.	275.00
Figurine, Chinese Lady, 7 In.	195.00
Figurine, Christ, Europe, 18th Century, 6 1/8 In.	180.00
Figurine, Crocodile, Fighting Tiger, Cane Handle, 7 In.	75.00
Figurine, Elephant With Howda, 19th Century, 6 In. ....*Illus*	190.00
Figurine, Elizabethan Woman Peasants, Instruments, 3 Piece, 6 In.	385.00
Figurine, Eskimo, Fossilized, Okvik, Oval Head, Incised Torso, 4 In.	225.00
Figurine, Fisherman & Fisherwoman, Carved, 6 In., Pair	200.00
Figurine, Indian, Krishna, Group	185.00
Figurine, Lady & Gentleman Standing, Japan, Signed, 5 1/6 & 5 1/8 In.	70.00
Figurine, Mice, Pushing Egg, Mahogany Base, 13 1/4 In.	325.00
Figurine, Musical Band, Children, Continental, 16 Piece, 6 1/2 In.	1980.00
Figurine, Nude Woman Standing In Garden, 6 1/4 X 3 1/2 In.	215.00
Figurine, Okimono, Bijiin, Son On Back, 5 In.	110.00
Figurine, Old Man & Child, 19th Century, 6 In.	275.00
Figurine, Samurai, Barefoot, Holding Spear, 20th Century, 5 1/4 In.	125.00
Figurine, Tanto, Karako Playing, Carved Leaves, Meiji Period, 11 In.	880.00

Figurine, Wolf, Fighting 2 Baboons, 4 In. 65.00
Frame, Easel, Engraved Dragons, Back Closure, 1 3/8 X 1 1/2 In. 90.00
Group, Fisherman, 2 Children Cleaning Fish, Signed, 5 1/2 In. 250.00
Horn, Figurine, Bird, 15 In. 20.00
Match Safe, Double Sided, Berlin, 1887 .... 110.00
Netsuke, Dragon, Coiled Tail, Signed, 2 In. 50.00
Netsuke, Skull, Coiling Snake, Frog At Back, Meiji Period, 2 In. 660.00
Okimono, Laughing Chinese Boy, Japan, C.1900, 6 In. ....*Illus* 275.00
Portrait, Empress Elizabeth, Austria, Tortoise Frame, C.1870, 5 In. 290.00
Portrait, Fanny Eisler, Actress, C.1870, Tortoise Frame, 5 1/2 In. 290.00
Portrait, Gentleman, 14K Gold Frame, JH Initials, 1784–1827, 3 In. 425.00
Portrait, Nude Standing, Garden, Ivory Frame, Painted, 6 X 3 1/2 In. 135.00
Seal, Desk, Brass, Earl's Crest 125.00
Sleigh, Wheel Drawn, Eskimo, Kamchatka, Incised, Peg Joined, 4 In. 45.00
Tankard, Continental, Alexander The Great In Battle, 16 1/4 In. 5500.00
Tool, Back Scratcher, China 40.00
Tusk, Elephant, Curved, 2 X 23 In. 175.00
Tusk, Narwhal, 5 Ft. 7 In. 3500.00
Tusk, Panels, Male, Female At Cemetery, Obelisk, C.1850, 14 1/2 In. 600.00
Vase, Long Legged Birds, Picking Berries, 8 In. 175.00
Whalebone, Needle Case, Shield Shape 32.00
Whalebone, Sewing Basket, Openwork 9350.00

Jack Armstrong, the all–American boy, was the hero of a radio serial from 1933 to 1951. Premiums were offered to the listeners until the mid–1940s. Jack Armstrong's best–known endorsement is for Wheaties.

JACK ARMSTRONG, Airplane, Punch–Out & Assemble, 1944 .... 110.00
Answer Box, Magic 35.00
Cereal Bowl, Wheaties, 1939 .... 35.00
Explorer Telescope, 1938 .... 25.00
Flashlight, Red 40.00
Hike–O–Meter ....12.50 To 25.00
Hike–O–Meter, Original Mailer 28.00
Light, Torpedo 15.00
Magic Answer Box, 1938 .... 45.00
Manual, Future Champs, 1944 .... 38.00
Shooting Plane, Radio Premium, Boxed 65.00
Telescope, Explorer, 1937 ....15.00 To 32.00
Viewer, Movie, Original Box 25.00
Whistle Ring, Egyptian, 1938 .... 28.00

Jack–in–the–pulpit vases were named for their odd trumpetlike shape that resembles the wild plant called jack–in–the–pulpit. The design originated in the late Victorian years. Vases in the jack–in–the–pulpit shape were made of ceramic or glass.

JACK–IN–THE–PULPIT, Vase, Applied Flower, Green Opalescent, 9 In. 88.00
Vase, Applied Flowers, Amber Branches, 6 X 6 7/8 In. 135.00
Vase, Green Ruffle, Embossed Design, Green, Opaque, 9 In. 88.00
Vase, Hobnailed & Maroon Rim, Opaque Blue, 6 3/4 In. 95.00
Vase, Petal Feet, Ruffled, Vaseline, 3 7/8 X 9 3/8 In. 80.00
Vase, Petal Top, Pink & White Spatter, 5 X 8 In. 75.00
Vase, Pink Spiral Trim, Swirl, Vaseline, 7 3/4 In. 88.00
Vase, Rigaree Around Body, Cranberry, 7 In., Pair 155.00
Vase, Ruffled, Green & White Spatter, 5 3/4 X 9 3/8 In. 88.00
Vase, Shaded Red Frilled Edge, 7 3/4 In., Pair 350.00
Vase, White Loopings, Frosted Feet, Green, 7 1/2 In. 135.00

Jackfield ware was originally a black glazed pottery made in Jackfield, England, from 1750 to 1775. A yellow glazed ware has also been called Jackfield ware. Most of the pieces referred to as "Jackfield" today are black–glazed, red–clay wares made at the Jackfield Pottery in Shropshire, England, in Victorian times.

JACKFIELD, Creamer, Covered, Cow, Black, Gilt Trim, 4 3/4 In. 65.00

Creamer, Covered, Cow, Black, Gilt Trim, 5 In. 35.00
Creamer, Cow, Oval Base, Gold Trim, 7 1/4 X 5 1/2 In. 125.00
Pitcher, Water, Green Ivy Leaves, Gold, 7 1/2 In. 125.00
Sugar, Creamer, & Teapot, Miniature 125.00

> *Two different minerals, nephrite and jadeite, are called jade. Nephrite is the mineral used for most early Oriental carvings. Jade is a very tough stone that is found in many colors from dark green to pale lavender. Jade carvings are still being made in the old styles, so collectors must be careful not to be fooled by recent pieces.*

JADE, Bowl, Covered, Chrysanthemum Shape, Stand, 16th Century, 5 1/4 In. 2900.00
Bowl, Green & Brown Striated, Round, Chinese, 1 1/2 X 4 In. 110.00
Clock, Buddha, Symbols, Round, 8 In. 60.00
Dish, White, Chrysanthemum Center, Scalloped, China, 4 3/4 X 3 1/16 In. 500.00
Figurine, Buddha, 3 In. 128.00
Figurine, Sage & Deer, White & Green, Late 19th Century, 2 1/4 In. 90.00
Figurine, Sage, With Toad, White, Gama Sennin, 19th Century, 4 In. 230.00
Figurine, Standing Figure, White, Wooden Base, Guanyin, China, 7 1/2 In. 250.00
Junk, Mottled Green, Tan, 2 Figures, Wooden Base, China, C.1900, 5 In. 275.00
Pendant, Carved, Birds, Flowers, 14K Gold Loop, C.1900 .... 85.00

> *Japanese Coralene is a ceramic decorated with small raised beads and dots. It was first made in the nineteenth century. Later wares made to imitate coralene had dots of enamel. There is also another type of coralene that is made with small glass beads on glass containers.*

JAPANESE CORALENE, Vase, Dogwood, Blush Apricot, Royal Kinjo, 1910, 8 In. 150.00
Vase, Floral, Burnt Orange To Rust, Handles, 13 1/2 In. 525.00
Vase, Gold, Gold Handles, Pat.Mark, 8 In. 245.00

> *There are two types of jasperware. Some pieces have raised designs of white or a contrasting color made from colored clay. Other pieces are made by decorating the raised portions with a color.*

JASPERWARE, see also various art potteries; Wedgwood
JASPERWARE, Pitcher, Green, Classical, Rope Handle, Wedgwood, 6 1/4 In. 295.00
Pitcher, White Grecian Figures, Blue Ground, 5 In. 15.00
Syrup, Classical Design, Lavender, 9 In. 145.00

Jewelry, Brooch, Coral, Diamond,
Black Enamel, Safety Chain

Jewelry, Brooch & Earring Set, Coral Scarab, Gold

Jewelry, Brooch, Earrings, Enameled,
Pearl, C.1870, Gold Frame

Jewelry, Brooch & Earrings, Fluted Design, Granulation

Jewelry, if made from gold and precious gems or plastic and colored glass, is still popular with collectors. Values are determined by the intrinsic value of the stones and metal and by the skill of the craftsmen and designers. Victorian and older jewelry has been popular since the 1950s. More recent interests are Art Deco and Edwardian styles, Mexican and Danish silver jewelry, and beads of all kinds. Copies of almost all styles are being made.

JEWELRY, Bar Pin, 3 Diamonds, Set In Starburst, 14K Gold, 2 X 1 1/2 In.	122.00
Bar Pin, Art Deco, Diamonds Set In Starburst, 14K Gold, 2 In.	122.00
Beads, Jadite, Green, Graduated, 18 In.	300.00
Bracelet, Arm, Topaz Stones, Sphinx On Each Side, Large	375.00
Bracelet, Art Nouveau, French Enamel, Pearl	975.00
Bracelet, Bangle, Coiled Snake, Diamond, 15K Gold, Garnet Eyes	550.00
Bracelet, Bangle, Sterling Silver, C.1910	35.00
Bracelet, Cabochon Garnet, Openwork, Gilt–Silver, Austro–Hungarian	200.00
Bracelet, Cabochon, Red Stone, Gilt–Silver Links, Austro–Hungarian	100.00
Bracelet, Diamond, Rope Twist Pattern, 15K Gold, C.1850 ....*Illus*	550.00
Bracelet, Double Row Bar Link, 3 Spinels, 2 Diamond Collets, 1900s	425.00
Bracelet, Garnet, Silver Mount, Rosette Set, 8 Garnets, Pearl	200.00
Bracelet, Mesh Band, Victorian, 14K Gold, Pair	2200.00
Bracelet, Oval Linked, 18K Gold, C.1920	95.00
Bracelet, Silver Dollar Mounted, Indian Silver, C.1926	72.00
Bracelet, Silver Rectangle Links, Swans, Leaves, G.Jensen, 7 1/2 In.	195.00
Bracelet, Tapered Hinged Gold Mount, Heart Shape, Sapphire, C.1940	1200.00
Bracelet, Turquoise & Enamel, Rosette Shaped Links, Red Stones	100.00
Bracelet, Victorian, Garnet, 14K Gold, Pierced Bangle	175.00
Bracelet, Victorian, Gold Filled	90.00
Brooch & Earring Set, Coral Scarab, Gold ....*Illus*	500.00
Brooch & Earrings, Fluted Design, Granulation ....*Illus*	450.00
Brooch, Gray Lava Cameo, Child In Hat, Lamb, 18K Gold Frame, 1870	200.00
Brooch, Agate Pebble, Silver Wreath, Scottish, Mid–19th Century	350.00
Brooch, Bar, 3 Rows Oriental Pearls, Gold, C.1910	150.00
Brooch, Beetle, Garnet & Diamond, Gold, Faberge, C.1900, 1 1/8 In.	2850.00
Brooch, Cameo, Engraved 10K Gold, 1885	225.00
Brooch, Cameo, Gone With The Wind, Lux	150.00
Brooch, Cameo, Rebecca At The Well, Original Frame, 2 X 1 1/2 In.	75.00
Brooch, Cameo, Shell, Figurine, Madonna, Signed, 1 1/4 X 1 In.	30.00
Brooch, Cameo, Solid Gold Frame, C.1870	200.00
Brooch, Cameo, Victorian, 10K Gold Filigree Frame, Large	250.00
Brooch, Cameo, Victorian, 10K Gold Frame	200.00
Brooch, Cameo, Young Lady, Engraved 10K Gold Frame, C.1860	250.00
Brooch, Coral, Diamond, Black Enamel, Safety Chain ....*Illus*	175.00
Brooch, Diamond & Platinum, Bow Shape, Edwardian, 55 Carats	1600.00

Brooch, Earrings, Enameled, Pearl, C.1870, Gold Frame ....*Illus*   900.00
Brooch, Enameled Tiger, Handset Marcasites, Sterling Silver 65.00
Brooch, Florentine, Boxer, Ruby Eye, Diamond Collar, Gold, C.1910 ....   700.00
Brooch, Gold, Oriental Pearl Bar, 3 Rows Of Pearls 150.00
Brooch, Lava Cameo & Gold, Grey Lava Cameo, Child Wearing Hat 200.00
Brooch, Leaf, Victorian, Gun Metal, Marcasite Type, Stones, 3 5/8 In. 25.00
Brooch, Memorial, Onyx, Pearl, & Gold, Seed Pearls Bar, 19th Century 350.00
Brooch, Painting, Lady, 18K Gold ....*Illus*   250.00
Brooch, Scottish Agate Pebble, Silver Wreath 350.00
Brooch, Shell Cameo, Victorian, Beaded Gold Frame 200.00
Brooch, Snow Baby, 1 1/4 In. 40.00
Brooch, Turquoise, Diamond & Gold Ibis, C.1820 ....*Illus*   2500.00
Case, Calling Card, Tortoiseshell & Silver 200.00
Case, Cigarette, 14K Gold Inlay, 4 X 3 In. 100.00
Chain & Whistle, Gold, Victorian, 18K Gold 130.00
Chain, 10K Gold, 16 In. 25.00
Chain, Antique Gold, Double Links, 47 In. 475.00
Chain, Herringbone, 14K Gold 1200.00
Chain, Watch, 14K Gold, 14 3/4 In. 110.00
Chain, Watch, Cast Faces, Filigree, Sterling Silver 75.00

Jewelry, Brooch, Painting, Lady,
18K Gold

Jewelry, Brooch, Turquoise, Diamond
& Gold Ibis, C.1820

Jewelry, Cuff Links, Coral, Carved, Bacchus

Jewelry, Choker, Floral,
Interlocking Links, 18K Gold

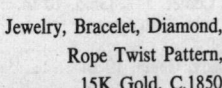

Jewelry, Bracelet, Diamond,
Rope Twist Pattern,
15K Gold, C.1850

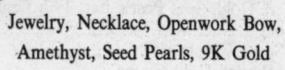

Jewelry, Necklace, Openwork Bow,
Amethyst, Seed Pearls, 9K Gold

Jewelry, Necklace, Amethyst,
Gold Openwork, Link Chain

Jewelry, Necklace, 18K Gold Chain, Hallmark, 80 In.

Chain, Watch, Figural Lion Fob, 18K Gold Inset, Brass	45.00
Chain, Watch, Slide Clasp, Yellow Gold Filled	75.00
Chain, Watch, Twisted Link, Yelow Gold Filled	55.00
Charm, Watch, Walrus Tooth, 14K Gold Deer's Head, Victorian	75.00
Chatelaine, Potpouri Flask, Stopper, Chain, Attachments	25.00
Choker & Bracelet, Leaves, Silver, Georg Jensen	350.00
Choker, 18K Gold Mess & Buckle, 2 Mine Cut Diamonds, Victorian	700.00
Choker, Floral, Interlocking Links, 18K Gold *Illus*	1100.00
Choker, Freshwater Pearl & Coral Beads, Rice Shape Pearls	250.00
Choker, Victorian Diamond & 18K Gold, Buckle, Mine Cut Diamonds	700.00
Cigar Cutter, Heart Shape, 14K Gold, Marked, 1 1/4 X 1 In.	85.00
Circle Pin, Carved Scrolled & Enamel Trim, English, 14K Gold	440.00
Cuff Links, 18K Gold, Mythological Scenes	375.00
Cuff Links, Coral, Carved, Bacchus *Illus*	500.00
Cuff Links, Diamond, Agate Scarab, 18K Gold	400.00
Cuff Links, Mythological Scene, 18K Gold, Box, L.Schlesinger, Berlin	375.00
Cuff Links, Sterling Silver, Unger Bros.	45.00
Dress Clip, Cinnabar	35.00
Earrings, Brass Filigree, Pierced Ear, Stones, Victorian, 3 1/4 In.	32.00
Earrings, Drop Shape Garnet Carbuncle, Pearl, Late 19th Century	150.00
Earrings, Gold, 6 Garnet Each, Pierced, C.1890	45.00
Earrings, Mother-Of-Pearl Cameo, Stud, Friction Post, 14K Gold	35.00
Earrings, Pendant, Diamond & 15K Gold, Georgian	650.00
Earrings, Rose Cut Diamonds, Georgian, 19th Century, Gold Mount	350.00
Earrings, Silver, Siamese, Bali Dancer, Screwback	15.00
Earrings, Turquoise And Gold Pendant, Flowers & Leaves *Illus*	225.00
Hatpin, Victorian, 14K Gold, 6 In.	55.00
JEWELRY, INDIAN, see Indian	
Key Chain, Lion, Sterling Silver, Victorian, 1880	48.00
Key Chain, Victorian, Solid Sterling Silver, Lion, C.1885	35.00
Lavaliere, Double Drop, Seed Pearl, Diamond Center, 14K Gold, 10 In.	90.00
Lavaliere, Pave Linked Bow Top, Diamond, Chain, 18th Century	475.00
Locket, 4 Mine Cut Diamonds, 14K Gold, 1890	200.00
Locket, Art Nouveau, Gold Plated Head Of Lady, Chain, 19 In.	65.00
Locket, Floral Design, Oval, 18K Gold	125.00
Locket, Silver Star, Diamond, Emerald, 18K Gold, Victorian	400.00
Necklace, 18K Gold Chain, Hallmark, 80 In. *Illus*	1000.00

Necklace, 2 Pearl Doves, Peridot Wings, Bow, Victorian, 14K Gold	450.00
Necklace, Alternating Onyx, Jade & Pearl Beads, 40 In.	45.00
Necklace, Amethyst, Gold Openwork, Link Chain ....*Illus*	170.00
Necklace, Art Deco, Snake, Safety Lock, 14K Gold, 15 1/2 In.	395.00
Necklace, Bellflower, Enameled, Green, Gold Washed, 15 1/2 In.	350.00
Necklace, Cherry Amber Beads, Graduated, Faceted, 29 In.	200.00
Necklace, Cherry Amber, Faceted, Graduated, 23 1/2 In.	95.00
Necklace, Honey Amber, Faceted, Graduated Ovals, 29 In.	85.00
Necklace, Jade, 13 Multicolor Beads, Golden Thread Knots	190.00
Necklace, Link Chain Design, Collet Set Diamonds, Platinum Mount	425.00
Necklace, Openwork Bow, Amethyst, Seed Pearls, 9K Gold ....*Illus*	225.00
Necklace, Tourmaline, Pink & Green, 14K White Gold	425.00
Pendant, 4 Section, 4 Diamonds, Blue Baroque Pearl Drop, 2 In.	199.00
Pendant, Coin, Franz Josep, Hungarian, Gold, C.1898	160.00
Pendant, Diamond, Enameled, French, Hallmarked, C.1880	1800.00
Pendant, Jade, Lavender, Carved, 14K Gold	750.00
Pendant, Lady's Enameled Face, Russian Hallmark	425.00
Pendant, Marcasite Cluster, Sapphire Center, Chain	60.00
Pendant, Openwork Flower, Enameled Gold, Pearl Drop ....*Illus*	325.00
Pendant, Owl, Filigree, 14K Gold	15.00
Pendant, Pearl & Diamond, Heart Shape, 14K White Gold	525.00
Pendant, Pierced Tree Design, Silver, Mother-Of-Pearl, Turquoise	900.00
Pendant, Victorian, Shield Shape, Beaded, Gold Chain, 2 Gold Tassels	375.00
Pendant, Victorian, Woven Hair, Marked Papa To Mary, Enameled	100.00
Pendant, Whistle, Fluted Link Chain Necklet, 18K Gold, Fred Paris	130.00
Pin, Bar, Victorian, Onyx, Gold Frame, Leaves	150.00
Pin, Blue Spade Leaves, Green Ground, Sterling Silver, 1908, 1 In.	100.00
Pin, Cameo, Lady's Head, Pink Ground, Scrolled Edge, Safety Clasp	50.00
Pin, Cat, Diamond, Black Enamel Jacket, 18K Gold ....*Illus*	375.00
Pin, Cat, Ruby, Sapphire, Diamond, 18K Gold ....*Illus*	300.00
Pin, Crescent, Diamond, Victorian	525.00
Pin, Dogwood, Kalo, Notched Leaves, Node Center, Sterling Silver	160.00
Pin, Enameled Eastern Center, 14K White Gold Filigree	45.00
Pin, Etched Brass, Cabochon, Green, Forest Craft Guild, 2 3/4 In.	55.00
Pin, Filigree, 14K White Gold, Enameled Easter Star	45.00
Pin, Gold Circle, Diamonds & Cultured Pearls, 14K Gold	250.00

Jewelry, Pin, Cat, Diamond,
Black Enamel Jacket,
18K Gold

Jewelry, Pin, Cat, Ruby,
Sapphire, Diamond,
18K Gold

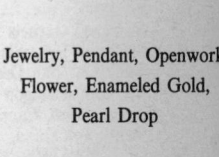

Jewelry, Pendant, Openwork
Flower, Enameled Gold,
Pearl Drop

Pin, Knot, Victorian, Gold Plated, 1 3/4 In. 25.00
Pin, Leaf & Flower, Silver, Bezel Set Lapis Stone, Jensen, 1 1/2 In. 160.00
Pin, Mourning, Hair, Oval, 1 1/8 In. ....20.00 To 28.00
Pin, Onyx, Pearl, Gold Branch, Purple Stone, Victorian 35.00
Pin, Scarf, Silver, Double Scroll Leaf, Georg Jensen, 3/4 In. 55.00
Pin, Silver, Full Figure Bird, Leaves, Berries, Georg Jensen, 2 In. 125.00
Pin, Silver, Scalloped, Scrolling Leaves, Beading, Jensen, 1 3/4 In. 135.00
Pin, Triangular, Spread Winged Eagle, Brass, Frost, 3 X 1 5/8 In. 22.00
Pin, Tulip, Silver Scroll & Fruit, G.Jensen, 1 3/4 In. 130.00
Pin, Violet, Figural, Unger Bros., Sterling Silver, Round, 1 In. 60.00
Ring, 22 Full Cut Diamonds, 1/8 In.Band, Platinum, 1930s 750.00
Ring, Baby's, Seed Pearl Center, Garnet Either Side, 10K Gold 20.00
Ring, Baby's, Victorian, Wide, 10K Gold 25.00
Ring, Belt & Buckle, 9K Gold, England, Victorian 99.00
Ring, Black Onyx, Floral Design, Sterling Silver, 1880 .... 25.00
Ring, Boy's, Oval Cut Garnet, 14K Gold, 7/8 In. 66.00
Ring, Cameo, 14K Yellow Gold, Oval, 1 1/4 X 1 In. 175.00
Ring, Cat's–Eye, 4 Diamonds Each Side 780.00
Ring, Cluster, Marcasite, 10 Garnets 55.00
Ring, Cocktail, 7 Garnets, 14K Yellow Gold Mounting 160.00
Ring, Coral Cameo, 6 Diamonds Around, Yellow Gold Setting 965.00
Ring, Diamond & Ruby, Crossover Design, 18K Gold 1300.00
Ring, Diamond, 18K White Gold, Pierced, Victorian 150.00
Ring, Dinner, 11 Diamonds, Art Deco, 14K White Gold, 3/4 In. 199.00
Ring, Hammered 18K Gold Mount, Rectangular Shape, David Webb 900.00
Ring, Jet, Diamond & 18K Gold, 19th Century, French 425.00
Ring, Lady's, 15 Mm.Garnet Center, Floral Design On Sides, 14K Gold 122.00
Ring, Lady's, 3 Rubies, 15K Gold, Victorian 125.00
Ring, Lady's, Amethyst, 18K Gold, Victorian 125.00
Ring, Lady's, Diamond, 10K Gold, C.1900 .... 45.00
Ring, Lady's, Diamond, 14K Gold, C.1895 .... 45.00
Ring, Lady's, Diamond, 1878 .... 475.00
Ring, Lady's, Opal, 10K Gold, Victorian 45.00
Ring, Lady's, Pearl, 14K Gold, Victorian 85.00
Ring, Lady's, Sapphire, Diamonds, Filigree, White Gold, Victorian 125.00
Ring, Lady's, Signet, Victorian, 15K Gold 50.00
Ring, Lady's, Victorian Sunburst Top Set, Opal Center, 14K Gold 58.00
Ring, Man's, Amethyst Stone, 18K Gold 200.00
Ring, Man's, Carnelian Cameo, Greek Warrior, 18K Gold, Victorian 275.00
Ring, Man's, Gold Mercury, Profile Of Mercury 1270.00
Ring, Man's, Gypsy, Ceylon Sapphire, 14K Gold, 3/8 In. 290.00
Ring, Man's, Onyx Intaglio, Young Warrior, 10K Gold 175.00
Ring, Natural Pearl, Diamond, 18K Gold, Oriental Pearl 450.00
Ring, Opal & Gold, Gypsy Set, Opal 260.00
Ring, Snake, Ruby Eyes, Sapphire In Head, 9K Gold 195.00
Ring, Wedding Set, Diamond, 10K Gold, C.1915 .... 40.00
Ring, Wedding, Diamond, C.1890 .... 95.00
Stickpin, Bell Shape, 9 Pave Diamonds, Sapphire Baguettes, 14K 335.00
Stickpin, Boy Profile, Enamel, Diamond, 18K Gold, Guilloche, Limoges 170.00
Stickpin, Case, Eagle 20.00
Stickpin, Case, Eagle Atop Globe 10.00
Stickpin, Garnets In Crescent, Large Garnet Center 40.00
Stickpin, Iowa State Teacher's Assoc., 1913 .... 12.00
Stickpin, John Deere 22.00
Stickpin, Octagon Soap 10.00
Tiara, Coral, Carved Fruit & Flowers, Victorian, Gold 325.00
Toothpick Case, George III, Inscription, I.A.London, 1798, 3 1/8 In. 500.00
    JEWELRY, WATCH, see Watch
Watch Chain, Alternating 14K Yellow & White Gold Links, 13 In. 130.00
Watch Chain, Hair, Hanging Fob, Crossbar, 12 1/2 In. 45.00
Watch Chain, Waldemere, 14K White & Yellow Gold, Dated 1925, 16 In. 131.00
Watch Chain, Waldemere, 14K Yellow, White Gold Links, 13 In. 131.00
Whistle, 14K Gold 40.00

Judaica,
Casket, Silver,
Continental,
Filigree, 4 In.

Judaica, Cup,
Kiddush, Silver,
Vienna, 1884,
3 1/2 In.

Judaica, Torah Finial, Polish Silver,
3–Tiered Form, 15 1/2 In.

 *John Rogers statues were made from 1859 to 1892. The originals were bronze, but the thousands of copies made by the Rogers factory were of painted plaster. Eighty different figures were made. Similar painted plaster figures were made by some other factories. Never repaint a Rogers figure because this lowers the value to collectors.*

JOHN ROGERS, Group, Council Of War 350.00
    Group, Rip Van Winkle At Home 200.00

Any memorabilia that refers to the Jews or the Jewish religion is collected. Interests range from newspaper clippings that mention eighteenth– and nineteenth–century Jewish Americans to religious objects, such as menorahs or spice boxes. Age, condition, and the intrinsic value of the material, as well as the historic and artistic importance, determine the value.

JUDAICA, Book, Prayer, Bezalel, Bronze Plaque Of Temple Cover, 1930 .... 80.00
    Box, Esrog, Olivewood, Painted Scenes, Brass, Palestine, 7 In. 80.00
    Box, Esrog, Plated, Bombe Shape, Swags, 4 Scrolled Feet, German, 7 In. 325.00
    Box, Esrog, Silver, Repousse, Foliage, Hebrew, 6 In. 200.00
    Box, Esrog, Sterling Silver, Stones, Filigree Borders, 9 In. 125.00
    Case, Scribe, Brass, Near Eastern, 13 In. 230.00
    Casket, Silver, Continental, Filigree, 4 In. ....*Illus* 200.00
    Cup, Kiddush, Silver, Cylindrical, Scrolls, Polish, 3 In., 2 1/2 Oz. 100.00
    Cup, Kiddush, Silver, Vienna, 1884, 3 1/2 In. ....*Illus* 225.00
    Kauffmann, Plate, Warrior & Lady, Green, Openwork Rim, Signed, 9 In. 84.00
    Knife, Bread, Sabbath, Pearl Handle 45.00
    Lamp, Hanukah, Oil Jug, Crown, Birds, Silver, Poland, 1889, 7 In. 1100.00
    Lamp, Hanukah, Silver, Fluted Columns, Servant Light, Jug, 10 In. 1200.00
    Lamp, Hanukah, Silver, Lions Flanking Candelabrum, Jug, 14 In. 1150.00
    Lamp, Sabbath, Brass, Racher, Pendant Drip Pan, Continental, 12 In. 250.00
    Menorah, Acanthus Leaves, Star Of David Center, Silver, 7 X 6 In. 430.00
    Torah Finial, Polish Silver, 3–Tiered Form, 15 1/2 In. ....*Illus* 325.00
    Torah Shield, Brass, Repousse, Lions, Crown, 16 In. 140.00

Jugtown Pottery refers to pottery made in North Carolina as far back as the 1750s. In 1915, Juliana and Jacques Busbee set up a training and sales organization for what they named "Jugtown Pottery." In 1921, they built a shop at Jugtown, North Carolina, and hired Ben Owen as a potter in 1923. The Busbees moved the Village Store where the pottery was sold and promoted to New York City. Juliana Busbee sold the New York store in 1926 and moved into a log cabin near the Jugtown Pottery. The pottery closed in 1958. It reopened and is still working near Seagrove, North Carolina.

JUGTOWN, Bowl, Deep Red, Chinese Blue Spots, Marked, 5 In. 286.00
Bowl, Flared Base, Chinese Blue Glaze, 8 3/4 X 4 In. 130.00
Creamer, Blue Design On Rim, Gray, 4 In. 40.00
Jug, Brown & Green, Handle, 4 1/2 In. 22.00
Vase, Chinese Red Glaze, 4 In. 250.00
Vase, Chinese White Glaze, 3 3/4 In. 80.00
Vase, Mottled Green Top, Brown Clay Bottom, Marked, 5 3/4 In. 132.00

Kate Greenaway, who was a famous illustrator of children's books, drew pictures of children in high-waisted Empire dresses. She lived from 1846 to 1901. Her designs appear on china, glass, and other pieces. Figural napkin rings depicting the Greenaway children are also to be found listed under Napkin Ring, Figural.

KATE GREENAWAY, Figurine, Boy In Top Hat, Wire Glasses, Bisque, 8 1/2 In. 75.00
Figurine, Boy, Carrying Basket, Silver Plated, 4 1/2 In. 245.00
Figurine, Girl & Tambourine, Tree Trunk, Hadley, 1884, 9 In. 420.00
Figurine, Girl And Boy, Tin Umbrellas, 2 In., Pair 90.00
Figurine, Girl, Fan In Right Hand, Bisque, 7 1/2 In. 55.00
Figurine, Grandma With Glasses, Pastel Shades, Bisque 68.00
Lamp, 3 Children On Fence, Bronze Seashell Base, Milk Glass 300.00
Powder Jar, Child With Dog, Covered 175.00
Rattle, Girl With Movable Hat, Happy & Sad Face 45.00
Saltshaker, Girl In Long Coat & Bonnet, 4 In. 60.00
Toothpick, Girl Holding Up Plated Toothpick, Tufts 100.00

"Kauffmann" refers to the type of work done by Angelica Kauffmann, a painter and decorative artist for Adam Brothers in England between 1766 and 1781. She designed small-scale pictorial subjects in the neoclassic manner. Most porcelains signed "Kauffmann" were made in the 1800s. She did not do the artwork on all pieces signed with her name.

KAUFFMANN, Box, Figures Painted Inside & On Cover, Round, Signed 35.00
Dresser Jar, Brass Collar 70.00
Planter, Bulb, Women, Brown To White, Marked, 6 1/4 In. 125.00
Plaque, 4 Ladies, Golds & Reds, 12 In. 125.00
Plate, 3 Women, Signed, 8 In. 55.00
Urn, 2 Scenes, Gold Embossed, Handles, Signed, 12 In. 200.00
Vase, 2 Scenes, Pastel, Signed, 8 1/2 In. 55.00
Vase, Portrait, Cobalt, Marked, 19 In. 285.00
Vase, Teal & Gold Scene, Signed, 8 In. 55.00
KAYSERZINN, see Pewter

KELVA

Kelva glassware was made by the C. F. Monroe Company of Meriden, Connecticut, about 1904. It is a pale, pastel-painted glass decorated with flowers, designs, or scenes. Kelva resembles Nakara and Wave Crest, two other glasswares made by the same company.

KELVA, Box, Beaded Ribbon, Pink Floral Top, Round, Signed, 3 1/2 In. 425.00
Box, Blown Out Maple Leaf Top, Green, Lining, Octagonal, Marked, 5 In. 400.00
Box, Flowers, Beading, Mottled Ground, Round, Covered, Signed, 3 In. 239.00
Box, Jewel, Green Mottled, Floral, Hinged Lid, Marked, 8 In. 750.00
Box, Jewel, Robin's Egg Blue, Apple Blossoms, Marble Ground, Marked 245.00
Box, Jewel, Shaded Poppies, Green Ground, Ormolu Base, Round, Covered 425.00

Jar, Cigar, Apple Green, Pink Roses, Enameled Cigars, Covered, Signed 450.00

> *Kemple glass was made by John Kemple of East Palestine, Ohio, and Kenova, West Virginia, from 1945 to 1970. The glass was made from old molds. Many designs and colors were made. Kemple pieces are usually marked with a "K" on the bottom. Many milk glass pieces were made with or without the mark.*

KEMPLE, Dish, Cow Cover 67.50
Slipper, Blue 15.00

> *Kewpies, designed by Rose O'Neill, were first pictured in the "Ladies' Home Journal." The pixielike figures were a success, and Kewpie dolls started appearing in 1911. Kewpie pictures and other items soon followed. Collectors search for all items that picture the little winged people.*

KEWPIE, Bell, Figural, Brass ....45.00 To 49.00
Camera, Kewpie Kamera No.3, Boxed, 1915 .... 25.00
Candy Container, Barrel 55.00
Card Holder, Bisque 110.00
Celluloid, On Stick, Feathers, 9 In. 18.00
Charm, Celluloid 4.00
Clock, Japserware, Signed Rose O'Neill, Germany, 4 1/2 In. 245.00
Creamer, 3 Kewpies, Floral Border, Rose O'Neill 135.00
Creamer, Farmer & Carpenter Cavorting, Rose O'Neill 125.00
Cup & Saucer, 8 Action Kewpies, Rose O'Neill 125.00
Cup & Saucer, Baseball Player, Rose O'Neill 95.00
Doll, Bisque, Arms Raised, Sticker On Back, 2 In. 95.00
Doll, Bisque, Heart Label On Chest, Stamped On Foot, 9 In. 495.00
Doll, Bisque, Hugger, Marked Rose O'Neill, 3 3/4 In. 175.00
Doll, Bisque, Jointed Arms, Eyes To Left, Shirt, Marked, 6 In. 150.00
Doll, Bisque, Jointed Arms, Straight Legs, Marked O'Neill, 5 1/2 In. 145.00
Doll, Bisque, Thinker, Signed Rose O'Neill, 5 3/4 In. 255.00
Doll, Bisque, Thumb In Mouth, Sitting, Marked, 4 1/2 In. 40.00
Doll, Blue Wings, World's Fair, Dressed, 1930s, Rose O'Neill, 25 In. 500.00
Doll, Bride & Groom, Wedding Clothes, 4 1/2 In., Pair 195.00
Doll, Bride & Groom, Jointed Arms, Marked O'Neill, 4 1/2 In. 275.00
Doll, Celluloid, Arms Out To Side, 2 1/4 In. 20.00
Doll, Celluloid, Pink Ribbon, Ring, Paper Label, 4 3/4 In. 85.00
Doll, Composition, Blue Wings, Movable Arms, Label, 11 In. 85.00
Doll, Painted, Chalk Hands Under Chin, Rose O'Neill, Germany, 4 In. 12.00
Doll, Reading Book, Two, 3 1/2 In. 495.00
Doll, Vinyl, Thinker, Marked Rose O'Neill, Cameo, 4 In. 25.00
Door Knocker, Brass 70.00
Figurine, Bisque, 5 In. 125.00
Figurine, Bisque, Rose O'Neill, 9 In. 150.00
Figurine, Bride & Groom, Crepe Paper Dressed, Japanese 110.00
Figurine, Thumb In Mouth, Sitting, Marked, 4 1/2 In. 40.00
Jar, Blue Jasperware, Metal Lid, Signed Rose O'Neill, 3 In. 175.00
Letter Opener, Stamped, Marked In Hearts, Pewter 55.00
Measure, Sifter, Tin, 1 Cup 8.00
Mug, 4 Kewpies, Rose O'Neill 95.00
Mug, Child's, 4 Kewpies & Bird, Etched & Chased, Mathews Silver Co. 390.00
Night–Light, Sitting, Bisque, Metal Base, 4 1/2 In. 125.00
Perfume, Figural, German 25.00
Pin, Marked 15.00
Pitcher, Kewpie Design, Rose O'Neill, 3 In. 48.00
Plate, 3 Kewpies Cavorting, Signed Rose O'Neill, Green, 5 1/2 In. 65.00
Plate, 9 Action Kewpies, Green Foliage, Rose O'Neill, 7 In. 165.00
Plate, Wilson, Bavaria, 7 In. 95.00
Salt & Pepper, Rabbits, 3 In. 750.00
Sand Pail, Scootles, Tin, Rose O'Neill 150.00
Stickpin, Black, Celluloid, 1 1/4 In. 65.00
Tea Set, German, Metallic Luster, Marked O'Neill 125.00
Thimble, Marked ....35.00 To 39.00

Toothpick, Sitting Beside Cornucopia 59.00
Tray, Cloverleaf, Green Jasperware, Pink Kewpies, Rose O'Neill, 7 In. 275.00
Tray, Ice Cream, Tin 85.00
Valentine, Celluloid Trim, Large, 1910 .... 35.00
　　　KIMBALL, see Cluthra
　　　KING'S ROSE, see Soft Paste

　　　　　All types of kitchen utensils, from eggbeaters to bowls, are collected
　　　　　today. Handmade wooden and metal items, like ladles and apple
　　　　　peelers, were made in the early nineteenth century. Mass-produced
　　　　　pieces, like iron apple peelers and graniteware, were made in the
　　　　　nineteenth century. Other kitchen wares are listed under
　　　　　manufacturers' names or under Iron; Store; Tool; or Wooden.

KITCHEN, Iron, Asbestos, 1900 .... 30.00
Iron, Charcoal, Brass, Cloisonne Handle, Small 24.00
Iron, Charcoal, Iron Handle, Wooden Knob, Cenkov DSR No.2, 8 In. 65.00
Iron, Charcoal, Rooster Finial 50.00
Iron, Charcoal, With Crimper 10.00
Iron, Charcoal, Wooden Handle, Deco Lady's Head, Latch, 7 1/2 In. 75.00
Iron, Child's, Cast Iron, 1 Piece 25.00
Iron, Dragon Relief, Wooden Handle, Chinese 55.00
Iron, Fluting, Geneva, 1866 .... 35.00
Iron, Fluting, Mrs.Knox's, Gilt Stenciling, Logo 145.00
Iron, Gas, Coleman, Blue Granite 25.00
Iron, Goffering, Arched Feet, 18th Century, Brass & Iron 325.00
Iron, Pleating, 4 Tubes, 3 1/2 In. 140.00
Iron, Sleeve, Cast Iron 15.00
Iron, Sunbeam, Electric, Fireproof Case, Dated 1925 .... 65.00
Iron, Taylor No.1, Unused 60.00
Apple Corer, Boye, Wooden 16.50
Apple Corer, Handmade, Tin 6.00
Apple Corer, T Handle, Tin 20.00
Basket, Egg, Chicken Shape, Tin 28.00
Basket, Egg, Collapsible, Wire ....16.00 To 22.00
Basket, Egg, Wire, Chicken Shape, Tin 28.00
Basket, Parsley, Wire 14.00
Basket, Potato Boiling, Wire 65.00
Bin, Porcelain, Wall, Hinged Wooden Lid, Mehl 60.00
Bin, Stencil Design, Tin, 27 In. 40.00
Blender, Pastry, Jenny Wren Flour 8.50
Board, Cutting, Daisies, Leaves, & Foliage, Porcelain, 5 7/8 X 10 In. 75.00
Board, Cutting, Pig Shape 12.00
Board, Noodle, Scalloped Sides, Hanging Hook, Pine 50.00
Board, Owl & Rabbit Carving, 4 X 7 In. 80.00
Board, Pastry, Camelback Top, Hanging Hole, 32 1/2 X 20 In. 95.00
Board, Pastry, Red Paint, Camelback Top, 38 X 20 In. 95.00
Bowl, Bennington–Type, Graduated Sizes 7, 8, 9 In. 225.00
Bowl, Chopping, Maple, Oblong, 20 3/4 X 11 1/2 In. 65.00
Bowl, Chopping, Wooden, Round, 21 1/2 In. 130.00
Bowl, Mixing, Advertising, Leisitkow's, Hand Painted Apples 45.00
Bowl, Sugar, Treenware, 5 X 5 In. 250.00
Box, Dough, Lid, Dovetailed, Hardwood Legs, Poplar, 19 X 34 X 29 In. 200.00
Box, Dough, Stained Lid, Pine & Poplar, 16 X 31 1/4 In. 125.00
Box, Spice, Tin, 6 Containers 50.00
Bread Maker, Tin, Universal 22.00
Bread Pan, Morton Salt, Embossed Old Kentucky Recipe 5.00
Bread Raiser, Pierced Lid 24.00
Broiler, Fireplace, Iron, Rotating, 21 X 12 In.Diam. 170.00
Bucket, Sugar, Lid, Copper Nails, 9 1/2 X 10 In. 65.00
Butter Carrier, Wooden, Green Paint, Wire Bail, Wooden Handle 140.00
Butter Roller, Chip Carved, Fish Tail Handle, Sheaf Of Wheat, 7 In. 295.00
Butter Stamp, Leaf, 4 In. 38.00
Butter Stamp, Pineapple, 4 1/2 In. 40.00
　　　KITCHEN, BUTTER, MOLD, see Kitchen, Mold, Butter

Use a timer on your lights at all times, even when you are at home. This will set a pattern of certain lights going on and off each day. When you are away, the house will appear to have normal activity. If possible, when you are away, park a car near the front of the house. The car will block your driveway so a burglar cannot load up through your garage.

Coffee Grinder, Table Model, Cast Iron,
    Wooden Drawer, 12 × 6 In.

Cabbage Cutter, Steel Blade, Maple Frame	20.00
Cabbage Cutter, Wooden	55.00
Cabinet, Spice, 8 Drawers, Tin, Germany, Blue Stencil On White	150.00
Cake Maker, Universal, Mechanical, Pat.1896	30.00
Cake Tester, Daniel Webster Flour, Celluloid, Brass Holder	6.00
Can Opener, Bull's Head, Cast Iron, 6 1/4 In.	68.00
Can Opener, Corkscrew, Iron, King, 1908	11.00
Can Opener, Figural, Fish, Iron, Ball Ended, 19th Century, 5 3/4 In.	58.00
Can Opener, Sure–Cut, Pattern 7/19/04	5.00
Can Opener, Wall, Nickel Plated, Corkscrew, 1930s	43.00
Canister Set, 10 Jars, Oil & Vinegar, Pearlized, Gold Trim	165.00
Canister Set, Covers, Porcelain, German, 6 Piece	95.00
Canister, Tea, Tin, White Paint, Gold Stencil	22.00
Canner, Steam, Inserts, Tin	20.00
Charcoal Iron, Wooden Handle, Bearded Man, Slide Over Hole, Iron	32.00
Cheese Cutter, Porcelain	25.00
Cheese Press, Wooden Toothed Gear, Painted Red, 19 X 46 In.	375.00
Cherry Pitter, Advertising, Dated	30.00
Cherry Pitter, Double, Goodell, Clamp Type	45.00
Cherry Pitter, Enterprise	29.00
Cherry Pitter, Enterprise, Clamp, Iron, Dated 1883	25.00
Cherry Pitter, Goodall, Double	35.00
Cherry Pitter, Holman, Clamp, Iron	25.00
Cherry Pitter, Home, August 7, 1917	40.00
Cherry Pitter, New Standard, Mt.Joy, Pa.	20.00
Cherry Pitter, Rollman	18.00
Cherry Seeder, Enterprise	27.00
Cherry Seeder, Rollman No.3	15.00
Chopper, Food, Dated 1892	8.00
Chopper, Food, Enterprise, Iron	25.00
Chopper, Food, Green Depression Glass Base	20.00
Chopper, Food, Moon Blade, Wooden Handle	9.00
Chopper, Food, Offset Wooden Handle, 7 1/2 In.	49.00
Chopper, Food, Steel, Wooden Handle, 18th Century	85.00
Chopper, Food, Winchester	35.00
Chopper, Food, Wooden Arched Handle	25.00
Chopper, Food, Wooden Frame, Handle That Slides, Guillotine Style	35.00
Chopper, Meat, Enterprise No.10, Tin, 1887	35.00
Chopper, Universal Food & Meat Chopper, No.1, Attachments, Box	25.00
Churn, Cylindrical, Green Paint	165.00
Churn, Dazey No.40	37.50
Churn, Dazey, 1/2 Gal.	75.00

Churn, Dazey, Complete, 1922 .... 35.00
Churn, Dazey, Decal, Unused 80.00
Churn, Dazey, Glass, 3 Qt. 56.00
Churn, Dazey, Model B, Glass, Oval Red Iron Egg Top, 4 Qt. 45.00
Churn, Dazy, No.4, Wooden Paddles, 4 Qt. 28.00
Churn, Glass, 1 Gal. 26.50
Churn, Handmade, Tin, 19th Century, Complete, 15 In. 295.00
Churn, Original Dasher, Tin 25.00
Churn, Pine, Tin Liner, Iron Crank, Blue, 13 X 31 1/2 In. 190.00
Churn, Rocking, Light Blue & Red Paint, 15 1/2 In. 110.00
Churn, Screw On Cast Iron Top, Handle, Glass, Wooden Paddles 85.00
Churn, Splash Cup, Dasher, 2 Handles, Tin, Small 295.00
Churn, Tole Type Handle, Insert, Tapered, 24 In. 200.00
Churn, Windsor Legs, Old Blue 425.00
Churn, Wooden, 3 Gal. 90.00
Cleaver, Meat, No.9, Signed, L.& I.J.White, 1837, Buffalo, N.Y. 16.00
Clothes Dryer, Wooden, Expandable Arms, 34 In. 25.00
Coffee Dispenser, Tin, Painted 22.00
KITCHEN, COFFEE GRINDER, see Coffee Grinder
Coffee Roaster, Iron, C.1870 .... 35.00
Coffee Server, Jewel Tea, 8 1/2 In. 45.00
Coffeepot, Electric, Dated 1925, Unused 35.00
Coffeepot, Nickel Over Copper, 1890s 50.00
Colander, Redware 235.00
Cookie Board, 11 Carvings, Animals, Birds, 19th Century, 4 X 24 In. 125.00
Cookie Board, 2 Full Figures Each Side, 5 1/4 X 23 1/4 In. 180.00
Cookie Board, 2 Song Birds, Carved, Pine, 7 1/2 X 10 In. 170.00
Cookie Board, 4 Carved Teddy Bears, Backpacks, Plaid Pants, 25 In. 95.00
Cookie Board, 6 Carvings, Basket, Adam & Eve, 4 1/4 X 26 1/2 In. 115.00
Cookie Board, 6 Carvings, People & Animals, 3 3/4 X 23 1/2 In. 85.00
Cookie Board, 7 Animal Carvings, 3 1/4 X 23 In. 85.00
Cookie Board, 8 Relief Carvings, 4 1/2 X 22 1/2 In. 105.00
Cookie Board, 8 Wreaths, Animal Or Bird In Each, 4 1/2 X 8 1/4 In. 70.00
Cookie Board, Carved, Rooster, 2 Men, 4 1/2 X 15 3/4 In. 150.00
Cookie Board, Flowers & Leaves In Circle, Pine, 6 1/2 X 10 In. 130.00
Cookie Board, Lion, C.1880, 12 X 12 In. 100.00
Cookie Board, Poodle With Basket In Mouth, 3 3/4 X 4 In. 55.00
Cookie Gun & Pastry Decorator, Weriver, Box, Set 20.00
Cookie Press, Tin, Cylinder, Wooden Handle 30.00
Cover, Fly Screen, 8 1/2 In. 35.00
Cover, Fly Screen, 9 1/2 In. 45.00
Cover, Pie, Tin, 1899 .... 22.00
Cover, Toaster, Mammy 12.50
Cream Separator, Aluminum Bowl, 10 X 11 X 16 In. 80.00
Cream Separator, Brass Bowl, Wooden Base, 11 X 12 X 17 In. 300.00
Crimper, Pie, 1 Brass & 1 Iron Wheel, Pat.Sept.11, 1886 .... 72.00
Crimper, Pie, Brass, 5 In. 33.00
Crimper, Pie, Brass, Wooden Handle 22.00
Crimper, Pie, Early 19th Century, Brass, 4 In. 35.00
Crimper, Pie, Forged Iron 10.00
Crimper, Pie, Pennsylvania, Brass 27.50
Crimper, Pie, White Porcelain, Wooden Handle, 2 In.Wheel, 7 1/2 In. 40.00
Crimper, Pie, Wooden 35.00
Cup, Measure, Swansdown Cake Flour, Tin 10.00
Curd Breaker, Cheese, Crank & Roller Hopper, Wooden Teeth 130.00
Curler, Butter, Hand Carved, Tiger Maple 175.00
Cutter, Cake, Petit Four, Assorted Patterns, Set Of 10 .... 50.00
Cutter, Cookie, Baby's Hand, Tin, 2 1/2 X 3 1/2 In. 210.00
Cutter, Cookie, Bird In Flight, Tin, 4 In. 22.50
Cutter, Cookie, Bird, Tin .... 8.00 To 39.00
Cutter, Cookie, Blondie & Dagwood 35.00
Cutter, Cookie, Boot, Tin, 4 In. 27.50
Cutter, Cookie, Chick, Tin, C.1880 .... 15.00
Cutter, Cookie, Chicken, Handle, Tin 8.50

Cutter, Cookie, Christmas Tree, Tin, 6 In. 20.00
Cutter, Cookie, Cornucopia, Rolled Edges, Tin, 3 1/2 In. 45.00
Cutter, Cookie, Diamond, Flat Back, Handle, 4 In. 13.00
Cutter, Cookie, Dog, Standing, Tin, 3 1/4 In. 12.00
Cutter, Cookie, Dog, Tin 39.00
Cutter, Cookie, Dog, Tin, 7 3/4 X 10 In. 65.00
Cutter, Cookie, Dove, Tin, C.1880 .... 15.00
Cutter, Cookie, Duck, Flat Back, Handle, 4 In. 18.00
Cutter, Cookie, Dutchman, Tin, 5 1/4 In. 20.00
Cutter, Cookie, Eagle, Primitive, Tin, 5 1/4 In. 22.50
Cutter, Cookie, Eagle, Tin, 6 1/2 In. 85.00
Cutter, Cookie, Ear Of Corn, Tin, 5 7/8 In. 65.00
Cutter, Cookie, Elephant, Tin 22.00
Cutter, Cookie, Fat Baby Chick, Flat Back, Handle, 4 In. 20.00
Cutter, Cookie, Fish, Flat Back, Tin, 5 1/2 In. 65.00
Cutter, Cookie, Fish, Tin, 4 7/8 In. 15.00
Cutter, Cookie, Flag, Tin 12.50
Cutter, Cookie, Gingerbread Man, Back Handle, 10 1/2 In. 55.00
Cutter, Cookie, Giraffe, Tin, 5 3/4 In. 105.00
Cutter, Cookie, Heart Shape 15.00
Cutter, Cookie, Horse & Rider, Tin, 6 3/4 In. 175.00
Cutter, Cookie, Horse, Tin, 4 3/8 In. 40.00
Cutter, Cookie, Horse, Tin, 7 In. 42.50
Cutter, Cookie, Lady, Tin, 5 In. 35.00
Cutter, Cookie, Lion, Flat Back, Handle 15.00
Cutter, Cookie, Lion, Tin, 4 1/2 In. 10.00
Cutter, Cookie, Lovebirds, Tin, German 14.00
Cutter, Cookie, Man & Woman, Standing, 1 Hole, Tin, 4 3/4 X 5 In., Pr. 36.00
Cutter, Cookie, Oak Leaf, Tin 39.00
Cutter, Cookie, Pig, Tin, 6 In. 65.00
Cutter, Cookie, Primitive Chicken, Tin, 4 1/4 X 5 1/4 In. 20.00
Cutter, Cookie, Rabbit, Flat Back, Handle, 5 In. 25.00
Cutter, Cookie, Rabbit, Sitting, Hole, Tin, 4 In. 10.00
Cutter, Cookie, Rabbit, Tin, C.1880 .... 15.00
Cutter, Cookie, Raggedy Ann & Raggedy Andy 28.00
Cutter, Cookie, Snowman, Handle, Tin 14.00
Cutter, Cookie, Squirrel, Sitting On Haunches, Tin, 3 1/2 In. 20.00
Cutter, Cookie, Standing Horse, 2 Holes, Tin, 5 3/8 In. 20.00
Cutter, Cookie, Standing Woman, 2 Holes, Tin, 6 In. 22.00
Cutter, Cookie, Stylized Big Bird, Tin, Handle, 5 1/2 In. 40.00
Cutter, Cookie, Stylized Rooster, Tin, 4 In. 25.00
Cutter, Cookie, Teardrop, 11 Nested Cutters, Tin, 1900s, Tin Box 50.00
Cutter, Cookie, Tulip, Tin, German 10.00
Cutter, Cookie, Turkey, Tin, C.1880 .... 15.00
Cutter, Cookie, Woman, Tin, C.1880 .... 15.00
Cutter, Doughnut, Knob Handle, Wooden 85.00
Cutter, Doughnut, Rumford ....6.75 To 12.50
Drainer, Cheese, Solid Slanted Sides, Slat Bottom 120.00
Drainer, Cheese, Wooden Bands, Round, 10 X 6 In. 50.00
Dryer, Corn, 10 Hooks 10.00
Dryer, Herb, Woven Splint, Bentwood Rim, 24 X 4 In. 55.00
Dryer, Stocking, Tiger Maple, 1 Piece, 37 In. 25.00
Drying Rack, Pine, Shoe Feet, Old Red, English, 43 X 13 X 48 In. 200.00
Dutch Oven, Covered, Griswold 25.00
Dutch Oven, Fixed Bail, Swivel Ring, Original Lid, 13 1/2 X 7 In. 300.00
Dutch Oven, Gray Graniteware, Red Lid, Premium, 1940s 10.00
Egg Carrier, Gander, Wood & Wire, 2 Doz. 45.00
Egg Carrier, Original Cardboard Cover, 12 Sections 50.00
Egg Cooker, Copper, Composition, Chicken, Revere 35.00
Egg Cooker, Insert, Hankscraft 45.00
Egg Poacher, Tin, 1885 .... 25.00
Egg Separator, Boston Market, Tin 6.50
Eggbeater, Cast Iron, Dated 1888 .... 27.50
Eggbeater, Cyclone, Steel, 1902 .... 14.00

Eggbeater, Dover, 1891 ....12.00 To 21.00
Eggbeater, Dover, 1904 .... 18.00
Eggbeater, Push, A & I, Pat.October 1907 .... 18.00
Eggbeater, Single Up & Down Spiral Motion, 13 In. 18.00
Eggbeater, Taplin, Cast Iron ....17.50 To 18.00
Eggbeater, Whip, Arthur Beck Co., Box 5.00
Fish Slicer, Copper, Pierced, Flat Paddle, 1 Piece, Hole, 10 1/2 In. 95.00
Flue Cover, Girl With Big Hat 17.00
Flue Cover, Pretty Woman, Oval 22.00
Flue Cover, Tinsel, Woman & Children Peeling Apples, Large 18.00
Flue Cover, Victorian Child, 6 In. 18.00
Fork, Keen Kutter 4.00
Fork, Meat Roasting, Iron, Wooden Handle, 18th Century, 35 In. 75.00
Freezer, Ice Cream, 1910 .... 25.00
Freezer, Ice Cream, Arctic, Wooden Pail, Paddles, Pat.Dec.1889, 1 Qt. 60.00
Freezer, Ice Cream, Glass, 1902 .... 30.00
Freezer, Ice Cream, White Mountain, Wooden Bucket, 2 Qt. 45.00
Funnel, Filling Fruit Jars, Brass, Oval, 5 1/2 X 7 In. 36.00
Funnel, Kenny Co., Metal 25.00
Funnel, Papier-Mache, C.1870 .... 22.00
Funnel, Treenware, Maple, 7 3/4 In. 89.00
Grater, Chocolate, Pierced, Patent 1891 .... 195.00
Grater, Climax, Iron & Tin 24.00
Grater, Fels Naptha Soap Advertising 7.50
Grater, Food, Hanging, Wood & Tin, 12 In. 27.50
Grater, Frame With Drawer, 4 1/2 X 6 X 9 In. 74.00
Grater, Gilmore, Hanging, Tin, 1897 .... 12.00
Grater, Half Round, Hand Pierced, On Board, Handle, Tin, 17 In. 65.00
Grater, Hand Hewn Board, Tin, Pierced 47.00
Grater, Houchin, Tin & Iron 38.00
Grater, Iron, Rotary Tin, Clamp On 12.00
Grater, Nutmeg, 2 Wooden Handles 30.00
Grater, Nutmeg, Edgar, 2 Wooden Handles, Pat.1896 .... 37.00
Grater, Nutmeg, France, Tin 10.00
Grater, Nutmeg, Green Handle 9.00
Grater, Nutmeg, Iron Cup, Tin Pierced Disc, Crank Knob 65.00
Grater, Nutmeg, Iron, Round Disc, Hinged Top, Wooden Center Handle 65.00
Grater, Nutmeg, Little Edgar 30.00
Grater, Nutmeg, Marked MTE Co., Graniteware, Gray 43.00
Grater, Nutmeg, Nickel Plated, M T E & Co. 3 1/2 In. 55.00
Grater, Pierced Tin, Frame, Drawer Below, 4 1/2 X 6 X 9 In. 75.00
Grater, Schoeter 10.00
Grater, Soap, Fels Naptha 5.00
Grater, Tin Mounted, Wooden Back, 4 X 11 In. 42.00
Grater, Tin, Open Handle Top, 7 1/2 X 11 1/2 In. 30.00
Grater, Tin, Wooden & Iron, Blue 35.00
Grater, Wooden, Box, 8 1/2 In. 10.00
Grinder, Food, Diamond Edge 10.00
Grinder, Food, Griswold, No.1110 .... 35.00
Grinder, Meat, Keen Kutter, No.21 .... 20.00
Grinder, Meat, Winchester 40.00
Grinder, Poppy Seed, Table Mount, Iron & Brass 35.00
Grinder, Sausage, 4 Discs, Iron, Wooden Plunger 20.00
Grinder, Sausage, Keen Kutter 45.00
Grinder, Sausage, Shapleigh, Cast Iron 6.50
Grinder, Spice, Wall Mount 25.00
Grinder, Wheat Krinker, Grinding Gears Below Hopper, Base Drawer 40.00
Holder, Rolling Pin, Wire ....15.00 To 19.00
Holder, Straw, Amber 295.00
Holder, String, Beehive, Cast Iron 45.00
Hot Plate, Pottery, J.S.Stahl, October 3, 1945 .... 35.00
Huller, Strawberry, F.A.Walker, Boston, Brass, 1894 .... 17.00
Huller, Strawberry, Tin, 1906 .... 8.00
Ice Cream Scoop, Brass, Cone Shape, Mosteller 55.00

Ice Pick, Prong Type, Wooden Handle 6.00
Ice Shaver, Metal, Gem 7.00
Ice Tongs, Iron 15.00
Ice Tongs, Marked Philadelphia Inquirer 5.00
Icebox, 2 Glass & 2 Wooden Doors, Oak 475.00
Icebox, 2 Glass & 2 Wooden Doors, Oak, 45 X 64 In. 475.00
Icebox, Lift Top, Paneled & Pressed Sides, Early 1900s, Miniature 440.00
Icebox, Oak, 4 Doors, Vitrolite Side, Tile Floor, Brass Hardware 1500.00
Icing Set, Double Handled Tube, 4 Heads, Tala 20.00
Ironing Board, Wood, Folding 25.00
Jar Opener, Canning, Schaefer Fruit Jar Rubber Co. 5.00
Jar, Apple Butter, 48 In. 14.00
Jar, Covered, Green, Provision, 3 Graduated Sizes 65.00
Kettle, Leafy Foliage, Reticulated Top, Cast Iron, 11 3/4 In. 30.00
Kettle, Witch's Pot Type, Iron, 3–Footed 35.00
Knife & Fork Set, 3–Tine, Ivory Handle, Piroth Sr., Set Of 6 .... 65.00
Knife Sharpener, Dazey Sharpit 15.00
Knife Tray, 2 Sections, Old Red Paint, Pine 95.00
Knife, Bread, Beveled Edge, Brass Rivets, Pig Imprint 18.00
Ladle, Butter, Hook End, Tiger Maple 120.00
Ladle, Butter, Maple, Hand Carved, Hook End, Wooden 29.00
Ladle, Skimmer, Brass 52.50
Ladle, Tin, Cream Top, 1925 .... 7.00
Lemon Squeezer, Iron 10.00
Lifter, Milk Cap, Wooden Handle, Coal Advertising 15.00
Marker, Pastry, Flowers, Wooden Handle, Diamond Pattern, Ironstone 35.00
Masher, Porcelain, White, Wooden Handle 15.00
Masher, Potato, Cast Iron 10.00
Masher, Potato, Wooden .... 8.50 To 14.00
KITCHEN, MATCH SAFE, see Match Safe
Measure, Cream, Tin, J.Coovers, Pat.Oct.22, '72, 7 In., Set Of 4 .... 36.00
Measuring Cup, Kellogg's, Pink, Depression Glass 22.00
Melon Scoop, Tin, 1916 .... 8.00
Mixer, Dough, Metal, Marked Pat.Jan, 1902, 13 X 8 In. 50.00
Mixer, Glass, Up And Down Spring Motion, Wooden, 11 In. 13.00
Mixer, Roberts Lighting, White Porcelain Knob, 8 In. 13.00
KITCHEN, MOLD, see also Pewter, Mold; Tinware, Mold
Mold, Beeswax, Flower Pattern, Wooden, Handle, 5 Sections, 2 X 10 In. 130.00
Mold, Butter, 2 Sides, Starflower & Foliage Design, 5 In. 415.00
Mold, Butter, Acorns, 2–Part 65.00
Mold, Butter, Beaver, Wooden 80.00
Mold, Butter, Carved Star 65.00
Mold, Butter, Child's, Pine 16.00
Mold, Butter, Conical Blossom, 4 3/4 In. 115.00
Mold, Butter, Cow, Round Case, 4 In. 360.00
Mold, Butter, Cow, Wooden 110.00
Mold, Butter, Cow, Wooden Handle, Glass 45.00
Mold, Butter, Eagle & Star, Turned Handle, Round, 3 1/2 In. 225.00
Mold, Butter, Floral, Pine 40.00
Mold, Butter, Flower & Leaves 60.00
Mold, Butter, Flower Pattern 65.00
Mold, Butter, Flower, Brass Fittings, 2–Part 38.00
Mold, Butter, Flowers & Leaves, Hand Carved, 3 1/2 X 3 1/2 In. 95.00
Mold, Butter, Leaf Design, Wooden, 3 3/4 In. 30.00
Mold, Butter, Lollipop, Pennsylvania Pinwheel, 9 3/4 In. 400.00
Mold, Butter, Maple Leaf, Round 48.00
Mold, Butter, Palm Leaf 20.00
Mold, Butter, Pineapple .... 56.00 To 75.00
Mold, Butter, Primitive, Simple Line Carving, Handle, 10 3/4 In. 50.00
Mold, Butter, Rectangular Shape 15.00
Mold, Butter, Sheaf, Separate Plunger Block, 3 5/8 X 5 7/8 In. 55.00
Mold, Butter, Star Pattern 38.00
Mold, Butter, Star, Plunger, 2 In. 40.00
Mold, Butter, Starflower, 4 5/8 In. 50.00

Mold, Butter, Strawberry, Wooden ....85.00 To 95.00
Mold, Butter, Swan, 1 3/4 X 1 1/2 In. 65.00
Mold, Butter, Swan, Pine ....125.00 To 145.00
Mold, Butter, Tree, Round 35.00
Mold, Butter, Tulip, Round, 3 1/2 In. 55.00
Mold, Butter, Walnut, 3 Piece 175.00
Mold, Cake, Bundt, Tinned, Copper, American, 1800s, 10 1/2 X 5 In. 140.00
Mold, Cake, Lamb, Blue Enamel, Cast Iron, 14 1/2 In. 75.00
Mold, Cake, Lamb, Cast Iron, 2–Part 37.50

KITCHEN, MOLD, CANDLE, see Tinware, Mold, Candle

Mold, Cheese, Wooden, 9 In. 24.00
Mold, Chocolate, 2 Baby Chicks, Tin, Hinged, Germany, 2–Part, 5 In. 25.00
Mold, Chocolate, 3 Bears, 9 1/2 X 12 In. 100.00
Mold, Chocolate, Bulldog, Small 55.00
Mold, Chocolate, Christmas, Jaburg Bros., NYC, 4 X 8 In. 95.00
Mold, Chocolate, Covered Wagon, Tin 4.25
Mold, Chocolate, Egg With Grapes, Large 68.00
Mold, Chocolate, Father Christmas, Full Figure 225.00
Mold, Chocolate, Fish, Large 180.00
Mold, Chocolate, Hen On Nest, Tin, 3–Part, Germany, 3 In. 17.50
Mold, Chocolate, Indian, Copper 18.00
Mold, Chocolate, Lamb, Large 125.00
Mold, Chocolate, Lamb, Small 45.00
Mold, Chocolate, Little Girl, Big Bow 40.00
Mold, Chocolate, Owl, Small 68.00
Mold, Chocolate, Rabbit, 6 In. 75.00
Mold, Chocolate, Rabbit, Sitting, Hinged, 10 In. 75.00
Mold, Chocolate, Rabbit, Standing, With Basket, 18 In. 85.00
Mold, Chocolate, Rooster, 10 In. 135.00
Mold, Chocolate, Santa Claus With Pack, Tree, Tin, Dresden, 6 1/4 In. 65.00
Mold, Chocolate, Squirrel, With Acorn, Bushy Tail, 15 In. 175.00
Mold, Chocolate, Swan, 10 1/2 X 8 1/2 In. 195.00
Mold, Chocolate, Swan, Small 45.00
Mold, Chocolate, Turkey, 3 Hinged Sections, Tin, 4 In. 5.00
Mold, Chocolate, Turkey, U.S.A., 5 1/2 X 6 In. 72.00
Mold, Cookie, Turkey, Wooden, 10 X 6 In. 24.00
Mold, Cornstick, Griswold, No.273 ....12.00 To 20.00
Mold, Cornstick, Wagner, Tea Size ....25.00 To 50.00
Mold, Cutlet, Lamb Chop Shape, Tin, Set Of 12 .... 45.00
Mold, Fish, 12 1/2 In. 10.00
Mold, Fish, Tin, Germany, 12 1/4 In. 10.00
Mold, Food, Dolphin Shape, Ironstone 21.00
Mold, Food, Embossed Rabbit, Oval, Tin, 3 3/4 In. 17.50
Mold, Food, Sheaf Of Wheat, Copper On Tin 85.00
Mold, Food, Tin, Copper, Rose & Leaves, 6 3/4 In. 70.00

KITCHEN, MOLD, ICE CREAM, see Pewter, Mold, Ice Cream

Mold, Jell–O, Gray Graniteware, 8 In. 29.00
Mold, Maple Sugar, 3 Sections, 4 1/2 X 23 In. 165.00
Mold, Maple Sugar, 4 Squares, 12 In. 50.00
Mold, Maple Sugar, Fish 8.00
Mold, Maple Sugar, Tin, Fluted ....3.00 To 15.00
Mold, Maple Sugar, Turkey 28.00
Mold, Meat Patty, Griswold, Box 115.00
Mold, Melon, Tin, Design, English 33.00
Mold, Melon, Tin, Kreamer 18.00
Mold, Pudding, Ear Of Corn, Tinned Copper, Oval, 5 In. 30.00
Mold, Pudding, Fluted, Embossed Fruits, Tin 30.00
Mold, Pudding, Kreamer, Cover, Tin 28.00
Mold, Pudding, Sheaf Of Wheat, 6 X 7 X 5 In. 89.00
Mold, Pudding, Tin 21.00
Mold, Turk's Head, 8 In. 35.00
Mortar & Pestle, Cast Iron 10.00
Noodle Maker, Crank, Italian 125.00
Paddle, Apple Butter, Pine, Primitive 22.00

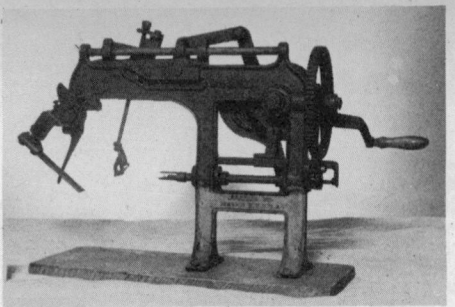

Kitchen, Peeler, Apple, Cast Iron, Goodell
Co., 12 X 18 In.

Knife, Hunting, U.S.,
Leather Case, Model 1880

Paddle, Butter, Lollipop, Hand Carved, 7 1/2 X 3 1/4 In.	495.00
Paddle, Jelly	7.00
Paddle, Lard, Curved, Metal	3.50
Pan Holder, Wooden Handle, Dentel's, Ackley, Iowa	17.50
Pan, Baking, Signed Granite Iron Ware, Gray, Dated July 3, 1877	38.00
Pan, Bread, Folding Ends, Tin, Early 1900s	6.50
Pan, Cake Swansdown Flour, Patent Dec.18, '23	20.00
Pan, Cake, Angel Food, Swansdown Flour	24.00
Pan, Cake, Santa Claus Head, Tin, 9 In.	15.00
Pan, Cake, Swansdown Flour, Patent Dec.18, '23	15.00
Pan, Copper, 49er, Eureka Savings, 1955, 6 In.	12.50
Pan, Corn Fritter, Miracle Maize	12.00
Pan, Cornstick, Iron, Wagner, 1920	17.00
Pan, Cornstick, No.8, Cast Iron	12.00
Pan, Cornstick, Wagner, Glass	25.00
Pan, Frying, Joe's Service Station, Pomeroy, Iowa, 6 In.	17.50
Pan, Lady Finger, 12 Fingers, Tin	14.00
Pan, Lady Finger, 6 Compartments, Kreamer	10.00
Pan, Lady Finger, Tin, Kreamer	30.00
Pan, Muffin, Griswold, No.10, Iron	28.00
Pan, No.7, Griswold, Enamel Interior, Gray Sides, Cast Iron	12.50
Pan, Sauce, Hand Forged Iron Handle, Copper, 3 Qt.	130.00
Pea Huller, Vaughan, Box	12.00
Pea Splitter, Holmes	28.00
Peanut Butter Maker, Mr.Peanut, Boxed	12.00
Peel, Hearth, Pine, 52 In.	110.00
Peel, Maple, 10 1/4 X 16 In.	49.00
Peel, Wooden, Short Handle, 15 1/2 In.	65.00
Peeler, Apple, 4–Gear, Hudson Parer Co., Dated 1882	48.00
Peeler, Apple, Baldwin, 1800s	35.00
Peeler, Apple, Cast Iron, Goodell Co., 12 X 18 In. ....*Illus*	110.00
Peeler, Apple, Harbster Bros., Mechanical, Iron, 1867	50.00
Peeler, Apple, Hudson, Cast Iron, Pat.1862	65.00
Peeler, Apple, Iron, Reading Hardware Co, Pa.	78.00
Peeler, Apple, Keen Kutter ....45.00 To	59.00
Peeler, Apple, Keyes, Iron, 1856	40.00
Peeler, Apple, Little Star	25.00
Peeler, Apple, Lockey, 1800s	34.00
Peeler, Apple, Reading Apple Peeler, Original Box	50.00
Peeler, Apple, Reading, No.78, Box	65.00
Peeler, Apple, Sargeants & Foster, Board Mounted, Patent 1856	110.00
Peeler, Apple, Sinclair Scott Co., Baltimore, 8–Gear, Heart Design	42.50
Peeler, Potato, Helinite, 1920	30.00
Pepper Mill, Wooden, Peugeot Freres Brevets Metal Top, 3 5/8 In.	10.00

Pie Bird, Beaumont	38.50
Pie Bird, Black Crow	22.50
Pie Bird, Duck	275.00
Pie Carrier, Woven Wire, 1900s	15.00
Pie Carrier, Woven Wire, Single	17.50
Pie Cooler, Wire, Holds 3 Pies	40.00
Pie Plate, Up & Up Flour, Tin	4.50
Pie Tin, Dark Tin, Swivel Loosener, Hetty Harper's Mix	4.00
Pie Trimmer, Sealer, Wooden & Metal, Green	8.00
Pie Wheel, Curved Handle & Crimper, Hand Forged Iron, 4 1/4 In.	145.00
Pitcher, Measuring, Flared Sides, Haystack Form, Handle, Copper	85.00
Pitcher, Tin, Attached Funnel, 1/2 Gal.	22.00
Pitcher, Utility, Jewel Tea, Pink	18.50
Place Card, Green & Amber Glass, Set Of 6	80.00
Poacher, Egg, Tin, 6–Part, Round	45.00
Popcorn Machine, Oak	650.00
Popper, Popcorn, Electric, Top Red Light, Clown, 19 X 8 In.	125.00
Popper, Popcorn, Pat. 1897	65.00
Popper, Popcorn, Wire, Cast Iron, Wooden Handle	15.00
Pot Pusher & Puller, Hearth, Hand Forged Iron, Arch Back Handle	95.00
Pot, Covered, Kendrick, Straight Handle, Iron, 1 Qt.	95.00
Potato Ricer, Foley Food Mill	8.00
Press, Lard, Marked Pat'd Aug.14, 1877	95.00
Press, Meat, Dated 1884, H.R.Osborne, 7 1/2 In.	45.00
Press, Sausage, Enterprise	192.50
Rack, Cooling, Baker's, 6 Shelves, Red Paint, Poplar, 22 3/4 X 63 In.	250.00
Rack, Pie Cooling, Wire	45.00
Rack, Potato Baking, Tin, 1909	27.00
Rack, Rolling Pin, Holds 3	46.00
Rack, Rolling Pin, Wire	39.00
Rack, Utensil, Graniteware, Gray	65.00
Rack, Wire, Pie Cooling	35.00
Raisin Seeder, Clamp, Enterprise, Philadelphia, Pat.1905	50.00
Raisin Seeder, Enterprise Mfg., No.36	32.00
Raisin Seeder, Enterprise, Iron, Dated 1895	25.00
Raisin Seeder, Mechanical, Gem, 1895	35.00
Reamer, Lemon, Bird Shape, Silver Plated, 4 1/2 In.	25.00
Roaster, Chestnut, Copper, Turned Wooden Handle, 9 In.	40.00
Roaster, Coffee Bean, Wooden Handle	22.00
Roaster, Coffee, Stove Top, Pierced Hole Lid, Handle, Tin	75.00
Roaster, Turned Legs, Iron, 17 1/2 In.	180.00
Roaster, Wagner Ware, Drip Drop Baster, Round	35.00
Rolling Pin, Advertising, Brown Stripes, Crockery, Iowa	160.00
Rolling Pin, Advertising, C.Herbrecht, Charles City, Iowa, Crockery	135.00
Rolling Pin, Advertising, Charles Dettmer, Marco Grocer, Stripe	165.00
Rolling Pin, Advertising, John J.Merrit, Groceries, Mt.Vernon, Iowa	150.00
Rolling Pin, Advertising, Jos. Blink, Gen, Merchandise, Iowa	145.00
Rolling Pin, Advertising, Kelvinator, China	70.00
Rolling Pin, Advertising, Nebraska, Stoneware	165.00
Rolling Pin, Advertising, O.E.Bing, Neb., Brown Bands, Stoneware	135.00
Rolling Pin, Advertising, Polar Bear Flour, Tulsa Feed Store	110.00
Rolling Pin, Advertising, Wild Flower	165.00
Rolling Pin, Black Amethyst	85.00
Rolling Pin, Blown Amethyst	150.00
Rolling Pin, Blue & White, Cameoware, Harker	68.00
Rolling Pin, Cameo Pattern, China, Blue & White	68.00
Rolling Pin, Child's, Wooden	12.50
Rolling Pin, Clear Glass, Screw Cap	8.00
Rolling Pin, Clear, Cambridge, O., July 25, 1921	45.00
Rolling Pin, Cookie, 14 In.	12.00
Rolling Pin, Curly Chestnut, 25 3/4 In.	50.00
Rolling Pin, Curly Maple	52.00
Rolling Pin, Elongated Knob Handles, Cherry, 18 1/2 In.	20.00
Rolling Pin, Glass, Green, Red Looping, American, 14 In.	45.00

Rolling Pin, Glass, Screw Cap End 12.00
Rolling Pin, Green Handles ....6.00 To 7.00
Rolling Pin, Harker, Pettipoint 65.00
Rolling Pin, Kelvinator, White 60.00
Rolling Pin, Maple Handles, Tin 65.00
Rolling Pin, Maple, 1 Piece 14.00
Rolling Pin, Marble, Ash Handles, 20 In. 65.00
Rolling Pin, Milk Glass, Wooden Handles 50.00
Rolling Pin, Nailsea, Rose & White Swirl 200.00
Rolling Pin, Pastry, Wooden, Vining Foliage Design, 13 3/4 In. 125.00
Rolling Pin, Pennsylvania Dutch, Wooden, Bar Handle 165.00
Rolling Pin, Rafioli 85.00
Rolling Pin, Royal Household Flour 75.00
Rolling Pin, Springerle, Animal Designs 37.50
Rolling Pin, Springerle, Fork Type Wooden Handle 50.00
Rolling Pin, Springerle, Pinned Yoke, Daisy Pattern, Hand Carved 150.00
Rolling Pin, Springerle, Signed Germany 35.00
Rolling Pin, Springerle, Wooden, 20 Carved Designs, 18 In. 295.00
Rolling Pin, Stoneware 75.00
Rolling Pin, Stoneware, Blue & White 135.00
Rolling Pin, Tapered, Button End, Maple 27.00
Rolling Pin, Tiger Maple, Knob Handles, 1 Piece 75.00
Rolling Pin, Tin ....150.00 To 175.00
Rolling Pin, Turned Wooden, 20 3/4 In. 35.00
Rolling Pin, Turning Handles, Maple 14.00
Rolling Pin, Woman With Spinning Wheel, China 65.00
Rolling Pin, Wooden Handles, Blue & White Stoneware 35.00
Rug Beater, Double Wire Loop, Wooden Handle, 27 1/2 In. 10.00
Rug Beater, Victorian, Wire, Fancy 22.00
Sadiron, Flip Back Handle, R.W.Weidas, Pat.1870, Oval, 3 X 6 In. 55.00
Sadiron, Fluters, 1871 .... 65.00
Salt & Pepper, Acme Beer 20.00
Salt & Pepper, Ball Fruit Jar, Original Box 50.00
Salt & Pepper, Esso 10.00
Salt & Pepper, Guckenheimer Whiskey 6.00
Salt & Pepper, Mammy, Luzianne Coffee 36.00
Salt & Pepper, Nipper Dog, RCA Victor, Lenox 20.00
Salt & Pepper, Schlitz Beer, Box 10.00
Salt & Pepper, Sealtest Milk 14.00
Salt & Pepper, Sunshine Bakers 11.00
Salt & Pepper, Texaco Gasoline Pump, Figural, Miniature 20.00
Salt & Pepper, Willie & Millie Penguin 10.00
Sausage Maker, Tin, Wooden 27.50
Scoop, Airy Fairy Cake Four, Metal 7.00
Scoop, Butter, Curly Maple, 8 3/4 In. 35.00
Scoop, Flour, Al Calazar, Tin, 2 In. 22.50
Scoop, Ice Cream, Brass, Indestructo, Size 40, 1923 .... 32.00
Scoop, Ice Cream, Cone Shape, Nickel Over Brass, Twisted Handle 48.00
Scoop, Ice Cream, Dairy Fresh, Brass, 2 1/2 In.Bowl 25.00
Scoop, Ice Cream, Dover, 2 Way Action 140.00
Scoop, Ice Cream, Dover, Cheater Cut–Off Knife 350.00
Scoop, Ice Cream, Gilchrist 30.00
Scoop, Ice Cream, Gilchrist No.31 .... 35.00
Scoop, Ice Cream, Ici Pi Ice Cream, Unused 65.00
Scoop, Ice Cream, Indestructo, No.5 .... 30.00
Scoop, Ice Cream, Kinger, 1894 .... 125.00
Scoop, Ice Cream, Quick & Easy 65.00
Scoop, Ice Cream, Tin 16.00
Scoop, Ice Cream, Tin, Size 4 .... 25.00
Scoop, Ice Cream, Trojan 50.00
Scoop, Tin, 1868, Small 17.00
Scoop, Flour, Tin, Painted Red, Flat Handle, 7 In. 15.00
Scraper, Dough, Brass Handle 30.00
Scraper, Dough, Pennsylvania, Brass Handle 375.00

Scraper, Dough, Wooden	10.50
Scraper, Pot, Advertising, Penn	35.00
Scraper, Pot, Kenkel's Flour	75.00
Scrub Stick, Tiger Maple, 1 Piece, Open Arched Handle, 38 1/2 In.	285.00
Shovel, Grain, Ash Wood, 16 In.	195.00
Shovel, Wooden, Shallow, 54 In.	139.00
Sieve, Advertising, National Stove	10.00
Sifter, Flour, Blood's Patent, Wooden	240.00
Sifter, Flour, Blood's, Paper Label, Patent 1861	265.00
Sifter, Flour, Child's, Tin	10.00
Sifter, Flour, For Hoosier Cabinet, Slide In	15.00
Sifter, Flour, Shaker Brand, Tin, C.1885	20.00
Sifter, Flour, Watkins, Triple	25.00
Sifter, Flour, Wooden, 16 1/2 In.	30.00
Sifter, Flour, Wooden, 1861	150.00
Sifter, Sugar, Dome Screen Bottom, Crank Handle, 4 1/2 X 7 In.	175.00
Skillet, 3 Short Legs, Cast Iron, 12 1/4 In.	10.00
Skillet, Copper, Iron Handle, Tin Lined, 10 In.	85.00
Skillet, Griswold, No.8	10.00
Skillet, Middletown Stoves, Cast Iron, 2 In.	7.50
Skimmer, Cream	5.00
Skimmer, Sorghum, Long Handle, Primitive	20.00
Skimmer, Tallow, Hand Hewn & Pierced, 18th Century, 18 In.	220.00
Skimmer, Tin	5.00
Sleeve Board, Clamp On Table, 1903	15.00
Slicer, Cheese, 3 Blades, Crank Handle, Mounted, 1800s, Wheel 14 In.	260.00
Slicer, Vegetable, Catawissa, Patent 1898	50.00
Smoothing Board, Roller, Maple, Handle, 19th Century	40.00
Soap Holder, Wire, Spring Handle, Wall	6.00
Spatula, Heart Shape, Iron, 12 In.	150.00
Spatula, Rumford Baking Powder, Metal	12.00
Spice Box, 5 Drawers, Pennsylvania, Old Rust Paint, 19th Century	995.00
Spice Box, 6 Inner Decorated Boxes, Tin	55.00
Spice Box, 8 Inner Spice Canisters, Round, Wooden	195.00
Spice Box, Chatauqua Spices, 7 Covered Tins, Round, Tin	65.00
Spice Box, Hanging, 4 Drawers, Oak	100.00
Spice Box, Original Spices, Tin, Set Of 6	75.00
Spice Cabinet & Salt Box, Pine, Slanted Lid, Drawers, 11 X 10 In.	85.00
Spice Cabinet, 8 Drawers, Original Stenciling Of Letters	135.00
Spice Cabinet, Hanging, 8 Drawers, Wooden	122.00
Spoon, Baker's Cocoa	40.00
Spoon, Borden's Ice Cream	1.25
Spoon, Cream Dip, Tin, Dated 1924	12.50
Spoon, Cream Whipper, Rumford	12.00
Spoon, Draining, Rumford, Wholesome Baking Powder	10.00
Spoon, Heinz	40.00
Spoon, Kellogg, Tony The Tiger	5.00
Spoon, Knox Gelatin	10.00
Spoon, Model Dairy, Cream Top	18.00
Spoon, New York Times, Victors Co.	20.00
Spoon, Rolex Watches, Lion In Bowl	28.00
Spoon, Slotted, Rumford	7.50
Spoon, Tasting, Hole For Hanging, 7 1/2 In.	50.00
Spoon, Tasting, Rattail Curled Handle, 9 1/2 In.	75.00
Spoon, Towle's Log Cabin	25.00
Stamp, Butter, 6–Pointed Star, Hand Carved, Round, 18th Century	130.00
Stamp, Butter, Eagle	185.00
Stamp, Butter, Fan Design Of Leaves, Handle, Wooden, 3 1/2 In.	25.00
Stamp, Butter, Flower	38.00
Stamp, Butter, Intertwined Double Heart, Knob Handle, 3 1/2 In.	150.00
Stamp, Butter, Primitive Starflower, 5 In.	120.00
Stamp, Butter, Rose, Turned Inserted Handle, 2 7/8 In.	60.00
Stamp, Butter, Sheaf With Leaves, Semicircular, 3 3/8 In.	75.00
Stamp, Butter, Sheaf, Wooden, Round, 4 1/2 In.	55.00

Stamp, Butter, Song Bird, Hand Carved, Round, Knob Handle, 1 Piece 280.00
Stamp, Butter, Star, Wooden, Handle, 3 In. 60.00
Stamp, Butter, Stylized Flower & Foliage, Wooden, Handle, 4 In. 55.00
Stamp, Butter, Stylized Flower, Fishscale Design, Handle, 4 3/8 In. 100.00
Stamp, Butter, Stylized Flower, Stars, Handle, 5 In. 195.00
Stamp, Butter, Tulip, Knob Handle, 18th Century, 4 In. 250.00
Stirrer, Apple Butter, Pierced Paddle, 43 In. 55.00
Stirrer, Apple Butter, Wooden 15.00
Stool, Milking, 3 Legs 50.00
Stove Dampener, Griswold, 1916 .... 9.50
Strainer, Curd, Tin 6.50
Strainer, Sink, Mrs.Vrooman, Tin, 1903 .... 20.00
Strainer, Tea Leaf, Tetley Tea, Embossed Tea Leaf On Handle, 1920s 20.00
Strainer, Tea, Williams, Hammered Handle Design 7.75
String Holder, Bell Shape, Emerald Green, Glass 150.00
String Holder, Cast Iron, 6 X 6 In. 30.00
Tamper, Butter, Right Angled Handle, 18th Century 85.00
Tamper, Cheese, Tin, Signed H, Early 1900s 18.00
Teakettle, Cast Iron, Black 50.00
Teakettle, Gooseneck, Flat Iron Bail, Ribbed Lid, Cast Iron, C.1810 .... 175.00
Teakettle, Hand Forged Iron Bail, Gooseneck, 18th Century 220.00
Teakettle, Nickel Plated Copper 22.50
Teakettle, Tilt, Iron, Conn., Cylindrical, Swing Handle, 18th Century 350.00
Teapot, Long Spout, Jewel Tea, 7 In. 85.00
Tenderizer, Diamond Points, 3 X 3 In.Head 22.00
Tenderizer, Meat, 2-Ended, Iron, Wooden Handle, Pat.Oct.1892, 10 In. 20.00
Tenderizer, Meat, Porcelain, White, Wooden Handle 15.00
Thermometer, Candy, Taylor, Box 4.00
Toaster, Bread, Lady Dover 8.00
Toaster, Electric, Ornate Pull Down Lids, 1918 .... 15.00
Toaster, Knoblock Pyramid, Pat.1909 .... 28.00
Toaster, Marion Flip Flop, 1914 .... 10.00
Toaster, Pyramid Shape, Wire Racks 9.00
Towel Bar, Nickel & Brass Ends, White, 1908 .... 25.00
Utensils, Green Handles, Unused, Original Box, Set Of 3 .... 18.00
Vacuum Cleaner, Original Paint, Pat.1911 .... 75.00
Wafer Iron, Geometric Design, Loop Handle, 3 1/4 X 14 In. 195.00
Wafer Iron, Stylized Floral Design, Center Letter C, 33 1/2 In. 150.00
Waffle Iron, Bakelite Handles, Manning Bowman 18.00
Waffle Iron, Belmont 20.00
Waffle Iron, Cast Iron, Pat.1910 .... 50.00
Waffle Iron, Crusco No.8, Holder 35.00
Waffle Iron, French, On Granite Stand, 22 In. 62.00
Waffle Iron, Griswold, American No.8 .... 55.00
Waffle Iron, Griswold, Dated 1893 .... 30.00
Waffle Iron, Griswold, Hearts & Star 75.00
Waffle Iron, Griswold, No.9, Patent 1880 .... 75.00
Waffle Iron, Heart & Star, Griswold, Patent May 18, 1920 .... 50.00
Waffle Iron, Manning Bowman, Bakelite Handles 18.00
Waffle Iron, Parrot Design, Porcelain Lid 50.00
Waffle Iron, Puritan, No.8 .... 25.00
Waffle Iron, Stand, Stover, Cast Iron 18.00
Waffle Iron, Wagner, Pat.Feb.22, 1910, Square 50.00
Wash Boiler, Tin Lid, Copper 95.00
Wash Stick, 2-Prong, 24 In. 15.00
Wash Stick, Corrugated, 4 X 28 In. 95.00
Washboard, Baby Grand 10.00
Washboard, Brushbilt 35.00
Washboard, Child's, Victory, Glass 12.00
Washboard, Child's, Wooden Frame, Zinc, 5 X 11 In. 7.00
Washboard, Glass 15.00
Washboard, Glass, Small 10.00
Washboard, Graniteware, Blue ....57.00 To 65.00
Washboard, Mellow Patina, 16 X 24 In. 95.00

Washboard, Mitten, Patent 1916, Tin 12.00
Washboard, Mother Hubbard 95.00
Washboard, National Washboard Co., Pat.1897 .... 11.00
Washboard, Threaded Screw Wooden Rollers, Directions, 12 X 22 In. 130.00
Washboard, Wooden Rollers, Mother Hubbard, 12 X 22 In. 130.00
Washboard, Wooden, Brass, Sunset, 12 1/2 X 24 In. 25.00
Whip, Cream, Norwegian, Wooden 22.00
Whip, Cream, Presto, Turbine Blades 18.00
Whip, Cream, Red & White Swirl Handle, 14 In. 24.00

In the 1960s, the government passed a law that required knife manufacturers to mark their knives with the country of origin. This seemed to encourage the collectors, and knife collecting became an interest of a large group of people. All types of knives are collected, from top quality twentieth-century examples to old bone or pearl-handled knives in excellent condition.

KNIFE, Anheuser-Busch, Sterling Silver 195.00
 Animal Bone Handle, Running Stag, Blade Etched With Turkey 25.00
 Army, German, World War II 115.00
 B.F.Goodrich, Pocket 12.00
 Boarding, Whaling, Carved Wooden Handle, Hand Forged Iron, 5 Ft. 650.00
 Bowie, Marked Plum, Bristol, German Silver Guard, C.1860, 8 1/4 In. 225.00
 Bowie, Sheath, California, Etched Panel, Silver Throat, C.1850 .... 1250.00
 Bowie, Sheath, German Silver Crossguard & Ferrule, C.1850, 16 In. 395.00
 Bowie, Sheath, Marked J.Nicholson & Sons, Late 1840s, 15 In. 1600.00
 Bowie, Stag Handle, Brass Guard, Leather Sheath, Handmade 50.00
 Bread, World's Fair 1692-1892 .... 15.00
 Butcher, Winchester No.1035, 12 1/2 In. 55.00
 Camillus, Pocket, Large 25.00
 Carving Set, Emily Dickinson Sheffield, Bone Handle, 3 Piece 85.00
 Case, No.5121, Stag Handle, Original Box 60.00
 Cattaraugus, Kitchen 3.00
 Cattaraugus, Sheath, No.2250 .... 115.00
 Dagger, Figural, Nude Handle, Art Deco, Sheath 50.00
 Dagger, Horn Handle, Brass Shank, Marked Mexico, 15 In. 75.00
 Dagger, Islamic, Iranian, Silver, 23K Gold Inlay, C.1900, 12 In. 275.00
 Dagger, Silver, Pierced, Geometric, Steel Blade, Near East, 14 In. 190.00
 Draw, Keen Kutter, 5 In. 28.00
 Draw, Simmons 30.00
 Draw, Violin Maker's, Brass, 1 X 3 3/4 In. 140.00
 Gravity, Nazi Paratrooper, World War II .... 95.00 To 140.00
 Half & Half Pipe Tobacco, Folding Tamper 6.00
 Hand, Civil War, Marked WE 60.00
 Hay .... 5.00 To 10.00
 Hunting, Bone Duck Shaped Handle, Scrimshaw Elk Horn Sheath 150.00
 Hunting, Folding, Antler Handle, Marked A.Rouge, Cavaillon, 6 3/4 In. 75.00
 Hunting, Marbles, Folding, Stag Handle, Carrying Pouch With Compass 350.00
 Hunting, Marbles, Original Sheath 35.00
 Hunting, Remington 65.00
 Hunting, Tooled Antler Grip, Leather Sheath, 11 In. 115.00
 Hunting, U.S., Leather Case, Model 1880 .... *Illus* 250.00
 Hunting, W.R.Case Tested, 6 In.Bowl Shaped Blade, Sheath 150.00
 Hunting, West-Cut, Boulder, Colo., 8 1/2 In. 15.00
 Imperial Frontier, Hunting, Unused 6.50
 Ivory Handle, American Revolution Period, Pocket 95.00
 Jack, Remington, No.R282, 4 In. 24.00
 Jack, Single Blade, Design Of Cornucopia, Fruit, Coin Silver 55.00
 Keen Kutter, Pocket 20.00
 Leg, Ka-Bar, Lady's 90.00
 Machete, Folding, Black Handle, 15 In. 40.00
 Pen, Gold Filled 15.00
 Pen, Stainless Steel 12.50

Pocket, American Boy, Magazine	12.00
Pocket, American United Life Ins., Raised Bulldog	14.00
Pocket, Bone Handle, Shoe Button Hook	12.00
Pocket, Camping, 2 Blades, Fork, Spoon, Corkscrew, Bottle Opener, Japan	30.00
Pocket, Canoe, Red Bone, Case XX USA	45.00
Pocket, Case XX Bulldog No.5172	150.00
Pocket, Case, 1 Blade, Buffalo Model, Walnut Handle	50.00
Pocket, Century Of Progress, Brass	38.00
Pocket, Daddy Barlow, Red Bone, Case XX 6143	45.00
Pocket, Franklin Fires Insurance, Silver	7.70
Pocket, German SS, World War II	25.00
Pocket, Hen & Rooster Brand, Pearl Handle	100.00
Pocket, Hibbard Spencer Bartlett No.9779, Pearl Handle	85.00
Pocket, Ka–Bar, Union Cut Co., 3 Fold Fish, Black Handle	150.00
Pocket, Ka–Bar, Dog's Head, Stag Handle	150.00
Pocket, Keen Kutter, No.K209	40.00
Pocket, Klein Bros., Chicago	10.00
Pocket, Nazi SS, Hitler Signature Blade, Ormolu Sides, World War II	275.00
Pocket, Nu–Grape	12.00
Pocket, Ralston Purina	10.00
Pocket, Remington, Daddy Barlow No.1240, Bone Handle	150.00
Pocket, Remington, Franklin Fire Insurance, 1929	35.00
Pocket, Remington, No.2295	50.00
Pocket, Remington, No.698	40.00
Pocket, Schrade, Everlastingly Sharp, Black Felt, Yellow Letters	149.50
Pocket, Stag, Folding Hunter, Case XX 5565	125.00
Pocket, Victorian, Gold Filled	20.00
Purina, Pocket	21.00
Race, Speckled Burl Handle, Brass Ferrule	110.00
Red Goose Shoes	25.00
Remington, Moby Dick	17.50
Remington, No.3565, Box	97.50
Remington, R.H.73	150.00
Sailor, Buffalo Handle, English, 1850s	50.00
Sash, Arabian Sheik, Damascus Steel, Inscription, 12 3/4 In.	625.00
Shrade, Chas.Hollenbach Meats, Louisville, Ky.	35.00
Skinning, Remington	22.50
Steak, Dresden Handle, Sheffield, Original Box, Set Of 6	30.00
Traveler's Insurance, Pocket	95.00
Ulster, Bird Emblem, Mess Kit Type	12.00
V–42, Case, U.S.Devil's Brigade, World War II	475.00
Valley Forge Cutlery Co., Newark, Nickel Silver Handle, 3 1/4 In.	175.00
Winchester, 2 Blades, Pocket	5.00

KNOWLES, TAYLOR & KNOWLES, see KTK; Lotus Ware

The name "Koch" is signed on the front of a series of plates decorated with fruit, vegetables, animals, or birds. The dishes date from the 1910 to 1930 period and were probably decorated in Germany.

KOCH, Berry Bowl, Peaches & Water Background, 5 1/2 In.	27.00
Bowl, Fruit, Apples, Signed	68.00
Bowl, Fruit, Grapes, Signed	68.00
Cake Plate, Open Handles, Grapes, Gold, Signed, 11 In.	45.00
Celery, Apples, Open Handle, 11 1/2 X 5 1/4 In.	40.00
Plate, Grapes, Signed, 8 1/2 In.	30.00

KOREAN WARE, see Sumida

It is safest to use distilled water for the final rinse when washing textiles.

Most dealers and collectors use the term "KPM" to refer to Berlin porcelain, but the same initials were used alone and in combination with other symbols by several German porcelain makers. They include the Konigliche Porzellan Manufaktur of Berlin, initials used in mark 1823-47; Meissen, 1723-24 only; Krister Porzellan Manufaktur in Waldenburg, after 1831; Kranichfelder Porzellan Manufaktur in Kranichfeld, after 1903; and the Kister Porzellan Manufaktur in Scheibe, after 1838.

KPM, Berry Bowl, Pink Luster, Roses	45.00
Bowl, Bunches Of Violets, 9 In.	45.00
Bowl, Covered, Footed, Egg Shape, Enameled, Angel, Rabbit, Gold Trim	185.00
Candlestick, White, 2 1/2 In., Pair	15.00
Cup & Saucer, Gold Trim, Demitasse	20.00
Figurine, Cupid, Bows & Arrows, Marked, 14 5/8 In.	605.00
Figurine, Ruth, Signed, 11 X 19 In.	2800.00
KPM, LITHOPHANE, see Lithophane	
Mustache Cup & Saucer	45.00
Plaque, Nun In Chamber, 19th Century, Scepter Mark, 13 1/8 X 7 7/8 In.	1320.00
Plaque, Ruth, Wheat Field, 19th Century, Scepter Mark, 9 1/4 X 6 3/8 In.	825.00
Plaque, Titled, Signed R.Dittrich, 10 X 12 In.	1700.00
Plate, Fruit Center, Lappet Border, Scepter Mark, 8 5/8 In., Set Of 8	1100.00
Plate, Fruit, Gilded, Marked, C.1870, 8 1/2 In.	185.00
Platter, Prussian Eagle, Pink, White, Scalloped, Open Handles, Marked	65.00
Stein, Porcelain Relief, C.1880, 1/2 Liter, Pair	275.00
Vase, Etch, Cobalt Blue, 9 In.	65.00
Vase, Jeweled, Blue, Caduceus Mark, 8 In.	1100.00

KTK are the initials of the Knowles, Taylor and Knowles Company of East Liverpool, Ohio, founded by Isaac W. Knowles in 1853. The company made many types of utilitarian wares, hotel china, and dinnerwares. They made the fine bone china known as Lotus Ware from 1891 to 1896. The company merged with American Ceramic Corporation in 1928. It closed in 1934. Lotus Ware is listed in its own category in this book.

KTK, Cake Plate, Floral, Center Gold Design, 12 1/4 In.	35.00
Cup & Saucer, Bluebird, Signed, Demitasse	12.00
Cup & Saucer, Child's, Bluebirds, Marked, Set Of 8	65.00
Dinner Set, Child's, Nursery Rhymes, Cup, Saucer, Plate, Sugar & Creamer	175.00
Soap Dish, Original Rest, Cover, Round, White	27.50

Any items relating to the Ku Klux Klan are now collected because of their historic importance. Literature, robes, and memorabilia are available. The Klan is still in existence, so new material is found.

KU KLUX KLAN, Application, Membership, Dues Record, Ideals, 1920	6.00
Box, Candy, Cloth, Paper, Label, 11 In.	150.00
Buckle, Belt, Signed Tiffany & Daniel Lowe, Salem Witch	65.00
Card, Membership, Chicago, 1928	25.00
Clip, Money	30.00
Knife, Pocket, Brass Handle, Emblem	6.85
Record, Label With Burning Cross, 1920	25.00
Sheet Music, Daddy Swiped Our Sheet & Joined, Ottawa, Ks.	65.00

Kutani ware is a Japanese porcelain made after the mid-seventeenth century. Most of the pieces found today are nineteenth century. Collectors often use the term "kutani" to refer to just the later, colorful pieces decorated with red, gold, and black pictures of warriors, animals, and birds.

KUTANI, Bowl, Women & Lake Scene, Green, Border, Marked, 1 1/2 X 5 In.	50.00
Creamer, Red & Gold Brocade, People, Marked	35.00
Jar, Covered, Bird Handles, Dragon Finial, 19th Century, 13 In., Pr.	725.00
Jar, Covered, Bird, Red Ground, Gilt, Japan, Late 19th Century, 10 In.	150.00
Mustard Pot, Attached Saucer, Diapering, Red Script Mark	30.00
Pitcher, Diapering, Red Script Mark, 5 In.	38.00

Pitcher, Raised Gold Reserve, Children, 6 Sides, Red Mark, 7 In.	65.00
Plate, Birds, Multicolored, 10 In.	65.00
Plate, Oriental Scenes, Serving Pieces, C.1948, Set Of 6	225.00
Plate, Rooster, C.1900, 8 1/2 In.	250.00
Relish, Diapering, Red Script Mark, 7 1/2 X 4 1/2 In.	18.00
Salt & Pepper, Diapering, Bulbous, 6 Sided, Red Script Mark	22.00
Sugar & Creamer, People & Lake Scene, Cobalt, Gold Trim, Marked	140.00
Tea Caddy, Raised Gold Reserve, Children, 6 Sides, Red Mark, 6 In.	58.00
Tea Set & Tea Caddy, Melon Ribbed, Nishikide Diapering, Gold, 10 Pc.	185.00
Tea Set, Gold Reserve, Children, Melon Ribbed Teapot, Red Mark	125.00
Tea Set, Gold Trim, Figures, 19 Piece	395.00
Teapot, 4 Cups & Saucers, Akaji Kinja, Gold Birds, Red	115.00
Teapot, Allover Design Of 1, 000 Figures, 4 1/4 X 6 In.	190.00
Teapot, Bulbous, Signed, 4 1/2 In.	35.00
Teapot, Floral, Gold Ground, C.1910	57.50
Vase, 4 Scenes, Gold Trim, Brownish Orange, 7 In.	60.00
Vase, Flowers, Black Ground, Signed, 12 1/2 In.	145.00
Vase, Stick, Birds, Flowers, Fan Shape, Bittersweet, Gold, & White	125.00
Vase, Stick, Floral, 9 3/4 In.	200.00

Lacquer is a type of varnish. Collectors are most interested in the Chinese and Japanese lacquer wares made from the Japanese varnish tree. Lacquer wares are made from wood coated with many coats of lacquer. Sometimes the piece is carved or decorated with ivory or metal inlay.

LACQUER, Box, Leather, Red, Applied Gold Designs, Brass, 11 X 29 X 19 In.	375.00
Box, Picnic, Trailing Vines, Gold, Red, 17 3/4 In.	300.00
Chest, Storage, Animals, Zodiac, Silver Mounted, 14 X 13 X 9 In.	3190.00
Inro, Brocade Bag, Tea Caddy Design, 4 Case, 17th Century	880.00
Inro, Carved Chinese Cash, Gold Design, Wood, 2 Case	990.00
Inro, Family, Chrysanthemums, Gold & Silver, Signed Kajikawa	1650.00
Inro, Samurai Watching Dancer, 4 Case, Signed, Shokosai	550.00
Inro, Scholars, Attendant, Wooden Pavilion, Diaper Ground	1100.00
Inro, School, Gold Quail, 4 Case, Signed Yamada	300.00
Inro, Sheaf Filled Boats, Lake, 3 Case, Signed Koma Kansai	1210.00
Tabouret, Black, 15 In.	10.00
Tea Caddy & Tray, Genre Scenes, Pewter Container, Tray 18 1/2 In.	110.00
Tray, Breakfast, Bird Flying, Chrysanthemums, Black, 4 Legs, 16 In.	200.00

Lalique glass was made by Rene Lalique in Paris, France, between the 1890s and his death in 1945. The glass was molded, pressed, and engraved in Art Nouveau and Art Deco styles. Pieces were marked with the signature "R. Lalique." Lalique glass is still being made. Pieces made after 1945 bear the mark "Lalique."

LALIQUE, Ashtray, Frieze Of Archers Rim, Frosted Black, Signed, 4 1/4 In.	1210.00
Atomizer, Perfume, Frosted Dove Each Side, Signed, Suede Case	325.00
Bar Pin, Frosted Ground, Gold Foil Lining, 2 3/4 In.	495.00
Bookends, Hirondelle	375.00
Bookends, Kneeling Angel, Frosted, Signed, 7 1/2 In.	660.00
Bottle, Cologne, Cobalt, Worth Dans La Nuit, Marked, 5 1/2 In.	145.00
Bottle, Perfume, 3 Different Bird Stoppers, Set Of 3	195.00
Bottle, Perfume, 6 Nudes, 7 In.	200.00
Bottle, Perfume, Air De Temps, Frosted Dove Stopper, 32 Oz., 12 In.	725.00
Bottle, Perfume, Art Deco Design, Yellow Orange, Signed, 4 1/4 In.	400.00
Bottle, Perfume, Black, Nouveau Lady Corners, Square, Signed, 5 In.	450.00
Bottle, Perfume, Blue Crystal, Turquoise Stopper	95.00
Bottle, Perfume, Cactus, Enameled	135.00
Bottle, Perfume, Chardon Pattern, Thistle Leaves, Square, 5 In.	350.00
Bottle, Perfume, Clairfontaine	115.00
Bottle, Perfume, Dans La Nuit, Worth	250.00
Bottle, Perfume, Double Flower	98.00
Bottle, Perfume, Flask Shape, Stopper, Nina Ricci Label, 3 5/8 In.	27.50
Bottle, Perfume, Heart Shape, 4 1/2 In.	160.00
Bottle, Perfume, Heart Shape, Cour Joie, Box, 3 1/4 In.	200.00

Bottle, Perfume, Heart Shape, For Nina Ricci, 3 1/2 In. 275.00
Bottle, Perfume, Mold Of Continuous Swallows, Stopper 125.00
Bottle, Perfume, Nudes In Relief, 3 In. 295.00
Bottle, Perfume, Nudes With Garland Of Flowers, Brass Atomizer 275.00
Bottle, Perfume, Nudes, Garlands Of Flowers, Brass Atomizer, 3 In. 275.00
Bottle, Perfume, Original Stopper, Turquoise, Marked Worth, 3 In. 95.00
Bottle, Perfume, Purse, Twined Hearts Pattern, Chamois Bag, Signed 67.00
Bottle, Perfume, Tzigana, Corday, Paris, Marked, 7 In. 225.00
Bottle, Perfume, Worth, 6 In. ....125.00 To 135.00
Bottle, Perfume, Worth, Blue, 2 1/2 In. 80.00
Bowl, Allover Tulips, 11 In. 65.00
Bowl, Coquilles Pattern, Signed, 4 X 10 In. 250.00
Bowl, Fish Frieze, 5 In. 105.00
Bowl, Fish, Opalescent Water, Bubbly Center, Marked, 2 X 11 3/4 In. 350.00
Bowl, Frosted Cosmos Floral, Relief, Block Letter Mark, 10 X 4 In. 400.00
Bowl, Hobnail, Enamel Dot At Point Of Hob, Signed, 9 1/2 In. 225.00
Bowl, Lily, Footed, 1894, Signed, 10 1/2 In. 600.00
Bowl, No.3249, Signed, 9 X 3 In. 325.00
Bowl, Opalescent Swirl, Raised Circles, 10 In. 195.00
Bowl, Opalescent, 12 In. 195.00
Bowl, Swirled Feather, Opalescent, 10 In. 225.00
Box, Floral D'Orsay, Brown Stain, 4 In. 110.00
Box, Powder, 3 Dancing Nudes, Signed D'Orsay 165.00
Box, Powder, Emiliane Pattern, Flowers, Round, Signed, 4 In. 185.00
Box, Powder, Nudes Dancing On Cover, Leaf Design, Marked, 3 3/4 In. 225.00
Brandy Glass, Band Of Fish, Signed, Blue Satin, 2 3/4 In. 85.00
Car Mascot, St.Christopher, Block Letters, Signed 1950.00
Cordial, Enfants 22.00
Crucifix, Molded With Brambles, Silk Cord, 1 3/4 In. 110.00
Cup & Saucer, Black Enameled Cactus Pattern, Signed 150.00
Decanter, Black Enameled Grape Clusters, Stopper, Signed, 11 In. 55.00
Decanter, Frosted, Kneeling Muse Stopper, Nude Figures, 11 1/2 In. 150.00
Dish, Leaf Pattern, Signed, 6 In., Pair 150.00
Figurine, 2 Birds, Frosted 75.00
Figurine, Bird, 4 X 5 In. 70.00
Figurine, Buffalo 225.00
Figurine, Fish, Blue Green 85.00
Figurine, Woman, Robe & Headdress Of Molded Leaves, Signed, 18 In. 1430.00
Fish, Signed, 2 1/2 In. 60.00
Flacon, Globular Form, Molded Butterflies, Stopper, Marked 495.00
Hood Ornament, Longchamps, Horse's Head, Frosted, Signed, 6 In. 1760.00
Hood Ornament, Rooster's Head, Purple, Signed, 7 In. 6600.00
Menu Card, Frosted Glass, Molded Menu & Grapes On Vine, 6 In. 350.00
Paperweight, Rooster Form, Pale Yellow, Signed, 3 1/2 In. 50.00
Pendant, Nymph Kneeling On Branches, Silk Cord, Marked, 1 1/4 In. 250.00
Plate, Annual, 1968, Gazelle 98.00
Plate, Annual, 1976, Eagle ....80.00 To 135.00
Plate, Bicentennial, Signed 250.00
Plate, Black Embossed Stylized Tree, Signed, 10 1/2 In. 75.00
Plate, Year 1965 Through 1976, Set Of 12 .... 1800.00
Ring Holder, 2 Swans, Saucer Bottom, 4 In. 155.00
Rooster, Opalescent 1050.00
Shade, Lamp, Hanging, Dandelion 135.00
Tumbler, Zigzag Design, Frosted Band At Base, Flared, Set Of 11 .... 750.00
Vase, 2 Squirrels Form Stem, Sitting On Acorns, Signed, 10 In. 1045.00
Vase, 3 Rows Crystal Flowers, Marked Block Letters, 6 1/4 In. 550.00
Vase, 4 Projecting Fins, Columns Of Leaves, Signed, 9 In. 1320.00
Vase, 8 Angled Panels, 5 Nude Children, Flowers, Signed, 3 1/2 In. 235.00
Vase, Blue Stain Band, Molded Leaves, Art Deco Shape, Marked, 7 In. 425.00
Vase, Cylindrical Shape, Intaglio Molded Into Sides, Signed, 6 In. 595.00
Vase, Esterel Pattern, Clusters Of Branches, Signed, 6 In. 475.00
Vase, Etched Thistles, Fluted Base, Cylinder, Marked, 14 In. 350.00
Vase, Eucalyptus, 7 In. 250.00
Vase, Eucalyptus, Opalescent, Signed, 6 1/2 In., Pair 950.00

Vase, Fish Design, No.925, Ruby, Spherical, Signed, 9 3/4 In. 900.00
Vase, Flared Cylinder, Band Of Antelopes & Stars, Signed, 7 3/4 In. 880.00
Vase, Large Spiralled Handles, Cylinder, Signed, Purple, 6 1/4 In. 11000.00
Vase, Molded As Coiled Cobra, Signed, 10 In. 3850.00
Vase, Molded With Fish, Etched, Signed, 11 1/2 In. 2860.00
Vase, Nudes Picking Grapes, Signed, 5 1/4 In. 265.00
Vase, Opalescent Reeded, Frog's Egg Pattern, Signed 985.00
Vase, Pairs Of Parakeets Amid Branches, Signed, Ovoid, Blue, 10 In. 4620.00
Vase, Poppies, Buds, Leaves, Signed, 6 In. 350.00
Vase, Rampillon, Opalescent, Signed, No.991 .... 510.00
Vase, Stacked Zipper Design, Frosted Birds, Marked, 6 3/4 In. 250.00
Vase, Stylized Heads Of Wheat, 7 In. 440.00
Vase, Thistle, Blue Wash, 8 In. 850.00
Vase, Thistle, Charcoal With Orange Stain, Signed 700.00
Wine, Black Enameled Rooster On Stem, Signed, 4 3/4 In. 110.00

*Interest is strong in lamps of every type, from the early oil–burning
Betty and Phoebe lamps to the recent electric lamps with glass or
beaded shades. Fuels used in lamps changed through the years; whale
oil (1800–40), Argand (1830), lard (1833–63), camphene (1828),
turpentine and alcohol (1840s), gas (1850–79), kerosene (1860), and
electricity (1879) are the most common. Other lamps are listed by
manufacturer or type of material.*

LAMP, Alabaster, Figural, Golden Retriever, Globe, Enameled, 15 X 8 In. 135.00
Alacite, Table, Chartreuse & Cream, Finial, Electric, Pair 70.00
Aladdin, Alacite, Cupid, Pair 200.00
Aladdin, B– 26, Simplicity,, 401 Shade, Burner, Ivory Alacite, Decal 210.00
Aladdin, B– 28, Rose Simplicity, Nashville Burner, Unused 200.00
Aladdin, B– 29, Simplicity, Green 75.00
Aladdin, B– 39, Washington Drape, Original Glass Shade, Clear 85.00
Aladdin, B– 41, Washington Drape, Amber 95.00
Aladdin, B– 47, Washington Drape, Clear, Bell Stem, Burner 70.00
Aladdin, B– 53, Washington Drape, Tripod, Clear 45.00
Aladdin, B– 62, Drape, Ruby 350.00
Aladdin, B– 62, Lincoln Drape, Ruby, Short 340.00
Aladdin, B– 76, Lincoln Drape, Cobalt, Scalloped Foot, Tall 400.00
Aladdin, B– 82, Beehive, Dark Amber, Burners 90.00
Aladdin, B– 83, Beehive, Ruby ....225.00 To 245.00
Aladdin, B– 88, Vertique, Yellow 270.00
Aladdin, B– 90, Diamond Quilt, White, Black Base, 701B Shade 200.00
Aladdin, B– 91, Diamond Quilt, White, Rose Base 65.00
Aladdin, B– 92, Vertique, Green 120.00
Aladdin, B– 93, Vertique, White 250.00
Aladdin, B–101, Corinthian, Amber Crystal, Burners ....50.00 To 78.00
Aladdin, B–102, Cathedral, Green 55.00
Aladdin, B–104, Corinthian, Clear Font, Black Base, Burner 100.00
Aladdin, B–105, Corinthian, Green 40.00
Aladdin, B–108, Cathedral, Green 65.00
Aladdin, B–110, Cathedral, White Burners 155.00
Aladdin, B–110, Cathedral, White, Burners 110.00
Aladdin, B–115, Corinthian, Green Moonstone 75.00
Aladdin, B–116, Corinthian, Rose ....85.00 To 115.00
Aladdin, B–122, Majestic, Green, Burners 100.00
Aladdin, B–124, Corinthian, White, Black Base 90.00
Aladdin, B–125, Corinthian, White, Green Base 75.00
Aladdin, B–125, Corinthian, White, Green Moonstone Base, Brass, 9 In. 90.00
Aladdin, G–211, Candelabra, Alacite 80.00
Aladdin, G–333, Bridegroom, Gray 95.00
Aladdin, Muncie 95.00
Aladdin, Night–Light, Perfume, Arab Woman Kneeling, 7 In. ....110.00 To 125.00
Aladdin, No.100, Venetian, White 40.00
Aladdin, No.104, Colonial, Clear, Burners 70.00
Aladdin, No.106, Colonial, Amber 125.00
Aladdin, No.109, Cathedral, Amber 70.00

Alcohol, Blue, Miniature 45.00
Angle, Brass, Old Glass 145.00
Angle, Double, Embossed Brass, Opalescent Swirl Shades 495.00
Argand, Blown & Frosted Shade, Prism Band, Brass, 19 In. 100.00
Argand, Cut & Frosted Shades, Pair 715.00
Art Deco, Blue Frosted Glass, Lady Laying, Shade, Pair 135.00
Art Deco, Chrome & Black, 11 In. 24.00
Art Deco, Night–Light, Black, Aluminum, 12 In. 30.00
Art Nouveau, Girl, Flowing Dress, Signed La Pensee, 22 In. 275.00
Art Nouveau, Glass, Floral, Vaseline, Urn Shape, America, 35 In. 475.00
Art Nouveau, McClelland Barclay, Lily Pad, Frog, Bronze Finish, 12 In. 225.00
Art Nouveau, Peasant Girl, Hand Sickle, Leaves, 2–Light, 17 In. 125.00
Astral, Cornelius & Co., C.1843, Gothic Design, Brass, 16 In. 175.00
Astral, Washington & Eagle, Gilt & Brass 700.00
Banquet, Bulging Loop, Pink, Miniature 125.00
Banquet, Cupid Stem, Ball Shade 195.00
Banquet, Onyx, Brass, Yellow Gold Cased Globe, Pole Wired, 29 1/2 In. 325.00
Betty, Holder, Glazed Pottery 18.00
Betty, Iron, Brass Hinge, Whale Oil, Mary Manfser, John Leony, 1855 .... 825.00
Betty, Old Gold Paint, Sheet & Wrought Iron, 3 In. 45.00
Betty, Wrought Iron, Hanger, 3 3/4 In. 30.00
Betty, Wrought Iron, Hinged Font Lid, Black Paint, 7 In. 225.00
Bicycle, Brass 30.00
Boudoir, Fortune Teller Doll, Composition Head, Inset Eyelashes 135.00
Boudoir, Orange Parrot, Tiffin 295.00
Boy Artist In Metal, Frosted Shade, Paris, Incised Madnat, 7 In. 150.00
Bozo The Clown, Full Figure 15.00
Bracket, Iron, Cranberry Shade 320.00
     LAMP, BRADLEY & HUBBARD, see Bradley & Hubbard, Lamp
Brass, Hammered Base, Pierced Shade, 20 In. 242.00
Brass, Hammered, Boudoir, Ball Finial Shade, Square Base, 11 1/4 In. 125.00
Brass, Single Spout, Saucer Base, 4 1/2 In. 45.00
Bronze, 2 Girls Dancing On Base, Crackle Glass Shade, Hiller 200.00
Bronze, Figural, Pavillion & Tribesman, Bronze, Austrian, 10 In. 650.00
Bronze, Frosted Glass, Pedestal, Square Base, C.1900, 33 In. 300.00
Bronze, Louis XV, Foliate Finial, Round Foot, Signed Paris, 25 In. 300.00
Bronze, Oriental Figures, Holding Umbrella, Electrified, 11 In., Pair 500.00
Buffalo, Lily, 18–Light, Green Shade 1900.00
Bull's–Eye, Clear, Hand Painted Flowers On Font 35.00
Bull's–Eye, Double, 8 In. 350.00
Bull's–Eye, Green, 10 In. 165.00
Cameo, Orange, Floral Shade, Mushroom Shape, Bronze Base, 14 In. 1450.00
Camphene, Sparking, Brass, Inverted Funnel Shape, Ring, Chain, Cap 57.00
Camphene, Sparking, Ring Handle, Single Burner Chain & Cap 57.00
Camphene, Twin Burners & Caps, Pewter, 6 1/2 In. 260.00
Candle, Double Arm, Ormolu, Pink Glass Shade, Onyx Base, C.1900, 20 In. . 275.00
Candle, Miner's, Folding, Patent 1865 .... 95.00
Carbide, Miner's, Bail Nickeled Over Brass, 9 In. 110.00
Carbide, Miner's, Justrite, Nickel Over Brass Bail, 9 In. 110.00
Carriage, Magnifying Lens, Marked Coach 6224, 13 1/2 In., Pair 95.00
Carriage, Neverout, Safety 38.00
Carriage, Tole, Silvered Copper, Glass Panels, Hexagonal, 1840, 17 In. 90.00
Chandelier, 6–Light, Pendant Chain & Lustres, Bronze, Crystal, 36 In. 1650.00
Chandelier, 12–Light, Faceted Glass & Gilt Bronze, French, 44 In. 2310.00
Chandelier, Candle, Wooden, Iron, 6 Curved Branch Arms, 10 1/2 X 18 In. .. 1400.00
Chandelier, Empire, Crystal Swags, Dome Shape, Hanging Crystals, French .. 270.00
Chandelier, Empire, Waterfall, 5 Scroll Arms, Bronze, Crystal 350.00
Chandelier, Gilt Metal, Cut Glass, & Rock Crystal, Drip Pans, 40 In. 6050.00
Chandelier, Teardrops, Faceted Florets, Silvered Metal, French, 32 In. 1320.00
Coleman, Gas, White Milk Glass Shade, Telephone Style, 20 X 8 In. 55.00
Copper Painted Metal, Clip On Shade, Greist Mfg.Co., 10 1/2 In. 33.00
Desk, Chrome, Chase 90.00
Duncan, Bar Pan, 8 In. 75.00
Electric, Deer & Castle, Ruby 195.00

Electric, Mushroom Shade, Ruffled Top, Flowers, Silver Plate, 17 In. 295.00
Electric, Nephrite, Carved, HU Form, Faces, Bronze Mounted, China, 22 In. 475.00
Electric, Rayo, Brass 85.00
Emeralite, Architect, Clamp On 375.00
Emeralite, Desk, 1916 .... 245.00
Emeralite, Desk, Adjustable Arm, Square Molded Base, 14 1/2 In. 170.00
Emeralite, No.8734, Type B, No Shade 90.00
Fairy, Baby Head, Emerald, Frosted, Clear Clarke Base, 4 1/2 In. 165.00
Fairy, Bisque, 3–Faced Owl 95.00
Fairy, Bohemian Glass, Flat, Stained Red To Clear Satin 250.00
Fairy, Burmese, Clear, Clarke, 4 In. 175.00
Fairy, Burmese, Diamond Point Base, England, 5 In. 140.00
Fairy, Burmese, Epergne, Clarke Holder, Dome Shade, 9 7/8 In., Pair 1100.00
Fairy, Burmese, Folded Sides, Holder Signed Clarkes Fairy, 7 In. 535.00
Fairy, Burmese, Ruffled Reversible Base, Marked Clarke Cup, 5 3/4 In. 550.00
Fairy, Burmese, Salmon To Yellow, Acid Finish, Clarke Base, 3 5/8 In. 165.00
Fairy, Canadian Bull's–Eye, Footed, Green 165.00
Fairy, Chartreuse, Frosted, Ruffled, Dome Shade, Verre Moire, 6 1/2 In. 450.00
Fairy, Christmas, Bisque Shade, Marked Clarke Base, 4 3/4 In. 250.00
Fairy, Clarke Base, Blue Overlay, 3 5/8 In. 110.00
Fairy, Clarke Signed Base, Cobalt Blue, 4 In. 43.00
Fairy, Clarke, Ormolu Mount, Chimney, Cricklite, 15 3/4 In., Pair 400.00
Fairy, Cranberry, Clear Applied Petals, Pyramid Clarke Base & Candle 295.00
Fairy, Crown Shape, Royal Blue, Clear Marked Clarke Base, 4 1/2 In. 195.00
Fairy, Diamond–Quilted, Mother–Of–Pearl, Blue, Clarke Base, 3 5/8 In. 145.00
Fairy, Diamond–Quilted, Sapphire Blue, Chimney, Rope Handle, 4 3/4 In. 75.00
Fairy, Drape Pattern, Sapphire, Clark, 4 1/4 In. 135.00
Fairy, Embossed Daffodils, Flat, Green Custard 225.00
Fairy, Frosted Cranberry Verre Moire, Ruffled Bowl, Loopings, 5 In. 495.00
Fairy, Green Overlay Shade, White Lining, Clark Base, 4 1/2 In. 98.00
Fairy, Made For Queen Victoria 1887 Jubilee, Royal Blue, 4 1/2 In. 175.00
Fairy, Olive, Frosted, Clear, Clarke Mark, Dome Shade, 3 7/8 In. 95.00
Fairy, Opalescent Swirl Shade, Thorny Feet, Pink, 4 In. 225.00
Fairy, Open Windows, Footed, Black Base, White 375.00
Fairy, Ormolu Jeweled, Footed, Ring Handle, Bezel Set Jewels, 18 In. 135.00
Fairy, Overshot Glass, Ruffled Rim Bowl, Applied Clear Scallop Shells 350.00
Fairy, Picket, Footed, Amber 225.00
Fairy, Puffy Diamonds, Marked Clarke Base, Pink, 4 In. 88.00
Fairy, Pyramid Pattern, Clarke, Verre Moire 250.00
Fairy, Red, White, Verre Moire 295.00
Fairy, Reticulated Ormolu Brass, 3 Feet, Bezel Jewels, 4 1/4 In. 160.00
Fairy, Ruffled, Burmese Base, Marked Cricklite 650.00
Fairy, Snowflake, Flat, Cranberry 425.00
Fairy, Snowflake, Flat, White 225.00
Fairy, Star Embossed Shade, Pink Interior, Cased In White, 6 1/4 In. 435.00
Fairy, Verre Moire, Fluted Base, Marked Clarke Insert Cup, 5 1/4 In. 450.00
Fairy, Verre Moire, Red & White 295.00
Fairy, Windows, Flat, Cranberry 425.00
Figural, Lady, Colonial, Flowers Extended From Body, 12 In. 28.00
Figural, Pan, Holding Bird, Signed T.Campajola, Art Glass Shade, Bronze 3000.00
Figural, Parrot, Porcelain Base, 12 1/2 In. 245.00
Finger, Brass, Nutmeg Pattern, Cobalt Blue Shade, Milk Glass 75.00
Finger, Brass, Nutmeg Pattern, Ruby Shade, Milk Glass 75.00
Finger, Bulbous Waist, Clinch Collar, Blue 85.00
Finger, Clear Handle, Cranberry, Large 85.00
Finger, Dated 1879 .... 32.00
Finger, Georgia Pattern, Sapphire Blue 135.00
Finger, Kerosene, Deep Blue, Crimped, Rib, Petal 165.00
Finger, Oil, Finger, Ruffled Bull's–Eye 15.00
Finger, Optic Spatter, Blue Finger Grip, Blue & White 300.00
Finger, Pink Overlay, Red Roses, Clear Handle, 6 1/2 In. 145.00
Finger, Rainbow Glass, Swirled, Reeded Handle 200.00
Finger, Shield Emblem Around Bowl, Applied Handle 125.00
Finger, Snowflake Pattern, Cranberry 425.00

Finger, Torpedo, Burner & Chimney 58.00
Floor, 3–Socket, Shade, Mask Base, Brass, 67 In., Pair 275.00
Floor, Baluster Standard, Shade, Brass, 50 In. 65.00
Floor, Louis XVI, Mahogany, Adjustable, 2–Light Oval Top, Tripod Base 260.00
Floor, Wicker ....160.00 To 475.00
Gas, Hanging, Store Type, Nickel Over Brass, White Shade 150.00
Gone With The Wind, Cosmos, Electrified 450.00
Gone With The Wind, Cranberry Coin Dot, Miniature 350.00
Gone With The Wind, Fleur–De–Lis, Raised Enameled Design, 25 In. 350.00
Gone With The Wind, Floral, Putti Design, C.1900, 23 1/2 In. 275.00
Gone With The Wind, Flowers, 16 In. 95.00
Gone With The Wind, Gas Lights, Blown Out Design, C.1904, 25 In. 800.00
Gone With The Wind, Hanging, Brass Font, Green Satin Ball Shade 795.00
Gone With The Wind, Oil, Blue Flowers 225.00
Gone With The Wind, Pastel Flowers On White Ground 175.00
Gone With The Wind, Pigeon Blood 750.00
Gone With The Wind, Red Satin Glass, Grape Pattern, 25 In. 750.00
Gone With The Wind, Red Satin Glass, Raised Flowers, Electric 395.00
Gone With The Wind, Roses, 23 In. 215.00
Gone With The Wind, Roses, Brass Font, Filigree Base, C.1895, 25 In. 125.00
Gone With The Wind, Ruby 750.00
Gone With The Wind, Satin Glass, Rose, Burner, Chimney, 9 In. 250.00
Gone With The Wind, White Satin, Peaches & Iris, 23 In. 610.00
Grease, 4 Wick, Weighted Tin Base, Box Copper Font, Japanned, 7 3/8 In. 105.00
Grease, Cast Iron, Double Wick, Scalloped Saucer Base, 6 In. 320.00
Grease, Pottery, Buff Clay, 4 3/8 In. 45.00
Hall, Hobnail, Pear Shape, Cranberry, Pair 425.00
Hall, Pull Down Canopy, Cranberry Opalescent 295.00
Hall, Pull Down, Oil Font, Burner & Chimney, Cranberry 195.00
Hand, Collidge Drape, Footed 95.00
Hand, Flat, Brass Collar, Applied Handle, Blue, 4 In. ....*Color* 300.00
Hand, Ripley, Clambroth Base, Handle, Light Blue Font, 5 1/4 In. 35.00
    LAMP, HANDEL, see Handel, Lamp
Hanging, Bull's–Eye Shade, Brass Eagles, Cranberry 1200.00
Hanging, Cast Iron, Star Font, Brass Chicken Finial, Trim, 30 In. 150.00
Hanging, Chrysanthemums & Leaves On Shade, Brass Frame, 14 In.Shade 365.00
Hanging, Cranberry Hobnail, Electrified 1000.00
Hanging, Petal, Green Slag Glass Shade, Victorian, 24 In. 350.00
Hanging, Pull Down, Opalescent Cranberry, Oil Burning 195.00
Hanging, Single Spout, Sheet Brass, Drip Pan, Hinged Lid, 7 1/2 In. 25.00
Hanging, Store Type, Gas, Nickel Over Brass, White Shade 150.00
Hanging, Store, Tin Shade, Milk Glass Insert 30.00
Hanging, Store, Waffle Pattern, Brass & Copper 180.00
Hanging, Tin, Open Font, 4 Curved Spouts & Bale, 9 3/4 In. 75.00
Jefferson, Oil, Reverse Painted Shade, C.1925 .... 1950.00
Jefferson, Reverse Painted Scene, Glass Base, Signed 1450.00
Jefferson, Reverse Painted, Domed Landscape Shade, C.1920, 16 In. 425.00
Jewelers, Sept.14th, 1880 Molded Into Glass, Metal Holder, Amber 65.00
Kerosene, Acme, Reflector, Edward Miller Co., Original Shade, Miniature 67.50
Kerosene, Acorn Font, Black Amethyst Base, Brass Connector, Sandwich 225.00
Kerosene, Baccarat Type, Prisms, Shade, Large 180.00
Kerosene, Beaded Heart, Green Stem, Clear Font, Frosted Hearts, 10 In. 225.00
Kerosene, Blue Alabaster, Handle, Ribbed, Star Flowers, Star Bottom 125.00
Kerosene, Bridges, Inverted Teardrop Band, Clear Font, Iron Base 85.00
Kerosene, Bright–As–Day, Fry Glass Shade 125.00
Kerosene, Bristol Ball Base, Farm Scene, Glass Font, Ribbed Brass Neck 55.00
Kerosene, Cosmos, Banquet 475.00
Kerosene, Cranberry Overlay, Clear Thumbprint, Signed Chimney 275.00
Kerosene, Electrified, Embossed Florals On Shade, Burmese, 15 In. 1250.00
Kerosene, Eyewinker, Clear, Stemmed, 8 In. 125.00
Kerosene, Green Paint, Tin, Large Reflector, Horizontal Font, 12 In. 30.00
Kerosene, Hamilton With Leaf, Sandwich, No.1, Flint, Late 1860s 80.00
Kerosene, Honeycomb Pattern, 8 In. 35.00
Kerosene, Lindsey No.62, Glass, 9 Shields On Font, 1873, 7 In. 110.00

Lamp, Oil, Egyptian Revival, Urn

Shape Globe, Tin, 31 1/2 In., Pr.

Parchment lamp shades can be cleaned with a cloth soaked in milk. Then wipe dry with a clean cloth.

To protect your investment in household furnishings, rewire any lamps in your home that are 15 or more years old. Cords crack and are a fire hazard.

Kerosene, McKee, Victor, Finger	45.00
Kerosene, Moon & Star Pattern	65.00
Kerosene, Petal, Eagle Burner, 9 1/2 In.	40.00
Kerosene, Pink Quilted Bottom, Thorn Pattern Shade, Miniature	98.00
Kerosene, Princess Feather	60.00
Kerosene, Ripley, 2 Handed, Marked	95.00
Kerosene, Stepped Base, Fluted Column, Petal Font, Clear Flint, 12 In.	75.00
Kerosene, Stoneware, Mottled Blue	85.00
Kerosene, Table, Clear Ribbed Stem, Emerald Green Font	37.50
Kerosene, Thumbprint, Beaded, Crystal, 8 1/2 In.	57.50
Kerosene, Vaseline Glass, Thousand Eye Base, Adams, 1860–71, 21 1/2 In.	1200.00
Kerosene, White, Porcelain, Pink Satin Glass Half Shade, 18 In.	575.00
Kerosene, Wreath & Torch, Embossed Riverside Clinch Collar, No.2	55.00
Lard, Maltby & Neal Pat.Tubular Burners, 5 1/2 In.	85.00
Library, Hanging, Prism Band, Bluebird Pattern, 14 In.	795.00
Library, Hanging, Prism Band, Cranberry Shade, Jewel Font, Frame, 14 In.	1150.00
Library, Hanging, Prism Band, Matching Shade, Bluebird Pattern	795.00
Library, Matching Font & Shade	350.00
Miner's, Candle, Sticking Tommy, Iron, Twisted Shaft, 12 In.	190.00
Miner's, Carbide, Justrite	45.00
Miner's, Emergency, Patent September 1840	65.00
Miner's, Mongahela City, Clip On	37.00
Miner's, Safety, Iron, Brass, Carrying Ring, F.W.D., 11 In.	72.00
Miner's, Sticking Tommy, Spring Held Candle Socket, Jab & Hook, Iron	150.00
Mission, Slag Shade, Oak Base, 14 X 18 X 6 In. ....*Color*	525.00
Nursing, Tin, Copper Double Top, Brass Hinges, Badger Burner, 9 In.	150.00
Oil, Amethyst, Gilt Design, Smither No.260, Miniature	225.00
Oil, Banquet, Opalescent Diagonal Blue Stripes, 12 3/4 In.	450.00
Oil, Bronze Openwork Base, Amber Font, Hand Blown Chimney, 2885, 21 In.	195.00
Oil, Bull's-Eye, Green	95.00
Oil, Cable With Ring, Hand	175.00
Oil, Chamber, Good Night, Chrome On Brass, 7 3/4 In.	50.00
Oil, Circle & Ellipse, 8 1/2 In.	175.00
Oil, Coolidge Drape	75.00
Oil, Corn, 7 1/2 In.	75.00
Oil, Currier & Ives	65.00
Oil, Double Semicircles, Milk Glass	115.00
Oil, Double, Diamond Cluster	115.00
Oil, Egyptian Revival, Urn Shape Globe, Tin, 31 1/2 In., Pr. ....*Illus*	1800.00
Oil, Empress, Glass, Green	135.00
Oil, Figural, French Maiden Base, Pressed Green Glass, Pair	225.00

Oil, Finger, Footed, Seneca Loop, Original Burner 135.00
Oil, Flattened Sawtooth, 18 In. 125.00
Oil, Flint Font On Marble Base, Hamilton 165.00
Oil, Foyer, Pull Down, Blue Swirl Shade 195.00
Oil, Glass, Sandwich Star Font, D.Symonds Pat.Mar.7, 1865, Flint, 11 In. 275.00
Oil, Greek Key, Blue Trim, Miniature 85.00
Oil, Greek Key, Matching Chimney, Miniature 70.00
Oil, Illuminator, Sandwich Glass 125.00
Oil, Lincoln Drape 75.00
Oil, Little Buttercup, Cobalt, Applied Handle, 3 1/4 X 2 1/2 In. 110.00
Oil, Lomax, Hand, Pat.Dec.10, 1870 ....55.00 To 90.00
Oil, Moon & Stars, Crystal & Amber, Heavy Mantel 250.00
Oil, Opalescent Base, Clear Font, Plume & Shield Design, 10 In. 65.00
Oil, Original Burner & Chimney, Sapphire Blue, Miniature 95.00
Oil, Parlor, Pull Down, Hand Painted Dome Shade, Prisms 300.00
Oil, Plume & Atwood Burner & Font, 1890s, Green & White 345.00
Oil, Prince Edward Font, Yellow Opaque, Sailboat Scene, Umbrella Shade 395.00
Oil, Princess Feather, 9 1/2 In. 75.00
Oil, Princess Feather, Large 100.00
Oil, Pull Down, Hall, Swirl Pattern, Cranberry 160.00
Oil, Ruby Hobnail, 11 1/2 In. 125.00
Oil, Torpedo, 7 1/2 In., Pair 125.00
Oil, Victorian, Brass, Gilt, Yellow Globe, Griffin Handles, 40 In. 250.00
Oil, Waffle, 11 1/2 In. 175.00
Oil, Wall, Crystal Etched Font & Globe, Cast Iron, 10 In. 68.00
Oil, Washington, Glass, Iron Base 125.00
Oil, White Opalescent Coin Spot Font, Black Base 55.00
Opalescent Vaseline Shade, Copper & Brass Base, 7 3/4 In. 195.00
Opalescent, Coin Spot, Clear, Blue, Handles, Marble Base, 9 In., Pair 50.00
    LAMP, PAIRPOINT, see Pairpoint, Lamp
Peg, Brass Fixtures, Blown Glass, Wooden Base, 6 1/2 In. 160.00
Peg, Cranberry Font, Brass Candlestick Base, 12 In. 150.00
Peg, Mushroom Shade, Brass Holder, Yellow Embossed, Pattern, 17 3/4 In. 595.00
Peg, Pink Overlay, Mother-Of-Pearl Satin Glass Shade 225.00
Peg, Violets On Porcelain Font, Prisms, Pair 175.00
Peg, Whale Oil Burner, Brass, Flared Base, 5 In. 95.00
Perfume, Figural, Owl, 1920, Glass Eyes, Ceramic, 10 In. 85.00
Perfume, Figural, Owl, Black Glass Base, 7 In. 145.00
Piano, Painted Globe, Brass Base, Marble Shelf, Adjustable 950.00
Pinup, Black Mammy 45.00
Pool Table, Caramel & Opalescent Panels, Oak Frame, 4 Light, 54 In. 550.00
Pull-Down, Prisms, Flowers, Oil 310.00
Safety, Wolf, Brass 110.00
Skater's, Perko, Wonder Junior 35.00
Skater's, Tin 38.00
Soapstone, Tan, Urn Shape, Foo Dog Handle, China, 10 In., Pair 100.00
Student, Brass, Generator, Adjustable, Emeralite Shade, 1880, 21 1/4 In. 250.00
Student, Brass, Harvard Style Base, Green & White Shade, 10 1/2 In. 300.00
Student, Roses Pattern, Amber, 19 In. 185.00
Student, Single Arm, C.1870, American 325.00
Student, Single Arm, Nickel Plated, Milk Glass Shade, Chimney, 22 In. 275.00
Table, Colt, Glass Globe, Wire Protector, Brass Top, Marked, 15 In. 150.00
Table, Mushroom, Burmese 600.00
Table, Pittsburgh, Painted Glass Dome Shade, Flared Base, 16 X 19 In. 250.00
Table, Reverse Painted Floral Shade, Red Flowers, Miller, Shade 12 In. 250.00
Table, Reverse Painted, Domed Base, Bronze Base, Classique, 23 In. 1650.00
Table, Reverse Painted, Domed Shade, Pittsburgh Lamp, 20 X 14 In. 800.00
Table, Slag Glass, Cylindrical Shade, Marked Salem Bros., 16 1/2 In. 175.00
Table, Slag Glass, Gilt Metal, C.1910, Gothic Panels, 23 1/2 In. 175.00
Table, Slag Glass, Iron, Oak Base, Lantern Shape, 21 X 12 In. 225.00
Table, Venetian Style Glass, Green, Rust & White Swirls, 37 In. 30.00
    LAMP, TIFFANY, see Tiffany, Lamp
Torchere, 3 Tiers, Putto Raising Light, Gilt Bronze, 5 Ft. 4 In. 9350.00
Torchere, 7-Light, Scrolled Arms, Gilt Wood & Bronze, 46 1/2 In., Pr. 2200.00

Torchere, Pricket, Flower Stem, Trifid Base, Iron, 5 Ft.7 In., Pr. 475.00
Trolley Car, Headlight, Golden Glow 225.00
Vapo–Cresolene, Dated 1898, Milk Glass Chimney, Vapo–Cresolene Bottle 55.00
Vapo–Cresolene, Original Box 40.00
Verdelite, Rolltop Desk, Embossed Base, 1917 .... 425.00
Wall, Bracket, Pattern Lamp, Beaded, Chimney, Iron 75.00
Wall, Leaded Glass, Star Form, 2 Wooden Putti Carvings 175.00
Whale Oil, Ball Fonts, Domed Saucer Base, Outfolded Rim, Pair 675.00
Whale Oil, Brass, Striped Fire Gilt, Burners, 4 1/2 In., Pair 370.00
Whale Oil, Bronze Standard, Marble Base, Sandwich, 12 In. 125.00
Whale Oil, Clear Glass, Faceted Cut Font, Burner, 1830, 9 1/2 In. 250.00
Whale Oil, Clear, Hex Paneled, Floral Cutting, No Burner, 9 1/2 In. 40.00
Whale Oil, Deep Blue, Pair 1000.00
Whale Oil, Hand, Brass, Saucer Base, Lemon Shape Fonts, 5 7/8 In., Pair 140.00
Whale Oil, Horn Of Plenty, Sandwich Glass ....195.00 To 295.00
Whale Oil, Light Blue, Pair 650.00
Whale Oil, Loop Pattern, Bell Shape, Pewter Top, Tube Burner, 4 1/2 In. 90.00
Whale Oil, Pear Shape Font, Sandwich, Mass., C.1835, 10 1/2 In., Pair 130.00
Whale Oil, Petticoat, Tin, Conical Font, Cast Ear Handle, 3 5/8 In. 82.50
Whale Oil, Pink, Dolphin Base 115.00
Whale Oil, Punty & Loop 85.00

A lantern is a special type of lighting device. It has a light source,
usually a candle, totally hidden inside the walls of the lantern. Light
is seen through holes or glass sections.

LANTERN, Barn, Brown & Camp Hardware Co., Des Moines 17.50
Barn, Dietz No.30 .... 75.00
Barn, Little Wizard, Blackened Tin 15.00
Buggy, International Harvester, Electrified 45.00
Candle, Folding, Embossed Stonebridge, Tin, Mica Shade, Dated 1908 .... 50.00
Candle, Pierced Tin & Glass, Ring Handle 95.00
Candle, Pierced Tin, Half Round, Glass Front, 18th Century, 18 In. 395.00
Candle, Pine, Hinged Door, 4 Sides Glass, Tin Vent, 9 X 9 X 14 In. 195.00
Carved Bone, Pedestal, 3 Monkeys, Birds, Roof, Signed, 6 1/2 In. 350.00
Coach, Kerosene Burner, Curved Beveled Glass, Convex Lens, 12 In. 52.00
Coach, Kerosene Burner, Red Jewel Lens, Brass, 12 1/4 In. 40.00
Copper, Side Mount, Green Patina, 21 In. 55.00
Dietz No.30 .... 75.00
Dietz, Acme Inspector 55.00
Dietz, Jr., Buggy, Bull's–Eye 60.00
Dietz, Night Watch 18.00
Dietz, No.60, Kerosene, Tin, Beacon Light, New York, Painted, 21 In. 185.00
Dietz, No.8, Kerosene 20.00
Dietz, Wagon, Red Lens 35.00
Kenlite, Kerosene, Red Metal, 3 Red Lenses, 5 X 5 X 15 In. 25.00
Kerosene, Crimped Top, Wire Bail, Inside Chimney, 12 In. 195.00
Magic, Tin, Nickle Plated Trim, Black Paint, Case, Slides, 10 3/4 In. 45.00
Norleigh Diamond, 14 In. 12.50
Pebble Glass On 4 Sides, Metal, Ring, 16 X 9 In. 132.00
Porcelain, Pierced, Electric, Baluster, Floral, China, 17 1/2 In., Pr. 250.00
Shapleigh Hardware 25.00
Street, Ham, No.9 .... 195.00
Tin, Pierced, Conical Top, Cylindrical, Hinged Door, Ring, 28 In. 100.00
Wall, Metal & Slag Glass, 4 Arms Hold Shade, 12 3/4 X 5 3/4 In. 242.00

Leather is tanned animal hide and it has been used to make
decorative and useful objects for centuries. Leather objects must be
carefully preserved with proper humidity and oiling or the leather will
deteriorate and crack. This damage cannot be repaired.

LEATHER, Bag, Church Collection, Long Handle, Bell, 63 In. 70.00
Bag, Marble, Full, 7 X 5 In. 55.00
Bank Bag, Canvas, W.F.& Co. 45.00
Blackjack 32.00
Case, Calling Card, Ostrich Skin 8.00

Cigarette Case, Fatima, Brown, Cross Country Club, 19 In. 15.00
Figurine, Elephant, Rearing, Trunk Up, 20 X 21 In. 70.00
Holster, For 1860 Colt, Allover Design, C.1860 .... 125.00
Holster, For 5 1/2 In.Barrel, Hand Tooled, Cowboy On Horse 50.00
Holster, Gun, 1918 .... 48.00
Holster, Heiser 49.50
Holster, Quick Draw, California Style, For S.A.A., Border Design 60.00
Horse Collar, Hames 50.00
Model, Antelope, Hide, Glass Eyes, Painted, Horns, Hoofs, 12 1/2 In. 35.00
Pouch, Hunting, Hide Flap, 7 X 8 In. 150.00
Pouch, Powder & Shot, 19 In. 65.00
Saddle Bags, Cavalry 85.00
Saddle, Circus Dog, Western Style 59.50
Saddle, Side, Lady's, White, Red Stitching, Double Horn 295.00
Saddle, Trick Riding, Pat.March 27, 1883 .... 235.00
Saddle, Western, Cut Design 125.00
Strap, Harness, Parade, Multiple White Graduated Hoops, Pair 75.00
Strop, Retractable, Horsehide, Silver Plate Cylinder, C.1890 .... 65.00
Vest, Latigo Stich, Cowboy & Buffalo Picture, Size 36–38 .... 90.00

LEEDS POTTERY. *Leeds pottery was made at Leeds, Yorkshire, England, from 1774 to 1878. Most Leeds ware was not marked. Early Leeds pieces had distinctive twisted handles with a greenish glaze on part of the creamy ware. Later ware often had blue borders on the creamy pottery.*

LEEDS, Bowl, Gaudy Design, Blue & Ocher, 12 3/8 X 3 3/4 In. 275.00
Carpet Ball, Blue & White Concentric Circles 140.00
Coffeepot, Domed Lid, Gaudy Blue & White, 10 1/4 In. 150.00
Creamer, Gaudy Cobalt Leaves, Cream, Applied Handle, C.1810, 4 In. 40.00
Cup & Saucer, Handleless, King's Rose Pattern, Scalloped 325.00
Cup & Saucer, Handleless, Mustard Yellow Strawberries 210.00
Cup & Saucer, Handless, Gaudy Floral Design 45.00
Cup Plate, Blue & White Floral, Gaudy, 3 3/4 In. 235.00
Pepper Pot, Blue Feather Trim, Creamware, C.1780 .... 145.00
Plate, 4–Color Floral Design, Green Feather Edge, 9 3/8 In. 45.00
Plate, Black Transfer, House, Lady & Sheep, Octagonal, 6 1/2 In. 55.00
Plate, Blue Feather Edge, Strawberry Design, 7 1/2 In. 300.00
Plate, Blue, Blue Border, 5 1/2 In. 105.00
Plate, Floral Design, Blue Trim, Scalloped, 9 1/2 In., Set Of 6 .... 275.00
Plate, Green, Border, Flower Center, 6 1/2 In. 280.00
Plate, Peafowl, Green Feather Edge, 8 In.Diam. ....*Illus* 125.00
Plate, Toddy, Green Feather Rim, 5–Color Peafowl, 5 1/2 In. 265.00
Plate, Toddy, Tulip, Orange Berries, Blue Border, 5 1/4 In. 190.00

Leeds, Plate, Peafowl,
Green Feather Edge, 8 In.Diam.

Lindbergh, Coin–Operated
Machine, Lindy Striker

Platter, Floral, Gaudy Blue & White, Oval, 16 In.	250.00
Platter, Light Blue, 6 In.	15.00
Platter, Rose Center, Orange & Green Leaf Border, Oblong, 6 In.	400.00
Sugar & Creamer, Covered, Child's, Floral Band, Pearlware	285.00
Sugar, Applied Floral Finial, 3 Colors, 5 In.	25.00
Teapot, Floral Design, Multicolor, 12 In.	275.00
Teapot, Gaudy Floral, Blue, Yellow Underglaze, 7 1/4 In.	85.00
Teapot, Yellow, Blue, Orange, & Brown, 12 In.	275.00
Urn, Creamware, Pistol Handle, Yellow, Red, Blue, Marbelized Base	90.00

The Geo. Zoltan Lefton Company has imported porcelains to be sold in America since 1940. The pieces are often marked with the Lefton name. The firm is still in business. The company mark has changed through the years and objects can be dated accurately by the shape of the mark.

LEFTON, Chocolate Set, Red Roses, Tan Ground, 3 Piece	95.00
Cup & Saucer, Floral, Crown Mark	18.00
Figurine, Bobwhite, Hand Painted, Marked KW 2002, 5 1/2 In., Pair	28.00
Figurine, Hen & Rooster, Black & White, Glazed, 9 In.	16.00
Figurine, Mother Hubbard	20.00
Figurine, Old King Cole	20.00
Figurine, Old Man, Little Boy, Butterfly On Man's Head, Bisque, 8 In.	22.00
Luncheon Set, Allover Roses, 3–Tier Serving Tray, 17 Piece	95.00
Pitcher, Lincoln, 5 In. ....*Color*	25.00
Pitcher, Washington, 4 In.	35.00
Salt & Pepper, Red Roses, Tan Ground	20.00
Tea Set, Sprays Of Wheat, 8 Piece	50.00

Legras was founded in 1864 by Auguste Legras at St. Denis, France. It is best known for cameo glass and enamel–decorated glass with Art Nouveau designs. Legras merged with Pantin in 1920 and became the Verreries et Cristalleries de St. Denis et de Pantin Reunies.

LEGRAS, Rose Bowl, Cameo, Fruit Design, Opaline, Marked, C.1900, 3 7/8 In.	215.00
Vase, Birds In Flight, Red, Dark Brown, Signed	625.00
Vase, Cameo, Russet Grapevine, Peach Ground, Marked, 16 In.	500.00
Vase, Green & Blue Overlay House & Trees, Signed, 6 In.	500.00
Vase, Lake Scene, Forest, Orange, Green, & Brown, Signed, 14 In.	750.00
Vase, Lavender Floral, Enameled, 5 In.	275.00
Vase, Pink–Orange, Blue, Hydrangeas, Signed, 9 In.	850.00
Vase, Seaweed, Light Brown To Tan, 14 In.	1250.00
Vase, Trumpet, Bulbous Base, Fruit Laden Cherry Boughs, 10 7/8 In.	175.00

Walter Scott Lenox and Jonathan Cox founded the Ceramic Art Company in Trenton, New Jersey, in 1889. In 1906, Lenox left and started his own company. The company makes a porcelain that is similar to Irish Belleek. The marks used by the firm have changed through the years and collectors prefer the earlier examples.

LENOX, see also Ceramic Art Co.

LENOX, Ashtray, Harvest	20.00
Ashtray, Shenango II	22.00
Ashtray, Shriner	18.00
Bookends, Art Deco Woman's Head, Bisque	125.00
Bottle, Perfume, Cream Finial, Blue Cover, 1 Atomizer, DeVilbiss, Pair	145.00
Bouillon Cup, Underplate, Ming	16.00
Bowl, Cabbage Leaf, Green Mark, 7 1/2 X 4 1/2 In.	135.00
Bowl, Salad, Ivory, Crimped, Sculptured Sides, Green Mark, 10 X 4 In.	125.00
Bowl, Shell Shape, Scalloped Edge, Green Wreath Mark, Pink, 12 In.	45.00
Box, Cigarette, White Relief Leaves, Tied With Tassel, 3 1/2 X 5 In.	45.00
Box, Cover, Soft Green, White Raised Design, Green Mark, 3 X 5 In.	45.00
Box, Dresser, Hattie Carnegie	80.00
Bread & Butter, Washington Wakefield	8.00
Bust, Art Deco, 9 In.	175.00
Butter, Covered, Ming	175.00
Cake Set, Mimosa Pattern, 10 1/2 In.	145.00

Candlestick, Dolphin, 10 In., Pair	100.00
Candy Dish, Shell Shape, Pink	28.00
Cider Set, Grapes, 5 Piece	275.00
Compote, Silver Overlay, 11 In.	75.00
Creamer, Aurora	17.50
Creamer, Covered, Green Wreath	50.00
Cup & Saucer, Coral, Gold, S.A.Gamp	65.00
Cup, Cretan	8.50
Cup, Demitasse, Sterling Holder	24.00
Cup, Sterling Silver Holder, Gold Band, Ivory, Demitasse, Set Of 6	225.00
Dish, Pin, Gold & Pastel Border, Pink Roses, Purple Mark, 6 In.	125.00
Dish, Rose Design, Leaf Shape, Gold Trim, 5 1/2 X 9 1/4 In.	35.00
Dish, Scalloped Rim, Shallow, 7 In.	16.00
Eggcup, Double, Ming Pattern	25.00
Figurine, Angel	145.00
Figurine, Bird In Tree	85.00
Figurine, Bird, Coral, Green Wreath	95.00
Figurine, Bulldog	350.00
Figurine, Colonial Lady	175.00
Figurine, Head, Art Deco, Cream Glaze, 8 1/2 In., Pair	400.00
Figurine, Penguin	110.00
Figurine, Robin, Pink, 3 1/2 In.	45.00
Figurine, Swan, 5 In.	28.00
Honey Pot, Gold Bee	15.00
Honey Pot, Underplate, Cover, Bee	50.00
Jar, Honey, Beehive, Silver Bees	135.00
Jar, Perfume, Pallet Mark	225.00
Lamp, Coral Pedestal, Urn Shape, Cream, Floral, Pair	300.00
Lamp, White Bisque, Swan Figural, Marked, 10 In.	350.00
Mug, 3 Handles, Crockery Board Of Trade, Gold Floral, Blue Dot	185.00
Mug, Friendship, 3 Handles, Blue Dot Florals, 1896 Mark	135.00
Pitcher, Backward C Handle, Cream, 5 In.	45.00
Pitcher, Colonial, Blue, White Handle, Green Wreath, 5 In.	25.00
Pitcher, Pink, White Handle, Blue Mark, 5 1/2 In.	50.00
Pitcher, Romeo & Juliet, Ispansky, 10 In.	125.00
Pitcher, White Handle, Pink, Blue Mark, 5 1/2 In.	50.00
Plate, Christmas, 1976, Douglas Fir, Box	32.00
Plate, Coronado, C.1922, Black Mark, 10 1/4 In., 12 Piece	220.00
Plate, Dinner, Kingsley	30.00
Plate, Dinner, Mystic, Black Mark, Set Of 8	240.00
Plate, Dinner, Platina, Maroon	35.00
Plate, Dinner, Rhodora	22.00
Plate, Dinner, U.S.Seal, Gilt & Cream, 41 Piece	850.00
Plate, Fish, Gold Etched Border, Signed Morley	45.00
Plate, Fruit, Still Life Of Fruit, Pink Ground, Signed Morley	85.00
Plate, Gold Band, 7 1/4 In., Set Of 6	57.00
Plate, Indian Tree Pattern, 9 In., Set Of 10	185.00
Plate, Ornate Silver Overlay, Handles, Square, 8 1/2 In.	98.00
Plate, Serving, Rhodora Pattern	20.00
Plate, Transfer Of Aga Khan, Horse, 10 In.	45.00
Plate, Virginian, 8 In.	50.00
Salt, Ruffled, Palette Mark	20.00
Salt, Swan, Green Mark	18.00
Sherbet, Pedestal, Gold Flowers	135.00
Soup, Bouillon, Renaissance Pattern, Underliner	22.00
Stein, Green Monk, Sterling Silver Top Rim, 1/2 Liter	104.00
Strainer, Tea, Lavender Mark	200.00
Sugar, Open, Green Wreath	30.00
Swan, 11 In.	150.00
Swan, Pink, Gold, 4 1/2 In.	28.00
Tea Set, Art Nouveau, Sterling Silver Overlay, 13 Piece	700.00
Tea Set, Mt.Vernon, 3 Piece	275.00
Teapot, Green Mark, Individual, 5 1/2 In.	32.00
Teapot, Ming	150.00

Teapot, Mistress Mary, 1/2 Handle 375.00
Tobacco Jar, No.328, Owl & Pinecone Design, 7 1/2 In. 150.00
Toby Jug, William Penn, Indian Head Handle, Marked, 7 In. 175.00
Vase, Birds On Branches, Artist Signed, Palette Mark, 15 1/2 In. 300.00
Vase, Butterscotch Ground, White & Red Roses, Handles, 15 In. 450.00
Vase, Cobalt, 10 In. 85.00
Vase, Coral Enamel, 8 In. 125.00
Vase, Cornucopia, Gold Design, Coral, 8 1/4 In., Pair 215.00
Vase, Cornucupia, White, Green Mark, 4 1/2 In. 34.00
Vase, Cream & Coral, Swan Handle, 10 In. 65.00
Vase, Pink Base, Cream Top, Cone Shape, Flowers, Black Mark, 10 In. ... 75.00
Vase, Roses In White & Red, Gold Handle, Butterscotch Ground, 15 In. .. 450.00
Wine, Crystal, Stemmed, Platinum Rim, 3 Sizes, 18 Piece 150.00

Letter openers have been used since the eighteenth century. Ivory and silver were favored by the well-to-do. In the late nineteenth century, the letter opener was popular as an advertising giveaway and many were made of metal or celluloid. Brass openers with figural handles were also popular.

LETTER OPENER, Alligator, Celluloid 8.00
Ball Perfect Mason, Handle Shape Of Ball Jar, Brass 125.00
Beebe Check Protector Co., Minn., Ruler Back, Celluloid 20.00
Black Figure On End, Celluloid 22.00
Borden's Prescription Products 15.00
Budweiser, Anheuser-Busch Eagle End, Brass 45.00
Cloisonne, Bronze Blade 34.00
Detroit Stove Works 24.00
Dip Pen, Mother-Of-Pearl, Gold Nib 10.00
Evans, Patent Attorneys, Brass 4.00
Figural, Embalming Fluid, Metal Arts, Rochester 30.00
Figural, Yale Lock 65.00
Golden Gate International Exposition, 1939 .... 8.50
Jackknife, Viking Forge Co., Brooklyn 24.00
Lion Bonding & Surety, Omaha 12.00
Mantel, Welsback 50.00
Mother-Of-Pearl & Sterling Silver 27.50
Nail File, Lilly Pharmaceuticals & Biologicals 24.00
Oakland Car 30.00
Phillips Milk Of Magnesia, Magnifying Glass Top, Metal 20.00
Pipestone 15.00
Stag Handle, Curved 9.00
Sword Shape, Cast Iron 18.00
Turkey Foot Shaped Handle, Blade Advertising, Bronze 32.50

Libbey

The Libbey Glass Company has made glass of many types since 1892. Libbey made cut glass and tablewares that are collected today. The stemwares of the 1930s and 1940s are once again in style. The Toledo, Ohio, firm was purchased by Owens-Illinois in 1935 and is still working under the name "Libbey" as a division of that company.

LIBBEY, see also Amberina; Cut Glass; Maize
LIBBEY, Basket, Amber Handle, Amberina, Signed, 7 1/4 In. 1500.00
Bowl, Brilliant Cut, Signed, 9 3/4 X 2 1/4 In. 155.00
Bowl, Copper Wheel Engraved Floral Border, Signed, 8 1/2 In. 235.00
Bowl, Cut Glass, Signed, 8 In. 55.00
Bowl, Flowers & Bull's-Eye, Signed, 9 In. 150.00
Bowl, Kimberly Pattern, Brilliant, 10 X 4 In. 270.00
Celery, Vintage, Polished & Matte Intaglio, Marked, 11 1/2 In. 175.00
Champagne, Squirrel Stem, Opalescent, Signed 70.00
Cocktail, Crow Stem 15.00
Cocktail, Eagle Stem 15.00
Cocktail, Kangaroo Pattern, Opalescent Stem 110.00
Cordial, Harvard Pattern, Fluted Stem, Faceted Knob, Signed, Set Of 6 .. 385.00
Cruet, Panel Cut, Latin Engraving, Toledo Church, Marked 58.00
Decanter, Copper Wheel Engraved, Teardrop Stopper 215.00

Decanter, Sawtooth Rim, Panels, Prisms, C.1910, Signed, 9 1/2 In. 700.00
Decanter, Teardrop Stopper, Intaglio Cut 215.00
Dish, Ruffled, Holly Engraving, Signed, 7 In. 95.00
Finger Bowl, Amberina, 1917, 2 1/2 In. 550.00
Goblet, Cat Stem 160.00
Goblet, Cut Glass, Teardrop Stem, Blown Pontil, Marked, Set Of 8 .... 500.00
Goblet, Silver Foliage 1.25
Ice Tub, Golden Foliage 8.00
Muffineer, Maize, Yellow Leaves, 6 In. 160.00
Plate, Santa Maria Ship, 1893 World's Fair, Mt.Washington, 7 3/4 In. 385.00
Salt, Footed, Signed 65.00
Sherbet, Sharp Cut, Floral, Ribbed Bowl, Stemmed, 4 X 3 1/2 In. 5.00
Sugar & Creamer, Scalloped Rims, Concave Sides, Signed 60.00
Tumble–Up, Clear, Signed 38.00
Tumbler, Cut Glass, Brilliant, Heavy, Marked, Set Of 5 .... 300.00
Tumbler, Maize, Green & Brown Leaves 120.00
Tumbler, Star & Feather Pattern, Signed 30.00
Vase, Amberina, Applied Amber Handles, C.1917, 9 1/2 In. 445.00
Vase, Amberina, C.1917, 11 In. 450.00
Vase, Amberina, Fuchsia Top, 2 Handles, Marked, 1917, 9 1/2 In. 445.00
Vase, Crystal, Dark Green Applied Prunts, Footed, Signed, 3 In. 110.00
Vase, Intaglio, Cut, Footed, 12 In. 175.00
Vase, Ruby To Amberina, Floriform, Footed, Marked, 1917, 11 1/4 In. 495.00
Vase, Trumpet, Iris & Leaves, Intaglio, Marked, 12 In. 250.00
Water Set, Cut Glass, Pitcher, 5 Tumblers, Signed 700.00
Water Set, Signed, 7 Piece 500.00
Water Set, Thistle Pattern, Pitcher & 6 Tumblers 500.00
Wine, Cut Glass, Acid Etched, Signed, 8 In. 100.00
Wine, Old Crow 50.00
Wine, Rawleigh 4.00

*Cigarettes became popular in the late nineteenth century and with the
cigarette came matches and cigarette lighters. All types of lighters are
collected, from solid gold to the first of the recent disposable lighters.
Most examples found were made after 1940.*

LIGHTER, Cigar, Greek Woman, Running, Original Paint 650.00
Cigar, Midland, Jump Spark 300.00
Cigar, Salty Sailor, Eyes Light Up Blue, Pipe Has Element 295.00
Cigarette, Aladdin Lamp Type, Urn Shape, Occupied Japan 9.00
Cigarette, Elgin, Case, Boxed 35.00
Cigarette, Figural, Pair Of Boots, Occupied Japan 35.00
Cigarette, Figural, Pistol, Occupied Japan 15.00
Cigarette, Figural, Winston Churchill Bulldog, Derby, Cigar 125.00
Cigarette, Foxhole, Instructions, Original Box, World War II 15.00
Cigarette, Los Angeles Angels, 1 Side Gene Autry, A's Symbol Other 17.00
Cigarette, Oriental Scene, Sterling Silver 15.00
Cigarette, Pistol, Original Case, Occupied Japan .... '18.00
Cigarette, Pocket, Music Box, Kitty Clover Potato Chips 24.00
Cigarette, Pocket, Tape Measure At Side 20.00
Cigarette, Revolver Shape, Brass, Dated 1914 .... 30.00
Cigarette, See Through Base, Contains Dice, Shake & Play 20.00
Cigarette, Statue Of Liberty 15.00
Cigarette, Table, Aladdin, Victorian Silver 40.00
Cigarette, Table, Dunhill, Silent Flame, Nude On Top 15.00
Cigarette, Table, Horse Hoof, Silver Plated Mounts, 1898 .... 65.00
Cigarette, Table, Ronson, Chrome & Bakelite 550.00
Cigarette, War Souvenir, Okinawa, Case 25.00
Cigarette, World War I, Trench, German 30.00
Cigarette, World War II, Chrome 10.00
Cigarette, Zenith, Jesters, Art Deco, Enameled, Chrome 40.00
Cigarette, Zippo, Brass Coca–Cola Bottle On Front 20.00

Lightning rods were placed on barns and wooden houses to protect the building from fire. The lightning rods are now favored by the folk art collectors, although most were commercially made. The glass balls added to the rods were for decorative purposes only. The earliest glass balls for lightning rods date from the 1840s. Today most lightning rods use plastic instead of glass balls.

LIGHTNING ROD, Ball, 10 Sided, Blue Milk Glass	30.00
Ball, Electra, 2 Clear Balls, Opaque Blue	35.00
Ball, Hawkeye Embossed, Amber	25.00

Limoges porcelain has been made in Limoges, France, since the mid-nineteenth century. Fine porcelains were made by many factories including Haviland, Ahrenfeldt, Guerin, Pouyat, Elite, and others. Modern porcelains are being made at Limoges and the word "Limoges" as part of the mark is not an indication of age. Haviland is listed as a separate category in this book.

LIMOGES, Asparagus Set, Mauve Tones, Marked	450.00
Basket, Sugar, Raised Scrolls, Gold, Purple Flowers, Marked	125.00
Basket, White Flowers, Handles, Peach, 6 X 4 In.	42.00
Bonbon, Pierced Handle, Heavenly Cherubs	27.00
Bowl, Coronet, Gold, Bright Anemones	55.00
Bowl, Portrait, 10 1/2 In.	42.00
Cake Plate, Pink Roses, Hand Painted, Gold Handles, 11 In.	35.00
Cake Plate, Pink Roses, Pierced Gold Handles, 10 In.	30.00
Charger, Gold Medallion Center, Gold Rim, 11 1/4 X 3 1/4 In.	90.00
Charger, Gold Rococo Edge, Full Nude Portrait, 12 1/2 In.	155.00
Charger, Grapes, Vines, Scalloped Rim, Marked, 12 1/2 In.	95.00
Charger, Hand Painted Maidens, Signed Bretan	415.00
Chocolate Pot, Peach Blossoms, Branches, Gold Trim	125.00
Chocolate Pot, Roses In Gold, 11 1/4 In.	250.00
Chocolate Set, Cherries, Floral Design, 19 Piece	295.00
Chocolate Set, Scalloped Gold Rim, Poppies, Dated 1906, 14 Piece	445.00
Chop Plate, Green Ground, Pink & Peach Roses, Gold Edge, Marked	110.00
Chop Plate, Raised Gold Border Design, Coronet, 12 In.	45.00
Cider Set, Crab Apples, Gold, Pitcher, Mugs, Artist Signed, 1920	225.00
Cider Set, Hand Painted Cherries, Green, 5 Piece	235.00
Compote, Golden Bird	48.00
Cracker Jar, Cream To Yellow Brown, Blue, Gilt Floral Panel, 7 In.	85.00
Cracker Jar, Pastel Floral, Gold, China	72.50
Cracker Jar, Pink & White Florals, Off White Ground, Handle, Marked	195.00
Cracker Jar, Underplate, Hand Painted, Signed, 8 In.	195.00
Creamer, Purple Flowers, Gold Trim, 3 1/4 In.	35.00
Cup & Saucer, Autumn Leaf	15.00
Cup & Saucer, Bouillon, Gold Trim, White	9.00
Cup & Saucer, Elite Pattern, Pink Roses	16.00
Cup & Saucer, Game Birds In Flight	14.00
Cup & Saucer, Gold Design, Demitasse	22.00
Dinner Set, Cobalt & Blue, C.1890, Service For 12, Complete	2800.00
Dinner Set, Yellow Greek Key Border, Gilt Trim, Haviland, 160 Piece	450.00
Dish, 3–Section, Irregular Gold Edge, Gold Handle, White, 12 In.	125.00
Dish, Cookie Corner, Bluebirds In Pond, Square, 7 In.	65.00
Dish, Gold Stand–Up Handles, Scalloped, Oval, 10 1/2 In.	40.00
Dish, Vegetable, Removable Drain Tray, Gold Leaf Handle, 12 1/2 In.	85.00
Dresser Tray, Hand Painted, Signed Sciota 1916, 10 3/4 X 8 In.	35.00
Dresser Tray, Roses, Gold, Blakemen & Henderson, 13 1/4 X 9 In.	65.00
Ewer, Hand Painted Violets, Gold Trim, 6 In.	65.00
Game Set, Gold Border, Platter, 16 X 14 In., 4 Plates, 10 In.	259.00
Game Set, Green, Gold Design, 16 In.Platter, 4 Plates, 10 In.	235.00
Hair Receiver, Flowers & Butterflies, Off–White Ground, Gold Trim	65.00
Hair Receiver, Hatpin Holder, Powder Jar, Hand Painted, Marked	65.00
Hair Receiver, Violet, Blue	45.00
Holder, Condensed Milk Can, 3 Piece	45.00
Humidor, Indians Smoking Peace Pipe, Gold, Orange	275.00 To 450.00

Ice Cream Set, Butterflies & Flowers, Gold Trim, Service For 12	450.00
Ice Cream Set, Thistle Design, Gold, 13 Piece	275.00
Loving Cup, Hand Painted, Cupids, 50th Anniversary, 1853–1903, 6 In.	72.00
Match Holder, Attached Saucer, Floral Design	48.00
Mug, Acorns, Fall Colors, 5 1/2 In.	45.00
Mug, Floral, Gooseberries Cascading Down Sides, Tankard, 4 1/2 In.	70.00
Mug, Fruit, Rust With Gold Band, G.Moser, 5 1/2 In.	35.00
Mug, Indian Warrior Bust, Hand Painted	125.00
Mug, Shaving, Gold Lettering	20.00
Mug, Strawberry Design, Gold Handle, 3 3/4 In.	65.00
Oyster Plate, Figural, Marine, Hand Painted, 9 In.	45.00
Oyster Plate, Gold Design, Weimar, Germany, 8 1/4 In., Set Of 6	95.00
Oyster Plate, Gold Trim, 5 Sections & Center Well, Set Of 7	325.00
Pin Tray, Violets	25.00
Pitcher, Chestnuts & Leaves, Beige Ground, Artist Signed, 11 In.	145.00
Pitcher, Cider, Apples & Leaves, Gold Handle	155.00
Pitcher, Cider, Hand Painted Pastel Asters	95.00
Pitcher, Tankard, Floral, Signed Knowles 1901	125.00
Pitcher, Walter Lily Design, Gold Trim, Beaded Handle, 5 In.	165.00
Plaque, Allegorical, Death Of Devil, Knight On White Horse, 7 In.	375.00
Plaque, Fish, Gold Rococo Rim, 2 Large Fish, Marked, 13 In.	115.00
Plaque, Fish, Rococo Border, Marked, 11 3/4 In.	110.00
Plaque, Flying Bird, Gold Edge, Blakemen & Henderson, 13 In.	145.00
Plaque, Full Portrait Of Ballerina, Hand Painted, Gold Leaf Frame	800.00
Plaque, Game, 12 In.	167.00
Plaque, Game, Gold Rococo Border, Signed, 13 1/2 In. ....239.00 To	249.00
Plaque, Napoleon Battle Scene, Gold Border, 10 1/2 X 11 In.	375.00
Plaque, Portrait, Artist Signed, 13 In.	185.00
Plate, 2 Hummingbirds, Rococo Gold Edge, Signed, 12 In.	140.00
Plate, 3 Clusters Currants, Russet, Artist Signed	20.00
Plate, Christmas, 1970, Partridge	90.00
Plate, Country Scene, Blue, Artist G.Trave, Pierced, 11 1/2 In., Pair	350.00
Plate, Deer & Doe, Gold Scalloped Rim, Signed, 10 In.	90.00
Plate, Duck, Rococo Gold, Signed Coronet, 9 3/4 In.	65.00
Plate, Fish, Cobalt, Gold Scalloped Border, 10 In.	80.00
Plate, Fish, Rococo Gilt Rim, Water Lilies, Grasses, 2 Fish, 9 In.	70.00
Plate, Fish, Signed Henry, 9 In.	75.00
Plate, Floral Wreath, Cobalt & Gilt Border, Scalloped, Set Of 12	450.00
Plate, Floral, Gilded, 10 In.	25.00
Plate, Fruit, Green Ground, Artist Barbet, 10 1/4 In.	145.00
Plate, Game, Bird, Gold Trim, Coronet, Signed L.Cudert, 10 In.	95.00
Plate, Game, Bird, Hand Painted, Scalloped, Marked, 10 1/4 In.	110.00
Plate, Game, Cobalt Gilt Border, Marked, 9 1/2 In., 22 Piece	825.00
Plate, Game, Hanging, Earth Tones, Signed J.Mongars, 9 1/2 In., Pair	150.00
Plate, Game, Pheasant, Artist F.Dartigeas, 11 1/2 In.	225.00
Plate, Game, Transfer Print, Scottish Grouse, Handle, 13 In.	235.00
Plate, Gold & White Oyster, 8 1/4 In.	60.00
Plate, Grapes, Peach, Gold Edge, Artist Signed, 12 1/2 In.	225.00
Plate, Green Ground, Lilies, Gold Edge, Coronet, 8 In.	35.00
Plate, Green, Holly Berries, Leaves, White Center, Marked, Set Of 6	150.00
Plate, Hanging, Floral, Yellow, Tan, Artist Golse, 11 5/8 In., Pair	265.00
Plate, Hanging, Gold Edge, Roses & Leaves, Marked, 13 1/2 In.	245.00
Plate, Hanging, Hand Painted Roses, Rococo Edge, Marked, 13 1/2 In.	245.00
Plate, Hanging, Winter & Summer Scenes, Scalloped, 14 1/2 In., Pair	495.00
Plate, Hummingbird, Rococo Gold Edge, Marked, 12 In.	140.00
Plate, Lady & Unicorn, 1977	85.00
Plate, Man & Woman Scene, Rococo Scalloped, 13 3/4 In., Pair	550.00
Plate, Pair Of Fowl, Gold Border, Signed J.Mongahs, 10 In.	75.00
Plate, Peaches, Hand Painted, Scalloped, 9 1/2 In.	28.00
Plate, Portrait, Bearded Man, Signed, 11 In.	30.00
Plate, Portrait, Cavalier, Gold Rim, Artist Signed, 9 3/4 In.	45.00
Plate, Roses In Basket Pattern, Hand Painted, 10 In.	32.00
Plate, Scalloped, Cottage Scene, 1 Winter, 1 Summer, 14 1/8 In., Pair	450.00
Plate, Shaggy Mums, Raised Gold, Leaves Around Edge, 8 1/2 In.	45.00

Plate, Women Of The Century, D'Arceau, Guneau, Box, Set Of 12	185.00
Plate, Yellow Poppies, Marked, 8 1/4 In.	35.00
Platter & 4 Plates, Undersea Design, Shells, Haviland	250.00
Platter, Fish, Hand Painted Fish & Lily Pads, LePacot, 23 1/2 In.	125.00
Platter, Red, Blue, Green & Yellow Rim, Guerin, C.1891, 14 X 17 In.	100.00
Platter, Touraine Pattern, 18 In.	35.00
Powder Box, Allover Clusters Pink Roses, 8 In.	95.00
Powder Box, Cover, Violets, Blue	50.00
Powder Box, Hand Painted Apple Blossoms, Alice Blue	45.00
Punch Bowl, Stand, Roses Inside & Out, Scalloped	675.00
Ramekin, Pink Rose Garland	30.00
Relish, 3–Section, Handle, Cerise Edge, Applied Gold Flowers, 12 In.	135.00
Ring Tree, Hand Shape, Colored Blossoms, Hand Painted	40.00
Rose Bowl, Roses, Pink Ground, 3 Gold Feet, Ruffled, 5 3/4 In.	55.00
Salt & Pepper, Pink Roses	22.50
Salt, Pedestal, Cupid Standard, Enameled, Griffin Handles, 5 X 6 In.	400.00
Shaving Mug, BPOE, Elk's Head, Owner's Name	75.00
Sugar & Creamer, Stacking, Dickens Scene, Sandland Ware	25.00
Sugar & Creamer, Sugar Is Basket, Raised Scrolls, Gold Trim	125.00
Tankard, Cavalier Portrait, Hand Painted, Marked Baumy, 13 1/2 In.	450.00
Tankard, Currants, Leaves, Artist Signed & Dated 1908, 11 In.	130.00
Tankard, Floral Design, Artist Signed, 15 In.	215.00
Tankard, Grape Clusters, Pastel Ground, Serpent Handle, 15 1/2 In.	150.00
Tankard, Grape, 15 In.	185.00
Tankard, Grapes, Hand Painted, Cylindrical, Marked, 13 1/2 In.	175.00
Tankard, Mug, Grapes, Gold & Green, 14 In.	295.00
Tankard, Purple & Red Cherries, Signed, 13 In.	225.00
Tankard, Red Cherries, Purple Ground, Signed, 13 In.	145.00 To 225.00
Tea Set, Art Nouveau, Silver & Gold Trim, Pickard Design, 3 Piece	175.00
Teapot, Roses, Gold, 4 Gold Feet, 5 1/2 X 8 In.	68.00
Tray, Art Nouveau, Free Form, Artist Signed, Dated 1896, 18 X 12 In.	58.00
Tray, Dresser, 8 X 7 1/2 In.	28.00
Tray, Dresser, Acorns & Foliage, Tan & Cream, 13 1/2 X 11 3/4 In.	145.00
Tray, Dresser, Spray Of Roses, Gold Trim, White Ground, 12 In.	45.00
Tray, Floral, Gold, Oval, 14 In.	50.00
Tray, Perfume, Scalloped Rim, Brown Ground, Pansies, 9 1/2 X 12 In.	35.00
Tray, Perrier, 6 In.	22.00
Tray, Raised Gold Handles, Wisteria, Green Mark, 15 1/2 In.	320.00
Tray, Serving, Star Design, Flowers, Ivory Ground, 13 In.	55.00
Tureen, Covered, Floral, Gilt	58.00
Tureen, Covered, Scroll Design, Pink Roses, Oval	65.00
Tureen, Cream Ground, Quilted, Flowers, Gold Trim	70.00
Tureen, Soup, Flowers, Leaves, Ribbon Handles, Lid Finial, 11 X 7 In.	90.00
Urn, Allover Red, Green & Gold, Dove Center, Metallic Luster, 14 In.	99.00
Vase, Bird Design, 10 In.	90.00
Vase, Floral, 12 1/2 In.	175.00
Vase, Gold Mum, Gold Legs & Handle, 9 In.	125.00
Vase, Green & Red Floral, Wm.Guerin No.2, C.1895, 15 1/2 In.	495.00
Vase, Hand Painted Floral, C.1895, 15 1/2 In.	495.00
Vase, Hand Painted, Couple In Meadow, Raised Florals, 7 1/2 In.	100.00
Vase, Red & Blue Florals, Hand Painted, Wm.Guerin Co., 15 1/2 In.	495.00
Vase, Roses, Gold Dragon Handles, 8 In.	95.00
Water Set, Grapes On Gold & Green, Tankard & 4 Mugs, 14 In.	295.00

In 1927, Charles Lindbergh, the aviator, became the first man to fly across the Atlantic Ocean. He was a national hero. In 1932, his son was kidnapped and murdered, and Lindbergh was again the center of public interest. He died in 1974. All types of Lindbergh memorabilia are collected.

LINDBERGH, Airplane, Hubley, Lindy, Spirit Of St.Louis, 1928	750.00
Airplane, Spirit Of St.Louis, Celluloid, 5 1/2 X 6 In.	55.00
Bookends, Portrait, Bronze	60.00
Bookends, The Aviator, Iron	28.00 To 90.00
Bottle, Whiskey, Spirit Of St.Louis Shape	145.00

Candy Container, Good Will To Latin America, 4 1/4 In. 150.00
Coin–Operated Machine, Lindy Striker ....*Illus* 475.00
Cover, Pillow, Dated, Our Hero 10.00
Decanter, Spirit Of St.Louis, Ceramic, Rem Orig.No.3, 7 In. 300.00
Pencil Box, Tin 37.50
Postcard, Picture Of Lindy & Plane 10.00
Sheet Music, Eagle Of The U.S.A. 15.00
Sheet Music, Like An Angel, Pictures 12.50
Tapestry, Wall, French, C.1927, 58 X 19 1/2 In. 65.00
Towel, Embroidered, 30 In. 62.00

> *Lithophanes are porcelain pictures made by casting clay in layers of various thicknesses. When a piece is held to the light, a picture of light and shadow is seen through it. Most lithophanes date from the 1825–75 period. A few are still being made. Many lithophanes sold today were originally panels for lampshades.*

LITHOPHANE, Cup & Saucer, Moriage 135.00
Cup & Saucer, Mormon Tabernacle 20.00
Cup, Saki, Faces Appear When Filled With Liquid, Set Of 6 .... 65.00
Lamp, 3 Mountain Scenes, Castles, Impressed Germany, Miniature 215.00
Lamp, Landscape Scene, Cherub Base, Germany, C.1900, 10 In. 500.00
Lamp, Night, 4 Seasonal Scenes, Children, Copper Frame, 5 7/8 In. 200.00
Lamp, Piano, 4 Courting Scenes, Brass, Iron, 55 In. 625.00
Lamp, Table, Landscapes, Multicolor, 6–Pane 700.00
Panel, Castle Scene, Leaded Frame, KPM, 5 3/4 X 7 1/2 In. 100.00
Panel, Madonna, Child, & St.John, 19th Century, 7 3/8 In.Diam. 45.00
Panel, Wm.Penn Treaty With Indians, 19th Century, 6 1/2 X 8 In. 240.00
Plaque, Beggar Girl, Guitar On Arm, Dog At Feet, 4 1/4 In. 140.00
Plaque, Couple Crossing Stream, Woods, 5 X 4 In. 95.00
Plaque, Girl By Tree, Basket Of Flowers, Boy On Path, 5 In. 140.00
Plaque, Hunter Leaving Bridge, Girl Looks At Him, Trees, 5 In. 140.00
Shade, 5–Sided, President's House, Fisherman, Lady & Friend 650.00
Stein, Deer In Woods, Dancing Couple, 1/2 Liter 122.50
Stein, Man From War, Wife With Child, House Behind, 1/2 Liter 105.00
Stein, Nun, Black, Head Is Lid, Pewter Rest, Priest, Lady 325.00
Stein, Occupational, Blacksmith 285.00
Stein, St. Louis Fair, 1904, Palace Of Liberal Arts, 5 1/2 In. 160.00
Tea Set, Luster, Dragons, 13 Piece 135.00
Tea Set, Oriental, Geisha, Dragons, 21 Piece 185.00
Tea Set, Sugar & Creamer, Teapot, Cups, Plates, Koshida 95.00
Tea Warmer, 4 Scenic Panels 265.00
Toddy Warmer, 4 Landscapes, Brass Cover, Scroll Feet, 5 3/4 In. 120.00
Warmer, Pot, White 230.00

> *Liverpool, England, was the site of several pottery and porcelain factories from 1716 to 1785. Some earthenware was made with transfer decorations. Sadler and Green made print–decorated wares from 1756. Many of the pieces were made for the American market and feature patriotic emblems, such as eagles, flags, and other special–interest motifs.*

LIVERPOOL, Jug, Black Transfer, Jack Spritsail Coming On Shore, 10 In. 200.00
Jug, Black Transfer, Washington's Tomb, Motto, 11 3/4 In. 350.00
Jug, Commodore Prebles' Squadron Attacking City Of Tripoli 1430.00
Jug, Creamware, Black Transfer, Washington City, 1800, 9 1/4 In. 600.00
Jug, Creamware, Black Transfer, Washington, Dated 1802, 10 7/8 In. 1000.00
Jug, Inscribed Boston Frigate, American Map Design 1980.00
Jug, Portrait Of John Jay 1430.00
Jug, Telling Fortune In Coffee Grounds, Dancers On Reverse 125.00
Mug, 1790 American Census 3080.00
Mug, Black Transfer, Prosperity To U.S.Of America, 1880, 5 In. 2800.00
Pitcher, Black Transfer, Peace & Plenty Independence, 10 1/4 In. 675.00
Pitcher, Black Transfer, Peace & Plenty, Ship, Girl, Anchor, 10 In. 675.00
Pitcher, Commodore Bainbridge & Victory Achieved, 8 In. 600.00

⚓
LLADRÓ°

Juan, Jose, and Vicente Lladro opened a ceramics workshop in Almacera, Spain, in 1951. They soon began making figurines in a distinctive, elongated style. In 1958 the factory moved to Tabernes Blanques, Spain. The company makes stoneware and porcelain vases and figurines in limited and nonlimited editions.

LLADRO, Figurine, Ballerina, K–8, MY	155.00
Figurine, Balloon Seller, No.5141	78.00
Figurine, Boy Soccer Player, No.5135	89.00
Figurine, Girl Soccer Player, No.5134	89.00
Figurine, Graceful Duo, No.2073	689.00
Figurine, Hamlet, 16 In.	600.00
Figurine, Harlequin With Guitar, No.1247	495.00
Figurine, Hebrew Student, No.4684	107.00
Figurine, Hunters, No.1048	305.00
Figurine, Napping, No.5070	155.00
Figurine, Nude, No.4511	129.00
Figurine, Portrait, No.4942	499.00
Figurine, Pottery Seller & Donkey, No.4859	350.00
Figurine, Reminiscing, No.1270	670.00
Figurine, Soccer Players, No.1266	2900.00
Figurine, Victorian Girl On Swing, No.1297	715.00
Figurine, Wheelbarrow With Flowers, No.1283	211.00
Plaque, Boy's Head With Wings	35.00

Locke Art is a trademark found on glass of the early twentieth century. Joseph Locke worked at many English and American firms. He designed and etched his own glass in Pittsburgh, Pennsylvania, starting in the 1880s. Some pieces were marked "Joe Locke," but most were marked with the words "Locke Art." The mark is hidden in the pattern on the glass.

LOCKE ART, Brandy, Flowers & Leaves, Paper Sticker, 3 1/4 In.	92.00
Butter Chip, Gooseberries, Leaves, Pedestal	35.00
Goblet, Etched With Poppies, Signed, 6 1/2 In.	75.00
Salt, Pedestal, Vintage Pattern, Signed, 2 1/4 X 1 1/4 In.	55.00
Sherbet, Grapes, Foliage, Signed, 3 1/2 In.	185.00
Sherbet, Turned Up Base Forms Underplate, Signed, 3 1/2 In.	185.00
Sherbet, Underplate, Grape & Leave Design	185.00
Sherbet, Vintage Pattern, Turned Up Rim, Signed, 3 3/4 In.	150.00
Tumbler, Grape & Vine, Crystal, Signed	60.00

Johann Loetz–Witwe bought a glassworks in Austria in 1840. He died in 1848 and his widow ran the company; then in 1879, his grandson took over. Loetz glass was varied. Most collectors recognize the iridescent gold glass similar to Tiffany, but many other types were made. The firm closed during World War II.

LOETZ, Basket, Brides, Green, Fluted, Brass Frame, 11 In.	575.00
Bowl, Centerpiece, Honeycomb Texture, Fluted Rim, Rainbow Spots, 4 In.	150.00
Bowl, Green Swirl, Iridescent, Ruffled, 2 1/2 X 6 In.	125.00
Bowl, Light Green Center, To Forest Green, Wide Scallops, 12 In.	140.00
Bowl, Pinched Sides, Folded Rim, Rainbow Iridescent, Spots, 9 1/2 In.	280.00
Bowl, Scalloped, Forest Green Over White, 8 X 12 In.	125.00
Bowl, Silver Bronze Iridescent Over Green, Bulbous, 6 In.	80.00
Bowl, Silver Bronze Over Green, 6 In.	100.00
Bowl, White, Pink Overlay, Piecrust Edge, 7 In.	40.00
Bowl, White, Pink Overlay, Piecrust Edge, 11 1/2 In.	140.00
Bride's Bowl, Ruffled, Cranberry To Mottled Green Rim, 12 In.	400.00
Cake Stand, Pedestal, Etched, Flint	100.00
Decanter, Church, Ruby To Clear, Marked, 8 In.	175.00
Decanter, Ruby Cut To Clear, Signed, 8 In.	175.00
Inkwell, Brass Lid, Brass Lily Pad Holder, Cranberry	295.00
Lamp, Amber Glass Domed Base, Holly & Women's Faces Shade, 63 In.	3300.00
Pendant, Iridescent Turquoise On Yellow, Gold Fittings, 1 1/2 In.	130.00
Planter, Green, 3 Twisted Feet, 4 X 8 In.	100.00

Shade, Tulip, Mottled Iridized Gold, Set Of 3 .... 325.00
Vase, Amethyst, Gold, Turquoise, 13 In., Pair 285.00
Vase, Amethyst, Iridescent, 8 1/2 In. 395.00
Vase, Amethyst, Oil Spot Swirl Design, Bulbous, 5 In. 75.00
Vase, Apricot, Platinum Feather, Cased White Interior, Marked, 8 In. 500.00
Vase, Ball Type, Multicolored, 8 1/2 In. 475.00
Vase, Baluster, Bands Of Yellow & Gold Waves, Ruby Ground, 8 In. 220.00
Vase, Bands Of White & Beige, Blue Silver Waves, Ruby, 8 In. 418.00
Vase, Black & Red Pattern, Sterling Silver Collar, Signed, 2 1/4 In. 375.00
Vase, Cobalt Blue, Twisted Form, Gold Foliage, 8 In. 285.00
Vase, Cylindrical, Flared Rim, Ground Pontil, Green, 5 1/2 In. 185.00
Vase, Cylindrical, Footed, Quad Lipped, Thread On Platinum, 4 In. 235.00
Vase, Enameled Flowers, Gold Leaves, Signed, 3 1/4 X 4 In. 115.00
Vase, Fan, Crimped, Ribbed, Green, Amethyst, Gold, Turquoise, 8 In. 115.00
Vase, Flower Form, Green, Amethyst Rim, 6 1/2 In. 165.00
Vase, Gold Iridescent, Green Base, 5 3/4 X 5 In. 450.00
Vase, Gold Splotching, Floriform, Gold Snake Around Body, 8 1/2 In. 375.00
Vase, Gold Thumbprint Indent, Iridescent, Flared, 3 1/4 In. 149.00
Vase, Gourd Form, Platinum Raindrops, Silver Overlay, Mark, 5 1/4 In. 1300.00
Vase, Green Glass, Optic Rib, Iridescent, Cylindrical, 12 X 4 1/2 In. 425.00
Vase, Green Iridescent, Ruffled Neck, Signed, 4 1/4 In. 220.00
Vase, Green With Silver Oil Spot, Signed, 7 In. 325.00
Vase, Green, Lavender Threaded, Crimped Top, Squat, 4 In. 120.00
Vase, Iridescent Green, Amethyst, Ruffled, Signed, 10 In. 245.00
Vase, Light Blue & Green Tone, 13 1/2 In. 1500.00
Vase, Misshapen, Twisted Form, Gold Foliage, 8 In. 285.00
Vase, Oil Spots, Wavy Lines, Ruffled Top, 7 1/4 In. 250.00
Vase, Optic Ribs, Pinched Neck, Flared Throat, Spots, Green, 4 1/4 In. 135.00
Vase, Ovoid, Openings In Neck, Iridized Yellow, 11 In. 660.00
Vase, Pinched Bulbous Base, 4 7/8 In. 195.00
Vase, Purple Tones, Silver Overlay, 6 In. 390.00
Vase, Ribbed Body, Flared Neck, Platinum Iridescent, 8 1/2 In. 325.00
Vase, Ruffled Top, Iridescent Green & Amethyst, Signed, 10 In. 245.00
Vase, Silvery Blue Overlay, Irregular Crater Effect, 4 X 3 1/2 In. 95.00
Vase, Spider Web Design, Amethyst, Corset Shape, 10 1/2 X 5 1/2 In. 180.00
Vase, Threaded, Amethyst & Green, Signed, 10 1/2 In. 155.00
Vase, Treebark, Green Ruffled Rim, 11 In. 175.00
Vase, Twisted Body, Green To Blue, Veined Gold Design, Signed, 13 In. 395.00
Vase, Urn Shape, Applied Platinum Circular Handles, Lavender, 4 In. 265.00
Vase, White Abstract Line Design, Flared Rim, 14 In. 100.00

The Lone Ranger is a fictional character introduced on the radio in 1932. Over three thousand shows were produced before the series ended in 1954. In 1938, the first Lone Ranger movie was made. Television shows were started in 1949 and are still seen on some stations. The Lone Ranger appears on many products and was even the name of a restaurant chain for several years.

LONE RANGER, Badge, Deputy, Star Shape 10.00
Badge, Hi–Ho Silver, Tin Litho, 1938 .... 25.00
Book, Big Little Book, Secret Of Somber Cavern 12.00
Book, Paint, Whitman, 1940 .... 25.00
Book, Somber Canyon, Better Little Book 9.00
Booklet, Bond Bread Roundup News, Vol.11, August 1939 .... 35.00
Certificate, Silvercup Bread Safety Club, 1938 .... 35.00
Cowgirl Outfit, Official, Esquire Novelty Co., Box 85.00
Doll, Cloth, 1974 .... 12.00
Figurine, Chalkware, 1940s, 15 In. ....18.00 To 55.00
Figurine, Lone Ranger & Horse, Composition, 1936 .... 15.00
Flashlight, Signal Siren, Box 30.00
Fob & Ribbon 12.50
Game, 1935 .... 25.00
Game, Ball Puzzle 18.00
Game, Parker Brothers, 1938 ....20.00 To 35.00
Game, Target Sign, Marx, Tin, 1938, 16 X 27 In. 75.00

Guitar 95.00
Gun, Stamped 15.00
Gun, Target, Original Box 65.00
Hairbrush, Wooden 15.00
Handkerchief 5.00
Holster & Guns, Leather 35.00
Kit, First Aid, With Contents 30.00
Knife, Pocket, Silver Bullet, Hi Ho Silver 40.00
News, Roundup, Bond Bread, Vol.1 .... 35.00
Outfit, Cowgirl, Official, Esquire Novelty Co., Box 85.00
Paint Box, Unused 15.00
Pedometer ....15.00 To 20.00
Pencil Case 30.00
Pin, Safety Scout 20.00
Pinball Game, Pocket Size 15.00
Pistol, Clicker, Tin 20.00
Poster, Serial Movie, Spanish Writing, Lee Powell 10.00
Puzzle, Clayton Moore, Jay Silverheels, & Silver 9.00
Radio 225.00
Ring, Atomic Bomb ....22.00 To 35.00
Ring, Flashlight, 1940 ....25.00 To 50.00
Ring, Six–Shooter, 1948 ....33.00 To 60.00
Ring, Weather 20.00
Target, With Stand, Metal, Marx, 16 X 27 In. ......60.00 To 125.00
Toy, Hi–Ho Silver, Windup, Tin, Litho, Marx, Original Box, 8 In. 350.00

The Longwy Workshop of Longwy, France, first made ceramic wares in 1798. The workshop is still in business. Most of the ceramic pieces found today are glazed with many colors to resemble cloisonne or other enameled metal. The factory used a variety of marks.

LONGWY, Bowl, Allover Floral On Burgundy Red, Blue Interior, 5 1/2 In. 55.00
Bowl, Floral On Blue Interior, Light Blue Exterior, 3 3/4 In. 38.00
Tile, Allover Geometric Design, Coat Of Arms Center, Footed, 8 In. 125.00
Vase, Cylindrical, Bird On Flowering Branch, 6 1/2 In. 160.00
Vase, Cylindrical, Floral On Blue, Border At Top, 7 1/4 In. 155.00
Vase, Flowers On Black Purple, 2 X 4 1/2 In. 55.00

The Lonhuda Pottery Company of Steubenville, Ohio, was organized in 1892 by William Long, W. H. Hunter, and Alfred Day. Brown underglaze slip-decorated pottery was made. The firm closed in 1896. The company used many marks, the earliest included the letters "LPCO."

LONHUDA, Vase, Cream, Flowers, 6 In. 100.00
Vase, Floral, Green, Brown, Hand Painted, 8 In. 160.00

Lotus Ware was made by the Knowles, Taylor & Knowles Company of East Liverpool, Ohio, from 1890 to 1900. Lotus Ware is a thin, Belleek–like porcelain. It was sometimes decorated outside the factory. Other types of ceramics that were made by Knowles, Taylor & Knowles Company are listed under "KTK."

LOTUS WARE, Candy Dish, Seaweed, Coral Feet, All White, 5 1/2 X 7 1/2 In. 195.00
Creamer, Molded Floral, All White, Small 115.00
Creamer, Shade Of Lemon 95.00
Creamer, Violets, Signed 125.00
Ewer, Daisies & Buttercups, Gilt Spout, Twig Handle, Signed 585.00
Pitcher, Milk, Pansies All Around, Signed, 5 1/2 X 7 1/2 In. 365.00
Vase, 6 In. 850.00
Vase, Floral, Handles, Signed, 7 1/2 In. 275.00

J.&J.G.LOW *Low art tiles were made by the J. and J. G. Low Art Tile Works of Chelsea, Massachusetts, from 1877 to 1902. A variety of art and other tiles were made. Some of the tiles were made by a process called "natural," some were hand–modeled, and some made mechanically.*

LOW, Tile, Man's Head, Brown, 4 In. 25.00

Tile, Woman's Head, Green Glaze, Marked, Round, 6 In. 22.00

> *The Lowestoft factory in Suffolk, England, worked from 1757 to 1802. They made many commemorative gift pieces and small, dated, inscribed pieces of soft paste porcelain.*

LOWESTOFT, see also Chinese Export
LOWESTOFT, Bowl, Pink Flowers, Blue Underglaze, 9 In. 300.00
Cup, Blue & White Flowers 50.00
LOY–NEL–ART, see McCoy

> *Lunch pails and lunch boxes have been used to carry lunches to school or work since the nineteenth century. Today, most collectors want either early advertising boxes or children's lunch boxes made since the 1930s. The original Thermos bottle must be inside the box for the collector to consider it complete.*

LUNCH BOX, All In Family 6.00
Bachelor Father 6.00
Bonanza ....7.00 To 20.00
Brotherhood Tobacco 45.00
Cameron & Cameron, Humidor Top, Red 125.00
Camerons Finest Tobacco, Red, Ilsley 90.00
Dixie Queen Plug Cut, Tin 65.00
Dixie Queen, Portrait 110.00
Fashion Tobacco ....115.00 To 125.00
Fat Albert 12.00
Football, Figural, Tin, Decoware, 2 Handles 12.00
George Washington Tobacco, Light Blue 25.00
Just Suits 28.00
Lunch Wagon, Porky's, Dome Lid, Thermos, 1959 .... 10.00
Main Brace 65.00
Miner's, Complete With Trays 27.00
Model Airplanes On Sides, World Globe Top, Green Metal 12.00
Patterson Seal 30.00
Peter Rabbit, Candy 47.00
Peter Rabbit, Easter Greeting, Small 48.00
Pictures Of Children & Cat, Red & Green, Oblong 12.50
Planet Of Apes 10.00
Plow Boy Tobacco ....95.00 To 115.00
Plow Boy, Silver 250.00
Rifleman, Thermos 12.00
Robin Hood 14.00
Santa Claus Pictured, C.1930 .... 37.50
School Bus, Disney 75.00
Star Trek, Thermos 6.00
Tiger, 7 X 10 X 10 In. 45.00
Union Leader Cut Plug, Tin 25.00
Vox Wagon, 1960 .... 35.00
Warnick & Brown 65.00

> *Luneville, a French faience factory, was established in 1731 by Jacques Chambrette. It is best known for its fine biscuit figures and groups and for large faience dogs and lions. The early pieces were unmarked. The firm was acquired by Keller and Guerin and is still working.*

LUNEVILLE, Plate, Musicians, Black Transfer, 10 In. 25.00
Vase, Floral Relief, Brown Glaze, Bulbous, Long Neck, 14 In. 200.00

> *Lusterware was meant to resemble copper, silver, or gold. It has been used since the sixteenth century. Most of the luster found today was made during the nineteenth century. The metallic glazes are applied on pottery. The finished color depends on the combination of the clay color and the glaze.*

LUSTER, Black, Jug, Garlands Of Flowers, Queen Victoria Portraits, 1897 .... 120.00
Blue, Tea Set, Plates Have 2 Bluebirds, 23 Piece 55.00

Luster, Pitcher, Mother & Child Playing, Copper, Pair, 7 1/2 In.

Canary, Cup & Saucer, Handleless, Gaudy Floral Enameling	250.00
Canary, Plate, Embossed Floral Rim, Enameling, 7 3/8 In.	275.00
Canary, Saucer, Woman & Music Scene, Black Transfer, 5 3/16 In.	70.00
Copper, Beaker, Blue Band, Foliage, Cream Berries, 3 In.	10.00
Copper, Creamer, Blue Band	28.00
Copper, Creamer, Polychrome Enameled Head Of Bacchus, Inside Frog	105.00
Copper, Creamer, Polychrome Floral Design, 3 1/2 In.	25.00
Copper, Goblet, Blue Band, Bird & Flower Design, 5 In.	70.00
Copper, Goblet, Canary Band, Reserves Of Mother & Child, C.1825	135.00
Copper, Goblet, Footed, England, C.1830, Set Of 7	125.00
Copper, Jug, Brown, War Of 1812, Black Transfer, 5 1/2 In.	750.00
Copper, Mug, Blue & Green Bands	42.00
Copper, Mug, Blue & Tan Stripes, 3 In.	25.00
Copper, Pitcher, Blue & Copper Rings, Bird, Flower, Eagle Handle	280.00
Copper, Pitcher, Blue Band, England, 4 3/4 In.	40.00
Copper, Pitcher, Blue Floral Band, 6 3/4 In.	35.00
Copper, Pitcher, Blue, Basket Of Flowers, Father Time Spout, 6 In.	105.00
Copper, Pitcher, Blue, Bird, Eagle Head Handle, Large Spout, 8 In.	280.00
Copper, Pitcher, Canary Band, Young Lady & Child Playing, 6 1/2 In.	80.00
Copper, Pitcher, Enameling, C.1870, 7 In.	75.00
Copper, Pitcher, Hanley, Miniature	32.50
Copper, Pitcher, Iridescent Band & Design, 5 In.	95.00
Copper, Pitcher, Mask Spout, 5 1/8 In.	45.00
Copper, Pitcher, Putty Band, Purple Luster Foliage, 5 1/2 In.	30.00
Copper, Pitcher, Raised Floral, Polychrome Enameling, 5 3/4 In.	32.50
Copper, Pitcher, Rust Transfer, Woman & Child, Canary Band, 4 In.	45.00
Copper, Pitcher, Yellow Band, Design, 7 In.	65.00
Copper, Pitcher, Yellow Band, White Reserves, Scenes, 5 3/4 In.	60.00
Copper, Pitcher, Yellow Design Band, 7 In.	80.00
Copper, Plate, Cup, & Saucer	25.00
Copper, Salt & Pepper, Figural, Cristopan	80.00
Copper, Shaving Mug, Cobalt Design	45.00
LUSTER, COPPER, TEA LEAF, see Tea Leaf Ironstone	
Copper, Teapot, Floral Design, Footed	195.00
Copper, Toby Jug, Man Seated, Pipe, Tricorn Hat, English, 4 1/2 In.	125.00
Copper, Tumbler, Cream Band, Raised Flower Design, 2 3/4 In.	25.00
LUSTER, FAIRYLAND, see Wedgwood	
Gold, Dinner Set, Child's, Tea Leaf, 24 Piece, Service For 8	1650.00
Pearl, Cup & Saucer, Japan ....*Color*	15.00
Pink, Basket, Winged Cupid, 4 1/2 In.	8.00
Pink, Bowl, House, 2 Story, 6 X 2 1/2 In.	58.00
Pink, Bowl, Medallions Of Bird & Flowers, 5 7/8 In.	65.00

Pink, Cup & Saucer, Children Scene, Hand Painted 20.00
Pink, Cup & Saucer, Dixon Impressed 38.50
Pink, Cup & Saucer, Folk Art Floral Design, Handleless 45.00
Pink, Cup & Saucer, Handleless, Black Transfer 30.00
Pink, Cup & Saucer, Staffordshire, Pink 25.00
Pink, Jug, Names Over 3 Children, Dated 1828, 9 3/8 In. 770.00
Pink, Luncheon Set, Printed Scene, Women In Garden, C.1825, 3 Piece 50.00
Pink, Plate, Scroll & Flowers, 7 1/4 In. 20.00
Pink, Tea Set, Child's, Noah's Ark 150.00
Pitcher, Lady & Cat In Relief, Blue Band, England, 3 1/2 In. 32.00
Pitcher, Mother & Child Playing, Copper, Pair, 7 1/2 In. ....*Illus* 325.00
Purple, Cup & Saucer, New Hall, Handleless, 1810 .... 80.00
Silver, Creamer, English, 6 In. 58.00
Silver, Cup & Saucer, Resist, Rose & Berry Design 45.00
Silver, Goblet, Copper Luster Interior, 5 In. 5.00
Silver, Jug, Resist, C.1815, 6 3/8 In. 715.00
Silver, Pitcher, Brown Roses, Signed St.Albans, 6 In. 135.00
Silver, Pitcher, Enameled, Elliptical Grooves, Head In Relief, 5 In. 195.00
Silver, Pitcher, White Interior, 13 In. 12.00
Silver, Shaker, 3 5/8 In. 35.00
Silver, Shaker, Toby, 4 7/8 In. 65.00
Silver, Tea Set, Classical Figures, Dark Brown, 3 Piece 275.00
    LUSTER, SUNDERLAND, see Sunderland
Yellow, Waste Bowl, Red & Green Floral Design, 6 3/4 X 3 5/8 In. 70.00

Lustre Art Glass Company was founded in Long Island, New York, in 1920 by Conrad Vahlsing and Paul Frank. The company made lampshades and globes that are almost indistinguishable from those made by Quezal. Most of the shades made by the company were unmarked.

LUSTRE ART, Prisms, Trumpet Body, Knob Stem, Blue To White, 10 5/8 In., Pair 325.00
Shade, Bell Shape, Gold Bands On Opalescent, 5 In., Set Of 4 .... 375.00
Shade, Conical, Gold Threading Over White, Signed, 5 X 4 1/2 In. 75.00
Shade, Gold Feather, Green Edge, Gold Lined, Scalloped Rim 125.00
Shade, Gold Zipper & White Wavy Pulled Design, Marked, 5 In. 150.00
Shade, Opalescent Feather, Green Edge On Gold, Marked, Set Of 3 .... 375.00
Shade, Ribbed, Signed, Gold Iridescent 42.50

Lustres are mantel decorations, or pedestal vases, with many hanging glass prisms. The name really refers to the prisms, and it is proper to refer to a single glass prism as a lustre. Either spelling, luster or lustre, is correct.

LUSTRES, Vase, Pedestal, Girl Portrait, Cut Prisms, White, 14 1/2 In., Pair 350.00

Nicolas Lutz worked at the Boston and Sandwich Glass Company from 1869 to 1888. He made delicate and intricate threaded glass of several colors. Other similar wares made by other makers are now known by the generic name "Lutz."

LUTZ, Epergne, 3 Flower 250.00

Petrous Regout established the De Sphinx pottery in Maastricht, Holland, in 1836. The firm was noted for its transfer-printed earthenware. Many factories in Maastricht are still making ceramics.

MAASTRICHT, Bowl, Footed, Dark Blue & White, 4 In. 25.00
Bowl, Timor Pattern, 7 1/2 In. 28.00
Compote, Pa Jong, Oriental Scene & Figures, Gold Rim, 8 1/4 In. 55.00
Plate, Colorful Fruit, Regout Mark, 9 In. 10.00
Plate, Portrait, Roosevelt, Large 29.00
Soup, Dish, Regout's Flower, Blue, C.1900, 9 In. 68.00
Tray, Gaudy Floral, Round, 12 In. 40.00

Maize glass was made by W. L. Libbey & Son Company of Toledo, Ohio, after 1889. The glass resembled an ear of corn. The leaves were usually green, but some pieces were made with blue or red leaves. The kernels of "corn" were light yellow, white, or light green.

MAIZE, Bowl, Centerpiece, Leaf Design, Libbey, White, 8 3/4 X 4 In.	165.00
Cruet, Stopper	135.00
Spooner	65.00
Sugar Shaker, Pearlized Luster, Yellow Leaves, Libbey, 5 1/2 In.	160.00
Syrup, Blue Tint Leaves At Base, Clear Handle, C.1889, 7 1/2 In.	385.00
Toothpick, Blue Leaves	295.00

 *Majolica is a general term for any pottery glazed with an opaque tin enamel that conceals the color of the clay body. It has been made since the fourteenth century. Today's collector is most likely to find Victorian majolica. The heavy, colorful ware is rarely marked. Some famous makers include Wedgwood; Minton; Griffen, Smith and Hill (marked "Etruscan"); and Chesapeake Pottery (marked "Avalon" or "Clifton").*

MAJOLICA, Ashtray, Black Boy	45.00
Basket, Double Fish, English Registry Mark, 9 In.	55.00
Bird, Branch, Picket Fence, Frame, Beige & Aqua, C.1900	65.00
Biscuit Barrel, Silver Mounts, Ivory Knob, White Figures	220.00
Bowl, Begonia, 6 In.	25.00
Bowl, Bird & Fan, 5 In.	35.00
Bowl, Classical Series, Etruscan, 9 In.	39.00
Bowl, Daisies, Leaves, Handles, Turquoise, 11 In.	78.00
Bowl, Embossed Cabbage Leaves, Green, Wedgwood, 6 In.	35.00
Bowl, Green, Stand, Wedgwood, 12 X 8 In.	45.00
Bowl, Morning Glory, Footed, Red, Pink, Blue, White, 10 In.	115.00
Bowl, Pink Flowers, Green, 10 X 5 In.	30.00
Bowl, Pond Lily, Holdcraft, 11 In.	130.00
Box, Seated Cow Finial, Bucket Shape	70.00
Butter Chip, Little Leaf, Marked GSH, Set Of 4	20.00
Butter, Covered, Shell, Seaweed, & Waves	150.00
Cake Plate, Etruscan, Open Handle, Pink Napkin In Center, 11 In.	85.00
Cake Plate, Handles, 13 In.	45.00
Cake Set, Blue–Green Ground, Impressed Czechoslovakia, Set Of 7	75.00
Cake Stand, Maple Leaves, Etruscan, Tree Trunk Foot	145.00
Charger, Figural Center, Floral Border, German, 20 In., Pair	200.00
Charger, Floral, Dark Green, Ground, Pink, Lavender, Tulips, 14 In.	175.00
Charger, Floral, Tulips, Daisies, Steidlzarin, 14 In., Pair	175.00
Cider Set, Corn, Signed Cusick, 5 Piece	225.00
Coffeepot, Shell & Seaweed, Etruscan	250.00
Compote, Bellflower, Cobalt, 5 1/4 X 9 1/2 In.	142.00
Compote, Daisies, Leaves, Handles, Turquoise	95.00
Compote, Daisy, Etruscan, Blue, 9 X 5 In.	165.00
Compote, Etruscan, Rose	65.00
Compote, Grape Leaf, Etruscan, Pink, 9 1/2 In.	140.00
Compote, Grape Leaf, Griffen, Smith & Hill 1879 Mark, 9 In.	145.00
Compote, Grape Leaf, Vine, Footed, Griffen, Smith & Hill, 9 1/4 In.	140.00
Compote, Open, Fern & Floral Bowl, Low Pedestal, Marked, 9 1/2 In.	85.00
Compote, Pink, Classical, Etruscan	75.00
Creamer, Albino	150.00
Creamer, Coral Pattern	275.00
Creamer, Corn, Marked	65.00
Creamer, Embossed Grapes & Leaves, Green, Wedgwood, 5 In.	45.00
Creamer, Pink, Shell & Seaweed, Etruscan	80.00
Creamer, Shell & Seaweed, Etruscan	135.00
Creamer, Shell & Seaweed, Marked, 3 1/2 In.	460.00
Cup & Saucer, Bamboo & Fern, Set Of 10	465.00
Cup & Saucer, Bird & Fan	110.00
Cup & Saucer, Coffee, Shell & Seaweed, Etruscan	125.00
Cup & Saucer, Pineapple	45.00

Majolica, Figurine, Fish, Bass,
Open Mouth, 12 X 9 In.

Majolica, Pitcher, Blue,
Red, Italy, 6 In.

Majolica, Platter, Fish, Shell, Coral,
Rose, Green, Brown, 19 In.

Cuspidor, Acanthus Leaves	75.00
Decanter, Duck, France, 13 In.	5.00
Dish, Basket Weave, Leaves In Center, 7 X 10 In.	35.00
Dish, Begonia Leaf, 5 1/2 In.	435.00
Dish, Begonia Leaf, 8 1/2 In.	27.00 To 55.00
Dish, Blue, Pink Roses, 8 In.	40.00
Dish, Leaf Shape, Raised Buds, Brown Handle, 12 X 9 1/4 In.	80.00
Dish, Leaf, Green Edge, Mottled Brown & Yellow, 12 In.	55.00
Dish, Leaf, Green, Pink, Yellow, Raised Buds, 12 X 9 In.	80.00
Ewer, Roman Scene, Blue Interior, Burgundy, 12 In.	75.00
Ewer, Rose, Flowers & Leaves, 11 In.	75.00
Figurine, Armorial Knights, Steeds, Signed, C.1900, 12 1/2 In., Pr.	475.00
Figurine, Camel, Standing, Oriental Mark, 6 X 5 1/2 In.	58.00
Figurine, Cock, 31 In.	175.00
Figurine, Fish, Bass, Open Mouth, 12 X 9 In. ....*Illus*	70.00
Figurine, Hunting Dog, 28 X 11 1/2 In.	450.00
Figurine, Psyche, Seated On Rock, Wedgwood, 8 In.	1150.00
Garden Seat, Figural, Tree Trunk	125.00
Goblet, Entwined Sea Monster, Sirens, Centaurs, 10 In. ....125.00 To 135.00	
Hair Receiver, Begonia Leaves, Colored Top	32.00
Humidor, Advertising, Gail & Ax	165.00
Humidor, Art Deco, Floral Design, Figural Pipe	50.00
Humidor, Figural, Frog	70.00
Inkwell, Cats Riding Unicycles, Floral, Maroon, Footed, 8 In.	95.00
Jar, Tobacco, Bowler With Ball, German, Medium	95.00
Jar, Tobacco, Smiling Monk With Cigarette, Pink, Blue, German	95.00
Jardiniere, Pedestal, Green	265.00
Jardiniere, Raised Floral Design, Green & Browns, 7 X 9 In.	43.00
Jardiniere, Sea Animal Handles, Italian, 18 In.	50.00
Jardiniere, Shell Design, English, 6 In.	90.00
Jardiniere, Stand, 9 1/2 X 16 In.	125.00
Medallion, Poor Maria, 1800, 2 In.	50.00
Mustache Cup, Saucer, Shell & Seaweed, Etruscan	125.00
Oyster Plate, Fishscale Ground, Turquoise, Yellow, Brown	65.00
Oyster Plate, Shell Shape, Burgundy Rim, 8 1/2 In., Set Of 8	255.00
Pitcher, Basket Weave & Bamboo, Banks & Thorley, 8 1/2 In.	100.00
Pitcher, Basket Weave, Floral, Lavender Interior, Marked, 5 1/4 In.	115.00
Pitcher, Begonia Leaf On Bark, 7 1/2 In.	78.00
Pitcher, Bird In Branches Both Sides, Pink Inside, 7 In.	65.00
Pitcher, Blackberry & Picket Fence, 7 1/2 In.	65.00
Pitcher, Blackberry, 6 1/2 In.	100.00
Pitcher, Blue, Red, Italy, 6 In. ....*Illus*	35.00
Pitcher, Burgundy Leaves, Flowers, & Berries, Albino Type, 6 In.	95.00
Pitcher, Cobalt Blue, Sheaf Of Wheat Design, 6 In.	78.00
Pitcher, Cobalt Pink, Brown, White, Stork, Fan, Oriental, Square	150.00
Pitcher, Cobalt, Hawthorn, 5 1/4 In.	100.00

Pitcher, Corn, 9 In. 160.00
Pitcher, Cream Ground, Floral Spray, Blue Lining, 6 3/4 In. 95.00
Pitcher, Edward & Alexandra, Horseshoe Design, Wedgwood, 5 1/2 In. 225.00
Pitcher, Figural, Corn, 8 1/2 In. 70.00
Pitcher, Figural, Cucumber, Green, 9 1/4 In. 90.00
Pitcher, Figural, Duck, Cattails Form Handle, 12 3/4 In. 90.00
Pitcher, Figural, Fish, 10 In. 85.00
Pitcher, Figural, Parrot, 12 1/2 In. .... 85.00 To 90.00
Pitcher, Figural, Rooster, Marked St.Clement, 11 In. 95.00
Pitcher, Floral, 6 In. 35.00
Pitcher, Flowers, 5 1/4 In. 70.00
Pitcher, Girl & Dog, Pewter Lid, 8 In. 125.00
Pitcher, Leaf Design, 7 In. 55.00
Pitcher, Made In Japan, 5 1/2 In. .... *Color* 25.00
Pitcher, Milk, Fern Design 170.00
Pitcher, Nautilus, Coral Handle, 5 In. 125.00
Pitcher, Owl & Fan, Triangular, Yellow Ground 85.00
Pitcher, Owl, Morley & Co., 8 1/2 In. 183.00
Pitcher, Palm Tree, Green, Brown Bark, Marked, 8 In. 75.00
Pitcher, Pineapple, Marked, 6 1/2 In. 95.00
Pitcher, Rooster, 12 In. 50.00
Pitcher, Rooster, Figural, Marked, 11 In. 95.00
Pitcher, Rooster, Pouring, French, 9 1/2 In. 100.00
Pitcher, Roses & Leaves, Green Ground, 7 1/2 In. 65.00
Pitcher, Shell & Seaweed, 5 3/4 In. 185.00
Pitcher, Shell & Seaweed, Marked, 3 3/4 X 5 1/4 In. 135.00
Pitcher, Syrup, Sunflower, Pewter Lid 200.00
Pitcher, Water Lily, 8 In. 65.00
Planter, Allover Shell & Seaweed, England, 6 In. 80.00
Plaque, Fish Shape, Multicolor, 15 In. 35.00
Plaque, Fish, Muskellunge, 2 Perch, Oak Base, 25 In. 550.00
Plaque, Green & Blue Leaves, Fish & Seashells, 7 1/2 In. 75.00
Plate, Avadon, 10 In. 40.00
Plate, Bamboo, Etruscan, 8 In. 75.00
Plate, Banks & Thorley, Fern & Bowl, Marked, 8 1/2 In. 50.00
Plate, Begonia Pattern, Hand Painted, 8 In. 15.00
Plate, Begonia, 8 1/2 In. 55.00
Plate, Birds & Fans, 10 In. 50.00
Plate, Blue, Pink Flowers, Green Leaves, Gold Center, 8 In. 35.00
Plate, Cabbage Leaf, Etruscan, 8 3/4 In. 70.00
Plate, Cherries & Butterflies, Turquoise, 7 In. 35.00
Plate, Cobalt, Brown, Greek Key Design, Green, 10 In. 100.00
Plate, Daisies, Leaves, Turquoise, 7 In. 35.00
Plate, Etruscan, Blackberry & Basket Weave, 8 1/4 In. 75.00
Plate, Fish, Figural, Marked, 9 X 11 In. 160.00
Plate, Grape Leaf, Pink Edge, 9 In. 60.00
Plate, Green Flower, Lily Of The Valley On Brown, 12 In. 75.00
Plate, Leaf, Etruscan, 8 3/4 In. 65.00
Plate, Leaf-Shape Flowers, Lily Of The Valley, Brown, 12 In. 115.00
Plate, Lettuce Leaf, 7 1/4 In. 17.00
Plate, Lily Pad, 9 In. .... 50.00 To 135.00
Plate, Moss Green, Flowers, Aqua, Head Of Queen Victoria, 8 In. 40.00
Plate, Portrait, 11 In. 50.00
Plate, Shaggy Dog & Doghouse, 11 In. 65.00
Plate, Shell & Seaweed, Light Green, Minton, Impressed Mark 175.00
Plate, Strawberry, Etruscan, White, 9 In. 75.00
Plate, Sunflower, 7 In. 32.50
Plate, Turquoise, White Pond Lilies, 11 3/4 In. 50.00
Plate, Various Centers, Burgundy, 8 1/2 In., Set Of 6 .... 58.00
Plate, Vines, Blossoms, & Berries, Central Design, 7 In. 60.00
Plate, Waste Not Want Not, Brown, Raised Pears, 12 1/2 In. 45.00
Platter, Begonia Leaf Shape, 12 In. 32.00
Platter, Begonia Leaf, Green Interior, White Framing, 12 X 8 In. 59.00
Platter, Brown Edge, Cobalt Fan, Butterflies, Oval 95.00

Platter, Cherries & Butterflies, Turquoise, 11 In.	65.00
Platter, Dog & Doghouse, Scalloped Edge, 11 In.	95.00
Platter, Fan & Butterfly, Oval, Blue, 13 1/4 In.	135.00
Platter, Fish, Shell, Coral, Rose, Green, Brown, 19 In. ....*Illus*	145.00
Platter, Molded Relief Design, Scalloped, Open Handles, 12 X 9 In.	55.00
Platter, Mottled Center, Oval, 14 In.	125.00
Platter, Multicolored Leaves & Grapes, Signed, Dated 1883, 12 In.	45.00
Platter, Oak & Acorn, Green, Open Twig Handle	100.00
Sauce, Etruscan, 8 1/2 In.	125.00
Shaving Mug, Divided, Lavender Interior, English Registry Mark	148.00
Shelf, Oak Leaf Design, Relief Carved	395.00
Spittoon, Brown, Green, Seashell, 8 In.	110.00
Spittoon, Etruscan, Pineapple	120.00
Spittoon, Roses On Lattice, Cobalt Blue Trim	175.00
Spooner, Corn	95.00
Spooner, Shell & Seaweed, Etruscan	125.00
Spooner, Shell Handles	350.00
Stein, Motto, Lid, 1871, 10 In. ....350.00 To	420.00
Sugar & Creamer, Picket Fence	80.00
Sugar & Creamer, Shell & Seaweed, Etruscan	175.00
Sugar, Etruscan, Bamboo, Signed, 6 In.	95.00
Syrup, Coral Pattern, Pewter Top	375.00
Syrup, Etruscan, Bamboo, Pewter Lid	395.00
Syrup, Etruscan, Cobalt Sunflowers	335.00
Syrup, Etruscan, Shell & Seaweed, Pewter Top, 7 In.	145.00
Syrup, Maple Leaf Design, Marked	130.00
Syrup, Pewter Lid, Marked Bennet, Birds On Holly Design	85.00
Teapot & Sugar, Pineapple Tree Design, Etruscan	250.00
Teapot, Bamboo Pattern, Impressed Registry Mark, English, 1884	135.00
Teapot, Bird & Fan, 4 1/2 In.	105.00
Teapot, Cauliflower Form	260.00
Teapot, Pewter Lid, Twigs, Leaves, & Squirrels, 5 1/2 X 7 In.	135.00
Teapot, Shell & Seaweed ....275.00 To	295.00
Tile, Fronds & Floral, Aqua, Wedgwood, 8 X 8 In.	195.00
Tobacco Jar, Black Boy	121.00
Tobacco Jar, Clown	95.00
Tobacco Jar, French Man's Head, 5 In.	40.00
Tobacco Jar, Man With Beard, Leaves For Hair	60.00
Tobacco Jar, Snake Coiled At Bottom Of Lid, Pipe On Cover	32.00
Tobacco Stand, Figural Indian, For Cigarettes, Matches, 10 1/2 In.	135.00
Tray, Banana Leaf, 13 1/2 In. ....95.00 To	135.00
Tray, Begonia Leaf, 11 1/2 In.	80.00
Tray, Begonia, 7 X 11 In., Pair	60.00
Tray, Bread, 12 In.	145.00
Tray, Etruscan Oak Leaf, 12 In.	85.00
Tray, Leaf Shape, Snail, Green & Blue, 2 X 7 In.	145.00
Tub, Kittens Peering Over Top, Yellow Band, Flowers, 6 X 3 1/4 In.	110.00
Vase, Brown To Rose, Thistle Design, Marked, 9 1/2 In.	95.00
Vase, Cream Ground, Magenta Leaves, Green Leaves, 7 In.	65.00
Vase, Floral, Branch, Ivory, Avalon Ware, Chesapeake, 7 3/4 In.	55.00
Vase, Flower & Leaf, Rose, Gold, Avalon Ware, Chesapeake, 7 1/2 In.	33.00
Vase, Green, Pedestal, Signed France PV, 8 1/2 In., Pair	135.00
Vase, Multicolor Floral, 7 1/2 In.	55.00
Vase, Nouveau, Ornate Handles With Iris, 8 1/2 In.	50.00
Vase, Poppies, Lattice Neck, Scroll Handles, Marked, 12 1/2 In.	70.00
Vase, Raised Thistle Design, Columnal Shape, Marked, 9 1/2 In.	95.00
Vase, Serpent Handles, Impressed Number, 8 In.	75.00

Maps of all types have been collected for centuries. The earliest known printed maps were made in 1478. The first printed street map showed London in 1559. The first road maps for use by drivers of automobiles were made in 1901. Collectors buy maps that were pages of old books, as well as the multifolded road maps popular in this century.

MAP, Along Alaska's Great River, 1898, Foldout, 426 Pages	11.00
Atlas, 1930	22.00
B.& O.Penn.R.R.	32.00
Bell Telephone, U.S., Canada, Cloth, Wood Rolls, Dated 1909, 54 X 80 In.	125.00
Book, American Social Civil Engineer, Volume 13, 1884	20.00
Book, Boston Water Works, Additional Supply From Sudbury River, 1882	40.00
British Isles, Hand Colored, J.Cry, C.1833, Boxed	225.00
Bullfrog Mining District, Nye County, Nev., C.1908, Mines & Mining Caps	35.00
Carte Topographique Des Environs, Plan De Paris, Framed, 19 X 24 In.	120.00
City Of New York, 1834, Original Leather Case	85.00
Civil War, Post, All Battles During War, Set Of 28	225.00
Coachilla Valley Date Growers, 1912, 16 Page	4.00
Colorado, Dept.Of Interior, Linen Backed, C.1881, 26 1/2 X 34 In.	37.50
Colton World, C.1855	250.00
Detroit Lakes, 17 X 22 In.	2.50
Ducatum Brabantia, Hand Colored, Framed, 23 1/4 X 25 1/4 In.	35.00
Eastern & Middle States, Hand Drawn & Tinted, C.1840, 18 3/4 X 23 In.	250.00
Globe, Wooden, D.C.Murdock, W.Boylston, Ma., 3 Turned Legs, C.1850, 5 In.	400.00
Goodrich Tire, Parrish, Slipcase, 1924	40.00
Jefferson County, New York, 1944, 11 X 14 In.	4.00
Mining, Quebec, Copper & Gold	6.00
New Amsterdam, Manhattan Island, N.Visscher, C.1651, 18 X 21 3/4 In.	1450.00
New England Soconyland, 1930	6.00
New England, Mobilgas, 1949	2.50
New England, New Amsterdam, Indian Tribes, Framed, 18 X 20 In.	295.00
New England, Socony, 1931	3.50
Ohio, 1914, Railroad, 28 X 32 In.	12.00
Plan Of Boston, Hand Colored, 1864	9.50
Plan Of Cincinnati & Vicinity, Hand Colored, 1864	9.50
Rennsalaer Country, New York, 20 X 20 In.	2.50
Star, Radium, Glows At Night, 1921, Opens To 12 1/2 X 51 1/2 In.	50.00
Street Number Guide, City Railway Directory Of Chicago, 1923	10.00
Texas, Oregon, & California, Published 1846, Engraved, 22 1/2 X 24 In.	100.00
Tool, Quadrilateral Rule, American, 19th Century, 0 To 1,000 Ft., Signed	240.00
Venezuela, C.1950, Esso	2.00
World Air, T.W.A., 4 Planes In Flight	20.00
World, Embroidered, Floral & Ribbon Cartouche, Framed, 24 X 26 In.	400.00

Marble is used in many ways on antiques. Marble tops are popular for tables because they resist stains and damage. Listed here are marble carvings, large or small figurines, and groups of people or animals that have been a special art form since the time of the ancient Greeks. Reproductions, especially of large Victorian groups, are being made of a mixture using marble dust. These are very difficult to detect and collectors should be careful. Other carvings are listed under Alabaster.

MARBLE CARVING, Bust, Apollo, Head Turned Down, Hair In Ringlets, 18 3/4 In.	3100.00
Bust, Marie Antoinette, White, Variegated Base, 28 In.	825.00
Bust, Mother & Child, Base, French, Signed, 18 In.	850.00
Bust, Sultana, Young Woman, Jeweled Turban, A.Piazza, 23 In.	325.00
Bust, U.S.Grant, C.1900, Porcelain Base, 12 In.	135.00 To 165.00
Bust, Woman, Low Cut Ruffle, Pedestal, 2 Piece, 34 In.	1650.00
Figurine, Aphrodite, Philippe Fiaschi, C.1900, 21 1/2 In.	1200.00
Figurine, Child, Seated On Tree Stump, White, 13 In.	450.00
Figurine, Elephant, Black, Pair	525.00
Figurine, Venus, Canova, Square Base, C.1890, 4 Ft. 11 In.	2200.00
Fountain, 4 Lion Masks, Fruit Garlands, Continental, 5 Ft.	4950.00
Mug, Child's, Dated 1881	20.00
Nest Egg	5.00
Pedestal, Verdean Antico, Octagonal, Baluster, 4 Ft.2 In.	880.00
Urn, Cover, Variegated, Gilt Bronze Mounted, 24 1/4 In., Pr.	1045.00

The game of marbles has been popular since the days of the ancient Romans. American children were able to buy marbles by the mid-eighteenth century. Dutch glazed clay marbles were least expensive. Glazed pottery marbles, attributed to the Bennington potteries in Vermont, were of a better quality. Marbles made of pink marble were also available by the 1830s. Glass marbles seem to have been made later. By 1880, Samuel C. Dyke of South Akron, Ohio, was making clay marbles and The National Onyx Marble Company was making marbles of onyx. The Navarre Glass Marble Company of Navarre, Ohio, and M. B. Mishler of Ravenna, Ohio, made the glass marbles. Ohio remained the center of the marble industry and the Akron-made Akro Agate brand became nationally known. The most expensive marbles collected today are the sulfides. These are glass marbles with frosted white figures in the center.

MARBLE, Akro Gate, 3 In., Set Of 16 .... 45.00
  Bennington, 1 1/4 In. 12.00
  Bennington, Original Box, 7/8 In., 24 Piece ....22.50 To 25.50
  China, Unglazed, 1 In. 35.00
  China, Unglazed, 3/4 In. 10.00
  Comic, Emma 35.00
  Comic, Moon Mullins 85.00
  Ribbon Core Swirl, 1 3/4 In. 65.00
  Sulfide, Bear, 1 1/2 In. 60.00
  Sulfide, Boar 68.00
  Sulfide, Dog, 1 7/8 In. 100.00
  Sulfide, Eagle, 1 1/2 In. 140.00
  Sulfide, Fish, 1 3/4 In. 125.00
  Sulfide, Fox, 1 3/4 In. 80.00
  Sulfide, Lamb 68.00
  Sulfide, Lion, 2 In. 60.00
  Sulfide, Papoose, 2 In. 200.00
  Sulfide, Poodle, 1 1/4 In. 85.00
  Sulfide, Rooster 75.00
  Sulfide, Squirrel, 1 7/8 In. 100.00
  Sulfide, Standing Lamb, 1 1/2 In. 68.00
  Sulfide, Standing Lamb, 1 3/4 In. 90.00
  Swirl, 2 In. 50.00
  Swirl, 3/4 In. 10.00

 *The Marblehead Pottery was founded in 1905 by Dr. J. Hall as a rehabilitative program for the patients of a Marblehead, Massachusetts, sanitarium. Two years later it was separated from the sanitarium and it continued operations until 1936. Many of the pieces were decorated with marine motifs.*

MARBLEHEAD, Bookends, Owl, Brown 135.00
  Bowl, Light Blue To Gray Speckled, Yellow Flowers, Marked, 4 In. 605.00
  Bowl, Yellow Flowers, Blue, Speckled Gray, Marked, 3 1/4 X 6 In. 605.00
  Candlestick, Blue Gray, Single, Marked, 3 In. 40.00
  Creamer, 2 Tone Blue, 3 In. 60.00
  Pitcher, Dark Green Matte, Brown Flecks, Handle, A.E.Baggs, 8 In. 395.00
  Tile, Sailing Ship, Green Shades, Brown, Marked, Round, 5 In. 412.00
  Tile, Sailing Ship, Oyster White Against Blue, Marked, 4 3/4 In. 110.00
  Tile, Ship, 6 3/4 In. 65.00
  Vase, 5 Blue Rabbits, Line Design Around Vase, Gray, 3 1/2 In. 350.00
  Vase, Blue, Pale Green Stemmed Design, C.1910, 6 In. 400.00
  Vase, Blue, V Shape, 6 In. 110.00
  Vase, Brown, 3 1/2 X 4 In. 50.00
  Vase, Bud, Gray Matte, 6 In. 50.00
  Vase, Cylinder, Pink, 6 In. 65.00
  Vase, Dark Blue, Full Bodied Shape, Marked, 7 In. 132.00
  Vase, Dark Green, Marked, 8 1/2 In. 176.00
  Vase, Floral & Leaves, Green To Yellow, Blue Matte, 5 In. 525.00
  Vase, Grapevine Design, Green Yellow, Marked, 3 1/2 In. 418.00

Vase, Gray Speckles, Branches & Clusters Design, Marked, 7 In. 715.00
Vase, Green Glaze, Blue Striations, C.1910, Signed AEB, 5 3/4 In. 50.00
Vase, Green Yellow, Grapevine Design, Blue Grapes, Marked, 4 In. 418.00
Vase, Lavender, 8 In. 55.00
Vase, Matte Brown Exterior, Sand Colored Interior, Marked, 2 In. 77.00
Vase, Matte Deep Green, Marked, 4 1/2 In. 110.00
Vase, Multicolored Geometric Design, Gray, A.E.Baggs, 4 1/2 In. 675.00
Vase, Trees With Berries, Blue, Marked, C.1910, 8 3/4 In. 650.00
Wall Pocket, Blue, 6 In. 55.00
Wall Pocket, Pink Matte, 6 In. 85.00

R W Martin London   *Martinware is a salt–glazed stoneware made by the Martin Brothers of Middlesex, England, between 1873 and 1915. Many figural jugs and vases were made by the three brothers. Of special interest are the fanciful birds, usually made with removable heads.*

MARTIN BROTHERS, Figurine, Chimpanzee, Pedestal, 5 In. ....200.00 To 225.00
Pitcher, Scalloped Shells, Dragon Spine Handle, 13 In. 235.00
Stein, Blue Foliage, Monogram, 5 In. ....105.00 To 125.00
Vase, Comical Grotesque Fish, 4 In. 165.00
Vase, Cylindrical, Flying Swallows, 9 In. ....135.00 To 175.00
Vase, Dragons & Swallows, 14 In. 300.00
Vase, Flying Swallows, Cylindrical, 9 In. ....150.00 To 159.00
Vase, Incised Flowers, 6 In. 90.00
Vase, Seaweed Design, Nov.1905, 10 1/2 In. 475.00
Vase, Squash, Red & Brown Streaked, 6 In. 150.00
Vase, Streaked Red & Brown, Luster, 5 X 7 In. 175.00

Mary Gregory glass is identified by a characteristic white figure painted on dark glass. It was made from 1870 to 1910. The name refers to any glass decorated with a white silhouette figure and not just to the Sandwich glass originally painted by Miss Mary Gregory. Many reproductions have been made and there are new pieces being sold in gift shops today.

MARY GREGORY, Bottle, Barber, Amethyst 195.00
Bottle, Barber, Cobalt 115.00
Bottle, Barber, Teal 125.00
Bottle, Wine, Stopper, Girl Holding Spray, Cranberry, 9 In. 150.00
Bowl, Amethyst, 9 X 3 1/2 In. ....*Illus* 130.00
Box, Amethyst, 7 In. ....*Illus* 725.00
Box, Girl In White On Lid, Sprays On Sides, Lime Green, 3 In. 145.00
Box, Girl, Foliage, Hearts, Amber, Hinged, 4 X 4 In. 145.00
Box, Hinged Cover, Girl, Amethyst, Dots, 5 1/2 X 4 1/2 In. 205.00

Mary Gregory, Box, Amethyst, 7 In.

The marble top of a table can be shined with putty powder (zinconium oxide) from a cemetery monument works. Put the powder on a piece of damp felt and rub the marble until it shines.

Mary Gregory, Bowl, Amethyst,   Mary Gregory, Vase, Glass, Cranberry, 7 1/2 In., Pair
9 X 3 1/2 In.   Mary Gregory, Vase, Glass, Tennis Players, Amethyst,
8 X 5 3/4 In.

Box, Hinged Lid, Girl, Brass Rings, Cobalt Blue, 4 X 4 1/4 In.	235.00
Box, Jewel, Boy, Hinged Lid, Cranberry, 4 1/4 X 5 1/4 In.Diam.	375.00
Box, Lift Off Lid, Girl, Melon Shape, Emerald Green, 3 In.	110.00
Box, Lime, White Enameled Boy, Hinged, 1 3/4 X 2 3/8 In.	135.00
Box, Sapphire, Hinged, Girl Holding Pitcher, Round, 2 3/8 In.	195.00
Box, Sprays On Sides, Girl & Bird On Cover, Cobalt Blue, 5 In.	395.00
Box, White Dots On Sides, Girl, Lid, Sapphire Blue, 3 1/4 In.	145.00
Box, Young Boy, White Panel, Hinged Cover, Lime Green, 4 In.	135.00
Cordial, Set Of 4	125.00
Creamer, Girl With Fishing Hook, Emerald Green, 6 In.	135.00
Decanter, Crystal, Boy With Bouquet, 10 In.	65.00
Decanter, Green, Clear Stopper	160.00
Figurine, Angel, White, Black Amethyst, Pair	165.00
Glass, Emerald Green, White Figure	45.00
Jar, Dresser, Fan Stopper, Mottled Ground, Gold Tracery	275.00
Jewelry Casket, Blue, Boy Scene, Hinged, Ormolu Feet, 5 In.	450.00
Jewelry Casket, Periwinkle, Young Boy, Bird, 5 1/2 X 3 1/2 In.	425.00
Lamp, Oil, Black, White Girl & Butterfly, Electrified, 31 In.	395.00
Lamp, Table, Blue	325.00
Mug, Child's, Girl With Basket	75.00
Patch Box, Cranberry, Boy Figure, 1 3/4 In.	175.00
Patch Box, Hinged, Young Girl, Lime Green, 2 1/8 X 1 3/8 In.	135.00
Patch Box, Little Boy, Cobalt Blue, 2 X 1 1/8 In.	165.00
Pitcher, Boy In Sailor Suit, Cranberry, Handle, 6 5/8 In.	175.00
Pitcher, Boy With Sailboat, Sapphire Blue, 6 In.	225.00
Pitcher, Cranberry, Boy & Sailboat, Clear Handle, 6 5/8 In.	195.00
Pitcher, Dark Blue, Girl, Dark Hair, Picking Flower, 12 In.	350.00
Pitcher, Deep Blue, Thumbprint, Bulbous, 1930s	90.00
Pitcher, Girl In Garden, Watering Can, Honey Amber, 12 3/4 In.	195.00
Pitcher, Girl Placing Flowers On Wall, Ruffled, Cranberry	650.00
Pitcher, Girl With Basket Of Flowers, Emerald, 3 5/8 In.	95.00
Pitcher, Girl With Basket, Sapphire, Reeded Handle, 12 In.	375.00
Pitcher, Girl With Butterfly, Blue & Amber, Handle, 9 1/4 In.	120.00
Pitcher, Sapphire, Amber Handle, Girl With Basket, 12 In.	375.00
Pitcher, Tankard, Emerald, Young Girl With Basket, 3 1/2 In.	95.00
Pitcher, Tinted Girl With Flower, Dark Blue, English, 12 In.	350.00
Plate, Brass Stand, Mounted On 3 Brass Rings, 6 1/4 In.	150.00
Plate, Girl With Butterfly Net, Compote Stand, 6 1/4 X 4 In.	150.00
Rose Bowl, Cranberry, Girl Scene, 8 Crimp Top, 3 X 3 1/4 In.	225.00
Spittoon, Orange, White, 3 In.	55.00
Stein, Boy, Butterfly, Sapphire Blue, Pewter Top, 5 In.	175.00
Syrup, White On Cobalt Blue	125.00
Tea Warmer, Children Scenes, Nickel Plated Alcohol Burner	285.00
Tray, Dresser, Double Figure, Cranberry, 6 3/8 X 9 1/4 In.	225.00

Tray, Dresser, Oval, Cranberry, 8 1/4 X 10 1/2 In. 245.00
Tumbler, Cupid Blowing Horn, Green, 3 1/2 In. 35.00
Tumbler, Girl In White With Tree, Aqua Blue, 5 In. 35.00
Tumbler, Juice, Young Girl, Cranberry, 4 In. 52.00
Tumbler, Spa, Girl With Basket, Flattened, Amber, 4 1/4 In. 98.00
Tumbler, White Figure, Emerald Green 45.00
Vase, 1 Boy, 1 Girl, Light Blue, 8 In., Pair 135.00
Vase, Angel With Cello, Blue, Gold Trim, Crimped, 9 1/4 In. 125.00
Vase, Boy & Girl Playing, Pink, Gold Trim, 10 1/2 In., Pair 350.00
Vase, Boy In Hat Running, Cranberry, 9 X 3 3/4 In. 165.00
Vase, Boy On Ladder Near Tree, Cranberry 650.00
Vase, Boy On Swing, Cranberry, 8 1/2 In. 275.00
Vase, Boy With Butterfly Net, Amethyst, 8 1/4 In. 295.00
Vase, Boy With Hat, Cranberry, 3 1/2 X 7 3/4 In. 125.00
Vase, Boy, Cobalt Blue, 7 1/4 In. 110.00
Vase, Girl & Pitcher Of Water, Blue, White, 12 In. 325.00
Vase, Girl Scene, Reverse Amberina, 10 In. 295.00
Vase, Girl With Basket Of Flowers, Cranberry, 11 In. 145.00
Vase, Girl With Cap, On Rock, Shaded Rose To Pink, 8 7/8 In. 365.00
Vase, Glass, Cranberry, 7 1/2 In., Pair ....*Illus* 250.00
Vase, Glass, Tennis Players, Amethyst, 8 X 5 3/4 In. ....*Illus* 360.00
Vase, Little Boy, Bulbous, Cranberry, 2 5/8 In. 89.00
Vase, Winged Cherub On Leaves, Green, 4 In. 100.00
Vase, Young Boy With Hat, Cranberry, 7 3/4 In. 125.00
Vase, Young Girl, Cranberry, Bulbous, Square Top, 8 1/2 X 4 In. 165.00
Wine, Girl Holding Spray, Bubble Stopper, Cranberry, 9 In. 150.00

Modern Freemasonry started in seventeenth–century England. The fraternal order was introduced in the American colonies in the 1730s. Symbols, including the trowel, square, level, plumb rule, pillars, columns, arches, the letter "G," beehive, five–pointed star, compass, and eye, have special meaning and are often pictured on Masonic material. Masonic Shrine glassware was made from 1893 to 1917.

MASONIC, Apron, Doeskin, Hand Painted, 19th Century 110.00
Ashtray, Emblems 22.00
Banner, Pictorial, Symbols, Green Ground, 94 X 36 In. 140.00
Beer Glass, Ruby, Masonic Temple, Chicago, Miniature 8.00
Bookmark, Lincoln Centennial, Feb, 12, 1909, Image Of Lincoln 4.00
Cane, Carved 70.00
Chalice, Shriner, 1908 .... 50.00
Champagne, Shriner, 1911 .... 55.00
Champagne, Syria Shrine, Pittsburgh, Alligator Handles, 1910 .... 50.00
Champagne, Syria Shrine, Rochester & Pittsburgh, 1911 .... 100.00
Chart, Hand Colored, Framed, 1885 .... 35.00
Cigar Cutter, 10K Gold 48.00
Coverlet, Masonic K.T.Ribbons, 36 X 80 In. 100.00
Cup & Saucer, Eastern Star .... 8.00 To 27.50
Dish, Nut, Design, Ceramic Art Co., Oval, 5 3/4 In. 65.00
Earrings & Pin, Emblems 12.00
Figurine, Fraternal Symbol, Wooden, 14 1/2 In. 25.00
Goblet, Etched Shrine Symbol & Los Angeles, Crystal, 1907 .... 95.00
Jewelry, Eastern Star, 4 Piece 15.00
Knife, Pewter, Pocket 35.00
Knife, Pocket, 10K Gold 85.00
Lamp Base, Shriner's Bust, Atlantic City, 1927 .... 125.00
Lamp, Wall, Elks, Figural, Brass 48.00
Lapel Pin, Sterling & Enamel, Grand Lodge Of Ohio, 25 Years 5.00
Locket, Masonic Designs, Geo.B.Newton, Lilly, Chaplain, 1856 .... 25.00
Locket, Sunburst & Triangle, Initials, Hiram Lodge No.7, Gold, 1798 .... 2200.00
Matchbox Holder 6.00
Mug, Atlantic City, Fish Handle, 1904 .... 50.00
Mug, Atlantic City, July 13, 1904, Fish Handle, Syrian Sword On Side 125.00
Mug, Indian Head In Relief, Saratoga, Glass, 1903 .... 35.00 To 95.00
Mug, Shrine, 1934 Kosair, Louisville, Ky., Roseville 68.00

Nodder, Mystic Shrine Decal On Fez, Papier–Mache, 7 In.	30.00
Pamphlet, 1862	22.00
Paperweight, Masonic Symbol, Banner, Spatter Ground, Sandwich, Round	295.00
Penny, Chartered Aug.17, 1871, Warren, Pa.	8.50
Penny, Golden Jubilee 1896–1946, Long Beach Lodge	4.50
Pin, Beads, Cut Glass, Black, 20 In.	8.00
Pin, Enameled, Guarding The Land We Love, Minute Women, 2 X 1 In.	15.00
Pin, Shriner, Small Diamonds, Marked Johonsten Jewelers, 1 3/4 In.	75.00
Pitcher, Tankard, Northern 25, 60th Anniversary, 1853–1913, 12 In.	115.00
Plate, B.P.O.Elks, Grand Lodge Reunion, Phila.July 15–20, 1907, Tin	50.00
Plate, Comic, Desert Scene Around Edge, Signed Shenango	45.00
Plate, Drunken Shriner, Palm Tree Border	45.00
Plate, Ft.Duquesne Center, 1912, Octagonal, 8 In.	22.50
Plate, Knights Of Columbus, Vienna Art	50.00
Plate, Shriner, 1906	50.00
Plate, Shriner, Los Angeles, 1906, 6 In.	35.00
Plate, Worcester, 1908	35.00
Print, Shriner's First Pin, 1908, Framed	25.00
Ring, 10K Gold	65.00 To 75.00
Ring, 32nd Degree, Zircon, 10K Gold	125.00
Salt & Pepper, Eastern Star	7.50
Shaving Mug	49.00
Stein, Elk's Temple Court House, Detroit, Mich., Beige & Dark Green	60.00
Syllabub Set, Etched Masonic Symbols, 7 Piece	1250.00
Teaspoon, Home, Utica, N.Y., March 14, 1895, Sterling Silver	35.00
Tumbler, Atlantic City, Fish Handle	50.00
Tumbler, Syria Temple, 3 Sided, White, 3 1/2 In.	50.00
Tumbler, Syria Temple, Pittsburgh, Grasshopper Pictured, 1901	30.00

J.MASSIER fils

> *Massier pottery is iridescent French art pottery made by Clement Massier in Golfe–Juan, France, in the late nineteenth and early twentieth centuries. It has an iridescent metallic luster glaze that resembles the Weller Sicard pottery glaze. Most pieces are marked "J. Massier."*

MASSIER, Jug, Persian Design, Gold Ground, Handles, Signed, 12 In.	350.00
Tile, Flowers, Beige Ground, Signed Jerome Massier	145.00
Vase, Cabinet, Purple, Metal Floral Mounted, Signed, 4 3/4 In.	400.00
Vase, Fish Swimming In Sea Of Waves, Signed, 13 1/2 In.	950.00
Vase, Mottled Glaze, Wasps At Top, Red Bodies, Signed, 10 In.	850.00

> *Large wooden matches were used in the nineteenth and twentieth centuries for a variety of purposes. The kitchen stove and the fireplace or furnace had to be lit regularly. One type of match holder was made to hang on the wall, another was designed to be kept on a tabletop. Of special interest today are match holders that have advertisements as part of the design.*

MATCH HOLDER, 3–Pocket, Scratch Sides, Metal	16.00
Acorn, Tilting, Iron, Decal Front, Pat.Jan.21, 1863, 4 1/2 In.	89.00
American Brewing Co., Stoneware, Eagle Design	110.00
Banner Bubbles, Tin	250.00
Bear & Honey Pail, Victorian, Brass	65.00
Born Steel Ranges, Tin, Wall	240.00
Boy With Tall Basket, Striker, Staffordshire, 4 In.	25.00
Brumbach's Shoes, Wall	42.00
Bull's Head, Green Paint, Tin	45.00
Buster Brown Bread, Tin, Wall	700.00
Cherub, Bisque, Flower Form, 4 In.	25.00
Cloisonne, Floral	12.00
Clover Brand Shoes, Tin, Wall	100.00
Colonial Lady, Striker, Incised Mold Number, Staffordshire	67.50
Columbia Mill Co., Diecut, Tin, Wall	375.00
Coors, Saucer Type	13.50
Cutout & Crimped Crest, Old Black Paint, Tin, Wall, 7 In.	25.00
De Laval, Mounted On Wooden Frame, Wall	55.00

De Laval, Tin 75.00
Devil Head, Wall, Cast Iron 75.00
Double Slipper, Iron 16.50
Double Urn, Cast Iron, Dated 1871 .... 24.00
Double Urn, Striker, Cast Iron, Dated 1887 .... 30.00
Double, Scroll Cut, Walnut, 10 X 7 In. 35.00
Double, Slipper 16.50
Double, Turkey & Hen House, Asbury Park, Striker, Germany 45.00
E.O.Webber Lumber Co. 52.00
Edgeworth Tobacco 75.00
Egg On Cushion, Baby Popping Out Of Egg, German 17.00
Father & Children Resting At Wayside, Cast Iron, C.1890 .... 75.00
Figural, Monk 65.00
Girl Washing Clothes Scene, Striker, Staffordshire, 3 3/4 In. 85.00
Gnome Head, Snaggle Toothed, Wall 50.00
Gold Floral, Brown, Black, Nippon, M In Wreath 30.00
Green River Whiskey, Ashtray 35.00
Hanging, Cover, Tin 10.00
Harper Whiskey, Embossed Glass, Held Box 16.00
Indian Head, Wall 20.00
Judson Whiskey, Tin, Wall .... 65.00 To 110.00
Juicy Fruit Gum, Wall .... 45.00 To 90.00
Kitchen, Says Matches, Blue Custard Glass 24.00
Kool Cigarettes, Penguin Smoking, Tin, Wall 15.00
Lovebirds, On Log, Hollow Stump Holds Matches, Parian, 8 In. 79.00
Man's Head, Wearing Night Cap, Chin Strap, Majolica, 4 1/2 In. 55.00
Man, Standing, Barrel On Back, Silver Plated, J.Tufts, 7 In. 65.00
Mother's Worm Syrup, Tin, Wall 425.00
Norton Co., Worcester, Mass. 18.00
Old Hickory Wagons, Tin 85.00
Parrot, On Top Of Red Tole Tray, 7 1/4 X 12 1/2 In. 185.00
Porcelain, Brown, Striker, 2 X 3 In. ....*Illus* 30.00
Rockford Watch 195.00
Ruesink's Jack Sprat Store, Cherry Grove, Minn. 17.50
Sharpels, Wall 150.00
Sheaf Of Wheat, Brass, For Kitchen Matches 35.00
Shoe Shape, Brass 7.00
Snow Eagles, Cast Iron, C.1865 .... 39.00
Solarine Metal Polish 55.00
Stoneware, American Brewing Co., Rochester 125.00
Sunny Brook Whiskey, Tin 25.00
Tannhauser Troper Bitters, Tin 36.00

Match Holder, Porcelain, Brown, Striker, 2 X 3 In.

Tartanware	18.00
Telephone, Wall, Cast Iron	90.00
Top Hat Shape, Scratch Side, Blue Glass	34.00
Turkey, Bone China, Striker Body, White	35.00
Universal Stoves	65.00
Urn Shape, Cast Iron, Dated 1878	18.00
Victorian Boy & Girl, Next To Baskets, White, Bisque, 4 In.	60.00
Vulcan Plows, Wall	200.00
White Furniture Co., Detroit, Double Flip Lid	20.00
Wolbach, Nebraska, Tin, Wall	18.00

*Early matches were made with phosphorous and could ignite
unexpectedly. Match safes were designed to be carried in the pocket.
The matches were safely stored in the tightly closed container.
Examples were made in sterling silver, plated silver, or other metals.
The English call these "vesta boxes."*

MATCH SAFE, 9K Gold	100.00
Acorn & Leaf Shape, Brass	26.00
Art Nouveau, Head Of Woman, Flowing Hair, Silver, French	55.00
Art Nouveau, Lady's Head, Florals, Marked Sterling	55.00
Art Nouveau, Nude Lady On Waves, Sterling Silver	70.00
Art Nouveau, Pullman Automobiles, Deer On Reverse	35.00
Art Nouveau, Sterling Silver	65.00
Book Design, Brass, 2 In.	40.00
Carved, Game Pouch, 2 Birds & Powder Horn, Walnut, 6 1/4 In. ...	95.00
Chrome, Irish Setter Center, Pearlized Trim	55.00
Compliments Of Las Dos Nacinoes Cigar Co.	75.00
Dated Oct.3rd, 1914, Sterling Silver	95.00
De Laval, Tin	55.00
Embossed Dragons, Tin	36.00
Engraved Christmas, 1900, Sterling Silver	75.00
Everdry, Waterproof	30.00
Face Of Lion, Sterling Sivler	89.50
Figural, Pornographic, Brass	195.00
Fish, Sterling Silver	89.50
Full Figure Nude, Scrolls, Sterling Silver, Marked	75.00
Gillette Blades	5.00
Hanging, Crimped Shell Top, Open Slat Front	65.00
Hercules Gun Powder	65.00
High Button Boot, On Legged Iron Platform, Cast Iron	40.00
Horse & Rider, Sterling Silver	79.50
Hunter Baltimore Rye, Celluloid & Nickel Over Brass	25.00
Judson Whiskey	85.00
Juicy Fruit Gum	50.00
K. Of C., 1919	95.00
Labrador Head, Repousse, Plain Case, Sterling Silver, Large ...	125.00
Owl, Figural, Glass Eyes, Brass	55.00
Pabst, Brass	20.00
Pearlized Celluloid Trim, Dog In Center	45.00
Pocket, Army	2.10
Pocket, U.S.Army	2.10
Red Riding Hood & Wolf On Lid, Striker, Staffordshire	85.00
Scroll & Geometric, Scalloped, Iron, Hanging, 2 Tier, Pat.1870 ...	65.00
Sea Monsters, Floral, Sterling Silver, Large	125.00
Shepherdess With Sheep On Lid, Striker, Staffordshire	85.00
Shoe, Lady's, High, Cast Iron, Rectangular Pedestal Base, 5 In. ...	47.00
Silver, Enameled Nude Lady, Cupid, Reed & Barton, 2 1/2 In. ...	400.00
Snaps Open, Button On Side, Striker On Bottom, 14K Gold, 2 In. ...	396.00
Soccer Ball	125.00
Tortoiseshell, Pocket, Embossed 2 Sides	65.00
Victorian Bowling Scene, Sterling Silver	110.00
When Clothing Store, Nov.9, 1896, Pant Shape, 2 3/4 In.	50.00
World's Fair, 1904, Lewis & Clark	75.00
Wylie Coal, Dated 1890, Brass	20.00

Matsu–no–ke was a type of applied decoration for glass patented by Frederick Carder in 1922. There is clear evidence that pieces were made before that date at the Steuben glassworks. Stevens & Williams of England also made an applied decoration by the same name.

MATSU–NO–KE, Mug, Crystal, Footed, Green Decoration & Handle, Steuben, 6 In. 225.00

McCoy pottery is made in Roseville, Ohio. The J. W. McCoy Pottery was founded in 1899. It became the Brush McCoy Pottery Company in 1911. The name changed to the Brush Pottery in 1925. The word "Brush" was usually included in the mark on their pieces. The Nelson McCoy Sanitary and Stoneware Company, a different firm, was founded in Roseville, Ohio, in 1910. The firm made art pottery after 1926. In 1933 it became the Nelson McCoy Pottery. Pieces marked "McCoy" were made by the Nelson McCoy Company.

MCCOY, Basket, Hanging, Bronze	20.00
Basket, Pinecone	25.00
Bean Pot, Tan & Green	9.00
Berry Bowl, Pale Green ....18.00 To	19.00
Bookends, Floral	12.50
Boot, Drinking, Figural, 8 In.	32.00
Bowl, Leaf Shape, Handle, Signed	22.00
Bowl, Mt.Pelee, Charcoal Iridescent	325.00
Box, Mixing, Brown Stripe, Ivory, 10 1/4 In.	8.00
Cake Plate, Gold Trim, With Server, 12 1/4 In.	35.00
Canister Set, Carved Eagle, 4 Piece	30.00
Canister, Chef	14.00
Chocolate Set, Sunburst Gold, 3 Piece	85.00
Cookie Jar, Animal Crackers	25.00
Cookie Jar, Bobby Baker ....15.00 To	27.00
Cookie Jar, Brown Bear	65.00
Cookie Jar, Bugs Bunny	35.00
Cookie Jar, Caboose	50.00
Cookie Jar, Chef's Head	45.00
Cookie Jar, Chipmunk ....28.00 To	60.00
Cookie Jar, Christmas Tree	65.00
Cookie Jar, Churn	12.00
Cookie Jar, Circus Horse	65.00
Cookie Jar, Clown Bust	25.00
Cookie Jar, Clown In Barrel ....22.00 To	30.00
Cookie Jar, Coalby Cat	69.00
Cookie Jar, Cookie Barrel	10.00
Cookie Jar, Cookstove, Black	25.00
Cookie Jar, Cookstove, White	14.00
Cookie Jar, Corn ....48.00 To	65.00
Cookie Jar, Covered Wagon ....30.00 To	40.00
Cookie Jar, Dalmations	55.00
Cookie Jar, Dog	18.00
Cookie Jar, Drum ....14.00 To	28.00
Cookie Jar, Dutch Treat Barn	20.00
Cookie Jar, Football, With Player	22.00
Cookie Jar, Fortune Cookie	25.00
Cookie Jar, Frontier Family ....20.00 To	40.00
Cookie Jar, Fruit & Nut On Front	12.50
Cookie Jar, Fruit Basket	27.00
Cookie Jar, Globe ....40.00 To	60.00
Cookie Jar, Grandfather Clock	35.00
Cookie Jar, Granny	48.50
Cookie Jar, Green Pepper	55.00
Cookie Jar, Hamm's Bear	55.00
Cookie Jar, Hobbyhorse	45.00
Cookie Jar, Honey Bear	25.00
Cookie Jar, House	40.00
Cookie Jar, Jack-O'-Lantern	175.00

Cookie Jar, Kangaroo, Yellow Tan Underglaze 130.00
Cookie Jar, Kissing Penquins 35.00
Cookie Jar, Kitten, Basket Weave 28.00
Cookie Jar, Kookie Kettle 15.00
Cookie Jar, Liberty Bell, Bronze 15.00
Cookie Jar, Locomotive, Black 65.00
Cookie Jar, Log Cabin ....15.00 To 35.00
Cookie Jar, Mac Dog 35.00
Cookie Jar, Mammy, Covered, Cauliflower 55.00
Cookie Jar, Mary, Mary 20.00
Cookie Jar, Monk, Brown 15.00
Cookie Jar, Monkey, On Stump 20.00
Cookie Jar, Mother Goose ....50.00 To 55.00
Cookie Jar, Mouse On Clock 25.00
Cookie Jar, Mr.Owl 25.00
Cookie Jar, Mrs.Owl 25.00
Cookie Jar, Nabisco 70.00
Cookie Jar, Oaken Bucket 10.00
Cookie Jar, Pelican, Yellow 55.00
Cookie Jar, Pineapple 20.00
Cookie Jar, Pup Holding Sign 35.00
Cookie Jar, Puppy, Brown 14.00
Cookie Jar, Rabbit, Pink Trim 20.00
Cookie Jar, Rooster ....25.00 To 55.00
Cookie Jar, Snow Bear 25.00
Cookie Jar, Squirrel On Log 20.00
Cookie Jar, Teepee ....68.50 To 110.00
Cookie Jar, Tilt Pitcher 20.00
Cookie Jar, Touring Car 35.00
Cookie Jar, Tudor House 65.00
Cookie Jar, Turkey ....65.00 To 75.00
Cookie Jar, W.C.Fields ....55.00 To 60.00
Cookie Jar, Windmill ....28.00 To 35.00
Cookie Jar, Wishing Well 15.00
Decanter, Apollo ....12.00 To 25.00
Decanter, Train Engine 35.00
Jardiniere, Basket Weave, 12 In.Diam. 35.00
Jardiniere, Pedestal, Green Woodland, 26 1/2 In. 295.00
Jug, Vat 69 .... 22.50
Lamp, Cowboy Boot, Pair 35.00
Pitcher & Bowl, Brown & Tan 25.00
Pitcher, Gold Berry Leaf Design, 9 In. 13.00
Pitcher, Green, Dolphin Handle, Brush, C.1935 .... 35.00
Pitcher, Parrot 25.00
Pitcher, Stoneware, Green 68.00
Pitcher, W.C.Fields 35.00
Planter, Alligator 16.00
Planter, Auto, Floraline 10.00
Planter, Duck 12.50
Planter, Five Scotties 15.00
Planter, Frog & Lily Pad, 7 1/2 In. 35.00
Planter, Shape Of Cross 3.00
Planter, Spinning Wheel 20.00
Planter, Squirrel 12.50
Planter, Tulip, Birds, Double 8.00
Planter, Turtle ....10.00 To 12.50
Planter, Wishing Well ....8.00 To 10.00
Reamer, Yellow 65.00
Sprinkler, Cat 20.00
Sprinkler, Elephant 12.00
Sprinkling Can, Poodle 20.00
Tea Set, Ivy 35.00
Tea Set, Pinecone, 3 Piece ....27.00 To 40.00
Teapot, Pinecone 20.00

Vase, Berries, Leaves, Handles, Loy–Nel–Art, 10 1/2 In.	185.00
Vase, Experimental, Loy–Nel–Art, 13 In.	225.00
Vase, Grecian, Handles, 9 In.	25.00
Vase, Handles, Pink & Green, 10 In., Pair	25.00
Vase, Hyacinth, 8 In., Pair	20.00
Wall Pocket, Apple	10.00
Wall Pocket, Banana	10.00
Wall Pocket, Cuckoo Clock	15.00
Wall Pocket, Horn Of Plenty, Basket Weave	12.50
Wall Pocket, Lady's Head, Wearing Bonnet	7.00
Wall Pocket, Lily, Signed N.M.	65.00
Wall Pocket, Owl	80.00
Wall Pocket, Owl, Trivet	12.00
Wall Pocket, Rustic Glaze	95.00
Wall Pocket, Whisk Broom Shape, Butterfly	12.00

PRESCUT

The McKee name has been associated with various glass enterprises in the United States since 1836, including J. & F. McKee (1850), Bryce, McKee & Co. (1850 to 1854), McKee and Brothers (1865), and National Glass Co. (1899). In 1903, the McKee Glass Company was formed in Jeanette, Pennsylvania. It became McKee Division of the Thatcher Glass Co. in 1951 and was bought out by the Jeanette Corporation in 1961. Pressed glass, kitchenwares, and tablewares were produced.

MCKEE, see also Custard Glass

MCKEE, Batter Bowl, Jadite, 7 In.	10.00
Bowl, Laurel, 5 In.	3.00
Bowl, Laurel, French Ivory, 11 In.	15.00
Butter, Dome	49.00
Canister, Covered, Marked Cereal, 6 In.	28.00
Creamer, Sunbeam, Red Rim	18.00
Cup, Punch, Nortec	5.00
Dish, Swan, Covered, Open Neck, Marked	200.00
Figurine, Squirrel, Split Ribbed Base, Milk Glass, 5 1/2 In.	110.00
Goblet, Rock Crystal, Footed, 8 Oz.	13.50
Iced Tea, Rock Crystal, 11 Oz.	13.50
Jug, Batter, Ruby	95.00
Measure, Milk Glass, 2 Cup	12.00
Mixing Bowl, 7 In.	8.00
Mug & Bowl, Tom & Jerry, Set Of 12	40.00
Plate, Doltec, 6 In.	2.50
Plate, Laurel, 9 In.	7.00
Plate, Ruby, Scalloped, 9 1/2 In.	32.50
Punch Bowl & Pedestal Base, Nortec	85.00
Punch Bowl, Wiltec	50.00
Reamer, Jadite Green	20.00
Reamer, Skokie Sunkist	16.50
Sugar, Ivory, Laurel, Tall	6.00
Syrup, Apollo Pattern, Pewter Top, Pink	68.00

MECHANICAL BANK, see Bank, Mechanical

All types of equipment used by doctors or hospitals are included in this section. Medical office furniture, operating tools, microscopes, thermometers, and other paraphernalia used by doctors are included. Medicine bottles are listed under "bottle." There are related collectibles listed under Dental.

MEDICAL, Abbe Test Plate, Zeiss, Signed Case, 19th Century	165.00
Amputation Set, Knife & Saw, English, Signed, C.1780, Set	550.00
Amputation Set, Weedon, Maple Case, Saw By MAW 16 1/2 X 5 1/2 In.	850.00
Apothecary Chest, Oak, Bottles, Scale, Ointment Pot, English	1050.00
Artificial Leg, Handmade, Pivoting Ankle, 17 In.Stump, 40 In.	150.00
Bag, Filled With 60 Cures, Alligator	98.00
Bleeder, 3 Blades, Fiber Board Case	69.00
Bleeder, 12 Blades, Brass	175.00

Bleeder, Hand Forged, Iron, 5 1/2 In. 45.00
Book, Kalogynomia Or The Laws Of Female Beauty, T.Bell MD, 1821 .... 275.00
Book, New Family Physician, King, 1127 Pages, 1860 .... 20.00
Book, Science & Art Of Surgery, Ericksen, 1885 .... 12.00
Box, Pill, Willow Wood, Label, C.1800 .... 65.00
Box, Slide, 72 Slides, 12 Trays, Paper Labels, French, C.1870 .... 175.00
Box, Wood's Emergency, Tin 38.00
Brace, Trepanning, Conical Steel, Hardwood Hand, Stamped Paris, 1760 .... 1400.00
Cabinet, Apothecary, Oak, 6 Ft. 2 In. 1850.00
Cabinet, Specimen, Ebony Sliders, Mahogany Box, English, C.1780 .... 695.00
Carrying Case, For Dead Body, Wicker, Full Size 400.00
Case, Apothecary, 30 Drawers, Old Gray Paint, Brasses, Pine, 30 In. 625.00
Case, Microscope Slides, 12 Trays, 6 Compartments, English, C.1880 .... 180.00
Case, Veterinarian, Leg Vaccinating Box Inside, Brass Trim, Oak 99.50
Chest, Medicine, 6 Bottles, Balance & Weights, Mahogany, C.1840 .... 750.00
Chest, Ship, Maynard & Noyes, Boston, Red, C.1840, 10 X 11 X 17 In. 250.00
Chest, Slide, Double Door, American, 57 Drawers, 9 X 8 X 5 In. 580.00
Depressor, Tongue, Sterling, Pediatric, Monogrm DMF, London 1900 .... 175.00
Depressor, Tongue, Sterling, S.Mordan, Hallmarked London 1893 .... 225.00
Device, Quack, Renulife, Internal, External, Violet Ray, Ozone 85.00
Drill, Trepanning, Corneal, Spring Wound, Nickel Plated, Case, 1910 .... 550.00
Drill, Trephine & Archimedian, Steel & Brass, 14 In. 85.00
Ear Horn, C.1890 .... 65.00
Ear Trumpet, Tin, Curved End By Ear, Disc, Other End, 20 In. 95.00
Equipment, Energex, Quack 45.00
Eyecup, Cobalt Blue 18.50
Eyecup, John Bull, 1917 .... 14.00
Eyecup, John Bull, Clear 15.00
Eyecup, John Bull, Cobalt Blue 40.00
Eyecup, Marked Wyeth, Blue ....4.00 To 9.50
Feeder, Infant, Blue Numbers On Side, Ironstone 30.00
Glass Eyes, 50 In Velvet Lined Wooden Case, C.1880, 12 1/2 X 7 In. 495.00
Hammer, Doctor's, Square Head, Expands To Round Face, 5 1/2 In. 38.00
Hearing Aid, Otophone, Meyrowitz, Pictorial Box Top, 1895 .... 75.00
Hot Water Bottle, Baby's, ABC & Numbers 18.00
Hot Water Bottle, Old Woman In Shoe, Embossed 10.00
Hypodermic Syringe, Glass, Needle, Coxeter, London, C.1850, 5 In. 395.00
Jar, Sponaceous Tooth, Dr. Bowditch, 19th Century 45.00
Kit, Caponizing, Dovetailed Oak Box, Instruments 55.00
Lamp, Heating, Alcohol, Brass, 1863 .... 15.00
Lamp, Microscope, Bockett, English, Brass 75.00
Lamp, Poser Slit, Bausch & Lomb, 1938 .... 150.00
Lancet, Brass Spring, Original Case 125.00
Leg Brace, Key Adjusting 95.00
Leg Brace, Notched Elevation Support, Wood Screws 150.00
Machine, Pill Making, Brass & Marble, 14 Rollers 215.00
Machine, Pill Making, Mahogany & Brass, 16 Rollers 200.00
Mannikin, Female Body, Lithograph, Dr.Minder's, N.Y., 1900, 19 In. 95.00
Measure, Apothecary, Glass, 4 In. 18.00
Microscope Set, Ring, 1946, Unused 55.00
Microscope, Chain Drive, American, C.1870, 10 To 14 1/2 In. 595.00
Microscope, Collapsible, Bausch & Lomb, No.170791, 1920, Pocket Size 240.00
Microscope, Culpeper, Brass, Wood Base, English, 1790–1800, 15 In. 950.00
Microscope, Dissecting, American, C.1890, J.Zentmayer, Brass 295.00
Microscope, Dissecting, English, C.1870, Brass, Swivel Arm, 3 Oculars 295.00
Microscope, Drum, French, Brass, C.1880 .... 60.00
Microscope, English, Brass, C.1880, 23 In.Draw Tube, 14 In. 580.00
Microscope, English, Field & Son, Dated 1855, Nickel–Iron Base 1250.00
Microscope, English, Lacquered Brass, Ivory Handle, Case, 2 1/2 In. 225.00
Microscope, French, Storage Drawer, Case, C.1875, 11 In. 550.00
Microscope, Gundlach, Brass, 1890 .... 345.00
Microscope, Martin Drum Type, Bronze, Case, C.1890, 6 In. Folded 95.00
Microscope, No.44030, Bausch & Lomb, Brass 125.00
Microscope, O.Bagger, Quebec, Brass & Cast Iron Base, 10 In. 395.00

Microscope, Petrographical, Swift, Magnifier, 360 Degree, C.1890 .... 875.00
Microscope, Spencer No.188300, 3–Turret, Extra Lens, Case 45.00
Microscope, Stand, Single, Compound, Aquatic, & Compass, C.1800 .... 2550.00
Microscope, W.Ekein, Wetzlar, Germany, Enamel, Nickel, 1933, 11 In. 160.00
Microscope, With Varley Stage, Brass, Iron Base, Bar–Limb, C.1875 .... 325.00
Microscope, Zeiss Oculars, U Shaped Foot & Rack, C.1860, 12 In. 600.00
Monocular, Student, Iron Base & Arm, C.1880, 12 In. 145.00
Mortar, Apothecary, Bronze, Late 18th Century, 4 In. 45.00
Nose Cup, Glass, Pat.Nov.19, 1901, 1 3/4 X 3 1/2 In. 28.00
Ophthalmometer, Iron Base, General Optical Co., C.1915, 23 In. 275.00
Ophthalmoscope, Morton's, Curry & Paxton, Ivory Handles, C.1885 .... 245.00
Pen, Swan, Eye Dropper 35.00
Perimeter, J.E.Limeburner & Co., 1800s 75.00
Perimeter, Table, American Optical Brombach, 1937 .... 150.00
Pill Finisher, Turned Walnut, C.1880 .... 45.00
Post Mortem Set, By Tiemann, Ebony Handles, C.1860, 11 X 5 1/2 In. 1000.00
Pump, Breast, Monogram, Original Box 20.00
Scarificator, 12 Blades, Brass, C.1820 .... 145.00
Scarificator, 13 Blades, Brass, C.1800 .... 175.00
Scarificator, 16 Blades, 2 Bleeding Bowls, Wien 800.00
Sign, Quarantine, Scarlet Fever 12.50
Sign, Quarantine, Smallpox 12.50
Skull, Poison Bottle Inside, Full Size 49.50
Slide Case, 2 Drawers, Mahogany, C.1860, 8 1/2 In. 185.00
Slide Set, Petroligic, German, Labeled, Case, Late 19th Century 180.00
Spatula, Pharmacist, Signed MAW, C.1880 .... 30.00
Stethoscope, Ivory, C.1860 .... 150.00
Stethoscope, Monaural, Fruitwood & Ivory, C.1850, 9 1/2 In. 375.00
Sugar Bowl, Covered, U.S.Army Medical Dept., Carr China 15.00
Surgical Set, Ear, H.Reiner, Vienna, Ebony Handle, 6 Tools, Case 325.00
Surgical Set, Ebony, Brass Case, Shepard–Dudley, C.1870, 10 Pc. 950.00
Syringe, Hard Rubber, Goodyear's Pat.May 7, 1851, 6 In. 39.00
Syringe, Hard Rubber, Goodyear, 1851, 6 In. 55.00
Telescope, 4–Section, Lens Cap, Leather Cover 159.00
Telescope, Selsi, Paris, Table Stand, 2 Drawers, Brass, Box., 16 In. 450.00
Tester, Vibration, English, Brass 125.00
Testing Set, Optometrist 95.00
Thermometer, Bath, Dr.Forbes Specifications, C.1900, 8 In. 30.00
Thermometer, Large Bulb, Pascal Amarante, Menton, France, Case 150.00
Tin, Opium, Powdered, Poison Mark, Picture Of Factory, 3 1/2 X 2 In. 50.00
Tool, Veterinarian's, Leather Satchel 89.00
Urinal, Glass 8.00
Vaporizer, Inhaler, Brass, Copper, Dr.C.Coulter, Ont., C.1890, 19 In. 220.00
Vaporizer, Simplex, Pierced Tin, Burner 25.00
Violet Ray Set, Quack, Leather Suitcase, Book, Cures 30.00

*Meerschaum pipes and other pieces of carved meerschaum, a soft
mineral, date from the nineteenth century to the present.*

MEERSCHAUM, Holder, Cigar, 3 Dogs 68.00
Holder, Cigar, Carved Dog, Original Case ....38.00 To 50.00
Holder, Cigar, Figural, Buxom Lady, Seated On Lounge, 3 3/4 In. 65.00
Pipe, Amber Stem, Silver Band, 1896 Carved Bowl, Original Case 100.00
Pipe, Carved Fox, Original Leather Case, 3 In. 32.00
Pipe, Carved Lion Head Bowl, Amber Stem, 3 1/2 X 6 1/2 In. 95.00
Pipe, Carved Nude Lady, 8 1/2 In. 150.00
Pipe, Carved Turk's Head Bowl 130.00
Pipe, Figural, Eagle & Ball, Amber Stem, Fitted Case, 12 1/4 In. 725.00
Pipe, Full Figure Hindu With Rifle, Leather Case, Silver Band 50.00
Pipe, Horse With Dog, Case 75.00
Pipe, Lion At St.Mark, Carved 90.00
Pipe, Mermaid, Amber Stem, C.1940, 12 In. 150.00
Pipe, Tuba Shape, Sherlock Holmes Type 35.00
Pipe, Turk's Head, Amber Stem 95.00

Meissen, Figurine, Man & Woman, Pair,
6 1/2 & 7 3/8 In.

Milk Glass, Dish, Log Cabin, Painted,
Westmoreland, 4 In.

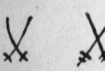

Meissen is a town in Germany where porcelain has been made since 1710. Any china made in the town can be called Meissen, although the famous Meissen factory made the finest porcelains of the area. The crossed swords mark of the great Meissen factory have been copied by many other firms in Germany and other parts of the world.

MEISSEN, Bottle Top, Vinegar, Figural, Lady's Capped Head 385.00
Bowl, Flowers, Gold Trim, 14 In., Pair 450.00
Bowl, Fruit Design, White, Gold Trim, Crossed Swords, 12 In. 175.00
Bowl, White, Gold Ivy Leaf Border, 11 In. 135.00
Candelabra, Putti, 4 Seasons, 4–Light, Crossed Swords, 19 In., Pr. 1320.00
Candleholder, Lady, Holding Child, C.1880, Crossed Swords, 12 In. 385.00
Chandelier, 3 Classic Ladies, Pierced, Latticework, 9–Light, 45 In. 4400.00
Charger, Raised Gold, Cobalt Blue Ground, Crossed Swords, 11 In. 250.00
Clock, Mantel, Grape Vines, C.1900, Crossed Swords, 16 In. 715.00
Clock, Mantel, Stand, Floral, Top Couple, Crossed Swords, 23 1/2 In. 1320.00
Coffee Mill, Marked 175.00
Coffee Set, White, Gold, Crossed Swords, 2 Cups & Saucers, 8 Pc. 400.00
Cup & Saucer, Jewels, Bouquets Of Flowers, Medallion 105.00
Cup & Saucer, Scenic Panels, Cobalt, Gold Floral, Crossed Swords 145.00
Dish, Serving, Rose Onion, Child Holding Cornucopia Knob, 13 In. 200.00
Ewer, Shell, Scroll, 19th Century, Putti With Fruit, 14 1/2 In., Pair 400.00
Figurine, 18th–Century Couple, Cupids, 9 1/2 In. 450.00
Figurine, Allegorical, Odin, Flags, Gold Rococo Base, Marked, 7 In. 800.00
Figurine, Allegorical, Putto, Day, Night, Marked, 7 In., Pair 1210.00
Figurine, Bird Catcher, C.1869, Crossed Swords & Number, 7 X 7 In. 475.00
Figurine, Bounty Of Hunt, Female, C.1890, Marked, 12 In., Pair 750.00
Figurine, Boy, Barefoot, Frock Coat, Against Tree Stump, 5 3/4 In. 250.00
Figurine, Ceres, Cupids, Crossed Swords, No.193, 20 3/8 In. 1210.00
Figurine, Cherub, Making A Rude Gesture, 19th Century, 8 In. 290.00
Figurine, Finch, Green & Yellow, Repaired, C.1800, 3 3/4 In., Pair 75.00
Figurine, Frightened Harlequin, Crossed Swords, 6 1/2 In. 385.00
Figurine, Gentlemen, Crossed Swords, C.1860 .... 463.00
Figurine, Group, Oval Base, Gold Trim, Hand Painted In Japan 50.00
Figurine, Lady's Bust, Hat, 5 1/2 In. 275.00
Figurine, Lovers Under Tree, Crossed Swords Mark, 10 5/8 In. 715.00
Figurine, Man & Lady On Couch, Musical, Crossed Swords Mark 1000.00
Figurine, Man & Woman, Pair, 6 1/2 & 7 3/8 In. ....*Illus* 500.00
Figurine, Monkey Band, With Orchestra Leader, 8 Piece 2900.00
Figurine, Oriole, Golden, Mounted, Pair 33000.00
Figurine, Oyster Seller, Green & White Dress, Crossed Swords, 6 In. 550.00
Figurine, Peasant, 11 1/2 In., Pair 475.00

Figurine, People Eating, Dancing, Crossed Swords D.96, 18 3/4 In. 1650.00
Figurine, Swan, Samson, 7 In., Pair 400.00
Figurine, Venus, Standing Nude, Flowing Hair, 5 3/4 In. 150.00
Figurine, Young Gardener, C.1900 .... 350.00
Gravy Boat, Floral Design, Diaper Pattern, Spoon, 10 In. 125.00
Group, 18th-Century Men & Women, Pillar Fragment, 13 In. 400.00
Group, 2 Astronomers, Telescope, Putto, Crossed Swords, 8 In. 1980.00
Group, 6 Figures Frolicking On Rock Base, Crossed Swords, 19 In. 550.00
Group, Man & Woman, Musical Instruments, Crossed Swords, 5 7/8 In. 1320.00
Group, Shepherd & Shepherdess, Sheep, Dog, 8 X 8 In. 350.00
Group, Venus, Swan Drawn Chariot, Cupid, Crossed Swords, 15 3/8 In. 1870.00
Lamp Base, Lady, Gentlemen 110.00
Lamp, Fairy, Onion Pattern, Lithophane & Porcelain, 19th Century 500.00
Mirror, Basket Of Flowers, Cartouche Shape, 2 Putti, Floral, 55 In. 7700.00
Mug, Aus Dankbarkeit, Monogram, 3 Claw Feet ....75.00 To 100.00
Nodding Pagoda, Head, Tongue & Hands Move, Crossed Swords, 7 In. 1650.00
Plate, Dessert, Center Cherub, 20th Century, 9 In., Set Of 6 .... 375.00
Plate, Hand Painted Fruit Center, Relief Leaves, 12 In. 125.00
Plate, Lovers Scenes, Lattice, Crossed Swords, 10 1/4 In., Set Of 12 .... 6600.00
Plate, Man Courting Woman, Blue & Gold Rim, H.Wolfjohn, 9 1/2 In. 350.00
Plate, Yellow & White Panels, 8 1/2 In. 75.00
Platter, Fish, 2 Piece Drain, C.1900, 22 1/2 X 11 1/4 In. 475.00
Sconce, Garden Scene, Cupid, 3 Lights, Crossed Swords, 18 In., Pr. 605.00
Shaving Mug, Blue, Crossed Lines, H Mark 35.00
Soup, Dish, Underplate, Blue Onion, Crossed Swords, Set Of 3 .... 140.00
Stopper, Boy Wearing Fez 65.00
Tray, Rococo Gold Edge, Handles, Crossed Swords, 11 1/2 X 6 In. 190.00
Urn, Coiled Snake Handles, Yellow Ground, White Design, 15 In., Pair 1000.00
Urn, Covered, French Silver Spigot, C.1773, Marked, 13 3/4 In. 660.00
Vase, Bud, Gold Laurel Wreath, Flowers, Insects, Marked, 3 1/2 In. 65.00
Vase, Cobalt Glaze, Serpent Handles, Crossed Swords, 15 In., Pair 522.00
Vase, Lover Panel, Floral, Campana Form, Crossed Swords, 25 1/2 In. 2750.00

*Mercury, or silvered glass, was first made in the 1850s. It lost favor
for a while but became popular again about 1910. It looks like a
piece of silver.*

MERCURY GLASS, Bottle, Cork & Metal Stopper, Grape Leaves, C.1840, 7 1/2 In. 145.00
Candle, Red Flame Tip, 10 In., Set Of 4 .... 50.00
Carafe, Vacuum, Mushroom Stopper, Dated 1909, 12 In. 45.00
Knob, Grape Design, Pair 45.00
Pitcher, Water, Clear Paneled Neck, Lacy Florals, 9 3/4 In. 195.00
Salt, Master, Pedestal, Gold Lining, 2 5/8 In. 88.00
Tieback, Embossed Flowers, Pewter End, 3 1/2 In., Pr. 3.00

*Mettlach, Germany, is a city where the Villeroy and Boch factories
worked. Steins from the firm are known as Mettlach steins. They date
from about 1842. PUG means "painted under glaze." The steins can
be dated from the marks on the bottom which include a date-number
code. Other pieces may be listed in the Villeroy & Boch category.*

METTLACH, Beaker, No.2327/1023, 1/4 Liter, Fiddler 20.00
Beaker, No.2327/1024, 1/4 Liter, Flute Player 20.00
Beaker, No.2327/1050, 1/4 Liter, Serving Girl 70.00
Beaker, No.2327/1200, 1/4 Liter, Nurnberg 34.00
Beaker, No.2368/1093, 1/4 Liter, Mandolin Player 34.00
Coaster, No.1032, Dwarf Design, German Saying, Set Of 6 .... 400.00
Cup & Saucer, Relief Flowers, Blue, Gray, & Silver 67.00
Goblet, No.2954/1194, Cherubs, 1/4 Liter, PUG 400.00
Holder, Cigar, No.136, Figural, Tree Stump, Applied Base Leaf, 5 In. 44.00
Humidor, No.1231, Cow Scene, Hinged Lid, 9 In. 475.00
Mug, Bartholomay's Rochester, Tan 135.00
Mug, Hunter With Dog 175.00
Mug, Minneapolis Brewing Co., 1897, B.P.O.E. 95.00
Mug, No.3095, Hires Root Beer 150.00
Mug, No.3287, 1/2 Liter, Sons Of The Revolution, Feb.22, 1910 .... 70.00

Mug, Powers Motel, Rochester, N.Y., Advertising 125.00
Pitcher, Raised Flowers, Fruit, Scrolls, & Birds, Gray, 10 3/4 In. 225.00
Plaque, No.1044/162, Germania Monument, PUG, 14 In. 137.00
Plaque, No.1108, Castle, 17 In. 993.00
Plaque, No.1365, Castle Scene, 17 In. 770.00
Plaque, No.1696, Butterfly Girl, 16 1/2 In. 938.00
Plaque, No.2112 & 2113, Dwarfs In Tree, 16 In., Pair 3042.00
Plaque, No.2195, Castle Scene, 17 1/2 In. 770.00
Plaque, No.2596 & No.2597, Art Nouveau Woman, 16 In., Pair 1595.00
Plaque, No.7072, Lady Holding Flowers, 6 X 8 In. 375.00
Plate, Christmas, 1977, Box 55.00
Punch Bowl, No.1158, 16 Liter, Lid Of Bearded Man 845.00
Punch Bowl, No.1888, 6 Liter, Imperial Eagle, State Shields 990.00
Stein, No. 6, 3 Liter, 3 Panels 140.00
Stein, No. 24, 1/2 Liter, 4 Panels 425.00
Stein, No.1132, 1/2 Liter, Fiddler & Dancing Crocodile 650.00
Stein, No.1266, 1/2 Liter, 3 Panel Drinking Scene 230.00
Stein, No.1394, 1/2 Liter, German Playing Cards 450.00
Stein, No.1403, 1/2 Liter, Bowling Scene 330.00
Stein, No.1467, 1/2 Liter, 4 Panels 165.00
Stein, No.1520, 1/2 Liter, Prussian Eagle & Soldiers 525.00
Stein, No.1526, 1/2 Liter, Town Scene, PUG 155.00
Stein, No.1566, 1/2 Liter, Man On High Wheeler 607.00
Stein, No.1642, 1 Liter, Drinking Man 425.00
Stein, No.1675, 1/2 Liter, Heidelberg 485.00
Stein, No.2002, 1/2 Liter, Munich 365.00
Stein, No.2007, 1/2 Liter, Black Cat 550.00
Stein, No.2057, 1/4 Liter, Dancing Peasants 175.00
Stein, No.2076, 3 Liter, Coat Of Arms 275.00
Stein, No.2082, 1 Liter, William Tell 1550.00
Stein, No.2097, 1/2 Liter, Musical Notes 350.00
Stein, No.2107, 1 1/2 Liter, Gambrinus Rex, Signed H.Schlitt 1050.00
Stein, No.2179/962, 1/4 Liter, Pewter Lid, Gnomes Drinking, PUG 150.00
Stein, No.2182, 1/2 Liter, Bowlers 250.00
Stein, No.2190, 1/2 Liter, Bicycles 650.00
Stein, No.2210, 3 1/4 Liter, Bowling Scene 585.00
Stein, No.2227/900, 4 1/2 Liter, Military, Eagle Finial, PUG 1900.00
Stein, No.2238, 1/2 Liter, 7th Regimental Armory, Eagle & Flag 1200.00
Stein, No.2246, 3/10 Liter, Dancing Peasants 200.00
Stein, No.2373, 1/2 Liter, St.Augustine Florida, Plain Handle 675.00
Stein, No.2373, 1/2 Liter, St.Augustine, Florida, Alligator Handle 450.00
Stein, No.2382, 1/2 Liter, Drinking Knight 570.00
Stein, No.2478, 5 Liter, Hildebrand 1430.00
Stein, No.2520, 1 Liter, Student & Barmaid 900.00
Stein, No.2524, 4 1/5 Liter, Knight In Castle 2550.00
Stein, No.2547, 1 Liter, 3 Panels 200.00
Stein, No.2662, 1/2 Liter, Dreaming Student, Mice 925.00
Stein, No.2690, 1 1/2 Liter, 3 Drinking Cavaliers 1250.00
Stein, No.2721, 1/2 Liter, Cabinetmaker 900.00
Stein, No.2726, 1/2 Liter, Goldsmith 1400.00
Stein, No.2773, 3/10 Liter, Lovers 1580.00
Stein, No.2828, 1/2 Liter, Wartburg 1550.00
Stein, No.2829, 1/2 Liter, Rodenstein 1650.00
Stein, No.3177, 1/5 Liter, Hunting 990.00
Tile, Warrior, Blue, 3/1/4 X 5 3/4 In. 190.00
Tumbler, Rearing Horse In Shield, Top Band With Legend, 1/4 Liter 65.00
Vase, No.1537, 4 Panels, Children, 14 1/2 In., Pair 750.00
Vase, No.1749, Maidens, 13 In. ....255.00 To 300.00

*Milk glass was named for its milky–white color. It was first made in
England during the 1700s. The height of its popularity in the United
States was from 1870 to 1880. It is now correct to refer to some
colored glass as blue milk glass, black milk glass, etc. Reproductions
of milk glass are being made and sold in many stores.*

MILK GLASS, Banana Stand, Openwork Base, Triple Spit Stem, 11 X 8 In. 38.00
  Basket, Blue, 2 Handles, 3 In. 22.50
  Bell, Handle, 5 1/2 In. 25.00
  Bottle, Dresser, Scroll Bottom, Original Stopper, White, 9 In. 30.00
  Bottle, Lion Heads, Scrolls, Enameled, Stopper, 9 In., Pair 65.00
  Bottle, Urbana Wine Co., Figural, Black Bear 145.00
  Bottle, Vinegar, Advertising 1939 World's Fair, Globe Shape 20.00
  Bowl, 3 Dolphin Feet, Shell Garlands, Covered, 5 1/2 X 6 In. 46.00
  Bowl, Beaded Rib, Open Work Top, 10 In. 60.00
  Bowl, Ceres, Covered, 8 In. 35.00
  Bowl, Flame, Citizen's Bank, Wheeling, 1924, 9 In. 50.00
  Bowl, Flared Top, Beaded Rib, 10 1/2 In. 45.00
  Bowl, Fruit, Roses, 3–Footed, 11 In. 35.00
  Bowl, Lattice, Flared, 10 X 4 In. 70.00
  Bowl, Trumpet Vine, Lattice Edge, 9 In. 55.00
  Box, Dresser, Actress, Covered, 10 1/2 In. 45.00
  Box, Figural, Wooden Trunk Shape, Covered, 3 7/8 X 2 5/8 In. 30.00
  Box, Hen, Covered, Westmoreland, 2 1/2 In. 14.00
  Bread Plate, Rope Handles, Give Us This Day, Dated 6/30/30 .... 45.00
  Breakfast Set, Flattened Diamond, Child's 40.00
  Butter, Apple Blossom 65.00
  Butter, Child's, Cloud Band, Covered 135.00
  Butter, Child's, Wild Rose, Covered 28.00
  Butter, Child's, Winged Scroll, Pink, Covered 45.00
  Butter, Cosmos, Covered ....160.00 To 225.00
  Butter, Diamond & Scroll, Gold Trim, Pink, Covered 55.00
  Butter, Pink, Diamond & Scroll, Covered 55.00
  Butter, Roman Cross, Covered 45.00
  Cake Plate, Beaded Rib, Short Pedestal, Hand Painted Center 35.00
  Cake Plate, Victorian, Lace Edge, 14 X 5 In. 32.00
  Calling Card Receiver, Jewish Star Center 22.00
  Candlestick, 7 1/2 In. 16.00
  Candlestick, Black, 8 1/4 In. 38.00
  Candlestick, Dolphin, 9 1/4 In., Pair 85.00
  Candlestick, Embossed Rosebuds, Leaves, 6 1/2 In., Pair 29.00
  Compote, Atterbury, Scalloped, Atlas 65.00
  Compote, Blackberry, Covered 70.00
  Compote, Cut Log, Pink, 6 X 9 In. 45.00
  Compote, Diamond Point & Leaf, Footed, Flint 65.00
  Compote, Dolphin Stemmed, 5 In. 19.00
  Compote, Entwined Fish Cover, Red Glass Eyes 110.00
  Compote, Jelly, Ball & Swirl, Signed Westmoreland, Covered 12.00
  Compote, Lattice Edge, 7 3/8 In. 12.00
  Compote, Sawtooth, Hexagonal Finial, Covered, 6 X 8 1/2 In. 165.00
  Compote, Sawtooth, White, 5 1/2 In. 35.00
  Compote, Sculptured Scrolls, Blue, 6 X 6 1/4 In. 55.00
  Compote, Shell, Dolphin Stem, 8 In. 50.00
  Compote, Strawberry, Flint, 8 X 8 In. 65.00
  Console Set, Child's, 3 Piece 30.00
  Cookie Jar, Tree Of Life 46.00
  Creamer, Child's, Wild Rose 30.00
  Creamer, Gooseberry 25.00
  Creamer, Owl, Eyes 25.00
  Creamer, Paneled Wheat 48.00
  Creamer, Scroll & Button, Blue 45.00
  Creamer, Wheat Pattern 45.00
  Cruet, Forget–Me–Not, Challinor, Taylor 98.00
  Cup, Fleur–De–Lis & Grape 15.00
  Decanter, Bulbous, Shell & Roses Pattern, Original Paint, 10 In. 85.00
  Decanter, Original Stopper, Bristol, 10 In., Pair 85.00
  Dish, Battleship Maine Cover ....40.00 To 50.00
  Dish, Boar's Head Cover 650.00
  Dish, Boar's Head Cover, With Eyes 950.00
  Dish, Camel Resting Cover 110.00

Dish, Cat Cover, Blue & White, White Ribbed Base	45.00
Dish, Cat Cover, Dated, Atterbury	120.00
Dish, Cat Cover, Ribbed Base, Blue	70.00
Dish, Chick & Eggs Cover, Pedestal, Base Dated 1889	125.00
Dish, Covered Wagon Cover	80.00
Dish, Crawfish Cover	145.00
Dish, Cruiser Ship Cover	45.00
Dish, Deer Cover, Flaccus, Signed	250.00
Dish, Dewey Cover	35.00
Dish, Dog Cover, Blue & White, Blue Ribbed Base	45.00 To 85.00
Dish, Dog On Nest Cover, White Face, Blue	50.00 To 60.00
Dish, Duck Cover, Dated	150.00
Dish, Duck Cover, Grass Base	45.00
Dish, Duck Cover, Swimming	55.00
Dish, Fish Cover	50.00
Dish, Fish On Skiff Cover	35.00
Dish, Fox Cover, Dated, Atterbury	125.00 To 135.00
Dish, Fox Cover, Glass Eyes, Westmoreland	35.00
Dish, Hand & Dove Cover, Dated, Atterbury	85.00
Dish, Hen Cover, Blue Base, White Top, Blue Head	45.00
Dish, Hen Cover, Lacy Base, Amber Eyes, Blue Head, Atterbury	155.00
Dish, Hen Cover, Open Tail, Head Turned, 7 1/2 In.	35.00
Dish, Hen On Sleigh Cover, 5 1/4 X 3 1/4 X 5 In.	50.00
Dish, Lion Cover, Dated, Atterbury	115.00 To 130.00
Dish, Log Cabin, Painted, Westmoreland, 4 In. ....*Illus*	55.00
Dish, Pickle, Double Fish, Dated	45.00
Dish, Pintail Duck Cover	55.00
Dish, Rooster Cover, White Head, Rope Edge	50.00
Dish, Santa Claus On Sleigh Cover	105.00
Dish, Stagecoach Cover	85.00
Dish, Swan Cover	38.00
Dish, Swan Cover, Black	30.00
Dish, Swan Cover, Eyes, White	170.00
Dish, Uncle Sam Cover	50.00
Eggcup, Rooster, Stemmed	20.00
Figurine, Owl, Glass Eyes, Original Paint, 5 1/2 In.	65.00 To 100.00
Figurine, Rabbit, Atterbury, White, 9 In.	100.00
Figurine, Rabbit, Dated, Blue, 6 1/4 In.	250.00
Flask, Klondike, Gold Nugget	77.00
Flower Pot, Dated 1877, Roses & Bluebells	99.00
Fruit Jar, Owl	135.00
Goblet, Snow, Straight Top, 6 In.	12.50
Gravy Boat, Dolphin	45.00
Guttate, Salt & Pepper, Green, Opaque	75.00
Guttate, Salt & Pepper, Pink Cased, Original Cover	90.00
Hatchet, Chillicothe, Mo., Clear Handle, Gold Head, 6 In.	25.00
Hatchet, Hastings, Nebraska, Hand Painted Flower On Head, 6 In.	25.00
Humidor, Brass Top, Roses	35.00
Indian, Draped Beading, 7 In.	20.00
Jar, Hobnail, Scalloped, Covered, 11 In.	15.00
Lamp, Blue, Miniature	350.00
Lamp, Cupid Decals & Birds, 19 In.	150.00
Lamp, Gold Trim, Miniature	195.00
Lamp, Green–Gold, Miniature	125.00
Lamp, King Edward, No.1, Blue, 12 In.	600.00
Lamp, Oil, Cosmos Variant, 8 In.Shade	275.00
Lamp, Oil, Yellow Floral	165.00
Match Holder, Advertising, Farm Boy Writing In Snow	37.50
Match Holder, Basket, Blue Opaque, Millard 148A, English Mark	28.50
Match Holder, Snaggle Toothed Gnome Head	50.00
Mug, Bleeding Heart	35.00
Mug, Child's, Red Pigs	10.00
Mug, Peacock	25.00
Mug, Washington & Lafayette, 3 1/4 In.	25.00

Paperweight, Rabbit	12.00
Pitcher, Grapes & Horn, Imperial, 8 1/2 In.	23.00
Pitcher, Grapes, Westmoreland, 8 In.	18.00
Pitcher, Milk, Horn Of Plenty	95.00
Pitcher, Water, Coreopsis	125.00
Pitcher, Water, Cosmos	250.00
Pitcher, Water, Owl, Glass Eyes	150.00
Plate, Black S Border, Square, 9 In.	13.00
Plate, Club & Shell, Battleship Maine, 7 1/4 In.	20.00
Plate, Club & Shell, Ribbon & Stamp Design, 9 In.	10.00
Plate, Club & Shell, Waffle Center, 9 In.	8.00
Plate, Columbus, Medallion Framed, 1892, 9 3/4 In.	38.00
Plate, Columbus, Openwork Border, Dated 1892, 9 3/4 In.	29.00
Plate, Cream Grapes, 7 1/2 In.	35.00
Plate, Cupid & Maiden, 7 1/2 In.	20.00
Plate, Cupid Playing Violin, Gold Trim, 7 In.	30.00
Plate, Double C, Blue, Millard, 5 1/4 In.	15.00
Plate, Fleur–De–Lis, Flag & Eagle, Gilt Edge, 7 1/4 In.	32.00
Plate, Floral, Hand Painted, 12 In.	30.00
Plate, Gothic, 7 1/4 In.	12.00
Plate, Gothic, Black, 9 In.	13.00
Plate, Half Pinwheel, 7 1/2 In.	25.00
Plate, Heart Edge, 7 In.	16.00
Plate, Keyhole Variant, Gilt & Color Border, 7 1/4 In.	25.00
Plate, Leaf & Chain, Triangular, 8 In.	30.00
Plate, One–O–One, 5 In.	5.00
Plate, One–O–One, 9 In.	9.00
Plate, Open Lattice, Floral Center, 10 1/2 In.	28.50
Plate, Peg Border, Dewey In Color, 7 1/4 In.	20.00
Plate, S Border, Square, 8 1/4 In., Set Of 8	85.00
Plate, Scroll & Eye, 8 In.	7.00
Plate, Scroll & Eye, 10 In.	28.00
Plate, Serenade, 6 In.	30.00
Plate, Wicket Border, 7 1/2 In.	16.00
Plate, Yacht & Anchor, 7 1/4 In.	32.00
Platter, Fish, 13 1/2 X 10 1/4 In.	85.00
Platter, Retriever, 13 1/4 X 9 3/4 In.	165.00
Punch Cup, Little Red Riding Hood	20.00
Salt & Pepper, G.E.Refrigerator	24.00 To 32.50
Saltshaker, Embossed Swirls, Flowers, Hand Painted	35.00 To 48.00
Spooner, Child's, Cloud Band	75.00
Spooner, Horse Head Handles	10.00 To 12.00
Spooner, Wild Rose	40.00
Stein, Child's, Monk	55.00
Sugar & Creamer, Daisy & Button	25.00
Sugar & Creamer, Randolph, Pale Pink, Fostoria	70.00
Sugar & Creamer, Strutting Peacock, Westmoreland, 6 In.	42.00
Sugar & Creamer, Wreathed Cherry, Opalescent	45.00
Sugar Shaker, Apple Blossom, Northwood	125.00
Sugar Shaker, Cone, Green	55.00
Sugar Shaker, Grape	27.00
Sugar Shaker, Original Corn Top	55.00
Sugar Shaker, Swirled Beading	32.00
Sugar, Child's, Lamb Cover	195.00
Sugar, Dahlia, Covered	15.00
Sugar, Georgian, Covered, Pink, Large	25.00
Sugar, Roman Cross	45.00
Syrup, Alba, Enamel Stain, Original Lid	55.00
Syrup, Currier & Ives	45.00
Syrup, Enamel Design, Bulbous Base, Original Lid	45.00
Syrup, Morning Glories, Hand Painted	85.00
Syrup, Raised Flowers, Colored Berries, Covered	47.50
Table Set, Ribbed, Lacy Edge, Atterbury, 4 Piece	145.00 To 165.00
Table Set, Wild Rose, 4 Piece	195.00

Toothpick, Beggar's Hand	22.00
Toothpick, Bulbous Body, Straight Neck, Blue & Pink Design	16.00
Toothpick, Cornucopia	12.00
Toothpick, Diagonal Bars	15.00
Toothpick, Dog In House	22.00
Toothpick, Elephant's Hand	25.00
Toothpick, Gamma Butterfly	30.00
Toothpick, Hand & Fan	12.00
Toothpick, Horseshoe & Clover	25.00 To 30.00
Toothpick, Indian, Full Headdress, Divided	45.00
Toothpick, Keg, Gold Hoops	15.00
Toothpick, Kneeling Boy With Marble	25.00
Toothpick, Leaf Design, 3-Footed	22.00
Toothpick, Man, Basket On Back	30.00
Toothpick, Owl, Souvenir Hot Springs, S.D., Original Paint	70.00
Toothpick, Owl, Wings Spread, Westmoreland	15.00
Toothpick, Parrot On Hat	25.00
Toothpick, Rabbit & Chick, Embossed	23.00
Toothpick, Ringed Plug Hat	18.00
Toothpick, Scroll Shell	30.00
Toothpick, Shell & Seaweed	35.00
Toothpick, Standing Butterfly	28.00
Toothpick, Uncle Sam	18.00
Toothpick, Urn, Square Footed, 3 In.	6.50
Tray, Beaded Design, 8 1/2 X 11 In.	25.00
Tray, Chick With Broken Egg, Oval, 5 In.	28.00
Tray, Pin, Scalloped, Blue, Gold Paint, 4 1/2 X 9 In.	10.00
Tumbler, Souvenir, Louisiana Purchase, 5 In.	12.00
Vase, Fan, Crimped, 4 X 4 In.	6.00
Vase, Fan, Mandarin Red, 8 In.	95.00

Millefiori means, literally, a thousand flowers. It is a type of glasswork popular in paperweights. Many small flowerlike pieces of glass are grouped together to form a design.

MILLEFIORI, Cruet, Frosted Handle, Clear Faceted Stopper	70.00
Figurine, Poodle	35.00
Lamp, Fairy, Spherical Shade, Clear Cup, Italy, 10 7/8 In.	125.00
Muffineer, Frosted Applied Handle, 4 1/2 In.	475.00
Paperweight, C.1910	85.00
Vase, Allover Design Of Millefiori, Handles, 8 In.	195.00
Vase, Yellow, Green, Red Dots, Bulbous, Long Neck, 11 In.	110.00

Minton china has been made in the Staffordshire region of England from 1793 to the present. The firm became part of the Royal Doulton Tableware Group in 1968, but the wares continued to be marked "Minton." Many marks have been used. The one shown dates from about 1873 to 1891, when the word "England" was added.

MINTON, Berry Bowl, Willow, Flow Blue, 1891-1902, 8 1/4 In.	69.00
Bowl, Flower Bouquets, Turquoise Ribbons, Large	650.00
Bowl, Fruit, Willow, Scalloped, Dated 1926, 9 In.	79.50
Box, Covered, Heart Shape, Hand Painted, Enameled, 2 X 1 1/2 In.	35.00
Chamber Pot, Red Mark, 3 Piece	125.00
Cup & Saucer, Blue & White	35.00
Dinner Set, Royal Blue Border, Raised Gilt Design, C.1925, 120 Piece	700.00
Figurine, 2 Men Carrying Wicker Basket, Majolica, Dated 1863, 19 In.	2860.00
Figurine, Little Red Riding Hood, Parian, Impressed Mark, Dated 1853	115.00
Garden Seat, Baluster, Majolica, Dated 1898, Moss Green, 20 5/8 In.	440.00
Garden Seat, Monkey, Holding Cushion, Majolica, C.1870, 18 1/2 In.	4950.00
Plate, Denmark Pattern, Rust, Octagonal, 7 3/4 In.	10.00
Plate, Gold, White Fruit	15.00
Plate, Hand Painted Flowers, Ruby Border, Signed, 11 In., 12 Pc.	420.00

Plate, Maiden & Cupid Scene, White Ground, Gray, Marked, 1911, 12 Pc. 2530.00
Plate, Roses Center, Turquoise Rim 265.00
Plate, Scenic Center, Turquoise Rim, Pair 550.00
Plate, Service, 3 Oval Reserves Of Psyche & Cupid, Signed 400.00
Plate, Wide Gold Rim, Enamel & Pink Rosebuds, 9 1/2 In., Set Of 6 .... 210.00
Platter, Pineapple 275.00
Tea Set, Japonisme, Yellow, Gold, 3 Piece ....Color 225.00
Teapot, Gold Design, Pink Flowing White, 1900s 150.00
Teapot, Underplate, Hand Painted Dogs' Heads, 1891 Mark, 4 In. 165.00
Tile, Stoke On Trent, Sunflower Pattern, Signed, 6 X 6 In. 25.00
Tile, Stylized Floral, Green, Blue, Yellow & White, 6 X 6 In. 45.00
Tray, Red Roses, Hand Painted, Artist Signature, 12 X 9 In. 95.00
Tureen, Cover, No.8667 .... 125.00
Vase, Embossed Flowers, 4 In. 125.00
Vase, Rosebuds, Gilt Jewels & Swags, Turquoise Reserves, 8 In. 175.00
   MIRROR, see Furniture, Mirror

> *Mochaware is an English–made product that was sold in America
> during the early 1800s. It is a heavy pottery with pale coffee-and-
> cream coloring. Designs of blue, brown, green, orange, black, or white
> were added to the pottery.*

MOCHA, Bowl, Black Stripes, Embossed Green Rim, Cream Band, 4 3/4 In. 85.00
Bowl, Dark Brown Band, White Slip, Blue & Tan Stripes, 5 X 10 1/2 In. 395.00
Bowl, Seaweed & Translucent Green Bands, 4 1/2 In. 345.00
Chamber Pot 255.00
Creamer, Blue & Brown Bands, Applied Acanthus Leaf Handle, 5 1/2 In. 195.00
Creamer, Blue Stripes, White & Gray Blue, 3 7/8 In. 75.00
Creamer, Cat's–Eye Pattern, Putty & Brown Stripes, 3 3/4 In. 450.00
Cup & Saucer, Handleless, Black Seaweed, Tan Ground 425.00
Cup, Beige Design, Brown, 4 X 4 1/4 In. 48.00
Jar, Earthworm Design On Lid, Blue & White, 6 1/4 In. 215.00
Mug, Black Seaweed Design, Orange, Blue Rim, 3 5/8 In. 525.00
Mug, Brown Seaweed Design, Orange Ground, Embossed Borders, 5 3/4 In. 525.00
Mug, Brown Stripes, Seaweed Design, Gray Green, 6 In. 325.00
Mug, Colored Stripes, 5 In. 180.00
Mug, Seaweed, Brown Center Band, Blue Top Band, 6 3/8 In. 88.00
Mug, Stripes, Cream, Brown & White, Cat's Eyes, Green Rim, 4 5/8 In. 400.00
Pepper Pot, Brown, Tan, Green, Bulbous 250.00
Pepper Pot, Seaweed Design, Yellow 175.00
Pitcher, Black Stripes, Blue & White, 5 1/8 In. 40.00
Pitcher, White Slip, White Ground, Blue, Tan & Dark Brown, 6 In. 300.00
Salt, Master, Earthworm Design 250.00
Shaker, Blue, Black & White, Narrow Stripes, 4 1/8 In. 150.00
Shaker, Circle Design, Orange & Black, 4 In. 225.00
Shaker, Ochre & White Cat's Eye Design, Blue & Black, 4 1/4 In. 300.00
Syrup 245.00
Tankard, Tan, Black, White Sprigwork Swags, Green Reed Top, 4 1/2 In. 325.00
Waste Bowl, Earthworm, Stripes, White Grounds, 6 1/2 X 3 1/4 In. 160.00

> *Monmouth Pottery Company started working in Monmouth, Illinois,
> in 1892. The pottery made a variety of utilitarian wares. They became
> part of Western Stoneware Company in 1906. The maple leaf mark
> was used until 1930. If the word "Co." appears as part of the mark,
> the piece was made before 1906.*

MONMOUTH, Pitcher, Blue, 1 Pt. 17.50
Vase, Green, Feather Glaze, Urn Shape, Handles, 9 In. 35.00
Vase, Lotus, Blue 65.00
Vase, Up & Down Design, Blue Glaze Inside, 11 1/2 In. 85.00
Vase, White, No.251, Pair 20.00
Wall Pocket, Aztec Pattern, Marked, 12 1/2 In. 35.00
   MONT JOYE, see Mt. Joye

William Moorcroft managed the art pottery department for James MacIntyre & Company of England from 1898 to 1913. In 1913, he started his own company, Moorcroft Pottery, in Burslem, England. He died in 1945, but the company continues. The earlier wares are similar to those made today, but color and marking will help indicate the age.

MOORCROFT, Ashtray, Fish Design	240.00
Bowl, Avocado, Coral, 6 In.	35.00
Bowl, Enameled Orchid, Indigo Blue Ground, Original Label, 4 In.	70.00
Bowl, Flambe, Orchid, 7 1/2 In.	350.00
Bowl, Florian, 4 In.	90.00
Bowl, MacIntyre Aurelian Ware, Handles, Silver Plate Lid, 6 In.	200.00
Bowl, Pomegranate, 9 In.	100.00
Bowl, Waving Corn, Matte, 11 In.	150.00
Box, Cigarette, Covered, Cobalt Blue	85.00
Butter Chip, Blue & Red, 3 In.	30.00
Butter Chip, Floral	25.00
Candlestick, Floral, Olive, Black Letters Impressed, 8 In., Pair	40.00
Canister, Pomegranate, Covered, 6 1/2 In.	150.00
Cup & Saucer, Blue On Blue, Gilded	210.00
Cup, Saucer, & Dessert Plate, Pansy On Cobalt Blue Ground	75.00
Dahlia Pot, 3 In.	45.00
Dish, Amaryllis, Queen Mark, 4 1/2 In.	65.00
Ewer, Yellow Tulips, Jug Handle, 11 3/4 In.	550.00
Jam Jar, Tudric Pewter Lid, Black, Red	195.00
Jar, Ginger, Pink Popcorn Design, Green, Incised, Covered, 8 In.	80.00
Lamp, Flambe, Base Only, 13 In.	250.00
Lamp, Flambe, Grapes, Leaves, Cover, 4 In.	175.00
Lamp, Table, Cobalt, Floral, Shade, Paper Label, 27 In.	450.00
Pitcher, Cobalt, Orchids, Marked In Script, H.M.The Queen, 5 In.	165.00
Vase, 7 Pomegranates, Navy, Full Baluster, Incised Mark, 9 1/2 In.	115.00
Vase, Anemones, Florian, Blue Green, 4 In.	175.00
Vase, Anemones, Handles, 9 In.	100.00
Vase, Cobalt, Purple, Pink Flowers, 6 In.	75.00
Vase, Dahlias, 13 In.	125.00
Vase, Deep Blue Outlined Flowers, Blue Ground, Signed, 10 In.	425.00
Vase, Flambe, Columbine, Squat, 3 In.	65.00
Vase, Flambe, Cornflower, 8 1/2 In.	350.00
Vase, Floral, Blue, Cream, Rust, Bulbous	195.00
Vase, Florian Ware, 3–Color, 5 In.	235.00
Vase, Florian Ware, 6 In.	200.00
Vase, Florian Ware, Anemones & Ivy, 12 In.	350.00
Vase, Hazeldene, Moonlight Blue, 6 1/2 In.	375.00
Vase, Multicolor Florals, Shaded Blue, 5 In.	125.00
Vase, Orange Luster, 5 In.	45.00
Vase, Pansies On Cobalt, 7 1/2 In.	150.00
Vase, Pomegranate, Squat, 3 In.	50.00
Vase, Poppies, C.1920, 6 In.	325.00
Vase, Purple & Pink Flowers, Cobalt Ground, 6 In.	75.00

Some types of Japanese pottery and porcelain are decorated with a special type of raised decoration known as moriage. Sometimes pieces of clay were shaped by hand and applied to the item; sometimes the clay was squeezed from a tube in the way we apply cake frosting. One type of moriage is called dragonware and is listed under that name.

MORIAGE, Basket, Marbelized Medallion, Jeweling, 9 In.	275.00
Box, Ring, Florals, Green Wreath Mark, 3 1/2 X 1 1/2 In.	20.00
Candlestick, Figural, Winged Griffin, 8 1/4 In.	50.00
Elephant, Match Holder Side Pack, Ashtray Saddle, Brown	12.00
Ewer, Poppies	65.00
Hair Receiver, Lilacs, Green Beaded Ground, Footed, 4 X 2 1/2 In.	125.00
Manicure Set, 3 Tools, Buffer, Trinket Box, Set	150.00
Smoking Set, Medallions Of Roses, Green Ground, 3 Piece	195.00

Spooner, Green Ground, Raised Turquoise Beading, 5 In. 235.00
Sugar, Covered, Poppies, Pagoda Shape, Beading 65.00
Tankard, Warriors, 14 1/2 In. 200.00
Tea Set, Dragon, 6 Cup & Saucer 250.00
Tea Set, Hand Painted, Demitasse, Victoria China, 17 Piece 85.00
Tray, Dresser, Pastel, 10 In. 65.00
Urn, Allover White Slip, Green Ground, Pedestal, Handles, 8 1/2 In. 295.00
Vase, Autumn Colors, 4 Handles, 10 1/2 In. 150.00
Vase, Hand Painted Violets, Low Handle, Light Green, 9 1/4 In. 180.00
Vase, Raised Design, Handle, Blue Ground, 1 1/2 X 2 3/4 In. 35.00
Vase, Raised Flowers & Birds, Pink, 10 In. 200.00
Vase, Violets, Green Slip Work, Low Handles, 9 In. 179.00

The Mosaic Tile Company of Zanesville, Ohio, was started by Karl Langerbeck and Herman Mueller in 1894. Many types of plain and ornamental tiles were made until 1959. The company closed in 1967. The company also made some ashtrays, bookends, and related gift wares. Most pieces are marked with the entwined MTC monogram.

MOSAIC TILE CO., Ashtray, Tile, Figural, Airdale, Multicolor 95.00
Figurine, Bear, Black, 6 X 10 In. 110.00
Figurine, Bear, Navy Blue, Semiglass Glaze, 5 3/4 X 9 In. 117.00
Lincoln, Blue & White 22.00
Plaque, 9 Rome Scenes, Micro, Pantheon, 19th Century, Italy 450.00
Tile, Map Of Mt.Desert Island 12.00
Tile, Monkeys & Owls, Square, 6 In. 25.00
Tile, Windmill, Ship, Blue, 4 1/2 In. 25.00

Moser glass is made by Ludwig Moser und Sohne, a Bohemian glasshouse founded in 1857. Art Nouveau–type glassware and iridescent glassware were made. The most famous Moser glass is decorated with heavy enameling in gold and bright colors. The firm is still working in Czechoslovakia. Few pieces of Moser glass are marked.

MOSER, Berry Set, Enameled, Signed, Cranberry, 7 Piece 400.00
Bottle, Malachite, Slab Polished Sides & Top, 6 1/2 In. 225.00
Bottle, Perfume, Amazon Women, High Relief, Gold Amber Atomizer 475.00
Bottle, Perfume, Cranberry To Clear, Signed, 9 1/2 In. 235.00
Bottle, Perfume, Opalescent Pink, Gold, Blue, White, Signed, 5 In. 250.00
Bowl, Amethyst To Clear, Ruffled Edge, Marked, 3 In., Pair 485.00
Bowl, Green, Enameled, Working Insects, Marked, 4 In. 120.00
Bowl, Raised Enameled Gold Vines, Allover Pattern, 10 In. 250.00
Bowl, Ruffled Edge, Enameled Rose, Green Stem, Amethyst To Clear, Pair 485.00
Bowl, White Enamel Flying Cranes, Signed, Italian Green, 4 1/2 In. 165.00
Box, Colored Enamels, Pink Opalescent, Signed, 3 1/2 X 2 In. 350.00
Box, Gold & Silver Trim, Amber, 4 3/4 X 5 1/2 In. 175.00
Cocktail Set, Rubina Glass, 7 Piece 695.00
Compote, Black Amethyst Cut To Clear, Signed, Covered, 11 In. 265.00
Cordial, Enameled Floral, Gold, Green Ground, 2 1/4 In., Set Of 4 .... 135.00
Decanter Set, Gold Trim, Cranberry Windows, Marked, 4 Cordials 850.00
Decanter, Body & Stopper Cut Poppy Design, 10 1/2 In. 850.00
Decanter, Oak Leaves, Cranberry Windows, Crystal Stopper, Signed 795.00
Decanter, Oak Leaves, Crystal, Cranberry, Stopper, 4 Cordials, Marked 795.00
Ewer, Cranberry Glass, Clear Applied Handle, Scale Band, 15 1/2 In. 800.00
Figurine, Parrot, Perched, Branch, 3 Acorns, Leaves, Signed, 7 3/4 In. 885.00
Glass, Juice, Raised Gold Branches, Enamel Leaves, Gold Band, 4 In. 185.00
Goblet, Cranberry, Floral Design, Lady Bug & Dragonfly, 4 1/4 In. 245.00
Goblet, Water, Cut Green To Crystal, Set Of 6 .... 500.00
Goblet, Wine, Amber, Grape & Strawberry Design, Signed Stem, Set Of 6 .... 995.00
Horn Of Plenty, Pulled By Brass Dwarf, Glass Horn 299.95
Lemonade Set, Pitcher, 3 Tumblers, Enameled, Blue Applied Handle 695.00
Pitcher, Cranberry Ground, Berries, Leaves, Reeded Handle, 6 In. 495.00
Pitcher, Enameled Salamander & Foliage, Signed, 14 In. 295.00
Pitcher, Inverted Thumbprint, Blue, 5 In. 295.00
Plate, Alexandrite, Marked, 8 In. 75.00

Salt, Signed, Footed, Blue, 4 1/2 In. 275.00
Tumbler, Cranberry Glass, Allover Gold Filigree, Floral, 4 In. 180.00
Tumbler, Cranberry, Juice, Raised Gold, Enameled Leaves, 4 In. 185.00
Tumbler, Light Amethyst, Gold Filigree, 4 In. 180.00
Vase, 7 Multicolored Enameled Salamander, Footed 375.00
Vase, Alexandrite, 3 In., Pair 125.00
Vase, Allover Coralene Design, Cranberry, Signed, 13 1/4 In. 1250.00
Vase, Amber, Enameled Flowers & Reeds, Signed, 14 In. 595.00
Vase, Applied Enameled Plants & Flowers, Bug, Amber, 10 1/2 In. 395.00
Vase, Applied Salamander Wrap To Form Feet, Honey Amber, 7 In. 385.00
Vase, Bud, Flared, Intaglio Flowers, Gold Rim, 8 In. 165.00
Vase, Cameo, Amber, Gold Band, Allegorical Figures, Marked, 7 1/2 In. 225.00
Vase, Cameo, Jungle Scene, Purple To Clear & Frosted, Signed, 12 In. 850.00
Vase, Deep Ruby, Enameled Butterflies, 15 In. 1750.00
Vase, Electric Blue, Red Set Jewels, Signed, 7 X 7 In. 1450.00
Vase, Enameled Flowers, Green, Signed, 10 In. 185.00
Vase, Enameled Long Stemmed Flowers, Lace Trim, Signed, 14 1/2 In. 395.00
Vase, Encrusted Enamel Butterflies, Dragons, & Flowers, Ruby, 15 In. 1750.00
Vase, Frieze Band, Gold Encrusted Warriors, Amber, 6 In. 175.00
Vase, Gold Band Of Etched Amazon Warriors, Amethyst, 6 3/4 In. 200.00
Vase, Gold Frieze, Amethyst, 11 In. 250.00
Vase, Green To Clear, Intaglio Wood Lily, Gold Trim, 4 1/2 In. 85.00
Vase, Jewels, Electric Blue Enamel, Signed & Numbered, 7 1/2 In. 1450.00
Vase, Pale Blue Purple, Facets, Trumpet Shape, C.1900, Signed, 13 In. 175.00
Vase, Paneled, Gold Band, Etched Amazon Warriors, Signed, 6 3/4 In. 200.00
Vase, Pink To Clear, Parrot Enameled, Oval, Signed, 7 1/2 X 2 1/2 In. 885.00
Vase, Pouch Type, Electric Blue, Enameled, Applied Amber Glass String 185.00
Vase, Set Jewels, Gold Rigaree Up Sides, Signed, 7 X 7 1/2 In. 1450.00
Wine Set, Decanter, 6 Tumblers, Signed 375.00
Wine, Amber, Facet Cut, Stem, 4 3/4 In., Set Of 12 .... 900.00
Wine, Cranberry, Enameled Floral Design, Dragonfly, 4 1/4 In. 250.00
Wine, Red & Gold Enameling, Emerald Green, 12 In., Set Of 6 .... 495.00

*Moss rose china was made by many firms from 1808 to 1900. It has
a typical moss rose pictured as the design. The plant is not as popular
now as it was in Victorian gardens, so the fuzz-covered bud is
unfamiliar to most collectors. The dishes were usually decorated with
pink and green flowers.*

MOSS ROSE, Dinner Set, Child's, 29 Piece, 4 Place Set 65.00
Tureen, Covered, Underplate, Child's, Girl With Bunnies, 2 Pc. 22.00
Tureen, Covered, Underplate, Gravy, Child's, 2 Pc. 24.00

*Mother-of-pearl glass, or pearl satin glass, was first made in the
1850s in England and in Massachusetts. It was a special type of
mold-blown satin glass with air bubbles in the glass, giving it a
pearlized color. It has been reproduced. Mother-of-pearl shell objects
are listed under Pearl.*

MOTHER-OF-PEARL, Basket, Herringbone, Rose To Pink, Thorn Handle, 7 1/2 In. ... 350.00
Bowl, Blue, Diamond-Quilted, 4 Applied Feet, 5 X 8 In. 285.00
Bowl, Diamond-Quilted, Satin Glass, Star Shaped Rim 500.00
Bowl, Tricorn, Crystal Feet, Cream Lining, 5 X 4 1/2 In. 595.00
Box, Dresser, Diamond-Quilted, Hinged Cover, 5 X 3 3/4 In. 200.00
Castor, Pickle, Diamond Quilted, Red 375.00
Creamer, White Lining, Frosted Handle, Blue, 4 1/2 In. 225.00
Decanter, Stopper, Pinched Sides, Signed LCT 415.00
Ewer, Herringbone, Blue, Frosted Handle, Crimped, 8 X 4 In. 225.00
Ewer, Herringbone, Blue, Handle, White Lining, 8 1/2 In. 198.00
Fairy Lamp, Diamond-Quilted, Rose, Leaves, Signed, 7 1/4 In. 785.00
Lamp, Diamond-Quilted, Brass Foot, Square Shade, 11 1/2 In. 695.00
Lamp, Fairy, 19th Century, Ruffled Base, Pink, 5 3/4 In. 150.00
Lamp, Fairy, Ruffled Base, Diagonal Threading, 5 In. 175.00
Pitcher, Diamond-Quilted, White Lining, 5 1/2 In. 175.00
Rose Bowl, Herringbone, 8 Crimps, Blue, 4 In. 99.00

MOTHER–OF–PEARL, SATIN GLASS, see Satin Glass; Smith Brothers; etc.

Tumbler, Diamond–Quilted, Yellow To White	85.00
Vase, American Beauty Rose, Acorn Pattern, 5 3/4 In.	398.00
Vase, Apple Green, Raindrop Pattern, Crimped Rim, 8 In.	295.00
Vase, Bud, Herringbone, Blue, Ruffled, 7 In.	195.00
Vase, Diamond–Quilted, 7 In.	225.00
Vase, Diamond–Quilted, Blue To Lavender, Satin, 13 1/4 In.	520.00
Vase, Diamond–Quilted, Frosted Thorn Handles, Blue, 8 In.	185.00
Vase, Diamond–Quilted, Ruffled Trim, Rose To White, 8 In.	135.00
Vase, Flared Ruffled Rim, Lavender To Blue, 13 1/4 In.	375.00
Vase, Herringbone, Frosted Handles, Shaded Blue, 7 3/8 In.	210.00
Vase, Herringbone, Peach, Ruffled, 9 1/4 In.	175.00
Vase, Ruffled, Frost Edge, Blue	130.00
Vase, Ruffled, White Lining, Thorn Handle, 7 In.	225.00

MOUSTACHE CUP, see Mustache Cup

Mont Joye is an enameled cameo glass made in the late nineteenth and the twentieth centuries by Saint–Hilaire Touvoir de Varraux and Co. of Pantin, France. This same company made De Vez glass. Pieces were usually decorated with enameling. Most pieces are not marked.

MT. JOYE, Vase, Burnt Orange, Gilt Poppies, Green Ground, 11 In.	225.00
Vase, Hand Painted Flowers, Leaves, Signed, Cranberry, 11 3/4 In.	1200.00

The Mount Washington Glass Works started in 1837 in South Boston, Massachusetts. In 1869 the company moved to New Bedford, Massachusetts. Many types of art glass were made there to the 1890s. These included Burmese, Crown Milano, Royal Flemish, and others.

MT. WASHINGTON, Bottle, Peachblow, Mums & Foliage, 3 1/4 X 6 3/8 In.	265.00
Bowl, Daisy & Butterflies, 1909, Diamond Base, 8 1/2 In.	225.00
Bowl, Melon–Ribbed, Hand Painted Flowers, 3 3/4 X 2 1/2 In.	105.00
Bowl, Peppermint, Star On Base, 8 3/4 X 2 5/8 In.	185.00
Bowl, Winged Birds, Flowers, Reed & Barton Holder, 8 In.	845.00
Box, Violet Design, Covered, 6 In.	195.00
Bride's Basket, Pink Custard Glass, Floral, Silver Frame	200.00
Bride's Bowl, Signed Pairpoint Holder, Daisies, Bluebells	575.00
Compote, Butter & Daisy, Starred & Diamond Base, 6 1/2 In.	350.00
Cracker Jar, Burmese	650.00
Cracker Jar, Napoli, Brownie Design, Signed, 6 In.	725.00
Cracker Jar, Paneled Cranberry, Bird On Branch	550.00
Cracker Jar, Tomato Shape, Pansies	135.00
Creamer, Inverted Thumbprint, Crystal Handle, 5 1/2 In.	225.00
Cruet, Burmese, Ribbed, Yellow Handle, 7 In.	795.00
Cruet, Burmese, Satin Finish, 6 1/2 In.	785.00
Cruet, Deep Fuchsia To Amber, Venetian Diamond Design	285.00
Ewer, Honeycomb Design, Cut Velvet, 5 X 4 1/2 In.	325.00
Ewer, Mother–Of–Pearl, Herringbone, Gold Gilded, 11 In.	375.00
Flower Holder, Blue Forget–Me–Not	150.00
Jug, Verona Pattern, Allover Gold Fish, 6 1/2 X 6 In.	900.00
Muffineer, Burmese, Colored Dots Form Flowers, 4 1/2 In.	585.00
Muffineer, Clear, Daisies, Satin Finish, Dime Size Top	285.00
Muffineer, White, Bittersweet Dots, Satin, Burmese, 4 1/2 In.	585.00
Pitcher, Oak Leaves, Vines, Gold Trim, Handle, Burmese, 9 In.	1450.00
Pitcher, Tankard, Ocean Seed, Handle, Gold Trim, 8 3/4 In.	1000.00
Pitcher, Verona Pattern, Blossom Outlined In Gold	675.00
Pitcher, Water, Burmese, C.1880, 8 1/2 X 7 1/2 In.	1050.00
Pitcher, Water, Burmese, Hobnail, Signed, 9 3/4 In.	750.00
Pitcher, White Lily, Cranberry Crackle Glass, 5 1/2 In.	265.00
Plate, Chimney, Hand Painted Country Scene, 10 In.	55.00
Plate, Hand Painted Roses, Lusterless White, 9 1/2 In.	35.00
Plate, Lusterless, 10 In.	25.00
Rose Bowl, Burmese, Queen's Design Blossoms, 5 X 2 1/4 In.	945.00
Rose Bowl, Tea Roses, Buds, Leaves, Gold Trim, 5 In.	375.00
Salt & Pepper, Acorn, Pink Shading To White, Brass Top, Pair	60.00

Salt & Pepper, Egg Shape, Flat Ends, Original Tops	130.00
Salt & Pepper, Egg Shape, Lavender, Pansies	75.00
Salt & Pepper, Fig Shape, Blossoms, Shades Of Green	335.00
Salt & Pepper, Fig Shape, Yellow Blossoms, White Blossoms	185.00
Salt & Pepper, Fig, Pair	145.00
Salt & Pepper, Floral, Melon Shape, C.1880, 2 3/4 In., Pair	175.00
Salt & Pepper, Melon, Original Tops, Enameled Flowers	75.00
Salt & Pepper, Melon–Ribbed, Pewter Tops, Pair	100.00
Salt & Pepper, Shrimp, Green Berries, Original Top	28.00
Salt & Pepper, Tomato Shape	150.00
Salt, Chicken Head	275.00
Salt, Custard, Floral, Egg Shape, Flat Base	55.00
Salt, Figural, Unfinished Burmese	180.00
Salt, Lay Down, Egg Shape, Pink Body, White & Orange Flowers	65.00
Salt, Melon–Ribbed, Violets	39.00
Saltshaker, Blue, Floral Design, Melon Shape	60.00
Saltshaker, Cockleshell, Pink & Blue	195.00
Saltshaker, Egg Shape, Floral, Pink To White	75.00
Saltshaker, Egg, Enameled Daisies, Blue, Original Top	48.00
Saltshaker, Egg, Flat Side, Apple Blossoms, Blue, Pair	75.00
Saltshaker, Tomato, Enamel Design	45.00
Shade, Burmese, Satin Finish, 5 1/4 X 3 3/4 In.	185.00
Sugar & Creamer, Applied Handle, Open Bowl, Burmese	585.00
Sugar & Creamer, Bull's–Eye & Notched Prism Pattern, C.1890	300.00
Sugar Shaker, Egg	142.00 To 155.00
Sugar Shaker, Egg, Blue & White Enameled Flowers	295.00
Sugar Shaker, Egg, Daisies, Original Top	215.00
Sugar Shaker, Egg, Original Top, Blue Jeweling, Orange Floral	225.00
Sugar Shaker, Egg, Unfinished Burmese	100.00
Sugar Shaker, Lemon Ground, Daisies	280.00
Sugar Shaker, Melon–Ribbed, Floral, Original Top	110.00
Sugar Shaker, Ostrich Egg, Egg Top	275.00
Sugar Shaker, Ostrich Egg, White Satin	225.00
Toothpick, Enamel Design Of Violets, Lobe Shape, 1 7/8 In.	200.00
Toothpick, White, Lusterless, Leaves, Hat Shape, 2 1/8 In.	235.00
Tumbler, Burmese	225.00
Tumbler, Burmese, Ivy Leaf Design	300.00
Tumbler, Water, Burmese, 4 1/4 In.	300.00
Tumbler, Whiskey, Diamond–Quilted, Acid Finish, 2 3/4 In.	175.00
Vase, 3 Shades Of Gold Enamel, Burmese, 4 3/4 In.	685.00
Vase, Blue & White Swirl, Satin Glass, 7 In.	475.00
Vase, Bud, Bronzed Metal Crane, Dragonfly, C.1870, 13 1/2 In.	385.00
Vase, Bud, Burmese, Dots Of Autumn Foliage & Berries, 9 In.	585.00
Vase, Bud, Lusterless White, Corn Shape, 9 In.	65.00
Vase, Bud, White, Cone Shape, Scallop Top, 9 In.	65.00
Vase, Burmese, Autumn Foliage, Dots Of Berries, Gold, 9 In.	585.00
Vase, Burmese, Dimpled, 4 1/2 In.	300.00
Vase, Burmese, Jack–In–The–Pulpit, 12 1/2 In.	745.00
Vase, Burmese, Sacred Ibis In Flight, Pyramids, 12 In.	3450.00
Vase, Burmese, Spray Of Daisies, Verse, Butterfly, 10 3/4 In.	1950.00
Vase, Burmese, Squat, 5 X 4 1/2 In.	285.00
Vase, Burmese, Swirl Ribbed, 4 In.	275.00
Vase, Butterfly & Daisies, Montgomery Verse, Burmese, 12 In.	2300.00
Vase, Country Lane Scene, Enameled, Signed Ambero, 9 In.	745.00
Vase, Enamel Of 4 Ducks Flying, Field Of Gold, Signed, 17 In.	3250.00
Vase, Enameled Dragonflies, Sprays, Lusterless, 10 1/2 In.	550.00
Vase, Enameled Forget–Me–Nots, Mushroom Shape, Blue & White	150.00
Vase, Jack–In–The–Pulpit, Crimped Top, Burmese, 12 1/2 In.	745.00
Vase, Lava, 2 Applied Handles, 4 1/2 X 5 In.	1500.00
Vase, Lava, Colored Chips, 2 Applied Handles, 9 In.	985.00
Vase, Mother–Of–Pearl, Clear Thorn Handle, Apricot & White	425.00
Vase, Napoli, Interior Frog Design, Gold Outlining	785.00
Vase, Optic Trumpet Form, Rose Amber, 16 In.	1250.00
Vase, Peachblow, Flower Top, 2 1/2 X 6 1/4 In.	1100.00

Vase, Peachblow, Flower Top, 3 X 3 1/4 In.	895.00
Vase, Sacred Ibis In Flight, Deep Blush, Gold, Burmese, 12 In.	2950.00
Vase, Spray Of Daisies, Verse By J.Montgomery, 10 3/4 In.	1950.00
Vase, Trumpet, Satin Finish, Burmese, 10 In.	345.00
Vase, Zipper, C.1875, 10 1/2 In.	600.00
Whiskey, Burmese, Diamond–Quilted, 2 3/4 In.	325.00

Mud figures are small Chinese pottery figures made in the twentieth century. The figures usually represent workers, scholars, farmers, or merchants. Other pieces are trees, houses, and similar parts of the landscape. The figures have unglazed faces and hands but glazed clothing. They were originally made for fish tanks or planters. Mud figures were of little interest and brought low prices until the 1980s. When the prices rose, reproductions appeared.

MUD FIGURE, 2 Men, Seated, Table, Flute & Fan, 4 1/2	35.00
Boy, Holding White Bird, Green Enamel Clothes, 10 In.	40.00
Chinese, Pair	30.00
Elder, Holding Fan & Book, Green Robe	20.00
Fisherman, 4 In.	30.00
Fisherman, Impressed China, 10 In.	15.00
Girl, Holding White Ball, Green Enamel Clothes, 10 In.	40.00
Man Sitting On Stump, With Fan, 5 1/2 In.	65.00
Man With Fishing Pole, Marked China, 3 1/2 In.	25.00
Man, Bearded, Holding Bundle, 3 1/2 In.	25.00
Man, Bent Over, Working On Basket, Base, 3 X 2 In.	35.00
Man, Chartreuse Robe, Holding Book, 6 In.	45.00
Man, Fishing Pole & Fish, Marked China, 3 1/2 In.	25.00
Man, Fishing, 4 In.	28.00
Man, Holding Book, Chartreuse Robe, 6 In.	45.00
Man, Holding Book, Cobalt Blue Robe, 6 In.	45.00
Man, Standing, Green Robe, 10 3/4 In.	100.00
Man, Standing, Yoke, 6 In.	40.00
Seated Buddha, 1 1/2 In.	20.00

Mulberry ware was made in the Staffordshire district of England from about 1850 to 1860. The dishes were decorated with a transfer design of a reddish brown, now called "mulberry." Many of the patterns are similar to those used for flow blue and other Staffordshire transfer wares.

MULBERRY, Bread Platter, Track Border	30.00
Candlesticks, No.549, Jade, 10 In., Pair	60.00
Creamer, Tavoy	85.00 To 105.00
Cup & Saucer, Davenport, C.1850	45.00
Cup & Saucer, Handleless, Kyber, Marked	65.00
Cup Plate, Cyprus, Davenport	35.00
Cup Plate, Rhone, W.Adderly, Red, 4 1/2 In.	20.00
Cup, Handleless, Corean	20.00
Cup, Handleless, Jeddo	16.00
Cup, Syllabub, Corean	70.00
Dish, Soap, Cover, Marble	58.00
Mug, Children In Period Dress, 2 1/2 In.	55.00
Pitcher & Bowl, Panama	175.00
Pitcher, Milk, Raised Cherubs, Grapes, & Grape Leaves, 1 Qt.	95.00
Plate, Pelew, 9 In.	20.00
Plate, Rose, Podmore Walker, 10 In.	40.00
Plate, Temple, 8 In.	30.00
Plate, Temple, Podmore Walker, 7 In.	20.00
Plate, Temple, Podmore Walker, 10 In.	30.00
Plate, Vincennes, 10 1/2 In.	55.00
Platter, 16 In.	125.00
Platter, Athens, 13 1/2 In.	145.00
Platter, Corean	105.00
Platter, Corean, 12 1/2 In.	40.00
Platter, Staffordshire, 14 1/2 X 12 In.	72.50

Platter, Washington Vase, 13 3/4 In. 65.00
Sauce, Corean, 5 In. 27.00
Soup, Dish, Scinde, 10 1/2 In. 25.00
Tea Set, Peru, Holdcroft, 29 Piece 795.00
Teapot, Peruvian Scene 200.00
Teapot, Rhone 85.00
Vase, Washington, 5 1/2 In. 20.00
Vegetable, Open, Rose, 10 In. 55.00
Vegetable, Open, Temple, 7 X 5 1/2 In. 55.00
Wash Pitcher, Marble 95.00
Waste Bowl, Avon 55.00
Waste Bowl, Corean 45.00

Muller Freres, French for Muller Brothers, made cameo and other glass from the early 1900s to the late 1930s. Their factory was first located in Luneville, then in nearby Croismaire, France. Pieces were usually marked with the company name.

MULLER FRERES, Vase, Cameo, Poppies, Gold, Flat Bulbous, Marked, 9 3/4 In. 2250.00
Vase, Cameo, Yellow Flecks, Trees, Purple Base, Signed, 4 In. 495.00
Vase, Lemon Yellow, Parrots, Signed, 10 In. 1100.00
Vase, Luneville Roses, Frosted Pink Ground, Signed, 7 3/4 In. 1200.00
Vase, Mottled Base, Roses, Acid Cuttings, Signed, 7 1/4 In. 1650.00
Vase, Red To Yellow Roses, 5 Cuttings, Pink, Signed, 7 1/2 In. 1100.00
Vase, Stork Scenic, Frosted Gold, Signed, 7 1/2 In. 1495.00
Vase, Tiered Cylindrical, Geometric Design, Signed, 9 1/2 In. 990.00
Vase, Tree Landscape, Maroon To Rose, Frosted, 8 5/8 In. 695.00

The Muncie Clay Products Company was established by Charles Benham in Muncie, Indiana, in 1922. The company made pottery for the florist and gift shop trade. The company closed by 1939. Pieces are marked with the name "Muncie" or just with a system of numbers and letters like "1A."

MUNCIE, Pitcher, Ball, Glossy 35.00
Pitcher, Ball, Glossy Tan Drip 45.00
Vase, Blue To Lavender, Small 11.00
Vase, Lavender To Blue, 4 In. 12.50
Vase, Turquoise Matte, 4 In. 11.50
Vase, Turquoise Matte, 4 Lobed Top, 4 In. 17.00
Vase, Turquoise Matte, Pinched 4 Petal Top 11.00

Music boxes, musical instruments, and sheet music are listed in this section. Phonograph records, jukeboxes, and phonographs are listed in other sections in this book.

MUSIC, Accordion, Child's, Brown Pearlized Finish, 1 Key Missing, Italy 95.00
Accordion, Rosati, Mother-Of-Pearl Panels, Leather Case 300.00
Accordion, Tanzbar, Roll Operated 650.00
Album, Bing Crosby, Autographed Picture Of Bing Inside Cover 20.00
Album, Photograph, Paisley Print Celluloid Cover, Lady, 1900 .... 175.00
Autoharp, Zimmerman 85.00
Automaton, Birds, Cage, Heads, Tails, Beaks Move, Whistle, Brass, 20 In. 850.00
Automaton, Singing Bird, Enameled, Hand Painted Box, France, 3 1/4 In. 900.00
Automaton, Singing Bird, Turns Alone, Gilt Bars, 15 X 22 In. 1450.00
Band Organ, Limonaire, 34 Key, 8 Books Of Music 5000.00
Banjo, Bacon, Silver Bell, Tenor 1250.00
Banjo, Howard & Davis, No.5, Square Bottom 1800.00
Banjo, Yale's Banjo Club, Original Case, Books, Photo Of Members 95.00
Bassoon, Rosewood, C.1890 .... 350.00
Baton, Conductor's, Ebony, Monogram, Ivory Handle, Boxed, 17 1/2 In. 55.00
Bazooka, Bob Burns 20.00
Box, 3 Singing Birds, Windup, 22 In. Cage 1000.00
Box, Album, German, Celluloid Covers, Lady Pictured 200.00
Box, Birdcage, Wooden Slat, 6 X 5 In. 18.00
Box, Bremond, Standing Cylinder, Inlaid Lid, Ebonized Rims, Tune Card 3250.00
Box, Carousel Animals, Switzerland, 12 X 10 In. 175.00

Box,	Columbia, Coin–Operated, Original Horn	2300.00
Box,	Cremona, A Roll Frame	250.00
Box,	Criterion, Double Comb, 20 Discs, Oak Table & Cabinet, 15 1/2 In.	3400.00
Box,	Criterion, Table Model, Cabinet, Double Comb, 20 Discs	3400.00
Box,	Cylinder, Rosewood Veneer, 8–Tune, Bells, Drum, Swiss, 10 1/2 In.	1800.00
Box,	Cylinder, Swiss Sublime Harmony, 12–Tune, Cylinder, 16 5/8 In.	1600.00
Box,	Double Comb, Serpentine Mahogany, 15 1/2 In.Disc	4400.00
Box,	Ducommon–Girod, Keywind, Pianoforte Cylinder	2500.00
Box,	Edelweiss, Hand Crank, 17 Discs	485.00
Box,	Euphonia, Disc 11 5/8 In.	1100.00
Box,	Figural, Organ Grinder With Monkey, Bisque	135.00
Box,	French, Lullaby, 2–Tune, Porcelain Hand Crank	75.00
Box,	Home, Hot Time In Old Town, C.1892	575.00
Box,	LeCoultre, 10–Tune, Bells & Butterflies, C.1870	1250.00
Box,	Mermod Freres, France, 8–Tune, Pat.1888, 17 1/2 X 9 X 6 In.	895.00
Box,	Mira Grand, Thirty 18 1/2 In.Discs, Stand	4500.00
Box,	Mira, Console, 50 Discs, Oak Cabinet	3800.00
Box,	Mira, Grand, Double Comb, 31 Discs, Cabinet, 18 1/2 In.	4500.00
Box,	Necessaire, Maple, Handle, Brass Work, Mirror, 2 3/4 X 4 1/4 In.	100.00
Box,	Oak, Cylinder, Crank, 12–Tune, Switzerland, 7 1/4 X 21 3/4 In.	800.00
Box,	Orchestral Regina, Upright, 27 In.	6500.00
Box,	Paillard, 12–Tune Roll, Inlaid Floral & Bird Design, C.1900	900.00
Box,	Perfection, 2 Discs, Oak Case, 14 In.	1250.00
Box,	Polyphone, Floor, 42 Discs, 19 3/4 In.	3500.00
Box,	Porcelain, Organ Grinder & Monkey, 2 Street Urchins, 11 In.	100.00
Box,	Regina Orchestra Corona, 27 In.Disc, 7 Ft.	6500.00
Box,	Regina, Art Glass & Clock, Automatic Changer	15500.00
Box,	Regina, Automatic Changer, Carved Dragon, 27 In.	11000.00
Box,	Regina, Double Comb, 1904, 19 Discs, 22 1/2 X 20 X 35 1/2 In.	4800.00
Box,	Regina, Floor Model, Serpentine Mahogany Case, Carved Dragons	4400.00
Box,	Regina, No. 9, Rococo, Carved Base, Gilded Finish	4000.00
Box,	Regina, No. 19, Black Walnut, Disc Double Comb, 6 Discs	1950.00
Box,	Regina, No. 19, Double Comb, Carved Art Nouveau Case	2500.00
Box,	Regina, No. 26, Casket Model, 20 3/4 In.Disc	4200.00
Box,	Regina, No. 31, Corona Changer, 20 3/4 In.	10500.00
Box,	Regina, No. 36, Front Changer, Flat Front, Coin–Operated	8900.00
Box,	Regina, No.240, Floor Model, Carved Lion's Heads, 32 Discs	4000.00
Box,	Regina, No.551, Princess	450.00
Box,	Regina, Orchestral, Upright	6500.00 To 7000.00
Box,	Regina, Orchestral, Upright, 20 Discs, 27 In.	995.00
Box,	Regina, Single Comb, Oak Case, 15 1/2 In.	1600.00
Box,	Regina, Upright, Oak Case, 20 In.	5250.00
Box,	Rococo, Gilded Design, Double Comb, 15 1/2 In.	4000.00
Box,	Stella, Scroll Front Over Drawer, 19th Century, 28 1/4 X 14 In.	1200.00
Box,	Sublime Harmonie, Song Card, 10–Tune	1055.00
Box,	Swiss, Inlaid Case, 3–Tune	145.00
Box,	Tin, Black Transfer, Girls Playing With Dolls, 2 7/8 In.	65.00
Box,	Whistler, Street Light, Windup, Hand Carved, German, 19 In.	130.00
Bugle,	Scout Rexcraft, Red Tassel Felt Case	85.00
Calliope,	44–Note, Hand Or A Roll Operation, Brass, Oak Cabinet	8950.00
Calliope,	Cozatt, 44 Brass Pipes, Keyboard Or Roll	9500.00
Calliope,	Pipes & Keyboard, Steam Operated	5000.00
Calliope,	Tangley, 43–Note, Roll Or Hand Played	7500.00
Catalog,	Victor, 1924	7.00
Catalog,	Victor, June, 1917	3.50
Clarinet,	Holton, Silver, Leather Case, 1920s	35.00
Clarinet,	Music Holder, Gladiator, White Co., Silver Plate, 24 In.	26.00
Clarinet,	Otello Lederer, Case	40.00
Clarino		325.00
Concertina,	Bardonian, Wooden, Leipzig, C.1906	325.00
Coronet,	French, 1900	75.00
Coronet,	King, Original Hard Case	75.00
Criterion,	Single Comb, Carved Mahogany Case, 15 1/2 In.	2000.00
Drum,	Hollow Spit, African, Handmade	425.00

Dulcimer, American, Heart Cutouts, Painted, 19th Century, 35 In. 300.00
Dulcimer, Handmade, Walnut, C.1910 .... 130.00
Fife, 6 Finger Holes, 6 Keys, Ivory Insets, Civil War 67.00
Figurine, Nipper, RCA, Bronze 65.00
Flute, Claude Laurent, Paris, Glass, 9–Key, 1838 .... 4400.00
Flute, Sterling Silver 395.00
Flute, Wooden, Metal, Wooden Case, Leather Cover, 26 In. 60.00
French Horn, Brass 150.00
Graphophone, Columbia Phonograph Co.Pat.1887, 1888, 1894, Case, Horn 225.00
Guitar, Civil War, Zogbaum & Fairchild, Pinewood Box 595.00
Guitar, Gibson, Dated 1940 ....300.00 To 350.00
Guitar, Symphonic, 1938 .... 250.00
Harmonica, Chromatic, Hohner, Original Case 38.00
Harmonica, Echo, M.Hohner, Original Box, Pre–1940 .... 15.00
Harmonica, Hohner, Navy, Box 20.00
Harmonica, Hohner, Pat.1926, Germany, Original Box 40.00
Harmonica, Marine Band, Hohner, No.1896, Instruction Book, Box 45.00
Harp, Black, Gilt, 1894 .... 35.00
Harp, Concert, Lyon & Healy, Single Action, Gold 2800.00
Harp, Erard Co., Bird's–Eye Maple & Gilt Gesso, C.1850, 69 1/2 In. 1400.00
Harp, French, Pedal, Gold & Ebony, 18th Century 1750.00
Harp, Inlaid Giltwood, P.I.Browne & Co., 19th Century, 5 Ft.9 In. 2200.00
Harp, Lyon & Healy, Single Action, Concert, Gold 2800.00
Harp, Sebastian Erard, London, Stenciled, Giltwood, C.1807 .... 3850.00
Horn, Fox Hunt, Brass 45.00
Jukebox, Seeburg Model 147MA, Blue Mirror Front, Free Play 1350.00
Jukebox, Wurlitzer, Model 1100, 78 Record, 1947 .... 1700.00
Mandolin Harp, Instructions, Original Box 50.00
Mandolin, Child's, Tortoiseshell Inlay Guard Plate, C.1875, 13 In. 150.00
Mandolin, Gibson 350.00
Mandolin, Inlay Work Of Butterfly & Flowers 100.00
Melodeon, C.1850 .... 585.00
Melodeon, Folding, Rosewood 500.00
Melodeon, G.A.Prince & Co., Detachable Legs, Pedals, Rosewood, 30 In. 750.00
Melodeon, Prince & Co., Buffalo, N.Y., Rosewood, Dated 1846 .... 1800.00
Melodeon, Rosewood Veneer, Octagonal Legs 1750.00
Melodeon, Rosewood, C.1870 .... 850.00
Melodeon, Rosewood, Folding Legs 60.00
Metronome, Maelzel, Chimes First Beat Of Every Measure 35.00
Metronome, Seth Thomas 37.50
Metronome, Wooden, German 35.00
Nickelodeon, 10–Tune, Beveled Glass, Tiger Oak 4500.00
Nickelodeon, Coinola, Cupid 3700.00
Nickelodeon, Nelson Wiggen, Casino–X, Original Art Glass 6000.00
Nickelodeon, Pipes, Style K 9500.00
Nickelodeon, Seeburg, Model A, Oak 6500.00
Nickelodeon, Seeburg, Model E, Flute Pipes 8000.00
Nickelodeon, Seeburg, Model E, Stained Glass, 8 Rolls, Mahogany 6000.00
Nickelodeon, Western Electric, Mascot, 1925, 36 X 22 X 51 In. 7200.00
Ocarina, Blue & White Onion Pattern, Meissen, 7 In. 200.00
Ooga Horn, Hand Klaxonet 75.00
Orchestrelle, Aeolian, Style A, 25 Rolls 3400.00
Orchestrion, Khul & Klatt, Pneumatic Model, Percussion, Accordion 3500.00
Orchestrion, Losche, Keyboard Piano, Accordion 5500.00
Orchestrion, Pneumatic Model, Full Percussion 3500.00
Orchestrion, Poppers Welt Jazz 6500.00
Organ, 1887 Gem, Cob 475.00
Organ, Aeolian, Pipe, 116–Note, 2 Manuals 1400.00
Organ, Band, Wurlitzer, No.125, Military 15000.00
Organ, Band, Wurlitzer, No.143, Rolls 20000.00
Organ, Barrel, 46 Metal Pipes, 16 Wooden Pipes, English, C.1835 .... 10500.00
Organ, Beckwith, No.C–915, Folding 35.00
Organ, Chapel, Farrand, Pump, Oak 1600.00
Organ, Chord, Estee, Revival 600.00

Organ, Clariona, Paper Roll, 11 Rolls 275.00
Organ, Crank Barrel, Longman & Brodripp, 10 Tune Barrels, Stand 5400.00
Organ, Crown, Parlor, High Back, 11 Stops, Stool, Walnut 1200.00
Organ, DeCap Dance, Restored 9500.00
Organ, Fairground, Bruder, 52 Keys, 217 Pipes, Book Music 17000.00
Organ, Farrand, Pumper, Chapel, Oak 1600.00
Organ, Gem, Roller, 5 Cobs 450.00
Organ, Gem, Table, 15 Cobs 500.00
Organ, Grand Roller, 4 Cobs 2400.00
Organ, Mason Hamlin, Walnut, Top Folds Down Over Keys, 1800s 750.00
Organ, Pipe, Kilgen, No., 3891, C.1933 .... 1000.00
Organ, Player, Aeolian, Model 1250 .... 2000.00
Organ, Pump, Chicago, Cottage, Claw Foot, Glass Ball Stool 3000.00
Organ, Pump, D.F.Beatty, Fruitwood, Swivel Stool, C.1890 .... 1100.00
Organ, Pump, Kimbal, Maple Finish, 42 X 48 In. 650.00
Organ, Pump, Kimbal, Oak, Beveled Mirror 1200.00
Organ, Pump, Lyon & Healy, Walnut, 48 X 24 X 52 In. 750.00
Organ, Pump, Mason & Hamlin, C.1880 .... 1000.00
Organ, Pump, Story & Clark, Walnut Case 495.00
Organ, Pump, Victorian, Mirror Back Canopy, Walnut 875.00
Organ, Pump, Victorian, Walnut, Mirror Back Canopy ....750.00 To 875.00
Organ, Pump, Victorian, Walnut, Mirror Back Canopy, Matching Stool 975.00
Organ, Pump, Windsor, Beveled Mirror, 7 Ft. 850.00
Organ, Reed, Beckwith, Church Type 450.00
Organ, Reed, Estey, 2 Manuals, Full Pedals, 15 Stops, 500 Reeds 850.00
Organ, Roller, Table Top, 9 Rollers 1650.00
Organ, Seeburg, Player Pipe, Pedal Board, 2 Manuals, 4 Ranks, Rolls 3875.00
Organ, Steinway, Duo–Art, Pipe, 6 Ft. 1 In. 9000.00
Organ, Symphonia, 18 Rolls 650.00
Organette, Musette 475.00
Organette, Oriston, Plays Flat Fiber Records, Germany 725.00
Orphenion, Upright, Coin–Operated 4500.00
Piano, Aeolian, Duo–Art, Upright, Reproducer, Bench 3800.00
Piano, Aeolian, Upright, Reproducer, Duo–Art, Bench 3800.00
Piano, Ampico, Art Cased, Harpsichord Shaped Case, 5 Ft.4 In. 15000.00
Piano, Bradbury, Spinet, Lyre Shaped Pedal Support, 38 1/2 X 57 In. 125.00
Piano, Busch & Gerts, Parlor, Gilded, Carved, Rosewood, 28 X 58 In. 3000.00
Piano, Bush & Gerts, Hand Carving, Pillars, C.1903, 54 In. 2200.00
Piano, Chickering, Grand, Square, Rosewood, C.1877 .... 950.00
Piano, D.L.Fry, Square, Rosewood, 1870s 4000.00
Piano, Duo–Art XR, Grand Player, 6 Ft.1 In. 6995.00
Piano, Emperiale, Model 310 60, 38 Keys, 40 X 41 1/2 X 22 In. 225.00
Piano, Empire, Mahogany, Gilt Bronze Mount, Triangular Top, 7 Ft. 4400.00
Piano, Farrand, Upright 7200.00
Piano, Fisher, Ampico, Spinet, 1937 .... 4800.00
Piano, Franklin Ampico Reproducer, Upright, 1928, Bench & Rolls 4000.00
Piano, Kranich & Bach, Grand, Rosewood, Square, C.1870 .... 6000.00
Piano, Kranich & Bach, Grand, Serial No.25880, Ivory, Ornate Legs 55000.00
Piano, Kranich & Bach, Parlor Grand, Ivory Keys 5500.00
Piano, Mason & Hamlin Ampico, Model A, African Mahogany, 1927, 7 Ft. 15000.00
Piano, Mother–Of–Pearl Inlay, Lacquered Design, Upright, C.1875 .... 1850.00
Piano, Player, Busch & Gerts, Roll Cabinet, Bench, C.1909 .... 5500.00
Piano, Player, Hamilton, Manualo, 300 Rolls 800.00
Piano, Player, Hammond, Tiger Oak, 24 Rolls, C.1919 .... 3500.00
Piano, Player, Kline, Recordo Player System, Walnut, Bench, 1920s 2750.00
Piano, Player, Knabe, Ampico A Player, Complete Roll Collection 4950.00
Piano, Player, Peerless, With Mandolin Bar & Bellow 9995.00
Piano, Player, Pump Or Coin–Operated 1850.00
Piano, Player, Smith Lyraphone, C.1905, Rolls 600.00
Piano, Player, Steinway, Duo–Art XR, Grand, 6 Ft. 1 In. ....6995.00 To 7200.00
Piano, Player, Steinway, Grand, Duo–Art XR, 6 Ft.1 In. 6995.00
Piano, Reproducer, Melvin Clark Co., Electrified 2000.00
Piano, Seeburg, Type L, Coin–Operated 6000.00
Piano, Steinway, Grand, Ebonized Wood, 76 In. 3800.00

Piano, Steinway, Grand, Model B, No.122229, Satinwood	4500.00
Piano, Steinway, Grand, Model M, 1924, Walnut, 5 Ft. 7 In.	6000.00
Piano, Steinway, Grand, No.0, Mahogany, 5 Ft.11 In.	8900.00
Piano, Steinway, Grand, No.1880, Square, Rosewood	5500.00
Piano, Steinway, Grand, Parcel Gilt & Painted, C.1890, 6 Ft.4 In.	5500.00
Piano, Steinway, Grand, Square, Rosewood, Claw Foot Stool, C.1897	5000.00
Piano, Steinway, No.1876, Square Grand, Organette, Musette, 4 Cobs	475.00
Piano, Steinway, No.1880, Square Grand, Rosewood	5500.00
Piano, Steinway, Reproducer, Duo–Art Mechanism, Upright Grand	9900.00
Piano, Steinway, Upright Grand, 1893, 54 In.	5600.00
Piano, Stoddard, Ampico, Upright	2500.00
Piano, Weber, Duo–Art, 5 Ft. 8 In.	9000.00
Piano, Weber, Grand, Walnut & Mahogany, 6 Ft.6 In.	8000.00
Piano, Welte Farrand, Upright	7200.00
Pianoforte, Sheraton, Mahogany, Plaque, A.Babcock, C.1820, 34 X 67 In.	2400.00
Pianoforte, Stand, 2 Sections, Charles Tans, 1794, Mahogany, 5 Ft.	3300.00
Pianolodeon, Chein, 5 Roll, 20 X 20 1/4 In.	250.00
Pianolodeon, Electric, 6 Rolls, Original Box, 1950s	180.00
Record Brush, Decca	9.50
Record Brush, RCA Dog & Horn	12.50
Record Brush, Victor, Oblong Shape, Gold Leaf Nipper On Blue, 1900s	25.00
Rollmonica, 2 Rolls	65.00 To 100.00
Saxophone, Harwood, Silver Plate, Case	155.00
Stand, Adjustable, Electrified Candleholders, Rosewood	275.00
Stand, Solid Brass, 48 In.	180.00
Tambourine, Red Wood	9.00
Tuning Fork, C, 4 1/2 In.	12.00
Ukelele, Harmony	35.00
Viola D'Amore, Leandro Bisiach, Milan, Cupid Head, C.1904	3575.00
Viola D'Amore, Prague, Red Brown Varnish, 1740	8800.00
Violin Bow, Gold–Mounted, Albert Nurnberg, Markneukirchen	935.00
Violin Bowl, Silver–Mounted, French, Stamped Paejot, Amt	550.00
Violin, Amati, Bow, Case	550.00
Violin, Germany, Hand Carved Wooden Case, C.1740	500.00
Violin, Karl August Berger, New York, Orange Varnish, 1922	1540.00
Violin, Lorenzo Ventapane, Naples, Gold Brown Varnish, C.1816	5225.00
Violin, Sherl & Roth, Case	95.00
Violin, Stainer Style, Handmade, Scrimshaw Trim, Wooden Case, C.1860	975.00
Violin, Stradivarius Copy, Case, 22 In.	100.00
Xylophone, Western Electric, Style X	2900.00
Zither, P.R.Richter, Munchen, Instruction Book, C.1860	90.00

The mustache cup was popular from 1850 to 1900 when the large, flowing mustache was in style. A ledge of china or silver held the hair out of the liquid in the cup. This kept the mustache tidy and also kept the mustache wax from melting. Left–handed mustache cups are rare but are being reproduced.

MUSTACHE CUP, Colonial Couple Scene, Sponge Design, Kettle Shape, 4–Foot	125.00
Design, Green Tones	30.00
Engraved Florals, Silver Plate, Saucer	75.00
Floral Design, White, Germany, Saucer	35.00
Floral, Gilt, Saucer	50.00
Flowers, Gold Trim	50.00
Gold & White Raised Leaf Design, Saucer, Germany	35.00
Grape Design, Polo Scene, China	13.50
Kind Regards, Gold Trim, Saucer	35.00
Pink Luster, Floral Band, Saucer	45.00
Remember Me, Raised Gold	25.00
Saucer, Applied Floral Around Uneven Edge, Silver Plate	95.00
Saucer, Floral Engraved, Silver Plate, Marked	80.00
Saucer, Pink & Gold, Ornate	28.00
Shaded White To Pink, Transfer Of Pink & Yellow Mums	32.00
White, Ribbon Of Applied Flowers, For A Gift Inscription	95.00

"MZ Austria" is the wording on a mark used by Moritz Zdekauer on porcelains made at his works from about 1900. The firm worked in the town of Alt–Rohlau, Austria. The pieces were decorated with lavish floral patterns and overglaze gold decoration. Full sets of dishes were made as well as vases, toilet sets, and other wares.

MZ AUSTRIA, Chocolate Pot, Floral Finial, Pearl Ground, Ovide, Marked, 10 In.	90.00
Dish, Fruit, Flower, 8 In.	35.00
Hairpin Holder, Roses, 6 In.	25.00

Nailsea glass was made in the Bristol district in England from 1788 to 1873. It was made by many different factories, not just the Nailsea Glass House. Many pieces were made with loopings of either white or colored glass as decoration.

NAILSEA, Basket, Pink & White Loops, 4 X 6 In.	75.00
Biscuit Jar, Cranberry & White, Bird, Butterflies, 6 1/4 In.	375.00
Epergne, Mirrored Plateau, 4 Lights, Center Fairy Lamp, 14 X 10 In.	325.00
Flask, Candy Stripe Glass, 6 In.	130.00
Flask, Clear, Pink Looping, White Casing, 9 In.	90.00
Flask, Double Gemel, Clear, Red & White Looping, 10 1/2 In.	70.00
Flask, South Jersey, Opalescent Loops, Cranberry, C.1820	450.00
Perfume Bottle, Deep Blue On Opaque White, 6 1/2 In.	125.00
Shade, White Loopings, Ruffled Rim, 5 1/2 X 4 7/8 In.	75.00
Sugar Shaker, Pear Shape, Blue, White Looping, Diagonal Bands, 5 In.	90.00
Vase, Blue, White Loops, Applied Flowers & Leaves, 9 In.	95.00
Walking Stick, Blown, Hollow, 22 In.	175.00

NAKARA

Nakara is a trade name for a white glassware made about 1900 by the C. F. Monroe Company of Meriden, Connecticut. It was decorated in pastel colors. The glass was very similar to another glass made by the company called "Wave Crest." The company closed in 1916. Boxes for use on a dressing table are the most commonly found Nakara pieces. The mark is not found on every piece.

NAKARA, Box, Blown–Out Pansy, Lined, Blue Ground, 3 3/4 In.	350.00
Box, Collars & Cuffs, Puffy, 7 In.	695.00
Box, Hinged Lid, Square, Signed, 4 In.	400.00
Box, Hinged Mirror Inside Cover, Crown Mold, 8 1/2 In.	695.00
Box, Jewel, Full Portrait Of Queen Louise, 8 In. ....875.00 To	1475.00
Box, Lid, Mirror, Burmese, Daisies, Yellow To Pink, Signed, 6 1/2 In.	575.00
Box, Pink Floral Design On Lid, Blue Ground, 4 3/4 In.	265.00
Casket, Crown Mold, Mirror Lid, Enameled Floral, Marked, 8 1/2 In.	750.00
Holder, Whiskbroom, Pink Flowers, Signed	850.00
Toothpick, Hand Painted Flowers, 3–Footed, Ormolu Base, Beaded Rim	100.00

Nanking is a type of blue–and–white porcelain made in Canton, China, since the late eighteenth century. It is very similar to Canton, which is listed under its own name in this book. Both Nanking and Canton are part of a larger group now called "Chinese Export" porcelain. Nanking has a spear–and–post border and may have gold decoration.

NANKING, Dish, Hot Water, Inclined Pines, Blue, White, 1790–1810, 15 1/2 In.	700.00
Tureen, Soup, Flower Finial, Strap Handles, 19th Century, 10 1/2 In.	1300.00

Napkin rings were in fashion from 1869 to about 1900. They were made of silver, porcelain, wood, and other materials. They are still being made today. The most popular rings with collectors are the figural napkin rings of silver plate. Small, realistic figures were made to hold the ring. Good and poor reproductions of the more expensive rings are now being made and collectors must be very careful, especially when buying any of the Kate Greenaway rings.

NAPKIN RING, Art Nouveau, Sterling Silver, Ladies, Unger Bros.	65.00
Cloisonne, Butterflies & Floral, Rust Ground	35.00
Cloisonne, Dragon Design, Openwork	45.00
Figural, Angel Pushing Ring, Butterfly On Top	159.00

Figural, Attached Bud Vase, Girl With Mirror, Silver Plate 75.00
Figural, Bird & Fan, Silver Plate 145.00
Figural, Boy Pushes Hoop, Meriden 85.00
Figural, Bud Vase Above Pedestal, Birds On Ring, Silver Plate 85.00
Figural, Bulldog, Dirigo Boy's State Seal, Silver Plate 125.00
Figural, Cat, Arched Back, Front Of Ring, Silver Plate 110.00
Figural, Chick On Wishbone, Silver Plate, Derby 55.00
Figural, Chicken On Wishbone, Quadruple Plate 38.00
Figural, Chicken, Sterling Silver 35.00
Figural, Cupid Standing 125.00
Figural, Double Eagles, Silver Plate 99.00
Figural, Double Wishbone, Silver Plate 98.00
Figural, Eagles, Silver Plate, Meriden 85.00
Figural, Eagles, Spread Wings 120.00
Figural, Elephant, Pewter 50.00
Figural, Kate Greenaway Girl Holding Stick, Silver Plate 225.00
Figural, Lily Pad, Silver Plate 55.00
Figural, Lion Pulling Car, Wheels Revolve 195.00
Figural, Naked Black Boy, Silver Plate, 3 1/2 In. 160.00
Figural, Ostrich & Kangaroo, Standing, Boomerang, Australia 115.00
Figural, Prancing Horse Hitched To Wheels, Silver Plate 75.00
Figural, Prancing Horse Pulls Wheeled Ring, Sterling Silver 245.00
Figural, Rabbits Leaning On Ring, Sterling Siver 245.00
Figural, Romping Dog, Full–Bodied, Silver Plate, 3 1/2 In. 85.00
Figural, Swan Pulling Ring, Boy On Top 250.00
Figural, Twin Seated Cherubs 65.00
Figural, Wishbones, Straddle Ring, Best Wishes, Silver Plate 37.00
Floral Leaf, Flower In Relief, Silver Plate 47.00
Ivory, Dragon, Carved 15.00
Ivory, Serpent, Carved 40.00
Ivory, Snake Curved Around Elephant's Tusk 45.00
Lacquer, Russian, Pair 125.00
Oak Leaves, Silver Plate 65.00
Porcelain, Roses & Snowballs, RS Germany 45.00

Nash glass was made in Corona, New York, after 1919 by Arthur Nash and his sons. He worked at the Webb factory in England and for the Tiffany Glassworks in the United States.

NASH, Bowl, Red Chintz, Signed, Gray On Blood Red, 10 X 3 1/2 In. 425.00
Bowl, Silver Chintz Pattern, Red, Marked, 4 X 10 In. 475.00
Candlestick, Green & Blue Stripes, Signed 85.00
Vase, Chintz Pattern, Art Deco Shaped, Signed, 11 1/2 In. 425.00
Vase, Chintz Pattern, Blue & Green, Trumpet Shape, Signed, 10 In. 395.00
Vase, Chintz Rose, Signed, Yellow Pattern, No.RD85X, Signed, 12 In. 725.00
Vase, Gold Iridescent, Blue Interior, Ribbed Bottom, Signed, 4 1/4 In. 225.00
Vase, Gold Iridescent, Signed, 5 In. 285.00
Vase, Gray Chintz Pattern, Red Pedestal, Signed, 5 1/2 In. 625.00

Nautical antiques are listed in this section. Any of the many objects that were made or used by the seafaring trade, including ship parts, models, and tools, are included. Other pieces may be found listed under Scrimshaw.

NAUTICAL, Almanac, 1882, Tides, List Of U.S.Lighthouses, 300 Pages 19.50
Anemometer, Inman's, English, Collapsible Wind Vane, C.1865, 9 In. 380.00
Bell & Barometer Set, Chelsea, Nickel 775.00
Bell, Bracket, 16 X 12 In. 550.00
Bell, Chelsea, Phenolic 375.00
Book, Passenger List, Queen Mary, 1937 .... 10.00
Bowl, Norwegian America Line, Vistafjord Sagafjord, Silver 18.50
Box, Sailor's, Inlaid, 19th Century 300.00
Butter Chip, Great Lakes Steamer, North West, Duluth, Embossed 28.00
Canoe, Birchbark 2400.00
Card, Clipper Ship, Advertising Ship, 3 1/2 X 6 1/2 In. 275.00
Card, Clipper Ship, Walter Lord Perkins, Itinerary, 1859, 6 In. 55.00

Chart Dividers, Single Handed, English, 19th Century, 7 In. 195.00
Chest, Papered Inside, St.Croix Minstrel Show Flyers 137.50
Chronometer, Hamilton, 3–Part Gimbal Box 1200.00
Chronometer, Hamilton, Model 21, Gimbal Box 1095.00
Chronometer, Hamilton, Model 22, Gimbal Box 495.00
Coaster, McCormick–Moore Shiplines, Blacks Loading Coffee 15.00
Compass, Diptych Dial, Geringer, Folding, Fruitwood, 3 1/2 In. 295.00
Compass, Dry Card, Maine, 128 Divisions, C.1830 .... 195.00
Compass, Ivory & Wood Diptych Dial, German, C.1700, 2 X 1 1/4 In. 980.00
Compass, Keuffer & Esser, Mahogany Box 38.50
Compass, Marine, New Bedford, J.Kehew, Wooden Case, 7 X 7 X 5 In. 175.00
Compass, Sperry Gyro, Chrysler Corp., Floor Style, 1919, 52 In. 500.00
Course Reckoner, Maine, Signed J.W.Strange, Brass, C.1880, 16 In. 185.00
Cup & Saucer, Cunard Line, Floral 34.00
Desk Set, Barometer, Thermometer, Hygrometer, Bronze, Base 65.00
Display Board, Ornamental Knots, 12 Examples, 33 1/2 X 27 In. 550.00
Divider, Beam, Geared, English, 19th Century, 24 In. 400.00
Eagle, Hand Carved, From Stern Of Ship, 19th Century 800.00
Eagle, Pilothouse, Signed F.L.Bailey, Gilt, 51 In. 1900.00
Gaff, Salmon, Telescopic Brass, Steel, & Rosewood, English, C.1850 .... 280.00
Galvanometer, Clamp Screw, English, Dated 1913, 14 In. 325.00
Globe, Terrestrial, Mounted In Cast Iron Circle, C.1895 .... 295.00
Hat, Sailor, U.S.S.Grant 24.00
Lamp, Ship, Brass Cage, Ruby Globe, 10 In. 95.00
Lantern, Brass, Tin, Labeled Port & Starboard, 11 1/8 In., Pair 165.00
Lantern, Channel Marker, Gas, Brass & Copper, C.1880, 36 In. 1500.00
Lantern, Helvios, Red & Blue Wind Directionals, Brass 40.00
Lantern, Night Watch, Dietz, Red, 8 1/2 In. 55.00
Lantern, Ship, Brass Lamp, Base, Green Glass, Triangular, 8 In. 25.00
Menu, Ivernia, Cunard, 1910 .... 6.00
Menu, Normandie Liner, 1939 .... 10.00
Menu, Normandie, French & English, Pictorial Cover, 1936 .... 12.00
Menu, S.S.Juanita, 1910 .... 30.00
Micro–Spectroscope, With Micrometer, English, C.1897 .... 550.00
Micrometer, Screw Drive, Silver Readout Scale, 19th Century, 7 In. 225.00
Model, 3–Masted Schooner, Half Model, Waves, Case, 21 1/2 X 40 In. 300.00
Model, Battleship, Cast Lead Fittings, Solid Wood Bodies, 1948 .... 175.00
Model, British Frigate H.M.S.Unicorn, Case, 33 X 30 In. 1760.00
Model, Clipper Ship, Wooden, Primitive, Black & White Paint, 28 In. 70.00
Model, Great Republic, Hull Cut Away, 1933 .... 150.00
Model, Heavy Cruiser, Handmade, Lead Fittings, Solid Wood Bodies 150.00
Model, Sailboat, Single Mast, Joseph DeYound, Halifax, 4 Ft. 2 In. 1050.00
Model, Sailing Ship, 3 Full Masts, Sails, Wicker 65.00
Model, Single Mast Sailboat, 19th Century, 43 In. 275.00
Model, Whaling Brig Viola, Fully Rigged, Case, 33 X 24 In. 4180.00
Note Cards, S.S.Lurline, Matson Lines, Unused, Set Of 10 .... 7.50
Octant, English, Signed Charles Jones, 3 Trade Labels, 14 In. 895.00
Octant, Signed Spencer, Browning, London, Box, 18th Century 975.00
Ring Dial, German, Gilt & Silvered Brass, Zodiacal Scale 3600.00
Sector, Portuguese, 18th Century, Folding, Opens To 11 15/16 In. 650.00
Sextant, Binocular, Monocular, Prismatic, German, Case, C.1925 .... 650.00
Sextant, Double Frame, Troughton, London, Complete, C.1815 .... 2200.00
Sextant, Double, T.Jones, English, Box, C.1830, Miniature 2150.00
Sextant, Flat Frame, English, No.1090, Brass, Wooden Case, C.1791 .... 6200.00
Sextant, Plath, German, Wooden Case, Manifest Papers, Early 1900s 500.00
Sextant, Signed Hughes, English, Mahogany Box, 19th Century 575.00
Sextant, Silver Scales, Magnifier, Filters, Pocket 220.00
Ship Log, Stamped E. & G.W.Blunt, New York, Brass, Mechanical, 1840 .... 450.00
Spectroscope, Rainband, English, 19th Century 190.00
Sundial, Augsburg Dial, Signed L.Grasl, Folding, Equinoctial, 2 In. 850.00
Telegraph, With Bells, Brass 350.00
Telegraph, World War I Marine Ship, Brass, Large 675.00
Telescope, 9 Drawers, Dancer, English, 19th Century, 7 To 42 In. 465.00
Telescope, Brass, 23 In. 65.00

Telescope, Brass, 39 In.	160.00
Telescope, Captain's, Brass, 42 In.	250.00
Telescope, Harris & Son, England, 1 Extension, Oak & Brass	250.00
Telescope, L.Ulrich, Paris, Filter, Focus By Drawtube	1050.00
Telescope, Set Of 60 Slides, Assembly Of Telescope, 1930s	420.00
Telescope, Ship, Brass, 1900s, 42 In.	175.00
Telescope, Silver Fittings, Mahogany Tube, 10 To 42 In.	750.00
Transit, Wm.J.Young, Philadelphia, No.3194, Brass	1495.00
Watch, Deck, Hamilton, Model 22, Box	495.00
Whistle, Bosuns, Silver, Miniature, 1 3/4 In.	145.00
Wine, Norwegian–American Lines, Signed NAL	10.00

Small ivory, wood, metal or porcelain pieces were used as buttons on the end of the cord that held a Japanese money pouch. These were called "Netsuke." The earliest date from the sixteenth century. Many are miniature, carved, works of art.

NETSUKE, Fishing Creel, Containing Fish, Signed	60.00
Frog, Upside–Down Dog, Signed Masayuki, 2 X 1 1/8 In.	135.00
Ivory, 2 Figures With A Tortoise, Signed, 1 1/2 In.	750.00
Ivory, Barnyard Scene, Cockerel, Millstone, Metal Inlaid, Koku	550.00
Ivory, Cat Lying On Large Fish, Signed, 3 In.	450.00
Ivory, Cat Pursuing Mouse In Paper Lantern, Signed, 19th Century	325.00
Ivory, Cat, Standing On Hind Legs, Viewing Opening Venus Clam	1045.00
Ivory, Dragon, Coiled Tail, Signed, 2 In. ....50.00 To	150.00
Ivory, Dutchman, Dancing, 1 Leg Raised, Domed Hat, Inlayed Eyes	600.00
Ivory, Elephant, Man Climbing On Back, Man Along Side, With Staff	135.00
Ivory, Fuku–Rokujo, Seated, Knee Raised, Engraved Robe, 18th Century	550.00
Ivory, Group Of Karako, Fancy Robe, Playing Drum, Signed Hakuunsai	300.00
Ivory, Group Of Oni, Demon Seated, Tiger Skin Pants, Tomomasa	715.00
Ivory, Hotei Wearing Robe, Carrying Karako, Signed Masatomo	990.00
Ivory, Hotei, Staff & Bag, Polychromed	85.00
Ivory, Ikaku Sennin, Carrying Woman Of Bernares, Hidemasa	385.00
Ivory, Kakio, Digging Up Gold, Wife & Child, Signed Tomochika	550.00
Ivory, Kirin, Seated On Haunches, Hooves Together, Tail Raised	770.00
Ivory, Monk, Holding Alms Bowl With Dragon, 18th Century	495.00
Ivory, Monkey & Young, Adult Seated On Hind End, Baby Under Paws	770.00
Ivory, Monkey, Seated, Wearing Spectacles, Signed Meigyokusai	1100.00
Ivory, Oni, Holding Gong, Umbrella On Back, Signed Mitsuharu	550.00
Ivory, Oni, Seated, Cross Legged, Tiger Skin, Signed Meigyokusai	1045.00
Ivory, Ota Dokwan & Girl, Signed Shounsai, 1 1/2 In.	650.00
Ivory, Poets, In Greenhouse, Black & Red Details, Signed Jusai	330.00
Ivory, Pot Of Gold, Signed Tomochika, 1 3/4 In.	900.00
Ivory, Puppy, Playing With Bamboo Stalk, Signed Kaigyokusai	2200.00
Ivory, Puppy, Resting On Belly, Paws Resting On Shell, 18th Century	660.00
Ivory, Sarumawashi & Mondey, 2 In.	1600.00
Ivory, Shishi, Signed Ishimitsu, 1 In.	1500.00
Ivory, Squirrel, Standing On Hind Legs, Bunch Of Grapes, Large Tail	600.00
Ivory, Thunder Gods, Signed Gyokuun, 1 1/2 In.	1000.00
Ivory, Turtle & Young, Emerging From Shell, Small One On Top	330.00
Ivory, Ushiwakamaru, Signed Tomochika, 1 1/4 In.	1400.00
Ivory, Woman In Kimono Holding Mask, Bare Breast, 2 In.	75.00
Whale Tooth, Blindman On Elephant, Balancing, 18th Century	360.00
Wood, Badger, Signed Yoshiaki, 1 1/4 In.	1400.00
Wood, Cat Scratching Ear, Signed	90.00
Wood, Cat With Bird In Mouth, Cat With Kitten, Set Of 2	125.00
Wood, Dancer, Standing, 1 Foot Raised, Holding Fan, Signed Hoju	440.00
Wood, Jurojin, Wearing Cap, Resembles Tortoise, Long–Headed	330.00
Wood, Monkey, 1 3/4 In.	2000.00
Wood, Okame, Signed Josetsu, 1 In.	1750.00
Wood, Rat, 1 1/2 In.	1750.00
Wood, Sneezer, Seated, Cross Legged, Robe Falling Off, Singed Hokkei	360.00
Wood, Toad, Seated On Hind Legs, On Wooden Bucket, Signed Masanao	440.00
Wood, Turtles, 2 In.	1200.00

The New Martinsville Glass Manufacturing Company was established in 1901 in New Martinsville, West Virginia. It was bought and renamed the Viking Glass Company in 1944 and is still producing fine glasswares.

NEW MARTINSVILLE, Ashtray, Chrome Wall Hanger, Moondrops, Ruby 25.00
Ashtray, Enameled Flowers, Crystal, 3 1/2 In. 25.00
Ashtray, Moondrops, Ruby, Chrome Wall Hanger 25.00
Basket, Janice, Blue, 12 1/2 In. 50.00
Basket, Light Blue, Janice, 12 In. ....50.00 To 75.00
Bookends, Elephant, Crystal, Pair 59.00
Bookends, Horse, Jumping, Crystal, 10 X 3 In. 65.00
Bookends, Wolfhound 85.00
Bowl, Radiance, Pedestal, Blue, 10 In. 45.00
Bride's Bowl, Peachblow, 10 3/4 In. 125.00
Bride's Bowl, Peachblow, Frilly, Base, 13 1/2 In. 140.00
Candleholder, 2–Light, Prelude 20.00
Candy Dish, Moondrops, 3–Section, Metal Holder 38.00
Compote, Moondrops, 4 1/2 In. 33.00
Cordial, Moondrops ....17.00 To 18.00
Cup, Moondrops, Red, Footed 7.00
Decanter, Moondrops, Beehive Stopper 55.00
Decanter, Moondrops, Ruby 95.00
Dish, Swan Cover, Amber, 5 In. 10.00
Figurine, Baby Bear 45.00
Figurine, Chick 18.00
Figurine, Elephant, Pair 168.00
Figurine, Hunters, Round Base, Pair 235.00
Figurine, Pony, Long Legged, Oval Base, Solid, 11 3/4 In. 60.00
Figurine, Rooster, Solid ....35.00 To 40.00
Figurine, Russian Wolfhounds, Crystal, 9 X 7 1/4 In., Pair 70.00
Figurine, Seal 22.00
Figurine, Swan, Emerald, 7 1/2 In. 18.00
Mayonnaise Set, Radiance, Etched Flower Basket, 3 Piece 35.00
Plate, Janice, Ruby, 11 1/2 In. 30.00
Plate, Moondrops, Ruby, 14 In. 30.00
Sherbet, Rock Crystal, Red 5.00
Sugar & Creamer, Janice, Etched Canterbury, Blue 62.50
Sugar & Creamer, Moondrops 25.00
Sugar & Creamer, Moondrops, Individual 12.00
Swan, Black, Clear Neck, 5 In. 15.00
Toothpick, Etched Birds 24.00
Tumbler, Moondrops, Ruby, 2 Oz. 10.00
Tumbler, Rock Crystal, Concave, Amber, 10 Oz. 20.00
Tumbler, Ruby, Footed 12.00
Vase, Bird, Frosted Seal, 9 In. 38.00
Vase, Cobalt, Enameled Floral, 9 In. 45.00
Vase, Radiance, Red Crimp, 12 In. 55.00
Water Set, 64 Oz. Pitcher, Red, 7 Piece 300.00
Water Set, Moondrops, Ruby, 7 Piece ....245.00 To 300.00
Wine, Moondrops, Ruby, 4 Oz. 18.00

Newcomb Pottery was founded by Ellsworth and William Woodward at Sophie Newcomb College, New Orleans, Louisiana, in 1896. The work continued through the 1940s. Pieces of this art pottery are marked with the printed letters "NC" and often have the incised initials of the artist as well. Most pieces have a matte glaze and incised decoration.

NEWCOMB, Bowl, Pink To Purple, Floral Design Top, Simpson, 4 1/2 X 6 1/2 In. 575.00
Bowl, White & Yellow Daffodils, Blue, Leaves, H.Bailey, 8 1/2 In. 350.00
Bowl, Yellow Buds, Leaves, Blue Glaze, Marked, 2 3/4 X 4 1/2 In. 200.00
Plaque, Heart Map, Named For Human Emotions, Marked, 5 X 6 In. 325.00
Vase, Black Shiny Glaze, Signed Joseph Meyer, 6 In. 350.00
Vase, Blue Green Ground, Floral Design Top, Alma Mason, 5 In. 750.00

Vase, Blue Matte, Bulbous, 5 1/4 In.	245.00
Vase, Bud, Closed Crinum Lily, Bailey, 8 In.	425.00
Vase, Floral Design, Signed, Blue Gray, 5 In.	225.00
Vase, Floral Design, Signed, Matte Blue Ground, 6 In.	325.00
Vase, Glossy Green Over Red Clay, Finger Marks, Marked, 5 1/2 In.	308.00
Vase, Green Drip Glaze Over Red Clay, JM & FR, 6 In.	725.00
Vase, Hand Turned, Handles, Green Drip, Red Body, 5 In.	308.00
Vase, Landscape, Willow Trees, Rising Moon, Shades Of Blue	1000.00
Vase, M.Morel, High Glaze, 5 1/2 In.	365.00
Vase, Maroon Matte, 5 1/2 X 5 1/2 In.	450.00
Vase, Moss Design, Blue Band At Top & Bottom, S.Irvine, 4 1/2 In.	1025.00
Vase, Pink Flowers, Unusual Shape, Blue & Green, H.Bailey, 8 X 4 In.	450.00
Vase, Scene Of Moss & Moon, Blue Matte, S.Irvine, 4 3/4 In.	650.00
Vase, Scenic, Blue Matte, Sadie Irvine, 3 3/4 In.	375.00
Vase, Ultramarine Blue, Pink Blossoms, Leaves, Marked, 3 1/4 X 3 In.	375.00
Vase, White Floral, Blue Ground, 6 In.	425.00
Vase, Yellow Green, Gunmetal Around Top, Finger Marks, Marked, 5 In.	242.00

Niloak Pottery (Kaolin spelled backward) was made at the Hyten Brothers Pottery in Benton, Arkansas, between 1909 and 1946. Although the factory did make cast and molded wares, collectors are most interested in the marbelized art pottery line made of colored swirls of clay. It was called "Mission Ware."

NILOAK, Ashtray, Swirl, 5 In.	45.00
Bowl, Blue, Squat, Impressed Block, 3 1/2 X 7 In.	20.00
Bowl, Green, Squat, Scalloped, Impressed Block, 3 X 5 1/2 In.	12.50
Candlestick, 6 X 10 In.	175.00
Candlestick, 8 1/2 In., Pair	195.00
Compote, 2–Tone, Signed Hywood By Niloak, 6 1/2 In.	35.00
Cornucopia, Blue	6.00
Creamer, Mauve With Green Overlay, Raised Mark, 4 3/4 In.	12.00
Ewer, Blue, Raised Mark, Factory Label, 6 3/4 In.	18.00
Ewer, Mauve With Green Overlay, Raised Mark, 6 3/4 In.	15.00
Jar, Strawberry, Light Blue	7.00
Pitcher, Eagle, 6 In.	15.00
Pitcher, Water, Geometric, White	35.00
Planter, Elephant	15.00
Planter, Figural, Bullfrog, White, Matte Glaze, 4 1/2 X 5 In.	20.00
Planter, Pink Deer, Marked	20.00
Planter, Squirrel	12.50
Planter, Swan, White, Small	8.00
Planter, Yellow Swan, Marked	20.00
Toothpick, Marbelized	95.00
Urn, Grecian, Mauve With Green Overlay, Handles, Raised Mark, 6 In.	15.00
Vase, 4 Open Tulips, Grays & Pinks	32.00
Vase, Bud, Marbelized, Blues, Brown, & Cream, 7 In.	60.00
Vase, Bud, Ribbed Rings Around Center, 8 In.	75.00
Vase, Bulbous, White, Marbelized, Terra Cotta Beige & Blue, 3 In.	65.00
Vase, Double, Marbelized, Bulbous, Signed, 12 In.	50.00
Vase, Marbelized, 3 In.	27.00
Vase, Marbelized, 5 In.	45.00
Vase, Marbelized, 8 In.	60.00 To 75.00
Vase, Marbelized, 10 In.	95.00
Vase, Marbelized, 12 In.	210.00
Vase, Marbelized, 14 In.	255.00 To 350.00
Vase, Marbelized, Brown, Blue, Rust, Cream Swirl, 2 1/2 X 7 1/2 In.	45.00
Vase, Marbelized, Brown, Red, Blues, Bulbous, Cuff, 5 1/2 In.	65.00
Vase, Marbelized, Earth Tones, Red & Brown, Extended Lip, 5 In.	65.00
Vase, Marbelized, Hourglass Shape, Marked, 4 1/2 In.	45.00
Vase, Marbelized, Marked, Sticker, 4 1/4 In.	35.00
Vase, Marbelized, Red & Brown Swirl, 6 In.	35.00
Vase, Marbelized, Reddish Brown, 4 1/2 In.	25.00
Vase, Marbelized, Rust, Blue, & Cream, 5 1/2 In.	22.00
Vase, Marbelized, Turned Over Edge, 9 X 4 1/2 In.	110.00

Vase, Marbelized, Turquoise, 12 Flower Holes, Bulbous, Marked, 6 In.	75.00
Vase, Painted Floral Design, Circular Stamp, 5 X 6 In.	65.00
Vase, Scalloped Rim, Double Handles, 7 1/2 In.	48.00
Wall Pocket, Gopher	20.00

Nippon–marked porcelain was made in Japan from 1891 to 1921. "Nippon" is the Japanese word for "Japan." A few firms continued to use the word "Nippon" on ceramics after 1921 as a part of the company name more than as an identification of the country of origin. More pieces marked Nippon will be found in the Noritake category.

NIPPON, Ashtray, Beaded Rim, Picture Of Ho–O Bird, Bisque, 4 1/2 In.	65.00
Ashtray, Leaf Shape, Scenic, Turquoise Jeweled Design, Marked	49.00
Ashtray, Lion Design, Enameled, Jewel Trim, 2 Handles	65.00
Ashtray, Pipe & Match Design, Green Wreath Mark, 5 In.	350.00
Ashtray, Scenic, House, Trees, Green Wreath	35.00
Ashtray, Turquoise Jewels, Scenic Center, 3 Rests	50.00
Ashtray, Water Scene, Beading, Green Mark, 4 1/2 In.	95.00
Asparagus Set, Blue & Gold Border, Tray 12 In., 6 Plates, Marked	359.00
Basket Server, Nile Scene, Gold	75.00
Basket, Blown–Out Nut, Browns, 8 In.	225.00
Basket, Moriage, Violets, Round, 5 In.	80.00
Basket, Violets, Gold Design, Handle, 6 1/2 In.	85.00
Berry Set, Blossoms, Gold Trim, Red Mark, Handled Bowl, 7 Piece	45.00
Berry Set, Pink Dogwood, Gold Beading, Ruffle Shape, 7 Piece	185.00
Bowl, 8 Panels Of Roses, Gold Medallion, Marked, 9 In.	110.00
Bowl, 8 Point, Roses, Green Mark, 7 1/2 In.	55.00
Bowl, Acorns, Leaves, Vines, Clover Shape, Jeweled, Wreath, 6 In.	75.00
Bowl, Blown–Out Walnuts, Extended Handles, M In Wreath, 7 1/2 In.	95.00
Bowl, Blue, Hazel Nuts, Square, Blown Out, 7 In.	95.00
Bowl, Chestnuts & Flowers, Leaves, 7 X 5 In.	28.00
Bowl, Cobalt & Gold On White, 2 Handles, 8 In.	97.50
Bowl, Coral Flowers, Jewels, 4 Gold Feet, Oblong, 8 In.	90.00
Bowl, Corner, Flowers, Scene, Raised Design, Green Mark, 6 In.	50.00
Bowl, Country Scene Interior, Hand Painted, 4 1/2 In.	20.00
Bowl, Dogwood Blossoms, Covered, 9 In.	60.00
Bowl, Floral, Gold Ground, Marked, 6 1/2 In.	95.00
Bowl, Floral, Hand Painted, Footed, Rising Sun Mark, 5 In.	35.00
Bowl, Flowers, Leaves On Inside, Gold Rim, Green Wreath, 9 1/2 In.	45.00
Bowl, Fruits, Flowers, & Bluebird Inside, Handles, Wreath Mark, 10 In.	120.00
Bowl, Full Figure, Blown–Out Squirrel, 9 In.	395.00
Bowl, Gold Handles Join Leaf Of Bowl, Gold Rim, Rising Sun, 7 In.	60.00
Bowl, Gold Roses, Pierced Gold Handles, Cobalt Trim, 8 In.	35.00
Bowl, Inside Roses, Sepia Ground, Gold Handles, Wreath, 5 1/2 In.	45.00
Bowl, Jeweled Handles, Cones, Pine Inside, Clover Shape, Wreath, 6 In.	75.00
Bowl, Lakeside Scene, Bisque, Matte Border, Pierced Handles, 6 In.	40.00
Bowl, Nut & Flowers, 3 Jeweled Feet, 5 In.	65.00
Bowl, Nut, 3 Feet, Applied Hazel Nuts, Scenic Ground, 7 1/2 In.	85.00
Bowl, Nuts, Leaves, Brown Matte Rim, 9 1/2 In.	100.00
Bowl, Pink Flowers, Green Leaves, Gold Trim, Marked, 9 In.	45.00
Bowl, Poppies, Gold Feet, Elongated, 8 In.	60.00
Bowl, Raised Flower, Scene, 6–Corner, Green Mark, 6 1/2 In.	50.00
Bowl, Roses Outlined In White Beading, Gold Rim, Footed, 7 1/2 In.	45.00
Bowl, Roses, Cobalt, Gold, 9 1/2 In.	125.00
Bowl, Roses, Gold Beaded Ground, Blue Rim, Marked, 9 In.	65.00
Bowl, Ruffled, Grapes, Daisies, Oblong, Green Mark, 7 1/2 In.	50.00
Bowl, Thistle & Floral, Bisque, 10 In.	27.50
Bowl, Underplate, Pink, Gray Flowers, Footed, White Ground, 4 1/2 In.	25.00
Bowl, Washington, D.C. Scene, Gold Trim, Octagonal, 7 In.	35.00
Bowl, Woodland Scene, 7 1/2 In. ....125.00 To 225.00	
Bowl, Yellow Poppies, Marked, 8 In.	10.00
Bowl, Yellow Roses, Brown Ground, 2 Gold Handles, 7 In.	30.00
Box, Sardine, Fish, Seaweed Design, 3 Piece	90.00
Box, Sardine, Underplate, Fish Handle, Floral Edge	90.00

Box, Tobacco, Egg Crate, Pink Clover, Gold Lettering, Pink 550.00
Cake Plate, Hand Painted Flower Border, 9 1/2 In. 18.00
Cake Plate, Persian Design, Browns, Rust, & Gold, 9 In. 55.00
Cake Set, Blue & Gold Floral, 6 Piece 50.00
Cake Set, Pink Roses, Gold Trim, Marked, 7 Piece 100.00
Candlestick, Gold Floral Upper Column, Gold Rims, Wreath, 6 In., Pair 110.00
Candlestick, Gold Overlay, Trim On White 95.00
Candlestick, Gold, Floral Medallions, 9 1/2 In. 175.00
Candy, Boat Scene, Mediterranean Ground, Handles, 7 In. 35.00
Carafe, Inverted Thumbprint, Hand Painted, Flowers, Gold 95.00
Celery Set, Master With Stalk Of Celery, 13 1/2 In., 5 Salts 95.00
Cheese & Cracker Set, Morning Glories, Vine, 2-Tier, Marked Sample 35.00
Chocolate Pot, Pink, Blue Cherry Blossoms, Gold Tracery, Green Mark 100.00
Chocolate Pot, Roses In Oval, Gold Trim, Cobalt, Marked 175.00
Chocolate Pot, Sunflowers, Art Deco Border, Green Wreath 85.00
Chocolate Pot, Terra Cotta, Bird, Floral, Blue & Gold, 9 In. 85.00
Chocolate Set, Blue Forget-Me-Nots, Signed, 9 Piece 145.00
Chocolate Set, Bluebirds, Marked 125.00
Chocolate Set, Floral, Rising Sun Mark 150.00
Chocolate Set, Geisha Girls, Orange, 9 Piece 75.00
Chocolate Set, Hand Painted Blue Forget-Me-Nots, Signed, 9 Piece 149.00
Chocolate Set, Hand Painted Roses, Rising Sun Mark, 6 Piece 105.00
Chocolate Set, Pink & Blue Floral, 9 1/2 In., 6 Cups 145.00
Chocolate Set, Raspberry & Blueberry Bands, 3 Cups & Saucers 115.00
Chocolate Set, Royal Satsuma, Gold Trim, Teapot, 3 Cups & Saucers 250.00
Chocolate Set, Tree In Meadow, Scenic, Green Wreath, 9 Piece 80.00
Chocolate Set, Yellow Flowers, Beaded Trim 160.00
Coaster, Scene Of Dutch Man Smoking Pipe At Water's Edge 25.00
Cocoa Set, Coral Pink Roses, Cream Ground, Leaves, 5 Cups & Saucers 295.00
Cocoa Set, Roses, Yellow Ground, Green Wreath, 13 Piece 355.00
Coffee Set, Allover Floral Design, Yellow, Gold Beading, 9 Piece 225.00
Coffee Set, Yellow Ground, Floral Design, Lavender & Gold Trim 225.00
Compote, Design Inside & Out, Forest Scene, Green Wreath Mark 325.00
Compote, Enamel Finish Resembling Pottery, Footed, 8 1/2 In. 150.00
Compote, Florals, Gold Trim, Pink, Green M In Wreath 15.00
Condiment Set, Tray, Green Mark, 5 Piece 39.00
Cracker Jar, Azalea, Artist Signed 150.00
Cracker Jar, Cobalt, Pink & Lavender Roses, 8 In. 95.00
Cracker Jar, Floral & Gold On White, Double Handle, Mark 35.00
Cracker Jar, Hand Painted Multicolored Currants, Gold, Green Mark 135.00
Cracker Jar, House On Hill, Cone Shape, 8 1/2 In. 275.00
Cracker Jar, House Scene, Cone Shape, Handle, 9 1/2 In. 350.00
Cracker Jar, Raised Floral, Footed, Gold Design 95.00
Cracker Jar, Rural Scenes, Bisque, Green Wreath Mark 75.00
Cracker Jar, Small Jewels, Glow Under Light 195.00
Creamer, Child's, Satsuma, Children Playing 30.00
Creamer, Googly-Eyed Boy Face, Blue Mark, 3 In. 50.00
Cup & Saucer, Azalea 15.00
Cup & Saucer, Bouillon, Ferncroft Pattern 40.00
Cup & Saucer, Butterlfies, Orange Ground, Demitasse, Set Of 6 .... 85.00
Cup & Saucer, Cake Plate, Gold Dragons, Oho, Lithophane 29.00
Cup & Saucer, Floral Design, Blue Rising Sun Mark, Set Of 8 .... 58.00
Cup & Saucer, Scenic With Swan, Signed 30.00
Cup, Bouillon, Raised Gold On Black, Roses, Gold Handles 225.00
Cup, Geisha, Red 7.50
Cup, White, Gold Band 8.50
Demitasse Set, 11 Piece 175.00
Demitasse Set, Deep Rose & White, Gold, Mark No.84, 11 Piece 165.00
Dish & Mug, Feeding, Girls Playing Badminton 75.00
Dish, Basket Shape, Handle, Miniature, Hand Painted 25.00
Dish, Boat Shape, Red Flowers, Gold Outlined, Green Mark, 7 In. 45.00
Dish, Cheese & Cracker, Pink & Gold Roses, 2-Tier 40.00
Dish, Hand Painted Roses, Trimmed In Gold, Beading, Marked, 6 1/2 In. 45.00
Dish, Nut, Scalloped Rim, 3 Legs, Florals Outlined, Raised, E-OH Mark 45.00

Dish, Sardine, Underplate, Gold Finial Fish On Lid 75.00
Dish, Serving, 2–Tier, Gold Trim, Marked, 9 In. 60.00
Dish, Underplate, & Ladle, Floral, Green Mark 40.00
Dish, Woodland Scene, Ruffled, 4 Enameled Feet 135.00
Eggcup, Double, Violets, Gold Trim, Marked, 3 1/2 In. 35.00
Ewer, Floral, Gold Outlining, Blue Mark, 13 In. 175.00
Ewer, Gaudy, Roses & Flowers, Beading, Green Base, 8 In. 65.00
Ewer, Moriage, Pastel Flowers, Maple Leaf Mark, 7 In. 245.00
Ewer, Woodland Scene, Blue Maple Leaf, 7 In. 225.00
Ferner, Roses, Gold Trim, Footed, Green M In Wreath, 5 1/4 In. 35.00
Ferner, Scenic 125.00
Figurine, 3 Brown Monkeys, Speak, See, Hear No Evil 145.00
Hair Receiver, Country Scene, Cobalt, Turquoise Jewels, Gold Design 75.00
Hair Receiver, Sage Green, Roses 30.00
Holder, Match, Woodland Scene 195.00
Holder, Playing Card, Floral 35.00
Humidor, 7 Ducks, Sky, Grass, Water 150.00
Humidor, Blown–Out Arab On Camel 1100.00
Humidor, Blown–Out Owl 150.00
Humidor, Covered, Blown–Out Indian & Bear 1000.00
Humidor, Egyptian Figures On Panels, 6–Sided 250.00
Humidor, Egyptian Symbols 75.00
Humidor, Gemometric, Horse Head Design 200.00
Humidor, Gold Florals & Leaves, Squirrel Finial 75.00
Humidor, Moriage, Marked Royal Moriye Nippon 475.00
Humidor, Swan Scene, Marked, 5 1/2 In. 95.00
Humidor, Woodland & Water Scene, Signed, Light Blue Ground 175.00
Ice Cream Set, Pink Apple Blossoms, 7 Piece 35.00
Ice Cream Set, Platter & 6 Plates, Apple Blossoms 40.00
Inkwell, Black Flower Design, Beige, Gold, Marked, Square, 4 In. 125.00
Inkwell, Pen Rest, Blue Flowers, Gold Trim, Insert 150.00
Jelly Jar, Violets, Enamel Design, Underplate 45.00
Jug, Whiskey, Sailboat Design 195.00
Jug, Whiskey, Windmill & Sailboat Scene, Enamel & Jewel Trim, 8 In. 425.00
Lamp, Gold Loops & Flowers Over Mountain Scene, 20 In. 250.00
Lamp, Scenic, Gold, 22 In. 275.00
Lazy Susan, Sailboat, Island Scene, Papier–Mache, No.7 Mark, 7 Piece 125.00
Lazy Susan, Sailing Ships, Bisque, Papier–Mache Box 50.00
Lemonade Set, Blown–Out Stag, Maple Leaf Mark, 7 Piece 4200.00
Lemonade Set, Scenic 115.00
Letter Rack, Colored Scenic, Gold Trim 175.00
Luncheon Set, Bird, Flowers, Gold Open Handle Tray, Green Mark, 7 Pc. 139.00
Luncheon Set, Royal Sometuke, Phoenix Bird, White & Blue, 20 Piece 115.00
Match Holder, Attached Saucer, Washington, D.C. Scene 35.00
Match Holder, Attached Tray, Woodland Scene 195.00
Match Holder, Indian Woman, Green Mark, 2 1/2 In. 100.00
Matchbook Holder, Bisque, Beaded Trim, Profile Of Indian 100.00
Mayonnaise Set, Azalea, 3 Piece ....25.00 To 45.00
Mayonnaise Set, Purple Pansies, Green Leaves, Gold Trim, 3 Piece 45.00
Mayonnaise Set, Rose, Gold Trim, Hand Painted, 2 Piece 35.00
Muffineer, Florals, Gold Overlay, 4 1/2 In. 85.00
Muffineer, Pink Flowers, Leaves, Maple Leaf Mark, 4 1/2 In. 65.00
Mug, Jeweled Dragon 165.00
Mug, Stag 240.00
Mug, Tropical Scene, Matte, Jeweled Handle, M In Wreath, 4 3/4 In. 85.00
Mustache Cup, Saucer, Scenic 75.00
Mustard, Attached Plate, Enameled Flowers, Gold Beading Handles 38.00
Mustard, Attached Plate, Tan Blue Border, Pink Roses 27.00
Mustard, Covered, Handles, Gold Trim 20.00
Napkin Ring, Gaudy, Floral, Footed, Scenic 55.00
Nut Cup, Moriage Leaves, 3 Feet, Set Of 6 .... 30.00
Nut Set, 3 Ball Feet, 7 Piece 125.00
Nut Set, Diamond Shape, Indian In Canoe, 5 Piece 145.00
Nut Set, Floral, Marked, 7 Piece 60.00

Nut Set, Indian Canoe Design, Diamond Shape, 5 Piece 145.00
Nut Set, Pink Flowers, 6 Trays, 8 In. Bowl 35.00
Nut Set, Pink Roses, Aqua & Gold Band, Mark No.47, 7 Piece 65.00
Nut Set, Scenic, Nuts, Enamel Trim, Footed, 7 Piece 38.00
Pancake Server, House & Tree Scene, Pastels, Matte Finish 75.00
Pitcher, Covered, Egyptian Sailing Ship, Moriage Beaded Trim 95.00
Pitcher, English Riding Scene, 7 In. 275.00
Pitcher, Milk, Flowers, Gold Trim, 5 In. 30.00
Pitcher, Pink Roses, Green & White Ground, Gold Handle, 9 1/4 In. 75.00
Pitcher, Red Roses, Gold, Cobalt, Gold Border, Maple Leaf, 13 1/4 In. 225.00
Pitcher, Water, Gold Over Cobalt, Red & White Flowers, 8 In. 150.00
Planter, Brownware, Medallion, Flower Holder, Footed, 10 X 5 In. 85.00
Plaque, American Indian, Horseback, Relief, Green M, 10 1/2 In. 925.00
Plaque, Bisque, Blue Flowers,, 7 3/4 In. 75.00
Plaque, Bisque, Scenic Background, Roses In Front, 7 In. 45.00
Plaque, Blown–Out Bison, 10 1/2 In. 585.00
Plaque, Blown–Out Buffaloes 775.00
Plaque, Blown–Out Indian In Water, Storm Clouds, Geese, 10 1/2 In. 775.00
Plaque, Blown–Out Indian, Turkey On Shoulder, Green Mark, 10 1/2 In. 995.00
Plaque, Blown–Out Lions, Dark, Night Scene, 10 1/2 In. 575.00
Plaque, Bluebird Amid Moriage, Painted Pinecones, 7 3/4 In. 90.00
Plaque, Brown Matte, Palm Tree, Lakeside, Sunset, 10 In. 125.00
Plaque, Fish, Scallions, 12 1/2 In. 145.00
Plaque, Floral & Fruit, Wicker Basket, 11 1/2 In., Pair 285.00
Plaque, Floral, Green, Gold Trim, Blue Mark, 10 In.Diam. 185.00
Plaque, Hand Painted Center Fruits, Egyptian Rim, Blue Maple, 10 In. 195.00
Plaque, Hanging, Moose Head, 10 In. 225.00
Plaque, House Scene, 7 1/2 In. 60.00
Plaque, Indian Chief, Cream & Brown, Green Mark, 10 In. 650.00
Plaque, Indian, Green Mark, 10 In. 350.00
Plaque, Jeweling Around Scene, Blue Maple, 10 In. 175.00
Plaque, Medallion Of Dogs' Heads Center, Moriage Border, 10 In. 350.00
Plaque, Riders On Horses, Green Wreath, 10 In. 150.00
Plaque, Roses, Leaves Outlined In Black, Gold Swag Border, 9 In. 100.00
Plaque, Windmill, 10 In. 175.00
Plaque, Windmill, Gold Flowers, Cream, White, Purple, Marked, 9 In. 125.00
Plate, Apple Blossoms, Gold Beading Outline, Blue Maple, 8 1/2 In. 45.00
Plate, Azalea, 7 1/2 In. 10.00
Plate, Child's, Sunbonnet Girl & Teddy Bear Border, 6 1/2 In. 30.00
Plate, Cobalt, Gold Beading, Webbing, 7 3/4 In. 175.00
Plate, Indian & Palm Tree, 7 3/4 In. 150.00
Plate, Indian In Canoe, Green Mark, 7 1/2 In. 75.00
Plate, Pink Dogwood, Gold Trim, 9 In. 22.00
Plate, Pink Morning Glories, Blue, Hand Painted, 6 1/2 In. 10.00
Plate, Roses & Leaves Outlined Black, Gold Edge, Blue Maple, 9 In. 95.00
Plate, Scenic Indian, 8 In. 55.00
Plate, Tier, Dip & Chip, Blue Dragons, Yellow 60.00
Plate, Trees, House, & Lake, White Rim, Crown Mark, 8 In. 40.00
Platter, Cream & Mauve, Scalloped, Oval 120.00
Platter, Violets, Gold, Scalloped, 12 X 8 In. 55.00
Powder Dish, Covered, Butterflies, & Floral, 4 1/2 In. 50.00
Relish, Hand Painted, Handles, Artist Signed, Roses 45.00
Relish, Multicolored Florals, Beaded Gold Rim, 5 X 9 In. 48.00
Ring Holder, Roses, Gold, Green, Designed Hand, Blue Maple Mark 60.00
Ring Tree, Figural, Green Wreath Mark, 3 1/2 In. 30.00
Ring Tree, Gold Hand, Hand Painted Floral, Gold Beading, Marked 55.00
Ring Tree, Hand, Ship Scene, Gold Edge 60.00
Ring Tree, Roses, Greens, Ribbons & Gold, Blue Maple Leaf 45.00
Salt & Pepper, 2 In. ....*Color* 15.00
Salt & Pepper, Cobalt, Gold Beading 37.00
Salt & Pepper, Crane On Red, White Ground, Egg Shape 50.00
Salt & Pepper, Gold Ground, Raised Turquoise Beading, Pink Roses 125.00
Salt & Pepper, Raised Turquoise Beading, Gold, Roses 119.00
Salt Dip, Floral Band, Gold Trim, Magenta M In Wreath, Boat Shape 10.00

Salt, Floral, Gold Design 20.00
Salt, Open, Pink Flowers, Gold Trim, Set Of 6 .... 90.00
Sauce, Floral, Green, Ladle, Underplate, Footed, Marked 39.00
Server, Pancake, Cover, Roses, Green Garlands, Blue Maple Leaf Mark 95.00
Shaving Mug, Arab, Browns 155.00
Shaving Mug, Pastoral Floral 60.00
Shoe, Floral Trim At Opening, Green Wreath Mark, 3 1/2 In. 42.00
Stein, Bisque, Signed, 7 In. 300.00
Sugar & Creamer, Azalea 30.00
Sugar & Creamer, Covered, Man In Boat Scene, Blue, Marked 65.00
Sugar & Creamer, Floral, Cobalt Border, Green Wreath Mark 85.00
Sugar & Creamer, Gold Trim, Violets & Gold, Green M In Wreath 25.00
Sugar & Creamer, Orange Luster, Blue Band, Florals, Hand Painted 12.00
Sugar & Creamer, Pink Roses, Blue & Gold Trim 40.00
Sugar & Creamer, Pink Roses, Gold Trim, Green M In Wreath 25.00
Sugar & Creamer, Raspberries, Melon Shape, Green Wreath 55.00
Sugar & Creamer, Swans, Art Nouveau, Gold Trim 75.00
Sugar, Art Deco, White, Gold & Green 30.00
Sugar, Covered, Pink & Red Roses 15.00
Syrup, Pink Flowers, Gold Design, Covered, M Wreath Mark 22.00
Syrup, Underplate, Pink Roses, Gold Trim, Marked 50.00
Tankard Set, Blown–Out Elk Stag 2750.00
Tankard, Grapes, Background Of Fall Trees, Gold Rim, Wreath, 11 In. 200.00
Tankard, Moriage Design, Panels Of Roses, 10 In. 300.00
Tankard, Yellow & Purple Grapes, Fall Trees, Handles, 11 In. 195.00
Tea Set, 6 Window Scenes, Gold Brown, Green Wreath Mark, 17 Piece 785.00
Tea Set, Aladdin–Type, Violets, 10 Piece 110.00
Tea Set, Child's, Flowers & Gold Trim, 23 Piece 160.00
Tea Set, Child's, White, Pink Border, 5 Piece 40.00
Tea Set, Gold Over Green, Ruffle Shaped Teapot, 3 Piece 160.00
Tea Set, Hand Painted Floral, Green Wreath Mark, 3 Piece 85.00
Tea Set, Stylized Multicolored, Floral Gold Highlights, Marked 95.00
Tea Set, White Egrets, Blue, Blue Leaf Mark, 11 Piece 115.00
Tea Strainer, Red & Pink Roses, Gold Trim, Signed 75.00
Tea Strainer, Undercup, Violets, Light Blue Trim, White Jewels 45.00
Teapot, Beaded Gold & Violet Design, 4 1/2 In. 55.00
Teapot, Roses, Pierced Gold Handle, Hand Painted, 6 In. 85.00
Tobacco Jar, Moriage, Black Dotting, Red Jewels, Green Mark, 7 In. 195.00
Toothpick, 2 Landscape Panels, Gold Beading 35.00
Toothpick, Acorns, Gold Handles 20.00
Toothpick, Gold, 3 Handles, Marked 37.00
Toy, Cannon, Metal, 17 X 5 In. 10.00
Tray, Dresser, Green & Gold Border, 10 1/2 X 7 1/2 In. 45.00
Tray, Dresser, Poppies, Cream Ground, Rising Sun Mark, 9 1/2 X 6 In. 45.00
Tray, Figural, Nipper Dog, Souvenir, Colorado Springs, Colo. 250.00
Tray, Pin, Pink, Blue, & Gold, Green M In Wreath 15.00
Tray, Scenic, Gold & Enamel Border, Bisque, 12 X 9 In. 150.00
Urn, Covered, Gaudy Cobalt, Blue Maple Leaf Mark, 14 In. 375.00
Vase, 3 Men Rowing Boat, Handles, Hand Painted, 13 In., Pair 275.00
Vase, 4 Panels Of Roses, Allover Gold Trim, Marked, 8 3/4 In. 95.00
Vase, Azalea, Mauve, 9 1/2 In. 115.00
Vase, Blown–Out Beggar, Green Mark, 10 In. ....1300.00 To 1500.00
Vase, Bulbous, Brown Roses & Blue Flowers, Gold Scrolls, 6 1/2 In. 85.00
Vase, Camel Rider Scene, Egyptian Design, Cobalt Trim, 8 1/2 In. 250.00
Vase, Center Band Of Marigolds, Vines, Cross Stitch, Wreath, 11 In. 125.00
Vase, Coralene, Gold With Lavender Tulips, 7 In. 125.00
Vase, Coralene, Shades Of Blue, Lavender & White, 8 1/4 In. 225.00
Vase, Coralene, Yellow Dandelions, 10 1/2 In. 275.00
Vase, Cowboy, Horse Silhouette, Sunset, Square, 2 Handles, 6 1/2 In. 175.00
Vase, Dragon Design, Nasturtiums, Beaded Base, Green Maple, 8 In. 100.00
Vase, Encrusted In Gold Dots, Mums, 11 3/4 In. 325.00
Vase, Floral, Brown, Olive, Handles, 6 1/4 In. 90.00
Vase, Fluted Shoulders, Geometric & Floral, Green Wreath, 10 1/4 In. 115.00
Vase, Forest Scene, Dogs & Moose, Beaded Handles, 6 1/2 In. 650.00

Noritake, Vase, Scene Of Sailboats,
Lake, Cottage, 12 In., Pair

Nippon, Vase, Maple Leaves,
Blown Out, 9 1/4 In.

Vase, Gaudy, Red & Pink Roses, Bulbous, 2 Handles, 6 X 5 In.	65.00
Vase, Geometric, Floral Design, Blue & Pink Thistles, Marked, 10 In.	125.00
Vase, Green & Pink Flowers, Gold Trim, Marked, 7 In.	150.00
Vase, House & Bridge Scene, Blue, Gold, 12 1/2 In.	85.00
Vase, House & Indian Border, Gold & Enamel Trim, 11 In.	125.00
Vase, Indians At Lake, Scenic, Imperial Mark, 8 1/2 In., Pair	350.00
Vase, Indians, Sitting, Standing, Palm Tree, Signed, 8 In.	350.00
Vase, Jeweled Leaves & Trees, Leaves At Base, Gold Handles, 15 In.	450.00
Vase, Lavender Floral, Handles, Footed, Green Wreath Mark, 8 1/2 In.	60.00
Vase, Magenta & Pink Roses Allover, Gold Swirls, Beading, 11 1/2 In.	145.00
Vase, Maple Leaves, Blown Out, 9 1/4 In. ....*Illus*	300.00
Vase, Moriage, Geese Design, 10 In.	125.00
Vase, Moriage, Pastel Flowers, Maple Leaf Mark, 9 In.	245.00
Vase, Mountain Scene, Gold Design Form Panel, 11 In.	135.00
Vase, Nautilus, Gold Jewels & Beading, Blue Leaf Mark, 8 In.	160.00
Vase, Overlapping Poppies, Gold Trim, Blue Leaf Mark, 8 X 5 3/4 In.	175.00
Vase, Pastoral Scene, Gold & Jewels, 14 In.	375.00
Vase, Peonies, Vines, & Twigs, Green Ground, EE Mark, 12 In.	150.00
Vase, Pink, Purple Orchids, Green Foliage Ground, Gold Rim, 15 In.	295.00
Vase, Red Floral, Black & White Panel, Bulbous, Handle, 6 3/4 In.	42.00
Vase, Red, Black & White Panels, Scenic Center, 6 In.	85.00
Vase, Ring Handle, Yellow Rose, Marked, 10 In.	65.00
Vase, Roses & Gold Leaf, Hand Painted, Green Ground, 12 1/2 In.	165.00
Vase, Roses, Pink, Orange, Yellow Ground, Brown Foliage, Marked, 8 In.	95.00
Vase, Roses, Pond Scene, Serpent Handles, 8 In.	175.00
Vase, Roses, Poppies, Fluted Neck, Gold Handles, Maple Leaf, 8 X 6 In.	225.00
Vase, Roses, Shaded Leaves, Bisque Finish, Green Wreath, 7 3/4 In.	85.00
Vase, Roses, White Ground, Gold Handles, Blue Mark, 14 1/2 In.	150.00
Vase, Scenic Center, Blue Top & Bottom, 11 1/2 X 8 In.	185.00
Vase, Scenic, Blue Ground, Gold, 2 Handles, 8 In.	75.00
Vase, Scenic, Dragon Handles, Gold Overlay, 5 1/2 In.	245.00
Vase, Scenic, Farmhouse, Green Mark, 11 1/2 In.	150.00
Vase, Scenic, Floral, Bulbous, 10 1/2 In.	175.00
Vase, Scenic, Handles, Matte Finish, Green Wreath Mark, 6 In.	55.00
Vase, Stylized Art Nouveau Florals, Gold Leaves, Gold Wreath, 9 In.	225.00
Vase, Swans In Lake, Trees, Cottage, Green Wreath, 7 In., Pair	200.00
Vase, Trees Frame Lake View, Gold Handles, Blue Maple, 9 In.	200.00
Vase, White Flowers, Gray Green Ground, Gold Trim, 2 Handles, 16 In.	195.00
Vase, Windmill Scene, Jeweled Handle, Green Wreath Mark, 4 1/2 In.	45.00
Vase, Yellow & Pink Nasturtiums, Dark Green Ground, Beaded, 8 In.	95.00
Vase, Yellow, Pink, Red Roses, Moriage, Handles, Scalloped Base, 8 In.	275.00
Wall Pocket, Dragon Coiling Design, Hand Painted	85.00

Nodders, or nodding figures, or pagods, are porcelain figures with heads and hands that are attached to wires. Any slight movement causes the parts to move up and down. They were made in many countries during the eighteenth and nineteeth centuries. A few Art Deco designs are also known. Copies are being made.

NODDER, Andy Gump, Bisque, 1930s, 4 In.	135.00
Andy Gump, Germany	65.00
Ashtray, Black Baby Boy	35.00
Ashtray, Black Turk In Turban	65.00
Ashtray, Girl, Swinging Legs	25.00
Birds, Salt & Pepper	22.00
Black Man, On Fence, Holding Rifle, Metal	120.00
Black, Girl, Bisque, 7 In.	175.00
Boy, Blue & White Suit & Cap, Bisque, Germany, 3 1/2 In.	65.00
Bulldog, Glass Eyes, Papier–Mache	35.00
Buttercup, Bisque, German	175.00
Candleholder, Bisque, Black Face & Hands, Male & Female, Pair	575.00
Chinese Man, Sitting, Blue & White Clothes, Red Pipe, 3 X 2 In.	68.00
Clown, Sitting, Head & Legs Nod, Large	75.00
Comical Man, Side Whiskers, Bulbous Eyes, Polychrome, German, 8 In.	35.00
Daddy Warbucks, Germany	95.00
Dogs, Bisque, Poodle & Bulldog, 4 3/4 In.	135.00
Doll, Bisque, White Clothes, Red Trim, Base, 4 1/2 In.	65.00
Donkey, Celluloid	17.50 To 27.50
English Barrister, White, Gold Trim, China, 6 In.	135.00
Group, Ladies At Tea Party, Heads Nod, Seated At Table, Bisque, 4 In.	275.00
Happy Hooligan, Cast Iron	175.00
Happy Hooligan, Papier–Mache, 4 1/2 In.	48.00
Herbie, Bisque, Germany	40.00
Houston Astro, Composition, C.1960	15.00
Jester, Bisque, Peach & White Clothes, Cap, 3 3/4 In.	75.00
Kissing Chinese Figurines, 8 In.	20.00
Lord Plushbottom, Bisque, German	125.00
Man Sitting Under Tree, Bisque, 5 1/2 X 2 1/2 In.	125.00
Mickey Mantle	50.00
Musician, Monkey, Sticks Out Tongue, Bisque, Occupied Japan	85.00
Oriental Figure Pulling Cart, Bisque, French, 7 1/4 X 3 X 5 In.	145.00
Oriental Lady, Standing, Robe, Blond Hair, Carries Jar, 4 7/8 In.	75.00
Oriental Man, Blue & White Clothes, Hat Holds Dagger, Bisque, 6 In.	135.00
Oriental Man, Sitting, Bisque, Blue, Pink Clothes, 2 5/8 X 1 5/8 In.	65.00
Orphan Annie, Bisque, German	85.00
Perry Winkle, Bisque	100.00
Police Dog, Glass Eyes, 8 In.	35.00
Rabbit, Playing Banjo, Musical, 13 1/2 In.	260.00
Retractable Tongue, French Parian, C.1860	295.00
Sandy, Bisque, German	65.00
Santa Claus, Japan	22.00
Seated Oriental Sage, Holding Dagger, Blue & White Clothes, Bisque	85.00
Skeezix, Bisque, 1930s, 2 3/4 In.	110.00
Spanish Couple, Papier–Mache	20.00
Sultan & Sultaness, Bisque, Green, Pink Robes, Gold Trim, 4 In., Pair	175.00
Uncle Bim, Bisque, German	125.00
Uncle Walt, Bisque, 1930s, 3 1/2 In.	100.00 To 110.00
Uncle Walt, Bisque, Germany	50.00
Winnie Winkle, Bisque, German	100.00
Woman, On Chaise, Bra, Shorts, Fanning, Legs Move, Japan Sticker	60.00
Woman, Red Nose, Husky Peasant, Carrying Pitcher, 7 1/4 In.	125.00
Woman, Turkish, Bisque	225.00

Noritake–marked porcelain was made in Japan after 1904 by Nippon Toki Kaisha. The best–known Noritake pieces are marked with the M in a wreath for the Morimura Brothers, a New York City distributing company. This mark was used until 1941. Another famous Noritake china was made for the Larkin Soap Company from 1916 through the 1930s. This dinnerware, decorated with azaleas, was sold or given away as a premium. There may be some helpful price information in the Nippon category since prices are comparable.

NORITAKE, Ashtray, 2 Blown–Out Horses Center	175.00
Ashtray, Figural, Girl	200.00
Ashtray, Figural, Yellow Bird, 3 1/2 In.	50.00
Ashtray, Floral Band, Art Deco, Blue	35.00
Ashtray, Yellow, Flower Medallions, Stripes, Cobalt Trim, 4 In.	35.00
Basket, Floral Bouquet In Center Of Each Section, Gold Rim, 8 In.	35.00
Basket, Multicolored Flowers, Scalloped Gold Edge, 2 1/2 In.	18.00
Basket, Tree In Meadow, Handle	65.00 To 80.00
Bottle, Perfume, Flower Stopper	75.00
Bouillon & Underplate, Indian Tree Pattern, Handle	12.00
Bowl Set, Lake & Sunset Scene, Gold Trim, Handles, 4 Sauce	65.00
Bowl, 4 Medallions Intertwined, Deco Rim, Gold Handles, 8 1/2 In.	30.00
Bowl, Azalea Pattern, 9 1/2 In.	75.00
Bowl, Bird Design, 2 Handles, Square, 8 1/2 In.	35.00
Bowl, Blown–Out Walnut, Signed, 7 1/2 In.	52.00
Bowl, Center Scene Of River, Fields, Pierced Handles, Luster, 8 In.	40.00
Bowl, Corn Mold In Relief, Side Hats, Green Wreath	75.00
Bowl, Figural, Squirrel	100.00
Bowl, Grapefruit, Azalea, No.185	95.00
Bowl, House & Tree Scene, 5 In.	17.00
Bowl, Lake, Mountains, & Field Center, Floral Rim, 9 In.	50.00
Bowl, Medallion Inside, White & Gold Band, Gold Handles, 5 1/2 In.	25.00
Bowl, Orange Luster Around Deco Medallion, Square, 6 1/2 In.	30.00
Bowl, Paneled, Medallions & Bouquets, Gold Rim, 3 Handles, 8 In.	35.00
Bowl, Purple, Florals, Black & White Striped, 8 In.	30.00
Bowl, Scenic Lake In Sunset, 3 Feet, 5 1/2 In.	25.00
Bowl, Stylized Moriage Flowers, Panels, Greek Key Rim, 7 X 3 In.	60.00
Bowl, Vegetable, Arvana, 10 1/2 In.	25.00
Bowl, Vegetable, Tree In Meadow, Oval, 9 1/4 In.	28.00
Butter Chip, Azalea, Set Of 6	210.00
Butter Tub, Moss Rose	8.00
Cake Plate, Azalea	25.00 To 45.00
Cake Plate, Butterfly, Orange, Handle, Green Wreath Mark, 9 In.	45.00
Cake Plate, Orange Luster, Floral Center, Marked, 9 In.	45.00
Cake Plate, Tree In Meadow, Pierced Handles	18.00
Cake Set, Green & White Luster, Gold Trim, 9 In.Plate, 6 Plates	25.00
Cake Set, Tree In The Meadow, Sailboat, 7 Piece	125.00
Candlestick, Butterfly Design, 5 1/2 In., Pair	95.00
Candlestick, Gold Lotus Blossom, Black & Gold, Marked, 8 1/4 In.	55.00
Card Holder, Victorian Boy, Dog In Circle, 5 X 5 In.	32.00
Casserole, Covered, Azalea, Round, 10 In.	50.00
Casserole, Covered, Shell & Seaweed	65.00
Celery, Azalea, 10 In.	235.00
Celery, Celery Stalk Design	25.00
Celery, Poppies, Green Trim	12.00
Chalice, Spanish Galleon, Simulated Waves, Gold Trim, 6 In.	45.00
Chocolate Set, Ming Tree, Gold, Pink Ground, Art Deco, 12 Piece	145.00
Compote, Hand Painted, Allover Fruit, 2 Piece	200.00
Condiment Set, Blue Luster, Japanese Lantern Trim, 4 Piece	65.00
Condiment Set, Tray, Azalea	60.00
Condiment Set, Tree In Meadow, On Tray	27.00
Cracker Jar, Cobalt Blue Trim, Desert Scene	250.00
Creamer, Azalea	10.00
Cruet, Azalea, 6 1/4 In.	160.00
Cup & Saucer, Arvana	17.00

Cup & Saucer, Azalea 10.00
Cup & Saucer, Bouillon, Flying Turkey, Howo 18.00
Cup & Saucer, Firenze 15.00
Cup & Saucer, Tree In Meadow 8.00
Demitasse Pot, Azalea 425.00
Demitasse Set, Gold Continental Design, Cream Ground, Rust, Gold 300.00
Demitasse Set, Rosamor, 17 Piece 55.00
Dessert Set, Anemone Pattern, 6 Cups & Saucers 135.00
Dinner Set, Crest Pattern, 21 Piece 60.00
Dinner Set, Mikado Pattern, 32 Piece 195.00
Dinner Set, Rose Marie Pattern, Platinum Band, 56 Piece 150.00
Dinner Set, Waverly Pattern, White With Gold Edge Band, 55 Piece 150.00
Dish, Child's Feeder, Teddy Bear, Dog, Marked 38.00
Dish, Lemon, Tree In Meadow, Ring Handle, 5 1/2 In. 10.00
Eggcup, Azalea 42.00
Flower Holder, Figural, Bird 95.00
Fruit Set, Disneyana, Tea Set, Mickey Mouse, Marked, 23 Piece 100.00
Fruit Set, Strawberries, Cherries, Gold Trim, Blue Luster, 7 Piece 125.00
Fruit Set, Tray & 6 Handled Bowls 175.00
Gravy, Attached Plate, Azalea Pattern 50.00
Holder, Cigarette, Bell Shaped, Bird Finial, Blue Luster 85.00
Holder, Teaspoon, Floral, 2 Handles, 8 In. 35.00
Humidor, Blown–Out Raccoon 600.00
Humidor, Owl, Blown–Out Pattern No.442 .... 600.00
Inkwell & Tray, Figural, Owl 150.00
Inkwell, Bulbous, Flowers On Gold Top, Gold Butterfly, 4 In. 65.00
Inkwell, Figural, Dresser Doll, Molded Holder, Tan Luster, 5 In. 225.00
Jam Set, Bird Finial, 4 Piece 40.00
Jug, Bearded Arab, Blue Interior, 6 In. 48.00
Jug, Smiling Fat Man, Blue Interior, Green Base, Miniature 25.00
Match Holder, Bear, Sitting On Top 35.00
Matchbox Holder, Figural, Bear, Outstretched Arms, Silver Luster 75.00
Mustard, Covered 10.00
Mustard, Covered, Cobalt Trim 15.00
Napkin Ring, Art Deco Portrait 18.00
Napkin Ring, Bird On Lilac, Blue, & Apricot Iridescent Ground 15.00
Napkin Ring, Woman In Ermine 28.00
Nut Cup, Humpback Trunk Case, Set Of 6 .... 60.00
Nut Set, Nut Center, Hand Painted, Green Mark, 7 Piece 45.00
Nut Set, Tree In Meadow, Chestnut, Square Master 7 In., 7 Piece 40.00
Pitcher, Honey, Liner, Green Wreath 25.00
Pitcher, Milk, Flying Turkey, Howo, 6 In. 35.00
Pitcher, Red & Yellow Berries, Cobalt, Shorter & Sons, 6 In. 55.00
Pitcher, Trees, Birds, & Lake, 4 3/4 In. 47.50
Plaque, Indian Brave On Horse, Green M In Wreath, 10 1/2 In. 525.00
Plaque, Lady Harem Dancer, Luster, 8 1/2 In. 96.00
Plate, Dinner, Towne House, White Lace 8.00
Plate, Flowers, Handle, 5 1/4 In. 14.00
Plate, Tree In Meadow, 7 1/2 In. 7.50
Platter, Azalea, No.186, 16 In. 300.00
Platter, Indian Tree Pattern, 18 In. 70.00
Powder Jar, Figural, Dresser Doll, Marked 225.00
Ramekin, Flying Turkey, Figure Three Border 12.50
Relish, Apricot Luster, Mythical Ram's Head Handles 18.50
Relish, Azalea Pattern, Oval, 8 1/4 In. 32.00
Relish, Azalea, 2 Piece 210.00
Relish, Azalea, Divided .... 25.00 To 45.00
Relish, Azalea, Gold Trim, Large 50.00
Relish, Figural, Bird 75.00
Salt & Pepper, Bulbous Pedestal, Tree In Meadow 15.00
Salt Dip, Blue Design, Roses, Gold, Pointed Ends, Green M, Set Of 6 ..... 25.00
Smoke Set, Clover Shaped Tray, Jar & Ashtray, 6 Piece 185.00
Smoke Set, Majolica, Monk, 3 Barrels, Cigars, Matches 98.00
Spooner, Azalea, Flat, Handles 72.00

Sugar & Creamer, Azalea, Individual	70.00
Sugar & Creamer, Floral, Gold, Footed, RC Mark	70.00
Sugar & Creamer, Flowers, Deep Pink Ground, Gold Trim	35.00
Sugar & Creamer, Gold Luster, Hand Painted Florals & Lanterns	30.00
Sugar & Creamer, Hand Painted Daisies & Poppies, Green Wreath	33.00
Sugar & Creamer, Ranier Pattern	35.00
Sugar & Creamer, Roseara	25.00
Sugar & Creamer, Tree In Meadow	35.00
Sugar Shaker, Figural, Girl, 6 In.	175.00
Sugar, Azalea, Covered	55.00
Sugar, Covered, Tree In Meadow	10.00
Tea Set, Anemone, 6 Cups, Gravy & Underplate, Sugar & Creamer	135.00
Tea Set, Bamboo Pattern, 15 Piece	68.00
Tea Set, Bird Finial On Lids, Basket Of Fruit Pattern, 3 Piece	125.00
Tea Set, Child's, Basket Of Roses, Pink Rim, C.1900, 20 Piece	110.00
Tea Set, Happy Birthday, Service For 4	175.00
Tea Set, Tree In Meadow, 11 Piece	110.00
Tea Set, Tree In Meadow, Scenic, 21 Piece	150.00
Tea Tile, Azalea	29.00
Teapot, Azalea, Gold Finial	300.00
Teapot, Scenic, Water, Tree, & House	23.00
Teapot, Tree In The Meadow	55.00 To 80.00
Toast Rack, Figural, Bird, 4–Slice	55.00
Vase, 3–Horned, Tulips, White & Tan Luster, 8 In.	110.00
Vase, Autumn, Gold Handles, Ruffled Top, 6 1/2 In.	45.00
Vase, Double, Bird Perched In Middle, 7 1/4 In.	150.00
Vase, Florals, Gold Trim Overall, Handles, Red M In Wreath, 11 In.	135.00
Vase, Gold Outlined Roses, Gold Handles, Rim, & Base, 8 In.	100.00
Vase, Green Border, Floral Medallions, 6 1/2 In.	28.00
Vase, Mythical Dragons, Fruit & Flowers, Howo Bird, 6 1/2 In.	65.00
Vase, Pink & White Roses, 7 1/4 In.	75.00
Vase, Scene Of Sailboats, Lake, Cottage, 12 In., Pair ....Illus	125.00
Vase, Swan In Lake, Double Gold Top Bands, Cobalt Blue, 5 In.	95.00
Vegetable, Azalea Pattern, 9 1/2 X 7 1/2 In.	70.00
Vegetable, Open, Azalea, 9 1/2 In.	20.00
Wall Pocket, Applied Bees & Flowers, Red, 5 In.	12.50
Wall Pocket, Art Deco, Cleopatra Sailing The Nile	95.00
Wall Pocket, Figural, Flowers, Bee, & Butterfly, 5 In.	38.00
Wall Pocket, Scenic Band, 8 1/4 In.	55.00
Wall Pocket, White & Blue, Red Poppies, 8 1/2 In.	409.00

The Norse Pottery Company started in Edgerton, Wisconsin, in 1903. In 1904 the company moved to Rockford, Illinois. The company made a black pottery which resembled early bronze relics of the Scandinavian countries. The firm went out of business in 1913.

NORSE, Bowl, Linear Design, 6 In.	100.00
Bowl, Serpent Handles, Effigy Feet, 8 In.	150.00
Candlestick, Curvy Snakes At Base, Gold Trim, Black, 11 3/4 In., Pair	80.00
Jardiniere, Faces, Footed	250.00
Mug	155.00
Vase, Geometric Design, Black, Gold, 4 1/2 In.	96.00
Vase, Incised Design, 9 In.	150.00

The North Dakota School of Mines was established in 1892 at the University of North Dakota. A ceramics course was included and pieces were made from the clays found in the region. Students at the university made pieces from 1909 to 1949. Although very early pieces were marked "U.N.D.," most pieces were stamped with the university seal.

NORTH DAKOTA SCHOOL OF MINES, Ashtray, Green	14.00
Bowl, Farm Ladies, Green To Brown, 3 1/2 In.	375.00
Bowl, Green, Drip Blue, 3 In.	60.00
Bowl, Turkeys, Green To Brown, 3 1/2 X 4 In.	275.00
Cup, Custard, 6–Color Band	60.00

Paperweight, Rebekan Design, 3 1/2 In.	85.00
Rose Bowl, Beige, Marked, 3 X 4 1/2 In.	350.00
Sugar & Creamer, Turquoise	63.00
Tile, 6 Colors, Carved, Mattson, Dated 1928	450.00
Tile, Incised Girl, Blue Gray, 5 In.	85.00
Tile, Parent's Day, 1940, 3 1/2 In.	60.00 To 90.00
Tile, Scenic, Carved, 6 Colors, Mattson, 1928	450.00
Vase, Black Indian Design, Marked, 4 1/2 In.	275.00
Vase, Blue, Signed Summers, 2 1/2 In.	65.00
Vase, Brown Design, Cable, 6 1/2 In.	132.00
Vase, Carved Indians, Horses, Mattson, 9 In.	375.00
Vase, Floral Design, Flecks Of Brown, 4 In.	170.00
Vase, Green, Brown Speckles, 1938, 6 1/2 In.	77.00
Vase, Incised Leaves, 6 1/2 X 7 In.	250.00
Vase, Incised Line & Dot Design, 1950, 3 In.	60.00
Vase, Milk Chocolate, Brown Design, 6 1/2 In.	132.00
Vase, Red To Blue, Artist Initials, 3 3/4 In.	35.00
Vase, Turkeys, Green, Brown, Mattson, 3 In.	275.00

The Harry Northwood Glass Company was founded by Harry Northwood, a glassmaker who worked for Hobbs, Brockunier and Company, La Belle Glass Company, and Buckeye Glass Company before founding his own firm. He opened one factory in Sinclaire, Pennsylvania, in 1896, and another in Wheeling, West Virginia, in 1902. Northwood closed when Mr. Northwood died in 1923. Many types of glass were made including carnival, custard, goofus, and pressed. The underlined N mark was used on some pieces.

NORTHWOOD, Base, Applied Cherries & Flowers, Peach Blow, 13 1/2 In.	2200.00
Basket, Electric Blue, Carnival, Round	115.00
Bell, Alamo, Gold Band, San Antonio, Texas, 1718	95.00
Berry Bowl, Drapery, Blue	30.00
Berry Bowl, Grape, Pedestal, Small	45.00
Berry Bowl, Master, Chrysanthemum & Sprig, Blue, 1890	385.00
Berry Bowl, Master, Singing Birds, Clear, Blue Enamel	85.00
Berry Set, Cherry Lattice, 7 Piece	85.00
Bottle, Cologne, Grape & Cable, Clear Stopper, Nutmeg, Pair	300.00
Bowl, Grape Frieze, 3–Footed, Emerald, Bold Design, 10 1/2 In.	100.00
Bowl, Peacock At The Fence, Blue Opalescent, Ruffled, 8 1/2 In.	75.00
Butter, Beaded Swirl, Green, Gold Design	95.00
Butter, Cherry Lattice, Covered	85.00 To 95.00
Butter, Cherry Thumbprint, Covered	85.00 To 95.00
Butter, Covered, Croesus, Gold Trim, Green	105.00
Butter, Covered, Frog, Amber	150.00
Butter, Covered, Near Cut, Clear, Marked	75.00
Butter, Covered, Paneled Holly	85.00
Butter, Covered, Paneled Sprig, Silver Trim	24.00
Butter, Covered, Regal	65.00
Butter, Covered, S Repeat, Gold Trim, Amethyst	65.00
Candlestick, Grape & Cable, Green, Pair	75.00
Compote, Inverted Thumbprint, Green, 6 1/2 In.	30.00
Compote, Twig Base, Blue Stretch Glass, 6 In.	40.00
Creamer, Cherry & Lattice	45.00
Creamer, Frosted Klondyke, Amberette, A.J.Beatty Co., Ohio	250.00
Creamer, Inverted Fan & Feather, Green, Gold	35.00
Creamer, Leaf Medallion, Green	35.00
Creamer, Regent, Green	35.00
Cruet, Alaska, Vaseline	200.00
Goblet, Grape & Gothic Arches, Nutmeg, Set Of 6	275.00
Pitcher, Milk, Raspberry, Marigold, N Mark	125.00
Pitcher, Regal Pattern, C.1901	85.00
Pitcher, Water, Apple Blossom, White	150.00
Pitcher, Water, Cherry Lattice, Clear, Gold & Red Design	110.00
Pitcher, Water, Near Cut, Green, Gold Design	125.00
Pitcher, Water, Peach Pattern, Green, Gold	125.00

Puff Box, Covered, Fluted Scrolls, Vaseline	45.00
Punch Cup, Cherry & Cable, Pedestal, Clear	20.00
Punch Cup, Grape & Cable, Marigold, Set Of 5	50.00
Punch Cup, Memphis, Purple	20.00
Rose Bowl, Royal Ivy, Frosted Rubina	95.00
Rose Bowl, Threaded Rubina	45.00
Salt & Pepper, Leaf Umbrella, Original Lids, Dark Cranberry	75.00
Sauce Boat, Fan, Handle, Opalescent Green	35.00
Spooner, Delaware, Green	45.00
Sugar & Creamer, Plum & Cherry	125.00
Sugar Shaker, Apple Blossom, Milk Glass, White	95.00
Sugar, Covered, Paneled Sprig, Silver Trim	19.00
Sugar, Open, Grape & Cable, Light Nutmeg	45.00
Syrup, Threaded Rubina	225.00
Table Set, Colorado, Green, 3 Piece	250.00
Table Set, Grape & Cable, Clear, Gold & Red Paint, 4 Piece	225.00
Table Set, Memphis, Clear, Gold, 4 Piece	195.00
Toothpick, Memphis, Crystal	70.00
Tumbler, Cattails & Lilies, Clear Blue	20.00
Tumbler, Gold Rose, Green	20.00
Tumbler, Oriental Poppy, Blue, 4 Piece	145.00
Tumbler, Oriental Poppy, Green & Gold	25.00
Vase, Diamond Point, Green Opalescent, 10 In.	32.00
Vase, Peach Blow, Appliqued Cherries & Flowers, 13 1/2 In.	2200.00
Water Set, Cherry Lattice, Clear, Gold & Red Design, 7 Piece	195.00
Water Set, Golden Peach, Green, 7 Piece	225.00 To 325.00
Water Set, Grape & Gothic Arches, Gold Trim, Green, 7 Piece	235.00
Water Set, Jeweled Heart, Clear, 5 Piece	115.00
Water Set, Memphis, Clear, Gold, 6 Piece	225.00
Water Set, Memphis, Gold Trim, Green, 6 Piece	215.00
Water Set, Oriental Poppy, Green & Gold	350.00
Water Set, Peach, Gold Trim, Ruby, 7 Piece	225.00
Water Set, Purple Flower, Gold Leaves, 7 Piece	280.00
Water Set, Red & Gold Roses, Leaves, Marked, 7 Piece	260.00
Water Set, S Repeat, Ice Green, Gold Design, 7 Piece	325.00

NU–ART   *Nu–Art was a trademark registered by the Imperial Glass Company of Bellaire, Ohio, about 1920.*

NU–ART, Ashtray, Scotty Sitting On Tray, Metal, Glass Insert Missing	42.50
Decanter, Golden Harvest, Stopper, Purple	385.00
Plate, Homestead, Amber, Marigold, 10 1/2 In.	750.00
Shade, Blue	20.00
Shade, Fishscale, Marigold, Pair	65.00
Shade, Green	20.00
Shade, Marigold, Marked	20.00
Shade, Paneled, Carnival Glass, Fitter, 2 3/4 In.	35.00

Nutcrackers of many types have been used through the centuries. At first the nutcracker was a fancy hammer; but by the nineteenth century, many elaborate and ingenious types were made. Levers, screws, and hammer adaptations were the most popular. Because nutcrackers are still useful, they are still being made, some in the old styles.

NUTCRACKER, Alligator, Brass, China, 8 1/2 In.	32.00
Alligator, Iron, 9 In.	89.00
Alligator, Iron, Green, 16 In.	100.00
Althoff Dog, On Base, Bronze	85.00
Bear's Head, Carved Wood, Glass Eyes	75.00
Betel Nut Indonesian Lady, Full Dress, Brass	95.00
Cat's Head, Hand Carved	95.00
Dog On Base, Bronze, L.A.Althoff & Co.	135.00
Dog, Cast Iron	50.00 To 75.00
Fagin & Bill Sykes, Brass	45.00

Lady's Legs Shape, Wooden, 7 1/2 In.	25.00
Lady's Legs, Bronze, 18th Century	55.00
Lady's Legs, Cast Iron	75.00
Lion's Head, Hand Carved, 19th Century	95.00
Old Man With Cap, Hand Carved, Wooden	40.00
Parrot, Brass, 5 1/2 In.	17.50
Parrot, Cast Iron, Gilt, 6 In.	110.00
Peasant Character, Hand Carved	65.00
Pecans, Clamp On, Waco, Texas, Dated 1914	42.00
Punch & Judy, Brass	45.00
Rooster's Mouth, Brass	12.50
Rooster, Brass	10.00
Squirrel On Leaf, Black, Iron	35.00
Squirrel, Iron, Full Figure, 5 1/2 In.	100.00
Squirrel, Sitting, Wooden	160.00
St.Bernard, 8 3/4 In.	50.00

The Nymphenburg porcelain factory was established at Neudeck–ob–der–Au, Germany, in 1753 and moved to Nymphenburg in 1761. The company is still in existence. Modern marks include a checkered shield topped by a crown, and a crowned CT with the year and a contemporary shield mark on reproductions of eighteenth–century porcelain.

NYMPHENBURG, Figurine, Child, Ermine Robe, Winter, Charcoal Brazier, 4 In.	50.00
Figurine, Chinese Boy, With Torch & Dagger, 5 In.	125.00
Figurine, Rooster, 3 3/4 X 5 3/4 In., Pair	55.00

The words "Occupied Japan" were used on pottery, porcelain, toys, and other goods made during the American occupation of Japan after World War II, from 1945 to 1952. Collectors now search for these pieces. The items were made for export.

OCCUPIED JAPAN, Ashtray, Statue Of Liberty Figure	7.50
Bowl, Floral & Vines, Black, 10 In.	10.00
Bowl, Fruit, Red, Slotted, Metal Base, 15 1/2 In.	50.00
Bowl, Orange, Crown Derby Type, Cobalt, Hokutosha, 8 In.	50.00
Cookie Jar, Mammy, Miniature	20.00
Cookie Jar, Tomato, Large	20.00
Cup & Saucer *Color*	18.00
Cup & Saucer, Blue, Yellow, Leaf & Stems, Gold Outlines	35.00
Cup & Saucer, Cherry China *Illus*	18.00
Cup & Saucer, Footed, Gold Outlined, Leaves, Demitasse	35.00
Cup & Saucer, Moriage, Demitasse	14.00

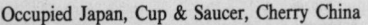

Occupied Japan, Cup & Saucer, Cherry China

Occupied Japan, Cup & Saucer, Orange, Red Flowers

Cup & Saucer, Orange, Red Flowers ....*Illus*	15.00
Figurine, 1940 American Girl & Muff, Mauyama, 8 1/2 In.	75.00
Figurine, 2 Boys & Girl Fishing, Shelf Sitter, 3 Piece	110.00
Figurine, Blue Boy, Marked, 6 1/2 In.	35.00
Figurine, Boy Next To Tree Stump, Rabbit, 4 In.	10.00
Figurine, Boy Riding Snail, 4 1/2 In.	15.00
Figurine, Bride, 4 In.	25.00
Figurine, Collie, 3 1/4 X 5 1/2 In.	10.00
Figurine, Colonial Couple, Mandolin By Side, 4 1/2 In.	37.00
Figurine, Colonial Girl, Bisque, Long Skirt, 10 3/4 In.	35.00
Figurine, Colonial Lady, Holding Closed Parasol, 7 1/2 In.	15.00
Figurine, Colonial Man, Holding Rose, 9 1/2 In.	30.00
Figurine, Dancing Girl, 5 1/4 In.	35.00
Figurine, Gentleman & Lady, Holding Bird, Rabbit, Gold, 9 In.	50.00
Figurine, Groom, 4 In.	25.00
Figurine, Lady Sitting In Chair, 4 1/2 In.	15.00
Figurine, Lady With Accordion, Porcelain, 10 In.	22.50
Figurine, Lady, Bisque, 11 In.	38.00
Figurine, Man & Woman Peasant, 6 1/2 In., Pair	22.00
Figurine, Man Playing Flute, 8 In.	28.00
Figurine, Oriental Girl, 10 In.	20.00
Figurine, Oriental Male Dancing, Bisque, Hadson, 6 1/2 In.	50.00
Figurine, Oriental Man, Gray Beard, Yellow Robe, 5 In.	18.00
Figurine, Young Woman, Summer Dress, Russian Wolfhounds	69.00
Incense Burner, Seated Oriental, Metal	20.00
Lamp, Colonial Man & Lady, Shade, Pair	80.00
Lighter, Hand Gun, Automatic, Metal	25.00
Mug, Bulldog, 2 3/4 In.	15.00
Mug, General MacArthur, 4 In.	22.50
Mug, Old Charley, 4 1/2 In.	20.00
Planter, Motorboat, 4 1/2 X 8 X 3 In.	22.50
Planter, Oriental Boy, 4 In.	10.00
Plaque, Colonial, Bisque, Chase Mark, Pair	35.00
Plaque, Dutch Girl	18.00
Plate, Lovers In Country, Pierced, 9 1/4 In., Pair	55.00
Salt & Pepper, Billikens	22.00
Salt & Pepper, George & Martha Washington	9.50
Salt & Pepper, Hugging Bears	12.00
Salt & Pepper, Old King Cole On Throne	12.00
Salt & Pepper, Peruvian Ladies	15.00
Smoking Set, Metal, Tray, 4 Ashtrays, Match Holder	45.00
Sugar & Creamer, Honeycomb, Bee Finial	20.00
Tea Set, Child, White, Flowers, 24 Piece	105.00
Tea Set, Dragon Scene, 17 Piece	125.00
Tea Set, House Shape, 3 Piece	40.00
Teapot, Brown Enamel	20.00
Toby Jug, Admiral, 3 Cornered Hat	30.00
Vase, Dresden Design, Cupids, Roses, White & Blue Ground	225.00
Vase, Wall, Hand Painted, Grapes, Apples, Round, 5 In., Pair	25.00

G. E. OHR,
BILOXI.

George E. Ohr, a true eccentric, made pottery in Biloxi, Mississippi, between 1883 and 1918. The pottery was made of very thin clay that was twisted, folded, and dented into odd, graceful shapes. Some pieces were lifelike models of hats, animal heads, or even a potato. Some pieces were decorated with folded clay "snakes." Although reproductions would be almost impossible to make, there have been some reworked pieces appearing on the market. These have been reglazed, or snakes and other embellishments have been added.

OHR, Candlestick, Dark & Light Mottled Green, Classic Form, Marked, 4 In.	154.00
Candlestick, Hand–Turned, Classical Form, Mottled Green, Marked, 4 In.	154.00
Candlestick, Twisted Body, Gunmetal Black, 4 1/2 In.	412.00
Chamberstick, Purple, Green Blue, Handle, Signed, 3 1/2 X 3 3/4 In.Diam.	295.00
Cup, Jefferson's Quote, Olive, Blue Interior, Handle, Signed, 8 1/4 In.	295.00
Mug, Handle On Lower Section, Gray Splotches, Marked, 4 3/4 In.	225.00

Mug, Mottled Yellow, Green Band, Handle, Incised Mark, 4 3/4 In. 340.00
Pitcher, Relief Design, Dated 1892, Handle, 10 1/2 In. 275.00
Vase, Blue Matt Glaze, Ruffled, Bulbous, Incised Mark, 5 1/4 X 5 1/2 In. 240.00
Vase, Brown Glaze, Red & Block Dots, Classic Shape, Signed, 5 1/2 In. 295.00
Vase, Crimped, Incised Lines At Top, Signed, Brown To Black, 3 1/2 In. 325.00
Vase, Globs Of Crystal Allover, Crimped, Green, Signed, 5 In. 295.00
Vase, Light & Dark Shaded Greens, Marked, 4 1/2 In. 715.00
Vase, Light Brown, Speckled Gold, Twisted Form, Marked, 4 In. 385.00
Vase, Metallic Purple, Blue, Dots On Apple Green Interior, 3 In. 325.00
Vase, Mottled Green, Ruffled, Pinch Sides, Impressed Mark, 5 1/2 In. 430.00
Vase, Rust & Gray Glaze, Round, Signed, 4 X 3 In.Diam. 295.00
Vase, Shaded Greens, Rose Spots, Twisted Neck, Marked, 4 3/4 In. 715.00
Vase, Specks Of Greenish Color Inside Ruffled, Marked Biloxi, 3 In. 240.00

OLD IVORY
84

*Old Ivory china was made in Silesia, Germany, at the end of the
nineteenth century. It is often marked with the crown and the word
"Silesia." Some pieces are also marked with the words "Old Ivory."
The pattern numbers appear on the base of each piece.*

OLD IVORY, Berry Bowl, No.11, Chloron Pattern, 10 In. 65.00
Berry Set, No.7, 6 Piece 135.00
Berry Set, No.84, 7 Piece 340.00
Berry Set, With Sugar & Creamer, Killarney Rose Pattern, 9 Piece 275.00
Bouillon, Underplate, Thistle, Germany 24.00
Bowl, 4 3/4 In. 7.25
Bowl, 8 1/2 In. 14.95
Bowl, No.16, 9 1/2 In. 55.00
Bowl, No.82, Silesia, 9 1/2 In. 75.00
Bowl, No.84, 10 1/4 In. ....20.00 To 78.00
Bowl, Salad, No., 28, 6 1/2 In., Set Of 6 .... 160.00
Cake Plate, No.84 ....65.00 To 98.00
Celery, Clarion No.11, 11 1/2 In. 75.00
Chocolate Pot, No.15 .... 135.00
Cracker Jar, Heart Shape, Silesia, Marked, Roses 95.00
Creamer, No.84 .... 45.00
Cup & Saucer, Chocolate, No.84 .... 45.00
Cup & Saucer, Fleur–De–Lis Mark 40.00
Cup & Saucer, No.15 .... 210.00
Cup & Saucer, No.16 ....38.00 To 60.00
Cup & Saucer, No.200 .... 40.00
Dish, Pickle, No.84, 7 3/4 In. 80.00
Muffineer, Copper, English, Silesia 60.00
Plate, 6 1/2 In. ....27.00 To 49.00
Plate, 7 3/4 In. ....31.00 To 57.50
Plate, 9 1/2 In. 5.75
Plate, Beige Roses, Clover Border, Marked, 8 1/2 In. 28.00
Plate, No.16, Silesia, 6 3/4 In. ....17.00 To 20.00
Plate, No.28, 10 In. ....20.00 To 130.00
Plate, No.75, 6 1/2 In. 27.00
Plate, No.84, 10 1/2 In. ....8.00 To 130.00
Plate, Thistle, 8 In., Set Of 4 .... 58.00
Platter, No.84, 13 1/2 In. 150.00
Relish, 6 1/4 X 4 1/2 In. 55.00
Saltshaker, No.75, Silesia Mark ....35.00 To 40.00
Spoon Holder, Lay Down 95.00
Sugar & Creamer, No.28 ....85.00 To 155.00
Sugar & Creamer, No.84 ....95.00 To 155.00
Sugar, Covered, La Touraine, Bellflowers, Gold Trim, Silesia 35.00
Tray, No.84, 11 1/2 X 7 In. 110.00
OLD SLEEPY EYE, see Sleepy Eye

Onion pattern, originally named "bulb pattern," is a white ware decorated with cobalt blue or pink. Although it is commonly associated with Meissen, other companies made the pattern in the late nineteenth and the twentieth centuries. A rare type is called "red bud" because there are added red accents on the blue and white dishes.

ONION, Bowl, Scalloped, German Mark, 8 1/2 X 3 1/2 In.	55.00
Butter Chip, Meissen	20.00
Butter, Covered	75.00
Butter, Meissen	85.00
Canister	29.00
Cup & Saucer, Cross Swords	35.00
Cutting Board, Meissen, Crossed Swords, 6 X 10 In.	135.00
Dish, Invalid	35.00
Dish, Leaf, Handle, Meissen, 7 In.	85.00
Dutch Shoe, Meissen, Crossed Swords, 2 1/4 X 7 In.	95.00
Eggcup, Meissen	20.00
Feeder, Sick, Cup Shape, Trivet, Meissen	35.00
Funnel, Meissen	75.00
Juice Set, Signed Kalk, Germany, 5 Piece	180.00
Mug, Advertising, Fred Sehring Brewing Co., Joliet, Dated 1907	110.00
Mug, Red Mark, Bavaria	35.00
Planter, Bulb	28.00
Rolling Pin, Marked Germany	135.00
Salt & Pepper, Blue	15.00
Sauceboat, Attached Underplate, Handles, Meissen, Swords	190.00
Spice Set, Canister, 4 Piece	120.00
Spoon Rest, Meissen, Crossed Swords, Signed	48.00 To 65.00
Strainer, Blue, Meissen	68.00
Teapot, Meissen, Crossed Swords, 6 Cup	325.00
Trivet, Footed, Crossed Swords	45.00

Opalescent glass is translucent glass that has the bluish–white tones of the opal gemstone. It is often found in pressed glassware made in Victorian times. Some dealers use the terms "opaline" and "opalescent" for any of the bluish–white translucent wares.

OPALESCENT, Basket, Dot Optic, Cranberry, 7 In.	85.00
Basket, Hobnail, Blue, Clear Handle, 6 In.	65.00
Basket, May, Victorian, Green, Looped Handle, 6 In.	40.00
Basket, Vaseline To Cranberry, Art Glass, Twisted Handle, 6 In.	175.00
Berry Bowl, Argonaut, Blue, 7 In.	75.00
Berry Bowl, Circled Scroll, Clear, 8 1/4 In.	55.00
Berry Bowl, Fluted Scroll, Vaseline	28.00
Berry Bowl, Iris, Blue, Meander	95.00
Berry Bowl, Master, Beatty Swirl, Clear	40.00
Berry Bowl, Master, Honeycomb & Clover, Blue	35.00
Berry Bowl, Master, Wreath & Shell, Vaseline	75.00
Berry Bowl, Scroll With Acanthus, White	12.00
Berry Bowl, Seaweed, White	45.00
Berry Bowl, Town Pump, Vaseline	65.00
Berry Bowl, Vaseline, Opalescent, Hobbs	35.00
Berry Set, Scroll With Acanthus, Clear, 5 Piece	110.00
Berry Set, Wild Bouquet, Clear, Goofus Design, 7 Piece	225.00
Berry Set, Wreath & Shell, Vaseline, 7 Piece	185.00
Bottle, Barber, Fern, Square	115.00
Bottle, Barber, Hobnail, Blue	135.00
Bottle, Barber, Polka Dot, Blue	125.00
Bottle, Barber, Polka Dot, Cranberry	125.00
Bottle, Barber, Seaweed, Cranberry, No Stopper	150.00
Bottle, Barber, Stars & Stripes, Blue	165.00
Bottle, Barber, Stars & Stripes, Clear	155.00

Bottle, Cologne, Blue Swirl, Black Flower Stopper, Fenton, 6 In. 90.00
Bottle, Perfume, Plumes, White, 4 1/2 In. 12.00
Bowl, Abalone, White, 2 Handles, 7 1/2 In. 20.00
Bowl, Astro, Ruffled, Vaseline, 8 1/2 In. 37.00
Bowl, Basket Weave, Yellow, Scalloped, Square, 4 3/4 In. 24.00
Bowl, Beatty Swirl, White, 5 In. 20.00
Bowl, Blocked Thumbprint & Beads, White, 5 1/4 In. 15.00
Bowl, Blossom & Webb, Clear, Ruffled, 8 1/2 In., Diam. 30.00
Bowl, Blue, Footed, Applied Trim, Oval 125.00
Bowl, Caribbean, Blue, Flat, Shallow, 7 In., Duncan & Miller 45.00
Bowl, Carousel, Blue, Goofus Center & Feet 45.00
Bowl, Cashews, Ruffled, Flat, White, 9 In. 20.00
Bowl, Fluted Scrolls, Blue, Turned Down Side, 7 1/2 In. 45.00
Bowl, Fluted Scrolls, White 17.50
Bowl, Greek Key & Ribs, White, Ribbon Candy Edge, 8 1/2 In. 30.00
Bowl, Greek Key & Scales, Footed Blue 35.00
Bowl, Greek Key & Scales, Ruffled, Blue, 8 In. 30.00
Bowl, Hobnail, Blue, Ruffled, 10 X 4 1/2 In. 59.00
Bowl, Holly, Purple 45.00
Bowl, Honeycomb & Clover, Green, 9 In. 35.00
Bowl, Jefferson Wheel, Blue, 3 1/2 X 8 1/2 In. 55.00
Bowl, Keyhold, Ribbon Edge, Blue, Footed, 8 1/2 In. 37.00
Bowl, Many Loops, Fluted, 8 In. 20.00
Bowl, Many Loops, Ruffled, Green, 7 1/2 In. 29.00
Bowl, Reflecting Diamonds, Green, 8 In. 20.00
Bowl, Ruffles & Rings, Green, Ribbon Candy Edge, Footed, 9 In. 38.00
Bowl, Shell & Wild Rose, Green, 3 Feet, Northwood, 7 1/2 In. 25.00
Bowl, Spiral, White, Flared, Ribbed, 9 1/2 In. 35.00
Bowl, Water Lily With Cattails, Ruffled Amethyst, 9 1/2 In. 22.00
Bowl, White, Fluted, Scalloped, Star Bottom, 9 1/4 X 6 In. 40.00
Bowl, Willow Oak, Blue, 8 In. 15.00
Bride's Bowl, Double Crimped, Cased Teal Blue, Painted Roses 45.00
Butter Chip, Fairy Villas 24.00
Butter, Covered, Alaska, Blue 225.00
Butter, Covered, Alaska, Vaseline 295.00
Butter, Covered, Beatty Swirl, Blue 150.00
Butter, Covered, Diamond Spearhead, Vaseline 185.00
Butter, Covered, Everglades, Blue, Gold 250.00
Butter, Covered, Everglades, Blue, Gold, Northwood 250.00
Butter, Covered, Fluted Scroll, Enamel Design, Gold, Blue 195.00
Butter, Covered, Fluted Scroll, Enameled Flowers, Blue 215.00
Butter, Covered, Fluted Scrolls, Blue 115.00
Butter, Covered, Intaglio, Gold Trim, Green 165.00
Butter, Covered, Iris With Meander, White 100.00
Butter, Covered, Iris With Meander, White 50.00
Butter, Covered, Regal, Gold Trim, Green 135.00
Butter, Covered, Regal, Green 160.00
Butter, Covered, Spirea Band, Sapphire Blue, 6 X 4 In. 55.00
Butter, Covered, Swag & Brackets, White 75.00
Candlestick, Dolphin & Petticoat, Blue, 6 1/2 In., Pair 150.00
Candlestick, Swirled, White, 3 1/2 In. 18.00
Candy Dish, Inverted Fan & Feather, White, Footed 32.00
Carafe, Water, Seaweed, Clear 120.00
Celery, Alaska, Vaseline 75.00
Celery, Cranberry, Paneled, Victorian, 6 1/2 In. 135.00
Celery, Reverse Swirl, Blue 68.00
Celery, Wreath & Shell, White 85.00
Compote, Beaded Rib, White, Crimped, Beaded Stem, 7 X 4 In. 25.00
Compote, Covered, X–Ray, Amber 60.00
Compote, Dolphin, Footed, Blue 40.00
Compote, Jelly, Argonaut Shell, Blue 100.00
Compote, Jelly, Blue, Northwood 100.00
Compote, Jelly, Diamond Spearhead, Vaseline 45.00
Compote, Jelly, Everglades, Green 40.00

Opalescent, Pitcher, Water, Acorn & Leaf,
Blue, 8 In.

The rarest pieces of Azalea pattern Nippon china are said to be the fluted square plates, the scalloped and footed mayonnaise, the pancake jug, and the ashtray.

Compote, Jelly, Iris With Meander, Vaseline	30.00
Compote, Jelly, Swag & Bracket, Green	15.00
Compote, Jelly, Swag & Bracket, Vaseline	35.00 To 38.00
Compote, Jelly, Wild Bouquet, Blue	85.00
Compote, Maple Leaf, Green	30.00
Compote, Pearl & Scales, Green, 7 In.	38.00
Compote, Spearpoint Band, Ruby, 4 1/2 X 5 In.	59.00
Compote, Tokyo, Blue, 5 In.	37.00
Compote, Tokyo, Green, Stemmed, 5 In.	20.00
Console Set, Diagonal Lace, French, 3 Piece	45.00
Creamer, Alaska, Blue	85.00
Creamer, Alaska, Vaseline	55.00 To 85.00
Creamer, Beaded Block, Vaseline	15.00
Creamer, Beatty, Clear	40.00
Creamer, Blue, Fenton, 4 1/2 In.	12.00
Creamer, Child's, Twist, Blue	50.00
Creamer, Diamond, Blue, Pedestal, 5 In.	48.00
Creamer, Fluted Scrolls, Blue	40.00
Creamer, Fluted Scrolls, Clear To White	35.00
Creamer, Fluted Scrolls, Yellow, 5 In.	45.00
Creamer, Intaglio, White	30.00
Creamer, Jewel & Flower, Blue	45.00
Creamer, Regal, Blue	55.00
Creamer, Scroll With Acanthus, Blue	45.00
Creamer, Shell, Green	85.00
Cruet, Coin Dot, Cranberry, 6 In.	85.00
Cruet, Daisy & Fern, Clear Stopper, Blue	50.00
Cruet, Daisy & Fern, Northwood Mold, Original Stopper, White	45.00
Cruet, Hobnail, Blue Handle & Stopper, Blue	210.00
Cruet, Scroll With Acanthus, Blue	135.00
Cruet, Seaweed, Frosted Handle, Blue	165.00
Cruet, Swirl, Original Stopper, Cranberry	145.00 To 160.00
Decanter, Blue, Ribbed, Gold Enameled Faces, 11 In.	95.00
Dish, Jelly, Maple Leaf, Blue	45.00
Dish, Jelly, Scroll With Acanthus, Blue	30.00
Dish, Jelly, Swag Bracket, Green	25.00
Dish, Sweetmeat, Applied Trim, Silver Plated Holder, 6 3/4 In.	100.00
Finger Bowl, Daisy & Fern, Blue	30.00
Hat, Spiral Optic, French, 4 X 6 In.	75.00
Hat, Swirl, 7 X 11 In.	125.00
Lamp, Cranberry, Dot, Umbrella Shade, Wright	99.00
Lamp, Oil, Blue, Snowflake, Scalloped Base, 9 In.	520.00

Lamp, Spiral Optic, Cranberry, 22 In. 225.00
Muffineer, Ribbed Lattice, Blue 70.00
Mug, Alphabet, Milk Glass, Blue 40.00
Mug, Polychrome Floral Enameling, Remember Me, 4 1/8 In. 25.00
Mug, Singing Birds, Aqua, Northwood 875.00
Nappy, Leaf Rays, Peach, 7 In. 29.00
Nappy, Sea Spray, Blue, 6 1/2 In. 29.00
Pitcher, Swirl, Square Top, White, 8 1/2 In. 75.00
Pitcher, Vaseline, Reeded Handle, Enameled Flowers, 7 1/2 In. 145.00
Pitcher, Water, Acorn & Leaf, Blue, 8 In. ....*Illus* 75.00
Pitcher, Water, Alaska, Blue 185.00
Pitcher, Water, Beatty Swirl, Blue 165.00
Pitcher, Water, Christmas Snowflake, Handle, Cranberry, 8 In. 365.00
Pitcher, Water, Daffodils, White 145.00
Pitcher, Water, Daisy & Fern, Blue, 3 Spout, Square, 8 1/2 In. 155.00
Pitcher, Water, Drapery, Blue, Northwood 165.00
Pitcher, Water, Fluted Scrolls, White 55.00
Pitcher, Water, Green, Striped, Handle, Heat Check 50.00
Pitcher, Water, Palm Beach, Blue 400.00
Pitcher, Water, Polka Dot, Burlington Mark 110.00
Pitcher, Water, Reverse Swirl, Bulbous, Vaseline 145.00
Pitcher, Water, Swag & Brackets, Blue ....285.00 To 325.00
Pitcher, Water, Swirl, Clear Handle, Quadrafoil Top, Cranberry 185.00
Pitcher, Water, Swirl, Square Top, Handle, Cranberry, 9 1/4 In. 165.00
Plate, Leaf, Blue, 8 1/2 In. 35.00
Plate, Vintage, Blue, 7 7/8 In. 22.00
Powder Jar, Fluted Scrolls, Blue 48.00
Puff Box, Fluted Scrolls, Vaseline 45.00
Rose Bowl, Beaded Cable, Straight Sides, Blue 65.00
Rose Bowl, Fancy Fantails, Blue To Cranberry, White 65.00
Rose Bowl, Fluted Scrolls, Vaseline 50.00
Rose Bowl, Optic, Hand Painted Design, Ground Pontil 45.00
Rose Bowl, Pearl Flowers, Dark Green, 5 In. 35.00
Rose Bowl, Spiral, Cranberry, Fenton 55.00
Salt, Beatty Rib, White, Individual 22.00
Salt, Master, Alaska, White 25.00
Salt, Ribbed, Holder, Rigaree Trim, Ruffled, 4 1/2 In. 100.00
Salt, Wreath & Shell, Yellow, Individual 60.00
Sauce, Alaska, Blue 40.00
Sauce, Circled Scroll, Blue, 4 1/2 In. 28.00
Sauce, Drapery, Northwood, Blue 25.00
Sauce, Idyll, Green 20.00
Sauce, Intaglio, Blue, Footed 22.00
Sauce, Regal, Blue, Flat, Northwood, 4 1/2 In. 29.00
Sauce, Shell, Blue 25.00
Sauce, Vaseline 20.00
Saucer, Wreath & Shell, Footed, Vaseline 20.00
Shade, Swirl, Cranberry, Miniature 95.00
Shade, Swirled Overlay, Blue Lace Border, 5 1/2 In., Pair 65.00
Shaker, Swirl, C.1890, Blue, 4 In. ....*Color* 65.00
Slipper, Cane & Fine Cut, Blue, 5 X 2 1/2 In. 45.00
Spittoon, White, Crimped, Fenton, Small 19.00
Spooner, Alaska, Blue ....40.00 To 65.00
Spooner, Alaska, Vaseline 55.00
Spooner, Criss–Cross, Rubina 80.00
Spooner, Diamond Pattern, Blue, Footed, Lattice Edge 35.00
Spooner, Diamond Spearhead, Green 40.00
Spooner, Diamond Spearhead, Vaseline 45.00
Spooner, Dolly Madison, Green 45.00
Spooner, Everglades, Gold Trim, Blue 75.00
Spooner, Flora, Vaseline 40.00
Spooner, Fluted Scroll, Blue 50.00
Spooner, Fluted Scroll, Vaseline 40.00
Spooner, Hobnail Thumbprint, Blue 60.00

Spooner, Hobnail With Paneled Thumbprint, Vaseline	50.00
Spooner, Hobnail, White, Northwood	30.00
Spooner, Idyll, Green	75.00
Spooner, Intaglio, Blue	42.00 To 60.00
Spooner, Monkey, White	135.00
Spooner, Palm Beach, Vaseline	75.00
Spooner, Regal, Green	55.00
Spooner, Ribbed Spiral, Blue	60.00
Spooner, Scroll With Acanthus, Blue	60.00
Spooner, Scroll With Acanthus, Inside Ribbing, Green	50.00
Spooner, Scroll With Acanthus, Vaseline	45.00
Spooner, Swag With Brackets, Blue	50.00 To 60.00
Spooner, Swag With Brackets, Vaseline	40.00
Spooner, Tokyo, White	45.00
Spooner, Twist, White, Miniature	35.00
Spooner, Water Lily & Cattails, Blue	50.00
Spooner, Wreath & Shell, Vaseline, Footed	82.00
Sugar & Creamer, Alaska, Covered, Vaseline	225.00
Sugar & Creamer, Alaska, White	70.00
Sugar & Creamer, Everglades, White & Gold	90.00
Sugar & Creamer, Green, Striped, Cobalt Handle	100.00
Sugar & Creamer, Wreathed Cherry, Vaseline, Ruffled	75.00
Sugar Shaker, Coin Dot, Blue	85.00
Sugar Shaker, Daisy & Fern, Northwood, Cranberry	110.00
Sugar Shaker, Reverse Swirl, Blue	115.00
Sugar Shaker, Ribbed Lattice, Blue	90.00
Sugar Shaker, Ribbed Lattice, Cranberry	110.00
Sugar, Covered, Alaska, Blue	120.00 To 125.00
Sugar, Covered, Drapery, Clear To White	55.00
Sugar, Covered, Everglades, Blue	120.00 To 145.00
Sugar, Covered, Tokyo, White	75.00
Sugar, Open, Alaska, Vaseline	95.00
Syrup, Coin Dot, Cranberry	145.00
Syrup, Daisy & Fern, Blue	55.00 To 115.00
Syrup, Dot	65.00
Syrup, Ribbed Lattice, Blue	175.00
Syrup, Windows, Blue	135.00
Table Set, Drapery, Clear To White, 4 Piece	255.00
Table Set, Fluted Scrolls, Blue	350.00
Tankard, Green Fronds, Gold Trim, Satin Finish, Handle, 11 In.	380.00
Toothpick, Beatty Waffle, Blue	45.00
Toothpick, Chrysanthemum Swirl, Cranberry	90.00
Toothpick, Daisy & Button, White	15.00
Toothpick, Diamond Spearhead, Blue	90.00
Toothpick, Diamond Spearhead, Vaseline	39.00
Toothpick, Iris & Meander, Green	45.00 To 55.00
Toothpick, Windows, Blue	45.00
Toothpick, Windows, Cranberry	95.00
Tray, Card, Argonaut Shell, White, 9 In.	25.00
Tray, Card, Nautilus, Vaseline	35.00
Tray, Water, Beatty Swirl, White	65.00
Tumbler, Alaska, Green	40.00
Tumbler, Button & Braids, Blue	30.00
Tumbler, Buttons & Braids	22.00
Tumbler, Collard Base, Vaseline	65.00
Tumbler, Drapery, Blue	25.00
Tumbler, Iris With Meander, White	37.00
Tumbler, Poinsettia, Blue	35.00
Tumbler, Reverse Swirl, Vaseline	38.00
Tumbler, Stars & Stripes, White	45.00
Tumbler, Twist, Cranberry	70.00
Tumbler, Water, Peach, White Flowers, Gold Leaves, 4 In.	35.00
Tumbler, Windows, White	25.00
Vase, Aurora Borealis, Blue, 6 In.	30.00

Vase, Aurora Borealis, Novelty, White, 6 In.	25.00
Vase, Baluster Stem, Ribbed Bowl, Blue, 12 In.	400.00
Vase, Block, Vaseline, Ruffled, Northwood, 8 In.	35.00
Vase, Blue & White Swirl, C.1925, 6 3/4 In., Pair	70.00
Vase, Diamond Point, Green, Northwood, 10 In.	48.00
Vase, Diamond Point, White, 10 1/2 In.	22.00
Vase, Jack–In–The–Pulpit, Stemmed, White Top, 11 In.	65.00
Vase, Pulled, Blue, Vertical Rib, Scalloped, 13 In.	28.00
Vase, Reticulated Diamond Point, Blue, Footed, 5 1/4 In.	22.00
Vase, Reverse Swirl, Cranberry, Handles, 6 1/4 In.	48.00
Vase, Ribbed, Ruffled, Blue, Northwood, 11 In.	45.00
Vase, Ripple, Blue, 13 1/2 In.	35.00
Vase, Simple Simon, White, Ruffled, 6 In.	22.00
Vase, Squirrel & Acorn, Green, 9 In.	60.00
Vase, Swirl, Fluted, Ruffled Top, Cranberry Edge, Green, 6 In.	38.00
Vase, Thumbprint, Blue, 8 1/2 In.	85.00
Vase, Treebark, Green, 11 1/2 In.	28.00
Vase, Wide Rib, Peach, 11 In.	36.00
Waste Bowl, Beatty Rib, Blue	35.00
Water Set, Iris & Meander, Blue, 7 Piece	350.00
Water Set, Rib, Green, Fenton, 7 Piece	275.00
Water Set, Wreath & Shell, Vaseline, 7 Piece	650.00

Opaline, or opal glass, was made in white, green, and other colors. The glass had a matte surface and a lack of transparency. It was often gilded or painted. It was a popular mid–nineteenth–century European glassware.

OPALINE, Bottle, Cologne, Bubble Stopper, Scrolls & Fan Design, 8 In.	165.00
Bowl, French Blue, Gilt, Shallow, 3 Footed, 3 3/4 In.	58.00
Cup, Everted Rim, Low Foot, Wooden Stand, Rose, 2 1/4 In.	25.00
Goblet, Sky Blue, 6 1/2 In., Set Of 6	175.00
Mug, Souvenir, Panora, Iowa, Lacy Medallion, 3 3/4 In.	12.00
Pitcher, Applied Handle, Label, Blue, 6 1/2 In.	50.00
Stein, Cut & Enameled Floral Design, Pewter Base Rim, 3/10 Liter	247.00
Tumbler, French Blue, Gilt, 2 1/4 In.	28.00
Tumbler, Souvenir, Minot, N.D., Button Arches Pattern, 3 In.	12.00
Vase, Corset Shape, 13 X 4 1/2 In.	45.00
Vase, French Blue, Gilt, 4 1/4 In.	40.00

The stage is a long way from some of the seats at a play or an opera, so the patrons sometimes carried special opera glasses in the nineteenth and early twentieth centuries. Mother–of–pearl was a popular decoration.

OPERA GLASSES, 3X, Occupied Japan	50.00
Extension Handle, Paris	85.00
Gold, Lens Overlay Diamond Set Monogram, Case, 3 1/2 In.	3300.00
Li Ville, Paris, Pearl Handle	17.00
Mother–Of–Pearl & Brass	65.00
Mother–Of–Pearl, Chevalier Optician, Paris, Gilt Trim	85.00
Mother–Of–Pearl, Marked Tiffany, Velvet Case	125.00
Mother–Of–Pearl, Mermod Jaccard, Leather Case	38.00
Mother–Of–Pearl, Paris, Brass	35.00
Paris, Leather Case, 1800s	25.00

Little Orphan Annie first appeared in the comics in 1924. The redheaded girl and her friends have been on the radio and are still on the comic pages. A Broadway musical show and a movie in the 1980s made Annie popular again and many toys, dishes, and other memorabilia are being made.

ORPHAN ANNIE, Ashtray, Lusterware, 1930s	75.00
Ashtray, Sandy, Bisque	65.00
Badge, Decoder, 1935 & 1938, Pair	20.00
Bandana	45.00
Book, Big Little, Orphan Annie & The Mysterious Shoemaker	20.00

Book, Circus, Cherry, Envelope, Uncut	247.50
Book, In The Circus, 1927	25.00
Book, Puffed Wheat Comic	15.00
Decoder, 1935 ....25.00 To	30.00
Decoder, 1936 ....10.00 To	15.00
Doll, Rag, White Eyes, 17 In. ....27.50 To	28.00
Doll, Stuffed, 7 In.	15.00
Game, Annie's Treasure Hunt, Board, Envelope	59.50
Game, Board, Treasure Hunt, Ovaltine Premium	22.00
Holder, Toothbrush, Bisque, Sandy, 1930s	175.00
Manual, Secret Society, 1939 ....16.00 To	65.00
Mug, Annie Jumping Rope With Sandy, Brown, 1937	50.00
Mug, Beetleware ....16.00 To	30.00
Mug, Ceramic, 1932	45.00
Mug, Knickerbocker Applesauce, Annie & Sandy, 1982	18.00
Mug, Ovaltine ....32.00 To	39.00
Mug, Shake Up, 2 Measuring Cups, Beetleware	10.00
Nodder, 1930s, Bisque, 3 1/2 In.	135.00
Nodder, Sandy, Bisque	38.50
Paper Doll, Cut & Uncut Clothes, 12 In.	35.00
Pin, Bronze	14.00
Pin, Secret Society	10.00
Poster, Coronet Orphan Annie Commando, 1943	12.00
Poster, Junior Commando, 1943	20.00
Puzzle, 1940	25.00
Ring, Face Of Annie	50.00
Ring, Star, Silver	15.00
Salt & Pepper, Chalkware, Annie & Sandy	27.00
Secret Society Manual, Radio, Full Color, 1939	65.00
Sheet Music, Ovaltine, 1931	20.00
Song Sheet, 1930–31, Radio	25.00
Star Pin, Silver	20.00
Stove, Electric, Pressed Steel, Painted, Decals, 9 1/2 In.	30.00
Stove, Pictures Of Annie & Sandy	37.00
Toy, Windup	135.00
Vase, Wall	95.00
Wristwatch, Boxed ....125.00 To	175.00

The Orrefors Glassworks, located in the Swedish province of Smaaland, was established in 1916. The company is still making glass for use on the table or as decorations. There is renewed interest in the glass made in the modern styles of the 1940s and 1950s. Most vases and decorative pieces are signed with the etched name.

ORREFORS, Bottle, Perfume, Stopper, Clear, Eve & Serpent Etched, 1936, 5 In.	40.00
Bowl, Pink Bottom, Blue On Clear, Signed, 5 X 2 1/2 In.	225.00
Candleholder, Ball Shape, Pair	40.00
Champagne, Crystal, Band Of Cut Diamonds, Set Of 8	80.00
Goblet, Sunrise, Footed	15.00
Tazza, Interior Colored Design, Expo 358–74, 7 1/8 In.	595.00
Vase, 3 Irregular Pink Patches, Spherical, Signed, 6 1/2 In.	285.00
Vase, Art Deco, Semi Nude Lady, Engraved, Signed, Clear, 8 In.	175.00
Vase, Bubble Design, Smoky Gray, Signed Edvin Ohrstrom, 7 In.	550.00
Vase, Cranberry, Signed, 10 1/2 In.	110.00
Vase, Fish Design, Signed Edvard Hald, 5 1/2 In.	795.00
Vase, Kneeling Woman Holding Bouquet, Octagonal, Signed, 11 In.	352.00
Vase, Nude Swimmer, Lindstrand, 1931, 8 1/2 In.	350.00
Vase, Paneling Design, Lead Crystal, Ofors 1242 Yared, 8 1/2 In.	135.00
Vase, Paperweight, Purple Fish Swimming, Signed, 6 In.	300.00
Vase, Signed Fa.W.Johansson, Cranberry, 10 1/2 In.	110.00
Vase, Undulating Rim, Engraved Kneeling Nude, Signed, 8 3/4 In.	495.00

Ott & Brewer Company operated the Etruria Pottery at Trenton, New Jersey, from 1863 to 1893. It was under the direction of William Bromley, Sr., who had worked at the Belleek factory at Belleek, Ireland, from 1883. The firm used a variety of marks that incorporated the initials O & B.

OTT & BREWER, Chocolate Pot, Dragon Spout, Gold Floral, Green & Cream 1095.00
Cup & Saucer, Pink 150.00
Ewer, Bulbous, Ribbed, Thistles 895.00
Ewer, Reticulated Handle, Hand Painted Lilacs, 10 1/2 In. 675.00
Jar, Gold Floral, Covered, 4 3/4 In. 300.00
Plate, Boy Fishing, Tree, House, Burgundy Edge, 8 In. 895.00
Sugar, Open, Gold Leaves, Twig Handle 175.00
Vase, 2 Gold Handles, Gold Paste Design, Cobalt Blue, 4 In. 300.00
Vase, Morning Glory Sculpture, 6 X 7 In. 795.00
Vase, Orchid, Mottled Green, 12 In. 375.00
Vase, Yellow Pansies, 10 In. 695.00

The four Overbeck sisters started a pottery in Cambridge City, Indiana, in 1911. They made all types of vases, each one-of-a-kind. Small, hand-modeled figurines are the most popular pieces with today's collectors. The factory continued until 1955 when the last of the four sisters died.

OVERBECK, Figurine, Bluebird, Blue Glaze, Brown, C.1936, Signed, 2 In. 100.00
Figurine, Bride, 5 In. 315.00
Figurine, Dog, Brown & Black, 4 X 4 1/2 In. 295.00
Holder, Flower, 4 Colors, 3 1/4 X 3 1/4 In. 185.00
Vase, Brown, Trees, Stylized Design, Green Ground, Signed, 4 In. 550.00

OWENS UTOPIAN *Owens Pottery was made in Zanesville, Ohio, from 1891 to 1928. The first art pottery was made after 1896. Utopian Ware, Cyrano, Navarre, Feroza, and Henri Deux were made. Pieces were usually marked with a form of the name "Owens." About 1907, the firm began to make tile and discontinued the art pottery wares.*

OWENS, Bottle, Utopian, 6 In. 120.00
Canister Set, Forest Green, Glass, 3 Large & 4 Small, 7 Piece 60.00
Jardiniere, Cyrano, 9 1/2 In. 200.00
Jardiniere, Standard Glaze, 12 In. 150.00
Jug, Honey, Indian Portrait, Handle, Artist Delores Harvey, 7 In. 675.00
Lamp, Sudanese, Mirror Black Ground, Art Nouveau Design, 14 In. 165.00
Lemonade Set, Fruit Tree Design, Green, Pitcher & 6 Mugs, C.1900 .... 200.00
Mug, Cherries 110.00
Mug, Currants, Standard Glaze, 5 In. 135.00
Pitcher, Aqua Verdi, Small 65.00
Pitcher, Lotus, Sandpiper Standing On One Leg, 8 In. 350.00
Planter, Painted Design, High Glaze Over White, Round, 4 X 2 In. 35.00
Planter, Straight Sides, Molded Design, Shield Mark, Round, 7 X 3 In. 175.00
Plate, Verdi, Aqua, Incised Design, 6 In. 85.00
Tile, Large Leaf, 6 In. 55.00
Tile, Matte Green, Relief Leaves, 6 X 6 In. 95.00
Vase, Brown Gloss Ground, Tulip Design, C.1900, 16 In. 100.00
Vase, Double Gourd, Opalescent Copper, Floral, 14 In. 250.00
Vase, Feroza, Violet Black Luster, Handle, 6 In. 135.00
Vase, Floral, Dark Brown High Gloss, 11 1/2 In. 75.00
Vase, Lady's Portrait, Henri Deux, 6 In. 195.00
Vase, Malachite, Opalescent, Floral Inset, 13 In. 475.00
Vase, Nasturtium Design, Brown Glaze, C.1900, 16 In. 75.00
Vase, Opalace Utopian, 13 In. 525.00
Vase, Orange Flowers, Design, Brown Glaze, 10 In. 60.00
Vase, Pansies, Conical, Marked, 10 1/2 In. 105.00
Vase, Utopian, Brown, Tan, Signed TS, 5 In. 125.00
Vase, Utopian, Matte, 11 In. 160.00
Vase, Utopian, No.125, Bulbous, Standard Glaze, 10 1/2 In. 200.00
Vase, Utopian, Pansies, 3 1/2 In. 95.00

Vase, Utopian, Yellow Floral Design, Bullet Shape, No.1032, 10 In.	65.00
Vase, Venetian, Yellow, Metallic Gold Glaze, Handle, 5 X 7 In.	88.00
Vase, Woman's Head Profile, Incised, Brown, Gold Accent, 6 3/4 X 9 In.	198.00
Water Set, Green Matte, 7 Piece	200.00

Oyster plates were popular from the 1880s. Each course at dinner was served in a special dish. The oyster plate had indentations shaped like oysters. Usually six oysters were held on a plate. There is no greater value to a plate with more oysters although that myth continues to haunt antiques dealers. There are other plates for shellfish including cockle plates and whelk plates. The appropriately shaped indentations are part of the design of these dishes.

OYSTER PLATE, Gold Script No.2730, Brown On White, 8 In., Set Of 6	250.00
Plate, Minton, Green	90.00
Scalloped, Gold On White, Rose Garland, Limoges, 8 1/2 In.	50.00

Paden City Glass Manufacturing Company was established in 1916 at Paden City, West Virginia. It is best known for glasswares but also produced a pottery line. The firm closed in 1951.

PADEN CITY, Bookend, Squirrel, Clear, 5 1/2 In.	85.00
Bowl, Light Blue, Large, 9 In.	15.00
Bowl, Yellow, Handles, 9 3/4 In.	17.50
Candlestick, Light Cobalt, 3–Light, Pair	100.00
Candy Dish, 3–Section, Gazebo Etched, Covered	22.00
Candy Dish, Crystal, Covered, Footed, Round	20.00
Casserole, Cupid Pattern, Covered, 13 In.	60.00
Compote, Cobalt, Orchid Etch	28.00
Compote, Peacock	18.00
Cup & Saucer, Crow Pattern, Red, Footed, Square	8.00
Cup & Saucer, Penny Line Pattern, Ruby	15.00
Decanter, Silver Overlay Hunt Scene, Ruby	47.00
Dish, Mayonnaise, Underplate, Ruby	38.00
Figurine, Chinese Pheasant, Light Blue	60.00 To 85.00
Figurine, Pony, Standing	50.00
Goblet, Georgian, Cobalt Blue	24.00
Goblet, Low, Penny Line Pattern, Footed, Green, 10 Oz.	8.00
Plate, Crown, Red, 8 In.	8.00
Plate, Penny Line Pattern, Ruby, 8 In.	10.00
Plate, Willow Pattern, 7 1/4 In.	15.00
Platter, Roses, 12 In.	12.50
Relish, 2–Section, Gazebo Etched, 7 In.	18.00
Salt & Pepper, Cobalt	35.00
Soup, Cream, Crow Pattern, Red	10.00
Sugar, Penny Line Pattern, Ruby	10.00
Tray, Swan Neck Handles, Silver Overlay, 11 In.	45.00
Tumbler, Penny Line Pattern, Footed, Amethyst, 5 In.	10.00
Vase, Etched Tulips, Green, 11 3/4 In.	55.00

The paintings listed in this book are not works by major artists but rather decorative paintings on ivory, board, or glass that would be of interest to the average collector. To learn the value of an oil painting by a listed artist you must contact an expert in that area.

PAINTING, On Board, At The Hearth, O.Johansson, Dated 1911, 1 1/2 X 6 In.	150.00
On Board, Cardinal & Friend At Chess, H.Desportes, 15 X 19 In.	850.00
On Board, Country House, F.C.Mathewson, 1900, 10 X 14 In.	110.00
On Board, Narrative Of A.Gordon Pym, Arthur E.Becher, 19 X 12 In.	250.00
On Board, Oil, Blustery Day, Harbor Scene, E.Jayar, 4 1/2 X 7 In.	150.00
On Board, St.Florian Quenching The Fire, Oval, 21 1/2 X 16 In.	350.00
On Board, Woman Portrait, Ruffled Bonnet, Oval Gold Frame, C.1850	100.00
On Ivory, Andrew Jackson, 3 1/2 X 4 In.	400.00
On Ivory, Bust, Lady, Roses & Ribbons In Hair, Signed, 3 3/4 In.	175.00
On Ivory, Dutch Gentleman, Koldije Antiquair, Frame, 2 1/2 In.	125.00
On Ivory, Fashionably Dressed Woman, Brass Frame, 4 X 4 7/8 In.	95.00

On Ivory, Gentleman In Formal Clothes, Gold Bezel, Frame, 6 In. 100.00
On Ivory, Gentleman, Velvet Case, Gilt Liner, Square, 9 1/2 In. 135.00
On Ivory, Girl In Round Glass Dome, My Brother Wm.Henry Owen 90.00
On Ivory, Girl, Light Blue Dress, Primitive, Framed, 2 1/2 X 2 In. 105.00
On Ivory, Gray Haired Gentleman, 19th Century, England, 2 1/2 In. 300.00
On Ivory, John Quincy Adams, 3 1/2 X 4 In. 400.00
On Ivory, Lady, Front Face, Signed Smant, Oval, England, 2 X 2 In. 100.00
On Ivory, Lady, Oval Gold Bezel, Recessed In Wooden Frame, 5 In. 100.00
On Ivory, Lady, Pearls, England, 18th Century, 2 1/4 X 1 7/8 In. 350.00
On Ivory, Man, Profile, Back Signed Rossini, C.1810, 2 3/8 In. 125.00
On Ivory, Napoleon's Son, Signed R.Krauss, 3 1/4 X 5 1/4 In. 350.00
On Ivory, Nobleman, Armor Vest, Cross, Frame, 4 1/4 X 5 1/8 In. 235.00
On Ivory, Queen, Lace Collar, Crown On Head, Oval, 3 In. 55.00
On Ivory, Theodore Roosevelt, 3 1/2 X 4 In. 400.00
On Ivory, Woman, Black Dress, Lace Collar, C.1830, 2 1/4 In. 125.00
On Ivory, Woman, Under Eglomise Glass, Framed, 3 1/2 X 4 1/8 In. 55.00
On Ivory, Woman, White Nightcap, Empire Dress, Framed, 4 In. 75.00
On Leather, Hunting Scene, Horse, Dogs, Framed, 16 X 14 In. 175.00
On Panel, 4 Seasons Coaching Scene, Rowland, C.1794, 6 X 11 In. 2500.00
On Panel, Algerian Arab Horsemen On Move, A.Nakache, 8 X 12 In. 550.00
On Panel, Boy With Bird, R.Gosminski, 1952, Framed, 35 X 23 In. 500.00
On Panel, Breaking Waves, W.J.Peters, 1898, 14 X 22 1/2 In. 75.00
On Panel, European Scenes, Bonheur, Dated 1671, 9 X 15 In., Pair 800.00
On Panel, German Man In Pub, T.Urbain, Framed, 10 1/4 X 8 1/4 In. 425.00
On Panel, Man In Pub, Young Maid, C.Ferrand, Framed, 10 X 8 In. 500.00
On Panel, Portrait Of Dog, Anton Weinberg, 1887, 13 X 10 In. 550.00
On Panel, Portrait, Gentleman With Ruffled Collar, 25 X 21 In. 800.00
On Panel, Putto With Monkey, 8 1/4 X 10 1/2 In. 350.00
On Panel, Winter Bouquet, P.Travis, Dated 1964, Framed, 32 X 22 In. 450.00
On Porcelain, Last Supper, Gold Frame, Artist Signed, 5 X 9 In. 225.00
On Porcelain, Long Haired Maiden, Draped Gown, Oval, 4 1/8 X 3 In. 185.00
On Porcelain, Long-Haired Beauty, Ormolu Frame, 3 1/2 In. 230.00
On Porcelain, Madonna & Child, Decorated Frame, 6 1/2 X 5 In. 130.00
On Porcelain, Napoleon, 1 1/2 X 1 1/4 In. 95.00
On Porcelain, Nude Woman, Framed, H.Rucker, C.1900, 5 X 3 1/2 In. 135.00
On Porcelain, Primitive Woman At Well, Signed Angelo, 10 X 15 In. 245.00
On Porcelain, Women, Gold Leaf Frame, Signed Epanouissemient Asti 210.00
On Tin, Fishing Boat On Open Sea, Spanish School, 4 3/4 X 3 In. 125.00
On Tin, Girl Feeding Parrot, Walter Dexter, 1840-55, 9 1/4 X 8 In. 350.00
On Tin, Moonlit Landscape, Cabin, By Lake, Primitive, 14 X 20 In. 25.00
On Velvet, Lilacs In Basket, 14 X 19 1/2 In. 145.00
On Wood, Ancestor Portrait, Woman, Framed, C.1840, 10 X 11 1/2 In. 110.00
On Wood, Elderly Gentlemen, Framed, 4 1/2 X 5 1/2 In., Pair 350.00
Reverse On Glass, Abraham Lincoln, Bust, Framed, C.1860, 17 In. 65.00
Reverse On Glass, Andrew, Floriana Jackson, Framed, 10 1/2 X 7 In. 500.00
Reverse On Glass, Basket Of Fruit, Framed, 11 X 13 In. 25.00
Reverse On Glass, Bearded Man, Seated, Holding Sword, 20 1/2 In. 125.00
Reverse On Glass, Bonbon, Bust Of Napoleon, C.1850, 2 5/8 In. 195.00
Reverse On Glass, Country Scene, Artist Signed, 9 X 15 In., Pair 150.00
Reverse On Glass, Fisherman, Tower, Russian, 7 5/15 X 9 1/2 In. 50.00
Reverse On Glass, George Washington, Framed, 10 X 7 In. 990.00
Reverse On Glass, Goddess Of Liberty, Mother-Of-Pearl, Oval Frame 35.00
Reverse On Glass, Home Sweet Home, Foil, Gold Frame, 16 X 9 In. 35.00
Reverse On Glass, Midsummer Magic, R.Atkinson Fox, 24 X 15 In. 55.00
Reverse On Glass, Napoleon, Empire Gilt Frame, 16 X 20 1/2 In. 550.00
Reverse On Glass, Sheep In Field, George Oyston, 9 X 12 In. 75.00
Reverse On Glass, Statue Of Liberty, Frame, 22 X 16 In. 65.00

The Pairpoint Manufacturing Company started in 1880 in New Bedford, Massachusetts. It soon joined with the glassworks nearby and made glass, silver plated pieces, and lamps. Reverse-painted glass shades and molded shades known as "puffies" were part of the production until the 1930s. The company reorganized and changed its name several times but is still working today.

PAIRPOINT, Ashtray, Floral, Controlled Bubble 65.00
Berry Bowl, Peppermint Stick, 7 In. 45.00
Bottle, Perfume, Red Flower Top, Clear, 8 1/2 In. 165.00
Bottle, Perfume, Ruby, Flowers, Pointed Stopper, Marked, 7 In. 65.00
Bowl, Cherry Leaf, 9 In. 30.00
Bowl, Console, Vintage, Amber, Pedestal, 12 X 7 In. 145.00
Bowl, Peppermint, Star Base, 8 3/4 X 2 5/8 In. 185.00
Bowl, Ruby, Double Bubble Ball Pedestal, 4 X 12 In. 68.00
Cake Basket, Raised Fruit, Ornate Bail, Silver Plate, Footed 55.00
Candleholder, Intaglio Etch, Clear, 8 1/2 In., Pair 60.00
Candlestick, Amber, Urn Socket, Baluster, Round Foot, 12 In., Pair 80.00
Candlestick, Intaglio Grape, Vaseline 115.00
Candlestick, Mushroom Top, Bubbles, Green, 4 1/2 In., Pair 95.00
Candlestick, Mushroom Top, Controlled Bubble, 4 In., Pair 95.00
Castor, Pickle, Enameled Floral, Diamond Quilted, Tongs, Covered 265.00
Centerpiece, Light Green, Bubble Ball Connector, 7 X 11 In. 115.00
Coffeepot, Footed, Monogram, Ebony Handle, Silver Plate, 9 In. 85.00
Compote, Amber, Controlled Bubble, 6 1/2 X 12 In.Diam. 125.00
Compote, Black, Sterling Silver Overlay Top & Base, 7 1/2 In. 285.00
Compote, Diamond Quilted, 9 X 8 In. 135.00
Compote, Mansfield Pattern, Covered, Mint Green, 10 1/4 In. 225.00
Compote, Paperweight Base, Controlled Bubble, Amber, 6 1/2 In. 125.00
Compote, Red Amber 88.00
Compote, Ruby, Clear Bubble Base, 7 In. 68.00
Compote, Wine 135.00
Console Set, Emerald Green, Clear Bubble Ball Stem, 3 Piece 275.00
Console Set, Ruby, Clear Bubble Vase 185.00
Cruet, Marina Scene, Blue 58.00
Cup, Bryden, Peachblow, Handle 85.00
Dish, Salad, Clear, Etched Grapevines Border, 8 In., Set Of 6 .... 75.00
Dish, Sweetmeat, Metal Rim, Enameled Florals, Signed, 4 1/2 In. 50.00
Ewer, Lotus Branch Handle, Green Shades, Gold, Limoges, 6 1/4 In. 750.00
Figurine, Swan, Amberina, 5 1/2 In. 35.00
Goblet, Rouge Flambe 32.00
Goblet, Wine, Rouge Flambe 22.00
Hat, Burmese 110.00
Ladle, Punch, Hobstar, S–Diamond Fan, Teardrop, Marked, 15 In. 250.00
Lamp, Art Nouveau Base, Brass Shade, Red Jewels, Signed 1250.00
Lamp, Base, Puffy, Signed, Dated 1907, 11 In., Pair 2200.00
Lamp, Base, Tree Trunk, Puffy, 8 In. 175.00
Lamp, Boudoir, Tree Trunk, Puffy, Reverse Painted Shade, 8 In. 700.00
Lamp, Brass, Square Foot, Reverse Painted Shade, No.83016, 16 In. 625.00

Pairpoint, Lamp, Puffy   Pairpoint, Lamp, Reverse Painted Shade,
                                Jungle Scene, 21 In.

Lamp, Garden Of Allah ....2000.00 To 2400.00
Lamp, Harp, Etched Silver, Marked, 22 In. 350.00
Lamp, Pear Shape, Dome Shade, Trees, 3–Light, Marked, 22 In. 1475.00
Lamp, Puffy ....*Illus* 725.00
Lamp, Puffy, 21 In. 2300.00
Lamp, Reverse Painted Glass Domed Shade, Poppies,, 21 In. 2400.00
Lamp, Reverse Painted Shade, Brass Base, Curved Arms, 21 1/2 In. 2200.00
Lamp, Reverse Painted Shade, Jungle Scene, 21 In. ....*Illus* 1250.00
Lamp, Reverse Painted Shade, Pheasant, Bronze Base, Signed, 15 In. 650.00
Lamp, Reverse Painted Shade, Silver Acorn Finial, Signed 795.00
Lamp, Reverse Painted, Floral, Brass Base, Signed, 23 In. 1300.00
Lamp, Stratford Apple Blossom Shade, Puffy Base, Signed, 8 In. 975.00
Paperweight, Burmese Rose, Bryden 275.00
Paperweight, Elephant On Bubble Glass, 8 In. 50.00
Paperweight, Fish, Clear, Controlled Bubbles, Sticker, 7 In. 30.00
Plate, Grape, Leaves & Vines Etched Border, Clear, 8 In., Set Of 6 .... 75.00
Shade, Garden Of Allah, Signed 2500.00
Table Set, 4 Piece 55.00
Toothpick, Child On Turtle Holding Umbrella, Silver Plate 160.00
Tray, Footed, Handles, 7 1/2 X 4 In. 30.00
Vase, Cobalt Blue Swirls And Feet, Fluted Top, 11 In. 80.00
Vase, Controlled Bubble Ball Connector, Cranberry, 12 In. 175.00
Vase, Jack–In–The–Pulpit, Sapphire Blue, Enameled Daisies 35.00
Vase, Ruby Base & Top, Controlled Bubble Connector, 13 In. 110.00
Vase, Trumpet Shape, Art Deco, 14 In. 35.00
Vase, Trumpet, Ruby, Bubble Ball Stem, 12 In. 140.00
    PALMER COX, BROWNIES, see Brownies

> *The first paper dolls were probably the pantins, or jumping jacks,*
> *made in eighteenth–century Europe. By the 1880s, sheets of printed*
> *paper dolls and clothes were being made. The first paper doll*
> *books were made in the 1920s. Collectors prefer uncut sheets or books or*
> *boxed sets of paper dolls. Prices are about half as much if the pages*
> *have been cut.*

PAPER DOLL, Air, Land, & Sea, Military, 1943 .... 215.00
  Ann Sothern, Uncut 45.00
  Arlene Dalton, Story Princess, 1957 .... 25.00
  Artistic Series No.22, 4 Dresses, 4 Hats, Tuck 35.00
  Baby Bunting, 1940s, Uncut 6.50
  Baby Sparkle Plenty, Book, Saalfield, 1948 .... 32.00
  Baby's Ball, Art Fabric, 1900, Large, Uncut 185.00
  Badgett Sisters, Joan, Joyce, Jeraldine, Jeanette, 1941, Uncut 98.50
  Barbie 12.50
  Barbie Boutique, 1973, Uncut 5.00
  Bear, 1950s, Uncut 12.00
  Belle Of Newport, Tuck, Original Folder, 4 Outfits, Dated 1894 .... 67.00
  Betsy McCall, 1960s 14.00
  Betsy McCall, 1971 .... 6.00
  Beverly Hillbillies, Folder, Cut, 4 Changes, C.1964 .... 15.00
  Biddle Peep, Cut 25.00
  Big Jim & Big Jake, 1976, Uncut 5.50
  Bobbsey Twins, Dust Jacket 12.50
  Bobby Butterick 6.00
  Bond Bread, Original Envelope, C.1915, Uncut 20.00
  Bridal Party, 6 Cardboard Dolls, 37 Changes, Whitman, 1966, Cut 8.00
  Bride & Groom, Wonder, 1975 .... 5.00
  Buffy & Jody, 1976, Boxed 7.50
  Canadian Spool Cotton, Wedding Series 60.00
  Caroline, Magic Wand, 1963, Boxed 25.00
  Children Around The World, 1955, Uncut 22.00
  Cinderella, 4 Outfits With Hats, Raphael Tuck 35.00
  Cinderella, Wonder, 1975 .... 5.00
  Circus, 1910, Uncut 14.00
  Claire McCardell, Whitman, 1956, Uncut 30.00

Clark Gable, Gone With The Wind 18.00
Clark's Spool Thread, 5 1/2 In. 15.00
Claudette Colbert, 9 Outfits 20.00
Debbie Darling, Uncut, Boxed 19.00
Debbie Reynolds, Cut 25.00
Dennis The Menace, 1960 .... 10.00
Diana Jemima, Holding Doll, Wade Davis, Envelope, 2 Dolls, Uncut 120.00
Dinah Shore, 1958 .... 40.00
Dionne Quintuplets, Palmolive, Uncut 65.00
Dolls Around The World, Clothes To Color, 1960 .... 4.00
Dolls From Storyland, 1948 .... 10.00
Dolly Dingle, 10 Pages, Pictorial Review, 1920s, Uncut 45.00
Dolly Dingle, 1927, Uncut 18.00
Double Wedding, Cut 24.00
Elizabeth & Her Pretty Clothes, 1963 .... 6.00
First Ladies Of White House, Uncut 45.00
Flintstones 10.00
Flying Nun, Artcraft, 1969 .... 12.50
Gale Storm, 1959, Uncut 40.00
German, Names & Stands, 100 Pieces, Original Box ....75.00 To 85.00
Glamour Models, 1950s, Uncut, Book 12.00
Gulliver's Travels, Book, Uncut 85.00
Happy Family Moving Dolls 75.00
Jackie & Caroline, Magic Wand, 1962, Boxed 25.00
Jill, Arbuckle Coffee, 1931, Uncut 55.00
Joan & Bobby, 1929 .... 37.50
Joan Walsh Angland, Wrap Paper Doll Clothes 2.50
Judy Garland, Cut 15.00
Lettie Lane, Journal, 1909 .... 25.00
Linentex, Jean & Alice, Saalfield, 1927, Uncut 25.00
Little Dressmakers, Saalfield, 1949 .... 22.50
Little Red Riding Kiddle, Cut 25.00
Lorraine Day, Uncut 40.00
Magic Mary Lou, Bradley, 1972 .... 3.50
Mammy, Cook & Thanksgiving Dinner, Carolyn Chester, 1912, Uncut 18.00
Mary, Mary, Quite Contrary, 1971 .... 4.00
Miss Hollywood, 1942, Uncut 20.00
Miss Malt–O–Rice, Uncut 100.00
Movie Land, 1947, Uncut 18.00
Movie Starlets, 1950s, Uncut, Book 12.00
N.Y.World's Fair, 1964 .... 8.00
Nanny & Professor 18.00
Natalie Wood 25.00
None–Such Mince Meat 22.50
Orphan Annie, Cut & Uncut 35.00
Pat Boone, Cut 25.00
Pat Nixon & Daughters 14.00
Patience & Prudence, Celebrity, Uncut 25.00
Peggy Pryde's Cousin Carrie, Sheet 8.00
Playmates, 1940s 6.00
Playtime Pals, 1946 .... 8.00
Polly Pratt, 3 Wooden Dolls, Clothes Uncut, Milton Bradley 38.00
Polly Pratt, School, Seashore, Uncut 16.00
Quaker Crackles, Advertising, Uncut 65.00
Raggedy Ann & Andy, Misprint On Dress, Saalfield, 1944 .... 18.00
Rudolph Valentino, 1979, Uncut 5.75
Shirley Temple, No.1789 .... 45.00
Shirley Temple, No.5110, Folding Doll, 18 In., Uncut 60.00
Shirley Temple, No.S2425, 1942, Uncut 125.00
Snow White & 7 Dwarfs, 1970 .... 8.00
Snow White, Grace Drayton, 1914 .... 30.00
Southern Belle, 4 Gowns & Hats, Raphael Tuck 35.00
Southern Belles, Uncut, Saalfield 18.00
Style Shop, Saalfield, C.1943, Uncut 14.00

Paper, Magazine, Playboy, 1st Issue,
  M. Monroe, 1953–54, 7 Issues

Do not mount old maps, prints, etc.,
on cardboard. The acid in the cardboard causes stains. Use an all rag
board. (An art store can help.)

A miniature painting should not be
washed. Most miniatures are painted
on ivory and the paint will wash off.

Sweathogs, Toy Factory, 1977, Boxed	6.00
Sweetheart, 1943	25.00
Tricia Nixon	10.00
Tuesday Weld, 1960, Boxed	15.00
Twiggy, 1967	7.50
Twinkle Twin, Uncut	12.00
Winking Winnie, 1964	5.00
Yellow Kid, 1896, 6 In.	30.00

*Paper collectibles, including almanacs, children's books, catalogs,
stock certificates, and other paper ephemera, are listed here. Paper
calendars are listed separately under Calendar.*

PAPER, Album, Photograph, St.Louis, 1880s	45.00
Almanac, 1914, Marshall's Cigarettes	5.00
Almanac, Farmer's, 1934, 1946, Pair	2.25
Almanac, Happiness In The Home, Dr.Pierce, 1928, 32 Pages	3.00
Almanac, Herb Doctor & Medicine Man, Lists Herbs & Medicines	15.00
Almanac, Hood's, 1905, 14 Pages	10.00
Almanac, J.C.Ayer & Co., Dated 1905	4.00
Almanac, Kate Greenaway, 1888	85.00
Almanac, Kate Greenaway, 1925	85.00
Almanac, Paine's Celery Compound, 32 Pages	20.00
Almanac, Rawleigh, 1927, 64 Pages	4.00
Baptism & Marriage Record, 1756–1778, German Calligraphy, 13 In.	770.00
Birth & Baptismal Certificate, 1845, English Script, 15 X 12 In.	467.00
Birth Certificate, Birds & Angels, John Ritter, Reading, 1847	27.50
Book, 50 Years Of Schwinn–Built Bicycles, Copyright 1945	60.00
Book, Alphabet, Kate Greenaway, C.1885	45.00
Book, An Old Sweetheart Of Mine, Christy Illustrated	30.00
Book, Big Little Book, Billy The Kid	15.00
Book, Big Little Book, Bringing Up Father	15.00
Book, Big Little Book, Capt.Frank Hawks Air Ace & League Of Twelve	10.00
Book, Big Little Book, Jungle Jim	15.00
Book, Big Little Book, Jungle Jim & The Vampire Woman	6.00
Book, Big Little Book, Laughing Dragon Of Oz	60.00
Book, Big Little Book, Mr.District Attorney On The Job	15.00
Book, Big Little Book, Phantom, 1936	35.00
Book, Big Little Book, Skippy & Sooky, Jackie Cooper	12.00
Book, Big Little Book, Terry & War In The Jungle	15.00
Book, Blackstone Secrets Of Magic, Tootsie Rolls, Mailer, 1947	30.00
Book, Coloring, Ceresota Flour, 1912	37.50
Book, Coloring, Jack Webb, Safety Squad, 1955	22.00

Book, Coloring, Lassie, Whitman, 1973 .... 4.00
Book, Coloring, Lucille Ball, 1950, 5 Pages, 11 X 15 In. 18.00
Book, Comic, Archie, Book No.1 .... 225.00
Book, Dodge Bros.Electric Equipment, 1924 .... 10.00
Book, Dr.Harter's Dream Book, 1890, 12 Pages 3.50
Book, Easy Steps In Sewing For Little Girls, 1913 .... 15.00
Book, Echels Anatomical Aid For Embalmer, Flip Pictures, Valice, 1903 .... 148.00
Book, First Dixie Reader, Moore, Raleigh, C.1863, 4 1/2 X 5 1/2 In. 295.00
Book, Fowl Breeder 18.50
Book, Frank In The Mountains, 1896 .... 7.00
Book, Goldilocks, Pop–Up, 1934 .... 75.00
Book, Heritage Of The Shakers, 1923 .... 25.00
Book, Horatio Alger Jr., Do & Dare 12.00
Book, IMA Labor Union Dues, Stamps, 1924 .... 15.00
Book, Jack Frost Painting & Drawing, Hamming Pub., Hard Cover, 1905 .... 12.50
Book, Knave Of Hearts, Illustrations By Parrish 450.00
Book, Light Side Of Egypt, Lance Thackeray, 36 Colored Plates, 1908 .... 25.00
Book, Little Red Riding Hood, Frances Brundage Cover, Saalfield, 1928 .... 20.00
Book, Manual Of Infantry & Rifle Tactics, Richmond Va., 1861 .... 95.00
Book, Manual Training Course In Wood Work, High School, 1905 .... 13.00
Book, Minnesota Farmers Institute Annual, 1895 .... 12.00
Book, Mother Goose, Kellogg's Singing Lady, Radio Premium, 1933 .... 25.00
Book, Mrs.Winslow's Soothing Syrup Recipe, 1872, 32 Pages 15.00
Book, Mushrooms Of America, Prang Co., 12 Colored Pages, 1885 .... 30.00
Book, Pied Piper Of Hamelin, Illustrations By Greenaway 75.00
Book, Poems Of A Childhood, Eugene Field, Illustrations By Parrish 65.00
Book, Pop–Up, Nister Model Menagerie, 6 Animals In Cages 125.00
Book, Pop–Up, Pinocchio, 1922, 4 Pages 125.00
Book, Queerie Queers, Palmer Cox Illustrations 25.00
Book, Raggedy Ann's Lucky Pennies, 1932 .... 40.00
Book, Sketches & Cartoons, C.D.Gibson, 1898 .... 125.00
Book, Storm Mountain, 1889 .... 7.00
Book, Tuck Dolly In Town, Doll Shape, 1896 .... 35.00
Book, York's English Grammar Revised For Southern Schools, 1864 .... 150.00
Brochure, Financial Review By Henry Clews, 4 Pages, May 20, 1916 .... 9.00
Catalog, Alaska Refrigerator, Ice Box, 1922 .... 40.00
Catalog, Albert Pick, Saloon Supplies, 1907 .... 827.00
Catalog, California Perfume Co., Soft Cover, 1920s, 32 Pages 250.00
Catalog, Guns & Ammo, Winchester, 1913, 212 Pages, 5 1/2 X 8 1/2 In. 65.00
Catalog, Keen Kutter, 1930, 2090 Pages 250.00
Catalog, Lionel Train, Original 1959 Issue, 56 Full Color Pages 8.00
Catalog, Modern Woodmen Of America, 1915 .... 18.00
Catalog, Perfection Weigher, Threshing Machines, 1889 .... 10.00
Catalog, Remington Typewriter Line, 37 Pages, 1927 .... 35.00
Catalog, Sears Fall & Winter, 1935 .... 22.00
Catalog, Sears Roebuck, Hard Cover, Order Blank, Envelope, 1902 .... 150.00
Catalog, Shapleigh's, 1935, 2546 Pages 125.00
Certificate, Marine, Samuel Godfrey, July 1798, Framed, 9 1/2 X 15 In. 450.00
Certificate, North American Land Co., Signed By J.Marshall, R.Morris 800.00
Certificate, Stock, Winchester, 1929 .... 65.00
Chart, Survey, Geodetic, South Carolina, 1900–30, 22 X 44 In. 5.00
Contract, Option, Emperor's India Co., 1730 .... 2600.00
Dairy, Don McNeill's Breakfast Club, Facts & Pictures, 1949, 64 Pages 50.00
Deed, English, Handwritten, Parchment, Dated 1825, Framed, 32 X 36 In. 30.00
Deed, Trustees, St.Paul & Pacific Railroad, 1899, 11 X 17 In. 16.00
Document, Confederate Orders, S.Cooper, Richmond, Va., Jan.12, 1863 .... 15.00
Document, Land Purchase S.Carolina, 1821, Framed 45.00
Flyer, Renowned Two–Headed Lady, Millie Christine, Colored, C.1875 .... 35.00
Fraktur, Angels & Birds, Susanna Detter, Dated 1821 .... 32.50
Fraktur, Birth, Ink, Watercolor, Pa., 1810, Framed, 17 1/2 X 19 1/2 In. 180.00
Fraktur, Birth, Lecha County, Pa., Colored, Framed, 13 3/4 X 16 3/4 In. 95.00
Fraktur, Geburts & Taufschein, Lancaster County, 1792, 16 X 19 In. 100.00
Fraktur, Horse, Capital Letters, Birds, Nov.23, 1798, 15 1/2 X 19 In. 800.00
Fraktur, John Ritter, Geburts Und Taufschein, 15 1/2 X 18 1/2 In. 55.00

Fraktur, Martin Brechall, Pen, Ink, & Watercolors, Birth Record, 1797 .... 900.00
Fraktur, Mary Hall, Barkhamsted, Born Oct.24, 1838, 12 X 15 3/4 In. 115.00
Fraktur, Ohio, English Inscription, 1841, Framed, 14 3/4 X 15 1/2 In. 55.00
Fraktur, Tulip Design, Inscription 725.00
Handbook, Columbian Exposition, 1893 .... 5.00
Handbook, For Mechanics, Millers Falls Tools, 1916, 63 Pgs., 4 X 7 In. 20.00
House Blessing, Pa.German, Isaac Palm, Lancaster Co., 1860, 15 X 18 In 150.00
Ledger, D.U.McCunn's Day Book, Ohio, Oct.19, 1839, 6 1/2 X 15 In. 70.00
Ledger, Penn.Area, Quill Written, 1789-1813 .... 60.00
Ledger, Township Treasurer, Ohio, 1881 To 1904 .... 25.00
Magazine, Ford Owner & Dealer, Dated 1922 .... 7.00
Magazine, Playboy, 1st Issue, M. Monroe, 1953-54, 7 Issues .... *Illus* 200.00
Pattern, Clothing, Dress, 1920s 6.00
Prescription, Doctor's Prescription For Whiskey, 1928 .... 10.00
Program, 1932 Olympics, 32 Pages 35.00
Program, Ballet Russe, 1916, Illustrated 20.00
Program, Birth Of A Nation 75.00
Program, Buffalo Bill's Wild West, 1909 .... 35.00
Program, Buffalo Bill, 1895, 65 Pages 45.00
Program, Football, Yale Vs.Columbia, October 1900 .... 15.00
Program, Gone With The Wind, Colored Photos, 1939 .... 35.00
Program, Great Lakes Exposition, 1936 .... 10.00
Program, King Of Kings, Cecil B.DeMille, 1938 .... 25.00
Program, National Air Races, Cleveland, 1932 .... 12.00
Program, Ringling Bros., 1937 .... 12.50
Program, What Price Glory, 1920s 25.00
Program, World Series, Cubs & Tigers, 1935 .... 75.00
Ration Book, Stamps, War, Original Folder 6.00
Register, Family, Calligraphic, Goodwin Family From 1793 To 1863 .... 44.00
Register, Marriage, Higgins Family, By Ann Currier, 1853, 9 X 14 In. 25.00
Stock Certificate, American Deforest Wireless Telegraph Co., 1905 .... 69.50
Stock Certificate, Bellevue Pipe & Foundry Co., 1907 .... 12.95
Stock Certificate, Chicago, Burlington & Northern Railroad, 1888 .... 19.95
Stock Certificate, Deluxe Mining & Milling Co., Colo., 1897 .... 28.95
Stock Certificate, Hannibal & St.Joseph Railroad, 1855 .... 149.50
Stock Certificate, Jacksonville, Alton & St.Louis Railroad, 1857 .... 109.50
Stock Certificate, Parke, Davis Drug Co., 1927, 8 1/2 X 11 In. 10.00
Stock Certificate, Silver Mining Co., Buena Vista, Colo., Blank 20.00
Stock Certificate, Sioux City Railroad Co., Picture Of Old Train 25.00
Stock Certificate, Smuggler Gold Mining & Milling Co., 1889 .... 29.95
Stock Certificate, State Of Iowa, Iowa Falls & Sioux City R.R.Co. 50.00
Ticket, Admission, Chicago Expo, 1893 .... 25.00
Travel Brochure, Hindenburg, 12-Page, Dated 1936 .... 115.00

> *Paperweights must have first appeared along with paper in ancient*
> *Egypt. Today's collectors search for every type from the very expensive*
> *French weights of the nineteenth century to the modern artist weights*
> *or advertising pieces. The glass tops of the paperweights sometimes*
> *have been nicked or scratched and this type of damage can be*
> *removed by polishing. Some serious collectors think this type of repair*
> *is an alteration and will not buy a repolished weight; others think it is*
> *an acceptable technique of restoration that does not change the value.*
> *Baccarat paperweights are listed separately under Baccarat.*

PAPERWEIGHT, 7-Point Starfish Style, Convex Center, Clear, 5 In. 20.00
Advertising, Beaver, Compliments Danville Stove Co., Iron, 1898 .... 22.00
Advertising, Berkshire Life Insurance, Golf Ball, Iron, 3 In. 40.00
Advertising, Dutch Boy Paints, Lead 17.50
Advertising, Gould, Agent, Bee Building, Omaha, Neb., Clear 28.00
Advertising, MoPac Observation Car, Glass, Colored 10.00
Advertising, Schoenecker Boot & Shoe Co. 24.00
Apple, Green Stem, Leaves, Art Glass, Cornflower Blue, Venetian 55.00
Apple, New England Glass Co., Stem, 19th Century, 2 1/2 In. 275.00
Army WAC, Snow 19.00
Art Glass, Mt.St.Helen's 35.00

Ayotte, Cardinal Head, Clear 400.00
Ayotte, Magnolia Warbler, Raspberries, Clear 350.00
Banford, Dragonfly, Blue & White Flower, Faceted, 2 1/2 In. 600.00
Banford, Snake, Red Rose, On Pebbled Ground, Signed, 2 1/2 In. 500.00
Beehive, Crystal Blown, Flower Base 75.00
Bell Shape, Local & Long Distance, Missouri & Kansas 95.00
Bell Telephone, Logo 15.00
Black Cat, Iron, C.1940 .... 15.00
Bohemian, Doorknob, Red & White Canes, 1 7/8 In. 95.00
Book Form, Marble 5.00
Brookville Glove Co., Air Bubbles, Tortoiseshell Coloring 45.00
Caithness, Flower In The Rain, Red 75.00
Coin Glass, 1892 Dollar, Faceted Sides & Top 250.00
Columbian Exposition Scene, Signed Libbey Glass Co. 32.00
Concentric Millefiori, Tuft Arrangement, Gillinder, 3 1/4 In. 1250.00
D'Albret, Astronauts 100.00
D'Albret, John J.Audubon 50.00
D'Albret, Pinchbeck, Sir Winston Churchill, Silver, 3 3/8 In. 150.00
DiNardo, Anisari Design, Black On Red Overlay, 3 5/8 In. 160.00
Dog, Renown, Iron 12.00
Dragonfly, Orient, Crystal, Cased, Flume, Signed 70.00
Dutch Girl, Snow 12.00
Elvis Presley, Cut Windows, Red Flashed 50.00
Figrual, Buffalo, Pan American Exposition, Bronze, 1901 .... 45.00
Figural, Hand Holding Cup, Turtle Above, Frosted, 4 1/2 X 3 In. 225.00
Fire Hydrant, Base, Cast Iron, Insurance Ed.Datty, 5 In. 135.00
Flowers, Vines, Millefiori, Orient, Crystal, Cased, Oval, Signed 60.00
Glass, Frosted Dog On Clear Cushion, Raised Fluted Edge 100.00
Globe, Glass, Signed 320 Medek, 4 In. 385.00
Globe, Signs Of Zodiac, Compass, & Ruler, Brass, Onyx Base, 6 In. ... 40.00
Illinois Central R.R., Brass 18.00
J.Glass, Millefiori, Pattern, 7 Canes, 1980 .... 125.00
Kaziun, Flower, Red & White Arrowhead Cane, K Signed, 2 In. 650.00
Kewpie, Star Shape, Signed Rose O'Neill 35.00
Kosta, Albert Schweitzer 70.00
Life Of Georgia, Bronze 22.00
Lincoln, Bronze, Kraueter & Co. 42.00
Lyre, Brass, 6 In. 20.00
Mason–Scotia, Manta Ray, Limited Edition 280.00
Memorial Hall, Centennial, 1776–1876 .... 195.00
Millefiori Canes, Clear Dome, Red, White, & Blue, 3 1/2 In. 175.00
New England, Crown, 18 Twists, 2 7/16 In. 600.00
Olma, Poinsettia, Clear, 3 5/8 In. 75.00
Orient & Flume, Blues, Dated 1976, Signed 65.00
Orient & Flume, Floral, 1977 .... 75.00
Pan American, Figural, Bronze, Buffalo, 1901 .... 45.00
Paul Revere, Gray Overlaid, Cristal D'Albret, 1969 .... 150.00
Perthshire, Blue & White Flower, Garland, Faceted, 1976 .... 95.00
Perthshire, Sunflower, Golden Amber Base, Garland, 1979 .... 195.00
Pharmacy, Blue 48.00
Phillips Milk Of Magnesia, Glass 25.00
Poinsettia, 12 Red Petals, Green Leaves, Round, Sandwich 295.00
Presentation, Marion, Ind., Hand Blown, C.1920, 3 1/2 In.Diam. 45.00
Rabbit, Milk Glass 12.00
Red Eagle, Fenton 18.00
Rosenfeld, Flowers & Buds, Clear 200.00
Rudolph The Red Nosed Reindeer, Snow 15.00
Scales, Scoop Shape, Iron & Brass, Fairbanks 78.00
Scotia, Millifiori, Thistle, Garland 105.00
Scotia, Springtime, Color Scramble, Bubbles 36.00
Scotty Dog, Hamilton, Foundry, Iron 15.00
Seal, Crystal, Large 30.00
St.Bernard, Brass, English 22.00
St.Louis, Eagle, Sulfide, Double Overlay, Blue 250.00

St.Louis, Fuchsia, Latticinio Ground, 1976, 3 In. 350.00
St.Louis, George Washington On Horse, Gold Incrustation, 1976 .... 230.00
St.Louis, Millefiori, Red & White Cane, Garland, 3 In. 650.00
St.Louis, Pope John Paul II, Sulfide, 1981 .... 250.00
St.Louis, Upright Bouquet, On White Spiral Torsade 2800.00
Standard, Braided Bouquet, Berries 1000.00
Studebaker, Revolving, Brass, C.1885 .... 95.00
Studebaker, Wooden 40.00
T.C.Wheaton Co., 1888–1936 .... 20.00
Tabucco, Sweet Peas, 1981 .... 350.00
Union Terminal Tower, Glass, Color 10.00
Western Pottery, Oak Life, Stoneware 18.00
Whitefriars, Millefiori, Concentric, Faceting, 1977 .... 200.00
Whitefriars, Millefiori, Radial Garden, Spiral Twist, Faceted 95.00
Whittmore, Bottle, Blue Rose, Blue & White Twist In Stopper 300.00
Wine Railway Appliance Co., Bronze, Round 30.00
Wright Swan Denver Municipal R.R.Bonds, Brass 20.00
Yellow Kid, Cast Iron 375.00

Papier–mache is made from paper mixed with glue, chalk, and other ingredients, then molded and baked. It becomes very hard and can be painted. Boxes, trays, and furniture were made of papier–mache. Some of the nineteenth–century pieces were decorated with mother–of–pearl.

PAPIER–MACHE, Ball, Polychrome, Girl, Deer & Woods, Opens At Center 27.50
Box, Alms, Man Praying, Mechanical, Wooden, Paper Label, 11 In. 100.00
Box, Bracelet, Mother–Of–Pearl Inlay, Gold Trim, 4 3/4 X 3 In. 195.00
Box, Candy & Nodder, Chicken, Dressed, German, 6 In. 20.00
Box, Candy & Nodder, Uncle Sam Riding Firecracker, 3 1/2 In. 125.00
Box, Candy, Duck, Dressed, German, 6 3/4 In. 30.00
Box, Candy, Poodle, Glass Eyes, Cover, German, 6 In. 225.00
Box, Candy, Rabbit Clown, Glass Eyes, German, 7 In. 60.00
Box, Candy, Rabbit, Hat, Scarf, Glass Eyes, 7 1/2 In. 50.00
Candy Container, Santa Claus, 5 In. 32.00
Candy, Apple Singing, 3 3/4 In. 175.00
Doll, Boy & Girl, Straw Body, Glass Eyes, Pair 200.00
Figurine, 9 Indians, Base, Bowling Ball, Germany, 1900, 9 In. 775.00
Figurine, Dachshund, Original Brown Paint, 27 1/2 In. 135.00
Figurine, Dog, Marked Sell's Columbus, Brown & White, 22 In. 175.00
Figurine, Man In Turk Costume, Autoperipetetikos, 12 In. 1000.00
Head, Santa Claus, 18 In. 69.00
Marionette, Child's, Japan, 1900, 3 In. 36.00
Match Holder, Striker Side, Gold Figures & Scene, 7 In. 30.00
Nodder, Bulldog, Growler, 9 In. 350.00
Nodder, Cat, Striped Orange & White, 9 1/2 In. 195.00
Nodder, Duck, 7 In. 10.00
Owl, Glass Eyes, 16 1/2 In. 48.00
Pumpkin, Paper Face, German, 4 In. 45.00
Puppet, Foxy Grandpa, German 125.00
Roly Poly, Clown, Hat, 5 In. 95.00
Roly Poly, Clown, Weight Loose, 7 In. 65.00
Roly Poly, Clown, Wooden, 15 3/4 X 9 In. 350.00
Roly Poly, Foxy Grandpa, 4 In. 100.00
Roly Poly, Mama Katzenjammer, 3 In. 50.00
Santa Claus, 3 1/2 In. 65.00
Snuffbox, Litho Of Napoleon, 1780 .... 465.00
Toy, Horse, Machine Made 40.00
Toy, Horse, On Wheels, Germany, 12 In. 95.00
Tray, Gold Design, Black Ground, Stand, 19th Century, 18 In. 1325.00
Tray, Stand, Cartouche Form, Horse & Rider, 31 1/2 X 18 In. 2860.00
Turkey, 7 In. 20.00
Whistle, Rooster, Tin, 5 1/2 In. 35.00
PARASOL, see Umbrella

Parian is a fine–grained, hard–paste porcelain named for the marble it resembles. It was first made in England in 1846 and gained in favor in the United States about 1860. Figures, tea sets, vases, and other items were made of Parian at many English and American factories.

PARIAN, Bust, Apollo, Marked, 7 X 5 In.	75.00
Bust, George Washington, 5 In.	12.00
Bust, Lady, 12 In.	30.00
Bust, Longfellow, Name & Verse On Reverse, 10 3/4 In.	85.00
Bust, Sir Walter Scott, 5 In.	40.00
Bust, William Shakespeare, 5 In.	50.00
Ewer, Grape & Leaves, 9 In.	80.00
Figurine, Can't You Talk, Child With Dog, R.J.Morris, C.1870, 16 In.	750.00
Figurine, Girl, Basket Of Flowers, Robinson & Leadbeater, 16 In.	275.00
Figurine, Girl, Kneeling, Impressed Minton, 9 X 9 3/4 In., Pair	150.00
Figurine, Grecian Goddess & Cupid With Arrows, 9 In.	165.00
Figurine, Man Seated On Rock, Holding Birds, Dog At Feet, 9 1/2 In.	135.00
Figurine, Owls, Dated August 2, 1871, Registry Mark, 7 1/2 In.	275.00
Figurine, Psyche, Seated, Cupid Floating Behind, 9 In.	165.00
Figurine, Ruth, Oval Base, 13 In.	175.00
Figurine, Woman, Hands In Front Of Lamp, Skull On Ground, 7 In.	125.00
Group, Boy Against Tree Stump, Stroking Bird, Signed, C.1865, 8 In.	135.00
Jug, Embossed Water Lilies, Branch Handle, Lavender, 1850, 7 1/2 In.	125.00
Lamp, Fairy, Clear Cup, Magenta Rose, 19th Century, 3 3/4 In.	65.00
Lamp, Fairy, Pale Pink, 19th Century, 3 3/4 In.	160.00
Loving Cup, Bacchus & Women, Blue, White, Charles Meigh, 1840, 7 In.	295.00
Pitcher, Boy Climbing Tree, Blue, Branch Handle, 1850, 7 In.	225.00
Pitcher, Embossed Canterbury Bells, Copeland, 9 In.	30.00
Pitcher, Embossed Ribbed Design, Rope Twist Handle, 5 3/4 In.	30.00
Pitcher, Seashell Design, 3 3/4 In.	22.00
Plaque, Advertising, North Carolina Smoking Tobacco, Frame, 12 In.	150.00
Teapot, Domed Cover, Squirrel Finial, Bennington, C.1859, 5 In.	350.00
Vase, Everted Rim, Bacchanalian Frieze, 4 1/2 In.	60.00
Vase, Spill, Mayers Longport, Babes In Woods Scene, C.1850	110.00

Vieux Paris, or Old Paris, is porcelain ware that is known to have been made in Paris in the eighteenth or early nineteenth century. These porcelains have no identifying mark but can be identified by the whiteness of the porcelain and the lines and decorations.

PARIS, Cup & Saucer, Hand Painted, C.1860, Oversize	250.00
Cup & Saucer, M Monogram For President Monroe	1875.00
Tureen, Painted Floral Sprays, White, Early 19th Century, 10 1/4 In.	450.00
Urn, Handles, Masks, Oriental Figures, Black, Electrified, 15 In.	300.00
Vase, Bands Of Coral, Gold Rim, Portrait Panel, French Lady, 8 3/4 In.	90.00
Vase, Napoleon Panel, Campana Shape, Gilt, Handles, 18 In., Pair	1100.00

Pate–de–verre is an ancient technique in which glass is made by blending and refining powdered glass of different colors into molds. The process was revived by French glassmakers, especially Galle, around the end of the nineteenth century.

PATE–DE–VERRE, Ashtray, Flower Form, Curling Petals At Back, Signed	1200.00
Lamp, Art Deco	1750.00
Paperweight, Butterfly Wings At Top, Signed, Square, 4 In.	2500.00

Pate–sur–pate means paste on paste. The design was made by painting layers of slip on the ceramic piece until a relief decoration was formed. The method was developed at the Sevres factory in France about 1850. It became even more famous at the English Minton factory about 1870. It has since been used by many potters to make both pottery and porcelain wares.

PATE–SUR–PATE, Box, Cherubs & Lion Pulling Chariot, Limoges, 3 3/4 In.	120.00
Plate, Cabinet, Maiden Center, White, Minton, 1911, Set Of 12	2530.00
Vase, Baluster Celadon, Handles, Electrified, 19 In., Pair	1760.00

Paul Revere pottery was made at several locations in and around Boston, Massachusetts, between 1906 and 1942. The pottery was operated as a settlement house program for teen–aged girls. Many pieces were signed "S.E.G." for Saturday Evening Girls. The artists concentrated on children's dishes and tiles. Decorations were outlined in black and filled with color.

PAUL REVERE, Bowl, Black Line Around Top, Blue, 1 3/4 In.	80.00
Bowl, Brown, Repeating Goose Design, Label, 5 X 11 1/2 In.	100.00
Bowl, Landscape Scene, Chicks, White, Interior Band, 6 X 2 In.	395.00
Bowl, Light Blue Drip Over Blue, 4 X 5 In.	40.00
Jar, Covered, Green Brown Glaze, Chick, S.E.G., 4 1/2 In.	495.00
Jar, Insects, Yellow Band, White Ground, Date 1/12/14, 5 1/4 In.	1800.00
Jar, Yellow Chick Band, Brown Green Ground, Marked, 4 1/2 In.	160.00
Paperweight, Goose Design, 8–Sided, S.E.G.	95.00
Plate, 15 Outlined Chicks Border, Cream, S.E.G., 10–21, 8 In.	295.00
Plate, Goose, Yellow, Edith Brown, Dated 4–23, 7 1/2 In.	75.00
Plate, Green Hills & Trees, S.E.G., 7 3/4 In.	100.00
Plate, Green, Blue, 10 Outlined Geese, S.E.G., 44–7–12, 7 In.	250.00
Tile, Border Landscape, Blue, Green, Edith Brown, 5 1/2 In.	154.00
Tile, Landscape, Blue & Green, Round, 1926, 5 1/2 In.	154.00
Tile, Revere On Horse, Blue, Green, Brown, White, 1911, 6 In.	440.00
Tile, Sailing Ship On Water, Marked In Circle, 6 In.	200.00
Tile, Yellow Tulip, Black Outlined, Dated 6–14, Round	295.00
Vase, Blue & Green Band, C.1923, 6 1/2 In.	160.00
Vase, Gloss Black, Label, 10 In.	75.00
Vase, Yellow Matte, Artist Signed, 4 1/2 X 3 1/2 In.	60.00
Wall Pocket, Turquoise	65.00

Peachblow glass originated about 1883 at Hobbs, Brockunier and Company of Wheeling, West Virginia. It is a glass that shades from yellow to peach. It was lined with white glass. New England peachblow is a one–layer glass shading from red to white. Mt. Washington peachblow shades from pink to blue. Reproductions of all types of peachblow have been made. Some are poor and easy to identify as copies, others are very accurate reproductions and could fool the unwary.

PEACHBLOW, Bowl, Cream Gloss Interior, Webb, 4 In.	265.00
Bowl, Cut Velvet, 5 In.	300.00
Bowl, Flared, Scalloped, New England Glass Co., 2 3/4 X 5 1/2 In.	745.00
Bowl, Melon, Hand Painted Berries, Crimped Top, 10 X 9 In.	350.00
Bowl, New England, 4 1/2 X 2 3/4 In.	435.00
Bowl, Porridge, Shiny, New England Glass Co., 2 3/4 X 4 1/2 In.	435.00
Creamer, Ribbed	350.00
Creamer, Wheeling	400.00
Darner, New England	120.00
Darner, Pink Ball, White Handle, 6 In.	140.00
PEACHBLOW, GUNDERSON, see Gunderson	
Lamp, Peg, Brass Socket, 4 In., Pair	60.00
Muffineer	425.00
Pitcher, Mahogany To Cream, Applied Amber Handle, Wheeling, 7 In.	200.00
Pitcher, Water, Applied Amber Handle, 9 1/2 In.	1250.00
Pitcher, Water, Wheeling, Amber Handle, 9 In.	450.00
Pitcher, Water, Wheeling, Applied Amber Handle, Large	1250.00
Pitcher, Wheeling, Applied Amber Handle, Square Top, 4 5/8 In.	500.00
Punch Cup, New England, Reeded Loop Handle, 2 1/2 In.	160.00
Relish, 3–Part, Farber Chrome Holder With 3 Shame Nudes, 8 In.	67.00
Rose Bowl, 3 In.	135.00
Salt, Satin, Wheeling, 3 In.	495.00
Shade, Gaslight, Ruffled, 4 1/2 X 6 1/4 In.	385.00
Shade, New England, Shiny Finish, 4 1/2 In.	385.00
Sugar, 2 Handles, Label, Mt.Washington, 2 1/2 In.	1600.00
Sugar, New England, 2 Handles, World's Fair, 1893	450.00
Syrup, Blown–Out Drapes, Rows Of Buttons	185.00

Tumbler, New England, Acid Finish 195.00
Tumbler, New England, Wild Rose Color In Upper Half, 3 3/4 In. 385.00
Tumbler, Water, Fuchsia To Yellow, Wheeling, 3 7/8 In. 300.00
Tumbler, Wheeling, 3 1/2 In. 250.00
Tumbler, Wheeling, White Lining, 3 3/4 In. 325.00
Vase, Dark Mahogany Top To Yellow Bottom, Wheeling, 7 In. 1100.00
Vase, Dragonfly, Bee, Gold, Silver Leaves, Webb, 5 X 4 1/2 In. 320.00
Vase, Enameled Flowers & Leaves, 6 X 12 In. 185.00
Vase, Enameled Flowers, TW & Sons, 6 In. 369.00
Vase, Floral, Gold Bands, Cream Lining, Webb, 7 1/2 In. 895.00
Vase, Gold Floral Overall, Webb, 7 1/2 X 4 3/8 In. 895.00
Vase, Lily, New England, Paper Label, 8 1/4 In. 845.00
Vase, Mahogany To Mustard, Bulbous, Long Neck, Wheeling, 9 In. 650.00
Vase, New England, Rose, Paper Label, 8 1/4 In. 845.00
Vase, Pink To Blue, Ruffled, Footed, Mt.Washington, 10 1/2 In. 3200.00
Vase, Wheeling, Fuchsia To Honey Amber, 6 X 10 1/2 In. 1025.00
Vase, Wheeling, Mahogany To Mustard Yellow, 9 In. 650.00
Vase, Wild Rose Color, New England, Paper Label, 8 1/4 In. 845.00
Water Set, Wheeling, 6 Piece 925.00
    PEACHBLOW, WEBB, see Webb Peachblow

> *Listed under Pearl are items made of the natural mother-of-pearl
> from shells. The glassware known as mother-of-pearl is listed by that
> name. Opera glasses made with natural pearl shell are listed under
> Opera Glasses. Natural pearl has been used to decorate furniture and
> small utilitarian objects for centuries.*

PEARL, Fruit Knife, Silver Plated Blade, Small, Set Of 12 .... 650.00
  Pen, Gold Point 20.00

> *Peking glass is a Chinese cameo glass first made popular in the
> eighteenth century. The Chinese have continued to make this layered
> glass in the old manner; and many new pieces are now available that
> could confuse the average buyer.*

PEKING GLASS, Bowl, Plain, Everted Rim, Footed, Amethyst, 19th Century, 8 In. 90.00
  Candlestick, Metal Oak Leaf Top, Jade Green, 5 3/4 In., Pair 85.00
  Goblet, Thick Stem, Marked China, Amethyst, 6 1/4 In. 85.00
  Goblet, Water, Thick Stem, Amethyst, Marked China, 6 1/4 In. 85.00
  Vase, Red, 8 In., Pair 250.00
  Vase, Yellow On White, 9 In., Pair 600.00

To take desirable cards from an old scrapbook or to remove old wallpaper from a box, soak the entire piece in warm water until the paste loosens. Most types of early ink will survive this method, but test ink on hand-written pages before soaking. Test dark wallpapers.

Peloton, Plate, Enameled Polychrome Floral Design,
5 1/2 In.

Peloton glass is a European glass with small threads of colored glass rolled onto the surface of clear or colored glass. It is sometimes called spaghetti, or shredded coconut glass. Most pieces found today were made in the nineteenth century.

PELOTON, Bowl, Boat Shape	325.00
Cracker Jar, Ribbed, Yellow, Blue, Red String, Satin, Bail Lid, Handle	750.00
Cruet, Amber Glass, Clear Handle, Bulbous, 6 1/4 In.	325.00
Pitcher, Pink, Blue & Yellow Strings, Applied Handle, 5 1/4 In.	485.00
Pitcher, Water, Shades Of Pink, White, Blue, & Green, 5 X 12 In.	550.00
Plate, Enameled Polychrome Floral Design, 5 1/2 In. ....*Illus*	80.00
Rose Bowl, 6–Crimp, Coconut Strings Allover Body, White Cased	265.00
Rose Bowl, White Cased, Coconut Strings Allover, 2 1/4 X 2 3/8 In.	265.00
Sugar Shaker	95.00
Vase, Blue, Rose, Yellow Threads On White, Clear Rigaree Foot, 4 In.	130.00
Vase, Ribbed Design, Coconut Strings, Tricorn Top, 5 3/4 X 7 In.	325.00

The first steel pen point was made in England in 1780 to replace the hand–cut quill as a writing instrument. It was 100 years before the commercial pen was a common item. The fountain pen was invented in the 1830s but was not made in quantity until the 1880s. All types of old pens are collected.

PEN, Ambassador, Super Point, Write Fine	12.00
Bakelite, Celluloid, Orange, Black & White	50.00
Chancellor Cigars	20.00
Conklin, Brown Marbled Case, Dated 1925	25.00
Conklin, Fountain, Dated 1918	35.00
Conklin, Rolled Gold	275.00
Desk Set, Parker Vacuumatic, Pencil & Pen, White Marble	60.00
Eversharp, Bronze, Green Gold Seal Signature, 5 1/2 In.	150.00
Eversharp, Pen & Pencil Set, 14K Gold	310.00
Eversharp, Pen & Pencil Set, White Dot, C.1923, Boxed	65.00
Eversharp, Skyline	20.00
Grieshaber, 10K Gold, Cup	750.00
Parker Parkette Bakelite, Fountain	10.00
Parker, 14K Cover	65.00
Parker, 51, Pen, Original Box, Set	25.00
Parker, Black, Silver Streaked Case	18.00
Parker, Duofold, Jr., Orange	10.00
Parker, Duofold, Jr., Red, Pencil	95.00
Parker, Duofold, Lady's, Green	18.00
Parker, Lucky Curve, Green, Large	35.00
Parker, Model 21, Box	18.00
Pavicer, Vacuumatic, Gold Stripes	28.00
Pearlette, Pencil, Set	10.00
Salz, Diamond Metal Pin, 14K Gold Nib	25.00
Shaeffer, Pencil, Desk Set, Marble Base, White Dot, 14K Gold Nib	55.00
Sheaffer Lifetime Desk Set, Green Onyx Base	20.00
Sheaffer, Dry–Proof, Pencil, Set	65.00
Sheaffer, Feathertouch, Brown & Gold Striped	25.00
Sheaffer, Feathertouch, Red & Black Striped	25.00
Sheaffer, White Dot 777, 1970	50.00
Sheaffer, White Dot Imperial Triumph, 1972	125.00
Wahl Eversharp, Gold Seal, Black & Pearl, 1928	75.00
Wahl Eversharp, Green Marble Case	20.00
Wahl, 1925	75.00
Wahl, Gold Filled	40.00
Wahl, Tempoint, Lady's, 14K Gold	250.00
Waterman, 14K Gold, No Tube	75.00
Waterman, Commando	20.00
Waterman, Ideal, Art Nouveau, 14K Gold	225.00
Waterman, Ideal, Fountain	20.00
Waterman, Ink View, Flat End, Silver Trim Band, Black With Amber Trim	20.00
Waterman, No.0512 1/2, Lady's, Gold Filigree	250.00

Waterman, Ripple, Man's, Orange	95.00
Wearever, Fountain	3.00

The pencil was invented, so it is said, in 1565. The eraser was not added to the pencil until 1858. The automatic pencil was invented in 1863. Collectors today want advertising pencils or automatic pencils of unusual design.

PENCIL, 10K Gold, Case Fob, English	75.00
Armstrong Tires, Rhinoceros Figure Inside Butting Tire	10.00
Eversharp, Gold Seal, Black & Pearl, 1930	50.00
Mechanical, Figural, Joe DeMaggio	25.00
Mechanical, Pointer, Chrome	6.50
Milwaukee Railroad, 1940s	15.00
Parker, Duofold Sr., Mottled Green	75.00
Parker, Lady's, Red	50.00
Parker, Mechanical, Pearl & Black	35.00
Wahl Eversharp, Gold Filled	20.00
Wahl Eversharp, Sterling Silver, Floral Engraving	40.00
Winchester, Bullet Shape	38.00

Pennsbury Pottery — *The Pennsbury Pottery worked in Morrisville, Pennsylvania, from 1950 to 1971. Full sets of dinnerware were made as well as many decorative items.*

PENNSBURY, Figurine, Rooster, 12 In.	125.00
Figurine, Rooster, Chicken, Brown & Beige, Large, Pair	185.00
Pitcher, Eagle, Large	42.00
Pitcher, Milk, Rooster	36.00
Sugar & Creamer, Covered, Rooster & Hex Design	38.00
Tray, B.& O.R.R., 8 In.	30.00

Pepsi–Cola, the drink and the name, was invented in 1898 but was not trademarked until 1903. The logo was changed from an elaborate script to the modern block letters in the 1970 Pepsi label. All types of advertising memorabilia are collected and reproductions are being made.

PEPSI–COLA, Bottle, Green, Embossed, Hourglass Shape, Script, 6 1/2 Oz.	12.50
Bottle, Red, White, Blue Painted Label, Double Dot Script, 12 Oz.	5.00
Cooler, 2–Section Lid, Logo & Revives You On End Panels, 1920s	350.00
Dispenser, Draught, Musical Tap	325.00
Fan, 2 Policemen, Old Logo, 1940	15.00
Pen, Fountain	35.00
Sign, Black People At Party, Tin On Cardboard, 1960s, 8 X 12 In.	21.00
Sign, Bottle Cap, 28 In.Diam.	40.00
Tap Knob, Musical, Plays Jingle, Chrome & Celluloid, C.1930	125.00
Thermometer, 1950s, 8 X 27 In.	35.00
Thermometer, Girl, Sipping Straw	125.00
Tray, Beach Scene, Round	15.00
Tray, C.1904	995.00
Tray, Change, Victorian Lady, Soda Fountain, Oval, 4 X 6 In.	225.00

Cut glass, pressed glass, art glass, silver, metal, enamel, and even plastic or porcelain perfume bottles have been made. Although the small bottle to hold perfume was first made before the time of ancient Egypt, it is the nineteenth– and twentieth–century examples that interest today's collector. Examples with the atomizer top marked "Devilbiss" are listed under that name. Glass or porcelain examples will be found under the appropriate name such as Lalique, Czechoslovakia, etc.

PERFUME BOTTLE, 15K Gold, Ruby, Spring Release Cap, English, 1840–50	450.00
Amethyst, Hexagonal, Stopper, 3 1/2 In.	30.00
Art Deco Design, Footed, Stopper, Pink Glass, 5 1/4 In.	20.00
Art Deco, Enameled Chrome Fittings, Satin Glass, 4 1/2 In.	50.00
Art Deco, Pink, Frosted, Plunger, 3 1/2 In.	8.00
Art Deco, Red Cased, Enameled, Dore Bronze, Square Stopper	295.00

Blue Milk Glass Insert, Sterling Silver Holder, C.1904 .... 75.00
Brass Sunflower Stopper, Brass, Germany, 5 1/2 In. 85.00
Cobalt To Clear, Brass Top, 2 1/2 In. 58.00
Colorado, Clear, Gold Feet & Stopper 195.00
Cranberry, Floral, 3 1/8 In. 60.00
Crystal, Faberge, French Label 55.00
Crystal, Silver Overlay, Sterling Funnel, Set 59.00
Cut Flowers, Sterling Silver Stopper, 5 In. 40.00
Cut Glass, Atomizer, Oval Thumbprint, Stars, 4 1/4 In. 58.00
Cut Glass, Diamond Shape, Stopper, 4 1/2 In. 25.00
Cut Glass, Large, Faceted Stopper 210.00
Cut Glass, Pink, Stopper, Czechoslovakia 25.00
Cut Glass, Sapphire, Ormolu, Marble Base, Ruffled, 6 In., Pair 165.00
Cylindrical, Notched Ribbed, Rayed Center, Dabber, 4 1/4 In. 68.00
Dark Blue, Cut To Crystal, Atomizer Round, Squeeze Ball 38.00
Depression Glass, Peach, Hand Painted Flowers, Footed, 5 In. 35.00
Diamond Point Panels, Plunger Type, Flowers, Green 20.00
Diamond–Quilted Atomizer, 3 In. 22.00
Double Lay Down, Octagonal, Green, Silver Cap, English 40.00
Enameled Allover Floral, Leaves, Brilliant Blue, 6 1/2 In. 70.00
Enameled Flowers, Frosted Ball Stopper, 4 1/4 In. 95.00
English Cameo, White, Blue, Morning Glory, Vines, 1 1/4 In. 685.00
Evening In Paris, Large 10.00
Fan Shaped Stopper, San Francisco Exposition, 1940, 10 In. 50.00
Figural, Colonial Lady, Czechoslovakia, 3 1/2 In 65.00
Figural, Lady, French, 2 1/2 In. 25.00
Floral, Quintuplets, Box 18.00
Frosted Squirrel Top, Crystal Dabber, Czechoslovakia, 6 In. 150.00
Gold Metal & Glass, Hinged Top, Opalescent Lime, 3 1/4 In. 65.00
Golliwog, 3 In. 89.00
Golliwog, 6 In. 145.00
Green, Allover Cut Design, 4 3/4 In. 85.00
High Button Shoe, Clear, 4 In. 16.00
Hobnail, Opalescent, Cranberry 45.00
Jeweled, Czechoslovakia, Purse Size 30.00
Jeweled, Yellow Cased, Stopper, Gold Trim, 5 1/2 In. 95.00
Lacy Gold Design, Original Green Stopper, Base Scallops 95.00
Lavender Roses & Trim, Mushroom Stopper, Toilet Water 75.00
Lay Down, Cranberry, Victorian, Stopper, English, 11 In. 110.00
Loop Pattern, Trefoil Scalloped Base, Stopper, Canary, 3 In. 55.00
Millefiori, Trumpet Shape, Round Stopper 50.00
Napoleon III, Painted Opaline Glass, Footed, Dore Bronze 275.00
Oval Cutting, Sterling Silver Cap, Birmingham, 1 5/8 In. 145.00
Pink Glass, Brass Lid, Mesh Bulb Atomizer, 2 1/2 In. 22.00
Pink, Dabber, Clear Cut, Pink, 4 In., Pair 120.00
Porcelain, Windmill, Movable Blade, Blue, White, 4 In. 35.00
Red Dots, Squat Round Base, Feather Stopper, 4 1/2 In. 75.00
Rick Secker Sweet Cologne, Spatter, Handles, 8 1/2 In. 60.00
Sandwich, Smoky, Flowers, Tulip Stopper, Jar, 8 In., 3 Piece 110.00
Satin Glass, Green, Butterflies On Stopper, France, Set Of 3 .... 75.00
Schaparelli, Purse, 2 5/8 In. 12.00
Screw Top, Bulbous, Small Holes On Top, 6 In. 40.00
Set, Art Deco, Pagoda, Lavender, Tray, Porcelain, 4 Piece 195.00
Silver Overlay, Stopper, Gorham, 5 In. 150.00
Skyscraper Shape, Clear, Wooden Lady Head Top, Set Of 5 .... 35.00
St.Louis, Crystal, Deep Blue Overlay, Atomizer, Set Of 2 .... 195.00
St.Louis, Faceted Stopper, Gold Star 250.00
Tiffany, Sterling Silver, On Keychain 100.00
Triangular, Plunger Style, Plastic Rose, Austria, Glass 20.00
U.S.Glass Co., No.40, Clear, Gold Feet, Colorado 195.00
Victorian, Glass, Gold & Black Enameled, Panel Cut Stopper 55.00
Wembdon Lavender, 1936 .... 15.00
White Enameling, Green Satin Glass, 5 In. 60.00
With Atomizer, Steuben, Swirl Pattern, Devilbiss Top 425.00

PERFUME, Lamp, Colonial Lady, Marked Japan, 5 1/2 In.	40.00
Stork Club, Advertising, Original Contents	20.00
Victorian Tear, Gild, 6 1/2 In.	35.00

Peters & Reed Pottery Company of Zanesville, Ohio, was founded by John D. Peters and Adam Reed in 1897. Chromal, Landsun, Montene, Pereco, and Persian are some of the art lines that were made. The company became Zane Pottery in 1920, Gonder Pottery in 1941, and closed in 1957. Peters & Reed was unmarked.

PETERS & REED, Basket, Hanging, Moss Aztec	28.00 To 35.00
Bowl, Butterfly, Green	16.00
Bowl, Mottled Blue, Gray, Beige, 6 X 2 In.	35.00
Bowl, Pereco, Laurel Branches & Berries, 9 In.	65.00
Bowl, Raised Laurel Branches, Matte Green Interior	60.00
Bowl, Swirling Blue & Gray Design, 6 X 2 In.	30.00
Bowl, Vines & Berries, Brown Tints, Green, 8 X 3 In.	35.00
Jardiniere, Pedestal, 31 In.	275.00
Jug, Ball, Grapes & Leaves, Brown Glaze, 6 1/4 In.	75.00
Jug, Sprigged On Ear Of Corn, Single Handle, Glaze, 5 1/2 In.	95.00
Mug, Applied Grapes, Aventurine Glaze	35.00
Pitcher & Mug, Cavalier Heads, Brown High Gloss	125.00
Pitcher, Grapes & Leaves, Brown Glaze, 12 In.	90.00
Powder Box, Covered, Landsun, Marked	30.00
Vase, Aztec Nude, 9 In.	15.00
Vase, Brownware, 11 In.	35.00
Vase, Bud, Teapot Shape, Floral	35.00
Vase, Landsun, Bulbous, Marked, 6 1/2 In.	35.00
Vase, Montene, 12 In.	225.00
Vase, Moss Aztec, Floral, Cone Shape, Ferrell, 8 In.	35.00
Vase, Shadow Ware, Blue Drip, Ivory Ground, 9 In.	85.00
Vase, Sprigged Floral, Squat, Footed	35.00 To 40.00
Wall Pocket, Egyptian Profile, Asp, Green, 8 In.	65.00
Wall Pocket, Moss Aztec, 8 1/2 In.	45.00
PETRUS REGOUT, see Maastricht	

The Pewabic Pottery was founded by Mary Chase Perry Stratton in 1903 in Detroit, Michigan. The company made many types of art pottery including pieces with matte green glaze and an iridescent crystalline glaze. The company continued working until the death of Mary Stratton in 1961. It was reactivated by Michigan State University in 1968.

PEWABIC, Ashtray, Blue Iridescent, 5 In.	125.00
Bowl, Green Drip, 4 1/2 In.	135.00
Cup & Saucer, Iridescent	150.00
Dish, Turquoise Over Lime, Scalloped, Round	125.00
Plate, Zodiac, Tube Lined, Crackle & Blue Iridescent	165.00
Tile, Raised Center White Flower, Turquoise, Paper Label, 5 In.	99.00
Vase, Beige, Globe Form, High Gloss, Incised Mark, 8 1/4 X 8 In.	125.00
Vase, Blue Matte, Backward Impressed Mark, 3 3/4 In.	210.00
Vase, Blue Streaked, Fold Over Lip, Incised, 6 In.	130.00
Vase, Green & Yellow Glaze, Deep Green Luster Drip, 2 1/2 In.	295.00
Vase, Hourglass Shape, Flared Rim, Pedestal, Label, 1925, 5 1/4 In.	550.00
Vase, Squat, Blue Metallic Luster, 4 X 2 1/2 In.	225.00

Pewter is a metal alloy of tin and lead. Some of the pewter made after 1840 has a slightly different composition and is called "Britannia metal." This later type of pewter was worked by machine; the earlier pieces were made by hand.

PEWTER, Ashtray, Woman's Face	20.00
Basin, Communion, American	192.50
Basin, Compton, Thomas & Townsend, London, 10 1/2 X 2 5/8 In.	175.00
Basin, Hammered Booge, English, 7 3/4 In.	105.00
Basin, Incised Line Bottom, Eagle Mark, T.D.B., 19th Century, 7 In.	50.00

Basin, Samuel Hamlin, Scroll Mark, 7 7/8 In. 550.00
Beaker, 3 Handles, 3 In. 75.00
Beaker, Glass, Vienna Cathedral, 1/4 Liter 33.00
Beaker, Trask, 5 In. 320.00
Bedpan, Screw Off Handle, Evans & Mathews, 11 1/4 In. 50.00
Board, Springerle, Animals 45.00
Bottle, Cologne, Barrel, Brass Spigot, 1900, 3 1/4 X 2 1/4 In. 54.00
Bottle, Nurser, English, C.1800, 5 1/4 In. 150.00
Bowl, 5 In. 25.00
Bowl, 7 3/4 X 1 In. 40.00
Bowl, Footed, American, 5 1/2 In. 50.00
Bowl, Footed, Britannia, 4 3/8 In. 95.00
Bowl, Shallow, German, Oval, 8 X 1 1/4 In. 40.00
Bowl, Vaughan, 3 3/4 X 7 1/4 In. 22.00
Box, Cigar, Liberty & Co., Tudric, Hammered Turquoise Matrix, 8 In. 150.00
Box, Cigarette, Wood Lined, Chase, 7 1/4 X 3 1/4 In. 45.00
Box, Cigarette, Wood Lined, Wooden Hinged Lid, 6 X 3 3/4 In. 18.00
Box, Desk, Double Hinged Lid, Round Legs 35.00
Cake Tray, Hammered, Handles, 10 In. 45.00
Candle Snuffer, Stylized Designs, Nekrasoff 15.00
Candlestick, 9 1/2 In., Pair 155.00
Candlestick, Beaded, Cylindrical, Drip Pan, L.K., London, 8 In., Pair 300.00
Candlestick, Bobeche, 7 1/2 In. 40.00
Candlestick, Ejector, Lewis & Cowles, Saucer Base, 4 5/8 In. 190.00
Candlestick, Fuller & Smith, 8 1/4 In., Pair 795.00
Candlestick, Handled Saucer, 6 7/8 In. 140.00
Candlestick, Push–Up, Meriden, 1860 .... 75.00
Candlestick, Saucer Bobeche, Vase Stem, Ohio, C.1840, 9 3/4 In., Pair 100.00
Candlestick, Single, R.Gleason, 6 7/8 In. 295.00
Candlestick, T.B.M. Co., 6 3/8 In., Pair 775.00
Candlestick, Wm.Bartholdt, Willimsburgh, Long Island, 8 7/8 In., Pair 775.00
Canister, Tea, 20 In. 195.00
Castor, Rosworth Gleason, Dated 1854 .... 98.00
Chalice, Boardman, 7 In., Pair 600.00
Chalice, Footed, I.Trask, 5 3/4 In., Pair 750.00
Chalice, German, Knopped Stem, Marked, C.1760, 7 1/4 In. 280.00
Chalice, Marked Boardman & Co., New York, 11 1/4 In. 1300.00
Chalice, Reed & Barton, 7 1/4 In. 95.00
Chalice, Scotland, C.1800, 8 3/4 In. 295.00
Charger, English, 16 In. 325.00
Charger, Gabriel Charton, Dated 1690, 13 In. 125.00
Charger, J.Mettery, 9 In. 50.00
Charger, Rim Stamped A.S., English, 15 In. 150.00
Charger, Samuel Danforth, Hartford, Connecticut, 13 1/4 In. 850.00
Charger, T.Letherbarn, 16 1/2 In. 165.00
Charger, Thomas Deacon Of London, C.1678, Hallmarked, 18 1/4 In. 425.00
Cocktail Shaker, Fruit Finial, Hammered, Domed Cover, 13 1/2 In. 25.00
Coffeepot, Calder, Lighthouse Style, 10 7/8 In. 435.00
Coffeepot, D.Curtiss Mark 210.00
Coffeepot, Etched Dates, Flowers, & Leaves, Swedish, Dated 1856 .... 68.00
Coffeepot, J.B.Woodbury, Eagle Mark, 11 1/8 In. 375.00
Coffeepot, Lighthouse Shape, F.Porter 365.00
Coffeepot, Massachusetts, Wood Finial, Pear Shape, C.1835, 11 1/2 In. 275.00
Commode, Birch & Villers, Birmingham, 7 1/4 In. 42.50
Compote, Art Deco, Geometric, Stylized Ram Finial, Swedish 165.00
Compote, Flagg & Homan, Marked, C.1842 .... 100.00
Creamer, Whitlock, Troy, N.Y., 5 1/4 In. 155.00
Cup, Church, Raised Design, Trask, 3 In. 95.00
Cup, Drinking, English, 3 In. 20.00
Cup, Measuring, Tulip Shape, Handle, V & Crown, Yates, 1/2 Pt. 57.00
Cuspidor, Signed Josiah Danforth 70.00
Dipper, Ball Shape, Wooden Handle 32.50
Dish, Deep, Thomas Danforth, Philadelphia, C.1800, 11 1/2 In.Diam. 330.00
Dish, English, 3 In. 20.00

Dish, English, 4 In. 12.00
Dish, Footed, Kayserzinn, 10 In. 50.00
Dish, Tudric, Scroll Design, Flared Base, Handles, Signed, 3 X 13 In. 100.00
Dish, Twig Handles, No.4065, Kayserzinn, 10 In. 50.00
Ewer, Liberty, Tudric, 14 In. 150.00
Figurine, Deer, Chinese, 28 1/2 In. 275.00
Flagon, Eben Smith, Beverly, Massachusetts, 1813–56, 1 Qt. 1100.00
Flagon, I.Trask, 10 1/2 In. 695.00
Flagon, Tappit Hen, Incised Design, Dome Cover, Handle, 10 1/2 In. 275.00
Goblet, Reed & Barton 20.00
Hot Plate, Touchmark, London, Handles, 8 3/8 In. 45.00
Ink Pot, English, 19th Century, 3 1/4 X 2 3/8 In. 115.00
Inkwell, Hinged Lid, Flat Base, 5 1/2 In. 60.00
Jar, Spice, Screw Top, English, 4 In. 90.00
Ladle, Gravy, Long Handle, Side Spout 50.00
Ladle, Marked Savage, 12 1/2 In. 95.00
Lamp, Aladdin, No.4439, Kayserzinn, Complete, 10 In. 160.00
Lamp, Bull's-Eye, 8 1/2 In. 390.00
Lamp, Copper Wick Support, Drip Pan, Repaired, 9 1/4 In. 95.00
Lamp, Petticoat, Bell Shape, Scrolled Ear Handle, American, 5 1/2 In. 85.00
Lamp, Whale Oil, Bull's-Eye 395.00
Lamp, Whale Oil, Ring Handle, American, C.1840, 5 1/2 In. 110.00
Lamp, Whale Oil, Saucer Base, 7 1/2 In. 50.00
Loving Cup, Animal Scenes, Handles, Kayserzinn, 1900, 9 1/2 X 10 In. 85.00
Measure, Gaskell & Chambers, 2 In. 35.00
Measure, Handle, James Yates V & Crown, 1 Qt. 94.00
Measure, Initial C M Left Of Handle, English, 1770–90, 1 Qt. 490.00
Measure, James Yates, 19th Century, 1 Gill 62.00
Measure, James Yates, 19th Century, 1 Qt. 245.00
Measure, James Yates, 19th Century, 1/10 Pt. 42.00
Measure, James Yates, 19th Century, 1/2 Pt. 90.00
Measure, James Yates, 19th Century, 1/4 Gill 32.00
Measure, Scotland, Crested Tappit Hen, 12 In. 775.00
Measure, Tankard, Gloucester, Imperial Quart, 7 In. 40.00
Measure, Tankard, Hinged, Thumbpiece Marked Imperial Gill, 4 In. 105.00
Measure, Yates, 1 Qt. 75.00
Mold, Candle, 4-Tube, Set Into Stand 440.00
Mold, Candle, 12-Tube, Footed Stand, 12 In. 450.00
Mold, Candle, 18-Tube, Pine Frame, D.Francis, Buffalo, N.Y. 700.00
Mold, Chocolate, Heart 5.00
Mold, Chocolate, Rabbit 75.00
Mold, Chocolate, Rabbit, Sitting, Clamps, 6 In., 2 Piece 70.00
Mold, Chocolate, Turkey 65.00
Mold, Ice Cream, 2 Tiny Morning Glories, Miniature 45.00
Mold, Ice Cream, 3-Part, Santa Claus, Standing, 12 In. 325.00
Mold, Ice Cream, American Beauty Rose K582 .... 27.50
Mold, Ice Cream, Asparagus 40.00
Mold, Ice Cream, Baby ....38.00 To 45.00
Mold, Ice Cream, Ball 25.00
Mold, Ice Cream, Banana 55.00
Mold, Ice Cream, Basket Of Flowers, 2 7/8 In. 30.00
Mold, Ice Cream, Battleship 120.00
Mold, Ice Cream, Bride & Groom 40.00
Mold, Ice Cream, Bunch Of Grapes 55.00
Mold, Ice Cream, Candle, Jack Be Nimble 130.00
Mold, Ice Cream, Car 85.00
Mold, Ice Cream, Cauliflower, French, 1 Qt. 125.00
Mold, Ice Cream, Chicken, Small 25.00
Mold, Ice Cream, Child On Bicycle, C & M., 4 1/2 In. 50.00
Mold, Ice Cream, Chinaman 75.00
Mold, Ice Cream, Christmas Tree E1154 .... 45.00
Mold, Ice Cream, Corn 29.00
Mold, Ice Cream, Cupid & Heart 34.00
Mold, Ice Cream, Cupid On Puffy Heart, Hinged 30.00

453

Mold, Ice Cream, Dahlia, E & Co. 37.50
Mold, Ice Cream, Eagle 85.00
Mold, Ice Cream, Floral No.13 .... 20.00
Mold, Ice Cream, Floral No.240 .... 20.00
Mold, Ice Cream, Floral No.554 .... 20.00
Mold, Ice Cream, Football 26.00
Mold, Ice Cream, Heart 45.00
Mold, Ice Cream, Hen 34.00
Mold, Ice Cream, Lily ....26.00 To 60.00
Mold, Ice Cream, Mandolin 90.00
Mold, Ice Cream, Masonic Symbol ....12.00 To 25.00
Mold, Ice Cream, Peach Half With Seed 22.00
Mold, Ice Cream, Potato 16.00
Mold, Ice Cream, Pumpkin, E & Co. 37.50
Mold, Ice Cream, Pumpkin, No.600 .... 30.00
Mold, Ice Cream, Puss 'N Boots 42.00
Mold, Ice Cream, Rabbit 37.00
Mold, Ice Cream, Rooster, Small 160.00
Mold, Ice Cream, Rose 65.00
Mold, Ice Cream, Santa Claus K427 .... 45.00
Mold, Ice Cream, Santa Claus, E & Co. 65.00
Mold, Ice Cream, Sedan 42.00
Mold, Ice Cream, Spade 20.00
Mold, Ice Cream, Squirrel 140.00
Mold, Ice Cream, Stork 75.00
Mold, Ice Cream, Turkey ....18.00 To 65.00
Mold, Ice Cream, Wedding Bell 80.00
Mug, Alleys Ale 50.00
Mug, Boardman, 1/2 Pt. 95.00
Mug, Child's, Danforth, 2 1/2 In. 240.00
Mug, Danforth, Family Initials On Front, 1 Pt. 295.00
Mug, English, 1 Pt. 20.00
Mug, James Yates, English, Owner's Initials, 19th Century, 1 Pt. 115.00
Mug, Joseph Morgan, 1/2 Pt. 50.00
Mug, Palethorpe, Philadelphia, 1 Pt. 425.00
Mug, Tulip Shape, Gerardin & Watson, London, 19th Century, 1 Pt. 130.00
Pitcher, Marked X, 9 In. 650.00
Pitcher, Samuel S. Hersey 2145.00
Pitcher, Tavern, Side Spout, English 110.00
Pitcher, Water, Covered, Boardman, 2 Qt. 295.00
Pitcher, Water, English, 9 In. 295.00
Pitcher, Water, Open, Boardman, Lion Mark, 1 Gal. 650.00
Pitcher, Water, Open, R.Dunham, 2 Qt. 450.00
Planter, Hanging, Bow Front, 11 1/2 In. 25.00
Plate, Ashbil Griswold, 7 7/8 In. 350.00
Plate, Blakeslee Barns, 1812–17, 7 7/8 In. 175.00
Plate, Collection, Boardman Warranted, 10 3/4 In. 495.00
Plate, Compton, London, 7 3/4 In. 55.00
Plate, England, Washington Crest, Marked SE, 8 1/4 In. 225.00
Plate, Francis Basset, Beaded Rim, Marked, 9 7/16 In. 595.00
Plate, Jacob Whitmore, Middletown, Ct., 7 7/8 In. 275.00
Plate, John Skinner, Boston, 1760–90, Hallmark, 9 1/8 In. 400.00
Plate, Lily–Of–The–Valley, Nude, Art Nouveau, Signed WMFB AS, 10 In. 300.00
Plate, Multiple Reed, Ralph Marsh, Family Initials, C.1680, 9 1/8 In. 175.00
Plate, R.A.Boston, 1792–1817, 7 7/8 In. 315.00
Plate, Richard Yates Mark, 8 In., Pair 150.00
Plate, Rim Stamped R.T., English, 9 1/2 In. 70.00
Plate, Samuel Danforth, Eagle Mark, 8 In. 355.00
Plate, Samuel Ellis Mark, English, 7 3/4 In. 55.00
Plate, Semper Eadem, Boston, Marked, 18th Century, 8 1/2 In. 350.00
Plate, Thomas Badger, Boston, Late 18th Century, 8 1/2 In. 375.00
Plate, Thomas D.Boardman, Marked, 8 3/8 In. 265.00
Plate, W.Scott, English, 9 3/4 In., Set Of 11 .... 300.00
Platter, Flower, Crown, Name & Dated 1690, Knife Marks, 12 1/2 In. 195.00

Porringer, Basin Type, Boardman, 4 In. 260.00
Porringer, Basin Type, Danforth, 3 5/8 In. 230.00
Porringer, Basin Type, Lee, 3 5/8 In. 270.00
Porringer, Heart & Moon Design, Initial R, 4 1/8 In. 255.00
Porringer, N.E.& N.Y., Old English Pattern, 4 In. 265.00
Porringer, Pierced Handle, Marked Stede, Bowl, 4 In. 52.00
Porringer, Pierced Handles, Marked T.D. & S.B., 3 1/4 In. 400.00
Porringer, Robert Bush, Sr., Crown Handle, 1770–80, 4 In. 325.00
Porringer, Trefoil Handle, Heart Cutout, 3 7/8 In. 85.00
Porringer, Vine Design, Lee, 2 In. 295.00
Pot, Wooden Handle & Finial, James Dixon & Sons, 12 1/2 In. 135.00
Salt, English, 18th Century, 3 3/8 X 3 In. 155.00
Salt, Master, Cobalt Blue Liner, James Dixon & Sons 75.00
Salt, Viking Ship Shape 20.00
Saltshaker, T.Wilkenson & Sons 50.00
Sealer, Wax, Woman, Art Nouveau 20.00
Snuffbox, Floral Design, American, 1810 .... 85.00
Spittoon, Ring Handle, American, 7 In.Diam. 60.00
Spoon, Touchmark L.B., Heart Design Back Of Bowl, 8 In., Set Of 5 .... 125.00
Stein, Eagle Beak Spout, Wings On Base, Kayserzinn, 13 1/2 In. 495.00
Stein, Hinged Cover, Applied Cartouche, Monogram, Dated 1771, 8 In. 100.00
Stein, Hinged Top, Friedrich Ferdinand Braune, German, 1797, Initials 85.00
Sugar, Covered, Square Base 45.00
Sugar, Creamer, & Tray, Flagg & Homan, Marked, American, C.1842 .... 225.00
Syrup, Hall & Cotton, 6 In. 175.00
Syrup, Mug Form, Connecticut, C.1840, 5 3/4 In. 235.00
Tankard, Domed Cover, Tulip Shape, Double C Scroll Handle, 8 1/4 In. 200.00
Tankard, Fleur–De–Lis Crest, Dolphin Thumbpiece, Continental 85.00
Tankard, Hinged Lid, Thumbpiece, 4 1/4 In. 35.00
Tankard, Measure, English, Side Spout, 1 Qt. 40.00
Tazza, Hammered, Sheffield 50.00
Tazza, Hammered, Studded, Griffin, Handles 90.00
Tea Caddy, Fluted, Chased Banding, Initials In Oval, Oval, English 265.00
Teapot, Acorn Top, T.Danforth & S.Boardman, Hartford, 9 1/2 In. 210.00
Teapot, American, Marked D.W.K., Connecticut, 7 3/4 In. 250.00
Teapot, Boardman, Eagle & Double X Mark 535.00
Teapot, Conical Cover, Spherical Body, Marked I.Curtiss, 9 In. 250.00
Teapot, Continental, Individual, 7 1/4 In. 95.00
Teapot, D.Curtiss, Scroll Touch, 8 In. 210.00
Teapot, Dome Top, Bulbous, Marked, 6 3/4 In. 50.00
Teapot, Foo Dog Finial, Japanese, Seal On Bottom, C.1800, 9 In. 150.00
Teapot, Gooseneck, 19th Century, 6 1/2 In. 48.00
Teapot, H.Yale & Co., Wallingford 320.00
Teapot, Melon Sectioned, Marked Dixon & Sons, English, 7 1/4 In. 110.00
Teapot, Melon Shape, Wooden Knob & Handle, 6 1/2 In. 60.00
Teapot, Queen Anne Style, Charles Yale, C.1825, 7 In. 100.00
Teapot, Roswell Gleason .... 325.00 To 475.00
Teapot, Sellew & Co., Cincinnati, Wooden Lid Finial, 7 1/4 In. 325.00
Teapot, Tea Caddy, Japanese, Seal On Bottom, C.1820, 5 In. 75.00
Teapot, Thomas D.Boardman, Eagle With Initials, 9 In. 135.00
Tray, Dragonflies, Fish, Lilies, Stamped Kayserzinn, 24 1/2 In. 225.00
Tray, Leaf Shape, Nekrassoff, 16 In. 45.00
Tray, Tea, 2 Handles, Leaf Design, Signed Tudric, C.1901, 20 In. 100.00
Vase, Bullet Shape, 3 Handles, Liberty & Co., C.1902, 11 1/2 In. 350.00
Wine Server, Spout, Abraham Ganting, 12 1/2 In. 1000.00

*Phoenix Bird, or Flying Phoenix, is the name given to a blue–and–
white kitchenware popular between 1900 and World War II. A
variant is known as Flying Turkey. Most of this dinnerware was made
in Japan for sale in the dime stores in America. It is still being made.*

PHOENIX BIRD, Cup & Saucer 30.00
Cup & Saucer, Demitasse 22.00
Dish, Moriage, Fish Shape 40.00
Eggcup, Double 12.00

Plate, 6 In.	3.00
Strainer, Tea, China	26.00
Syrup, No Lid, 5 In.	65.00
Teapot, Stick Handle, Demitasse, 6 In.	140.00

Phoenix Glass Company was founded in 1880 in Pennsylvania. The firm made commercial products such as lampshades, bottles, and glassware. Collectors today are interested in the sculptured glassware made by the company from the 1930s until the mid-1950s. The company is still working.

PHOENIX, Bowl, Lovebirds, Bronze, Iridescent Lining, 10 1/4 X 5 In.	125.00
Compote, Fish, Amber	65.00
Lamp, Berries & Foliage, Aqua & Orange On White, 24 In.	75.00
Lamp, Foxglove, Orange, Aqua, & White, 14 In.	145.00
Lamp, Foxglove, Salmon, Green, & White, 10 1/2 In.	100.00
Lamp, Peony, Pink, Green, Brown, & White, 6 1/2 In.	70.00
Lamp, White & Yellow Mums, Marble Base, 13 In.	110.00
Lamp, Woodrow Wilson, Doughboys, Liberty Bell Shade, Marked, 16 In.	115.00
Rose Bowl, Sculptured Flowers, Rose Pink Ground, Label, Large	125.00
Shade, Lamp, Ribbed, 6 1/4 In.	24.00
Vase, Amethyst Owls, 5 1/2 In.	70.00
Vase, Blown-Out Nudes, Blue & White, Label, 14 1/2 In.	475.00
Vase, Blue Fish, Tails On Yellow Ground, 8 X 9 1/2 In.	250.00
Vase, Blue Flowers, Cream Satin Ground, 9 1/2 In.	95.00
Vase, Brown, White, Bluebells, 7 In.	50.00
Vase, Cream, Blue Berries, Brown Leaves, 9 3/4 X 4 1/2 In.	120.00
Vase, Dancing Nudes, Flesh & White, 12 In.	395.00
Vase, Dancing Nudes, Frosted, 12 In.	95.00
Vase, Dogwood Blossoms, Paper Label, 11 In.	125.00
Vase, Dogwood, Tan, Green, Custard, 10 1/2 X 6 1/2 In.	90.00
Vase, Fan, Grasshopper, Amber, Frosted, 8 1/2 8 X 3 3/4 In.	80.00
Vase, Frosted Emerald Green, Allover Floral, 12 In.	140.00
Vase, Grasshoppers & Leaves, Purple, 8 X 7 In.	85.00
Vase, Lovebirds, Pillow, Brown, 6 1/4 X 5 1/2 In.	68.00
Vase, Madonna, Cream Ground, White Sculptured Head, 10 In.	225.00
Vase, Madonna, Sculptured Head Back & Front, Cream, 10 1/4 In.	225.00
Vase, Madonna, Sculptured Head, Cream Ground, 10 In.	235.00
Vase, Molded Flowers, Wisteria Blue, Satin Glass, Bulbous, 11 In.	275.00
Vase, Nude Design, Triangular, Green, 7 1/2 In.	35.00
Vase, Opalescent Purple Owls, Pillow Shape, 5 3/4 In.	32.50
Vase, Pink Birds On Each Side, Light Ground, 6 X 4 1/2 In.	75.00
Vase, Praying Mantis, Pillow, Amethyst, 7 In.	110.00
Vase, Sculptured Lovebirds, Cream Ground, 10 1/2 In.	180.00
Vase, Star Flowers, Ball Shape, Pink Ground, Label, 7 In.	65.00
Vase, Tan Owls, Turquoise Boughs, White Ground, 6 In.	75.00
Vase, Turquoise Leaves, Red Berries, White Opaque Ground, 10 In. ...	85.00
Vase, White Daisies On Brown, Label, 10 X 10 In.	125.00

The tin cases that held phonograph needles are collected today by music and phonograph enthusiasts and advertising addicts. The tins are very small, about 2 inches across, and often have attractive graphic designs lithographed on the tin.

PHONOGRAPH NEEDLE, Tin, Bell Tower, Red	10.00
Tin, Britain Best, Red	7.00
Tin, Compagnion, Green	8.00
Tin, Dog & Baby, Red	15.00
Tin, Greyhound, Green	12.00
Tin, Meritone, Green	8.00
Tin, Nita, Red	10.00
Tin, Ondulette, Blue	15.00
Tin, Parrot, Red	14.00
Tin, R.C.A., Yellow	12.00
Tin, Songster, Yellow	7.00
Tin, Zenith, Green	12.00

The phonograph, invented by Thomas Edison in the 1880s, has been made by many firms. This section also includes other items associated with the phonograph. Records and jukeboxes are listed in their own sections.

PHONOGRAPH, Busy Bee Disc	450.00
Camerphone, Black	175.00
Capital Cuff, Style D, Coin–Operated, 21 Cuffs	3800.00
Columbia, AB, McDonald	1200.00
Columbia, AF	1200.00
Columbia, AN	400.00
Columbia, AU	475.00
Columbia, Lyric Reproducer	75.00
Columbia, Model B1, Oak Horn	1600.00
Columbia, Oak, 2 Minute Cylinder, Black, Brass Horn	395.00
Columbia, Regent, Desk	285.00
Dancing Doll, Fit On Disc, Ragtime Rastus	85.00
Dancing Doll, Ragtime Rastus & Boxing Darkies, Nat'L.Toy	510.00
Doll, Mae Starr	385.00
Edison Amberola 30	230.00
Edison, 2 Heads, Model C–250	225.00
Edison, Amberola 30, Oak Case, Inside Horn, 4 Minute Cylinder	295.00
Edison, Amberola 75, Oak Case	450.00
Edison, Concert, Crane, Black & Brass Horn, 5 Records	2000.00
Edison, Cylinder, Brass Horn, Crank	575.00
Edison, Ediphone, Voice Writer, Cylinder Shaver, Accessories	500.00
Edison, Gem A, Banner Decal, Keywind	350.00
Edison, Gem, 4 Minute Attachment	335.00
Edison, Gem, Cylinder	495.00
Edison, Home, Cignet Horn, Oak	1250.00
Edison, National, Tin Morning Glory Horn, Records, 13 1/2 In.	375.00
Edison, Radio, C4 Model	700.00
Edison, Standard Cylinder, Horn, 31 In.	285.00
Edison, Standard, Morning Glory Horn	425.00
Edison, Standard, Outside Horn	285.00
Edison, Triumph, Oak Horn ....750.00 To	1600.00
Edison, Windsor Model, Floor Model, Coin–Operated	7500.00
Gem Edison, Cylinder, Oak, Horn, Crank, 1906, 8 1/4 X 10 In.	300.00
Harmony, Horn ....135.00 To	425.00
Hexaphone, Regina, With Sign	4500.00
Jay–O–Phone, Glass Window Front, Mahogany	595.00
Jukebox, Bing Crosby Jr.	225.00
Jukebox, Chicago, Coin–Operated	700.00
Jukebox, Mills, Ferris Wheel, 78	1000.00
Jukebox, Risteaucrat, Counter Top	250.00
Jukebox, Seeburg, KT	11000.00
Jukebox, Seeburg, Library Model, Oak	250.00
Jukebox, Victor Orthophonics, Model10–50X	1000.00
Jukebox, Victor VTLA, Serial 1933, 1st Upright Model	850.00
Jukebox, Wurlitzer, 1942, Model 850A	7500.00
Jukebox, Wurlitzer, Counter Model	3500.00
Jukebox, Wurlitzer, Model 61, Countertop	875.00
Jukebox, Wurlitzer, Model 1015 ....4500.00 To	5000.00
Jukebox, Wurlitzer, Model 1100, 1947	1700.00
Jukebox, Wurlitzer, Model 1400	975.00
Jukebox, Wurlitzer, Model L	5500.00
Lamp, Organophone, No Shade	975.00
Music Master, Speaker, Wooden Horn	100.00
Music Master, Wooden Horn, Mahogany Case	600.00
Pathe, Leather Horn	750.00
Pathe, Oak, 15 Records	650.00
Seeburg, Nickelodeon, EX, With Accordion	9600.00
Thorens, Portable, Brown Leather, Folds	115.00
Victor I, Matching Small Oak Wooden Horn	1500.00

Victor III, Oak Horn ....1500.00 To 1800.00
Victor IV, Mahogany Wooden Horn 1800.00
Victor, Columns & Press Carving 450.00
Victor, English O, Black Metal Horn, 78 RPM 495.00
Victor, Model D, Nickel Horn 950.00
Victor, Model M, Wooden Horn 900.00
Victor, Model MS, Metal Horn, Oak Case 850.00
Victor, Model V, Petal Horn 1200.00

The first photograph was a view from a window in France taken in 1826. The commercially successful photograph started with the daguerreotype introduced in 1839. Today all sorts of photographs and photographic equipment are collected. Albums were popular in Victorian times. Cartes de visite were cardboard-mounted photographs popular in the years after the Civil War. Stereo views are listed under Stereo.

PHOTOGRAPHY, Album, Actor Photographs, Set Of 60, C.1896 .... 75.00
Album, Leather, Dated 1885 .... 75.00
Ambrotype, Black Women 55.00
Ambrotype, Civil War, Full Standing View Soldier, Gilt Frame 64.50
Ambrotype, Dead Baby Girl, Holding Bouquet, Cased 65.00
Ambrotype, Young Man, Blue Velvet Case, Scroll Edge, 2 1/4 In. 65.00
Cabinet Card, 5 Men With Bicycles, C.1890 .... 12.50
Cabinet Card, Apache Women & Children, Captivity, Mobile, 1890s 65.00
Cabinet Card, Captain Bogardus, Sons, World Champion Shooters 50.00
Cabinet Card, Ferris Wheel At Columbian World's Fair 25.00
Cabinet Card, Giant Girl With Mother & Father, Sept.1897 .... 12.50
Cabinet Card, Girl & Boy At Tea 12.50
Cabinet Card, Indian Papoose In Backboard 30.00
Cabinet Card, Major & Mrs.Ray, Midget 15.00
Cabinet Card, Pomo Indians 65.00
Cabinet Card, Princer Tinymite, Midget 10.00
Cabinet Card, Running Antelope, Indian Police, 1880s 125.00
Calculator, F/Stops, Exposure Times, Sterling Silver Case 220.00
Camera, Ansco Shur-Shot Jr., Original Box 5.00
Camera, Ansco, No.10, Model A, Red Bellows 30.00
Camera, Argus, 44, 35 Mm 48.00
Camera, Argus, C-3, 35 Mm, Leather Case 60.00
Camera, Brownie, Junior 6, 16 .... 14.00
Camera, Brownie, Small, Canada, Original Box 10.00
Camera, Century, No.10-A, Betax No.4 Lens, Century Tripod 650.00
Camera, Ensign Greyhound, Dark Gray, Case 32.00
Camera, Ernmann, Double Bellows, 2 Original Film Holders 250.00
Camera, Filmagraph Corp., S.Easton, Mass., USA, 16 Mm, Metal Case 100.00
Camera, Gunblach Korona VII 75.00
Camera, Jiffy Kodak, Instructions 10.00
Camera, Kodak Bullet, Box 18.00
Camera, Kodak Duaflex Reflex 25.00
Camera, Kodak, 3A Model C, Autographic 22.50
Camera, Kodak, Box, Brown Target 616 .... 6.00
Camera, Kodak, Folding, Vest Pocket, 1902 .... 32.00
Camera, Kodak, No.1-A, Folding, Pocket, Weather Bellows, Pat.1908 .... 32.50
Camera, Kodak, Vigilant 620 .... 1.00
Camera, Lucida, Double Prism, French, Case, C.1880 .... 160.00
Camera, Lucida, Leitz, Wezlar, 2 Swing-Away Filters, C.1910 .... 100.00
Camera, Minox C, Miniature, Case 85.00
Camera, Movie, Bell & Howell, Film 45.00
Camera, Polaroid Land, No.240, Automatic 12.00
Camera, Polaroid, Model 80A, Flash, Meter, Original Case 18.00
Camera, Polaroid, Model 95, Leather Case 35.00
Camera, Remington, Miniature 15.00
Camera, Rochester, Wood 75.00
Camera, Seneca Camera Co., Rochester, N.Y., Case, 4 Wood Slides 75.00
Camera, Seneca Scout, Original Box 75.00

Camera, Speed Graphic, 120 Mm	175.00
Camera, Trumpfreflex, Meyer Gorlitz, 3.5 Lens, Compur Shutter	40.00
Camera, Voigtlander, Bessa 1, 120 Film	25.00
Camera, Welta, Superfecta, 100 Mm, Horizontal, Vertical, C.1934	300.00
Camera, Wollensak Optical Co., Jar.Model, Original Case, 1901	125.00
Camera, Zeiss Ikon, Kalart Sync.Range Finder	40.00
Carte De Visite, Black Girls, Lynchburg, Va., C.1880, Set Of 3	25.00
Carte De Visite, Black People	9.00
Carte De Visite, Booth In Top Coat & Gloves	65.00
Carte De Visite, Dead Child, J.Reid, Patterson, N.J., C.1862	8.00
Carte De Visite, Edwin Hay Cameron, Cameron	175.00
Carte De Visite, Entrance Burlington Photo Co.Studio, Vt.	65.00
Carte De Visite, John Wilkes Booth, Sitting With Cane	27.50
Carte De Visite, Robert E.Lee, Profile, Vannerson, 1864	150.00
Carte De Visite, Tom Thumb & Wife, Mathew Brady, Photographer	68.00
Carte De Visite, Tom Thumb's Wedding	20.00
Carte De Visite, Union Soldier, Heimbach's, Allentown, Pa.	22.50
Carte De Visite, Wild Bill Hickok, 1870s	125.00
Daguerreotype, Boy, Staffordshire Dog On Table, 1/6 Plate	100.00
Daguerreotype, Elderly Woman, Bonnet, Stamped, Cased, 1/6 Plate	35.00
Daguerreotype, Man, Fraternal Pin On Neckerchief, 1/6 Plate	50.00
Daguerreotype, Niagara Falls, Platt Babbitt, Oval, Full Plate	3630.00
Enlarger, Signed Thornton Pickard, Altrincham, England	375.00
Magic Lantern, 150 Slides	190.00
Magic Lantern, 50 8–In.Slides	275.00
Movie, Kellogg's Jungleland, 1909	25.00
Photograph, Arizona Indian, Orange Mount, C.1885	25.00
Photograph, Beach, Santa Cruz, G.Webb, Early 1900s, 5 X 7 In.	10.00
Photograph, Buffalo Bill Wild West Show	480.00
Photograph, Caboose, Oriental Ltd., Pre–1920, 5 1/4 X 4 In.	4.50
Photograph, Charles Lindbergh, 2 Pilots & Plane, 1920s	35.00
Photograph, Charles Lindbergh, Spirit Of St.Louis, 1927	125.00
Photograph, Child, White Dress, Tinted, 33 1/2 X 26 In.	180.00
Photograph, Connecticut National Guard, Red Cross, 1890s	30.00
Photograph, Cotton Market, Montgomery, Ala., 1890s	35.00
Photograph, Dinner, National Football League, 1934, 11 X 18 In.	18.00
Photograph, Gettysburg Battlefield, W.H.Tipton, Ivory, 1890	25.00
Photograph, Indian Chief, 5 X 7 In.	58.00
Photograph, Jamestown, N.D.Boy's Band, Framed, 1927, 6 X 15 In.	15.00
Photograph, Las Cruces, El Paso, Mexican Border, Military, 1916	30.00
Photograph, Man & Woman, Boat, Santa Cruz, G.Webb, 7 1/2 X 5 In.	10.00
Photograph, Marie McDonald, Autographed, 1956	35.00
Photograph, Marilyn Monroe, Autographed Back, 1956	85.00
Photograph, Pier & Fishermen, Santa Cruz, G.Webb.4 X 5 1/2 In.	7.50
Photograph, Rebel Works, Atlanta, Ga., No.5, Barnard View	350.00
Photograph, Sol Smith Russell, Autographed, 1880	12.00
Photograph, Victorian Woman, Sepia, Framed, 1890, 23 X 19 In.	80.00
Photogravure, Curley, Custer Scout, 1913	55.00
Photogravure, Indian Portrait, E.S.Curtis, 1900	135.00
Projector, Kerosene, Magic Lantern, 13 Slides, Lens	145.00
Projector, Movie, Keystone, Child's, Movie Bills, Tickets, 1928	58.00
Projector, Postcard, Radio Junior, Tin, North Bennington, Vt.	65.00
Screen, Movie, Kodak, No.I, Dovetailed Wooden Box	50.00
Stand, Camera, Collapsible, Wooden	24.00
Tintype, 2 Butchers Holding Implements, 3 1/2 X 2 1/2 In.	14.00
Tintype, 2 Civil War Men In Full Uniform, 2 1/2 X 3 In.	20.00
Tintype, 6 Men Scene, 1 Playing Violin	8.00
Tintype, Card Players, 1/6th Plate, Case	30.00
Tintype, Cowboy Wearing Boots, Holding Straw Hat	20.00
Tintype, Girl With Large Doll	35.00
Tintype, Horse & Buggy	20.00
Tintype, Little Black Girl, Case, Dated 1857	70.00
Tintype, Man Playing Violin, 2 X 3 In.	7.50
Tintype, President Franklin Pierce, Full Uniform With Sword	3850.00

Tintype, Union Officer, 3/4 Seated View, 2 1/2 X 3 In.	84.50
Tintype, Union Sergeant, Cased	65.00
Tintype, Union Soldier, Battlefield, 3 X 4 In.	45.00

About 1880, the well–decorated home had a shawl on the piano. Bisque piano babies were designed to help hold the shawl in place. They range in size from 6 to 18 inches. Most of the figures were made in Germany. Reproductions are being made.

PIANO BABY, Blond Girl Sitting, Bonnet, Pulling Off Socks, Heubach, 6 In.	275.00
Crawling, Foot In Air, Green & White Bonnet, Heubach, 7 In.	195.00
Hertwig & Co., C.1910, 2 1/2 In.	195.00
Holding Sock, 8 In.	125.00
Laying On Back, Touching Toes, Marked, 4 In.	95.00
Laying On Stomach, Ready For Thumb In Mouth, White Gown, 9 In.	325.00
Legs Crossed, Arms Raised, White Gown, Pink Trim, Marked, 10 In.	400.00
Lying, Rattle In Hand, Dog Climbing On Her, 9 In.	195.00
Nude Blond Boy, Squatting, Holding Toes, Heubach, 6 In.	375.00
Nude, Sitting, Intaglio Googly Eyes, Arms Away, Heubach, 5 In.	145.00
On Back, Hands Touching Left Foot, Aqua, 8 1/2 In.	325.00
Sitting, Feeding Cat From Dish, Bald Head, German, 8 1/2 In.	175.00
Sitting, Girl Holding Puppy, Pacifier In Mouth, 11 In.	250.00
Sitting, Hand To Ear, Nude, 4 1/2 In.	35.00
Sitting, Holding Gold Watch To Ear, Gown, German, 7 In.	145.00
Sitting, Lacy Dress, Jeweled Moth On Skirt, German, 10 In.	225.00
Sitting, Playing With Toes, White Shift, Blue Trim, 3 3/4 In.	80.00
Sitting, Touching Toes, White Gown, Aqua Trim, Marked, 9 1/2 In.	375.00

Pickard China Company was started in 1898 by Wilder Pickard. Hand–painted designs were used on china purchased from other sources. In the 1930s, the company began to make its own china wares. The company now makes many types of porcelains including a successful line of limited edition collector plates.

PICKARD, Bonbon, Garden Scene, Roses, Scalloped, 1912, Signed, 7 In.	75.00
Bowl, Coufall, Autumn Ground, Gold Rim, Pedestal, Marked, 11 X 5 In.	385.00
Bowl, Enchanted Garden Scene, Octagonal, Artist Signed, 9 In.	150.00
Bowl, Gold Ground, Fruits In Center, Signed, 10 1/2 In.	255.00
Bowl, Gold Interior, Scene Around Outside, 6 3/4 In.	295.00
Bowl, Oranges In Foreground, Artist Vokral, 4 In.	35.00
Bowl, Poppy Pattern, Signed, 9 In.	65.00
Bowl, Red Poppies, Gold Trim, 10 In.	160.00
Bowl, Roman Garden Scene, Signed, Handles, 7 3/4 X 6 1/4 In.	140.00
Bowl, Scenic, Gold Interior, Matte Finish, Signed, 6 3/4 In.	295.00
Box, Covered, Design, Signed Beautlich, 8 In.	150.00
Cake Plate, Fruit On Blue Gold Center, Signed, Handles, 12 In.	110.00
Cake Plate, Gold Center, Strawberries, Signed, 12 In.	130.00
Candy Dish, Divided, Covered, Handles, 6 1/4 In.	45.00
Celery, Violets, Gold Trim, Boat Shape, 12 In.	65.00
Coffeepot & Creamer, 1912–19	55.00
Coffeepot & Creamer, Enameled Bands & Gold Flowers, 1912	75.00
Compote, Grapes & Leaves Inside & Out, Gold Trim, Artist Signed	150.00
Compote, Grapes & Leaves, Signed, Marked	150.00
Creamer, Stylized Lilies, Signed, 4 1/2 In.	85.00
Cup & Saucer, Leon, Signed	95.00
Cup & Saucer, Souvenir, 1910, Full Size	30.00
Cup, Child's, Humpty–Dumpty	10.00
Cup, Child's, Little Boy Blue	10.00
Dessert Set, Donatello Pattern, Signed, 12 Piece	250.00
Dish, Dessert, American Buffalo	138.00
Pitcher, Fruit & Blossoms, Gilded Top & Bottom, Signed, 7 3/8 In.	225.00
Pitcher, Red Currants, Leaves, Gold Border, Handle, Signed, 9 1/2 In.	245.00
Plate, 3 Hand Painted Birds, Gold Trim, 8 1/2 In.	55.00
Plate, Blues, Moon, Trees, Matte Finish, Signed, 8 1/2 In.	195.00
Plate, Branch Of Gold, Nuts On Pastel Ground, 1905 Mark, 7 1/2 In.	35.00
Plate, Floral, Max Klipphan, 8 1/2 In.	77.00

Plate, Garden Scene Wall, Pierced Handle, 7 In.	225.00
Plate, Gold Center, Fruit & Floral Border, Leaf Mark, 10 3/4 In.	30.00
Plate, Gold, Random Edge, Open Handles, 10 1/2 In.	40.00
Plate, Oriental Poppies, Gold Trim, Signed Gasper, 9 In.	145.00
Plate, Pink Oak Leaves, Gold Design, Marked, C.1912, 6 3/4 In., Pair	35.00
Plate, Poppies, Yellow Ground, Artist F.James, Circle Mark, 9 In.	125.00
Plate, Purple, Violets, Leaves, Signed, 6 1/2 In.	24.00
Plate, Scalloped Gold Edge, Violets, 9 In.	58.00
Plate, Scenic, Blues, Matte Finish, Signed James, 8 3/4 In.	189.00
Plate, Scenic, Gold Etched Border, Signed Marker, 10 In.	125.00
Plate, Scenic, Moon, Trees, Signed James, Matte Finish, 8 3/4 In.	195.00
Plate, Shamrock & Gold Band Design, 10 In.	65.00
Plate, Violets, Gold Trim, Artist Signed, 9 In.	70.00
Punch Set, Shaded Leaves, Gold Border, 10 Cup, Artist M.Rosti Leroy	1250.00
Relish, Violets In & Out, Gold, Boat Shape, Circle Mark, 8 3/4 In.	45.00
Salt & Pepper, Ora Lorgenta, Signed Hess	28.00
Saltshaker, Poppy Design, Gold, Artist Signed Fox	65.00
Sugar & Creamer, Floral, Challinor	30.00
Sugar & Creamer, Open, Gondola Type, Handles, Artist Signed, 1898	100.00
Sugar Shaker, Violet Design, Coin Gold Top, Artist Signed, 1910	195.00
Tray, Open Handles, Square, 9 1/2 In.	45.00
Vase, 3 Lilies, Gold Collar, Signed, 8 3/4 In.	135.00
Vase, Art Nouveau, Gold, Signed, 10 1/2 In.	225.00
Vase, Floral, Water Lilies, Silver Band, Signed Osborne, 7 In.	150.00
Vase, Grecian Shape, Pheasant, Gold & Black Ground, Signed, 8 In.	225.00
Vase, Italian Garden Scene, Challinor, Maple Leaf Mark, 12 3/4 In.	595.00
Vase, Lake Scene, Gold Handles, Signed Markel, 6 In.	145.00
Vase, Lake Scene, Trees, Signed E.Challinor, Maple Leaf, 5 1/4 In.	395.00
Vase, Stylized Flowers, Trailing Leaves, Gold Trim, 6 1/2 In.	145.00
Vase, Water Lily Pattern, Artist Signed, 7 1/2 In.	295.00

PICTURE FRAME, see Furniture, Frame

Pictures like silhouettes and small decorative pictures are listed here. Some other types of pictures are listed under Print or Painting.

PICTURE, Cutout, Birds & Leaves, 14 1/2 In.	75.00
Cutout, Garden, Framed, 15 In.	75.00
Hair, Floral Wreath, Harriet Nelson, Nevada City, 1870, Framed	400.00
Mourning, Cutwork, Miss Wonson, Boston, April, 1827, 10 X 8 In.	1320.00
Silhouette, 2 Children & Dog, Baltimore, 1840, 12 3/4 X 15 3/4 In.	700.00
Silhouette, A.Lincoln, 6 X 8 In.	10.00
Silhouette, Child, Full, Gilt Highlights, Frame, 7 3/4 X 12in.	210.00
Silhouette, Child, On Plaster, Geo.Breece, Edinburgh, 4 X 5 In.	95.00
Silhouette, Double, Laughing Gentleman & Lady, 6 1/2 X 5 1/2 In.	165.00
Silhouette, Gentleman, Eglomise, Oval Frame, 3 3/4 X 4 1/2 In.	85.00
Silhouette, Gentleman, Full Length, Aug.Edouart, 1828, 8 X 12 In.	120.00
Silhouette, Gentleman, Ink & Pencil, Frame, 3 7/8 X 4 7/8 In.	45.00
Silhouette, Gentleman, Ink, Watercolor, Framed, 10 1/2 X 13 In.	170.00
Silhouette, Gentleman, Matthew Smith, 5 3/4 X 6 3/4 In.	70.00
Silhouette, George & Martha Washington, Pair	25.00
Silhouette, George Johnson & Family, Edouart, 1836, 11 X 8 1/2 In.	425.00
Silhouette, Lady With Lace Bonnet, Collar, Oval Center, Black Frame	90.00
Silhouette, Man & Woman, Walnut Frame, 5 1/4 X 6 3/8 In., Pair	200.00
Silhouette, Man With Top Hat, Oval Center, Black Frame	60.00
Silhouette, Man, 3 1/2 X 5 1/2 In.	40.00
Silhouette, Man, Pam K, 3 X 4 In.	45.00
Silhouette, Man, Pigtail, Colored Dress Suit, Oval Center, Frame	40.00
Silhouette, Preacher At Lecturn, Apr.30, 1836, 9 1/4 X 11 1/4 In.	185.00
Silhouette, Printed On Linen, Embroidered, 10 X 13 In.	105.00
Silhouette, S.Littlefield, Children, Edouart, 1841, 11 X 8 1/2 In.	425.00
Silhouette, Two New Englanders At Ease, 7 1/2 X 9 In.	575.00
Silhouette, Woman Sitting On Chair, 11 In.	35.00
Silhouette, Woman, Bonnet, Frame, Peale Museum, 5 1/2 X 7 1/2 In.	145.00
Silhouette, Woman, Ink & Pencil, Frame, 3 7/8 X 4 3/4 In.	47.50
Silhouette, Young Woman, Ink, Framed, 4 1/4 X 5 1/4 In.	45.00

Tinsel, Reverse Painted Floral, Frame, 4 7/8 X 5 7/8 In. 40.00

The Pigeon Forge Pottery was started in Pigeon Forge, Tennessee. Red clay found near the pottery was used to make the pieces. Molded or thrown pottery with matte glaze and slip decoration was made. The pottery is still working.

PIGEON FORGE, Candle Bowl, Mottled Browns, 5 In.Diam. 12.00
Flower Frog, Green, 5 In. 30.00
Jug, 7 1/2 In. 19.00
Pitcher, Green, Lady Slipper Incised, 4 In. 12.00
Tile, Flower, Green Rim, Round, 5 In. 30.00
Wall Pocket, 4 In. 22.00

The Pilkington Tile and Pottery Company was established in 1892 in England. The company made small pottery wares like buttons and hatpin heads but soon started decorating vases purchased from other potteries. By 1903, the company had discovered an opalescent glaze that became popular on the Lancastrian pottery line. The manufacture of pottery ended in 1937 but decorating continued until 1948.

PILKINGTON, Vase, Lapis Ware, Globular, 10 In. 60.00
Vase, Lapis Ware, Royal Lancastrian, Globular, 10 In. ....50.00 To 55.00
Vase, Lapis Ware, Straight Sides, 10 In. 75.00

The pincushion doll is not really a doll and often was not even a pincushion. The top half of a doll was made of porcelain. The edge of the half-doll was made with several small holes for thread, and the doll was stitched to a fabric body with a voluminous skirt. The finished figure was used to cover a hot pot of tea, a powder box, a pincushion, a whiskbroom, or a lamp. They were made in sizes from less than an inch to over 9 inches high. Most date from the early 1900s to the 1950s.

PINCUSHION DOLL, Arms Away, Japan, 4 1/4 In. 25.00
Arms Away, Lady Holding Mirror, German 75.00
Art Deco, Black Hair, Green Gown, 6 3/4 In. 70.00
Art Deco, Pierrette Head As Powder Puff, French, Box 95.00
Art Deco, Porcelain Torso, Legs, Satin Cushion, Lace, 7 In. 85.00
Bisque, Half, Satin & Lace 35.00
Blond Hair, Cellophane Wrapped, Orchid Gown 20.00
Blond Molded Hair, Hands At Face, Pink Bodice 25.00
Bride, 1 1/4 In. 38.00
Dancing Girl, China 24.00
Dog, Full Figure 48.00
Dressel Kister, 2-Faced 135.00
Egg Head, Art Deco, Full Figure 45.00
Flapper, Arms Extended, Hat, Beads, Green Blouse, 4 1/4 In. 295.00
Flapper, On Broom 18.00
Flapper, Wearing Cloche, German 42.00
Flapper, With Compact, 4 1/2 In. 185.00
Girl, Full Figure, Blue Suit, Germany, 3 3/4 In. 95.00
Girl, Gold Bra, Original Cushion, 4 In. 275.00
Girl, Mardi Gras, Marked Germany, 3 In. 75.00
Head, Bald, Movable Arms, Germany, 5 In. 225.00
Jenny Lind, Goebel, 3 1/2 In. 95.00
Jester Head, Sew Holes, Artist Mark, 2 1/2 In. 65.00
Lady, Gray Hair, Hand To Hair, Germany, 3 3/4 In. 30.00
Lady, Orange Hat, Marked Deutschland, 4 In. 165.00
Lady, Top Hat, Holding Flowers, Germany, 3 In. 45.00
Lady, White Hair, Arms Away, Germany, 18th Century, 4 In. 98.00
Pierrette, Pink, White Ruffle, 3 In. 65.00
Porcelain, Blond, Blue Hair Ribbon, Germany, 3 In. 25.00
Senorita, Spanish, 5 In. 95.00
Spanish Dancer, With Comb, Earrings, Castanets, 11 In. 225.00
Spanish Senorita, Blue Comb, Black Lace, Germany, 8 3/4 In. 75.00

With Skirt, German, 5 1/2 In. 25.00
PINK SLAG, see Slag, Pink

Pipes have been popular since tobacco was introduced to Europe by Sir Walter Raleigh. Meerschaum pipes are listed under Meerschaum.

PIPE, Amber, Leather Case 25.00
   Black Man, Poking Alligator In Bowl, Hand Carved, 10 In. 150.00
   Carved, Figural, Climbing Dog, Wooden 12.00
   Dog, Clay, Miniature 14.00
   Dunhill, 1939 Receipt, Original Box 100.00
   German Military Commemorative, Motto, Porcelain, C.1890, 2 Piece 250.00
   Graf Zeppelin Shape, Bakelite Stem, Briarwood Bowl, 5 1/2 In. 130.00
   Holder, F. Jones Ales, Clay 50.00
   Italian Briar, Elephant Head, Glass Eyes, Tusks, C.1925 .... 25.00
   Ivory Bowl, Ivory & Amber Stem, 2 1/4 In. 8.00
   Opium, Bamboo Stem, Malachite Bit & Bowl, 6 3/4 In. 89.00
   Porcelain, Man & Dog, Hand Painted, German 79.00
   Red Clay, Bearded Man, Tooled Hair, Molded, 2 5/8 In. 30.00
   Rosewood, Carved Stag On Bowl, Victorian 100.00
   Stag On Bowl, Carved Band, Rosewood 100.00
   Tamp, Britannia, Brass, 2 7/8 In. 25.00
   Tamp, Bust Of Sir Walter Drake, Brass, 2 3/8 In. 15.00
   Tamp, Dickens Character, Man & Woman, Pair 75.00
   Tamp, Leg, Pewter 55.00
   Tamp, Medallion Tip, Bust Of Mater Jesu Christie, Sole Clarior, Brass 20.00
   Tamp, Robin Hood, Marked England, Brass, 2 1/4 In. 30.00

Pirkenhammer is a porcelain manufactory started in 1802 by Friedrich Holke and J. G. Lilst. It was located in Bohemia, now Brezova, Czechoslovakia. The company made tablewares usually decorated with views and flowers. Lithophanes were also made. The mark of the crossed hammers is easy to remember as the Pirkenhammer symbol.

PIRKENHAMMER, Vase, Avant Garde, Gold Foliage, Portraits, C.1850, 19 In., Pair 595.00
   Vase, Renaissance Portrait, C.1850, 19 In., Pair 650.00

Pisgah pottery pieces that are marked "Pisgah Forest Pottery" were made in North Carolina from 1926. The pottery was started by Walter R. Stephen in 1914, and after his death in 1941, the pottery continued in operation. The most famous types of Pisgah Forest ware are the cameo type with designs made of raised glaze and the turquoise crackle glaze wares.

PISGAH FOREST, Candlestick, 4 In. 45.00
   Pitcher, Blue Glaze, 3 1/2 In. 15.00
   Sugar & Creamer, Blue 22.00
   Teapot, Turquoise, 1941 .... 65.00
   Vase, 1937, Turquoise, 4 1/2 In. 36.00
   Vase, Blue Over Ivory, Pink Interior, Signed, 7 In. 100.00
   Vase, Cameo, Stagecoach Scene, Signed Stephen, 8 In. 265.00
   Vase, Glossy Green, 1942, 3 In. 20.00
   Vase, Turquoise Crackle, Cream Interior, 1933, 8 In. ....20.00 To 50.00
   Vase, Turquoise To Aubergine, 5 1/2 In. 35.00

Planters Nut and Chocolate Company was started in Wilkes–Barre, Pennsylvania, in 1906. The Mr. Peanut figure was adopted as a trademark in 1916. National advertising for Planters Peanuts started in 1918. The company was acquired by Standard Brands, Inc., in 1961. Some of the Mr. Peanut jars and other memorabilia have been reproduced; and, of course, new items are being made.

PLANTERS PEANUTS, Ashtray, Mr.Peanut, Ceramic 60.00
   Ashtray, Mr.Peanut, Glass 30.00
   Bag, Shopping, An American Tradition, 1940 .... 25.00
   Bank, Hard Plastic, Red 5.00
   Book, Coloring, Presidents, Unused, 1963 .... 10.00

Book, Paint, Mr.Peanut, Historical, 1949 .... 10.00
Can, Pennant Brand, 10 Lb. 175.00
Canister, Pennant Brand, No Lid, 10 Lb. 40.00
Container, Peanut Shape, Papier–Mache, 11 In. 55.00
Dish, Mr.Peanut Center, Metal, 4 1/2 In. 30.00
Display, Full Figure, Eyes Light Up, Plaster Of Paris 2500.00
Figurine, Mounted On Fence Post, Cast Iron, 38 In. 2450.00
Funnel, Oil, 2 Piece 15.00
Hat, Halloween, Rubberized 58.50
Holder, Mr.Peanut, Papier–Mache, 12 1/2 In. 185.00
Jar, Barrel Shape, 100 Label 230.00
Jar, Barrel, Embossed Mr.Peanut, Silvering, 1930, 12 In. 70.00
Jar, Barrel, Peanut Finial Lid, Silvering, 1930, 12 1/4 In. 60.00
Jar, Bulbous Peanuts & Peanut Finial Lid, Round, 14 In. 185.00
Jar, Clipper 75.00
Jar, Fishbowl, Label 100.00
Jar, Leap Year 50.00
Jar, Nut Lid, Square 38.00
Jar, Pennant Salted Peanuts, Octagonal, C.1930, 12 1/2 In. 40.00
Jar, Running Man ....120.00 To 125.00
Jar, Square ....45.00 To 65.00
Jar, Storage, Relief Peanut Corner, 1920, 13 3/4 In. 110.00
Jar, Store, Glass Lid, Peanut Finial, Square 50.00
Knife, Figural, 7 In. 35.00
Lamp 100.00
Marbles, Unopened Bag, Mr.Peanut On Top 35.00
Mug, Figure Of Mr.Peanut 10.00
Mug, Red 3.50
Nut Chopper, Tin 15.00
Pen, Figural, Mr.Peanut 8.00
Pencil 20.00
Pencil, Mechanical, Mr.Peanut Floating In Liquid 20.00
Pencil, Mr.Peanut 10.00
Salt & Pepper, 4 In. 10.00
Salt & Pepper, Mr.Peanut, 3 In. 7.50
Scoop, Serving, Tin 45.00
Server, Peanut On Rim, Silver Plate 12.00
Tin, 10 Lb. 75.00
Toy, Jumbo Blocks, Box 10.00
Tumbler, Embossed, Peanut Finial, Square 50.00
Whistle, Figural 15.00
Wristwatch, Mr.Peanut 30.00

> *Plated amberina was patented June 15, 1886, by Edward D. Libbey*
> *and made by the New England Glass Works. It is similar in color to*
> *amberina, but is characterized by a cream–colored or chartreuse*
> *lining (never white) and small ridges or ribs on the outside.*

PLATED AMBERINA, Vase, 6 In. 1700.00

> *Plique–a–jour is an enameling process. The enamel is laid between*
> *thin raised metal lines and heated. The finished piece has transparent*
> *enamel held between the thin metal wires. It is different from*
> *cloisonne because it is transparent.*

PLIQUE–A–JOUR, Bowl, Green Ground, Swimming Goldfish, Seaweed, 5 In. 695.00

> *All types of political memorabilia are collected from buttons to*
> *banners. Items related to presidential candidates are the most popular,*
> *but collectors also search for material related to state and local*
> *offices. Many reproductions have been made.*

POLITICAL, Armband, Repeal & Roosevelt, Red Felt, Framed, 3 X 16 In. 47.50
Badge, Inauguration, Harry S.Truman & Alban W.Barkley, 1949 .... 600.00
Badge, Sheriff, Republican National Convention, Enamel Center 17.50
Badge, Shield Shape, Nixon & Agnew, 1969, Eagle Top, White House 250.00
Badge, Wages For Debs 134.00

Bandanna, Hancock, White, Red, Black, Framed, 1880, 19 X 21 In. 145.00
Bandanna, Washington, Grant Head, Framed, 1876, 25 X 30 In. 100.00
Bank, John F. Kennedy, Bust 10.00
Bank, Pocket, Wilson & Marshall, 3 Dimensional 770.00
Banner, Alfred Smith 52.50
Banner, Clay & Frelinghuysen, C.1844 .... 2600.00
Banner, Cleveland & Thurman 160.00
Banner, Douglas & Herschel Johnson, Glazed Cotton 4100.00
Banner, Douglas & Johnson, C.1860 .... 800.00
Banner, Grover Cleveland, Flag, Oval Bust, Framed, 24 X 31 In. 300.00
Banner, Lincoln & Hamlin 8250.00
Banner, McKinley Portrait, Blue, White Stars, Framed, 17 X 23 In. 125.00
Bar, Silver, Watergate, Nixon, See No Evil, Case, Louise Aleo 95.00
Book, St.Onge Inaugural Address, John Kennedy, Miniature 18.00
Book, Vantage Point, Lyndon Johnson, First Editon, Signed, 1971 .... 150.00
Booklet, LaFollette Campaign, 1920 .... 8.00
Bookmark, Woodrow Wilson, Lines Of Poetry, Convention Of 1912 .... 35.00
Bottle, General Ulysses S.Grant 20.00
Bottle, Humphrey & Muskie, Green, 1968 Campaign 20.00
Bottle, John F.Kennedy 25.00
Bottle, Nixon & Agnew, Amber, 1968 Campaign 20.00
Bust, President Grant, Pewter, 4 In. 25.00
Bust, President Kennedy, Bronze Finish 25.00
Button, All The Way With Adlai 15.00
Button, Barry Goldwater For President, Picture, 6 In. 5.00
Button, Bryan, Keaton, Jugate, Sepia, 1908 .... 350.00
Button, Byron, Sewall, Jugate 85.00
Button, Carter, Set Of 3 .... 1.00
Button, Corregan, Cox, Jugate 440.00
Button, Debs & Hanford, Jugate, Socialist Party, 1904 .... 150.00
Button, Downtown Tammany Club, Star, Ribbon, 1 In. 15.00
Button, For President Wm.M.Taft, Picture, 1 1/4 In. 38.00
Button, Ford, Set Of 3 .... 1.00
Button, Franklin D. Roosevelt, 5/8 In. 12.00
Button, Geraldine Ferraro, 3 1/2 In. 3.00
Button, Hubert Humphrey, Caricature, 7/8 In. 2.00
Button, Hughes & Bruce Jugate, 7/8 In. 28.00
Button, Ike, Dick, Jugate, They're For You, 1 In. 8.00
Button, Inaugural, Hoover, Picture, 1929, 1 1/4 In. 22.00
Button, John Davis, 7/8 In. 95.00
Button, Johnson, Humphrey, Jugate, Vote Democratic, 7/8 In. 1.50
Button, Keep America Strong, Reagan '84, Bodybuilder 3.00
Button, Mamie Eisenhower, Oval, 3/4 In. 4.00
Button, McKinley Eclipse, Clouds Around Portrait, 1 1/4 In. 175.00
Button, McKinley, Hobart, Jugate 55.00
Button, Minnesota Truman Club, 2 1/4 In. 45.00
Button, Missouri Minute Men For Roosevelt 20.00
Button, Nixon & Lodge, Jugate, Celluloid, 5/8 In. 5.00
Button, Nixon Now, Celluloid, 5/8 In. 4.00
Button, Nixon, Agnew, Jugate, Striped Ground, 3/4 In. 1.35
Button, President Wilson, Portrait 10.00
Button, Rockefeller For President, Picture, 6 In. 6.00
Button, Ronald Wilson Reagan, Cowboy Hat, 1980 Inaugural, 1 In. 3.50
Button, Roosevelt, Babcock, Jugate 50.00
Button, Senior Citizens For Kennedy, 5/8 In. 1.50
Button, Stevenson, 1960, Picture, 7/8 In. 50.00
Button, Taft, Art Nouveau, Peach Ground, 3/4 In. 50.00
Button, Teddy Roosevelt, 2 In. ....10.00 To 22.00
Button, Truman, Barkley, 3 1/4 In. 175.00
Button, Truman, Jugate, 1 1/4 In. ....99.00 To 119.00
Button, U.S.For Ike, Picture, Striped Shield, 6 In. 18.00
Button, Women For Mondale In '84, 1 In. 1.00
Calligraphy, John C.Fremont, Republican, James Buchanan, Democrat 220.00
Campaign Hat, Teddy Roosevelt, Original Silk Ribbon, Tan Felt 275.00

Canteen, Lincoln, Garfield, McKinley, Ceramic, Portraits, 5 3/8 In.	85.00
Car Attachment, Roosevelt For All Mankind, Red, White, & Blue, Tin	15.00
Cigar Box, FD Roosevelt	27.50
Cigar, Hoover	12.00
Cigarette Silk, For Governor Wm.Randolph Hearst, 1 In.	6.00
Cigarette Silk, Wm.McKinley, 3 1/4 In.	18.00
Clock, Electric, F.D.R.At Helm, Bronze Spelter, 14 X 9 In.	135.00
Compact, I Like Ike	29.50
Cookbook, Congressional, Congressman Wives Recipes, C.1933	22.00
Doll, Barry Goldwater, Plastic	12.00
Doorstop, Capitol Design, Picture Of F.D.Roosevelt, Bronze	305.00
Flag, Benjamin Harrison, Silk, Framed, 1892, 10 X 13 3/4 In.	235.00
Flag, Roosevelt, Battle, 1912	45.00
Gum Card Set, Kennedy	20.00
Hat, Nixon, Campaign, Lodge	8.00
Hatchet, Carrie Nation Your Loving Home Defender	65.00
Horseshoe, Bryan, Kern, 1908, Brass	20.00
Invitation & Program, Goldwater & Brown Reception, 1961	11.00
Invitation, Eisenhower Inaugural Ball, Envelope	25.00
License Plate, Wallace, 1968, Metal	5.00
Mirror, Pocket, Hoover, Iowa, 2 1/8 In.	200.00
Mug, F.D.Roosevelt, New Deal	15.00
Mug, Nixon & Agnew, Frankoma, 1973	20.00
Nodder, Teddy Roosevelt, C.1904	355.00
Pamphlet, Life Of William McKinley, Memorial Edition, 1901	10.00
Paperweight, Herbert Hoover, Bronze, Box	39.00
Parade Torch, 1868, Wood Staff, Tin, Grant Campaign	95.00
Peanut, Jimmy Carter, Windup	10.00
Pencil Box, Herbert Hoover	50.00
Pennant, Landon & Knox, Small	8.00
Photograph, Woodrow Wilson, Autographed, At Desk, 9 1/2 X 13 In.	275.00
Pin, Alf Landon, Sunflower, Picture, 1 1/4 In.	9.00
Pin, Inaugural, Ribbon, Eisenhower & L.B.J.	15.00
Pin, McKinley Memorial, Picture	9.00
Pin, Truman Inauguration, Picture	10.00
Pin, Welcome Home Ike, Ribbon, Picture	5.00
Pin, Welcome Teddy, Printed On Teeth Of Animal, Tin	75.00
Plaque, Teddy Roosevelt, Bronze	35.00
Plate, 1956 Republican National Convention, Vernon Kilns	35.00
Plate, McKinley, Protection & Plenty, 45 Stars, 7 1/4 In.	55.00
Plate, Portrait, McKinley, White, Gold Trim, 8 In.	20.00
Plate, Roosevelt, Bears Digging Panama Canal, Verse, Pink, 6 In.	47.50
Plate, Roosevelt, Bears, Dancing, Molly Coddles, Verse, 7 In.	47.50
Plate, Teddy Roosevelt Center Transfer, Death Date, 9 1/2 In.	25.00
Plate, Wilson Center Transfer, Gold Trim, Brown & White, 6 In.	30.00
Portrait, On Ivory, 24 Presidents, W.A.Patterson, 1865–1939	1600.00
Poster, Coolidge, Economy, 21 X 30 In. ....*Color*	350.00
Poster, Geraldine Ferraro, Liberty	25.00
Poster, Herbert Hoover For President, Portrait, 1928, 18 X 23 In.	15.00
Poster, Wilson Fights For America & Humanity, 1917, 20 X 18 In.	90.00
Poster, Wilson, Lincoln & Washington Medallions, Framed	55.00
Presidential Fact Finder Wheel, Kennedy & Johnson, Paper	8.50
Program, Roosevelt & Fairbanks Inaugural, 1905	30.00
Program, Truman Inaugural, 1949	16.00
Puzzle, Administration, Blaine In, Harrison Get Him Out, Blocks	100.00
Ribbon, Fisk & Brooks, Third Party, 1888	165.00
Ribbon, Harrison & Morton	90.00
Ribbon, Harrison Tippecanoe Club	100.00
Ribbon, Inaugural, Nixon	5.00
Ribbon, Lincoln, By Matt Brady, 1860	400.00
Ribbon, Martin Van Buren, Silk	425.00
Ribbon, Portrait, Grover Cleveland, Dated 1888, 1 1/2 X 4 In.	20.00
Ribbon, Young Men's Democratic Club, 1892	15.00
Ring, Al Smith	20.00

Ring, Hoover, Elephant Insignia, 1928	28.00
Salt & Pepper, Figural, John Kennedy In Rocking Chair, 1962	22.00
Salt & Pepper, Lyndon Johnson And Lady Bird	15.00
Sheet Music, Coolidge & Dawes	10.00
Spoon, Washington To F.Roosevelt, Rogers, Silver Plate, 31 Piece	47.50
Teapot, Ronald Reagan, Hall China	40.00
Textile, Horace Greeley, B.Gratz Brown, Dec.12, 1871, 33 X 38 In.	2625.00
Thimble, Coolidge, Dawes	12.00
Thimble, Hoover	15.00
Token, Herbert Hoover For President, Brass, 1928	15.00
Torch, Campaign, Tin	10.00
Torch, Parade, Red, White, & Blue	300.00
Toy, Tricky Dick, Figural	25.00
Toy, Wm.Gladstone & Lord Palmerston, Figure, Papier–Mache, Wooden	225.00
Trash Can, Spiro Agnew, Chein, 1970s	20.00
Trivet, President & Mrs.Kennedy	15.00
Tumbler, Beer, Ike Eisenhower, 1953	10.00
Tumbler, McKinley, Etched	21.50
Umbrella, Sun, McKinley & Hobart, Red, White & Blue Panels	525.00
Watch Fob, Bust Of Lincoln, Republican National Convention, 1920	20.00
Watch Fob, Cox, Roosevelt, 1920	60.00
Watch Fob, Roosevelt, 1912–16, Brass	22.00
Watch Fob, Woodrow Wilson For President, Celluloid, 5 1/2 In.	55.00
Watch, Nixon, I'm Not A Crook	1550.00
Wristwatch, Spiro Agnew	75.00

Pomona glass is a clear glass with a soft amber border decorated with pale blue or rose–colored flowers and leaves. The colors are very, very pale. The background of the glass is covered with a network of fine lines. It was made from 1885 to 1888 by the New England Glass Company. First grind was made from April 1885 to June 1886. It was made by cutting a wax surface on the glass, then dipping it in acid. Second grind was a less expensive method of acid etching that was then developed.

POMONA, Bowl, Cornflower, Crimped Rim, 2nd Grind, 8 In.	255.00
Cruet, Toed Base, 2nd Grind, Original Stopper	265.00
Cup, Cornflower Design, First Grind	40.00
Decanter & 6 Wines, Gold Band Design	35.00
Finger Bowl, Ruffled, Amber Edge, 2nd Grind, 6 In.	100.00
Finger Bowl, Thumbprint	35.00
Finger Bowl, Underplate, Amber Rim, Ruffled, 2nd Grind	75.00
Pitcher, Clear, Square Top, 1st Grind, 4 1/2 In.	150.00
Pitcher, Water, Thumbprint, 3 Tumblers	225.00
Toothpick, 1st Grind	35.00
Toothpick, Amber Top, Ruffled Ring Collar	210.00
Toothpick, Tricornered	130.00
Tumbler, Blue Cornflowers, Leaves, 3 3/4 In.	145.00
Tumbler, Cornflower, Amber, 2nd Grind	75.00
Tumbler, Juice, Amber, Acanthus Leaves, 2nd Grind	114.00
Tumbler, Juice, Hobnail Design, Tapered, 3 3/4 In.	67.50
Tumbler, Lemonade, Handle	50.00
Water Set, 1st Grind, 6 3/4 In. Pitcher, 7 Piece	750.00
PONTYPOOL, see Tole	

Popeye was introduced to the Thimble Theater comic strip in 1929. The character became a favorite of readers. In 1932, an animated cartoon featuring Popeye was made by Paramount Studios. The cartoon series continued and became even more popular when the old movies were used on television starting in the 1950s. The full–length movie with an actor as Popeye was made in 1980.

POPEYE, Bank, Dime, 1956	38.50
Bank, Dime, C.1929	20.00 To 50.00
Book, Pop–Up, Popeye With The Hag Of The Seven Seas	125.00
Book, Popeye & The Pirates, Comic, Julian Wehr, Copyright 1945	85.00

Bottle, Soap, King Features, Colgate Palmolive Co., Plastic 5.00
Bubble Set, Pipe, Tin Soap Dish, Box, 1936 .... 10.00
Case, Pencil, Picture, Cardboard, 1934, 10 1/2 X 4 1/2 In. 17.50
Charm, Celluloid, Popeye Rolling Up Sleeve, 1930s, 1 1/4 In. 8.00
Charm, With Pipe, Celluloid, 1 1/8 In. 10.00
Christmas Lights, Original Box, 1930s 150.00
Cookie Jar, Blue Hat Cover, Features Outlined In Black Paint 250.00
Doll, Celluloid 15.00
Doll, Jointed, 5 In. ....42.00 To 60.00
Doll, Popeye & Olive, Rubber, Action Poses, 8 In., Pair 85.00
Doll, Vinyl Face & Hands, Stuffed Body, 14 In. 35.00
Figure, Jointed, Wood, 1930s, 5 1/2 In. 65.00
Figurine, Chalkware, 14 In. 25.00
Game, Bingo, 1929, 5 1/8 X 3 1/2 In. ....30.00 To 50.00
Game, Bubble Target, Metal, 1935 .... 95.00
Game, Card, 1934, Boxed 25.00
Game, Juggler 55.00
Game, Pipe Toss 22.00
Game, Sling Dart 22.00
Handkerchief, Picture Of All Characters 22.00
Kazoo 15.00
Lamp, 1935, No Shade 75.00
Lunch Box 10.00
Napkin Ring 30.00
Night–Light, Iron Boat, 1935 .... 385.00
Pail, Dinner, Thermos 10.00
Pail, Sand, Popeye At The Beach, Pictures Olive & Sweet Pea 60.00
Paint Box 23.00
Pencil Box, Cardboard 10.00
Pencil Sharpener, Figural 28.00
Pencil, Lead, Boxed 50.00
Pin, Enameled, Popeye & Olive Oyl 60.00
Puppet, Hand ....10.00 To 15.00
Puppet, With Olive Oyl, Strung, Pair 45.00
Puzzle, 1963, In Can 12.00
Puzzle, Set Of 2, Original Box, 1932 .... 35.00
Record, Blow The Man Down & Popeye The Sailor Man, Sleeve 15.00
Rug, Popeye & Sweet Pea, Hooked, White Ground, Red, Blue, 30 X 36 In. 27.50
Soap, 1930s, 5 Piece 15.00
Sparkler, 1930s 120.00
Spoon, Packaged, 1950s 14.00
Toy, With Parrots, Windup, Tin, Litho, 8 In. 70.00
Toy, Balancing Chair, Olive Oyl On His Chin, Windup, Tin, Linemar 850.00
Toy, Carrying Parrot Cages, Windup 125.00
Toy, Dippy Dumper, Linemar 325.00
Toy, Dippy Dumper, Windup, Tin, Litho, Marx, 8 1/2 In. 450.00
Toy, Dipsy Airplane, Orange Wings, Yellow 410.00
Toy, Donald Duck Duet, Marx 94.00
Toy, Drummer, 1932, Chein 450.00
Toy, Express, Overhead Plane, Box 585.00
Toy, Jigger, Windup, Tin, Litho, Marx, Original Box, 9 In. 375.00
Toy, Paddle Wagon, Corgi, Box 95.00
Toy, Pistol, Boxed, 1929 .... 110.00
Toy, Popeye & Olive Oyl, On Roof ....450.00 To 550.00
Toy, Puncher, Battery Operated 230.00
Toy, Punching Bag 395.00
Toy, Roller Skates 385.00
Toy, Sailboat, Wooden, King Features Syndicate, 1929 .... 230.00
Toy, Tank, Turnover, Windup, Tin, Litho, Marx, Original Box, 3 3/4 In. 220.00
Toy, Turnover Tank, Linemar ....95.00 To 110.00
Toy, Walking Popeye ....160.00 To 165.00

Porcelain, Figurine, Boy, Mandarin, Japan, 4 In.   Porcelain, Figurine, Dog, Japan, 5 In.

Major porcelain factories are listed in this book under the factory name. This section lists pieces that are by the less well-known factories.

PORCELAIN, Basket, Pink, Yellow & Blue Flowers, Union, Oblong, 4 3/4 In.	35.00
Bedpan, Eureka, England, 1890, 11 In.	12.00
Biscuit Jar, Hand Painted, Deer Hunter, Silver Plate, English	225.00
Bowl, Copper Rim, Mountain Landscape, Chinese, 8 1/8 In.	400.00
Bowl, Household Scenes, Polychrome Enamel, Oriental, 7 1/4 In.	170.00
Bowl, Ming Dynasty, Interior Cloud & Medallion, Stand, 6 In., Pair	575.00
Box, Cowl, Gilt Trim, 6 In.	55.00
Cake Plate, Indian, Reddish Orange, Royal Saxe, 9 3/4 In.	400.00
Cake Set, Polychrome Floral Spray, Scalloped, England, 15 Piece	425.00
Candlestick Urn, Covered, Baluster Shape, Gilt Design, 11 In., Pr.	250.00
Canister Set, White, Germany, 8 In., Set Of 6	115.00
Carpet Ball, Pink & White Sponged Design	95.00
Celery, Pink Roses, Green & Gold Trim, Scalloped, Austrian, 12 In.	43.50
Charger, Carp Design, Japanese, C.1880, 23 1/2 In.	950.00
Charger, Cloisonne On Tree Bark, Butterflies, Totai, 1890, 18 In.	725.00
Charger, Dragon Design, Chinese, 19th Century, 12 3/4 In.	1000.00
Charger, Spider Mum Design, Dark Blue Ground, Europe, 18 3/4 In.	275.00
Cheese Dish, Windsor, Beige, Floral, Crown Devon, 5 X 7 In.	80.00
Chocolate Set, Hand Painted, Jul.H.Brauer, Florals, 11 Piece	300.00
Condiment Set, 3 Musicians, Pastel, Germany, 2 1/4 In., 3 Piece	35.00
Creamer, Cow, Standing, Brown, 7 In.	35.00
Cup & Saucer, Dog, Pink, 3 1/2 In. ....*Color*	65.00
Cup & Saucer, Fortune Telling, England, Paragon	40.00
Cup & Saucer, Handleless, Floral Enameling, English	35.00
Cup & Saucer, Handleless, Floral Sprays, English	7.50
Cup & Saucer, Munich Child Scene	65.00
Cup & Saucer, Polychrome Enameling, Faith, Hope, Charity, English	10.00
Cup & Saucer, Russian, Kornilov Factory, 19th Century	135.00
Cup, Regimental, 166th Infantry	44.00
Dinner Set, Turquoise, Border, For E.V.Haughwout & Co., 75 Piece	440.00
Egg, Last Supper & Annunciation, Gilt Ground, Russian, 3 In., Pair	350.00
Ewer, Bacchus Head Is Spout, Pink Roses, Brown To Caramel Ground	150.00
Figurine, Boy & Girl, 18th–Century Clothes, 5 3/8 In., Pair	375.00
Figurine, Boy, Mandarin, Japan, 4 In. ....*Illus*	12.00
Figurine, Bulldog, Wearing Union Jack Flag, Crown Devon, 6 In.	65.00
Figurine, Clown, Signed Cappe, 12 In.	299.00
Figurine, Dachshund, Brown, Signed Hardie, 6 X 4 In.	35.00
Figurine, Dog, Japan, 5 In. ....*Illus*	15.00

Figurine, Fallen Drunken Man, Wife, Gardner, 19th Century, 7 In. 715.00
Figurine, Girl, Riding Side Saddle, Enameling, 3 1/4 In. 55.00
Figurine, Half Egg On Sled, Lily Of Valley, 2 1/2 In. 145.00
Figurine, Hand, Clomal Co., 1958, 5 1/2 In. 32.00
Figurine, Hippo, Standing, 1 1/2 X 3 1/2 In. 75.00
Figurine, Lady, Torch & Swan, Blue M Mark, 19th Century, 11 In. 375.00
Figurine, Madame Recamier, Signed Wagner, 2 X 1 5/8 In. 85.00
Figurine, Man, Marked China, 9 In. 145.00
Figurine, Old Couple Playing Cards, 10 X 7 In. 90.00
Figurine, Pekinese On Cushion, Tan & Brown, 4 1/4 In. 90.00
Figurine, Pillow Boy, Coral & Black Clothing, Chinese, 16 In. 200.00
Figurine, Retriever, Standing, Gray, White, Germany, 77 X 6 1/2 In. 48.00
Figurine, Sleeping Cupid, Crossed Swords Mark, 3 1/8 In. 98.00
Figurine, Temple God, Arita, Blue, Chinese, 19th Century, 10 In. 225.00
Figurine, Whippet, Sleeping, Impressed Artist Signature, 11 In. 85.00
Figurine, Woman Playing Spinet, Popov, 19th Century, 7 1/2 In. 770.00
Fish Bowl, Famille Noire, Polychrome Lotus, Lily & Duck, 16 In. 375.00
Flask, Sake, Japanese, Kakiemon, 4–Sided, Stopper, C.1800, 10 In. 115.00
Garden Seat, Blue Design, Maddock Works, 15 X 14 In. 325.00
Ginger Jar, Chinese, 8 In. ....*Color* 85.00
Humidor, Basket Weave, Figural Pipe On Lid, German, 6 X 7 In. 70.00
Jar, Covered, Celadon Finish, Gustavsberg, Sweden, 5 1/2 In. 600.00
Jardiniere, White, Orange Floral Design, Stand, England, 33 In. 400.00
Jug, Musical, John Peel, Brown Fox Handle, Crown Devon, 8 1/4 In. 195.00
Jug, Stacks Of Corn, Gilded, W.& E.Evans, C.1850, 14 In. 550.00
Lamp, Perfume, Colonial Lady, Japan, 5 1/2 In. 40.00
Lamp, Perfume, Colonial Lady, Japan, 7 In. 30.00
Mug, Polychrome Floral Design, German Inscription, Dated 1826 .... 10.00
Mug, Portrait, Ship, Caesar & Helene In Script, F.G.Hauthal & Co. 140.00
Mug, Stag Heads, Foliage, Earth Tones, Blown Out 45.00
Plaque, 19th–Century Nobleman Wearing Medals, 3 3/4 X 3 In. 150.00
Plaque, Head Of Spaniel, Greenery, Signed C.B.White, 15 X 17 In. 290.00
Plaque, Retriever Head, Black & White, 7 X 7 In. 45.00
Plaque, Tyrolean Tavern Scene, C.Bauer, 1900, Framed, 14 X 14 In. 2200.00
Plate, Cupids, Hand Painted, French 20.00
Plate, Portrait, Sitting Bull, Royal Saxe, 8 1/2 In. 125.00
Shoe, Green, 5 In. 20.00
Shoe, Pink, 5 In. 20.00
Soap Dish, Covered, Strainer, Blue & White Floral, Round 25.00
Spoon, Medicine, Germany 9.00
Sugar, Covered, Chinoiserie, Chinese Boy, 1765–75, 3 3/4 In. 1650.00
Teapot, Blue & White, Fruit & Foliage Design, Oriental, 5 3/4 In. 65.00
Teapot, Floral, Red Enameled, Gilt, Fluted, Oval, 6 5/8 In. 45.00
Tray, Hand Painted, Roses, Green Circular Band, Gilded, 15 3/4 In. 100.00
Tureen, Turtle Form, Chinese, 12 In. 110.00
Umbrella Stand, Blue, White Ground, Gold Dots, Oriental, 24 In. 120.00
Umbrella Stand, Blue, White, Brown Glaze, Molded Rim, 21 In. 80.00
Urn, Portrait, Maroon, Handles, Bulbous, K.Weingel, German, 12 In. 130.00
Vase, Amatory Scene, Hound, Gilt Lozenge, C.1790, 9 3/4 In., Pair 1100.00
Vase, Brown Water Lily, Slender Neck, Rosenburg, 3 X 6 1/2 In. 345.00
Vase, Butterflies, Floral Sprays, Mounted As Lamps, 14 In., Pair 200.00
Vase, Chein Lung, Calligraphy, Red Mark, 6 In. 310.00
Vase, Classical Maidens, Figural Handle, Royal Saxe 175.00
Vase, Covered, Portrait Reserves, Green, Electrified, Vienna 175.00
Vase, Imperial Yellow, 19th Century, 24 In. 900.00
Vase, Portrait, Victorian Women, Handles, Austrian 65.00
Vase, Purple Red Glaze, Footed, Bulbous, China, 14 1/2 X 10 In. 500.00
Vase, Sang De Boeuf Glaze, Lamp Mounted, Shade, Oriental, 18 In. 100.00
Vase, Thousand Flower, C.1900, 12 1/2 In. 825.00
Vase, Venus & Cupid In Relief, Korschann, Louchet, Bronze Mount 1875.00
Vase, Wheel Carved Floral Design, Red, Band, 5 In. 44.00

Postcards were first legally permitted in Austria on October 1, 1869. The United States passed postal regulations allowing the card in 1873. Most of the picture postcards collected today date after 1910. The amount of postage can help to date a card. The years the rates changed and the rates are: 1872 (1 cent), 1917 (2 cents), 1919 (1 cent), 1925 (2 cents), 1928 (1 cent), 1952 (2 cents), 1959 (3 cents), 1963 (4 cents), 1968 (5 cents), 1973 (8 cents), 1975 (7 cents), 1976 (9 cents), 1978 (10 cents), 1981 (12 cents), 1981 (13 cents).

POSTCARD, American Express Co., C.1900, 3 X 5 In.	3.50
American Legion Parade, San Francisco, 1923	2.00
American Rocket Airplane Flight, Feb.23, 1936	10.00
Baby, Photograph, Eli Lilly, Pre–1920s	8.00
Bears Photographing Couple In Tree, Frightened, C.Russell, 1908	15.00
Beautiful Children, Signed MEP	5.00
Beauty & The Beast, Evelyn Nesbit, Hand Tinted, Postmarked 1907	25.00
Birthday, Embroidered	10.00
Birthday, Pillow	7.50
Black, Set Of 8	8.50
Booklet, Flowers	5.00
Broadway, Denison, Iowa	4.00
Buck Jones With Horse, 1920s	12.00
Cat Dressed As Baby, Pre–1920	5.00
Chesterfield Cigarette, Joe Louis, Black & White	8.80
Christmas Kewpie, Signed	30.00
Christmas, 1900–20, Set Of 5	4.00
Christmas, 1900–20, Set Of 12	6.00
Christmas, C.1896	3.50
Christmas, Hold To Light, Set Of 2	40.00
Christmas, Santa Claus, Set Of 10	30.00
Cigar Store Interiors, Davenport, I A	17.00
Columbia River Highway, Set Of 20	15.00
Comic, Dirigible	5.00
Comic, Dog	2.00
Comic, Kitten	2.50
Comic, Steamship	4.00
Coney Island	3.50
Cracker Jack	15.00
Dawson, N.M.Railroad Yards, Photograph, Pre–1910	6.50
Destruction Of Verdun, France, World War I	3.00
Durant Car Factory	17.00
Easter, 1900–20, Set Of 6	4.00
Easter, 1910	3.00
Easter, Woolson Spice Co., Lion Coffee, 5 X 7 In.	8.00
Eli Lilly Baby Powder, Pre–1920s	6.00
Elsie & Twins, Borden, Set Of 3	2.00
Enrico Caruso Memorial, 1921	10.00
Esmond, S.D., Main Street, Photograph, Pre–1910	7.00
Fire Station, Set Of 7	85.00
Firehouse, Firefighters	5.00
Florida, Pre–1920, Set Of 50	35.00
Golden Gate Exposition, 1939	1.50
Halloween	6.00
His Majesty, Gutmann	15.00
Indian & Teepee, Indian Pull-Out Picture, Oklahoma, 1909	9.00
Indian Presenting Decorative Baskets, Photograph, Pre–1920	20.00
Iowa Towns, 1900–20, Set Of 6	4.00
Jamestown Exposition, 1907, Set Of 6	25.00
Jenny Lind	15.00
Joan Crawford, Black & White, Glossy, 1930s	15.00
Kathy Kruse, Doll Scene, Signed	3.00
Lincoln Funeral Car	12.00
Logging, State Of Oregon	7.00
Logging, State Of Washington	7.00

Los Angeles Olympic, 1932 .... 3.50
Memorial, Civil War 5.00
Milwaukee Parade Locomotive, Photograph, 1941 .... 4.00
Mining Towns & Mines, Set Of 18 .... 43.00
Mother–In–Law, Paul Finkenrath, Set Of 6 .... 30.00
Nursery Rhymes, Signed ABJ 4.00
Papa's Boy, Squeeze 28.00
Parrish, Broadmoor Hotel 25.00
Parrish, Palace Hotel, San Francisco 70.00
Phonograph, Edison 3.00
Picture Of Kaiser & Crown Prince, Captive In Horse Drawn Jail 75.00
Quebec, Set Of 13 .... 8.00
Quick Meal Gas Stove, 1908 .... 6.00
Railroad Depot, Findley, Ohio 5.00
Roosevelt Bear 15.00
San Diego, 1912, 5 1/2 X 31 In. 15.00
Santa Claus In Airplane 12.00
Santa Claus, 1910, 3 In Red Suit, 1 In Brown Suit, Set Of 4 .... 10.00
Santa Claus, Full Suited, C.1910 .... 10.00
Santa Claus, Pre–1920 .... 4.00
Santa Claus, Silk Suited, On Balcony, Horn & Clock Tower, Germany 22.00
Sarah Bernhardt 12.00
Sleepy Eye, Pipe Of Peach, Unused 50.00
Song Card, Music Staff & Lyrics, 1906 .... 2.50
Stereoview, Kansas City Flooded Railroad Yards, 1903, Set Of 2 .... 12.00
Sunbonnet Babies 7.00
Swift & Co., Children, C.1909, Set Of 3 .... 27.00
Teddy Bear Christmas, 1907 .... 10.00
Thanksgiving, C.1910 .... 3.00
Thanksgiving, Set Of 4 .... 2.00
Thousand Islands, Set Of 10 .... 12.00
Three Kittens In Sewing Basket, 1910–14 .... 2.50
Train Wreck, C.M.& P.R.R. 5.00
Valentine, 1896 .... 3.50
Valentino, On Horse 10.00
W.C.T.U. 15.00
Workers Alongside R.R. Handcar, Back Of Depot 5.00
World War I, Army Airplanes, Pre–1920s 10.00
World War I, Army, Set Of 5 .... 2.00
World War I, Fort McDowell, C.1918 .... 2.00
Zeppelin, Bust Of Count Zeppelin, German, 1918 .... 50.00

> *Posters have informed the public about news and entertainment events*
> *since ancient times. Nineteenth–century advertising or theatrical*
> *posters and twentieth–century movie and war posters are of special*
> *interest today. The price is determined by the artist, the condition,*
> *and the rarity. Other posters are listed under Store, World War I,*
> *and World War II.*

POSTER, 1,000 In War Stamps, Will Build Mystery Ship, Framed, 26 X 20 In. 20.00
5 Sullivan Brothers, Dated 1943, 22 X 28 In. 12.00
8 Bells, Dancing Women, Sailor Suits, Litho, C.1910, 49 X 30 In. 110.00
Air Mail, Movie, Douglas Fairbanks Jr., W.Baxter, Framed, 38 X 24 In. 410.00
Anchor Line, Frank Harrison, 1927, 25 X 40 In. 325.00
Anne Shirley, Chasing Yesterday, 18 X 13 In. 8.00
Audie Murphy, Movie 20.00
Battle–Wise Infantryman, World War II, Schlairker 1944, 27 X 19 In. 27.00
Between The Acts, Tobacco, Portrait Of Lillian Russell 965.00
Black Cat, Bella Lugosi & Karloff, Universal, 20 X 29 In. 85.00
Black Cat, Silk Hosiery, 22 X 31 In. 700.00
Blue Jeans, Play By Joseph Arthur, 1905, 19 X 27 In. 60.00
Buy The McCormick, Farm Machinery, Trade Card, Framed, 14 X 16 In. 295.00
Buy War Bonds, World War II, Dated 1942, 14 1/2 X 20 In. 8.50
Campbell's Horse Foot Remedies, Axtell, 1890, 26 X 19 In. 155.00
Circuit Des Ardennes Belges 1906–Duray, E.Montaut, 17 3/4 X 35 In. 230.00

Poster, Oxford County Fair,
Couple In Sinking Auto, C.1910

> Advertising card collectors should be careful how the cards are displayed. Don't use photo albums with plastic envelopes and a sticky cardboard backing (sometimes called "magnetic" albums). The cards will stick and the backs will be ruined. Pure pharmacy acetone, carefully dripped under the corner of the card, will help free it with minimal damage. Do not use nail polish remover.

Circus, 3 Girls On Trapeze, 40 X 55 In.	45.00
Circus, Animal Trainer, Bareback Rider, Clowns, & Horses, 40 X 56 In.	55.00
Circus, Christiana Bros., Circus Logo, 1950s, 41 X 27 In.	25.00
Circus, Tiger & Lion, Sitting, 40 X 55 In.	40.00
Crusader Tobacco, Stone Litho, 1890s, 7 X 13 In.	20.00
Cursa Internacional De Voiturettes, Spanish, C.1922, 34 X 48 In.	210.00
Dupont Powder Co., 1906, 30 X 21 1/2 In.	140.00
DuPont, Various Game Birds, 1920	165.00
Epco Giants 5 Cent Cigar, Picture Of Large Cigar, 1920s, 8 X 22 In.	15.00
Favor, Cycles Et Motos De Grande Luxe, Chromo, France, 47 X 33 In.	90.00
Feed The Guns With War Bonds, 1918, Framed, 20 X 30 In.	180.00
Fibber McGee & Molly, Pet Milk, 15 X 24 In.	25.00
Ginger Rogers, Romance In Manhattan, 18 X 13 In.	8.00
Green Hornet, 1939	35.00
Handy Package Dyes, 14 X 18 1/2 In.	150.00
Hart–Schaffner & Marx, Full Figure Of Man, 1902, 18 X 24 In.	15.00
Herbert Hoover For President, Portrait, Daltaraff, 1928, 23 X 18 In.	15.00
Hercules Powder, Right In The Blind, 1922	150.00
Hires RJ Root Beer, Lady, 34 X 54 In.	65.00
Humphrey Bogart, On African Queen, Gordon's Gin, 16 X 22 In.	10.00
Hupfels Sons Of Old Beer, Hunter, 3 Dogs, 1800s, 19 1/2 X 28 1/2 In.	165.00
Imperial Airways, Fly Through Europe, Signed Schurich, 38 X 24 In.	85.00
Irving The Magician In Oriental Oddities, 14 X 41 In.	15.00
Isos, Pare A Tout Sans Amortisseurs, Paris, Shrink Wrap, 13 X 23 In.	110.00
John Wayne, Rio Lobo	20.00
Join The Air Service, Give 'er The Gun, Framed, 1918, 20 X 30 In.	375.00
Kar–Mi The Magician, Advertising Feats, Board, 28 1/2 X 40 1/2 In.	45.00
Kit Carson Jr.Broadside, Celebrated Texan Ranger, 1878, 29 X 10 In.	50.00
Kola Pop, Color, Mid–1940s, 13 1/2 X 10 1/2 In.	4.00
Lautz Bros.Soap, 25 1/2 X 20 In.	45.00
Lobby, Ballad Of Josie, Doris Day, 22 X 28 In.	10.00
Lobby, Fighting Caravans, Gary Cooper, 14 X 35 1/2 In.	20.00
Lobby, Frenzy, Alfred Hitchcock, 27 X 40 In.	35.00
Lobby, In Like Flint, James Coburn, Lee Cobby, 22 X 28 In.	10.00
Lobby, Jack In The Bean Stalk, Play, 1930s, 30 X 42 In.	60.00
Lobby, James Bond, You Only Live Twice	20.00
Lobby, John Wayne, Legend Of The Lost, 14 X 36 In.	40.00
Lobby, Little Red Riding Hood, Play, 1930s, 30 X 42 In.	75.00
Lobby, Sad Sack, Jerry Lewis, 1958, 14 X 35 1/2 In.	15.00
Lobby, Tyrone Power & Errol Flynn, 14 X 36 In.	25.00
Lucky Teter, 1940s, 26 X 42 In.	20.00
Maude Banks, Theater, Litho By Forbes, C.1872, 78 X 40 1/2 In.	100.00

Oxford County Fair, Couple In Sinking Auto, C.1910 ....*Illus* 160.00
Pears Soap, Bubbles, Chrome Printed On Cardboard, 1890 .... 245.00
Peter's Union Pneumatic, Litho, Weismann, Paris, 1902, 48 X 35 In. 110.00
Real Coffee We Know How To Make It, 1920s, Framed, 20 X 28 In. 65.00
Red Sox–Champions 1912, Team Photo, Pennant, Framed, 13 3/4 X 21 In. 400.00
Remember December 7th, Dated 1942, 13 7/8 X 9 7/8 In. 8.50
Rice's Seeds, Cabbage Man, 22 X 28 In. 175.00
Ringling Bros.Circus, Bust Pictures, Banner, 1937, 12 X 16 In. 65.00
Schmidt's Beer, Rockwell, Full Color, C.1935, 22 X 28 In. 10.00
Service–Courteous, Thoughtful, 1920s, Framed, 20 X 28 In. 65.00
Sir Walter Raleigh, Illustration Of Can, 1940s, 14 X 20 In. 20.00
Smash Japanese Aggression, R.Nolkulch, 1942, Framed 21 X 31 In. 200.00
Snow White, Cardboard, 1938, 6 X 8 In. 15.00
Tarzan & Leopard Woman, Johnny Weismuller, RKO, 18 X 20 In. 85.00
Tarzan The Fearless, 1933 .... 35.00
Uncle Tom's Cabin, Silk Screen On Cardboard 22.50
Wilbur's Stock Food, 6 Horse Team, Framed, 1904, 32 X 16 In. 135.00
Winchester, Junior Rifle Corps, Sample Powder Can, 2 X 1 7/8 In. 150.00

> *Pottery and porcelain are different. Pottery is opaque; you can't see through it. Porcelain is translucent. If you hold a porcelain dish in front of a strong light you will see the light through the dish. Porcelain is colder to the touch. Pottery is softer and easier to break and will stain more easily because it is porous. Porcelain is thinner, lighter, and more durable. Majolica, faience, and stoneware are all pottery. Many types of pottery are listed in this book under the factory name.*

POTTERY, Basket, Kate Greenaway, Figure, Floral Scroll Design, 4 X 7 In. 100.00
Beater Jar, Blue Band 50.00
Berry Set, Oval, Knox, New Wharf, Plate & 5 Dishes 75.00
Bookend, Dog, 7 In. 15.00
Bowl, A.Bigot, Studio Piece, 3 1/2 In. 225.00
Bowl, Blue, White, Enameled, 8 Immortals, Daoguang Seal Mark, 9 In. 440.00

Never touch the surface of a daguerreotype or an ambrotype.

Use eyeglass cleaning tissues to clean
the glass on small pictures.

Pottery, Figurine, Dog,
Morton, Brown, 6 1/2 In.

Pottery, Shoe, Brown, 3 In. Long

Bowl, Green Glaze, Irregular Oval Sides, Han Dynasty, 7 1/8 In.	165.00
Bowl, Pitcher, Chamber Pot, Blue, White Windmill, Empire Ware, 3 Pc.	225.00
Bowl, White Glaze, Ring Foot, Juluxian Type, Song Dynasty, 5 1/2 In.	110.00
Butter, Blue Cow, Handle	165.00
Butter, Blue Daisy, Trellis	125.00
Cake Dish, Sponge, Glazed, 9 3/4 In.	90.00
Candlestick, Stylized Flowers, Wiener Werkstatte, 8 3/4 In.	175.00
Chamberstick, Cloron, Green Matte, Artist Signed	85.00
Cooler, Iced Tea, & Ice Crock, Signed, 2 Gal.	85.00
Creamer, Dark Glaze, 5 In.	70.00
Dish, Cheese, Cover, Denman Pattern, Keeling & Co., 9 7/8 In.	85.00
Figurine, Dog, Morton, Brown, 6 1/2 In. ....*Illus*	25.00
Figurine, Horse, Green, Cream Yellow Glazed, Ming, 12 1/2 In.	715.00
Figurine, Horse, Iridescent Aubergine Glaze, Stand, 5 In., Pair	605.00
Figurine, Horse, Polychrome Design, Mahogany Stand, China, 13 In.	2000.00
Holder, Toothbrush, Beaded Panel, Flemish, Blue	115.00
Honey Pot, Relief Bee On Flower Lid, Vallon Star, Pink & Black	17.50
Humidor, Tobacco, German Gentleman Shape, Marked J.W.R., 9 In.	95.00
Jar, Brown Glaze, Ribbed, Song Dynasty, 3 3/4 In.	550.00
Jar, Rim Spout, Handle, Green Ash Glaze, 12 X 11 In.	50.00
Jug, Green Glaze, Incised Signature Lanier Meaders, 10 1/2 In.	130.00
Jug, Grotesque, Impressed Brown Pottery, Contemporary, 7 In.	55.00
Jug, Red Apple & Yellow Pear, Purington	15.00
Jug, Water, Old Curiosity Shop, Universal	15.00
Jug, Yellow Bands, Running Circular Top To Base, Shelley, 7 3/8 In.	59.00
Mold, Fish, Green, John Bell, 10 In.	1000.00
Mug & Plate, Child's, Decorated, Canonsburg, Pa., 2 Piece	25.00
Mug, Catalina Island, Matte Green, Incised Mark	35.00
Mug, Monk, Flemish, Blue & Gray	90.00
Ocarina, Sweet Potato, Gold Seal, Austria	85.00
Pitcher, Blue Bird, Gal.	295.00
Pitcher, Classic Figures, Leaves, Rope Handle, Blue, Dudson, 7 In.	68.00
Pitcher, Embossed Hunt Scene, Buff, Handle, Turner, 9 3/8 In.	80.00
Pitcher, Flemish, Hunting Scene, Blue & Gray	265.00
Pitcher, Lemonade, Peacock Pattern, Goodwin Pottery, C.1850, Large	37.50
Pitcher, Parrot, Wade–Heath, English, 1930s ....*Color*	65.00
Pitcher, Tan, Brown, 4 In.	20.00
Pitcher, Witch Scene, Gypsy, Beige, Jones & Walley, Dated 1842, 9 In.	115.00
Planter, Bust Of Woman Shape, 1940s Attire, Block Pottery, 1940	15.00
Plaque, Blue & Green Moorish Design, Spain, 15 1/4 In.	45.00
Plate, Floral, Blue, Tin Glazed, Pair	150.00
Plate, Parmerende, Art Nouveau Moths, Upturned Corners, 6 3/4 In.	95.00
Pot, Brown Glaze, Bulbous, Small Neck, Mettinger	150.00
Pot, Glazed, Handle, Spout, 5 1/4 X 6 1/4 In.	75.00
Salt, Blue, Hanging	125.00
Shoe, Blue & Green, 4 In., Pair ....*Color*	50.00
Shoe, Brown, 3 In.Long ....*Illus*	25.00
Stand, Umbrella, Daffodil Design, Standard Glaze, 23 X 10 1/4 In.	300.00
Stein, 1/2 Liter, Hinged Pewter Top, Incised Violets, Leaves, 8 In.	110.00
Stein, 1/2 Liter, Monk	273.00
Sugar, Covered, Stahl, Dated 1946	22.50
Syrup, Lid, Pastel Tulips, Silver Trim	15.00
Teapot, Applied Design, Present From George To R.Blackwell, 1898	192.50
Vase, Bird, Grass Scene, Painted, Tan Ground, Morgan, 1883, 14 1/4 In.	3500.00
Vase, Chinese Transition Glaze, Coldrum, R.Wells, 4 1/4 In.	195.00
Vase, Figurine With Urns, Japan, 9 In. ....*Color*	17.50
Vase, Floor, New Jersey Pottery, 16 1/2 In.	60.00
Vase, Green Leaves, Blue, Tonverhe Kandern, M.Hauger Style, 8 In.	185.00
Vase, Painted, House Scene, Heart Shape, Artist Signed, 4 1/2 In.	20.00
Vase, Stripes, Teardrop Shape, Small Pointed Top Opening, 7 In.	20.00
Water Cooler, Blue Bands, Love Field Potteries, Dallas, Tx., 2 Gal.	50.00

Pratt, Pitcher, Men Smoking
& Drinking Scene, 1780, 8 In.

To test the age of engraving on glass, place a white handkerchief on the inside. If the engraving is old, the lines will usually show up darker than the rest of the glass. New engraving has a bright powderlike surface.

Powder flasks and powder horns were made to hold the gunpowder used in antique firearms. The early examples were made of horn or wood, later ones were of copper or brass.

POWDER FLASK, British Carved, Drinking Men, Spiral Spout, Motto, C.1830	595.00
Colt, Eagle & Shield, Crossed Revolvers, Brass, 4 1/2 In.	350.00
Double Compartment, Plunger Charger, Ball Section, 5 1/4 In.	175.00
Eagle & Shield, Crossed Revolvers, Motto, Copper, 3 3/4 In.	110.00
Eagle, Motto, Mermaid, Cannon, Allegorical Figures, Dated 1813	135.00
Fleur–De–Lis Embossed, Metal, Brass Fittings	38.00
Full Figure Seated Nude, Male Holding Rabbit, French, 8 In.	145.00
Hunter In Knee Britches, Firing Gun, Dog, Copper, 7 In.	60.00
Hunter Leaning On Horse, Scroll & Leaf Panel, 6 1/2 In.	110.00
Lanthorn, Cross Spring Charger, Cow Horn, Hunter, 7 1/2 In.	395.00
Pistol, Shell Design Center & Bottom, Copper, 6 In.	57.50
Relief Seated Fox In Trap, French, Copper, 7 In.	165.00
Relief Vase Holding Flowers, Card Center, Copper	31.50
Rifle, Violin Shape, Lily Leaf Bordering Center, Copper	57.50
Runaway Horse, Rider Grasping Limb, French, 7 1/2 In.	195.00
Running Dog In Field, Oval Panel, Copper, 6 1/2 In.	39.50
Sailing Ship, Fish, Birds, Trees, C.1758, 10 In.	495.00
Semibag Shape, Copper, Miniature	145.00
Shell Design, German Silver, Hallmarks, 4 1/2 In.	175.00
U.S.Navy, Anchor Both Sides, Copper, Marked Stimpson 1845	185.00
POWDER HORN, 2 Wide Sides, Wooden Stopper, Octagonal, 8 1/2 In.	55.00
Carving, 12 In.	60.00
Eagle, Wings Down, On Hummock, Both Sides, Copper, 4 In.	97.50
Engraved Horse & Peacock, 9 1/2 In.	125.00
Engraved Map, River & New London, Waterbury, U.M., 15 1/4 In.	475.00
Fort, Pinwheels, C.1756, 12 In.	660.00
Landscape, House, Deer, Tiger, Vessel, Ladies, 13 3/4 In.	225.00
Measure On End, Spring Latch, Brass Trim, 14 In.	55.00
Mermaids, Soldier, Horse, Crown Mark, C.1758, 14 In.	990.00
Nova Scotia, Designs & Signed	550.00
Ship, Castle, Large Owl, C.1758, 10 1/4 In.	825.00
Ships, Fish, Flags, Birds, Tom Solomon, 12 1/2 In.	175.00
Standing Stag, Surrounding Oak Leaf Wreath, Fox Head Bottom	89.50
Turned Spout, Chip Carved Wooden End, 12 1/4 In.	155.00
Turned Wooden End, Threaded Tip, 17 In.	90.00
White Looping, Applied Rings, & Lip, Green Interior, 9 1/2 In.	195.00
Wooden, Engraved, J.Emmons, Was.B.Inye, 1804, 16 1/2 In.	325.00

PRATT
FENTON

Pratt ware means two different things. It was an early Staffordshire pottery, cream–colored with colored decorations, made by Felix Pratt during the late eighteenth century. There was also Pratt ware made with transfer designs during the mid–nineteenth century in Fenton, England. Reproductions of the transfer-printed Pratt are being made.

PRATT, Bowl, Interior Scene, Polychrome Enameling, Dr.Syntax, 9 7/8 In.	95.00
Bowl, Matte Black, Classical Transfers, 4 In.	35.00
Box, Gang Of Boys On Lid, Wolf & Lamb, 4 In.	65.00
Cradle, Hooded, Child, Yellow Glaze, Blue Highlights, Miniature	325.00
Figurine, 4 Seasons, Ladies, 1780–90, 8 1/2 To 8 7/8 In., Set Of 4	2970.00
Figurine, Faith, 1800, 7 In. ....135.00 To 145.00
Figurine, Hope, 1800, 7 In. ....125.00 To 135.00
Figurine, Prince Albert, On Horse, 1840, 8 In.	175.00
Figurine, Soldier's Dream, 1850, Miniature	75.00
Pitcher, Men Smoking & Drinking Scene, 1780, 8 In. ....*Illus*	225.00
Pitcher, Molded Scenes In Heart Reserve, Titles, 19th Century, 8 In.	150.00
Pitcher, Old Greek, Classical Figures, Black, Fenton, 5 1/2 In.	150.00
Potlid, Polychrome Transfer Scene Of Fish Seller, 4 In.	55.00
Potlid, Polychrome Transfer Scene, Village Wedding, 4 1/4 In.	75.00
Snuff Jar, Black Transfer Men & Animals, Blue	25.00
Tea Set, Enameled Flowers, Black Glazed Tea Kettle, 1860, 3 Piece	135.00

Pressed glass was first made in the United States in the 1820s after the invention of glass pressing machines. Hundreds of patterns of pressed glass were made in complete table settings. Although the Boston and Sandwich Works was the most famous of the pressed glass factories, there were about sixteen other factories making pressed glass from 1830 to 1850, and still more from 1850 to 1900, when pressed glass reached its greatest popularity. It is now being widely reproduced.

1000–EYE, see Thousand Eye
101, see One–O–One
ACANTHUS, see Ribbed Palm
ACME, see Butterfly With Spray
ACORN MEDALLION, BEADED, see Beaded Acorn Medallion

PRESSED GLASS, Acorn, Goblet	20.00
Acorn, Salt & Pepper, Pink	35.00
Acorn, Spooner ....15.00 To 35.00
Actress, Bottle, Dresser, Original Paint, Stopper	75.00
Actress, Bowl, Footed, 6 In.	30.00
Actress, Bread Plate, Pinafore	115.00

Actress

Arched Fleur–De–Lis

Actress, Celery 155.00
Actress, Compote, 11 In. 160.00
Actress, Compote, Covered, 11 1/2 X 7 In. ....110.00 To 140.00
Actress, Compote, Open, 7 1/4 X 7 1/4 In. 145.00
Actress, Creamer 50.00
Actress, Dish, Oval 95.00
Actress, Plate, Miss Nelson 100.00
Actress, Sauce, Footed, 4 X 2 1/2 In. 45.00
Admiral Dewey, Pitcher ....55.00 To 75.00
Admiral Dewey, Tumbler 25.00
Adonis, Compote, Covered, Yellow, 6 1/4 In. 88.00
Adonis, Plate, 10 In. 18.00
Adonis, Spooner, Vaseline 40.00
Alabama, Creamer, Individual 13.00
Alabama, Pitcher, Water 95.00
Alabama, Spooner 35.00
Alabama, Toothpick 45.00
Alaska, Berry Bowl, Master, Emerald, Enameled Forget–Me–Nots 130.00
Alaska, Creamer, White 32.00
Alaska, Cruet, Green 95.00
Alaska, Spooner, Blue 40.00
Alaska, Sugar & Creamer, Yellow 185.00
Alaska, Tumbler, Opalescent Vaseline 65.00
Alaska, Water Set, Opalescent Vaseline 450.00
Almond Thumbprint, Wine 15.00
Amazon, Bowl, 7 In. 15.00
Amazon, Cake Stand, 10 In. 40.00
Amazon, Creamer ....26.00 To 35.00
Amazon, Creamer, Child's ....20.00 To 35.00
Amazon, Dish, Covered, Oval, 9 In. 23.00
Amazon, Nappy, Lion Handle 24.00
Amazon, Spooner ....20.00 To 35.00
Amazon, Sugar, Covered, Etched 28.00
Amazon, Tumbler 15.00
Amazon, Wine 33.00
        AMBERETTE, see Klondike
American Beauty, Pitcher, Water 50.00
Anthemion, Plate, Ruffled, 10 In. 25.00
Anthemion, Sugar, Covered 39.00
Anthemion, Tumbler 15.00
Apollo, Goblet 45.00
Apollo, Tray, Water 45.00
Apple Blossom, Goblet 25.00
Apple Blossom, Pitcher, Blue Band 110.00
Aquarium, Pitcher, Water, Green 295.00
Arabesque, Goblet, Flint 25.00
Arched Fleur–De–Lis, Spooner 18.00
Arched Grape, Celery Vase 39.00
Arched Leaf, Plate, 10 In. 28.50
        ARGONAUT SHELL, see Nautilus
Argus, Tumbler, Bar 65.00
Argus, Wine 22.00
Arrow Sheaf, Pitcher, Water 40.00
Arrowhead In Oval, Creamer, Child's 8.00
Arrowhead In Oval, Sugar, Covered, Child's 18.00
        ART NOVO, see Dogwood
Art, Banana Stand 140.00
Art, Basket, Fruit 165.00
Art, Butter, Covered, Ruby Stained 65.00
Art, Cake Stand, 10 In. 40.00
Art, Celery Vase 48.50
Art, Compote, Open, 9 In. ....40.00 To 50.00
Art, Sugar, Covered ....34.00 To 35.00
Artichoke, Bowl Set, Ice Cream, Master, & 6 Bowls, 5 1/4 In. 110.00

Artichoke, frosted   Ashburton   Atlas

Artichoke, Cruet, Original Stopper, Clear & Frosted 75.00
Artichoke, Finger Bowl, Underplate 14.00
Artichoke, Goblet 30.00
Ashburton, Eggcup, Flared 24.50
Ashburton, Goblet, Flaring Top, Flint 50.00
Ashburton, Jar, Toddy, Covered, Flint 110.00
Ashburton, Wine, Flared, Flint 20.00
Atlanta, Bowl, Square, 8 1/2 In. 25.00
Atlanta, Cake Stand 80.00
Atlanta, Compote, Jelly, Clear Lion 28.00
Atlanta, Goblet .... 9.00 To 10.00
Atlanta, Pitcher, Water 85.00
Atlas, Cake Stand, 8 1/2 In. 25.00
Atlas, Creamer, Flat, Etched 22.50
Atlas, Goblet, Etched ....35.00 To 40.00
Atlas, Toothpick 25.00
Atlas, Tray, 12 1/2 In. 29.00
Atlas, Wine, 5 1/2 In. 18.50
Austrian, Goblet 42.00
Austrian, Punch Cup ....14.50 To 20.00
Austrian, Sugar, Covered ....32.00 To 35.00
Austrian, Wine ....15.00 To 25.00
Baby Face, Compote, Covered, 5 1/4 In. 125.00
Baby Face, Compote, Open, 7 X 8 In. 45.00
    BABY THUMBPRINT, see Dakota
    BALDER, see also Pennsylvania
Balder, Bowl, Gold Trim, 8 1/2 In. 24.50
Balder, Goblet, Gilt Top 25.00
Balder, Tumbler, Water 18.50
Balder, Whiskey ....12.00 To 13.50
Balder, Wine ....15.00 To 18.50
    BALKY MULE, see Currier & Ives
Ball & Bar, Tumbler, Amber 19.00
Ball & Swirl, Spooner 22.50
Ball, Cruet 15.00
Balloon, Sugar, Covered 250.00
Baltimore Pear, Sugar & Creamer 50.00
    BAMBOO, see Broken Column
Band & Fan, Spooner 20.00
    BANDED BEADED GRAPE MEDALLION, see Beaded Grape Medallion,
    Banded
Banded Buckle, Spooner ....26.50 To 28.50
Banded Buckle, Tumbler, Bar 26.00
Banded Buckle, Wine 15.00
    BANDED FINE CUT, see Fine Cut Band
Banded Fleur–De–Lis, Wine 18.00

Banded Icicle, Celery Vase, Pedestal 40.00
Banded Icicle, Goblet 25.00
Banded Paneled Stippled Bowl, Goblet 9.50
    BANDED PORTLAND, when flashed with pink, is sometimes called
    "Maiden Blush."
Banded Portland, Goblet 30.00
Banded Portland, Powder Box 12.00
Banded Portland, Powder Jar, Original Lid 35.00
Banded Portland, Relish, Maiden Blush, 6 1/2 In. 20.00
Banded Portland, Table Set, Cranberry, Gold Trim, 6 Piece 285.00
Banded Portland, Vase, Maiden Blush, 6 In. 30.00
Banded Portland, Wine 15.00
Banded Prism Bar, Goblet 15.00
    BANDED RAINDROP, see Candlewick
Banded Variance Panels, Goblet 23.00
    OTHER BANDED PATTERNS, see under name of basic pattern: e.g.
    Banded Honeycomb, see Honeycomb, Banded
Banner, Butter, Covered, Clear 110.00
    BAR & DIAMOND, see Kokomo
Barberry, Butter, Covered 42.00
Barberry, Celery Vase ....22.00 To 30.00
Barberry, Compote, Covered, Low Stand 42.00
Barberry, Compote, Open 25.00
Barberry, Dish, Oval, 8 In. 33.50
Barberry, Plate, 6 In. ....17.50 To 22.50
Barberry, Salt, Master, Footed 22.00
Barberry, Spooner ....20.00 To 35.00
    BARLEY & OATS, see Wheat & Barley
    BARLEY & WHEAT, see Wheat & Barley
Barley, Bread Plate 30.00
Barley, Cake Stand, 9 1/2 In. 22.00
Barley, Goblet ....18.00 To 23.50
Barley, Pitcher, Water ....45.00 To 50.00
Barley, Pitcher, Water, Bulbous, Applied Handle 75.00
Barley, Wine 25.00
Barred Forget–Me–Not, Goblet 25.00
Barred Hobnail, Goblet 15.00
    BARRED OVALS, see Banded Portland
Barrel Ashburton, Wine 41.50
Barrel Excelsior, Goblet, Flint 42.50
    BARREL HONEYCOMB, see also Honeycomb
Barrel Thumbprint, Tumbler 30.00
Barrel Thumbprint, Wine, Flint 45.00
    BARRELED BLOCK, see Red Block
Basket Weave, Bread Plate 18.00
Basket Weave, Goblet, Amber ....18.00 To 30.00

Barberry

Beaded Grape Medallion

Beaded Grape

Basket Weave, Goblet, Canary 33.00
Basket Weave, Pitcher, Water 48.00
Basket Weave, Pitcher, Water, Vaseline 70.00
Basket Weave, Syrup, Blue 90.00
Basket Weave, Toothpick, Amber 20.00
Bead & Scroll, Cruet 20.00
Bead & Scroll, Mug 21.00
Bead & Scroll, Pitcher, Water, Enamel Design 60.00
Beaded Acanthus, Pitcher, Milk 25.00
Beaded Acorn Medallion, Goblet 43.00
Beaded Band, Creamer 18.00
Beaded Band, Goblet 28.00
Beaded Band, Wine 18.00
    BEADED BULL'S—EYE & DRAPE, see Alabama
Beaded Chain, Compote, Open 15.00
Beaded Circle, Spooner, Green, Gold Trim 28.00
Beaded Dahlia, Salt & Pepper, Pink 33.00
Beaded Dewdrop, Cake Stand 45.00
Beaded Dewdrop, Goblet 35.00
Beaded Dewdrop, Pitcher, Water 65.00
Beaded Dewdrop, Relish ....20.00 To 25.00
Beaded Dewdrop, Wine ....45.00 To 55.00
Beaded Grape Medallion, Butter, Covered 39.00
Beaded Grape Medallion, Creamer 50.00
Beaded Grape Medallion, Goblet ....16.00 To 20.00
Beaded Grape Medallion, Spooner ....24.00 To 28.50
Beaded Grape, Bread Plate 25.00
Beaded Grape, Butter, Covered 65.00
Beaded Grape, Butter, Covered, Green ....85.00 To 95.00
Beaded Grape, Cruet 48.00
Beaded Grape, Dish, Square, Green, 5 1/4 X 5 1/4 In. 15.00
Beaded Grape, Salt & Pepper 30.00
Beaded Grape, Sauce, Square, Green, Set Of 4 .... 20.00
Beaded Grape, Toothpick, Green 30.00
Beaded Grape, Tumbler, Green 25.00
Beaded Loop, Butter, Covered, Flat 50.00
Beaded Loop, Cake Plate, 5 In. 28.00
Beaded Loop, Pitcher, Water, Pedestal 52.00
Beaded Ovals In Sand, Cruet, Original Stopper, Green 125.00
Beaded Ovals In Sand, Table Set, Green, Gold, Enameled, 4 Pc. 375.00
    BEADED STAR, see Shimmering Star
Beaded Swirl, Berry Set, Gold Trim, Green, 7 Piece 155.00
Beaded Swirl, Creamer, Green 35.00
Beaded Swirl, Cruet, Stopper 28.00
Beaded Swirl, Sugar, Covered, Child's 25.00
Beaded Tulip, Wine 16.00
Bear Climber, Goblet 65.00
    BEARDED MAN, see Viking
Beatty Honeycomb, Toothpick, White 34.00
Beatty Rib, Pickle Castor, Blue Opalescent 175.00
Bedford, Sugar & Creamer 77.00
Bellflower With Loops, Goblet 225.00
Bellflower, Champagne, Knob Stem, Single Vine, Flint 115.00
Bellflower, Compote, Open, Scalloped, 8 X 4 3/4 In. 50.00
Bellflower, Creamer, Ribbed Top 158.00
Bellflower, Eggcup, Flint 35.00
Bellflower, Goblet, Flint ....40.00 To 45.00
Bellflower, Pitcher, Double Vine, Applied Handle, 7 1/4 In. 410.00
Bellflower, Plate, 6 In. 60.00
Bellflower, Salt, Covered, Beaded Top, Single Vine, Flint 75.00
Bellflower, Sauce, Flat 12.50
Bellflower, Spooner 32.00
Bellflower, Sugar, Covered 45.00
Bellflower, Wine, Flint 50.00

Bellflower   Bethlehem Star   Bird & Strawberry

Belted Icicle, Goblet 15.00
BENT BUCKLE, see New Hampshire
Berry Cluster, Creamer 26.50
Bessimer Flute, Goblet 15.00
Bethlehem Star, Creamer 28.50
Bethlehem Star, Cruet ....18.00 To 25.00
Bethlehem Star, Pitcher, Water 52.00
Bethlehem, Wine 15.00
Beveled Diamond & Star, Cracker Jar 45.00
Beveled Diamond & Star, Cruet, Original Stopper 20.00
Beveled Diamond & Star, Sugar, Covered 31.50
Beveled Star, Butter, Covered, Green 85.00
Beveled Star, Cake Plate 38.00
Beveled Star, Compote, Open, Flint, 8 3/4 X 9 In. 185.00
BIG BLOCK, see Henrietta
Birch Leaf, Eggcup 12.00
Bird & Roses, Champagne, Etched 34.00
Bird & Roses, Goblet, Etched 55.00
Bird & Strawberry, Bowl, 3 Footed, 5 1/2 In. 25.00
Bird & Strawberry, Bowl, 7 1/2 In. 25.00
Bird & Strawberry, Cake Stand ....35.00 To 45.00
Bird & Strawberry, Compote, 5 7/8 X 7 3/4 In. 70.00
Bird & Strawberry, Punch Cup ....18.00 To 22.00
Bird & Strawberry, Sauce, 5 1/2 In. 14.50
Bird & Strawberry, Sugar, Open 30.00
Bird & Strawberry, Tumbler ....22.50 To 55.00
Bird & Strawberry, Wine ....45.00 To 50.00
Bird & Tree, Mug, Blue 60.00
BIRD IN RING, see Butterfly & Fan

Bleeding Heart   Block & Fan   Broken Column

Birds At Fountain, Goblet 30.00
Bismarc Star, Goblet ....15.00 To 30.00
Blackberry, Celery Vase ....50.00 To 75.00
Blackberry, Goblet 27.00
Bleeding Heart, Bowl, Covered, 9 1/2 In. 55.00
Bleeding Heart, Cake Stand 85.00
Bleeding Heart, Compote, Covered 65.00
Bleeding Heart, Creamer 38.00
Bleeding Heart, Goblet ....25.00 To 40.00
Bleeding Heart, Honey 10.00
Bleeding Heart, Mug 28.00
Bleeding Heart, Pitcher, Water, Applied Handle ....85.00 To 110.00
Bleeding Heart, Tumbler ....65.00 To 85.00
Block & Circle, Celery Vase 22.00
Block & Circle, Goblet 12.00
Block & Fan, Celery Vase ....27.00 To 30.00
Block & Fan, Sauce, Footed 12.00
Block & Fan, Sugar Shaker 45.00
        BLOCK & FINE CUT, see Fine Cut & Block
Block & Honeycomb, Goblet 22.00
        BLOCK & STAR, see Valencia Waffle
Block With Fan, Sauce, Footed, Set Of 8 .... 75.00
Block With Sawtooth Band, Wine 12.50
        BLOCK WITH STARS, see Hanover
Block With Thumbprint, Wine 20.00
Block, Creamer, Frost With Amber 40.00
Block, Pitcher, Water, Red 175.00
Block, Syrup, Ruby 140.00
Block, Tumbler 5.00
        BLOCKADE, see Diamond Block With Fan
Blocked Thumbprint, Tumbler, White, Gilt Bands 20.00
        BLOCKHOUSE, see Hanover
        BLUEBIRD, see Bird & Strawberry
Bohemian, Sugar, Individual 29.00
Bosworth, Goblet 8.50
Bow Tie, Butter, Covered 65.00
Bow Tie, Cake Stand, 9 In. 59.00
Bow Tie, Compote, 10 1/2 X 10 1/4 In. 70.00
Bow Tie, Goblet 45.00
Bow Tie, Jam Jar, Covered ....40.00 To 45.00
Bow Tie, Pitcher, Tankard, 6 In. 65.00
Bow Tie, Relish, 4 1/4 X 7 In. 22.00
Bow Tie, Salt, Master 30.00
Bow Tie, Sugar, Covered 55.00
Britannic, Berry Bowl, Master, Gold 30.00
Broken Column, Banana Stand, Footed 95.00
Broken Column, Bowl, 7 1/2 In. 25.00
Broken Column, Cake Stand ....59.50 To 70.00
Broken Column, Compote, Covered, Square, 10 1/4 In. ....40.00 To 55.00
Broken Column, Compote, Jelly, Covered, Red Notches ....118.00 To 225.00
Broken Column, Creamer 40.00
Broken Column, Cruet, Original Stopper 55.00
Broken Column, Goblet ....29.00 To 52.00
Broken Column, Pitcher, Water ....55.00 To 95.00
Broken Column, Tumbler ....33.00 To 45.00
Broughton, Berry Bowl 10.00
Broughton, Berry Set, Child's, 5 Piece 75.00
Broughton, Pitcher 30.00
Broughton, Tumbler 9.00
        BRYCE, see Ribbon Candy
Buckle & Star, Sugar, Open 18.00
Buckle With Shield, Goblet 14.00
Buckle, Eggcup 28.00
Buckle, Goblet ....19.00 To 24.00

Buckle   Bull's–Eye & Daisy   Bull's–Eye with Diamond Point

Buckle, Spooner, Flint	40.00
Buckle, Sugar, Covered	85.00
Budded Ivy, Creamer, Applied Handle	60.00
Budded Ivy, Goblet	27.00
Bull's–Eye & Daisy, Nappy, Purple Eyes	21.50
Bull's–Eye & Daisy, Tumbler	24.00
Bull's–Eye & Diamond Panels, Goblet	19.00
Bull's–Eye & Drape, Sugar, Covered	37.00
BULL'S–EYE & FAN, see Daisies in Oval Panels	
Bull's–Eye & Fan, Wine, Gold Trim	15.00
Bull's–Eye & Wishbone, Goblet	150.00
BULL'S–EYE BAND, see Reverse Torpedo	
BULL'S–EYE VARIANT, see Texas Bull's–Eye	
Bull's–Eye With Diamond Panels, Tumbler, Bar	26.00
Bull's–Eye With Diamond Point, Celery Vase	100.00
Bull's–Eye With Diamond Point, Goblet, Flint	75.00
Bull's–Eye With Diamond Point, Pitcher, Water, Ruby Owl	95.00
Bull's–Eye With Diamond Point, Salt, Master, Flint	85.00
Bull's–Eye With Fleur–De–Lis, Goblet, Flint	65.00
Bull's–Eye, Compote, Open	25.00
Bull's–Eye, Cruet, Stopper	28.00
Bull's–Eye, Dresser Set, Amber, Paris, 1913, 4 Piece	150.00
Bull's–Eye, Goblet, Flint	60.00
Bull's–Eye, Shade, Gas, Blue, 5 X 5 X 7 In.	105.00
Bull's–Eye, Spooner	50.00
Bungalow, Goblet, Etched	24.00
Bunker Hill, Bread Plate	65.00
Butterfly & Fan, Bread Plate	40.00
Butterfly & Fan, Spooner	25.00

Bull's–Eye   Cabbage Rose   Cable

| Canadian | Cardinal Bird | Cathedral |

Butterfly With Spray, Goblet 18.00
Butterfly With Spray, Mug, Child's 45.00
Butterfly, Dish, Oblong, 7 X 10 In. 90.00
Button & Star, Cruet 95.00
Button Arches, Creamer, Individual 17.00
Button Arches, Pitcher, Banded, Ruby, 12 In. 165.00
Button Arches, Toothpick 25.00
Button Arches, Tumbler, Banded, Ruby 23.00
Button Band, Basket, Handle, 10 1/2 X 11 In. 125.00
Button Panel, Spooner, Yellow Opalescent 42.50
Buttons & Braids, Pitcher, Water, Blue Opalescent 155.00
Cabbage Leaf, Butter, 4 X 6 1/2 In. 145.00
Cabbage Leaf, Butter, Covered, Frosted ....95.00 To 145.00
Cabbage Rose, Celery Vase ....35.00 To 50.00
Cabbage Rose, Compote, Covered 120.00
Cabbage Rose, Goblet 46.00
Cabbage Rose, Tumbler ....35.00 To 45.00
Cable, Compote, Open, 8 X 4 1/2 In. 35.00
Cable, Goblet, Flint ....60.00 To 75.00
Cactus, Toothpick 45.00
    CALIFORNIA, see Beaded Grape
    CAMEO, see Ceres
    CANADIAN DRAPE, see Garfield Drape
Canadian, Butter, Covered 85.00
Canadian, Creamer 30.00
Canadian, Sugar, Covered 67.50
Canadian, Wine ....35.00 To 41.50

> *There is also a pattern called "Candlewick" which has been made by Imperial Glass Corporation since 1936. It is listed in this book under Imperial, Candlewick.*

    CANDY RIBBON, see Ribbon Candy
Cane & Rosette, Celery Vase 29.00
Cane & Rosette, Spooner 25.00
Cane Horseshoe, Wine 15.00
Cane, Goblet ....10.00 To 15.00
Cane, Pitcher, Water 65.00
Cane, Plate, Toddy, Amber 14.00
Cane, Salt & Pepper, Blue 38.00
Cane, Syrup, Blown 65.00
Cape Cod, Compote, Covered, 8 In. ....115.00 To 130.00
Cape Cod, Cruet, Squat Form ....12.00 To 15.00
Capitol Building, Champagne 25.00
Capitol Building, Goblet ....27.00 To 39.00
Cardinal Bird, Creamer 32.50
Cardinal Bird, Goblet ....29.00 To 50.00

Cardinal, Creamer 32.50
Cardinal, Goblet ....30.00 To 35.00
    CARMEN, see Paneled Diamond & Finecut
Carolina, Creamer 20.00
Cathedral, Berry Bowl, Amber, 8 1/4 In. 48.00
Cathedral, Butter, Covered 50.00
Cathedral, Compote, Ruffled, Amber 35.00
Cathedral, Cruet, Original Stopper, Amber 65.00
Cathedral, Pitcher, Water 85.00
Cathedral, Wine, Amber ....35.00 To 39.00
Celtic Cross, Celery Vase 35.00
    CENTENNIAL, see also Liberty Bell; Washington Centennial
Centennial, Goblet, 1876 .... 35.00
Centennial, Relish, Bear Paw Handles 50.00
Ceres, Mug 15.00
Ceres, Sugar, Open 8.50
Chain & Shield, Bread Plate 22.00
    CHAIN WITH DIAMONDS, see Washington Centennial
Chain With Shield, Pitcher, Water 50.00
Chain With Star, Bread Plate 32.00
Chain With Star, Butter, Covered, Flat 30.00
Chain With Star, Compote, Fruit, 9 3/8 In. 29.00
Chain With Star, Goblet ....17.50 To 55.00
Chain With Star, Sugar, Covered 35.00
Chandelier, Cake Plate, 7 X 10 In. 75.00
Chandelier, Celery Vase 41.50
Chandelier, Goblet ....35.00 To 46.50
Checkerboard, Butter, Covered 42.50
Checkerboard, Cruet 10.00
Checkerboard, Pitcher, Milk 35.00
Checkerboard, Wine 12.00
Cherry Lattice, Berry Set, Northwood, 7 Piece ....100.00 To 125.00
Cherry Lattice, Butter, Covered ....100.00 To 110.00
Cherry Lattice, Plate, Rosette Handle 25.00
Cherry Thumbprints, Berry Bowl, Northwood 15.00
Cherry Thumbprints, Butter, Northwood ....100.00 To 110.00
Cherry Thumbprints, Creamer 35.00
Cherry Thumbprints, Spooner, Northwood ....40.00 To 45.00
Cherry, Goblet ....25.00 To 40.00
Chilson, Goblet 175.00
Chrysanthemum Sprig, Cruet, Blue, Stopper 595.00
Chrysanthemum, Pitcher, Tankard, Speckled Lemon, Handle 165.00
    CHURCH WINDOWS, see Tulip Petals
Circle, Cruet, Original Stopper 48.00
Classic Medallion, Creamer 22.00
Classic Warrior, Bread Plate 95.00

Ceres   Classic   Columbian Coin

Classic, Celery Vase 140.00
Classic, Compote, Covered, Log Feet, 7 1/2 In.Diam. 250.00
Classic, Creamer, Log Feet, Frosted & Clear 110.00
Classic, Pitcher, Milk, Log Feet, 8 1/2 In. 395.00
Classic, Sauce, Open Feet 25.00
Classic, Spooner, Log Feet, Frosted & Clear .... 90.00 To 150.00
Classic, Spooner, Open Feet ....85.00 To 100.00
Classic, Sugar, Covered 75.00
Classic, Sugar, Open, Log Feet 150.00
Cleat, Pitcher, Applied Handle, Flint, Clear, 9 1/4 In. 85.00
Cleveland & Thurman, Plate, Rectangular 250.00
Clover & Daisy, Goblet ....14.00 To 15.00
    COIN SPOT, see Coin Spot Category
Colonial, Tumbler, Flint, 3 1/4 In. 35.00
Colonial, Wine, Gold Trim 20.00
Colorado, Berry Bowl, 9 In. 42.00
Colorado, Bowl, Green, Footed, 8 1/2 In. 35.00
Colorado, Butter, Covered, Green, Gold Trim ....100.00 To 125.00
Colorado, Celery Vase, Green, 12 1/2 In. 80.00
Colorado, Creamer, Green, Individual ....20.00 To 29.00
Colorado, Creamer, Souvenir, Gold Trim, Individual 35.00
Colorado, Cup, Souvenir, Gold Trim 30.00
Colorado, Sauce, Fluted, Cobalt Blue 40.00
Colorado, Sherbet, Green ....18.00 To 22.00
Colorado, Sherbet, Green, Gold Trim 35.00
Colorado, Spooner 20.00
Colorado, Spooner, Green, Gold Trim 55.00
Colorado, Sugar, Covered, Green 95.00
Colorado, Sugar, Open 20.00
Colorado, Table Set, Butter, Sugar & Creamer, Green, Gold Trim 250.00
Colorado, Toothpick 30.00
Colorado, Tumbler, Gold Trim, Souvenir 30.00
Colorado, Wine 18.00
Colossus, Goblet 29.00
Columbia, Berry Bowl, Master 25.00
Columbia, Bread Plate 125.00
Columbia, Compote, Jelly, Stem 14.00
Columbian Coin, Butter, Covered 45.00
Columbian Coin, Celery 48.00
Columbian Coin, Compote, 7 In. 85.00
Columbian Coin, Creamer ....20.00 To 60.00
Columbian Coin, Pitcher, Water 110.00
Columbian Coin, Saltshaker, Clear 95.00
Columbian Exposition, Goblet, Ring Stem 45.00
Comet, Goblet, Flint ....65.00 To 75.00
    COMPACT, see Snail
Constitution, Bread Plate 80.00
Continental, Bread Plate ....40.00 To 55.00
Corcoran, Tumbler 225.00
Cord & Tassel, Butter, Covered 48.00
Cord & Tassel, Double Salt, Pink ....*Color* 45.00
Cord & Tassel, Goblet ....24.00 To 25.00
Cord & Tassel, Wine ....27.00 To 34.00
Cord Drapery, Cake Plate 50.00
Cord Drapery, Pitcher, Water, Amber 165.00
Cord Drapery, Spooner 40.00
Cordova, Celery Vase 45.00
Cordova, Pitcher, Milk 40.00
Cordova, Punch Cup 5.00
Cordova, Spooner 25.00
Cordova, Sugar & Creamer 35.00
Cordova, Syrup 85.00
Cornucopia, Cordial 30.00
Cornucopia, Pitcher, Green, Gold, 6 In. ....*Color* 25.00

Croesus

Crossed Discs

Cupid & Venus

Cornucopia, Pitcher, Water ....40.00 To 50.00
  COSMOS, see Cosmos Category
Cottage, Cake Stand 50.00
Cottage, Compote, Cover, 7 In. 30.00
Cottage, Creamer 35.00
Cottage, Goblet 25.00
Cottage, Plate, 6 In. 15.00
  CRANE, see Stork
  CRISSCROSS, see Rexford
Croesus, Berry Bowl, Green, 6 1/4 In. 95.00
Croesus, Berry Bowl, Purple, Gold Trim, Small 45.00
Croesus, Butter, Covered, Green ....95.00 To 135.00
Croesus, Butter, Green, Gold 115.00
Croesus, Creamer, Purple 150.00
Croesus, Creamer, Purple, Gold Trim, Individual 90.00
Croesus, Cruet, Green, Gold Trim 85.00
Croesus, Cruet, Original Stopper, Green & Gold 145.00
Croesus, Pitcher, Water, Emerald Green 150.00
Croesus, Plate, Amethyst, 7 1/2 In. 119.00
Croesus, Salt & Pepper, Green 160.00
Croesus, Spooner, Green ....60.00 To 85.00
Croesus, Spooner, Purple 85.00
Croesus, Sugar, Covered, Green 119.00
Croesus, Table Set, Green, Butter, Sugar, Creamer, 6 Piece 495.00
Croesus, Toothpick, Green, Gold Trim 85.00
Croesus, Tray, Condiment, Curved, Green, 9 In. 20.00
Croesus, Tumbler, Amethyst 52.00
Croesus, Water Set, Green, Gold Trim, 7 Piece ....595.00 To 850.00
Crossed Discs, Sauce, Footed 6.50
Crossed Pressed Leaf, Creamer 25.00
Crossed Pressed Leaf, Spooner 25.00
Crowfoot, Cake Stand, 9 In. 48.00
Crowfoot, Compote, Tall 42.00
Crowfoot, Creamer 21.00
Crowfoot, Goblet ....25.00 To 37.00
Crowfoot, Pitcher, Water 55.00
  CROWN JEWELS, see Chandelier; Queen's Necklace
Crystal Rock, Pitcher, Water, Pink & Blue Trim 50.00
Crystal Wedding, Compote, Covered, 13 In. 85.00
Crystal Wedding, Compote, Open, 6 1/2 In. 24.00
Crystal Wedding, Spooner 30.00
Cube & Daisy, Mug 12.00
  CUBE & DIAMOND, see Milton
  CUBE & FAN, see Pineapple & Fan
Cube, Bowl, Apple Green 85.00
  CUPID & PSYCHE, see Psyche & Cupid

Cupid & Venus, Bread Plate ....20.00 To 29.50
Cupid & Venus, Butter, Covered 65.00
Cupid & Venus, Celery Vase 38.00
Cupid & Venus, Compote, Open, 9 3/4 In. 95.00
Cupid & Venus, Creamer 30.00
Cupid & Venus, Dish, Dessert, Footed, Set Of 4 .... 110.00
Cupid & Venus, Pitcher, Milk ....40.00 To 58.00
Cupid & Venus, Pitcher, Water ....45.00 To 80.00
Cupid & Venus, Plate, Amber, 10 In. 115.00
Cupid & Venus, Spooner ....30.00 To 38.00
Cupid & Venus, Wine 60.00
Cupid's Hunt, Relish 25.00
Currant, Cake Stand, 11 1/2 In. 50.00
Currant, Celery Vase 36.00
Currant, Creamer 25.00
Currier & Ives, Bread Plate, Balky Mule, 9 1/2 In. 45.00
Currier & Ives, Cake Set, 8 Piece 20.00
Currier & Ives, Compote, Covered, Pedestal 95.00
Currier & Ives, Decanter, Stopper 55.00
Currier & Ives, Goblet ....18.00 To 30.00
Currier & Ives, Plate, Adams, 10 1/2 In. 22.00
Currier & Ives, Saltshaker, Vaseline ....50.00 To 55.00
Currier & Ives, Sauce, 4 1/2 In. 6.00
Currier & Ives, Tray, Water, Balky Mule, 12 In. 50.00
Currier & Ives, Tumbler 23.00
Currier & Ives, Water Set, Pitcher & 6 Goblets 175.00
Curtain Tieback, Butter, Covered 38.00
Curtain Tieback, Goblet ....15.00 To 18.00
Curtain, Celery Vase ....28.00 To 45.00
Cut Log, Cake Stand, 9 In. ....60.00 To 63.00
Cut Log, Celery Vase 25.00
Cut Log, Compote, Covered, 9 In. 45.00
Cut Log, Creamer ....12.00 To 16.00
Cut Log, Cruet, Original Stopper ....35.00 To 45.00
Cut Log, Goblet 45.00
Cut Log, Mug ....10.00 To 15.00
Cut Log, Pitcher 75.00
Cut Log, Sugar, Covered ....55.00 To 65.00
Cut Log, Wine ....22.50 To 28.00
Dahlia, Bread Plate 45.00
Dahlia, Goblet 30.00
Dahlia, Pitcher, Footed, 9 In. 20.00
Dahlia, Plate, Amber, 6 7/8 In. 40.00
Dahlia, Sugar 20.00
Dahlia, Wine 40.00
Daisies In Oval Panels, Bowl, Green, 3 1/2 X 5 In. 14.00

Curtain

Dahlia

Daisies in Oval Panels

Daisy & Button   Daisy & Button   Deer & Dog
with Crossbar   with Thumbprint

Daisies In Oval Panels, Creamer 10.00
Daisies In Oval Panels, Goblet ....15.00 To 21.50
Daisies In Oval Panels, Pitcher, Lemonade, Gold Trim 70.00
Daisies In Oval Panels, Syrup, Metal Cover 28.00
Daisies In Oval Panels, Table Set, Gold Trim, 4 Piece 150.00
Daisy & Block, Goblet 28.00
Daisy & Button With Crossbar, Berry Set, Blue, 5 Piece 45.00
Daisy & Button With Crossbar, Butter, Covered, Blue 35.00
Daisy & Button With Crossbar, Celery, Vaseline 50.00
Daisy & Button With Crossbar, Creamer, Blue 35.00
Daisy & Button With Crossbar, Cruet, Vaseline 110.00
Daisy & Button With Crossbar, Goblet, Amber ....35.00 To 45.00
Daisy & Button With Crossbar, Pitcher, Water 46.00
Daisy & Button With Crossbar, Water Set, Amber, 9 Piece 185.00
Daisy & Button With Crossbar, Wine 25.00
Daisy & Button With Narcissus, Goblet 15.00
   DAISY & BUTTON WITH OVAL PANELS, see Hartley
Daisy & Button With Thumbprint, Basket, Cake, Yellow, 7 In. 125.00
Daisy & Button With Thumbprint, Goblet 35.00
Daisy & Button With Thumbprint, Sugar, Covered, Blue 40.00
Daisy & Button With V–Ornament, Celery 25.00
Daisy & Button With V–Ornament, Spooner, Blue 37.50
Daisy & Button With V–Ornament, Toothpick, Blue 35.00
Daisy & Button, Berry Set, 11 1/2 In.Bowl, 10 Piece 145.00
Daisy & Button, Berry Set, Sapphire Blue, 7 Piece 95.00
Daisy & Button, Bowl, Oval, 11 X 6 1/2 In. 20.00
Daisy & Button, Canoe, Amber, 13 3/4 In. 60.00
Daisy & Button, Canoe, Blue, 11 1/2 In. 28.00
Daisy & Button, Castor Set, Toothpick Final, 3 Bottles 50.00
Daisy & Button, Creamer, Child's 10.00
Daisy & Button, Cruet ....15.00 To 20.00
Daisy & Button, Dish, Hand Shape 65.00
Daisy & Button, Goblet, Vertical Amber Thumbprint Panels 65.00
Daisy & Button, Hat, 3 1/2 X 2 1/2 In. ....6.50 To 8.00
Daisy & Button, Hat, Amber, 2 1/2 In. 10.00
Daisy & Button, Match Holder, Blue, Bulbous, Flared, 2 1/2 In. 18.00
Daisy & Button, Plate, Square, 7 In. 11.00
Daisy & Button, Salt, Vaseline 15.00
Daisy & Button, Sauce, Blue, Scalloped, 4 1/2 In. 14.00
Daisy & Button, Shoe, Amber, 5 3/4 In. 18.00
Daisy & Button, Shoe, Roller Skate, Amber, 5 1/4 X 3 1/4 In. 35.00
Daisy & Button, Slipper, 4 3/4 In. 10.00
Daisy & Button, Spooner, Vaseline, Triangular 35.00
Daisy & Button, Sugar, Amber, Covered ....35.00 To 40.00
Daisy & Button, Toothpick, Flared Rim, Amber 35.00
Daisy & Button, Toothpick, Pink 25.00

Daisy & Button, Vase, Red, Hand 49.00
Daisy, Creamer, 4 In. 24.00
Dakota, Butter, Covered, Etched ....25.00 To 68.00
Dakota, Butter, Covered, Piecrust Base 65.00
Dakota, Cake Stand, 9 1/2 In. 38.00
Dakota, Celery Vase, Etched 45.00
Dakota, Compote, Covered, 7 X 11 In. 40.00
Dakota, Compote, Open, 8 X 8 In. 31.50
Dakota, Creamer, Etched ....35.00 To 56.00
Dakota, Cruet, Child's 49.00
Dakota, Dish, Jelly, Covered 46.00
Dakota, Goblet, Etched ....20.00 To 35.00
Dakota, Pitcher, Water, Ruffled ....115.00 To 135.00
Dakota, Pitcher, Wheel Engraved Fish 100.00
Dakota, Spooner, Etched ....22.00 To 49.00
Dakota, Tray, Water, Fluted, 12 1/4 X 12 1/4 In. ....160.00 To 165.00
Dakota, Tumbler 50.00
Dakota, Tumbler, Etched 45.00
Dakota, Wine, Etched ....25.00 To 35.00
Deer & Dog, Butter, Covered, Frosted Dog Finial 90.00
Deer & Dog, Goblet, Etched ....65.00 To 95.00
Deer & Dog, Sugar, Covered, Frosted Dog Finial 85.00
Deer & Oak Tree, Pitcher, Water ....115.00 To 125.00
Deer & Pine Tree, Bread Plate 45.00
Deer & Pine Tree, Butter, Covered 115.00
Deer & Pine Tree, Compote, Covered, Large ....95.00 To 145.00
Deer & Pine Tree, Goblet ....40.00 To 55.00
Deer & Pine Tree, Tray, Amber, 8 X 13 In. 85.00
Deer & Pine Tree, Tray, Apple Green, 8 X 13 In. 78.00
Deflating Balloon, Goblet, Flint 20.00
Deflating Balloon, Wine, Set Of 4 .... 50.00
Delaware, Banana Boat, Green, Gold Trim, 11 1/2 In. 65.00
Delaware, Berry Bowl, Boat Shape, Green, Gold Trim 28.00
Delaware, Berry Bowl, Master, Boat Shape 50.00
Delaware, Bowl, Amethyst, Gold Trim, 12 X 7 In. 125.00
Delaware, Bowl, Green, Gold Trim, 8 1/2 In. ....32.00 To 55.00
Delaware, Butter, Covered, Green, Gold Trim ....100.00 To 125.00
Delaware, Celery Vase, Green, Gold Trim ....35.00 To 65.00
Delaware, Creamer ....35.00 To 40.00
Delaware, Jug, Wine, Green ....175.00 To 195.00
Delaware, Pitcher, Tankard, Green, 9 1/2 In. 195.00
Delaware, Pitcher, Water, Rose, Gold Trim 110.00
Delaware, Punch Cup, Green ....25.00 To 29.50
Delaware, Ring Tree, Ivory 65.00
Delaware, Sauce, Boat Shape, Green, Gold Trim 28.00
Delaware, Spooner 42.00
Delaware, Spooner, Green, Gold Trim ....38.00 To 50.00
Delaware, Sugar, Open, Green, Gold Trim 65.00
Delaware, Toothpick, Rose, Gold Trim 300.00
Delaware, Tumbler, Cranberry, Gold Trim ....45.00 To 50.00
Delaware, Water Set, Green, Gold Trim, 7 Piece 285.00
Dew & Raindrop, Butter, Covered 55.00
Dew & Raindrop, Creamer, Child's 40.00
Dew & Raindrop, Goblet, Cordial 5.00
Dewberry, Goblet, Gold Trim 12.50
Dewdrop Band, Goblet ....12.00 To 20.00
Dewdrop In Points, Goblet 12.50
Dewdrop With Sheaf Of Wheat, Bread Plate 35.00
Dewdrop With Star, Cake Stand 45.00
Dewdrop, Goblet 20.00
    DEWEY, see also Admiral Dewey
Dewey, Butter, Covered, Canary 95.00
Dewey, Celery Vase, Green, 5 1/2 In. 22.00
Dewey, Pitcher, Water ....55.00 To 85.00

Dewey, Relish, Serpentine Shape 50.00
Dewey, Sugar, Covered, Vaseline 65.00
Diagonal Band & Fan, Creamer 22.50
Diagonal Band & Fan, Goblet 16.00
Diagonal Band & Fan, Plate, 8 In. 9.00
Diagonal Band, Celery Vase 25.00
Diagonal Band, Creamer ....18.00 To 22.50
Diagonal Band, Goblet ....15.00 To 19.00
Diagonal Band, Pitcher, Water ....25.00 To 30.00
Diagonal Band, Sugar & Creamer 35.00
Diagonal Block & Fan, Goblet 35.00
    DIAMOND, see Umbilicated Sawtooth
Diamond & Long Sunburst, Plate, 7 1/4 In. 6.00
    DIAMOND & SUNBURST, see also Flattened Diamond & Sunburst
Diamond & Sunburst, Compote, Scalloped, 8 1/2 X 9 In. 20.00
Diamond & Sunburst, Sugar Shaker 22.00
Diamond Block With Fan, Celery Vase, Pedestal 30.00
Diamond Cut With Leaf, Sugar, Covered, Amber 45.00
    DIAMOND LACE, see Hobstar
Diamond Medallion, Butter, Covered 35.00
Diamond Medallion, Cake Stand, 9 1/2 In. 35.00
Diamond Medallion, Creamer ....16.00 To 32.00
Diamond Medallion, Goblet ....18.00 To 25.00
Diamond Medallion, Pitcher, Water 27.50
Diamond Medallion, Spooner 25.00
    DIAMOND POINT DISCS, see Eyewinker
Diamond Point, Champagne 45.00
Diamond Point, Creamer 138.00
Diamond Point, Eggcup, Clambroth 115.00

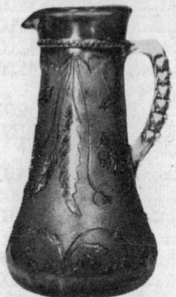

Delaware   Diagonal Band & Fan   Diagonal Band

Diamond Point   Diamond Thumbprint   Double Ribbon

Diamond Point, Spooner 55.00
Diamond Prisms, Jar, Covered 40.00
Diamond Quilted, Celery, Amberina, Square Top, 6 1/4 In. 275.00
Diamond Quilted, Tumbler, 3 1/2 In. 50.00
Diamond Quilted, Wine, Vaseline 20.00
Diamond Ridge, Cracker Jar, Covered 75.00
Diamond Ridge, Punch Cup 8.00
Diamond Rosettes, Dish, Sweetmeat 65.00
Diamond Shield, Goblet 13.00
Diamond Sunburst, Compote, Jelly 20.00
Diamond Sunburst, Cup Plate 30.00
Diamond Sunburst, Goblet .... 8.00 To 22.00
Diamond Sunburst, Spooner 21.50
Diamond Sunburst, Toothpick 35.00
Diamond Thumbprint, Compote, 4 1/2 X 7 1/2 In. 75.00
Diamond Thumbprint, Creamer 125.00
Diamond Thumbprint, Decanter, Stopper, Flint, Quart 125.00
Diamond Thumbprint, Sugar, Covered 125.00
Diamond Thumbprint, Tumbler, Bar, 3 3/4 In. 75.00
Diamonds With Double Fans, Wine 48.00
Diana, Cup & Saucer, Child's, Gold Trim 3.00
Dice & Block, Cruet, Original Stopper, Amber 45.00
Divided Block With Sunburst, Creamer 12.00
Divided Stem, Celery Vase, Etched 45.00
Dog & Rabbit, Bread Plate, Baby Falling From Cart 44.00
Dogwood, Banana Boat, Gold Trim, Green 30.00
Dogwood, Goblet 15.00
Dogwood, Sugar, Gold Trim 35.00
    DORIC, see Feather
Double Beaded Band, Wine 20.00
Double Beetle Band, Goblet .... 25.00 To 35.00
Double Beetle Band, Wine 18.00
Double Beetle Band, Wine, Blue 42.00
Double Dahlia & Lens, Banana Boat, Oval, Gold Trim 45.00
    DOUBLE DAISY, SEE ROSETTE BAND
Double Fan, Celery 30.00
Double Leaf & Dart, Goblet, Diamond Ornament 21.50
    DOUBLE LOOP, see Double Loop & Dart
Double Loop & Dart, Goblet 14.00
Double Ribbon, Champagne, Frosted 35.00
Double Snail, Rose Bowl 20.00
Double Spear, Butter 18.00
Double Spear, Eggcup 21.00
Double Spear, Sugar & Creamer 55.00
Double–Eye Hobnail With Decorative Band, Pitcher, Water 39.00
Dragon, Bowl, Open, Pedestal, 5 In. 140.00

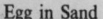

Egg in Sand   Egyptian   Fan with Diamond

Drapery Band With Stars, Goblet 20.00
Drapery, Spooner 28.50
Drum, Creamer, Child's 55.00
Drum, Spooner, Child's 25.00
Duchess, Creamer, Green, Gold Trim 25.00
Duchess, Relish 30.00
    DYNAST, see Radiant
    EARL, see Spirea Band
Early Thumbprint, Celery Vase 98.00
Edgerton, Spooner 12.00
Egg In Sand, Bread Plate, 8 X 12 In. 37.50
Egg In Sand, Goblet ....28.00 To 35.00
Egg In Sand, Pitcher, Water 50.00
Egg In Sand, Relish, Rectangular 17.00
Egg In Sand, Spooner 25.00
Egg In Sand, Tray, Water, 11 1/2 In. 55.00
Egyptian Pyramid, Bread Plate ....40.00 To 55.00
Egyptian, Berry Set, 7 Piece 95.00
Egyptian, Bread Plate, Cleopatra, Give Us This Day ....42.50 To 45.00
Egyptian, Butter, Covered ....55.00 To 80.00
Egyptian, Celery Vase 65.00
Egyptian, Compote, Open, Sphinx Base, 8 In. 65.00
Egyptian, Creamer ....32.00 To 43.00
Egyptian, Goblet ....30.00 To 53.00
Egyptian, Spooner ....26.00 To 37.50
Elegant, Wine 25.00
Elephant, Cookie Jar 25.00
Elmino, Goblet, 3 Line Etched 12.50
Emblem, Mug, Epluribus Unum 90.00
Empress, Creamer, Green, Gold Trim 65.00
Empress, Pitcher, Water, Emerald Green, Gold 135.00
Empress, Pitcher, Water, Gold Trim 82.00
Empress, Sugar & Creamer, Covered, Gold Trim 75.00
Empress, Water Set, Gold Trim, 5 Piece 130.00
    ENGLISH HOBNAIL CROSS, see Klondike
English Hobnail, Cruet, Child's 12.00
Esther, Cruet, Emerald Green, Stopper, 5 3/4 In. 145.00
Esther, Dish, Ice Cream, Green 45.00
Esther, Plate, Green, Gold, 12 1/2 In. 65.00
Esther, Salt & Pepper, Green 98.00
Esther, Tray, Ice Cream, Green 150.00
    ETCHED BAND, see Dakota
    ETCHED DAKOTA, see Dakota
Eugenie, Wine 35.00
Eureka, Bread Plate 40.00
Eureka, Compote, Jelly, Ruby Stained 85.00
Eureka, Goblet, Flint 20.00
Excelsior, Goblet, Barrel, Flint 42.50
Eyewinker, Butter, Covered 40.00
Eyewinker, Cake Stand 75.00
Eyewinker, Celery Vase 49.00
Eyewinker, Compote, Open, 7 In. 35.00
Eyewinker, Spooner 26.50
    FAGOT, see Vera
    FAN, see also Butterfly & Fan
Fan & Pineapple, Cruet 25.00
Fan Band, Creamer, Footed, 6 In. 14.00
Fan With Diamond, Eggcup 15.00
Fan With Diamond, Goblet 22.50
Fan With Diamond, Pitcher, Water 50.00
Fan With Diamond, Spooner ....18.00 To 30.00
Fancy Cut, Butter, Covered, Child's ....30.00 To 35.00
Fancy Cut, Pitcher, Water, Child's 25.00
Fancy Cut, Sugar, Covered, Child's 20.00

Fine Cut & Block   Fine Cut   Flattened Diamond & Sunburst

Fancy Loop, Celery ....35.00 To 40.00
Fancy Loop, Toothpick, Green 95.00
Feather Duster, Pitcher, Water 24.00
Feather Swirl, Celery Vase 30.00
Feather Swirl, Shaker 18.00
Feather, Cake Stand, 4 1/2 X 8 In. ....30.00 To 55.00
Feather, Celery Vase, Scalloped Rim 35.00
Feather, Compote, Jelly ....15.00 To 18.00
Feather, Cruet, Original Green Stopper, Emerald Green 185.00
Feather, Goblet 45.00
Feather, Pitcher, Water ....30.00 To 58.00
Feather, Sugar, Covered ....37.00 To 55.00
Feather, Tumbler ....40.00 To 45.00
Feather, Wine, Maiden's Blush Stain 40.00
Feathered Doric, Butter 30.00
Feathers & Arches, Punch Bowl, Child's 18.00
Feeding Swan, Butter, Covered, Etched 75.00
Feeding Swan, Cake Stand 65.00
Ferris Wheel, Goblet 17.00
     FESTOON & GRAPE, see Grape & Festoon
Festoon, Cake Stand 40.00
Festoon, Creamer 15.00
Festoon, Plate, 9 1/4 In. 42.00
Festoon, Spooner, 4 In. 24.00
Festoon, Tray, Water ....18.00 To 35.00
Festoon, Tumbler 22.50
Festoon, Water Set, Tray, 6 Piece 195.00
Fickle Block, Goblet 15.00
Fine Cut & Block, Compote, Open, 8 In. 28.00
Fine Cut & Block, Creamer, Amber Blocks, Jewel Tray 85.00
Fine Cut & Block, Creamer, Blue 48.00
Fine Cut & Block, Pitcher, Water, Amber 85.00
Fine Cut & Block, Pitcher, Water, Pink Blocks 125.00
Fine Cut & Block, Saltshaker, Yellow 24.00
Fine Cut & Block, Spooner 42.00
Fine Cut & Panel, Goblet, Amber 35.00
Fine Cut & Panel, Goblet, Blue, 5 3/8 In. 52.00
Fine Cut & Panel, Spooner, Vaseline 30.00
Fine Cut Bar, Compote, Jelly 15.00
     FINE CUT MEDALLION, see Austrian
Fine Cut, Creamer, Blue 40.00
Fine Cut, Goblet 21.00
Fine Cut, Pitcher, Water, Amber 95.00
Fine Cut, Spooner, Green, Roses 38.00
Fine Cut, Wine, Parisian 42.00
Fishbone, Goblet 18.00

Fishscale, Berry Bowl ....15.00 To 16.50
Fishscale, Butter, Covered 40.00
Fishscale, Cake Stand, 9 In. ....28.00 To 32.00
Fishscale, Celery Vase 35.00
Fishscale, Compote, Jelly 18.00
Fishscale, Creamer 32.50
Fishscale, Goblet ....26.00 To 28.00
Fishscale, Pitcher, Milk 35.00
Fishscale, Plate, 8 In. 28.50
Fishscale, Plate, Square, 9 In. 32.50
Fishscale, Sauce ....4.00 To 5.00
Flamingo Habitat, Cheese Dish, Cover, Underplate 125.00
Flamingo Habitat, Goblet, Etched 25.00
Flamingo, Salt 20.00
FLAT DIAMOND & PANEL, see Lattice & Oval Panels
Flat Diamond, Spooner, Flat 26.50
Flattened Diamond & Sunburst, Celery Vase 30.00
Flattened Diamond & Sunburst, Punch Bowl, Child's 20.00
Flattened Diamond & Sunburst, Punch Bowl, Child's, 5 Cups 50.00
Fleur–De–Lis & Drape, Plate, 9 In. 15.00
Fleur–De–Lis & Tassel, Celery Vase 30.00
Fleur–De–Lis & Tassel, Compote, Covered, 9 1/2 In. 55.00
Fleur–De–Lis & Tassel, Compote, Jelly 23.00
Fleur–De–Lis & Tassel, Spooner 25.00
Fleur–De–Lis, Cake Stand, 9 3/4 In. 55.00
Fleur–De–Lis, Carafe, Water 30.00
Fleur–De–Lis, Toothpick ....10.00 To 20.00
Flora, Cruet, Clear Stopper, Green 25.00
Flora, Water Set, Green, Gold Trim, 7 Piece 195.00
Floradora, Sugar, Covered, Green, Gold Trim 125.00
Floral Oval, Wine 18.00
    FLORIDA, see Herringbone
Florida Palm, Cake Stand, 10 1/2 In. 25.00
Florida Palm, Compote, Open ....28.00 To 35.00
Florida Palm, Tumbler 28.00
    FLANGE, see Dewey
Flower Medallion, Pitcher, 6 Tumblers, Tray 140.00
    FLOWER PANELED CANE, see Cane & Rosette
Flute, Eggcup, Flint 18.00
Flute, Goblet, Flint 28.00
Flute, Mug, Applied Handle, Flint, Emerald Green 175.00
Fluted Scrolls, Pitcher, Water, Blue Opalescent 195.00
Fluted Scrolls, Spooner, Vaseline 35.00
    FLYING ROBIN, see Hummingbird
    FORGET–ME–NOT IN SNOW, see Stippled Forget–Me–Not
Forget–Me–Not, Cruet, Stopper, Milk Glass 33.00

Frosted Eagle

Frosted Stork

Garfield Drape

Forget–Me–Not, Salt & Pepper, Pink & Green 38.00
Forget–Me–Not, Salt & Pepper, White 27.00
Forget–Me–Not, Sugar Shaker, Green 125.00
Four Petal, Sugar & Creamer, Flint 135.00
Fringed Drape, Spooner, Green 30.00
    FROSTED PATTERNS, see also under name of main pattern
    FROSTED CRANE, see Frosted Stork
Frosted Eagle, Creamer ....40.00 To 42.00
Frosted Foot, Compote, Open, Etched ....35.00 To 40.00
Frosted Fruits, Pitcher, Water 70.00
Frosted Fruits, Tumbler 35.00
Frosted Leaf, Goblet, Flint 65.00
Frosted Lion, Bread Plate, Solid Handles, 12 In. 130.00
Frosted Lion, Celery Vase ....45.00 To 80.00
Frosted Lion, Compote, Covered, 8 X 9 In. 80.00
Frosted Lion, Compote, Open, 6 1/4 In. 45.00
Frosted Lion, Compote, Open, 7 1/2 In. ....55.00 To 75.00
Frosted Lion, Goblet ....55.00 To 60.00
Frosted Lion, Jam Jar, Crouching Lion Finial 55.00
Frosted Lion, Sauce, 4 In. 22.00
Frosted Lion, Spooner ....40.00 To 48.00
Frosted Ribbon, Goblet ....20.00 To 27.00
Frosted Ribbon, Pitcher 45.00
Frosted Ribbon, Sauce 7.00
Frosted Stork, Bread Plate, Round 70.00
Frosted Stork, Creamer 60.00
Frosted Stork, Finger Bowl, Iowa City Glass 90.00
Frosted Stork, Waste Bowl ....40.00 To 45.00
    FROSTED WAFFLE, see Hidalgo
Fruit Panels, Goblet, Colored Flashing 28.00
Fuchsia, Spooner ....22.00 To 25.00
G.A.R., Bread Plate 135.00
G.A.R., Goblet 55.00
Gaelic, Goblet 15.00
Galloway, Butter, Covered 45.00
Galloway, Celery Vase, 12 In. 18.00
Galloway, Creamer ....16.00 To 25.00
Galloway, Dish, Rectangular, 5 3/8 X 3 1/4 In. 25.00
Galloway, Sugar, Covered, Maiden's Blush & Clear 75.00
Galloway, Syrup, Original Top 65.00
Galloway, Toothpick 23.00
Garden Fern, Goblet 20.00
Garden Fruits, Compote, Covered, Etched, 8 In. 38.50
    GARDEN OF EDEN, see Lotus & Serpent
Garfield Drape, Bread Plate, We Mourn Our Nation's Loss 42.50
Garfield Drape, Compote, Covered, Footed, Large 98.00
Garfield Drape, Creamer ....25.00 To 38.50
Garfield Drape, Goblet 40.00
Garfield Drape, Pitcher, Water ....72.50 To 95.00
Garfield Drape, Plate, 10 In. 60.00
Garfield Drape, Sugar, Covered 65.00
Garfield Memorial, Bread Plate, 11 In. 55.00
Gathered Knot, Compote, Open, 7 1/4 In. 20.00
Geddes, Goblet 5.00
Geneva, Berry Bowl, Master, Northwood, Green 125.00
Geneva, Goblet 15.00
George Washington, Bread Plate, Frosted Center 125.00
Georgia, Compote, Open, 7 In. 30.00
Giant Sawtooth, Goblet, Flint 85.00
Giant Thumbprint, Footed, Flint, 4 1/2 In. 45.00
Gibson Girl, Creamer 115.00
Giraffe, Goblet, Etched 85.00
Goat's Head, Spooner 85.00
    GOOD LUCK, see Horseshoe

Grape & Festoon with Shield   Grape & Festoon   Hairpin with Rayed Base

Gooseberry, Butter, Covered 35.00
Gooseberry, Creamer 28.00
Gooseberry, Mug ....25.00 To 34.00
Gothic, Butter, Covered 65.00
Gothic, Celery Vase, Flint 95.00
Gothic, Goblet 60.00
Gothic, Sugar, Covered 85.00
Gothic, Wine, Flint 58.00
    GRACE, see Butterfly & Fan
    GRAND, see Diamond Medallion
    GRAND ARMY OF THE REPUBLIC, see G.A.R.
Grant, U.S., Bread Plate, Let Us Have Peace ....35.00 To 50.00
    GRAPE, see also Beaded Grape; Beaded Grape Medallion; Magnet &
    Grape
Grape & Festoon With Shield, Mug 24.00
Grape & Festoon With Shield, Mug, Blue, 3 1/4 In. 35.00
Grape & Festoon, Compote, Covered 65.00
Grape & Festoon, Spooner, Footed 20.00
Grape & Festoon, Sugar, Covered, Acorn Finial 65.00
Grape & Gothic Arches, Tumbler, Emerald Green, Gold Trim 22.00
Grape Band, Goblet ....13.00 To 15.00
Grape With Thumbprint Band, Celery Vase 38.50
Grape With Thumbprint, Goblet ....22.00 To 40.00
Grape, Bread Plate, It Is Pleasant To Labor, Handle, 10 In. 35.00
Grasshopper, Butter, Covered, No Grasshoppers 60.00
Grasshopper, Compote, Covered 50.00
Grasshopper, Goblet 85.00
Grasshopper, Pitcher, Water 60.00
Greek Key, Cruet, Clear, Polished Pontil 18.00
Greek Key, Goblet, Flint 45.00
Greek Key, Plate, 9 In. 40.00
Greek Key, Sugar, Open 30.00
Gridley, Pitcher, Water 85.00
Hairpin With Rayed Base, Spooner 36.50
Halley's Comet, Goblet ....28.00 To 45.00
Halley's Comet, Pitcher, Tankard, Etched 99.00
Halley's Comet, Wine ....15.00 To 25.00
    HAMILTON WITH CLEAR LEAF, see Hamilton with Leaf
Hamilton With Leaf, Compote, Open, High Standard 85.00
Hamilton, Goblet, Flint 48.00
Hamilton, Spooner 35.00
Hamilton, Tumbler 75.00
Hamilton, Wine 90.00
    HAND, see Pennsylvania Hand
Hanover, Celery Vase 25.00
Hanover, Goblet ....25.00 To 35.00

Hanover, Pitcher, Water 55.00
Hanover, Pitcher, Water, Amber 90.00
Harp, Butter, Covered, Flint 85.00
Harp, Goblet 658.00
Hartley, Berry Bowl, Vaseline 9.00
Hartley, Bowl, Footed, 8 1/4 In. 21.00
Hartley, Creamer 23.00
Hartley, Goblet 22.00
Hartley, Wine, Blue 35.00
Harvard, Sugar, Pea Green, 2 1/4 In. 20.00
Harvard, Toothpick, Green, Souvenir 41.00
Hawaiian Lei, Butter 35.00
Hawaiian Lei, Salt & Pepper, Tin Tops 25.00
Hawaiian Lei, Sugar 35.00
Hawaiian Lei, Table Set, Signed 72.00
Heart Band, Mug 12.00
Heart Band, Toothpick ....25.00 To 30.00
Heart Stem, Celery Vase 40.00
Heart With Thumbprint, Banana Boat 75.00
Heart With Thumbprint, Berry Set, Ruffled, Gold Trim, 7 Piece 130.00
Heart With Thumbprint, Berry, Master 22.00
Heart With Thumbprint, Bowl 25.00
Heart With Thumbprint, Bowl, Gold, Turned Up, 4 1/2 In. 18.00
Heart With Thumbprint, Celery Vase, Green, 6 1/2 In. 65.00
Heart With Thumbprint, Creamer 28.00
Heart With Thumbprint, Cruet, Faceted Stopper 60.00
Heart With Thumbprint, Goblet ....45.00 To 55.00
Heart With Thumbprint, Ice Bucket ....35.00 To 65.00
Heart With Thumbprint, Plate, 6 1/2 In. 25.00
Heart With Thumbprint, Plate, Gold Trim, 6 In. 23.00
Heart With Thumbprint, Punch Cup 15.00
Heart With Thumbprint, Saltshaker 45.00
Heart With Thumbprint, Sugar, Green, Individual 28.00
Heart With Thumbprint, Sugar, Open, Individual 24.00
Heart With Thumbprint, Tray, Card, Gold Trim ....20.00 To 21.00
Heart With Thumbprint, Tumbler 35.00
Heart With Thumbprint, Wine ....35.00 To 49.00
Heart, Creamer 150.00
HEARTS OF LOCH LAVEN, see Shuttle
Helene, Sugar, Covered 70.00
Henrietta, Celery Vase, Pedestal 35.00
Henrietta, Creamer, 3 1/2 In. 10.00
Hercules Pillar, Syrup, Amber 115.00
Hercules Pillar, Syrup, Original Lid, Blue 35.00
Hercules Pillar, Tumbler, Flint, 4 In. 65.00
Heron, Pitcher, Water, Etched 135.00
Herringbone, Bowl, Green, 9 In. 30.00
Herringbone, Cake Stand, Green 42.00
Herringbone, Celery Vase 35.00
Herringbone, Compote, Ruby Flashed, Square, 8 1/2 In. 75.00
Herringbone, Creamer, Green 28.00
Herringbone, Cruet, Emerald Green, Original Stopper 85.00
Herringbone, Goblet, Etched ....25.00 To 35.00
Herringbone, Goblet, Green 28.00
Herringbone, Pitcher, Water, Emerald Green ....50.00 To 65.00
Herringbone, Spooner 25.00
Herringbone, Sugar, Covered, Green 39.00
Herringbone, Water Set, Emerald Green, 7 Piece 225.00
Hexagon Block, Berry Bowl, Master 65.00
Hexagon Block, Creamer 75.00
Hexagon Block, Tankard 85.00
Hexagonal Bull's-Eye, Compote, Open, 8 1/4 X 10 In. 45.00
Hickman, Breakfast Set, Gold Trim, 4 Piece 175.00
Hickman, Cake Plate, 9 In. 23.00

Hickman, Goblet ....18.00 To 35.00

Hickman, Ice Bueket 55.00

Hickman, Pitcher, Milk 30.00

Hickman, Sugar & Creamer, Green, Individual ....38.00 To 39.00

Hidalgo, Celery Vase, Frosted 48.00

Hidalgo, Goblet, Etched ....15.00 To 20.00

    HOBNAIL, see Hobnail category

    HOBNAIL & BARS, see Barred Hobnail

Hobnail With Thumbprint Base, Butter, Covered, Blue 65.00

Hobstar, Celery Vase 20.00

    HOLBROOK, see Pineapple & Fan

Holly, Spooner 55.00

    HONEYCOMB, see also Loop & Honeycomb

Honeycomb With Ovals, Goblet, Flint 22.50

Honeycomb, Butter, Covered, Flint 45.00

Honeycomb, Celery Vase, 9 In. 45.00

Honeycomb, Claret, Flint 15.00

Honeycomb, Compote, Open, Scalloped, 5 1/2 X 7 In.Diam. 22.00

Honeycomb, Goblet 16.00

Honeycomb, Mug 15.00

Honeycomb, Pitcher, Water, Bulbous 85.00

Honeycomb, Powder Jar, Sterling Silver Lid 85.00

Honeycomb, Wine 5.00

Hooks & Eyes, Goblet 25.00

Hops Band, Goblet ....10.00 To 21.00

Hops Band, Sauce 5.00

Horn Of Plenty, Compote, Open, 19 X 9 In. 145.00

Horn Of Plenty, Eggcup, Flint ....35.00 To 42.00

Horn Of Plenty, Goblet, Flint 55.00

Hamilton   Hidalgo   Holly

Horn of Plenty   Horseshoe   Inverted Fern

Horn Of Plenty, Honey 15.00
Horn Of Plenty, Tumbler 75.00
Horn Of Plenty, Whiskey, Handle, Flint 235.00
Horse & Cart, Match Holder, Amber 55.00
Horseheads Medallion, Spooner, Child's ....20.00 To 45.00
Horseshoe, Bread Plate ....32.50 To 39.00
Horseshoe, Cake Stand, 9 In. 50.00
Horseshoe, Celery Vase, Pedestal 40.00
Horseshoe, Compote, Open, 9 X 9 In. 20.00
Horseshoe, Creamer ....28.50 To 29.50
Horseshoe, Goblet, Fancy Stem 37.50
Horseshoe, Goblet, Knob Stem ....36.50 To 40.00
Horseshoe, Tray 45.00
Horseshoe, Wine 145.00
Hotel Argus, Wine 14.00
Huber, Goblet, Flint 10.00
    HUCKLE, see Feather Duster
Hummingbird, Goblet 32.50
Hummingbird, Pitcher, Water, Blue ....85.00 To 125.00
Hummingbird, Tumbler 35.00
Hummingbird, Water Set, Amber, 7 Piece 358.00
Humpty–Dumpty, Mug, Child's 45.00
    IDA, see Sheraton
    IDAHO, see Snail
Idyll, Butter, Apple Green, Gold Trim 120.00
Idyll, Creamer, Apple Green 45.00
Idyll, Spooner, Apple Green 50.00
Illinois, Basket, Rope Handle, 7 In. ....45.00 To 65.00
Illinois, Butter, Covered ....36.00 To 45.00
Illinois, Creamer 35.00
Illinois, Plate, 7 In. 22.50
Illinois, Spooner ....35.00 To 48.00
Imperial No.9, Goblet 15.00
    INDIAN TREE, see Sprig
    INDIANA SWIRL, see Feather
Intaglio Sunflower, Pitcher, Water, 10 In. 45.00
Intaglio Sunflower, Wine, Gold Trim 18.00
Intaglio, Creamer, Green ....85.00 To 95.00
Interlocked Hearts, Cruet 15.00
Interlocking Crescents, Compote 20.00
Inverted Fern, Goblet, Flint ....28.00 To 37.00
Inverted Fern, Sugar, Covered, Flint 60.00
Inverted Fern, Tumbler, Flint, 3 3/8 In. 95.00
Inverted Prism, Goblet, Etched 25.00
Inverted Thumbprint & Star, Goblet, Blue 55.00
Inverted Thumbprint, Carafe, Hand Painted Flowers, Amber 95.00
Inverted Thumbprint, Cruet, Blue, Clear Stopper, 6 1/2 In. 145.00
Inverted Thumbprint, Goblet 10.00
Inverted Thumbprint, Pitcher, Square Top, 4 1/4 In.Diam. 150.00
Inverted Thumbprint, Punch Cup, Amber 12.00
Inverted Thumbprint, Spooner, Vaseline 22.00
Inverted Thumbprint, Sugar, Covered, Amber 40.00
Iowa City, Cheese Dish, Covered, Girl At Play 155.00
Iowa, Goblet, Gold Trim 23.00
Iowa, Toothpick, Gold Trim 18.00
Iris With Meander, Sugar & Creamer, Gold Trim, Electric Blue 225.00
Iris, Goblet 15.00
Ivanhoe, Compote, 8 In. 35.00
Ivy In Snow, Cake Stand, 8 In. 20.00
Ivy In Snow, Goblet 66.00
Ivy In Snow, Wine 15.00
Jacob's Coat, Creamer, Sapphire Blue 45.00
Jacob's Coat, Pitcher, Water, Rose 75.00
Jacob's Ladder, Butter, Covered 38.00

Jacob's Ladder, Celery Vase ....25.00 To 49.00
Jacob's Ladder, Compote, Open, 7 1/2 In. 38.00
Jacob's Ladder, Compote, Scalloped, 6 3/4 X 8 1/4 In. 29.00
Jacob's Ladder, Creamer ....30.00 To 32.00
Jacob's Ladder, Cruet, Maltese Cross Stopper 75.00
Jacob's Ladder, Goblet ....55.00 To 58.00
Jacob's Ladder, Pitcher, Water ....135.00 To 155.00
Jacob's Ladder, Salt, Master ....22.50 To 25.00
Jacob's Ladder, Sugar & Creamer 55.00
Jacob's Ladder, Wine ....29.50 To 40.00
Jefferson Davis, Bread Plate 65.00
Jefferson Optic, Table Set, Emerald, Sugar & Creamer, Spooner 65.00
Jersey Swirl, Cake Stand, Amber ....55.00 To 75.00
Jersey Swirl, Celery Vase, Amber 50.00
Jewel & Dewdrop, Berry Set, Bowl, 6 Flat Sauce 75.00
Jewel & Dewdrop, Pitcher, Water ....40.00 To 55.00
Jewel & Dewdrop, Relish 20.00
Jewel & Dewdrop, Tumbler, Handle 40.00
    JEWEL & FESTOON, see Loop & Jewel
    JEWEL BAND, see Scalloped Tape
Jeweled Heart, Water Set, Green, Gold Trim 450.00
Jeweled Moon & Star, Celery Vase ....35.00 To 45.00
Jeweled Moon & Star, Compote, 6 3/4 In. 55.00
Jeweled Moon & Star, Goblet 20.00
    JOB'S TEARS, see Art
    JUBILEE, see Hickman
Jumbo & Barnum, Head Handle, Etched 125.00
Jumbo & Barnum, Sugar, Cover, Elephant Finial, Face Handle 275.00
Jumbo, Butter, Covered, Round 475.00
Jumbo, Castor Set 95.00
Jumbo, Creamer 250.00
Jumbo, Goblet, One–O–One Border 400.00
    KAMONI, see Pennsylvania
    KANSAS, see Jewel & Dewdrop
Kentucky, Cruet 20.00
Kentucky, Wine 25.00
Kentucky, Wine, Green 30.00
King's 500, Tumbler 45.00
King's Crown, Bowl, Bell Shape, 8 3/4 In. 25.00
King's Crown, Celery Vase ....25.00 To 60.00
King's Crown, Compote, Open 30.00
King's Crown, Creamer ....50.00 To 80.00
King's Crown, Goblet 32.00
King's Crown, Goblet, Green Eyes 22.00
King's Crown, Salt, Master, Oblong, 2 1/2 X 7/8 In. 25.00
King's Crown, Sugar, Covered 60.00

Jacob's Ladder   Jeweled Heart   Jumbo

Leaf & Dart   Liberty Bell

King's Crown, Toothpick, Etched ....25.00 To 40.00
King's Crown, Tumbler 37.00
King's Crown, Wine 25.00
King's Royal, Toothpick, Ruby & Clear 35.00
Kitten, Plate, Iowa City 95.00
Kitten, Spooner, Marigold 42.00
Klondike, Berry Set, Gold Band, Frosted, 5 Piece 385.00
Klondike, Bowl, Flat, 8 In. 55.00
Klondike, Celery Vase, 8 1/4 In. 125.00
Klondike, Punch Cup 110.00
Klondike, Tumbler, Amber Stained, Clear & Frosted 135.00
Knobby Bull's-Eye, Goblet 35.00
Knobby Bull's-Eye, Tumbler 14.00
Kokomo, Goblet ....18.00 To 45.00
Kokomo, Muffineer 40.00
Kokomo, Tray, Condiment 35.00
     LACE, see Drapery
Lacy Daisy, Berry Set, 7 Piece 60.00
Lacy Daisy, Syrup, Pittsburgh 48.00
Lacy Medallion, Sugar, Open, Green 15.00
Lacy Medallion, Toothpick, Green, Gold Trim 35.00
     LACY SPIRAL, see Colossus
Ladder With Diamonds, Plate, 9 In. 25.00
Ladder-To-The-Stars, Holder, Condensed Milk 40.00
Lady Hamilton, Compote, Covered 69.00
Lakewood, Goblet 18.00
Laredo Honeycomb, Goblet, Flint 18.00
Later Prisms With Diamond Point, Goblet, Buttermilk 32.00
Later Prisms With Diamond Point, Spooner 24.50
Lattice & Oval Panels, Punch Bowl, Child's 25.00
Lattice, Celery Vase 18.50
Lattice, Compote, 8 In. 20.00
Lattice, Sugar, Covered 22.50
Lattice, Syrup 40.00
Leaf & Dart With Round Ornaments, Butter, Covered 85.00
Leaf & Dart, Eggcup ....18.00 To 28.00
Leaf & Dart, Goblet ....20.00 To 40.00
Leaf & Dart, Salt ....24.50 To 25.00
Leaf & Dart, Tumbler, Footed 15.00
Leaf & Flower, Berry Set, Amber, Master & 4 Sauce 110.00
Leaf & Flower, Spooner 42.00
Leaf & Flower, Spooner, Amber 30.00
Leaf & Flower, Sugar & Creamer, Amber ....75.00 To 125.00
Leaf & Flower, Syrup, Frosted & Clear 100.00
Leaf & Flower, Table Set, Clear, Frosted, Amber Stain, 4 Pc. 235.00
Leaf & Flower, Tankard, Amber 85.00

Leaf & Rib, Tumbler, Amber 32.00
Leaf Medallion, Creamer, Green 55.00
Leaf Mold, Salt & Pepper, Vaseline, Frosted, Brass Top 125.00
Leaf, Goblet 15.00
Lee, Wine 125.00
    LENS & STAR, see Star & Oval
    LEVERNE, see Star in Honeycomb
Liberty Bell, Berry Bowl, Flat Bottom 15.00
Liberty Bell, Bread Plate, 13 Colonies ....75.00 To 135.00
Liberty Bell, Bread Plate, Oval, 1776-1876, Signers ....75.00 To 85.00
Liberty Bell, Bread Plate, Oval, Shell Handles, 1776-1876 .... 55.00
Liberty Bell, Butter, Covered 110.00
Liberty Bell, Creamer, Applied Handle 80.00
Liberty Bell, Creamer, Rope Handle, Pedestal 125.00
Liberty Bell, Goblet ....25.00 To 65.00
Liberty Bell, Plate, 8 In. 75.00
Liberty Bell, Relish 40.00
Liberty Bell, Spooner 80.00
Liberty Bell, Sugar, Covered ....95.00 To 110.00
Liberty, Goblet 40.00
Liberty, Wine 25.00
Lily-Of-The-Valley, Cruet, Pedestal, Original Stopper 95.00
Lily-Of-The-Valley, Goblet 20.00
Lincoln Drape With Tassel, Goblet 128.00
Lincoln Drape, Goblet 65.00
Lincoln Drape, Spooner, Flint 30.00
    LION, see also Frosted Lion
Lion In Jungle, Goblet, Stag 110.00
Lion With Cable, Compote, Covered, 8 In. 94.00
Lion's Head, Compote, Open, Square, 1895, 10 1/2 In. 85.00
Lion's Head, Cup & Saucer, Child's 87.50
    LION'S LEG, see Alaska
Lion, Butter, Covered, Child's 115.00
Lion, Celery Vase, Frosted Base, Rope Edge, Pedestal 95.00
Lion, Compote, Covered, Lion Head Finial, 8 In. 115.00
Lion, Creamer, Etched 40.00
Lion, Cup & Saucer, Child's 55.00
Lion, Cup, Child's ....29.00 To 35.00
Lion, Goblet 55.00
Lion, Spooner, Child's 35.00
Lion, Sugar, Covered, Rampant Lion Finial 95.00
    LIPPMAN, see Flat Diamond
Little Lamb, Sugar, Open, Child's 35.00
Locket On Chain, Compote, Open, Beaded Rim, 8 In. 145.00
Log Cabin, Bowl, 3 1/4 X 2 1/4 In. 35.00
Log Cabin, Butter, Covered 125.00

Lily-of-the-Valley   Lincoln Drape   Maine

Log Cabin, Creamer .... 65.00 To 150.00
Log Cabin, Jam Jar, Covered, Vaseline 675.00
Log Cabin, Spooner 85.00
Log Cabin, Sugar, Covered .... 85.00 To 200.00
    LOOP, see also Seneca Loop; Yuma Loop
Loop & Dart With Diamond Ornament, Butter, Covered 35.00
Loop & Dart With Diamond Ornament, Goblet 18.50
Loop & Dart With Round Ornament, Eggcup ....27.00 To 28.00
Loop & Dart, Celery Vase ....35.00 To 40.00
Loop & Dart, Goblet ....17.00 To 25.00
Loop & Honeycomb, Goblet 17.00
Loop & Jewel, Creamer, Individual 18.50
Loop & Jewel, Spooner 28.00
Loop & Moose Eye, Wine 24.00
Loop & Petal, Candlestick, Canary, Pair 295.00
Loop With Dewdrop, Goblet 26.00
Loop With Dewdrop, Pitcher, Water 65.00
    LOOP WITH STIPPLED PANELS, see Texas
Loop, Celery Vase, Flint 50.00
Loop, Goblet 20.00
Loop, Sugar, Covered, Flint, 7 1/2 In. 38.00
Loop, Wine, Barrel Shape 12.00
    LOOPS & DROPS, see New Jersey
Loops & Fans, Goblet 25.00
Lotus & Serpent, Bread Plate 45.00
Lotus & Serpent, Compote, Covered, 7 1/2 X 6 In. 55.00
Lotus & Serpent, Mug 45.00
Lotus & Serpent, Pitcher, Water 95.00
Lotus, Bread Plate 35.00
Lotus, Dish, Oval, 9 X 6 1/2 In. 12.00
Lotus, Plate, 6 In. 20.00
Louise, Bowl, Teal Green, Footed 40.00
Louise, Cake Stand, 4 1/2 X 9 1/2 In. 75.00
Louise, Punch Cup 8.00
Louisiana Purchase, Tumbler 15.00
Louisiana, Toothpick 30.00
Louisiana, Tumbler 20.00
Magnet & Grape, Compote, Open, Frosted, 8 X 6 1/2 In. 68.00
Magnet & Grape, Goblet, Frosted Leaf, Knob Stem, Flint 65.00
Magnet & Grape, Spooner 35.00
Magnolia, Cruet, Stopper 15.00
Magnolia, Pitcher 55.00
    MAIDEN BLUSH, see Banded Portland
Maine, Berry Bowl, Green 35.00
Maine, Jelly, Covered, Green 65.00
Maine, Pitcher, Milk, Emerald Green 85.00
Maine, Sugar, Green, Covered 60.00
Majestic, Cruet 20.00
Majestic, Pitcher, Water, Green 40.00
Maltese Cross, Goblet, Flint 42.00
Manhattan, Bowl, 7 In. .... 12.00 To 20.00
Manhattan, Bowl, 9 In. 10.00
Manhattan, Cake Stand 60.00
Manhattan, Plate, 6 In. 9.00
Manhattan, Punch Bowl 95.00
Manhattan, Toothpick, Gold Trim 35.00
Manhattan, Wine 25.00
Maple Leaf, Creamer, Cobalt Blue, Gold Trim 60.00
Maple Leaf, Goblet, Amber .... 95.00 To 125.00
Maple Leaf, Goblet, Tree Stem, Amber 140.00
Maple Leaf, Spooner, Cobalt Blue 60.00
Maple Leaf, Sugar, Covered, Cobalt Blue 85.00
Mardi Gras, Spooner, Child's, Gold Horizontal Ribs 45.00
Mardi Gras, Wine, Gold Trim 22.50

Marquisette, Celery Vase 55.00
Marquisette, Goblet 22.00
Martha's Tears, Goblet ....12.00 To 25.00
Martyrs, Mug 45.00
Maryland, Goblet 24.50
Mascotte, Butter, Covered, Etched 48.00
Mascotte, Creamer, Etched ....32.50 To 38.00
Mascotte, Goblet, Etched 45.00
Mascotte, Sauce, Footed, 4 In. 5.50
Mascotte, Spooner, Etched 32.00
Masonic, Celery Vase 27.50
Massachusetts, Bottle, 11 In. 80.00
Massachusetts, Butter, Covered ....25.00 To 45.00
Massachusetts, Celery Vase, Trumpet Shape 28.00
Massachusetts, Plate, 8 1/4 In. 25.00
Massachusetts, Sugar 17.50
Massachusetts, Teapot, Large 65.00
Master Argus, Tumbler, Flint 35.00
McKinley Memorial, Bread Plate, His Will Be Done ....37.50 To 65.00
McKinley, Cup, Covered 65.00
Medallion Sunburst, Berry Set 25.00
Medallion Sunburst, Cake Plate, Square 9.00
Medallion Sunburst, Creamer, Individual 10.00
Medallion Sunburst, Cruet ....18.50 To 25.00
Medallion Sunburst, Plate, Square, 7 In. 6.50
Medallion Sunburst, Sugar & Creamer, Individual 15.00
Medallion, Cake Stand, 6 3/4 X11 In. 125.00
Medallion, Creamer, Green ....45.00 To 55.00
Medallion, Goblet 23.00
Medallion, Goblet, Amber 28.00
Medallion, Pitcher, Water, Blue 90.00
Medallion, Spooner, Green 45.00
Medallion, Sugar, Covered, Green 60.00
Melrose, Cake Stand 25.00
Melrose, Celery Vase ....22.00 To 25.00
Melrose, Wine 16.00
Memphis, Creamer, Gold Trim 70.00
Memphis, Pitcher, Water, Green, Gold Trim 100.00
Memphis, Spooner, Gold Trim 70.00
Memphis, Table Set, Gold Trim, 4 Piece 225.00
Memphis, Tumbler, Gold Trim 20.00
Memphis, Water Set, Green, Gold Trim, 6 Piece 215.00
Michigan, Compote, Jelly 23.00
Michigan, Goblet 25.00
Michigan, Pitcher, Child's 22.00
Michigan, Relish 17.00
Michigan, Spooner, Yellow, Painted Flowers 38.00
Michigan, Toothpick, Blue On Top, Enamel Trim 65.00
Michigan, Tumbler 20.00
Milton, Goblet 16.00
Minerva, Bread Plate ....35.00 To 95.00
Minerva, Butter, Covered 65.00
Minerva, Cake Stand, 11 In. 100.00
Minerva, Creamer ....35.00 To 48.50
Minerva, Goblet 70.00
Minerva, Plate, Handles, 7 1/2 In. 50.00
Minerva, Spooner ....30.00 To 45.00
Minnesota, Carafe, Water ....24.00 To 35.00
Minnesota, Compote, 9 In. 38.00
Minnesota, Cruet, Original Stopper 35.00
Minnesota, Goblet 35.00
Minnesota, Toothpick, 3 Handles 20.00
Minnesota, Wine ....25.00 To 35.00
Minor Block, Celery Vase, Etched 35.00

| Mitered Diamond | Moon & Star | New England Pineapple |

Mioton, Goblet	10.00
Mioton, Pleat Band, Goblet, Flint	40.00
Missouri, Cake Plate, 8 1/4 In.	35.00
Missouri, Pitcher, Water, Green	87.00
Missouri, Wine	35.00
Missouri, Wine, Green	35.00
Mitered Bars, Spooner	20.00
MITERED DIAMOND POINT, see Mitered Bars	
Mitered Diamond, Condiment Set, 5 Piece	65.00
Mitered Diamond, Water Set, Blue, 6 Piece	150.00
Mitered Frieze, Celery Vase, Pedestal	23.00
Model Peerless, Wine	10.00
Monkey, Bowl, Scalloped Edge, 8 X 4 1/2 In.	400.00
Monkey, Mug	65.00
Monkey, Pitcher, Water	425.00
Monkey, Spooner	50.00 To 95.00
Moon & Star, Cake Stand, 10 In.	55.00
Moon & Star, Celery Vase	68.50
Moon & Star, Compote, Covered, 10 In.	28.00
Moon & Star, Compote, Open, 8 In.	32.00 To 35.00
Moon & Star, Compote, Open, Frosted To Clear, High, 8 In.	25.00
Moon & Star, Goblet	32.50 To 36.50
Moon & Star, Spooner	35.00
Moon & Star, Tray, Ice Cream	35.00
Moon & Star, Tumbler, Flint	65.00
MOON & STORK, see Ostrich Looking At The Moon	
Moose–Eye In Sand, Goblet	18.00
Morning Glory, Goblet, Flint	165.00
My Lady's Workbox, Goblet	30.00 To 33.00
Nail, Creamer, Ruby	45.00
Nail, Pitcher, Water	65.00 To 75.00
Nail, Spooner	75.00
Nailhead, Butter, Covered	46.50
Nailhead, Cake Stand, 9 1/2 In.	20.00 To 24.00
Nailhead, Goblet	25.00 To 40.00
Nailhead, Pitcher, Water	32.00 To 60.00
Nailhead, Plate, 9 In.	12.00 To 25.00
Nailhead, Wine	18.00 To 20.00
Narcissus Spray, Pitcher, 8 1/2 In.	115.00
Narcissus Spray, Tumbler	34.00
Naturalistic Blackberry, Goblet	50.00
Nautilus, Berry Set, White, Northwood, 5 Pc.	250.00
Near Cut, Compote, Jelly	35.00
NEBRASKA, see Bismarc Star	
Nellie Bly, Bread Plate, Scalloped	45.00
Nelly, Wine	15.00

Nestor, Spooner, White Enameling 55.00
New England Pineapple, Compote, Open, Flint, 7 In. 45.00
New England Pineapple, Goblet, Flint ....35.00 To 50.00
New England Pineapple, Spooner 38.00
New England Pineapple, Sugar, Covered, Flint 75.00
New England, Eggcup 38.00
New Era, Compote, Jelly, Covered 30.00
New Hampshire, Cake Stand 40.00
New Hampshire, Toothpick 32.00
New Hampshire, Wine, Flared 9.00
New Jersey, Berry Set, 7 Piece 57.50
New Jersey, Butter, Covered 90.00
New Jersey, Cake Plate 30.00
New Jersey, Compote, Open, Beaded Rim, 5 In. 35.00
New Jersey, Creamer, Gold Trim 35.00
New Jersey, Cruet, Stopper 45.00
New Jersey, Goblet, Clear, Gold Trim 35.00
New Jersey, Pitcher, Water, Ruby Flashed 125.00
New Jersey, Relish 15.00
New Jersey, Sugar, Covered ....40.00 To 45.00
New Jersey, Toothpick, Gold Trim 40.00
New Jersey, Tumbler ....12.00 To 25.00
New Jersey, Water Set, 7 Piece 165.00
New York Honeycomb, Eggcup, Flint 18.00
New York Honeycomb, Salt, Master, Etched 29.00
New York, Goblet, Flint 15.00
Niagara Falls, Bread Plate 130.00
Nursery Rhymes, Butter, Covered, Child's 85.00
Nursery Rhymes, Creamer, Child's ....25.00 To 40.00
Nursery Rhymes, Punch Set, Child's, Milk Glass, 7 Piece 295.00
Nursery Rhymes, Tea Set, Child's, 12 Piece 175.00
Nursery Rhymes, Tumbler ....18.00 To 20.00
Oak Leaf Band, Goblet 17.00
Odd Fellows, Goblet 30.00
Ohio Inverted Thumbprint, Goblet, Green 19.00
Ohio Star, Butter, Covered, Millersburg 95.00
Ohio Star, Vase, Millersburg, 9 1/2 In. 95.00
Oklahoma, Candlestick, Double Handles 45.00
Oklahoma, Goblet 35.00
Oklahoma, Pitcher, Water 60.00
       ONE HUNDRED ONE, see One–O–One
One–O–One, Bread Plate, Give Us Our Daily Bread, Implements 45.00
One–O–One, Butter, Covered, Clear Stork Finial 65.00
One–O–One, Cake Stand, 10 In. 65.00
One–O–One, Goblet ....30.00 To 50.00
One–O–One, Plate, 7 In. ....8.00 To 22.00
One–O–One, Spooner ....18.00 To 27.00
One–O–One, Sugar & Creamer 75.00
       ONE–THOUSAND EYE, see Thousand Eye
Open Rose, Creamer 60.00
Open Rose, Eggcup ....22.00 To 24.50
Open Rose, Goblet 20.00
Open Rose, Relish, Scalloped Rim, Floral Design On Bottom 15.00
Open Rose, Tumbler ....26.00 To 65.00
Opposing Pyramids, Celery Vase 35.00
Opposing Pyramids, Goblet 24.50
Opposing Pyramids, Wine ....12.00 To 15.00
       OREGON, see also Beaded Loop
Oregon, Bread Plate 35.00
Oregon, Compote, Open, 7 In. 20.00
Oregon, Syrup 45.00
Oregon, Tumbler 35.00
Oriental, Spooner 25.00
Oriental, Sugar & Creamer 100.00

ORION, see Cathedral
Orion Inverted Thumbprint, Goblet 16.50
Ornate Star, Wine 18.00
Ostrich Looking At The Moon, Goblet ....65.00 To 85.00
OVAL LOOP, see Question Mark
Oval Miter, Spooner, Flint 36.50
Oval Panels, Goblet, Amber 16.00
Oval Star, Berry Set, 7 Piece 75.00
Oval Star, Butter, Covered, Child's 35.00
Oval Star, Punch Set, 7 Piece 75.00
Oval Star, Water Set, Gold Trim, Clear, 7 Piece 125.00
Overshot, Mug 29.50
Overshot, Tumbler 25.00
Ovoid Panels, Goblet, Flint 50.00
OWL, see Bull's–Eye with Diamond Point
Owl & Possum, Goblet ....90.00 To 125.00
Owl & Pussy Cat, Cheese Dish 200.00
Paddlewheel, Butter, Covered 35.00
Paddlewheel, Wine 10.00
Paisley, Relish, Purple Dots 12.00
Paling, Sugar, Covered 25.00
Palm Leaf Fan, Cruet 25.00
Palm Leaf, Salt, Turquoise 12.00
Palm Stub, Goblet 25.00
Palmette, Compote, Covered, 8 In. 40.00
Palmette, Cup Plate 45.00
Palmette, Goblet 39.50
Palmette, Spooner, Footed 22.50
Panama, Pitcher 60.00
Panama, Wine 80.00
Paneled 44, Berry Set, Green Flashed, Gold, Master, 6 Bowls 135.00
Paneled Acorn Band, Goblet 26.50
Paneled Cane, Goblet 10.00
Paneled Cane, Sugar, Open 32.00
Paneled Dewdrop, Creamer ....14.00 To 25.00
Paneled Dewdrop, Sugar, Open 30.00
Paneled Diamond & Finecut, Cake Stand, 9 In. 25.00
Paneled Diamond & Flowers, Goblet 26.00
Paneled Diamond Point, Goblet, Blue 35.00
PANELED DOGWOOD, see Dogwood
Paneled Forget–Me–Not, Bread Plate 24.00
Paneled Forget–Me–Not, Cake Stand 55.00
Paneled Forget–Me–Not, Celery Vase ....30.00 To 32.00
Paneled Forget–Me–Not, Compote, Covered, 8 In. ....45.00 To 55.00
Paneled Forget–Me–Not, Goblet ....35.00 To 38.00
Paneled Forget–Me–Not, Pitcher, Milk ....35.00 To 38.00

Open Rose   Oval Miter   Paneled Forget–Me–Not

Pennsylvania   Pleat & Panel   Princess Feather

Paneled Heather, Table Set, Hand–Painted Flowers, 4 Piece	175.00
Paneled Heather, Tumbler	13.00
Paneled Herringbone, Goblet, Green	38.00
Paneled Herringbone, Mustard, Covered	22.50
Paneled Herringbone, Pitcher, Water	35.00
Paneled Hexagons, Compote, Jelly, Blue	23.50
Paneled Hobnail, Plate, 7 In.	7.00
Paneled Iris, Pitcher, Water	38.00
Paneled Jewels, Goblet	18.00
Paneled Jewels, Goblet, Amber	25.00
Paneled Jewels, Wine, Vaseline	35.00
Paneled Long Jewels, Goblet	22.00
Paneled Nightshade, Goblet	10.00 To 22.50
Paneled Nightshade, Goblet, Amber	40.00
Paneled Nightshade, Wine	12.00 To 28.00
Paneled Sagebrush, Goblet	18.00
PANELED STAR & BUTTON, see Sedan	
PANELED STIPPLED BOWL, see Stippled Band	
Paneled Sunflower, Goblet	20.00 To 30.00
Paneled Thistle, Basket, Applied Handle	35.00
Paneled Thistle, Creamer	22.50
Paneled Thistle, Pitcher, 7 1/2 In.	35.00
Paneled Thistle, Rose Bowl, Footed, Bee Mark, 4 In.	50.00
Paneled Thistle, Salt & Pepper	55.00
Paneled Waffle	16.00
Paneled Wee Blossoms, Pitcher, Water	30.00
Pansy, Sugar & Creamer, Marigold	45.00
Pathfinder, Cake Stand	25.00
Pathfinder, Cruet	32.00
Pathfinder, Pitcher, Water	32.00
Pathfinder, Tumbler	15.00
PATTEE CROSS, see Broughton	
Pavonia, Butter, Covered, Footed	65.00
Pavonia, Celery Vase, Etched	30.00 To 40.00
Pavonia, Goblet	16.00 To 22.00
Pavonia, Goblet, Pineapple Stem, Etched Maple Leaf	35.00
Pavonia, Pitcher, Water	75.00
Pavonia, Salt, Master	28.00
Pavonia, Spooner	22.00
Pavonia, Sugar, Covered, Ruby	78.00
Pavonia, Tankard, Etched, 13 In.	90.00
Pavonia, Tumbler, Etched Maple Leaf	20.00 To 30.00
Pavonia, Water Set, Etched, 5 Piece	258.00
Pea Pods, Pitcher, Water	40.00
Pea Pods, Tumbler, Green, Gold	35.00
Peacock At The Fountain, Salt, Open, Blue & White	95.00

Peacock Feather, Compote, Low 27.00
Peacock Feather, Cruet 25.00
Peacock Feather, Decanter, Stopper 30.00
Peacock Feather, Sauce 5.00
    PEACOCK'S EYE, see Peacock Feather
    PEERLESS, see also Model Peerless
Peerless, Spooner 30.00
    PENNSYLVANIA, see also Balder; Pennsylvania Hand
    PENNSYLVANIA HAND, see also Pennsylvania
Pennsylvania Hand, Jam Jar, Covered 35.00
Pennsylvania, Creamer .... 14.00 To 26.00
Pennsylvania, Creamer, Gold Trim 7.50
Pennsylvania, Goblet 30.00
Pennsylvania, Hand, Pitcher, Water 50.00
Pennsylvania, Mustard, Pewter Top 40.00
Pennsylvania, Sugar, Open 12.00
Pennsylvania, Tumbler .... 15.00 To 30.00
Pennsylvania, Wine 9.00
Petal & Loop, Compote, Open, 9 X 6 In. .... 62.00 To 65.00
Philadelphia Centennial, Goblet .... 36.00 To 55.00
Picket, Goblet 35.00
Picket, Pitcher, Water 95.00
Picket, Salt, Master 30.00
Picket, Toothpick 25.00
Pigs In Corn, Goblet .... 50.00 To 90.00
    PILLAR & BULL'S–EYE, SEE THISTLE
Pillow Encircled, Bowl, Ruby Flashed, 8 In. 56.00
Pillow Encircled, Cruet 24.00
Pillow Encircled, Pitcher, Tankard 95.00
Pillow Encircled, Sugar & Creamer 45.00
Pillow Encircled, Sugar Shaker 15.00
Pillow Encircled, Water Set, Etched, 6 Piece 115.00
    PINAFORE, see Actress
Pineapple & Fan, Bottle, Cologne 15.00
Pineapple & Fan, Carafe, Water 29.00
Pineapple & Fan, Celery Vase, Cone Shape, 7 1/2 In. 10.00
Pineapple & Fan, Relish, Oval, 8 1/2 In. 8.00
Pineapple & Fan, Toothpick 35.00
Pineapple & Fan, Tray, Ice Cream, 12 7/8 X 7 1/4 In. 25.00
Pineapple & Fan, Whiskey 6.00
Pineapple, Goblet 20.00
Pioneer's Victoria, Butter, Covered 95.00
Pioneer's Victoria, Goblet, Etched 45.00
    PITT HONEYCOMB, see also Honeycomb
Plain Sunburst, Goblet 10.00
Pleat & Panel, Bread Plate .... 29.00 To 45.00
Pleat & Panel, Butter, Covered, Handles, Pedestal 55.00
Pleat & Panel, Celery Vase .... 25.00 To 35.00
Pleat & Panel, Compote, Covered, High Standard, Square, 6 In. 45.00
Pleat & Panel, Dish, Covered, Oblong, 7 X 4 1/2 In. 35.00
Pleat & Panel, Goblet .... 19.00 To 35.00
Pleat & Panel, Saltshaker 25.00
Pleat & Panel, Spooner 25.00
Plume, Celery Vase 30.00
Plume, Compote, Open, High Standard, 7 In. 32.00
Plume, Creamer 25.00
Plume, Spooner .... 25.00 To 26.50
Pointed Cube, Wine 15.00
Pointed Jewel, Compote, Jelly, 4 1/2 X 4 1/2 In. 55.00
    POINTED PANELED DAISY & BUTTON, see Queen
    POINTED THUMBPRINT, see Almond Thumbprint
Polar Bear, Goblet .... 85.00 To 185.00
Polar Bear, Goblet, Frosted & Clear .... 75.00 To 115.00
Polar Bear, Pitcher, Water, Ohio, Late 19th Century, 9 3/8 In. 110.00

Popcorn, Butter, Covered 50.00
Popcorn, Cake Stand, 11 In. ....65.00 To 90.00
Popcorn, Pitcher, Raised Ears, Bulbous 75.00
Popcorn, Wine 35.00
    PORTLAND WITH DIAMOND POINT BAND, see Galloway; Virginia
Portland, Compote, 7 X 5 1/4 In. 45.00
Portland, Creamer ....16.00 To 16.50
Portland, Cruet ....32.50 To 42.00
Portland, Goblet ....22.00 To 40.00
Portland, Spooner 20.00
Portland, Toothpick 15.00
Portland, Wine ....12.00 To 19.00
Post Script, Goblet, Footed, Gold Trim, 4 In., Set Of 6 .... 115.00
Post, Creamer, Etched 40.00
Post, Goblet, Etched 35.00
Post, Spooner 17.00
Powder & Shot, Sugar, Covered, Flint 60.00
    PRAYER RUG, see Horseshoe
Pressed Diamond, Compote, Open 32.00
Pressed Diamond, Spooner, Vaseline 27.00
Pressed Leaf, Goblet 18.00
Pressed Leaf, Wine, Flint 30.00
    PRINCESS FEATHER, see also Lacy Medallion
Princess Feather, Celery Vase 30.00
Princess Feather, Compote, Covered 45.00
Princess Feather, Creamer 45.00
Princess Feather, Goblet ....19.00 To 30.00
Princess Feather, Goblet, Buttermilk 18.50
Princess Feather, Relish, Shaped As Pickles With Open Stems 17.50
Princess Feather, Spooner ....25.00 To 28.00
Printed Hobnail, Eggcup 28.50
Priscilla, Berry Bowl, Master, 9 In. 35.00
Priscilla, Cake Stand 55.00
Priscilla, Compote, Covered, 9 1/2 X 6 In. ....55.00 To 65.00
Priscilla, Creamer, Individual, 3 1/2 In. 30.00
Priscilla, Pitcher, Water 85.00
Priscilla, Relish, 3 Section 28.00
Priscilla, Spooner ....22.00 To 45.00
Priscilla, Sugar, Open, Individual, 2 3/4 In. 12.00
Priscilla, Tumbler 28.00
Prism & Broken Column, Goblet 14.50
Prism & Bull's-Eye, Goblet 30.00
Prism & Clear Panels, Butter, Covered 25.00
Prism & Diamond Band, Goblet 20.00
Prism Arc, Celery Vase 20.00
Prism Band, Celery Vase, Pedestal 25.00

Prism with Diamond Points   Psyche & Cupid   Rexford, goblet

Ribbon Candy   Roman Rosette

Prism Band, Wine	9.75
Prism With Diamond Points, Salt, Master, Footed	25.00
Prism With Diamond Points, Spooner	40.00
Prism, Spooner, Flint	36.50
Prisms & Hexagons, Goblet	30.00
Prize, Wine	12.00
Psyche & Cupid, Bread Plate	32.00
Psyche & Cupid, Celery Vase	37.50
Psyche & Cupid, Goblet	35.00
QUEEN ANNE, see Viking	
Queen's Necklace, Vase, Findlay, 8 3/4 In.	40.00
Queen, Goblet, Amber	35.00
Question Mark, Celery Vase	26.50
Radiant, Celery Vase	22.00
Radiant, Goblet	36.00
Railroad Train, Bread Plate	70.00
Raindrop, Eggcup, Double	27.00
Rayed Flower, Cake Stand	25.00
Rayed Flower, Creamer	15.00
Reaper, Bread Plate	85.00
RECESSED OVALS WITH BLOCK BAND, see Recessed Ovals	
Recessed Ovals, Goblet	30.00
Red Block, Berry Bowl, Master	60.00
Red Block, Butter, Covered	50.00
Red Block, Goblet	40.00
Red Block, Pitcher, Water	115.00
Red Block, Spooner	25.00 To 40.00
Red Block, Sugar & Creamer	60.00
Red Block, Table Set, Ruby, 4 Piece	185.00
REGENT, see Leaf Medallion	
Reverse 44, Bowl, Platinum, Flashed, 7 In., 5 Cup	95.00
Reverse 44, Butter, Covered, Gold Trim, Green Enamel	65.00
Reverse 44, Pitcher, Amethyst, Gold Trim	55.00
Reverse 44, Pitcher, Red, Gold Trim, Pedestal	75.00
Reverse 44, Tankard, Amethyst, Footed, Gold Trim	70.00
Reverse 44, Water Set, Footed, 6 Piece	185.00
Reverse Torpedo, Banana Stand	110.00
Reverse Torpedo, Bowl, Ruby Stained Edge, Crimped, 8 X 3 In.	65.00
Reverse Torpedo, Compote, Jelly	25.00 To 35.00
Reverse Torpedo, Honey, Covered	65.00
Reward, Celery Vase, 6 1/4 In.	95.00
Rexford, Cake Stand, Child's	25.00 To 35.00
Rexford, Creamer, Child's	15.00
Rexford, Cruet, Stopper	22.00

Rexford, Toothpick 15.00
Rexford, Water Set 150.00
Rib Band, Celery Vase, Pedestal 25.00
Ribbed Acorn, Sauce 15.00
Ribbed Forget–Me–Not, Breakfast Set, 4 Piece 175.00
Ribbed Grape, Goblet, Flint 35.00
Ribbed Grape, Plate, Flint, 6 In. 25.00
Ribbed Ivy, Bowl, 6 In. 15.00
Ribbed Ivy, Goblet, Flint ....40.00 To 58.00
Ribbed Ivy, Spooner, C.1850 .... 40.00
Ribbed Ivy, Wine, Flint 28.00
    RIBBED OPAL, see Beatty Rib
Ribbed Palm, Goblet, Flint ....28.00 To 38.00
Ribbon Candy, Creamer 15.00
Ribbon, Butter, Covered, Frosted 49.50
Ribbon, Celery Vase, Frosted 45.00
Ribbon, Compote, Dolphin Stem, Rectangular 225.00
Ribbon, Creamer 32.00
Ribbon, Fruit Bowl, Clear, 10 In. 16.50
Ribbon, Goblet 35.00
Ribbon, Spooner, Frosted 20.00
    RIPPLE BAND, see Ripple
Ripple, Cake Plate, 12 In. 35.00
Ripple, Goblet 20.00
Rising Sun, Goblet, Green Suns 19.50
Rising Sun, Pitcher, Water, Gold Suns ....32.00 To 35.00
    ROCHELLE, see Princess Feather
Rock Of Ages, Bread Plate, Milk Glass Center ....195.00 To 225.00
Roman Key, Goblet, Clear & Frosted 30.00
Roman Key, Goblet, Flint ....25.00 To 48.00
Roman Key, Spooner, Frosted 36.00
Roman Rosette, Creamer 31.00
Roman Rosette, Goblet 37.00
Roman Rosette, Salt & Pepper 32.00
Rope & Thumbprint, Creamer, Vaseline 30.00
Rope & Thumbprint, Syrup, Blue, Dated Top 80.00
Rope Bands, Cake Stand, 9 1/2 In. 28.00
Rose In Snow, Butter, Covered 65.00
Rose In Snow, Compote, Covered, Low Pedestal 55.00
Rose In Snow, Creamer ....29.50 To 70.00
Rose In Snow, Dish, Pickle 18.50
Rose In Snow, Goblet ....20.00 To 34.00
Rose In Snow, Plate, Handles, 10 In. 28.00
Rose In Snow, Relish 9.00
Rose In Snow, Sugar, Open 48.00
Rose In Snow, Tumbler ....37.50 To 50.00

Rose in Snow

Rose Sprig

Royal

Scroll with Flowers   Sawtooth   Shell & Jewel

Rose Leaves, Goblet 23.00
Rose Point Band, Wine 20.00
Rose Sprig, Cake Stand, Pedestal, 10 In. 45.00
Rose Sprig, Celery Vase, Pedestal ....25.00 To 36.50
Rose Sprig, Goblet ....22.00 To 48.00
Rose Sprig, Relish, Blue, Boat Shape ....28.00 To 50.00
Rose Sprig, Sauce, Blue, Finger Grip, 4 X 5 1/2 In. 12.00
Rose Sprig, Wine 49.50
Rosette Band, Creamer 15.00
    ROSETTE MEDALLION, see Feather Duster
Rosette With Palms, Compote, 6 5/8 X 8 In. 21.00
Rosette With Palms, Plate, 9 In. 9.00
Rosette With Pinwheels, Pitcher, Water 55.00
Rosette With Pinwheels, Spooner 15.00
Rosette, Cake Stand, 9 In. 12.50
Rosette, Goblet ....24.50 To 27.00
Rosette, Pitcher, Milk 40.00
Rosette, Spooner 25.00
Rosette, Sugar 25.00
Royal Crystal, Carafe, Water 65.00
Royal Ivy, Berry Bowl, Frosted, Small 30.00
Royal Ivy, Butter, Covered, Frosted, Rubena 200.00
Royal Ivy, Cracker Jar, Covered 85.00
Royal Ivy, Creamer, Frosted 35.00
Royal Ivy, Cruet, Frosted, Rubena 280.00
Royal Ivy, Pitcher, Water, Clear & Frosted 125.00
Royal Ivy, Pitcher, Water, Clear To Cranberry 165.00
Royal Ivy, Salt, Clear To Cranberry 18.00
Royal Ivy, Spooner, Frosted, Rubena 75.00
Royal Ivy, Sugar Shaker, Clear & Frosted 58.00
Royal Ivy, Sugar, Covered, Frosted 65.00
Royal Ivy, Toothpick, Frosted, Clear To Cranberry 75.00
Royal Ivy, Water Set, Clear To Cranberry, 6 Piece 425.00
Royal Oak, Butter, Frosted Cover, Cranberry 95.00
Royal Oak, Creamer, Frosted & Clear, Rubena 275.00
Royal Oak, Pitcher, Frosted, Rubena ....315.00 To 375.00
Royal Oak, Sugar, Open, Frosted 60.00
Royal Oak, Tumbler, Frosted, Rubena 85.00
Royal, Compote, Covered, Low, 8 In. 55.00
    RUBY ROSETTE, see Pillow Encircled
    RUBY THUMBPRINT, see King's Crown
S—Repeat, Cruet, Apple Green 85.00
S—Repeat, Tumbler, Green, Gold Trim 30.00
S—Repeat, Water Set, Sapphire Blue, 7 Piece 175.00
Sandwich Ivy, Sugar & Creamer, Loaf, Set 129.00
Sandwich Star, Decanter, Bar 75.00

Sawtooth & Star, Water Set, 5 Piece 85.00
    SAWTOOTH BAND, see Amazon
Sawtooth, Butter, Covered, Child's 45.00
Sawtooth, Celery Vase, 9 3/8 In. ....25.00 To 58.00
Sawtooth, Compote, Covered, 8 In. ....30.00 To 35.00
Sawtooth, Compote, Open, 9 1/2 X 4 1/2 In. 45.00
Sawtooth, Creamer, Rayed, Handle, 5 5/8 In. 73.00
Sawtooth, Dish, Footed, 7 X 4 3/4 In. 15.00
Sawtooth, Goblet, Flint ....22.00 To 28.00
Sawtooth, Spooner ....25.00 To 37.00
Sawtooth, Sugar, Covered 44.00
Sawtooth, Wine, Flint 30.00
Scalloped Swirl, Wine, Etched 42.00
Scalloped Tape, Celery Vase 24.00
Scalloped Tape, Goblet 20.00
Scroll With Acanthus, Compote, Jelly, Clear To Opal 12.00
Scroll With Cane Band, Berry Bowl, Master, Amber 45.00
Scroll With Flowers, Spooner 18.50
Scroll, Eggcup ....12.50 To 16.00
Scroll, Goblet ....13.00 To 16.00
Scroll, Spooner 12.50
Sedan, Creamer 19.00
Sedan, Wine 12.00
Selby, Goblet ....12.00 To 16.00
Seneca Loop, Goblet ....12.50 To 18.00
Seneca Loop, Pitcher, Water, Applied Handle ....110.00 To 170.00
Sequoia, Salt & Pepper, Handles, Footed, Vaseline 38.00
    SHEAF & DIAMOND, see Fickle Block
Sheaf Of Wheat, Bread Plate, 10 In. 25.00
Shell & Jewel, Pitcher & 5 Tumblers 140.00
Shell & Jewel, Pitcher, Water ....17.00 To 45.00
Shell & Jewel, Sugar, Covered 50.00
Shell & Jewel, Tumbler 17.00
Shell & Tassel, Bowl, 12 X 6 1/2 In. 45.00
Shell & Tassel, Bowl, Amber, 10 In. 75.00
Shell & Tassel, Creamer, Square 35.00
Shell & Tassel, Pitcher, Water 35.00
Shell & Tassel, Salt & Pepper, Square ....40.00 To 150.00
Shell & Tassel, Sauce, Seashell Handles 20.00
Shell, Creamer, Footed, Opalescent Green 85.00
Shell, Spooner, Blue, Gold Trim 55.00
Sheraton, Bowl, Amber, 6 5/8 X 4 7/8 In. 23.00
Sheraton, Bread Plate, Blue, 10 1/2 X 8 In. 25.00
Sheraton, Compote, 6 3/4 X 5 1/4 In. 20.00
Sheraton, Goblet, Blue 22.00
Sheraton, Pitcher, Water 30.00

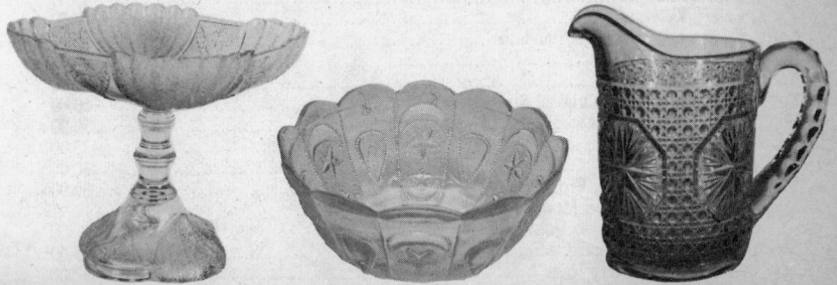

Shell & Tassel   Shrine   Star Medallion

Sheraton, Spooner 18.00
Sheraton, Sugar, Covered, Amber 40.00
Sheraton, Wine ....15.00 To 16.00
Shimmering Star, Sauce 25.00
Shimmering Star, Sugar & Creamer 55.00
Short Ribs, Goblet 14.00
Shoshone, Butter, Covered, Ruby Flashed 125.00
Shoshone, Butter, Covered, Yellow Flashed 50.00
Shoshone, Cake Plate, 9 In. 24.00
Shoshone, Compote, Open, Green, 5 1/4 X 3 In. 20.00
Shoshone, Cruet, Green ....75.00 To 90.00
Shoshone, Saltshaker, Gold Trim 25.00
Shovel, Goblet 15.00
Shrine, Pitcher, Water 50.00
Shrine, Relish 14.50
Shrine, Sugar, Covered 55.00
Shrine, Tumbler 43.00
Shuttle, Cake Stand, 10 In. 85.00
Shuttle, Pitcher, 6 In. 35.00
Shuttle, Punch Cup 10.00
Shuttle, Wine ....9.00 To 10.00
Snail, Berry Bowl, Master 35.00
Snail, Cake Stand 60.00
Snail, Celery Vase, Etched 75.00
Snail, Cruet, Stopper 32.00
Snail, Goblet 65.00
Snail, Relish, Oval 22.00
Snail, Salt, Individual ....18.00 To 20.00
Snake Drape, Goblet ....17.00 To 20.00
Snakeskin & Dot, Plate, 9 In. 12.00
Snow Band, Goblet 13.00
Snowflake, Bowl, 9 In. 18.00
Southern Ivy, Pitcher, Water 50.00
    SPANISH AMERICAN, see Admiral Dewey
    SPANISH COIN, see Columbian Coin
Spearhead, Goblet, Buttermilk 25.00
Spearpoint, Sugar 38.00
Spinning Star, Toothpick, Footed, Gilt 30.00
Spiraled Ivy, Butter, Covered 25.00
Spiraled Ivy, Creamer 20.00
Spiraled Ivy, Spooner 12.00
Spiraled Ivy, Sugar, Covered 25.00
Spiraled Ivy, Tumbler 10.00
Spirea Band, Creamer, Amber 36.50
Spirea Band, Goblet, Amber ....22.00 To 32.50
Spirea Band, Spooner, Amber 26.50
Sprig In Snow, Salt & Pepper, Clear 30.00
Sprig, Butter, Covered, Pedestal 60.00
Sprig, Cake Stand 45.00
Sprig, Celery Vase 36.50
Sprig, Compote, Open, High Standard 30.00
Sprig, Goblet 26.00
Sprig, Pitcher, Water 30.00
Squat Pineapple, Cruet, Original Stopper, Green 50.00
Squirrel In Bower, Goblet 250.00
Squirrel, Goblet 425.00
Star & Oval, Celery Vase 30.00
Star & Oval, Celery Vase, Frosted 30.00
    STAR & PUNTY, see Moon & Star
    STAR BAND, see also Bosworth
Star Band, Berry Set, Footed, Master & 5 Bowls, 4 In. 35.00
Star In Bull's—Eye, Celery Vase 30.00
Star In Bull's—Eye, Creamer, Ruby Top 15.00
Star In Bull's—Eye, Goblet 10.00

Star Medallion, Celery 25.00
Star Medallion, Spooner 14.00
Star Of David, Pitcher 125.00
Star, Sugar, Child's, Oval 13.50
Starred Cosmos, Water Set, 6 Piece 125.00
Stars & Bars, Cruet, Stopper, Amber 55.00
Stars & Bars, Goblet, Emerald Green, 5 3/4 In. ....40.00 To 65.00
Stars & Stripes, Goblet, Set Of 4 .... 80.00
    STATES, see The States
Stippled Band, Spooner 15.00
Stippled Chain, Goblet ....14.00 To 22.00
Stippled Chain, Spooner 24.00
Stippled Cherry, Plate, 6 In. 12.50
Stippled Cherry, Plate, 9 1/4 In. 18.00
    STIPPLED DAHLIA, see Dahlia
Stippled Daisy, Creamer 15.00
Stippled Dart & Balls, Goblet 16.00
Stippled Double Loop, Celery Vase 60.00
Stippled Fleur–De–Lis, Tumbler, Sapphire Blue 25.00
Stippled Forget–Me–Not, Tumbler 26.00
Stippled Grape & Festoon, Creamer, Clear Leaf 38.50
Stippled Grape & Festoon, Goblet 40.00
Stippled Grape & Festoon, Spooner, Clear Leaf 28.50
Stippled Ivy, Goblet 30.00
Stippled Ivy, Plate, 7 In., Set Of 6 .... 85.00
Stippled Ivy, Sugar, Covered ....25.00 To 32.00
Stippled Maidenhair Fern, Goblet 25.00
Stippled Medallion, Eggcup 23.00
    STIPPLED PANELED FLOWER, see Maine
Stippled Peppers, Goblet ....25.00 To 30.00
    STIPPLED SCROLL, see Scroll
Stippled Star, Celery Vase 15.00
Stippled Star, Spooner ....22.00 To 25.00
    STORK LOOKING AT THE MOON, see Ostrich Looking At The Moon
Stork, Butter, Covered 65.00
Stork, Creamer 42.00
Stork, Tray, Frosted, One–O–One Border 58.00
Strawberry & Currant, Goblet ....20.00 To 23.00
Strawberry With Roman Key Band, Berry Set, 6 Piece 110.00
Strawberry, Goblet ....15.00 To 32.00
Strawberry, Pitcher, Water, Bulbous 110.00
Strigil, Pitcher, Water 85.00
Sunbeam, Tumbler 25.00
Sunbeam, Wine 25.00
Sunburst & Tepee, Butter, Covered 38.00
Sunburst, Creamer 12.75
Sunflower, Spooner 10.00
Sunk Daisy, Plate, 8 In. 6.00
Sunk Honeycomb, Creamer, Individual 30.00
Sunk Honeycomb, Cruet 90.00
    SUNKEN BUTTONS, see Mitered Diamond
Sunken Primrose, Celery, Flat, Ruby & Amber 65.00
Sunken Primrose, Creamer, Ruby Flashed 20.00
Sunken Primrose, Spooner 65.00
    SUNRISE, see Rising Sun
Swag With Brackets, Cruet, Amethyst 100.00
Swan, Jam Jar, Bird Finial 37.50
Swan, Jam Jar, Slot In Cover, Amber 55.00
Swan, Tray, Oval 165.00
Sweetheart, Butter 35.00
Sweetheart, Spooner 30.00
Sweetheart, Sugar 35.00
Sweetheart, Table Set, Child's 130.00
Swirl & Cable, Compote, Covered, 12 1/2 X 8 1/2 In. 145.00

Strawberry   Thistle   Three Face

Swirl Band, Cake Stand, Etched, 9 1/2 In. 32.50
Sylvan, Sugar, 3 Handles 14.00
Tacoma, Spooner, Ruby 45.00
Tandem Bicycle, Goblet ....22.00 To 45.00
Tappan, Butter, Child's 25.00
Tappan, Creamer, Blue, Child's 25.00
Tappan, Spooner, Child's 15.00
Tappan, Sugar, Covered, Blue, Child's 30.00
Teardrop & Tassel, Butter, Covered, Cobalt Blue 135.00
   TEARDROP & THUMBPRINT, see Teardrop
Teardrop, Celery Vase 37.50
Teardrop, Goblet ....18.00 To 30.00
Tennessee, Bread Plate 25.00
Tennessee, Pitcher, Water 65.00
Tennessee, Salt & Pepper 28.50
Tennessee, Spooner 35.00
Tepee, Punch Cup ....8.00 To 8.50
Tepee, Salt & Pepper 28.50
Texas Bull's–Eye, Tumbler 57.50
Texas Bull's–Eye, Wine 20.00
Texas Star, Cruet, Original Stopper 55.00
Texas Star, Cup & Saucer 15.00
Texas Star, Toothpick ....16.00 To 35.00
Texas, Creamer, Gold Trim 14.00
Texas, Spooner 45.00
Texas, Sugar & Creamer, Open, Individual, Gold Trim 20.00
Texas, Toothpick ....22.00 To 38.00
The States, Berry, Master 125.00
The States, Berry, Master, Green 100.00
The States, Celery Vase ....30.00 To 35.00
The States, Creamer, Gold Trim 24.50
The States, Goblet, Gold Trim 40.00
The States, Relish, 7 1/4 X 5 1/4 In. 20.00
The States, Sugar & Creamer 40.00
The States, Tumbler 22.00
The States, Water Set, 7 Piece 125.00
The States, Wine ....7.00 To 22.00
Theodore Roosevelt, Bread Plate 95.00
Thistle Shield, Goblet 26.00
Thistle, Cake Stand, 10 1/2 In. 60.00
Thistle, Compote, 8 X 7 1/2 In. ....35.00 To 40.00
Thistle, Goblet, Flint ....60.00 To 70.00
Thistle, Salt 10.00
Thistle, Wine, Flint 55.00
Thousand Eye, Bowl, 8 In. 35.00
Thousand Eye, Bread Plate, Square, 10 In. ....15.00 To 22.00

Thousand Eye, Celery, 3 Knob 40.00
Thousand Eye, Compote, Jelly, Blue, 6 In. 35.00
Thousand Eye, Cruet, Apple Green, 3 Knob Stopper, 6 1/2 In. 110.00
Thousand Eye, Cruet, Yellow 65.00
Thousand Eye, Pitcher, Water, Apple Green 85.00
Thousand Eye, Plate, Square, Amber, 8 In. 25.00
Thousand Eye, Salt & Pepper, Blue 81.00
Thousand Eye, Sauce, Footed .... 8.00 To 12.00
Thousand Eye, Syrup, Pewter Lid, Dated 1884 .... 85.00
Thousand Eye, Tray, Apple Green, 14 In. 85.00
Thousand Eye, Tumbler, Blue 27.00
Thousand Eye, Vase, Ruffled Top, 5 1/2 In. 15.00
Thousand Eye, Wine 30.00
Thousand Eye, Wine, Apple Green .... 40.00 To 42.50
Threaded, Goblet 25.00
Three Face, Compote, Covered, 6 1/2 In. 75.00
Three Face, Goblet, Etched 95.00
Three Face, Jam Jar, Frosted Quail Finial 45.00
Three Face, Salt & Pepper, Frosted & Clear, Original Covers 85.00
Three Face, Sugar Shaker 60.00
    THREE GRACES, see also Three Face
Three Graces, Bread Plate .... 45.00 To 78.00
Three Panel, Bowl, Low Pedestal, Blue, 7 1/2 In. 55.00
Three Panel, Celery Vase, Amber, Straight Top 35.00
Three Panel, Creamer, Vaseline .... 28.00 To 29.00
Three Panel, Goblet, Amber 27.00
Three Panel, Mug, Blue 35.00
Three Panel, Spooner 23.00
Three Panel, Spooner, Vaseline 25.00
Three Presidents, Bread Plate .... 35.00 To 85.00
Three Presidents, Goblet, Etched 225.00
    THREE SISTERS, see Three Face
Three Stories, Mug, Blue 25.00
Thumbprint, Ale, Giant, Flint 40.00
Thumbprint, Berry Bowl, Master, Boat Shape, Etched, Ruby 155.00
Thumbprint, Celery Vase 41.50
Thumbprint, Goblet, Flint 40.00
Thumbprint, Pitcher, Blue, Ruffled Lip, 9 In. 90.00
Thumbprint, Spooner .... 48.00 To 55.00
Thumbprint, Spooner, Flint .... 48.00 To 48.50
Tiny Finecut, Wine, Dark Green 20.00
Tiny Lion, Pitcher, Water, Etched 45.00
    TOM THUMB, see Humpty–Dumpty
Torpedo, Bowl, 9 1/2 In. .... 35.00 To 55.00
Torpedo, Butter, Covered, Etched 65.00
Torpedo, Compote, 5 X 5 In. 45.00

Thumbprint   Tree of Life   Tulip with Sawtooth

Torpedo, Compote, Jelly, 4 3/4 In. ....40.00 To 43.00
Torpedo, Creamer ....25.00 To 40.00
Torpedo, Goblet ....42.00 To 45.00
Torpedo, Goblet, Etched 45.00
Torpedo, Pitcher, Milk, Ruby 90.00
Torpedo, Pitcher, Water 85.00
Torpedo, Salt, Individual 22.00
Torpedo, Syrup, Metal Top, Ruby 135.00
Torpedo, Tray, Water, Round, 10 In. 75.00
Tree Of Life, Butter, Green, 3 In.Diam. 22.00
Tree Of Life, Cake Stand, Infant Samuel, Signed Davis 200.00
Tree Of Life, Creamer, Silver Plated Holder 20.00
Tree Of Life, Saltshaker 25.00
Tree Of Life, Sugar, Silver Plated Cover 20.00
Tree Of Life, Tumbler, Lemonade, 5 1/2 In. 35.00
Triangular Prism, Compote, Open, 7 1/2 X 5 In. 30.00
Triangular Prism, Compote, Open, McKee, 4 In. 25.00
Triple Triangle, Butter, Covered, Ruby 75.00
Triple Triangle, Goblet, Ruby 38.50
Trophy, Toothpick 25.00
Truncated Cube, Creamer, 3 In. 10.00
Truncated Cube, Cruet, Stopper 15.00
Truncated Cube, Toothpick, Ruby Flashed 19.00
Tulip & Honeycomb, Punch Bowl, 8 Cups, Child's 80.00
Tulip & Honeycomb, Spooner, Child's ....15.00 To 24.00
Tulip & Honeycomb, Sugar, Covered, Child's ....20.00 To 25.00
Tulip Band, Compote, 4 3/4 X 6 1/2 In. 65.00
Tulip Petals, Goblet ....12.00 To 22.00
Tulip With Sawtooth, Celery Vase, Pedestal ....60.00 To 85.00
Tulip With Sawtooth, Eggcup, 3 3/8 In. 5.00
Tulip With Sawtooth, Salt, Master, Flint 25.00
Tulip With Sawtooth, Wine 18.00
Twin Leaves, Creamer, Pedestal 30.00
Twin Snowshoe, Creamer, Child's ....20.00 To 55.00
Twin Teardrops, Plate, 9 1/2 In. ....18.00 To 24.00
TWINKLE STAR, see also Utah
Two Band, Compote, Covered, 7 X 7 In. 32.00
Two Band, Compote, Covered, Pheasant Finial, 6 X 8 In. 90.00
Two Panel, Goblet, Blue 30.00
Two Panel, Goblet, Vaseline 36.00
Two Panel, Spooner, Blue 35.00
Two Panel, Spooner, Vaseline 32.50
Two Panel, Table Set, Vaseline, 4 Piece 185.00
Two Panel, Wine, Blue 40.00
U.S.Rib, Toothpick, Green, Gold Trim ....30.00 To 35.00
U.S.Thumbprint, Goblet 18.00
Umbilicated Hobnail, Goblet 15.00
Umbilicated Sawtooth, Eggcup, Flint 28.00
Utah, Butter, Covered 34.00
Utah, Wine 35.00
Valencia Waffle, Cake Stand 70.00
Valencia Waffle, Celery Vase ....35.00 To 40.00
Valencia Waffle, Goblet 10.00
Valencia Waffle, Salt, Master, Amber 22.00
Valencia Waffle, Spooner, Blue 25.00
Valencia Waffle, Table Set, 4 Piece 95.00
Vera, Spooner, Frosted 20.00
Vermont, Celery, Flat 27.00
Vesta, Spooner, Vaseline 35.00
Viking, Celery Vase 35.00
Viking, Compote, Covered, 12 In. 150.00
Viking, Jar, Covered, Viking Face As Feet 110.00
Viking, Mug, Lemonade, Handle 65.00
Viking, Pitcher, Water ....80.00 To 85.00

Waffle & Thumbprint   Washington Centennial   Wedding Ring

Viking, Sugar, Covered 50.00
Viking, Vase, Covered, Amber, Pineapple Finial, 10 In. 29.50
Vine & Beads, Creamer, Child's, Stippled, Teal Blue 85.00
Vine & Beads, Spooner, Child's 25.00
    VIRGINIA, see also Galloway
Virginia, Pitcher, Water 26.00
Virginia, Plate, 7 In. 20.00
Virginia, Spooner 17.50
Virginia, Sugar, Covered 30.00
Waffle & Star Band, Toothpick 30.00
Waffle & Thumbprint, Goblet 50.00
Waffle & Thumbprint, Goblet, Bulb Stem, Flint 65.00
Waffle, Creamer, Applied Handle, Footed, Flint .... 85.00 To 135.00
Waffle, Eggcup, Flint 24.50
Waffle, Sugar, Covered, Flint .... 85.00 To 125.00
Waffle, Tumbler, Light Green Slag 60.00
Waffle, Wine, Square 15.00
Wahoo, Goblet 30.00
    WASHBOARD, see Adonis
Washington Centennial, Bread Plate, Frosted Bust .... 100.00 To 110.00
Washington Centennial, Butter, Covered 30.00
Washington Centennial, Cake Stand 45.00
Washington Centennial, Eggcup 40.00
Washington Centennial, Goblet .... 35.00 To 52.00
Washington Centennial, Pitcher, 7 In. 80.00
Washington Centennial, Relish, Claw Handles, 9 In. .... 30.00 To 35.00
Washington Centennial, Spooner 35.00
Washington Centennial, Sugar, Covered 30.00
Washington, Cruet, Stopper 57.50
Washington, Goblet, Flint .... 70.00 To 95.00
Washington, Wine 20.00
    WATER LILY, see Rose Point Band
Way's Currant, Goblet 17.50
Wedding Bells, Cruet, Original Stopper 50.00
Wedding Bells, Toothpick, Alternating Clear & Gilt 28.00
Wedding Ring, Banana Stand 75.00
Wedding Ring, Cake Stand 65.00
Wedding Ring, Compote, 8 X 6 1/2 In. 28.00
Wedding Ring, Creamer, Octagonal 35.00
Wedding Ring, Goblet, Flint .... 38.50 To 60.00
Wedding Ring, Sugar, Covered, Fruit Knob 35.00
Wee Branches, Sugar, Covered, Child's 60.00
Wee Branches, Table Set, Child's, 4 Piece 425.00
Westmoreland, Butter, Covered 48.00
Westmoreland, Celery Vase 14.50
Westmoreland, Sugar 26.50

Westward Ho, Butter, Covered ....75.00 To 210.00
Westward Ho, Compote, Covered, 6 In. 225.00
Westward Ho, Compote, Covered, 8 In. ....120.00 To 275.00
Westward Ho, Compote, Covered, Tall Pedestal, 6 In. 175.00
Westward Ho, Goblet ....60.00 To 75.00
Westward Ho, Pitcher, Water, Dog's Head Handle 185.00
Westward Ho, Sauce, Footed, 4 In. 25.00
Westward Ho, Sugar & Creamer 175.00
Wheat & Barley, Butter, Covered ....35.00 To 40.00
Wheat & Barley, Goblet 25.00
Wheat & Barley, Goblet, Blue 40.00
Wheat & Barley, Jam Jar, Covered 50.00
Wheat & Barley, Pitcher, Milk, Blue 65.00
Wheat & Barley, Plate, Blue, 7 In. 30.00
Wheat & Barley, Plate, Blue, 10 In. 20.00
Wheat & Barley, Salt & Pepper 30.00
Wheat & Barley, Sauce, Amber, Stem 15.00
Wheat & Barley, Spooner 18.00
Wheat & Barley, Sugar, Covered ....32.00 To 40.00
Wheat & Barley, Tumbler, Amber 40.00
Wheat Sheaf, Punch Bowl, Child's 25.00
Whirligig, Goblet, Footed, 6 In. 15.00
Whirligig, Punch Set, Bowl, 4 Cups, Child's 65.00
Wild Bouquet, Spooner, White 28.00
Wild Rose With Bow–Knot, Tumbler, Gold Trim 45.00
Wild Rose, Bowl, Green, Footed, 7 In. 30.00
Wildflower, Bowl, Square, 8 In. 12.00
Wildflower, Champagne, Amber 40.00
Wildflower, Creamer, Blue 30.00
Wildflower, Plate, Green, 10 In. ....30.00 To 45.00
Wildflower, Sauce, Footed, 3 5/8 In. 10.00
Wildflower, Spooner ....12.00 To 15.00
Wildflower, Tray, Amber, 9 1/4 X 4 1/4 In. 25.00
Wildflower, Tumbler, Blue 25.00
Wildflower, Tumbler, Green 29.00
Willow Oak, Bowl, 7 In. 12.00
Willow Oak, Cake Stand, Amber 60.00
Willow Oak, Celery Vase, Pedestal 50.00
Willow Oak, Compote, Open, High Standard, Blue 60.00
Willow Oak, Creamer 28.00
Willow Oak, Creamer, Blue 40.00
Willow Oak, Goblet 32.00

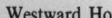

Westward Ho

Wildflower

Willow Oak, Pitcher, Water, Blue 65.00
Willow Oak, Plate, 9 1/4 In. 22.50
Windflower, Pitcher, Water 60.00
Winged Scrolls, Box, Trinket, Souvenir, Green 50.00
    WINONA, see Barred Hobnail
    WISCONSIN, see Beaded Dewdrop
Wooden Pail, Butter, Covered, Blue .... 90.00 To 120.00
Wooden Pail, Pitcher, Water, Amber .... 75.00 To 80.00
Wooden Pail, Pitcher, Water, Amethyst 150.00
Wooden Pail, Pitcher, Water, Blue 110.00
Wooden Pail, Spooner 50.00
Wooden Pail, Sugar, Covered 35.00
Wooden Pail, Sugar, Covered, Vaseline 65.00
Wooden Pail, Table Set, 4 Piece 195.00
Wyoming, Cake Stand 38.00
Wyoming, Pitcher, Milk 60.00
X–Ray, Celery Vase, Green, Gold Trim 45.00
X–Ray, Jam Jar, Green 75.00
X–Ray, Pitcher, Water, Green, Gold Trim 70.00
X–Ray, Sugar, Covered, Gold Trim .... 50.00 To 60.00
X–Ray, Table Set, Green, Gold Trim, 4 Piece 125.00
X–Ray, Toothpick, Gold Trim 20.00
X–Ray, Toothpick, Green 55.00
    YALE, see Crowfoot
Yoke & Circle, Celery Vase 30.00
Yoked Loop, Goblet, Flint 20.00
York Herringbone, Cake Stand, Etched 48.00
Yuma Loop, Goblet 20.00
Zipper, Celery Vase, Pedestal .... 20.00 To 25.00
Zipper, Cruet, Original Top 38.00
Zippered Block, Goblet 35.00

> Print, in this listing, means any of many printed images produced on
> paper by one of the more common methods, such as lithography. The
> prints listed here are those of interest to the average collector not the
> art collector. Many of these prints were originally part of books. Other
> prints will be found in the sections headed Currier & Ives, Store, and
> Poster.

PRINT, Alken, Grouse Shooting 150.00
Alken, Quorn Hunt, Plate No.7 .... 195.00
Audubon, American Red Fox, 1846, 22 1/8 X 28 1/2 In. 1200.00
Audubon, American Robin, 1832, 16 X 19 In. 320.00
Audubon, American Wildcat, Hand Colored, 1842, 22 X 28 1/2 In. 1250.00
Audubon, Autumnal Warbler, Plate 88, Original 1000.00
Audubon, Black Billed Cuckoo, Plate No.7, 19 1/2 X 23 In. 360.00
Audubon, Blue Winged Yellow Warbler, Engraver R.Havell, 16 X 19 In. 550.00
Audubon, California Gray Squirrel, 1843, 22 X 28 1/2 In. 500.00
Audubon, Camas Rat, 21 X 27 5/8 In. 125.00
Audubon, Canada Lynx, 1843, 22 X 28 1/2 In. 1500.00
Audubon, Collared Peccary, 1844, 22 X 28 1/2 In. 1550.00
Audubon, Common American Deer, 1845, 22 1/4 X 28 1/2 In. 2100.00
Audubon, Cougar, Female & Young, 1846, 21 3/8 X 27 3/8 In. 1000.00
Audubon, Gray Fox, 1843, 22 X 28 1/2 In. 2600.00
Audubon, Key West Dove, 1833, 19 1/2 X 12 3/4 In. 360.00
Audubon, Louisiana Heron, 1834, 19 1/2 X 23 In. 240.00
Audubon, Mallard Duck, 1834, 19 1/2 X 23 In. 240.00
Audubon, Mexican Marmot Squirrel, 1847, 22 X 28 1/2 In. 225.00
Audubon, Northern Hare, 1843, 22 X 28 1/2 In. 675.00
Audubon, Orange Bellied Squire, 1845, 22 X 28 1/2 In. 425.00
Audubon, Raven, No.21, 16 X 19 In. 280.00
Audubon, Rocky Mountain Hare, 1842, 22 X 28 1/2 In. 925.00
Audubon, Sharp Tail Grouse, 1837, 19 1/2 X 12 3/4 In. 240.00
Audubon, Shoveller Duck, 1836, 19 1/2 X 12 3/4 In. 240.00
Audubon, Tawny Weasel, 1848, 22 1/16 X 28 1/2 In. 275.00

Audubon, Townsend's Rocky Mountain Hare, 1842, 22 X 28 1/2 In. 925.00
Audubon, Trumpeter Swan, 1838, 19 1/2 X 12 3/4 In. 240.00
Audubon, Wilson's Meadow Mouse, 1844, 22 X 28 3/8 In. 1700.00
Avery, Murmuring Brook, 16 X 20 In. 30.00
Baillie, Eliza 50.00
Baillie, Family Register, Columns For Names & Dates 25.00
Baillie, General George Washington, Curly Maple Frame 45.00
Barry, Indian, Custer, Indian Chief, Framed, Signed, Set Of 31 .... 1500.00
Benton, Down The River, Matted, 1939, Signed, 10 X 12 1/2 In. 1980.00
Benton, Frisky Day, Matted, Signed, 12 X 8 In. 880.00
Benton, Letter From Overseas, Framed, 1943, Signed, 9 1/2 X 13 In. 880.00
Benton, Morning Train, Matted, 1943, Signed, 13 1/2 X 9 1/4 In. 1540.00
Benton, Music Lesson, Framed, 1943, Signed, 10 X 12 3/4 In. 2090.00
Bowen, Indian Print, Hand Colored, Framed, 14 X 12 In. 50.00
Bruckman, Madonna & Child, Framed 75.00
Chandler, Ship, Moon & Sea Scene, Framed, Signed, 10 1/2 In. 22.00
Christy, The Cotillion, 10 X 14 In. 22.50
Davidson, Heart's Desire, Original Frame, Signed, 12 X 16 In. 15.00
DeLangpre, Home Sweet Home, Clover & Daisies, Framed, 39 In. 37.50
Dineen, World War I Fighter Planes, Original Frame, 29 X 35 In. 35.00
Dufner, Summer Evening, 7 X 9 In. 25.00
Ferris, George Washington's Last Birthday Party, 1799, 9 X 13 In. 18.00
Fildes, Village Wedding, Oak Frame, 1885, 25 X 38 In. 48.00
Fisher, Greatest Moments Of Girl's Life, Framed, Signed, 28 X 10 In. 95.00
Fisher, Sweetheart Girl, Lacy Hat, Framed, 1909, 13 X 17 In. ....30.00 To 35.00
Fisher, Sweetheart, Original Frame, 13 X 17 In. 40.00
Fisher, The Six Senses, New Baby, Original Gold Frame, 27 1/2 X 9 In. 75.00
Fox, Afternoon Call, Dogs, Horses, Dated 1924, 17 X 22 In. 45.00
Fox, Dreamland, Original Frame, 9 X 13 In. 35.00
Fox, Dreamland, Original Frame, Signed, 24 X 16 In. 55.00
Fox, Field Of White Flowers, Original Frame, Signed, 10 X 24 In. 38.00
Fox, Girl Seated On Balcony, Master Art Pub., Signed, 15 X 9 1/4 In. 35.00
Fox, Glorious Vistas, 32 X 20 In. 40.00
Fox, Home Sweet Home, Framed, 12 X 8 In. 25.00
Fox, Hunters Canoeing In Whitewaters, 14 X 12 In. 25.00
Fox, Lady On Balcony, 12 X 20 In. 43.00
Fox, Love's Paradise, 8 X 14 In. 24.00
Fox, Moonlight & Roses, Signed, Framed, 19 1/2 X 15 1/2 In. 37.50
Fox, Mother Holding Infant, Signed, 19 1/2 X 11 1/2 In. 22.00
Fox, Mother Lying Holding Babe Up, 1925, 12 X 20 In. 44.00
Fox, Nature's Grandeur, 22 X 18 In. 52.00
Fox, Old Fashioned Garden, Framed, 18 X 30 In. 75.00
Fox, Perfect Day, Framed, Signed, 21 1/2 X 15 1/2 In. 55.00
Fox, Spirit Of Youth, 18 X 30 In. 65.00
Fox, Spring Beauties, 25 1/2 X 11 1/2 In. 55.00
Fox, Sunset Dreams, Signed, 8 X 15 In. 35.00
Frost, A Flaw In The Title, 10 X 14 In. 22.50
Gatlin, Indian, Wild Horse, Buffalo Hunt, Set Of 6 .... 300.00
Gilbert, Romeo & Juliet, 11 X 15 In. 45.00
Goodwin, Battle Of Manila, 1898, 20 X 16 In. 45.00
Goodwin, Two Men In Canoe, C.1920, 14 3/4 X 12 1/8 In. 28.00
Gozzard, At Break Of Day, C.1880, Framed, 18 X 25 In. 225.00
Gutmann, Awakening, Baby, Round, 15 1 /2 In. 35.00
Gutmann, Butterfly, Original Frame, 15 X 19 In. 30.00
Gutmann, Chilly Day, Lady Tending Fire, 11 X 13 In. 18.00
Gutmann, Contentment, Oval, 8 In. 25.00
Gutmann, Double Blessing, Twins, 15 X 21 In. 145.00
Gutmann, Fairest Of The Flowers, Bride, 12 X 16 In. 70.00
Gutmann, Good Night, Toddler & Toy Monkey, Matted, C.1945, 16 X 20 In. 55.00
Gutmann, Home Builders, Framed, 16 X 12 In. 65.00
Gutmann, Little Bit Of Heaven, 16 X 11 In. 20.00
Gutmann, Little Bit Of Heaven, 21 X 15 In. 65.00
Gutmann, Message Of The Roses, Maiden, 12 X 16 In. 110.00
Gutmann, On Dreamland's Border, 16 X 23 In. 35.00

Print, Japanese, Woodblock, Winter Scene,
8 1/2 X 13 1/2 In.

Print, Japanese, Woodblock,
C.1920, 14 X 9 1/2 In.

Gutmann, On Dreamland's Border, 20 X 15 1/2 In.	45.00
Gutmann, Rosebud, Baby, 15 X 19 In.	25.00
Gutmann, The New Love, Oval, Original Frame, 9 X 5 In.	38.00
Gutmann, The Reward, 20 X 16 In.	45.00
Helck, Climb To The Clouds, 1946, Matted & Framed, 25 X 20 In.	125.00
Helck, New York To Paris 1908, 1946, Matted & Framed, 25 X 20 In.	125.00
Helck, The Brighton 24 Hour, 1946, Matted & Framed, 25 X 20 In.	125.00
Humphrey, Child Seated, Church, Original Frame, 1898, 12 3/4 X 16 In.	150.00
Humphrey, Kitty's Bath, Fairbanks Co., 1899, 13 X 23 1/2 In.	225.00
Humphrey, Miss Muffet's Christmas Party, 14 1/2 X 10 1/2 In.	135.00
Icart, Best Friends, Signed, 17 X 14 In.	600.00
Icart, Hortensia, Oval, Copyright 1919, 16 X 20 In.	700.00
Icart, Symphony In Blue, Copyright 1936, 23 X 19 In.	950.00

*Japanese prints are listed as follows: Print, Japanese, name of artist,
title or description, type, and size. Dealers use the following terms:
Tate-e is a vertical composition. Yoko-e is a horizontal composition.
The words Aiban (13 by 9 inches), Chuban (10 by 7 1/2 inches),
Hososban (12 by 6 inches), Oban (15 by 10 inches), and Koban (7 by
4 inches) denote size.*

Japanese, Hasui, Evening At Itako, 1932, 6 X 14 In.	80.00
Japanese, Hasui, May Rain On Ara River, 1932, 10 X 15 In.	140.00
Japanese, Hasui, Snow Over The Ferry, 1932, 6 X 14 In.	80.00
Japanese, Hasui, Winter Moon, 1931, 10 X 15 In.	140.00
Japanese, Koitsu, Night Rain At Ushigome, 1939, 11 X 16 In.	125.00
Japanese, Koitsu, Wisteria At Kameido, 1933, 11 X 16 In.	125.00
Japanese, Kurosaki, Lunar Eclipse, 13 X 19 In.	120.00
Japanese, Kurosaki, Melancholy B, 13 X 19 In.	120.00
Japanese, Sadanobu III, Dancing Girl In Black Kimono, 10 X 15 In.	90.00
Japanese, Sadanobu III, Samurai On A White Horse, 11 X 17 In.	90.00
Japanese, Tokuriki, Black Cat & Butterfly, 16 X 21 In.	250.00
Japanese, Tokuriki, Irises & Dragonfly, 10 X 11 In.	60.00
Japanese, Tokuriki, Woman Combing Her Hair, 10 X 16 In.	150.00
Japanese, Utamaro, Standing Geisha, Framed, 18 3/8 X 9 5/16 In.	325.00
Japanese, Woodblock, C.1920, 14 X 9 1/2 In. ....*Illus*	45.00
Japanese, Woodblock, Winter Scene, 8 1/2 X 13 1/2 In. ....*Illus*	40.00
Japanese, Yoshida, From The Ryogoku Bridge, 1938, 8 X 10 In.	85.00
Japanese, Yoshida, Lidabashi, 1939, 8 X 10 In.	85.00
Kellogg, American Scenery, Connecticut River Valley	130.00
Kellogg, Battle Of Chattanooga, Tenn., Nov.24, 1863	120.00
Kellogg, Death Of Zachary Taylor	90.00
Kellogg, Lady Of The Lake	50.00

Kenyon, Indian Maiden 45.00
Leigh, Upright Bear, Fallen Hunter With Gun, Signed, 23 X 16 In. 65.00
Lithograph, Elephant, Castle, Brighton Road, Pollard, 21 X 30 In. 250.00
Lithograph, Harper's April, E.Penfield, 9 3/4 X 8 3/4 In. 25.00
Lithograph, Moonlit Landscape, German, 20th Century, 27 X 37 In. 125.00
Masseria, Roseanna & Eduardo, Framed, Set Of 6 .... 4500.00
Millet, Between Two Fires, Signed, Framed, 19 X 22 In. 32.00
Nutting, A Bit Of Sewing, 11 X 13 1/2 In. 90.00
Nutting, A Garden Of Larkspur, 9 1/2 X 12 In. ....35.00 To 40.00
Nutting, A Joyous Anniversary, Signed, 11 X 13 In. 35.00
Nutting, A Sip Of Tea, Framed, Signed, 15 X 8 In. ....75.00 To 115.00
Nutting, A Stitch In Time, Framed, 11 1/2 In. 70.00
Nutting, A Warm Spring Day, 12 X 20 In. 135.00
Nutting, Blooms At The Bend, 12 X 21 In. 25.00
Nutting, Blossoms At The Bend, Framed, 13 X 16 In. 20.00
Nutting, Decked As A Bride, Framed, 19 X 22 In. 52.50
Nutting, Honeymoon Stroll, 5 X 7 In. 30.00
Nutting, Joy Path, 9 1/2 X 12 In. 40.00
Nutting, Larkspur, 5 X 7 In. 28.00
Nutting, Lichfield Minster, Cathedral, Flowers, Framed, 11 X 12 In. 65.00
Nutting, The Book Settle, Interior Scene, Framed, 12 X 18 In. 50.00
Parkinson, Cupid Asleep, 11 X 14 In. 25.00
Parkinson, Cupid Awake, Original Oak Frame, 1897, 7 1/2 X 9 1/2 In. 20.00
Parrish, Air Castles, Original Frame, 12 X 16 In. ....90.00 To 110.00
Parrish, Asleep Or Awake, Black Cupid, Tin Frame, 5 X 7 In. 225.00
Parrish, Cleopatra, Framed, 10 X 11 In. 75.00
Parrish, Cupid Watching, Brown Feather Grain Oval Frame, 12 X 18 In. 150.00
Parrish, Daybreak, Original Frame, 10 X 6 In. 45.00
Parrish, Dinkey Bird, Original Oak Frame, 11 X 15 In. 85.00
Parrish, Garden Of Allah, Signed, Dated 1918, Framed, 15 X 30 In. 125.00
Parrish, House Of Art, Framed, Hilltop Label, 7 X 11 1/4 In. 95.00
Parrish, Lone Wolf, Framed, 19 X 14 In. 35.00
Parrish, Perfect Day, Framed & Matted, 12 X 14 In. 75.00
Parrish, Seeing Things At Night, Black & White, Framed, 18 X 15 In. 35.00
Parrish, The Canyon, 12 X 15 In. 85.00
Parrish, Under Summer Skies, Signed, 18 X 15 1/2 In. 75.00
Prana, Indians On Hill, 1906, Framed, 13 X 16 In. 125.00
Reece, Sailfish, Original Frame, 16 X 12 1/2 In. 65.00
Schile, Smith Rescued By Pocahontas, Framed, 26 1/2 X 32 1/2 In. 200.00
Tidler, Tennis Girl, With Racquet, Oak Frame, 1909, 10 1/2 X 17 In. 65.00
Ulman, Sunbonnet, To Market, 1906, 15 X 6 1/2 In. 46.50
Waugh, Blond Girl, Original Ivory Frame, Signed, 14 1/2 X 13 In. 95.00
Wood, February, Matted, 1940, Signed, 8 3/4 X 11 3/4 In. 2475.00
Wood, Fertility, Matted, 1929, Signed, 11 3/4 X 9 In. 1870.00
Wood, Midnight Alarm, Matted, 1939, Signed, 12 X 7 In. 880.00
Wyeth, Elizabethan Galleons, 12 X 9 1/2 In. 55.00

How to carry a handkerchief and lipstick is a problem today for every woman, including the Queen of England. The purse has been recognizable since the eighteenth century. Leather and needlework purses were preferred. Beaded purses became popular in the nineteenth century, went out of style, but are again in use. Mesh purses date from the 1880s and are still being made.

PURSE, Alligator, Suede Lining 20.00
Art Nouveau, Florals, Sterling Silver, Brass Frame, Inner Purse 35.00
Bag, Beaded, Silver Bugle, Kid Lining, German Silver Frame, C.1910 .... 45.00
Bag, Mesh, Gold, Whiting Davis 35.00
Beaded Reticule, Victorian, Both Ends Dated 1919 .... 35.00
Beaded, 5 Rows Beaded Loops, Beaded Tassel, 4 X 7 1/2 In. 35.00
Beaded, Brass Top & Chain, Blue 65.00
Beaded, Carnival Glass, Evening 65.00
Beaded, Clutch, White, Gray Art Deco, Zipper, Czechoslovakia, 5 X 7 In. 12.00
Beaded, Floral Pattern, 5 Colors, No Strap 50.00
Beaded, Floral, White Ground, Fringe, Silver Plated Frame, 10 X 6 In. 45.00

Beaded, Gray & White 45.00
Beaded, Seed Pearls, Multicolored, Overall Floral & Leaf, French 30.00
Beaded, Tortoise Chain Handle & Frame, Geometric, Blue, Black, Fringe 35.00
Beaded, White Envelope, Seed Pearls On Sequins, 5 X 8 In. 14.00
Beaded, White, Multicolored Flowers, Beaded Fringe, Chain Handle 45.00
Black Velvet, Bead Rimmed 7.00
Black, Red Rose, Metal Frame, Silk Lining, Chain Handle 35.00
Brocade, Jeweled Clasp, Twin Mirror Inset, Satin Lined 16.00
Bronze Beaded, Art Deco, 1940s 30.00
Change, Abalone Sides, Chain 27.00
Child's, Piglets Peeking Out, China, 4 X 5 In. 25.00
Coin, Beaded, C.1910 .... 45.00
Coin, Elaine Christmas, 1916 Carved On Case, Chain, Sterling Silver 40.00
Copper Beaded, Tortoiseshell Frame 45.00
Drawstring Bag, Mesh, Gun Metal, Iridescent Beads, On Silk, 7 X 4 In. 24.00
Drawstring, Pouch, Beaded, Tassel, Black, Blue 18.00
Envelope, Braid Design, Velvet, Brown 9.50
Envelope, Pearls & Beaded, Zipper 6.00
Evening, Blue Sequined, Chain, Small 6.00
Evening, Gold Mesh, Whiting & Davis, Box ....10.00 To 27.00
Evening, Victorian, Petit Point, Roses On Silk, 48 Stones 125.00
Flame Stitched, Velvet Rim, Linen Lining, 5 1/2 X 6 In. 245.00
Lucite, Etched Flower Design, Cylinder Shape 12.50
Mesh, Art Nouveau Frame, German Silver, 8 X 6 1/2 In. 45.00
Mesh, Basket Of Flowers, Fringe, Whiting & Davis, ElSah, 7 X 8 In. 95.00
Mesh, Black & White Pattern, Whiting & Davis 35.00
Mesh, Coin, Patent 1890 .... 28.00
Mesh, Design, Chain Handle, Early 1900s 40.00
Mesh, Enameled, Picture Of Cockatoo 65.00
Mesh, Evening, Gold, Braided Handle 45.00
Mesh, Jewels On Reticulated Frame, Chain, 5 1/4 X 6 In. 35.00
Mesh, Marcasite, Enameled Silver, Art Deco, Bracelet, Whiting & Davis 250.00
Mesh, Tassels, Scroll, Floral Frame, Sterling Silver 115.00
Metal, Silver & Black, Whiting & Davis, 3 1/2 X 6 1/2 In. 45.00
Miser, Steel Bead Trim, Black 50.00
Petit Point On Silk, Brass Frame, 48 Stones, Victorian 85.00
Red Beaded, Diamond Shape, Beaded Fringe, Brass Closure, Chain Handle 50.00
Samorodok, Silver, Chain, 2 Cabochon Thumbpiece, 1910, Russian, 9 In. 550.00
Silver Metal Discs, Tortoise Handle, Whiting & Davis, 12 X 11 In. 75.00
Suede, Black, Marcasite Ornament 28.00
Tapestry, Scenic, Chain 12.00
Tatted, Drawstring, Velvet Lined 11.50

Quezal
Quezal glass was made from 1901 to 1920 by Martin Bach, Sr., in Brooklyn, New York. Other glassware by other firms, such as Loetz, Steuben, and Tiffany, resembles this gold-colored iridescent glass. After Martin Bach's death in 1920, his son continued the manufacture of a similar glass under the name "Lustre Art Glass."

QUEZAL, Saltshaker, Gold Iridescent, Ruffled Edge, Set Of 6 .... 135.00
Shade, Bell Form, Signed, Gold, 5 1/2 In. 175.00
Shade, Bulbous Shape, Golds, 7 In. 375.00
Shade, Flared, Roberts 66, Signed, 7 X 5 In., Set Of 5 .... 695.00
Shade, Gold Feather, Gold Lining, 5 1/2 In., Set Of 4 .... 475.00
Shade, Gold Iridescent, Pulled Feathers, Signed, 6 X 4 1/2 In, Pair 335.00
Shade, Gold, Bell Shaped, Ribbed, Signed, Set Of 3 .... 250.00
Shade, Green Feather, Calcite, Gold Interior, 6 1/2 In. 210.00
Shade, Iridescent Green Feather, Ribbed, Signed, 4 1/2 In. 125.00
Shade, Pulled Feather, Green, 6 X 4 In. 150.00
Vase, Candle, Gold Luster, Signed, 11 In. 195.00
Vase, Floriform, Ruffled Rim, Gold Interior, C.1910, Signed, 5 3/8 In. 600.00
Vase, Gold & Green Swirls, Cream, Marked, 8 1/4 In. 575.00
Vase, Gold Pink, Maroon Highlights, Signed, 8 In. 400.00
Vase, Gold Scrollwork, Gold Interior, Signed, Ovoid, 12 1/2 In. 550.00
Vase, Green & Gold Feathers, Gold Interior, Signed, 5 1/2 In. 895.00

Vase, Jack–In–The–Pulpit, Gold, 10 In. 300.00
Vase, Pearlized Vine & Leaf Design, Iridescent Blue, Signed, 10 In. 875.00
Vase, Pulled Green Feathers, Bordered In Gold, Signed, 5 1/2 In. 985.00
Vase, Trumpet, Bulbous Base, Gold, Pink Highlights, Signed, 10 In. 525.00
Vase, Trumpet, Gold, Pink Highlights, 10 In. 495.00
Vase, Trumpet, Pulled Green Feathers, Gold Outline, Signed, 5 1/2 In. 985.00

> *Quilts have been made since the seventeenth century. Early textiles were very precious and every scrap was saved to be reused. A quilt is a combination of fabrics joined to a filler and a backing by small stitched designs known as quilting. An appliqued quilt has pieces stitched to the top of a large piece of background fabric. A patchwork, or pieced, quilt is made of many small pieces stitched together. Embroidery can be added to either type.*

QUILT, Amish, Bar, Homespun, Blue, Purple, Green, Diamond Quilting, 64 X 76 In. ... 605.00
Amish, Bar, Red, Green, Purple, Diamond Quilting, 84 X 76 In. 385.00
Amish, Central Diamond, Patchwork, Mrs.Marvin Grober, 45 X 45 In. 115.00
Amish, Crib, Blind Pattern, Chain Links, Blue & Pink, 40 X 48 In. 150.00
Amish, Crib, Vine, Chain Links & Diagonal, Blue, Pink, 40 X 48 In. 130.00
Amish, Cross & Square, Purple, Jade, Green, Pink, Black, 80 X 60 In. 495.00
Amish, Double Irish Chain, Gray, Jade, Maroon, 76 X 82 In. 700.00
Amish, Double Monkey Wrench, Maroon, Gray, Blue, 64 X 64 In. 770.00
Amish, Lone Star, Emma Schwartz, 43 X 43 In. 135.00
Amish, Pine Cone, Blue, Brown, Green, 88 X 88 In. 1540.00
Amish, Star Pattern, Burgundy, Black, 8 Point Cut Out, 74 X 88 In. 650.00
Appliqued, 6 Bird Design, Sunman, Indiana, 1854, Crib 4600.00
Appliqued, Bunnies, Birds, Butterflies, Tulip, Child's, 35 X 58 In. 95.00
Appliqued, Butterflies, Multicolor, 82 X 70 In. 120.00
Appliqued, Chintz, Trapunto Wreath, 1846, 105 X 105 In. 3000.00
Appliqued, Dogwood, Chartreuse, Yellow & Green, 84 X 87 In. 200.00
Appliqued, Flying Geese, Reds & Blacks, 74 X 66 In. 145.00
Appliqued, Green & Purple Tulip, 66 X 75 In. 185.00
Appliqued, Lily, Pots Of Vining Flowers, 76 1/2 X 91 In. 725.00
Appliqued, Reverse Buttonhole Stitches, 1853, Square, 80 In. 2800.00
Appliqued, Shaded Roses, Buds, Scalloped Edge, 76 X 88 In. 250.00
Appliqued, Stylized Floral, Feather Stitched Edge, 100 X 100 In. 950.00
Appliqued, Stylized Floral, Sawtooth Border, Homespun, 87 X 88 In. 525.00
Appliqued, Stylized Florals, Vining, Calico & Homespun, 84 X 85 In. 500.00
Appliqued, Sunbonnet Babies, 72 X 104 In. 350.00
Appliqued, Sunbonnet Babies, Each Different, Handmade, 59 X 95 In. 225.00
Appliqued, Sunbonnet Babies, Red & White Border, 72 X 104 In. 450.00
Patchwork, 9 Stars, Calico, Sawtooth Border, 82 X 86 In. 350.00
Patchwork, 9 Pinwheels, Stylized Leaves, 78 X 89 In. 525.00
Patchwork, Bar Design, Plaids & Homespun, 102 X 112 In. 395.00
Patchwork, Blind Pattern, Leaves, Flowers, Pink, White, 81 X 92 In. 225.00
Patchwork, Blossom & Bud, Calico, Green, Pink, Yellow, 88 X 88 In. 330.00
Patchwork, Bow Tie, Calico, Green, Brown, Red, Blue, 68 X 85 In. 550.00
Patchwork, Bow Tie, White Homespun, 64 X 82 In. 150.00
Patchwork, Briar, Stitched, 1, 763 Squares, 88 X 84 In. 200.00
Patchwork, Broken Star, Yellow, Pink, Beige, White Ground, 80 X 80 In. 350.00
Patchwork, Bud & Leaf, Calico, Pink, White, Green, 1852, 80 X 84 In. 550.00
Patchwork, Central Star, Multicolored Diamonds, 94 X 94 In. 300.00
Patchwork, Checkerboard, Doll's, 1920s, 20 X 16 In. 15.00
Patchwork, Cherry Branch, Red & Beige, 76 X 76 In. 715.00
Patchwork, Columbia Puzzle, Blue, White, 1920, 65 X 70 In. 140.00
Patchwork, Compass, White Ground, Calico, 77 X 88 In. 100.00
Patchwork, Crazy, Black, Maroon, Tan, Man, Chicken, 1870, 96 X 76 In. 990.00
Patchwork, Crazy, Rowena & Sara Bowen, C.1880, 98 X 89 In. 700.00
Patchwork, Crazy, Silks & Satins, Feather Stitched, 90 X 102 In. 98.00
Patchwork, Crazy, Silks, Satins, Velvets, Feather Stitched, 80 X 65 In. 110.00
Patchwork, Diamond, Red, Yellow, Green, Blue, White, 76 X 88 In. 660.00
Patchwork, Double Irish Chain, Yellow, Brown, Green, 70 X 82 In. 150.00
Patchwork, Double Star, Green, Yellow, Maroon Patches, 76 X 76 In. 880.00
Patchwork, Double Wedding Ring, White Ground, 72 X 88 In. 100.00

Patchwork, Dresden Plate, 60 X 80 In.	85.00
Patchwork, Dresden Plate, Scalloped Edge, 70 X 74 In.	225.00
Patchwork, Embroidered Squares, 1899, Red & White, Crib	65.00
Patchwork, Feather Quilted Wreaths, Scalloped, 80 X 96 In.	175.00
Patchwork, Field Of Diamonds, Aqua Ground, 80 X 84 In.	150.00
Patchwork, Floral & Berry, Leaf & Wine Edge, 76 X 80 In.	715.00
Patchwork, Floral Center, Grape Ivy Edge, Chintz, 81 X 94 In.	550.00
Patchwork, Flower Basket, Trapunto, Calico, 100 X 100 In.	1210.00
Patchwork, Flower Garden, Flowers, Green, Pink Back, 75 X 90 In.	250.00
Patchwork, Flower Garden, Green Ground, Double Bed	215.00
Patchwork, Flying Geese, Homespun Back, 70 X 90 In.	375.00
Patchwork, Geometric Diamonds & Squares, Calico, 88 X 80 In.	467.00
Patchwork, Grandmother's Flower Garden, Yellow Centers, 68 X 80 In.	125.00
Patchwork, Hexagonal Blocks, Stars, Calico, 73 1/2 X 93 1/2 In.	335.00
Patchwork, Irish Chain, White, Floral Medallions, 81 X 86 In.	100.00
Patchwork, Jacob's Ladder, Pink Calico, White, Signature, 89 X 71 In.	150.00
Patchwork, Jacob's Ladder, Red, White, Blue, Red, Calico, 70 X 72 In.	165.00
Patchwork, Jacob's Ladder, Red, Yellow, White Ground, 88 X 74 In.	110.00
Patchwork, Kate Greenaway, Figures, Embroidered, Bolster, 84 X 88 In.	350.00
Patchwork, Lady Of Lake, Green Calico, Wild Goose Border, 76 X 80 In.	175.00
Patchwork, Lightning Bolt Bars, Green Calico, Crib	275.00
Patchwork, Lilies, Sawtooth Edge, Appliqued, 87 X 108 In.	285.00
Patchwork, Little Stars Of Bethlehem, 58 X 76 In.	85.00
Patchwork, Log Cabin, Each Square Has Center H, 78 X 82 In.	475.00
Patchwork, Log Cabin, Red Squares & Diamonds, 88 X 92 In.	195.00
Patchwork, Lone Star, Blue Floral, Peach Ground, 64 In.	100.00
Patchwork, Monkey Wrench, Red & White, 77 X 72 In.	90.00
Patchwork, Pieced Star, Red, Orange, White Ground, 92 X 70 In.	225.00
Patchwork, Pieced, Sawtooth Snowflakes, 13 Diamonds, 81 X 81 In.	750.00
Patchwork, Quadruple Diamond Border, Yellow, White, Twin, Pair	595.00
Patchwork, Red Stars, White Ground, 70 X 80 In.	185.00
Patchwork, Red, Green, Yellow, Blue, Calico, C.1850, 112 X 112 In.	3520.00
Patchwork, Red, White, & Blue Design, Stars, 80 X 84 In.	350.00
Patchwork, Reel & Flying Geese, Calico & Chintz, 88 X 88 In.	1045.00
Patchwork, Repeated Bethlehem Stars, Floral Corners, 84 X 84 In.	935.00
Patchwork, Snowball, Body	500.00
Patchwork, Sprig & Heart Pattern, D.Smith & M.A.Beck, 80 X 80 In.	825.00
Patchwork, Star & Octagon, Red, Maroon, Green, Pink, 76 X 88 In.	495.00
Patchwork, Star Design, Blue & White, Blue Binding, 69 X 78 In.	250.00
Patchwork, Star Of Bethlehem, Blue & White, 77 X 72 In.	135.00
Patchwork, Star Of Bethlehem, Yellow, Red, Green, Brown, 108 X 100 In.	1210.00
Patchwork, Star Of David, White Ground, 86 X 84 In.	125.00
Patchwork, Starflower, Hearts, Scissors Edge, 76 X 80 In.	170.00
Patchwork, State Bird, 48 Birds On Gold, 82 X 106 In.	450.00
Patchwork, Stylized Flowers, 35 Squares, 76 X 100 In.	250.00
Patchwork, Stylized Tulip Medallions, Green Border, 78 X 78 In.	250.00
Patchwork, Texas Star, Calico, Red Polka Dot Ground, 93 X 90 In.	350.00
Patchwork, Triple Irish Chain, Blue & White, 72 X 80 In.	400.00
Patchwork, Wild Goose Chase, Pink & Calico Squares, 80 X 70 In.	80.00
Patchwork, Wild Goose Chase, Pink, Calico, American, 80 X 70 In.	80.00
Patchwork, Windowpane, Blue & White, 72 X 88 In.	190.00

Tin-glazed, hand-painted pottery has been made in Quimper, France, since the late seventeenth century. The earliest firm, founded in 1685 by Jean Baptiste Bousquet, was known as HB Quimper. Another firm, founded in 1772 by Francois Eloury, was known as Porquier. The third firm, founded by Guillaume Dumaine in 1778, was known as HR or Henriot Quimper. All three firms made similar pottery decorated with designs of Breton peasants and sea and flower motifs. The Eloury (Porquier) and Dumaine (Henriot) firms merged in 1913. Bosquet (HB) merged with the others in 1968. The factory is now called Les Faienceries de Quimper. It was sold to a United States family in 1984.

HR.
Quimper

QUIMPER, Bowl, Man, Flowers, Pedestal, Ruffled, Spatter Handles, 7 X 4 1/2 In.	42.00

Box, Portrait Of Man, Wide Brim Hat, Signed, 3 1/2 X 5 X 1/12 In.	235.00
Cruet, Oil & Vinagar, Peasant Design, Signed, 6 In.	125.00
Cup, Custard, Peasants, Handles, Henriot	35.00
Figurine, Boy & Girl, Dancing, Artist Signed, 6 1/2 In.	375.00
Holder, Letter, 4 Compartment, Deco Trim, 5 X 8 In.	325.00
Inkwell, Figural, Pig, Green Mottled Spots, Yellow, Signed, 4 X 3 In.	85.00
Inkwell, Scalloped Edge, 5 In.	50.00
Knife Rest, Peasant Woman Center, Signed	40.00
Oil & Vinegar, Double, Stopper, Peasants, Signed H.Quimper, 6 In.	125.00
Pitcher, Figural, Flemish Woman, Signed C.Maillard, 7 5/8 In.	250.00
Pitcher, Man With Basket	65.00
Pitcher, Peasant Man, Left Handle, Yellow, 5 X 5 In.	85.00
Plate, 8 1/4 In.	45.00
Plate, Brittany Woman, Odetta	275.00
Plate, Dutch Fraktur, 1882	95.00
Plate, Lady Scene Center, Yellow & Blue Bands, 9 3/8 In.	70.00
Plate, Signed, Blue & Yellow, 4 In.	30.00
Tea Set, Tray, Quimper Mark, 4 Piece	900.00
Teapot, Peasant Design, Octagonal, Signed Henriot Quimper	75.00
Wall Pocket, Art Deco Riche Border	450.00

Radford pottery was made by Alfred Radford in Broadway, Virginia, Tiffin and Zanesville, Ohio, and Clarksburg, West Virginia, from 1891 until 1912. Jasperware, Ruko, Thera, Radera, and Velvety Art Ware were made. The jasperware resembles the famous Wedgwood ware of the same name.

RADFORD, Jardiniere, Jasperware, Florals, 8 1/2 X 10 1/4 In.	155.00
Vase, Thera, 12 1/2 In.	215.00

The first radio broadcast receiving sets were sold in New York City in 1910. They were used to pick up the experimental broadcasts of the day. The first commercial radios were made by Westinghouse Company for listeners of the experimental shows on KDKA Pittsburgh in 1920. Collectors today are interested in all early radios, especially those made of Bakelite plastic or decorated with blue mirrors.

[THERA]

RADIO, Airline, Model 54K, Wooden Case	25.00
Andrews, Battery, Art Deco Panel, Type II	325.00
Apex, Metal Cabinet, External Speaker	150.00
Arvin, Coral Tint, Metal	37.00
Atwater Kent, Cathedral, Model 135	75.00
Atwater Kent, Model 20, Horn	150.00
Atwater Kent, Model 33, Wooden, Speaker	55.00
Atwater Kent, Model 48	65.00
Atwater Kent, Model 60, Kiel Table	400.00
Bendix, Marbelized Green & Black Bakelite	185.00
Con, Sodium, 1 Tube	160.00
Crosley Ultra, Musicone Speaker	60.00
Crosley, Bandbox Model 601, External Speaker	110.00
Crosley, Model 4–29, Battery	135.00
Crosley, Model 506, Small	18.00
Crosley, Model B, Type 5	85.00
Crosley, Musicone, Metal Cabinet, External Speaker	130.00
Crosley, Pup, Battery	245.00 To 265.00
Crystal Set, Steinite Laboratories	95.00
Crystal, On Wooden Base	20.00
Deforest D–01A, Tube, Box	15.00
Doron Bros., Hamilton, Ohio, Crystal Set	85.00
Emerson, Clock, Round, 15 In.	95.00
Fada, Art Deco, Mustard Yellow, Red Trim, Handle, 1935, 6 X 10 1/2 In.	225.00
General Electric, Plastic, 1950s	65.00
Hallicrafter, S–38 Model, AM & Shortwave To 30 Megacycle	50.00
Philco, Beehive, Model 60	115.00
Philco, Cathedral, Model 70	215.00
Philco, Model 45, Table	45.00

Radiola, Battery Box	135.00
RCA, Cathedral, No.128	250.00
RCA, Wooden, Gold Coast Super, 1930s	85.00
Silvertone, Model 1809, Amateur, Art Deco	35.00
Silvertone, Model 7033, 3–Band, Phonograph Jack	18.00
Spartan, Blue Mirrored Glass	650.00
Steinite A.C.–l	165.00
Trav–Ler Beehive	45.00
Zenith, Consoltone, Green	95.00
Zenith, Model 6 S 330, Police Band, Shortwave, Automatic	28.00

Railroad enthusiasts collect any train memorabilia. Everything is wanted, from oilcans to whole train cars. The Chessie system has a store that sells many reproductions of their old dinnerware and uniforms.

RAILROAD, Ashtray, C.& O., Chessie	70.00 To 79.00
Ashtray, New York Central, Bird, China, 7 In.	25.00
Ashtray, Paper, Folding, Chicago, Milwaukee, St.Paul, & Pacific	5.00
Ashtray, Union Pacific R.R., Blue Glass	20.00
Badge, Cap, Missouri Pacific Lines, Red Porcelain, Emblem	40.00
Badge, Porter's, Santa Fe, Atchison, & Topeka, Emblem	70.00
Baggage Cart, U.P.R.R.	200.00
Bell, Crossing, 12 In.Diam.	100.00
Bell, Iron Yoke & Ringer, D & GR R.R., Brass, 18 1/2 X 19 1/2 In.	600.00
Bell, Locomotive, 10 1/2 In.Diam.	400.00
Bell, Locomotive, Bronze, No Mount, 12 In.Diam.	150.00
Bell, Locomotive, C&NW RR, Yoke & Cradle, Bronze, 13 In.Diam.	850.00
Bell, Steam Locomotive, Yoke & Cradle, Bronze, 15 In.Diam.	875.00
Bench, Depot, 2–Sided, Bentwood Seat, Oak, 8 Ft.	450.00
Bib, Paper, Union Pacific, Set Of 5	12.00
Blotter, Northern Pacific	5.00
Book, Pocket List Of Railroad Officials, 1931	20.00
Book, Tour, Great Western Railway, England, Shakespeare's Country	10.00
Bottle, Thermos, Lettered Pullman, Stainless Steel	75.00
Bowl, Vegetable, N.Y.C., DeWitt Clinton	40.00
Box, Engineer, P.R.R.Red, Gold Paint, Marked No.124, Phila.Div.	50.00
Butter Chip, L.& N. R.R., Silver Plate	45.00
Butter Chip, Santa Fe, Membrena	25.00
Butter Chip, Union Pacific, Winged Streamliner	12.00
Calendar, Missouri Pacific R.R., Tin	85.00
Can, Kerosene, D.& R.G.R.R.	55.00
Can, Kerosene, Union Pacific	25.00
Can, Oil, Rock Island	30.00
Cap, Trainman, Badge, Side Buttons, Cord Trim, C.1910	85.00
Card, Playing, Atchison & Topeka, Front View Of Diesel, Red	8.00
Cards, Playing, Alaska Railroad, Boxed Double Deck	13.00
Cards, Playing, Algoma Central, Bear Logo, Boxed Double Deck	15.00
Cards, Playing, B.& O., Sleep Like A Kitten, Set Of 2 Decks	25.00
Cards, Playing, Bangor & Aroostook R.R., Blue On White	4.00
Cards, Playing, Double Deck, Frisco	15.00
Cards, Playing, Milwaukee	14.00
Cards, Playing, Rio Grande R.R.	25.00
Cards, Playing, Rock Island R.R.	9.00
Cards, Playing, Santa Fe, Double Deck, Color	10.00
Cards, Playing, Southern Pacific, Streamlined Train Scene, Box	15.00
Cards, Playing, Vista Dome, California Zephyr, Mountains, Pair	24.00
Cards, Playing, Washington & Pacific Northwest, Picture Of Faces	30.00
Cart, Baggage, 40 X 118 X 36 In.	500.00
Cart, Baggage, Railway Express Agency, Wooden	475.00
Cart, Station, Oak, 1906, 10 X 36 Ft.	295.00
Celery Dish, B.& O., Gold	125.00
Celery Dish, U.P.R.R.Harriman, Blue	49.00
Chair, Swivel, Lounge, Pennsylvania Railroad Observation Car	250.00
Chisel, N.P.R., 9 In.	7.50

Cocktail Shaker, Art Deco Chrome, Red Knob, Century NYC	35.00
Cocoa Pot, N.Y.C., Mercury	75.00
Creamer, N.K.P., Ft.Wayne, Individual	150.00
Creamer, Southern Pacific, Sunset On Tracks Logo, Individual	50.00
Crossing Sign, Cast Iron, Yellow, 18 In.Diam.	90.00
Cup & Saucer, Chicago, Milwaukee, St.Paul, Haviland	90.00
Cup & Saucer, Erie R.R., Starucca, Demitasse	165.00
Cup & Saucer, Olympian R.R.	80.00
Cup, B.& O.	45.00
Cup, Bouillon, N.Y.C.R.R., DeWitt Clinton	42.00
Cup, Bouillon, P.R.R., Broadway	15.00
Cup, Canadian Pacific RR Hotel, Leaves & Bows	32.50
Cup, Lackawanna Railroad, Route Of Phoebe Snow	10.00
Cuspidor, Pullman Co., Nickel Silver	55.00
Diary, Pocket, Rhode Island	6.00
Eggcup, Chicago Northwestern, Black & Red Logo	22.00
Figurine, Cat, Chessie	18.00
Flag Kit, Conductor, Shoulder, Metal	10.00
Flare, A.T.& S. R.R., Brass Ends, Steel Center, 12 In.	60.00
Funnel, C.& E.I. R.R.	16.50
Gauge, Air, Locomotive, 4 1/2 In.	25.00
Gauge, Steam, Utica Steam Gauge Co., Utica, N.Y., 1865., 4 1/2 In.	135.00
Globe, D.& H., Tall Logo	50.00
Goblet, Crystal, Great Northern Logo	25.00
Goblet, Etched Great Northern Logo, 8 In.	37.50
Gravy Boat, B.& O., Centenary	40.00
Hair Receiver, Pullman, Embossed Hair On Lid, Fits Into Sink Top	65.00
Handbag, N.P., Nomad Logo, Vinyl	15.00
Hat, Badge, Conductor	15.00
Hat, Conductor's, T.P.& W.	40.00
Hatchet, N.Y.C.C. R.R.	45.00
Hatchet, Station Agent, Marked D.& R.G.W.	69.50
Ice Tong, N.Y.C.R.R.	35.00
Invitation, Line Completion Party, La Crosse & Milwaukee, 1855	16.00
Jug, Deodorizer, Pullman, Stoneware	65.00
Key, Lock, Switch, C.& N.W. Railway, Brass	15.00
Knife, Rock Island, Logo, Pocket	15.00
Lamp, Caboose, Inside, D.T.& I.	47.00
Lamp, Carbide, Oxwell R.R.	65.00
Lamp, Oil, Hanging, Parlor	60.00
Lantern, A.T.& S.F.R.R., Etched Red Globe	50.00
Lantern, Adlake Reliable, G.N.R.Y.On Lid, Clear Globe	55.00
Lantern, Adlake, C.M.& S.T.Pry, Globe, 1913, 5 3/8 In.	65.00
Lantern, Adlake, Frame, Globe, B.M.R.R.	85.00
Lantern, Adlake–Kero, Rock Island R.R., Dated 1913, Signed	37.50
Lantern, B. & O. R.R. Logo, Tall Globe	120.00
Lantern, B.& O.R.R., Red Glaze, Original Torpedoes	70.00
Lantern, Brass, Gem Cold Blast, C.T.Ham	85.00
Lantern, Carbide	25.00
Lantern, Conductor's, Brass	175.00 To 265.00
Lantern, Conductor's, Nickel Plated, B.B., Clear Globe	145.00
Lantern, D.L.& W. R.R.	32.00
Lantern, Dietz Vesta, N.Y.C.S., Red Cast Globe	22.00
Lantern, Dietz Veta, Boston & Albany, Clear Globe	45.00
Lantern, Flag Globe, Wabash R.R., 5 3/8 In.	140.00
Lantern, Hand, Universal Metal Co., Brass	200.00
Lantern, Inspector's, Dietz Acme	45.00
Lantern, Inspector, Marked P.R.R.	50.00
Lantern, Kerosene, Adlake, New York Central R.R.	45.00
Lantern, Kerosene, Missouri Pacific	65.00
Lantern, Marked PRR On Lid, Red Globe	40.00
Lantern, N.Y.C.S., Clear, Unmarked Globe	20.00
Lantern, Post, Kerosene, English	75.00
Lantern, Signal, Adlake, 4–Light, 16 In.	150.00

Lantern, Signal, Battery Operated, Genesy 22.00
Lantern, Switch, Bull's-Eye 100.00
Lantern, Switch, C.M.& S.T.P.R.Y., Brass Top, Clear Globe, 1895 .... 95.00
Lantern, Tin, Feurer Hand, Atom, Germany, Red Globe, 6 1/8 In. 20.00
Lantern, Tin, Green Paint, C.Eastgate & Son, Birmingham, 13 In. 15.00
Lantern, United Ry., 5 3/8 In. 120.00
Lock, Iron, Key Embossed B.R.& P.Co. 30.00
Lock, Key, Burnished Brass, HV R.R., Heart Shape 125.00
Lock, Key, Rock Island R.R., Brass 32.50
Lock, Switch, B.& O., Brass Key 17.00
Lock, Switch, B.& O.R.R., Brass, Heart Shape 25.00
Lock, Switch, D.T. & I., Steel 12.00
Lock, Switch, Signed New York 35.00
Lunch Box, Brass Handled, Square, Marked Black Diamond 15.00
Map, Ohio, 1914 .... 15.00
Map, Southern Pacific R.R. 25.00
Match Holder, Wall, Brass, Pennsylvania R.R., Embossed 80.00
Match Holder, Wall, Cast Iron, I.C.R.R. Miller 80.00
Matches, Book, Rock Island, Red & Black Logo, Pkg.Of 6 .... 2.00
Menu, American Export Line, 1935 .... 5.00
Menu, Breakfast, U.P.R.R., Sun Valley, 1949 .... 6.00
Mustard Pot, Green Stripe, N.Y.C., Logo In Blue Circle 24.00
Mustard, New York Central 35.00
Notebook, Rock Island, 3-Ring, Logo, Operations 8.00
Oil Can, Long Spout 25.00
Oil Can, N.P.R.Y., Small 8.00
Oil Can, Rock Island Lines, 15 In. 35.00
Oil Can, Tin & Brass, 27 1/2 In. 20.00
Oiler, Long Spout, C.M.St. & P. 37.00
Oyster Dish, Rock Island R.R. 47.00
Padlock, N.& W.Ry.Co., Key 40.00
Pencil, Illinois Central, 10 Piece 4.00
Pencil, Mechanical, B.& O., Blue Logo, Pearlized 15.00
Plate, 1847, Train Center, N.Y.C., Buffalo China, 8 1/2 In. 39.00
Plate, Atlantic Coast Lines RR, 9 In. 40.00
Plate, B.& O., Centenary, 10 1/2 In. 35.00
Plate, Missouri Pacific, State Flowers, Diesel 325.00
Plate, N.Y.C. R.R., Salmon, 10 In. 45.00
Plate, N.Y.C., DeWitt Clinton, 7 3/4 In. 25.00
Plate, R.I. R.R., LaSalle, 10 1/2 In. 140.00
Plate, Souvenir, Engine Scene, New York Central, Cedar Point, 1951 .... 20.00
Plate, Wabash, Banner, 5 In. 75.00
Plate, Wabash, Banner, 7 1/2 In. 90.00
Platter, Brown, Southern Serves The South, Buffalo China 100.00
Platter, Missouri Pacific, Silver Plate, 8 1/2 In. 20.00
Platter, Monon R.R., Oval, 7 In. 110.00
Platter, Southern Railway, Brown Band, Logo, Buffalo China 100.00
Platter, Steak, Violets & Daisies, Burlington, 9 In. 85.00
Print, Great Northern, R.R., Indian, W.Reiss, Framed, 32 X 12 In. 125.00
Print, Pecunnie Blackfoot Indian, Great Northern R.R., Set Of 8 .... 225.00
Rack, Luggage, Brass, New South Wales 200.00
Receipt, Cleveland & Toledo, Dated 1857, 5 3/4 X 7 In. 2.00
Rule, Minn.& St.Paul R.R., Metal 10.00
Scissors, Santa Fe R.R., Marked 15.00
Server, Seafood, Union Pacific, Silver Plate, 3 Piece, Set Of 4 .... 265.00
Sherbet, B.& O.R.R., Capital Pattern 55.00
Sherbet, Missouri Pacific, Eagle, Silver Plate 25.00
Sign, Rutland R.R., Watch Out For Locomotive, Iron, 14 X 24 In. 125.00
Spittoon, Union Pacific R.R., Brass 18.00
Spoon, Sterling Silver, Mt.Tom Railway, Holyoke, Mass. 42.50
Step Stool, Conductor's, Missouri Pacific 90.00
Step Stool, Pullman 65.00
Stock Certificate, B.& O.Wagon Train Engraving, Framed, 1901 .... 20.00
Stock Certificate, Illinois Central, 400 Shares, 1948, Signed 60.00

Sugar & Creamer, Union Pacific, Silver Plate	125.00
Sugar Tongs, U.P. R.R., Silver Plate, Large	18.00
Switch Key, N.Y.C.	25.00
Switch Lamp, Dressel, 2 Red, 2 Blue Lenses, 17 In.	95.00
Switch Lock, Signed N.Y. N.H.& H.	35.00
Teapot, Missouri Pacific, Silver Plate, 11 Oz.	25.00
Teapot, Pennsylvania R.R., International Silver, Keystone Logo	150.00
Teapot, Union Pacific, Winged Streamliner	45.00
Teaspoon, Iced Tea, Erie R.R., Silver Plate	12.00
Telegraph Sounder, Pa.R.R.Altoona Shop, 2 Brass Hand Keys	260.00
Thermos, Pullman, Stainless Steel	50.00
Timetable, B.& O., Nov.13, 1927	10.00
Timetable, Pennsylvania R.R., 1937	6.00
Timetable, Union Pacific R.R., 1945	8.00
Tray, Panama Pacific, Pewter, 1915	28.00
Tray, Tip, N.Y.C., Silver Plate, Round, 6 1/2 In.	35.00
Tumbler, Soda, Santa Fe, White Logo	6.00
Vase, Blue Glass, Minneapolis & St.Louis Railway, McKee, 7 1/2 In.	275.00
Water Container, Soo Line, Tin, Galvanized	25.00
Whistle, Backup, Caboose, A.T.& S.F.	40.00
Whistle, Missouri Pacific, Caboose, Backup, Unused	55.00
Whistle, Steam, Brass, Valve, 6 X 23 In.	500.00
Whistle, Union Pacific Sherburne, Caboose, Backup, Brass	65.00
Wrench, Chicago, Burling, Quincy	10.00

The razor was used in ancient Egypt and subsequently wherever shaving was in fashion. The metal razor used in America until about 1870 was made in Sheffield, England. After 1870, machine–made hollow–ground razors were made in Germany or America. Plastic or bone handles were popular. The razor was often sold in a set of seven, one for each day of the week. The set was often kept by the barber who shaved the well–to–do man each day in the shop.

RAZOR, Corn, Griffin XX, Original Box, 3 1/2 In.	22.00
English Rolls, Original Box	20.00
Fox, Embossed Running Fox, Celluloid Handle	15.00
Gem Eveready	8.50
Gem Junior, Parade Model, Box	6.00
Gillette, Original Box	15.00
Keen Kutter, Blades, Box	25.00
Kit, Barber's, 11 Straight Razors	70.00
Rolls Imperial, Original Box	14.00
Safety, Gillette, Box	15.00
Safety, Keen Kutter, Box	31.50
Safety, Larkin, Brass Pocket Case	12.00
Sharpener, Blade, Kriss Kross, Single Edge, Original Box	20.00
Simmons Barber's Pet, Case	26.00
Star, Model 100, Box	7.00
Straight, Art Nouveau Design, Lady's Head	25.00
Straight, Boker & Co., Horn Handle, S.S.St.Louis On Blade, Box	55.00
Straight, Bone Handle, Train On Blade, English, Art Deco Lady	25.00
Straight, Celebrated Wade & Butcher, Wostenholm, Faux Ivory Handle	30.00
Straight, Chicken Claw Both Sides, German	26.00
Straight, Germany, Box	10.00
Straight, Green Peacock On Celluloid Handle	30.00
Straight, Henckel, Platinum, Celluloid Picture Of Little Kids	30.00
Straight, Horn Handle, Angel & Horn Of Plenty Etched On Blade	50.00
Straight, Horn Handle, Statue Of Liberty Etched On Blade	50.00
Straight, Imperial Razor Co., Horn Handle, Old Car Etched On Blade	45.00
Straight, Ivory Celluloid, Elk & Trees	35.00
Straight, Ka–Bar, Box	27.50
Straight, Keen Kutter, Box	27.50
Straight, Otto Deutsch, Green Transparent Handle	48.00
Straight, Roger Cutlery, German, Ivory Case	20.00
Straight, Wade & Botcher, Brass Spline, Etched Stage Coach, C.1840	45.00

Straight, Wester Bros., White Handle, Case	25.00
Straight, Winchester, No.8425	55.00
Straight, Wooden Handle, Steel, 25 1/2 In.	65.00
Strop, U.S.Cavalry	25.00
Valet Autostrop, Metal Case, Model C	10.00 To 15.50

Reamers, or juice squeezers, have been known since 1767, although most of those collected today date from the twentieth century. Figural reamers are among the most prized.

REAMER, Clown	18.00 To 28.00
Figural, Orange Spout & Handle, White Top, 2 Piece	28.00
Fry, Pearl Glass	38.00
Fry, Sunkist	60.00
Lemon, Arcade, No.2, Cast Iron	65.00
Lemon, Hand, Dark Beech, 11 In.	45.00
Lemon, Wooden	30.00 To 110.00
Lime, Zinc Plated	8.00
Pink, No.310	85.00
Pump Log, Iron	30.00
Red Wing, Cup, Yellow	95.00
Sunkist, Caramel	200.00
Sunkist, Custard Yellow	40.00
Sunkist, Jadite, Large	30.00
Sunkist, No.3, Yellow	65.00
Sunkist, Pink	26.50 To 40.00
Sunkist, White, Milk Glass	22.00

The cylinder-shaped phonograph record for use with the early Edison phonograph was made about 1889. Disc records were first made by 1894; the double-sided disc by 1904. The high-fidelity records were first issued in 1944, the first vinyl disc in 1946, the first stereo record in 1958. The 78 rpm became the standard in 1926 but was discontinued in 1957. In 1932, the first 33 1/3 rpm was made but was not sold commercially until 1948. In 1949, the 45 rpm was introduced.

RECORD, Doris Day, 45, Picture Sleeve, 1950s	5.00
Holiday Greetings From Bunch At Orange, Edison Speaks	1000.00
Johnny Cash, Sings Hank Williams, 45, Sun Label	15.00
Pat Boone, 45, Picture Sleeve, 1950s	8.00
Perry Como, Set Of 10	10.00
Shirley Temple, Golden, On The Good Ship Lollipop	5.00
Stan Kenton, 45, 1950s	7.50

The Red Wing Pottery of Red Wing, Minnesota, was a firm started in 1878. It was not until the 1920s that art pottery was made. It closed in 1967. Rumrill pottery was made for George Rumrill by the Red Wing Pottery and other firms. It was sold in the 1930s.

RED WING, Ashtray, Minnesota Twins, World Series, 1965, 12 1/2 X 6 In.	60.00
Ashtray, Wing, Maroon	27.50
Bean Pot, Signed Minnesota Stoneware, Brown, 8 In.	35.00
Beater Jar, Advertising, Titonka, Iowa	75.00
Beater Jar, Gray Line, Signed	98.00
Beater Jar, Jorgenson Bros., Alden, Iowa	75.00
Beater Jar, Tracer, Minnesota	80.00
Beater Jar, Yellowware	65.00
Berry Bowl, Dutch Boy & Girl	30.00
Beverage Server, Stopper	20.00
Bowl Set, Nested, Blue & Rust, Sponge, 7 Piece	400.00
Bowl, Advertising, Kluckhorn's, Klemme, Iowa, Signed, 7 In.	75.00
Bowl, Bail Handle, Signed Minnesota Stoneware Co., 10 1/2 In.	55.00
Bowl, Blue & Rust, 11 In.	80.00
Bowl, Console, Brown, Top Band, Turquoise Inside, 11 In.	35.00
Bowl, Console, Ivory, Deer Flower Frog, No.926	10.00
Bowl, Console, Turquoise Top Band, Art Glaze Finish, 11 1/2 In.	35.00

Bowl, Glade Ketchren, Hartley, Iowa, 7 1/2 In. 45.00
Bowl, Greek Key Band, Luhman & Sanders, Postville, Iowa, 8 In. 55.00
Bowl, J.D.Cutling, Byron, Rock Dell, 7 In. 30.00
Bowl, Marquardt & Son, Cambria, Wisc., Blue Stripe, 7 1/2 In. 32.50
Bowl, Minnesota Stoneware Co., Bail Handle, 10 1/2 In. 55.50
Bowl, Red, Blue, & Cream, Marked, 7 In. 45.00
Bowl, Rounded Square, Rust Exterior, Green Interior, Large 12.00
Bowl, Saffron Ware, Signed, No.6 .... 70.00
Bowl, Salad, Bobwhite 45.00
Bowl, Sponge Band, Signed, Gray, 7 In. 75.00
Bowl, Westend Grocery, Waukon, Iowa, Sponge Band, 8 X 5 In. 145.00
Butter, 4 Lb. 40.00
Butter, Covered, Bird 15.00
Butter, Covered, Bobwhite 25.00
Candleholder, Mottled Blue, Pair 18.00
Casserole, Covered, Dancing People 45.00
Casserole, Covered, Gray Line 85.00
Casserole, Covered, Sponge Band, 8 1/2 In. 85.00
Casserole, Freeman, Emmetsburg, Iowa, Sponge Band, Marked, 7 1/2 In. 135.00
Casserole, Gray, 4 1/2 In. 470.00
Casserole, Lid, Sponge Band, W.B.Freeman, Emmetsburg, Ia., 7 In. 150.00
Churn, Birch Leaves All Around, Zinc Glaze, 2 Gal. 550.00
Churn, Dated December 21, 1915, Large Wing, 2 Gal. 150.00
Churn, Large Wing, 5 Gal. 195.00
Churn, Lazy 8, No Dasher 110.00
Churn, Salt Glaze, Minnesota Stoneware Co., 3 Gal. 850.00
Coffee Set, Cup & Saucer Of Different Colors, 9 Piece 65.00
Cookie Jar, Baker, Yellow ....27.00 To 33.00
Cookie Jar, Bobwhite ....30.00 To 40.00
Cookie Jar, Dutch Girl, Blue ....35.00 To 45.00
Cookie Jar, Dutch Girl, Yellow ....30.00 To 35.00
Cookie Jar, French Chef, Yellow 35.00
Cookie Jar, Goldilocks 85.00
Cookie Jar, Katrina, Blue 30.00
Cookie Jar, King Of Hearts 75.00
Cookie Jar, Monk, Green 40.00
Cookie Jar, Monk, Yellow & Brown 26.00
Cookie Jar, Pineapple, Aqua 28.00
Cookie Jar, Winnie Pig 70.00
Cooler, Iced Tea, Original Spigot & Lid, 3 Gal. 275.00
Cooler, Water, 5 Gal. 200.00
Creamer, Bird 20.00
Creamer, Bobwhite 20.00
Crock, Cobalt Blue Leaf, Salt Glaze, 6 Gal. 95.00
Crock, Handles, Patent 1915, 10 Gal. 45.00
Crock, R.W.Union, 5 In.Wing, 40 Gal. 310.00
Crock, R.W.Union, 60 Gal. 250.00
Crock, Small Wing, 5 Gal. 75.00
Crock, Spongeware, 7 In. 30.00
Crock, Union, 5 Gallon 25.00
Cup, Bobwhite 5.00
Cup, Bobwhite, Large 8.50
Dish, Candy, Rooster Cover, Blue 17.50
Dispenser, Juleps, Cattail Design 85.00
Egg, Baby Face On One Side, Buttocks On Other, Pair 100.00
Feeder, Water, Chicken 60.00
Figurine, Cow & Calf, Spotted, 4 X 6 In. 250.00
Figurine, Cowgirl, Pensive Pose, Red Hair, Hand Painted, 10 1/2 In. 85.00
Fruit Jar, Union Stoneware Of Red Wing, 1/2 Gal. 110.00
Hors D'Oeuvres Holder, Bobwhite 35.00
Jar, Batter, Advertising, Winterset, Iowa 60.00
Jar, Beater, Sponge Band 65.00
Jar, Canning, Applesauce, Spring, Clamp Top, 3 Gal. 100.00
Jar, Canning, Mason, 1/2 Gal. 95.00

Jar, Canning, Union Stoneware, 1 Qt. 85.00
Jar, Lab, Cover, Spigot, Float Device, 5 Gal. 125.00
Jar, Pantry, 3 Gal. 1900.00
Jar, Pantry, No.1 .... 225.00
Jug, Ball Lock, Small Wing, 5 Gal. 145.00
Jug, Beehive, Birch Leaves & Oval, 5 Gal. 125.00
Jug, Beehive, Large Wing, 5 Gal. ....120.00 To 125.00
Jug, Brown Beehive, Name Incised On Bottom, 1/2 Gal. 35.00
Jug, Colfax Mineral Water, Colfax, Iowa, 5 Gal. 100.00
Jug, Minnesota Stoneware Co., Zinc Glaze, C.1896, 1/2 Gal. 50.00
Jug, Shoulder, Brown Top, Wing & Oval, 5 Gal. 225.00
Jug, Union Stoneware, Signed 65.00
Jug, Wide Mouth, Signed, 6 1/2 In. 37.50
Mug, Bobwhite 5.00
Mug, Hamms 58.00
Mug, Salt Glaze, Handle Broken, G.Schatola 1894 Mark, 2 Gal. 575.00
Pail, Butter, Sponge Band, 5 Lb. 300.00
Pitcher, Blue, Spongeware, Schatola Marked 125.00
Pitcher, Blue, Spongeware, Squat 90.00
Pitcher, Bobwhite, 60 Oz. ....27.50 To 30.00
Pitcher, Chartreuse 17.50
Pitcher, Cherries & Leaves 190.00
Pitcher, Cherry Band, 1914 .... 215.00
Pitcher, Dutch Boy & Girl 340.00
Pitcher, Dutch Children & Windmill 175.00
Pitcher, Gothic Greek Design, Brown & Green, 8 In. ....75.00 To 98.00
Pitcher, Grapes, Brown, 9 1/2 In. 135.00
Pitcher, Green Craquelle Glaze, Deco Shape, Marked 30.00
Pitcher, Gross Mercantile Co., Bridgewater, S.D., Cherry Band 67.50
Pitcher, I.M.Bump, Rockford, Iowa, Cherry Band, Large 265.00
Pitcher, Ridgeway Dairy, Charles City, Iowa, Phone 238, 4 1/2 In. 30.00
Pitcher, Sponge Band, St.Paul Advertising 130.00
Pitcher, Spongeware Band 95.00
Pitcher, Water, Lily 175.00
Pitcher, Yellowware, 7 In. 75.00
Planter, Swan, Yellow 8.00
Planter, White, Aqua Interior, Gold Holder 34.00
Plate, Bobwhite, 11 In. 12.00
Plate, Capistrano 8.00
Plate, Dinner, Bobwhite ....10.00 To 12.00
Plate, Lexington 10.00
Platter, Bobwhite, 13 1/2 In. 18.00
Platter, Bobwhite, 14 1/2 In. 17.50
Platter, Bobwhite, 20 In. 40.00
Platter, Capistrano, 15 In. 14.00
Roaster, Cover, Brown, Green Glaze, Cover, Large 45.00
Salt & Pepper, Bobwhite ....20.00 To 25.00
Salt & Pepper, Damask 5.00
Saucer, Bobwhite 6.00
Shoe, High Button, Green, 10 In. 85.00
Soap Dish, Salt Glaze 65.00
Sugar, Cover, Bird 20.00
Teapot, Art Deco Turquoise Design 15.00
Teapot, Bobwhite 50.00
Tray, Sandwich, Blue, Chevron, 15 In. 20.00
Trivet, Bobwhite 170.00
Urn, Cherubs, Green & Brown, Signed 60.00
Vase, Cattails, 10 In. 35.00
Vase, Fan, Deco Design, Red–Orange, 8 1/2 In. 35.00
Vase, Fan, Matte Green, 12 In. 20.00
Vase, Gardenia, White, Brown Highlights, 10 1/2 In. 25.00
Vase, No.1175, Lady Between Pillars, 10 1/2 In. 45.00
Vase, White, Turquoise, Cactus Design, Geometric Handles, 8 In. 45.00
Wall Pocket, Raised Bird On Grapevine, Gray Green 15.00

China can be washed in warm water with mild soapsuds. The addition of ammonia to the water will add that extra sparkle.

Figurines are often damaged. Examine the fingers, toes, and other protruding parts for damage or repairs.

Redware, Vase, Black, Albany,
Slip Design, 7 In.

Water Cooler, Small Wing, Lid, 5 Gal. 225.00

> *Redware is a hard, red stoneware that originated in the late 1600s and continues to be made. The term is also used to describe any common clay pottery that is reddish in color.*

REDWARE, Bowl, Clear Glaze With Brown Spots, Applied Handles, 8 1/4 In. 155.00
Bowl, Floral Design, Yellow Glaze, 6 1/2 X 14 1/2 In. 50.00
Bowl, Green Rust Glaze, Footed, 10 1/2 X 11 1/2 X 5 3/4 In. 85.00
Bowl, Milk, Arch Design, Dripping Yellow Slip, Europe, 12 1/4 In. 30.00
Bowl, Milk, Yellow Slip Design, 7 X 2 1/2 In. 15.00
Charger, 4 Puddles Of Yellow Slip, Coggled Edge, 13 In. 325.00
Charger, Dished Form, Notched Rim, Cross–Comb, Yellow, 13 In. 495.00
Churn, Brown Glaze, Gordy's Pottery, Greenville, Ga., 16 In. 105.00
Cooler, Water, Barrel Shape, Pennsylvania, 19th Century, 13 3/4 In. 400.00
Creamer, Figural, Lady's Head, Twisted Handle, 4 7/8 In. 35.00
Crock, Flower & Leaves, Signed Harrington Lyons, Blue Gray, 2 Gal. 220.00
Dish, Loaf, Breininger, For York Historical Society, 17 In. 60.00
Figurine, Dog's Head, Molded, Olive Amber Glaze, 4 In. 75.00
Figurine, Turk's Head, 3 1/2 In. 85.00
Flowerpot, Saucer Base, Green Clear Glaze, White Slip, 5 In. 150.00
Inkwell, Dark Brown Glaze, 3 3/8 In. 30.00
Inkwell, Helmet Shape, Advertising Label, Original Stopper, 4 In. 75.00
Jar, Beaded Band, Olive Amber Glaze, Brown Flecks, Ovoid, 3 7/8 In. 45.00
Jar, Brushed With Dark Brown, 6 X 9 1/2 In. 145.00
Jar, Cylindrical, Lid, Coggle Wheel & Scratch Design, 9 1/2 In. 990.00
Jar, Double Ear Handles, Incised Bird On Branch, Ovoid, 6 In. 250.00
Jar, Ovoid, Interior Glaze, 8 In. 30.00
Jar, Scalloped Lid, Tooled Band Of Wavy Lines, Ovoid, 9 1/2 In. 90.00
Jar, Strap Handle, Brown Sponging, 5 1/2 In. 95.00
Jug, Dark Brown Glaze, 4 In. 75.00
Jug, Incised Band, Strap Handle, Spotted Glaze, 2 7/8 In. 35.00
Jug, John Bell, Waynesboro, Brown Speckled, 8 In. 450.00
Jug, Olive Green Glaze, E.J.Brown, Impressed, 4 1/2 In. 40.00
Jug, Opaque Green Glaze, Brown Splotches, Ovoid, 7 1/4 In. 35.00
Jug, Pouring Spout, Handle, Bloomfield, N.Y., 1 Gal. 130.00
Jug, Puzzle, Incised A.K.Pinka, North Western Pottery, 7 3/4 In. 215.00
Jug, Ribbed Strap Handle, Shiny Glaze, 10 In. 10.00
Jug, Rust Glaze, Bulbous, Ovoid, Squat, 1 Qt. 135.00
Jug, Strap Handle, Ovoid, 7 In. 20.00
Lion, Recumbent, Iridescent Dark Brown, 7 1/4 In. 440.00
Match Holder, Open Acorn, Old Paint, Round 130.00
Mold, Cake, Swirled 130.00

Mold, Turk's Head, Brown Speckled Glaze, 5 3/4 In. 25.00
Mug, Black Speckled Glaze, Hand Tooling, Applied Handle, 4 3/4 In. 55.00
Mug, Mottled Green Glaze, Signed Thomas Stahl, 1941, 3 In. 49.00
Pan, Baking, Turk's Head, Brown Sponging, 8 1/4 In. 35.00
Pan, Loaf, Coggled Edge, 3 Line Slip Design, Oval, 12 X 15 1/2 In. 500.00
Pie Plate, 9 1/8 In. 135.00
Pitcher, Brown Glaze, 13 1/2 In. 45.00
Pitcher, Clear Glaze, Brown Splotches, 2 1/2 In. 55.00
Pitcher, Incised, C.1840, 1 Gal. 950.00
Pitcher, Olive Green Glaze, Orange Spots, 6 5/8 In. 105.00
Pitcher, White Marbelized Slip, Butterscotch Glaze, 4 1/2 In. 115.00
Plate, Coggled Edge, Yellow Slip Design, 7 3/4 In. 350.00
Pot, Coggle Wheel Design, Winged Eagle, 1900, 6 1/4 In. 915.00
Pot, Small Handles, Ovoid, 8 1/4 In. 17.50
Pot, Straight Sides, 6 X 6 In. 95.00
Salt Bucket, Brown Glaze, Cream Foliage, 19th Century, 11 3/4 In. 50.00
Salt, White Slip, Under Clear Glaze, Running Green, 3 1/2 In. 155.00
Spill Holder, Smiling Upturned Face Shape, Mahogany, 3 5/8 In. 50.00
Spittoon, Lady's, Scroll Design, Lead Glaze, 5 In. 110.00
Vase, Black, Albany, Slip Design, 7 In. ....Illus 300.00

REGOUT, see Maastricht

"Richard" was the mark used on acid–etched cameo glass vases, bowls, night–lights, and lamps made in Lorraine, France, during the 1920s. The pieces were very similar to the other French cameo glasswares made by Daum, Galle, and others.

RICHARD, Jar, Castle Mountain Lake, Orange & White, Covered, Signed, 6 In. 595.00
Vase, Dancing Lady, Hands In Air, Scarf, Signed, 9 7/8 In. 995.00
Vase, Mountains, Trees, Castle, Orange Ground, Signed, 10 1/2 In. 915.00

Ridgway pottery has been made in the Staffordshire district in England since 1808 by a series of companies with the name Ridgway. The transfer–design dinner sets are the most widely known product. They are still being made. Other pieces of Ridgway are listed under Flow Blue.

RIDGWAY, Bone Dish, Yellow & Orange 15.00
Bowl, Eloped, Coaching Days, 9 In. 75.00
Creamer, Coaching Days 40.00
Dessert Set, 3 Square, 3 Shell Fruit Dishes, 13 Plates 6000.00
Jug, Coaching Days, Squatty, Black Scenes, Caramel, 5 In. ....29.00 To 48.00
Mug, Gulf Of Venice, Large 38.00
Pitcher, Hunting Scene, High Relief, Hound Handle, 1835 .... 100.00
Pitcher, Scene Of Congressional Library, Luster Band, Tan 70.00
Pitcher, Tankard, Coaching Days, Black, Caramel, Marked, 12 In. 145.00
Pitcher, Tavern Scene, Mustard Ground, Dated 1835, 6 In. 65.00
Plaque, Coaching Days, In A Snowdrift, Yellow Ground, 12 In. 100.00
Plate, Brown, White, Bird, Bow Mark, 1880 .... 25.00
Plate, Child's, Blue Boy In Straw, 7 In. 10.00
Plate, Medina Pattern, Blue Ink, Incised, 9 1/4 In. 12.00
Plate, Niagara Falls, 1920 .... 22.00
Platter, Boston & Bunker Hill, Blue, White, 1884, 15 3/4 In. 165.00
Tea Set, People Scenes, Puce, 1820, 37 Piece ....125.00 To 165.00
Tile, Tea, Royal Vista 35.00
Tray, Coaching Days, Scalloped Edge, A Christmas Visitor, 12 In. 100.00

A rifle is a firearm that has a rifled bore and that is intended to be fired from the shoulder. Other firearms are listed under Gun.

RIFLE, Allen & Thurber, Percussion Side Hammer, Muzzle Loading, 31 In. 450.00
Burnside, 54 Caliber Carbine, Civil War, Gray Metal, 4th Model 395.00
Flintlock, Sutton Under Eagle, U.S. In Oval In Talons, 1812 .... 500.00
Flintlock, Tiger Maple Stock 625.00
Frank Wesson, Sporting, 38 Caliber 210.00

Gallager, Percussion Carbine, Civil War 550.00
Jacob Kickert, 45 Caliber, Flintlock, Signed 3500.00
Kentucky Half Stock, Converted To Percussion, Patch Box 325.00
Kentucky, Percussion Lock, Curly Maple Half Stock, 46 In. 175.00
Kentucky, Percussion Lock, Curly Maple Stock, 43 In. 250.00
Military, Bolt Action, Continental, Bottle Neck 50.00
Musket, Percussion, Muzzle Loading, Brass 100.00
Percussion, Jas.Golcher, Curly Maple, Half Stock, Silver Inlay, 50 In. 450.00
Percussion, T.C.Mortimer, George St., Half Stock, Short Barrel, 36 In. 225.00
Sharp, Carbine, Model 1863, Dated September 13, 1848, L.W. 400.00
Smith Percussion Carbine, Civil War 750.00
Springfield Trapdoor, Cavalry Carbine, 45–70, Saddle Tin 795.00
Springfield, 58 Cal., Bayonet, Contract W.C. & Stn., C.1864 .... 475.00
Springfield, Trap, 1878 .... 200.00
Styer, Military, 1895 .... 37.50
Whitney, Phoenix Sporting, 40–70 Caliber, 26 In. 450.00
Winchester 1886, 45–90 Caliber, Crescent Butt, 26 In. 2750.00
Winchester Repeating, 1897 .... 500.00
Winchester, Carbine, 44–40, Model 1873, No.17790, 1st Model 850.00
Winchester, Model 1873, Cal.38–40, 1886, 24 In. 325.00
Winchester, Model 1873, Saddle Ring Carbine, Ca.44–40, 1876, 20 In. 550.00

Riviera dinnerware was made by the Homer Laughlin Co. of Newell, West Virginia, from 1938 to 1950. The pattern was similar in coloring and in mood to Fiesta and Harlequin. The Riviera plates and cup handles were square.

RIVIERA, Baker, Green, 9 In. 10.00
Bowl, Mauve Blue, 6 In. 6.00
Bowl, Vegetable, Oblong, Yellow, 9 In. 5.00
Butter, Ivory, 1/4 Lb. 35.00
Casserole, Green, Covered 38.50
Casserole, Mauve Blue, Covered 23.00
Creamer, Ivory 5.00
Gravy Boat, Old Ivory 9.00
Jug, Green, Covered, 8 In. 60.00
Pitcher, Juice, Yellow 55.00
Plate, Green, 10 In. 5.00
Plate, Old Ivory, 9 In. 3.50
Platter, Ivory, Square, 11 1/2 In. 14.50
Platter, Mauve Blue, 11 1/2 In. 6.00
Platter, Yellow, Oval, 13 1/4 In. 18.50
Salt & Pepper, Red, Pair 10.00
Saucer, Old Ivory 2.00
Shaker, Ivory, Pair 4.00
Soup, Dish, Ivory 3.00
Sugar & Creamer, Green 18.50
Sugar & Creamer, Mauve Blue, Covered 15.00
Syrup, Red, Covered 45.00
Teapot, Yellow, Covered 22.00
Tumbler, Juice, Red 27.50
Tumbler, Juice, Yellow 26.00

Roblin Art Pottery was founded in 1898 by Alexander W. Robertson and Linna Irelan in San Francisco, California. The pottery closed in 1906. The firm made faience with green, tan, dull blue, or gray glazes. Decorations were usually animal shapes. Some red clay pieces were made.

ROBLIN, Vase, Brown, 6 In. 200.00

Rockingham, in the United States, is a brown glazed pottery with a tortoiseshell–like glaze. It was made from 1840 to 1900 by many American potteries. Mottled brown Rockingham wares were first made in England at the Rockingham factory. Other types of ceramics were also made by the English firm.

ROCKINGHAM, Bottle, Building Shape, 7 1/2 In. 25.00
Bottle, Coachman, 9 1/2 In. 95.00
Bottle, Embossed Busts Of Queen Victoria & Duchess Of Kent 55.00
Bottle, Figural, Woman With Elongated Neck, 8 1/4 In. 125.00
Bottle, Figural, Woman With Scroll, Spirit Of...., 6 3/4 In. 35.00
Bottle, Shoe Shape, 7 In. 55.00
Bottle, Toby Barrel, End Marked 2, 9 1/2 In. 125.00
Bowl, 8 7/8 X 4 In. 45.00
Bowl, 9 5/8 X 4 3/8 In. 20.00
Candlestick, 9 1/4 In. 85.00
Crock, Peacock At Fountain, Brick Base Design 57.00
Cup, Stirrup, Fox Head, 4 3/4 In. 25.00
Cuspidor, 7 1/4 X 4 1/8 In. 25.00
Cuspidor, 8 In.Diam. 20.00
Dish, Octagonal, 7 3/4 In. 40.00
Dish, Scrolled Rim, 8 3/4 In. 150.00
Doorknob, Glazed, Pair 14.00
Figurine, Cat, Seated, Late 19th Century, 14 In. 425.00
Figurine, Dog, Seated, Shell Designs On Base, 10 1/2 In. 75.00
Flask, Satchel Shape, Brown Glaze, Cork, John Turner, 5 7/8 In. 95.00
Inkwell, Sleeping Youth, 5 3/4 In. 55.00
Mold, Food, Vintage Design, Oval, 5 1/2 X 7 3/4 In. 105.00
Ornament, 3-Story Cottage ....325.00 To 600.00
Ornament, Tudor Cottage, Octagonal, Detachable Roof 625.00
Pie Plate, 11 In. 85.00
Pitcher, 7 1/2 In. 55.00
Pitcher, Cottage Design With Ivy, 6 7/8 In. 85.00
Pitcher, Hound Handle, Embossed Eagles & Deer, 8 3/4 In. 45.00
Pitcher, Hound Handle, Mask Spout, Game, 9 1/2 In. 65.00
Pitcher, Paneled, 7 7/8 In. 205.00
Pitcher, Peacock Design 75.00
Pitcher, Toby, 5 7/8 In. 35.00
Pitcher, Toby, Brown, 10 1/2 In. 110.00
Plate, Paneled Rim, 8 1/2 In. 30.00
Platter, 9 5/8 X 12 3/4 In. 65.00
Teapot, Rebecca At Well, 10 In. 88.00
Teapot, Toby, 9 1/4 In. 85.00
ROGERS, see John Rogers

Rookwood pottery was made in Cincinnati, Ohio, from 1880 to 1960.
All of this art pottery is marked, most with the famous flame mark.
The R is reversed and placed back to back with the letter P. Flames
surround the letters. After 1900, a Roman numeral was added to the
mark to indicate the year. The name and some of the molds were
purchased in 1984; new items will be clearly marked.

ROOKWOOD, Ashtray, 5 X 5 In. ....55.00 To 85.00
Ashtray, Bat, Green Wax Matte, 1928, 2 X 6 In. 190.00
Ashtray, Bird, Brown, 6 In. 65.00
Ashtray, Central Trust Cincinnati, Pink 32.00
Ashtray, Fish Shape, Green 50.00
Ashtray, Fox, Cream 85.00
Ashtray, Indian Sahib, Riding Elephant, No.6068 .... 75.00
Ashtray, Maroon, High Glaze, Nude, 1950 .... 75.00
Ashtray, Nude, White, 4 1/2 In. 65.00
Basket, Handle, Satin Blue, 4 X 3 1/2 In. 45.00
Basket, Handle, Turquoise With Glaze Drip, 5 1/2 X 5 In. 95.00
Bookends, Dog, Beige, 1929, 8 In. 95.00
Bookends, Dog, Droopy Ears, Head Bent, 1928, Blue Gray Finish 250.00
Bookends, Elephant, Amber Glaze, 1919, Marked 175.00
Bookends, Elephant, Slate Gray 105.00
Bookends, Elephant, White, 1921 .... 85.00
Bookends, Girl Reading Books, No.6037, 1929 .... 175.00
Bookends, Rooks, Green, 1922, Large 185.00
Bookends, Water Lilies In Various Stages Of Bloom, 3 3/4 In. 90.00

Bowl, Butterflies, Matte, 1901	125.00
Bowl, Faience, California, 3 Colors, Chinese, 12 In.	275.00
Bowl, Molded Flower Design, 1921, 6 X 3 In.	17.50
Bowl, Molded Lily Design, Blue High Glaze, 1945, 6 X 4 1/4 In.	110.00
Bowl, Mums, Rose Caramel, Amelia Sprague, 1889, 8 1/2 X 1 3/4 In.	250.00
Bowl, Rose, Copper Green Relief Border, 1930, 7 1/2 In.	46.00
Bowl, Vegetable, Ships, Blue, 11 In.	70.00
Bowl, Vellum, Blue, Violets, Geometric Border, 1930, 6 X 5 In.	425.00
Bust, Young Woman, 1925, White, 8 X 7 In.	170.00
Candleholder, Matte Glaze, Powder Blue, 1920, 6 1/2 In., Pair	110.00
Candleholder, Seahorse In Corners Of Triangular Base, 4 In.	35.00
Candleholder, Turquoise, Floral, 1921, Pair	60.00
Candlestick, Royal Blue To Umber, 1916, 13 In., Pair ....*Illus*	225.00
Cider Set, Halloween Design, 6 Piece	2320.00
Creamer, Butterfly Handle, Honeysuckles, E.R.Felton, 1900	225.00
Creamer, Vellum, 1918	60.00
Ewer, Clover Shape, Orange, Yellow, Olive Flowers, 1902, 3 X 5 In.	550.00
Ewer, Floral, 1891, 10 In.	185.00
Ewer, Nasturtium, Sage Green, Albert Valentien, 1890, 11 1/2 In.	850.00
Ewer, Nasturtiums, Wm.Klemm, 1899, 6 1/4 In.	295.00
Ewer, Tulips, Light, Dark Brown Ground, Anna Valentien, 10 1/2 In.	600.00
Ewer, Yellow Nasturtium Design, Bulbous, Fluted, C.1892, 7 1/2 In.	275.00
Figurine, Egret, Gray, Brown, White, 9 In.	195.00
Figurine, Elephant, Blue Matte Glaze, No.649, 1941	75.00
Figurine, Polar Bear, Beige Glaze, C.1929, 4 1/2 X 6 1/2 In.	65.00
Flower Frog, Black Glaze, 5 X 4 1/4 In.	95.00
Flower Frog, Black, 1923, 6 In.	175.00
Flower Holder, Pan & Turtle, Black Glaze, 1921, 7 In.	150.00
Jar, Blue, Matte, Egyptian Style, C.1911, 5 In.	55.00
Jardiniere, Royal Blue Glaze, Yellow Interior, 1921, 11 1/4 In.	88.00
Jug, Flowers, Butterflies, Green, Handles, Stamp, 1883, 4 1/2 In.	100.00
Lamp, Allover Rose On Beige Blossoms, Brass Fittings, 1935, 12 In.	300.00
Lamp, Gone With The Wind, Cranberry, Shirayamadani, 1887, 19 In.	600.00
Marmalade, Underliner, Cover, Ships, Blue	85.00
Mug, Advertising Club Of Cincinnati, 1949, Maroon	75.00
Mug, Black Grapes, Matte Green, 1905, 5 3/4 In.	150.00
Mug, Matte Glaze, Green, 1903	65.00
Mug, Matte Green, Deep Carved Black Grapes, Coyne, 1905, 6 1/2 In.	120.00
Mug, Swimming Frog, Blue To White, 3 Handles, Wareham, 4 1/2 In.	1900.00
Paperweight, Clipper Ship, Teal	90.00
Paperweight, Dog, White Matte Glaze, 4 3/4 In.	135.00
Paperweight, Duck, Blue	95.00

Rookwood, Candlestick, Royal Blue
To Umber, 1916, 13 In., Pair

Wooden items should be kept off the sunny windowsill. Direct sunlight will harm wood finishes.

If using an old wooden bowl for a salad, treat it with an edible oil, not a normal wood polish.

Paperweight, Elephant, Standing, White	90.00
Paperweight, Nude	175.00
Paperweight, Nude, White	150.00 To 175.00
Paperweight, Rabbit, White	100.00
Paperweight, Rooster, Multicolor, McDonald, 1928	145.00
Paperweight, Seated Nude, 1928	95.00
Paperweight, White Owl On Book, 1935	150.00
Paperweight, Yellow Flower	60.00
Paperweight, Yellow High Glaze, 1949, 2 3/4 In.	30.00
Pitcher, Bird, Grasses, Blue Ground, Angled Handle, 1885, 8 In.	125.00
Pitcher, Cherries, 9 1/2 In.	35.00
Pitcher, Iridescent Lemon Lime Glaze, 1915, 4 In.	75.00
Pitcher, Persian, Yellow, Incised Flowers, Vines, H.Wenderoth, 1884	750.00
Pitcher, White Breasted Bird In Flight, A.M.Bookbinder, 6 1/4 In.	450.00
Pitcher, White Mums, Blue Bisque, Ruffled, M.Daly, 1884, 11 In.	875.00
Pitcher, Yellow, 1949, 3 In.	22.50
Plaque, Quiet Waters, L.Asbury, Paper Label, 1919, 8 X 10 1/2 In.	1320.00
Plaque, River Road Scene, Vellum, Blue, Brown, 8 X 6 In.	1500.00
Plaque, River Scene, Blue Sky & Water, 1920s, L.Asbury, 13 X 10 In.	1850.00
Plaque, Titled Reflections, F.Rothenbush, Framed, 6 X 9 In.	1200.00
Plate, Mermaids, Artist, W.Hentschel, K Mark, 10 In.	240.00
Plate, Vellum, Harbor Scene, 1909, Dark Ground, Drilled, 9 In.	395.00
Pot, Posey, White To Pink, Blossoms, Iris Glaze, Asbury, 2 X 5 In.	450.00
Rose Jar, Reticulated Lid, Turquoise High Glaze, 3 Piece	125.00
Saucer, Porridge, Fox, Rabbits, Saying, Fluted, 1885, 6 1/2 In.	308.00
Sugar & Creamer, Blue Pirate Ship, White Ground	50.00
Sugar & Creamer, Pink, 1949	35.00
Sugar & Creamer, Ships, Blue, Covered	60.00
Tea Set, Butterfly Handles, Berried Branches, Signed, C.1891	100.00
Teapot, Ships, Blue, Covered	100.00
Tile, Dog Portrait, Signed	975.00
Tile, Faience, Geometric, 3 Color, 4 X 4 In.	75.00
Tile, Faience, Hand Design, 6 In.	65.00
Tile, Geometric, 3 Colors, Faience, 4 In.	75.00
Tile, Tea, Parrot On Branch	85.00
Tile, Tea, Pink Parrot, 1920–21	80.00
Tray, Pin, Nude, Maroon	65.00
Tray, Rook With Open Wing On Edge, Blue Glaze, Dated 1939	150.00
Tray, White Matte Glaze, Female Nude, Dated 1936, 4 X 3 In.	125.00
Urn, Celadon Glaze, Ornate Handles, 19 In.	350.00
Urn, High Gloss, Reticulated Outer Lid, Dated 1922, 13 1/2 In.	575.00
Urn, No.2079	75.00
Vase, 3 Handles, Blue Matte, 1928, 5 In.	30.00
Vase, Allover Floral, Dragonflies, A.R.Valentien, 1883, 10 3/4 In.	950.00
Vase, Aqua Base To Yellow Top, 1930, 3 In.	31.50
Vase, Art Deco, Green Blue Ground, Wm.E.Hentschel, 1921, 6 In.	600.00
Vase, Art Deco, Ivory Wax Matte, 1945, 8 In.	42.50
Vase, Band Of Rooks, 1922, 7 In.	46.00
Vase, Beige, Bulbous, Crimped, 7 In.	27.00
Vase, Blue & Brown Leaves, Aqua Ground, Wm.Hentschel, 6 In.	349.00
Vase, Blue Glaze, Carved Flowers, Leaves, Marked, 6 In.	400.00
Vase, Blue Ground, Vivid Flowers, Cover, 1921, 10 In.	295.00
Vase, Blue Matte Glaze, Molded Women, L.Abel, 1925, 13 1/4 In.	150.00
Vase, Blue Matte, Molded Fish, Birds, Frogs, 1935, 8 In.	125.00
Vase, Blue, Birds Flying, 1934, Signed, 5 In.	95.00
Vase, Brown & Gold, Glazed, C.1898, F.D.H.Othenbusch, 8 1/4 In.	250.00
Vase, Bud, 1946, Pink	25.00
Vase, Bud, Blue, Molded Flowers, 1919, 7 In.	85.00
Vase, Bud, Gray, Brown & White Glaze, 1943, 7 1/4 In.	35.00
Vase, Bud, Iris, Cherry Blossoms, Blue To Pink, Signed, 8 1/2 In.	300.00
Vase, Bud, Pink & Green, Molded Peacock Feather, 1922, 8 In.	150.00
Vase, Burnt Amber, Narcissus, Marked, 1898, 8 In.	150.00
Vase, Cylindrical Shape, Brown Bottom Band, 1910, 9 1/2 In.	650.00
Vase, Dark Red, Dark Green Crackle Glaze, Maple Leaves, 1904, 6 In.	375.00

Vase, Deer, Willows, 1932, 7 1/2 In. 65.00
Vase, Demarest, 5 In. 395.00
Vase, Dragonfly, Blue Green, No.6218, 7 In. 65.00
Vase, Floral Band, Plum Glaze, Blue, Red, Green Highlights, 5 In. 195.00
Vase, Floral, Yellow, Signed, 1915, 8 1/2 In. 425.00
Vase, Flower Band, Purple, Cylindrical, Impressed 2435, 1922, 7 In. 25.00
Vase, Flower Garden, 50th Anniversary, 1930, E.T.Hurley, 5 In. 650.00
Vase, Flowers, Green, 6 In. 45.00
Vase, Glossy Brown Floral, Marked LNL, 1903, 6 X 6 3/4 In. 385.00
Vase, Grapevine, Howard Altman, 1903, 7 1/2 In. 275.00
Vase, Greek Key, Matte Blue Green, 1902, 9 In. 45.00
Vase, Green & Blue Scroll, Medium Brown Ground, E.Barrett, 6 In. 325.00
Vase, Green & Yellow, C.1906, 5 In. 30.00
Vase, Harbor Scene, Vellum, Blue, 1924, C.Schmidt, 7 1/2 In. 3000.00
Vase, Horses, Brown, No.6498, 5 In. 45.00
Vase, Incised Geometric Design, Brown Over Blue, 5 In. 135.00
Vase, Iris Glaze, Rose & Blue Ground, Flying Rooks, 7 In. 650.00
Vase, Iris, Rose & Blue Ground, Flying Rooks, 1904, 6 1/2 In. 670.00
Vase, Iris, Rothenbusch, 7 3/4 In. 375.00
Vase, Lavender, Blue Ground, C.1929, 7 1/4 In. 550.00
Vase, Leaves, Flowers, Red Inside, Butter Fat Glaze, 1925, 5 1/2 In. 500.00
Vase, Magnolia Tree, Floral, Turquoise Glaze, 1915, 7 1/2 In. 60.00
Vase, Molded Berry & Holly Design, 1922, Yellow, 6 3/4 In. 37.50
Vase, Molded Rooks Band, Green Wax Matte, 1921, 7 In. 150.00
Vase, Monkey Scene, Red & Orange Currents, Shirayamadani, 9 In. 1200.00
Vase, Night Scene, Silhouettes Of Figures At Lake, 1909, 11 In. 1375.00
Vase, No.2862, 9 In. 125.00
Vase, Orange Poppies, Brown Glaze, J.D.Wareham, 1895, 7 In. 695.00
Vase, Orange To Green, Carnations, Foertmeyer, 1893, 8 1/2 In. 550.00
Vase, Oval, Glossy, Kay Ley, 1946 .... 325.00
Vase, Pink To Gray Blend, 5 In. 28.00
Vase, Pink To Gray, Allover Sweet Peas, Iris Glaze, Steinle, 7 In. 895.00
Vase, Poppies, Green Pods, Brown, Green, Amber, M.Nourse, 14 In. 1760.00
Vase, Raspberry Glaze, 1921, 5 1/2 In. ....48.00 To 50.00
Vase, Red Matte, Molded Flowers, Green At Top, 1915, 6 1/2 In. 75.00
Vase, Scenic Vellum, Brown Mountains, L.Epply, 1917, 11 3/4 In. 850.00
Vase, Scroll Design, Pastel Green & Blue Ground, Signed, 6 In. 80.00
Vase, Shirayamadani, 1945, 7 3/4 In. 485.00
Vase, Slip Painted Florals, Handles, Signed, 1905, 4 1/2 In. 345.00
Vase, Snow Scene, Pink & Lavender Ground, S.Coyne, 1923, 7 1/4 In. 1350.00
Vase, Standing Poppies, Brown & Green, Signed, 5 1/2 In. 375.00
Vase, Swans In Relief, Bulbous, 4 In. 40.00
Vase, Trumpet Shape, Turquoise To Blue, Flowers, 1925, 8 In. 375.00
Vase, Vellum Scenic, Gray Blues, Creams, Marked, 9 3/4 In. 400.00
Vase, Vellum, Cream To Lavender, Buds, S.E.Coyne, C.1905, 10 1/2 In. 325.00
Vase, Vellum, Scenic, 9 In. 925.00
Vase, Wax Matte, Rim Splotched, Barret, 1926, 5 In. 245.00
Vase, White Matte, Aqua Interior, Flared Rim, 1928, 5 In. 45.00
Vase, Yellow Daisy, Brown Glaze, C.Schmidt, 1897, 4 1/4 In. 325.00
Vase, Yellow Rose, Brown Glaze, 2 Handles, C.T.Hurley, 1899, 3 In. 325.00
Vase, Yellow, 1937, 4 3/4 In. 31.50
Wall Pocket, Stylized Flowers At Top, Gray Over Green, 11 1/2 In. 85.00
    ROSALINE, see Steuben

 *Rose bowls were popular during the 1880s. Rose petals were kept in the open bowl to add fragrance to a room, a popular idea in a time of limited personal hygiene. The glass bowls were made with crimped tops, which kept the petals inside. Many types of Victorian art glass were made into rose bowls.*

ROSE BOWL, Crimped, Satin Glass, Blue 35.00
   Egg Shape, Cherubs, Floral Wreath, Yellow, 5 In. 135.00
   Enamel Design, Frosted Leaf Feet, Gold Buds, Blue, 4 1/2 In. 69.00
   Green Random Thread Overlay, Pontil, Green, 7 Clear Rigaree Legs 50.00
   Mother–Of–Pearl, Germany 40.00

Rose Medallion, Garden Seat,
Genre Scene, Barrel Shape, 18 1/4 In.

Rosenthal, Figurine, Dancer,
Korean, 1919, 16 In.

Mother–Of–Pearl, Yellow Coralene Seaweed, 3 1/2 In.	300.00
Satin Glass, Pink, 4 In.	30.00
Silver Design In Glass, Pink Cased, 3 1/2 In.	155.00
Silver Design, Pink Cased, 3 1/2 In.	155.00

Rose Canton china is similar to Rose Medallion, except no people are pictured in the decoration. It was made during the nineteenth and twentieth centuries in greens, pinks, and other colors.

ROSE CANTON, Butter Chip	40.00
Plate, 9 3/4 In.	75.00 To 85.00
Platter, Butterflies & Flowers, 14 In.	250.00
Teapot, In Cosy Basket	125.00
Teapot, Twisted Handle	285.00

Rose Medallion china was made in China during the nineteenth and twentieth centuries. It is a distinctive design picturing people, flowers, birds, and butterflies. Pieces are colored in greens, pinks, and other colors.

ROSE MEDALLION, Bowl, 10 X 1 3/4 In.	75.00
Bowl, 7 1/2 In.	85.00
Bowl, Polychrome & Gilt Figural Design, Large	450.00
Bowl, Rice	45.00
Bowl, Salad, Butterfly, Bouquet Each Side, 11 1/4 X 5 In.	550.00
Charger, Butterflies, Peonies, Gilt Rim, C.1875, 12 3/4 In.	200.00
Creamer, China	55.00
Cup & Saucer, Coffee	45.00 To 68.00
Cup & Saucer, Demitasse	45.00
Cup & Saucer, Handle Comes To Point At Top	73.00
Cup & Saucer, Hexagonal	30.00
Cup & Saucer, Tea	28.00
Cup & Saucer, Wishbone Handle	75.00
Dish, Covered, C.1840, 8 1/2 X 9 1/2 In.	450.00
Dish, Vegetable, Covered, C.1890	175.00
Dish, Warming, Genre Scene, Birds, Butterflies Panels, 10 In.	200.00
Garden Seat, Genre Scene, Barrel Shape, 18 1/4 In. ....*Illus*	2100.00
Incense Burner, Figural Top, Chinese, C.1900, 10 In.	95.00
Plate, 5 1/2 In.	17.00
Plate, 6 In.	40.00
Plate, 7 In.	45.00
Plate, 8 In.	35.00
Plate, 9 5/8 In.	60.00 To 65.00
Plate, Rooster, 19th Century, Square, 7 1/8 In.	175.00

Plate, Scalloped, 9 3/4 In.	75.00
Platter, Footed, 15 In.	440.00
Platter, Liner	330.00
Platter, Oval, 19 In.	357.00
Platter, Warming, Domed Cover, Gilt Pod Finial, 11 3/4 In.	1400.00
Punch Bowl, 16 In.	1800.00
Punch Bowl, Chien Lung Mark, 14 In.	1400.00
Punch Bowl, Genre Scenes, Floral Panels, 15 1/2 X 6 3/4 In.	900.00
Saucer, 6 In.	25.00
Soup, Dish, C.1880, 8 1/2 In.	75.00
Sugar, Covered	65.00
Tea Set, 47 Piece	425.00 To 450.00
Teapot, 4 5/8 In.	70.00
Teapot, Cord Wrapped Handles, Ladies Scene	100.00
Teapot, Dome Lid, China, 6 1/2 In.	75.00
Teapot, Lined Wicker Carrying Basket, 2 Cups	175.00
Tureen, Covered, C.1840	700.00
Vase, 12 In., Pair	300.00
Vase, Applied Salamanders, Foo Dog Handles, 8 In., Pair	500.00
Vase, Flowers & Birds, Handles, 7 3/4 In.	135.00
Vase, Genre Scenes, Floral Panels, Ovoid Body, 12 1/2 In.	325.00

ROSE O'NEILL, see Kewpie

Rose Tapestry porcelain was made by the Royal Bayreuth factory of Tettau, Germany, during the late nineteenth century. The surface of the porcelain was pressed against a coarse fabric while it was still damp and the impressions remain on the finished porcelain. It looks and feels like a textured cloth. Very skillful reproductions are being made that even include a variation of the Royal Bayreuth mark, so be careful when buying.

ROSE TAPESTRY, Basket, Blue Mark, 5 In.	210.00 To 295.00
Basket, Braided Handle, Blue Mark, 5 X 5 In.	300.00
Basket, Marked, 6 1/2 In.	325.00
Basket, Pink Roses, Handle, Blue Mark, 6 1/2 X 3 3/4 In.	300.00
Basket, Reticulated Handle & Bottom, Footed, 5 X 5 In.	300.00
Basket, Royal Bayreuth, 5 In.	295.00
Basket, Royal Bayreuth, Blue Mark, 6 3/4 In.	325.00
Bowl, Royal Bayreuth, 10 1/2 In.	695.00
Cake Plate, Open Handle, 3–Color Roses, 10 1/4 In.	365.00
Cake Plate, Pink Roses, Royal Bayreuth, 10 1/2 In.	195.00
Chamberstick, Chrysanthemum Pattern, Handles, Blue Mark	325.00
Chocolate Pot, 3–Color Roses	1050.00
Creamer, 3–Color Roses, 4 In.	220.00 To 230.00
Creamer, Blue Mark	175.00
Creamer, Castle & Hill	250.00
Creamer, Corset, Roses, Beaded Border, 3 3/4 In.	155.00 To 195.00
Creamer, Dogs, Swimming Moose, Marked, 4 In.	250.00
Creamer, Royal Bayreuth, 4 3/4 In.	185.00 To 225.00
Cup, Chocolate, Royal Bayreuth, Blue Mark	95.00
Dish, Trefoil, Ring Handle, Blue Mark	140.00
Dresser Tray, Christmas Cactus, Royal Bayreuth	185.00
Hair Receiver, 2–Color Roses, Royal Bayreuth	192.00
Hair Receiver, 3 Gold Feet, Pink & Yellow Roses, Marked	178.00
Hair Receiver, 3–Color Roses, 3 Gold Feet, Blue Mark	155.00
Hair Receiver, Gold Legs, Blue Mark	150.00
Hatpin Holder, Pink Roses, Yellow & White Flowers	225.00
Pitcher, Corset Shape, Beaded, 3 3/4 In.	185.00
Pitcher, Goats, Blue Mark	198.00
Pitcher, Gold Handle, Blue Mark, 5 3/4 In.	265.00
Pitcher, Milk, Pinch Spout, Blue Mark	145.00
Planter, Bulbous Base, Fluted Rim, Blue Mark, Miniature	175.00
Planter, Bulbous Base, Handles, Fluted Top Rim, Blue Mark	185.00
Plate, Royal Bayreuth, 7 1/2 In.	195.00
Powder Box, 3 Gold Feet, Blue Mark, 4 1/2 In.	210.00

Powder Box, 3–Color Roses, Covered, Footed, Royal Bayreuth	179.00
Powder Box, Blue Mark, Footed, Covered	175.00
Toothpick, Castle Scenic, Royal Bayreuth	125.00
Tray, Blue Mark, 7 1/2 X 10 In.	185.00
Vase, Cows & Mountains, Oval, Blue Mark, 4 1/4 In.	125.00
Vase, Royal Bayreuth, 3 In.	155.00
Vase, Royal Bayreuth, Blue Label, 6 In.	225.00
Vase, Woodland Scene Allover, French, 4 1/2 In.	78.00

MARKE

Rosenx̌thal

Rosenthal porcelain was made at the factory established in Selb,
Bavaria, in 1880. The factory is still making fine–quality tablewares
and figurines. A series of Christmas plates was made from 1910.
Other limited edition plates have been made since 1971.

ROSENTHAL, Bowl, Delft Type, Blue, Delft–Savoy–Germany, 13 X 8 3/4 In.	150.00
Bowl, Fruit, Orange, Ivory Poppies, Scalloped, 12 In.	95.00
Bowl, Lion D'Or, Poppies, Openwork Border, Yellow, Breidel, 6 In.	75.00
Box, Ring, Blue Florals	15.00
Box, Trinket, Pink Roses, Blue Forget–Me–Nots, 2 1/2 In.	16.00
Candleholder, 3 Arms, Gilt Trim	75.00
Charger, Scenic, Blue, 15 In.	160.00
Coffeepot, Sansouci	50.00
Cup & Saucer, Antoinette	18.00
Cup & Saucer, Empress Flower Pattern	22.00
Cup & Saucer, Gold Band, Demitasse, Set Of 8	80.00
Cup & Saucer, Medallion Portrait, Demitasse	45.00
Cup & Saucer, Pompadour	30.00
Dessert Set, Floral Design, Square Cake Plates, 48 Piece	170.00
Figurine, American Redheaded Woodpecker, Artist Signed, 7 In.	75.00
Figurine, Bahamian Policeman, 7 In.	45.00
Figurine, Ballerina, 7 In.	250.00
Figurine, Bear, Standing Erect On Hind Legs, Brown, 5 1/4 In.	130.00
Figurine, Blackamoor, Signed H.Meisel, 7 In., Pair	275.00
Figurine, Bulldog, Puppy, Sitting, Signed, White & Tan, 7 1/4 In.	325.00
Figurine, Child Holding Flowers, Deer, Signed Lote, 6 1/2 In.	225.00
Figurine, Child, Holding Flowers, Baby Deer In Front, 6 1/2 In.	185.00
Figurine, Dachshund, 7 1/4 In.	150.00
Figurine, Dancer, Korean, 1919, 16 In. *Illus*	800.00
Figurine, Dog, Bulldog, White, Black Spots, 6 X 4 In.	100.00
Figurine, Dog, English Springer Spaniel, Bird In Mouth, 9 X 5 In.	135.00
Figurine, Dog, Pointer, Black & White, 8 X 6 In.	125.00
Figurine, Elephant	185.00
Figurine, Fairy, Riding Back Of Snail, 3 1/2 X 3 1/2 In.	185.00
Figurine, Flying Seagull, Rolling Waves, Signed, 9 In.	140.00
Figurine, Lizard, Porcelain, 1/2 X 2 1/2 In.	40.00
Figurine, Nubian, Playing Mandolin, White	150.00
Figurine, Otter, White Glazed	55.00
Figurine, Pekingese, On Pillow	85.00
Figurine, Pelican, Perched Over Tray, Water Lilies, 7 1/2 In.	135.00
Figurine, Poodle, Standing, White, Collar, Artist Signed, 8 1/2 In.	235.00
Figurine, Princess, Bending Over Frog, 8 1/2 In.	190.00 To 235.00
Figurine, Snail, A.Caassmann	110.00
Lamp Base, Green & Gold Spatter, Early Mark, 11 In.	95.00
Mug, Wreath Of Purple Grapes, Vines, 5 In.	40.00
Plaque, St.Jerome, Reading, C.1910, Marked, 9 7/8 X 7 7/8 In.	550.00
Plate, Christmas, 1910	250.00
Plate, Christmas, 1922	75.00
Plate, Grape Design, Relief	40.00
Plate, Maria Pattern, 12 In.	20.00
Plate, Portrait, Young Lady, Gold, Malmaison–Bavaria, 10 In.	70.00
Plate, Sculptured Beaded Edge, Red & Gold On Ivory, 9 In.	24.00
Plate, Serving, Antoinette, Handle	45.00
Plate, Serving, Handle	45.00
Relish, Sansouci, 10 In.	22.00
Soup, Cream, Underplate, Antoinette	18.00

Soup, Flat, Louis XIV, White, 9 3/4 In. 23.00
Tea Set, Tray, Floral, Scalloped Edges, 8 Piece 175.00
Urn, Cover, Portrait, 2 Handles, 10 1/2 In. 185.00
Urn, Portrait, Covered, 19 1/2 In. 225.00
Vase, Floral, 11 In. 85.00
Vase, Free–Form, White Satin Finish, 3 In. 35.00

Roseville
U.S.A.

> *The Roseville Pottery Company was organized in Roseville, Ohio, in
> 1890. Another plant was opened in Zanesville, Ohio, in 1898. Many
> types of pottery were made. Early wares include sgraffito, Olympic,
> and Rozane. Later lines were often made with molded decorations,
> especially flowers and fruit. Pieces are marked "Roseville."*

ROSEVILLE, Ashtray, Fatima ....
Ashtray, Florentine, Fleck 120.00
Ashtray, Magnolia 35.00
Ashtray, Pine Cone, Brown 35.00
Ashtray, Snowberry 50.00
Ashtray, Zephyr Lily, Green & Brown 35.00
Basket, Apple Blossom, Pink, 8 In. ....40.00 To 65.00
Basket, Bleeding Heart, Blue, 10 In. 65.00
Basket, Bleeding Heart, Pink, 10 In. 55.00
Basket, Bushberry, Blue, 12 In. 95.00
Basket, Bushberry, Brown, 12 In. 65.00
Basket, Capri, Sandalwood Yellow, 10 In. 75.00
Basket, Clematis, Blue, 10 In. ....45.00 To 145.00
Basket, Cosmos, Handle, Impressed Mark, Tan, 10 In. 75.00
Basket, Dogwood II, 6 In. 50.00
Basket, Dogwood, 8 In. 45.00
Basket, Foxglove, Green 75.00
Basket, Freesia, Brown, 7 In. ....45.00 To 55.00
Basket, Freesia, Green, 10 In. 55.00
Basket, Fuchsia, Blue 110.00
Basket, Gardenia, Gray 45.00
Basket, Gardenia, Green, 10 In. ....50.00 To 80.00
Basket, Hanging, Bittersweet, Green & Orange, No Chain 40.00
Basket, Hanging, Bushberry, Blue 60.00
Basket, Hanging, Clematis, Green ....50.00 To 58.00
Basket, Hanging, Dahlrose ....65.00 To 75.00
Basket, Hanging, Dogwood I 175.00
Basket, Hanging, Futura, Brown, 5 In. 135.00
Basket, Hanging, Futura, Pink Gray Tones, Chain, Small 120.00
Basket, Hanging, Imperial I 75.00
Basket, Hanging, Jonquil 225.00
Basket, Hanging, Magnolia, Blue, 11 In. 60.00
Basket, Hanging, Moss, Blue 125.00
Basket, Hanging, Snowberry, Green ....45.00 To 70.00
Basket, Hanging, Snowberry, Pink, Chain 52.00
Basket, Hanging, Sunflower 125.00
Basket, Hanging, Zephyr Lily, Green 58.00
Basket, Iris, Blue, 8 In. 53.00
Basket, Ixia, Pink, 10 In. 65.00
Basket, Ixia, Yellow Brown, 10 In. 55.00
Basket, Magnolia, Blue, 10 In. 50.00
Basket, Magnolia, Green, 7 In. ....42.00 To 45.00
Basket, Mayfair, Tin, 10 In. 26.00
Basket, Ming Tree, Green, 12 In. 60.00
Basket, Ming Tree, White, 8 In. 55.00
Basket, Peony, Green, 6 In. 35.00
Basket, Peony, Yellow, 8 In. 45.00
Basket, Pine Cone, Blue, 6 In. 60.00
Basket, Pine Cone, Brown, 11 In. 73.50
Basket, Snowberry, Green, 7 In. ....35.00 To 40.00
Basket, Vista, 6 3/4 In. 60.00
Basket, Water Lily, Blue, 12 In. ....75.00 To 90.00

Basket, White Rose, Green, 10 In. 65.00
Basket, White Rose, Pink & Green, 12 In. 65.00
Basket, Wincraft, Green, 12 In. 45.00
Basket, Wincraft, Tan, 8 In. 45.00
Basket, Zephyr Lily, 7 In. 44.00
Basket, Zephyr Lily, Blue, 10 In. 60.00
Basket, Zephyr Lily, Brown, 7 In. 45.00
Basket, Zephyr Lily, Green, 8 In. 55.00
Bleeding Heart, Green, 4 In. 23.00
Bookends, Apple Blossom, Blue 85.00
Bookends, Bittersweet, Gray 95.00
Bookends, Burmese, Green 70.00
Bookends, Clematis, Blue, 5 In. 10.00
Bookends, Dawn, Pink, 5 In. .... 75.00 To 135.00
Bookends, Dawn, Yellow 55.00
Bookends, Ming Tree, White 110.00
Bookends, Pine Cone, Green 75.00
Bookends, Water Lily, Pink & Green 60.00
Bowl, Baneda, Handles, Green, 8 1/2 In. 100.00
Bowl, Blackberry, Handles, 6 1/2 In. 295.00
Bowl, Cherry Blossom, Brown, 12 In. 32.00
Bowl, Clematis, Green, 5 In. 45.00
Bowl, Console, Apple Blossom, Blue, 16 In. 35.00
Bowl, Console, Apple Blossom, Blue, Boat Shape, 10 In. 39.00
Bowl, Console, Bushberry, Brown, 13 In. 100.00
Bowl, Console, Egypto, 3 Handles, 3 1/2 X 9 In. 32.00
Bowl, Console, Florentine, 2 Handles, 3 X 9 X 6 In. 60.00
Bowl, Console, Freesia, Brown, 14 In. 40.00
Bowl, Console, Fuchsia, Green, 10 In. 18.00
Bowl, Console, Magnolia, Green, 10 3/4 X 3 1/4 In. 40.00
Bowl, Console, Moderne, Turquoise, 10 In. 75.00
Bowl, Console, Monticello, Turquoise & Tan, 7 1/2 X 13 1/4 In. 42.00
Bowl, Console, Moss, 12 In. 37.00
Bowl, Console, Peony, Pink, 10 In. 55.00
Bowl, Console, Pine Cone, Blue, 9 In. 53.00
Bowl, Console, Pine Cone, Green, 9 In. 35.00
Bowl, Corinthian, 8 In. 125.00
Bowl, Cremona, Green, 12 In. 35.00
Bowl, Dahlrose, Handles, Oval, Paper Label, 8 1/2 X 5 1/2 In. 57.50
Bowl, Donatello, 10 In. 40.00
Bowl, Donatello, Frog, 2 3/4 X 10 In. 190.00
Bowl, Donatello, Inside Design, Low, 10 In. 45.00
Bowl, Earlam, Handles, 10 X 4 In. 225.00
Bowl, Falline, Blue, 6 1/2 In. 20.00
Bowl, Florane, Green 35.00
Bowl, Florentine, 7 In. 25.00
Bowl, Gardenia, Gray, 6 In. 175.00
Bowl, Imperial II, Blue & Gold, 8 In. 30.00
Bowl, Iris, Pink, Sticker, 4 In. 72.00
Bowl, Jonquil, 5 1/2 In. ....60.00 To 80.00
Bowl, Laurel, 13 In. 50.00
Bowl, Ming Tree, Green, 10 In. 20.00
Bowl, Mostique, 7 In. 175.00
Bowl, Panel, Nude Fan, 6 In. 38.50
Bowl, Persian, Double Handles, Velmoss, 8 1/2 X 5 1/4 In. 40.00
Bowl, Pine Cone, Blue, 9 In. 90.00
Bowl, Pine Cone, Brown, 2 Handles, Oval, 11 X 5 In. 23.00
Bowl, Pine Cone, Green, 3 In. 32.00
Bowl, Rosecraft Vintage, 4 1/2 X 2 1/2 In. 25.00
Bowl, Rosecraft, Dusty Rose, 6 In. 45.00
Bowl, Sunflower, Handles, Pink Ground, 10 In. 850.00
Bowl, Tourist, 3 1/2 X 7 In. 32.00
Bowl, Tuscany, Gray, Pedestal, Handle, Black Paper Label, 7 In. 40.00
Bowl, Volpato, 9 1/8 X 3 7/8 In. ....

Item	Price
Bowl, Water Lily, Brown, Handles, Bulbous, 6 In.	45.00
Bowl, Wisteria, Red Crayon Marks, Blue, 6 1/2 X 2 1/4 In.	40.00
Bowl, Zephyr Lily, Handles, 8 In.	45.00
Candleholder, Blackberry, Pair	65.00
Candleholder, Carnelian II, Pink, Pair	30.00
Candleholder, Earlam, 2 1/2 In., Pair	55.00
Candleholder, Ixia, Double, Tan, Pair	58.00
Candleholder, Ixia, Green, 5 In., Pair	25.00
Candleholder, Lotus, Burgundy & Yellow, 2 1/2 In., Pair	39.00
Candleholder, Magnolia, 2 3/4 In., Pair	35.00
Candleholder, Moderne, Lavender, Pair	40.00
Candleholder, Moss, Pair	20.00
Candleholder, Pine Cone, Blue, 4 In., Pair	35.00
Candleholder, Zephyr Lily, Brown & Green, Flat	12.50
Candlestick, Azurine	750.00
Candlestick, Carnelian I, Green, 3 In., Pair	28.00
Candlestick, Cosmos, Green, 4 1/2 In., Pair	40.00
Candlestick, Creamware, Blue Band, 2 In.	100.00
Candlestick, Dahlrose, 3 1/2 In., Pair	70.00
Candlestick, Donatello, Finger Loop, 7 In., Pair	125.00
Candlestick, Falline, Brown, Pair	175.00 To 185.00
Candlestick, Foxglove, Blue, 5 In., Pair	35.00
Candlestick, Fuchsia, 5 1/2 In.	78.00
Candlestick, Pine Cone, Brown, Pair	90.00
Candlestick, Primrose, Pink, Pair	125.00
Candlestick, Rosecraft, 10 In., Pair	85.00
Candlestick, Rozane Woodland	300.00
Candlestick, Rozane, 1917, 8 In.	55.00
Candlestick, Velmoss Scroll, 8 In.	32.00
Candlestick, Wisteria, Brown, 4 1/2 In., Pair	95.00
Chamber Pot, Child's, Lid	260.00
Chamber Pot, Dutch, Child's	190.00
Cider Set, Pine Cone, Blue, Jug & 4 Mugs	395.00
Cigar Holder, Dutch, Boy & Girl With Cat	65.00
Coffeepot, Raymor, Charcoal, Swinging	155.00
Coffeepot, Tally Ho, Creamware	425.00
Compote, Donatello, Nude Children Frolicking, 7 1/2 X 9 1/2 In.	85.00
Console Set, Apple Blossom, Diamond Shaped Bowl, Pink, 4 Piece	55.00
Console Set, Bushberry, Blue, 3 Piece	75.00
Console Set, Freesia, Candleholders, Green	85.00
Console Set, Imperial II, Flower Frog, 4 Piece	175.00
Console Set, Ming Tree, Blue, 3 Piece	65.00
Cookie Jar, Clematis, Blue	57.00
Cookie Jar, Freesia, Blue	95.00
Cookie Jar, Magnolia, Brown	150.00
Cookie Jar, Water Lily, Brown	80.00
Cornucopia, Bittersweet, Gray, 8 In.	40.00
Cornucopia, Bushberry, Green	30.00
Cornucopia, Clematis, Handle, Blue, 6 In.	32.00
Cornucopia, Foxglove, Green	45.00
Cornucopia, Pine Cone, Brown, 6 In.	60.00
Cornucopia, Primrose, Brown, 6 In.	25.00
Cornucopia, Russco, White Outside, Blue Inside, Label, 8 3/8 In.	25.00
Cornucopia, Snowberry, Green, 8 1/4 In., Pair	48.00
Cornucopia, Water Lily, Pink, 8 In.	40.00
Cornucopia, Wincraft, 5 In.	27.00
Creamer, Medallion, 3 1/2 X 3 1/2 In.	48.00
Cup & Saucer, Raymor	20.00
Cuspidor, Donatello, 6 1/2 X 5 In.	75.00
Dish, Egypto, 3 Handles, 8 1/2 X 3 In.	100.00
Dish, Feeding, Chicks Around Inside Rim, Words On Rolled Rim	50.00
Dish, Pine Cone, Orange Lining, Blue, 7 X 6 In.	26.00
Eggcup, Child's	110.00
Ewer, Apple Blossom, Branch Handle, Pink, 8 In.	50.00

Ewer, Bleeding Heart, Blue, 6 In.	50.00
Ewer, Carnelian I, Red, Pink, 15 In., Pair	375.00
Ewer, Clematis, Brown, 10 In.	50.00
Ewer, Clematis, Green, 6 In.	35.00
Ewer, Cosmos, Green, 15 In.	175.00
Ewer, Freesia, Brown, 15 In.	115.00 To 118.00
Ewer, Freesia, Fat, Blue, 6 In.	40.00
Ewer, Freesia, Green, 15 In.	75.00
Ewer, Gardenia, Brown, 15 In.	75.00
Ewer, Magnolia, Green, 6 In.	40.00
Ewer, Ming Tree, White, 10 In.	70.00
Ewer, Peony, Gold, 6 In.	35.00
Ewer, Peony, Pink, 10 In.	75.00
Ewer, Pine Cone, Blue, 10 In.	175.00
Ewer, Poppy, Green, Large	250.00
Ewer, Rozane, Flowers, Brown Glaze, 1900, 9 1/2 In.	225.00
Ewer, Silhouette, 6 In.	40.00
Ewer, Silhouette, Bluish Green, 10 In.	55.00
Ewer, Snowberry, Blue, 10 In.	75.00
Ewer, Water Lily, Brown, 15 In.	175.00
Ewer, White Rose, Pink, 6 In.	35.00
Ewer, Wincraft, Tan, 6 In.	28.00
Ewer, Zephyr Lily, Brown, 10 In.	55.00
Ewer, Zephyr Lily, Green, 6 In.	40.00
Flower Frog, Bleeding Heart, Angular Handle, Blue, 3 1/2 In.	18.00
Flower Frog, Clematis, Blue, 5 1/2 In.	18.00
Flower Frog, Fuchsia, Green, 3 X 5 In.	48.00
Flower Frog, Futura	55.00
Flower Frog, Ixia, Yellow	24.00
Flower Frog, White Rose, Pink	24.00
Flower Pot, Corinthian, Saucer	75.00
Flower Pot, Donatello, Saucer, 6 1/2 X 7 In.	85.00
Flower Pot, Florane II, Capri Glaze, Experimental	26.00
Flower Pot, Futura, 4 In.	85.00
Flower Pot, Ixia, Green	45.00
Flower Pot, Magnolia, Green, Saucer	30.00
Flower Pot, Poppy, Gray	30.00
Flower Pot, Water Lily, Pair	30.00
Flower Pot, Zephyr Lily, Brown, Saucer	45.00
Jar, Bittersweet, Pedestal, Rose & Gray, 24 In.	375.00
Jardiniere, Apple Blossom, 6 In.	50.00
Jardiniere, Blackberry, 9 In.	250.00
Jardiniere, Blackberry, 28 1/2 In.	600.00
Jardiniere, Bleeding Heart, Pedestal, Blue, 8 In.	125.00
Jardiniere, Bushberry, Pedestal, 30 In.	750.00
Jardiniere, Cherry Blossom, Brown, 5 In.	85.00
Jardiniere, Creamware, Liner	85.00
Jardiniere, Dahlrose, 6 In.	60.00 To 75.00
Jardiniere, Dogwood I, 6 1/2 X 7 In.	48.00
Jardiniere, Donatello, Ink Stamp, 5 In.	40.00 To 48.00
Jardiniere, Donatello, Pedestal, 28 In.	485.00
Jardiniere, Florentine, 12 X 9 In.	150.00
Jardiniere, Florentine, Brown, 9 In.	80.00
Jardiniere, Foxglove, Pedestal, Blue, 24 In.	225.00
Jardiniere, Futura, 6 In.	110.00
Jardiniere, Futura, Gray & Pink Leaves, 10 In.	115.00
Jardiniere, Heron & Cattails, Paint Over Red Clay	98.00
Jardiniere, Ixia, Green	28.00 To 29.00
Jardiniere, Luffa, Green, 6 In.	75.00
Jardiniere, Normandy, 6 3/4 X 7 3/4 In.	150.00
Jardiniere, Normandy, 9 1/2 In.	125.00
Jardiniere, Pine Cone, 2 Handles, 3 In.	35.00
Jardiniere, Roman Scene With Gladiator, Horses, Footed, 10 In.	145.00
Jardiniere, Rosecraft, Blended, 4 X 6 In.	35.00

Jardiniere, Rozane, White, 1917, 10 1/4 In. 175.00
Jardiniere, Thornapple, Pedestal, 8 In. 125.00
Jardiniere, Volpato, 6 X 6 In. 70.00
Jardiniere, Wisteria, Brown, 8 In. 185.00
Jardiniere, Zephyr Lily, Pedestal, Brown 295.00
Jug, Thornapple, Brown 35.00
Lamp, Carnelian, Dark Drip From Top, Fixtures, 9 1/2 X 8 In. 125.00
Lamp, Cosmos, Blue, 8 In. 90.00
Lamp, Falline, Ceramic, Brass Stand, Brown, 7 In., Pair 275.00
Lamp, Tuscany, Gold Brushed Top, Green, Original Fittings 175.00
Mostique, Bowl, Textured, Pink, Green, Yellow Glaze, 9 In., Pair 50.00
Mostique, Vase, Arrow Design, Cobalt Blue Glaze, 11 3/4 In. 45.00
Mug, Chloron .... 90.00 To 100.00
Mug, Creamware, Loyal Order Of Moose, Howdy Pap, 5 In. 68.00
Mug, Dutch, Boy & Girl Fishing 65.00
Pitcher, Bleeding Heart, Pink, 8 In. 60.00
Pitcher, Carnelian, Corn, Blue, 6 In. 75.00
Pitcher, Cider, Bushberry, Green .... 80.00 To 90.00
Pitcher, Cider, Bushberry, Russet .... 80.00 To 90.00
Pitcher, Cider, Clematis, Blue 85.00
Pitcher, Cider, Magnolia, Green 115.00
Pitcher, Donatello, Nude Children Playing Instruments, 6 1/2 In. 65.00
Pitcher, Dutch, Creamware, 8 In. 125.00
Pitcher, Freesia, Green, 10 In. 140.00
Pitcher, Imperial II, Mottled Green, Glaze Rub Handle, 12 In. 65.00
Pitcher, Pine Cone, Ice Lip, Blue 75.00
Pitcher, Water, Magnolia, Ice Lip, Blue 165.00
Pitcher, Water, Moss, R Mark 70.00
Pitcher, Wine, Egypto, 12 In. 57.50
Planter, Bittersweet, Gray, 8 In. 190.00
Planter, Chloron, Footed, 4 1/2 X 5 In. 34.00
Planter, Lotus, Burgundy, Yellow, 10 1/2 In. 95.00
Planter, Peony, 6 In. 72.00
Planter, Pine Cone, Brown, 6 In. 27.00
Planter, Silhouette, Red, 15 In. 45.00
Planter, Wincraft, Blue, 10 In. 40.00
Planter, Zephyr Lily, Brown With Green, 10 In. 45.00
Plate, Dutch, 11 In. 37.50
Plate, Juvenile, Chicks, 7 In. 35.00
Plate, Juvenile, Duck With Hat, Rolled Edge 32.00
Plate, Juvenile, Hickory Dickory Dock 32.00
Plate, Juvenile, Jack Horner, 8 In. 30.00
Plate, Juvenile, Little Bopeep, Creamware 38.00
Plate, Juvenile, Old Woman, 7 In. 60.00
Plate, Juvenile, Piper's Son, Rolled Edge, 8 In. 68.00
Plate, Juvenile, Rabbits, 7 In. 35.00
Plate, Juvenile, Sunbonnet Babies 35.00
Powder Jar, Donatello 75.00
Rose Bowl, Foxglove, Pink, Handles, 6 In. 115.00
Shelf, Wall, Iris, Pink, 8 In. 39.00
Sign, Dealer's, Blue Script 85.00
Soap Dish, Dutch, Covered .... 340.00 To 400.00
Soap Dish, Juvenile, Covered 130.00
Spittoon, Carnelian 110.00
Sugar & Creamer, Peony, Brown 100.00
Tankard, Rozane, Artist T.S., 10 1/2 In. 35.00
Tea Set, Apple Blossom, Pink, 3 Piece 300.00
Tea Set, Magnolia, 3 Piece 105.00
Tea Set, Peony, Pink, 4 Piece 90.00
Tea Set, Snowberry Rose, Green, 3 Piece 125.00
Tea Set, White Rose, 3 Piece 120.00
Teapot, Apple Blossom, Pink 115.00
Teapot, Dutch, 1916 .... 80.00
Teapot, Freesia, Green Lid 125.00
 .... 55.00

Teapot, Landscape, Brown Decal	115.00
Teapot, Peony, Yellow	85.00
Teapot, Snowberry	50.00 To 65.00
Tray, Pine Cone, Blue, 12 In.	55.00
Trivet, Raymor, 8 1/2 In.	20.00
Tumbler, Pine Cone, Green	125.00
Umbrella Stand, Florentine, Paper Label	225.00
Urn, Baneda, Red, 7 In.	75.00
Urn, Falline, 6 In.	140.00
Urn, Mostique, 12 In.	45.00
Urn, Rosecraft, Black, 5 In.	65.00
Urn, Russco, 7 In.	58.00
Urn, Sunflower, 4 In.	50.00 To 55.00
Urn, Sunflower, 8 In.	80.00
Urn, Topeo, Original Label, 6 In.	75.00
Urn, Wisteria, Brown, Green, 5 In.	95.00
Vase, Apple Blossom, Green, 15 In.	125.00
Vase, Apple Blossom, Pink, Cuff, 8 In.	45.00
Vase, Aztec, Blue, White, Ochre & Rust, 11 In.	295.00
Vase, Aztec, Shiny, 10 In.	200.00
Vase, Baneda, Green, 4 In.	48.00
Vase, Baneda, Green, 8 In.	65.00
Vase, Baneda, Ovoid, Green, 6 In.	55.00
Vase, Baneda, Pink, 6 In.	60.00
Vase, Bittersweet, 7 In.	35.00
Vase, Bittersweet, Green, Low Handles, 14 In.	155.00
Vase, Bittersweet, Yellow, 8 In.	35.00
Vase, Blackberry, 6 X 8 In.	160.00
Vase, Blackberry, Bulbous, Handles, 5 1/2 In.	85.00 To 110.00
Vase, Bleeding Heart, Pink, 4 In.	20.00
Vase, Boneda, Ovoid, Green, 6 In.	50.00
Vase, Bushberry, Blue, 4 In.	20.00
Vase, Bushberry, Blue, 12 In.	160.00
Vase, Bushberry, Brown, 6 In.	30.00 To 35.00
Vase, Bushberry, Green, 8 In.	40.00
Vase, Capri, Brown, 10 In.	42.00
Vase, Carnelian I, Fan, Beige, 5 In.	22.00
Vase, Carnelian I, Olive Over Turquoise, Handles, 7 1/2 In.	40.00
Vase, Carnelian, Blue, 5 1/4 In.	35.00
Vase, Cherry Blossom, 4 In.	85.00
Vase, Cherry Blossom, Blue & Pink, 7 In.	95.00
Vase, Cherry Blossom, Spherical Shape, Handles, Orange, 8 In.	225.00
Vase, Chloron, 12 In.	125.00
Vase, Chloron, Footed, 4 1/2 In.	90.00
Vase, Clemana, Bowling Ball Shape, Handles, Flowers, Marked, 6 In.	100.00
Vase, Clemana, Brown, 9 1/2 In.	120.00
Vase, Clemana, Small Handles, Green, 6 1/4 In.	85.00
Vase, Clematis, Green, 15 In.	18.00
Vase, Columbine, Pink, 9 In.	45.00
Vase, Corinthian, 10 In.	80.00
Vase, Cosmos, Beige, 4 In.	25.00
Vase, Cosmos, Blue, 18 In.	150.00
Vase, Cosmos, Green, 7 In.	35.00
Vase, Cremona, Green, 8 In.	25.00
Vase, Crocus, Floral Design, Dark Blue Ground, High Glaze, 8 In.	375.00
Vase, Dahlrose, 6 In.	22.00 To 24.00
Vase, Dahlrose, Double Bud, 8 In.	30.00
Vase, Dahlrose, Triangular Handles, 6 In.	18.00
Vase, Dawn, Pink, 6 In.	24.00
Vase, Donatello, 12 In.	100.00
Vase, Earlam, Blue, 4 1/2 In.	32.00
Vase, Earlam, Handles, Blue, 6 In.	40.00
Vase, Ferrella No.2, Handles, Raspberry, 9 In.	295.00
Vase, Ferrella, Handles, Brown, 4 1/2 In.	135.00

Vase, Ferrella, Handles, Raspberry, 9 In. 250.00
Vase, Ferrella, Red, 5 1/2 In. 245.00
Vase, Florentine, 6 In. 30.00
Vase, Foxglove, Blue, 6 In. 15.00
Vase, Freesia, Blue, 8 In. ....22.00 To 35.00
Vase, Freesia, Blue, 12 In. 65.00
Vase, Freesia, Brown, 7 In. 36.00
Vase, Freesia, Bud, 7 In. 30.00
Vase, Freesia, Green, 8 1/2 In. 24.00
Vase, Freesia, Urn Style, Signed, Blue, 8 In. 35.00
Vase, Fuchsia, Blue, 6 In. 33.00
Vase, Fuchsia, Brown, 15 1/2 In. 175.00
Vase, Fuchsia, Green, 9 In. 60.00
Vase, Futura, Ball, 7 1/2 In. 70.00
Vase, Futura, Blue Squared Handles, Blue Band Top & Bottom, 6 In. 115.00
Vase, Futura, Pink & Gray, 8 In. 195.00
Vase, Futura, V Design, Square, 7 In. 150.00
Vase, Gardenia, Gray, 8 In. 33.00
Vase, Gardenia, Tan, 10 In. 38.00
Vase, Holly, Urn Shape, Blue, 4 In. 45.00
Vase, Imperial I, Slant Top, 8 1/2 In. 48.00
Vase, Imperial II, Turquoise Trim, 7 In. 150.00
Vase, Iris, Blue, 4 In. 26.00
Vase, Ixia, Green, 7 In. 34.00
Vase, Ixia, Tan, Yellow, & Purple Flowers, 8 In. 40.00
Vase, Jonquil, 8 In. ....65.00 To 67.50
Vase, Jonquil, Gold Paper Label, 5 3/4 X 6 In. 55.00
Vase, Laurel, Yellow, 8 In. ....65.00 To 66.00
Vase, Lotus, Pillow, Brown & Yellow, 10 In. 88.00
Vase, Luffa, 2 Handles, 6 1/2 X 7 X 4 1/4 In. 55.00
Vase, Luffa, Brown, 12 In. 155.00
Vase, Magnolia, 2 Handles, Grayish Ground, 6 1/2 X 12 1/2 In. 75.00
Vase, Magnolia, Blue, 6 In. 35.00
Vase, Magnolia, Blue, 12 In. 55.00
Vase, Magnolia, Brown, 6 In., Pair 48.00
Vase, Magnolia, Green, Handles, 12 In. 58.00
Vase, Mayfair, Light Brown, 10 1/2 In. 25.00
Vase, Ming Tree, 7 In. 35.00
Vase, Mock Orange, Fan, Yellow, 9 In. 38.00
Vase, Moderne, Blue, 6 In. 35.00
Vase, Moderne, Lavender, 12 In. 88.00
Vase, Moderne, White & Rust, 7 1/2 In. 50.00
Vase, Monticello, Blue, 6 In. 45.00
Vase, Monticello, Brown, 8 In. 75.00
Vase, Monticello, Terra-Cotta, 8 In. 95.00
Vase, Morning Glory, Green, 7 In. ....100.00 To 145.00
Vase, Morning Glory, Mold White, Color, 9 1/2 In. 285.00
Vase, Moss, Pillow, Blue, 8 1/2 In. 42.00
Vase, Mostique, 2 Handles, Glazed, 12 X 8 In. 100.00
Vase, Mostique, 6 In. 35.00
Vase, Orian, Handles, Brown Green, 10 1/2 In. 65.00
Vase, Orian, Tan, 7 In. 55.00
Vase, Orian, Yellow & Turquoise, 9 1/2 In. 78.00
Vase, Panel, 4 Nudes, Brown, 10 1/2 In. 45.00
Vase, Panel, Pillow, Green, 6 1/2 In. 38.00
Vase, Peony, Ball Shaped, Green, 6 In. 32.00
Vase, Peony, Conch Shell, Green, 9 1/2 In. 45.00
Vase, Peony, Green, 4 In. 22.00
Vase, Peony, Orange, 6 In. 17.00
Vase, Pine Cone, Blue, 8 1/2 X 6 1/2 In. 85.00
Vase, Pine Cone, Brown, 12 In. 135.00
Vase, Pine Cone, Gold, 12 In. 125.00
Vase, Pine Cone, Green, 8 In. 28.00
Vase, Pine Cone, Pillow, Brown, 10 X 8 1/2 In. 145.00

Vase, Poppy, Handles, Green & Ivory, 11 In. 65.00
Vase, Rosecraft, Blue, 11 1/2 In. 45.00
Vase, Rosecraft, Brown, 10 In. 85.00
Vase, Rosecraft, Bud, Yellow, 8 1/4 In. 23.00
Vase, Royal Capri, Gold, 7 In. 225.00
Vase, Royal Rozane, Dark Brown, Yellow Floral, Signed, 8 In. 95.00
Vase, Royal Rozane, Open Rose, White & Gray, 8 In. 135.00
Vase, Rozane, Aqua, 15 In. 125.00
Vase, Rozane, Blue, Green, 10 In. 39.00
Vase, Rozane, Navy High Gloss, 8 1/2 In. 35.00
Vase, Rozane, Violets, Artist E.C., 3 3/4 In. 135.00
Vase, Rozane, Yellow, 1917, 8 In. 40.00
Vase, Savona, Handles, 6 1/2 In. 58.00
Vase, Silhouette, Aqua, 7 In. 18.00
Vase, Silhouette, Fan, Nude, 7 In. 115.00
Vase, Silhouette, Fan, White & Green, 7 In. 1254.00
Vase, Snowberry, Green, 18 In. 225.00
Vase, Snowberry, Pink, 12 1/2 In. ....60.00 To 70.00
Vase, Sunflower, 6 In. 52.00
Vase, Sunflower, 10 In. 110.00
Vase, Teasel, 8 In. 35.00
Vase, Thornapple, Blue, 8 1/2 X 12 In. 145.00
Vase, Topeo, Green To Blue, 9 1/2 X 6 In. 100.00
Vase, Topeo, Red, 8 1/4 In. ....100.00 To 135.00
Vase, Tourmaline, Burnt Orange, 8 In. 40.00
Vase, Tuscany, 2 Handles, Gray, 4 X 6 1/2 In. 30.00
Vase, Velmoss I, Bud, 2 Handles, 6 1/2 X 8 1/2 In. 45.00
Vase, Velmoss II, Blue, Green, Yellow, 7 In. 30.00
Vase, Velmoss II, Raspberry, 8 In. 65.00
Vase, Vista, 15 In. 140.00
Vase, Volpato, 6 1/2 In. 55.00
Vase, Water Lily, Orange, 9 In. 40.00
Vase, Water Lily, Pink, Handles, 8 In. 35.00
Vase, Water Lily, Rose, 9 In. 37.50
Vase, White Rose, 6 In. 18.00
Vase, White Rose, Pink, Green, 7 In. 15.00
Vase, Wincraft, Blue, 15 In. 110.00
Vase, Wincraft, Green, 7 In. 38.00
Vase, Wincraft, Panther, 10 In. 135.00
Vase, Windsor, Blue, 5 In. 90.00
Vase, Windsor, Brown, Geometric, Handles, 5 1/2 In. 85.00
Vase, Wisteria, Blue, 8 In. 80.00
Vase, Wisteria, Brown, 7 1/2 X 8 1/4 In. 155.00
Vase, Zephyr Lily, Blue, 18 In., Pair 475.00
Vase, Zephyr Lily, Pillow, Blue, 7 In. 32.00
Wall Pocket, Apple Blossom, 8 1/2 In. 42.00
Wall Pocket, Blackberry, 6 In. 95.00
Wall Pocket, Carnelian I, Blue, 8 In. 42.00
Wall Pocket, Carnelian I, Dark Green, 7 1/2 In. 42.00
Wall Pocket, Cherry Blossom, Blue 275.00
Wall Pocket, Corinthian, 8 In. 45.00
Wall Pocket, Dahlrose, 9 In. 45.00
Wall Pocket, Donatello, 10 In. 60.00
Wall Pocket, Earlam, 7 In. 65.00
Wall Pocket, Florentine, Brown, 7 In. 48.00
Wall Pocket, Freesia, Green, 8 In. 25.00
Wall Pocket, La Rose, 8 1/2 In. 62.00
Wall Pocket, Mayfair, Green, 8 In. 40.00
Wall Pocket, Morning Glory, Double, Original Sticker 350.00
Wall Pocket, Nude Panel, Green, Marked 200.00
Wall Pocket, Snowberry, 8 In. 35.00
Wall Pocket, Sunflower 285.00
Wall Pocket, Triple, Pine Cone, Green 95.00
Wall Pocket, Wincraft, Ball Shape, Blue, 6 In. 90.00

Wall Pocket, Zephyr Lily, Green	55.00
Water Set, Bushberry, Brown, 6 Mugs	375.00
Window Box, Artwood	40.00
Window Box, Clematis, Handles, 10 1/2 In.	40.00
Window Box, Ming Tree, Green, 10 In.	50.00

Rowland & Marsellus Company is a mark which appears on historical Staffordshire dating from the late nineteenth and early twentieth centuries. Rowland & Marsellus is believed to be the mark used by the British Anchor Pottery Co. of Longton, England, for some pieces made for export. Many American views were made. Of special interest to collectors are the rolled edge, blue and white plates.

ROWLAND & MARSELLUS, Jug, Discovery Of America, Handle, 8 In.	165.00
Plate, Charles Dickens, Rolled Rim, Marked	45.00
Plate, Portland, Ore., Blue	30.00
Plate, Providence, Blue	35.00
Plate, Robert Burns, Blue	48.00
Plate, Souvenir Of Allentown, Pa., Blue, 10 In.	48.00
Plate, Souvenir Of Chicago, Blue, 10 1/2 In.	35.00
Plate, Souvenir, Atlantic City	60.00
Plate, Statue Of Liberty, 6-Scene Border	48.00
Plate, Teddy Roosevelt	60.00
Plate, Valley Forge, Blue	45.00

Roy Rogers was born in 1911 in Cincinnati, Ohio. In the 1930s, he made a living as a singer; and in 1935, his group started work at a Los Angeles radio station. He appeared in his first movie in 1937. From 1952 to 1957, he made 101 television shows. Roy Rogers memorabilia is collected, including items from the Roy Rogers restaurants.

ROY ROGERS, Bank, Boots, With Trigger, Metal	20.00
Book, Big Little Book, Doom Comet	40.00
Book, The New Cowboy, Little Golden Books	9.00
Book, The Raiders Of Sawtooth Ridge	8.00
Breakfast Set, Bowl, Mug, Dish, Trigger, Ceramic	40.00
Camera, No.620	20.00
Cap Pistol, Shootin' Iron, Repeating, Box	35.00
Card, Arcade, With Gabby Hayes	10.00
Clock, Ingraham, Animated	110.00
Comic Book, Roy Rogers & Trigger In The Rebel Rider No.1	8.00
Cup, Face Pictured	7.50
Dinner Set, Roy & Dale Evans, Western, Ideal, 1958 .... 40.00 To 75.00
Flashlight, Roy & Trigger, Signal Siren	60.00
Game, Horseshoe Set, Box .... 30.00 To 40.00
Gloves, Cowboy, Child's	48.00
Guitar, Board	90.00
Gun, Repeating Cap Pistol, Boxed	35.00
Harmonica, Roy & Trigger Picture	15.00
Harmonica, Unopened, Original Display Card	25.00
Holster Set, 2 Guns	125.00
Horseshoe, Lucky, Red Rubber .... 10.00 To 20.00
Jacket, Corduroy, Size 4	25.00
Jigsaw Puzzle, 1952	9.00
Lamp, Chalkware, Hand Painted	35.00
Lantern, Tin, Ohio Art	22.50
Lunch Box, Thermos, Wagon Shape	50.00
Mug, Cereal Bowl, & Sauce Dish	45.00
Mug, Quaker Cereal	18.00
Notebook, Pad, Dale Evans	12.50
Pail, Dinner, Dale Evans, Double R Ranch	18.00
Pinback, Trigger	7.00
Puzzle, Cardboard, Tray	6.00
Puzzle, Jigsaw, Boxed	9.00
Record Album, 78 Rpm, Set Of 4 Records	15.00

Spurs, Jewels, Leather	22.00
Thermos, Original Box	40.00
Toby Mug, Plastic, Signed	15.00
Toy, Hauler & Van Trailer	90.00
Toy, Robot, Green Litho Sparks In Chest, Japan, 5 1/2 In.	55.00
Wristwatch, Dale Evans, Leather Band	55.00

The Royal Bayreuth factory was founded in Tettau, Bavaria, in 1794. It has continued to modern times. The marks have changed through the years. A stylized crest, the name "Royal Bayreuth," and the word "Bavaria" appear in slightly different forms from 1870 to about 1919. Later dishes may include the words "U.S. Zone," the year of the issue, or the word "Germany" instead of "Bavaria."

ROYAL BAYREUTH, see also Rose Tapestry; Sand Babies; Snow Babies; Sunbonnet Babies

ROYAL BAYREUTH, Ashtray, Cow Scene, Cigarette Rests	50.00
Ashtray, Devil's Head, Red	115.00
Ashtray, Elk, Blue Mark	85.00
Ashtray, Equestrian Scene, Blue Mark	45.00
Ashtray, Hunter With Dog, Heart Shape	55.00
Bell, Girl & Dog, Blue Mark	125.00
Bowl & Ladle, Poppy Shape, 2 1/2 X 7 3/4 In., 2 Piece	100.00
Bowl, Grape Cluster, Pearl Luster, Stem Handles, 9 1/2 In.	250.00
Bowl, Pastel, Sheep, Scalloped, 10 1/2 In.	45.00
Bowl, White, Floral, Gold Trim, Blue Mark, 3 1/4 X 10 1/4 In.	195.00
Box, Pin, Covered, White Flowers, Gold Outlines, Blue Mark	48.00
Box, Pin, Lilac Tapestry, 3 1/2 X 2 In.	150.00
Box, Pin, White Flowers, Pink Ground, Marked, 2 1/2 In.	48.00
Candleholder, Clown, Marked	175.00
Candleholder, Devil & Cards, 3 1/2 X 6 In., Pair	265.00
Candleholder, Little Bopeep, Blue Mark	75.00
Candleholder, Pansies & Roses, Hooded, Marked	60.00
Candy Dish, Devil & Cards	250.00
Chamberstick, Fox Hunt Scene, Shield Back	145.00
Chamberstick, Roses, Pansies, Forget-Me-Nots	45.00
Chocolate Pot, Roses, Reticulated Draped Bottom, Blue Mark	200.00
Chocolate Set, Barnyard Scene, 9 Piece	550.00
Chocolate Set, Boy & 3 Donkeys Scene, Signed, 5 Piece	275.00
Compote, Sheep, Blue Mark, 6 X 2 3/4 In.	40.00
Creamer, Alligator, Blue Mark	155.00
Creamer, American Flag & Tennis Design, Blue Mark, 4 In.	90.00
Creamer, Apple, Blue Mark	55.00
Creamer, Arab Scene, Blue Mark, 3 1/2 In.	60.00
Creamer, Bell Ringer, Blue Mark	155.00 To 190.00
Creamer, Bird Of Paradise, Figural	175.00
Creamer, Black Cat, Blue Mark	90.00
Creamer, Black Crow, Blue Mark	80.00
Creamer, Black Water Buffalo	120.00 To 125.00
Creamer, Boy & Turkeys, Blue Mark, 3 1/2 In.	60.00
Creamer, Brittany Scene, Blue Mark, 4 In.	65.00
Creamer, Buffalo, Blue Mark	100.00
Creamer, Bull, Blue Mark	150.00
Creamer, Bull, Brown & Black, Red Horns	125.00
Creamer, Bull, Gray	100.00
Creamer, Bull, Red, Blue Mark	165.00
Creamer, Castle & Hill, Rose Tapestry	350.00
Creamer, Cat, Black, Blue Mark	90.00
Creamer, Cat, Black, Green Mark	140.00
Creamer, Children Playing On Beach	75.00
Creamer, Clown, Blue, Marked	105.00
Creamer, Clown, Red, Blue Mark	145.00
Creamer, Coachman, Blue Mark	145.00 To 165.00
Creamer, Cockatoo, Marked	140.00
Creamer, Cow Scene, Blue Mark, 3 In.	60.00

Creamer, Cow, Red Highlights	185.00
Creamer, Crow, Black, Blue Mark	90.00 To 140.00
Creamer, Devil & Cards, Blue Mark, 3 3/4 In.	145.00
Creamer, Devil & Cards, Green Mark	95.00
Creamer, Duck	65.00 To 75.00
Creamer, Farmer & Turkeys	40.00
Creamer, Farmer, Chickens, Corset Shape, 4 In.	65.00
Creamer, Fish	125.00
Creamer, Fishing Scene, Blue Mark, 2 1/2 X 3 In.	45.00
Creamer, Fox Hunt, Blue Mark	60.00
Creamer, Frog, Green, Figural	95.00 To 110.00
Creamer, Girl With Pitcher, Red, Marked	295.00
Creamer, Lemon, Blue Mark	65.00
Creamer, Lettuce Leaf	75.00
Creamer, Lobster, Blue Mark	75.00
Creamer, Lobster, Green Mark	65.00
Creamer, Man In Boat, Square Foot, Blue Mark, 3 1/2 In.	65.00
Creamer, Melon, Blue Mark	135.00 To 165.00
Creamer, Milkmaid, Signed	275.00
Creamer, Monk	250.00
Creamer, Monkey & Girl With Water Jug, Marked	225.00
Creamer, Moose	45.00
Creamer, Moose Head	65.00
Creamer, Nursery Rhymes	50.00
Creamer, Orange, Signed	105.00
Creamer, Owl	275.00
Creamer, Pansy, Blue Mark	125.00
Creamer, Parakeet, Blue Mark	165.00
Creamer, Pelican	75.00
Creamer, Pig, Blue Mark	250.00
Creamer, Poodle, Black, Blue Mark	185.00
Creamer, Poodle, Gray, Blue Mark	135.00 To 165.00
Creamer, Poppy, Blue Mark	85.00 To 125.00
Creamer, Purple Pansy, Green Mark	145.00
Creamer, Robin, Blue Mark	175.00
Creamer, Rooster, Blue Mark	145.00
Creamer, Rose Tapestry	115.00 To 185.00
Creamer, Santa Claus	485.00
Creamer, Seal, Blue Mark	165.00
Creamer, Sheep Grazing, Blue Mark, 3 1/2 In.	60.00
Creamer, Sheep Grazing, Pinched Spout, 4 In.	115.00
Creamer, Shell	35.00
Creamer, Sunflower, Blue Mark	175.00
Creamer, Tomato, Blue Mark	40.00
Creamer, Tomato, Green Mark	29.00
Creamer, Water Buffalo, Blue Mark	130.00
Creamer, Yellow Roses, Blue Mark	75.00
Cup & Saucer, Devil & Dice, Demitasse	160.00
Cup & Saucer, Red Rose, Signed	195.00
Cup, Hand Holding Table Tennis Paddle, Marked	32.00
Dish, Candlemas Girl, Miniature, 2 In.	45.00
Dish, Feeding, Little Boy Blue	80.00
Dish, Fishing Scene, Handles, Rolled Edge, 5 3/4 X 3 1/4 In.	55.00
Dish, Leaf Pattern, Handle, 4 In.	14.00
Dresser Set, Blue Floral, Hair Receiver, Jar, Tray, Blue Mark	195.00
Ewer, Lady's Portrait, 5 In.	125.00
Ewer, Polar Bear Scene, Bulbous	85.00
Ewer, Swans, Blue Mark, 6 1/2 In.	85.00
Figurine, Crow, Black, 4 3/4 In.	75.00
Flower Holder, Roses, Clusters On Base, Blue Mark, 4 In.	88.00
Hair Receiver, Lady, Ducks, Yellow Ground, 4 1/4 X 2 1/2 In.	95.00
Hair Receiver, Roses, Blue Mark	58.00
Hatpin Holder, Penguin, 5 In.	300.00
Holder, Cigar, Horses, Rider, Dog, Blue Mark	175.00

Holder, String, Figural, Rooster	155.00
Humidor, Covered, Card & Devil, Blue Mark ....275.00 To	550.00
Humidor, Troubadours, Signed Dixon	225.00
Jar, Hunting Scene, Footed, Covered, 4 1/2 In.	150.00
Loving Cup, Allover Mountain Scene, 3 Deer, Blue Mark, 7 In.	90.00
Match Holder, Clown, Blue Mark ....155.00 To	240.00
Match Holder, Enameled Storks, Yellow Glaze, Blue Mark	295.00
Match Holder, Shell	60.00
Mug, Drinking Scene, Yellow, Marked, Set Of 4	295.00
Mug, Nursery Rhymes, Handle, Blue Mark, 2 In.	55.00
Mustard, Apple	50.00
Mustard, Grape, Pink Mother–Of–Pearl, Blue Mark	125.00
Mustard, Grape, Yellow, Blue Mark ....90.00 To	125.00
Mustard, Poppy, Mother–Of–Pearl, Pink, Blue Mark	185.00
Mustard, Purple Grape, Blue Mark	65.00
Mustard, Tomato, Green Leaf Underplate, Blue Mark	57.50
Nappy, Cabbage Leaf, Handles, Blue Mark, 4 1/4 In. ....25.00 To	35.00
Nappy, Heart Shape, Handle, 5 1/4 In.	148.00
Nappy, Shell, Scalloped, Marked	45.00
Pitcher, Cabbage, Green & Orange, 5 1/2 X 6 1/2 In.	225.00
Pitcher, Castle In Mountains, Tapestry, Blue Mark, 5 In.	145.00
Pitcher, Castle Scene, Green, Gold Handle, 4 1/2 In.	55.00
Pitcher, Coachman, Blue Mark, 7 In.	375.00
Pitcher, Cockatoo, Blue Mark, 5 In.	200.00
Pitcher, Conch Shell, Coral Handle, 5 In. ....50.00 To	150.00
Pitcher, Cow Scene, Gold Handles, Bulbous, 5 In.	65.00
Pitcher, Cows In Pasture Scene, Blue Mark, 4 1/2 In.	45.00
Pitcher, Devil & Cards, 5 In.	190.00
Pitcher, Devil & Cards, Green Mark, 7 In.	380.00
Pitcher, Dutch Scene, 5 In.	85.00
Pitcher, Elk, Blue Mark, 7 In.	175.00
Pitcher, Fish Head, Blue Mark, 5 In.	155.00
Pitcher, Hunt Scene, 7 1/4 In.	125.00
Pitcher, Jack & Jill, Hand Painted, Double Handle, 5 In.	165.00
Pitcher, Lemonade, Fish Head, 8 In.	250.00
Pitcher, Little Boy Blue, Blue Mark	105.00
Pitcher, Little Miss Muffet, Blue Mark, 4 1/2 In.	75.00
Pitcher, Lobster, Blue Mark, 7 In.	175.00
Pitcher, Musicians, Blue Mark, 7 In.	160.00
Pitcher, Musicians, Dickens, Blue Mark, 3 X 3 In.	62.50
Pitcher, Rooster, 6 1/2 In.	185.00
Pitcher, Shell, Blue Mark, 7 In.	300.00
Pitcher, Shell, Coral Handle, 5 In.	45.00
Pitcher, Standing Trout, 7 In.	300.00
Pitcher, Tapestry, 3 Dogs & Moose Swimming, Blue Mark, 4 In.	200.00
Pitcher, Tavern Scene, Blue Mark, 4 1/2 In.	80.00
Pitcher, Tomato, Blue Mark, 7 In.	200.00
Pitcher, Watermelon, Blue Mark, 5 In.	165.00
Planter, Man & Turkey, Handles, Blue Mark, 3 1/2 In.	65.00
Plate, Deer Crossing River, 6 In.	30.00
Plate, Donkey Boy, Marked, 13 In.	115.00
Plate, Goose Girl, 6 In.	55.00
Plate, Hunter Shooting Ducks Scene, 9 In.	125.00
Platter, 12 1/2 X 7 1/2 In.	40.00
Powder Jar, Cover, Poppy, Mother–Of–Pearl	175.00
Powder Jar, Elk Scene On Lid	85.00
Salt & Pepper, Grape, Iridescent White, Blue Mark	110.00
Salt & Pepper, Grape, Purple, Blue Mark	65.00
Salt, Master, Devil & Cards, Blue Mark	195.00
Salt, Twin, Dutch Scene, Blue Mark	100.00
Shoe, Man's, Black, Hightop, Blue Mark	80.00
Shoe, Man's, Hightop, Cinnamon Stitching, Eyelets	45.00
Sugar & Creamer, Corinthian, Signed	125.00
Sugar & Creamer, Grape Cluster, Covered, Blue Mark	175.00

Sugar & Creamer, White Poppy, Mother-Of-Pearl, Open 145.00
Sugar, Conch, Open 12.50
Tankard, Arab & 2 Horses, Blue Mark, 8 In. 150.00
Tea Set, Sugar & Creamer, Salt & Pepper, Tomato, Blue Mark 175.00
Teapot, Shell, 7 1/2 In. 195.00
Teapot, Silver On Glazed Body, Chinoiserie Figures, C.1730 .... 385.00
Teapot, Sunset Landscape, Covered, Blue Mark, 3 X 4 1/8 In. 95.00
Tobacco Jar, Hunt Scene, Blue Mark 195.00
Toothpick, Brittany Girl, Blue Mark 95.00
Toothpick, Coachman 195.00
Toothpick, Oyster & Pearl, 3 Handles, Blue Mark 195.00
Toothpick, Portrait Of Girl & Dog, Footed, Handles 90.00
Tray, Dresser, Devil & Cards 475.00
Tray, Dresser, Roses Of 3 Colors 195.00
Tray, Goose Girl 140.00
Tray, Marmalade, Figural, Grape, Blue Mark 35.00
Tray, Pin, Penguin, Yellow Ground 75.00
Vase, Castle, Maids Swimming, Openwork Top, Blue Mark, 9 In. 80.00
Vase, Castle, Waterfall Scene, Blue Mark, 3 3/4 In. 95.00
Vase, Corinthian, Tangerine, 3 1/2 In. 35.00
Vase, Dutch Boy Flying Kite, Dog, Blue Mark, 4 1/4 In. 55.00
Vase, Fighting Cocks, 4 1/4 In. 75.00
Vase, Goats, Handles, Gold Trim, Blue Mark, 4 3/4 In. 88.00
Vase, Hunter & Animal In Forest, Blue Mark, 4 1/4 In. 279.00
Vase, Hunting Scene, Blue Mark, 4 X 5 X 3 In. 45.00
Vase, Musicians, 4 1/2 In. 40.00
Vase, Peasant Carrying Basket Of Fish, White Ground, Signed 75.00
Vase, Portrait, Gold Design, Blue Mark, 10 In. 210.00
Vase, Swan Scene, Pale Blue Ground, 7 1/2 In. 60.00
Vase, Yellow Carriage Scene, Blue Mark, 4 3/4 In. 50.00
Wall Pocket, Grape, Figural, Blue Mark 250.00
Wall Pocket, Mustard, White Grape, Marked 75.00
Wall Pocket, Two Men Fishing In Boat, Marked 75.00

Royal Bonn is the nineteenth- and twentieth-century trade name for the Bonn China Manufactory. It was established in 1755 in Bonn, Germany. A general line of porcelain was made. Many marks were used, most including the name "Bonn," the initials "FM," and a crown.

ROYAL BONN, Berry, Floral, Scalloped Gold Rim, C.1850 .... 7.50
Biscuit Jar, Floral, Silver Plate Top & Handle, Square, 7 In. 85.00
Bowl, Blue Leaves & Flowers, Collared Foot, 9 X 4 In. 45.00
Bowl, Chrysanthemum, Blue, Pedestal, 7 In. 65.00
Ewer, Beige, Gold, Hand Painted, 12 In. 185.00
Ewer, Persian Style, 14 In. 200.00
Ewer, Scenic, Peacock Feather Design, 14 1/2 In. 185.00
Plate, Chrysanthemums, Hand Painted, Raised Enamel, 8 1/2 In. 35.00
Powder Box, Madame Pompadour, Figural, Signed 65.00
Tile, Orchid Design, 7 In. 29.00
Urn, Cries Of London, Gold Tracery, Red Ground, 1875, 32 In. 1900.00
Vase, Bulbous, Allover Rose Design, Signed, 4 In. 85.00
Vase, Cavalier Portrait, 5 1/2 In. 185.00
Vase, Chrysanthemums, Raised Gold Borders, Marked, 10 1/2 In. 249.00
Vase, Floral & Bird, Gilt, 5 In. 48.00
Vase, Gilt Collar, Side Ring Handles, Gilt Tracery, 7 1/2 In. 225.00
Vase, Gold Neck, Handles, Cows & Farm Scene, Signed, 12 1/4 In. 175.00
Vase, Green Ground, Tulips, 8 In. 95.00
Vase, Handles, Gold Trim, Orchard, Signed, 11 In. 145.00
Vase, Orchids, Blue Bands, Gold Lines, Marked, 8 In., Pair 225.00
Vase, Roses, Hand Painted, 7 In. 82.00
Vase, Serpent Climbing Slender Neck, Tapestry, 12 1/2 In. 175.00
Vase, Tapestry, Floral Design, 8 1/2 X 11 In. 225.00
Vase, White, Farm & Cow Scene, Handles, Sticker, 12 1/4 In. 195.00

Royal Copenhagen porcelain and pottery have been made in Denmark since 1772. The Christmas plate series started in 1908. The figurines with pale blue and gray glazes have remained popular in this century and are still being made. Many other old and new style porcelains are made today.

ROYAL COPENHAGEN, Basket, Fruit, Stand, Flora Danica, Oval, Marked, 9 In.	1320.00
Candlestick, 4 3/4 X 2 In., Pair	35.00
Candlestick, No.910/3335, 2 1/4 In., Pair	60.00
Cup & Saucer, Cream Soup, Flora Danica, Marked, Set Of 12	4125.00
Cup & Saucer, Demitasse, Cactus Flower, Set Of 5	95.00
Decanter, Rosenborg Castle	60.00
Dinner Service, Blue Fluted, Open Lace Border, 99 Piece	2100.00
Eggcup, Blue Fluted	15.00
Figurine, 2 Birds, Blue, 4 In.	75.00
Figurine, Amager Girl, No.1251	126.00
Figurine, Bird, No.1040	95.00
Figurine, Bird, No.2144	95.00
Figurine, Blue Jay, 3 In.	20.00 To 30.00
Figurine, Cow On Stomach, Legs Under, No.1072, 6 In.	180.00
Figurine, Dog, Scotty, Green Slipper In Mouth, No.3476	85.00
Figurine, Duck, No.516	15.00
Figurine, Elephant, Walking, Trunk Raised, 4 X 5 In.	135.00
Figurine, Gibbon, 5 In.	55.00
Figurine, Goat, On Rocks, No.4760, 3 1/2 In.	87.50
Figurine, Goose Girl, No.527, 9 1/2 In.	180.00 To 235.00
Figurine, Lhasa Apso, Seated, No.1006, 4 1/2 X 5 1/2 In.	135.00
Figurine, Little Boy, Pointed Hat, Umbrella, No.1145, 6 In.	135.00
Figurine, Lovebirds, No.402	95.00
Figurine, Mouse, On Chestnut, No.511, White, 2 1/2 In.	65.00
Figurine, Nude, White, 6 1/2 In.	250.00
Figurine, Pan On Turtle, No.858, 3 3/4 In.	110.00 To 195.00
Figurine, Penguin Group, 4 In.	200.00
Figurine, Penguin, 2 3/4 In.	125.00
Figurine, Polar Bear Cub, Playing With Paws, 4 1/4 In.	145.00
Figurine, Pug, Puppy Sitting On Haunches, No.3169, 4 In.	115.00
Figurine, Robin, 2 1/2 In.	60.00
Figurine, Seal, 4 7/8 In.	200.00
Figurine, Shepherd, 8 In.	450.00
Figurine, Siamese Cat No.3281, 8 In.	110.00
Figurine, Sparrow, 4 In.	45.00
Figurine, Terrier, 7 X 7 1/2 In.	65.00
Plate, Blue, Gray Ground, Woven Border, 11/948B, 10 In.	30.00
Plate, Bread & Butter, Flora Danica, 6 1/2 In., Set Of 12	950.00
Plate, Christmas, 1945, Peaceful	209.00
Plate, Christmas, 1946, Church	97.00
Plate, Christmas, 1951, Angel	179.00
Plate, Christmas, 1959, Christmas Night	87.00 To 100.00
Plate, Flora Danica, 10 In., Set Of 14	2800.00
Plate, Flora Danica, 5 5/8 In., Set Of 5	650.00
Plate, Flora Danica, Marked, 10 1/4 In., Set Of 12	6875.00
Plate, Flora Danica, Model 20/3549, 10 1/4 In., Set Of 4	1540.00
Plate, Lobster, No.3277	95.00
Plate, Mother's Day, 1971	10.00 To 15.00
Plate, Rooster, 1923	50.00
Plate, Scandinavian Starburst, Magenta, Turquoise, 9 In.	65.00
Tazza, Flora Danica, Triangular, Footed, 4 1/2 In.	550.00
Tureen, Flora Danica, Cover, Handles, Marked, 13 1/4 In.	2200.00
Tureen, Soup, Cover, Flora Danica, Oval, Marked, 13 1/4 In.	2640.00
Urn, Cigarette, No.2688A	22.00
Vase, Carp, 1930, 7 1/2 In.	120.00 To 125.00
Vase, Pale Blue, Chestnut Blossom, Signed, 13 1/2 In.	230.00
Wine Cooler, Flora Danica, Handles, Marked, 7 1/4 In.	1045.00

Royal Copley china was made by the Spaulding China Company of Sebring, Ohio, from 1939 to 1960. The figural planters and the small figurines, especially those with Art Deco designs, are of great collector interest.

ROYAL COPLEY, Bank, Pig, Brown, 5 1/2 In. 22.00
Figurine, Cat, Black 25.00
Figurine, Cat, Purple 18.00
Figurine, Dutch Boy & Girl 33.50
Figurine, Parrot 20.00
Figurine, Pup With Suitcase 15.00
Figurine, Rooster, 8 1/2 In. 118.00
Flower Frog, Parrot 12.50
Planter, Black, Oval, 4 In. 6.00
Planter, Dog & Mailbox 33.50
Planter, Fish Shape, Open Center, Green 12.00
Planter, Mallard With Stump, 8 In. 15.00
Planter, Philodendron, Oval, 7 In. 7.00
Planter, Pony 12.00
Planter, Rooster, 7 In. 14.00
Planter, Spaniel 12.00
Planter, Star & Angel 12.00
Planter, Swallow, Extended Wings, 7 In., Pair 18.00
Plate, Children In Snow, Light Blue, Crown & Crossed Swords 100.00
Vase, Bow & Ribbon Pattern, 7 In. 10.00
Vase, Philodendron, 4 1/2 In. 6.00
Vase, Stylized Leaf, 5 1/2 In. 6.50
Vase, White Leaves, Dark Green, 8 In. 7.50
Wall Pocket, Boy, Holding Fishing Pole 7.00
Wall Pocket, Girl With Hat 7.00
Wall Pocket, Girl, Pigtails 11.00
Wall Pocket, Indian, 7 1/2 In. 20.00

Royal Crown Derby Company, Ltd., was established in England in 1876. There is a complex family tree that includes the Derby, Crown Derby, Worcester, and Royal Crown Derby porcelains. The Royal Crown Derby mark includes the name and a crown. The words "Made in England" were used after 1921.

ROYAL CROWN DERBY, Box, Lid, Orange Transfer, Blue, Quilt Trim, Oval, 4 In. 25.00
Can, Coffee, Cobalt, Rust, Gold 100.00
Coffeepot, 2 Pt. 395.00
Coffeepot, Imari Pattern, 2 Pt. 395.00
Cup & Saucer, Imari Pattern 70.00
Cup & Saucer, Imari Pattern, Demitasse ....69.00 To 79.00
Cup & Saucer, Imari Pattern, Lined Case, 6 Sets 225.00
Ewer, Cobalt, Light Blue Accent, Gold Flowers, 1890, 8 In. 195.00
Pitcher, Cobalt Blue Ground, Multicolor Floral, 1818 .... 125.00
Plate, Imari Pattern, 6 In. 39.00
Plate, Imari Pattern, 8 1/4 In. 69.00
Plate, Imari Pattern, 10 3/4 In. 95.00
Plate, Portrait, Women, Blue, Crown & Crossed Swords 100.00
Sugar & Creamer 350.00
Sugar & Creamer, Imari Pattern, Covered, Dublin Shape 295.00

"Royal Doulton" is the name used on Doulton and Company pottery made from 1902 to the present. Doulton and Company of England was founded in 1853. Pieces made before 1902 are listed under Doulton. Royal Doulton collectors search for the out-of-production figurines, character jugs, and series wares. For a complete listing, see "Kovels' Illustrated Price Guide to Royal Doulton."

ROYAL DOULTON, Ash Pot, Old Charley, D.5925 .... 95.00
Ash Pot, Parson Brown, D.6008 .... 95.00
Ash Pot, Sir Roger De Coverly 65.00
Ashtray, Old Charley ....95.00 To 110.00

Ashtray, Parson Brown 110.00
Biscuit Jar, Floral, Fuchsia, Gold Trim, Covered 45.00
Biscuit Jar, Tony Weller, Handle, 7 In. 395.00
Bookends, Bridesmaid, M 30 ....155.00 To 185.00
Bookends, Sweet Anne, M 6 ....200.00 To 210.00
Bottle, Ben Johnson 225.00
Bottle, Dewar's Whiskey, Bonnie Prince Charlie 225.00
Bottle, Old Crow 110.00
Bowl, Artful Dodger, 4 In. 60.00
Bowl, Coaching Days, 6 In. 40.00
Bowl, Dick Swiveller, Dickens Ware, 7 1/2 In. 135.00
Bowl, Mr.Pickwick, Dickens Ware, Square, Marked, 2 X 8 3/4 In. 85.00
Bowl, Robin Hood, Collared Foot, Marked, 3 3/4 X 7 1/2 In. 135.00
Bowl, Sam Weller, Dickens Ware, Australian, Octagonal, 9 In. 100.00
Bust, Mr.Micawber, D.6050 .... 60.00
Bust, Queen Elizabeth, Black Basalt 575.00
Cake Plate, Robin Hood, Under The Greenwood Tree, Handles 95.00
Candlestick, Bayeux Tapestry, 8 3/4 In. 75.00
Candlestick, Old Moreton, 6 1/2 In. 85.00

> *Character jugs are the modeled head and shoulders of the subject.*
> *They are made in four sizes: large, 5 1/4 to 7 inches; small, 3 1/4 to*
> *4 inches; miniature, 2 1/4 to 2 1/2 inches; and tiny, 1 1/4 inches.*
> *Toby jugs depict a seated, full figure.*

Character Jug, 'Ard Of 'Earing, Large 795.00
Character Jug, 'Arriet, A Mark, Large 160.00
Character Jug, 'Arriet, Tiny 180.00
Character Jug, 'Arry, Miniature 75.00
Character Jug, Auld Mac, Small, A Mark 32.00
Character Jug, Auld Mac, Tiny ....200.00 To 245.00
Character Jug, Beefeater, Miniature 55.00
Character Jug, Blacksmith, Large 75.00
Character Jug, Bootmaker, Small 22.00
Character Jug, Cap'n Cuttle Small ....92.50 To 95.00
Character Jug, Captain Hook, Large ....275.00 To 365.00
Character Jug, Cardinal, Large ....125.00 To 150.00
Character Jug, Cardinal, Tiny 245.00
Character Jug, Cavalier, A Mark, Large 140.00
Character Jug, Cliff Cornell, Blue, Small 225.00
Character Jug, Clown, Red Hair, Large ....3500.00 To 3650.00
Character Jug, Clown, White Hair, Large ....995.00 To 1200.00
Character Jug, Dick Turpin, Gun Handle, Miniature 50.00
Character Jug, Dick Turpin, Horse Handle, Miniature 25.00
Character Jug, Dick Whittington, Large 395.00
Character Jug, Falstaff, Large 45.00
Character Jug, Farmer John, Small 85.00
Character Jug, Fat Boy, Tiny ....86.00 To 135.00
Character Jug, Fortune Teller, Large ....350.00 To 450.00
Character Jug, Fortune Teller, Small ....295.00 To 325.00
Character Jug, Friar Tuck, Large ....365.00 To 375.00
Character Jug, Gaoler, Small 32.00
Character Jug, Gladiator, Miniature 325.00
Character Jug, Gondolier, Large ....425.00 To 535.00
Character Jug, Gondolier, Small ....340.00 To 355.00
Character Jug, Gone Away, Miniature ....22.00 To 25.00
Character Jug, Granny, A Mark, Large ....80.00 To 100.00
Character Jug, Granny, Small 30.00
Character Jug, Guardsman, Large ....45.00 To 75.00
Character Jug, Gulliver, Small 350.00
Character Jug, Jarge, Small ....165.00 To 185.00
Character Jug, Jockey, Large 175.00
Character Jug, John Barleycorn, Large ....140.00 To 175.00
Character Jug, John Barleycorn, Miniature 65.00
Character Jug, John Doulton, Small 35.00

Character Jug, John Peel, Miniature ....50.00 To 75.00
Character Jug, John Peel, Small 85.00
Character Jug, Johnny Appleseed, Large 295.00
Character Jug, Long John, Large 50.00
Character Jug, Lord Nelson, Large ....225.00 To 300.00
Character Jug, Lumberjack, Small 32.00
Character Jug, Mephistopheles, Large ....2500.00 To 3000.00
Character Jug, Mikado, Small 300.00
Character Jug, Mr.Micawber, Tiny ....85.00 To 92.50
Character Jug, Mr.Pickwick, A Mark, Large 150.00
Character Jug, Night Watchman, Miniature 28.00
Character Jug, Old Charley, Tiny ....80.00 To 92.50
Character Jug, Old King Cole, A Mark, Small 100.00
Character Jug, Old King Cole, Small ....80.00 To 120.00
Character Jug, Othello, Large 40.00
Character Jug, Paddy, Tiny 85.00
Character Jug, Parson Brown, A Mark, Large 140.00
Character Jug, Pied Piper, Miniature ....25.00 To 27.00
Character Jug, Porthos, Small 50.00
Character Jug, Punch & Judy Man, Small 425.00
Character Jug, Regency Beau, Small 425.00
Character Jug, Rip Van Winkle, Large 42.00
Character Jug, Robin Hood, Large, Plain Handle 125.00
Character Jug, Robinson Crusoe, Miniature 45.00
Character Jug, Sam Weller, A Mark, Tiny 80.00
Character Jug, Sam Weller, Small 55.00
Character Jug, Sam Weller, Tiny 80.00
Character Jug, Samuel Johnson, Large 200.00
Character Jug, Scaramouche, Large ....550.00 To 575.00
Character Jug, Sergeant Buz Fuz, Small 150.00
Character Jug, Simon The Cellarer, Large 130.00
Character Jug, Simple Simon, Large ....525.00 To 550.00
Character Jug, Smuggler, Large 55.00
Character Jug, St.George, Large 105.00
Character Jug, Toby Philpots, A Mark, Miniature 55.00
Character Jug, Tony Philpots, Large 125.00
Character Jug, Tony Weller, Miniature ....42.50 To 45.00
Character Jug, Tony Weller, Small 60.00
Character Jug, Touchstone, Large 210.00
Character Jug, Town Crier, A Mark, Miniature 145.00
Character Jug, Ugly Duchess, Large ....310.00 To 375.00
Character Jug, Ugly Duchess, Small 285.00
Character Jug, Uncle Tom Cobbleigh, Large ....350.00 To 395.00
Character Jug, Veteran Motorist, Large 50.00
Character Jug, Vicar Of Bray, Large 190.00
Character Jug, Walrus & Carpenter, Small 50.00
Character Jug, Yachtsman, Large 75.00
Cheese Dish, Robin Hood, Under The Greenwood Tree, Covered 350.00
Chocolate Set, Yellow & Pink Orchids, Signed, 13 Piece 140.00
Chop Plate, Jackdaw Of Rheims, 13 In. 95.00
Chop Plate, Treasure Island, 13 In. 90.00
Coffeepot, Applied Figures, Tavern Scene, Brown, 10 In. 140.00
Coffeepot, Gleaners 155.00
Coffeepot, Gnomes 180.00
Cookie Jar, Tapestry 475.00
Creamer, Juliet, C.1925, 3 1/4 In. 75.00
Cup & Saucer, Arcadia 12.00
Cup & Saucer, Bill Sykes, Dickens Ware, Saucer 5 1/2 In. 70.00
Cup & Saucer, Chelsea Rose, Green Mark 25.00
Cup & Saucer, Coaching Days 40.00
Cup & Saucer, Fagin, Dickens Ware, Saucer 5 1/2 In. 70.00
Cup & Saucer, Flambe, Landscape, Demitasse 75.00
Cup & Saucer, Nursery Rhymes, Hey Diddle Diddle 40.00
Cup & Saucer, Old Moreton 45.00

Cup & Saucer, Pomeroy, Pink	9.00
Cup & Saucer, Sam Weller & Fagin, Demitasse	65.00
Decanter, Mr.Pickwick	49.00
Dinner Set, Arcadia, 51 Piece	350.00
Dish, Child's, Feeding, Bunnykins	45.00
Dish, Coach Scene, Green Mark, 4 X 1 3/4 In.	30.00
Dish, Zunday Zmocks, 3 Section, Oval, 6 7/8 X 11 5/8 In.	95.00
	175.00
Figurine, A La Mode, HN 2544	375.00 To 520.00
Figurine, A'Courting, HN 2004	295.00
Figurine, Afternoon Tea, HN 1747	699.00
Figurine, Ajax, HN 2908	1550.00
Figurine, Alchemist, HN 1282	595.00
Figurine, Angelina, HN 2013	90.00
Figurine, Anna, HN 2802	235.00
Figurine, Annette, HN 1550	475.00 To 495.00
Figurine, Anthea, HN 1527	125.00
Figurine, Ascot, HN 2356	125.00
Figurine, Autumn Breezes, HN 1934	430.00
Figurine, Autumn, HN 2087	350.00
Figurine, Baby Bunting, HN 2108	215.00 To 300.00
Figurine, Bachelor, HN 2319	92.00 To 125.00
Figurine, Balloon Man, HN 1954	975.00
Figurine, Bather, Potted, HN 687	595.00
Figurine, Beggar, Potted, HN 526	225.00
Figurine, Bell O' The Ball	110.00 To 195.00
Figurine, Biddy, HN 1513	160.00
Figurine, Blacksmith Of Williamsburg, HN 2240	130.00 To 200.00
Figurine, Blithe Morning, HN 2021	165.00 To 175.00
Figurine, Blithe Morning, HN 2065	195.00 To 275.00
Figurine, Bonnie Lassie, HN 1626	250.00 To 565.00
Figurine, Breton Dancer, HN 2383	150.00 To 225.00
Figurine, Bride, HN 2166	250.00
Figurine, Bridesmaid, M 30	195.00 To 225.00
Figurine, Bridget, HN 2070	425.00 To 550.00
Figurine, Broken Lance, HN 2041	85.00
Figurine, Bulldog, HN 1072, White, 5 1/2 In.	575.00
Figurine, Butterfly, HN 720	65.00
Figurine, Cairn, Charming Eyes Champion, HN 1035	445.00 To 750.00
Figurine, Calumet, HN 1689	550.00
Figurine, Calumet, HN 2068	187.00
Figurine, Captain Cook, HN 2889	265.00 To 380.00
Figurine, Carolyn, HN 2112	450.00
Figurine, Cassim, HN 1231	275.00
Figurine, Cat, Flambe, 12 In.	350.00 To 500.00
Figurine, Cellist, HN 2226	445.00 To 595.00
Figurine, Charley's Aunt, HN 1703	100.00
Figurine, Child From Williamsburg, HN 2154	595.00
Figurine, Chinese Dancer, HN 2840	225.00
Figurine, Chloe, M 29	225.00
Figurine, Christmas Parcels, HN 2851	225.00 To 300.00
Figurine, Clockmaker, HN 2279	335.00
Figurine, Coachman, HN 2282	215.00 To 225.00
Figurine, Cobbler, HN 1706	175.00
Figurine, Cocker Spaniel & Pheasant, HN 1001, 6 1/2 In.	80.00
Figurine, Cocker Spaniel, HN 1109, Black & White, 5 In.	525.00 To 555.00
Figurine, Columbine, HN 1297	525.00
Figurine, Columbine, HN 1439	103.00 To 150.00
Figurine, Country Lass, HN 1991A	325.00
Figurine, Cradle Song, HN 2246	395.00
Figurine, Craftsman, HN 2284	335.00 To 355.00
Figurine, Curly Knob, HN 1627	695.00
Figurine, Cymbals, HN 2699	95.00
Figurine, Dachshund, HN 1129	245.00
Figurine, Dancing Years, HN 2235	

Figurine, Darby, HN 2024 .... 225.00
Figurine, Darling, HN 1319 ....92.00 To 110.00
Figurine, Dawn, HN 1858 .... 825.00
Figurine, Delight, HN 1772 ....135.00 To 185.00
Figurine, Delphine, HN 2136 ....225.00 To 235.00
Figurine, Derrick, HN 1398 ....355.00 To 495.00
Figurine, Detective, HN 2359 ....100.00 To 115.00
Figurine, Dinky Do, HN 1678 ....50.00 To 55.00
Figurine, Doctor, HN 2858 ....100.00 To 112.00
Figurine, Duke Of Edinburgh, HN 2386 .... 475.00
Figurine, Easter Day, HN 1976 .... 375.00
Figurine, Easter Day, HN 2039 .... 325.00
Figurine, Elephant, Flambe, 9 X 5 1/2 In. 110.00
Figurine, Embroidering, HN 2855 .... 112.00
Figurine, Enchantment, HN 2178 ....120.00 To 230.00
Figurine, English Setter, HN 1051 ....65.00 To 110.00
Figurine, Esmeralda, HN 2168 .... 265.00
Figurine, Fair Maiden, HN 2211 .... 200.00
Figurine, Family Album, HN 2321 .... 300.00
Figurine, First Steps, HN 2242 .... 500.00
Figurine, Fleurette, HN 1587 ....350.00 To 425.00
Figurine, Flower Seller's Children, HN 1342 .... 325.00
Figurine, Flute, HN 2483 .... 900.00
Figurine, Forty Winks, HN 1974 ....210.00 To 225.00
Figurine, Fox, Flambe, 5 1/2 In. 48.00
Figurine, Fox, Flambe, Sitting, 10 In. 225.00
Figurine, Friar Tuck, HN 2143 ....385.00 To 425.00
Figurine, Gay Morning, HN 2135 ....200.00 To 300.00
Figurine, Golden Days, HN 2274 .... 150.00
Figurine, Goody Two Shoes, HN 1905 .... 180.00
Figurine, Gossips, HN 1429 .... 425.00
Figurine, Gossips, HN 2025 .... 385.00
Figurine, Greta, HN 1485 .... 225.00
Figurine, Griselda, HN 1993 ....450.00 To 525.00
Figurine, Grossmith's Tsang Ihang, HN 582 .... 375.00
Figurine, Guy Fawkes, HN 98 .... 795.00
Figurine, He Loves Me, HN 2046 .... 185.00
Figurine, Heart To Heart, HN 2276 .... 275.00
Figurine, Helen Of Troy, HN 2387 ....595.00 To 725.00
Figurine, Henrietta Maria, HN 2005 ....355.00 To 595.00
Figurine, Her Ladyship, HN 1977 ....250.00 To 300.00
Figurine, Ibrahim, HN 2095 .... 750.00
Figurine, In Grandma's Days, HN 362 .... 595.00
Figurine, Irene, HN 1621 .... 300.00
Figurine, Irene, HN 1952 .... 475.00
Figurine, Irish Setter, HN 1056, 3 3/4 In. 110.00
Figurine, Janet, HN 1916 .... 250.00
Figurine, Janice, HN 2165 ....380.00 To 485.00
Figurine, Jean, HN 2032 .... 250.00
Figurine, Joan, HN 1422 ....225.00 To 275.00
Figurine, Judith, HN 2089 ....225.00 To 250.00
Figurine, June, HN 1690 ....315.00 To 325.00
Figurine, Juno & The Peacock, HN 2827 ....950.00 To 1199.00
Figurine, Kathleen, HN 1252 .... 550.00
Figurine, Kathleen, HN 1357 .... 600.00
Figurine, Katrina, HN 2327 ....195.00 To 270.00
Figurine, Lady Betty, HN 1967 ....300.00 To 350.00
Figurine, Lady Charmian, HN 1948 ....220.00 To 225.00
Figurine, Lady Charmian, HN 1949 .... 150.00
Figurine, Lady Clare, HN 1465 .... 430.00
Figurine, Lady Fayre, HN 1265 ....395.00 To 450.00
Figurine, Lady From Williamsburg, HN 2228 .... 135.00
Figurine, Lights Out, HN 2262 .... 150.00
Figurine, Lilac Time, HN 2137 .... 225.00

Figurine, Little Boy Blue, HN 2062 ....108.00 To 140.00
Figurine, Little Bridesmaid, HN 1433 .... 99.00 To 155.00
Figurine, Love Letter, HN 2149 .... 220.00
Figurine, Lucy Locket, HN 524 .... 425.00
Figurine, Madonna Of The Square, HN 594 .... 795.00
Figurine, Margaret Of Anjou, HN 2012 .... 475.00
Figurine, Mary Mary, HN 2044 .... 145.00
Figurine, Masquerade, HN 599 ....350.00 To 375.00
Figurine, Maytime, HN 2113 ....195.00 To 220.00
Figurine, Melody, HN 2202 .... 350.00
Figurine, Memories, HN 1855 .... 350.00
Figurine, Mephistopheles & Marguerite 895.00
Figurine, Mermaid, HN 97 .... 595.00
Figurine, Midinette, HN 2090 ....175.00 To 200.00
Figurine, Millicent, HN 1714 .... 795.00
Figurine, Minuet, HN 2019 ....225.00 To 250.00
Figurine, Miss Demure, HN 1402 .... 200.00
Figurine, Negligee, HN 1219 .... 800.00
Figurine, Newsboy, HN 2244 .... 500.00
Figurine, Noelle, HN 2179 ....310.00 To 425.00
Figurine, North American Indian Dancer, HN 2809 .... 595.00
Figurine, Old Balloon Seller, HN 1315 .... 195.00
Figurine, Old King Cole, HN 2217 ....575.00 To 695.00
Figurine, Old Mother Hubbard, HN 2314 ....215.00 To 250.00
Figurine, Orange Lady, HN 1759 ....195.00 To 220.00
Figurine, Orange Lady, HN 1953 ....165.00 To 185.00
Figurine, Owd Willum, HN 2042 ....200.00 To 245.00
Figurine, Paisley Shawl, HN 1987 ....195.00 To 210.00
Figurine, Paisley Shawl, HN 1988 ....115.00 To 200.00
Figurine, Pantalettes, M 15 .... 200.00
Figurine, Parson's Daughter, HN 564 ....300.00 To 400.00
Figurine, Patchwork Quilt, HN 1984 ....200.00 To 375.00
Figurine, Patricia, M 28 .... 250.00
Figurine, Patricia, M 8 .... 275.00
Figurine, Pearly Boy, HN 1547 .... 420.00
Figurine, Penelope, HN 1901 .... 340.00
Figurine, Perfect Pair 650.00
Figurine, Philippine Dancer, HN 2439 .... 595.00
Figurine, Phillippa Of Hainault, HN 2008 .... 325.00
Figurine, Phyllis, HN 1420 .... 350.00
Figurine, Pierrette, HN 643 .... 625.00
Figurine, Poacher, HN 2043 ....245.00 To 250.00
Figurine, Polka, HN 2156 .... 265.00
Figurine, Polly Peachum, HN 550 .... 495.00
Figurine, Potter, HN 1493 .... 240.00
Figurine, Pretty Lady, HN 70 .... 595.00
Figurine, Priscilla, HN 1337 ....295.00 To 325.00
Figurine, Priscilla, M 14 .... 185.00
Figurine, Punch & Judy Man, HN 2765 .... 147.00
Figurine, Puppetmaker, HN 2253 .... 465.00
Figurine, Queen Elizabeth II, HN 2878 ....210.00 To 475.00
Figurine, Queen Mother, HN 2882 .... 895.00
Figurine, Queen Of Sheba, HN 2328 .... 995.00
Figurine, Repose, HN 2272 ....145.00 To 150.00
Figurine, River Hog, HN 2663, Chatcull Range 125.00
Figurine, Romance, HN 2430 ....135.00 To 140.00
Figurine, Rose, HN 1368 .... 70.00
Figurine, Rosebud, HN 1581 ....475.00 To 500.00
Figurine, Ruth The Pirate Maid, HN 2900 .... 325.00
Figurine, Sabbath Morn, HN 1982 ....195.00 To 275.00
Figurine, Sailor's Holiday, HN 2442 .... 145.00
Figurine, Shepherd, HN 1975 ....175.00 To 200.00
Figurine, Shore Leave, HN 2254 ....150.00 To 165.00
Figurine, Southern Belle, HN 2229 .... 125.00

Figurine, Spring Flowers, HN 1807 .... 275.00
Figurine, Spring Morning, HN 1922 .... 209.00
Figurine, Spring, HN 2085 .... 400.00
Figurine, St.George, HN 2067 .... 1950.00
Figurine, Suitor, HN 2132 ....320.00 To 395.00
Figurine, Summer, HN 2086 ....335.00 To 430.00
Figurine, Summer, The Seasons, HN 313 .... 595.00
Figurine, Sunday Morning, HN 2184 .... 225.00
Figurine, Susanna, HN 1233 .... 700.00
Figurine, Sweet & Twenty, HN 1298 ....200.00 To 225.00
Figurine, Sweet & Twenty, HN 1589 ....165.00 To 225.00
Figurine, Sweet Anne, HN 1330 .... 325.00
Figurine, Sweet Anne, HN 1496 ....180.00 To 190.00
Figurine, Sweet April, HN 2215 ....295.00 To 335.00
Figurine, Sweet Lavender, HN 1373 ....325.00 To 330.00
Figurine, Sweet Maid, HN 2092 .... 275.00
Figurine, Sweeting, HN 1935 .... 120.00
Figurine, Symphony, HN 2287 .... 350.00
Figurine, Tete-A-Tete, HN 799 .... 800.00
Figurine, Toinette, HN 1940 .... 1250.00
Figurine, Top O' The Hill, HN 1834 ....85.00 To 120.00
Figurine, Top O' The Hill, HN 1849 ....145.00 To 175.00
Figurine, Town Crier, HN 2119 .... 225.00
Figurine, Toymaker, HN 2250 ....300.00 To 350.00
Figurine, Veronica, HN 1517 .... 295.00
Figurine, Viking, HN 2375 .... 212.00
Figurine, Virginia, HN 1693 .... 450.00
Figurine, Votes For Women, HN 2816 .... 175.00
Figurine, Wardrobe Mistress, HN 2145 ....325.00 To 375.00
Figurine, West Indian Dancer, HN 2384 ....250.00 To 565.00
Figurine, Wigmaker Of Williamsburg, HN 2239 .... 120.00
Figurine, Winter, HN 2088 ....275.00 To 430.00
Figurine, Wizard, HN 2877 ....107.00 To 126.00
Figurine, Wood Nymph, HN 2192 .... 215.00
Flask, Dewars, Vikings, Ships, Lion, No.181 .... 295.00
Hatpin Holder, Bill Sykes, Dickens Ware, 5 1/2 In. 140.00
Jam Jar, Gaffers, Covered 133.00
Jardiniere, Foliage, Stamped, 7 X 7 1/2 In. 165.00
Jardiniere, Ophelia & Hamlet, Shakespeare, 8 5/8 In. 325.00
Jug, Whiskey, Special Highland Whiskey, 7 In. 75.00
Jug, Whisky, Ben Jonson, Kingsware, Marked, 7 1/2 In. 195.00
Lighter, Cigarette, Lawyer 95.00
Lighter, Cigarette, Poacher 95.00
Lighter, Long John Silver ....95.00 To 105.00
Liquor Pot, Rip Van Winkle 120.00
Loving Cup, Burslem, Watteau, 3 Handles 225.00
Loving Cup, Queen Elizabeth Coronation, Portraits, 11 In. 375.00
Match Holder, Card Suit Design, Cream, Marked, 3 1/4 In. 55.00
Mug, Golf, Men In Knickers, Maxim, 5 1/2 In. ....395.00 To 450.00
Pitcher & Bowl, Dutch Scene, C.1910, Signed 595.00
Pitcher, Churchill, 8 1/2 In. 95.00
Pitcher, Coaching Days, 6 In. 100.00
Pitcher, Falstaff, C.1920, 6 3/4 In. 135.00
Pitcher, Gaffers, Signed Noke, 4 In. 125.00
Pitcher, Kingsware, Watchman, White Letters, 5 X 6 In. 200.00
Pitcher, May Day Children, Blue & White, 8 In. 110.00
Pitcher, Oriental Scene, Flowers On Handle & Spout, 7 In. 70.00
Pitcher, Sam Weller, Dickens Ware, Signed Noke, 7 In. 85.00
Pitcher, Sea Shanty, Limericks, 6 1/2 In. 125.00
Pitcher, Tony Weller, Dickens Ware, 6 In. 175.00
Pitcher, Watteau, 5 1/4 In. 100.00
Plate, Anne Hathaway's Cottage, 10 1/2 In. 35.00
Plate, Arabian Nights, Unknown Princess, Marked, 10 3/8 In. 95.00
Plate, Babes In Woods, Flow Blue, Marked, 9 1/4 In. 198.00

Royal Doulton, Vase, Stoneware,
Gray, Blue, H.S., 9 In.

Royal Dux, Vase, Merman & Mermaid
Rising From Waves, 13 1/2 In.

Plate, Castle Scene, 10 In.	35.00
Plate, Hay Cart & Chickens, Square, 7 1/2 In.	25.00
Plate, Itch Yer On Guvenor, Auto Scene, 10 3/8 In.	195.00
Plate, Kathyrn, 7 1/2 In.	10.00
Plate, Loch Ness, Hand Painted, 9 In.	25.00
Plate, Rochester Castle, 10 In.	45.00
Plate, Sailing Vessels, Dark Green Border, 10 In.	40.00
Plate, Shakespeare, 10 1/2 In.	52.00
Plate, Tower Of London, 10 In.	30.00 To 35.00
Plate, Turkey, Watteau, 10 1/2 In.	80.00
Plate, U.S.Capitol, Washington, D.C., Bowman, 10 In.	28.00 To 30.00
Powder Box, Tony Weller	70.00
Salt, Hunting Scene, Silver Rim	55.00
Sugar & Creamer, Autumn	55.00
Sugar & Creamer, Coaching Days	65.00 To 75.00
Sugar & Creamer, Malvern, Covered	20.00
Sugar, Tony Weller, Beswick	50.00
Tankard, Cheshire Cheese, Brown	45.00 To 60.00
Teapot, Bill Sykes, Dickens Ware, Marked, 6 X 4 1/2 In.	225.00
Teapot, Coaching Days	115.00
Teapot, Under The Greenwood Tree, 4 3/4 X 8 1/2 In.	295.00
Tile, Tea, Gleaners, 6 1/2 In.	55.00 To 65.00
Toby Jug, Churchill, Small	24.50
Toby Jug, Cliff Cornell, Blue, Large	225.00
Toby Jug, Falstaff, Large	52.50
Toby Jug, Sairy Gamp, A Mark, Small	65.00
Toothpick, Gallant Fishers	65.00
Toothpick, Under The Greenwood Tree	75.00
Tray, Rustic England, 5 X 10 1/2 In.	55.00
Tray, Sandwich, Zunday Zmocks, Marked, 5 X 11 In.	88.00
Tumbler, Child's, Mother Goose	25.00
Vase, Alfred Jingle, Dickens Ware, Handles, Marked, 9 3/8 In.	165.00
Vase, All Black Cricket Team, Marked, 2 1/2 In.	135.00
Vase, Artful Dodger, Dickens Ware, 4 In.	60.00
Vase, Babes In Woods, 7 1/2 X 6 In.	250.00
Vase, Babes In Woods, 8 1/2 In.	250.00 To 275.00
Vase, Babes In Woods, Blindman's Bluff, Flow Blue, 9 In.	298.00
Vase, Babes In Woods, Girl With Basket, Marked, 8 In.	325.00
Vase, Babes In Woods, Girls Looking At Forest, 10 3/4 In.	295.00
Vase, Babes In Woods, Girls, Firefly, Flow Blue, 7 In.	275.00
Vase, Coaching Days, Barrel Shape, 8 3/4 X 3 3/8 In.	165.00
Vase, Flambe, Bullet Shape, Landscape, Deer, Signed, 7 In.	225.00

Vase, Flambe, Sung, Brass Rim & Base, 5 In. 175.00
Vase, Flambe, Veined Sung, Pumpkin, Signed FM, 6 X 10 In. 550.00
Vase, Mr.Micawber, Dickens Ware, Handle, Marked, 5 7/8 In. 78.00
Vase, Stoneware, Gray, Blue, H.S., 9 In. ....*Illus* 125.00
Vase, Stoneware, H.S., 9 In. ....*Color* 150.00
Vase, Sydney Carton, Dickens Ware, Handles, Marked, 6 3/4 In. 135.00
Wall Mask, Jester, 11 In. 265.00
Washbowl & Pitcher, Lilacs, 8 Sided, Marked, C.1820, 7 1/2 In. 250.00

The Duxer Porzellanmanufaktur was founded in Dux, Bohemia, in 1860 by E. Eichler. By the turn of the century, the firm specialized in porcelain statuary and busts of Art Nouveau–style maidens, large porcelain figures, and ornate vases with three–dimensional figures climbing on the sides. After 1918, the word "Bohemia" was taken out of the mark because the city had become Duchcov, Czechoslovakia. The firm is still in business.

ROYAL DUX, Basket, Green, Bullet Shape, Marked 85.00
Centerpiece, 2 Entwined Art Nouveau Maidens Standing, 20 In. 600.00
Centerpiece, Shepherdess, Sheep, Water Hole, Triangle Mark, 14 In. 795.00
Figurine, Boy & Girl At Well, Pink Triangle, 24 In., Pair 1450.00
Figurine, Boy With Basket Of Fish, Pink Triangle Mark, 10 In. 200.00
Figurine, Classical Woman Carrying Jug, Marked, 20 In. 595.00
Figurine, Girl Holding Teddy Bear, 5 1/2 In. 75.00
Figurine, Greek Potter, Seated, 1900, 8 In. ....195.00 To 215.00
Figurine, Horse, Rearing, Cream, Gold Base, Marked, 16 X 15 In. 195.00
Figurine, Lady Reclining, Shell, Matte, Pink Triangle, 8 X 9 In. 450.00
Figurine, Lady With Water Jar, Cup, Blue 3F 1216–20 Mark, 18 In. 300.00
Figurine, Lady, Art Deco, Blue Dress, Pink Triangle Mark, 9 In. 295.00
Figurine, Lady, Art Deco, Slate Blue Dress, Signed, 9 3/4 In. 245.00
Figurine, Lady, Cupid On Shoulder, 1900, 14 In. 400.00
Figurine, Maiden With Cupid On Shoulder, Classical, 14 In. 400.00
Figurine, Mother With Young Boys, Triangle Mark, 16 1/4 In. 695.00
Figurine, Nude Leaning Against Rock Formation, 15 1/4 In. 350.00
Figurine, Nude, Pink Triangle Mark, 1940s, 8 In. 140.00
Figurine, Peasant Boy & Girl, C.1900, 13 In. 325.00
Figurine, Polar Bear, On All 4 Legs 160.00
Figurine, Polar Bear, Sitting 140.00
Figurine, Shepherdess, Rose Toga, Sheepskin Robe, 14 3/4 In. 575.00
Figurine, Stallion, Standing, Rectangular Base, 8 1/2 In. 65.00
Figurine, Tiger, Stalking, 21 In. 125.00
Figurine, Tiger, Stalking, Pink Triangle Mark, 19 X 9 1/2 In. 115.00
Figurine, Woman, Beige & Green Gown, Holding Bowl, 20 In. 550.00
Jar, Art Nouveau, Maiden Face, Character, 9 In. 400.00
Vase, 2 Protruding Roses, 8 Leaves, Handle, 6 In. 65.00
Vase, Cream Ground, Tan, Green Seashore Scene, Lady, Marked, 12 In. 595.00
Vase, Dutch Girl, Matte Finish, Marked, 12 In. 425.00
Vase, Floral, Relief, C.1900, 14 In. 160.00
Vase, Maiden, Art Nouveau, 17 In. 400.00
Vase, Merman & Mermaid Rising From Waves, 13 1/2 In. ....*Illus* 525.00
Vase, Relief Flowers, C.1900, 14 In. ....120.00 To 150.00
Vase, Sirens On Waves, Art Nouveau, 17 In., Pair 750.00
Vase, Woman Figure, Cream, Bronze, Gold, Pink Triangle, 14 3/4 In. 395.00

Royal Flemish glass was made during the late 1880s in New Bedford, Massachusetts, by the Mt. Washington Glass Works. It is a colored satin glass decorated with dark colors and raised gold designs. The glass was patented in 1894. It was supposed to resemble stained glass windows.

ROYAL FLEMISH, Cookie Jar, Grapes 795.00
Cookie Jar, Large Roses 1475.00
Cracker Jar, Pink, Mauve, & Maroon, Coins ....1500.00 To 2250.00
Vase, Bulbous, Squatty, Pansies, Gold Borders, 5 3/4 In. 1750.00
Vase, Gold Serpent & Falcon, Tan & Red, Bulbous, 10 1/2 In. 3500.00
Vase, Pansies, Gold Border & Tracery, 7 1/4 X 5 3/4 In. 1750.00

ROYAL HAEGER, see Haeger
ROYAL IVY, see Pressed Glass, Royal Ivy
ROYAL OAK, see Pressed Glass, Royal Oak
ROYAL RUDOLSTADT, see Rudolstadt

Royal Vienna was established in Vienna, Austria, by Claude Innocentius du Paquier in 1719. In 1744, the firm began using a shield mark taken from the coat of arms of the Hapsburg royal family. Viewed upside down, the shield looks like a beehive; it became known as the "beehive mark." The factory closed in 1864. Since then, many German, Austrian, and Japanese factories have reproduced Royal Vienna wares, complete with the original shield or "beehive" mark.

ROYAL VIENNA, see also Beehive

ROYAL VIENNA, Candlestick, 3 Angels, Florals, C.1860, 14 In.	450.00
Charger, Rape Of Daughters Of Leucippus, Label, 16 1/4 In.	2310.00
Clock, Mantel, Drum Movement, Cupids, Marked, C.1900, 15 1/8 In.	715.00
Cookie Jar, Hand Painted, Artist Signed	95.00
Ewer, Chariot Of Venus & Cupid, Stand, Marked, 23 1/4 In., Pair	1980.00
Figurine, 18th Century Lady & Gentleman, Marked, 35 In., Pair	3300.00
Figurine, Boy, Impressed Beehive & 837, 7 In.	285.00
Figurine, Neptune & Amphitrite, Seated, Marked, C.1755, 10 In.	330.00
Figurine, Young Boy, Enameled, Onyx Base, Beehive, 7 In.	285.00
Jardiniere, 2 Bust Portrait, Cobalt, Gold Feet & Handle	200.00
Lamp, Musicians In Medallion, Gold On Cobalt, Marked, 10 In.	145.00
Plate, Blue Mark, Signed Kroeller, Script Title, 9 1/2 In.	350.00
Plate, Center Medallion, 2 Women Gazing At Fire, 10 3/4 In.	125.00
Plate, Diana & Cupid, Border Panels, Marked, 9 7/8 In., Pair	550.00
Plate, Jeweled, Center Scene, Marked KPM, 10 In., Pair	1850.00
Plate, Marie Antoinette & Desdemona, 9 5/8 In., Pair	990.00
Plate, Painted Scene, Cobalt Rim, Raised Gold & White Jewels	650.00
Plate, Painted, Gilded, Title, Description, Beehive, 9 In.	300.00
Plate, Portrait, Lady, Raised Gold Border, Wagner, 9 1/2 In.	550.00
Sugar & Creamer, Pink & Gold, Portraits	85.00
Tray, Wine, Man & Woman Center, Border, Handles, 15 In.Diam.	175.00
Urn, Cover, Classic, Pink, Blue, Gold Handles, Beehive, 25 In.	1200.00
Vase, Cover, Courting Couple Panels, Marked, 20 1/4 In., Pair	550.00
Vase, Covered, Stand, Lohengrin & Elsa, Artist F.Holzl, 46 In.	3100.00
Vase, Cupid Scene, Cobalt, Reticulated Top, Handles, 5 1/2 In.	295.00
Vase, Girl & Putto, Pale Green, Gilt, Beehive Mark, 11 1/2 In.	225.00
Vase, Girl, String Instrument, Covered, Footed, Handles, 12 In.	750.00
Vase, Lid, Allover Frieze, Gilt, Marked, C.1900, 21 5/8 In., Pr.	1650.00
Vase, Nude Scene, Maroon & Gold, Pierced Lid, 9 In.	450.00
Vase, Portrait Of Girl, 2 Handles, Cover, 11 1/2 In.	750.00
Vase, Portrait, Gold, Bottle Shape, Wagner Teresita, 7 In.	595.00
Vase, Portrait, Raised Arabesque, Turquoise, Wagner, 13 In.	795.00
Vase, Portrait, Raised Gold, Signed, 15 1/2 In.	875.00
Vase, Queen Louise Descending Palace Steps, 10 3/4 In.	625.00

Worcester porcelains were made in Worcester, England, from about 1751. The firm went through many different periods and name changes. It became the Worcester Royal Porcelain Company, Ltd., in 1862. Today collectors call the porcelains made after 1862 "Royal Worcester." In 1976, the firm merged with W. T. Copeland to become Royal Worcester Spode. Some early products of the factory are listed under Worcester.

ROYAL WORCESTER, Basket, Gold Trim, Green Mark, 3 1/2 In.	120.00
Biscuit Jar, Floral, Silver Plate Top, Rim, Handle, 6 In.	265.00
Biscuit Jar, Flowers, Foliage, Silver Plated Top & Handle	265.00
Biscuit Jar, Gold Trim, Raised Pattern, Marked, 6 In.	195.00
Biscuit Jar, Mark, Beige & Aqua Satin, 1897, 6 In.	195.00
Biscuit Jar, Silver Plate Top & Handle, 1899 Mark, 7 In.	295.00
Biscuit Jar, Swirl Pattern, Daisies, Fuchsias, Marked, 7 In.	275.00
Bottle, Cologne, Pansies, Silver Cap, Dated 1887, 3 3/4in.	220.00

Cake Plate, Sterling Silver Band, Roses & Garlands, 11 In. 125.00
Candle Snuffer, Cook, White Apron, Pink, Purple Mark 75.00
Candle Snuffer, Mr. Caudle, C.1889 .... 175.00
Candle Snuffer, Mrs. Caudle, C.1889 .... 175.00
Candle Snuffer, Punch 45.00
Candlestick, Spiral, Neoclassical, Marked, 11 In., Pair 132.00
Chocolate Pot, Pitcher, Bird, Floral, Bulbous, 1750–70, 7 In. 500.00
Compote, Pierced Rim, 4 Putti Supports, C.1870, 12 3/4 In. 450.00
Creamer, Gold Design, Purple Mark 110.00
Cup & Saucer, Blue & White, Demitasse, C.1884 .... 25.00
Cup & Saucer, Floral Design, Gold Tracery, Demitasse 45.00
Cup & Saucer, Hyde Park 20.00
Cup, Lavinia, Demitasse 15.00
Cup, Pope's England Visit, 1982, Demitasse 25.00
Ewer, Floral, Acanthus Leaf, Turquoise, 15 1/2 In. 650.00
Ewer, Floral, Cream, Dragon Handle, Green Stamp, 11 1/2 In. 175.00
Ewer, Floral, Gilded, Bamboo Handle, Signed, 1889, 10 1/4 In. 250.00
Ewer, No.29115, 5 1/2 In. 75.00
Ewer, Purple Flowers, Cream Ground, Gold Trim, 9 In. 180.00
Figurine, Against The Wind, White, 1870, 12 In. 475.00
Figurine, Airedale, No.3026 .... 150.00
Figurine, Anne Boleyn, 8 In. 475.00
Figurine, Blond Girl, White Rabbits, F.G.Doughty, 5 5/8 In. 275.00
Figurine, Boy Carrying Basket, Marked, 9 In. 550.00
Figurine, Bullfinch Seated On Rock, 2 1/4 In. ....55.00 To 60.00
Figurine, Cairo Water Carrier, Stained Ivory, Marked, 9 In. 385.00
Figurine, Caroline, 7 1/2 In. 500.00
Figurine, Cricklite Water Carriers, 10 3/4 In., Pair 522.00
Figurine, Eastern Water Carriers, 20 In., Pair 17500.00
Figurine, First Cuckoo, F.G.Doughty, 6 1/2 In. 185.00
Figurine, Friday's Child 115.00
Figurine, Grandmother's Dress, No.3081, Purple Mark 145.00
Figurine, Grecian Water Carriers, Marked, 10 1/4 In., Pair 1650.00
Figurine, Hereford Bull, Doris Lindner 375.00
Figurine, John Bull, Shot Enamel, Gold, Marked, 1903, 7 In. 425.00
Figurine, Joy & Sorrow, Ladies & Birds, Marked, 9 In., Pair 895.00
Figurine, June, Boy On Rock Playing Harmonica, 6 In. 145.00
Figurine, Little Boy Blue, Lying Next To Sheep 50.00
Figurine, Mary Queen Of Scots, 8 In. 475.00
Figurine, Michael, No.2912 .... 125.00
Figurine, Noelle, 4 In. 115.00
Figurine, Peter Pan With Rabbit, Seated, 8 In. ....150.00 To 170.00
Figurine, Pomeranian, 5 1/2 X 5 1/4 In. 125.00
Figurine, Rabbit, Basket On Back, No.2514, Marked, 4 3/4 In. 450.00
Figurine, Scotsman, Enamel, Green & Gold, Marked, 1903, 6 In. 425.00
Figurine, Sorrow, Glazed, 9 In. ....175.00 To 200.00
Figurine, Sunday's Child, 4 1/2 In. ....89.00 To 110.00
Figurine, Wednesday's Child, 6 1/2 In. ....110.00 To 115.00
Figurine, Wind, 1916, 6 In. ....120.00 To 125.00
Figurine, Yankee, Dated 1906, 6 3/4 In. 425.00
Figurine, Yankee, Shot Enamel, Tan & Gold, Marked, 6 3/4 In. 425.00
Figurine, Young Farmer, No.3433, Signed F.S.Doughty 155.00
Flask, Geese, Dragonflies, Marked, 1878, 19 1/2 In., Pair 2310.00
Group, 3 Hounds, No.3132, 1930s, Doris Lindner 350.00
Jug, Gold, Man & Woman Head, 2 Sides, 1903, Marked, 11 In. 595.00
Jug, Mask, Figural 550.00
Lamp, Fairy, Gilded Water Carriers, Clarke, 17 In. 990.00
Mush Set, Child's, Florals On Deep Pink, 3 Piece 45.00
Pitcher, Beige Satin, Flowers, Gold Trim, Marked, 1902, 6 In. 135.00
Pitcher, Bird, W.Powell, 3 1/2 In. 59.00
Pitcher, Dolphin Handle, Yellow Ground, Leaves, 8 In. 295.00
Pitcher, Elephant Head Handle, 6 1/2 In. 275.00
Pitcher, Flat Back, Flowers, Cream Ground, 6 1/4 In. 145.00
Pitcher, Gold Florals, Cream Ground, 1889, 3 3/4 In. 60.00

Pitcher, Gold Mums, Red Outlined, 1888 Mark, 6 1/4 In. 145.00
Pitcher, Leaf Shape, Satin, Leaf Frond Handle, Marked, 7 In. 225.00
Pitcher, Yellow, Gold Vines, Dolphin Handle, 1885, 7 1/2 In. 295.00
Plate, Bird, Deep Blue, Signed, 9 In. 190.00
Plate, Blue Willow Pattern, C.1880, 11 In. 29.00
Plate, Enamel Rim, Stylized Florets, 12 1/2 In., Set Of 12 .... 240.00
Plate, Gold Rim, Floral Center, C.1880, 10 1/2 In., Set Of 6 .... 1500.00
Plate, Rabbit & Flying Geese, Cobalt Foliage, 10 In. 60.00
Plate, Tapestry Type Border, Floral Center, 10 In. 47.50
Salt & Pepper, Hand & Fishscale, Frosted 50.00
Sugar Shaker, Figural, Girl, No.1103, Marked, 7 1/2 In. 450.00
Sugar, Creamer, Cup & Saucer, Fruit Design, Artist Signed 500.00
Teapot, Floral, Beige Ground 250.00
Urn, Floral Reserves, Orange, Handles, 7 1/2 In., Pair 375.00
Vase, Autumn Colors, Pierced, Persian Shape, Marked, 12 In. 550.00
Vase, Bamboo & Gold, 2 1/2 In., Pair 65.00
Vase, Beige Satin, Flower, Gold Trim, Base, Marked, 7 In. 325.00
Vase, Bronze & Gilt Lily Pads, Base, 1882, Marked, 6 3/4 In. 192.00
Vase, Cornucopia, Scroll Base, Mark, Floral, 1898, 7 1/8 In. 335.00
Vase, Double Bamboo, 8 In. 225.00
Vase, Dragonfly & Roses, 4 In. 75.00
Vase, Enameled Dots, Butterflies, Signed, C.1890, 7 1/2 In. 950.00
Vase, Flared, Hand Painted Flowers, 1880 Mark, 16 1/4 In. 300.00
Vase, Floral, Beige Satin, 3 Opening, C.1913, Marked, 4 In. 158.00
Vase, Floral, Beige, Rope Handle, 1893, Marked, 5 1/2 In. 225.00
Vase, Flowers & Butterflies, 17 1/2 In. 750.00
Vase, Gold Dragon Handle & Flowers, 8 In. 345.00
Vase, Gold Outlined Leaves, Dragon Handle, 1887 Mark, 8 In. 435.00
Vase, Mums, Cream, Coin Gold, Dog Handles, 14 In., Pair 200.00
Vase, Oriental Vines, Ivory, Covered, Marked, 14 3/4 In. 605.00
Vase, Reticulated Gold Neck, Handles, Bird, 1885, 13 In. 495.00
Vase, Serpent Handles, Spattered Gold, 1890 Mark, 8 3/4 In. 498.00
Vase, Stylized Blossoms, Yellow, Gilt, Bulbous, 9 1/2 In. 85.00
Vase, Wicker, Blue Ground, Pink Flowers, Dated 1873, 8 In. 450.00

Roycroft products were made by the Roycrofter community of East Aurora, New York, in the late nineteenth and early twentieth centuries. The community was founded by Elbert Hubbard, famous philosopher, writer, and artist. The workshops owned by the community made furniture, metalware, leatherwork, embroidery, and jewelry. A printshop produced many signs, books, and the magazines that promoted the sayings of Elbert Hubbard.

ROYCROFT, Bean Pot, Cover, Brown, 4 In. 20.00
Bookends, Copper, Open Frame, Side Design, Marked, 8 1/2 In. 38.50
Bookmark, Suede, Fringed, Build Strong, Elbert Hubbard, 11 In. 22.00
Box, Mahogany, Copper Trim, Swing Handles, C.1911, 8 X 14 X 12 In. 1800.00
Candleholder, Mottled Green, Pair 95.00
Chamberstick, Brass Finish, Footed, Bobeches, 2 1/4 In., Pair 27.50
Chamberstick, Round Indents, Dark Patina, Marked, 3 In., Pair 44.00
Console Set, Steel, Polished, Acid Finished, Signed, C.1910 .... 100.00
Crumber Set 60.00
Frame, Oak, Holds 6 Pictures, Logo, C.1900, 11 X 37 1/2 In. 650.00
Frame, Picture, Incised Flower, Tracery, Art Nouveau, 5 X 6 In. 125.00
Frame, Standing, Brass Finish, Marked, 6 3/8 X 4 3/8 In. 33.00
Honey Pot 12.00
Jar, Tan, Cover, 4 In. 25.00
Jar, Tobacco, Cover, 6 Slots, Burnished Copper Finish, Marked, 8 In. 44.00
Jug, Handle, Logo In Base, Brown Glaze, 5 In. 18.00
Jug, Maple Syrup, Original Tag, 13 1/2 Oz. 25.00
Lamp, Bottle, Blue, Hexagonal, Brass Base, Marked, 18 1/4 In. 120.00
Lamp, Copper, Hammered, Pedestal, Dome Shade, Marked, 18 In. 412.50
Letter Opener, Buffalo Envelope Co., Copper 25.00
Mirror, Wall, Oak, Rectangular Frame, 23 X 29 In. 250.00
Plate, Logo Center, 8 In. 85.00

Sconce, Arrowhead Shape, 8 In.	95.00
Sconce, Hammered Copper, Medium Patina, Marked, 8 3/4 In., Pair	154.00
Tray, Hammered Brass, Handles, Octagonal, Marked, 9 3/4 In.	49.50
Tray, Pen, Hammered Copper, 11 In.	28.00
Vase, 6 1/2 In.	275.00
Vase, American Beauty, Copper, Hammered, Marked, 12 1/4 In.	330.00
Vase, Banded Design, Hammered Copper, Marked, 5 In.	220.00
Vase, Copper, Hammered, Applied Silver Band, Marked, 6 1/4 X 3 In.	467.50
Vase, Hammered Brass Finish, Marked, 4 5/8 In.	77.00
Vase, Silver Geometric Over Copper, 6 In.	235.00
Vase, Strap & Stud Details, Elongated Neck, Signed, 12 1/4 In.	225.00
Vase, Stylized Incised Bell Shaped Flowers, 10 3/4 In.	175.00

ROZANE, see Roseville

R. R. P. C.
U.S.A.
Roseville, O.

RRP is the mark used by the firm of Robinson–Ransbottom. It is not a mark of the more famous Roseville Pottery. The Ransbottom brothers started a pottery in 1900 in Ironspot, Ohio. In 1920, they merged with the Robinson Clay Product Company of Akron, Ohio, to become Robinson–Ransbottom. The factory is still working.

RRP CO., Cookie Jar, Wise Bird	35.00
Vase, Green, Brown Spaniel Dog, 6 In.	20.00

The RS Germany mark was used on porcelain made at the factory of Reinhold Schlegelmilch from about 1910 to 1956 in Tillowitz, Germany. It was sold decorated and undecorated. The Schlegelmilch family made porcelains marked in many ways. Each type is listed separately. See also ES Germany, RS Poland, RS Prussia, RS Silesia, RS Suhl, and RS Tillowitz.

RS GERMANY, Ashtray, Cox Brownies, 1913	45.00
Ashtray, Red Poppies	37.50
Berry Set, Yellow & Pink Roses, 7 Piece	135.00
Bonbon, Bird On Floral Branch, Handles, Blue Mark, 7 1/2 In.	65.00
Bowl, Floral, Shell Molded, 3 1/4 In.	16.00
Bowl, Flowers, Cream Ground, Gold Trim, Green Mark, 10 In.	80.00
Bowl, Iris, Steeple Mark, 10 In.	65.00
Bowl, Lilies, Leaves, Pale Beige, Green Ground, 9 In.	78.00
Bowl, Open Handles, Shell Molded Floral, 3 1/4 In.	16.00
Bowl, Pastel Morning Glories, Scalloped, 9 In.	46.50
Bowl, Peach Lilies, Green, White Ground, 9 1/2 In.	45.00
Bowl, Pierced Handles, Floral, 7 1/4 In.	22.00
Bowl, Salmon Roses, Gold Band, Black, 3 Handles, 6 1/2 In.	66.00
Bowl, Swans, Oval, 7 In.	45.00
Box, Trinket, Floral, Green Mark, 2 3/4 In.	35.00
Cake Plate, Tulips At Center, Green Ground, 10 In.	69.00
Cake Plate, White Azalea Blossoms, Pale Green, Handles, 9 In.	35.00
Cake Set, Yellow Roses, 7 Piece	65.00
Celery, Roses, 12 1/2 In.	52.00
Celery, Roses, Pink Ground, Blue Mark, 5 X 10 1/2 In.	60.00
Chocolate Pot, Floral Design, Blue Mark, 9 1/2 In.	155.00
Chocolate Pot, White Roses, Green Trim, Individual, Marked	75.00
Chocolate Set, Blossoms Over White Ground, Gold Band, 9 Piece	185.00
Chocolate Set, Grapes & Leaves, Marked, 7 Piece	450.00
Chocolate Set, Pink Rose, Gold Band, Blue Mark, 13 Piece	30.00
Compote, Scenic, Mill & Windmill, Pedestal, Large	275.00
Cracker Jar, Pink Roses, Handles	90.00
Creamer, Roses, Gold Knobby Handle, Scalloped Rim, 3 3/4 In.	65.00
Cup & Saucer, Iris Design, Large	35.00
Cup & Saucer, Pink Roses, Green Border	35.00
Cup & Saucer, Roses, Gold, Demitasse	30.00
Dish, Bone, Cherub Design, Blue Mark	25.00
Dish, Cheese & Cracker, Floral, Pale Green Rim, 10 In.	45.00
Dish, Red Peonies, Glossy Tan Ground, 3 Sections, Blue Mark	30.00
Dish, White, Gold Trim, Handle, Blue Mark	22.00
Fernery, 4–Footed, Ornate Mold, 7 In.	90.00

Hair Receiver, Pale Green, Flowers 40.00
Hair Receiver, Roses, Gold Leaves, Covered, Green Mark ....55.00 To 65.00
Hatpin Holder, 2 Bands Of Roses & Gold, Pink 50.00
Hatpin Holder, Calla Lilies 70.00
Hatpin Holder, Orange Poppies, Green Mark 50.00
Hatpin Holder, Peach Floral, Gold Highlights, Green Mark 65.00
Hatpin Holder, Roses, Blue Mark 55.00
Hatpin Holder, White Roses, Pastel Greens 60.00
Holder, Pencil, Roses, Compliments Omaha Crockery Co. 67.50
Mustard, Dogwood, Green & White 65.00
Nut Cup, Gold Trim, White, Set Of 6 .... 100.00
Nut Cup, White, Gold, Footed, Set Of 4 .... 25.00
Nut Set, Scalloped Gold Rims, Footed, Blue Mark, 9 Pieces 70.00
Plate, Carnations, Hand Painted, Open Handle, Green Mark, 9 In. 50.00
Plate, Carnations, Shaded Ground, 8 1/2 In. 35.00
Plate, Christmas Rose, White Roses, Blue Mark, 9 In. 27.00
Plate, Floral, Poppies, Hand Painted, 8 In. 45.00
Plate, Floral, White Ground, 8 1/2 In. 65.00
Plate, Green, Holly Red Berries, White Rose, 8 1/2 In. 55.00
Plate, Hand Painted, Open Handles, Carnations, 10 In. 40.00
Plate, Pink, White Carnation, Hand Painted, Open Handle 50.00
Plate, Roses, Green & White, Gold Trim, 8 In. 35.00
Plate, Tulip Design, Cream To Brown, Marked, 6 1/4 In. 17.50
Plate, White Tulips, Hand Painted, 6 1/4 In. 12.00
Powder Box, Pink Roses 25.00
Ramekin, Pink Roses, Satin Finish, Blue Mark 29.00
Salt & Pepper, Mustard, On Tray, 4 Piece 75.00
Salt, Footed, Pair 14.00
Shaving Mug, Floral, Steeple Mark 60.00
Sugar & Creamer, Chickadee & Bluebirds 90.00
Sugar & Creamer, Hand Painted Violets 45.00
Sugar & Creamer, Pink Roses, Gold Trim, 3 In. 100.00
Sugar & Creamer, White, Gold 25.00
Sugar, Cover, Floral, Green Mark 20.00
Syrup, Pale Roses, Green & White Ground, Gold Trim, Blue Mark 35.00
Toothpick, 2 Handles ....60.00 To 65.00
Toothpick, Peach Floral, Gold Highlights, 2 Handles, Green Mark 60.00
Toothpick, Roses, 3 Handles, Signed 45.00
Tray, Tulips, Gold, Handles, Oval, Marked, 7 3/4 In. 22.00
Trivet, Flowers, Leaves, Gold Tracing, Blue Mark, 6 1/4 In. 35.00
Vase, Blue, Floral, Green Ground, 6 In. 27.50
Vase, Parrots In Black Medallion, 8 In. 145.00
Wall Pocket, Parrot, Green Mark 85.00

The RS Poland (German) mark was used by the Reinhold Schlegelmilch factory at Tillowitz from about 1945 to 1956. This is one of many of the RS marks used. See also ES Germany, RS Germany, RS Prussia, RS Silesia, RS Suhl, and RS Tillowitz.

RS POLAND, Creamer, Florals, Red & Brown 55.00
Vase, Brown, Cream Ground, White Roses, Handles, Marked, 9 3/4 In. 145.00

"RS Prussia" is a mark that appears on porcelain made at the factory of Reinhold Schlegelmilch from the late 1870s to 1914 in Tillowitz, Germany, or on items made at the Erdmann Schlegelmilch factory in Suhl, Germany, from about 1910 to 1956. It was sold decorated or undecorated. The factories were owned by brothers. See also ES Germany, RS Germany, RS Poland, RS Silesia, RS Suhl, and RS Tillowitz.

RS PRUSSIA, Berry Bowl, Pink Roses, Shell Shaped 12.00
Berry Set, Blown–Out Iris Mold, Roses, 9 1/2 In.Bowl, 6 Piece 395.00
Berry Set, Blown–Out Lily Mold, Red Mark, 7 Piece 395.00
Berry Set, Green, Gold, Blue & White Ground, Marked, 7 Piece 350.00
Berry Set, Plume Mold, Reflected Flowers, Red Mark, 7 Piece 550.00
Berry Set, Red, Pink, & White Floral, Red Mark, 7 Piece 350.00

Berry Set, Roses & Snowballs, Red Mark, 7 Piece 600.00
Biscuit Jar, Portrait Both Sides, Lady, Flowers In Hair 575.00
Bowl, 6 Curved Panels, Center Roses, Footed, 10 1/2 X 3 1/2 In. 125.00
Bowl, 6–Sided Floral Molded–Out Border, Red Mark, Blue 145.00
Bowl, Barnyard Scene, Red Mark, Orange, 10 1/2 In. 750.00
Bowl, Blossoms, Scalloped Rim, Satin Finish, Red Mark, 6 1/4 In. 185.00
Bowl, Bluebird, Floral Center, Red Mark, 10 1/2 In. 425.00
Bowl, Cottage Scene, Green, Yellow, Orange, Sawtooth Mold, 10 In. 750.00
Bowl, Covered, Puffed Iris, Deep Green To Nile, 9 1/4 In. 260.00
Bowl, Daisy Scalloped Border, Hand Painted, Signed, Red Mark 175.00
Bowl, Fleur–De–Lis Rim, Gold Petals, Red Mark, 7 3/4 In. 140.00
Bowl, Floral Bottom, 30 Jewels, Black, Gold, Red Mark, 10 1/2 In. 325.00
Bowl, Floral Bowl Scene, 10 1/2 In. 200.00
Bowl, Floral, Grape Cluster, Marked, 10 In. 200.00
Bowl, Floral, Scalloped, Shell, Red Mark, 10 In. 150.00
Bowl, Flowers, White Ground, Marked, 11 1/2 In. 185.00
Bowl, Ice Cream, Floral, Aqua, Blown–Out Rim, 12 1/2 In. 225.00
Bowl, Ice Cream, Multicolor Roses & Daisies, Marked, 12 X 7 In. 230.00
Bowl, Icicle Mold, Flower Forms, Gold, Red Mark, 9 1/2 In. 175.00
Bowl, Iris Floral Design, Scalloped, Footed, Red Mark, 6 1/2 In. 52.00
Bowl, Iris Mold, Winter Season, Satin Finish, 10 1/2 In. 950.00
Bowl, Iris, Poppies, Shadow Flowers, Red Mark, 10 1/2 In. 275.00
Bowl, Iris, Puff Mold, Red Mark, 9 1/2 In. 205.00
Bowl, Lilac, Scalloped Rim, Red Mark, 6 1/4 In. 185.00
Bowl, Lilies, Green Ground, Red Mark, 10 1/2 In. 160.00
Bowl, Mill Scene, 8 In. 350.00
Bowl, Opalescent Jeweling, Flower, Oval, Red Mark, 13 In. 250.00
Bowl, Orchid Mold, Fluted Edge, Red Mark, Green, 11 In. 200.00
Bowl, Pink & White Roses, Carnation, Red Mark, 9 1/2 In. 195.00
Bowl, Pink Roses, Open Handles, Red Mark, 13 1/2 X 6 1/2 In. 165.00
Bowl, Pink Roses, Snowballs, Green & Cream, Red Mark, 10 1/2 In. 195.00
Bowl, Pink, White Roses, Scalloped, Gold Rim, Red Mark, 5 1/2 In. 110.00
Bowl, Poppies, Red Mark, 10 1/2 In. 225.00
Bowl, Poppy Center, Dark Pink To White, Red Mark, 9 1/4 In. 185.00
Bowl, Poppy, Poppies & Leaves Center, Red Mark, 9 1/4 In. 195.00
Bowl, Purple, Floral Center, Red Mark, 11 In. 200.00
Bowl, Raised Poppies & Daisies, Gold Trim, Red Mark, 10 1/2 In. 95.00
Bowl, Red & Gold Top Band, Pink Flowers, Red Mark, 10 1/2 In. 350.00
Bowl, Red Border, Opal Jeweling, Marked, 13 X 8 In. 250.00
Bowl, Red, Pink, & White Floral, Red Mark, 11 In. 185.00
Bowl, Reflection In Water, Red Mark, 10 In. 300.00
Bowl, Rose & Garland, Embossed Feather Mold, 11 1/2 In. 190.00
Bowl, Roses, Gold Beading, Red Mark, White Ground, 10 In. 200.00
Bowl, Roses, Heavy Red & Gold All Around, Red Mark, 10 1/2 In. 275.00
Bowl, Roses, Satin, Footed, Crown Mark, 6 1/2 In. 35.00
Bowl, Sawtooth, Green & Gold Rim, Floral Center, 10 1/2 In. 130.00
Bowl, Scenic & Florals, Red Mark, 11 In. 225.00
Bowl, Summer Season, Bowl In Bowl, 10 1/2 In. 875.00
Bowl, Summer, Iris, Red Mark, 10 In. 750.00
Bowl, Swan & Pine Trees, Scalloped, 12 Points, Red Mark, 10 In. 300.00
Bowl, Swan & Temple, 11 In. 485.00
Bowl, Swans With Bluebirds Overhead, Floral Rim, Marked, 11 In. 475.00
Bowl, Violets, Roses, Fluted, Scalloped, 11 In. 110.00
Bowl, White Roses, Gold Trim, 5 Panels, Marked, 11 In. ....175.00 To 200.00
Bowl, White, Green Leaves, Raised Grapes, 10 In. 150.00
Bowl, Winter, Iris Mold, Red Mark, 9 1/2 In. 1000.00
Bowl, Winter, Iris Mold, Red Mark, 9 In. 950.00
Bowl, Winter, Red Mark, 10 1/2 In. 750.00
Bread Plate, Pink & White Roses, 11 X 7 In. 125.00
Butter Chip, Floral, Red Mark 40.00
Butter, Cover, Porcelain Insert, Roses Allover, Raised Enamel 695.00
Cake Plate, Allover Design Of Roses & Leaves, Red Mark, 12 In. 115.00
Cake Plate, Icicle Mold, Satin Finish, Red Mark, 9 1/2 In. 225.00
Cake Plate, Jeweled, 11 3/4 In. 175.00

Cake Plate, Leaf Shape, 11 In. 125.00
Cake Plate, Lime Green To White, Cream Pink Roses, Marked 275.00
Cake Plate, Red Arches, Cream & Gold, Red & Yellow Roses, Marked 175.00
Cake Plate, Rose Garland Design, Jewels, Red Mark 160.00
Cake Plate, Roses, Handle, 10 In. 165.00
Cake Plate, Sunflower Mold, 11 In. 100.00
Cake Plate, Swan, Open Handle, Icicle Mold, Red Mark, 11 In. 395.00
Cake Plate, Swans, Gazebo Scene, Open Handle, 11 1/4 In. 485.00
Candy Dish, Footed, Roses, Red Mark 65.00
Celery, Peacock Design, Icicle Mold, Signed, 12 In. 375.00
Celery, Poppy & Daisy, Scalloped Rim, Cut Handles, 12 1/2 In. 125.00
Celery, Purple Violets, 12 In. 50.00
Celery, Scalloped Rim, Handles, Poppies, Red Mark, 12 1/2 In. 220.00
Celery, Stippled Florals, Roses, Cream & Green, Red Mark, 12 In. 175.00
Chocolate Pot, Floral Finial, 6 Molded Feet, Red Mark, 9 In. 349.00
Chocolate Pot, Lavender, Magenta, Cinnamon, Pedestal, Marked 265.00
Chocolate Pot, Magenta & Pale Yellow, White Floral, 10 1/2 In. 175.00
Chocolate Pot, Pink & White Roses, Gold Trim, Red Mark, 11 In. 200.00
Chocolate Pot, Puffy, Floral, Signed 110.00
Chocolate Pot, Raised Gold, Roses, Footed, Red Mark 260.00
Chocolate Pot, Ripple & Quilt Pattern, Red Mark, 11 3/4 In. 295.00
Chocolate Pot, Roses, Gold Beading, Red Mark, White Ground 395.00
Chocolate Pot, Violets, Pink, Gold Trim, Marked, 9 1/4 In. 375.00
Chocolate Set, Double Handles, Roses, Gold Trim, 11 Piece 825.00
Chocolate Set, Floral, Red Mark, 4 Sets 735.00
Chocolate Set, Lilies On Pond, Icicle Mold, Marked 595.00
Chocolate Set, Pink Roses, Ivory Satin Ground, 9 Piece 295.00
Chocolate Set, Roses, Pearlized Green, Yellow, Red Mark, 9 Piece 375.00
Cocoa Pot, Portrait, Flossie, Leaf Feet 425.00
Coffee Cup, Melon Eater, Red Mark 200.00
Coffee Cup, Swan, Red Mark 150.00
Compote, Iris, Scalloped, Beige & Gold Design, 4 1/2 X 7 In. 300.00
Compote, Lilies, Beige, Gold, Satin Finish, Red Mark, 4 X 7 In. 350.00
Cookie Jar, Ribbed, Footed, Red Mark 225.00
Cracker Jar, Allover Color, Floral, Red Mark 250.00
Cracker Jar, Allover Floral, Ornate Handles, Covered, Red Mark 225.00
Cracker Jar, Colonial Figures, Floral 380.00
Cracker Jar, Green, Cream & Gold Handles, 8–Sided, Marked 295.00
Cracker Jar, Groupings Of Roses, 4 Scallops, Red Mark 350.00
Cracker Jar, Leaf Mold, Leaf Curved Handles, 10 Leaf Footed 275.00
Cracker Jar, Lebrun Portrait Knob, Covered 195.00
Cracker Jar, Pink Roses, Red Mark, 8 1/2 X 3 1/2 In. 150.00
Cracker Jar, Roses, Leaves, Pink Ground, Red Mark, 7 3/4 X 5 In. 135.00
Cracker Jar, Scalloped Top, Mint Green, Red Roses, Marked 225.00
Cracker Jar, White Tulips, Shaded Green, Red Mark 195.00
Creamer, Castle Scene, Signed, 3 1/2 In. ....195.00 To 225.00
Creamer, Church, Footed, Green Tint, Red Mark 200.00
Creamer, Green Cottage Scene, Red Mark 235.00
Creamer, Lavender, Yellow Flowers, Gold, Bluebirds In Flight 105.00
Creamer, Mill Scene, 8 Scalloped Feet, Marked 150.00
Creamer, Portrait, Queen Louise, Leaf Feet 265.00
Creamer, Scalloped Rim, Flowers, Gold Trim, Footed, 4 In. 105.00
Cup & Saucer, Blown–Out Body, Scalloped, Pink Roses, Red Mark 115.00
Cup & Saucer, Blown–Out, Blue Border, Flowers, Red Mark 145.00
Cup & Saucer, Chocolate, Floral 50.00
Cup & Saucer, Dogwood Blossom, Footed, Red Mark 450.00
Cup & Saucer, Pink Roses, Green Ground 72.00
Cup & Saucer, Roses With Swags, Gold Design 75.00
Cup & Saucer, Roses, Red Mark 125.00
Cup & Saucer, Sunflower Mold, Red Mark 135.00
Cup & Saucer, Swan, Red Mark, Pink Satin, Demitasse 95.00
Cup, White Flowers, Soft Green Ground, Red Mark 75.00
Demitasse Pot, Pink Ribbon & Roses, Red Mark, Blue & White 225.00
Dish, Cheese, Marked 120.00

Dish, Leaf Shape, 6 In. 12.00
Dish, Pearl Luster, Scalloped Edge, Roses, Gilding, 7 In. 40.00
Ewer, Poppy, 10 1/4 In. 275.00
Figurine, Dog, Pointer, Staffordshire Type, 8 In. 10.00
Hair Receiver, Florals, Square, Large 100.00
Hair Receiver, Jewels Outlined In Gold On Cover, Red Mark 100.00
Hair Receiver, Orange Roses, Gold Tracings, Red Mark, 4 1/2 In. 100.00
Hair Receiver, Shocking Pink Legs, Roses, Gold Swirls, Marked 95.00
Hair Receiver, Yellow Flowers On Lid, Blue Shading, Red Mark 165.00
Hatpin Holder, 3–Footed, Floral Design, Red Mark, 4 1/2 In. 250.00
Hatpin Holder, Perry ....*Illus* 800.00
Holder, Clock, Iridescent, Orange Design, Hand Painted, 7 In. 35.00
Inkwell, Dog, Sitting, Hinged Lid, Shaped Well, Enamel Design 150.00
Lamp, Fairy, Owl 37.50
Muffineer, Mill & Cottage Scene, Aqua, Green, Brown, Satin 150.00
Mustache Cup, Beveled Mirror 200.00
Mustache Cup, Flowers, Gold Trim, Signed 85.00
Mustard, Cottage Scene, Spoon, Browns 150.00
Mustard, Figural, Swan, Red Mark 145.00
Mustard, Portrait, Blown–Out Flowers, Tiffany Red, Red Mark 150.00
Mustard, Spoon, Mums 45.00
Mustard, Yellow Roses, Red Mark 90.00
Pitcher, Cider, Lily Design 175.00
Plate, 6 Medallions, Green & Orange Shading, Red Mark, 11 In. 165.00
Plate, Bluebirds, Red Mark, 10 1/2 In. ....450.00 To 550.00
Plate, Carnation Mold, Gold, Red & Pink Roses Design, 8 1/2 In. 138.00
Plate, Castle Scene, Red Mark, 8 1/4 In. 645.00
Plate, Chain Of Flowers, Roses, Ivy, Handle, Marked, 11 In. 250.00
Plate, Dice Player, Rope Rimmed 400.00
Plate, Dice Players, Marked Wurfelspieler & Murillia, 9 In. 395.00
Plate, Dogwood, Green & White, 8 1/2 In. 100.00
Plate, Embossed Shells Inner Rim, Carnations, Red Mark, 11 In. 215.00
Plate, Fall Season, Keyhole, Red Mark, 9 In. 900.00
Plate, Floral, Grape Cluster, Marked, 10 In. 200.00
Plate, Floral, Green Ground, Hand Painted, Red Mark, 8 1 2/In. 135.00
Plate, Fruits, Open Handles, Red Mark, 10 In. 150.00
Plate, Greek Key Border, Pink Roses, Gold, Open Handle, 12 In. 140.00
Plate, Hydrangeas, Scalloped, Gold Stencil, Red Mark, 7 3/4 In. 95.00
Plate, Icicle Mold, Open Handles, Cerise, 10 In. 100.00
Plate, Keyhole, Spring Season, 9 In. 900.00
Plate, Melon Boys, Keyhole Handles, Red Mark, 8 1/2 In. 850.00
Plate, Melon Boys, Keyhole, Jeweled, Green, Red Mark, 8 1/2 In. 950.00

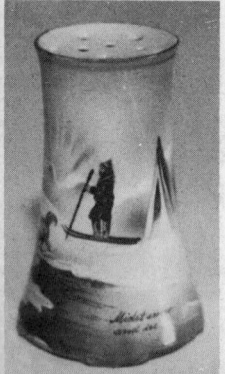
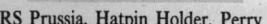

RS Prussia, Hatpin Holder, Perry   RS Prussia, Tray, Dresser, Fall Season

Plate, Old Man Of The Mountain, Red Mark, 10 1/2 In. 540.00
Plate, Open Handles, 4 Blown–Out Iris, Center Floral, 10 1/4 In. 225.00
Plate, Pink & White Iris, Gold Trim, Red Mark, 8 1/2 In. 85.00
Plate, Poppies, Daisies Reflected In Water, Red Mark, 8 1/2 In. 150.00
Plate, Poppies, Daisies, Gold Outline, Medallion, Red Mark, 11 In. 155.00
Plate, Portrait, 5 3/4 In. 10.00
Plate, Portrait, Keyhole, Marked, 9 In. 895.00
Plate, Puffed Artichoke, Florals, Handles, Red Mark, 11 5/8 In. 250.00
Plate, Roses, Hydrangeas, Ribbon & Jewel, Red Mark, 10 1/2 In. 185.00
Plate, Scalloped Rim, Gold, Red Mark, 6 In. 42.00
Plate, Sheepherder & Swallows, Red Mark, 11 In. 450.00
Plate, Snowbirds, Orange, Yellow, & Cream, Red Mark, 8 1/2 In. 950.00
Plate, Spring, Keyhole, Lavender, Red Mark, 9 In. .... 900.00 To 1000.00
Plate, Summer, Keyhole, Red Mark, 8 3/4 In. 800.00
Plate, Tigers, Open Handles, Red Mark, 10 1/2 In. 2700.00
Plate, Turkey, Red Mark, Black & White, 8 1/2 In. 550.00
Plate, Winter, Satin Finish, Red Mark, 10 1/2 In. .... 800.00 To 950.00
Platter, Yellow & Tan, 10 X 7 In. 45.00
Relish, Castle Scene, 8 Bluebirds, Open Handle, 8 X 4 In. 175.00
Relish, Floral, Red Mark 75.00
Relish, Medallion Mold, Reflecting Flowers, Red Mark 150.00
Relish, Pines & Pheasant, 12 X 6 In. 300.00
Relish, Red Roses, Red Mark, 9 1/2 In. 65.00
Relish, Scalloped, Handle, Gold Trim, Red Mark 50.00
Relish, Swan & Gazebo, Red Mark, 8 In. 150.00
Shaving Mug, Carnation, Shadow Flowers, Peach Roses, Red Mark 175.00
Sugar & Creamer, Castle Scene, Red Mark 450.00
Sugar & Creamer, Cover, Pedestal, Square Base, Red Mark 195.00
Sugar & Creamer, Mill & Cottage Scene, Green & White, Red Mark 350.00
Sugar & Creamer, Pink Roses, Leaves, Satin Finish, Covered 165.00
Sugar & Creamer, Red Roses, Cream Ground, Pedestal 175.00
Sugar & Creamer, Red Roses, Lavender 175.00
Sugar & Creamer, Roses With Shadows, Red Mark 165.00
Sugar & Creamer, Roses, Light Blue, 4–Footed, Ribbed, Red Mark 250.00
Sugar & Creamer, Swallows Over Water Lilies, Red Mark 385.00
Sugar & Creamer, Water Lilies, Light Blue, Icicle, Red Mark 250.00
Sugar & Creamer, Winter Scene, Green, Pedestal, Red Mark 450.00
Sugar Shaker, Colonial Figures, Red Mark 300.00
Sugar Shaker, Roses 98.00
Sugar Sifter, Red Roses, Bottom Handles, Red Mark 110.00
Sugar, Cover, Pink Floral, Ornate Handles, Red Mark 55.00
Sugar, Covered, Dogwood, Gold Trim, Red Mark 62.00
Sugar, Covered, Pink & White Poppies, Icicle, Red Mark 135.00
Sugar, Covered, Swan, Pearlized Finish, Marked 250.00
Sugar, Covered, Swan, Pearlized, Footed, Urn Shaped, Red Mark 200.00
Sugar, Dogwood Pattern, Beaded Rim, Gold Trim, Red Mark 65.00
Sugar, Peony, Handles 40.00
Sugar, Pink Roses, White Ground, Gold Tracery, Red Mark 50.00
Sugar, Raised Star, Crown Design On Lid 50.00
Syrup & Underplate, Swan 145.00
Syrup, Blown–Out Upper Body, Handle, Gold Stenciling, Red Mark 125.00
Syrup, Floral, Embossed Rim, C.1890, Red Mark 65.00
Syrup, Underplate, Point & Clover, Roses, Leaf Finial, Red Mark 225.00
Syrup, Underplate, Roses, Gold Edging, Red Mark 125.00
Tankard, 8 Ball Feet, Pink & Yellow Roses, Red Mark, 14 1/2 In. 625.00
Tankard, Ball & Leaf Mold, Handle, Spout, Red Mark, 10 1/2 In. 575.00
Tankard, Mill Scene, Brown & Tan, Acorn Mold, 11 1/2 In. 1700.00
Tankard, Pink & Yellow Roses, 8 Ball Feet, 14 1/2 In. 625.00
Tankard, Roses, Beaded Top, Red Mark, 13 1/2 In. 550.00
Tankard, Swan, White Ground, 2 Swans, Green Trees, Marked, 10 In. 350.00
Tea Set, Child's, 15 Piece 400.00
Tea Set, Pink Floral, Red Mark, 3 Piece 195.00
Tea Strainer, Red Mark, Turquoise 155.00
Toothpick, Carnation, Blue, White Ground, Roses, Handle, Red Mark 135.00

Tray, Bread, 2 Swans, Pink, Satin, Red Mark, 12 In. 300.00
Tray, Bun, Laurel Chain Pattern, Open Handles, Oblong, Red Mark 75.00
Tray, Bun, Mill Scene 495.00
Tray, Card, Basket Of Roses 60.00
Tray, Celery, Floral, Hand Painted, Red Mark 190.00
Tray, Dresser, Fall Season ....*Illus* 1650.00
Tray, Dresser, Fluted, Roses, Red Mark, 12 X 7 1/2 In. 135.00
Tray, Dresser, Poppies, Handles, Ruffled, Red Mark, 7 3/4 In. 235.00
Tray, Dresser, Red, Yellow Roses, 11 X 7 1/2 In. 139.00
Tray, Dresser, Scalloped, Handles, Roses, Marked, 12 X 7 1/2 In. 145.00
Tray, Dresser, Scalloped, Pierced Handles, 11 3/4 X 7 1/2 In. 75.00
Tray, Floral, Satin, Open Handle, Red Mark, 11 1/2 7 1/4 In. 145.00
Tray, Gold Border, Blown-Out Roses Border, 11 1/2 In. 135.00
Tray, Pin, Bouquet Of Flowers Hanging From Basket 95.00
Vase, Church, Green Tint, Red Mark, 4 In. 200.00
Vase, Dice Throwers Scene, Green, Jewels, Pedestal, Marked, 8 In. 550.00
Vase, Easter Lilies, Small Flower Clusters, Gold Trim, Red Mark 225.00
Vase, Lilies On Italian Green, Handles, Red Mark, 9 1/2 In. 375.00
Vase, Loving Cup Shape, Melon Eaters, Boy On Back, Marked, 5 In. 1200.00
Vase, Loving Cup Shape, Melon Eaters, Jeweled, 8 1/2 In. 1200.00
Vase, Melon Eaters, Jeweled, 2 Handles, Red Mark, 10 1/2 In. 1075.00
Vase, Open Sections, Easter Lilies, Red Mark, 9 In. 245.00
Vase, Peacock, Red Mark, 7 1/2 In. 395.00
Vase, Pheasant Handle, Red Mark, 9 In. 390.00
Vase, Pillow, Melon Eaters, Red Mark, 10 X 11 In. 2200.00
Vase, Pink Floral, Green Luster, 2 Jewels, Red Mark, 6 In. 95.00
Vase, Portrait, Lebrun, 10 In. 695.00
Vase, Roses, Handles, 10 1/2 In. 290.00
Vase, Roses, Pearl Jewels, Handles, Red Mark, 6 In. 275.00
Vase, Winter, Green, Gold Ground, Handle, Marked, 9 In. 295.00

The RS Silesia mark appears on porcelain made at the Reinhold Schlegelmilch factory in Tillowitz, Germany, from about 1920 to the mid-1930s. The Schlegelmilch family made porcelains marked in many ways. Each type is listed separately. See also ES Germany, RS Germany, RS Poland, RS Prussia, RS Suhl, and RS Tillowitz.

RS SILESIA, Plate, Pink Roses, 9 3/4 In. 15.00

RS Suhl was a mark used by the Erdmann Schlegelmilch factory in Suhl, Germany, from c. 1900 to the mid-1920s. The factory worked from 1861 to 1925. The Schlegelmilch family made porcelains in many places. See also ES Germany, RS Germany, RS Poland, RS Prussia, RS Silesia, and RS Tillowitz.

RS SUHL, Bowl, Iris Mold, Poinsettia, 10 In. 190.00
Vase, Daisies, Gray Ground, 12 In. 125.00

The RS Tillowitz mark was used by the Reinhold Schlegelmilch factory at Tillowitz, near Silesia, from about 1920 to the mid-1930s. Table services and ornamental pieces were made. See also ES Germany, RS Germany, RS Poland, RS Prussia, RS Silesia, and RS Suhl.

RS TILLOWITZ, Bonbon, Poppies, Pierced Handles, 6 1/4 X 7 1/4 In. 42.00
Bowl, Underplate, Roses & Violets, 9 1/2 In. 55.00
Flower Frog, 2-Part 37.00
Flower Frog, Mother-Of-Pearl, 2 Part 37.00
Tray, Dresser, Bird Of Paradise,, 4 X 13 In. 55.00
Vase, Floral Design, 8 In., Pair 85.00

Rubena Verde is a Victorian glassware that was shaded from red to green. It was first made by Hobbs, Brockunier and Company of Wheeling, West Virginia, about 1890.

RUBENA VERDE, Cheese, Covered, 5 3/4 In. 45.00
Finger Bowl, Threaded 80.00
Pitcher, Water, Thumbprint 165.00

Vase, Goblet Shape, Enameled Lady, 6 3/4 In. 225.00
Vase, Ruffled Top, Gold Enameling, 8 In. 70.00
Vase, Stick, 5 1/2 In. 50.00
Vase, Vaseline Applique, Footed, 4 X 8 1/4 In. 88.00

> *Rubena is a glassware that shades from red to clear. It was first made by George Duncan and Sons of Pittsburgh, Pennsylvania, about 1885. This coloring was used on many types of glassware. The pressed glass patterns of Royal Ivy and Royal Oak are listed under Pressed Glass.*

RUBENA, Berry Bowl, Honeycomb Pattern, Green To Red 85.00
  Bowl, Melon Shape, Ribbed, Hobbs, 9 In. 65.00
  Castor Set, 4 Bottles, Cut 495.00
  Compote, Honeycomb Pattern, Footed, 4 X 8 1/2 In. 150.00
  Condiment, Cranberry, Sugar Spoon, 3 Piece 205.00
  Creamer, Fluted Top, Swirl Bands, Clear Handle, 4 In. 65.00
  Cruet, Verde Thumbprint, Stopper, 6 3/4 In. 325.00
  Decanter, Wine, Threaded, Northwood 175.00
  Jug, Wine, Flowers, Pewter, Gold Wash, Hinged Lid, 12 3/4 In. 139.00
  Lamp, Hall, Frosted, Large 425.00
  Perfume Bottle, Cut Panels, Faceted Stopper, Cranberry To Clear 75.00
  Pitcher, Water, Optic, Hand Painted Flowers, Applied Handle 185.00
  Syrup, Inverted Thumbprint, Tapered 150.00
  Tumbler, Mother-Of-Pearl Herringbone 110.00
  Vase, Jack-In-The-Pulpit, Vaseline Edge, Cranberry To Clear, 11 In. 125.00

> *Ruby glass is the dark red color of the precious gemstone known as a ruby. It was a Victorian and twentieth-century glass. This dark red glass was shaped by many different processes to make many different types of ruby glass. It was a popular color in the 1940s.*

RUBY GLASS, see also Cranberry Glass; Pressed Glass; Souvenir
RUBY GLASS, Basket, Souvenir, State Fair, 1923, 5 1/2 In. 40.00
  Berry Bowl, New Hampshire 15.00
  Berry Bowl, Plume, Small 20.00
  Berry Set, New Jersey, 7 Piece 200.00
  Celery, Souvenir, Lambertsville, Pa. 55.00
  Compote, Fluted, Covered, 11 X 7 In. 20.00
  Compote, Huber, Scalloped, Flint 75.00
  Compote, Persian 45.00
  Compote, Thumbprint, 6 In. 45.00
  Creamer, Heart Band ....20.00 To 25.00
  Creamer, Mother 1916, Miniature 40.00
  Creamer, Nail 50.00
  Creamer, Pavonia ....40.00 To 45.00
  Creamer, Riverside, Miniature 35.00
  Creamer, Thumbprint, Applied Handle, Large 65.00
  Cruet, Snail, Flashed 225.00
  Cruet, Wimpole, Clear, Large, Original Stopper 135.00
  Cup, Souvenir, Oelwein, Iowa 20.00
  Goblet, Prism, Flint 30.00
  Goblet, Red Block 25.00
  Lamp, Toy, Fluted, Ball Shade, Wright 85.00
  Mug, Arched Ovals, Souvenir 35.00
  Mug, Bordered Ellipse ....20.00 To 30.00
  Mug, Root Beer, Alice, 2 In. 15.00
  Mug, Root Beer, Alma, 2 In. 15.00
  Mug, Souvenir, Syracuse, N.Y., Heart Band 30.00
  Mug, Sunk Honeycomb, Florence, Atlantic City 1907, 3 In. 22.00
  Pitcher, Heart, 4 3/4 In. 36.00
  Pitcher, Tankard, York Herringbone, 12 In. 95.00
  Pitcher, Water, Stars & Pinwheels, Crystal Overlay 125.00
  Pitcher, Water, Thumbprint With Vintage Engraving 135.00
  Salt & Pepper, Bulging Loops ....65.00 To 95.00
  Saltshaker, Beaded Swag, Pair 30.00

Saltshaker, Block & Lattice	35.00
Saltshaker, Florette, Pair	65.00
Saltshaker, Punty Band, Pair	30.00
Saltshaker, Truncated Cube	18.00
Sauce, Thumbprint, Round	30.00
Spill, Diamond Point, Flint	35.00
Spill, Horn Of Plenty, Flint	60.00
Spooner, Button & Arches	35.00
Spooner, Crystal Wedding	45.00
Spooner, Paneled Dogwood	45.00
Spooner, Pavonia	40.00
Spooner, Royal Crystal	45.00
Spooner, Spearpoint Band, Gold Trim, Frosted	45.00
Spooner, Thumbprint With Fern & Berry	50.00
Spooner, Thumbprint With Vintage Engraving	35.00
Spooner, Thumbprint, Etching	45.00
Spooner, Triple Triangle	25.00
Spooner, Truncated Cube	30.00
Sugar & Creamer, Deer & Castle Etched, Covered	95.00
Sugar, Cathedral, Covered	65.00
Sugar, Cherry & Cable, Flashed, Covered, Northwood	38.00
Table Set, Pavonia, Etching, 4 Piece	295.00
Table Set, Red Block, 4 Piece	225.00
Table Set, Riverside, 4 Piece	315.00
Table Set, Triple Triangle, 4 Piece	245.00 To 265.00
Tankard, Milk, Thumbprint, 8 1/2 In.	85.00
Toothpick, Atlantic City 1900, 2 1/2 In.	22.00
Toothpick, Button & Arches, Mother, 1947	15.00
Toothpick, Truncated Cube	30.00
Tumbler, Fleur–De–Lis, Gold Trim	38.00
Tumbler, Heart Band	20.00
Tumbler, Loop & Block	28.00
Tumbler, Pavonia	30.00
Tumbler, Souvenir, Chicago, 1904	35.00
Vase, Clear Applied Rigaree Neck, Bulbous, 5 In.	35.00
Vase, Jack–In–The–Pulpit, Westmoreland, 6 In.	15.00
Wine, Arched Ovals	30.00
Wine, Sunk Honeycomb	35.00

Rudolstadt was a faience factory in the Thuringia region of Germany from 1720 to about 1791. In 1854, Ernst Bohne began working in the area. From about 1887 to 1918, the New York and Rudolstadt Pottery made decorated porcelain marked with the RW and crown familiar to collectors. This porcelain was imported by Lewis Straus and Sons of New York, which later became Nathan Straus and Sons. The word "Royal" was included in their import mark. Collectors often call it "Royal Rudolstadt." Late nineteenth– and early twentieth–century pieces are most commonly found today.

RUDOLSTADT, see also Kewpie

RUDOLSTADT, Biscuit Jar, Royal, C.1890	150.00
Bowl, Floral, White, Gold Rim, Marked R W, 9 X 3 In.	55.00
Charger, Reticulated Edge, Rose Design, C.1870, Footed	85.00
Chop Plate, A.Koch, Royal	55.00
Creamer, Floral, Cream Ground, Royal, 5 1/2 In.	25.00
Creamer, Gold Handle, Feathering Gold Over Drape Pattern	45.00
Cup & Saucer, Golliwogs, Lechler	25.00
Dish, Roses, Handled, Royal	42.00
Dresser Set, Violets, Gold Trim, 3 Piece	125.00
Pitcher, Bird On Branch, Cream Ground, Marked, 8 X 5 In.	75.00
Planter, Floral, Round, 9 In.	55.00
Plate, Pastel Roses, Royal, 8 1/2 In.	30.00
Plate, Pink, Yellow, White Roses, Piecrust Edge, Royal, 8 In.	27.00
Plate, Roses, Royal, Artist Signed, 6 In.	20.00
Plate, Winter Scene, Ice Man, Sleighs, Marked Royal, 8 1/4 In.	65.00

Plate, Winter, Man & Sleigh Scene, 8 1/4 In.	58.00
Sugar, Floral	35.00
Sugar, Multicolored Flowers, Gold Handles, Dome Lid, Blue Mark	45.00
Tea Set, Pink & Purple Pansies, Gold Trim, Royal, 5 Piece	95.00
Tray, Day Lily Pattern, Cut Handles, Royal, 12 In.	67.50
Vase, Wine Ground, Melitha At Well, Marked Royal, 8 1/2 In.	395.00

> *Rugs have been used in the American home since the seventeenth century. The Oriental rug of that time was often used on a table, not on the floor. Rag rugs, hooked rugs, and braided rugs were made by housewives from scraps of material.*

RUG, Afghan Bokahara, 7 Ft. 4 In. X 10 Ft.	55.00
Aubusson, Central Gold Cartouche, 6 Ft. 4 In. X 5 Ft. 10 In.	5060.00
Aubusson, Floral Cluster, Cartouche, 6 Ft. 3 In. X 6 Ft.	6325.00
Aubusson, Flower Medallion, Pale Blue, Rinceaux Border, 108 X 70 In.	1100.00
Badshir, Herati, Guard Border, C.1860, 4 1/3 X 9 Ft.	1200.00
Bahktiari, Black, Ivory Flower, Red, Blue, 5 X 6 Ft.	650.00
Bahktiari, Concentric Medallions, 10 Ft. 4 In. X 12 Ft.	3000.00
Baluch, 3-Part Center Panel, 3 Ft. 3 In. X 4 Ft. 9 In.	145.00
Baluch, Allover Mina Khani Design, Red Border, 19th Century, 4 X 7 Ft.	800.00
Baluch, Diamond Trellis Center, Wide Open Border, 5 X 8 Ft.	1900.00
Baluch, Floral Grid, Ivory Accents, Red Border, 3 Ft. 2 In. X 6 Ft.	350.00
Baluch, Hooked Diamonds, Star Border, 2 Ft. 10 In. X 6 1/2 Ft.	250.00
Baluch, Woven Loops, Bag Face, 9 Ft. X 2 Ft. 1 In., Pair	225.00
Bidjar, Allover Herati Design, 8 Ft. 5 In. X 12 Ft.	5000.00
Bidjar, Allover Lateral Design, 11 Ft. 9 In. X 8 Ft. 10 In.	7000.00
Bidjar, Flower Medallions, Dark Blue, 6 Ft. 9 In. X 4 1/2 Ft.	425.00
Bidjar, Flowering Vines, Center Medallion, 3 Ft. 4 In. X 5 Ft. 2 In.	400.00
Bidjar, Forked Tendrils, Palmettes, Red, 18 Ft. 6 In. X 11 Ft.	6325.00
Bidjar, Red Field, Ivory & Blue Border, 14 Ft. 4 In. X 12 Ft.	5225.00
Bidjar, Red Ground, Green, Blue, Pink, Yellow, 5 X 8 Ft.	1200.00
Bidjar, Roses, Blue Field, Turtle Border, 4 Ft. 3 In. X 6 Ft.	900.00
Bokhara, 45 X 66 In.	1225.00
Brangwyn, Stylized Foliate Design, C.1930, 9 1/2 X 8 3/4 Ft.	3525.00
Bruhns, Alternating Parallel Lines, Dots, 140 X 98 1/2 In.	4400.00
Cabistan, 3 Ft. 1 In. X 5 Ft. 6 In.	725.00
Chinese, Center Medallion Of Flowers & Sprigs, 9 Ft. X 11 Ft. 7 In.	300.00
Chinese, Center Medallion, Stylized Vines, 4 Ft. 3 In. X 6 Ft. 8 In.	225.00
Chinese, Detached Blossoming Plants, 2 Ft. 8 In. X 5 Ft. 9 In.	300.00
Chinese, Floral Rondel, Floral Border, 13 Ft. 8 In. X 10 Ft.	850.00
Chinese, Gray Lavender, Sprigs, Blossoms, Blue Border, 19 X 12 Ft.	475.00
Chinese, Ivory & Beige, Blue Field, Wool, 14 Ft. 3 In. X 12 Ft.	500.00
Chinese, Pink & Blue Floral Sprays, Ivory Field, 107 X 73 1/2 In.	750.00
Coin Spot, Fringe, Late 1800s, 76 X 27 In.	137.50
Daghestan, Prayer, Pictorial, Camels, Riders, 3 Ft. X 3 Ft. 4 In.	2500.00
Ferahan, Allover Cartouche Trellis, Floral Border, 4 X 6 Ft.	1700.00
Gashgai, Hexagonal Field, Floral Trellis, 4 Ft. 9 In. X 6 Ft. 9 In.	2100.00
Gorevan, Geometric Design, Blue Ground, 7 X 10 Ft.	675.00
Hamadan, Bibkabad, Red Field, Floral Lattice, 21 Ft. X 5 In. X 12 Ft.	700.00
Hamadan, Center Medallion, Allover Floral, 2 Ft. 5 In. X 4 Ft. 1 In.	60.00
Hamadan, Gold Medallion, Floral Sprays, 3 Ft. 7 In. X 11 Ft.	210.00
Hamadan, Hexagonal Field, Stepped Medallions, 2 Ft. X 3 Ft. 10 In.	150.00
Hamadan, Mhina Khani Design, Blue Field, 5 Ft. 8 In. X 18 Ft. 2 In.	1200.00
Hamadan, Red Field, Allover Florals, 20th Century, 3 Ft. X 4 Ft. 10 In.	130.00
Hamadan, Red Lozenge, Blue Field, Florals, 4 Ft. 4 In. X 6 Ft. 6 In.	225.00
Hamadan, Runner, Red Field, Allover Florals, 2 Ft. 7 In. X 6 Ft. 9 In.	250.00
Hamadan, Vases, Rust Field, 4 Ft. 7 In. X 7 Ft. 3 In.	425.00
Heriz, Blue Medallion, Allover Floral, 9 Ft. 6 In. X 12 Ft. 2 In.	2250.00
Heriz, Flowers On Gold Stems, 19th Century, Turtle Border, 9 X 9 Ft.	3000.00
Heriz, Geometric Floral, 4 Borders, 3 Ft. 7 In. X 5 Ft. 2 In.	325.00
Heriz, Geometric Medallion, Ivory, Blue, 12 Ft. X 8 Ft. 9 In.	2200.00
Heriz, Persia, C.1875, 16 Ft. 8 In. X 12 Ft. 6 In.	7700.00
Heriz, Red Ground, Flowers, Diamonds, Blue, Brown, Ivory, 11 X 9 Ft.	1900.00
Heriz, Serapi, Flowers, Diamonds, Blue, Brown, Ivory, 11 X 9 Ft.	1900.00

Heriz, Wine, Dark Blue Medallion, Turtle Border, 6 Ft. X 4 Ft. 8 In. 600.00
Hooked, Allover Various Design, 12 Ft. 4 In. X 8 Ft. 10 In. 4400.00
Hooked, Beige, Red, Green, Black, Flowers, C.1900, 32 X 56 In. 550.00
Hooked, Branch With Leaves, 8 Butterflies, Swirling Ground, 26 X 36 In. 65.00
Hooked, Brown, Blue, Orange, White, Reindeer, 22 X 37 In. 495.00
Hooked, Calico Cat On Ottoman, Foliage Borders, 28 1/2 X 45 In. 220.00
Hooked, Center Medallion, American Shield Corners, 1898, 44 X 35 In. 450.00
Hooked, Dennis The Menace, 1950s, 3 X 5 In. 85.00
Hooked, Diamond Design, Basket Of Flowers, Blackbirds, 6 X 2 Ft. 250.00
Hooked, Dog & Cat Center, 1800s, Wool, 5 X 2 1/2 Ft. 135.00
Hooked, Dog Center, Beige Ground, Border Stripes, 17 1/2 X 38 1/2 In. 100.00
Hooked, Dog's Head, Gray Ground, Signed Alla, 31 1/2 X 33 In. 55.00
Hooked, Floral Center Medallion, Birds, Natural Ground, 40 X 51 In. 475.00
Hooked, Floral Design, Oval, 30 X 19 In. 12.50
Hooked, Fruit & Vegetables, 6 X 2 1/2 Ft. 125.00
Hooked, Geometric & Floral, Earth Tones, 8 Ft. 4 In. X 6 Ft. 245.00
Hooked, Hearth, Mosaic Tile Pattern, 3 Diamonds, 7 1/2 X 25 3/4 In. 495.00
Hooked, Kittens In Basket, Gray, Red, Brown, & Blue, 39 1/2 X 25 In. 250.00
Hooked, Lion On Cliff, Yarn, Mounted On Wooden Frame, 28 X 42 In. 325.00
Hooked, Newfoundland, Owl On Limb, 19th Century, 32 X 61 In. 150.00
Hooked, Pictorial, Spaniel In Landscape, 28 1/4 X 50 In. 1320.00
Hooked, Pink, Green, Yellow, Brown, Floral, 9 X 5 Ft. 412.00
Hooked, Pretty Kitty, 30 1/2 In. 450.00
Hooked, Rag, Brown Dog, Outlined In Black, Red Ribbon, 20 1/2 X 38 In. 170.00
Hooked, Rag, Floral Design, Olive Ground, 23 X 37 1/2 In. 65.00
Hooked, Rag, Foliage, Blue, Brown, White, Red, Olive Gray, 27 X 29 In. 55.00
Hooked, Rag, Geomtric Floral Design, 23 X 54 1/2 In. 70.00
Hooked, Rag, Multicolored Marbelized Design, 33 X 40 In. 195.00
Hooked, Rag, Quatrefoil Medallion, Beige, Black Border, 36 X 70 In. 115.00
Hooked, Rag, Scrolled Leaf Design Each Corner, 29 X 40 In. 10.00
Hooked, Rag, Stylized Deer Leaping Over Waves, 25 X 47 In. 275.00
Hooked, Striped Cat Center, Linear Squares Ground, 33 X 50 In. 1100.00
Hooked, Vegetables & Fruits, 39 X 68 In. 125.00
Hooked, Wool, Beige, Green Border, Floral Center, 1940s, 9 X 12 In. 25.00
India, Center Flower Clusters, 1940s, 10 Ft. 5 In. X 11 Ft. 8 In. 100.00
India, Floral Center Medallion, 20th Century, 14 Ft. 10 In. X 12 Ft. 275.00
India, Natural, Greek Key Border, 2 Green Circles, C.1910, 102 X 77 In. 75.00
Indo–Sarouk, Diamond, Maroon Ground, 5 X 3 Ft. 175.00
Iranian, Floral, Center Medallion, 2 Ft. 8 In. X 4 Ft. 8 In. 100.00
Iranian, Multicolored Floral, Green Ground, 1 Ft. 10 In. X 3 Ft. 200.00
Joval, 9 Patterned Border, 4 Ft. X 2 Ft. 5 In. 275.00
Joval, Mirror Guls, Hourglass Design, 3 Ft. 8 In. X 2 1/2 Ft. 275.00
Kashan, Floral Arabesques, Center Medallion, 4 1/3 Ft. X 6 Ft. 10 In. 3900.00
Kazak, 3 Medallions, Ivory Border, C.1880, 6 Ft. 8 In. X 4 Ft. 3 In. 1100.00
Kazak, Boteh & Vines, Star Border, 3 Ft. 9 In. X 8 Ft. 4 In. 1500.00
Kazak, Center Eagle Medallion, 19th Century, 5 Ft. 2 In. X 7 Ft. 2400.00
Kazak, Diagonal Striped Field, 3 Ft. 11 In. X 5 Ft. 9 In. 2400.00
Kazak, Medallions Enclosing S Forms, 4 Ft. 10 In. X 7 Ft. 10 In. 1500.00
Kazak, Red Field, Garden Keyhole Center, 7 Ft. 10 In. X 5 Ft. 6 In. 2400.00
Kazak, Reds & Blues, Blue Ground, 4 Ft. 2 In. X 6 Ft. 9 In. 900.00
Kazak, Row Of Medallions, Ivory Border, 4 Ft. 6 In. X 10 Ft. 5 In. 550.00
Kazvin, White Field, Floral Medallion, 8 Ft. 10 In. X 18 Ft. 6 In. 1200.00
Kerman, Cypress Design, Ivory Field, 6 Minor Borders, 12 X 9 Ft. 2600.00
Kerman, Floral On Pale Green Ground, 10 X 12 1/2 Ft. 800.00
Kerman, Floral Trellis Center, Cloud Band, 5 Ft. 3 In. X 20 Ft. 9 In. 200.00
Kerman, Magenta Field, Detached Floral Sprays, 4 Ft. 5 In. X 7 Ft. 150.00
Kerman, Magenta, Ivory Medallion, Floral Border, 2 1/4 X 3 1/2 Ft. 150.00
Kerman, Open Ivory Ground, Floral Medallion, 4 Ft. 3 In. X 8 Ft. 6 In. 375.00
Kerman, Saddle Cover, Pictorial, Urn, Game Animals, 3 Ft. X 3 Ft. 8 In. 550.00
Kuba, 3 Medallions, Blue Field, Georgian Border, 5 1/3 X 3 1/4 Ft. 425.00
Kuba, Center Design, Allover Medallions, 4 Ft. 3 In. X 5 Ft. 2 In. 2000.00
Kuba, Medallions Of Eagle Profiles, 4 Ft. 3 In. X 9 Ft. 5 In. 2500.00
Kuba, Trees, Speckled Chickens, 3 Ft. 1 In. X 4 Ft. 5 In. 4000.00
Kurdish, Bag Face, Blue Grid Of Diamonds, Ivory, 3 X 3 Ft. 375.00

Kurdish, Bag Face, Ovoid Forms In Border, 1 Ft. 8 In. X 2 Ft. 3 In. 125.00
Kurdish, Geometric Design, Mustard Borders, 6 1/3 X 3 2/3 Ft. 8 In. 100.00
Lillihan, Floral On Wine Ground, 2 Ft. 7 In. X 4 Ft. 75.00
Lillihan, Floral Spray, Red, Blue Border, 6 1/4 X 5 Ft. 2 In. 375.00
Luri, Corner Spandrels, Diamonds, Animals Center, 3 Ft. 10 In. X 7 Ft. 800.00
Pakistan, Terra Cotta, Medallions, White Border, 8 1/3 X 5 1/4 Ft. 160.00
Persian, Allover Herati Design, Corner Spandrels, 5 Ft. X 9 Ft. 4 In. 600.00
Persian, Field Of Stylized Floral Grid, 1850, 4 Ft. 6 In. X 7 Ft. 1900.00
Persian, Lattice Design, Brown, Brick Border, 106 X 93 In. 780.00
Persian, Runner, Floral Lattice Field, 3 Ft. 1 In. X 12 Ft. 8 In. 800.00
Sarouk, Allover Florals, Floral Border, 9 Ft. X 11 Ft. 10 In. 3000.00
Sarouk, Arabesque Medallion, Floral Edge, 14 Ft. 2 In. X 10 Ft. 5 In. 9075.00
Sarouk, Cross Shaped Flowers, Painted Maroon Field, 2 X 2 2/3 Ft. 80.00
Sarouk, Dark Navy Blue Ground, 4 Ft. 2 In. X 6 Ft. 7 In. 130.00
Sarouk, Ferahan, Central Rose, Floral Medallion, 12 Ft. 3 In. X 9 Ft. 7150.00
Sarouk, Floral Design, Red Ground, 6 Ft. 3 In. X 8 Ft. 9 In. 1500.00
Sarouk, Floral Design, Rose Ground, 1 Ft. 11 In. X 2 Ft. 4 In. 170.00
Sarouk, Floral Design, Salmon Red Ground, 8 Ft. 6 In. X 11 Ft. 8 In. 800.00
Sarouk, Floral Medallion, Dark Blue Ground, 12 X 20 Ft. 1200.00
Sarouk, Floral Sprays, Painted Maroon Field, 2 X 4 Ft. 250.00
Sarouk, Floral Sprays, Red, Palmette Border, C.1940, 9 X 11 1/2 Ft. 1800.00
Sarouk, Flower Filled Center Medallion, 10 Ft. 4 In. X 6 Ft. 8 In. 3850.00
Sarouk, Hanging Lamp Design, 2 Ft. 1 In. X 2 Ft. 9 In. 235.00
Sarouk, Intricate Floral Design, Red Ground, 4 Ft. 5 In. X 6 Ft. 5 In. 700.00
Sarouk, Midnight Blue, Yellow Medallion, Blue Border, 2 X 2 1/2 Ft. 50.00
Sarouk, Mulberry Red Field, Floral Sprays, 10 1/4 X 15 Ft. 2300.00
Sarouk, Red Medallion, Garden Wall Ends, Ivory, 4 1/2 X 6 2/3 Ft. 2600.00
Sarouk, Red Pink Field, Floral Sprays, Border, 2 X 2 1/2 Ft. 130.00
Senneh, Floral Sprays, Stylized Medallions, C.1910, 4 Ft. 7 In. X 6 Ft. 2100.00
Senneh, Saddle Cover, Herati Filled Spandrels, 3 Ft. 2 In. X 3 Ft. 2100.00
Serab, Open Camel Field, Trefoil Border, 9 Ft. 2 In. X 4 Ft. 4 In. 3740.00
Serab, Persia, C.1900, Overall Design, 13 Ft. 8 In. X 8 Ft. 9 In. 2750.00
Serapi, Persia, C.1900, Central Medallion, Blue, 13 Ft. 4 In. X 10 Ft. 9900.00
Shirvan, 1 Row Of Hooked Diamonds, Polygons, 3 Ft. 5 In. X 7 Ft. 6 In. 200.00
Shirvan, Blue Lattice, Ivory Field, Knotted Ends, 3 1/2 X 5 Ft. 950.00
Shirvan, Runner, Row Of Octagons, Medallions, 3 Ft. 6 In.X 9 Ft. 11 In. 750.00
Shirvan, Stylized Leaves, Flowers & Medallion Rows, Ivory, 38 X 61 In. 280.00
Shirvan, Yellow Field, Colored Polygons, 3 Ft. 11 In. X 5 Ft. 9 In. 1200.00
Soumak, Geometric Design, 1886, 8 Ft. 9 In. X 7 Ft. 2 In. 4950.00
Spanish, Ascending Floral Bouquets, Birds, 9 Ft. 11 In. X 7 Ft. 6 In. 5500.00
Sultanabad, Boteh & Cypress Design, 6 Ft. 5 In. X 4 Ft. 3 In. 300.00
Sultanabad, Overall Design, Palmettes, Vines, 10 Ft. 4 In. X 8 1/2 Ft. 3025.00
Tabriz, Center Arabesque Medallion, C.1900, 11 1/3 X 8 Ft. 10 In. 5500.00
Tabriz, Center Medallion, Corner Spandrels, 8 Ft. 7 In. X 12 Ft. 5 In. 3600.00
Tabriz, Geometric Designs, 2 Ft. 8 In. X 12 Ft. 8 In. 85.00
Tabriz, Medallion, Leaf Palmettes, 10 Ft. 2 In. X 8 Ft. 4 In. 4400.00
Tekke, Mafrash, 6 Guls, Geometric Border, 2 Ft. 10 In. X 1 Ft. 375.00
Torba, Rows Of Ashik Designs, Ivory Border, 2 2/3 X 1 Ft. 2 In. 175.00
Turkish, Double Ended Medallion, Mustard, Cartouche, 62 X 50 In. 320.00
Turkish, Prayer, Black & Plum Field, Floral, 3 X 5 1/2 Ft. 150.00
Turkish, Purple Field, Stars At Corners, 3 Ft. 4 In. X 4 Ft. 9 In. 150.00
Turkish, Red Field, Ivory Medallion, Star Border, 3 1/3 X 5 2/3 Ft. 110.00
Turkoman, Dyrnak Guls, Pinwheels, Pole Tree, 5 Ft. 7 In. X 10 Ft. 6 In. 2200.00
Turkoman, Trellis Of Ashik, Tasseled, 3 Ft. 11 In. X 2 Ft. 6 In. 1500.00
Yomud, Ensi, Blue Candelabra, Ivory Lattice, Red Field, 3 3/4 X 5 Ft. 700.00

Rumrill Pottery was designed by George Rumrill of Little Rock,
RumRill *Arkansas. From 1930 to 1933, it was produced by the Red Wing Pottery of Red Wing, Minnesota. In 1938, production was transferred to the Shawnee Pottery in Zanesville, Ohio. Production ceased in the 1940s.*

RUMRILL, Ewer, Dragon Handle, Grinning Gargoyle On Front, 10 In. 30.00
Jardiniere, Turtle Handles 20.00
Pitcher, Tilt, Ball, Blue Spatter, Ice Lip, 7 In. 18.00

Planter, Wall, Wishing Well 30.00
Vase, Fan, Mottled Blue, 6 1/4 In. 12.00

Ruskin is a British art pottery of the twentieth century. The Ruskin Pottery was started by William Howson Taylor; his name was used as the mark until about 1899. The factory, at West Smethwick, Birmingham, England, stopped making new pieces in 1933 but continued to glaze and sell the remaining wares until 1935. The art pottery is noted for the exceptional glazes.

RUSKIN, Vase, Green Foliage, Yellow Luster, 5 In. ....40.00 To 50.00
Vase, Green Foliage, Yellow Luster, 9 In. ....85.00 To 95.00
Vase, Mottled Red, Blue, Purple, 8 In. 75.00

Russel Wright designed dinnerwares in modern shapes for four companies. Iroquois China Company, Harker China Company, Steubenville Pottery, and Justin Therod and Sons made dishes marked "Russel Wright." The Steubenville wares, first made in 1938, are the most common today. This section lists the dinnerwares by Wright. He was a designer of domestic and industrial wares, including furniture, aluminum, radios, interiors, and glassware.

RUSSEL WRIGHT, Butter, Blue 35.00
Carafe, Nutmeg 30.00
Carafe, Wine, Iroquois, Blue 15.00
Casserole, Chartreuse, Covered 25.00
Casserole, Gray, Covered 35.00
Casserole, Pink, Grip Handle, Covered 15.00
Coaster, Coral 4.00
Creamer, Blue 5.50
Cup & Saucer, Pink 6.00
Cup, Pink, Iroquois Casual 4.00
Decanter, Turquoise 18.00
Dinner Set, Nutmeg, Iroquois, 33 Piece 95.00
Pitcher, Water, Gray 16.00
Plate, Pink, Iroquois, 10 In. 5.00
Plate, Seafoam Green, 10 In. 7.50
Relish, Chartreuse 30.00
Salt & Pepper, Pink 6.50
Sugar & Creamer, Coral 15.00
Sugar, Pink, Covered 10.00
Teapot, Chartreuse 35.00
Teapot, Gray, Iroquois ....28.50 To 29.00
Teapot, Light Green, Iroquois 20.00
Tray, Coral 30.00

Sabino glass was made in the 1920s and 1930s in Paris, France. Founded by Marius–Ernest Sabino, the firm was noted for Art Deco lamps, vases, figurines, and animals in clear, colored, and opalescent glass. Production stopped during World War II but resumed in the 1960s with the manufacture of nude figurines and small opalescent glass animals. The new pieces are a slightly different color and can be recognized.

SABINO, Figurine, Baby Bird On Stump, 4 In. 55.00
Inkwell, Snail, Open Top, Signed 65.00
Perfume Bottle, Nudes In Relief, France 110.00
Powder Jar, Covered, 4 In. 100.00
Sign, Prism 65.00

Salopian ware was made by the Caughley factory of England during the eighteenth century. The early pieces were blue and white with some colored decorations. Another ware called "Salopian" today is an elaborately color–transfer decorated tableware made during the late nineteenth century.

SALOPIAN, Creamer, White Stag, Polychrome 385.00
Jug, White Tobacco Leaf, Blue Chinoiserie Design 350.00

Night–Light, Teapot, Blue & White 3900.00
Saucer, Black Transfer, Deer, Polychrome Enameling 45.00
Waste Bowl, Brown Transfer Of Britannia, Florals, 6 3/8 In. 55.00
SALT & PEPPER, see Porcelain; Pressed Glass; etc.

Salt glaze has a grayish–white, pitted, orange–peel–textured surface. It is a method of decoration that has been used since the eighteenth century. Salt–glazed pieces are still being made.

SALT GLAZE, Box, Salt, Blue, Advertising 165.00
Churn, Palm Tree, 3 Gal. 140.00
Cooler, Wine, Embossed Angels, Family Crests, Pennsylvania Dutch 225.00
Creamer, Flowers, Eagle, Blue Striping, Castleford, 4 1/2 In. 50.00
Crock, Butter, Wire Bail 200.00
Jar, Rings At Neck, Ovoid, 8 1/2 X 7 1/2 In. 95.00
Jug, Argyle, Registry Mark, Blue & Gray, 7 7/8 In. 75.00
Jug, Embossed Eagle, 1 Gal. 100.00
Jug, Embossed Soldiers & Phoenix Birds, August 1856, 7 1/4 In. 120.00
Jug, Embossed Soldiers, Birds, Ridgway & Abington, 7 1/4 In. 118.00
Jug, Incised Cobalt Blue Swan, 1 Gal. 98.00
Jug, Lamson & Swasey, Portland, Maine, 1 Gal. 50.00
Jug, Mineral Spring Water, Embossed Wright Stoneware, 2 Gal. 85.00
Mug, Figural, Stag, Brown, Cobalt Blue Trim 110.00
Mug, Figural, Town Crier, Cobalt Blue & Gray 95.00
Pitcher, Molded Figures, Medium Blue, 9 In. 75.00
Teapot, Foo Dog Finial, Spherical, England, 4 1/2 In. 425.00
Toby Jug, Duke Of Wellington, White, 6 3/4 In. 25.00
Vase, Opening Leaves Pattern, White, 5 3/4 In. 45.00

ABCDE   *Samplers were made in America from the early 1700s. The best examples were made from 1790 to 1840. Long, narrow samplers are usually older than square ones. Early samplers just had stitching or alphabets. The later examples had numerals, borders, and pictorial decorations. Those with mottoes are mid–Victorian.*

SAMPLER, Adam & Eve, Animals, Alston, Age 13, 1831, 16 1/2 X 12 1/2 In. 750.00
Adam & Eve, Mary Taylor, Age 10, 23 3/4 X 28 1/2 In. 300.00
Alphabet & Numbers, Sarah B.Wiley, 1850, Unframed, 7 X 9 In. 130.00
Alphabet & Numerals, Hannah Bingham, 1788, 6 X 8 3/4 In. 125.00
Alphabet With Motto, Alice Dodge, 1827, Lyme, N.H., 9 X 15 In. 285.00
Alphabet, 1896, 10 X 10 1/2 In. 65.00
Alphabet, 1897, Signed, Framed, 8 X 13 In. 165.00
Alphabet, Flowers, Dog Over Fence, 1862, 18 X 14 1/2 In. 225.00
Alphabet, Rosa, 1881, 11 1/2 X 32 In. 70.00
Alphabet, Verse, Susanna Roland, Age 15, 1813, 9 5/8 X 11 5/8 In. 175.00
Alphabets, Flowers, Building, 1808, 16 3/4 X 18 1/4 In. 150.00
Alphabets, Martha Jane Reynolds, Ohio, July 4, 1835, 19 1/2 X 20 In. 775.00
Animals, Dancing Black Children, Banjo, Dated 1877, 20 X 20 In 145.00
Ann Hodges, Age 13, April 20th, 14 1/2 X 18 1/4 In. 1200.00
Black Family Saying Grace, God Bless Our Home, C.1910, 16 X 20 In. 80.00
Butterflies, House, Trees, Flowers, ABC, 1837, 12 1/2 X 14 In. 55.00
Dinah Cameron, Silk Thread, Linen, Frame, 1829, 17 3/4 X 15 In. 1650.00
Dogs, Deer, Houses, Trees, Flowers, 1839, 13 X 22 In. 60.00
Elizabeth M.Carson, Age 12, Frame, 1842, 10 1/4 X 18 1/4 In. 300.00
Family Register, Henry & Phebe Mathewson, 1818, Framed, 22 X 18 In. 225.00
Flowers In Urns, Birds, Isabella Robertson, Dated 1817 .... 400.00
Flowers, Trees, Birds, Martha Loving, Age 13, 1838, 17 X 21 In. 600.00
Hannah Whittier, Essex County, Mass., 1805, 15 X 12 1/4 In. 1980.00
House & Lawn, Lambs, Birds & Flowers, Verses, 1818 .... 2250.00
House, Trees, Saying, C.1830 .... 98.00
Lady, At Needlework Frame, Susanna H.White, 1806, 14 X 19 In. 1400.00
Linen, Elizabeth Moore, Age 20, April 20, 1780, 7 3/4 X 10 In. 390.00
Lydia T.I.Damon, Age 16, June 4, 1832, 16 X 14 1/4 In. 1500.00
Maria Cheever, Age 12, April 20, 1838, 26 X 17 1/2 In. 500.00
Mary Kent, Horncastle, Homespun, 1796, 14 1/4 X 16 1/2 In. 450.00
Memorial, Joan Damon, Born Feb.18, 1813, Scituate, Mass., 15 X 14 In. 800.00

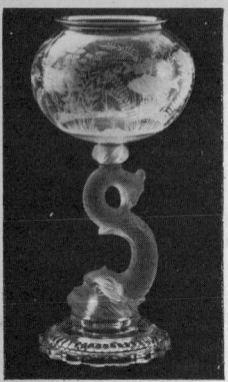

Sandwich Glass, Fishbowl,
Clear, Etched, C.1870, 16 1/2 In.

Any lithographed can with a picture is of more value to the collector than a lithographed can with just names.

Any paper-labeled can that can be dated before 1875 is rare.

Any ad that pictures an American flag or a black has added value. Known brand names are also of greater value.

Mennonite Symbol, ABC, Lancaster City, 1889, Framed, 10 X 8 In.	140.00
Multicolored Alphabets, Verse, E.Clarkson, 1799, 18 1/2 X 22 In.	675.00
Nancy Lenox, Cambridge, Mass., Verse, 1800, 16 X 12 1/4 In.	2640.00
Phebe Atherton, England, Landscape, 1829, 21 1/2 X 20 1/2 In.	350.00
Picture, Zebar Taylor, 1848, Framed, 14 X 18 In.	210.00
Pious Verse, Polly Archer, New England, 1788, 21 X 15 3/4 In.	2200.00
To Lucinda, By Cousin, C.P.Prudden, 1839, 19 1/2 X 20 1/2 In.	650.00
Tulips, Wreath, Dog & Trees, 1804, 8 X 8 In.	130.00
Verse, Flowers, Lucretia Abbott, Age 12, Detroit, 1829, 17 X 18 In.	1650.00
Vining Borders, A Friend In Need, April 12, 1854, 13 1/2 15 In.	75.00
Wedding, Edythe Crow–Frederic Vogel, C.1910, Framed, 13 X 17 In.	40.00

Samson and Company, a French firm specializing in the reproduction of collectible wares of many countries and periods, was founded in Paris in the early nineteenth century. Chelsea, Meissen, Famille Verte, and Chinese Export porcelain are some of the wares that have been reproduced by the company. The firm uses a variety of marks on the reproductions. It is still in operation.

SAMSON, Plate, Armorial, Oriental Export Style, Borders, Set Of 4	140.00
Platter, Scroll Borders, Armorial Center, 20 1/2 In.	130.00

Sand Babies were used as decorations on a line of children's dishes made by the Royal Bayreuth China Company. The children are playing at the seaside. Collectors use the names "Sand Babies" and "Beach Babies" interchangeably.

SAND BABIES, Creamer, Royal Bayreuth, 3 1/2 In.	75.00
Planter, 2 Handles, Royal Bayreuth, Blue Mark, 3 In.	110.00
Vase, 3 Handles, Royal Bayreuth, 3 5/8 In.	90.00
Vase, Handles, Royal Bayreuth, 3 1/2 In.	55.00

Sandwich glass is any one of the myriad types of glass made by the Boston and Sandwich Glass Works in Sandwich, Massachusetts, between 1825 and 1888. It is often very difficult to be sure whether a piece was really made at the Sandwich factory because so many types were made there and similar pieces were made at other glass factories.

SANDWICH GLASS, see also Pressed Glass, etc.

SANDWICH GLASS, Basket, Fruit, Floral & Butterfly Cut	150.00
Bottle, Cologne, Star & Punty, Vaseline	275.00
Bottle, Scent, Amethyst, 2 3/8 In.	50.00
Bowl, Dolphin Base, Etched, C.1870, 16 1/2 In.	500.00
Bowl, Horn Of Plenty, 7 1/2 In.	65.00
Bowl, Rayed Peacock Eye, 7 In.	65.00

Butter Chip, Set Of 6	75.00
Butter, Popcorn, Covered, C.1860	49.00
Butter, Sawtooth, Covered	75.00
Butter, Teal Blue, Covered, Indiana	150.00
Candlestick, Cobalt Blue, 9 In., Pair	500.00
Candlestick, Crucifix, Canary Tiered Base, Flint, 11 1/4 In.	350.00
Candlestick, Dolphin, Canary, 10 1/2 In., Pair	875.00
Candlestick, Double Step Dolphin, Vaseline, Pair	625.00
Candlestick, Vaseline, Hexagonal Base, 9 7/8 In., Pair	350.00
Celery, Tulip, Looped Rim, Facets, Lavender, 1840, 10 In.	425.00
Compote, Cable, Flint	48.00
Compote, Narrow Flute, Black & Gold Bands, Covered, 6 In.	65.00
Creamer, Stippled Woodflower	45.00
Dish, Peacock Eye Variation, Lacy, 5 1/4 X 1 3/8 In.	35.00
Dish, Pipes Of Pan, Lacy, Oblong, 8 In.	525.00
Dish, Roman Rosette, Lacy, 4 1/8 In.	30.00
Dish, Thistle, Lacy, 5 1/4 X 1 1/4 In.	20.00
Fishbowl, Clear, Etched, C.1870, 16 1/2 In. ....*Illus*	500.00
Goblet, Frosted Leaf	60.00
Goblet, Horn Of Plenty ....65.00 To	75.00
Goblet, New England Pineapple	75.00
Goblet, Ripple, Pair	50.00
Inkwell, Sapphire Blue, Hinged, Covered	100.00
Lamp, Cobalt Blue, Pair	1600.00
Lamp, Kerosene, Blackberry, Blue Alabaster, Hinged Burner	275.00
Lamp, Whale Oil, Horn Of Plenty	195.00
Lamp, Whale Oil, New England Pineapple	195.00
Mug, Child's, Dogs, Bird, & Trees	35.00
Pitcher, Applied Handle, 9 In.	110.00
Pitcher, Overshot, Ice Bladder, Rope Handle, 1875, 11 In.	300.00
Pitcher, Water, Rope Handle, Square Top, Amber	325.00
Plate, Diamond Optic, Ruffled, Cranberry Gold Shading, 8 In.	78.00
Plate, Toddy, Berry Border, Bird On Branch, Dark Blue, 4 In.	23.00
Salt, Lacy, Stipple Ground, Domed Cover, 3 1/4 In., Pair	625.00
Salt, Master, Double Beaded Scroll, Lacy, Flint	55.00
Salt, Master, Eagle, Scalloped	135.00
Salt, Master, New England Glass, Lacy, Flint	45.00
Salt, Master, Oblong With Scroll Ends, Lacy, Flint	20.00
Sauce, Rayed Peacock Eye	18.00
Spill Holder, Star, Canary	395.00
Spooner, Diamond Band	30.00
Spooner, Horn Of Plenty	38.00
Spooner, New England Pineapple	38.00
Spooner, Opalescent Opaque	175.00
Sugar, Horn Of Plenty, Covered	98.00
Swan, Ruby, 2 In.	60.00
Tieback, Opalescent, 4 In.	20.00
Tieback, Petal Design, Pewter Stem, 3 1/2 In., Pair	75.00
Tieback, Pewter Shank, 2 In., Set Of 4	135.00
Tieback, Pink, 3 In., Pair	16.50
Tray, Butterfly, Lacy, 8 In.	165.00
Tumbler, Horn Of Plenty	75.00
Vase, Lacy, C.1830, 8 1/2 In.	265.00
Vase, Loop, Emerald, Marble Base, 11 1/8 In.	435.00
Vase, Stick, Applied Clear Rigaree, Blue, 12 In.	80.00

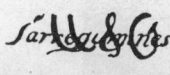

Utzschneider and Company, a porcelain factory, made ceramics in Sarreguemines, Lorraine, France, from 1770. Transfer-printed wares and majolica were made in the nineteenth century. The nineteenth-century pieces, most often found today, usually had colorful transfer-printed decorations showing peasants in local costumes.

SARREGUEMINES, Pitcher, Character, Head, Scotsman, Marked, 7 3/4 In.	58.00
Pitcher, Character, Head, Turk, Majolica, 7 1/2 In.	85.00

Pitcher, Character, Scotsman, Majolica 52.00
Plate, Apples On Leaf, 7 1/2 In. 30.00
Plate, Boy & Girl In Door Scene, 8 1/2 In. 25.00
Plate, French Clowns, Music Design, 8 In. 24.00
Plate, Majolica, Leaf Shape, Marked, 11 In. 50.00
Plate, Napoleon, Battle Scenes, 8 In., Set Of 6 .... 165.00
Plate, Strawberry, Blue, 8 In. 58.00

Satin glass is a late nineteenth–century art glass. It has a dull finish that is caused by a hydrofluoric acid vapor treatment. Satin glass was made in many colors and sometimes had applied decorations.

SATIN GLASS, Bell, Smoke, 8 In. 15.00
Bowl, Blue Ground, Maize Design, Crimped Top, 4 1/2 X 6 In. 50.00
Bowl, Diamond–Quilted & Ruffled, Cranberry Skirt, Shell Feet 325.00
Bowl, Diamond–Quilted, Mother–Of–Pearl, Blue, 5 X 5 3/4 In. 185.00
Bowl, Rainbow Colors, Ruffled, Enameled, 8 In. 195.00
Bowl, Rounding In At Top, Wavered Edge, 12 In. 125.00
Bowl, Sapphire Blue, Open Lace Edge, 11 In. 98.00
Candy Dish, Nude Stem, Covered, 10 In. 35.00
Celery, Swan Scene, Red Mark, 12 1/4 X 6 1/4 In. 295.00
Compote, Blue, Westmoreland, 7 In. 15.00
Creamer, Diamond–Quilted, Mother–Of–Pearl, Pink, 6 In. 110.00
Cruet, Applied Handle, Rainbow, 7 In. 310.00
Epergne, Birds & Floral, Hand Painted, 18 In. 250.00
Ewer, Melon Panel, Berries, Frosted Handle, Pedestal, 10 3/4 In. 135.00
Ewer, Peach, Frosted Handle, Floral, White Lining, 7 3/4 In. 95.00
Ewer, Pink Overlay, Enameled Flowers, Frosted Handle, 9 1/4 In. 98.00
Ewer, Pointed Rolled Lip, Enameled Flowers, Scrolls, 9 1/2 In. 95.00
Lamp, Beaded Drape, Soft Green, C.1890, 14 1/2 In. 185.00
Lamp, Fairy, Blue Overlay, Clear Clarke Base, 3 5/8 In. 100.00
Lamp, Fairy, Coralene Wheat Shade, 4 1/2 In. 110.00
Lamp, Kerosene, Floral Design, Small, Pair 85.00
Pitcher, Blue Raindrop, Frosted Handle & Rim, Oval, 7 In. 275.00
Pitcher, Bubble Lattice, Canary, 6 In. 125.00
Pitcher, Water, Blue ....*Illus* 225.00
Rose Bowl, Applied Flower, Petal Feet, Chartreuse, 3 5/8 In. 100.00
Rose Bowl, Blue, White Casing, Crimped, 6 In. 135.00
Rose Bowl, Brown Ribbon, Mother–Of–Pearl, White Lining, 3 In. 325.00
Rose Bowl, Chartreuse Ribbon, Mother–Of–Pearl, Prunus 275.00
Rose Bowl, Crimped Edge, Multicolors, 1885 .... 65.00
Rose Bowl, Optic Ribbed, White Lining, Lemon, 2 In. 65.00
Rose Bowl, White Ribbon, Mother–Of–Pearl, Floral, 2 1/2 X 3 In. 495.00

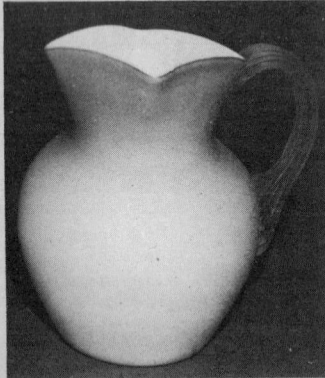

Satin Glass, Pitcher, Water, Blue

Satin Glass, Vase, Diamond–Quilted, Blue, Ruffled, 7 In.

Salt & Pepper, Guttate, Pink, Pair	122.00
Spittoon, Ladies, Cased White Over Light Blue	85.00
Sugar, Pink, Hand Painted, Covered	95.00
Toothpick, Bulging Loops, Pink	85.00
Toothpick, White, Pink Casing, Enameled	75.00
Tumbler, Blue Herringbone, White Lining, 4 1/4 In.	65.00
Tumbler, Diamond–Quilted, Mother–Of–Pearl, Daisies, 3 7/8 In.	195.00
Tumbler, Striped & Wavy Pattern, Blue	85.00
Vase, Blue Cased With White, 8 1/4 In.	185.00
Vase, Blue Overlay, White Enameled Flowers, 9 5/8 In.	88.00
Vase, Brown, Yellow Birds, Purple Flowers, Handle, 12 In.	225.00
Vase, Bud, Blue, Orange Floral, 5 1/2 In.	55.00
Vase, Bud, Herringbone, Blue, Ruffled, 7 1/4 In.	195.00
Vase, Bulbous, Ruffled Top, 10 1/2 In.	115.00
Vase, Coin Spot, Mother–Of–Pearl, Cream, Ruffled, 8 3/8 In.	165.00
Vase, Coin Spot, Ruffled, Floral, Webb, 11 7/8 X 6 1/2 In.	950.00
Vase, Diamond–Quilted, Apricot To Ruby, Bulbous, 10 X 5 1/4 In.	180.00
Vase, Diamond–Quilted, Apricot, Thorn Handle, 8 In.	225.00
Vase, Diamond–Quilted, Blue, Ruffled, 7 In. ....*Illus*	75.00
Vase, Diamond–Quilted, Cut Velvet, Blue, White Lining, 7 1/4 In.	118.00
Vase, Diamond–Quilted, Mother–Of–Pearl, Blue, 8 X 5 1/4 In.	180.00
Vase, Diamond–Quilted, Mother–Of–Pearl, Blue, Ruffled Top, 7 In.	85.00
Vase, Diamond–Quilted, Mother–Of–Pearl, Peach, 8 1/2 In.	145.00
Vase, Floral, Ruffled, Peach, Frosted Feet, 9 X 3 1/4 In.	225.00
Vase, Herringbone, Mother–Of–Pearl, Blue, Handles, 7 3/8 In.	225.00
Vase, Herringbone, Mother–Of–Pearl, Blue, Ruffled, 12 7/8 In.	225.00
Vase, Herringbone, Mother–Of–Pearl, Yellow, Handles, 8 1/8 In.	175.00
Vase, Jack–In–The–Pulpit, White, Dusty Rose Lining, 7 In.	55.00
Vase, Melon Ribbed, Blue Overlay, White Lining, 7 1/4 In.	110.00
Vase, Melon Ribbed, Ruffled Top, Pink, 11 1/2 In.	65.00
Vase, Quilted, Double Bulbous Shape, 6 Blow–Outs, 9 In.	425.00
Vase, Quilted, Ruffled, Blue To Light Blue, White Lining, 7 In.	75.00
Vase, Rainbow, Ruffled, Footed, Bulbous, America, C.1880, 7 In.	175.00
Vase, Raindrop, Blue, 6 Pinched Sides, 8 3/4 In.	125.00
Vase, Ribbed Pink, Bulbous, Ruffled Top, 10 1/4 In.	115.00
Vase, Ribbed Pink, White Frosted Ruffle, Bulbous, 10 1/4 In.	100.00
Vase, Scrolls, Floral, Ruffled, Peach, Leaf Feet, 9 1/4 In.	95.00
Vase, Swirl, Mother–Of–Pearl, Pink, Ruffled, Handle, 11 1/2 In.	275.00
Vase, White Flowers, Yellow & Gold Leaves, Handle, 10 In.	135.00

SATIN GLASS, WEBB, see Webb

Satsuma is a Japanese pottery with a distinctive creamy beige crackled glaze. Most of the pieces were decorated with blue, red, green, orange, or gold. Almost all the Satsuma found today was made after 1860. During World War I, Americans could not buy undecorated European porcelains. Women who liked to make hand-painted porcelains at home began to decorate plain Satsuma. These pieces are known today as "American Satsuma."

SATSUMA, Bottle, Double Gourd, Gold Center, Mums, Butterflies, C.1895, 6 In.	165.00
Bowl, Interior Bird Design, Chrysanthemum Border, Marked, 6 In.	200.00
Bowl, Polychrome Florals, Beige Ground, Low Feet, 7 In.	400.00
Bowl, Reserves Of Figures In Landscape, Florals, 4 3/4 In.	575.00
Bowl, Temple Scene, Meiji Period, 1880, 5 1/2 In.	575.00
Burner, Incense, Flowering Hawthorne Branches, Signed, 2 3/4 In.	275.00
Candlestick, Temple Scene, Crackled Glaze, Beige, 6 3/4 In., Pair	80.00
Cracker Jar, Feudal Lords, Florals, Butterflies, Diaper Rim, Signed	135.00
Creamer, Child's, Children Playing, Artist Signed	22.50
Cup & Saucer, Floral & Butterfly, Enameled	18.00
Flask, Moon, Foo Dog & Ring Handle At Neck, 8 1/2 In.	70.00
Incense Burner, Dragon Design, Calligraphic Signed, 2 3/8 In.	250.00
Jar, Deities, Gold Diaper Pattern, Blue & Red, Covered, 29 In.	170.00
Pin, Full–Fingered, Lady With Fan, Cinquefoil, 1 3/4 In.	75.00
Plate, 2 Feudal Lords, Diaper Pattern, C.1890, 8 1/2 In.	110.00
Plate, Birds, People, & Mountain, 9 1/2 In.	65.00

Scale, Balance, Brass, Weights
Stored In Base, C.1900, 40 X 30 In.

Scale, Counter, Cast Iron, Red Paint, Hand Stenciling, 16 In.

Plate, Feudal Lords, Gilt & Diaper Pattern, Meiji, C.1890, 8 1/2 In.	110.00
Plate, Warlord, Dragon, Black, Raised Gold, 7 1/2 In.	18.00
Salt, 3 Warriors, Marked	57.00
Salt, Wisteria	13.50
Sugar & Creamer, Overall Enamel Jeweling, Geisha & Lord Scenes	60.00
Tea Set, Wisteria, Lavender, Cream Ground, Gold Trim, 13 Piece	275.00
Teapot, Child's, Children Playing In Garden, Multifloral, Covered	650.00
Teapot, Dancer Scene	75.00
Toothpick, Kinkozan Leaves, Gilding, Teakwood Stand, Pair	300.00
Vase, Adults & Children Circle Body, Baluster, Marked, 9 3/4 In.	420.00
Vase, Chrysanthemums, 1920, 7 In.	40.00 To 50.00
Vase, Enameled Elephant, Cobalt Blue Flowers, 6 In.	35.00
Vase, Everted Neck, Convex, Figural Reserves, Butterfly Bands, 6 In.	200.00
Vase, Figural Scene, Latticework Panel, C.1900, Marked, 8 1/4 In.	400.00
Vase, Figural Scenes, Cobalt Round, Floral Design, Signed, 11 In.	700.00
Vase, Figural, Elephant Handles, 12 In.	200.00
Vase, Figures & Flowers, Gold Encrusted, 12 In.	210.00
Vase, Figures, 2 Panels, Signed, 3 1/2 In.	58.00
Vase, Floral, Gold, Crackle, 9 In.	130.00
Vase, Flowers, Polychrome, Baluster Shape, 19th Century, 3 5/8 In.	180.00
Vase, Foliage Design, Meiji Period, Gilded, 2 In., Pair	300.00
Vase, Garden Scene, Holy Men, Cobalt, 2 Panels, 9 In.	245.00
Vase, Geese In Flight, 1880, 8 In.	70.00
Vase, Gold Dust Clouds, Oriental Children, Signed, 2 1/2 In.	85.00
Vase, Hanging Wisteria, Gold Outline, Signed, 2 3/4 In.	80.00
Vase, Lady On Front, Gold Trim, 3 In.	45.00
Vase, Lavender Flowers, Cobalt Blue Collar & Base, 7 1/4 In.	325.00
Vase, Man & Woman On Front, Man On Rear, Gold Trim, 12 In., Pair	275.00
Vase, Moriage Flowers & Leaves, Double Handles, 13 In.	120.00
Vase, Petaled Rim, Bulbous, 6 1/2 In., Pair	220.00
Vase, Royal Lady, Geishas, Cobalt, Gold, Meiji Period, 14 1/2 In.	275.00
Vase, Scenic, Florals, Gold Handles, 12 In.	50.00
Vase, Swirling Dragon, Immortals Design, 8 In.	375.00
Vase, Warrior, C.1875, 16 In.	160.00 To 165.00
Vase, Warriors, Woman, Double Gourd, 1900, Signed, 4 5/8 In.	225.00

Special scales have been made to weigh everything from babies to gold. Collectors search for all types. Most popular are small gold-dust scales and special grocery scales.

SCALE, Acme Egg Grading, Pat.June 24, 1924	17.50
Aper Testing, Brass Pendulum, C.1878, 22 1/2 In.	995.00
Apothecary, Torsion Balance Co.	45.00
Baby, Advertising, Paragon Furniture	42.00
Baby, Pink & Blue Picture, Wicker Tray, 1940s	25.00

Balance, Brass Graduated Bar, Howl Scale, 1867, Cast Iron, 18 1/2 In. 80.00
Balance, Brass, Flat Bar, Sliding Weight, Bucket, 11 1/2 In. 135.00
Balance, Brass, Weights Stored In Base, C.1900, 40 X 30 In. ....*Illus* 330.00
Balance, Detecto, Brass Bar, 2 Round Plate, Weights 35.00
Balance, Gold Miner's, Weights, Walnut Box 38.00
Balance, Square Glass Platforms, Steel Base, Schaar & Co., 1915 .... 35.00
Balance, Storage Drawer, Oak, Cased Set 295.00
Bathroom, Detecto, Raised Platform, 1917 .... 20.00
Butter, Hanging, Wooden, Original Pans 6 X 9 In., Cords, 28 In. 225.00
Candy, Brass Pan, 1915 .... 55.00
Candy, Buffalo, Red, Gold Lettering, Brass Pan 50.00
Candy, Detecto, Gram, Brass Scoop 40.00
Candy, Fairbanks, Chicken Foot, Brass Tray 65.00
Candy, I.B.M. No.166, Fancy Trim Top & Middle 125.00
Candy, Imperial, 2 Lbs. 10.00
Candy, Pelouze 25.00
Candy, Toledo, Brass Pan, 14 In. 80.00
Candy, Toledo, Fan Shape, Scoop, 3 Lbs. 85.00
Candy, Toledo, Nickel 195.00
Chair, For Weighing Jockeys 950.00
Chatillon, Brass Face, 24 Lbs. 18.00
Chatillon, Brass, 50 Lbs. 12.50
Chatillon, No.2, Counter, Cast Iron, Brass Bar 55.00
Chatillon, Spring Balance, Brass Front, 25 Lbs. 12.00
Coin, Folding, Brass, Rosewood Case 125.00
Counter, Cast Iron, Red Paint, Hand Stenciling, 16 In. ....*Illus* 290.00
Counter, Iron Cross Balance, Brass Pan, C.1900, 9 1/2 In. 165.00
Counter, Openwork Iron Posts, Brass Bar, Weights, Scoop 75.00
Counter, Platform, Openwork, Iron Pillars, Brass Scoop Bar 45.00
Egg, Farm Master 27.00
Egg, Jiffy Way, Red & Green 18.00
Egg, Mascot 15.00
Egg, Premier 18.00
Excelsior Improved, Hanging, Brass 25.00
Fairbanks, 1878 .... 50.00
Fairbanks, Brass Tray & Measures, Stenciling, 4 Lbs. 85.00
Floor, Brass, Ivory Indicator, 2 Balances, 1900, 68 In. 1000.00
Floor, National, Claw Feet 975.00
Floor, Peerless, Lollipop, Porcelain, Blue 1150.00
Floor, Peerless, Printed Record Of Weight, Deco, 1 Cent 350.00
Gold, 3 Weights, Velvet Lined Box, Brass 57.00
Gold, Base Drawer, Wood Mounted 250.00
Gold, Brass, Folds In Oak Box, Weights, Dated 1862 .... 96.00
Gold, Design On Steel Beam, Brass Pans, 18th Century 75.00
Grain, Fairbanks, Brass, Bucket 170.00
Hanging, Brass Face, Spring Balance, 1867 .... 23.00
Hanging, Cast Iron Hook & Sliding Weight, 16 1/2 In. 40.00
Hanging, Chatillion's Improved Circular Spring Balance, Brass 75.00
Hanging, Detecto, Galvanized Basket 35.00
Hanging, Excelsior Improved, Brass 25.00
Hanging, Penn Scale, Basket 40.00
Hanging, Spring Balance, Brass Face, 1867 .... 23.00
Hanson Dairy 14.00
Henry Troemer, Wooden, Glass Case, Becker Bros., Weight Set 250.00
Iron, Victorian, Ornate, Porcelain Dial, Sweden, 1855 .... 65.00
Jewel, Ohaus 90.00
Jeweler's, Free Hanging, Small 16.00
Kitchen, Brass Tray, Design Reg.1900, 101 Lbs., 16 X 12 X 6 In. 90.00
Kitchen, Pelouze, Ivory 16.00
Kitchen, Simmons Hardware 18.00
Kitchen, Tin Pan, Green Enamel 18.00
Maple Syrup, Baume, Glass 5.00
Medical, Buffalo Scale Co., Brass, Cast Iron, Height Gauge 600.00
National, Speciality, 10 In. 250.00

Pelouze Mfg.Co., Glass Enclosed Dial, Pat.1903 .... 24.00
Pennsylvania Dutch, Hex Patterns, Signed, Nickel Plated Brass 240.00
Postal, Crescent, Tin, Blue, 1903, 3 In. 22.00
Postal, Gem, Black & Copper Design, Sheet Iron 34.00
Postal, Ideal, 3 Cent 30.00
Railroad Depot, 7 Ft. 750.00
Rockola, Cast Iron 225.00
Sidewalk, 1 Cent, Weight & Fortune 100.00
Spring, Brass Platform, Pedestal Disc, L.E.Brown, 1878 .... 150.00
Steelyard, 4 Hooks & Weights, 19 In. 25.00
Steelyard, Iron, 10 Pound 20.00
Store, Computing Scale Co., Dayton, O., Green Paint, 1937, 31 1/4 In. 45.00
Store, Fairbanks, Brass Scoop, 1877 .... 55.00
Timber, Maple, Simon C.Noyes, Lisbon, N.H., 36 In. 95.00
Tobacco, Speckled Beauty & Early Bird 37.50
Toledo, Lollipop, Open Face Type, Back Door 125.00

Schafer & Vater, makers of small ceramic items, are best known for their amusing figurals. The factory was located in Volkstedt, Germany, from 1890 to 1962. Some pieces are marked with the crown and R mark, but many are unmarked.

SCHAFER & VATER, Bottle, Figural, Comical Man Bowling, Marked, 6 1/8 In. 115.00
Bottle, Figural, Fireman With Hose, Stopper 70.00
Box, Jasperware, Nymph & Cupid, Blue, Oval, 5 In. 55.00
Creamer, Blue Cow In Dress, 3 3/4 In. 95.00
Creamer, Chinaman, Long Hair Forms Handle 68.00
Creamer, Clown With Lute 65.00
Creamer, Comical Black Man, 3 1/2 In. 95.00
Creamer, Dutch Maid Holding Pitcher 55.00
Creamer, Goose In Bonnet & Shawl, 5 1/2 In. 125.00
Creamer, Maid With Jug & Keys, 3 1/2 In. 95.00
Creamer, Seated Goat With Boutonnieres, 5 1/2 In. 110.00
Figurine, Dog, Wearing Cap, Why Be Unhappy? I'm Insured 135.00
Figurine, Keep Your Hair On, Man's Head, Open Mouth 95.00
Figurine, Waiting For The Tide, Man Wearing Cap, Pipe 135.00
Figurine, Woman, Sitting, Blue Dress, Movable Feet 135.00
Match Holder, Laughing Man 95.00
Nodder, Man, Sitting, With Cat 95.00
Pin Tray, Cameo Girl Heads, Pink, Emblem, 4 X 5 In. 30.00
Salt & Pepper, Smiling Apple & Pear 90.00
Striker, Match, 2 Dutch Figures 75.00
Teapot, Smiling Apple, Multicolor, 1 Cup 120.00
Urn, Grecian Lady, White Ship Design, Sage Green, 6 In. 110.00
Vase, Boy Facing Wall, I'm So Discouraged, 4 1/2 In. 130.00

Schneider Glassworks was founded in 1903 at Epinay–sur–Seine, France, by Charles and Ernest Schneider. Art glass was made between 1903 and 1930. The company still produces clear crystal glass.

SCHNEIDER, Bowl, Flared, Mottled, Orange, Signed, 9 In. 75.00
Bowl, Red Rim, Yellow Footed Center, Wrought Iron Holder, 6 In. 225.00
Compote, Mottled, Amethyst Stem, Wrought Iron Base, 15 In. 595.00
Compote, Royal Blue, Yellow, Orange, Green, Marked, 5 In. 85.00
Ewer, Mottled Amethyst To Red, Applied Handle, Marked, 6 1/2 In. 175.00
Rose Bowl, Cluthra Yellow To Brown, Marked, 3 1/2 In. 125.00
Vase, Art Deco, Opalescent Lavender Top Band, Signed, 8 1/2 In. 375.00
Vase, Blown Into Wrought Iron Base, C.1925, Signed, 5 1/2 In. 250.00
Vase, Brown, Green, & Orange Satin, 10 In. 85.00
Vase, Cluthra Crystal, Abstract Shape, 5 In. 125.00
Vase, Hand Painted Flowers, Gold Rim, Signed, C.1914, 14 In. 895.00
Vase, Marbelized, Pink & Yellow, Amethyst Base, Marked, 7 1/4 In. 375.00
Vase, Pink & Amethyst, Signed, 7 1/4 In. 295.00

Scrimshaw is bone or ivory or whale's teeth carved by sailors and others for entertainment during the sailing–ship days. Some scrimshaw was carved as early as 1800. There are modern scrimshanders making pieces today on bone, ivory, or plastic.

SCRIMSHAW, see also Nautical

SCRIMSHAW, Candlestick, Whales, Sailing Ship, Sailor On Base, 4 3/4 In., Pr.	900.00
Elephant Tusk, Missionary Arthur Mills, Nov.4, 1859, 24 In.	1750.00
Engraving Tools, Holder, Whalebone, Set Of 12	4400.00
Jagging Wheel, 3 Pierced Hearts, Ivory, C.1870, 8 1/4 In.	2750.00
Powder Horn, Man & 2 Women, Egrets Other Side, Motto	300.00
Swift, Original Mahogany Dovetailed Box	2500.00
Thimble, Ship & Flowers, Ivory	15.00
Tooth, American Eagle, Whaling Ship In Back, Dated 1830	250.00
Tooth, Aristocratic Lady, Holding Flowers, C.1840, 5 In.	330.00
Tooth, Bust Of Eskimo Girl, Western Dress, 5 1/2 In.	247.00
Tooth, Captain Lecturing Cabin Boy, 4 In.	85.00
Tooth, Country House, Cupola, Lady, C.1850, 5 1/2 In.	660.00
Tooth, Crochet Needle, Lady's Hand Holding Rose, 8 In.	605.00
Tooth, Fully Rigged Naval Ship, Fort, Flag, C.1860, 7 In.	330.00
Tooth, Lady, Depiction Of Sperm Whale, C.1840, 5 1/2 In.	467.00
Tooth, Peddler, Dancing, Walking Stick, Ship On Side, 5 In.	522.00
Tooth, Ship Flying British Flag, Polychrome, 5 X 8 In.	425.00
Tooth, Ship, Clouds, Gulls, Walnut Base, 2 1/4 In.	50.00
Tusk, Eagle, Shields, 1882, Whalers & Neptune's Boaters, 7 1/2 In.	300.00

Prescott W. Baston made the first Sebastian miniatures in 1938 in Marblehead, Massachusetts. More than 400 different designs have been made and the collectors search for the out–of–production models. The mark may say "Copr. P. W. Baston U.S.A.," or "P. W. Baston, U.S.A.," or "Prescott W. Baston." Sometimes a paper label was used.

SEBASTIAN MINIATURES, Aunt Polly, 1948	52.00
Brom Bones, The Headless Horseman, 1949	75.00
Charles Dickens, 1952	35.00
Colonial Kitchen, 1952	35.00
Corner Drugstore, 1940	65.00
Dan'l Boone & Mrs. Dan'l Boone, 1940, Pair	175.00
Deborah Franklin, 1939	75.00
James Monroe & Elizabeth Monroe, 1940, Pair	195.00
John Harvard & Mrs.Harvard, 1940, Pair	150.00
Mr.Obocell, Green & Silver, Marblehead Label, 1950	135.00
Nurse, 1967	25.00
Parade Rest, Signed, 1953	55.00
Patrick Henry & Sarah Henry, 1949, Pair	195.00
Pilgrims, 1947	35.00
Rip Van Winkle, 1950	30.00
Sam Houston & Margaret Houston, 1939, Pair	150.00

SEG, see Paul Revere Pottery

Sevres porcelain has been made in Sevres, France, since 1769. Many copies of the famous ware have been made. The name originally referred to the works of the Royal Porcelain factory. The name now includes any of the wares made in the town of Sevres, France. The entwined lines with a center letter used as the mark is one of the most forged marks in antiques. Be very careful to identify Sevres by quality, not just by mark.

SEVRES, Bowl, Maiden Pastoral Scene, Gilt Bronze Mount, Covered, 27 In.	3575.00
Bust, Boy, Waisted Socle, Gilded, Bisque, C.Tharaud, 16 In., Pair	522.00
Bust, Dante, Art Nouveau, C.1890	1100.00
Bust, Marie Antoinette, Gilt Bronze Base, Tajou, 18 3/4 In.	275.00
Bust, Peter & Catherine The Great, Blue, Bisque, 18 1/2 In., Pair	550.00
Casket, Jewel, Cupid & Putti Cover, Gilt Bronze Mounted, 10 3/4 In.	660.00
Casket, Leisure Scenes, Musicians, Gilt Bronze, Hinged, 13 3/4 In.	1650.00
Center Bowl, Panel Of Lovers, Gilt Border, Handles, 14 In., Pair	7700.00

Clock, Mantel, Figural, Floral Festoons, Figures Of Industry, 24 In. 1045.00
Clock, Mantel, Louis XVI, Gilt Bronze, Jewels, Toupie Feet, 20 1/2 In. 1650.00
Dish, Baroque Form, Lavender, Blue, Pink, Gold, Marked, 7 X 12 In. 225.00
Ewer, Gilt Over Bronze, Pointed, Footed, Artist Signed, 22 In., Pair 475.00
Jardiniere, Pastoral Scene, Ebonized, Bronze, Metal Liner, 27 In. 2200.00
Lamp, Oil, Gilt Bronze, Putti Frolicking, Border, G.Poitevin, 20 In. 600.00
Plate, Dessert, Chateau De F.Bleau & L.Phillipe Mark, 1847, Set Of 6 .... 600.00
Plate, Lady In Empire Gown, Gold Filigree Design, Marked, 9 1/4 In. 95.00
Plate, Maiden Churning Butter, Artist Dupoigny, 9 1/2 In., Pair 522.00
Plate, Portrait, Francois II 75.00
Plate, Portrait, Lady, Polychrome Floral, Signed Leber, 9 5/8 In. 160.00
Plate, Portrait, Madame De Monteipar 95.00
Plate, Portrait, Madame De Pamballe 75.00
Plate, Portrait, Mme.De Pompadour, Gold Border, Signed, 9 1/2 In. 225.00
Sugar & Creamer, Covered 375.00
Tea Caddy, Turquoise 50.00
Tea Set, Bird Medallions, Gold Trim, C.1780, 36 Piece 5785.00
Tea Set, Lover Panels, Gilt Border, Teapot, Milk Jug, Tray, 8 Piece 1045.00
Tobacco Jar, Hinged Lid, 6 In. 85.00
Urn, Acorn Finial On Domed Cover, Reserve Of Couple, 21 In., Pair 1100.00
Urn, Hunting Scenes, Gilt Medallions, C.1835, 15 In., Pair 625.00
Urn, Mantel, Domed Cover, Flower Bud Finial, Lion Head, 19 1/2 In. 800.00
Urn, Marked F On Base, Dated 1758, 19 In. 1250.00
Urn, Reclining Lovers, Gilt Bronze, Covered, Marked, 31 In., Pair 4600.00
Vase, C.1900, Black Clover Mark, 3 In. ....Color 35.00
Vase, Covered, Maiden & Cupid, Gilt Bronze Mount, J.Pascault, 58 In. 6875.00
Vase, Covered, Napoleon, Rivoli Battle, Artist A.Debarle, 39 In. 5500.00
Vase, Covered, Rustic Maiden, Lover, Apple Green, 23 3/4 In., Pair 1650.00
Vase, Covered, Shepherd Lovers, Greek Key Handles, 21 In., Pair 1320.00
Vase, Covered, Venus & Cupid Scene, Landscape Scene, Turquoise 950.00
Vase, Portrait, Cobalt Blue, 6 1/2 In. 110.00
Vase, Silvered Plaques, Ormolu Mount, Blood Red, 16 In. 700.00

Sewer tile figures were made by workers at the sewer tile factories in the Ohio area during the late nineteenth and early twentieth centuries.

SEWER TILE, Bank, Ball Shape, Tooled Dot, F.Exley, 1907, 3 5/8 In. 10.00
Bust, Gentleman With Goatee, Tooled, 4 3/4 In. 35.00
Dish, Incised Birds & Design, Hexagonal, 2 1/4 In. 15.00
Dog, Incised Face & Collar, 10 In. 150.00
Eagle, 7 1/4 In. 235.00
Figure, Head Of Smiling Boy, Tooled Hair, 5 1/4 In. 130.00
Figurine, Bear, Primitive, 5 1/4 In. 5.00
Figurine, Dog, Seated, White & Black Repaint, 8 In. 55.00
Frog, Tooled Features, Heart On Back, Stone Necklace, Eyes, 6 In. 115.00
House Surrounded With Trees & Hedge, 6 In. 135.00
House, With Landscaping, 6 In. 110.00
Parrot, 6 1/4 In. 195.00
Pitcher, Tree Trunk Surface, Bark Tooling With Knots, 8 1/2 In. 70.00
Planter, 3 Open Branches For Planting, Marked, 24 In. 125.00
Scotty, 5 1/2 In. 10.00
Strainer, Cylindrical, Handle, 10 1/2 X 11 1/2 In. 25.00
Stump, 4 In. 15.00

All types of sewing equipment are collected, from sewing birds that held the cloth to old wooden spools.

SEWING, Basket, Chinese Medallion Tassels, Beads, 8 3/4 In. 22.00
Basket, Chinese, Bead & Coin Trim, Covered, 9 In. 30.00
Basket, Sweet Grass, Covered, Thimble & Holder 9.50
Bird, 2 Pincushions, Blue, Pat.1867, 5 In. 130.00
Bird, 2 Pincushions, Brass, Dated 1853 .... 90.00
Bird, 2 Pincushions, Silver Plate 85.00
Bird, 2 Pincushions, Silvered Brass, Pat.Feb.15, 1853 ....125.00 To 145.00
Bird, Brass, Clamp-On, Dated 1852 ....105.00 To 140.00

Bird, Embossed Brass 285.00
Bird, Round Mirror On Side, Screw Type, Wooden, Design 90.00
Bird, Table Clamp, Patented Feb.15, 1858, Small Pincushion, Brass 115.00
Bobbin, Lace, Ivory 9.00
Box, Curly Maple Posts, Pincushion, Cherry & Pine, 6 1/2 X 9 1/2 In. 150.00
Box, Dovetailed, Dated 1889, Oak 13.00
Box, Figural, House, Pincushion Roof, 1940s 25.00
Box, Japanese, Bombe Sides, 2 Drawers, Red Lacquer, 15 3/8 In. 90.00
Box, Machine Attachments, Oak 9.25
Box, Painted Design, Handles, C.1835, American, 3 1/2 X 5 X 1 3/4 In. 225.00
Box, Pincushion Top, Drawer, Hearts & Diamonds, Maple, 5 1/2 X 8 In. 1500.00
Box, Poplar & Pine, Pencil Signed Wm.H.R., 1868, 5 1/4 X 9 In. 75.00
Box, Poplar, Walnut Lid, Gold Striping, Tray, 11 1/2 In. 17.50
Box, Rosewood Veneer, Inlaid Brass, Striping, England, 13 X 10 In. 140.00
Box, Thimble, Repousse, Sterling Silver, Strawberry Shape, Hinged Top 155.00
Box, Thread Caddy Lid, Signed C.G.Pease, Concord, Lake Co., O., Wooden 175.00
Box, Thread, Repousse, Sterling Silver, Shiebler, 1 1/8 X 1 3/4 In. 145.00
Box, Top For Spools, Holes For Thread, Lower Drawer, Bone Trim 125.00
Box, Walnut, Bottom Drawer, Ivory Rim Openings, For Thread, 9 X 6 In. 125.00
Box, Wooden, Inlaid, Scissors, Thimble 32.00
Chest, Wicker, White 45.00
Crochet Hook, Bone .... 9.00 To 15.00
Cutter, Thread, Knife Under Spring, Gilt Iron Stand, 1874, 3 In. 25.00
Darner, Aqua, Glass 22.00
Darner, Celluloid 6.00
Darner, Ebony, Silver Sterling Handle 25.00
Darner, Mrs.Griffith's Superior, Original Envelope 5.00
Darner, Sterling Silver Handle 29.00
Darner, Sterling Silver Top, Wooden 14.00
Darning Egg, Whalebone, Tiger Maple Handle, 19th Century, 9 3/4 In. 165.00
Eyelet Punch, Adjustable Gauge, Sterling Silver 22.00
Hem Marker, Boco, Iron Base, Wooden 12.50
Hook, Crochet, Ivory, Set Of 3 .... 22.00
Kit, Calvert Whiskey, Embossed Tin, Yellow Tassel 15.00
Kit, Figural, Jewel Casket, Pincushion Top, Opens To Contents, Brass 77.00
Kit, Lydia Pinkham Vegetable Compound, Brass 7.50
Kit, Lydia Pinkham, Nickel Cylinder Container .... 7.00 To 12.00
Kit, Sealtest Ice Cream, Cone Shape 20.00
Kit, Traveling, Art Nouveau 22.00
Lacer, Ribbon, Silver Sterling, Pat.1906 .... 15.00
Loom, Pine, Dovetailed, Sliding Lid Box, C.1880, 11 1/4 X 5 1/2 In. 250.00
Loom, Tape, 17 X 6 1/2 In. 125.00
Machine, Gateway Engineering Co., Salesman Sample, Painted 45.00
Machine, Howe, Treadle, 1870 .... 75.00
Machine, Wilcox & Gibbs, Portable, 1871 .... 35.00
Needle Book, New York, Occupied Japan 20.00
Needle Case, 1 Drawer, Label, Watson's Needles, 15 1/2 X 2 3/4 In. 45.00
Needle Case, 6 Hinged Compartments, Ormolu, Perry & Co., London 135.00
Needle Case, Art Nouveau, Sterling Silver 65.00
Needle Case, Beaded, Roses & Lyre, Silk Interior, Dated 1839 .... 95.00
Needle Case, Tin, Cylindrical, Various Size Needles, 11 In. 30.00
Needle Holder, Bone 30.00
Needles, Knitting, Whalebone, Inlaid Wood, 11 In., Pair 175.00
Pin, Casket, Sliding Leaf Cover, Lined, Perry & Son, Reddish 135.00
    SEWING, PINCUSHION DOLL, see Pincushion Doll category
Pincushion, 2 Pigs, Bronzed 15.00
Pincushion, Boot, Meriden, Silver Plate, 1890s 35.00
Pincushion, Bucket, Lift–Off Top, Mirror Inside, 2 In. 65.00
Pincushion, Canoe Shape, Brass 18.00
Pincushion, Celluloid Girl, Thimble Inside, Germany 20.00
Pincushion, China Boy With Fiddle 12.00
Pincushion, Diamond Shape, Victorian, Beaded .... 8.00 To 12.00
Pincushion, Dove, Beaded, Green, 1901 .... 18.00
Pincushion, Dutch Wooden Shoe, Silver Design, 4 1/2 In. 65.00

Pincushion, Flapper Skirt, Exposed Legs, 5 In. 24.00
Pincushion, Heeled Shoe, Silver Plate, 6 In. 15.00
Pincushion, Lady's Shoe, Mt.Vernon, Va. 9.00
Pincushion, Leather Shoe, Yugoslavia 14.50
Pincushion, Pelican & Sparrow, German 45.00
Pincushion, Pug Dog Beside Hexagonal Cushion, Marked J.B., 1920s 40.00
Scissors, Advertising, Star Brand Shoes 35.00
Scissors, Buttonhole, Germany, 4 1/2 In. 15.00
Scissors, Embroidery, Sterling Silver Handle 29.00
Scissors, Ivy, Germany, 5 1/2 In. 10.00
Shuttle, Lydia Pinkham 37.00
Shuttle, Ribbon, Wooden, 19th Century, English, 3 1/4 X 3 1/2 In. 35.00
Shuttle, Tatting, Celluloid 23.00
Shuttle, Tatting, Sterling Silver ....35.00 To 65.00
Sign, Singer Sewing Machine, 1940s, Glass, 5 X 12 In. 13.00
Sign, Singer, Porcelain, Multicolor, 24 X 36 In. 325.00
Spool Holder, Silver Plate, Victorian, James Tufts Co., Boston 112.00
Tape Measure, Carved Nut Ivory, Bone Spindle 55.00
Tape Measure, Colgate, Fab, Celluloid 18.00
Tape Measure, Curtis & Spindle Elastic Stockings, Aluminum 8.50
Tape Measure, Fab, Celluloid, Sunset Picture 25.00
Tape Measure, Figural, Basket Of Flowers 30.00
Tape Measure, Figural, Chinese Man's Head, Celluloid 37.00
Tape Measure, Figural, Clamshell, Metal 35.00
Tape Measure, Figural, Clock 40.00
Tape Measure, Figural, Colonial Man, Celluloid 35.00
Tape Measure, Figural, Dog Head, Hat, Kerchief, Tongue Is Tape, Metal 25.00
Tape Measure, Figural, Doll In Shoe, Plastic 10.00
Tape Measure, Figural, Fish, Silver Plate Over Brass ....40.00 To 47.00
Tape Measure, Figural, Pig, Advertising, Plastic 17.50
Tape Measure, Figural, Pig, Brass 45.00
Tape Measure, Figural, Pig, Silver Plate ....22.00 To 40.00
Tape Measure, Figural, Pig, White, Flowers, 2 In. 25.00
Tape Measure, Figural, Policeman, Pull Gun To Measure, Celluloid 45.00
Tape Measure, Figural, Rabbit 40.00
Tape Measure, Figural, Rooster, Celluloid 35.00
Tape Measure, Figural, Sailfish 22.00
Tape Measure, Figural, Sailing Ship 25.00
Tape Measure, Figural, Statue Of Liberty, Empire State Building 22.00
Tape Measure, Figural, Straw Hat, Silver Plate Over Brass 47.00
Tape Measure, Figural, Straw Hat, Tin 49.00
Tape Measure, Figural, Stuffed Teddy Bear, 3 In. 45.00
Tape Measure, Figural, Teakettle, Brass, Turning Lid Winds Tape 60.00
Tape Measure, Figural, Terrier With Puppy 28.00
Tape Measure, Figural, Turtle, Pull My Head 20.00
Tape Measure, Figural, Watch Fob 12.00
Tape Measure, Figural, Windmill, Brass 45.00
Tape Measure, Frigidaire, Celluloid 15.00
Tape Measure, G.E.Refrigerator, Celluloid 18.00
Tape Measure, Hill Top Poultry Medicine, Celluloid 20.00
Tape Measure, Horse, Celluloid, Red Saddle, Japan 18.00
Tape Measure, International Harvester, Small 5.00
Tape Measure, Jamestown Exposition 18.00
Tape Measure, John Deere 40.00
Tape Measure, Langenkamp Co., Indianapolis, Celluloid 18.00
Tape Measure, Mazda 15.00
Tape Measure, Millhouse 40.00
Tape Measure, Singing Tower, Lake Wales, Fla., German 15.00
Tape Measure, Spiked German Helmet, Brass, Black Maltese Cross, 1914 .... 65.00
Tape Measure, Stromberg Carburetor 20.00
Thimble Holder, Bird On Post, Round, Footed, Taunton Silver Plate 95.00
Thimble Holder, Brass Egg, Hanging Loop 47.00
Thimble Holder, Watering Can, Spout Holds Needles 67.00
Thimble, 14K Gold, Bright Cut Rim, Size 10 ....90.00 To 135.00

Thimble, Advertising, Prudential 6.00
Thimble, Advertising, Singer Sewing Machine ....4.00 To 7.00
Thimble, Advertising, Tastykake 5.00
Thimble, Aluminum, Just A Thimble Full, 2 In. 10.00
Thimble, Beading, Engraved Bell Shape Rim, 14K Gold, Size 7 .... 85.00
Thimble, Bird & Floral, Julia, Sterling Silver 25.00
Thimble, Double Row Cut Rim, 10K Gold, Size 7 .... 80.00
Thimble, Panels Of Flowers, Sterling Silver, Size 12 .... 25.00
Thimble, Raised Cat, Silver 42.00
Thimble, Scenic Band, 10K Gold 85.00
Thimble, Scrimshaw Ship, Ivory 15.00
Thimble, Silver Plate, Gold Wash Interior, Leather Case, 2 3/4 In. 22.00
Thimble, Sterling Silver, Incised Gold Band, Size 9 ....22.00 To 24.00
Thimble, Sterling, Floral, Band, Size 11 .... 24.00
Thimble, Straight Republican Ticket, Aluminum 10.00
Thimble, Sylvia, Raised Scroll Border, 14K Gold, Size 8 .... 100.00
Thimble, Tailor, Coin Silver 19.00
Thread & Thimble Holder, White Metal, Baby Figural, Footed Base 85.00
Thread Holder, Ivory, Barrel Shape, 2 In. 80.00
Threader, Lilly May's, Instructions, 1923 .... 5.00
Winder, Bobbin, Clamp–On Table, Marked Wm.H.Mains, Patent 1870 .... 60.00
Winder, Thread, Ivory Fish 5.00

Shaker–produced items are characterized by simplicity, functionalism, and orderliness. There were many Shaker communities in America from the eighteenth century to the present day. The religious order made furniture, small wooden pieces, and packaged medicines, herbs, and jellies to sell to "outsiders." Other useful objects were made for use by members of the community.

SHAKER, Almanac, 1882 .... 15.00
Almanac, 1897, Advertising, Recipes, Stories 15.00
Apron, Sister's, Woven Silk, Mixed Indigo & Red, 32 In. 250.00
Basket, Ash Splint, Hickory Handle, Square Bottom, 15 In. 450.00
Basket, Gathering, Oblong, Hoop Handle, Double Wrap Rim, 13 X 17 In. 175.00
Basket, Gathering, Sabbathday Lake, Round, 15 In. 550.00
Basket, Kittenhead, Green Silk Ribbon Edge, 1 X 2 1/4 In. 700.00
Basket, Laundry, 31 In. 797.50
Basket, Lid, Open Weave For Herb Drying, 6 1/2 X 13 In. 200.00
Basket, Maple Splint, For Draining Cheese, C.1850, 8 X 20 1/2 In. 300.00
Basket, Sewing, Lid, Round, Covered, Weaving On Top, 4 X 6 1/2 In. 400.00
Basket, Sewing, Original Ribbon Decoration, $1.00, First Price Tag 132.50
Basket, Sewing, Pink Satin Lining, Fitted, Signed, 5 1/2 In. 300.00
Bin, Grain, Pine, Original Gray Paint, Hinged Slant Door, 16 X 6 In. 1000.00
Board, Lap, Pine, Cutout For Waist, Inset Yardstick, 29 X 45 In. 100.00
Bonnet, Doll 225.00
Bonnet, Miniature, Silk, Black & Gray, 2 In. 200.00
Bonnet, Poplarware, Brown Calico Trim, Satin Ribbon, 8 X 10 In. 125.00
Bonnet, Quilted Indigo Blue, Beige Homespun Lined, 12 In. 125.00
Book, A Juvenile Guide Or Manual Of Good Manners, 1844 .... 95.00
Book, Daily Activities, Receipts & Suggestions, 1861–92 .... 850.00
Bowl, Chopping, Fruitwood, Carved Grips, Oval, 4 X 23 X 13 In. 200.00
Box, 16 In. 4620.00
Box, 3–Finger Construction, Copper Tacks, Oval, 6 X 9 X 3 1/2 In. 225.00
Box, 3–Finger, Maple & Pine, Original Mustard Paint, 2 X 5 In. 425.00
Box, 4–Finger, Maple & Pine, Oval, Red Stain, 4 1/2 X 12 In. 900.00
Box, 4–Finger, Red, 5 5/8 In. 1980.00
Box, 5–Finger, Red, Oval, 17 1/4 In. 2750.00
Box, Butter, Pine, Green, Isaac Bullrick, Hancock, Mass., 7 X 17 In. 275.00
Box, Cheese, Buttonhole Laps, Honey Color, Round, 12 1/4 In. 225.00
Box, Cheese, Staves, Copper Tacks, Sabbathday Lake, Maine, 17 X 7 In. 185.00
Box, Copper Tacks, No Lid, Oval, 7 1/2 X 9 3/4 In. 80.00
Box, Cover, Maple & Pine, Oval, Mustard Paint, 3 3/4 X 9 3/8 In. 500.00
Box, Fingered, Arched Handle, Oval, 6 In. 260.00
Box, Hickory & Pine, Original Red Paint, 8 X 17 In. 2500.00

Box, Knife, Ash, Chestnut, Cutout Divided Handle, Hinged Lids, 8 In. 225.00
Box, Knife, Cherry, Natural Finish, Carved Handle, 7 In. 175.00
Box, Knife, Walnut, Natural, 2 Lids, 2–Part, Trestle Handle, 6 1/2 In. 325.00
Box, Letter, Poplar, 9 Shelves, Scalloped, Red Finish, 18 X 11 1/4 In. 140.00
Box, Maple & Pine, Oval, Orange Red Paint, 2 1/2 X 6 In. 2750.00
Box, Oval, Maple & Pine, Orange Stain, Floral Design, 4 X 11 In. 300.00
Box, Painted Yellow Ocher, Oval, 4 Spools Inside, 4 1/2 In. 2700.00
Box, Pantry, Oval, Natural Finish, 5 In. 125.00
Box, Pill, Copper Fastener, Oval, Wooden, 3 1/4 In. 65.00
Box, Red Wash, Silk Lined, Pin Picked Inscription, 1837, 5 1/4 In. 1300.00
Box, Seed, Pine, Divided Interior, Red Finish, 11 1/2 X 23 1/2 In. 135.00
Box, Sewing, Movable Handle, Holes For Fittings, Maine, 5 1/4 X 8 In. 65.00
Box, Sewing, Oval, Swing Handle, Pink Material Interior, 2 X 7 In. 220.00
Box, Spit, Dovetailed Walnut, Enfield, 10 X 10 X 4 1/2 In. 45.00
Box, Storage, Pine, Original Gray Paint, Dovetailed, Lock, 8 X 17 In. 140.00
Box, Utility, Oval, Fitted Lid, Olive Green, 2 1/2 X 5 1/2 In. 990.00
Box, Veneer & Inlay In Maple & Walnut, Paper Lining, 8 X 11 In. 35.00
Box, Wooden, Natural, Oval, 4 X 3 X 1 1/2 In. 85.00
Box, Wooden, Oval, 4 X 3 X 1 /2 In. 85.00
Box, Wooden, Oval, Red Paint, 5 1/2 X 13 1/4 X 9 3/4 In. 900.00
Box, Woven Poplar, 1/2 Round 45.00
Broadside, Shaking Quakers, Glazed, Framed, October, 1846, 26 X 11 In. 600.00
Bucket, Bands, Lid, Wooden, Old Green Paint 28.00
Bucket, Berry, Pine, Whitewashed, Green Stenciled Design, Good Boy 250.00
Bucket, Berry, Whitewashed, 3 1/2 In. 275.00
Bucket, Green Paint, White Interior, Bail, Marked Viola, 4 1/2 In. 250.00
Bucket, Lid, Yellow Paint 475.00
Bucket, Pine, Chrome Yellow, Wire Bail, Turned Handle, 7 In. 350.00
Bucket, Pine, Red Stain, Enfield, N.H., 8 X 9 3/4 In. 300.00
Bucket, Sap, Old Red Paint 110.00
Bucket, Sap, Stave, Metal Bands, Aluminum Repaint, 11 3/4 X 9 1/4 In. 95.00
Butter Churn, Tabletop, Tin 195.00
Candy Box, Sabbathday Lake 18.00
Cape, Red Wool, Hooded, Shawl Collar, Checked Neckband, 28 In. 80.00
Carrier, 3–Finger, Enfield, N.H., Natural Finish, 14 1/2 In. 795.00
Carrier, 4–Finger, Enfield, N.H., Red, 11 In. 1980.00
Carrier, Mt.Lebanon, Natural Finish, Round, 13 1/4 In. 660.00
Carrier, Tiger Maple & Pine, Fixed Handle, 8 X 14 1/2 In. 725.00
Case, Display, Pine, Red Stain, Slide Lid, Glass, 8 X 10 In. 375.00
Case, Spool, Walnut & Pine, Drawer, Sliding Doors, Pat.1880, 9 1/2 In. 95.00
Cloak, Child's, Hooded, White Wool, Pink Satin Ribbons, 20 In. 200.00
Cloak, Hooded, Violet Wool, Shawl Collar, 46 In. 300.00
Clothespin, Oak, Hand Carved From 1 Piece, 6 In., Set Of 4 .... 150.00
Coffeepot, Side Spout, Classic Style, Tin, Black Finish, 9 1/2 In. 75.00
Dipper, Hancock, Mass., Maple 1100.00
Dipper, Maple, Chrome Yellow Paint, Carved From 1 Piece 1000.00
Dipper, Oak, Pine With Maple Handle, 7 X 12 In. 200.00
Doll, Roberta, Poplarware Bonnet, Gray Cloak, Taffeta Dress, 14 In. 350.00
Door, Pine, Oak Grained, Iron Hardware, Pegged, 6 Ft. 6 In. X 30 In. 90.00
Dustpan, Maple & Tin 220.00
Flyswatter, Splint, Oval 85.00
Footstool, Mt.Lebanon, 2–Step 595.00
Footstool, Pine, Blue Paint, Wire Nails, 7 7/8 X 11 7/8 In. 50.00
SHAKER, FURNITURE, see Furniture
Gloves, Brethren, Sheepskin, Brown Leather Palm, C.1870 .... 50.00
Hanger, Cloak, Tiger Birch, Pegged, 46 X 15 1/4 In. 25.00
Hanger, Dress, Wooden 20.00
Holder, Fire Tool, Walnut, Rack, 2 Iron Pegs, 23 X 4 In. 200.00
Lifter, Bonnet, Poplar, Short Handle, 32 X 24 In. 250.00
Lunch Pail, Bail Handle, Cover, 19th Century, 8 X 4 1/2 In. 225.00
Measure, Maple, 14 In.Diam. 62.00
Measure, Oak & Pine, Original Red Paint, 4 1/4 X 9 3/4 In. 225.00
Measure, Pine, Beech, Copper Rivets, 1870–90, 4 1/4 X 8 1/2 In. 70.00
Measure, Signed Sabbathday Lake, Wooden, 6 In. 95.00

Porcelain, Cup & Saucer, Dog, Pink, 3½ In.

Minton, Tea Set, Japonisme, Yellow, Gold, 3 Piece

Depression Glass, Moderntone, Bowl, Soup, Cream, Cobalt

Steuben, Compote, Stringing,
Signed, Green, 8 In.

Cruets: Plain Scalloped Panel,
Green; Pressed Optic, Vaseline

Pottery, Vase, Figurine With
Urns, Japan, 9 In.

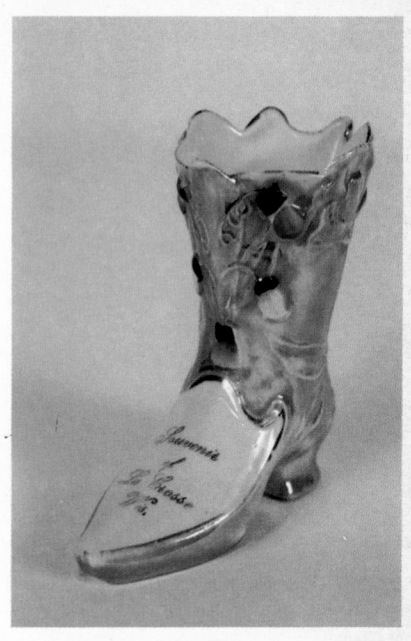

Souvenir, Boot, La Crosse,
Wisconsin, 4½ In.

Pottery, Shoe, Blue & Green, 4 In., Pair

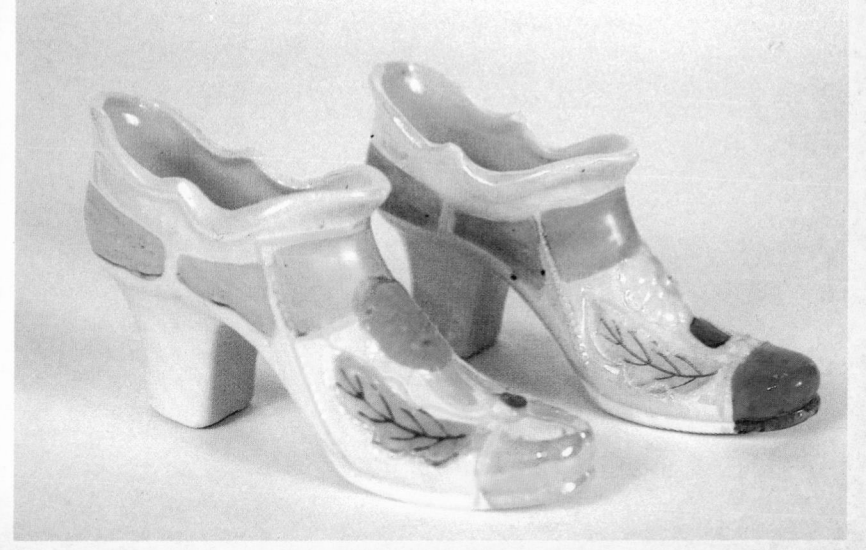

Luster, Pearl, Cup & Saucer, Japan

Haviland, Cup & Saucer, Demitasse,
Theodore Haviland

Sevres, Vase, C. 1900,
Black Clover Mark, 3 In.

Furniture, Chest, Mahogany, Miniature, C. 1840, 13 × 7 × 12 In.

Lamp, Mission, Slag Shade, Oak Base, 14 × 18 × 6 In.

Haviland Type, Vase, Raised
Flowers, 12 In.

Royal Doulton, Vase,
Stoneware, H.S., 9 In.

Pressed Glass, Cord & Tassel,
Double Salt, Pink

Grueby, Vase, Matte Green,
5½ In.

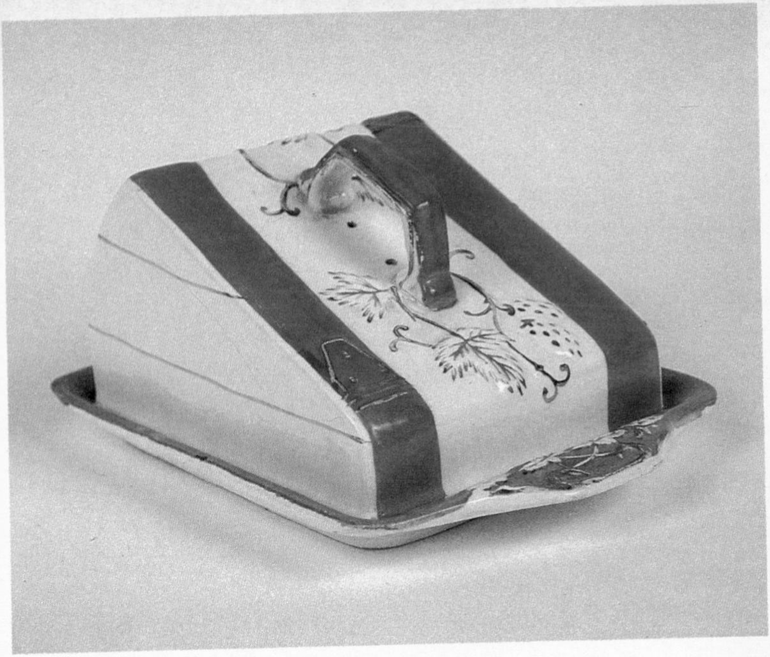

Staffordshire, Dish, Cheese, 10 × 4½ In.

Porcelain, Ginger Jar, Chinese, 8 In.

Store, Figure, Foot, George's Patent Corn & Bunion Shields, 9 In.

Toy, Monkey, Battery

Mirror, Hand, Shaker Medicine	125.00
Mortar & Pestle, Maple, Brown Finish, Turned & Scribed, 11 X 6 In.	60.00
Pail, Seed, Covered, Pine, Varnish, Iron Bands, Bail Handle, 8 In.	110.00
Pan, Dust, Maple & Tin, Turned Handle, 8 X 6 1/2 In.	200.00
Pie Lifter, Wooden Handle, 2–Tine, Brass Ferrule	30.00
Pincushion, Yellow	95.00
Print, Mode Of Worship, D.W.Kellogg, Framed, 18 X 20 In.	550.00
Rack, Drying, Apple, Poplar, Slatted, Nailed, 26 X 36 In.	235.00
Rack, Mortised Ladder, Hold Straining Cloth Over Tub, 12 X 28 In.	35.00
Rack, Spool, Loom, Poplar, Natural Finish, Steel Rods, 42 1/2 In.	275.00
Rail, Pine & Maple, Natural, 70 1/2 In.	200.00
Rug, Cotton, Woven, Multicolored Diagonals, C.1870, 32 X 54 In.	50.00
Rug, Flat Woven, Muted Tan, Red Stripes On Each End, 53 X 26 In.	65.00
Sander, Funnel Top, Punched Holes In Base, Tin, 8 In.	115.00
Sander, Maple, Lemon Yellow Stain, Star Design, 2 7/8 X 2 7/8 In.	175.00
Scoop, Cherry, Carved From 1 Piece, Enfield, N.H., 1870, 6 1/2 X 2 In.	300.00
Scoop, Flour, Maple, Ribbed Finger Grip, 1 Piece	85.00
Scoop, Hancock, Mass., Maple	825.00
Scoop, Maple, Open Handle, Carved From 1 Piece, 1840, 15 X 5 1/2 In.	750.00
Sewing Kit, Leather, Silk, 3 Needle Cases, Silver Thimble, Hancock	120.00
Shovel, Carved From 1 Piece Of Birch	935.00
Shovel, Pine, Green Paint, Carved Handle, Enfield, N.H., 45 In.	75.00
Sieve, Handle, Tin, 10 In.	10.00
Sieve, Horsehair, Bentwood, Sabbathday Lake, Maine, 14 1/4 In.	205.00
Sieve, Horsehair, Poplar, Single Wrap, Copper Nails, 4 1/2 In.	75.00
Sieve, Maple, Laminated Wrap, Copper Screening, 5 1/2 X 17 In.	150.00
Sleeve, Iron, Birch Handle, Iron Plate, 22 In.	85.00
Squeezer, Fruit, Maple, Brass Hinge & Screws, Chamfered Edges	175.00
Stretcher, Stocking, Maple, Size 10, 22 In.	40.00
Sweater, Man's, White Wool, Hart & Shepard, 1933	175.00
Swift, Maple & Basswood, Yellow Ochre Stain, C.1872, 25 In.	175.00
Tongs, Stove	35.00
Tool, Quilting Frame, Cherry Legs, Pine Rods, 36 X 35 1/2 In.	175.00
Tray, Poplar, Scalloped, White Kid Leather Edge, Canterbury	85.00
Tray, Winnowing, Arched Hickory Handles, 18th Century, 1/2 Round	395.00
Washtub, Pine, Mustard Paint, Handles, Lapped Hoop, 14 X 20 1/2 In.	800.00

Shaving mugs were popular from 1860 to 1900. Many types were made, including occupational mugs featuring pictures of men's jobs. There were scuttle mugs, silver plated mugs, glass–lined mugs, and others.

SHAVING MUG, B.P.O.E.Koken, Gold Name	95.00
Baseball Player, Harvard Uniform, Signed F.Earl Christy, 5 In.	45.00
Brush Rest, Bright Cut Flowers, Wallace, Silver Plate, 2 Piece	38.00
Buffalo Head, Matching Brush	225.00
Father In Raised Letters, Hand Painted	50.00
Floral, Coin Gold Handle, Hand Painted	24.00
Flower & Name In Gold, Limoges	45.00
Gold, Flowers, & Name, China	20.00
Golden Knight Shaving Soap, Ansehl, St.Louis, Glass	20.00
Indian Face	68.00
K Of P, Fraternal, Red Holly Berries, Green Leaves	40.00
Milk Glass, Emblem, Drape & Floral, 1930s	15.00
Occupational, Airplane, Ship, Train Transportation	95.00
Occupational, Automobile	1705.00
Occupational, Banjo, Full Name	175.00
Occupational, Barber Shop, Interior	550.00
Occupational, Bartender	225.00
Occupational, Baseball Team	825.00
Occupational, Brewer, Man, With Beard, Sitting High On Cart	195.00
Occupational, Caboose, Owner's Name	212.00
Occupational, Card Maker, Hand Holding Card, Brown & White	175.00
Occupational, Coal Miner	578.00
Occupational, Courtroom Scene, Lawyer, Judge, Policeman, Jurors	375.00

Occupational, Electrical Worker 319.00
Occupational, Engineer 100.00
Occupational, Express Wagon Driver 264.00
Occupational, Exterminator, Rat 1320.00
Occupational, Farmer Hoeing, 2 Horses ....150.00 To 225.00
Occupational, Fire Ladder Wagon 1265.00
Occupational, Fireman 100.00
Occupational, Hearse & Horses 688.00
Occupational, Horse Trader 235.00
Occupational, Horse, Covered Cart, Man, Home Made Bakery Wagon 175.00
Occupational, Hotel 578.00
Occupational, Mortician 242.00
Occupational, Printer & Printing Press, Full Name 300.00
Occupational, Railroad Worker, Locomotive, B.R.T., Gold Name 150.00
Occupational, Railroad, Bluefield, W.Va.& Va., Train, 1863 .... 65.00
Occupational, Telegrapher 95.00
Occupational, Trolley, Owner's Name 342.00
Occupational, Tugboat 770.00
Occupational, U.S.S.Maine 1485.00
Occupational, Waiter 743.00
Occupational, William Macrae, Driver In Phaeton, Gold Trim 150.00
Owl On Branch, Half Moon, C.D.Rich In Gold, Hand Painted 75.00
Polychrome, Flying Eagle, 2 Flags & Shield, Name, Limoges 195.00
Raised Figures Of Lady Barber & Man In Chair, 1930s 75.00
Raised Floral Design In Cobalt Blue, Gold Trim, White 35.00
S.Merrihew, Gold Trim 22.00
Scuttle Type, S Handle, Hinged Brush Holder, Silver 225.00
Silver Plate Overlay, German Reading, From Loving Papa, KPM 55.00
Soap Tray, Lid, Brush Holder, Forbes Silver Co., No.431, 4 Piece 70.00
Tea Leaf, Meakin 48.00

Shawnee
USA

The Shawnee Pottery was started in Zanesville, Ohio, in 1935. The company made vases, novelty ware, flowerpots, figurines, dinnerwares, and cookie jars. Shawnee produced pottery for George Rumrill during the late 1930s. The company stopped working in 1961.

SHAWNEE, Bank, Winnie 100.00
Bowl, Cereal, Corn King 12.00
Bowl, Fruits, Lid 8.00
Bowl, Mixing, Corn King, 5 In. 8.00
Bowl, Mixing, Corn King, 8 In. ....8.00 To 15.00
Bowl, Mixing, Corn Queen, 6 1/2 In. 12.00
Bowl, Mixing, Nested, Corn King, Set Of 3 .... 45.00
Butter, Corn King, Covered ....22.00 To 49.00
Butter, Corn Queen 30.00
Cabaret Set, Child's, Pre–1860, 7 Piece 95.00
Candleholder, Russet & Green 20.00
Casserole, Corn King, Individual 18.00
Casserole, Corn King, Large, 1 1/2 Qt. ....28.00 To 32.00
Casserole, Fruit Basket 25.00
Cookie Jar, Bear With Cookie 38.00
Cookie Jar, Blinking Owl 65.00
Cookie Jar, Clown ....40.00 To 75.00
Cookie Jar, Cookie House 115.00
Cookie Jar, Corn King ....40.00 To 60.00
Cookie Jar, Corn Queen ....60.00 To 65.00
Cookie Jar, Drummer Boy 85.00
Cookie Jar, Dutch Boy ....45.00 To 75.00
Cookie Jar, Dutch Girl ....35.00 To 52.00
Cookie Jar, Elephant, Pink 50.00
Cookie Jar, Farmer Pig ....40.00 To 45.00
Cookie Jar, Fruit Basket 70.00
Cookie Jar, Mugsey 25.00
Cookie Jar, Puss 'N Boots, Lady 55.00
Cookie Jar, Schoolhouse, Original Bell 35.00

Cookie Jar, Smiley Pig, Blue Bandana ....40.00 To 55.00
Cookie Jar, Smiley Pig, Green Bandana, Gold Trim, Flower Design 125.00
Cookie Jar, Winking Owl ....45.00 To 65.00
Cookie Jar, Winnie Pig, Green Collar, Red Closers On Hat & Body 65.00
Creamer, Cat, Gold & Green 20.00
Creamer, Chicken .... 7.00 To 18.00
Creamer, Corn King ....12.00 To 17.00
Creamer, Elephant .... 7.50 To 18.00
Creamer, Pig, Gold 35.00
Creamer, Puss 'N Boots, Green & Yellow ....14.00 To 20.00
Creamer, Smiley, Blue & Yellow, Gold Trim 45.00
Creamer, Spalding Pig 18.00
Cup & Saucer, Corn King 20.00
Cup, Corn King 20.00
Dish, Fruit, Corn King 14.00
Figurine, Chickadee, No.502, Black, Gray 15.00
Figurine, Rooster, No.503 .... 10.00
Jug, Tilt, Fruit 18.00
Jug, Water, Smiley Pig, 2 Qt. 37.00
Mug, Corn King 20.00
Pitcher, Boy Blue, Red Pants 26.00
Pitcher, Chanticleer, Gold ....18.00 To 125.00
Pitcher, Corn King ....12.00 To 30.00
Pitcher, Milk, Bopeep ....25.00 To 40.00
Pitcher, Milk, Corn King 32.50
Pitcher, Milk, Fruits 28.00
Pitcher, Milk, Smiley Pig ....22.00 To 30.00
Pitcher, Smiley Pig, Clover Flower 49.00
Pitcher, Smiley Pig, Gold Trim 90
Pitcher, Smiley Pig, Peach Flower, Gold Trim 115
Planter, Black Bull 29
Planter, Boy Going Fishing .... 5.00 To 10
Planter, Bulb 20
Planter, Bull 16
Planter, Burro, No.772 12
Planter, Butterfly ....
Planter, Caboose ....
Planter, Clown, Marked Supnick ....
Planter, Coal Car ....
Planter, Covered Wagon, Gold .... 7.00 To 2
Planter, Deer 1
Planter, Doe & Log, Light Green Log, Gold Trim, Marked Supnick 2
Planter, Donkey & Cart, Gold Trim, Marked Supnick ....
Planter, Elephant ....
Planter, Fawn & Doe ....
Planter, Fawn, Yellow ....20.00 To
Planter, Fish, Gold Trim ....
Planter, Gazelle, Marked Supnick ....
Planter, Locomotive .... 18.
Planter, Piano, Green, Marked Supnick 16.0
Planter, Polynesian Girl, Marked 15.0
Planter, Rabbit, Marked Supnick .... 15.
Planter, Ram ....
Planter, Rickshaw, Gold Trim, Marked Supnick .... 5.00 To
Planter, Rockinghorse, Original Gold Paint, Marked Supnick ....
Planter, Shoe Form, Elf On Rim ....
Planter, Toy Horse, No.660, White, Red Trim ....
Planter, Uncle Sam Hat, Marked Supnick ....
Planter, Wall Telephone ....
Planter, Water Mill, No.769 ....
Planter, Wishing Well ....
Plate, Corn King ....
Plate, Salad, Corn King ....
Platter, Corn King ....

Relish, Corn King 16.00
Salt & Pepper, Blinking Owl 12.00
Salt & Pepper, Chanticleer 20.00
Salt & Pepper, Cookie House 19.00
Salt & Pepper, Corn King, Large ....10.00 To 15.00
Salt & Pepper, Corn King, Small 8.00
Salt & Pepper, Corn Queen, Large 12.00
Salt & Pepper, Corn Queen, Small 8.00
Salt & Pepper, Daisy, Large 22.00
Salt & Pepper, Dutch Boy & Girl 22.00
Salt & Pepper, Elephant 5.00
Salt & Pepper, Farmer Pig ....8.50 To 12.00
Salt & Pepper, Jug, Labels 35.00
Salt & Pepper, Little Chef, Gold Trim 16.00
Salt & Pepper, Little Red Riding Hood 27.50
Salt & Pepper, Milk Can Shape 12.00
Salt & Pepper, Mugsey, Small ....8.50 To 10.00
Salt & Pepper, Puss 'n Boots ....15.00 To 21.00
Salt & Pepper, Smiley 10.00
Salt & Pepper, Swiss Children 14.00
Salt & Pepper, Watering Can 8.50
Saltshaker, Corn King 12.00
Saltshaker, Corn Queen 12.00
Saltshaker, Mugsey, 5 In. ....18.00 To 34.00
Saltshaker, Winnie & Pig Boy 15.00
Saucer, Corn King 6.00
Shaker, Milk Pail, Figural 9.00
Sugar & Creamer, Petalware, Red Trim 20.00
Sugar & Creamer, Polka Dots 23.00
Sugar, Corn King, Covered ....16.00 To 20.00
Teapot, Corn King, 1 Cup, No.65 ....28.00 To 62.50
Teapot, Corn King, 30 Oz. ....40.00 To 50.00
Teapot, Daisy, Gold ....20.00 To 30.00
Teapot, Elephant ....22.00 To 52.00
Teapot, Granny Ann, Green Apron ....35.00 To 49.00
Teapot, Tom Tom The Piper's Son, Covered ....12.50 To 45.00
Vase, Fairy Wood, Original Sticker, 9 1/4 In. 18.00
Vase, Pineapple, 5 In. 10.00
Vase, Swan, Yellow, Gold 10.00
Vase, Yellow Dove, No.829 .... 2.00
Wall Pocket, Bird House 10.00
Wall Pocket, Girl & Rag Doll 14.00
Wall Pocket, Grandfather Clock 14.00
Wall Pocket, Little Bopeep 12.00
Wall Pocket, Little Jack Horner ....12.00 To 12.50
Watering Can Shaker 8.00

The Shearwater pottery is a family business started by Mr. and Mrs.
G. W. Anderson, Sr., and their three sons. The local Ocean Springs,
Mississippi, clays were used to make the wares in the 1930s.

SHEARWATER, Bowl, Medium Green, Gunmetal Gray Brushed, Marked, 8 1/2 X 3 In.   33.00
Bowl, Warrior, Riding Black Horse, Indian Design, 9 1/2 In. 55.00
Cup & Saucer, Woodpecker Handle, Blue, Demitasse 35.00
Ewer, Marked, Silver Touches, Green, 5 In. 15.00
Mug, Woodpecker Handle, Figural, Green, Gray 38.00
Pitcher, Gray Drip, Green, 4 In. 30.00
Vase, Blue, Green, Metallic Gray, Marked, 6 In. 154.00
Vase, Ducks, Blue, Green, Metallic Gray Wash, Marked, 6 1/4 In. 154.00
Vase, Ribbed, Narrow Neck, Bulbous, Green To Gray, 7 In. 45.00

Sheet music from the past centuries is now collected. The favorites are examples with covers with artistic or historic pictures. Early sheet music covers were lithographed but by the 1900s photographic reproductions were used. The early music was larger than more recent sheets and you must watch out for examples that were trimmed to fit in a twentieth-century piano bench.

SHEET MUSIC, All My Life, Kenny Rogers, Photo, 1983	2.50
And They Called It Dixieland, Al Jolson	10.00
April Showers, The Jolson Story	4.50
Aquarius, Published By United Artists, 1968	1.50
Babylon Is Fallen, Litho, 7 Black Soldiers, Muskets, 1863	27.50
Bell Bottom Trousers, Pictures Dancing Sailors	5.00
Big Bad Wolf, Disney	12.00
Bing Crosby Minstrel Song Folio, 1943, 64 Pages	15.00
Buffalo City Guards Parade March, 1840s	35.00
Burning Of Rome, E.T.Paull, Matte	25.00
Cake Walk, Eli Green, 1899	8.00
Carry Me Back To Old Virginny, 1878	8.00
Coo Coo Song, Al Jolson	9.00
Count Your Blessings Instead Of Sheep, Rosemary Clooney, 1952	5.00
Cover, God Bless Our Home, Framed	115.00
Daddy Swiped Our Last Clean Sheet & Joined The Ku Klux Klan	65.00
Dance Of The Brownies, 1895	10.00
Dinah, Al Jolson	10.00
Djer Kiss, Parrish Front	165.00
Everybody's Teddy March, 1901	14.00
Everything I Have Is Yours, Joan Crawford, Clark Gable, 1933	15.00
Forward Pass, Douglas Fairbanks Jr., Framed, 1929	20.00
G.I.Jive, 1943	10.00
Going From De Cotton Fields	6.00
Goodnight Nurse, Mae West, 1912	15.00
Hail Arkansas, Lum & Abner Cover	6.00
Happy Days, Ralph W.Foote, 1919	2.00
Hello My Dearie, Color Cover, Raphael Kirchner	15.00
Hello, Aloha, Abel Baer, 1926	3.00
I'm A-Whistlin', Jack Berch Shoe Photo	3.50
If He Can Fight Like He Can Love, Goodnight, Germany	4.00
If I Knock The 'L' Out Of Kelly, 1916	4.00
Ivory Tower, 1956	3.00
Jenny Lind	26.00
Keep Your Eye On Your Heart. 1940	4.00
Kentucky Blues, 1921	3.50
King Of The Air, Glenn Curtis, Plane Over N.Y.City	12.00
Lavender Blue, From So Dear To My Heart	15.00
Like An Angel You Flew Into My Heart, Lindbergh Picture	15.00
Lindbergh, The Eagle Of The U.S.A., Picture	12.00
Little French Mother Goodbye, Rockwell Cover, 1917	20.00
Lucinda Cinda June, Supplement Chicago Chronicle, 1901	20.00
Lucky Lindy, 1926	32.00
Memorial, Custer	200.00
Mermaids' Dance, 1800s	5.00
Mickey Mouse's Birthday Party, 1936	15.00
Nigger Blues	20.00
On The Boardwalk In Atlantic City, 1946	5.00
Over The Top	10.00
Piano Music, Humoresque, 5th Nocturne, 1800s, 10 Sheets	15.00
Second Star From The Right, From Peter Pan, Disney	20.00
Sidewalks Of New York, Al Smith Cover	5.00
That Wonderful Something, 1929	15.00
Those Good Old Ku Klux Blues, Fox Trot, Horse, Rider	35.00
Three Caballeros	20.00
Thumper Song, Twitterpated, From Bambi, Disney	10.00
Tom, Dick, Harry, & Jack	10.00

Too Young, Nat King Cole, 1951 .... 1.50
Turkey In The Straw, Black Boy Climbing Turkey House, 1904 .... 15.00
We Don't Know Where We're Going, But We're On Our Way 10.00
Wedding Of The Painted Doll, 1929 .... 15.00
When You Wish Upon A Star, From Pinocchio, Disney 20.00
Yankee Doodle Boy, James Cagney 10.00
Zip A Dee Doo Dah, From Song Of The South, Disney 20.00
      SHEFFIELD, see Silver–English; Silver Plate

*Shirley Temple, the famous movie star, was born in 1928. She made
her first movie in 1932. Shirley Temple dolls, first made in 1934 by
Ideal Toy, Shirley Temple cobalt blue glass dishes, made by Hazel
Atlas Glass Company from 1934 to 1942, and thousands of other
items picturing Shirley were made. Many of these items are being
reproduced today.*

SHIRLEY TEMPLE, Book, Coloring, Saalfield No.1768 .... 40.00
  Book, Heidi, Saalfield 25.00
  Book, How I Raised Shirley Temple 24.00
  Book, Just A Little Girl 15.00
  Book, Littlest Rebel, Movie Version, Pictures 20.00
  Book, Now I Am Eight 27.50
  Book, Poor Little Rich Girl, 1936 .... 45.00
  Book, Rebecca Of Sunnybrook Farm, Movie Version, Pictures 20.00
  Book, Shirley Temple In Dimples 16.00
  Book, Spirit Of Dragonwood, 1945 .... 4.50
  Book, Through The Day, 1936, 32 Page 25.00
  Bowl & Mug, Blue, Picture, Signature 40.00
  Bowl, Pitcher, & Mug, Blue, Picture, Signature 90.00
  Carriage, Doll, Metal Chassis, Rubber Wheels, 1937 .... 180.00
  Creamer, Blue Ceramic 50.00
  Creamer, Blue, Picture, Signature ....28.00 To 34.00
  Doll, Composition, Original Clothes, Ideal, 1934, 18 In. 350.00
  Doll, Composition, Original Wig & Cloth, Marked, 27 In. 400.00
  Doll, Composition, Undressed, 16 In. 150.00
  Doll, Flirty Eyes, Original Clothes, 24 In. 500.00
  Doll, Heidi, Vinyl, Original Clothes, 19 In. ....180.00 To 195.00
  Doll, Original Dress, 1972 ....55.00 To 64.00
  Doll, Sleep Eyes, Open Mouth, Sailor Suit, Ideal, 1937, 15 In. 300.00
  Doll, Vinyl, Original, 1958, 19 In. 250.00
  Figurine, Shirley, Playing Drum, 4 1/2 In. 40.00
  Mirror, Pocket, 1937, 1 3/4 In. ....22.00 To 35.00
  Mirror, Pocket, Pink, Fox Film Corp.1935 .... 27.00

Sign, Scourene, Red, White, Blue,
2 Sides, Cardboard, 9 X 6 1/2 In.

Sign, Picaninny Freeze, Color,
Cardboard, 14 X 10 In.

Mug, Blue ....30.00 To 45.00
Paper Doll, Partially Cut, Saalfield, No.1715, 1935 .... 55.00
Paper Doll, Stand Up, Some Uncut Pages, 1935 .... 45.50
Paper Doll, Whitman, C.1972 .... 10.00
Pen, Fountain 75.00
Photograph, Bright Eyes, Promotional, Autograph, 8 X 10 In. 35.00
Picture, Nightgown, Stuffed Goose, Sepia, Framed, 12 X 15 In. 25.00
Pitcher, Blue, Picture, Round, Signature ....32.00 To 40.00
Postcard, Movie 15.00
Scrapbook, 160 Pictures 50.00
Scrapbook, 1935 ....20.00 To 23.00
Sheet Music, On The Good Ship Lollipop 8.00
Sheet Music, Poor Little Rich Girl 10.00
Song Album, 8 Pages Of Photographs 50.00
        SHRINER, see Masonic

SIGN, Butcher's Shop, Pig Form, Wood, Iron Tail, C.1930, 12 X 26 In. 1430.00
Picaninny Freeze, Color, Cardboard, 14 X 10 In. ....*Illus* 45.00
Scourene, Red, White, Blue, 2 Sides, Cardboard, 9 X 6 1/2 In. ....*Illus* 25.00

Silver deposit glass was made during the late nineteenth and early twentieth centuries. Solid sterling silver was applied to the glass by a chemical method so that a cutout design of silver metal appeared against a clear or colored glass. It is sometimes called silver overlay.

SILVER DEPOSIT, Carafe Set, Rooster, 6 Tumblers 45.00
Creamer & Sugar, Flowers, Porcelain 125.00
Decanter, Cockfight, Black Glass, Pair 200.00
Decanter, Fox Hunt, Black Glass, Rye, Scotch, Pair 300.00
Dish, Candy, Roses, Leaves 45.00
Plate, Amethyst Glass, Flowers, 9 In. 35.00

Listed in this section are many of the current and out-of-production silver and silver plated flatware patterns made in the past eighty years. Other silver is listed under Silver-American, Silver-English, etc. Most silver flatware sets that are missing a few pieces can be completed through the help of one of the many silver matching services listed in "The Kovels' Collectors' Source Book."

SILVER FLATWARE SILVER PLATE, Adonis, Knife, Oneida 3.00
Adoration, Cold Meat Fork, International 12.50
Adoration, Knife, International 4.50
Alhambra, Fork, International, 7 In. 12.50
Alhambra, Grapefruit Spoon, Rogers 4.00
Ambassador, Fruit Spoon, International 6.60
Anniversary, Carving Set, 10 1/2 In., 2 Piece 30.00
Arcadian, Demitasse Spoon, 1847 Rogers 10.00
Athena, Fruit Spoon, Wallace 3.50
Beaded, Strawberry Fork, Oneida 8.00
Berkshire, Fork, International 6.50
Berkshire, Pie Server, Rogers 12.00
Charter Oak, Oyster Fork, Rogers 15.00
Cheshire, Teaspoon, Oneida 2.50
Columbia, Knife, International 12.00
Concerto, Berry Spoon, National 6.50
Danish Princess, Berry Spoon, International 16.00
Debutante, Dinner Set, Rogers, 42 Piece 45.00
Enchantment-Bounty, Sauce Ladle, Oneida 6.00
Fleur De Lis, Dinner Knife, Community 14.00
Florida, Sugar Shell, Rogers 8.00
Fortune, Pie Server, Oneida 6.50
Heraldic, Butter, 1847 Rogers 4.00
Heritage, Pie Server, International 10.00
Ionic, Cake Knife, Rogers, 10 3/4 In. 50.00
La Touraine, Demitasse Spoon, International 3.00
La Vigne, Cold Meat Fork, Rogers 14.00

Lady Hamilton, Knife, Oneida	5.00
May Queen, Fork, International	4.50
Mayfair, Dinner Set, Rogers, 1923, 31 Piece	52.00
Mystic, Chipped Beef Fork, Rogers	9.00
Mystic, Soup Ladle, Rogers	40.00
New Century, Oyster Ladle, Rogers, 9 1/2 In.	28.00
New Century, Salad Set, Rogers, 2 Piece	24.00
New Century, Soup Ladle, Rogers, 10 3/4 In.	35.00
Normandy, Cream Spoon, Reed & Barton	3.00
Oak, Gravy Ladle, Rogers	11.00
Old Colony, Fork, International	4.00
Orange Blossom, Oyster Fork, Rogers	6.00
Paragon, Ice Cream Fork, American	12.00
Parisian, Pie Server, Reed & Barton	12.00
Priscilla, Fork, 1847 Rogers, 1900	3.00
Queen Bess, Knife, Oneida	4.00
Savoy, Cheese Scoop, Rogers	30.00
Saxony, Knife, Gorham	4.00
Silver Flowers, Cold Meat Fork, Oneida	5.50
Southern Splendor, Knife, International	3.50
Tiger Lily, Butter Server, Reed & Barton	8.00
Tudor, Food Pusher, Rogers & Hamilton	22.00
Tuxedo, Berry Spoon, International	10.00
Vintage, Berry Spoon, Rogers	27.00
Vogue, Teaspoon, Wallace	4.00

SILVER FLATWARE STERLING, Acorn, Dinner Set, Jensen, 78 Piece 8300.00

Adam, Asparagus Fork, Whiting	175.00
Alexandra, Sugar Shell, Lunt	26.00
Alexandra, Teaspoon, Lunt	17.00
American Federal, Cake Knife, Reed & Barton	15.00
Arabesque, Sugar Shell, Whiting	30.00
Atlantis, Olive Spoon, Tiffany	55.00
Autumn Leaves, Teaspoon, Reed & Barton	17.00
Bamboo, Luncheon Knife, Tiffany	28.00
Bead, Bonbon Spoon, Whiting, Pierced Bowl	16.00
Berain, Soup Ladle, Wallace	190.00
Bridal Rose, Luncheon Fork, Alvin	37.00
Bridal Rose, Teaspoon, Alvin	15.00
Brocade, Luncheon Fork, International	13.00
Buttercup, Sugar, Creamer, & Tray, Gorham, 9 In.	175.00
Buttercup, Teaspoon, Gorham	10.00
Calvert, Teaspoon, Kirk	15.00
Cambridge, Fish Server, Gorham	105.00
Camellia, Luncheon Knife, Gorham	12.00
Candlelight, 4 Piece, Towle, Service For 8	660.00
Candlelight, Sugar Tongs, Towle	25.00
Canterbury, Lettuce Fork, Towle	45.00
Cascade, Ladle, Towle, 5 3/4 In.	27.50
Cattails, Strawberry Fork	30.00
Chantilly, 5 Piece, Gorham, Service For 12	675.00
Chantilly, Carving Set, Gorham	95.00
Chantilly, Macaroni Server, Gorham	225.00
Chantilly, Pie Server, Gorham	28.00
Chantilly, Salad Set, Gorham	160.00
Chapel Bells, 6 Piece, Alvin, Service For 12	1240.00
Chapel Bells, Teaspoon, Alvin	14.00
Chateau, Ladle, Lunt, 5 In.	32.00
Chatelaine, Soup Spoon, Lunt	24.00
Chippendale, 6 Piece, Towle, Service For 8	890.00
Chrysanthemum Beading, Lettuce Fork, H.H.Curtis	38.00
Chrysanthemum, Butter Spreader, Stieff	16.00
Clover, Preserve Spoon, Towle, 7 In.	30.00
Colfax, Fork, Durgin	31.00

Countess, Master Butter, Frank M.Smith	13.00
Cupid, Dessert Spoon, Dominick & Haff	22.00
D'Orleans, Luncheon Fork, Towle	32.00
Damask Rose, 6 Piece, Heirloom, Service For 12	1265.00
Dancing Flowers, Cream Soup, Reed & Barton	23.00
Dancing Flowers, Teaspoon, Reed & Barton	18.00
Dauphine, Nut Spoon, Wallace	28.00
Debussy, 5 Piece, Towle, Service For 12	1410.00
Debussy, Fork, Towle	26.00
Della Robbia, Dinner Set, Alvin, Service For 8	895.00
Dundee, Soup Ladle, 1847 Rogers	23.50
Duvaine, Teaspoon, Unger	28.00
Edgewood, Cucumber Server, International	70.00
Eloquence, Dinner Set, Lunt, 56 Piece	1750.00
Elsinore, 5 Piece, International, Service For 6	475.00
English Gadroon, Dinner Set, Gorham, 69 Piece	995.00
Esplanada, 5 Piece, Towle, Service For 8	870.00
Etruscan, Dinner Set, Gorham, Service For 12	1400.00
Fairfax, Butter Knife, Durgin	9.00
Fairfax, Olive Spoon, Durgin, Pierced	28.00
Fairfax, Pickle Fork, Durgin	18.00
Faneuil, Fork, Tiffany	42.00
Fleur De Lis, Food Pusher, Alvin	45.00
Floral, Punch Ladle, Wallace	200.00
Florentine, Dinner Fork, Gorham	45.00
Francis I, Dinner Set, Reed & Barton, 72 Piece	1750.00
Francis, Fork, Reed & Barton	25.00
Frontenac, Teaspoon, International	14.00 To 18.00
Georgian, Teaspoon, Towle	15.00
Grand Victorian, Luncheon Fork, Wallace	33.00
Grande Baroque, 4 Piece, Wallace, Service For 8	795.00
Greenbriar, Butter, Gorham	16.00
Greenbrier, 5 Piece, Gorham, Service For 8	700.00
Homewood, Teaspoon, Steiff	17.00
Hunt Club, Knife, Durgin	16.00
Hunt Club, Tomato Server, Durgin	40.00
Inaugural, Butter, State House	12.00
Indian, Soup Ladle, Whiting	160.00
Joan Of Arc, Serving Spoon, International	35.00
John & Priscilla Alden, Fork, Westmoreland	18.00
John & Priscilla Alden, Knife, Westmoreland	16.00
Josephine, Cheese Scoop, Howard St.Co.	70.00
Josephine, Lettuce Fork, Whiting	48.00
King Albert, Fork, Whiting, Div.Gorham	30.00
King Cedric, Luncheon Fork, Oneida	23.00
King Cedric, Sugar Spoon, Oneida	17.00
King Edward, 4 Piece, Gorham, Service For 12	955.00
King Richard, 4 Piece, Towle, Service For 12	1230.00
King Richard, Ladle, Towle	95.00
La Reine, Dinner Set, Wallace, Service For 8	750.00
La Rocaille, Luncheon Fork, Reed & Barton	25.00
La Strada, Teaspoon, International	16.00
Lace Point, Dinner Set, Lunt, Service For 8	640.00
Lancaster Rose, Tomato Server, Gorham	95.00
Laureate, Crumb Scoop, Whiting, 12 In.	90.00
Legato, Luncheon Fork, Towle	29.00
Legato, Teaspoon, Towle	18.00
Lily, Dinner Fork, Whiting	45.00
Lily, Teaspoon, Whiting, Monogram	15.00
Lily–Of–The–Valley, Soup Ladle, Whiting	395.00
Lily–Of–The–Valley, Sugar Shell, Whiting	65.00
Lotus, 5 Piece, Wallace, Service For 8	815.00
Louis XIV, Carving Set, Towle	65.00
Louis XV, Asparagus Fork, Whiting, 8 1/2 In.	175.00

Louis XV, Asparagus Server, Whiting 185.00
Louis XV, Berry Spoon, Whiting 65.00
Love Disarmed, Teaspoon, Reed & Barton 80.00
Lucerne, Luncheon Fork, Wallace 26.00
Luxembourg, Knife, Gorham 22.00
Madame Jumel, Teaspoon, Whiting, Div.Gorham 12.00
Madrigal, Dinner Set, Lunt, 36 Piece ....695.00 To 800.00
Majestic, Sugar Tongs, Alvin 22.00
Majestic, Teaspoon, Alvin 15.00
Mandarin, Teaspoon, Whiting 9.00
Marie Antoinette, Fish Set, Gorham, 2 Piece 295.00
Marquise, Demitasse Spoon, Tiffany 15.00
Marquise, Teaspoon, Tiffany 22.00
Maryland, Dinner Set, Alvin, Service For 8 .... 635.00
Maryland, Tablespoon, Alvin 35.00
Mayflower, Luncheon Fork, Kirk 29.00
Meadow Song, 5 Piece, Towle, Service For 8 .... 805.00
Melbourne, Teaspoon, Oneida 15.00
Melrose, Luncheon Fork, Gorham 33.00
Mignonette, Dinner Set, Lunt, Service For 12 .... 1115.00
Modern Victorian, Carving Set, Lunt 75.00
Monticello, Luncheon Fork, Lunt 21.00
Monticello, Teaspoon, Lunt 14.00
Moonbeam, Dinner Set, Rogers, 58 Piece 600.00
Moonglow, Cream Soup, International 15.00
Moonglow, Luncheon Fork, International 25.00
Nautilus, Berry Spoon, Blackinton 55.00
Newbury, Bouillon Ladle, Towle 160.00
Norfolk, Luncheon Fork, Gorham 22.00
Old Colonial, Demitasse Spoon, Towle 15.00
Old English, Ice Cream Server, Towle 80.00
Old French, Ice Cream Fork, Gorham 15.00
Old Medici, Meat Fork, Gorham, 10 1/2 In. 100.00
Old Newbury, Toast Fork, Towle 200.00
Old Orange Blossom, Butter Spreader, Alvin 28.00
Old Rosalind, Dinner Fork, International 1810 .... 22.00
Old Rosalind, Tablespoon, International 1810 .... 38.00
Olfas, Knife, Durgin 16.00
Onslow, Fork, Tuttle 31.00
Orient, Fish Fork, Alvin 85.00
Palm, Fork, Tiffany 53.00
Persian, Sugar Sifter, Tiffany 165.00
Pomona, Pie Server, Towle 90.00
Promise, Fork, Royal Crest 18.00
Provence, Luncheon Fork, Tiffany 70.00
Provence, Teaspoon, Tiffany 45.00
Quadrille, Fork, Kirk 26.00
Quadrille, Teaspoon, Kirk 45.00
Queens Lace, Knife, International 16.00
Queens, Luncheon Fork, Gorham 16.00
Rambler Rose, Gravy Ladle 35.00
Rambler Rose, Sugar Spoon, Towle 23.00
Repousse, Ice Tongs, Kirk 95.00
Repousse, Pie Server, Kirk 22.00
Repousse, Soup Ladle, Jacobi & Jenkins 275.00
Rhapsody, Teaspoon, International 14.00
Richelieu, Butter, International 18.00
Richelieu, Teaspoon, International 21.00
Rose Cascade, Luncheon Fork, Reed & Barton 26.00
Rose Point, 5 Piece, Wallace, Service For 8 .... 835.00
Rose, Bacon Fork, Steiff 55.00
Royal Windsor, Cocktail Fork, Towle 11.00
Royal Windsor, Luncheon Fork, Towle 24.00
Scroll, Dinner Set, Jensen, Service For 12 .... 4300.00

Shell, Serving Fork, Williamsburg	125.00
Shepherdess, Pea Server, Continental, 7 1/2 In.	70.00
Sir Christopher, Teaspoon, Wallace	21.00
Spring Glory, Cream Soup, International	21.00
Spring Glory, Fork, International	20.00
Stardust, Carving Set, Gorham	65.00
Stradivari, 5 Piece, Wallace, Service For 8	820.00
Strasbourg, Fork, Gorham	41.00
Strasbourg, Teaspoon, Gorham	17.00
Tapestry, 5 Piece, Reed & Barton, Service For 12	1185.00
Tapestry, Cake Knife, Reed & Barton	25.00
Trianon, Fruit Spoon, Dominick & Haff	12.00
Trianon, Master Butter, International	16.00
Violet, Gravy Ladle, Wallace	82.00
Virginia Carvel, Luncheon Knife, Towle	16.00
Virginia Carvel, Teaspoon, Towle	9.00
Wakefield, Salad Spoon, Reed & Barton	49.00
Watson, Tongs, Towle	18.00
Wedding Bells, Luncheon Fork, International	27.00
Wedding Bells, Soup Spoon, International	19.00
William & Mary, Luncheon Fork, Lunt	24.00

Silver plate is not solid silver. It is a ware made of a metal, such as nickel or copper, that is covered with a thin coating of silver. The letters "EPNS" are often found on American and English silver plated wares. Sheffield silver is a type of silver plate.

SILVER PLATE, Ashtray, Ringling Circus	22.00
Basket, Nature Scene, Leaf Rim, Bail, Wilcox, 5 In.	50.00
Bookends, Figural, Bowlers	45.00
Bookends, Horse Head, Horseshoe Base, Marked PMC, 6 3/4 In.	68.00
Bottle, Wine, Figural, Caddy, Towle, Gadrooned Fluting, 7 In.	30.00
Bowl, Porringer Handle, 12 1/2 In., Pair	30.00
Bowl, Savoy, Double, Fluted, Rogers 1847, 15 In.	75.00
Box, Art Nouveau, Scrolled Feet, Floral, Europe, 4 X 5 3/4 In.	175.00
Butter, Covered, Embossed Flowers, Meriden	55.00
Butter, Covered, Liner, Handles, Knife Rest, James Tufts	55.00
Butter, Dome Top, Raised Rim Repousse, Scroll Handles, Knife	38.00
Butter, Roll Top, Elk Head, Feet, Etched, Knife Rest, Dated 1863	95.00
Cake Basket, Lily–Of–The–Valley Design, Rogers Smith, 9 In.	45.00
Cake Basket, Victorian, Cherubs, Derby	225.00
Candelabra, Reeded Branches, Rings, Sheffield, 19 1/2 In., Pair	100.00
Candlestick, Bobeche, Sheffield, 10 1/8 In., Pair	130.00
Candlestick, English, Bobeche, Swags, 10 3/4 In., Pair	200.00
Candlestick, Hammered, Derby, 7 In., Pair	26.00
Candlestick, Ornate, Dated 1883, 6 X 6 In., Pair	120.00
Candlestick, Ornate, Wilcox, 11 In.	28.00
Candlestick, Sailboat, People, Repousse, Base, 4 3/4 In., Pair	50.00
Casket, Jewel, Raised Roses, Footed, Rogers, 9 X 5 In.	60.00
Cocktail Shaker, Art Deco	29.00
Coffee Service, Coronation, 3 Piece	175.00
Coffeepot, Pomegranate Finial, Gadroon Feet, 1810, 11 5/8 In.	250.00
Coffeepot, Sheffield Walker & Hall, C.1895	195.00
Condiment Set, Figural, Acorn, Claw & Ball Feet, 3 Piece	45.00
Creamer, Repousse, Snake Handle, Elephant Feet, Individual	50.00
Cup, Child's, 7 Teddy Bears Frolicking	65.00
Dish, Chafing, Burner, Scalloped Edge, 12 1/2 X 6 1/2 In.	95.00
Dish, Double, Warming, Sheffield, C.1910, 8 1/2 X 8 1/2 In.	185.00
Egg Caddy, 4 Cups, Salt, Pepper, 8 X 5 1/2 In.	85.00
Flask, Cup Top, Engraved, Art Nouveau Lady, Initials, 6 In.	45.00
Fruit Stand, Roman Faces, Fox Bail, Reed & Barton, 1871, 10 In.	95.00
Holder, Playing Card, Cut Scroll On Front & Cards, Scalloped	25.00
Humidor, 4–Part, Meriden, 11 X 7 In.	185.00
Humidor, Cigar, Tobacco Leaves, 3 Part, Matches, Cigars, Ashtray	120.00
Humidor, Figural, Champagne Bottle, Cigars, Bristol, 10 In.	48.00

Ice Bucket, Eagle Symbol, Engraved, International	300.00
Kettle, Hot Water, Chinoiserie Figural, Stand, American, 16 In.	90.00
Kettle, Lampstand, Scrolling, Engraved, Elkington, 1865, 10 In.	100.00
Knife Rest, Cupid Playing Mandolin, Figural, 3 3/4 In.	38.00
Mirror, Plateau, Double Bevel, 14 In.	90.00
Mirror, Plateau, Floral Sprays, Fairy Masks, C.1810, 22 In.	1750.00
Mug, Floral, James W.Tufts, Boston, Quadruple Plate, 1885	45.00
SILVER PLATE, NAPKIN RING, see Napkin Ring	
Pitcher, Latticework Bands, Pierced Design, Stand, 18 In.	150.00
Pitcher, Repousse Pears, Leaves, Barbour Bros., 7 3/4 In.	45.00
Plate, Alms, Latin Inscription, Given In 1636, 12 3/8 In.	175.00
Plate, Child's, ABC Border, Oneida	85.00
Plate, Tied Reeded Edge, Bust Of Louis XVI Center, 11 In.	140.00
Platter, Dome, Gadrooned, Handles, Engraved, Sheffield, 18 In.	30.00
Platter, Eternally Yours, Well, Tree, Rogers, 19 In.	45.00
Punch Cup, Vintage, 1881 Rogers	8.00
Salt Dip, Lily On Leaf Base, Figural	28.00
Server, 3 Shell Sections, Handle, Walker & Hall, 9 1/2 In.	50.00
Spoon Holder, Bird Finial, 12 Hooks, Sheffield, 1923	90.00
Spoon Holder, Dome Lid, Inverted Thumbprint Bowl, Amber	120.00
Spoon Tray, Applied Flowers, Handle, Gold Wash, Footed, Marked	35.00
Spoon Warmer, Nautilus Shape On Rocks	135.00
SILVER PLATE, SPOON, SOUVENIR, see Souvenir, Spoon, Silver Plate	
Sugar, Manhattan, International, Marked, Dated	18.00
Syrup, Lion Finial, Footed, Reed & Barton, 7 1/2 In.	45.00
Syrup, Woman's Head Finial, Meriden, 1878	100.00
Tankard, Classical Figures, Mythical Pan Finial, 17 In.	320.00
Tea Ball, Hinged Top, Chain & Ring, Piercing, 1 3/4 In.	28.00
Tea Set, Embossed Band Of Diamonds, Wurttenbergische, 5 Piece	605.00
Tea Set, Rosewood Handle & Finials, French, C.1930, 5 Piece	770.00
Tea Urn, Gadrooned, Pedestal, Paw Feet, Sheffield, 1820, 14 In.	450.00
Toast Rack, 6 Slice, Center Ring Handle, English	55.00
Toothpick, Corset Shaped, Scalloped Beaded Flanged Rim	32.00
Tray, Coiled Snake, Art Nouveau, James Dixon, 12 In.	55.00
Tray, Engraved & Scroll Edge, Hallmarked, 25 1/2 X 15 1/2 In.	125.00
Tray, Floral Swag, Beaded Edge, Eagle, England, 17 3/4 In.	125.00
Tray, Leaf Scroll Design, Handles, Crescent Mfg., 24 In.	100.00
Tray, Meat & Vegetable, Victorian Rose, Oval, 22 X 16 In.	60.00
Tray, Openwork Handles, Stylized Florals, P.Follot, 24 1/4 In.	3850.00
Tray, Ornate Engraving, Footed, 9 X 7 In.	25.00
Tray, Pastry, Manhattan, International, 11 1/4 X 15 1/2 In.	110.00
Tray, Scroll & Fans, Handles, Footed, Crown & Star Mark, 25 In.	125.00
Tray, Tree Well, Victorian Rose, Oval, Wm.Rogers, 22 X 16 In.	60.00
Vase, Art Deco, Pear-Shaped, Kneeling Nudes Feet, 9 In.	65.00
Vase, Flared, Glass Flower Holder, Webb Corbett, 7 In.	45.00
Water Cooler, Stand, Porcelain Lined, Extension Holds Cups	155.00
Wine Cooler, Handles, C.1830, 12 In., Pair	975.00
SILVER, SHEFFIELD, see Silver Plate; Silver–English	

The silver listed in this book is subdivided by country. Silver–American is the first listing, followed by Silver–Chinese, Silver–Danish, etc. There are also other pieces of silver and silver plate listed under special categories, such as Napkin Ring or Tiffany, and under Silver Flatware.

SILVER–AMERICAN, see also Tiffany Silver; Silver–Sterling	
SILVER–AMERICAN, Basket, Circular, Handle, Woodside Sterling Co., 9 1/2 In.	260.00
Basket, Dessert, Shell Shape, Howard, 1908, 10 3/8 In., Pair	3650.00
Beaker, Armorial, Beaded Border, Jaccard, 1842–52, 3 1/2 In.	750.00
Bonbon, Full Figure Of King Henry VIII, Gorham, 9 In.	235.00
Bowl, Art Nouveau Borders, J.E.Caldwell, C.1901, 10 1/8 In.	1750.00
Bowl, Ladle In King's Pattern, R. & W.Wilson, 11 1/8 In.	400.00
Bowl, Scalloped Rim, Carp Trapped In Nets, 9 3/4 In.	715.00
Box, Cigar, Lid Engraved, 1898, Black, Starr & Frost, 10 In.	275.00
Bread Tray, Chantilly, Gorham, 12 In.	320.00

Silver–American, Coffeepot,
Joseph Richardson, C.1770

> Wash silver every time it is used. Before
> you polish, be sure to wash the silver to
> remove all dust. Small gritty pieces of
> dirt will scratch the silver.

Butter, Glass Insert, Gold Wash, Covered, Knife, Wilcox	125.00
Butter, Master, A.Coles, Coin, C.1860	65.00
Butter, Tazza, Pierced Liner, Covered, C.B. & Co., 7 In.	425.00
Caddy, Wine Bottle, Openwork, Scrolls, Whiting, 7 1/4 In.	95.00
Cake Basket, Filigree Handle, J.E.Caldwell & Co.	1540.00
Cake Plate, Trianon, Low Foot, International, 10 In.	150.00
Candelabra, Circular Branches, Gorham, 12 In., Pair	135.00
Candlestick, Baluster Stem, Art Deco, Norbert, 10 In., Pair	275.00
Candlestick, Fluted Stem, Tulip Candle Nozzle, 11 In., Pair	175.00
Candlestick, Repousse, S.Kirk & Son, 11 1/2 In., Pair	2000.00
Candy Dish, Rose Point, Wallace	85.00
Carving Set, Hollow Handle, Case, Gorham, 3 Piece	95.00
Coffee Set, After Dinner, Etruscan, Gorham, 3 Piece	720.00
Coffeepot, 8–Sided, Pedestal, Unger Bros., Demitasse	255.00
Coffeepot, Joseph Richardson, C.1770 ....*Illus*	10450.00
Coffeepot, Plymouth, Curved Spout, Gorham, 11 In.	140.00
Coffeepot, Swan Neck Spout, John Ewan, C.1825, 11 1/2 In.	1430.00
Compote, Allover Grapes & Leaves, W.Adams, N.Y., 4 X 6 In.	325.00
Creamer, Scrolls, Shells, Leaf Spout, Gorham, 1888, 7 In.	375.00
Decanter, Pinch, Silver Mounted, 9 In.	10.00
Demitasse Pot, 8 Panels, Ivory Handles, Unger Brothers	245.00
Dish, Windsor, Reed & Barton, Square, 8 1/2 In.	80.00
Epergne, Openwork, 3 Dish, Handles, Tiffany, C.1870, 10 In.	1100.00
Fish Slice, Olive Pattern, Jones, Ball, & Co., C.1850, 12 In.	300.00
Flask, Hip, Engraved Bands Of Reeding, International	120.00
Flask, Hip, Screw–On Hinged Cap, Oblong Shape, 7 1/2 In.	80.00
Flask, Pocket, Gibson Girl Head, Unger Bros.	265.00
Funnel, Wine, Marked WS, 1782, 4 1/2 In.	200.00
Hatpin, Figural, Bulldog Head, Jewel Eyes, Unger Bros.	125.00
Kettle, Lampstand, Swing Handle, Tiffany, C.1910, 14 In.	3950.00
Ladle, Christian Wiltberger, Philadelphia, C.1790, 14 In.	1100.00
Ladle, Mustard, A.G.Reed & Co., Fiddle	35.00
Ladle, Sauce, H.L.& E.J.Zahm, Brite Cut	65.00
Ladle, Soup, Fiddle, CIH In Script, John Wolfe Forbes, 1830	50.00
Mug, Cylindrical, Loop Handle, Crichton & Co., 3 1/2 In.	170.00
Mug, Reeded Rim, Scroll Handle, John Crawford, 3 1/2 In.	250.00
Pill Box, Lafayette Silver Dollar Top, C.1900, 2 1/8 In.	130.00
Pitcher, Bulbous, Inscription, T.Emery, 1808, 5 3/4 In.	600.00
Pitcher, Octagonal Vase Shaped, Unger Bros., 9 1/2 In.	175.00
Pitcher, Scroll Handle, Reed & Barton, 1930s, 10 In.	210.00
Pitcher, Square Loop Handle, Oval, Gorham, 9 In.	275.00
Pitcher, Water, Garden Flowers, Kirk, 11 In.	750.00

Pitcher, Water, Scroll Design, Gorham, 7 1/4 In.	440.00
Pitcher, Water, Scroll Handle, A.E.Warner, C.1835, 8 1/4 In.	5600.00
Pitcher, Water, Stand, Thermal, Wm.Wilson, C.1890, 13 1/2 In.	3300.00
Plate, Tea, Scroll Border, Monogram, Mauser, 6 In., Set Of 12	325.00
Porringer, Keyhole Handle, Monogram, John W.Forbes, C.1830	600.00
Powder Jar, Love's Dream, Unger Brothers, Covered	175.00
Punch Bowl, Civil War Presentation, Gorham, C.1865, 17 In.	3750.00
Salver, 3 Feet, Tompkins & Black, C.1840, 10 3/4 In., Pair	850.00
Saucepan, Richard Humphreys, C.1772	3600.00
Smoker Set, Tray, Horn, Cigar Lighter, J.F.Fradley, 6 Piece	500.00
Soup, Hyperion, Whiting, Monogram	33.00
Spoon, Baby, Carved Handle, Watrous Silver, 1898	35.00
Spoon, Dessert, A.B.Warden, Philadelphia, C.1845	30.00
Spoon, Dessert, N.W.Goddard, Fiddle	20.00
Spoon, Dessert, R.H.Bailey, Woodstock, Vt.	32.00
Spoon, Orange, N.Harding, Boston, C.1860	30.00
Spoon, Richard Humphrey, C.1780, 8 7/8 In.	300.00
Spoon, Serving, Ball, Black & Co., Coin, C.1850, 11 In.	400.00
Spoon, Serving, Coin Silver, E.P.Esoure, Philadelphia, 1830	60.00
Spoon, Serving, Coin Silver, Wilson McGrew, Cincinnati	60.00
Spoon, Serving, J.P. Trott, New London, Ct., C.1810	175.00
Spoon, Serving, Repousse, Fruits & Flowers, Kirk & Son	250.00
Spoon, Serving, Theophilus Bradbury, Newburyport, C.1815	40.00
Spoon, Trifid, Johannis Wys, 1695–1700	495.00
Sugar & Creamer, Hunter, Stag Scene, Covered, Kirk, C.1850	750.00
Sugar Basket, Swing Handle, Raised Foot, Kirk & Sons, 7 In.	325.00
Sugar Shell, Coin Silver, Butler & McCarthy, C.1845	60.00
Sugar Shell, King Pattern, Bailey & Co., C.1850, Coin	125.00
Sugar Sifter, Dominick & Haff, No.10	75.00
Sugar Tong, Clark & Anthony, Coin, C.1790	60.00
Sugar Urn, Covered, C.Wiltberger, C.1800, 10 1/8 In.	1750.00
Tablespoon, C.Young, Bridgeport, Ct., C.1830	55.00
Tablespoon, G.Aiken, Baltimore, C.1815	65.00
Tablespoon, Wood & Hughs, New York, C.1840	15.00
Tea & Coffee Set, Scroll Handles, Gorham, C.1865, 6 Piece	2750.00
Tea & Coffee Set, Scroll Handles, S.Kirk, 1830–46, 6 Piece	3500.00
Tea & Coffee Set, T.Warner, Baltimore, C.1800, 5 Piece	7000.00
Tea & Coffee Set, Tray, Georgian Style, Gorham, 6 Piece	3850.00
Tea & Coffee Set, Tray, Navarre, Watson, 6 Piece	2000.00
Tea Caddy, Fleur–De–Lis, Goodnow & Jenks, C.1900, 4 In.	120.00
Tea Caddy, Hand Engraved, Reed & Barton, C.1880, 8 In.	125.00
Tea Set, B.Gardner, C.1830, 3 Piece	1000.00
Tea Set, Gadroon Rims, Monogram, Lewis & Smith, 4 Piece	1500.00
Tea Set, Lobed Form, Wallace & Sons, Tray 22 In., 7 Piece	1250.00
Teapot, Hugh Wishart, New York City, C.1795	3800.00
Teapot, J.B.Jones & Co., Boston, Coin	425.00
Teaspoon, Asa Sibley, Coffin End	180.00
Teaspoon, Coffin End, Jesse Corbett	45.00
Teaspoon, G.Terry, Enfield, Ct., C.1790	55.00
Teaspoon, H.Evans, Newark, N.J., C.1825	38.00
Teaspoon, J.Coles, N.Y., Ct., & N.J., C.1830	25.00
Teaspoon, L.Young, Bridgeport, C.1837	18.00
Teaspoon, Samuel Drown II, Oval End, Feathered Edge	150.00
Teaspoon, Sigourney & Hitchcock, Watertown, N.Y., C.1850	18.00
Teaspoon, T.Bradbury & Sons, Newburyport	24.00
Teaspoon, T.K.Emery, Boston, Coin, C.1810	28.00
Teaspoon, Wilson, Philadelphia	30.00
Tongs, C.Youngs, Bridgeport, Ct., C.1830	85.00
Tongs, J.A.Willick, Baltimore, Md., 1811–22	135.00
Tongs, Sugar, Basket Of Flowers Design, C.1820, Coin, 6 In.	215.00
Tray, Bevelein, Boston, Raised Edge, Scroll Feet, 12 1/4 In.	225.00
Tray, Bread, Oval Leaf Shape, Reed & Barton, 12 In.	80.00
Tray, Card, Repousse Border, 3 Ball & Claw Feet, Kirk, 6 In.	150.00
Tray, Engraving, Centennial Lodge No.763, 1914, 18 In.	230.00

Tray, Fluted Border, Reed & Barton, 11 X 8 1/2 In. 110.00
Tray, Hampton Court, Cutout Handles, Reed & Barton, 16 In. 495.00
Tray, Raised Fluted Detail, Gardner, Mass., C.1920, 9 In. 225.00
Tray, Redlich & Co., New York, 20th Century, Round, 14 In. 245.00
Trophy Cup, Gorham Co., Engraved Inscription, 9 In. 140.00
Tureen, Covered, Dominick & Haff, 1887, 9 3/4 In., Pair 1050.00
Tureen, Ring Handles, Covered, J.E.Caldwell, 1875, 16 In. 2000.00
Vase, 8 Panels, Floral, Pedestal, Unger Bros., 14 In. 255.00
Vase, Lily Pattern, Flared, Gorham, 9 X 3 1/4 In. 200.00
Vase, Trumpet, 8 Panels, Florals, Unger Bros., 14 In. 255.00

SILVER–AUSTRIAN, Candlestick, Stylized Swags, Campana Sockets, 13 In., Pair 250.00
Platter, 11 Austrian Coins, Marked 800, 1920–37, 14 In. 225.00
Tray, Scroll Handles, Ribbed Rim, Oval, 22 1/4 In. 250.00

SILVER–BELGIAN, Teapot, Ribbed Body & Cover, Wooden Finial, Handle, Marked 60.00

SILVER–CHINESE, Tea Set, Twig Spout & Handles, Late 19th Century, 3 Piece 775.00
Vase, Hawthorne Design, 19th Century, 6 In. & 4 In., Pair 300.00

SILVER–CONTINENTAL, Box, Raised Cartouche Of Triton Cover, 5 3/4 X 3 In. 325.00
Snuffbox, Colored Stone & Hinged Lid, Penknife, 2 Piece 70.00
Tea Set, Foliate Design, Scroll Handles, C.1900, 5 Piece 1500.00
Tray, Reeded Border, Leaf Clad Handles, 21 In. 500.00

SILVER–DANISH, Box, Cigarette, Jensen, Signed Sigvard 395.00
Butter Knife, Georg Jensen, 5 1/2 In., Set Of 6 .... 475.00
Cheese Scoop, Parallel, Jensen 75.00
Compote, Openwork Leaf & Pod, Georg Jensen, C.1915, 7 In. 1100.00
Dish, Vegetable, Covered, J.P.Hertz, C.1930, 5 1/2 In. 375.00
Dresser Jar, Sterling Silver Figural Dolphin On Lid, Jensen 250.00
Fork, Dinner, Acorn, Jensen, 7 3/8 In. 55.00
Fork, Luncheon, Acanthus, Jensen, 6 1/2 In. 35.00
Fork, Pastry, Cactus, Jensen, 3 Tine 45.00
Mustard, Acorn, Cobalt Blue Liner, Ladle, Jensen 295.00
Poultry Shears, Acorn, Jensen 110.00
Salt & Spoon, Acorn, Curled Handles, G.Jensen, Pair 180.00
Serving Pieces, Art Nouveau Scroll Design Handles, Set Of 6 .... 160.00
Spoon, Tea Caddy, Acorn, Jensen 50.00
Spreader, Cheese, Jensen 75.00
Teaspoon, Acanthus, Jensen, 6 1/8 In. 38.00

SILVER–DUTCH, Basket, Lacy Openwork, Cobalt Glass Lining, 3 1/2 X 4 In. 160.00
Bell, Table, Fluted, Crown Finial, H.Nieuwenhuys, 5 1/8 In. 1650.00
Box, Chased Romantic Scenes, Coin Base & Lid, 1900, 4 In. 75.00
Box, Outdoor Scene In Repousse, 4 Ball Feet, 5 X 2 1/2 In. 175.00
Casket, Jewelry, Embossed Allover Scene, Hinged Lid, C.1900 .... 155.00
Creamer, Everted Rim, Scrolled Handle, Paw Feet, 3 1/2 In. 45.00
Decanter, Silver Stopper, Crystal, 12 In. 600.00
Inkstand, Tray, 2 Wells, Pen Tray, Initialed JH, 5 X 7 1/4 In. 250.00

*English silver is marked with a series of four or five small hallmarks.
The standing lion mark is the most commonly seen sterling quality
mark. The other marks indicate the city of origin, the maker, and the
year of manufacture. These dates can be verified in many good books
on silver.*

SILVER–ENGLISH, Beaker, Victorian, Heraldic Shield, 1865, 4 1/4 In. 200.00
Bowl, Domed Cover, Edwardian, 3 Ball Feet, Carrington, 5 In. 150.00
Box, Tobacco, Slip–On Cover, Crest, E.Cornock, 1717, 4 In. 1320.00
Box, William IV, J.Hardy, Covered, Crest, 1830, 2 1/2 In. 325.00
Bucket, Sugar, Pedestal, Bail Handle, Bateman, 5 In. 400.00
Cake Basket, Foliate, S.Herbert & Co., 1755, 13 1/2 In. 2750.00
Candlestick, Carter, Smith, & Sharp, 1778, 11 3/8 In., Pr. 4400.00
Candlestick, George II, P.Storr, 1815, 6 1/2 In., Pr. 5500.00

Card Tray, Chippendale Edge, C. Stuart Harris, 6 3/4 In. 100.00
Case, Cigarette, Hand Engraved Florals, Birmingham, 1923 .... 55.00
Castor Set, Tray, Strap Handle, C.1799, 10 X 8 In. ....*Illus* 510.00
Coaster, Grapevine Border, Sheffield, C.1830, 7 1/2 In. 25.00
Coaster, Sawn Pierced Floral Design, Wire, 1773, 5 3/8 In. 375.00
Coffeepot, Bright Cut, Martin & Hall, 1874, 10 3/4 In. 880.00
Coffeepot, Crest, Swan Neck Spout, G.Godfrey, 9 1/8 In. 1980.00
Creamer, Coat Of Arms, Ovoid Body, Chawner, 1792 .... 100.00
Creamer, Pear Shaped, Footed, Repousse, Marked TS, 1778, 4 In. 75.00
Creamer, Ribbon Swag Body, Bateman, C.1790, 4 1/2 In. 140.00
Fish Slice, Abstainando King, 1802, 12 1/2 In. 95.00
Fish Slice, Ivory Handle, W.Eley, London, C.1796, 10 1/2 In. 250.00
Flagon, Horn, London, 1881 .... 400.00
Funnel, Wine, Detachable Bowl, H.Bateman, 1783, 4 3/4 In. 275.00
Goblet, Floral, Fennel, Engraved June 1856, 6 5/8 In., Pair 975.00
Ice Spade, Shell Pattern, Crest, P.Storr, 1819, 9 1/2 In. 770.00
Inkstand, 4 Pad Feet, Acorn Finial, P.Storr, 1811, 13 1/4 In. 7425.00
Jug, Pear Shaped, Footed, Scroll Handle, 1767, 4 1/2 In. 100.00
Kettle, On Lampstand, Boat Shaped, Handle, Sheffield, 12 In. 350.00
Ladle, Crested, Geo.Smith & Wm.Fearn, C.1790, 12 3/4 In. 400.00
Ladle, Fine Ribbed Bowl, Feathered Edge, Dated 1776 .... 365.00
Ladle, Soup, George III, George Wintle, Shell Bowl, 1809 .... 200.00
Ladle, Soup, Rampant Lion Crest, London, 1766, 14 In. 365.00
Letter Opener, Curved Design, Silvered Bronze, 11 3/4 In. 440.00
Matchbox, American Indian Head, Leaf, Corn Husk 250.00
Muffineer, Octagonal, Covered, C.Adam, C.1713, 6 5/8 In. 450.00
Muffineer, Urn Finial, Gadrooned Cover, 1691, Marked, 7 In. 475.00
Mug, Baluster Form, Newcastle, John Langlands, 1757 .... 125.00
Mug, Baluster, Robert Alkin Cox, 1756, 3 1/2 In. 450.00
Mug, Christening, Farmyard Animals, Loop Handle, 1930 .... 90.00
Mustard, George III, Liner, P.Storr, 1817, 4 1/4 In., Pair 1870.00
Pitcher, Baluster, Scroll Handle, James Robinson, 8 1/2 In. 525.00
Plate, Beaded, Coronet, Garrards, 1894, 9 7/8 In., Set Of 12 .... 6325.00
Punch Bowl, Chased Scrolls, Martin Hall, 1900, 12 In. 1800.00
Salt, Rectangular, S.Adams II, 1813, 4 5/8 In., Pair 330.00
Salver, 6 Satyr Masks, Shell Feet, J.E.Terry, 1840, 24 In. 5500.00
Salver, Gadrooned, R.R.Cartouche, 1767, 13 1/2 In. 800.00
Salver, Scroll Border, 3 Scroll Feet, Chester, 1909, 9 In. 300.00
Salver, Shells & Scroll Rim, R.Abercromby, 1743, 21 1/4 In. 7700.00
Scoop, Cheese, Baccanalian, P.Storr, 1816, 9 In. 1210.00
Server, Pale Green Wooden Handle, Bateman, C.1792, 8 1/4 In. 300.00
Serving Spoon, George IV, W.Chawner, 1825, 8 3/4 In., Pair 100.00

Silver-English, Castor Set, Tray,
Strap Handle, C. 1799, 10 × 8 In.

Don't display silver on latex paint.

Don't wrap silver with rubber bands.

Felt gives off hydrogen sulphide,
which tarnishes silver. Do not use
felt liners in drawers or felt bags to
store silver.

> Clean silver with any acceptable commercial polish. Don't use household scouring powder on silver, no matter how stubborn the spot may be. Use a tarnish-retarding silver polish to keep your silver clean. It will not harm old solid or plated wares. Do not use "instant" silver polishes.

Silver–German, Table Ornament,

Nautilus Shell, C.1900, 14 In.

Snuffbox, Double, Oval, Crest, R.Biggs, 1796, 4 In.		825.00
Snuffbox, George IV, Chased Rosette, T.Newbold, 1823, 2 In.		110.00
Snuffbox, Textured, William Phillips, 1835, 2 5/8 In.		150.00
Snuffbox, Tricorn Hat, W.Fish, 1716, 3 In.		1650.00
Spoon Caddy, Hourglass, Jos.Willmore, 1838, 3 1/2 In.		90.00
Spoon, Basting, Marked J.G., C.1750, 12 1/2 In.		400.00
Spoon, Salt, Master, Reverse Tip, London, 1866		28.00
Spoon, Tea Caddy, Benjamin Davis, C.1828, 3 5/8 In.		125.00
Spoon, Tea Caddy, Bright Cut Bowl, Birmingham, 1834		85.00
Spoon, Tea Caddy, Shell & Scroll Handle, Birmingham, 1826		110.00
Stand, Cruet, Wreath Handles, 2 Etched Bottles, 1875, 7 In.		275.00
Sugar Shaker, Pear Form Cover, Laurel Swags, Beaded, 7 In.		325.00
Sugar Sifter, Reverse Tip, Pierced Bowl, 1836, 6 In.		70.00
Tankard, Roses & Shamrocks Bands, Covered, J.Tapley, 1836		2640.00
Tea & Coffee Set, Boat Shaped, 1940, 5 Piece		1300.00
Tea & Coffee Set, George II Style, Crichton Bros., 1915		4400.00
Tea Caddy, Beaded, Floral Swags, J.Denziloe, 1786, 5 3/4 In.		2970.00
Tea Caddy, Hinged Lid, Inside Lock, N.Hart, 1806, 6 1/2 In.		1650.00
Teapot, Bright Cut, Wood Handle, J.Robins, 1795, 6 5/8 In.		1650.00
Teapot, Duke's Coronet, P.Storr, 1837, 5 1/2 In.		3575.00
Teapot, Gadrooned Border, Ebonized Handle, 1898, 12 In.		275.00
Teapot, Turned Finial, Squat Dome Cover, P.Bennett, 1740		425.00
Teapot, Twig, Leaf Base, Twig Handle, P.Storr, 1830, 6 1/8 In.		3850.00
Teapot, Undertray, Ivory Handle, Daniel Pontifex, 1797		550.00
Toast Rack, Georgian Style, 6 Slice, Marked, 1920		110.00
Tray, Acanthus Handles, P.Rundell, 1820, 23 5/8 In.		4400.00
Tray, Pen, Gilt, Female Masks, 4 Winged Supports, 1802, 11 In.		160.00
Tureen, Sauce, Covered, P.Storr, 1799, 9 1/8 In., Pair		6600.00
Urn, Coffee, Loop Handles, Wm.Holmes, 1775, 39 In.		1100.00
Vinaigrette, Marked RB, 1818–19, 1/2 X 1 In.		100.00
Vinaigrette, Raised Floral Border, L.&C., 1820, 1 3/16 In.		175.00
SILVER–FINLAND, Tea Set, Walnut Handles, T.Wirkkala, 4 Piece		1980.00
SILVER–FRENCH, Candelabra, 3–Light, Quatrefoil Base, G.Keller, Set Of 4		1870.00
Candlestick, Spiral Flute, E.Moreau, 1776, 10 5/8 In., Pair		6600.00
Cigarette Case, Geometric Design, Lacquer & Eggshell, 4 In.		385.00
Coffeepot, Scrolls, Hinged Lid, Baluster, 1819–38, 11 In.		450.00
Plate, G.Keller, 20th Century, 9 In., Pair		160.00
Salt, Master, 3 Scroll Feet, Hallmarks, 2 1/8 In.		20.00
Snuffbox, Latticework Ground, A.Robert, 1762, 3 1/4 In.		450.00
Spoon, Jelly, Looped Rope Handle, Marked Paris		75.00

Tray, Scalloped, 4 Scrolled Feet, J.E.Puiforcat, 9 In., Pair 990.00
Vase, Kneeling Boy, Mother, Father, Nude, Boucheron, 6 1/2 In. 825.00
Vinaigrette, Gold Interior, Inner Hinged Cover, C.1830 .... 95.00

SILVER–GERMAN, Basket, Engraved, Dated 1906, 11 3/4 In. 385.00
Beaker, Winged Double Shells, C.B. In Shield Mark, 4 In. 3100.00
Box, Foliage, Pheasant Figure, Stones, Hinged Cover, 6 In. 90.00
Cup, Parcel Gilt, Infant Victory Stem, C.R., C.1680, 8 In. 1980.00
Dish, Rosewater, Monarchs On Horseback, 7 1/4 In. 90.00
Dish, Sweetmeat, Family In Carriage, I.K., C.1700, 6 3/8 In. 1760.00
Dresser Set, Enameled Peacocks, 3 Piece 125.00
Plate, Gadroon Rim, Hossauer, 1854, 10 1/4 In., Set Of 12 .... 5500.00
Purse, Coin, Chain, 3 X 4 1/2 In. 45.00
Table Ornament, Nautilus Shell, C.1900, 14 In. ....*Illus* 2100.00
Wine Taster, Profiles, Marked H.B., 17th Century, 5 1/8 In. 715.00

SILVER–HUNGARIAN, Platter, Game, Oval, Gadroon Border, Engraved, 15 In. 220.00
Platter, Meat, Gadroon Border, 19 In. 400.00
Tray, Engraved Fish, Oblong, 16 In. 375.00

SILVER–IRISH, Candlestick, R.Calderwood, 1760, 11 7/8 In., Pair 3300.00
Coffeepot, Side Handle, C.1730 .... 12500.00
Cup, Trophy, Engraved, James Scott, 1808, 11 In. 1500.00
Platter, Well & Tree, C.Marsh, 1833, 22 1/2 In. 2420.00
Spoon, Sam'l Neville, Horticultural Prize, C.1836, 7 In. 225.00

SILVER–ITALIAN, Inkstand, 3 Pots, Detachable Lids, Bell, 1771, 11 1/4 In. 5500.00
Peacocks, Articulated Wings, 13 In., Pair 1400.00

SILVER–MEXICAN, Bracelet, Aztec Design, 2 Band, Los Castillo 418.00
Bracelet, Hinged Concave, Rectangular Sections, Marked 275.00
Bracelet, Rectangular Sections, Sphere Separators, Marked 275.00
Bracelet, Stylized Leaves & Berries, Margot De Taxco 528.00
Coffee Set, Coffeepot, Sugar & Creamer, Tray, Signed Eddie's 1200.00
Earrings, Graduated Crescents, Beaded Links, Batilla 352.00
Figurine, Bull, Charging, 6 Sword Picks In Back, 3 In. 65.00
Necklace, Graduated & Peaked Pentagonal Sections, A.Pineda 1650.00
Needle Case, Engraved People 22.00
Tray, Reeded Border, Loop Handles, Oblong Shape, 35 In. 675.00

SILVER–NORWEGIAN, Ewer, Classic Engraved, C.1910, 11 1/2 In. 85.00

SILVER–ORIENTAL, Tea Set, Cased Birds & Blossoms, Bamboo, C.1900, 3 Piece 750.00

SILVER–POLISH, Candlestick, Baluster Stem, Chased Foliage, 15 In., Pr. 80.00
Cup, Bell–Shaped Bowl, Engraved Stem, 19th Century, 1 In. 30.00

SILVER–PORTUGUESE, Tray, Pierced Rim, 3 Paw Feet, A.P.Canaveses, 7 In. 170.00

Russian silver is marked with the cyrillic or Russian alphabet. The numbers 84, 88, or 91 indicate the silver content. Russian silver may be higher or lower than sterling standard. Other marks indicate maker, assayer, or city of manufacture. Many pieces of silver made in Russia are decorated with enamel.

SILVER–RUSSIAN, Candlestick, Floral, 3 Scroll Feet, C.1875, 13 3/4 In., Pair 525.00
Cigarette Case, Enameled Floral, 1907, 3 5/8 In. 550.00
Cup & Saucer, Enameled, Floral, Ivy Form Handle, C.1889 .... 1200.00
Flask, Parcel–Gilt, C–Scroll Handle, Chain, 1887, 8 3/4 In. 825.00
Kovsh, Enameled Floral, Blue Ground, C.1910, 5 1/2 In. 3000.00
Letter Opener, Figural, Nude, Ivory Handle, 10 1/4 In. 1045.00
Salt, Throne–Shaped Hinged Seat, Moscow, 1890, 2 In. 195.00
Spoon, Cloisonne Teardrop Bowl Back, Demitasse, Set Of 6 .... 325.00
Stein, Cupids, Finial, Hallmarked, C.1870 .... 1500.00
Sugar, Peasant Scene, Swing Handle, Ring Foot, 1910 .... 350.00

Tablespoon, Rococo Shell, Scrollwork, 7 In., Set Of 6 .... 200.00
Tazza, Enameled, Domed Base, Shallow Bowl, C.1895, 5 In. 1950.00
Tea Holder, Enameled Floral, Cane–Shaped Handle, C.1895 .... 770.00
Teaspoon, Rococo Shells, Flowers, 7 In., Set Of 6 .... 200.00
Tray, Kremlin Scene, Scroll Handles, C.1868, 18 3/8 In. 1375.00

SILVER–SCOTCH, Coffeepot, Rococo Design, J.McKay, 1836, 11 1/2 In. 2600.00
Ladle, Sauce, Alex Zeigler, C.1800, 6 In. 150.00
Ladle, Sheaf Of Wheat At Pointed Oval End, Marked, 15 In. 250.00
Spoon, Stuffing, Lothian & Robertson, 1746, Marked, 16 In. 230.00
Tablespoon, George III, Crest, Motto, 1793, 9 1/2 In., Pair 70.00

Sterling silver is made with 925 parts silver out of 1,000 parts of metal. The word "sterling" is a quality guarantee used in the United States after about 1860.

SILVER–STERLING, see also Silver–American; Silver–English; etc.
SILVER–STERLING, Basket, Cast Lion Head & Paw Feet, Peters & Co., 5 1/2 In. 110.00
Basket, Sugar, Pierced Swing Handle, Cobalt Blue Liner 48.00
Berry Spoon, Art Nouveau, Shiebler 275.00
Brush, Bonnet, Repousse Handle & Top 22.00
Buttonhook, Repousse Hollow Handle, 4 In. 10.00
Celery, Intaglio & Brilliant, Regal Pattern, 13 In. 200.00
Chalice, Raised & Chased Flowers, Presentation, 6 In. 375.00
Coaster, Glass, Sterling Rim & Holder, Set Of 8 .... 45.00
Coffeepot, Repousse, Medallion, E & S, 11 1/2 In. 500.00
Compact, Floral Design, 4 In. 70.00
Compote, Oval Top, Cellini Craft, 5 X 7 In. 600.00
Corkscrew, Ivory, Repousse, Marked, 6 1/2 In. 75.00
Cup, Wager, Woman Has Cup Above Head, Enameled, 10 1/2 In. 160.00
Cup, Wager, Woman Holding Cup, Repousse, 12 1/2 In. 330.00
Cutter, Cigar, Chased Design 25.00
Dish, Repousse, Waves, Mermaid, S.H.& Miller, 9 3/8 In. 195.00
Dog, Pug, Standing, Wearing Collar With Bells, 2 X 2 In. 125.00
Dresser Set, Art Deco, Pineapple Finials, 6 Piece 125.00
Dresser Set, Brush, Mirror, Comb, Monogram J, 1920s, 3 Piece 120.00
Dresser Set, Gorham, 15 Piece 1500.00
Figurine, King, Ivory Face & Hands, Stones, Sword, 7 1/2 In. 745.00
Figurine, Oriental Man, Vending, Revolving Wheel, 3 In. 65.00
Frames, Spectacle, 1776–1820, English 250.00
Glove Stretcher, Hallmark 32.50
Holder, Place Card, Peruvian Llamas, Set Of 12 .... 300.00
Holder, Stamp, Overall Repousse, Attached Ring 55.00
Manicure Set, Art Nouveau Style, Case, 8 Piece 125.00
Mirror, Hand, Art Nouveau, Blown–Out Daisy 95.00
Mirror, Hand, Art Nouveau, Blown–Out Flowers, Lady's Head 125.00
Mirror, Hand, Art Nouveau, Blown–Out Irises 100.00
Mirror, Hand, Victorian, Engraved, Beveled, C.1900 .... 125.00
Nail Buffer, Victorian, Large Handle 40.00
Rattle, Bunny With Teether, 2 In. 65.00
Rattle, Pearl Handle, Attached Bells, 19th Century 275.00
Seal, Wax, Black Boy, Alligator, Palm Tree, 2 1/4 In. 60.00
Shears, Grape 75.00
Soap Dish, Golden Medici, Cartier 85.00
Spoon, Serving, Engraved Lilies, Pierced, Gold Mixed, 9 In. 225.00
SILVER–STERLING, SPOON, SOUVENIR, see Souvenir, Spoon, Sterling Silver
Stamp Case, Hinged Top Ring, Embossed 42.00
Stirrup Cup, Fox Head, 3 1/2 In. 29.00
Sugar & Creamer, Georgian, Scroll Handle, Cabriole Legs 85.00
Sugar & Creamer, Scroll Design, Europe, C.1900, 2 In. 100.00
Sugar Shaker, Cartier, 8 1/4 In. 350.00
Sugar Tongs, Birmingham, 1887 .... 25.00
Tea Ball, 4 Blown–Out Heads Of Mephistopheles, Round 75.00
Tea Ball, Art Nouveau, Repousse Flowered Body, 2 1/4 In. 165.00

Tea Ball, Figural, Teapot, Chain & Ring 45.00
Tea Set, Repousse, Floral & Vines, Miniature, 4 Piece 500.00
Toast Rack, Georgian Style, C.1900, 6 Slice 110.00
Tray, Applied Grape & Scrolled Rim, Mauser Mfg.Co., 14 In. 130.00
Whisk Broom, Victorian, Set Of 2 .... 60.00
Yo–Yo, Gorham 88.00
Youth Set, Alhambra, Whiting, 3 Piece 55.00

SILVER–SWEDISH, Salt, Viking Ship, Cobalt Blue Insert, Spoon, 3 In., Pair 47.50
Sugar Box, Bombe Side, Leaf–Tip Border, Zethelius, 1829 .... 1320.00

SILVER–SWISS, Coffeepot, Baluster Form, J.Redart, C.1765, 8 1/2 In. 3300.00

> *Sinclaire cut glass was made by H.P. Sinclaire and Company of Corning, New York, between 1905 and 1929. He cut glass made at other factories until 1920. Pieces were made of crystal as well as amber, blue, green, or ruby glass. Only a small percentage of Sinclaire glass is marked with the S in a wreath.*

SINCLAIRE, Candlestick, Swirl Stem, Green, Signed, 10 1/4 In. ....65.00 To 85.00
Champagne, Teardrop Stems, Step Cut Bowl, Set Of 12 .... 300.00
Cheese & Cracker Set, Flute & Panel, 1910 .... 247.50
Compote, Adam II, Signed, 12 In. 700.00
Compote, Honey Amber, Small 80.00
Compote, Silver Threads, Hollow Foot, Marked, 8 X 8 In., Pair 850.00
Console Set, Signed, Amethyst, 3 Piece 250.00
Tumbler, Etched, Marked 25.00
Vase, Border Of 4 Griffins, Ivory Glass Trim, Marked, 9 1/2 In. 225.00
Vase, Floral, Engraved, Marked, 12 In. 185.00
Vase, Rose Bowl Shape, Floral Engraving, Signed, 8 X 5 In. 100.00

> *Slag glass resembles a marble cake. It can be streaked with different colors. There were many types made from about 1880. Pink slag was an American Victorian product of unknown origin. Purple and blue slag were made in American and English factories. Red slag is a very late–Victorian and twentieth–century glass. Other colors are known but are of less importance to the collector.*

SLAG, Blue, Dish, Squirrel On Acorn, Cover 145.00
Blue, Toothpick, Near Cut, Inverted Strawberry, Footed, 2 1/2 In. 10.50
    SLAG, CARAMEL, see Chocolate Glass
Green, Shade, Bead Fringe, Mottled 125.00
Green, Shade, Leaded, American, Purple Rose Border, C.1900, 28 In. 250.00
Lavender, Bowl, Orange, Gold Floral, Hand Painted, Scalloped, 10 3/4 In. 48.00
Pink, Lemonade Set, 8 In.Pitcher, 6 Tumblers 625.00
Pink, Sauce, Inverted Fan & Feather Pattern, Ball Feet, 4 1/2 In., Pair 575.00
Pink, Sauce, Inverted Fan & Feather, 4 5/8 In. 225.00
Pink, Tumbler, Water, Inverted Fan & Feather, 3 7/8 In. 395.00
Purple, Compote, Cover, Crown Majestic, Challinor 225.00
Purple, Compote, Crimped, 4 1/2 In. 65.00
Purple, Jelly, Threaded 45.00
Purple, Match Holder, Daisy & Button, 3 X 5 In. ....25.00 To 35.00
Purple, Mug, Singing Birds 35.00
Purple, Plate, Lattice Edge, 10 1/2 In. 100.00
Purple, Spooner, Leaf Pattern 45.00
Purple, Spooner, Scroll Acanthus 55.00
Purple, Sugar, Scrolled Flower Panels, Scalloped, Footed, Rings, 4 In. 90.00
Purple, Toothpick, Ribbed Kettle, Challinor & Taylor 36.00
Purple, Vase, Beads & Bark, Northwood, 6 In. 49.00
Red, Ashtray, Imperial, Label, 8 In. 22.00
Red, Bowl, Venetian, Footed, Fenton 125.00
Red, Compote, Bicentennial, Fenton 165.00
Red, Compote, Crimped, Imperial, 6 1/2 In. 57.00
Red, Cup, Figural, Rooster 35.00
Red, Pitcher, Windmill, Imperial, 1 Pt. 96.00

Sleepy Eye pottery was made to be given away with the flour products of the Sleepy Eye Milling Co., Sleepy Eye, Minnesota, from about 1893 to 1952. It is a heavy stoneware with blue decorations, usually decorated with the famous profile of the Indian. Reproductions of the pitchers are being made today. The original pitchers came in only five sizes: 4 in., 5 1/4 in., 6 1/2 in., 8 in., and 9 in. Sleepy Eye collectors also search for other advertising material related to the flour mill.

SLEEPY EYE, Blotter 40.00
Bowl, Salt, Blue & Gray, Weir ....225.00 To 650.00
Butter Crock, Covered, Blue, Gray, Weir, 5 X 6 1/2 In. ....375.00 To 425.00
Catalog, Western Stoneware Co., 1935 .... 75.00
Cookbook, Loaf Of Bread Shape 25.00
Flour Sack 35.00
Label, Barrel ....60.00 To 70.00
Lemonade Set, No.5 Pitcher, 6 Mugs 1000.00
Letter Opener, Bronze ....375.00 To 450.00
Mug, 5th Convention, 1980 .... 50.00
Mug, Blue On Gray, 1952 .... 220.00
Mug, Blue On White ....70.00 To 160.00
Mug, Blue On White, Blue Band ....145.00 To 170.00
Mug, Blue On Yellow 250.00
Mug, Verse, Minnesota Stoneware Co. 1500.00
Pillow Front, Linen, Meeting In Pres.Monroe's Office, 1824 .... 20.00
Pin, Membership, Blue & White .:.. 45.00
Pitcher, Blue & White, 1 Gal. 200.00
Pitcher, No.1, Blue & Gray, 4 In. ....85.00 To 160.00
Pitcher, No.1, Blue & White, 4 In. ....70.00 To 185.00
Pitcher, No.2, Blue & White, 5 1/4 In. ....65.00 To 170.00
Pitcher, No.2, Blue & White, Blue Rim, 5 1/4 In. 380.00
Pitcher, No.3, Blue & White, 6 1/2 In. ....150.00 To 195.00
Pitcher, No.4, Blue & White, 8 In. ....80.00 To 200.00
Pitcher, No.4, Blue & White, Blue Rim, 8 In. ....160.00 To 250.00
Pitcher, No.5, Blue & White, 9 In. ....30.00 To 170.00
Pitcher, No.5, Blue & White, Blue Rim, 9 In. 230.00
Pitcher, Odd Indian, Bennington Type 1000.00
Pitcher, Standing Indian, 1/2 Gal. ....895.00 To 995.00
Pitcher, Town Of Sleepy Eye, Souvenir, China 170.00
Postcard ....25.00 To 75.00
Poster, Advertising, Western Stoneware Co. 35.00
Sign, Flour, Tin, Chief Sleepy Eye In Oval, 19 X 13 1/2 In. 895.00
Spoon ....65.00 To 95.00
Spoon, Demitasse 135.00
Stein, Blue On Gray, 1952 .... 140.00
Stein, Blue On Gray, Stoneware, 7 3/4 In. 390.00
Stein, Blue On White, 7 3/4 In. 375.00
Stein, Board Of Directors, Blue & White 180.00
Stein, Brown On White, 7 3/4 In. 825.00
Stein, Brown On Yellow, 7 3/4 In. 550.00
Stein, Flemish, Handle Replaced 155.00
Stein, Solid Blue, 7 3/4 In. 650.00
Sugar, Open, Blue On White ....375.00 To 425.00
Teaspoon, Indian Handle 75.00
Thimble ....135.00 To 180.00
Tin, Flour 850.00
Vase, Cattail, Blue On Gray, 8 1/2 In. 200.00
Vase, Cattail, Blue On White, 8 1/2 In. 225.00
Vase, Cattail, Solid Blue 115.00
Vase, Cattail, Solid Green 430.00
Vase, Indian Head, Cattails, Blue & Gray, 8 1/2 In. ....110.00 To 150.00

Slip is a thin mixture of clay and water, about the consistency of sour cream, that is applied to pottery for decoration. It is a very old method of making pottery and is still in use.

SLIPWARE, Charger, Reverse, England, Notched Rim, 18th Century, 13 1/2 In. 1600.00
Pitcher, Albany, 5 In. 200.00
Plate, Redware, 10 In. ....120.00 To 200.00
    SLOT MACHINE, see Coin–Operated Machine

Smith Bros. Co.

Smith Brothers glass was made after 1878. Alfred and Harry Smith had worked for the Mt. Washington Glass Company in New Bedford, Massachusetts, for seven years before going into their own shop. They made many pieces with enamel decoration.

SMITH BROTHERS, Bowl, Rampant Lions, Melon Rib, Pansies, 3 3/4 X 2 1/2 In. 135.00
Bowl, White, Melon Shape, Pansy Design, Marked, 2 1/2 In. 225.00
Cracker Jar, Melon Rib, Signed 335.00
Dish, Sweetmeat, Ribbed, Silver Plated Lid, Signed 275.00
Humidor, Cream, Pansies, Silver Plated Lid, Marked, 7 In. 485.00
Jar, Tobacco, Pale Lemon To Deep Peach, Pansies, Signed 195.00
Muffineer, White, Purple Columbines, 3 X 4 In. 485.00
Sugar & Creamer, Gold Apple Blossoms, Leaves, Jewels, Signed 585.00
Sugar & Creamer, Gold Enameled Flowers, Swing Handle 500.00
Toothpick, Columned Ribs 95.00
Vase, Heron In Rushes, Pink Ground, 4 1/2 In., Pair 100.00
Vase, Herons In Reeds, Pink Ground, 10 In. 150.00
Vase, Painted Parrot, Flowers In Background, 10 In. 175.00
Vase, Parrot In Blue, Purple, Yellow, Green, Flowers, 5 In. 175.00
Vase, Swirl Design, Floral & Gold Gilt, Marked, 6 3/4 In. 450.00
Vase, Wisteria Blossoms, Oval Shape, 9 3/4 X 6 1/4 In. 485.00

Snow Babies, made from bisque and spattered with glitter sand, were first manufactured in 1864 by Hertwig and Company of Thuringia. Other German and Japanese companies copied the Hertwig designs. Originally, Snow Babies were made of candy and used as Christmas decorations. There are also Snow Babies tablewares made by Royal Bayreuth. Copies of the small Snow Babies figurines are being made today and can easily confuse the collector.

SNOW BABIES, Chamberstick, Blue Mark 125.00
Chocolate Pot, Royal Bayreuth, Blue Mark 190.00
Doll, Black, Standing, White Snowsuit, Hertwig & Co., C.1910 .... 350.00
Doll, Sitting On Red Sled, Marked, 1 3/8 In. 35.00
Figurine, Sitting, Open Arms 50.00
Mug, Handle, Blue Mark, 3 In. 75.00
On Sled, Germany 25.00
Pitcher, Milk, Royal Bayreuth 95.00
Plate, On Sled, Blue Mark, 8 In. 110.00
Tea Tile, Royal Bayreuth 145.00
    SNUFF BOTTLE, see Bottle, Snuff

Taking snuff was popular long before cigarettes became available. The snuff was kept in a small box. The gentleman or lady would take a small pinch of the ground tobacco or snuff in the fingers, then sniff it and sneeze. Snuffboxes were made of many materials, including gold, silver, enameled metal, and wood. Most snuffboxes date from the late eighteenth or early nineteenth century.

SNUFFBOX, Ashton Olde Hall, Oak 55.00
Columbian Exposition, Footed 29.00
Enameled, Hinged Cover, Picnic Scene, English, 1770, 2 1/8 In. 500.00
Enameled, Quail Shape, Hinged Cover, Hunting Scene, English, 3 In. 1540.00
Engine Turned, Enamel Floral Reserves, Silver Gilt, French, C.1800 .... 195.00
English, Sterling Silver, Gold Wash, 1884, 1 1/4 X 2 1/4 X 3/4 In. 145.00
Gold, Enameled Children & Dog Scene Lid, C.1820, 3 1/2 In. 2500.00
Horn & Tortoiseshell, English, 1 1/4 X 2 3/4 X 3/4 In. 65.00
Horn Lining, Horn Inlay On Lid, Oval, Wooden, Dated 1915, 3 1/8 In. 95.00
Horn, Death Of Napoleon, Bas–Relief, 19th Century, 3 5/8 In. 80.00
Horn, Elongated Oval, Carved Swivel Closure, 2 3/4 X 4 1/4 In. 105.00
Horn, Hinged Lid, Silver Plated Fittings, Thistle, 3 3/4 In. 35.00
Horn, Hinged Pewter Lid, Touchmark, Durie, 3 1/2 In. 65.00

Horn, Inlaid Tortoise & Ivory, 1 3/4 X 3 3/4 In. 50.00
Painting On Lid, Man Lifting Money Bag, Black Lacquer, 4 In. 45.00
Painting On Lid, Monk Stealing Kiss From Sister, Lacquer, 4 In. 95.00
Papier–Mache, Black Lacquer, Decoupage, Hunting Scene, French 15.00
Papier–Mache, Copenhagen, 3 1/2 X 1 1/2 In. 30.00
Russet Shade Agate, Brass Bound, Square, 1 1/4 In. 90.00
Sailboats, Building In Harbor, Black, Fluted Base, Oval, 2 1/4 In. 120.00
Ship, Lightning, Commemorative, Walnut, Gold Mounted, American, 1854 .... 715.00
Silver, Oval Shape, Engraved, Thomas Willmore, 1802, 3 In. 160.00
Sterling Silver, 2–Headed Eagle On Lid, Russian 110.00
Tooled Lid, Hinge, Brass, Oval, 3 1/2 In. 35.00
Tortoise Lined, Carved Building On Cover, Burl, 2 1/2 X 3 3/4 In. 45.00

Soapstone is a mineral that was used for foot warmers or griddles because of its heat-retaining properties. Soapstone was carved into figurines and bowls in many countries in the nineteenth and twentieth centuries. Most of the soapstone seen today is from China or Japan. It is still being carved in the old styles.

SOAPSTONE, Bookends, Elephant, 1890 .... 50.00
Bookends, Vase With Trailing Vines & Flowers 55.00
Box, Inlaid Pearl, Artist Signed, 3 X 5 In. 40.00
Cigarette Box, Match, Carved Floral Design, China 38.00
Figurine, Cupid & Psyche In Embrace, 19th Century, 29 1/2 In. 1650.00
Figurine, Lady, Mottled Tan & Rust, C.1900, 10 1/8 In. 65.00
Figurine, Man, Off–White With Pink, Stand 20.00
Figurine, Monkeys, Standing On Each Other's Head, Green, 5 In. 50.00
Figurine, Nanny Goat & Kids, 6 1/2 In. 55.00
Figurine, Seal, Foo Dog Surmounts, 6 1/2 In., Pair 50.00
Foo Dog, With Ball, Gilt, 19th Century, 5 1/2 In. 85.00
Incense Burner, Black, 19th Century, 8 In. 325.00
Teapot, 5 X 3 In. 350.00
Toothpick, Garden Of Gods 28.00
Toothpick, Monkey ....18.00 To 25.00
Vase, Carved Flowers & Leaves, 4–Footed, Pink, 7 In. 100.00
Vase, Triple, 5 In. 35.00

Soft paste is a name for a type of pottery. Although it looks very much like porcelain, it is a chemically different material. Most of the soft-paste wares were made in the early nineteenth century. Other pieces may be listed under Gaudy Dutch or Leeds.

SOFT PASTE, Bowl, Blue & White, Spongeware, English, 9 In. 45.00
Bowl, Blue Feather Edge, Oval, 10 1/4 X 13 3/8 X 2 1/8 In. 75.00
Bowl, Gaudy Floral Design, Leeds Type, 7 1/2 X 3 1/2 In. 285.00
Bowl, Oriental Design, Blue & White, 7 1/4 X 3 In. 70.00
Bowl, Waste, Strawberries, Pink Band Border, 5 5/8 X 2 3/4 In. 120.00
Burner, Incense, Cottage, Green Vegetation, 4 1/4 X 5 1/2 In. 50.00
Burner, Incense, Mill House, England, Polychrome, 6 1/2 In. 35.00
Charger, 5–Color Flowers, Scalloped Blue Feather Rim, 14 In. 425.00
Charger, 5–Color Urn Of Flowers, Blue Feather Edge, 15 5/8 In. 400.00
Creamer, Floral Design, Pink & Purple Luster, 4 3/4 In. 22.50
Cup & Saucer, Handleless, Bird In Sponged Foliage, 4 Colors 80.00
Cup & Saucer, Handleless, Gondola, E.Wood 35.00
Cup & Saucer, Handleless, Medium Blue Floral Transfer 40.00
Cup & Saucer, Handleless, Roses, Black Rim, Enameling, Miniature 25.00
Cup Plate, Historical, Dark Blue Transfer, Fruit, 3 5/8 In. 55.00
Cup Plate, Rust Transfer, Lafayette & Washington, 3 3/4 In. 375.00
Dish, Leaf Shape, Blue Feather Edge, 6 In. 95.00
Dish, Raised Vegetables, Blue Feather Edge, 4 3/8 In. 245.00
Dish, Serving, Eagle & Shield Design, 4 Colors, 8 3/4 X 11 In. 400.00
Figurine, Tiger, Yellow Ocher Enameling, Black Stripes, 3 In. 130.00
Jar, Embossed Artichoke Leaves, Blue Trim, 2 3/4 In. 250.00
Mug, Purple Luster Rim, Transfer Of Cock Robin, 2 1/2 In. 20.00
Mug, Purple Luster, House Design, 2 1/2 In. 12.50
Pitcher, 5 In. ....*Color* 125.00

Pitcher, Farming Tools, 5 1/2 In. 285.00
Pitcher, Gaudy Rose Design, Pink, Green, Blue, Yellow, Red, 6 In. 55.00
Plaque, Lions, Polychrome Enameling, Dated 1818, 10 3/4 In. 1200.00
Plate, Blue Feather Edge, Gaudy Floral, Leeds, 8 1/2 In. 325.00
Plate, Blue Transfer, Oriental Scene, Purple Luster Rim, 8 In. 25.00
Plate, Burnt Umber Leaf Design, White, English, 9 In. 25.00
Plate, Feather Edge, Floral Design Center, 9 7/8 In. 105.00
Plate, King's Rose, Pink Border, 8 1/4 In. 85.00
Plate, Lafayette, Welcome To Land Of Liberty, 6 3/4 In. 500.00
Plate, Mahogany Transfer, A Reward For Diligence, 6 3/8 In. 40.00
Plate, Strawberries In A Basket Design, 8 In. 155.00
Plate, Strawberries, Vine Border, 7 1/4 In. 75.00
Sauceboat, Blue Feather Edge, 2 7/8 In. 55.00
Shaker, Blue Stripes, 4 3/8 In. 60.00
Shaker, Medium Blue Transfer, Fishing Scene, 3 5/8 In. 45.00
Tea Set, Purple Luster Floral Band, Red Enameling, 8 Piece 250.00
Teapot, Black Transfer, Mother & Child, Pink Border, 5 In. 65.00
Teapot, Raised Strawberries, Rope Border 290.00

*What could be more fun than to bring home a souvenir of a trip?
Our ancestors enjoyed the same thing and souvenirs were made for
almost every location. Most of the souvenir pottery and porcelain
pieces of the nineteenth century were made in England or Germany,
even if the picture showed a North American scene. In the twentieth
century, the souvenir china business seems to have gone to the
Japanese, Taiwanese, English, and American makers. Another popular
souvenir item is the souvenir spoon, made of sterling or silver plate.
These are usually made in the country pictured on the spoon.*

SOUVENIR, Ashtray, Illinois Sesquicentennial 1818–1968, Ill. Shape, Brown 16.00
Ashtray, Tire Shape, International Exposition 1935 .... 19.00
Banner, Boston Braves, Full Roster, Indian Head, Black 22.00
Baseball Bat, Louisville Slugger, Ernie Banks, Small 12.50
Bear, Mischa, 1980 Olympics, Unwrapped 18.50
Boot, La Crosse, Wisconsin, 4 1/2 In. ....*Color* 25.00
Bowl, Atlantic City 1911, Elk, Blue, Carnival Glass 425.00
Button, 1932 Washington Bicentennial 3.75
Canteen, Brass, 26th Grand Annual Encampment 1892, GAR, 4 1/2 In. 30.00
Creamer, Individual, Green, 1917, 2 1/2 In. ....*Color* 25.00
Emblem, Good Fellows, William Thompson, Silver, July 2nd, 1844 .... 65.00
Figurine, Zeppelin, Coat Of Arms On Dirigible, English, 5 In. 40.00
Hatchet, Monmouth, Ill., Gold Trim, Milk Glass, White, 7 In. 20.00
Horseshoe, Sheriff's Badge, Dallas, Texas Centennial, 1936 .... 75.00
Mug, Elk's, Atlantic City Convention, 1911, Stoneware 28.00
Mug, Flashed Glass, Clay Center, 3 In. 15.00
Pan, New York State, Free Blown, Light Green, Pouring Lip, 7 In. 355.00
Pencil Sharpener, Olympics, 1936, Jesse Owens Running, 1 3/4 In. 65.00

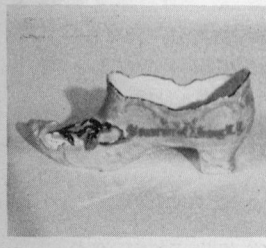

Souvenir, Shoe, Albany, 6 In.

Souvenir, Shoe, Bisque,
Blue & White, 5 In.

Souvenir, Shoe,
Harvard, 4 In.

Plaque, Buffalo, Bronze, Pan American Exposition, Buffalo, N.Y.1901	75.00
Plate, Airplane, Vernon Kilns, Convair Corp.	25.00
Plate, Dodgers National League Champions, 1952	25.00
Plate, Harpers Ferry, Blue	45.00
Plate, Iowa City, Be Playful Center, Stippled Bird Handles, 5 In.	95.00
Plate, Salt Lake City Scene, Tin, Souvenir Novelty Co., 1911	140.00
Plate, St.Bernard, I Bark–Morristown, Minn., 8 In.	30.00
Scarf, Pan American Expo, 1901	45.00
Scarf, Souvenir D'Egypt, 8 Portraits, British & Egyptian Rulers	185.00
Shoe, Albany, 6 In. ....*Illus*	18.00
Shoe, Bisque, Blue & White, 5 In. ....*Illus*	20.00
Shoe, Harvard, 4 In. ....*Illus*	25.00
Spoon, Kneeling Indian, Copper, College Of Mines, Houghton, Mi.	25.00
Spoon, Silver Plate, Arizona	6.00
Spoon, Silver Plate, Charlie McCarthy	8.00
Spoon, Silver Plate, Colorado	6.00
Spoon, Silver Plate, Electricity Building In Bowl	9.00
Spoon, Silver Plate, Gloria Swanson	8.00
Spoon, Silver Plate, Mary Pickford Handle, Embossed	30.00
Spoon, Silver Plate, Missouri	6.00
Spoon, Silver Plate, New York World's Fair	6.00
Spoon, Silver Plate, Niagara Falls	7.50
Spoon, Silver Plate, Pan American Exposition	15.00
Spoon, Silver Plate, President John Kennedy	6.00
Spoon, Silver Plate, Sesquicentennial Battle, Wyoming	9.00
Spoon, Sterling Silver, Army & Navy, Embossed Ship In Bowl, Gorham	85.00
Spoon, Sterling Silver, Army & Navy, Enameled Shield, Gorham	85.00
Spoon, Sterling Silver, Army/Navy Ship, Embossed Bowl, Gorham	85.00
Spoon, Sterling Silver, Asheville, N.C., Mountain View	28.00
Spoon, Sterling Silver, Atlantic City, Fishing Rod, Fish Handle	48.00
Spoon, Sterling Silver, Banff, Demitasse	15.00
Spoon, Sterling Silver, Battle Creek, Mich., Pattern Handle	9.50
Spoon, Sterling Silver, Berlin	98.00
Spoon, Sterling Silver, Black Boy, Oxen, Wagon, South Carolina	47.50
Spoon, Sterling Silver, Boston South Station Elevated Railway	37.50
Spoon, Sterling Silver, Boston, 1st Church Christ Sci., Demitasse	15.00
Spoon, Sterling Silver, Canada, Enameled	28.00
Spoon, Sterling Silver, Catalina Island, Gold Bowl, Tuna Handle	25.00
Spoon, Sterling Silver, Catskill Mountains, Indian Kneeling	65.00
Spoon, Sterling Silver, Chicago Fair, 1933	12.00
Spoon, Sterling Silver, Chicago, Indian In Headdress	65.00
Spoon, Sterling Silver, City Hall, Los Angeles, Ca., Demitasse	12.00
Spoon, Sterling Silver, Colorado Seven Falls	19.50
Spoon, Sterling Silver, Colorado Springs, Demitasse	15.00
Spoon, Sterling Silver, Cooperstown, N.Y., Picture In Bowl	28.00
Spoon, Sterling Silver, Denver, Colo., State Capitol On Handle	17.50
Spoon, Sterling Silver, Denver, Demitasse	15.00
Spoon, Sterling Silver, Detroit Post Office	15.00
Spoon, Sterling Silver, Detroit, Cut Out Handle, Grand Circus Park	30.00
Spoon, Sterling Silver, Detroit, Face Inside Flower	22.00
Spoon, Sterling Silver, Detroit, In Bowl, Watson	18.00
Spoon, Sterling Silver, El Paso, Texas, Swastika Handle	18.00
Spoon, Sterling Silver, Elgin, Ill., Name In Bowl	9.50
Spoon, Sterling Silver, Eugene Engraved In Bowl, Alvin	65.00
Spoon, Sterling Silver, First Congregational Church, Elyria, Ohio	15.00
Spoon, Sterling Silver, Flatiron Building, N.Y., Bowl Design	32.00
Spoon, Sterling Silver, Ft.Cumberland, Mo., Scroll Handle, 1765	35.00
Spoon, Sterling Silver, Graduate, Figural Head	19.00
Spoon, Sterling Silver, Grand Junction, Colorado	37.50
Spoon, Sterling Silver, High School, Paw Paw, Mich.	28.00
Spoon, Sterling Silver, John Wesley, World Is My Parish, Norway	18.00
Spoon, Sterling Silver, Junction Building, Kansas City, Mo.	28.00
Spoon, Sterling Silver, Kentucky State, Watson	25.00
Spoon, Sterling Silver, Knights Of Columbus	38.00

Spoon, Sterling Silver, Lansing, Mich., Mainelde Industrial School 20.00
Spoon, Sterling Silver, Lincoln, Nebraska, Cutout 15.00
Spoon, Sterling Silver, Los Angeles, Towle 18.00
Spoon, Sterling Silver, Manitou, Colo., Cog Road, Gorham, Demitasse 15.00
Spoon, Sterling Silver, Mannington, W.Va., Oil Fields 30.00
Spoon, Sterling Silver, Mary Baker Eddy 195.00
Spoon, Sterling Silver, Masonic Home, Utica, N.Y., Picture In Bowl 28.00
Spoon, Sterling Silver, Masonic Temple, Chicago 18.00
Spoon, Sterling Silver, Masonic, Wallace 29.00
Spoon, Sterling Silver, Merry Christmas, Demitasse 15.00
Spoon, Sterling Silver, Metropolitan Building, N.Y. 32.00
Spoon, Sterling Silver, Michigan, 1930 .... 15.00
Spoon, Sterling Silver, Miles City, Mont., Cowboy, Demitasse 12.00
Spoon, Sterling Silver, Missouri State, Mule, Motto 37.50
Spoon, Sterling Silver, Montana, Anaconda, Mont., Picture In Bowl 28.00
Spoon, Sterling Silver, Montana, Stanford, Enameled 27.00
Spoon, Sterling Silver, Munising, Mich., Waterfall, Picture In Bowl 28.00
Spoon, Sterling Silver, My Old Kentucky Home, Bowl Picture 50.00
Spoon, Sterling Silver, New Orleans, Demitasse 18.00
Spoon, Sterling Silver, New York, Flame, Wallace, Demitasse 14.00
Spoon, Sterling Silver, North Bay, Pattern Handle, Name In Bowl 9.50
Spoon, Sterling Silver, Oklahoma, State Seal 20.00
Spoon, Sterling Silver, Palestine, Ill., Floral Pattern 16.50
Spoon, Sterling Silver, Palm Beach, Fla., Alligator Handle 47.50
Spoon, Sterling Silver, Pantlind Hotel, Grand Rapids, Mich. 17.50
Spoon, Sterling Silver, Paris, Texas, Courthouse 20.00
Spoon, Sterling Silver, Plymouth, Mass., Demitasse 18.00
Spoon, Sterling Silver, Port Huron, Mich., Name In Bowl 9.50
Spoon, Sterling Silver, President McKinley 45.00
Spoon, Sterling Silver, Rebekah, May 22, 1903, Scrolled Handle 28.00
Spoon, Sterling Silver, Saratoga, Gold Wash Bowl 25.00
Spoon, Sterling Silver, Saugatuck, Michigan 12.00
Spoon, Sterling Silver, Scottish Rite, Winnepeg, 1929 .... 25.00
Spoon, Sterling Silver, Scottish Rite, Winnepeg, 1942 .... 25.00
Spoon, Sterling Silver, Seven Falls, Cheyenne Canyon, Demitasse 15.00
Spoon, Sterling Silver, Sheboygan, Wis., State Seal 20.00
Spoon, Sterling Silver, Sioux City, Demitasse 12.00
Spoon, Sterling Silver, Spain, Matador 22.00
Spoon, Sterling Silver, St.Joseph, Mo., Demitasse 12.00
Spoon, Sterling Silver, St.Louis Exposition, 1904 .... 55.00
Spoon, Sterling Silver, St.Louis Exposition, 1904, Set Of 3 .... 90.00
Spoon, Sterling Silver, Statue Of Liberty, Demitasse 45.00
Spoon, Sterling Silver, Texas, Engraved Bullfight 18.00
Spoon, Sterling Silver, Texas, Longhorn Steer 20.00
Spoon, Sterling Silver, Toronto, City Hall, Columbia Anchor On Top 20.00
Spoon, Sterling Silver, Toronto, Full Figure Indian, Maple Leaf 20.00
Spoon, Sterling Silver, Treaty, Philadelphia, Lenape Indians, 1882 .... 45.00
Spoon, Sterling Silver, Vermillion, Ohio, Name In Bowl 9.50
Spoon, Sterling Silver, Washington & American Eagle, Enameled 60.00
Spoon, Sterling Silver, Washington State, View Of Old Church 18.00
Spoon, Sterling Silver, Washington, D.C. ....12.00 To 32.00
Toothpick, Atlantic City, Ruby Glass, 1903 .... 15.00
Toothpick, Harrisburg, Pa., Ruby Glass 30.00
Toothpick, Revere Beach, Ruby Glass, 1905 .... 30.00
Tray, Indian, Buy Glassport Lots, 1903, Glass, 4 X 5 1/2 In. 40.00
Tumbler, Pewter, Pan American Expo.Buffalo 1901, 3 1/2 In. 35.00
Tumbler, St.Louis Exposition, Opaque White, 1904 .... 20.00
Vase, Custard Glass, Hannaford, N.Dak., 6 In. 45.00
Wine, Camden, Me., Ruby Glass 35.00

*Spangle glass is multicolored glass made from odds and ends of
colored glass rods. It includes metallic flakes of mica covered with
gold, silver, nickel, or copper. Spangle glass is usually cased with a
thin layer of clear glass over the multicolored layer.*

SPANGLE GLASS, see also Vasa Murrhina
SPANGLE GLASS, Box, Gold, Aventuring, Brass Fittings, Tortoiseshell Color 400.00
  Vase, Crimped Lip, White Lining, 7 In. 85.00
  Vase, Orange To Pale Gold, Enameled Bird, Webb, 9 1/2 In. 385.00

> *Spanish lace is a Victorian glass pattern that seems to have white lace on a colored background. Blue, yellow, cranberry, and clear glass was made with this distinctive white pattern. It was made in England and the United States after 1885. Copies are being made.*

SPANISH LACE, Epergne, Blue, Fenton, 10 In. 68.00
  Pitcher, Water, Cranberry 250.00
  Pitcher, Water, White Opalescent, Fenton 165.00
  Rose Bowl, Satin Glass, Blue 50.00
  Rose Bowl, White 30.00
  Rose Bowl, Yellow Opalescent 85.00
  Sugar Shaker, Blue Opalescent 110.00
  Tumbler, Cranberry Opalescent 45.00
  Vase, Bulbous, White Opalescent, Fenton, 11 In. 95.00

> *Spatter glass is a multicolored glass made from many small pieces of different colored glass. It is sometimes called "End–Of–Day" glass. It is still being made.*

SPATTER GLASS, Basket, Fan Shape, Pedestal, White Interior, 7 In. 165.00
  Basket, Red, Yellow, White Interior, Thorn Handle, 5 3/4 In. 65.00
  Bottle, Cologne, Leaf Mold, Cranberry, Vaseline 85.00
  Bottle, Liquor, Raised Swirl, Hexagonal, Cork, 11 1/2 In. 75.00
  Candlestick, Cased, 9 1/2 In., Pair 110.00
  Candlestick, Green & White Cased, 9 1/2 In. 40.00
  Centerpiece, Flowers At Sides, Blue, 13 3/4 X 18 In. 395.00
  Lamp, Fairy, Pyramid Form, Silver Plate Stand, 8 1/2 In. 50.00
  Lamp, Finger, Peach & White, Clear Handle, Chimney, 6 1/4 In. 110.00
  Lamp, No.367 Base, Miniature 280.00
  Pitcher, Bulbous, Ruffled, Clear Applied Handle, Amber 65.00
  Pitcher, Pink & White, Ruffled, Clear Reeded Handle, 8 In. 150.00
  Pitcher, Ruffled, Clear Handle, 7 7/8 In. 165.00
  Pitcher, Water, Green, White, Gold Mica, Bulbous, Reeded Handle 80.00
  Pitcher, Water, Swirl & Ribbed, White Interior, 8 In. 150.00
  Shoe, Applied Design 75.00
  Sugar Shaker, Ring Neck, Pink 67.00
  Tumbler, Royal Blue & White, 3 1/4 In. 32.00
  Tumbler, Water, Royal Blue & White, 3 3/4 In. 35.00
  Vase, Green & White Case, Clear Handles, 7 1/4 In. 35.00
  Vase, Jack–In–The–Pulpit, Quilted, Green & White, 9 1/4 In. 95.00
  Vase, Maroon, Green, Foil, White Lining, Silver Rim, 6 In. 75.00
  Vase, Maroon, Green, White Lining, Silver Rim, 5 1/4 In., Pair 75.00
  Vase, Pink, Brown, Buff, Clear Applied Handle, 4 1/2 In. 40.00
  Vase, Thorn Handles, 9 In. 95.00
  Vase, Yellow, Pink, 3 Rings Around Middle, Flared, 8 1/2 In. 45.00

> *The creamware or soft–paste dinnerware decorated with spatter designs in color is called, of course, spatterware. The earliest pieces were made in the late eighteenth century, but most of the spatterware found today was made from about 1800 to 1850 or is a late nineteenth– and twentieth–century form of kitchen crockery that has added spatter designs. The early spatterware was made in the Staffordshire district of England for sale in America. The kitchen type is an American product.*

SPATTERWARE, Bean Pot, Lid, Brown, Green, Cream 67.50
  Bowl & Pitcher Set, Peafowl, Blue, Adams, 13 3/8 X 11 In. 400.00
  Bowl, Advertising, Dickmann Readlyn, Iowa, 8 In. 55.00
  Bowl, Advertising, Jones Bros., Duncombe, Iowa, 7 In. 55.00
  Bowl, Blue & Rust, 8 In. 55.00
  Bowl, Blue Flowers, Stick Spatter Trim, Belgium, 11 In. 35.00
  Bowl, Blue Flowers, Tan & Light Blue, Spatter, German 55.00

Bowl, Blue, Rust, & Cream, 6 In. ....40.00 To 42.00
Bowl, Dark Flowers, Black Trim, Belgium, 11 In. 65.00
Bowl, Peafowl, Red, 3 X 5 1/4 In. 65.00
Creamer, 4 Buds, Blue Ground, 3 In. 230.00
Creamer, Blue & Lavender, 5 3/8 In. 50.00
Creamer, Fort Pattern, 4 5/8 In. 80.00
Creamer, Morning Glory, Red, 4 In. 35.00
Creamer, Red & Blue Flower, Green Stripe On Base, 4 In. 65.00
Creamer, Red & Green Rose, Brown, 3 7/8 In. 65.00
Cup & Saucer, Blue, Miniature 315.00
Cup & Saucer, Green Stripes, Blue, Miniature 10.00
Cup & Saucer, Handleless, Blue 65.00
Cup & Saucer, Handleless, Coxcomb Design, Blue 235.00
Cup & Saucer, Handleless, Peafowl, Red 225.00
Cup & Saucer, Handleless, Red ....30.00 To 60.00
Cup & Saucer, Handleless, Red & Purple 70.00
Cup & Saucer, Handleless, Red Clover, Black Stem 85.00
Cup & Saucer, Handleless, Rose On Saucer, Blue 65.00
Cup & Saucer, Handleless, Star Design, Blue 25.00
Cup & Saucer, Handleless, Stick, Purple, Gaudy Floral 37.50
Cup & Saucer, Handleless, Thistle, Red 25.00
Cup & Saucer, Pink & Yellow 270.00
Cup & Saucer, Purple, Miniature 85.00
Cup & Saucer, Red & Green, Miniature 50.00
Cup & Saucer, Schoolhouse, Green 295.00
Cup & Saucer, Schoolhouse, Red Border 125.00
Cup Plate, Black Panels, Tulip Design, Purple 400.00
Cup, Handleless, Rooster, Blue, Miniature 120.00
Cup, Peafowl, Red, Miniature 450.00
Dish, Bull's–Eye Center, Purple, 7 1/2 In. 45.00
Dish, Peacock Center, Blue Border, 5 In. 240.00
Mug, Blue, 3 7/8 In. 150.00
Mug, Stick, Gaudy Floral, Rabbits, 5 3/8 In. 345.00
Pitcher, Brown & Cream, 1 Qt. 60.00
Pitcher, Cow, Green & Tan, 8 In. 60.00
Pitcher, Eagle & Shield Design, Red, 7 In. 300.00
Pitcher, Paneled, Thistle, Yellow, 12 In. 250.00
Pitcher, Roses, Blue Ground, 5 In. 290.00
Plate, 4–Color Acorn, Blue, 8 3/8 In. 375.00
Plate, Brown Transfer, Cowboys, Green, 9 1/2 In. 85.00
Plate, Brown, Polychrome Floral Design, 7 3/8 In. 25.00
Plate, Bull's–Eye Center, Red & Purple, 9 1/2 In. 225.00
Plate, Bull's–Eye Design, Red & Green, 7 1/8 In. 26.00
Plate, Dahlia Center, Blue, 8 3/4 In. 145.00
Plate, Holly Berry Pattern, Blue, 6 3/8 In. 85.00
Plate, Peafowl, Green Ground, 7 In. 240.00
Plate, Peafowl, Red Ground, 5 1/2 In. 300.00
Plate, Peafowl, Red, 8 1/4 In. 85.00
Plate, Primrose, Red, 8 5/8 In. 110.00
Plate, Red Schoolhouse, Red Border, 8 1/2 In. 600.00
Plate, Soup, Gaudy Polychrome Design, 10 5/8 In. 75.00
Plate, Stick, Blue, Adams Rose Center, 8 5/8 In. 55.00
Plate, Thistle, Red, 8 1/2 In. 85.00
Plate, Toddy, Green Acorn, Purple, 5 1/8 In. 400.00
Plate, Tulip Center, Blue, 6 1/2 In. 55.00
Plate, Tulip, Blue, Impressed Cotton & Barlow, 8 3/4 In. 65.00
Platter, Red & Green, 15 3/4 In. 625.00
Platter, Watermelon, Blue & Lavender, 18 In. 700.00
Pot, Tall, Blue, Grape Finial, Octagonal, 10 In. 225.00
Sauce, Peacock Center, Red Spatter Border, 5 In. 290.00
Sauce, Peafowl, Red, 5 In. 245.00
Sugar, Black & Purple, 5 1/2 In. 45.00
Sugar, Covered, Rainbow, 5 3/8 In. 285.00
Sugar, Parrot, Blue, 4 7/8 In. 110.00

Spinning Wheel, Ivory
Fittings, Small

Moths can damage stored textiles. Use the
moth crystals such as paradichloroben-
zene. The vapors are heavier than air so
the crystals must be placed above the textiles, preferably in small cloth bags sus-
pended from the ceiling.

Sugar, Peafowl, Blue, 7 3/4 In.	175.00
Sugar, Peafowl, White Ground, 5 In.	160.00
Sugar, Red Star, Blue, 4 1/2 In.	25.00
Tea Set, Child's, Staffordshire, 16 Piece	90.00
Teapot, Peafowl, Green Ground, 6 In.	180.00
Teapot, Peafowl, Red Ground, 6 In.	200.00
Teapot, Rectangular Cut Corners, Stylized Red Flower	950.00
Vase, Cobalt Blue Ground, 5 In., Pair	65.00
Vase, Gold Trim, Hand Painted Flowers, Ruffled, 10 In., Pair	500.00
Washbowl, Blue, 13 5/8 In.	90.00
Washbowl, Peafowl, Red, 12 3/4 In.	85.00

*Spelter is a synonym for a zinc alloy. Figurines, candlesticks, and
other pieces were made of spelter and given a bronze or painted finish.
The metal has been used since about the 1860s to make statues,
tablewares, and lamps that resemble bronze. Spelter is soft and breaks
easily. To test for spelter, scratch the base of the piece. Bronze is
solid; spelter will show a silvery scratch.*

SPELTER, Bookends, Figural, Nude Figure Of Dicbolus, 1924, Signed, 7 In.	75.00
Figurine, Girl Feeding Cat, Marble Base, Pilet, 11 1/2 In.	225.00
Figurine, Lion, Coinchon, 8 3/4 X 6 1/2 In.	125.00
Figurine, Roman Soldiers, Gilded, Signed, 12 In., Pair	300.00
Figurine, Setter, 13 X 6 1/2 In.	165.00

*The old spinning wheel in the corner has been the symbol of earlier
times for the past 100 years. Although spinning wheels date back to
medieval times, the ones found today are rarely more than 200 years
old. Because the style of the spinning wheel changed very little, it is
often impossible to place an exact date on a wheel.*

SPINNING WHEEL, Chip Carved, Signed Mavin	135.00
Flax, Oak, Maple, H.R.Cut In Block, 35 In.	350.00
Foot Pedal & Attachment, Maple, 48 In.	275.00
Ivory Fittings, Small ....*Illus*	400.00
Pine Table, Pine Gear Mechanism, 27 X 45 In.	100.00
Primitive, Pad Feet, Signed F.W., C.1816, 36 1/2 In.	525.00
Turned Legs, Spokes, & Spindles, 28 In.	105.00
Wooden, Small	175.00

Spode pottery, porcelain, and bone china were made by the Stoke-on-Trent factory of England founded by Josiah Spode about 1770. The firm became Copeland and Garrett from 1833 to 1847, then W.T. Copeland or W.T. Copeland and Sons until 1976. It then became Royal Worcester Spode Ltd. The word "Spode" appears on many pieces made by the factories. Most collectors include all the wares under the more familiar name of Spode. Porcelains are listed in this book by the name that appears on the piece.

SPODE, see also Copeland; Copeland Spode

SPODE, Butter Chip, Wickerdale	8.00
Cheese Keeper, Angels, Trees, & Puppy, Acorn Finial, Green	142.50
Creamer, Tower, Blue, 4 In.	48.00
Cup & Saucer, Auld Lang Syne, Tower, Red Giant, 5 1/2 In.	45.00
Cup & Saucer, Blue & White, Copeland, 1 In.	55.00
Cup & Saucer, Coffee, Imari Pattern, Cobalt, Red, Gold, 1804	235.00
Cup & Saucer, Fairy Dell	22.00
Cup & Saucer, Hand Painted, C.1830	195.00
Feeding Set, Farm Animals, Marked, 3 Piece	45.00
Figurine, Pelican, Royal Jade, Art Deco, 3 1/2 In.	12.00 To 20.00
Ornament, Cottage, Octagonal, Marked Feldspar	775.00
Plate, Black & White American Scene, 1930s, 10 3/4 In.	10.00
Plate, Cowslip, 10 1/2 In.	22.00
Plate, Tower, Blue & White, Copeland, 10 1/2 In.	25.00
Platter, Camelia Pattern, Pink, 12 1/2 In.	30.00
Platter, City Of Corinth, Blue, Marked, 13 In.	110.00
Platter, Principal Entrance Of Harbor On Cacamo, Blue, 14 3/4 In.	150.00
Punch Bowl, Tower, Blue, 15 1/2 In.	140.00
Soup, Cream, Fairy Dell	12.00
Tea Set, Wickerdale Pattern, 62 Piece	500.00
Teapot & Tile Underplate, Floral, Animal Finial Lid, Signed	135.00
Toothpick, Camille, Copeland	15.00
Urn, Tower, Blue, 13 X 17 In.	695.00
Vase, Oriental Garden, Gilt Scalework, No.967, 1810–15, 10 1/4 In.	1210.00
Vase, Tower, Blue, 5 In.	42.00

Spongeware is very similar to spatterware in appearance. The designs were applied to the ceramics by daubing the color on with a sponge or cloth. Many collectors do not differentiate betwen spongeware and spatterware and use the names interchangeably. Modern pottery is being made to resemble the old spongeware, but careful examination will show it is new.

SPONGEWARE, Bean Pot, Blue & White	275.00
Bean Pot, Brown, Green, & Cream, 6 In.	90.00
Bottle, Red, White, & Green, 7 1/4 In.	50.00
Bowl, American, Blue & White, 10 In.	150.00
Bowl, Arches, Blue & White, 12 X 5 1/2 In.	185.00
Bowl, Blue & Tan, 11 1/2 In.	185.00
Bowl, Blue Over Yellow, 3 X 9 In.	65.00
Bowl, Blue, 6 1/4 In.	165.00
Bowl, Brown & Cream, 4 1/2 In.	16.50
Bowl, Cobalt, Rust, Nesting, Set Of 2	75.00
Bowl, Cream, Green, & Brown, 7 In.	24.00
Bowl, Gray, Band, Advertising, 8 In.	50.00
Bowl, Green & Brown, 10 In.	40.00
Bowl, Green & White, 10 1/4 X 5 3/8 In.	60.00
Bowl, Mixing, Blue & Rust, 10 1/2 X 6 In.	85.00
Bowl, Mixing, Blue & White, 11 X 4 1/4 In.	45.00
Bowl, Mixing, Blue Edge, Rust & Blue, 11 X 5 In.	95.00
Bowl, Pudding, Blue & White, 7 X 3 In.	155.00
Bread Plate, Open Handles, Blue On White, 10 1/4 In.	95.00
Butter, Covered, Blue & White	115.00
Butter, Covered, Good Luck Sign, Blue & White, 7 1/2 In.	180.00
Casserole, 3 In.	145.00

Casserole, Covered, Green & Brown On Cream 55.00
Cheese, Covered, 10–Petal Flower Form, Vent Cover, 8 1/4 In. 135.00
Cookie Jar, Cream & Green 45.00
Cup & Saucer, Handleless, Blue, C.1840 .... 130.00
Cup, Custard, Bennington, Set Of 5 .... 40.00
Cup, Custard, Blue & White, 2 3/8 In. 30.00
Cuspidor, Blue & White 129.00
Cuspidor, Gray & Blue 125.00
Custard, Brown On Yellow, 3 In. 20.00
Dish, Cake, Glazed, Wagner, Lehigh Valley, 7 In. 48.00
Dish, Cake, Molded Design Interior, Glazed, 11 In. 190.00
Dish, Cake, Wagner, Lehigh Valley, 8 1/2 In. 1300.00
Holder, Pipe, Blue & White 65.00
Mold, Food, Redware, 8 1/2 In. 70.00
Mold, Food, Redware, 9 1/2 In. 70.00
Mug, Blue & White, 3 1/2 In. 155.00
Pitcher & Bowl, Blue Band, Blue & White 400.00
Pitcher, Blue & White Sponge, 8 3/4 In. 80.00
Pitcher, Blue & White, 10 In. 115.00
Pitcher, Girl & Dog, Blue & White 395.00
Pitcher, Green & Brown On Cream 65.00
Pitcher, Spencer Cement Block Works, Green & Brown, 4 1/2 In. 44.00
Pitcher, Tankard, Blue, 2 Qt. 175.00
Pitcher, Water, Blue & White, 11 3/4 In. 175.00
Plate, Bread, Blue On White, Open Handles, 10 In. 95.00
Plate, Deep Blue Daubing On White, Cutout Handles, 10 In. 125.00
Platter, Blue & White, Cobalt Edge, Oblong, 13 X 10 In. 135.00
Spittoon, Blue & White 55.00
Spittoon, Brown & Yellow 45.00
Spittoon, Red & Blue 195.00
Teapot, Blue & White, 5 3/4 In. 175.00
Teapot, Wooden Handle, Pewter Lid, Brown & White 125.00
Vase, Red, Yellow, Blue, 6 1/2 In. 32.00

Pottery and porcelain have been made in the Staffordshire district in England since the 1700s. Hundreds of kilns are still working in the area. Thousands of types of pottery and porcelain have been made in the many factories that worked and still work in the area. Some of the most famous factories have been listed separately, such as Royal Doulton, Royal Worcester, Spode, Wedgwood, and others. Some Staffordshire pieces are listed under sections like Flow Blue, Shaving Mug, etc.

STAFFORDSHIRE, see also Flow Blue; Mulberry

STAFFORDSHIRE, Bank, Cottage Shape 300.00
Bank, Spaniel Head, Black & White, 3 3/4 In. 55.00
Bottle, Snuff, Queen Street Scene 25.00
Bowl, Pains Hill Surrey, Beaded Rim, Blue, Hall, 9 1/2 In. 250.00
Box, Cow, Black, Polychrome Enameling, 8 1/4 In. 115.00
Box, Enamel On Copper, Pink Blossoms, Brown, 1 X 1 1/2 In. 285.00
Box, Patch, Hand Painted Primroses, Marked 85.00
Box, Pink Blossoms, Yellow, C.1800, Top Is 1 3/4 In. 285.00
Centerpiece, Floral, 8 X 7 In. 45.00
Cheese Dish, Flow Blue Type, Marked 30.00
Coffeepot, Lafayette At Tomb Of Franklin, C.1825, 11 In. 950.00
Cottage, Floral Arched Trellis, Polychrome 150.00
Creamer, Covered, Cow, Rust & White, Gilt Trim, 4 1/4 In. 80.00
Creamer, Cow, Girl Milking, Sponge Spatter Design 110.00
Creamer, Hope, Charity 48.00
Creamer, Man & Boy, Horses, Dark Blue 150.00
Creamer, Sower, Adams, Pink & White 65.00
Creamer, Wadsworth Tower, 4 3/8 In. 225.00
Cup & Saucer, Beehive, Purple Transfer, Handleless, Adams 45.00
Cup & Saucer, Blue Scalloped Edge, Pink & White 155.00
Cup & Saucer, Brosley's Dragon, Handleless ....70.00 To 85.00

Cup & Saucer, English Steam Locomotive, Blue, Flower Border 320.00
Cup & Saucer, English View, Blue 320.00
Cup & Saucer, Floral & Urn, Dark Blue, Stubbs 85.00
Cup & Saucer, Gaudy Polychrome Floral, Handleless 17.50
Cup & Saucer, Harvest Home, Jackson, Pink & White 35.00
Cup & Saucer, Lafayette At Franklin's Tomb, Blue 425.00
Cup & Saucer, Lavender, Gold Rim, C.1900 .... 14.00
Cup & Saucer, Sower, Adams, Pink & White 45.00
Cup & Saucer, Wadsworth Tower, Handleless, Wood & Sons, Blue 185.00
Cup Plate, Buildings, Brown Transfer, 3 7/8 In. 15.00
Cup Plate, Flower, Blue Transfer, Rogers, 3 7/8 In. 40.00
Cup Plate, Flower, Dark Blue Transfer, Stubbs & Kent 85.00
Cup Plate, Garden Urn & Boat, Red Transfer, Adams, 4 1/4 In. 12.50
Cup Plate, Home Of R.Jordan, Light Blue 285.00
Dinner Set, Kent Pattern, Blue & White, 45 Piece 300.00
Dish, Cheese, 10 X 4 1/2 In. ....*Color* 85.00
Dish, Chicken On Nest, Glazed, Small 85.00
Dish, Chicken On Nest, Medium 100.00
Dish, Feeding, 18th Century, 6 3/4 In. 250.00
Dish, Footed, Square, 9 3/4 X 10 X 4 3/4 In. 650.00
Dish, Hen On Nest, Bisque, Tan, 9 X 7 3/4 In. 550.00
Dish, Hen On Nest, Covered, Black, White, & Gray, 7 1/2 X 6 In. 395.00
Dish, Soup, William Penn's Treaty, Blue, 9 1/4 In. 65.00
Dish, Vegetable, Columbus, Adams, Pink & White, 11 In. 70.00
Dish, Vegetable, Cover, Leaf Handles, Fruit Finial, 10 1/2 In. 300.00
Dish, Vegetable, Open, 10 1/2 X 12 1/4 In. 325.00
Ewer, Allegorical Design, Pewter Lid, Yellow, Booth, 13 In. 225.00
Figurine, 2 Dogs & House, Polychrome Enameling, 1 5/8 In. 45.00
Figurine, 3 Girls Standing, Blue Plaid Dresses, 7 1/2 In. 325.00
Figurine, Albert, Victoria, & Baby, On Throne, 8 In. 200.00
Figurine, Black Watch Guard & Woman, 14 In., Pair 150.00
Figurine, Boy & Girl Dancers, 8 In. 45.00
Figurine, Boy With Lamb, C.1840, 4 In. 95.00
Figurine, Cat Sitting In Draped Bed, Who Said Rats, 4 In. 110.00
Figurine, Cat, Brown & White, Blue Ribbons, 8 In., Pair 110.00
Figurine, Cat, Painted Flowers, 1860, 4 In., Pair 120.00
Figurine, Cat, Painted Flowers, 1860, 7 In., Pair 170.00
Figurine, Champion, Man On Horse, 9 X 5 1/2 In. 75.00
Figurine, Charlotte At Tomb Of Werther, C.1800, 9 In. 130.00
Figurine, Cobbler & Wife, 6 1/2 In. 135.00
Figurine, Diana, With Bow, 12 In. 155.00
Figurine, Dog, 11 In., Pair 65.00
Figurine, Dog, Black & White, Ochre Collar, 10 In., Pair 70.00
Figurine, Dog, Pebbled Trim, White, 4 In. 45.00
Figurine, Dog, Polychrome Features, Gilt Trim, 13 In., Pair 190.00
Figurine, Dog, Seated, Copper Luster Spots, 8 3/4 In., Pair 110.00
Figurine, Dog, Seated, Gold Collar & Lock, 9 1/2 In. 70.00
Figurine, Dog, White, Copper Luster, 11 In., Pair 275.00
Figurine, Duke Of Wellington, 10 X 6 In. 70.00
Figurine, Earl Of Lucan, On Horse, 1860, 14 In. ....110.00 To 135.00
Figurine, Edward & Alexandra, Pink, C.1900, 13 In., Pair 440.00
Figurine, Elijah & Raven, Wooden, 1790, 10 In. 225.00
Figurine, Fat Dignitary, 6 In. 240.00
Figurine, Greyhound, With Dead Rabbit, 8 1/2 In., Pair 260.00
Figurine, Hen On Basket, 9 X 7 In. 200.00
Figurine, Highlander, Standing, 12 In. 59.00
Figurine, Huntsman, 2 Pistols & Rifle, 17 In. 100.00
Figurine, Ireland & Britannia, Angel, Peace On Earth, 13 In. 295.00
Figurine, Jenny Lind, 10 In. 125.00
Figurine, King Edward, Sampson Smith, 12 In. 90.00
Figurine, Lion Slayer, Polychrome Enameling, 16 1/4 In. 95.00
Figurine, Lion, Recumbent Position, Brown, 12 In., Pair 195.00
Figurine, Lion, Soft Paste, Polychrome Enameling, 2 3/4 In. 100.00
Figurine, Lion, Standing, Glass Eyed, 13 X 10 In., Pair 325.00

Staffordshire, Pitcher, Rider On Horse, Black, 3 In.

The word "trademark" was used on English wares after 1855, but most of the pieces with the letters "LTD." were made after 1880.

Figurine, Maiden, Holding Cornucopia, Pratt, 11 In.	150.00
Figurine, Mary Had A Little Lamb, Vase Shape, 9 1/2 In.	100.00
Figurine, Mr.Pickwick Behind Chair, Marked, 6 In.	95.00
Figurine, Princess Helena & Prince Christian, 12 In., Pair	75.00
Figurine, Prodigal's Return, 15 In.	100.00
Figurine, Punch On Swing, 4 1/2 In.	75.00
Figurine, Rabbit, Polychrome Enameling, 3 1/4 In.	220.00
Figurine, Sailor, 9 In.	45.00
Figurine, Scotch Lassie With Lamb, 9 In.	125.00
Figurine, Scotch Shepherd, 8 In.	165.00
Figurine, Scottish Couple, Brown, Green, 12 In.	90.00
Figurine, Scottish Couple, Clock Face, C.1850, 14 In.	125.00
Figurine, Spaniel, 19th Century, 12 In., Pair	250.00
Figurine, Thomas Smith, William Collier, Combat, 13 In.	170.00
Figurine, Wellington Spaniel, Purple Luster, 6 In.	140.00
Figurine, Wesley, In Pulpit, 1850, 11 In.	120.00 To 125.00
Figurine, Wesley, White Robe, 8 In.	100.00
Figurine, Whippet, Lying On Blue Cushion, 7 X 5 In., Pair	70.00
Figurine, Whippet, Polychrome Enameling, Base, 4 3/8 In., Pair	170.00
Figurine, Whippet, Russet, Recumbent Position, 6 1/2 In., Pair	70.00
Figurine, Widow, 1810, 11 In.	175.00
Gravy Boat, Yanguesian Conflict, Don Quixote, Dark Blue	325.00
Group, Venus & Cupid, Shells On Base, C.1830, 10 1/4 In.	440.00
Holder, Spill, Scotch Lad With Swan	125.00
Inkwell, Figural, Mother & Girl Sitting On Fainting Couch	35.00
Jug, Constitution, Battle, Black Transfer, C.1815, 6 1/2 In.	750.00
Jug, Lafayette, Black Transfer, Copper Luster, 1825–30, 6 In.	715.00
Jug, Portrait, John Jay, Black Transfer, 1815–30, 5 1/2 In.	1425.00
Jug, Satyr, Multicolor, Pearlware, 5 In.	295.00
Ladle, Sauce, Country House, 6 1/4 In.	100.00
Ladle, Sauce, English Country Scene, 6 1/2 In.	135.00
Lamp, Tudor House, Glass Windows, 5 1/4 In.	60.00
Mug, Children Feeding Animals, 4–Line Verse, 2 1/2 In.	50.00
Mug, Children Playing, Green Transfer, Marked, 2 3/4 In.	5.00
Mug, Children Playing, Shuttlecock, Allerton, 2 1/2 In.	45.00
Mug, Feeding The Chickens, Pink Transfer, 2 3/4 In.	35.00
Mug, Gaudy Floral, Green & Copper Luster, 3 3/4 In.	35.00
Mug, Getting Ready For Walk, Green Transfer, 3 In.	55.00
Mug, Interior Frog, 4 1/2 In.	95.00
Mug, Pet Lamb, Black Transfer, Polychrome, 2 7/8 In.	35.00
Mug, Railroad Engine, Passenger Cars, Brown Transfer, 3 In.	15.00
Mug, Red Transfer, S & T, 2 3/8 In.	55.00

Mug, Salmon Fishing, Brown Transfer, 2 3/4 In. 30.00
Mug, Seated Cat & Running Zebra, Black Transfer, 3 1/2 In. 85.00
Mug, The Actors, 2 Children On Stage, Rose Transfer, 3 In. 35.00
Obelisk, Marbelized Glaze, 14 In. 135.00
Pastille Burner, Covered, Cottage, Floral, C.1835, 5 In., 2 Pc. 770.00
Pepper Pot, Landing Of Lafayette, Blue 800.00
Pitcher & Bowl, Franklin, Tomb, Adams, Bowl, 12 1/8 In. 1100.00
Pitcher, Baby & Dog, Gray, Incised Till, C.1850, 6 In. 95.00
Pitcher, City Hall, New York Hospital, Dark Blue, 6 In. 650.00
Pitcher, Cover, Morning Glories, Scroll Handle, Meakin, 8 In. 20.00
Pitcher, Mount Vernon, Washington's Seat, 8 1/4 In. 425.00
Pitcher, Oriental Scenes, Blue Transfer, Mask, 5 In., Pair 130.00
Pitcher, Portrait, Admiral Nelson & Captain Hardy, 6 3/8 In. 55.00
Pitcher, Rabbits, Putty, Black Transfer, 5 1/2 In. 65.00
Pitcher, Rider On Horse, Black, 3 In. ....*Illus* 30.00
Pitcher, Volunteer Rifle Corps, Soldier Scene, 7 5/8 In. 155.00
Pitcher, Young Girl & Deer, Pink, 2 3/4 In. 35.00
Plate, Abbey Pattern, G.Jones & Son, 10 1/2 In. 24.00
Plate, Almshouse New York, Stevenson, Dark Blue, 10 In. 625.00
Plate, America & Independence, Clews, 10 5/8 In. ....130.00 To 225.00
Plate, America & Independence, Dark Blue Transfer, 6 5/8 In. 125.00
Plate, Arms Of New York, Impressed Mayer, Blue, 10 In. 95.00
Plate, Aurora, Black, Colors, 10 In. 28.00
Plate, B & O On Level, Blue, Wood, 10 In. 425.00
Plate, Bank Of U.S.Philadelphia, Eagle Border, 10 In. 300.00
Plate, Beehive, Dark Blue, Flower Border, Stevenson, 8 1/2 In. 65.00
Plate, Blue Feather Edge, Embossed Florals, 10 In. 55.00
Plate, British Views, Dark Blue Transfer, 7 1/4 In. 45.00
Plate, Cabbage Rose, Red, Green, Yellow & Black, Gaudy, Pair 190.00
Plate, Canova, Red Edge, Green Center, 9 1/4 In. 50.00
Plate, Catholic Cathedral, New York, Dark Blue, 5 1/4 In. 1000.00
Plate, Catskill Mountain House, Adams, 10 1/4 In. 60.00
Plate, Chief Justice Marshall, Troy Line, Dark Blue, 10 In. 650.00
Plate, Chinese Pastimes, Pink, 9 1/2 In. 20.00
Plate, City Of Albany, New York, Dark Blue, 10 1/4 In. 450.00
Plate, Claremont, Clementson, Lavender, 1856, 8 In. ....35.00 To 48.00
Plate, Columbus, Adams, Pink & White, 6 In. 35.00
Plate, Columbus, Adams, Pink & White, 10 1/2 In. 55.00
Plate, Commodore Macdonough's Victory, Blue, Wood, 7 3/4 In. 200.00
Plate, Conova, Red Border, Green Center, 9 In. 50.00
Plate, Constitution And Guerierre, Blue, 10 In. 479.00
Plate, Couple In Park, Bird, Butterfly Rim, 7 1/4 In. 35.00
Plate, Cut, General Jackson, The Hero Of New Orleans, 3 In. 650.00
Plate, Dam, Water Works, Philadelphia, Blue, 10 In. ....110.00 To 425.00
Plate, Dancing On Deck Of Ship, Black Transfer, Adams, 8 In. 30.00
Plate, Dartmouth, Dark Blue, Shell Border, 9 1/4 In. 225.00
Plate, Delphi, Adams, Blue, 10 In. 25.00
Plate, Dr.Syntax, Scene, Floral Border, 10 1/4 In., 7 Piece 200.00
Plate, Embossed Daisy Rim, Polychrome Of December 22.50
Plate, Erie Canal At Buffalo, Red Transfer, 9 3/4 In. 45.00
Plate, Escape Of The Mouse, Wilkie's Design, 10 In. 150.00
Plate, Experience Keeps A Dear School, 6 In. 60.00
Plate, Fulham Church, Middlesex, Blue Transfer, 8 1/2 In. 35.00
Plate, Game Birds, Dark Blue Transfer, 7 3/4 In. 60.00
Plate, General Jackson, New Orleans, Black, 6 1/2 In. 350.00
Plate, Gilpin's Mills On Brandywine Green, Blue, 9 1/4 In. 195.00
Plate, Grecian Font, Mayer, Pink & White, 9 1/2 In. 20.00
Plate, Highland Jessie, Flat Back, 9 In. 115.00
Plate, Hudson River, Near Fishkill, Blue, 7 1/2 In. 85.00
Plate, Intemperance Produces Starvation, 6 In. 60.00
Plate, Isola Bell, Light Blue Transfer, Adams, 6 In. 28.00
Plate, Junction Of Sacandaga & Hudson, Brown, Clews, 7 In. 125.00
Plate, Landing Of Fathers At Plymouth, Medium Blue, 10 In. 140.00
Plate, Landing Of Lafayette, Blue, Clews, 10 In. ....135.00 To 190.00

Plate, Landing Of Lafayette, Blue, Clews, 7 3/4 In. 140.00
Plate, Lily, Sepia, 10 In. 16.50
Plate, Mahomedan, Mosque Tomb, Oriental Scenery, Hall, 10 In. 40.00
Plate, Montevideo, Conn., Pink & White, 7 In. 55.00
Plate, Near Fishkill, Hudson River, Clews, Blue, 7 1/2 In. 85.00
Plate, Near Fort Miller, Hudson River, Clews, 9 In. 98.00
Plate, New York City Hall, Dark Blue, 10 In. 195.00
Plate, New York, Pink & White, Adams, 5 3/4 In. 70.00
Plate, Peace & Plenty, Impressed Clews, Dark Blue, 9 In. 175.00
Plate, Poughkeepsie, N.Y., Various Scenes, Blue, 7 1/2 In. 38.00
Plate, Quadrupeds, I.Hall, 10 In. 95.00
Plate, Quadrupeds, I.Hall, Medium Blue, 9 3/4 In. 85.00
Plate, Queen's Rose, Mayer, Pink Band Border, 6 In. 55.00
Plate, Race Bridge Philadelphia, Jackson, 9 In. 85.00
Plate, Robinson Crusoe & Family Dining, Daisy Rim, 7 5/8 In. 35.00
Plate, Scene Of Florence, Medium Blue, 10 1/4 In. 25.00
Plate, Seasons, Mayer, Pink & White, 10 1/2 In. 55.00
Plate, Select Scenery, Clews, Dark Blue, 6 3/4 In. 75.00
Plate, Select Scenery, Fountain Abbey, Clews, 10 In. 85.00
Plate, Senate House, Cambridge, Light Blue Transfer, 7 In. 55.00
Plate, Shannondale Springs, Va., Pink & White, 8 In. 45.00
Plate, Soup, Blue, Fruit Center, 8 1/2 In. 40.00
Plate, Soup, Cows Grazing In Meadow, Dark Blue, Marked, 10 In. 98.00
Plate, The Escape Of The Mouse, 10 In. 125.00
Plate, Thistle, Blue Luster, White, 10 Sided, 9 In. 22.00
Plate, Toddy, Canova, Mayer, Pink & White, 5 In. 30.00
Plate, Toddy, Don Quixote Repose, Woods, Dark Blue, 5 3/8 In. 150.00
Plate, Toddy, Donkey Scene, Red Transfer, 4 7/8 In. 10.00
Plate, Vassar College, Taylor Hall, Adams, Blue, 7 1/2 In. 38.00
Plate, View Near Conway, N.H., Pink & White, 9 In. 35.00
Plate, View Near Philadelphia, Dark Blue, Clews, 10 1/2 In. 375.00
Plate, View Of Liverpool, Blue, Wood, 10 In. 190.00
Plate, Vincennes Pattern, Grayish Purple, 10 1/2 In. 225.00
Plate, Vincennes, Gray Purple, Alcock, 10 1/2 In. ....45.00 To 55.00
Plate, West Point, Hudson River, Black, Clews, 7 1/2 In. 85.00
Plate, Winter View Of Pittsfield, Mass., Clews, 10 1/2 In. 225.00
Plate, Winter View Of Pittsfield, Mass., Dark Blue, 8 3/4 In. 90.00
Plate, Wreck Kent East Indiaman, Blue, 9 1/4 In. 190.00
Platter, Blue Feather Edge, Clews, 17 In. 150.00
Platter, Boston & Bunker Hill, Slate Blue, Ridgway, 19 In. 265.00
Platter, Christianburg, Africa, Blue, Enoch Wood, 18 1/2 In. 1200.00
Platter, Columbian Star, Blue, 13 In. 220.00
Platter, English Country Scene, Blue Transfer, 19 1/2 In. 130.00
Platter, Hybla, Brougham & Mayer, 11 1/4 X 9 1/4 In. 35.00
Platter, LaConch, Well, Tree, Blue, 18 In. 290.00
Platter, Landing Of Lafayette, Blue, Clews, 17 In. 625.00
Platter, Little Falls At Luzerne, Black, 17 1/2 In. 250.00
Platter, Louisville, Kentucky, Dark Blue, Clews, 12 1/2 In. 2000.00
Platter, Niagara Falls, Dark Blue, Enoch Wood, 14 1/2 In. 1200.00
Platter, Oriental, Green, 15 In. 50.00
Platter, Pagoda, Medium Blue Transfer, 11 3/4 In. 70.00
Platter, Palestine, R.Stevenson, Medium Dark Blue, 10 5/8 In. 85.00
Platter, Tuscan Rose, Light Blue Transfer, 19 1/2 In. 40.00
Platter, Tuscan Rose, Sepia Tone, C.1840, 14 X 17 In. 75.00
Pot, Dome Top, Oriental Building, Floral, Blue, 10 In. 90.00
Soup Dish, Vue Du Chateau, Dark Blue, 10 In. 145.00
Soup, Dish, Caledonia, Black, Adams, 9 1/2 In. 36.00
Soup, Dish, Fruit Center, Blue, 8 1/2 In. 40.00
Spaniel, White With Gold Design, 10 In., Pair 130.00
Spill, Huntsman & Dog, 14 In. 110.00
Spill, Woman Standing With Rabbit & Dead Bird, 11 In. 65.00
Sugar & Creamer, Cottage Pattern 48.00
Sugar, Covered, Beehive, Purple Transfer, Adams 79.00
Sugar, Covered, Franklin Tomb, Wood, 6 3/4 In. 85.00

Sugar, Covered, Landing Of Lafayette, Blue, 5 1/2 In.	55.00
Sugar, Lafayette At Franklin's Tomb, Dark Blue Transfer	375.00
Sugar, River & Garden Folly, Marked Rogers, Soft Paste, Blue	10.00
Sugar, Sower, Adams, Pink & White	70.00
Tea Set, Child's, Little Mae, C.1890, 16 Piece	225.00
Tea Set, Peafowl At Fountain, Green Transfer, 9 Piece	135.00
Teapot, Chancellor Livingston, Dark Blue, Enoch Wood	750.00
Teapot, Franklin Tomb, Wood, 7 5/8 In.	225.00
Teapot, Garden Scene With Pagodas, Adams, 8 1/4 In.	105.00
Teapot, Green Center, Red Border	250.00
Teapot, Orange Design, White Ground, Soft Paste	225.00
Teapot, Sower, Adams, Pink & White	155.00
Teapot, Zamara, Blue Transfer, Polychrome ....135.00 To	145.00
STAFFORDSHIRE, TOBY JUG, see Toby Jug	
Toddy, Embossed Blue Rim, Clews, 4 5/8 In.	12.50
Toddy, Residence Of Late Richard Jordan, N.J., Red Transfer	45.00
Tureen, Underplate, Cambrian, Phillips, Green & White, 13 In.	90.00
Tureen, Underplate, R.Hall's Select Views, 16 1/4 In.	1150.00
Vase, Cows, Calf Nursing, 11 In., Pair	450.00
Vase, Spill, Deerslayer, 16 In.	225.00
Washington & Lafayette, Black Transfer, 5 In.	325.00
Waste Bowl, Christmas Eve, Dark Blue, 6 1/2 In.	275.00
Watch Holder, Scottish Man & Woman, Mid–19th Century, 7 In.	150.00

The Fulper Pottery had a long history that entwined with the Stangl Pottery in 1910 when Johann Martin Stangl started work. He bought into the firm in 1913, became president in 1926, and in 1929 changed the company name to Stangl Pottery. The pottery made dinnerwares and a line of limited–edition bird figurines. The company went out of business in 1972.

STANGL, ABC Set, Plate & Cup	55.00
Ashtray, Canada Goose	25.00
Ashtray, Pheasant, Oval, Red Clay, Marked, 11 X 7 3/4 In.	30.00
Ashtray, Sportsman, Jumping Deer	20.00
Ashtray, Wood Duck, Red Clay, Marked, 10 3/4 X 7 1/2 In.	30.00
Bird, Bird Of Paradise, No.3408 ....65.00 To	90.00
Bird, Blackpoll Warbler, No.3810	110.00
Bird, Bluebird, No.3276D	125.00
Bird, Bluebird, No.3276S ....75.00 To	80.00
Bird, Bluebirds, No.3276D, Double	125.00
Bird, Broadbill, No.3629	100.00
Bird, Broadtail Hummingbird, No.3626	95.00
Bird, Bunting, Painted, No.3452	125.00
Bird, Cardinal, No.3444	60.00
Bird, Cardinal, No.3596, Gray, Signed DM ....29.00 To	45.00
Bird, Cerulean Warbler, No.3456 ....50.00 To	65.00
Bird, Chestnut–Backed Chickadee, No.3811	60.00
Bird, Cliff Swallow, No.3852	36.00
Bird, Cockatoo, No.3405D, Pink, Pair	85.00
Bird, Cockatoo, No.3405S	45.00
Bird, Cockatoo, No.3580, Blue & Gray	95.00
Bird, Cockatoo, No.3580, Medium	95.00
Bird, Cockatoo, No.3584, 11 1/2 In. ....105.00 To	225.00
Bird, Duck, No.3250B	40.00
Bird, Evening Grosbeak, No.3813	135.00
Bird, Flying Duck, No.3443	250.00
Bird, Goldfinches Group, No.3635	150.00
Bird, Hen, No.3446, & Rooster, No.3445, Pair ....225.00 To	275.00
Bird, Hummingbird, No.3585	40.00
Bird, Hummingbird, No.3628	75.00
Bird, Kentucky Warbler, No.3598	45.00
Bird, Key West Quail Dove, No.3454	235.00
Bird, Kingfisher, No.3406S ....35.00 To	75.00
Bird, Lovebird, No.3400	40.00

Bird, Nuthatch, No.3593 .... 45.00
Bird, Oriole, No.3402S 35.00
Bird, Redstart, No.3490D 150.00
Bird, Rivoli Hummingbird, No.3627 .... 95.00 To 155.00
Bird, Rufous Hummingbird, No.3585 .... 34.00
Bird, Titmouse, No.3592 .... 30.00
Bird, Turkey, No.3275 .... 275.00
Bird, Wilson Warbler, No.3597 .... 45.00
Bird, Wren, No.3401S 37.00
Bird, Yellow Warbler, No.3447 .... 50.00
Bowl, Salad, Thistle Pattern, 10 In. 8.00
Butter, Covered, Thistle 5.00
Candlestick, Cube Shape, Mottled Green 11.00
Cup & Saucer, Bella Rosa 12.00
Cup & Saucer, Florette 12.00
Cup & Saucer, Orchard Song 7.00
Cup & Saucer, Thistle Pattern 8.00
Cup, Wild Rose 5.00
Figurine, Elephant, White Porcelain 6.00
Gravy Boat & Liner, Orchard Song 11.00
Pitcher, Curved Handle, Mottled Green 10.00
Pitcher, Green To Yellow Top, Art Deco Handle, Ribbed, Marked, 10 In. 35.00
Pitcher, Milk, Thistle 7.00
Plate, Bachelor Button, 10 In. 5.00
Plate, Gold Rim, Gold, Gray, & Blue Ground, 14 1/2 In. 35.00
Plate, Thistle, 8 In. 2.00
Platter, Brown, White Printing, Stangl Pottery Since 1805, 12 In. 330.00
Platter, Paisley, Round 20.00
Salt & Pepper, Hen & Rooster 55.00
Stand, Hat & Wig, Red Clay, Gold Tag, 15 In. 135.00
Stand, Wig, Brunette Lady, Wooden Base 80.00
Sugar & Creamer, Thistle 4.00
Teapot, Americana, Yellow 15.00
Tray, Art Deco, Deer, Mottled Green, 5 1/2 In. 35.00
Tray, Bread, Orchard Song 16.00
Vase, Blue & Green, 10 In. 30.00
Vase, Horsehead, Art Deco, Blue, 12 1/2 In. 185.00
Vase, Pillow, Sunflower, Lustrous Blue, Terra Rose, No.3502, 12 In. 30.00
Vase, Terra Rose, 12 In. 25.00
Vase, Terra Rose, 7 X 6 In. 25.00
Wall Pocket, Cosmos, Green, 8 In. 25.00

*We named Star Holly in an article in the 1950s. It was thought to be
an early nineteenth–century art glass, but it is really a type of milk
glass made by the Imperial Glass Company of Bellaire, Ohio, in 1957.
The pieces were made to look like Wedgwood jasperware. White holly
leaves appear against colored borders of blue, green, or rust. It is
marked on the bottom of every piece. Some identical molded glass
was made without the added color. Unfortunately, misinformation is
difficult to correct, and even some museums have mislabeled the Star
Holly as earlier than 1957.*

STAR HOLLY, Dish, Blue, 8 In. 85.00

*Steins have been used by beer and ale drinkers for over 500 years.
They have been made of ivory, porcelain, stoneware, faience, silver,
pewter, wood, or glass in sizes up to nine gallons. Although some were
made by Meissen, Capo–di–Monte, and other famous factories, most
were made in Germany. The words "Geschutz" or "Musterschutz" on
a stein are the German words for patented or registered design, not
company names. Steins are still being made in the old styles.*

STEIN, 3 Kings, Dumler & Breiden, 1/2 Liter 91.00
   109 Leib–Gren.Regt.Karlsrube 1901–03, 1/2 Liter, Roster 260.00
   Amber Glass, 1/4 Liter, Berry Prunts, Pewter, Handle, 6 3/4 In. 165.00
   Amber Glass, Deer In Forest, Hand Painted, C.1890, 1 1/2 In. 225.00

Amber Glass, Enameled German Ruler, State Shields, Humpen, 12 In. 374.00
Amber Glass, Enameled Munich Children, Prunts, 14 In. 495.00
Amber Glass, Pokal, Boot Shape, Silver Plate Spur & Lid, 13 In. 176.00
Austrian, Silver Plate Fittings, Blue Handle, Oval Reserve, 6 1/8 In. 500.00
Barrel, Wooden, Copper, Bands, 1/2 Liter 78.00
Beer, Germany, C.1920, 12 In. 125.00
Bisque, 1/2 Liter, Figural, Skull, E.C.S., Inscribed Hoffmann 1911 .... 655.00
Black Boy, Pottery, 1/2 Liter 440.00
Blown Glass, 25th Anniversary, Silver Panels, 1874–99, 11 In. 110.00
Blown Glass, Orange, Thread Design, Pewter Neck & Handle, 1 Liter 175.00
Blown, Blue Prunts, Green Thread Design, 1/2 Liter 120.00
Blown, Fluted, Porcelain Inlay Of Girl & Goat, 1/2 Liter 115.00
Bowling Pin, 1/2 Liter 145.00
Bowling Pin, Pottery, Boy & Pins Scene, 1/2 Liter, E.C.S.1134 .... 97.00
Bowling Scene, Print Over Glaze, Stoneware, 1/2 Liter 44.00
Brass, Glass Insert, Wilhelm I & II, Frederick III Panel, 1/2 Liter 264.00
Cavalier & Maiden, Copper, Hand Hammered, 4 Foot, 14 In. 128.00
Clock Tower, Pottery, 1/2 Liter, E.C.S.426 .... 110.00
Cut Glass, 1/2 Liter, City Scene, Marked B.Pruckner, 5 1/2 In. 175.00
Cut Glass, Crystal, Pewter Top, 8 In. 42.50
Drinking Cavalier, 2 Liter, J.W.Remy 85.00
Dwarfs At Keg, Etched, 1/2 Liter, Merkelbach & Wick 204.00
Elephant, Pottery, 1/2 Liter 97.00
Embossed Classical Figure, Pewter, Marked, 7 1/2 In. 175.00
Embossed Polychrome Tavern Scene, Pewter Lid, Stoneware, 8 In. 45.00
Engraved Floral Design, Westerwald, C.1890, 9 In. 109.00
Etched Pattern, Cobalt Blue Designs, Stoneware, 1/2 Liter 123.00
Falstaff Man, Squire, & Tavern Keeper, Floral Bands, 1 Liter, German 235.00
Famous Warriors, Brass, Hand Hammered Relief, 3 Liter 193.00
Flagon, Copper, Brass, 4 Footed, 18 In. 275.00
Floral Design, Amber Glass, German, 14 In. 245.00
Football Shape, Chicago Flag, Porcelain, Maddocks Sons, 12 In. 429.00
Freicorps, Iron Cross Lid, 1924, 1/2 Liter 325.00
German Transfer, Hinged Pewter Top, 5 In. 25.00
German, 4 Liter, Salt Glazed, Pewter Lid, 19th Century, 17 In. 175.00
Grecian Woman, Pewter, Relief, 1/2 Liter 239.00
Hunter Scene, Print Over Glaze, 1/2 Liter, Reinhold Hanke 93.00
Hunters, Pottery, Print Over Glaze, 1/2 Liter 114.00
Ironstone, 3 Figures, Legend, Etched, 1 Liter, German 85.00
Ivory, Classical Figures, 14 In. 1850.00
Judge, Porcelain, 1/2 Liter, Perkeo E.C.S. No.227 .... 690.00
Made For Schaefer Brewery, Stoneware, 1/2 Liter 54.00
Man In Countryside, Stoneware, 1/2 Liter 44.00
Marzi & Remy, 19 Infantry, Reg.Munich, 1/2 Liter 163.00
Men Watching Woman Dancing, Print Over Glaze, 1/2 Liter 55.00
Merkelbach & Wick, Bridge, Railroad Scenes, 1905–07, 1/2 Liter 915.00
Merkelbach & Wick, Eisenbahn Locomotive, Roster, 1901–03, 1/2 Liter 330.00
Merkelbach & Wick, Print Over Glaze, Cathedral, 1/2 Liter 44.00
Merkelbach & Wick, Prussian Flag, Enameled, 1/2 Liter 69.00
    STEIN, METTLACH, see Mettlach, Stein
Monk & Nun, Lithophane, 1/2 Liter, 6 3/4 In. 345.00
Monk Reading Newspaper, Print Over Glaze, 1/2 Liter, Columbian Art 96.00
Monk, Robe & Skull Cap, Blue & Gray Salt Glaze, 1/2 Liter, 7 1/2 In. 175.00
Monkey & Bear, Bear Handle, Blue, Gray, Maroon, 1/2 Liter, 8 3/4 In. 195.00
Monkey & Bear, Pottery, 1/2 Liter, Bear Handle, 8 3/4 In. 225.00
Munich Child, Print Over Glaze, 1/2 Liter 50.00
Munich, Rust, Green, Blue, & White, Brass Lid, 8 X 5 In. 495.00
Musical, Zeppelin Scene, Hand Painted, Metal Lid, German, 1909, 11 In. 300.00
Nurnberg Trichter, Musterschutz, Lithophane, 1/2 Liter 535.00
Oriental Scene, Hand Painted, 3/4 Liter, Nymphenburg, C.1850 .... 2541.00
Painted Stag In Forest, Pewter Top, 0/3 Liter 55.00
Pig, Pig With Pipe Cover, Musterschutz, 1/2 Liter 440.00
Porcelain, 22 Inft.Regt.Zweibvrucken 1904–06, 1/2 Liter, Roster 358.00
Porcelain, 2nd Infantry Reg. Munich, 1909–11, 1/2 Liter, Screw Lid 385.00

Porcelain, Regimental, 1901 .... 300.00
Pottery, Naval, S.M.S.Dresden, 1909–12, Side Roster, 1 Liter 1431.00
Pottery, Nazi, Print Over Glaze, 1 Liter 424.00
Puzzle, Raised Hunting Scene, Thorn Handle & Rim, 6 In. 85.00
Regimental, Cavalry, 13th Hussar 525.00
Regimental, Pewter Lid, Cannon Finial, Lithophane, Naked Lady 45.00
Salt Glaze, 1/2 Liter, C.1880 .... 55.00
Salt Glaze, Pewter Lid, 19th Century, 4 Liter, 17 In. 150.00
Soccer Players, 1/2 Liter 30.00
Stoneware, Blue Design, Pewter Top, 4 1/2 In. 40.00
Stoneware, Porcelain Insert, Hand Painted Lid, C.1840, 1 Liter 150.00
Stoneware, Pschorrbrau, Brewery Lid, Salt Glaze, 1 Liter 170.00
Tourist, Raised Relief Pottery, Cobalt, Germany, 4 In. 45.00
Trumpet Girls, Horse & Rider On Lid, Pewter, 19 In. 392.00
Wachgenheuser, Westerwalk, Stoneware, 1/2 Liter 253.00

Stereo cards that were made for stereopticon viewers became popular after 1840. Two almost identical pictures were mounted on a stiff cardboard backing so that, when viewed through a stereoscope, a three–dimensional picture could be seen. Value is determined by maker and by the subject. These cards were made in quantity through the 1930s.

STEREO CARD, 1876 Exposition, 10 Views 20.00
1899, Set Of 63 .... 50.00
Balloon, Zeppelin & Russo–Japanese War, World War I 10.00
High Bridge At Harlem, N.Y., 1855 .... 40.00
Mississippi Steamboat, 1890 .... 4.00
Niagara Falls, 12 Views 7.00
Trip Through Sears Roebuck & Co., 1915, Box Set Of 50 .... 60.00
World War I, Set Of 300 .... 300.00

The stereoscope, or stereopticon, was used for viewing stereo cards. The hand viewer was invented by Oliver Wendell Holmes, although more complicated table models were used before his was produced in 1859.

STEREOSCOPE, All Wooden, Hand Held, Adjustable, 20 Views 75.00
Brushed Aluminum, Polished Wood, 1900 .... 25.00
Hand Held, Adjustable, 20 Views 100.00
Oakwood, Underwood, Pat.1901 .... 25.00
Viewer, Walnut Stand 45.00
STERLING SILVER, see Silver–Sterling

Steuben glass was made at the Steuben Glass Works of Corning, New York. The factory, founded by Frederick Carder and T. C. Hawkes, Sr., was purchased by the Corning Glass Company. They continued to make glass called "Steuben." Many types of art glass were made at Steuben. The firm is still making exceptional quality glass but it is clear, modern–style glass.

STEUBEN, see also Aurene
STEUBEN, Atomizer, Blue Aurene, 6 1/4 In. 275.00
Atomizer, Blue Aurene, 7 1/2 In. 400.00
Atomizer, Gold Aurene, Signed, 7 1/2 In. 165.00
Bottle, Cologne, Green, Self Threaded Stopper, Pomona, 5 1/2 In. 125.00
Bowl, ABC, Plum Jade, 8 In. 1850.00
Bowl, Aurene, Gold Interior, Light Green Iridescent, 10 1/2 In. 375.00
Bowl, Blue Aurene, 10 In. 450.00
Bowl, Blue Aurene, Calcite, 8 1/4 X 2 In. 495.00
Bowl, Centerpiece, Alabaster Foot, Signed, Jade, 12 In. 135.00
Bowl, Centerpiece, Applied Yellow Threading, Signed, Oval, 14 In. 135.00
Bowl, Centerpiece, Fleur–De–Lis, Bristol Yellow, Footed, Signed 500.00
Bowl, Footed Base, Iridescent, Signed, 12 In. 400.00
Bowl, Gold Aurene On Calcite, 10 In. 295.00
Bowl, Gold Aurene, No.2879, 3 X 10 In. 150.00
Bowl, Gold, Calcite, Rolled Rim, Shallow, 1920, 9 1/2 In. 120.00

Bowl, Grotesque, Cranberry, 12 X 6 1/2 In.	275.00
Bowl, Grotesque, Ivory, Folded, Oval, 12 X 6 1/2 In.	225.00
Bowl, Jade Green, Alabaster Footed, Bulbous, 3 X 4 1/4 In.	50.00
Bowl, Jade, 10 In.	125.00
Bowl, Mica Flecked, Signed, Silverina, Air Trapped, 11 X 4 3/4 In.	700.00
Bowl, Scalloped, Ribbed Body, Signed, Selenium Red, 12 In.	150.00
Bowl, Thumbprint, Blue Threading, Fleur–De–Lis Mark, 12 In.	190.00
Bowl, Topaz Swirl, Ribbed, Green Pedestal, Signed, 4 1/4 X 5 1/2 In.	95.00
Bowl, Underplate, Daffodil, Celeste Blue	45.00
Bowl, Underplate, York Pattern, Green Jade Etched, Marked, 8 1/2 In.	175.00
Bowl, Verre De Soie, 14 In.	75.00
Candlestick, Acid Cut, Rose Pattern, Jade Green, Alabaster, 6 In.	380.00
Candlestick, Amber Swirl, Blue, 12 In.	125.00
Candlestick, Amethyst & Gold, No.2596, 10 In.	175.00
Candlestick, Aurene, Gold, Signed, 4 3/4 X 10 In., Pair	800.00
Candlestick, Baluster Standard, Alabaster Ring, 9 In., Pair	500.00
Candlestick, Blue Aurene, Twisted Stem, Signed & Dated, 10 In., Pr.	900.00
Candlestick, Gold Ruby Cased Over Crystal, Cut Flowers, 12 In., Pr.	1950.00
Candlestick, Ribbed Foot, Top, Signed, Selenium Red, 12 1/4 In., Pr.	400.00
Candlestick, Rose Pattern, 1920s, 6 In., Pair ....*Illus*	350.00
Champagne, Oriental Poppy, Signed, 6 1/4 In.	325.00
Cologne, Pink Petal Flower Design, Black Jade Stopper, 6 In.	500.00
Compote, Calcite, 4 1/2 In.	100.00
Compote, Calcite, Aurene, 6 X 4 In.	180.00
Compote, Clear & Green With Bubbles, Reed Under Rim, Signed, 7 In.	80.00
Compote, Green Swirl, Amber Feet, Fleur–De–Lis Mark, 10 3/4 In.	225.00
Compote, Jade Green, Alabaster Stem & Base, 8 X 10 In.	140.00
Compote, Stem, Green, Signed, 6 1/2 In.	75.00
Compote, Stringing, Signed, Green, 8 In. ....*Color*	125.00
Compote, Threaded Rim, Random Bubbles, Teardrop In Stem, 4 3/4 In.	75.00
Cordial, Aurene, Twisted Stem, 3 3/4 In.	185.00
Cordial, Celeste Blue	50.00
Cordial, Gold Aurene, Footed, Signed, 3 1/2 In., Set Of 6	1350.00
Creamer, Celeste Blue, Amber	75.00
Cup & Saucer, Gold Aurene, Signed	325.00
Darner, Stocking, Blue Aurene	625.00
Darner, Stocking, Gold Aurene	465.00
Dish, Nut, Green Threading, Pedestal, Signed, 3 X 1 1/2 In.	85.00
Figurine, Horse, Clear, 1939, Signed Sidney Waugh, 9 1/2 X 7 1/2 In.	575.00
Figurine, Koala Bear, Red Fitted Leather Case, 5 3/4 In.	1250.00
Figurine, Love, Stylized Couple, 4 1/4 In.	175.00
Figurine, Porpoise, Signed, 5 1/2 In.	450.00
Finger Bowl & Underplate, Gold Millefiori, Hearts & Vines, 5 In.	1750.00

Steuben, Vase, Oriental Jade,
Opaque White Swirl, 6½ In., Pair

Steuben, Candlestick, Rose Pattern, 1920s, 6 In., Pair

Finger Bowl & Underplate, Gold Millefiori, Ruffled Bowl, Signed 1750.00
Finger Bowl, Floriform Gold, Calcite Exterior 400.00
Finger Bowl, Rosaline, Swirled, Opalescent 145.00
Fixture, Hanging, Calcite Acid Etched, Acorn Shape Globe 225.00
Flower Frog, Buddha Figure In Double Row Base, Alabaster 250.00
Flower Frog, Female With Arms Out, Faceted Block, 14 1/2 In. 280.00
Glass, Lemonade, Pomona Green, Topaz Base, 5 In. 20.00
Goblet, Aurene, Twisted Stem, Signed, 6 In. 350.00
Goblet, Celeste Blue, Rose Stem, Signed, 8 In. 40.00
Goblet, Clear Top, Amethyst Twisted Stem, 9 In. 90.00
Goblet, Cobalt Blue, 5 In. 20.00
Goblet, Diamond–Quilted, Green Applied Threads, Clear, Marked, 8 In. 55.00
Goblet, French Blue, Stem, Controlled Bubbles, Signed, 9 In. 70.00
Goblet, Gold Ruby, Swirl, Clear Twisted Stem, 9 In. 30.00
Goblet, Pomona, Green, Signed, 6 In. 30.00
Goblet, Swirled Bowl, 8 In. 85.00
Goblet, Topaz, Signed, 8 In. 25.00
Goblet, Verre De Soie, 6 In. 50.00
Jar, Sweetmeat, Blue Aurene, Silver Plated Bail, Signed, 3 1/2 In. 450.00
Lamp, Aurene, Intarsia Banded Shade, Brown, 7 1/4 X 6 In. 650.00
Lamp, Dark Green Aurene, Platinum Applied Border, 10 In. 1900.00
Lamp, Floor, Art Glass Plaque Of Woman, Iron, Signed Carder, 68 In. 475.00
Lamp, Light Green Cut To Clear, Floral Design, Marble Base, 31 In. 300.00
Lamp, Light Green Glass, Oriental Floral Design, Acid Cut, 32 In. 425.00
Perfume Bottle, Blue Threaded 165.00
Perfume Bottle, Green Threaded, Signed 110.00
Perfume Bottle, Jade Green, White Stopper 115.00
Perfume Bottle, Rosaline Body, Alabaster Stopper & Foot, 8 In. 185.00
Perfume Bottle, Rosaline, Alabaster, Swirl Pattern Atomizer 425.00
Perfume Bottle, Verre De Soie, Emerald Green Stopper 250.00
Pitcher & Bowl, Cascading Rose Panels, Turquoise 185.00
Plate, Clear, Black Reeding, Signed, 8 In. 40.00
Plate, Cut To Alabaster, Signed, 7 1/2 In. 60.00
Plate, Jade Green, 8 3/4 In., Set Of 6 .... 200.00
Plate, Signed, Green, 8 1/2 In., Set Of 6 .... 115.00
Powder Jar, Rose, Opalescent, White Handle, Covered, 4 X 6 In. 150.00
Puff Box, Rosaline, Alabaster Knob, 5 X 5 1/2 In. 295.00
Salt, Aurene & Calcite, Pedestal 175.00
Salt, Clear, Green Threading, Pedestal, Signed, 3 In. 85.00
Salt, Rosaline, Alabaster Handle, 2 1/2 In. 65.00
Salt, Yellow, Pedestal, Bubbles, Threading, Signed, 1 1/2 In. 95.00
Shade, Aurene On Calcite, Leaf & Vine, Allover Green, 6 1/2 In. 950.00
Shade, Aurene, Ball Shape, 5 X 4 1/2 In. 140.00
Shade, Aurene, Gold Leaf & Vine, Gold Lined, Tan, Signed 165.00
Shade, Bell Shape, Verre De Soie, Signed 75.00
Shade, Calcite, Bell Shape, Pair 150.00
Shade, Dark Green Aurene, Platinum Applied Border, 10 In. 1900.00
Shade, Gold Aurene, Ribbed, 5 In., Pair 300.00
Shade, Gold, 10 Sides, 6 X 3 1/2 In. 85.00
Shade, Green Aurene On Calcite, Platinum Leaf, Vine, 6 1/2 X 6 In. 950.00
Shade, Melon Stripes & Platinum Applied Border, Signed, 10 In., Pr. 2250.00
Sherbet & Underplate, Cranberry Rim, Star, Signed, 8 1/2 In. 160.00
Tray, Controlled Bubble Stem, Gold Reeding, Marked, 7 In. 55.00
Tumbler, Red, 6 In. 60.00
Tumbler, Swirled Green Jade, Alabaster Handle, Signed, 5 1/2 In. 65.00
Urn, Blue Aurene, Signed, 2 In. 375.00
Vase, Acid Cut Back, Allover Flower Design, 7 1/2 In. 180.00
Vase, Alabaster, Black Jade Rim, M Shape Handles, Marked, 6 In. 450.00
Vase, Amber Reeding At Top, Bubbly Crystal, 8 In. 95.00
Vase, Amber Ribbed, Flared, Wafer Stem, Signed, 8 1/4 In. 85.00
Vase, Amethyst Ribbed, Pedestal, Signed, 8 1/4 In. 120.00
Vase, Aurene, Blue, Signed & Numbered, 3 1/2 X 10 In. 325.00
Vase, Black Jade Over Alabaster, Pussy Willow, Signed, 6 In. 1500.00
Vase, Blue Aurene, Iridescent, 8 1/2 In. 450.00

Vase, Blue Aurene, Marked, 4 In. 250.00
Vase, Blue Aurene, Ruffled Rim, Disc Foot, Signed, 6 In. 360.00
Vase, Bubbles Throughout, Amber Reeding At Top, Signed, 8 In. 95.00
Vase, Bud, Controlled Air Bubble Stem, Signed, 8 In. 180.00
Vase, Bud, Sheared Rim, Crystal, 10 In. 95.00
Vase, Calcite, Gold Aurene Interior, Ruffled, Signed Carder, 7 In. 285.00
Vase, Diagonal Ribbing, Round Foot, Blue, Signed, 7 3/4 In. 95.00
Vase, Diamond–Quilted, Green Threads, Signed, 6 In. ....65.00 To 95.00
Vase, Emerald, Silver Overlay, Art Nouveau, Tulips, Alvin, 12 In. 927.00
Vase, Fan Shape, Topaz Ribbed Top, Green Knobbed Stem, Signed, 8 In. 95.00
Vase, Fan, Controlled Bubbles, Threading, Green, 8 In. 115.00
Vase, Fan, Gold Design, Signed, 8 In. 1550.00
Vase, Fan, Wisteria, Pomona Green & Amber, 8 In. 85.00
Vase, Flared Ruffle Top, Gold Aurene Over Calcite, 8 1/2 In. 445.00
Vase, Floriform Shape, Clear To Deep Green, Marked, 19 In., Pair 675.00
Vase, Floriform, Ivory & Black, 12 In. 795.00
Vase, Gold Aurene Interior, Calcite, Flared, Paper Label, 6 1/4 In. 265.00
Vase, Gold Aurene, 10 In. 750.00
Vase, Gold Aurene, Highlights, Signed, 2 1/2 In. 175.00
Vase, Green & Gold Tiger Stripes, Footed, Marked, 12 In. 795.00
Vase, Green Aurene, Silver Pull–Up Design, C.1920, 8 In. 1700.00
Vase, Green Jade, Round Body, Footed, Signed, 6 In. 125.00
Vase, Green Jade, Swirl, 4 Sides, Upper, Round Base, 5 1/2 In. 120.00
Vase, Green Jade, Swirl, Ball Stem, Alabaster Foot, Marked, 9 1/4 In. 225.00
Vase, Green To Clear, Signed, 11 1/2 X 6 1/2 In. 250.00
Vase, Ivorene, Signed, 8 In. 275.00
Vase, Ivorene, Trumpet Shape, Footed, Signed, 6 In., Pair 600.00
Vase, Jade Green, Trumpet Shape, Opalescent White Base, 12 In. 160.00
Vase, Jade Green, White Lion's Head Handle, 7 1/2 In. 100.00
Vase, Jade Swirl, Signed, 7 In. 285.00
Vase, Lavender, Sterling Silver Rim, Hawkes Bird Design, 12 In. 245.00
Vase, Oriental Jade, Opaque White, Swirl, 6½ In., Pair .... *Illus* 350.00
Vase, Oriental Poppy, Tiffany Bronze Base, Signed, 19 In. 1900.00
Vase, Plum Jade, Squat, 3 3/4 In. 350.00
Vase, Pomona Green, Ribbed, Signed, 10 In. 115.00
Vase, Ribbed Topaz Crystal, Top & Bottom Rims, Signed, 8 In. 95.00
Vase, Rosaline, Engraved Floral Garland, Alabaster Foot, 9 1/4 In. 775.00
Vase, Selenium Red, Marked & No.2013, 5 In. 125.00
Vase, Silverina, Trapped Air Pockets, Pale Blue, Signed, 10 In. 475.00
Vase, Stick, Aurene, Blue & Pink, Signed, 3 X 8 In. 225.00
Vase, Stick, Aurene, Iridescent Blue, 6 In. 375.00
Vase, Stick, Jade & Alabaster, 12 In. 95.00
Vase, Stick, Signed & Numbered, Blue Aurene, 8 1/2 In. 295.00
Vase, Thorn, Emerald Green, 3 Prongs, Marked, 7 In. 235.00
Vase, Topaz Swirl, Block Letters Mark, 9 3/4 In. 95.00
Vase, Topaz, Footed, Ribbed, Marked, 6 In. 85.00
Vase, Topaz, No.938, 7 In. 85.00
Vase, Tree Stump, Signed, Gold Aurene, 6 In. 625.00
Vase, Tyrian, Signed, 13 1/2 In. 8000.00
Vase, Verre De Soie, Green Reeded, Iridescent, Footed, 6 In. 95.00
Vase, Wisteria, Ribbed, 4 3/4 In. 150.00
Wine, Clear Stem, Mica Throughout Top, Silverina, 7 In., Set Of 6 .... 1100.00
Wine, Crystal Stem, Green Applied Threading, Signed, 6 1/2 In. 30.00
Wine, French Blue, Stem, Controlled Bubbles, Signed, 6 1/2 In. 45.00
Wine, Green Bubble Glass, Signed ....55.00 To 75.00
Wine, Jade 75.00

> *Stevengraphs are woven pictures made like fancy ribbons. They were*
> *manufactured by Thomas Stevens of Coventry, England, and became*
> *popular in 1862. Most are marked "Woven in silk by Thomas*
> *Stevens" or were mounted on a cardboard that tells the story of the*
> *Stevengraph. Other similar ribbon pictures have been made in*
> *England and Germany.*

STEVENGRAPH, Bookmark, 3 Ladies Praying 55.00

Bookmark, A Blessing, Woven Silk	30.00
Bookmark, George Washington, Centennial	95.00
Bookmark, Home Sweet Home	100.00
Bookmark, To Mother, Signed	45.00
Centennial, Poem	95.00
Coronation	12.00
Death, Matted, Gold Leaf Frame, 8 1/2 X 11 1/4 In.	175.00
Finish, Framed	185.00
George Washington, J.B.Chamromy, Phila., Framed, 6 X 10 In.	55.00
Gladstone, Original Mat	175.00
John L.Sullivan	225.00
Last Rose Of Summer, Musical Notes & Lyrics, Oak Frame	75.00
Meet, Framed	185.00
Ribbon, Washington, Eagle, Centennial, 3 1/4 X 18 In.	50.00
Start, Framed	185.00
The Good Old Days, Framed	150.00
Water Jump, Framed	185.00

Stevens & Williams of Stourbridge, England, made many types of glass, including layered, etched, cameo, and art glass, between the 1830s and 1930s. Some pieces are signed "S & W." Many pieces are decorated with flowers, leaves, and other designs based on nature.

STEVENS & WILLIAMS, Bottle, Ivorene, Sterling Silver Collar, 8 In., Set Of 3	175.00
Cracker Jar, Ruby, Clear Applied Leaves On Body & Lid	250.00
Finger Bowl, Tricorner, Citron Threading	145.00
Finger Bowl, Tricorner, Rose To Amber, Diamond–Quilted	145.00
Lamp, Fairy, Matching Base, Diamond–Quilted, Chartreuse	340.00
Lamp, Fairy, Ruffled Base, Striped, Dome Shade, 6 In.	550.00
Lamp, Oil, Striped Font, Frosted, Brass, Shade, 12 In.	425.00
Pitcher, Applied Flowers, Cut Top, Off–White, 2 7/8 In.	165.00
Pitcher, Applique Flowers, Amber Handle, 2 7/8 In.	175.00
Plate, Shell, Ruffled, Mother–Of–Pearl Swirl, 4 1/2 In.	175.00
Rose Bowl, Applied Leaves, Pink Lining, Loop Feet, 5 In.	210.00
Rose Bowl, Blue Thorns Allover, Shell Feet, 3 3/4 In.	125.00
Rose Bowl, Box Pleated Top, Blue Opalescent, 4 3/8 In.	135.00
Rose Bowl, Mother–Of–Pearl, Blue, Saucer, 4 X 5 3/4 In.	485.00
Rose Bowl, Tray, Swirled Mother–Of–Pearl, 3 1/2 In.	450.00
Tumbler, Applied Fruit, Amber, 3 3/4 In.	225.00
Tumbler, Cone Shape, Pedestal, Tiny Horse In Clear Ball	39.00
Urn, Ruffled, Amber Handles, Dark Pink, 5 1/2 In., Pair	99.00
Vase, Amber Handle & Branch, Pink Square Top, 8 In.	100.00
Vase, Amber Ruffled Edge, Applied Nut, Blue, 10 1/4 In.	225.00
Vase, Applied Crystal Leaf, Blue Lined, Cream, 4 1/4 In.	125.00
Vase, Applied Flowers, Amber Ruffled Top, 10 1/4 In.	275.00
Vase, Applied Plums, White Cased, Pink Overlay, 7 In.	325.00
Vase, Applied Strawberry, Thorny Feet, 3 5/8 X 4 In.	210.00
Vase, Applique Flowers, Pink Inside, Amber Rim, 7 In.	135.00
Vase, Applique Flowers, Rose Interior, White, 6 3/4 In.	135.00
Vase, Applique Fruit & Leaves, Ruffled Top, 8 In.	125.00
Vase, Colored Applied Leaf, 8–Crimp Top, 6 3/4 In.	145.00
Vase, Cranberry Melon Ribbed, 5 Clear Feet, 4 1/2 In.	115.00
Vase, Cream, Pink Inside, Double Ruffled, 7 1/4 In.	395.00
Vase, Emerald Cut To Clear, Trumpet Shape, 10 In.	195.00
Vase, Fan, Pink Interior, Flowers, Amber Edge, 5 In.	265.00
Vase, Intaglio, Swans, Pink To Crystal, Band, 7 3/8 In.	650.00
Vase, Mahogany, White Interior, Jewels, O.Erard, 7 In.	385.00
Vase, Mother–Of–Pearl Swirl, White Interior, 5 3/4 In.	995.00
Vase, Opal, Ruby Lining, Acanthus Leaf, 3 Foot, 7 In.	110.00
Vase, Overlay, Applique Fruit, White, Amber, 8 In.	125.00
Vase, Pink Interior, Opaque, Applied Flower, 11 1/2 In.	265.00
Vase, Pompeiian Swirl, Cream Lining, 5 X 9 3/4 In.	900.00
Vase, Rose Bowl Shape, 4–Petal Top, Swirl Body, Large	275.00
Vase, Yellow, Opalescent, Applied Gooseberry, 4 In.	150.00

Henry William Stiegel, a colorful immigrant to the colonies, started his first factory in Pennsylvania in 1763. He remained in business until 1774. Glassware was made in a style popular in Europe at that time and was similar to the glass of many other makers. It was made of clear or colored glass and was decorated with enamel colors, mold blown designs, or etching. It is almost impossible to be sure a piece was made by Stiegel, so the knowing collector now refers to this glass as Stiegel type.

STIEGEL TYPE, Bottle, Bird Design, 5 1/2 In.	240.00
Bottle, Blown Glass, Enameled, Flowers, Lovebirds, 4 1/2 In.	290.00
Bottle, Flower Design, Enameled, Pewter Top, 6 3/4 In.	210.00
Bowl, 18 Vertical Ribs, Petal Foot, 2 3/4 In.	55.00
Bowl, Baptismal, Blue, Blown, Footed, Folded Rim, 5 1/2 In.	175.00
Creamer, Diamond–Quilted Pattern, Blue, Handle, 3 3/4 In.	325.00
Flask, Chestnut, Checkered Diamond Pattern, Clear, 6 In.	675.00
Flip, Blown, Enameled, Heart, Doves, German, 3 1/2 In.	290.00
Flip, Blown, Flower & Horse Design, Enameled, 3 1/4 In.	200.00
Flip, Floral Design, Enameled, Inscription, 3 1/4 In.	200.00
Flip, Flower, Building, Dove, Enameled, Fluted, Clear, 3 3/4 In.	250.00
Pitcher, 19 Vertical Ribs, Swirled At Flared Rim, 5 In.	235.00
Salt, 20–Diamond Mold, Opalescent Rim, 3 1/8 In.	225.00
Salt, Blue Checkered Diamond, Violet Blue, Sapphire, 2 7/8 In.	875.00
Salt, Diamond–Quilted, Lily Pad Base, 3 In.	110.00
Salt, Diamond–Quilted, Lily Pad Base, Clear, 2 3/4 In.	110.00
Salt, Violet Blue Diamond, Applied Foot, 3 In.	300.00
Tumbler, Distelfink, Floral Design, Translucent, 3 3/4 In.	130.00
Vase, Free–Blown Flip, Etched Floral Design, 12 X 9 1/4 In.	375.00
Wine, Conical, Ribbed, Blown	75.00

The Stockton Terra Cotta Company was started in Stockton, California, in 1891. The art pottery called Rekston was made after 1897. The company burned in 1902 and was never reopened.

STOCKTON, Mug, Floral Design, 3 Handles, 8–Footed, Marked, 5 1/2 In.	450.00

Stoneware is a coarse, glazed, and fired potter's ceramic that is used to make crocks, jugs, bowls, etc. It is often decorated with cobalt blue decorations. Stoneware is still being made.

STONEWARE, Ashtray, Western Stoneware, Monmouth, Ill.	37.50
Barrel, Ale, Incised Frank Jones, Blue Bands, Spigot, 5 Gal.	395.00
Basket, Dipping, Brown	175.00
Beaker, American Verse, Gerz, 1/4 Liter	48.00
Beater Jar, Blue Band, Keystone, Iowa	45.00
Beater Jar, Boscobel, Wisconsin	69.00
Beater Jar, F.J.Moeller, Artesian, Iowa, Blue Stripe	65.00
Beater Jar, Joe Huber, Ft.Atkinson, Iowa	65.00
Beater Jar, Osterdock, Iowa	79.00
Beater Jar, Trade With Vogt & Bahnser	60.00
Beater Jar, Wesson Oil	75.00
Berry Bowl, Flying Bird, Blue & White	70.00 To 95.00
Bird Feeder, Blue Leaf Design, 12 In.	250.00
Bottle, Beer, Cobalt Blue Blob Top, 1 Qt.	40.00
Bottle, Ink, Brown, 4 1/2 In.	9.00
Bottle, Pig, Albany Slip Glaze, 7 1/4 In.	85.00
Bowl, Blue Shaded, Keystone, Iowa, 7 1/4 In.	65.00
Bowl, Child's, Blue & Gray, 3 1/2 In.	22.50
Bowl, Cream, Blue & Orange, Ribbed, 7 In.	35.00
Bowl, Gray, Dough, 6 In.	18.00
Bowl, Strawberry Fair, Johnson Bros., Round, 8 In.	10.00
Bowl, Wedding Ring, Blue & White, 5 In.	45.00
Bowl, Wedding Ring, Blue & White, 10 In.	100.00
Bowl, Wedding Ring, Yellow & Green	30.00
Cake Crock, Blue Band	175.00
Candlestick, Rugby Football, Sterling Silver Rim	70.00

Canister, Blue Band, Beans 55.00
Canister, Coffee, Blue & White, Marked GMT Bros.Germany 45.00
Canister, Raisins, Original Lid 195.00
Canister, Spice, Wildflower, Cover 110.00
Chamber Pot, Beaded Rose, Blue & White 95.00
Chamber Pot, Blue And Gray, Blue Around Handle, Numbered 250.00
Chamber Pot, Fort Dodge Stoneware Co. ....98.00 To 125.00
Chamber Pot, Western Stoneware, Memphis Pattern, Cover 75.00
Churn, Brown & White, Side Handle, 4 Gal. 75.00
Churn, Brushed Cobalt Blue Floral, Marked 2 At Handles, 16 In. 145.00
Churn, Cobalt Blue, Ovoid, 18 1/2 In. 20.00
Churn, Cobalt Hen Silhouette, 5 Gal. 400.00
Churn, Cobalt Script, J.Fisher, Lyons, N.Y., Handles, 5 Gal. 210.00
Churn, Cobalt Tiger Head, Woodruff, Cortland, Handle, 5 Gal. 475.00
Churn, J.P.Parker, Jane Lew W.Va., Blue Stencil, 18 3/4 In. 250.00
Churn, Lion, J.Burger, Jr., Rochester N.Y., 8 Gal. 4000.00
Churn, Ottman Bros. & Co., Fat Bird On Stump, 4 Gal. 880.00
Churn, Table, J.Breck & Son, 1 Gal. 30.00
Coffeepot, Swirl Design, Blue & White 550.00
Cooler, Ears, Blue Floral, J.L.Floyd, June 30, 1857, 16 1/2 In. 2600.00
Cooler, Fort Edward, N.Y., Spout, 6 Gal. 400.00
Cooler, House & Deer, J.& E.Norton, Bennington, Vt., 5 Gal. 4000.00
Cooler, Water, Cobalt Bands, Blue Spigot Hole, Dated 1863, 5 Gal. 225.00
Crock, 3–Winged Cobalt Designs, Stamped Geddes, N.Y., 9 1/2 In. 195.00
Crock, Bangor Stoneware, Bangor, Maine, Bird On Branch, 11 3/4 In. 175.00
Crock, Beck's Pottery, Parish, Iowa, Brown, 1 Gal. 45.00
Crock, Beck's Pottery, Parish, Iowa, Brown, 2 Gal. 50.00
Crock, Beck's Pottery, Parish, Iowa, Brown, 3 Gal. 55.00
Crock, Blue Design, Emands & Co., Mass., 2 Gal. 100.00
Crock, Blue Floral Design, E.E.Hall & Co., 11 3/4 In. 125.00
Crock, Blue Floral Design, H.& S.Swank, Johnstown, Pa., 10 3/4 In. 125.00
Crock, Blue Flower, Marked Albany, 2 Gal. 205.00
Crock, Blue Parrot On Branch, Blue & Gray, New York, 2 Gal. 350.00
Crock, Blue, Gray, Burgher Bros., Rochester, N.Y., 3 Gal. 250.00
Crock, Brown Brothers, Huntington, Ovoid, Florals, 1 1/2 Gal. 220.00
Crock, Brown Red, 2 Handles, 4 Gal. 100.00
Crock, Burger & C., Rochester, N.Y., Handles, 11 1/4 In. 120.00
Crock, Butter, Basket Weave & Flowers, Lid, Bail, Blue & White 185.00
Crock, Butter, Blue Scrolls, Word Butter, Signed I.W., Lid 125.00
Crock, Butter, Brown Glaze Design, Stripes, New Geneva Pottery 285.00
Crock, Butter, Cover, Cobalt Floral Border, On Knob & Rim, Pa. 375.00
Crock, Butter, Cover, Embossed Swastikas, Blue & White, 7 1/2 In. 95.00
Crock, Butter, Daisy & Trellis, Blue 95.00
Crock, Butter, Daisy & Waffle, Blue & White, Original Lid 120.00
Crock, Butter, Daisy, Wooden Lid, Bail, Blue & White 95.00
Crock, Butter, Dragonfly & Flower, Lid, Bail, Blue & White 250.00
Crock, Butter, Fair Store, Rockwell, Iowa, Blue & White 120.00
Crock, Butter, Good Luck Pattern, Blue & White, Lid 95.00
Crock, Butter, Handles, Floral Border & Cover, Pennsylvania 375.00
Crock, Butter, Rolled Edge, Gold Stripe, Marked, 11 X 6 1/2 In. 52.00
Crock, Butter, Scott's Creamery, Bradford, Reddish Brown, 5 In. 25.00
Crock, Cobalt Bird On Stump, Wide Mouth, 3 Gal. 395.00
Crock, Cobalt Bird, J.Norton & Co., Bennington Vt., 1 Gal. 310.00
Crock, Cobalt Blue Flower & Quill Work, Handles, 11 3/4 In. 55.00
Crock, Cobalt Blue Slip, Double Flourish, Speckled, 11 1/2 In. 55.00
Crock, Cobalt Blue Spray, R.E.Hall, Boston, Mass., 3 Gal. 195.00
Crock, Cobalt Iris, W.A.MacQuaid & Co., New York, 1 1/2 Gal. 120.00
Crock, Cobalt Leaves, Lewis Huntington, Ovoid, 3 Gal. 340.00
Crock, Cobalt Lineal Dog, Basket, S.Hart, Fulton, Handles, 6 Gal. 1150.00
Crock, Cobalt Pecking Chicken, Troy, N.Y.Pottery, 4 Gal. 375.00
Crock, D.L.& A.K.Ballard, Burlington, Vt., Floral Design, 3 Gal. 120.00
Crock, Deer, Cobalt Blue, 3 Gal. 650.00
Crock, Double Bird Design, Norton, Signed, 10 1/4 X 12 1/4 In. 650.00
Crock, Double Crossed Fish, Havana, N.Y., 1 Gal. 4600.00

Crock, Double Flower, John Burger, Rochester, N.Y., 6 Gal. 1450.00
Crock, E. & L.P.Norton, Bennington, Leaf Design, 7 In. 185.00
Crock, E.Swasey Co., Portland, Me., Beige & Brown 40.00
Crock, Figure 8 & Flourish In Cobalt Blue, 16 In. 37.50
Crock, Floral Design, Impressed W.J. & E.G.Schrop, Ohio, 14 In. 85.00
Crock, Floral Design, J.& E.Norton, Ovoid, 2 Gal. 357.50
Crock, Floral Design, J.S.Taft & Co., 2 Gal. 100.00
Crock, Fort Dodge Stoneware Co., Brown, 1 Gal. 35.00
Crock, Gray Tan, Bulbous, 12 1/2 X 8 1/4 In. 55.00
Crock, Hancor Stoneware, Bangor, Maine, Salt Glaze, 4 Gal. 65.00
Crock, Haxston, Ottman & Co., Ft.Edward, N.Y., 11 3/4 X 9 In. 110.00
Crock, J.L.Cluskey, Lake Nam, Missouri, 2 Gal. 45.00
Crock, J.Norton & Co., Basket Of Flowers, 2 Gal. 650.00
Crock, John Burger, Rochester, Leaf Design, 3 Gal. 185.00
Crock, Large Design, Ballard Of Burlington 440.00
Crock, Lid, Sweetser Bros., Byfield, Mass., Eagle, 11 1/2 In. 80.00
Crock, Pacific Stoneware, Portland, 2 Gal. 35.00
Crock, Salt, Daisy, Original Lid, White 120.00
Crock, Salt, Eagle, Blue & White 245.00
Crock, Salt, Good Luck, Lid, Blue & Gray, 6 In. 100.00
Crock, Salt, H.Lourender, Petersburg, Va., Tree, 6 Gal. 1000.00
Crock, Salt, Hanging, Blue & Gray, Leaf Design 100.00
Crock, Salt, Hanging, Blue Band, Original Lid 125.00
Crock, Salt, Hanging, Butterfly, Blue & Gray 80.00
Crock, Salt, Master, Embossed Hunting Scene 50.00
Crock, Salt, Peacock, Lid, Blue & White 135.00
Crock, Salt, Swastika, Blue & White, Wooden Lid 75.00
Crock, Somerset, Blue Design, Ovoid 275.00
Crock, Stag, Fence, & Pine Tree, J. & E. Norton, 3 Gal. 2640.00
Crock, Stylized Flower, Frank Norton, Worcester, Mass., 2 Gal. 180.00
Crock, Western, Cobalt Lilies, Handles, 4 Gal. 40.00
Cup, Measuring, Blue & White 135.00
Cuspidor, Lady's, Blue & White 125.00
Cuspidor, Lady's, Rose Floral Design Top & Sides, 7 1/2 In. 85.00
Dispenser, Barrel, Spigot, F.Jones, Old Fashioned Ale, 6 Gal. 395.00
Dispenser, Cherryline, Blue Bands, Spigot 125.00
Ewer, Incised Fish, Lizard Handle, Frog Spout, 14 In. 235.00
Figurine, Poodle, Brown Glaze, 9 In. 235.00
Figurine, Tiger, Lying Down, German, 6 1/4 In. 38.00
Flask, Lord Brougham Reform, 1830, Bournes 190.00
Flask, Portraits Of Queen Victoria, Prince Albert, 1840 .... 120.00
Flask, Seagram's, 9 In. 140.00
Jar, Apple Butter, Ferns, Burger & Lang, Rochester, 2 Gal. 120.00
Jar, Bird On Branch, New York Stoneware Co., 3 Gal. 385.00
Jar, Brushed Cobalt Blue Foliage Band, 12 3/4 In. 60.00
Jar, Brushed Cobalt Blue Foliage, 10 1/2 In. 70.00
Jar, Canning, Blue Stenciled Label, A.P.Donagho, 5 1/2 In. 225.00
Jar, Canning, Cobalt Bird, Haxstun, Ottoman & Co., 3 Gal. 150.00
Jar, Canning, Cobalt Bird, Whites, Utica, 1 Gal. 225.00
Jar, Canning, Cobalt Flower, C.Hart & Son, Sherburne, 3 Gal. 45.00
Jar, Canning, Cobalt Flower, Holmes & Purdee, Dundee, N.Y., 3 Gal. 140.00
Jar, Canning, John Sexton Co., Cam Lever Seal, 1/2 Gal. 60.00
Jar, Canning, Sloping Shoulders, Flared Mouth, Tan, 9 1/4 In. 18.00
Jar, Chocolate Brown, J.W.Zieger, Eldors, Iowa, 3 Gal. 145.00
Jar, Cobalt Blue Floral Design, Ovoid, 13 1/2 In. 55.00
Jar, Cobalt Blue Tulip, Dillon Henry & Porter, Albany, 12 3/4 In 85.00
Jar, Cowden & Wilcox, Harrisburg, Pa., 2 Blue Flowers, 12 In. 155.00
Jar, Curved Shoulders, Brushed Cobalt Blue Design, Lid, 9 1/2 In. 60.00
Jar, F.Laufersweiler Empire City Pottery, 1 1/2 Gal. 230.00
Jar, H.F.Phillips & Stein, Richmond, Stenciled Label, 10 1/2 In. 42.00
Jar, Hamilton & Jones, Stenciled Flowers, 1 Gal. 110.00
Jar, L.H.Yeager & Co., Allentown, Pa., Blue Tulip, 9 X 6 3/4 In. 155.00
Jar, Mustached Face, Macquoid, New York City, 1 1/2 Gal. 880.00
Jar, P.Rodenbaugh, Brushed Cobalt At Handles, 13 1/2 In. 265.00

Jar, S.Purdy, Blue Flower, Ovoid, 9 1/2 In. 195.00
Jar, Sanford's Inks–Pastes, Wehr Type Lid, Blue & White 158.00
Jar, Stylized Federal Shield, Haxston, Ottman & Co., 2 Gal. 770.00
Jar, Thomas Commeraw, Corlears Hook, C.1810, 3 Gal. 550.00
Jar, Tooling At Neck, 2 Tooled Hearts, Charlestown, Ovoid, 13 In. 450.00
Jar, Vaughan & Mott, Glens Falls, Stylized Design, 4 Gal. 302.00
Jar, Western, Leaf, 2 Gal. 30.00
Jug, A.J.Gunther, Wholesale Liquors, Hot Spring, Ark., 1/2 Gal. 80.00
Jug, Adolph Goldhammer, Denver, Colo., Brown Cone Top, 1 Gal. 135.00
Jug, B.Cushman & Co., Albany, 3 Gal. 165.00
Jug, Ballard Bros., Burlington, Vt., 2 Gal. 695.00
Jug, Banner Liquor Store, Winona, Minn., All White, 1 Gal. 95.00
Jug, Banner Liquor Store, Winona, Minn., Brown Top, 2 Gal. 110.00
Jug, Batter, Cobalt Swatch Ear, Spout & Handle, 1 1/2 Gal. 50.00
Jug, Batter, Evan R.Jones, Pittston, Penn., Man In Moon, 2 Gal. 2200.00
Jug, Bellamine, Pear Shape, Snarling Face On Neck, 9 In. 125.00
Jug, Bellarmine, Molded Bearded Mask, Strap Handle, Brown, 17 In. 100.00
Jug, Bird On Branch In Cobalt Blue Slip, Impressed 3, 15 In. 345.00
Jug, Bird, Satterlee & Morey, Ft.Edward, N.Y., 2 Gal. 375.00
Jug, Brown Albany Slip, Ovoid, 9 1/4 In. 30.00
Jug, Brown Top, Turn Of Century, 5 Gal. 35.00
Jug, Brown, White, Madison, Ind., Wine & Liquor Store, 1/2 Gal. 48.00
Jug, Cobalt Blue Maple Leaf, Brown Top, White, 1 Gal. 35.00
Jug, Cobalt Flower, Harrington Lysons, Wide Mouth, Ears, 2 Gal. 220.00
Jug, Cobalt Flower, Impressed Label N.White, Utica, 15 In. 120.00
Jug, Cobalt Flower, J.& E.Norton, Bennington, Vt., 2 Gal. 175.00
Jug, Cobalt Flower, J.Pinkerton Wholesale Liquor Dealer, 3 Gal. 270.00
Jug, Cobalt Tulips, Handles, Wm.E.Warner, West Troy, 6 Gal. 60.00
Jug, Dark Green Black Ash Glaze, Handles, 15 1/2 In. 40.00
Jug, Double Ear Handles, Floral Design, Ovoid, 16 3/4 In. 235.00
Jug, Double Ear Handles, Stenciled U.S. 10, 24 In. 35.00
Jug, Drink Plezee, Greencastle, Ind., Brown Top, 1 Gal. 110.00
Jug, Edmunds & Co., Stylized Foliage, Impressed, 11 3/4 In. 115.00
Jug, Egyptian Embalmer For Preserving The Dead 265.00
Jug, Embossed Cobalt Swan, 1 1/2 Gal. 120.00
Jug, F.W.Pfortner, Pure Wines, Liquors, Madison, Ind., 1/2 Gal. 58.00
Jug, Fawn & Cream Whiskey, Paper Label, Brown & Co., 5 In. 45.00
Jug, Finn & Laskey, Detroit, Mich., Brown Cone Top, 1 Gal. 110.00
Jug, Floral Design, Cobalt Blue, Ovoid, 12 3/4 In. 90.00
Jug, Floral Design, H.R.Ross & Co., Sherburne, 2 Gal. 100.00
Jug, Floral Design, M.Tuller, Richfield Springs, 3 Gal. 175.00
Jug, Fort Edward Pottery Co., Cobalt Blue Floral, 15 In. 255.00
Jug, Fort Edward Pottery Co., Stylized Blue Floral, 13 3/4 In. 250.00
Jug, Fort Edward, N.Y., John Coyne, Utica, N.Y., Label, 14 In. 125.00
Jug, Gray, Blue Design, Williams & Reppert, Queensboro, Pa., 2 Gal. 90.00
Jug, Griesel Bros., Winona, Minn., Brown Cone Top, 1 Gal. 110.00
Jug, H.& G.Nash, Utica, Ocher Floral Design, Ovoid, 3 Gal. 50.00
Jug, H.A.Schunk, Pure Family Liquors, Dubuque, Iowa, 1/2 Gal. 68.00
Jug, H.Bonn Grocery Co., St.Louis, 1 Gal. 45.00
Jug, Hoffman House, Blended Whiskey, Corbin Co., Miniature 50.00
Jug, Hoffman House, Rye Whiskey, H.F.Corbin & Co., Miniature 110.00
Jug, I.M.Mead 2, Cobalt Blue, Handle, Ovoid, Label, 13 1/2 In. 80.00
Jug, I.W.Harper, Nelson Co., Kentucky, Brown & Cream, Miniature 40.00
Jug, Incised 4, Greenish–Brown Glaze, Southern, 18 3/4 In. 20.00
Jug, Incised Bird, Brushed Cobalt Blue Handle, Ovoid, 12 In. 450.00
Jug, Incised Lines On Shoulder, Ovoid, Marked Boston, 12 In. 190.00
Jug, J.Clark & Co., Troy, Ovoid, Cobalt Tulip Bud, 1 Gal. 170.00
Jug, J.H.Conradt & Co., Drydale, Mo., Brown, 1 Gal. 110.00
Jug, Jas.Benjamin Stoneware Depot, Stenciled Label, 13 3/4 In. 70.00
Jug, John Baum, Stillings, Mo., White, 1/2 Gal. 110.00
Jug, Kentucky Liquor House, Springfield, Mo., 1 Gal. 105.00
Jug, Leaf, Norton, Bennington, Vermont, Cobalt Blue, 1 Gal. 120.00
Jug, M.E.Vail & Son, Middletown, Vt., Bird, Blue, 15 1/2 In. 750.00
Jug, Manhattan Pickle, Chicago, 1 Gal. 35.00

Jug, Market Co., Providence, R.I., White, 1/2 Gal. 75.00
Jug, N.Clark & Co., Rochester, Cover, Cobalt Flowers, 2 Gal. 60.00
Jug, Old Joe, Oldest Distillery In Anderson, Founded 1818 .... 88.00
Jug, Onetto & Terrible, Buffalo, N.Y., Blue Label, 13 1/4 In. 95.00
Jug, R.Brand Old Sour Mash, Embossed Grain Stocks, 1 Qt. 85.00
Jug, Richardson Drug Co., Louisville, Ky., Beehive Top, 1 Gal. 140.00
Jug, S.H.Smith & Bro., Flemington, N.J., Tulip & Leaves, 5 Gal. 350.00
Jug, Simon & Lewis, Rock Island, Ill., 1 Gal. 140.00
Jug, Stern, Schloss & Co., Albuquerque, N.Mexico, 1 Gal. 185.00
Jug, T.P.Smith Co–Operative, New York, Free Hand, 4 Gal. 90.00
Jug, W.Roberts, Binghamton, N.Y., Floral, Impressed, 11 1/2 In. 115.00
Jug, Westerwald, Pewter Mounted, Bead Edge, Stags, 9 7/8 In. 440.00
Mug, Cattail, Blue & White 90.00
Mug, Flying Bird, Blue & White 195.00
Mug, Grape With Leaf Band, 5 1/4 In. 38.00
Mug, Leather Ware, Sterling Silver Rim, Black, 6 In. 70.00
Mug, Old Heidelberg, Raised Figures, Green 16.00
Mug, Vauxhall, Tudor Roses, Hunter & Hounds, Dated 1727, 8 1/8 In. 880.00
Pan, Milk, Lop, Nathan Porter, West Troy, 2 Gal. 80.00
Pie Pan, Blue & White, 2 Stenciled Birds 45.00
Pitcher, American Beauty Rose, Blue & White 195.00
Pitcher, Apricot & Blue 65.00
Pitcher, Arc & Leaf, Blue, 1 Pint 65.00
Pitcher, Avenue Of Trees, Brown, Small 43.00
Pitcher, Bluebird, Blue & Gray, 9 In. 215.00
Pitcher, Bulbous, Lid, Rib Swirl Pattern, Brown, 3 Qt. 65.00
Pitcher, Cattail, Blue & White 95.00
Pitcher, Cherry Band & Leaves, Blue & White 75.00
Pitcher, Cobalt Fantail Bird, 9 In. 260.00
Pitcher, Cobalt Heart–Shaped Leaf, 1 Gal. 40.00
Pitcher, Cobalt, Bouquet Of Flowers, Scalloped 325.00
Pitcher, Cow, Blue & White ....95.00 To 165.00
Pitcher, Cow, Cream & Green 75.00
Pitcher, Deer & Fawn, Blue & White ....70.00 To 195.00
Pitcher, Doe & Fawn, Blue 150.00
Pitcher, Dutch Boy & Girl Kissing, Blue & White ....50.00 To 145.00
Pitcher, Dutch Scene, Squatty, Blue & White 165.00
Pitcher, Flying Swallows & Lovebirds, Blue & White 75.00
Pitcher, Good Luck, Blue Sponging 95.00
Pitcher, Grape Pattern, Cream & Green, 8 1/4 In. 70.00
Pitcher, Impressed 3, Wooden Lid, Brown Albany Slip, 9 In. 15.00
Pitcher, Indian Boy & Girl, Blue & White ....250.00 To 275.00
Pitcher, Indian, Brown & White 195.00
Pitcher, Leaping Deer, Blue & White 145.00
Pitcher, Lovebirds, Blue & White 175.00
Pitcher, Lovebirds, Brown 55.00
Pitcher, Molasses, Cobalt Triple Tulip, Cortland, 2 Gal. 220.00
Pitcher, Painted Flowers, 1930s, 9 In. 35.00
Pitcher, Ribbed, Blue & White Floral, Embossed Base, 12 In. 149.00
Pitcher, Riveted Band, Seattle Export Co., Chicago, 7 In. 175.00
Pitcher, Sponging & Flower, Blue & White, 8 7/8 In. ....185.00 To 235.00
Pitcher, Stag & Pine Tree, Blue & Tan 135.00
Pitcher, Swan, Blue & White, 8 In. 185.00
Pitcher, Syrup, Blue & White Sponge, 3 1/2 In. 90.00
Pitcher, Tan & Brown, 7 In. 23.00
Pitcher, Vines, Berries, Brown & Green Glaze, 9 In. 37.50
Pitcher, Windmill & Bush, Blue & White ....65.00 To 165.00
Planter, Blue Design, Lehew, Strasburg, Va., 3 Gal. 345.00
Planter, Figural, Man's Head, Incised B.Rimmplin, 1877 .... 750.00
Plaque, Couple In Garden, Crommer, 15 1/2 In. X 11 3/4 In. 495.00
Plate, Loch Ness, Hand Painted, 9 In. 25.00
Rolling Pin, Mills Dept.Store 135.00
Rolling Pin, North Liberty, Iowa 165.00
Rolling Pin, The Boys, Denison, Iowa 55.00

Rolling Pin, Wildflower, 8 In. 135.00
Soap Dish, Beaded Roses, Blue & Gray 90.00
Soap Dish, Bowtie, Blue & White 40.00
Soap Dish, Dragonfly, Wright's Coaltar 55.00
Soap Dish, Lion Head, Blue & White 120.00
Soap Dish, Pedestal, Pierced Hole Base, Brown Glaze 200.00
Spittoon, Beaded, Blue 65.00
Spittoon, Cobalt Bands, Groups Of Brush Strokes 120.00
Tankard, Pewter Mounted, German, Globular, 18th Century, 8 In. 385.00
Toothbrush Holder, Bowtie Pattern, Blue & Gray 50.00
Toothbrush Holder, Open Rose, Blue & Gray 70.00
Toothpick, Swan, White, Pink, & Green 32.00
Tray, Frank Fehr Brewing Co., Round, Dated 1910 .... 275.00
Vase, Scrolling Plants, Frank Butler, 11 In. 115.00
Vase, Toothbrush, Bowtie Pattern, Blue & Gray 45.00

The old country store with the crackers in a barrel and a potbellied stove is a symbol of an earlier, less hectic time. The advertisements, containers, and products sold in these stores are now all collectibles. We have tried to list items in the logical places, so large store fixtures will be found under the Architectural category, enameled tin dishes under Graniteware, etc. Listed here are many of the advertising items. Other similar pieces may be found under the product name such as Planters Peanuts.

STORE, Ashtray, Blue Diamond Coal, Iron 12.50
Ashtray, Cigar Band, 5 1/2 In. 22.50
Ashtray, Copper–Armstrong, Tire 10.00
Ashtray, Dubonnet, Figural, Man Pouring Drink, Metal 15.00
Ashtray, Fleischmann's Malt, Chicago 18.00
Ashtray, G.E., Light Bulb, Maroon, Double Bulb 95.00
Ashtray, Goodrich, Silvertown, 6 In. 10.00
Ashtray, Goodyear, Tire 10.00
Ashtray, Greyhound Bus Co., Glass 7.00
Ashtray, Holophane, Oval 20.00
Ashtray, Iron Fireman, Figural 35.00
Ashtray, Kelly Heavy Duty Tire, Green 27.50
Ashtray, Labatts, Porcelain, Red & Beige 6.00
Ashtray, Mack Truck, Bulldog 25.00
Ashtray, Modern Barn Equipment, Model Of Cattle, Drinking Cup 150.00
Ashtray, National Foundry, Brooklyn, N.Y., Cast Iron, Iron Worker 24.00
Ashtray, Reinhart's Lager & Ale, Tin 10.00
Ashtray, Roxo Ice Cream, Rockford, Ill., Brass 15.00
Ashtray, Salem Cigarette, Tin 5.00
Ashtray, Sweeney's Ham On Rye, Orlando–Sanford, Fla., Picture 8.00
Ashtray, Twin Bears Store, Bears, Sign, Chalkware, Dated 1931, 4 1/2in. 45.00
Ashtray, White Horse Scotch, Horseshoe Shape, England 20.00
Bag, Moxie, Imprinted Moxie Kid, Paper 6.50
Banner, Falstaff, On Draught, Fringed, Rayon 150.00
Banner, San Felice Cigars, Cloth, 26 1/2 X 141 In. 65.00
Banner, Spider Monkey, Sideshow, Canvas ....*Illus* 275.00
Barrel, Independent Baking Co., Davenport, Iowa, Tin, 27 In. 47.50
Barrel, Pickle, Heinz, Original Paint 95.00
Barrel, Pickle, Monarch Teenie Weenie, Lion Design 80.00
Bean Pot, Heinz 57 .... 10.00
Beer Tap, Fehr's, Sterling Silver 18.00
Beer Tap, Schlitz, Figural, Nude 15.00
Beer Tap, Widemann's, Sterling Silver 18.00
Billhook, Austex, Celluloid 15.00
Bin, A & P, Wooden, Slant Hinged Lid, Gilt, Black, 17 X 27 X 25 In. 300.00
Bin, Bower & Bartletts Coffee, Boston Favorite, 19 X 18 In. 130.00
Bin, Campbell & Woods Coffee, Tin, Pre–1910, 14 X 18 X 17 1/2 In. 385.00
Bin, Ceresota Flour, Boy Picture, Norton Bros., 25 Lb. 675.00
Bin, Coffee, Wooden, Red Paint, Greek Key Edge, Slant Lid, 30 X 18 In. 90.00
Bin, Dwinell–Wright Co. Coffee, Tin, Hinged Top, Paper Labels, 19 In. 60.00

Bin, Game, Pheasants, Tobacco, 24 X 10 X 12 In. 275.00
Bin, Jersey Coffee, Original Red Paint, 16 X 21 X 32 In. 180.00
Bin, Munyon's Homeopathic Remedies, Litho Tin Over Wood, 13 1/2 In. 160.00
Bin, Pastime Tobacco, 14 X 10 X 3 In. 125.00
Bin, Perfection Flour, Original Red Paint, 18 In. 75.00
Bin, Polar Bear Tobacco, 1920s, 20 X 15 X 12 In. 275.00
Bin, Sweet Mist Tobacco, Round, 10 Lb. 110.00
Blackboard, Nature's Remedy 95.00
Blotter, Old Reliable Peanut Butter, Black Saying Some Butter 10.00
Blotter, Sunoco, Goofy Auto Repairs, Disney Enterprises, 1939 .... 10.00
Book, Punch–Out, Pillsbury Farina, Animated, 1936 .... 45.00
Book, Quaker Oats Premium, How To Play Baseball, Ethan Allen 55.00
    STORE, BOTTLE, see Bottle
Bottle Cap, Sunshine Beer, 1930s 2.50
Bottle Carrier, Carling's Red–Cap, Cardboard, 6 Bottles 11.00
Bottle Carrier, Moxie, Cardboard 4.00
Bowl, Peanut, The Nut House, Impressed House, 9 In.Globe 40.00
    STORE, BOX, see also Box
Box, Arm & Hammer, Unused, 1906, Sample 12.00
Box, Black Hawk Soap, Rock Island, Ill. 95.00
Box, Butterfly Indigo Washing Blue, 4 X 8 In. 37.50
Box, Calumet Baking Powder, Printing 3 Sides, 14 X 11 1/2 In. 20.00
Box, Carton, Chesterfield, Pictures A.Godfrey, B.Crosby, P.Como, 1940s 35.00
Box, Cheese, Borden's, Wooden 5.00
Box, Cheese, Kraft, Wooden 11.00
Box, Churn Baking Soda, Housewife Churning Butter, Unused, 1920s 10.00
Box, Clark, Pictures Bear, Candy Covering Globe 20.00
Box, Crossman Seeds, Wooden, Dovetailed, Original Contents 95.00
Box, Day's Soap, Wooden, Green Paint, Label, C.1875, 4 X 16 X 12 In. 70.00
Box, German's Sweet Chocolate, Walter Baker Co., 1906 .... 15.00
Box, Gillette Blades, Display, 13 X 5 1/4 In. 25.00
Box, Gold Dust Washing Powder, Unopened, 4 3/4 In. 10.00
Box, Goudy & Kent's Biscuit, Wooden, Paper Labels, 10 X 20 X 13 In. 65.00
Box, Greens Circle Brand Chewing Gum, Metal, Glass Lid 130.00
Box, Hat, Stetson Fedora Hat, Oval, 4 X 3 1/2 X 2 5/8 In. 28.00
Box, International Louse Killer, Cardboard, 7 X 3 In. 18.00
Box, Jap Rose Soap, Full Front, Lid, Oriental Woman, 50 Bars, Counter 95.00
Box, Keens Mustard, Wooden, 12 X 11 X 7 In. 18.00
Box, Kennedy Biscuit, Nabisco, Wooden 85.00
Box, Merlin's Washing Powder 20.00
Box, Mexican Heat Powder, Label, Round, Shaker Lid 5.00
Box, Queen Lill Chocolates, LaCrosse, Wi., Wooden, Etched, 6 X 3 In. 28.50
Box, Red Jacket Stomach Bitters 95.00
Box, Rees Cigars, 2 For 5 Cents, Wooden 3.00
Box, Richman's 5 Cent Cigar 25.00
Box, Soap, Pearline, Wooden, 20 X 8 In. 18.00
Box, Tea Balls, Ying Mee Co.Long Tuan Tea, Hong Kong, C.1900, Unopened 50.00
Box, Toilet Soap, Grandpa's Pine Tar, Embossed 10.00
Box, Walter Baker, Chocolate Lady Stencil, Wooden, 8 1/2 X 13 In. 18.00
Box, Washing Powder, Fun To Wash, Black Mammy, 1920s, Sample 32.00
Bread Box, Wheat Heart Brand, Metal 75.00
Brush, Kalamazoo Uniforms, Knight Picture 9.00
Brush, Record, Bank Co., Millheim, Pa., Celluloid, Blue 28.50
Cabinet, Bolt & Nut, Swivel, Octagonal Shape, 80 Drawers 700.00
Cabinet, Bolt, Hardware, 96 Drawers, Oak, 42 In. 650.00
Cabinet, Diamond Dyes, Children Scene, Tin, Wooden, 1910, 24 1/2 In. 275.00
Cabinet, Diamond Dyes, Fairies 750.00
Cabinet, Diamond Dyes, Girl With Ribbons 550.00
Cabinet, Dr.Daniel's Veterinary ....575.00 To 775.00
Cabinet, Humphrey's Veterinary Remedies, Tin Front, Barnyard Scene 900.00
Cabinet, Peerless Dyes, N.Spencer Thomas, Rolltop, Wooden, 31 3/4 In. 175.00
Cabinet, Pratt's Veterinary Remedies, Tin Door Panel, Wooden 275.00
Cabinet, Putnam Dyes, Lithograph Tin Of Men Riding Horse, Packettes 110.00
Cabinet, Ribbon, 24 Shelves, 28 Glass Pieces, 22 X 38 In. ....375.00 To 675.00

Store, Banner, Spider Monkey, Sideshow, Canvas

Store, Cabinet, Spool, C.1900,
37 X 19 1/2 X 19 1/2 In.

Cabinet, Spool, Belding Bros.& Co., Walnut, 2 Doors, 32 X 46 X 15 In.	450.00
Cabinet, Spool, Brainard & Armstrong, Oak, 12 Glass, 1900	522.00
Cabinet, Spool, Brainard & Armstrong, Oak, 3 Drawer, 16 X 16 X 8 In.	150.00
Cabinet, Spool, C.1900, 37 X 19 1/2 X 19 1/2 In. ....*Illus*	475.00
Cabinet, Spool, Clark's Spool Cotton, Oak, 1910, 16 X 24 In.	75.00
Cabinet, Spool, Clark's, 3 Drawers, Oak, 9 X 14 X 22 In.	98.00
Cabinet, Spool, Cortecelli, Oak, 18 X 21 X 15 In.	300.00
Cabinet, Spool, Corticelli, Oak, Decals, 18 X 23 X 33 In.	675.00
Cabinet, Spool, Daggett's Roll Braid, Walnut, 24 X 8 1/2 X 17 In.	200.00
Cabinet, Spool, Hemmingway, 11 Drawers, Oak	350.00
Cabinet, Spool, J.P.Coates, 6 Drawer, On Legs	645.00
Cabinet, Spool, Merrick Cotton, Cylindrical, Oak, 1900, 23 X 18 In.	225.00
Cabinet, Spool, Oak, Cylindrical, Glass Front, 1897, 20 X 18 1/2 In.	200.00
Cabinet, Veterinary, Sargents	225.00
Cabinet, Willimantic Spool Cotton, Composition, 19th Century, 15 In.	100.00
Cane Case, Victorian, Oak, Glass, Hinged Slant Top, 47 X 19 1/2 In.	300.00
STORE, CANISTER, see Store, Tin	
Case, Alfred J.Brown Seed Co., C.1890, Display, 4 1/2 In.	435.00
Case, American Candy, Nut, Walnut, Counter, 10 Compartments, Display	175.00
Case, Camillus Knives, Curved Glass Front, Display, Holds 24	75.00
Case, Cigar, 2 Doors, Morten & Co., N.Y., 8 Drawers, Golden Oak	350.00
Case, Collar, Display, German Sterling Silver Frame, 3 Rows Wide	285.00
Case, D.F.Foley & Co., Gold Pens, Etched, 20 X 12 In.	250.00
Case, Eagle Musical Strings For Banjo, Guitar, & Ukelele, Display	80.00
Case, F.X.Ganter, Nickel & Glass, Mirror, Label, Display, 13 X 35 In.	150.00
Case, Fry's Choice Chocolates, Impressed Advertising, C.1910, Wooden	425.00
Case, Keen Kutter, Pocket Knives, Scissors, & Shears, Display	575.00
Case, Pratt's Veterinary Remedies, Display, Oak, C.1890	285.00
Case, Remington, Counter, Slant Front, Knives, Display	125.00
Case, Rickseckeers Perfumes, Etched Glass, 46 X 12 In.	650.00
Case, Shell Motor Oil, Holds 16 Bottles, Hinged Cover	30.00
Case, Shrade Pocket Knife, Oak, Lettering, Glass, 22 X 10 In.	400.00
Chair, Duke Tobacco, Folding	225.00
Chair, Gravely Tobacco, Folding	295.00
Chair, Piedmont Cigarette	125.00
Change Receiver, Baby Ruth, Glass, Attached Gum Dispenser ....85.00 To 90.00
Change Receiver, Cuticura, Glass	35.00
Change Receiver, Don Digo Cigars, Glass	20.00
Change Receiver, Sybilla Cigar, Elegant Lady, Dated In Glass, 1895	75.00
Change Receiver, Tin Dispenser, Baby Ruth, Glass	85.00
Change Receiver, Wrigley's Gum, Glass, Square, 17 In.	75.00
Cigar Clipper, Automatic, Havana Cigars, Iron	225.00

Cigar Clipper, Match Holder, Yankee, Iron 325.00
Cigar Cutter, Boy Sitting On Rock, 7 In. 400.00
Cigar Cutter, Krank Cigars, Cart Shape 295.00
Cigar Cutter, Lord Stirling 165.00
Cigar Cutter, Man Singing, Painted, 8 In. 325.00
Cigar Cutter, Smoke Parsons 125.00
Cigarette Roller, Elephant, Cast Iron 95.00
Clothes Brush, Brush Your Troubles Away, Bensinger's, Louisville, Ky. 25.00
STORE, COFFEE GRINDER, see Coffee Grinder
Cooler, Dr Pepper, Metal 45.00
Counter, Candy, Oak, 5 Glass Drawers, C.1880, 6 Ft.X 3 Ft. 950.00
Counter, Milk Glass Panels, Oak, 10 Ft. 600.00
Crock, Butter, Lambrecht, 12 Cent Deposit, Since 1909, 1 1/2 Lb. 50.00
Crock, Heinz Baked Beans, Handle, Lid 150.00
Cup & Saucer, Drink Castor's Coffee, Avon Royal, Demitasse 35.00
Cup & Saucer, Nestle's, Red Logo On Beige 10.00
Cup & Saucer, Walgreen, Green Logo On White, Sterling China Co. 10.00
Cup, Breakfast Cheer Coffee, Demitasse 15.00
Cup, Measuring, Bromo Seltzer, Cobalt 27.00
Cup, Measuring, Elsie The Cow, Ceramic, 1/2 Cup 16.00
Cup, Measuring, Lettering, Cinnamon Drops, 1 Cent 12.00
Cutter, Cheese, Cleaver, Iron & Wood 250.00
Cutter, Wrapping Paper 12.00
Dish, Baby's, Haines Furniture Co., June 11, 1912, Triangular 66.00
Dish, Teaberry Gum, Pedestal, Green 35.00
Dish, Teaberry Gum, Pedestal, Vaseline Glass 45.00
Dispenser, Alka Seltzer, Ship's Wheel, Tin 99.50
Dispenser, Allen's Red Tame Cherry, Nickel Plated Base, 31 In. 950.00
Dispenser, Brazilla Syrup, Original Pump 950.00
Dispenser, Brookhill Ky., Sour Mash Whiskey, Scene Of Kentucky 900.00
Dispenser, Buckeye Syrup, Original Pump 550.00
Dispenser, Carnation Malted Milk, Glass 68.00
Dispenser, Cherry Chic Syrup, Globe, Silver Plate Pump, 11 1/2 In. 1450.00
Dispenser, Coffee, Oval, Brass, 9 1/2 X 23 In. 295.00
Dispenser, Dry Sherry, Tropical Scene, Brass Spigot, Pub, 13 1/4 In. 350.00
Dispenser, Fan Taz Syrup, Plunger Rod 800.00
Dispenser, Gillette Blue Blades, Tin, Look Sharp, Feel Sharp, Be Sharp 55.00
Dispenser, Gin, Pottery, Original Lid & Spigot, Pub, 12 X 9 1/2 In. 165.00
Dispenser, Grape–Ola Syrup, Dated 1914 .... 80.00
Dispenser, Hires Syrup, White Ceramic, Pat.1920, 14 1/4 X 8 1/2 In. 340.00
Dispenser, Liberty Dry Ginger Ale, Wooden, Banded Keg Shape, C.1920 .... 45.00
Dispenser, Liberty Root Beer, Barrel Shape 400.00
Dispenser, Mission Orange Syrup, 28 In. ....100.00 To 150.00
Dispenser, Mission Real Fruit Juice Syrup, Vaseline Glass, Chrome 95.00
Dispenser, Orange Crush, Spigot, Crushy On Front, 5 Gal., 16 X 12 In. 195.00
Dispenser, Orange–Julep Syrup, Orange Globe, C.1920, 14 1/2 In. 500.00
Dispenser, Schuster's Beverages, Pottery 100.00
Dispenser, Tetley Iced Tea, Embossed Ceramic Barrel 95.00
Dispenser, Vigorola Syrup 1250.00
Display Easel, Black & Decker Mfg.Co., Towson, Md., 68 1/2 In. 45.00
Display, Stroh Beer, Plastic, Blown–Out Backdrop, Saloon, 14 X 19 In. 58.00
Door Pull, Colonial Bread, Loaf Shape, Tin, 24 In. 75.00
Door Pull, Salada Tea, 2 Sides 45.00
Door Push, Hires Root Beer, Self–Framed, Tin, 4 X 14 In. 45.00
Door Push, Junge's Bread For Better Health, Yellow Ground, Porcelain 24.50
Door Push, Kist Beverages, 1940s, Tin, 3 X 12 In. 10.00
Door Push, Lyons Tea, 1930s, Metal, 3 X 5 1/2 In. 10.00
Door Push, Majors Cement–It Mends Everthing, Scrollwork, Die Cut, Pair 115.00
Door Push, Miss Sunbeam Bread, Bread Loaf Shape 65.00
Door Push, Polar Bear Tobacco, Bear, Mounting Holes, 3 1/2 X 7 In. 45.00
Door Push, Sunbeam Bread, Young Girl, Paper, 8 X 18 In. 55.00
Emblem, Keen Kutter, Metal, 4 In. 12.00
Figure, Antique Bourbon, Baseball Player, Composition, 44 1/2 In. 90.00
Figure, Beefeater Gin, Papier–Mache Scotsman, Spear, 16 1/2 In. 45.00

Figure, Bird, Red Goose Shoes, Chalkware, 4 1/2 In. 75.00
Figure, Clockwork, Black Boy Moving Eye, Original Clothes 960.00
Figure, Cow, Real Hide, 28 In. 795.00
Figure, Dog, RCA, Hard Rubber, 10 In. 250.00
Figure, Dr Pepper, Plastic Bottle, 1940s, 13 X 49 In. 375.00
Figure, Foot, George's Patent Corn & Bunion Shields, 9 In. ....*Color* 100.00
Figure, Goose, Red Goose School Shoes, Papier-Mache, 24 In. 475.00
Figure, Milk Bottle, Embossed Cow 1 Side, Bottle Other Side, 18 In. 235.00
Figure, Morton Salt Girl, Bisque, 3 1/2 In. 12.00
Figure, Nipper, RCA, His Master's Voice, Dog, Papier-Mache, 36 In. 350.00
Figure, Phillips Soles & Heels, Composition, Shoemaker, 1940, 12 In. 70.00
Figure, Red Goose, Chalkware, 5 In. 30.00
Figure, Schmidt's, Bronze Tone Bartender, 2 Mugs In Hand, Tub, 8 In. 28.00
Flue Cover, Doe-Wah-Jack, 10 X 10 In. 85.00
Globe, Traveller's Aid, Greyhound Bus Station, World Map 165.00
Holder, Broom, Revolving, Circular 65.00
Holder, Paper, Wrapping, Counter, Cutter 15.00
Holder, Straw, Bire-Ley's 18.00
Holder, String, Baker Boy 12.00
Holder, String, Beehive, Iron 25.00
Holder, String, Pat.Feb.14, 1860, Iron 70.00
Holder, String, Three S Tonic, Cast Iron 65.00
Holder, String, Victorian Lady, Iron 20.00
Holder, Sucker, Indian Chief Watta Pop ....110.00 To 125.00
Holder, Sucker, Statue Of Liberty ....190.00 To 200.00
Hook, Grab All, Grocery, Double Lever, Babbit's Soap 60.00
Humidor, Mail Pouch Tobacco, Counter Top 200.00
Ice Pick, Arcade 8.00
Ice Pick, Crystal Ice Co. 7.50
Ice Pick, Webster City, Iowa, Wooden 5.00
Jar, Bob's Peanut Butter Sandwiches, Albany Ga., Tin Hinged Lid 65.00
Jar, Cover, Bakers Chocolate, Picture, Counter 100.00
Jar, Curtiss Chicas, Spanish Peanuts, Tin, Glass, 11 1/8 In. 95.00
Jar, Eat Tom's Roasted Peanuts, 5 Cent, Glass, Lid 35.00
Jar, Globe Tobacco Co., Barrel Shape, Tin Screw Cap, Amber, 7 In. 75.00
Jar, Kis-Me Gum, Glass Covered, 11 In. 49.00
Label, Barrel, Heinz 57, 1920s, Full Color, 11 In. 5.00
Label, Cigar, Apollo, Sculptor Finishing Bust Of Apollo, 6 X 9 In. 14.00
Label, Cigar, Bull, Head Of Dog, 4 X 4 In. 15.00
Label, Cigar, Drummer, Little Boy Beating Drum, Horseshoe, 4 X 4 In. 12.50
Label, Cigar, Dutch Maid, Dutch Girl, Holding Stick, Tulips, 6 X 9 In. 9.00
Label, Cigar, Gentlemen Of Quality, Men In Formal Suits Sitting 45.00
Label, Cigar, Hand Made, Yellow, Red, Black, White, Embossed, 4 X 4 In. .... .50
Label, Cigar, Happy Hours, Woman Lying In Hammock, Umbrella, 6 X 9 In. 35.00
Label, Cigar, Innkeeper, Elderly Man Holding Box 22.00
Label, Cigar, K & P, Armored Knight On Horseback, 4 X 4 In. 28.00
Label, Cigar, La Flor De Magnolia, Large Flower 15.00
Label, Cigar, May Belle, Woman, Hat Of Flowers, 4 X 4 In. 9.00
Label, Cigar, Old King Cole, 2 Jesters, King Cole, Maxwell Parish 165.00
Label, Cigar, Our Little Prince, Boy In Red, Brown Hair, 4 X 4 In. 7.00
Label, Cigar, Peter Schuyler 2.00
Label, Cigar, Spirit Of St.Louis 6.00
Label, Cigar, Uncle Sam, Holding Globe, Tobacco Fields, 4 X 4 In. 12.00
Label, Food, Uncle Remus Syrup, Dated 1924, 6 3/4 X 20 In. 8.00
Label, Fruit Crate, Basketball, California Lemons, Girls Playing 35.00
Label, Fruit Crate, Columbia Bell, Apple, Miss Liberty Holding Apple 2.50
Label, Fruit Crate, Maywood Fruit Assoc., Lithograph Of Orchards 24.00
Label, Fruit Crate, Unicorn, Oranges, Tan & White Unicorns Running 15.00
Lighter, Cigar, Midland's Jump Spark, Davenport Mfg.Co., 1909 .... 395.00
STORE, LUNCH BOX, see Lunch Box

Pocket mirrors range in size from 1 1/2 to 5 inches in diameter. Most of these mirrors were given away as advertising promotions.

Mirror, Aetna, Montreal, Red, White, & Black, Pocket, 4 In. ....15.00 To 24.00

Mirror, American Druggist Fire Insurance, Pocket 9.00
Mirror, Angelus Marshmallows, Oval, Pocket ....36.00 To 40.00
Mirror, Beeman's Pepsin Gum, Pocket 60.00
Mirror, Boston Leaf Mfg. Co., Dated 1872, 3 In.Diam. 37.50
Mirror, Buckwalter Stoves, Fancy Stove, Pocket 65.00
Mirror, Buddy Brand, Black & White Dog, Pocket, Round, 3 In. 22.00
Mirror, Cascarets, Cherub On Potty, Pocket 20.00
Mirror, Cerosota Flour, Boy Sitting, Pocket, 2 In. 35.00
Mirror, Checkers Corn Confections, Pocket 70.00
Mirror, Clock Face, Out, Will Return At, Pocket 32.00
Mirror, Colby's Clothing House, Taunton, Ma., 1876, Pocket ....32.00 To 45.00
Mirror, Continental Cubes Tobacco, Beautiful Woman, Pocket 125.00
Mirror, Dueber Watch, Pocket 45.00
Mirror, Duffy's Malt Whiskey, Makes The Weak Strong, Pocket 20.00
Mirror, Duffy's Malt Whiskey, Oval, Pocket ....55.00 To 60.00
Mirror, Equitable Fire Insurance, Hanging 42.00
Mirror, Friedman's Shoes, Pocket 35.00
Mirror, Garland Stove Factory, Pocket 30.00
Mirror, Granite Trust Co., Photograph, Pocket, 3 1/2 In. 25.00
Mirror, Independent Order Foresters, Pocket 37.50
Mirror, John Morrells Meat Packing Co., Pocket 25.00
Mirror, Lawson Varnishes, Pocket 30.00
Mirror, Maccabees Insurance, Faces Of 2 Girls, Pocket 9.00
Mirror, Mascot Tobacco, Pocket 20.00
Mirror, Morton Salt, Pocket 18.00
Mirror, Munsingwear, Handle 30.00
Mirror, New King Snuff, Pocket 22.00
Mirror, Niagara Falls, Pocket 15.00
Mirror, Pacific Shoes, Pictures High Button Shoe, Pocket 35.00
Mirror, Plymouth Rock Chicken, Black & White, Footed, 12 In. 98.00
Mirror, Red Cross Stoves, Pocket 25.00
Mirror, Robin Hood, Red, White, Made From Washed Wheat, Pocket 45.00
Mirror, Schaefer Pianos, Pictures Upright Piano, Pocket ....35.00 To 40.00
Mirror, Shaving, Scissor Type Extention 25.00
Mirror, Universal Theaters, Pocket 12.00
Mirror, White Cat Union Suits, Cat Picture, Pocket ....22.00 To 30.00
Mirror, Whitehead & Hoad, Berry Brothers Toy Wagon, Kids, Pocket 120.00
Mirror, Yuengling, Pocket 90.00
Mug, Blatz Brewing, Barrel Shape 12.00
Mug, Buckeye Root Beer, White & Blue 12.00
Mug, Burnham's Clam Bouillon, Small 40.00
Mug, Carlings National Breweries, Horn Shape, White, Gold Trim, 6 In. 35.00
Mug, Coors, Ivory, 1 1/2 In. 12.00
Mug, Elsie The Borden Cow, Ceramic 14.00
Mug, Fred Sehring, Factory Picture, 1903 .... 90.00
Mug, Hires Root Beer, Boy Picture, Hourglass Shape, Marked Doulton 75.00
Mug, Hires Root Beer, Child Dressed In Formal Clothes 175.00
Mug, Hires Root Beer, Mettlach, Child In Bib 125.00
Mug, Leisy Beer, Desert Scene 125.00
Mug, Lowenbrau Beer 5.00
Mug, Oertels Real–Lager In Relief, Tan, White Interior 9.00
Mug, Pabst Beer, Elves Around Barrel 85.00
Mug, Richardson's Root Beer, Crystal 35.00
Mug, Richardson's Root Beer, Embossed 60.00
Mug, Rochester Root Beer 20.00
Mug, Shultz & Dooley Beer 8.00
Mug, Smith's Musty Ale, Philadelphia, Pa. 28.00
Mug, Stag Beer, Tin 9.00
Pail, Armour's Veribest Peanut Butter, Nursery Characters, 12 Oz. 85.00
Pail, Boon River Lard, Tin, 50 Lb. 20.00
Pail, Buffalo Brand Peanut Butter, 12 Oz. 55.00
Pail, Buffalo Fancy Salted Peanuts, 10 Lb. 125.00
Pail, Buffalo Peanut Butter, Standing Buffalo, Red, Gold, 20 Lb. 275.00
Pail, Daisy Lamp Oil, Glass, Bail Handle, Pat.April 26, 1881, 1 Gal. 100.00

Pail, Eight Brothers Tobacco, Litho, Dark Yellow 55.00
Pail, Fort Pitt Lard, 50 Lb. 20.00
Pail, Frazer Axle Grease, Tin, 2 In. 45.00
Pail, Jolly Time Popcorn, Red, Dated 1927, 16 Oz. 85.00
Pail, Miles Standish Mince Meat, Pilgrim Pictures, Covered, 30 Lbs. 45.00
Pail, Miners & Puddlers Tobacco 175.00
Pail, Monarch Peanut Butter, Teenie Weenies, 2 Lb. 175.00
Pail, Monarch Peanut Butter, Teenie Weenies, 3 Stand–Ups, 1 Lb. 125.00
Pail, Monarch Peanut Butter, Teenie Weenies, Dated 1926, 10 Oz. 50.00
Pail, Naphey's Lard, Bail Handle, Black Design, Miniature, 1876 .... 32.50
Pail, Nigger Hair, Brown, Tin ....115.00 To 125.00
Pail, Plow Boy Tobacco, Paper Label, Tin 35.00
Pail, Schepps Cocoanut, Tin, 4 1/4 X 4 1/2 In. 65.00
Pail, Schoolboy, Peanut Butter, 1 Lb. 65.00
Pail, Standard Oil Co., Mica Axle Grease, Metal, 24 In. 250.00
Pail, Sweet Cuba Cigar, Red, Yellow, Tin, Bail, Wooden Handle 32.50
Pail, Swift, Lard, 2 Lb. 6.00
Pail, Teddie, Peanut Butter 525.00
Pail, Toyland, Peanut Butter, 1 Lb. 95.00
Pencil Box, 9 Baseball Players Posing, 1870s 275.00
Pencil Box, Red Goose 75.00
Pencil Box, Scholar's Companion, Pat.1874, Tin 10.00
Pencil Sharpener, Baker's Chocolate, Figural ....20.00 To 40.00
Pitcher, Bovax Consomme Special, Monk Smelling Flowers 25.00
Pitcher, Cadillac, Crystal, Applied Handle, Etched Emblem 23.00
Pitcher, Davis Baking Powder, Embossed, 8 1/2 In. 75.00
Pitcher, Hiram Walker Bourbon Whiskey, Tan, Red, & Blue 20.00
Pitcher, Kellogg's, Embossed Correct Cereal Creamer 15.00
Pitcher, Mr.Boston, Plastic, Pearl White, Original Mailing Box 15.00
Plaque, Columbus Day Goods Co., Ohio, Germany, Bisque, 5 1/2 In. 20.00
Plaque, Hudepohl Brewing Co., Horse Drawn Coach, 21 In. 75.00
Plate, Citizen's Bank, Cat Lapping Milk, Early 1900s, 7 In. 26.00
Plate, Crosley Dishwasher, 10 In. 18.00
Plate, Dr Pepper, Woman In Low Cut Gown, Tin, 10 In. 110.00
Plate, Moxie, 9 1/2 In. 75.00
Platter, Bread, Pioneer Flour, 90th Anniversary 34.50
Postcard Rack, Tin, Hanging, Country Store, 8 Sides, 36 In. 85.00
Punchboard, Red Star, Unused, 6 X 8 In. 16.00
Rack, Alka Seltzer, Metal, Bright Colors, Holds Boxes, Counter 25.00
Rack, Autolite Battery, Cloth Curtain Backdrop, 3D 15.00
Rack, Boye Needle Threader, Tin, Thread On Top, 1908 .... 75.00
Rack, Chiclets, Holds 20 Boxes, 5 Cent 30.00
Rack, Golden Burst Popcorn, Tin, Colored, Ear Of Corn, 1935 .... 42.00
Rack, Lifesavers, 1920s 25.00
Rack, Piels Bros., Logo, Holds 2 Bottles, Metal, 8 X 8 1/2 In. 35.00
Rack, Princess Pat Makeup, Cardboard, 3 Box, 1927 .... 25.00
Rack, Wild Turkey, Metal, Embossed Name, Turkeys, Holds Bottle 50.00
Razor Blade Bank, Donkey, Listerine Premium 20.00
Sack, Buckwheat Flour, Stag On Front, 10 Lb. 2.50
Sack, Chief Rolled Oats, Picture Of Indian Chief, 100 Lb. 35.00
Sack, Crystal Sugar, Cloth, 10 Lb. 5.00
Sack, Domino Sugar, Cloth, 10 Lb. 5.00
Sack, Sea Island Sugar, Cloth, Doll Cutouts On Back, 10 Lb. 10.00
Sack, Whole Wheat Flour, Roller Mills, 10 Lb. 2.50
     STORE, SCALE, see Scale
Scoop, Henkel's Flour, Sure To Satisfy, Blue & Red Paint, Tin 30.00
Shot Glass, A.Eisler, Minn. 22.50
Shot Glass, F.Zimmerman & Co., Portland, Ore. 22.50
Shot Glass, Louis Bergholl Brewing Co. 35.00
Shot Glass, Sunny Brook Pure Food Whiskey, Inspector 12.00
Sign, Acme Beer, Stein, Wagon Wheel, Gold Pan, Framed, 28 X 22 In. 115.00
Sign, Adams & Ford Co., Shoes, 1905, Lady, Tin, 19 X 13 3/4 In. 150.00
Sign, Adkins Nut Brown Tobacco, Porcelain, 19 X 47 In. 65.00
Sign, Airplane Rides, 1930s, Stone Litho, 26 X 42 In. 300.00

Sign, Allen, Allen & Stroup, Law Offices, Sheet Metal, 17 1/2 X 30 In. 75.00
Sign, American Express Money Orders, Embossed, Tin, 24 X 32 In. 60.00
Sign, Antiseptic Cup, Brush & Soap, Framed, C.1910, 18 1/4 X 14 In. 350.00
Sign, Ask For Hires, Thank You, Call Again, 5 X 18 In. 42.00
Sign, August Flower For Dyspepsia, Liver, Reverse Glass, 18 X 12 In. 350.00
Sign, August Wolf Milling, Factory, Linen Mount, 1890, 21 X 31 In. 500.00
Sign, Ayers Sarsaparilla, Tin, Infant & Sea Scene, C.1890, 26 X 13 In. 2100.00
Sign, Baby Esmond 5 Cent Drink, 1930s, Tin, 20 X 28 In. 40.00
Sign, Baker's Cocoa, La Bell Chocolatiere, Tin, Framed, 22 X 28 In. 400.00
Sign, Bavarian Beer, Tin, Pictures Man, 5 X 10 In. 20.00
Sign, Beck's Hunting Tobacco, 1895, Tin, 14 X 6 In. 45.00
Sign, Beck's Hunting Tobacco, Tin, Yellow, Black, 1890, 13 X 6 In. 45.00
Sign, Berkley Knit, Man Wearing Tie, Cardboard, 1925, 8 X 10 In. 30.00
Sign, Blue Crown Spark Plugs, Metal, 19 X 14 In. 30.00
Sign, Boardwalk, 5 Cent Hotdog, Woman, Dog, Electric, 3 X 3 Ft. 850.00
Sign, Boot, Tin Edge, Wrought Iron Hangers, Wooden, 27 1/4 In. 375.00
Sign, Braem's Bitters, Bottle, Tin On Cardboard, C.1906, 7 X 13 In. 27.50
Sign, Bremen Fire Insurance Co., Hamburg, Germany, Glass, 28 X 20 In. 95.00
Sign, Buick, Wisconsin Dealer, Embossed, Tin, 13 X 19 In. 100.00
Sign, Bull Durham Tobacco, Lithograph, 1890, 21 X 27 In. 500.00
Sign, Burger Beer, 1940s, Men Fishing, Tin Over Cardboard, 15 X 20 In. 68.00
Sign, Burger Beer, Embossed Copper, 1940s, Framed, 10 X 14 In. 18.00
Sign, Burpee Seed, Nasturtiums, 1934 .... 135.00
Sign, Butcher, Gold Word Pork, Oval, Redwood, 31 X 20 In. 500.00
Sign, Call Again, 1930s, Embossed Tin, 12 X 32 In. 40.00
Sign, Carhartt, 1920s, Embossed Tin, 10 X 24 In. 30.00
Sign, Carling's Ale, Tin, Policeman, 9 Pints Of Law, 12 1/4 X 19 In. 25.00
Sign, Cascarets, Sleeping Hobo, Cardboard, 22 X 16 In. 35.00
Sign, Cetacolor Dye, Victorian Woman, C.1890, Oilcloth, 36 X 25 In. 59.50
Sign, Chesterfield Cigarettes, Tin, 3 X 14 In. 10.00
Sign, Chew Tomahawk Plug, Indians Battle, Chromolitho, 25 X 17 In. 160.00
Sign, Chicken Dinner Candy, 5 Cent, Stand–Up, Cardboard, 24 X 18 In. 35.00
Sign, Chief Two–Moon Bitter Oil, Cardboard, C.1930, 4 Ft.4 In. 80.00
Sign, Chiropractor, C.M.Link, Gold & Black Letters, Glass, 24 X 14 In. 30.00
Sign, Clabber Girl, 1952, Tin, 12 X 30 In. 25.00
Sign, Clark's ONT Thread, Cardboard, 14 X 21 In. 325.00
Sign, Clarke's Pure Rye, Old Man Pouring Shot, Ceramic, 1891, 11 In. 125.00
Sign, Climax Tobacco, Woman On Terrace, Cardboard, Round, 17 In. 85.00
Sign, Continental Trailway Bus Depot, Porcelain, 36 X 18 In. 150.00
Sign, Cott Ginger Ale, Metal, 9 1/2 X 28 In. 20.00
Sign, Cream Of Wheat, Cardboard, 11 X 16 In. 28.00
Sign, Creamery Marshmallow Drop, Tin, 12 X 12 X 17 In. 30.00
Sign, DeLaval Cream Separator, Tin, Chromolitho, 1910, 25 In.Diam. 150.00
Sign, DeLaval Dairy Equipment, Metal, 17 X 12 In. 20.00
Sign, DeLaval Dairy Equipment, Tin, 12 X 19 In. 19.00
Sign, DeLaval, Girl & Cow Scene, Green Ground, Tin, Framed, 41 X 30 In. 1050.00
Sign, DeLaval, We Use DeLaval Cream Separator, Porcelain, 12 X 16 In. 45.00
Sign, Dixon Lumber & Marking Crayons, Cardboard, 30 X 20 In. 35.00
Sign, Doe–Wah–Jack, Pressed Board, Round, 8 In. 125.00
Sign, Doe–Wah–Jack, Stove, Oak, Round, 8 In. 225.00
Sign, Dr Pepper, Tin, 11 X 30 In. ....50.00 To 85.00
Sign, Dr.Daniel's Horse & Dog Medicine, Tin, White, Blue, 30 X 20 In. 65.00
Sign, Dr.Drake's Cough Syrup, Die Cut, Framed, 18 X 16 In. 125.00
Sign, Dr.Lynas Hair Grower, Cures Diseases, Cardboard, 10 X 13 In. 5.00
Sign, Drink Sheffield Farms Fer–Mil–Ac, Reverse On Glass, Gold 425.00
Sign, Eagle Pure White Lead, Tin, Double Sided, 1905, 14 X 19 In. 225.00
Sign, Early Times Whiskey, Distiller In Relief, Plaster, 28 X 23 In. 325.00
Sign, Eat Chicken Dinner Candy 5 Cents, Tin, Yellow, 13 3/4 X 28 In. 65.00
Sign, Edgeworth Tobacco, Tin, Gold, Blue, Red, 32 X 8 In. 22.50
Sign, Egyptienne Straights Cigarettes, Cardboard, Frame, 31 In. 110.00
Sign, El Roi–Tan, Perfect Cigars, Chromolitho, Metal, 24 1/2 X 20 In. 100.00
Sign, El Wadora Cigar, Metal, 36 X 24 In. 20.00
Sign, Elk Head, Convex, Tin, C.1900, Round, 14 1/2 In. 25.00
Sign, Employers Liability Assurance, Self–Framed, Tin, 22 X 28 In. 125.00

Sign, English Tavern, Drummer In Carved Relief, 33 X 41 In. 250.00
Sign, Enjoy Gluek's Beer, Tin, 18 3/4 In.Diam. 15.00
Sign, Enjoy Gobel Bantam Beer, Tin, 14 X 11 In. 14.50
Sign, Eveready Spotlight, 1920s, Canvas, 59 X 39 In. 225.00
Sign, Ex–Lax, Porcelain, 20 In. 150.00
Sign, Export Beer, Tin, Yellow, Red, Round, 48 In. 70.00
Sign, F.W.Woolworth, Reverse On Glass, C.1900, 20 X 36 In. 475.00
Sign, F.W.Woolworth, Reverse On Glass, Red, Gilt Letters, 69 X 10 In. 275.00
Sign, Fatima Cigarette, Veiled Lady, Tin, Oval, 13 X 16 In. 175.00
Sign, Ferguson's Clocks & Watches, Iron, Zinc, Paint, 24 X 23 In. 175.00
Sign, Five–O Chocolate, 1930s, Tin, 10 X 27 In. 25.00
Sign, Garland Stoves, Porcelain, 38 X 38 In. 225.00
Sign, Gipp's Beer, Embossed Tin, Peoria, Ill., 16 X 20 In. 30.00
Sign, Glass, Ice Cream, 10 X 10 In. 65.00
Sign, Globe Wernicke, Bookcases, Tin, 29 X 40 In. 250.00
Sign, Glove, Oversized Top Hat, Metal, Painted, 32 X 33 1/2 In. 350.00
Sign, Goebels Meats, Porcelain, Round, 19 In. 65.00
Sign, Golden Orangeade, Paper, 4 X 14 In. 3.50
Sign, Grape–Nuts, Girl, Dog, Tin, C.1910, 30 1/2 X 20 In. ....475.00 To 800.00
Sign, Green River Whiskey, Tin Litho, Black Man & Mule Scene, 24 In. 500.00
Sign, Griesedieck Bros.Beer, Register Top, Foil Covered Board 32.00
Sign, Grocery Store, Cardboard, Chickens In Flowered Hat, 14 X 14 In. 45.00
Sign, Hair Grower, 1906, 2 Color, Cardboard, 10 X 14 In. 7.00
Sign, Harvard Beer, Ohio, Tin, Litho, Framed, 1910, 35 3/4 X 26 3/4 In. 550.00
Sign, Havoline Oil, Tin, Navy & Cream, 9 X 19 In. 19.00
Sign, Henley Bicycle, Victorian Girl, Paper Under Glass, 26 X 18 In. 395.00
Sign, Herald Ranges, Embossed Tin, C.1890, Detailed Cook Stove, Large 885.00
Sign, Hires Root Beer, Bottle Shape, Tin, 1950s, 48 In. 90.00
Sign, Hires Root Beer, Bug–Eyed Man, Tin, 9 X 17 1/2 In. 400.00
Sign, Hires Root Beer, Red, White, & Blue, Tin, Round, 12 In. 35.00
Sign, Hires Root Beer, Tin, 40 X 13 In. 25.00
Sign, Hires Root Beer, Tin, Black, Orange, & White, 27 X 10 In. 38.00
Sign, Hires Root Beer, Tin, Round, 9 In. 20.00
Sign, Hommel Wine, 1896, Stone Litho, 19 X 26 In. 150.00
Sign, Honeymoon Tobacco, Embossed Couple Scene, Tin, Oak Frame, C.1910 .... 375.00
Sign, Illinois Watch, Lincoln, Emblem, Linen, 1912, 10 X 6 1/2 In. 60.00
Sign, Insurance, Philadelphia, Reverse Glass, 34 X 26 In. 385.00
Sign, J.& P.Coats' Spool Cotton Is Strong, Litho, Framed, 16 X 20 In. 125.00
Sign, Jewelry Store, Glass Inserts With Name, Tin, Round, 24 In. 95.00
Sign, John P.Squire & Co., Boston, Sitting Pig, Tin, 24 X 19 1/2 In. 600.00
Sign, Kato Beer, Picture Eagle, Convex Glass, 15 In., Diam. 125.00
Sign, Keen Kutter, Tin, Multicolored, 10 X 28 In. 50.00
Sign, Kibbee's Candies, Brass, 9 X 8 In. 45.00
Sign, Kist Root Beer, 1940s, Embossed Tin, 16 X 26 In. 40.00
Sign, Kist, Tin, Color, 53 X 15 In. 65.00
Sign, Kitchel's Liniment, Children Scene, Cardboard, 13 X 7 In. 15.00
Sign, Kodak, Box Of Film, Blue, Tin, Arm Bracket, Hanging, 30 X 18 In. 75.00
Sign, Kraeuter Tool, Die Cut Pliers, Tin, 37 X 10 In. 595.00
Sign, Kraft, 1950s, Embossed Tin, 11 X 18 In. 90.00
Sign, Lafayette Life Insurance, Hanging, 1930s, Tin, 9 X 15 In. 60.00
Sign, Lee Overalls, Tin, Yellow & Blue, 3 1/2 X 23 In. 25.00
Sign, Leland Stanford Cigars, C.Shonk, Tin, 12 X 18 In. 375.00
Sign, Lemp Brewery, German Tavern Scene, Tin, Round, C.1910, 24 In. 60.00
Sign, Len Talisman, Fish, Tin, 21 X 9 In. 85.00
Sign, Lime Cola, Tin, Bottle, Color, 28 X 10 In. 55.00
Sign, Lipton Tea, Indian Women Picking Tea, Tin, 10 X 7 X 4 In. 55.00
Sign, Longines Wittnauer, Brass, 8 3/4 In. 48.00
Sign, Lux Fire Extinguishing, 2–Sided, Porcelain, 13 X 28 In. 65.00
Sign, Ma's Root Beer, 1940s, Tin, 13 X 23 In. 25.00
Sign, Manilla Anchor Brewing Co., Tin, 13 1/2 X 19 1/2 In. 325.00
Sign, Marc Anthony Jewelry, Zinc, Iron, 19th Century, 20 X 15 In. 345.00
Sign, Marseilles Soap, Mama's Darlings, Paper, Frame, 1900, 20 X 13 In. 130.00
Sign, McGowans, Rexall Drugs, Leaded Glass, Electric, 28 X 64 In. 625.00
Sign, Mellin's Food, Baby, Color, Framed, 18 X 26 In. 65.00

Store, Sign, Neon,
Red Goose Shoes, 24 In.

To restore old tools, wash wood with Murphy's oil soap, dry, sand with steel wool, apply two coats of Minwax or other oil, then use paste wax and buff. Clean metal parts, then coat with clear lacquer.

Sign, Merchant Tailors, Rose & Co., Metal, Litho, 1900, 26 1/2 X 18 In. 325.00
Sign, Merit Brand, Men & Boy Scene, Tin, C.1900, 23 X 17 1/2 In. 130.00
Sign, Minneapolis Moline Tractor, Tin, 13 X 19 In. 39.00
Sign, Moccasin Agency, Indian In Headdress, Tin, 10 X 10 In. 38.00
Sign, Mortar & Pestle, Jeweled, Electrified, C.1915, 3 1/2 Ft. 875.00
Sign, Morton Salt, Girl Under Umbrella, Tin, Blue & White, 12 X 8 In. 100.00
Sign, Moxie, Ted Williams, 1950s, Cardboard, 12 X 15 In. 150.00
Sign, Mt.Union Consolidated Mining Co., Paint, Wood, 23 1/2 X 30 In. 80.00
Sign, Murphy Da–Cote Enamel, Chromolitho, Tin, 27 X 19 In. 650.00
Sign, Mutual Biscuit Co., Tin, 10 X 10 X 11 In. 75.00
Sign, National Liberty Insurance, Chromolitho, Tin, 1910, 19 X 13 In. 175.00
Sign, National Lifeboat Association, Litho, Framed, 1872, 16 X 29 In. 40.00
Sign, National Lightning Rod Co., 1940, Embossed, Metal, 15 X 3 In. 8.00
Sign, Neon, Red Goose Shoes, 24 In. ....*Illus* 225.00
Sign, New England Organ Co., Chromolitho, Uncirculated, 24 X 34 In. 450.00
Sign, Nonesuch Mincemeat, Indian Chief, Metal, Frame, 1890, 28 X 20 In. 800.00
Sign, Nu Grape Soda, Tin, Self–Framed, Embossed Bottle, 17 X 43 In. 85.00
Sign, Oasis Cigarettes, Always Refreshing, Chromlitho, 30 X 19 In. 110.00
Sign, Oh Boy Gum, 1930s, Tin, 8 X 16 In. 90.00
Sign, Old Overholt Rye, Fisherman, Framed Canvas, 1913, 27 X 38 In. 400.00
Sign, Optometrist, Colored Glass Spectacle Form, Stand, 53 X 35 In. 990.00
Sign, Optometrist, Eyes Examined, Glasses Fitted, Reverse Glass, Light 275.00
Sign, Palmolive Flakes, Cardboard, Streetcar, Early 1930s 8.00
Sign, Park & Pollard Co., Lay Or Bust Feeds, Tin, 13 1/2 X 19 3/4 In. 50.00
Sign, Parrot Safety Match, Counter, Cardboard, 1900, 15 X 7 1/2 In. 550.00
Sign, Paul Jones Pure Rye, Tin, Lithograph, C.1903, Framed, 28 1/2 In. 225.00
Sign, Pears Soap, Bubbles, Chromo Print, Cardboard, 1890, 2 X 3 In. 245.00
Sign, Pepsi–Cola, Porcelain, 12 X 29 In. 25.00
Sign, Pepsi–Cola, Tin, Red, Yellow, & Black, 20 X 8 In. 25.00
Sign, Perambulators & Mail Carts, Red Letters, Enamel, 76 X 15 In. 150.00
Sign, Peter Pan Ice Cream, Tin, 9 X 10 In. 55.00
Sign, Pharmacy, Porcelain, Green, Scalloped, Dated 1932, 9 X 60 In. 145.00
Sign, Piedmont Cigarettes, Porcelain, Square, 12 In. 75.00
Sign, Piedmont Cigarettes, Tin, Washington & Mt.Vernon, Frame, 1916 .... 375.00
Sign, Players, Porcelain, 12 X 9 In. 24.00
Sign, Pocket Watch, Double–Sided, Cast Iron, 23 In. 285.00
Sign, Popsicle, Yellow, Orange & Black, Tin, 28 X 10 In. 65.00
Sign, Purity Flour, Porcelain, White, Yellow, Dark Blue, 36 X 24 In. 70.00
Sign, Railway Express Agency, Porcelain, 36 X 36 In. 100.00
Sign, Railway Express Agency, Porcelain, Gold & Black, 12 X 72 In. 175.00
Sign, Railway Express, Porcelain, Diamond Shaped, 3 Ft. 125.00
Sign, Rainbo Bread, Embossed Tin, 1940s, 3 X 14 In. ....10.00 To 12.00

Sign, Red Jacket Fire Equipment, Fire Pumper, Litho, 1850, 15 X 22 In. 175.00
Sign, Red Rose Feed, Porcelain, Yellow, Red, Blue, 36 X 48 In. 50.00
Sign, Remington, Cardboard, Lynn Boque Hunt, 1923 .... 325.00
Sign, Robertson's Silver Shred Marmalade, Porcelain, 10 X 30 In. 55.00
Sign, Royal Baking Powder, Tin Litho, 1920s, 20 X 26 In. 25.00
Sign, Royal Crown Cola, Bottle Shape, 1936, Tin, 12 X 30 In. 28.00
Sign, Royal Household, Porcelain, Blue, White, & Red, 32 X 16 In. 100.00
Sign, Rummy Soda Water, 1930s, Tin, Get Chummy With Rummy, 5 X 9 In. 25.00
Sign, Salada Tea, Canadian, Porcelain, French Writing, 7 X 15 In. 160.00
Sign, San Felice Cigars, Tin, 27 X 11 In. 18.00
Sign, Schlitz Brewery, Tin, Auto Scene, C.1915, Round, 24 In. 375.00
Sign, Schoep's Ice Cream, Glass, 16 X 12 In. 24.00
Sign, Seilheimer's, 1930s, Porcelain, Wood Frame, 11 X 22 In. 70.00
Sign, Silver Spring Ale, 1920s, Tin, Embossed, 19 X 9 In. 42.00
Sign, Silver Spring Ale, 1930s, Embossed Tin, 10 X 16 In. 15.00
Sign, Silver Spring Ale, 1930s, Tin, 11 X 17 In. 50.00
Sign, Smith's Overalls, Tin, Yellow, Black Lettering, 18 X 36 In. 65.00
Sign, Smoke 44, Tin, 13 X 19 In. 100.00
Sign, Spaulding Company, Pocket Watch Shape, Cast Iron, C.1890, 22 In. 350.00
Sign, St.Charles Milk, Gilt Letters, C.1920, 10 X 29 1/2 In. 130.00
Sign, Standard Portland Cement, Porcelain, Black, White, 12 X 20 In. 42.00
Sign, Stationery, Silver, Black Reverse On Beveled Glass, 8 X 30 In. 195.00
Sign, Streeter Shoe, Oil On Board, Chase Emerson, 13 1/2 X 17 In. 80.00
Sign, Sun Drop Golden Cola, Tin, 27 X 19 1/2 In. 15.00
Sign, Thieves Beware, Protection Service, Metal, 13 X 9 In. 10.00
Sign, Tip Top Stove, Porcelain, Curved, 16 X 18 In. 95.00
Sign, Turog Bread, Wooden, 6 In. 125.00
Sign, U.S.Shotgun Shells, Hunting Dog, Cardboard, 10 X 17 1/2 In. 95.00
Sign, Union Leader Tobacco, Red Pocket Tin, 10 Cents, 3 X 9 Ft. 275.00
Sign, Velvet Tobacco, Pictures Pocket Tin, 1920s, Tin, 48 X 12 In. 150.00
Sign, W.H.Smith's Lung & Cough Syrup, Cardboard, 11 X 14 In. 8.00
Sign, Walter Baker & Co.Ltd., Woman, Hot Chocolate, Tin, 44 X 32 In. 125.00
Sign, Welcome Visitors, 1920s, Football Player, Canvas, 30 X 36 In. 100.00
Sign, White Flyer Armour Laundry Soap Makes Dirt Fly, Tin, 1912 .... 225.00
Sign, White Label 5 Cent Cigar, Tin, 10 X 12 In. 50.00
Sign, Willard Storage Batteries, Porcelain, 15 X 30 In. 40.00
Sign, Wills Cigars, Tin, 8 1/2 X 11 1/2 In. 15.00
Sign, Wings, 1941, Cardboard, 20 X 26 In. 40.00
Sign, Wistars Cherry Balsam, Reverse On Glass, 1880, 15 X 32 In. 475.00
Sign, Wrigley's Spearmint Gum, Display Pack, Oversize 125.00
Sign, X–Ray Headache Tablets, 8 Cures, 10 Cents, Cardboard, 5 X 13 In. 8.00
Sign, Y–B Havana Cigars, Beautiful Woman, Tin, 10 In. 65.00
Spoon Holder, Ingman Matthews Range Co., Attaches To Pan, Tin 24.00
STORE, THERMOMETER, see Thermometer

> *The English language is sometimes confusing. Tin cans or canisters were first used commercially in the United States in 1819 and were called "tins." Today the word "tin" is used by most collectors to describe many types of containers, including food tins, biscuit boxes, roly poly tobacco containers, gunpowder cans, talcum powder sprinkle–top cans, cigarette flat–fifty tins, and more. This book also includes the following categories: Beer Can; Store, Bin; and Store, Canister. Things made of undecorated tin are listed under Tinware.*

Tin, 666 Salve, Sample 5.00
Tin, Acme Coffee, 1 Lb. 22.00
Tin, Adams Honey Chewing Gum, 9 X 5 X 1 In. 15.00
Tin, Akro Agate Marble, Boys & Girls Playing Marbles, 1920s 75.00
Tin, Allen's Foot Talcum 12.00
Tin, Angelus Shoe Polish, Green 3.00
Tin, Anusol Suppositories, Sample 6.00
Tin, Artstyle Chocolate Co., Victorian Scene 10.00
Tin, Astor House Coffee, Round, 1 Lb., 5 X 3 In. 70.00
Tin, Bagley's Old Colony Tobacco, Pocket 60.00
Tin, Baird & Peter's Tea, House Shape, Door Opens, Glass Windows 210.00

Tin, Baker's Cocoa, Picture Of La Belle Chocolatiere, C.1950 .... 29.50
Tin, Bank Note Cigars, Liberty Can Co., Canister, 6 X 5 In. 45.00
Tin, Big Ben Tobacco, Canadian, Clock Pictured, Canister ....20.00 To 29.00
Tin, Big Ben, Horse, Pocket 18.00
Tin, Biscuit, Bell, Huntley & Palmers, 1912 .... 50.00
Tin, Biscuit, Bluebird, English, 1911 .... 110.00
Tin, Biscuit, Book, English 65.00
Tin, Biscuit, Camera, Huntley & Palmers, 1913 .... 500.00
Tin, Biscuit, Coronation Coach, British, Original Box, 1936 ....*Illus* 625.00
Tin, Biscuit, Fairy Tree, William Crawford & Sons 100.00
Tin, Biscuit, Library, Huntley & Palmers, 1900 .... 250.00
Tin, Biscuit, Log, Huntley & Palmers, 1902 .... 450.00
Tin, Biscuit, Screens, Huntley & Palmers, 1913, Pair 250.00
Tin, Biscuit, Statue Of Liberty 24.50
Tin, Biscuit, William Crawford, Biplane Shape 1600.00
Tin, Biscuit, Yule Log, MacFarlane, Lang & Co. 160.00
Tin, Black Sheep Cigar, Pocket, 1915 .... 75.00
Tin, Blue Boy Frozen Foods, Canister, 30 Lb. 40.00
Tin, Bob White Baking Powder, Round 18.00
Tin, Bokar Coffee, Cup Picture, Canister, 1 Lb. 10.00
Tin, Bon Ami, Baby Chick, Housewife, Unopened, 1940s 10.00
Tin, Breakfast Call Coffee, Canister, 3 Lb. 44.00
Tin, Brocks Marshmallows, 5 Lb. 45.00
Tin, Buckingham Smoking Tobacco, Orange, 6 X 5 In. 35.00
Tin, Buckingham Tobacco, Sample, Pocket 125.00
Tin, Bull Dog Tobacco, Oval, Pocket 155.00
Tin, Bulmark, Man With Telescope Looking To Sea, 4 X 3 X 1 In. 35.00
Tin, Bunte Bros. Confections, Square, 5 Lb. 10.00
Tin, Burley Boy Tobacco, Pocket 375.00
Tin, Cadbury Chocolate Milk, Figural 45.00
Tin, Cadets, Condom, Contents 35.00
Tin, California Perfume Co., Baby Powder, 2 Nude Babies Playing 90.00
Tin, Calumet Baking Powder, Indian Picture, Red, Canister, 1 Lb. 8.00
Tin, Calumet, Round, 8 In. 15.00
Tin, Camel Cigar, 5 Cent, Oval 30.00
Tin, Camel Cigarettes, Round, 50 .... 40.00
Tin, Campbell Coffee, Round, 5 Lb. ....55.00 To 65.00
Tin, Campbell's Coffee, Canister, Bail Handle, Litho, 14 X 8 In. 70.00
Tin, Campfire Marshmallow, Round, 5 Lb. 25.00
Tin, Cashmere Bouquet, Sample, Box 15.00
Tin, Celestes, Nail Polishing Stone, Contents 6.00
Tin, Central Union, Small Top, Canister, 6 X 3 In. 200.00
Tin, Century Coffee, Scene, 1 Lb. 22.00
Tin, Champlain's Baking Powder, Paper Label, Round, 6 X 2 In. 18.00
Tin, Chase & Sanborn Coffee, Sample 35.00
Tin, Clabber Girl Baking Powder, Label, Round, 2 Lb. 16.00
Tin, Clarks Peanut Brittle, 15 Lb. 20.00
Tin, Cloverine Talcum Powder, Lady 150.00
Tin, Co–Re–Ga Dental Powder, Sample 6.00
Tin, Coffee, Royal Corona, Mexican & Burro, Round, 5 Lb. 75.00
Tin, Colgate's Florient Talcum Powder, Sample 20.00
Tin, Comfort Powder, Parke, Davis, Sample 25.00
Tin, Condor Tea, French, Green Ground, Yellow Lid, 8 1/2 X 6 1/2 In. 56.00
Tin, Cox's Best Waterproof, Japanned, Tin, Green, Small 10.00
Tin, Cross Country Motor Oil, Sears 20.00
Tin, Curtiss Candy, Butter Finger, Picture Of Whistle 14.50
Tin, Davis Baking Powder, Round, 5 Lb. 35.00
Tin, Dearest Baby Powder, Canada, Beige, Blue, 1935, 4 1/2 X 2 In. 15.00
Tin, Del Monte Coffee, Round, 6 X 3 In. 12.00
Tin, Dill's Best, Curved & Concave, Pocket 45.00
Tin, Dill's Best, Pocket, 4 X 2 In. ....12.00 To 20.00
Tin, Dix Coffeemeter, 1900s 18.00
Tin, Djer Kiss Talcum Powder 7.00
Tin, Dorsie Chocolate Can, Dutch Children, 4 Oz. 15.00

Tin, Doublets Cigarettes, Orange, Flat, 1942 .... 6.00
Tin, Dr.LeGear's Udder Ointment, Doctor & Cow's Udder Picture, 7 Oz. 15.00
Tin, Dream Girl Talcum 22.00
Tin, Dream Girl Talcum, Lady 25.00
Tin, Droste Cocoa, 3 3/4 In. 12.50
Tin, DuPont Gunpowder, Label Of Indian & Buffalo, 1924, 1 Lb. 37.50
Tin, Dutch Girl Tire Patches, 1930s 8.00
Tin, Dutch Girl Tire Patches, Forever Tight, Canister, 1930s 8.00
Tin, Edgeworth Tobacco, Pocket 6.00
Tin, Edgeworth Tobacco, Square, 4 In. 30.00
Tin, EF Kemp Salted Mixed Nuts, 1/2 Lb., 1926 .... 5.00
Tin, El Roi Tan Cigars, 5 X 3 1/2 In. 15.00
Tin, Epicure Green, Leaves, Square, 4 X 3 X 3 In. 75.00
Tin, Ex–Lax, Sample 7.00
Tin, Fairy Dell Coffee, 4 Lb. 32.00
Tin, Felber Malto Milk Biscuits, Blue, 5 Lb. 25.00
Tin, FFV Macaroon Krisps, Lb. 4.00
Tin, Fiebing's Castor Axle Oil, Round, Spout Cover, 4 7/8 In. 12.00
Tin, Fleischman's Yeast, Counter Top, 8 In. 11.00
Tin, Folger's Coffee, Vacuum, Round, 2 Lb. 12.00
Tin, Forest & Stream Tobacco, Key Open, Men In Canoe, Round, 4 X 4 In. 125.00
Tin, Forest & Stream Tobacco, Pocket, Fisherman ....20.00 To 30.00
Tin, Fox's Special, Upright Pocket, Paper Label, 1870 .... 50.00
Tin, Freeman's Face Powder, Sample 10.00
Tin, Friend's Smoking Tobacco, Dog, Round, Flip Top 15.00
Tin, Full Dress Tobacco, Gold, Orange, Flip Top, Pocket 100.00
Tin, Glicks Cabaret Mints, Girl, 10 Lb. 115.00
Tin, Golden Dome Coffee, Round, 1 Lb. 20.00
Tin, Granulated 54, Lithographed, Pocket 40.00
Tin, Grape Nuts, Yellow Lithographed, Removable Lid 50.00
Tin, Gravely, Flat, 4 X 6 In. 28.00
Tin, Gray Cadette Talc 62.00
Tin, Great West, Gold, Red, Canadian, 6 X 4 X 2 In. 16.00
Tin, Griffin ABC Shoe Polish 4.00
Tin, Guth Treasure Chest Of Chocolates, 1 Lb. 20.00
Tin, Half & Half Tobacco, Sample Pocket Tin, 1910 Stamp 60.00
Tin, Hanley & Kinsella Coffee, Canister, 3 Lb. 28.00
Tin, Heinrich Haberlein, Lebkuchen–Nurnberg, Cottage Shape, 7 1/2 In. 50.00
Tin, Herold Sardine, Red, Green, White, Gold Lettering, 12 X 12 X 3 In. 115.00
Tin, Hi–Plane Tobacco, Pocket, Twin Engine, 3 X 1 1/2 X 2 In. 30.00
Tin, Holiday Pipe Mixture, Pocket 15.00
Tin, Honest Labor, Red Arm, Pocket, 4 X 2 X 1 In. 25.00
Tin, Honey Moon, Pocket 40.00
Tin, Hoosier Boy Coffee, Round, 1 Lb. 155.00
Tin, Idle Hour Tobacco, Pocket, 4 X 2 In. 45.00
Tin, Imperial Ice Cream, Parkersburg, W.Va., Quart 9.00
Tin, Iron Biscuit Co., Animal Cookies, Toys On Wheels 100.00
Tin, Jack Sprat Coffee, Round, 4 Lb. 200.00
Tin, Jockey Club Pomade, Sample 6.00
Tin, Johnson's Milco–Malt, Round, 1 Lb. 8.00
Tin, Joseph Tetley & Co., Tea Caddy, 1 Lb. 10.00
Tin, Just Suits Tobacco, Canister, 7 X 4 In. 65.00
Tin, K.C.Baking Powder, 25 Oz. For 25 Cents 12.00
Tin, Kellogg's Drinket, Sample 80.00
Tin, King Syrup, Lion Picture, Round, 6 X 4 In. 22.00
Tin, Klutch Dental Adhesive, Sample 7.00
Tin, Korbel Sec Calif.Champagne, C.1930, 13 X 19 In. 150.00
Tin, La Fendrich Cigars, Box, 5 X 4 X 1 In. 20.00
Tin, Larkin's Orange Blossom Talc 15.00
Tin, Latona Coffee, 3 Horse Picture, 5 Lb. 75.00
Tin, Libby's Dill Pickles, Sample 22.00
Tin, Libby's Fruit Float, Strawberry Dessert, Sample 10.00
Tin, Lipton Tea, 2 Lb. 10.00
Tin, Lipton Tea, Indian Women Picking Tea, 10 X 7 X 4 In. 60.00

Tin, Little Kittens Candy, Tin 29.00
Tin, Log Cabin Syrup, Cabin Shape, Paper Label, Dated 1914, 14 Oz. 165.00
Tin, Long's Covered Wagon Syrup, Wagon Shape 150.00
Tin, Louisiana Perique Tobacco, Gold, 3 X 1 1/2 X 2 In. 25.00
Tin, Lucky Strike Cigarettes, Flat 50's, Green 4.50
Tin, Lucky Strike Cigarettes, Sample 45.00
Tin, Lucky Strike Cut Plug, 4 1/2 X 2 1/2 X 3 1/4 In. 18.00
Tin, Luer's Lard, Children Riding Tricycles, 4 Lb. 19.00
Tin, Luzianne Coffee, Black, Round, 1 Lb. 18.00
Tin, Luzianne Coffee, Black, Round, 2 Lb. 12.00
Tin, Lyon's Swansdown Marshmallow, 4 Oz. 55.00
Tin, Mapacuba Cigars, Pocket 55.00
Tin, Maryland Beauty, Oyster, Lady Pictured, 1 Pt. 8.00
Tin, Maryland Club Tobacco, Orange, Flat Lid, Pocket 125.00
Tin, Matador Granulated Mixture, Illinois Can Co., Square Corners 85.00
Tin, Mayo's Tobacco, 4 X 6 In. 30.00
Tin, McAleers Polish & Cleaner, Sample 12.00
Tin, McCormick Tea, Hinged Lid, 100 Bags, 1936 .... 10.00
Tin, McNess Humpty Dumpty Talc 30.00
Tin, Modjeska Talcum Powder 25.00
Tin, Monarch Cocoa, Sample 29.00
Tin, Monarch Light Of Asia, Tea 48.00
Tin, Monarch Tea, 8 Oz. 15.00
Tin, Monarch Teenie Weenie, Suitcase, 1922 .... 55.00
Tin, Montgomery Ward Coffee, Canister, 5 Lb. 19.00
Tin, Morrell's Snow Cap Lard, Round, 8 Lb. 15.00
Tin, Morse's Duchess Brand Tobacco, Victorian Woman, 5 Lb. 35.00
Tin, Mother Hubbard Flour, 5 Lb. 9.00
Tin, Mothers Joy Coffee, Round, Pound 8.00
Tin, Murad Cigarettes, Flat 50s, Canadian, 1897 Stamp, 5 1/2 X 3 In. 35.00
Tin, Mutual Biscuit Co., 10 X 10 X 11 In. 75.00
Tin, Natalie Cigars, Somers, Litho, Dated 1879, 4 1/2 X 4 1/2 In. 85.00
Tin, Nebia Coffee, Elephant Picture, Round, 3 Lb. 25.00
Tin, No–To–Bac, Cure For Tobacco Habit, Tin, Small 6.50
Tin, Nurnberg, Lithographed, Raised, Georg Goess ....*Illus* 15.00
Tin, Oak Hill Coffee, Scene, Round, 1 Lb. 55.00
Tin, Octagon Scouring Cleanser, Contents, Free Trial Size 12.00
Tin, Old Chum Virginia Flake Cut Tobacco, Montreal, Canada, 1/2 Lb. 17.50
Tin, Old Colony Root Beer, Cone Top 25.00
Tin, Old Colony Tobacco, Pocket 60.00
Tin, Old Crumb Tobacco, Pictures Pouch 40.00
Tin, Old English Curve Cut, 4 1/2 X 3 1/2 X 3 In. ....10.00 To 15.00

Store, Tin, Nurnberg, Lithographed,
    Raised, Georg Goess

Do not use Scotch tape or other sticky tapes on paper. Even if the tape is removed, the paper will eventually discolor from the contact with the glue.

To remove wrinkles from old paper, set a regular iron for cotton. Iron out the wrinkles from the wrong side of the paper. Be sure to iron quickly so you do not scorch the paper.

Tin, Old Master Coffee, Round, 3 Lb. ....50.00 To 55.00
Tin, Old Squire Tobacco, Canadian, Blue, Pocket 100.00
Tin, Optimo Cigars, Round, 6 X 5 In. 55.00
Tin, Orange Blossom Talc, 8 In. 6.50
Tin, Ovaltine, 1921 .... 20.00
Tin, Ox–Heart, No.15, Paper Label 25.00
Tin, P.C.W. Cough Drops, Somers, Red 50.00
Tin, Palmy Days, Gold Letters, Pocket 110.00
Tin, Pat Hand Tobacco, Oval, Pocket 110.00
Tin, Patterson's Seal, 7 X 5 In. 15.00
Tin, Peachey Tobacco, Pocket 40.00
Tin, Peak Coffee, Round, 1 Lb. 18.00
Tin, Perma–Grip Dental Powder, Sample 4.00
Tin, Peter Pan Peanut Butter, Sample, 2 X 1 In. ....40.00 To 65.00
Tin, Peter Rabbit On Parade, Oval Shape Box, 3 X 5 In. 40.00
Tin, Peter Rabbit Talcum ....90.00 To 125.00
Tin, Pickwick Coffee, No.5, Dated 1897 .... 49.00
Tin, Pickwick Coffee, Round, 1 Lb. 22.00
Tin, Picobac Tobacco, Canadian, Pocket, 4 X 2 In. 35.00
Tin, Pilot Cocoa, Airplane Picture 20.00
Tin, Plato Dental Powder, Sample 4.00
Tin, Players Gold Leaf, British, 2 X 2 X 1 In. 10.00
Tin, Postmaster Cigars, 3 For 5 Cents, Round, 3 1/2 X 6 In. 85.00
Tin, Postum, Sample 45.00
Tin, Pride Of The Chesapeake, Oyster, 1 Gal. 20.00
Tin, Prince Albert Tobacco, 1907 Patent, Round, 4 X 5 In. 12.00
Tin, Prince Albert, Pocket 3.50
Tin, Pure Spring Orange, Cone Top 20.00
Tin, Puritan, Canadian, Boat, Light Yellow, Pocket, 4 X 6 In. 60.00
Tin, Q Boid, Pocket, Curved 35.00
Tin, Radio Oil, Green & White, 5 X 5 In. 6.00
Tin, Rawleigh Salve 8.00
Tin, Rawleigh's Good Health Talc, Mother Goose Characters, 1 Lb. 35.00
Tin, Real Man Talc, Fisherman 35.00
Tin, Red & Gold Coffee, Canister, 1914, 3 Lb. 25.50
Tin, Red Bird Coffee, Round, 1 Lb. 22.00
Tin, Red Dot Jr.Cigar, 3 X 5 In. 24.00
Tin, Red Jacket, Pocket 30.00
Tin, Red Rose Coffee, Round, 1 Lb. 18.00
Tin, Repeater Tobacco, Canadian, Pocket 35.00
Tin, Richelieu Midas Brand Tea, Oriental Scenes, 4 In. 15.00
Tin, Richman's Segars, 5 Cent, 4 X 4 X 4 In. 25.00
Tin, Ridgway's Tea, Embossed, Safe–Tea First, Established 1836 .... 25.00
Tin, Riverside Country Club Coffee, Round, 3 Lb. 48.00
Tin, Roly Poly, Dutchman, Mayo ....350.00 To 450.00
Tin, Roly Poly, Mammy, Dixie Queen 400.00
Tin, Roly Poly, Mammy, Mayo ....225.00 To 450.00
Tin, Roly Poly, Mammy, Red Indian 165.00
Tin, Roly Poly, Mammy, U.S.Marine 525.00
Tin, Roly Poly, Satisfied Customer, Mayo 450.00
Tin, Roly Poly, Singing Waiter, Mayo 175.00
Tin, Roly Poly, Singing Waiter, U.S.Marine ....375.00 To 450.00
Tin, Roly Poly, Tobacco, Set Of 6 .... 3500.00
Tin, Rough Rider Baking Powder, Pictures Roosevelt On Horse, 5 Cent 15.00
Tin, Rountree Cocoa, 1902, Commemorative, Edward VII, Queen Alexandra 70.00
Tin, Royal Baking Powder, 1928, Round, 4 In. 10.00
Tin, Royal Baking Powder, Sample, Unused 15.00
Tin, Rumford Baking Powder, Round, 12 Oz. 8.00
Tin, Runkel's Cocoa, Paper Label, 1/2 Lb. 12.00
Tin, Sensible Tobacco, Box, 4 1/2 X 3 X 3 1/2 In. 15.00
Tin, Simoniz, Man Polishing Model T, Canister, 1920s 15.00
Tin, Sir Walter Raleigh Cigarettes, Pocket 10.00
Tin, Sir Walter Raleigh, Round, 5 X 5 In. 10.00
Tin, Solarine Metal Polish, Sample 40.00

Tin, Solitaire Peanut Butter, Pictures 3 Kids Eating, 5 Lb. 50.00
Tin, Southern Biscuit Co., Dated 1920, Negro Butler, 10 In. 45.00
Tin, Sozodont Tooth Powder 35.00
Tin, Spice, Bee Brand, Bee Pictured, Contents, Pair 10.00
Tin, Spice, Tray, Grand Union Tea Co., Amber, Japanned, Canister, 6 Pc. 75.00
Tin, Stag, Pictures Deer, Pocket, 1910, 3 1/2 In. 26.50
Tin, Starless Gall Salve, Litho Of Workhorses 8.00
Tin, Style King Talcum, Contents, 1940s 5.00
Tin, Sunshine Fruit Cake, Egyptian Lady's Head, Round, 9 In. 9.00
Tin, Superla Cream Separator Oil, Tin, Farm Scenes 24.00
Tin, Sure Shot Tobacco, 20 X 8 X 6 In. 120.00
Tin, Susie Q Hair Dressing Salve, Sample 12.00
Tin, Swee–Touch–Nee, 3 In. 3.50
Tin, Sweet Burley, Yellow, Canister 80.00
Tin, Sweet Cuba Chewing Tobacco, Hinged Lid, 12 X 18 In. 75.00
Tin, Sweet Cuba, Dark Blue, Round, 8 In. 58.00
Tin, Sweet Cuba, Green, Round, 8 In. 50.00
Tin, Sweetheart Talcum, Lady 25.00
Tin, Teriff's Talcum 250.00
Tin, Three States Tobacco, Pocket, Oval 265.00
Tin, Tiger Chewing Tobacco, Red, 12 X 8 X 6 In. 75.00
Tin, Tiger Red, Canister, 5 Lb. 150.00
Tin, Times Square Tobacco, Pocket, 4 X 2 In. 235.00
Tin, Tom Moore Cigars, 3 1/2 X 5 In. 18.00
Tin, Torrone Italian Candy, Multicolor, 8 X 7 X 2 In. 16.00
Tin, Trailing Arbutus Talcum, 1 Lb. 45.00
Tin, Tuxedo Tobacco, 4 X 2 X 2 In. 100.00
Tin, Twin Oaks, Pocket, Foldover Top, Press Here 35.00
Tin, Union Leader, Eagle, Pocket 22.00
Tin, Union Leader, Eagle, Round, 4 X 6 In. 30.00
Tin, Velvet Tobacco, Sample, Pocket 65.00
Tin, Velvet, Octagon, 6 X 4 In. 35.00
Tin, Verna Fleur Face Powder, 1925 .... 35.00
Tin, Victrola Needles, Nipper 10.00
Tin, Virginia Dare Tobacco, Box, 4 X 3 In. 50.00
Tin, Wagon Wheel, Pocket, Free Trial Package 200.00
Tin, Watkin's Egyptian Talcum 15.00
Tin, Watkin's Pepper, Yellow 22.00
Tin, Webster Cigars, 5 X 3 1/2 X 1 1/2 In. 20.00
Tin, Webster's Tobacco, Man's Face, Flat, 3 X 4 1/2 In. 18.00
Tin, Weldon Slice Tobacco, 4 1/2 X 5 In. 12.00
Tin, Wernet's Dental Powder, Sample, Boxed 6.00
Tin, White House Coffee, Pictures White House, Round, 1 Lb. 20.00
Tin, Whitman's Pleasure Island Chocolates, Pirate Pictures 10.00
Tin, Whitman's Salmagundi, Egyptian Lady, 1 Lb. ....15.00 To 18.00
Tin, Wigwam Spices, Indian Pictured, Small 5.00
Tin, Wild Cherry Sweet Scotch Snuff, Sample, Dated 1923 .... 28.50
Tin, William's Talcum Shaker, Toy Sized 4.00
Tin, Wood Fields, Oyster, Galesville, Md., 1 Gal. 20.00
Tin, Woolco Creamy Mints, 1/4 Lb. 7.00
Tin, World's Navy Tobacco, Canadian, 8 X 8 X 3 In. 40.00
Tin, Yankee Boy, Upright Pocket, Blond Baseball Player 175.00
Tip Tray, Almeda Cigar, Lady 45.00
Tip Tray, American Brewery 110.00
Tip Tray, Baby Ruth, Glass, Tin Gum Dispenser 90.00
Tip Tray, Ballantine 40.00
Tip Tray, Bartel's Nightwatchman 135.00
Tip Tray, Bartholomay, Girl On Winged Wheel 125.00
Tip Tray, Big Jo 75.00
Tip Tray, Budweiser, Negroes Loading Riverboat, St.Louis Levee 110.00
Tip Tray, Burroughes Furniture Co. 55.00
Tip Tray, Canada Bud Beer, Cartoon Scene 20.00
Tip Tray, Case & Martins Connecticut Pies 20.00
Tip Tray, Champagne Velvet 55.00

Tip Tray, Clysmic, King Of Table Waters, Girl, Stream, Deer, Oval 50.00
Tip Tray, DeLaval 750, 000, Litho, 4 1/4 In. 50.00
Tip Tray, DeLaval Cream Separators, Scenic, Round 65.00
Tip Tray, Dick Bros. 95.00
Tip Tray, Dixie Queen 60.00
Tip Tray, Dr.Daniel's Veterinary Medicines 30.00
Tip Tray, Dubbleware Overalls 34.00
Tip Tray, Eldredge 85.00
Tip Tray, Eye Fix Remedy, Woman & Cherub 75.00
Tip Tray, Fairy Soap, Blue ....40.00 To 65.00
Tip Tray, Fairy Soap, Orange, 4 1/4 In. 24.00
Tip Tray, Frank Jones Ale, Logo ....30.00 To 50.00
Tip Tray, Franklin Life Insurance, Springfield, Ill., Ben's Picture 11.50
Tip Tray, Gold Seal Champagne, Multicolored Bottle, Scene 40.00
Tip Tray, Grain Belt Beer 28.00
Tip Tray, Gravel Springs 65.00
Tip Tray, Grossvater Beer 200.00
Tip Tray, Heptol Splits, Cowboy, Bronco.1904 .... 225.00
Tip Tray, Home Of Stegmaier Beer, Oval, 6 In. 75.00
Tip Tray, Hommel's Champagne, 2 Bottles, Sandusky, Ohio, 1905, 4 In. 44.00
Tip Tray, Hupful Brewing, Raised Logo 45.00
Tip Tray, Hyroler Whiskey, Victorian Gambler ....35.00 To 65.00
Tip Tray, I.P.Thomas & Son, High Grade Fertilizer, Philadelphia 38.00
Tip Tray, Jacob Ruppert Beer, Pilgrim Scene, Oblong, C.1938 .... 125.00
Tip Tray, Jacob Ruppert's, Cartoon 40.00
Tip Tray, Laxol Castor Oil, 4 1/8 In. 25.00
Tip Tray, Liberty Beer, American Brewing Co., Indian Girl Head 90.00
Tip Tray, Lion Bee, Lion Pushing Barrel 85.00
Tip Tray, Lucky Lager, Western Hemisphere 25.00
Tip Tray, Maltosia 90.00
Tip Tray, Miller Beer, People, Carriage, Mansion, 1940s 24.00
Tip Tray, Monroe Brewing Co., King With Mug 100.00
Tip Tray, Monroe Brewing Co., Rochester, N.Y., King Toasting 135.00
Tip Tray, Monticello Whiskey, Fox Hunt Scene 85.00
Tip Tray, Moxie, Multicolored Woman, 6 In. 850.00
Tip Tray, Muehlebach 145.00
Tip Tray, National Cigar Stands Co. 110.00
Tip Tray, National Premium, Coats Of Arms 10.00
Tip Tray, Old Angus 9.00
Tip Tray, Old Crow Whiskey 8.00
Tip Tray, Peter Doelger Beer 80.00
Tip Tray, Phoenix Brewery, Picture 89.00
Tip Tray, Pittsburg Butchers, Packers, Beautiful Lady 65.00
Tip Tray, Pittsburgh Brewing, Bottle Of Tech Beer, 1913 .... 60.00
Tip Tray, Prudential Insurance, 2 1/2 X 3 1/2 In. 32.00
Tip Tray, Quevic, Roulette Wheel Design 45.00
Tip Tray, Red Raven Cigars, Little Girl 65.00
Tip Tray, Red Raven Splits, World's Fair 78.00
Tip Tray, Red Raven Whiskey, Woman & Raven 55.00
Tip Tray, Risinol Soap For All Skin Diseases 75.00
Tip Tray, Rockford Watches, Pictures Lady ....35.00 To 55.00
Tip Tray, S.Fernandez & Co., Tampa, Fla.Cigar Counter 75.00
Tip Tray, Sears, Roebuck & Co., Scales Of Justice, Home Office, 1920s 65.00
Tip Tray, Seitz Beer, Pictures Eagle, Easton, Pa. 89.50
Tip Tray, Standard Root Beer, Denver, 1931 .... 15.00
Tip Tray, Stegmaier Beer, Factory 175.00
Tip Tray, Stollwerck Chocolates, Cocoa 45.00
Tip Tray, Success Manure Spreader 50.00
Tip Tray, Sunshine Paints 25.00
Tip Tray, Tam O'Shanter Ale, Scotsman Holding Tumbler 125.00
Tip Tray, Tivoli Brewing Co., Detroit, Beer Bottle 55.00
Tip Tray, Tom Moore Cigars, Green & Black 22.00
Tip Tray, Ubero Coffee, Tole, Lithograph, 4 1/4 In. 25.00
Tip Tray, Union Brewing Co., Anaheim, Cal. 190.00

Tip Tray, Welsbach Mantels	30.00
Tip Tray, White Rock, World's Best Table Water, Winged Girl, Oval	35.00
Tobacco Cutter, Brighton	50.00
Tobacco Cutter, Brown Mule	48.00
Tobacco Cutter, Conway & Knickerbocker, Iron	50.00
Tobacco Cutter, Drummonds Good Luck	100.00
Tobacco Cutter, Enterprise 1889, 17 In.	43.00
Tobacco Cutter, Enterprise Champion, Incised Measure Mark	35.00
Tobacco Cutter, Enterprise, Iron	30.00
Tobacco Cutter, Good Luck, Good Cheer, Call Again, You Are Welcome	100.00
Tobacco Cutter, Iron, Dated 1885	55.00
Tobacco Cutter, Klug TCU 15 Master Workman	55.00
Tobacco Cutter, Leypoldt, Philadelphia, Pat.1860	35.00
Tobacco Cutter, Lorillard, Iron, C.1890, 17 1/2 In.	35.00
Tobacco Cutter, Mahogany Base, Brass, Steel, C.1860, 14 In.	280.00
Tobacco Cutter, Plug, Johnson Co., Ornate Side Plate, 1914	55.00
Tobacco Cutter, R.J.Reynolds Co., Enterprise, 18 1/2 X 8 In.	72.50
Tobacco Cutter, Star, C.1885	60.00
Tray, Altes Lager Beer, Bohemian Waiter, Detroit Tivoli Brewery, 1910	75.00
Tray, American Ice Cream	65.00
Tray, Anheuser Busch Beer	48.00
Tray, Anheuser Busch, Bevo Beverage	80.00
Tray, Anheuser Busch, Woman & Cherubs, Oval	620.00
Tray, Arrow Beer, King On Throne, Pub Scene, 18 1/4 In.Diam.	35.00
Tray, Artic Ice Cream, Round, 13 1/2 In.	165.00
Tray, Atlas Beer, Enamel, Eagle On Western Hemisphere, Panama	125.00
Tray, Ballantine Brewing, Glass Of Beer On Background Of Stars	26.00
Tray, Blackhorse Ale & Porter Beer, Clydesdale In Field, 12 In.	80.00
Tray, Blatz Milwaukee Beer, Logo	35.00
Tray, Braumeister Beer, Independent Milwaukee Brewery	35.00
Tray, Budweiser Beer, Dock Loading	49.00
Tray, Budweiser, Colonial Men By Fireplace	75.00
Tray, Budweiser, Levee, 1914	90.00
Tray, Buffalo, Tin, Beer	250.00
Tray, Burke's Ales, Long Island City, N.Y., 11 3/4 In.Diam.	35.00
Tray, Calumet Brewing Co., Chilton, Wi., Cavalier Scene, 12 X 17 In.	250.00
Tray, Carta Blanca, Lady & Man Dining	75.00
Tray, Cascade Beer, San Francisco, Uncle Sam & 5 Ethnics	650.00
Tray, Chero Cola, There's None So Good 5 Cent, Color, 1905	165.00
Tray, Christian Feigenspan Brewing Co., Lady, Artist, 13 1/4 In.	25.00
Tray, Cold Spring Brewing Co., Victorian Woman, Tiger, 13 1/2 In.	25.00
Tray, Congress Beer, Label	45.00
Tray, Crescent Brewing, Factory, Nampa, Idaho	450.00
Tray, Dawson's Ale & Lager, Lady & Man Dining	125.00
Tray, DeCoursey's Ice Cream, Kansas City	35.00
Tray, Deiber & Kerich Bros., 1908, Stag, Round	45.00
Tray, E.Folmer's Ice Cream	80.00
Tray, Eagle Brewery, Utica, N.Y., Eagle Center, Beer	45.00
Tray, Eagle Brewing, Jolly Gent With Mug	75.00
Tray, Fatima Cigarette, Veiled Woman, Turkish Blend, Tin, 1900, 16 In.	190.00
Tray, Fehr's Beer, King & Queen, 16 In.	40.00
Tray, Germania Brewing, Picture Of Stag	125.00
Tray, Gleuck's Beer	45.00
Tray, Grain Belt Beer, 50 Cents, 13 In.	18.00
Tray, Gretz Beer, Bicyclist	45.00
Tray, Gum Goods & Tailor Made Clothing, Tin, C.1900, Oval, 16 1/4 In.	50.00
Tray, H.Weinhard Beer, Factory, Oval	550.00
Tray, Hall's City Ice & Beverage Co., Louisville Ky., Beer, Sandwich	45.00
Tray, Hammondsport, N.Y.	35.00
Tray, Hampton Beer, Who Wants Handsome Waiter	65.00
Tray, Hires Root Beer, Round, 1915	250.00
Tray, Hornell Lager Beer, Crystal Ale, Hornell, N.Y.	55.00
Tray, Hudson & Swan Milling Co., Chicago, Building Picture, 12 In.	52.00
Tray, Hunnydew, Oval	125.00

Tray, International Brewing, Iroquois With Full Headdress 40.00
Tray, Iroquois Brewery, Large Indian Head 28.00
Tray, J.H.Cutter Whiskey, 17 In. 250.00
Tray, Kaumagraph Co., Bronze 29.00
Tray, Kemp Burpee Success Manure Spreader, Litho, 3 1/2 X 5 In. 55.00
Tray, Kippitz, Melcher's Pale Select Beer, 4 Seasons, Drinkers 295.00
Tray, Kist, Risque Bathing Beauty 78.00
Tray, Labbatts Beer, Porcelain 65.00
Tray, Londonderry Ale, Coach Scene, Jacob Hornung Brewing Co., Phila. 65.00
Tray, Miller High Life, Tin, Woman On Crescent Moon, C.1920, 13 In. 45.00
Tray, Monroe Brewing Co., King With Mug, Round, 12 In. 185.00
Tray, Murray Co., Sodawater Flavors, Boston, Ma., Tin.1900, 12 In. 50.00
Tray, Narragansett Lager & Ale, Picture Chief Pansett, Round 50.00
Tray, Nugrape, Oval, 10 1/2 X 13 In. 75.00
Tray, Orange Crush, Round 1948, 12 In. 38.00
Tray, Ortliebs Beer 36.00
Tray, Pacific Beer, Mt.Tacoma Scene, Round, 12 In. 110.00
Tray, Palisade Beer, Union City, Factory On Palisades, Oval 200.00
Tray, Prudential Insurance Co., 1900s, Pin, Tin 15.00
Tray, Quandt Brewing, Achilles On World 37.00
Tray, Red Raven Beer, Man 135.00
Tray, Red Raven, Early 1900s, Nude Little Girl, 12 In. 65.00
Tray, Rochester Brewing Co., Ricenzi, Brass, Round, 12 In. 85.00
Tray, Ruhstaller's Beer, Factory, Oval 450.00
Tray, Ruhstaller's Gilt Edge Lager, Sacramento, Ca.Touring Car 265.00
Tray, Ruppert Beer, 1938, 2 Steins Pictured, Oval 45.00
Tray, Ruppert's Beer, Art Deco Scene, Copyright Hans Flato, 13 In. 40.00
Tray, S.Bolton's Sons, Troy, N.Y., Monk Scenes, 18 1/2 X 15 In. 150.00
Tray, Savannah Brewing Co., Lady On Lion Rug, Round, 13 In. 145.00
Tray, Scheid's Washington Headquarters, Norristown, Pa., Beer 29.00
Tray, Simon Pure Beer, Winged Hops Center 35.00
Tray, Standard Brewing Co., Rochester, N.Y.Pie Shape, 1930s 25.00
Tray, Terre Haute Brewing, 18th Century Dining Scene, 15 X 12 In. 95.00
    STORE, TRAY, TIP, see Store, Tip Tray
Tray, Utica Club Beer, West End Brewery, Picture Of Old Brewery 18.00
Tray, Velvet Ice Cream 65.00
Tray, Virginia Dare Wine, Bottle With Girl 50.00
Tray, Weinhards's Portland Beer, Factory 550.00
Tray, Who's Having More Fun, Norman Rockwell, Tin 35.00
Tray, Wolverine Toy Co., 1920s, 4 X 6 In. ....65.00 To 85.00
Tray, Yuengling, Horse's Head 60.00
Tray, Zett's Beer, Pictures King 350.00
Tumbler, 7–Up, Hoofie, Set Of 4 .... 6.00
Tumbler, Adlerika Bowl Cleanser, Embossed, 2 In. 8.00
Tumbler, Anthony Kuhl Beer 30.00
Tumbler, Beer, Bartholomay Brewery, Winged Wheel Logo 18.00
Tumbler, Big Top Peanut Butter 2.50
Tumbler, Bromo–Seltzer, White On Blue Cobalt 15.00
Tumbler, Budweiser, Enameled With Hops, Set Of 4 .... 15.00
Tumbler, Buffalo Cooperative Brew Co., Buffalo Head, Flags 45.00
Tumbler, Cider, Clarksville 20.00
Tumbler, Colgate, Paper Label 20.00
Tumbler, Dr Pepper, Etched 20.00
Tumbler, Dr.Browns Celery Tonic, Etched, Set Of 3 .... 65.00
Tumbler, Dr.Graydon's Inhaler, Cincinnati 10.00
Tumbler, Germania Brewing Co., Frosted Lettering 35.00
Tumbler, Heinz Tomato Juice, Face Painted 7.00
Tumbler, Mah–Tay, Syrup Line, 4 1/2 Oz., Set Of 6 .... 60.00
Tumbler, Moxie, Embossed 25.00
Tumbler, Neoferrum 10.00
Tumbler, Pet Milk, 2 Spouts, Pet Scenes 15.00
Tumbler, Piel Bros.German Lager Beer 35.00
Tumbler, Pilsner, Etched Notre Dame 10.00
Tumbler, Purina Chick 10.00

Tumbler, Richardson's Root Beer, Bear On Front	21.00
Umbrella, For Clothing Trade With Emersons, Large	155.00
Whistle, Atwater Kent, Tin	10.00
Whistle, Red Goose Shoes, Tin	10.00
Whistle, Weatherbird Shoes, Tin	10.00
Yardstick, James Cushing & Son Co., Wooden, Square, Folding	15.00
Yardstick, Richardson's Tailor System, Dressmaker's	35.00
Yardstick, Winchester Store	50.00

Stoves have been used in America for heating since the eighteenth century and for cooking since the nineteenth century. Most types of wood, coal, gas, kerosene, and even some electric stoves are collected.

STOVE, Alcohol, Table Top, Universal, Copper Tank & Tea Kettle, Dated 1901	70.00
Charter Oak, No.103, Dated 1881, Salesman's Sample	1000.00
Cook, 6 Burners & Oven, Cast Iron & Porcelain, C.1940	550.00
Cook, Atlantic Silver Moon, No.11, Mica Windows, Nickel, Brass, 58 In.	1800.00
Cook, Bengal, Coal & Gas, Folding Table Top Covers, White Enamel	385.00
Cook, Service Stewart, Coal, 2 Overhead Gas Ovens, Fuller Warren	600.00
Cook, Wood Burning, 6 Lids, Center Oven, Reservoir, White Porcelain	550.00
Kerosene Heater, Bon Ami No.84B, Blue & Gray Granite, 22 1/2 In.	45.00
Parlor, Gothic Revival, Cast Iron, Cole, Davis & Co., C.1857, 22 In.	50.00
Parlor, Iron, Cabriole Legs, Co-Operative Foundry, N.Y., 1900, 49 In.	100.00
Royal, Miniature, Iron, Green	22.00
Shaker, Iron, Brother's Workshop, Mt.Lebanon, 18 X 35 1/2 In.	2200.00
Shaker, Iron, Straight Legs, Canterbury, N.H., 19 X 26 In.	300.00
Shaker, Mt.Lebanon, N.Y., Tool Holder & Tools	2200.00
Shaker, Wells, Maine, Iron, 19th Century, 29 1/2 X 16 1/2 In.	100.00
Shaker, Wood, Canterbury, N.H., Tin	650.00
Universal, Regal, Dragon Heads	1200.00

STRAWBERRY, see Soft Paste

Stretch glass is named for the strange stretch marks in the glass. It was made by many glass companies in the United States from about 1900 to the 1920s. It is iridescent. Most American stretch glass is molded; most European pieces are blown and may have a pontil mark.

STRETCH GLASS, Basket, White, 10 1/4 In.	95.00
Bowl, Blue, 10 X 3 In.	24.00
Bowl, Footed, Green, 7 1/2 X 3 In.	22.50
Bowl, Imperial Jewel, Pedestal, Green, 9 In.	35.00
Bowl, Red, 7 X 1 1/2 In.	94.00
Bowl, Ruffled Top, Cobalt Blue, 6 In.	35.00
Bowl, Square, Orange, Imperial, 7 1/2 X 3 1/2 In.	48.00
Bowl, Treebark Foot, Blue, 9 1/2 X 2 3/4 In.	22.00
Bowl, Vaseline, 11 X 3 In.	55.00
Bowl, Vaseline, Double Scalloped, 11 In.	45.00
Candlestick, Blue, 9 3/4 In., Pair	35.00
Candlestick, Colonial, Olive, 8 1/2 In., Pair	60.00
Candlestick, Green, White Enameled Design, 9 In., Pair	68.00
Candy Container, Covered, Pink, 9 1/2 In.	33.00
Candy Container, Covered, White, 5 1/4 X 6 In.	28.00
Candy Dish, Covered, Pink, 9 1/2 In.	30.00
Cheese & Cracker Set, Gray	29.00
Compote, Blue, 5 1/2 X 4 In.	18.00
Compote, Orange, 7 X 5 In.	35.00
Compote, Purple, 6 X 7 In.	45.00
Compote, Teal, Imperial, 7 3/4 X 7 1/2 In.	53.00
Compote, White, 4 1/2 X 9 In.	40.00
Console Set, Blue, Bowl 9 3/4 In., 3 Piece	85.00
Plate, Amberina, 8 1/4 In.	53.00
Plate, Brown & Orange, 10 In.	16.00
Plate, Purple, 8 In.	14.50
Plate, Sandwich, Gray, Center Handle, 10 1/2 In.	28.00
Vase, Amberina, Imperial, 8 1/2 X 5 7/8 In.	165.00

Vase, Bud, Blue, 11 3/4 In.	22.00
Vase, Fan, Vaseline, 7 In.	25.00
Vase, Pink, 6 X 6 In.	28.00
Vase, Red, 8 1/2 In.	60.00
Vase, Ribbed, Green, 5 1/2 In.	24.00
Vase, Vertical Cuttings, Green, 8 In.	35.00

> *Sumida, or Sumida Gawa, is a Japanese pottery. The pieces collected by that name today were made about 1895 to 1970. There has been much confusion about the name of this ware, and it is often called "Korean Pottery" or "Poo Ware." Most pieces have a very heavy orange–red, blue, or green glaze, with raised three–dimensional figures as decorations.*

SUMIDA, Bowl, 3 Men At Top Rim, Footed, 6 1/2 X 4 In.	145.00
Mug, Applied Animals, Blue Seal Signature	140.00
Tankard, Applied Children, 4–In.Enameled Neck, Seal Mark, 12 1/2 In.	595.00
Vase, Applied Pigs, Pinched, Glazed Neck, Seal Mark, 8 3/4 In.	159.00
Vase, Mottled Top, Embossed Man, Dragon, Mountain, Marked, 7 3/4 In.	110.00
Vase, Mottled Top, Raised Figure Of Boy, Orange Red, 6 5/8 In.	85.00
Vase, Raised Geisha Girl, Blue & Gray Top, Red, 4 5/8 In.	135.00
Vase, Raised Oriental Children Playing, Red, 9 1/2 X 4 1/2 In.	195.00
Vase, Raised Oriental Children, Red, 11 3/4 X 3 3/4 In.	225.00

> *Sunbonnet Babies were first introduced in 1902 in the "Sunbonnet Babies Primer." The stories were by Eulalie Osgood Grover, illustrated by Bertha Corbett. The children's faces were completely hidden by the sunbonnets. The children had been pictured in black and white before this time, but the color pictures in the book were immediately successful. The Royal Bayreuth China Company made a full line of children's dishes decorated with the Sunbonnet Babies. Some Sunbonnet Babies plates have been reproduced but are clearly marked.*

SUNBONNET BABIES, Bowl, Nut, 3 Scroll Feet, Fluted Edge, Sweeping, 4 3/4 In.	125.00
Cake Plate, Washing & Hanging, Blue Mark, 10 1/2 In.	250.00
Cake Set, 7 Piece	650.00
Creamer, Cleaning, Pinched, Blue Mark	195.00
Creamer, Washing & Ironing, Blue Mark	125.00
Cup & Saucer, Sweeping	165.00
Dish, Feeding, Mending, 8 In.	95.00
Dish, Pin, Washing & Ironing, Covered, 3 X 3 In.	150.00
Hair Receiver, Ruffled, Blue Mark	295.00
Handkerchief, Child's, Box, Pair	15.00
Mug, Sweeping	110.00
Pitcher, Sewing, Pinched Spout, Royal Bayreuth, 4 1/2 In.	175.00
Plaque, Girls With Elf, 9 1/2 X 7 1/2 In.	365.00
Plate, Mending, 9 In.	75.00
Plate, Thursday's Scrubbings, 6 1/4 In.	85.00
Postcard, 12 Months Of The Year, Framed	140.00
Postcard, 7 Days Of Week, 1905, Set	30.00
Print, Cleaning Day, Signed Corbett, Framed	20.00
Quilt, Dated 1932, 90 X 76 In.	350.00
Relish, Sweeping, Open Handles	135.00

> *Sunderland luster is a name given to a special type of pink luster made by Leeds, Newcastle, and other English firms during the nineteenth century. The luster glaze is metallic and glossy and appears to have bubbles in it.*

SUNDERLAND, Creamer, Scenic, 2 1/2 In.	45.00
Jug, Transfer Print, Ship Northumberland, C.1825, 7 In.	325.00
Masonic, Black Transfer, Polychrome Enamel, 7 In.	200.00
Pitcher, Luster, 8 In.	27.50
Saltshaker, Footed, 3 X 2 In.	65.00

Superman was created by two seventeen-year-olds in 1938. The first issue of "Action" comics had the strip. Superman remains popular and became the hero of a radio show in 1940, cartoons in the 1940s, a television series, and several major movies.

SUPERMAN, Button, Supermen Of America, 1947	10.00
Clock, Alarm, Animated, 1940s	550.00
Doll, Jointed, Wood, 1940s, Ideal Co.	345.00
Game, Card, Ideal, 1966	10.00 To 12.00
Goblet, Flying Over City At Night	10.00
Lunch Box, 1967	12.00
Puppet, Hand, Boxed, 1965	13.00
Ray Gun, Krypto, Daisy	95.00
Ring, Crusader, Boxed	135.00
Swim Fins, Official, Boxed	25.00
Toy, Krypton Rocket & Launcher, Instructions, Mailing Carton	85.00
Toy, Windup, Superman Chasing Airplane, Tin, Marx, 6 In.Wingspan	725.00
Valentine, 1940s	8.00

In 1933, the Kraft Food Company began to market cheese spreads in decorated, reusable glass tumblers. These were called "Swankyswigs." They were discontinued from 1941 to 1946, then made again from 1947 to 1958. Then plain glasses were used for most of the cheese, although a few special decorated Swankyswigs have been made since that time. A complete list of prices can be found in "The Kovels' Illustrated Price Guide to Depression Glass and American Dinnerware."

SWANKYSWIG, Bustlin' Betsy, Blue, 3 1/4 In.	2.25
Bustlin' Betsy, Green, 3 1/4 In.	2.25
Carnival, Green, 3 1/2 In.	8.00
Carnival, Yellow, 3 1/2 In.	8.00
Circle & Dot, Blue, 3 1/2 In.	4.00
Circle & Dot, Green, 3 1/2 In.	3.00
Posy, Jonquil	2.50 To 2.75
Sailboat No.2, Green, 3 1/2 In.	10.00
Star No.1, Green, 3 1/2 In.	3.50
Star No.1, Red	5.00
Tulip No.1, Blue, 3 1/4 In.	3.00
Tulip No.1, Red, 3 1/2 In.	3.00
Tulip No.2, Red, 3 1/2 In.	6.00
Tulip No.3, Yellow, 3 1/2 In.	2.00
Tulip No.3, Yellow, 3 7/8 In.	2.75

All types of swords are of interest to collectors. The military dress sword with elaborate handle is probably the most wanted. Be sure to display swords in a safe way, out of reach of children.

SWORD, American, Maple Grip, Silver Hilt, C.1760	70.00
Bayonet, Dress, Nazi, Sfilheimer, Leather Frog, World War II	65.00
Bayonet, German, Leather Sheath, World War II	25.00
Bayonet, Parade, Nazi, World War II	28.00
Bayonet, Ramrod, 1884 Springfield, 45–70	375.00
Bayonet, Scabbard, Nazi, World War II	15.50
Bayonet, Stag Handle, Nazi, World War II	70.00
Bowie & Sheath, Marked Marsh Bros & Co/Sheffield, Leather Sheath	195.00
Cavalry, Model 18660, Scabbard, Dated 1877	175.00
Civil War, Inscribed Scabbard, Eagle Head Pommel, C.1863, 38 1/2 In.	1850.00
Confederate, Brass Hilt, Boyle, Gamble & MacFee	595.00
Cutlass, Frolich, North Carolina	525.00
Cutlass, Gilt Design On Hilt & Blade, Leather Sheath	55.00
Cutlass, Revolutionary War, Sheet Iron Guard, Figure 8 Shape, 28 In.	295.00
Dagger, Dress, Nazi Officer's, Bat Blade, World War II	110.00
Dagger, Etched Motto, America & Liberty, 12 1/2 In.	375.00
Dagger, Nazi, Hanger, World War II	135.00
Dagger, Officer's, Navy, Miniature, U47, World War II	65.00

Dagger, SA, Nazi, World War II 100.00
Dagger, Scabbard, Luftwaffe, German, 1st Model, World War II 225.00
Dirk, Naval Officer's, Eagle Head, C.1820, Gilt Finish 450.00
Dress, Engraved Col.Samuel L.Smith, Marines, 1865 .... 550.00
Dress, Officer's, Naval, U.S., Engraved Blade, Leather Scabbard 35.00
Eagle Head, Artillery, 1830–49, British Made, Eagle & 13 Star Cluster 750.00
Infantry Officer's, Eagle Head, 1821–40, Design Of Indian, 32 In. 250.00
Knight Of St John & Malta, Ivory Handle, C.1717, Germany 1250.00
Leather Scabbard, Spanish, Arta Faba De Toledo, C.1894, 29 1/2 In. 75.00
Nazi, Police, World War II 150.00
Nazi, Scabbard & Knot, World War II 130.00
Officer's, Army, German, Blade Engraved, World War I 169.00
Officer's, Silver Hilt, Eagle Head Pommel, 1785–90, 25 In. 1750.00
Officer's, Silver Hilt, Lion Head Pommel, 1750–70, 24 In. 950.00
Saber Bayonet, Rem Zouave Rifle, Leather Sheath 225.00
Saber, Ames Mfg.Co., Metal Scabbard, U.S., C.1854 .... 295.00
Saber, Cavalry, Leather Grips, Copper Wire Wrap, Sheble & Fisher 250.00
Saber, Cavalry, Smith, Crane & Co., Leather Grips, Wire Wrapped, 1861 .... 650.00
Saber, Scabbard, Dragoon, Leather Grips, Marked Ames–1837, U.S. 395.00
Scabbard, Civil War, Sergeant's, Brass Hilt, Grips, Emerson & Trenton 150.00
Scabbard, German Cavalry, World War I 95.00
Scabbard, Japanese Police, World War II 45.00
Scabbard, Nazi, World War II, 37 1/2 In. 150.00
Scabbard, Staff Field Officer's, 1/2 Basket Guard, Brass Mounts 475.00
Scabbard, U.S. Diplomatic, Original Gilt, White Painted Finish 650.00
Short, Officer's, Navy, J.Gieve & Sons, English, World War I 220.00
U.S.N., 1861, Brass Hand Guard, Pair 300.00

SYRACUSE China *Syracuse is a trademark used by the Onondaga Pottery of Syracuse, New York. The company was established in 1871. It is still working. The name became the Syracuse China Company in 1966. It is known for fine dinnerware and restaurant china.*

SYRACUSE, Bowl, Cereal, Rose Marie 10.00
Creamer, Corabel 10.00
Cup & Saucer, Apple Blossom 22.50
Cup & Saucer, Corabel 12.00
Cup & Saucer, Rose Marie 20.00
Dinner Set, Governor Clinton, Service For 12 .... 325.00
Dinner Set, Old Ivory, Service For 8, 81 Piece 400.00
Dinner Set, Portland, 45 Piece 350.00
Dinner Set, Suzanne, 74 Piece 452.00
Plate, American Songbird, Set Of 8 .... 100.00
Plate, Indian Carrying Canoe, The Portage, Akron, O., 8 In. 24.00
Plate, Luncheon, Apple Blossom 10.00
Plate, Rosalie, 10 In., Set Of 10 .... 95.00
Platter, Apple Blossom, 14 In. 50.00
Platter, Corabel, Covered 25.00
Soup Dish, Corabel 10.00
Sugar, Corabel, Covered 20.00
     TANKARD, see Stein
     TAPESTRY, PORCELAIN, see Rose Tapestry

A tea caddy is a small box made to hold tea leaves. In the eighteenth century, tea was very expensive and it was stored under lock and key. The first tea caddies were made with locks. By the nineteenth century, tea was more plentiful and the tea caddy was larger. Often there were two sections, one for green tea, one for black tea.

TEA CADDY, Chased Acanthus Leaf Design, London Hallmarks, C.1903, 3 3/4 In. ... 65.00
Country, Bird's-Eye Maple 310.00
Hand Carved, Pewter Fittings, 18th Century, Chinoiserie Lacquer 385.00
Inlaid Ovals, Wood Veneer, Inside Compartments, 6 X 9 In. 65.00
Inlaid Sprays, Flower Filled Baskets, Tortoiseshell, Domed Lid 880.00
Inlaid With Shell, 2 Lidded Compartments, Mahogany, 4 1/4 In. 250.00
Painted Cupids, Quatrefoil Design, Porcelain, Beehive Mark, 5 In. 150.00

Tortoiseshell Panels, Silver Border, Hinged Lid, Silver Feet 550.00

There was a superstition that it was lucky if a whole tea leaf unfolded at the bottom of your cup. This idea was translated into the pattern of dishes known as "tea leaf." By 1850, at least twelve English factories were making this pattern; and by the 1870s, it was a popular pattern in many countries. The tea leaf was always a luster glaze on early wares, although now some pieces are made with a brown tea leaf.

TEA LEAF IRONSTONE, Bone Dish, Signed Shaw 20.00
Bowl, Oblong, 5 1/4 X 7 1/2 In. 30.00
Bowl, Vegetable, Bamboo, Square, Covered 60.00
Bowl, Vegetable, Square, Covered, Powell & Bishop, C.1878 .... 85.00
Butter Chip, Square 15.00
Butter, Covered, Mellor Taylor 145.00
Coffeepot, Wilkinson Hulme 150.00
Cup, Burslem 25.00
Nappy, Square 10.00
Pitcher, 7 In. 65.00
Pitcher, Bishop & Stonier, 12 In. 75.00
Pitcher, Milk, Alcock 125.00
Plate, 7 1/2 In. 7.00
Plate, 10 In. 20.00
Plate, Meakin, 8 3/4 In. 8.00
Plate, Meakin, 9 In. 13.00
Platter, J.E.Mayer, 14 In. 18.00
Platter, Meakin, 12 X 9 In. 39.00
Platter, Meakin, 14 In. 40.00
Shaving Mug, Meakin 48.00
Shaving Mug, Shaw 65.00
Soap Dish, Covered, Powell & Bishop 35.00
Soap Dish, Meakin 25.00
Soup Dish, Pink Luster Rim, Set Of 12 .... 295.00
Stand, Doughnut, Shaw 250.00
Sugar & Creamer 195.00
Sugar, Covered ....75.00 To 86.00
Teapot, Davenport, 9 In. 125.00
Teapot, Empress Shape, W.Adams, 1960 .... 110.00
Tureen, Covered, Anthony Shaw, 7 X 4 1/2 In. 85.00
Tureen, Soup, Burgess, 13 1/2 X 9 In. 295.00

Teco pottery is the art pottery line made by the Terra Cotta Tile Works of Terra Cotta, Illinois. The company was founded by William D. Gates in 1881. The Teco line was first made in 1902 and continued into the 1920s. It included over 500 designs made in a variety of colors, shapes, and glazes.

TECO, Jardiniere, Molded Leaf, Bulbous, Green Glaze, C.1905, 9 X 11 In. 950.00
Mug, Leaf Form, Silver Gray, Green Matte, 5 In. 198.00
Mug, Overlapping Leaves All Around, Matte Green, Gray, 5 3/4 In. 198.00
Pitcher, Silver Gray Speckled Glaze, Slanted Handle, Marked, 9 In. 154.00
Vase, 2 Handles, Matte Green, 10 3/4 In. 110.00
Vase, 4 Angled Handles, Impressed Mark, C.1908, 7 In. 210.00
Vase, Bulbous, Tapers To 4 Corners, Green Matte, 7 1/2 X 8 In. 375.00
Vase, Cylindrical, 2 Angled Ear Handles, 1908, Impressed Mark, 11 In. 175.00
Vase, Footed, Matte Green, Silver Specks, Marked, 13 1/2 In. 110.00
Vase, Tapered, Satin Green, 13 In. 148.00

The first teddy bear was a cuddly toy said to be inspired by a hunting trip made by Teddy Roosevelt in 1902. Morris and Rose Michtom started selling their stuffed bears as "Teddy bears" and the name stayed. The Michtoms founded the Ideal Novelty and Toy Company. The German version of the teddy bear was made about the same time by the Steiff Company. There are many types of teddy bears, all collected, and the old ones are being reproduced.

TEDDY BEAR, Angus The Scot, No.22/600, Nisbet 125.00
  Baloo, Disney 450.00
  Beige, Straw Stuffed, Glass Eyes, German, 11 1/2 In. 265.00
  Brown Shaggy, Glass Eyes, 21 In. 75.00
  Brown, German, 1905–10, 12 In. 225.00
  Brown, Glass Eyes, Musical, 14 In. 25.00
  Button Eyes, Red Nose, Bell Inside, 5 1/2 In. 225.00
  Celluloid, 16 In. 95.00
  Chenille, American, 1905, 12 In. 400.00
  Cinammon Mohair, 1930, 16 In. 225.00
  Cinammon Mohair, 23 In. 225.00
  Clockwork, France, Real Fur, Glass Eyes, 7 In. 150.00
  Elipuppen, German, 1950s, 22 In. 450.00
  Fully Jointed, Glass Eyes, Growler, 1920–30, 17 In. 250.00
  Hand Puppet, Chad Valley Bear, Black Ears, Stitch Nose, 10 In. 55.00
  Honey Mohair, 1930, 15 In. 95.00
  Humpback, C.1910, Mohair, 6 1/2 In. 225.00
  Humpback, Jointed, Mohair, Glass Eyes, Stumpy Arms, 1910, 14 In. 195.00
  Jointed, Glass Eyes, 1930s, 6 1/2 In. 75.00
  Jointed, Glass Eyes, 4 In. 26.00
  Jointed, Glass Eyes, Small Hump, 1920s, 12 In. 175.00
  Jointed, Mohair, 8 In. 85.00
  Jointed, Sheepskin, 14 In. 90.00
  Jointed, Straw Filled, Humpback, Honey Mohair, 22 In. 210.00
  Knickerbocker, Brown, 15 In. 30.00
  Mohair, Glass Eyes, Jointed, 16 In. 100.00
  Mohair, Glass Stickpin Eyes, Jointed, Straw Filled, Hump, 20 In. 485.00
  Mohair, Pointed Nose, Head Center Seam, English, 1930–40, 18 In. 175.00
  Mohair, Straw Filled, C.1900, 14 In. 225.00
  Mohair, Straw Filled, Jointed, Early 1940s, 12 1/2 In. 85.00
  Muff, 1930, Pink, 9 In. 75.00
  Musical, Clockwork, Germany, Mohair, Chain From Nose, 7 In. 150.00
  On Wheels, Cloth Covered, Glass Eyes, 1900, 6 1/2 In. 195.00
  On Wheels, Push Handle, 15 In. 425.00
  On Wooden Wheels, Mohair, Glass Eyes, Hump, Growler, 15 X 21 In. 750.00
  Open Felt Mouth, Mohair, Squeak, Glass Eyes, Peach Claws, 10 In. 95.00
  Outside Button Joints At Hips & Shoulders, 21 In. 120.00
  Plush, Gold, Long Snout, Jointed, Excelsior Stuffing, 15 In. 225.00
  Plush, Skinny, 14 In. 225.00
  Schucco, Yes–No, 1920s, 12 In. 450.00
  Steiff, 1950s, 9 1/2 In. 135.00
  Steiff, 1950s, 12 In. 175.00

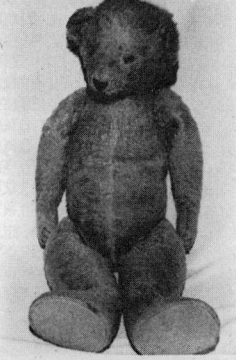

Teddy Bear, World's Fair, 1903

If you buy an old teddy bear that had been stored in a basement, be sure to treat it for insect infestation. Put the bear in a box with a stick insecticide and seal the box for sixty hours.

Steiff, 1950s, 21 In. 425.00
Steiff, Beige Mohair, Embroidered Nose, Glass Eyes, 13 In. 375.00
Steiff, Blank Button, 10 In. 275.00
Steiff, Clownie, Glass Eyes, Tag, 16 In. 175.00
Steiff, Fully Jointed, 3 1/4 In. 250.00
Steiff, Glass Eyes, Brown Nose, Felt Pads, 1920s, 13 In. 395.00
Steiff, Gold Mohair, 17 In. 175.00
Steiff, Mama & Baby, 1981, Box 175.00
Steiff, Mohair, 1950s, 13 In. 350.00
Steiff, Pads On Feet & Paws, Squeeze For Sound, 14 In. 300.00
Steiff, Papa, Mama, & Baby, Anniversary, 1980 .... 600.00
Steiff, Swivel Head, 1950s, 3 In. 49.00
Steiff, Zotty, Growler, 16 In. 75.00
Steiff, Zotty, Jointed, Button In Ear, Eyes, 8 1/2 In. 150.00
Straw Stuffed, Jointed, 28 In. 78.00
Straw, Jointed, Glass Eyes, Before 1915, 36 In. 950.00
White Mohair, Ear Button, Long Snout, Germany, 1906, 16 In. 850.00
World's Fair, 1903 ....*Illus* 2000.00

The first telephone may have been made in Havana, Cuba, in 1849, but it was not patented. The first publicly demonstrated phone was used in Frankfurt, Germany, in 1860. The phone made by Alexander Graham Bell was shown at the Centennial Exhibition in Philadelphia in 1876, but it was not until 1877 that the first private phones were installed. Collectors today want all types of old phones and phone parts.

TELEPHONE, Book, Birmingham, Ala., 1924, Yellow Cab Ad Cover 85.00
Booth, Pay Phone, Seat, Light, Sign, Oak 750.00
Booth, Wooden 385.00
Candlestick, Black, Dial, Jack 50.00
Candlestick, Brass 190.00
Candlestick, Chicago Police, Dispatcher's 65.00
Candlestick, Kellogg, Ringer Box 65.90
Candlestick, Kellogg, Western Electric Box 125.00
Candlestick, Stromberg Carlson, Miniature 165.00
Chair, Operator's, New England Tel.& Tel., Oak 110.00
Cradle Type, Stomberg Carlson 22.00
Crank, Wall, 1913, 26 In. 125.00
Desk, Crank On Side, C.1920 .... 45.00
Field, German, World War II 135.00
Field, Japanese, Leather Case, World War II 135.00
Intercom, Kress Store, Tulsa, 1940, 16 Depts. 68.00
Kellogg, Wall, Picture Frame Front, Signed, Oak, 19 In. 225.00
Railroad Station, Bakelite, Crank 50.00
Railroad, Dispatch, Santa Fe, Oak, 2 Piece 195.00
Sign, Bell System Public Telephone, Porcelain, Round, 7 In. 50.00
Sign, Flange, Bell System Public Telephone, Porcelain, 11 In. 45.00
Sign, Flange, Bell Telephone Co. Of Pa., Porcelain, 11 In. 145.00
Sign, Flange, Local & Long Distance Telephone, Porcelain, 17 In. 95.00
Sign, Intermountain Telephone Co., Yellow Bell, Porcelain 125.00
Sign, N.E.Telephone & Telegraph, Pay Station, Blue, White, 20 In. 110.00
Sign, Public Telephone, 2 Sides, Porcelain, 16 X 18 In. 50.00
Sign, Public Telephone, Pictures Bell, Porcelain, 7 In. 40.00
Switchboard Box, Walnut, Tin Front, 24 Push Buttons, Handset 35.00
Switchboard, Wooden 80.00
Wall, Crank, Ericsson, Complete 225.00
Wall, Crank, Wooden, 1913, 26 In. ....125.00 To 139.00
Wall, Hand Held Ear Piece, First Dial With Mouthpiece 75.00
Western Electric, 2 Boxes 125.00

Teplitz refers to art pottery manufactured by a number of companies in the Teplitz–Turn area of Bohemia during the late nineteenth and early twentieth centuries. The Amphora Porcelain Works and the Alexandra Works were two of these companies.

TEPLITZ, Basket, Gold Floral, Matte Green, Blown Out, R S & K, 7 X 9 1/2 In. 265.00
  Bowl, Signed, Amphora, 10 X 5 In. 75.00
  Compote, Art Deco, Amphora 35.00
  Figurine, Lady, Art Nouveau, Artist Doebrieh, 15 X 6 X 8 In. 650.00
  Mug, Fox & Bear Design, Austrian Crown, C.1891, Amphora, 5 3/4 In. 95.00
  Rose Bowl, Enameled Art Deco Flowers, Pebbly Ground, Blue Rim 70.00
  Vase, Art Deco, Sculptured Bird, Flower, Czech, Amphora, 1922, 13 In. 165.00
  Vase, Art Nouveau, Female Head, Pansies, Marked, 12 1/2 In. 600.00
  Vase, Bark Type Surface, Grape, Leaves, Handles, Amphora, 3 1/4 In. 85.00
  Vase, Bark Type Surface, Grape, Leaves, Handles, Amphora, 7 In. 100.00
  Vase, Branches, Flowers, Artist Signed, No.2228, Amphora, 7 In. 110.00
  Vase, Chestnuts & Berries, Amphora, Blue & White, 9 1/2 In. 170.00
  Vase, Cluster Of Grapes, Amphora, Cobalt, 8 In. 35.00
  Vase, Das Still, Slender, Signed C.Perelaer, C.1905, Amphora, 9 In. 195.00
  Vase, Enameled Stork, Pierced Handles, Amphora, 5 In. 80.00
  Vase, Girl's Face In Relief, Long Hair, Aqua, 8 In. 325.00
  Vase, Mermaid In Relief On Neck, Brown Band, Marked, 18 3/4 In. 595.00
  Vase, Mosaic Lovebirds, Art Deco, Amphora, 12 In. 135.00
  Vase, Polychrome Drummer Boy, Handles, Dark Green, 4 3/4 In. 95.00
  Vase, Poppy Pattern, Blue, 4 Handles, Red Crown Mark, 7 1/2 In. Pair 175.00
  Vase, Rose Floral, Gold Tracing, Yellow Ground, 10 1/2 In. 175.00
  Vase, Stylized Cosmos, Footed, Gold Leaf, Signed, Amphora, 16 In., Pair.............. 275.00

Terra–cotta is a special type of pottery. It ranges from pale orange to dark reddish–brown in color. The color comes from the clay, which is fired but not always glazed in the finished piece.

TERRA–COTTA, Figurine, Colonial Girl, Fan, French, 11 In. 135.00
  Figurine, Female, Reclining, Riding Dolphin, 11 In. 250.00
  Humidor, Tobacco, Churchill 49.50
  Owl, Leaves On Base, Evans & Howard, St.Louis, 28 In. 350.00
  Plaque, Monks Drinking, Jon Maresch, 13 In. ....184.00 To 242.00
  Plaque, No.9588, Castle Scene, W.S.& S, 13 In. 129.00
  Plaque, Relief Castle Scene, W.S.& S., 9 In. 83.00
  Umbrella Stand, Oriental, Relief Dragon, Cylindrical, 24 In. 50.00
  Vase, Flying Dragon Design, Oriental Signed, 11 1/2 In., Pair 135.00

Textile includes many types of printed textiles, table and household linens, and clothing. Some other textiles will be found under Coverlet, Rug, Quilt, etc.

TEXTILE, Afghan, Knitted Squares, Crocheted Edge, 63 X 41 In. 25.00
  Altar Cloth, Gold & Silver Embroidery, Turquoise, Silk, Calligraphy 350.00
  Apron, Tucks & Crochet Lace Bottom, White, Long 23.00
  Banner, Kelly Springfield Steam Road Rollers 90.00
  Banner, William Penn, Bicentennial 1882, Black & White, Flag Shape 80.00
  Bathing Costume, Black, Sateen, 2 Piece 35.00
  Bed Jacket, Lace Inserts & Trim, Eyelet 120.00
  Bedcover, Handworked, Crocheted Flowers, 7 Ft. 2 In. X 7 Ft. 8 In. 650.00
  Bedspread, Battenburg Lace, 90 X 90 In., Pair 350.00
  Bedspread, Candlewick, Floral Design, White, Signed, 88 X 102 In. 200.00
  Bedspread, Crocheted, 72 X 92 In. 135.00
  Bedspread, Crocheted, Geometric Design, Eggshell, 66 X 72 In. 69.50
  Bedspread, Crocheted, Hand Knotted, Fringe On 2 Sides, Large 165.00
  Bedspread, Crocheted, Pineapple Pattern, Fringed, 6 X 8 Ft. 75.00
  Bedspread, Hand Woven, Counterpane, 76 X 80 In. 110.00
  Bedspread, Marseilles Trapunto Style, Dated 1/21/19, Square, 83 In. 70.00
  Bedspread, Muslin, Hand Embroidered Peacocks, 76 X 86 In. 65.00
  Bedspread, Trapunto Style, White, Pat.Dated 1/21/19, 83 In. 70.00
  Bedspread, Trapunto, Marseilles, Crib 95.00
  Bedspread, Woven Stripes, Figures, Central Star, 88 X 102 In. 50.00
  Blanket, Canada, Hand Woven, Central Star, Wool, 68 X 101 In. 150.00
  Bloomers, Tatted Edge, Long 20.00
  Blouse & Skirt, Lace Trim, Long Skirt, White, 1800s 60.00
  Blouse, Embroidered Leaves, Lace Edging, White 14.00
  Blouse, Lady's, Batiste, Tucks & Lace 35.00

Blouse, Victorian, Crochet, Irish 210.00
Blouse, White Net Oversewn Lace, High Neck, Tight Wrists, C.1895 .... 125.00
Boa, Silver Fox, Glass Eyes 27.00
Bodice, Handmade Lace Insert & Trim, Ecru Silk, C.1850 .... 85.00
Bonnet, Chambray, Blue 30.00
Bonnet, Child's, Lace 35.00
Bonnet, Gray Check 24.00
Bonnet, Lady's, Amish, Wool, 1930s 55.00
Bonnet, Lady's, Velvet, 1900s 22.00
Bonnet, Pioneer, Silk, Black Quilted 30.00
Camisole, Crocheted Trim 18.00
Camisole, Tatting Trim, Satin, Pink 38.00
Cap, Prayer, Amish 10.00
Cape, Black Velvet, White Rabbit Fur Trim 25.00
Cape, Handmade, Black Satin, Wide Braided Lace, Beaded Neck 65.00
Cape, Lady's, Silk Brocade, Red Silk Lining, 1870 .... 55.00
Cape, Long, Black Velvet, 1930s 50.00
Cape, Long, Woolen, Brown, Monkey Fur Trim, Silk Lining, 1880s 85.00
Cape, Victorian, Jet Black Beading, Fur Trim, Black 30.00
Cloak, Velvet, Brown, Knotted Fringes, C.1860, 38 In. 55.00
Cloth, Bridge, Linen, Cutwork, Lace 22.00
Cloth, Embroidered Butterfly Design, Fringe, Round, 33 In. 38.50
Coat, Braiding, Black Velvet, 1905 .... 95.00
Coat, Child's, Victorian, Black, Crushed Velvet, Fur Buttons 38.00
Coat, Child's, White, Waffle Pique, Capelet, Trim, 1880, Size 2 .... 50.00
Coat, Fox Trim, Green Velvet, 1920s 70.00
Coat, Militia, Blue Wool, Seal Buttons, Chevrons On Cuff, C.1875 .... 250.00
Coat, Velvet, Shirred Collar & Sleeves, 1920s 50.00
Collar, Battenburg Lace 30.00
Cover, Table, Battenburg Lace Center, Cluny Edging, 40 In.Diam. 72.00
Doily, Crocheted, Butterflies, Ecru, Round, 15 In. 12.00
Doily, U.S.Army 12.00
Dress, Black Crepe, Beading, Bodice & Skirt, Padded Shoulders, 1940s 30.00
Dress, Black Crepe, Gored Skirt, 1940s 15.00
Dress, Bridesmaid, Street Length, Pink, Crepe, Lace, Hat, Mitts, 1940s 58.00
Dress, Brown Luster, Puffed Sleeves, Train, Copper Lining, 1860s 55.00
Dress, Calico, Brown 80.00
Dress, Christening, Embroidered Wool Petticoat, Bonnet, Victorian 125.00
Dress, Christening, Lace Collar & Sleeve Trim 28.00
Dress, Christening, Made In 1820, 43 In. 65.00
Dress, Christening, Matching Petticoat, Lace, Tucks 70.00
Dress, Christening, Victorian, Cotton, Embroidered Eyelet, 38 In. 75.00
Dress, Crushed Velvet, Brown, 1920s 28.00
Dress, Dinner, Long, French, Black Velvet, 1960s 25.00
Dress, Embroidery On Bodice, Sleeves, & Hem, Silk Satin, C.1905 .... 450.00
Dress, Evening, Bat Sleeves, Rhinestones, V Neck, Blue Velvet, 1930s 50.00
Dress, Evening, Tassels & Lace, C.1900 .... 150.00
Dress, Evening, Wide Skirt, Green Net, C.1913 .... 125.00
Dress, Flapper, Glass Beads On Netting, Blue Diamond Pattern 62.00
Dress, Girl's, Amish, Tan 30.00
Dress, Halter, Rayon, Paisley Skirt, 1950s 125.00
Dress, Lace, Pink, Separate Slip, Padded Shoulders, 1940s 18.00
Dress, Lady's, Black Wool, Applique, C.1890, 2 Piece 125.00
Dress, Lady's, Victorian, Gray, Modified Bustle, 2 Piece 40.00
Dress, Lawn, White, Lace Trim, Tucked, Victorian 185.00
Dress, Mini, Anne Fogarty, Gold Threaded, 1960s 35.00
Dress, Off Shoulder, Rhinestone Bodice, Black Velvet, 1940s 20.00
Dress, Sequins, Black Lace, 1930s 60.00
Dress, Silk, Lace, & Chiffon, Black, 1920s 85.00
Dress, Tea, Jacket, Oversewn Net, White, C.1915 .... 175.00
Dress, Tea, White, Embroidery, Net, C.1900, Size 10–12 .... 85.00
Dress, Victorian, Scalloped Trim On Top, White, Long 30.00
Duster, Driving, Cotton, Yellow 45.00
Duster, Driving, Lady's, Linen, Beige ....45.00 To 55.00

Embroidery, Betsy Ross Making Flag, Anderson Bros., 13 X 10 In. 100.00
Embroidery, Floral Wreath, 1856, Framed, 17 1/2 In. 200.00
Embroidery, On Silk, Oval, Framed, C.1810, 17 X 13 1/2 In. 375.00
Embroidery, Silk, Painted, Girl With Rake, Oval, C.1830 .... 95.00
Embroidery, Statue Of Liberty, White Satin, France, 16 In. 600.00
Gown, Evening, Lace, Net, Wine, Drop Waist, Wide Shoulders, 1935 .... 150.00
Gown, Evening, Strapless, Pink Net, Floor Length, 1950s 55.00
Gown, Servant's, Black & White Gingham, Full–Length 10.00
Gown, Tea, Pink & White Polka Dot, 1880s 36.00
Gown, Wedding, Beaded, Bustle Back, Headpiece, Veil, Shoes, 1940s 98.00
Gown, Wedding, Fan Lace, Cocktail Length, Hoop, Headpiece, 1950s 50.00
Gown, Wedding, Short Front, Long Back, Beaded Neckline, Satin, 1920s 85.00
Gym Suit, Bloomer, Black 30.00
Hair Bow, Black Velvet, Comb, Peck & Peck 5th Ave., Box 12.50
Handkerchief, England, Washington, Adams, & Jefferson, 32 X 25 In. 700.00
Handkerchief, Printed George Washington, Brown, Natural, C.1800 .... 425.00
Handkerchief, Raggedy Ann, Characters, Set Of 2 .... 20.00
Handkerchief, Skippy, 1930s 10.00
Hat, Campaign, Indian Wars, Wide Brim 300.00
Hat, Graduation, College, Tassel, Dated 1897 .... 10.00
Hat, Hattie Carnegie, Breton 28.00
Hat, Top, Folding, Black, Pop–Up Type, C.1890 .... 100.00
Hat, Velvet, Trimmed, 1880s 25.00
Hat, Visor, Spanish American War 58.00
Headdress, Set Of Ear Decorations, Beaded, Chinese 85.00
Homespun, Red, White, & Blue, 31 X 110 In. 270.00
Jacket & Vest, Cutaway Tails, Wool, Fancy Buttons, Dated 1914 .... 85.00
Jacket, Man's, Cutaway Tails, Wool, C.1900 .... 50.00
Jacket, Smoking, 1915 .... 35.00
Jock Strap, Johnson & Johnson, Little League, Boxed, 1940s 10.00
Kimono, Lined, Hand Printed & Embroidered Flowers, Silk 45.00
Kimono, Silk, Pastel Embroidered Butterflies, Light Ground 95.00
Kimono, World War II, Silk 25.00
Knickers, Boy's, Patterned, 1920s 8.00
Knickers, Man's, Linen 36.00
Needlepoint, Child With Dog, Satinwood Frame, 10 In. 165.00
Needlework, U.S.S.Cleveland, Matted, Framed, 18 X 22 1/2 In. 225.00
Net, Bu–Bee–Net, Crib, Original Envelope 30.00
Nightgown, Long, Short Sleeve, Voile, 1920s 24.00
Nightgown, Satin, 1930s 15.00
Nightgown, Wedding, Lace Bodice, C.1880 .... 20.00
Panel, Crocheted, Eagle & Stars, God Bless America, 17 X 19 In. 42.00
Panel, Door, Peacock, Lace, 1920–30 .... 16.00
Panel, Hawk, Needlepoint, Flowers, Mesh Ground, Frame, 30 X 22 In. 160.00
Panel, Pointe De Gaze Lace, Rose, 19th Century, 10 In.X 16 Ft. 400.00
Panel, Silk, Aubusson, Basket Of Flowers, Birds, French, 20 X 48 In. 260.00
Pantaloons, Black, Wool 10.00
Pantaloons, Lace On Lace 10.00
Pennant, Baltimore Orioles, 1970, World Champions 5.00
Petticoat, Child's, Crocheted Lace, 1930s 16.00
Petticoat, Organdy, Eyelet Ruffle, 1950s 25.00
Petticoat, Victorian, Batiste, Deep Ruffle, Large Size 45.00
Pillow Sham, Embroidered, Angels Sing Thee, Rest, Red, Pair 45.00
Pillow Sham, Good Morning 9.00
Pillow, Painted, Embroidered, Autumn Leaf Colors, Outlined, 18 In. 16.50
Robe, Chinese, Embroidered, Made For Bonwit Teller, China, 1920s 300.00
Robe, Embroidered Silk, Chinese, Figural Panels, 19th Century 200.00
Runner, Battenburg Lace, 18 X 52 In. 95.00
Runner, Battenburg Lace, 3 Squares Down Center, 19 X 52 In. 78.00
Runner, Battenburg Lace, Grape & Leaf Border, 24 X 80 In. 145.00
Runner, Christmas, People, Houses, Churches, Linen, Oval, 48 X 21 In. 12.00
Scarf, Bunnies, Easter Basket, Lace Border, 31 1/2 In. 22.00
Shawl, Embroidered Pink Floral On Light Pink Silk, 50 X 50 In. 80.00
Shawl, Fringe, Wool, 52 X 52 In. 25.00

Shawl, Paisley, Multicolor, 1900, 64 X 64 In. 60.00
Shawl, Piano, Embroidered Flowers, Black Silk, Square, 50 In. 150.00
Shawl, Pointe De Gaze Lace, Iris, Roses, 1800s, 21 X 8 Ft. 300.00
Shawl, White Embroidery On White Silk, Fringe, 24 X 58 In. 60.00
Shawl, Wool Paisley, 72 X 32 In. 78.00
Shirt, Man's, Collarless, White 6.00
Shoe, Boy's, Black, Brass Pegs, 1850 .... 36.00
Shoes, Baby, White, Tie, 1920s 10.00
Shoes, Gray Suede, C.1920, Size 6 1/2 .... 25.00
Shoes, Lady's, Black, Lace, High Top 35.00
Skirt, Felt, 1950s 23.00
Skirt, Poodle Holding Basket Of Flowers, Pink 85.00
Skirt, Ribbed Velvet, Green, Peacock Eyes Appliqued, C.1910 .... 95.00
Skirt, Walking, Victorian, Gray Linen 45.00
Smock, Farmer's, Wool, Blue, 18th Century 150.00
Suit, Boy's, White Corded, 2 Piece, 1860–80 .... 30.00
Suit, Uncle Sam, Cotton, Cutaway Coat, Applied Paper Stars & Pants 65.00
Sweater, Lone Star Rider, Cowboy, Unused, 1940s 10.00
Tablecloth, Battenburg Center, Satin Stitched Floral Edge, 40 In. 115.00
Tablecloth, Battenburg Lace, 28 X 28 In. 45.00
Tablecloth, Battenburg Lace, Round, 50 In. ....55.00 To 110.00
Tablecloth, Battenburg, 8 Napkins, White, 68 X 88 In. 200.00
Tablecloth, Crocheted, 52 X75 In. 40.00
Tablecloth, Crocheted, 72 X 92 In. 125.00
Tablecloth, Crocheted, 80 X 60 In. 125.00
Tablecloth, Crocheted, Cluny Lace, Butterfly Center, 52 X 74 In. 175.00
Tablecloth, Crocheted, Medallions, Ecru, 72 X 62 In. 89.50
Tablecloth, Crocheted, Pineapple, Round, 24 In. 10.00
Tablecloth, Crocheted, Rosette Design, Eggshell, 56 X 79 In. 79.50
Tablecloth, Crocheted, Wide Border, Linen Center, Round, 50 In. 125.00
Tablecloth, Cutwork & Lace, Linen, Round, 68 In. 115.00
Tablecloth, Drawnwork Center, Battenburg Lace, Square, 29 In. 115.00
Tablecloth, Embroidered, Cutwork, Italian, 12 Napkins, 66 X 122 In. 1500.00
Tablecloth, Floral Design, White, 72 X 102 In. 125.00
Tablecloth, Gold & White, Hand Hemming, Homespun, 40 X 67 In. 125.00
Tablecloth, Hand Crocheted, Lacy, White, 45 X 80 In. 85.00
Tablecloth, Hand Crocheted, White, 72 X 124 In. 50.00
Tablecloth, Hand Tatting Each End, Linen, 68 X74 In. 20.00
Tablecloth, Handwork, 12 Napkins, Unused, 66 X 132 In. 600.00
Tablecloth, Homespun, Wheat, Red Embroidery, 55 X 70 In. 90.00
Tablecloth, Lace Portrait Center, Round, 29 In. 40.00
Tablecloth, Lace, 58 X 76 In. 165.00
Tablecloth, Lace, Crocheted, 74 X 90 In. 100.00
Tablecloth, Lacy Openwork, 72 X 96 In. 30.00
Tablecloth, Needlework & Cutwork, Drawn Squares, Ecru, 8 Ft. 4 In. 175.00
Tablecloth, Overall Symmetrical Floral & Scroll, 11 X 5 1/2 Ft. 200.00
Tablecloth, Paisley, Brown & Red, 132 X 63 In. 65.00
Tablecloth, Polychrome Embroidered, Needlework Edge, Square, 7 Ft. 150.00
Tapestry Panel, Tree Landscape, Garden, Border, Belgium, 94 X 25 In. 425.00
Tapestry Panel, Waterfall Scene, France, 18th Century, 76 X 49 In. 475.00
Tapestry, Arabian Dancing Girl, Village Scene, 25 X 33 In. 50.00
Tapestry, Aubusson, Courting Couple, 5 Ft.4 In. X 7 Ft.4 In. 1870.00
Tapestry, Bride & Groom, Marriage Contract, C.1900, 58 X 34 In. 650.00
Tapestry, Cherub & Floral Pattern, Gold Fringe, 8 X 6 1/2 Ft. 50.00
Tapestry, Country Woman, Game, Wool, Silk, Beads, Framed, 19 X 38 In. 400.00
Tapestry, Deer & Forest Scene, Belgium, 48 X 72 In. 55.00
Tapestry, Pastoral Dancer & Friends, Petit Point, 27 X 35 In. 350.00
Tapestry, Spanish Courtyard Scene, Belgium, 37 1/2 X 19 In. 18.00
Tapestry, Temple Scene, People Inside Temple, 80 X 50 In. 200.00
Tapestry, Victorian Scene, Belgium, 27 X 37 1/2 In. 65.00
Tapestry, Watteausque Scene, Painted, Signed S.H.Fisher, 51 X 29 In. 30.00
Towel, Dated 1831 .... 325.00
Towel, Linen, Show, Elisa Bethwolf, Dated 1821 .... 50.00
Towel, Show, Peacocks, Floral, Elizabeth Binkley, Dated 1832, 58 In. 160.00

Wall Hanging, Lace, Discoverer,
Father Of Our Country, 36 × 36 In.

Thermometer, Doans,
Black & White, Wood,
C.1935, 20 In.

Trousers, Amish, Young Boy's, Drop Front	50.00
Underwear, Lady's, Feedsack, Homemade, 1 Piece	10.00
Uniform, British, Dress, Royal Artillery, C.1855, 3 Piece	110.00
Uniform, Maid's, Chambray, Gray, 1915	30.00
Uniform, TWA Stewardess, 1970s	30.00
Vest, Silk, Cream Brocade, Embroidered, Floral, Chinese, 19th Century	160.00
Wall Hanging, Appliqued, Flowering Vine, Birds, Ruffle, 6 Ft. 2 In.	450.00
Wall Hanging, Lace, Discoverer, Father Of Our Country, 36 X 36 In. ....*Illus*	55.00
Wall Hanging, Needlework, Flying Ducks, Trees, C.1930, 65 X 30 In.	70.00
Wall Hanging, Silk, Wax Resist, Woman, Dog, Brown, Green, 43 X 40 In.	150.00
Window Shade, Hudson Valley Painting, Linen	375.00

The thermometer was invented in 1731. It measures temperature of either water or air. All kinds of thermometers are collected, but those with advertising messages are the most popular.

THERMOMETER, 7–Up, Round	25.00
Arbuckles Coffee, Pound Package, Tin	185.00
Atlas Beer, Eagle On Western Hemisphere, Enamel	125.00
Biltrite Heels & Soles, Shoemaker, Heel, 4 X 13 In.	85.00
Buick Motor Cars	175.00
Carter's Ink, Porcelain	100.00
Dad's Root Beer, Box	20.00
DeLaval Cream Separator, C.1910, Wooden	235.00
Desk, Classical Woman Leaning On Pedestal, Bronze	75.00
Doans, Black & White, Wood, C.1935, 20 In. ....*Illus*	65.00
Doctor Scholl's, Porcelain, Hand Pointing To Foot, 1916	125.00
Drink Bireley's, 26 X 10 In.	45.00
Duffy's Pure Malt Whiskey, Picture Of Old Chemist	125.00
Ex–Lax, 8 X 39 In.	9.50
Ex–Lax, Porcelain, Prescriptions, Drugs, 36 In.	135.00
Ex–Lax, Red, White, & Blue, 3 Ft.	110.00
Figural, Black Man, Multiproducts, 1941	17.50
Fish, Brass	15.00
Fitger Brewing	18.00
Folger's Coffee, Pound Can, 9 In.	75.00
Great American Insurance Co., Capital 125, 000, Metal, 9 In.	45.00
Havoline, 1933	24.00
Hawthorne Coal, Choice Of Thrifty Buyers, 36 In.	70.00
Hills Bros.Coffee, Robed Turk Sipping Coffee	200.00
John Deere	8.00
Johnstown Bank, Brass, Round	35.00
Lucas Service Imported Cars	20.00

Mail Pouch Tobacco, Porcelain, 3 In.	55.00
Millington Naval Base, Memphis, Figural, Sea Captain, 4 In.	20.00
Mission Orange, 1950, 5 X 17 In.	20.00
Morton Salt, 6 X 16 In.	6.00
Nature's Remedy, Porcelain	125.00
Nehi, 15 In.	25.00
Nesbitts Orange Drink, 22 In.	40.00
None Such Pie, Figural, New England Mince Meat Pie, 1888	145.00
Old Dutch Root Beer, 1950s, 7 X 20 In.	35.00
Orange Crush, Wooden, 1937	30.00 To 37.50
Parodi Cigars, Kid, Bottle	30.00
Pollack Wheeling Stogies, Porcelain, 39 X 8 In.	85.00
Prestone Anti-Freeze, Porcelain, Round, Canada	85.00
R.C.Cola, Tin, 13 X 6 In.	10.00
R.R.Mills Snuff, 6 X 16 In.	6.00
Ramon's Pine Brownie Pills, Little Doctor Brings Happy Days	235.00
Red Goose Shoes	55.00
Red Top Wool, 16 X 27 In.	45.00
Rochester Brewing, Round, 12 In.	49.00
Saver's Flavoring Extracts, Wooden, Bottle, Box Picture	140.00
Squirt, Embossed Bottle, Squirt Kid, 5 X 13 In.	30.00
Stegmier Beer, Tin, Spring, 12 In.	42.50
Stethenson Union Suits, Porcelain, Man In Long Johns, 1916	245.00
Tuck's Chewing Tobacco, Tin, Pictures Package	115.00
Universal Batteries, Since 1899, 8 X 38 In.	65.00
Weatherbird Shoes, Tin	45.00
Yellow Cab, Wooden	35.00
Yuengling, Round, 12 In.	35.00

Tiffany glass was made by Louis Comfort Tiffany, the American glass designer who worked from about 1879 to 1933. His work included iridescent glass, Art Nouveau styles of design, and original contemporary styles. He was also noted for his stained glass windows, his unusual lamps, bronze work, pottery, and silver. Other types of Tiffany are listed under Tiffany Pottery, Tiffany Silver, or Tiffany. The famous Tiffany lamps are under Tiffany, Lamp. Reproductions of some types of Tiffany are being made.

TIFFANY GLASS, Bottle, Cologne, Double Lobed Stopper, Bulbous, Signed, 10 In. 750.00

Bowl & Tray, Gold, Fluted Tray, Signed, Bowl 9 1/2 In.	750.00
Bowl, 2 Flower Frogs, Iridescent Gold, 3 X 10 In. *Illus*	550.00
Bowl, Blue & Gold Iridescent, Scalloped, Signed, 8 1/2 In.	225.00
Bowl, Blue, 10 X 4 In.	540.00

Tiffany Glass, Bowl, 2 Flower Frogs,
Iridescent Gold, 3 X 10 In.

Tiffany Glass, Vase, Iridescent Gold,
Green Ivy, Marked, 7 In.

Bowl, Favrile, Blue, Green, Silver, Ribbed, 6 In. 500.00
Bowl, Favrile, Deep Ribs, Ruffled Top, Green, Silver, 2 1/2 In. 500.00
Bowl, Flower, Favrile, 2–Tier Holder, Signed, 2 X 11 1/2 In. 1250.00
Bowl, Gold Iridescent, Signed, 6 1/2 X 3 In. 255.00
Bowl, Gold, Marked, 8 In. 750.00
Bowl, Green & Silver Tones, Ribbed, Base, Blue 2 1/2 In. 500.00
Bowl, Green Leaves, Signed, 8 X 3 1/4 In. 800.00
Bowl, Pedestal, Gold Iridescent, Signed, 9 3/4 In. 325.00
Bowl, Ruffled, Purple Iridescent, Signed, 9 7/8 In. 650.00
Bowl, Scalloped, Gold Iridescent, Signed, 6 In. 375.00
Bowl, Shallow, Peacock Blue, Signed & Numbered, 5 In. 425.00
Bowl, Swirled Ribbed Design, Signed, 6 1/2 In. 325.00
Box, Open, Marbelized Pattern, Bronze Rim, Signed, 6 X 2 In. 300.00
Champagne, Faceted Stem, Foot & Cup Pattern, 5 In. 250.00
Champagne, Gold, Favrile, Signed 165.00
Compote, Band Of Intaglio Cut Vines, Signed, 4 1/2 In. 300.00
Compote, Favrile, Laurel Leaf, Clear Stem, Signed, 5 3/4 In. 525.00
Compote, Optic Pattern Of Laurel Leaves, Pastel, Signed 525.00
Compote, Pastel Turquoise, Signed, 4 1/2 In. 435.00
Compote, Rolled Rim, Twisted Stem, Signed, Label, 7 1/2 In. 450.00
Cordial, Applied Lily Pads, Stems Go To Bottom, Signed, 2 In. 135.00
Cordial, Gold Iridescent, Signed, Pair 295.00
Dish, Mint, Favrile, Punts, Gold, Red, & Violet, 5 1/2 In. 125.00
Dish, Nut, Favrile, Flared Top, Signed, 1 1/4 In. 125.00
Dish, Scalloped Rim, Signed, 7 1/4 In. 285.00
Dish, Scalloped, Edge, Gold Iridescent, Signed, 6 1/2 In. 110.00
Figurine, Scarab, Iridescent Red, 1 1/2 In. 135.00
Fingerbowl, Plate, Gold Iridescent, Signed L.C.T.1509 .... 375.00
Goblet, Faceted Stem, Foot & Cup In Pattern, 6 In. 275.00
Goblet, Gold, Signed, 3 3/4 In. 450.00
Goblet, Wisteria, Turquoise Ribbed Bowl, Signed, 8 3/4 In. 375.00
Inkwell, Spiderweb, Butterscotch 195.00
Jug, Claret, Monogram, Silver Mount, Hinged Cover, 10 In. 425.00
Parfait, Wisteria, Ribbed Foot, Signed, 6 1/2 In. 350.00
Pitcher, Corset Shape, Blue Iridescent, Signed, 4 1/4 In. 750.00
Plate, Aqua & Opalescent, Signed, 11 In. 245.00
Plate, Opalescent Rays From Center, Pink, Signed, 8 1/2 In. 275.00
Plate, Scalloped, Opalescent White, Signed, 11 In. 250.00
Punch Cup, Gold, Spreading Hollow Stem, Signed, 3 1/2 In. 140.00
Punch Cup, Heart Shaped Leaves, Vines, Gold, Green, Signed 285.00
Salt Dip, Blue Gold, Signed, 2 In. 165.00
Salt, 4 Spread Feet, Gold Iridescence, Signed, 2 1/2 In. 235.00
Salt, Blue Iridescent, Pedestal Foot, Signed, 2 In. 250.00
Salt, Favrile, 4 Spread Feet, Round Body, Signed, 1 1/2 In. 235.00
Salt, Favrile, Gold, Signed, 2 1/2 In. 400.00
Salt, Gold, Iridescent Interior, Pulled Feet, Marked 115.00
Sherbet, Rooster Stem, Cobalt, 4 In., Set Of 8 .... 160.00
Toothpick, Multigreen, Orange Gold Stripes, Signed, 2 In. 315.00
Toothpick, Pigtail Prunts, Gold 285.00
Toothpick, Stripe, Green To Iridescent Blue, 2 1/2 In. 300.00
Vase, Allover Green, Gold Feather, Aventurine Sparkles, 4 In. 725.00
Vase, Allover King Tut Damascene, Signed, Blue, 6 In. 1375.00
Vase, Allover Leaf & Trailing Vine, Signed, 9 In. 1600.00
Vase, Applied Glass Loops At Middle, Signed, 5 1/2 In. 650.00
Vase, Bud, Gold Iridescent, 8 In. 496.00
Vase, Bulbous, Round Foot, Gold Iridescent, Signed, 14 5/8 In. 450.00
Vase, Carved Leaves, Gold Ground, Green Vines, Signed, 9 In. 1750.00
Vase, Dimpled Center, Ribbed Neck, Blue To Black, 3 In. 575.00
Vase, Embossed Leaf, Sterling Silver Rim, Signed, 5 In. 150.00
Vase, Favile, Flower Form, Green Feather, Signed, 11 In. 1400.00
Vase, Favrile, Blue Iridescent, Raised Rib, Signed, 6 1/2 In. 550.00
Vase, Favrile, Flower Form, Green Feather, Ruffled, 11 In. 1400.00
Vase, Favrile, Round Bottom, Slender Neck, Signed, 5 1/2 In. 350.00
Vase, Favrile, Stand–Up Collar, Ribbed, Signed, 4 In. 400.00

Vase, Feather Design, Gold & Green, Signed, 3 3/4 In. 375.00
Vase, Flared At Shoulder, Narrow Neck, Gold, Signed, 3 3/4 In. 295.00
Vase, Flower Form, Blue, Marked, 17 1/2 In. 3000.00
Vase, Flower Form, Bronze Base, Ruffled, Signed, 16 In. 1250.00
Vase, Flower Form, Green Feather Design, Signed, 11 In. 1400.00
Vase, Flower Form, Jack–In–Pulpit, Gold, Marked, 17 In. 3500.00
Vase, Flower Form, Ribbed, Scalloped Rim, Signed, 11 1/2 In. 880.00
Vase, Flower Shape, Deep Gold, Footed, Signed, 9 3/4 In. 850.00
Vase, Funnel Type, Bronze Holder, Signed, Green, 14 1/4 In. 1800.00
Vase, Intaglio Cut Leaves, Vines, 3 Arms, Signed, 7 1/2 In. 2500.00
Vase, Inverted Trumpet, Green Leaves, Gold Luster, 8 1/2 In. 750.00
Vase, Iridescent Gold, Green Ivy, Marked, 7 In. ....*Illus* 750.00
Vase, Iridescent Green To Cobalt, Marked, No.9309, 6 1/2 In. 700.00
Vase, Leaves & Vines, Opal Ground, Narrow Neck, Signed, 5 In. 775.00
Vase, Opal, Pink, Green, & Gold Feathering, Signed, 4 In. 1250.00
Vase, Paneled Body, Iridescent Blue, Signed, 6 In. 550.00
Vase, Pulled Blue Design Over Ruby Ground, Signed, 3 1/4 In. 2100.00
Vase, Ribbed, Iridescent, Gold, Signed, 6 In. 385.00
Vase, Ribbed, Melon Shaped Body, Blue, Signed, 5 1/4 In. 650.00
Vase, Rose Bowl Shape, Leaves, Random Vines, Signed, 2 3/4 In. 625.00
Vase, Squat, Gold & Green Pulled Design, Signed, 4 1/4 In. 700.00
Vase, Striated Green Petals, Gold Outline, Signed, 9 1/2 In. 1550.00
Vase, Trumpet, Morning Glory, Ribbed, Knob Stem, Signed, 11 In. 825.00
Wine, Gold, Signed, 4 In. 150.00

TIFFANY POTTERY, Lamp, Ormolu Trim, Original Silk Shade, 45 In. 1000.00
Vase, Allover Blossoms, Textured, Signed, 5 1/4 In. 450.00
Vase, Deep Aqua, Hearts, Millefiori, Signed, 5 1/2 In. 2750.00
Vase, Inverted Mushroom Shape, Matte Top, Signed, 10 X 7 In 500.00
Vase, Metallic Glaze, Signed, 15 1/2 In. 500.00
Vase, Multishaded, Raised Ribs, Signed, 8 1/2 X 6 1/2 In. 500.00

TIFFANY SILVER, Ashtray, Cherub ....120.00 To 140.00
Box, Signed, 4 1/4 X 3 1/4 In. 195.00
Cake Basket, Filigree Handle 1540.00
Case, Cigarette, Coat Of Arms, Gilt On Silver 75.00
Chatelaine Holder, Art Nouveau, Signed 75.00
Cup, Bouillon, Pierced, Lenox Liner, 2 Handles, Set Of 4 .... 55.00
Cup, Traveling, Leather Case 45.00
Demitasse Set, Pot, Tray, Cream & Sugar 925.00
Dish, Mint, Leaf Shape 80.00
Dresser Set, Gilt, Monogram, 11 Piece 375.00
Flask, Floral Repousse, Marked, Small 160.00
Fork & Spoon, Serving, Flemish Pattern 325.00
Fork, Fish, 1860s 360.00
Fork, Ice Cream, Faneuil, 5 13/16 In., Set Of 8 .... 320.00
Fork, Renaissance, Seminude 95.00
Fork, Salad, Art Nouveau, Seminude 145.00
Goblet, Tall Stem, Domed Base, Conical Bowl, 8 In., Set Of 12 .... 1600.00
Jug, Hot Water, Floral Finial, Handle, 1902–07, 9 1/2 In. 200.00
Knife, Fruit, Boy, Paper Hat, Holding Sword, 1891–1902, 7 In. 50.00
Ladle, Punch, Wave Edge Design 320.00
Lamp, Wax, Handle, Marked 230.00
Loving Cup, Rococo, Handles, Engraved Front, 1891, 9 In. 500.00
Nut Pick, Old French 10.00
Ring, Man's, Scarab, Stamped, Size 8 1/2 .... 275.00
Salt, Repousse, Footed, Pair 250.00
Salt, Ruffled, Footed, Spoon 40.00
Salt, Ruffled, Signed, 2 1/2 In. 125.00
Salver, Little Bopeep, Repousse, Footed, C.1883, 12 In.Square 900.00
Sugar Sifter, Persian 325.00
Tazza, Crackled Iridescence, Footed, Signed, Blue, 9 3/4 In. 400.00

TIFFANY, Ashtray, Bronze, Gold Dore Finish, Signed, 5 1/4 X 4 3/4 In. 135.00

Ashtray, Bronze, Ribbed Handles, Signed, 4 In. 135.00
Ashtray, Curved Design, Cigarette Rest, Signed, 5 1/4 In. 135.00
Ashtray, Floor, Adjustable Height, Tray, Bronze, Signed, 26 In. 550.00
Ashtray, Floor, No.1695, Bronze & Glass, Marked 945.00
Ashtray, Match Safe, Spanish, Signed, 7 In. 195.00
Blotter Ends, Bronze, Zodiac, Gold Dore, 12 In. 87.00
Blotter Ends, Pine Needle, Signed, 2 1/4 In. 200.00
Blotter Ends, Spanish, Signed, 19 1/2 X 2 In. 250.00
Blotter Ends, Zodiac, 19 1/2 In. 150.00
Book Rack, Pine Needle Pattern, Adjustable, Bronze & Glass, Signed 650.00
Bookends, Abalone Shell Discs, Bronze, Signed, 5 1/2 X 5 1/2 In. 495.00
Bookends, Bookmark Pattern, 14K Gold Plate, Signed, 4 3/4 X 6 In. 350.00
Bookends, Patina Finish, Woman Buddha, Signed, 6 X 5 1/2 In. 350.00
Bookends, Woman Buddha, Dark Patina, Signed, 6 In. 350.00
Bowl, Gold Dore Finish, Marine Design, Bronze, Signed, 8 X 4 In. 225.00
Bowl, Grapevine, Bronze Over Green Slag, Signed 950.00
Box, 4 Dividers Inside, Bronze, Signed, 2 1/2 X 4 1/2 In. 95.00
Box, Adams, Polychrome, Bronze, Signed, 4 1/2 X 3 1/2 In. 165.00
Box, Azalea, Beaded Rim, Bronze & Glass, Signed, Square, 7 In. 750.00
Box, Cigarette, Bronze, Blue Enameled Highlights, 4 X 6 X 2 In. 160.00
Box, Copper, Hammered, 3 1/2 X 4 3/4 In. 125.00
Box, Desk, Zodiac, Bronze 115.00
Box, Grapevine Filigree, Green Glass Cover, Bronze, 8 In. 275.00
Box, Grapevine, Bronze & Glass, Signed, 6 1/2 X 4 X 3 In. 450.00
Box, Hammered Copper, Signed, 3 1/2 X 4 3/4 In. 125.00
Box, Hinged Lid, Ferns Over Green Glass, Signed, 5 1/2 X 2 In. 325.00
Box, Indian, Hinged Cover, Signed, 5 1/2 X 3 1/4 In. 295.00
Box, Jewelry, Chinese, Bronze, Signed, 10 X 5 1/2 In. 900.00
Box, Medallion, Gold Dore Finish, Cedar Lining, Hinged, Signed 350.00
Box, Openwork Leaf, Caramel Glass Liner, Hinged Cover, Bronze 425.00
Box, Pine Needle, Amber Glass, Bronze, Signed, 5 1/2 X 2 In. 225.00
Box, Pine Needle, Glass & Bronze, Green, Signed, 6 X 3 In. 450.00
Box, Stamp, Bronze, Marked, 1 3/4 X 2 3/4 In. 120.00
Box, Stamp, Venetian, Bronze, Original Insert ....195.00 To 210.00
Calendar, Desk, Zodiac, Dore 185.00
Candelabra, 4 Arms, Acorn Holder, Bronze, Marked, 14 In, ... 1100.00
Candelabra, Water Lily Base, Double, Bronze, Tiffany Studio, 9 In. 290.00
Candlestick, Bamboo Shoot Ending In 8 Flaring Feet, Bronze, 10 In. 550.00
Candlestick, Blown Glass, Bronze Openings, Signed, 8 1/2 In. 450.00
Candlestick, Blown-Out Glass & Bronze, C.1910, Green Glass, 20 In. 350.00
Candlestick, Bronze, Glass, 3 Ball Feet, Green, Signed, 8 1/2 In. 450.00
Candlestick, Dragon Dolphin Design, Bronze, C.1900, 11 In. 275.00
Chamberstick, Bronze, Glass, Fleur-De-Lis, 2 Arm, Snuffer, 9 In. 900.00
Charger, Blue, Green, & Yellow, Signed, 11 1/2 X 13 1/2 In. 450.00
Clock Garniture, Onyx & Gilt Bronze, 3 Piece 1650.00
Clock, Alabaster, Gilded Bronze Figurines & Trim, 18 X 24 In. 7500.00
Clock, Mantel, Gilt Bronze, Basalt, Moorish, Splayed Base, 26 In. 1265.00
Clock, Mantel, Louis XIV, Bronze, Open Dome Top, Winged Putto, 35 In. 1210.00
Clock, Mantel, Mahogany, Round Case, Scroll Base, 16 In. 600.00
Compote, Butterfly Design, Pedestal, 6 X 6 In. 475.00
Compote, Enamel & Bronze, Green & Yellow, Signed, 7 In. 250.00
Compote, Etched Design In Bronze, Signed, 5 3/4 In. 110.00
Desk Set, Abalone, Bronze, Inkwell, Letter Holder & Blotter 550.00
Desk Set, Bronze & Inlaid Abalone, C1910, 6 Piece 350.00
Desk Set, Zodiac, C.1900, Bronze & Glass, 4 Piece 300.00
Desk Set, Zodiac, Dore, Bronze, Signed, 6 Piece 795.00
Desk Set, Zodiac, Letter Rack, Pen Tray, Postage Scale, Bronze 550.00
Dish, Spider Web, Yellow Ochre & White Panels, Bronze, Glass, 14 In. 500.00
Fern Dish, Marigold, Bronze, Signed, 10 1/2 In. 1210.00
File Clip, Grapevine, Slag Glass, Initialed I.T.H. 135.00
File, Letter, Zodiac, Bronze 275.00
Frame, Desk, Zodiac, Dore 285.00
Frame, Grapevine, Bronze, Glass, Double, 9 1/2 X 8 In. 1500.00
Frame, Heraldic, Bronze, Enamel, Signed, 6 X 5 1/2 In. 225.00

To be sure you have a Tiffany lamp, you must find the words "Tiffany and Co." printed on the metal base. The glass shades were also marked "L. C. Tiffany," or just with the letters "L. C. T." According to the records of the Tiffany Company, all these lamps were marked.

Tiffany, Lamp, Desk, 3 Lily Light, Bronze, Marked, 8 1/4 In.

Frame, Ninth Century, Jeweled & Bronze, Signed 400.00
Frame, Oriental, Bronze, Chinese Scene, Signed, 9 X 6 1/4 In. 500.00
Frame, Pine Needle, Bronze, Glass, Signed, 12 X 14 1/2 In. 1000.00
Glue Jar, Pine Needle, Covered, Urn Body, Signed, 3 In. 225.00
Inkstand, Bronze, Dore, Octagon Shape, Signed 299.00
Inkstand, Bronze, Tiered Panels, Hinged Cover, Signed, 3 3/3 In. 1980.00
Inkstand, Spherical, Bronze Body, Opaque Glass In Openings, 7 In. 660.00
Inkwell & Pen Tray, Zodiac, Glass Insert, Bronze, Signed 750.00
Inkwell, American Indian, Glass, Brass, Signed ....285.00 To 295.00
Inkwell, Art Nouveau, Curved Tray, Signed, Bronze, 8 X 2 1/2 In. 1200.00
Inkwell, Byzantine, Bronze, Jewel, Signed, 4 1/2 In. 1500.00
Inkwell, Chinese, 6 In. 185.00
Inkwell, Crab, Bronze, Claws Open, Signed, Full Size 2800.00
Inkwell, Graduate, Hinged Cover, Bronze, Glass, Signed, Square 225.00
Inkwell, Grapevine, Bronze, Glass, Covered, Signed, 7 In. 600.00
Inkwell, Indian, Sculptured Lines, Masks, Bronze, Signed 300.00
Inkwell, Venetian, Double, 14K Gold Plate, Signed, 5 In. 2800.00
Inkwell, Zodiac, Bronze 225.00
Jar, Geometric, Bronze, Signed, 2 1/4 In. 95.00
Ladle, Mustard, Jeweled, Footed, Gaston Mold 195.00

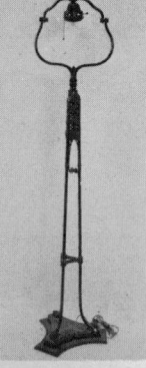

Tiffany, Lamp, Bridge, Harp Design, Marked, 55 In.

Tiffany, Lamp, Desk, Balance, Bronze, Marked, 14 X 7 In.

Lamp, 4 Gold Shades, Bronze Base, Signed, 30 In. 5500.00
Lamp, 7 Tulip Shades, Bronze Base, Water Lily Leaves, 21 In. 5000.00
Lamp, Acorn, Bronze, Signed, 19 In. 8750.00
Lamp, Bamboo Candlestick, 8 Tree Trunks, Signed, 15 In. 950.00
Lamp, Band Of Dragonflies, Wings, Signed, Glass & Bronze, 20 In. 17600.00
Lamp, Bridge, Harp Design, Marked, 55 In. ....*Illus* 500.00
Lamp, Bronze Base No.614, Drapery Glass Shade, Signed, Amber 1375.00
Lamp, Candle, Bronze, Red & Blue Shade, Signed, 18 1/2 X 5 1/2 In. 1050.00
Lamp, Candle, Domed Apricot Glass Shade, Filigree, Metal Overlay 125.00
Lamp, Candle, Favrile, Gold Iridescent, Ribbed Body, Signed, 16 In. 1000.00
Lamp, Candle, Gold, Damascene Shade, Signed, 1920, 12 1/2 In. 625.00
Lamp, Candle, Ruffled, Stretch Glass, Bronze Base, Signed, 18 1/2 In. 900.00
Lamp, Candle, Shade, Art Nouveau, Signed 250.00
Lamp, Candle, Twisted Ribbed Body, Flanged, Signed, Electric, 16 In. 1000.00
Lamp, Candle, Twisted Ribbed Body, Gold Iridescent, Signed, 13 In. 900.00
Lamp, Candle, Twisted Ribbed Body, Signed, Electric, 13 In. 900.00
Lamp, Candlestick, Bamboo, Bronze Base, Patina Finish, Signed, 15 In. 950.00
Lamp, Candlestick, Bronze Base, Pastel Shades, Signed, 15 In., Pair 1500.00
Lamp, Candlestick, Fitted Shade, Gold Feathers, Bronze, 18 In. 1050.00
Lamp, Candlestick, Turtleback Shades, 2 Arm, Signed, 19 X 19 In. 2500.00
Lamp, Desk, 3 Lily Light, Bronze, Marked, 8 1/4 In. ....*Illus* 650.00
Lamp, Desk, Balance, Bronze, Marked, 14 X 7 In. ....*Illus* 1300.00
Lamp, Desk, Bronze Base, Arms, Ribbed Foot, Glass Shade, 14 1/2 In. 2640.00
Lamp, Desk, Bronze Base, Gold Dore Finish, Bronze Finial, 14 1/2 In. 1200.00
Lamp, Desk, Bronze, Wire Mesh, Green, White, Blue Enameled, 17 1/2 In. 850.00
Lamp, Desk, Chinese Red, Gold Iridescent, 14 1/2 In. 1200.00
Lamp, Desk, Counter Balance, Signed, Glass & Bronze, 16 In. 3740.00
Lamp, Desk, Dragonfly Shade, Signed 22000.00
Lamp, Desk, Flared Red Iridescent Shade, Bronze Base, 14 1/2 In. 1200.00
Lamp, Desk, Gold Dore Finish, Elongated Shade, Signed & Numbered 650.00
Lamp, Desk, Liberty Bell, Bronze Base, Blue Glass, Signed, 14 3/4 In. 3500.00
Lamp, Desk, Ruffled Shade, Adjustable, Bronze Base, Signed 975.00
Lamp, Desk, Stretch At Lower Rim Of Shade, Bronze Base, 14 In. 1200.00
Lamp, Drapery Glass Shade, Amber, Bronze Base, Signed 1375.00
Lamp, Etched Bronze Base, 5–Footed, Glass Shade, Signed, 13 1/2 In. 1430.00
Lamp, Fleur–De–Lis, Leaded Shade, Bronze Beaded Border, 21 In. 6500.00
Lamp, Floor, Bronze Base, Ashtray, Geometric Pattern Shade, 56 In. 950.00
Lamp, Floor, Bronze, No.432, Harp On Standard, 3 Spade Feet, C.1910 .... 600.00
Lamp, Floor, Greek Key Rim On Shade, Tripod Platform, Signed 8500.00
Lamp, Floor, Turtleback Tiles, Green, Brass, Marked, 63 In. ....*Illus* 8000.00
Lamp, Gold Iridescent Shades, Signed, 7 1/2 In., Pair 1200.00
Lamp, Harp, American Indian, Bronze Base, Gold Shade, 7 In. 1500.00
Lamp, Kerosene, Gold Swirled Base, Damascus Shade, Green, 17 In. 1850.00
Lamp, Lily, 3 Gold Shades, Bronze Base, Signed, 13 In. 3500.00
Lamp, Mosque, Feathered Shade, Gold Dore Bronze, Signed, 8 1/2 In. 1800.00
Lamp, Shade, Etched Silver, Signed 2100.00
Lamp, Shade, Lily, Yellow, Ribbed, Scalloped, 4 1/2 In., Set Of 6 .... 4950.00
Lamp, Student, Adjustable, Bronze Base, Gold Shade, 19 1/2 In. 1375.00
Lamp, Student, Stick Bronze Body, Damascene Swirl Shade, 19 1/2 In. 2500.00
Lamp, Table, 65 Gold Prisms, Bronze Body, Signed, 24 In. 3500.00
Lamp, Table, Arrowroot, Green, White Blossoms, Signed, 25 In. 9000.00
Lamp, Table, Bronze Petal Platform, 3 Arms Hold Shade, Signed 800.00
Lamp, Table, Fleur–De–Lis, Green & White, Orange Pattern, 16 In. 4600.00
Lamp, Table, Greek Key, Leaded Shade, Bronze Base, Signed, 24 1/2 In. 5500.00
Lamp, Table, Peacock Blue, Amber, No.1474–44, 1910, 25 In. 5300.00
Lamp, Table, Woodbine, Green Leaves, Pink, Brown, Signed, 23 In. 8000.00
Lamp, Table, Yellow Blossoms, Mottled, Bronze Base, Signed, 21 In. 8000.00
Letter Opener, Abalone, Discs Set In Design, Signed, 10 In. 200.00
Letter Opener, Adam, Design On Curved Handle, Signed, 10 In. 165.00
Letter Opener, Ninth Century, Gold Dore, Signed, 10 1/4 In. 165.00
Letter Opener, Venetian, Gold Dore, Signed, 10 1/4 In. 165.00
Letter Rack, Grapevine, 2 Compartments, Signed, 6 1/2 X 10 In. 400.00
Letter Rack, Grapevine, Bronze, Glass, Signed, 7 X 8 In. 500.00
Letter Rack, Ninth Century, Bronze, Glass, Jewels, Signed 400.00
Letter Rack, Spider Web, Etched Glass 225.00

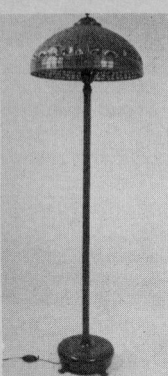

Tiffany, Lamp, Floor, Turtleback Tiles, Green, Brass, Marked, 63 In.

Tiffany, Shade, Leaded Glass, Dogwood Blossoms, 22 1/2 In.

Magnifying Glass, Chinese, Signed	275.00
Magnifying Glass, Graduate, Signed	275.00
Magnifying Glass, Venetian, Signed	275.00
Magnifying Glass, Zodiac, Gold Dore Finish, Signed	275.00
Match Hoder, Geometric Pattern In Corners, Bronze, 2 1/4 In.	65.00
Match Holder, Grapevine, Bronze, Initialed I.T.H., 2 1/2 In.	165.00
Match Safe & Ashtray, Zodiac, Signed & Numbered, Bronze	125.00
Match Safe, Bronze, Geometric Pattern, 2 1/4 In.	65.00
Match Safe, Fleur–De–Lis, Hinged, Blue, Pink Enamel, 1 1/2 In.	125.00
Mirror, Leaded Glass & Bronze, Peacock, Signed, 12 1/2 In.	7150.00
Note Pad Holder, Grapevine, Wood Backing, Signed, 7 3/4 X 5 In.	275.00
Note Pad Holder, Jeweled, Bronze, Signed, 17 X 4 In.	300.00
Paper Clip, Zodiac, Bronze, Gold Dore, Signed	90.00
Paperweight, Animal, Bronze, Shando, Signed, 2 1/4 X 3 1/2 In.	450.00
Paperweight, Figural, Bulldog, Bronze, Green Patina	300.00 To 350.00
Paperweight, Figural, Hippopotamus, Bronze	225.00
Paperweight, Figural, Lion, Bronze, Patina, Signed, 2 1/2 X 7 In.	650.00
Paperweight, Figural, Turtleback, Bronze Base, Signed, 6 In.	950.00
Paperweight, Pine Needle, Signed, 3 1/2 In.	325.00
Pen Brush, Grapevine, Signed, 1 1/2 X 2 1/4 In.	150.00
Pen Holder, Easel Style, Glass, Bronze, Pine Needle Pattern, 5 In.	350.00
Pen Tray, Adam, Gold Dore Finish, Signed, Oval, 4 X 3 In.	125.00
Pen Tray, Grapevine, 4 Bronze Ball Feet, Signed, 9 1/2 In.	150.00
Pen Tray, Mosaic & Bronze, Patina Finish, 7 X 3 In.	2200.00
Pen Tray, Pine Needle, 4 Ball Feet, Signed, 9 1/2 In.	150.00
Pen Tray, Venetian, Signed	150.00
Pen Tray, Zodiac, 9 1/2 X 3 In.	95.00 To 137.50
Pen Wiper, Zodiac	135.00
Platter, Gold Dore Finish, Deep Center Well, Bronze, Signed, 9 In.	95.00
Postage Scale, Grapevine, Slag Glass, Initialed I.T.H.	325.00
Shade, Leaded Glass, Dogwood Blossoms, 22 1/2 In. ....*Illus*	13000.00
Tray, Border Design, Bronze, Round, 14 In.	150.00
Tray, Enameled Flower Handles, Gold Door, 10 In.	95.00
Tray, Geometric Pattern Border, Bronze, Signed, 10 In.	225.00
Tray, Gold Dore Finish, Raised Border Design, Bronze, Signed, 12 In.	175.00
Tray, Serving, Bronze, Gold Dore Finish, Signed, 10 In.	225.00
Tray, Serving, Bronze, Gold Dore, Raised Border, Signed, 12 In.	175.00
Tray, Serving, Raised Edge, Gold Dore, Bronze, Signed, 14 In.	200.00
Vase, Bronze Base, Gold Outlined Feather, Signed, 11 3/4 In.	575.00
Vase, Bronze, Gold Finish, Raised Ribs, Signed, 7 In.	250.00
Vase, Foliate Border Rim, Gold Texture, Bronze, No.1767, 9 In.	50.00
Vase, Multicolor Glass, Vitreous Enamel, Signed, 7 In.	1000.00

The Tiffin Glass Company of Tiffin, Ohio, was a subsidiary of the United States Glass Co. of Pittsburgh, Pennsylvania, in 1892. The U.S. Glass Co. went bankrupt in 1963, and the Tiffin plant employees purchased the building and the inventory. They continued running it from 1963 to 1966, when it was sold to Continental Can Company. In 1969, it was sold to Interpace; and in 1980, it was closed. The black satin glass, made from 1923 to 1926, and the stemware of the last twenty years are the best–known products.

TIFFIN, Bottle, Perfume, Hand Painted Florals, Dabber, 6 In.	65.00
Cocktail, Cherokee Rose	12.00
Console Set, Blue Satin, Blown Out Poppies,, 4 Piece	85.00
Console Set, Gold Bands, Art Deco, Black Satin, 4 Piece	225.00
Console, Cherokee Rose, 12 In.	30.00
Goblet, Water, Cherokee Rose	12.00
Pipe, Opalescent, Souvenir Of Akron, Ohio	25.00
Pitcher, Black Satin, 10 In.	55.00
Punch Set, Williamsburg, 12 Cups	295.00
Rose Bowl, Black Satin, Poppies	50.00
Vase, Caralene Poppy, Black Satin, 9 X 8 In.	95.00
Vase, Poppies, Black Satin, 6 In.	30.00
Vase, Poppy, Black Ground, 9 In.	30.00
Vase, Poppy, Black Satin, Bulbous, 5 In.	35.00
Wine, Fuchsia	14.00

Tiles have been used in most countries of the world as a sturdy building material for floors, roofs, fireplace surrounds, and surface toppings. Many of the American tiles are listed in this book under the factory name.

TILE, Abraham Lincoln, Staffordshire, Dated 2/12/09, 6 X 9 In.	235.00
Bounty, Blue & Tan Glaze, Moravian, Square, 4 In.	65.00
Boy With Sheep, Trent, Gallimore, 6 X 18 In.	235.00
Calendar, 1894, Jones, Duffee, & Stratton	35.00
Calendar, McDuffie, M.I.T., 1916	65.00
Child & Lantern Design, Franklin	100.00
Faience, Persian Design, California	275.00
Fireplace, Dr.Becker & Prince, Alpha Factory, Staffordshire	150.00
Fireplace, King Edward, Sampson King, Staffordshire, 12 In.	65.00
Fireplace, Lady Lytteton & Princess, Staffordshire, 1848	150.00
Fireplace, P.Sarsfield, Earl Of Lucan, On Horse, Staffordshire, 14 In.	110.00
Fireplace, Pomona Holding Cornucopia, Staffordshire, 11 In.	115.00
Fireplace, Prince Albert On Horse, Staffordshire, 1840, 8 In.	145.00
Fireplace, Princess Helena & Prince Christian, Staffordshire, 12 In.	49.00
Fireplace, Queen Victoria, King Of Sardinia, Staffordshire, 14 In.	140.00
Fireplace, T.Smith & Wm.Collier In Mortal Combat, Staffordshire, 1860	170.00
Fireplace, Wesley In Pulpit, Staffordshire, 1850, 11 In.	135.00
Fireplace, Wesley, White Robe, Staffordshire, 1850, 8 In.	100.00
Fireplace, William III, On Horse, Staffordshire, 14 In.	110.00
Fireplace, Witch Riding Swan, Staffordshire, 1850, 8 In.	135.00
Floral Relief, Brown, High Glaze, 6 X 6 In.	30.00
Flowers, Batchelder, 7 X 12 In.	100.00
Geometric, Malibu, 6 X 6 In.	25.00
Geometric, S.& S., 6 X 6 In.	25.00
High Relief Heads In Profile, Brown Gloss, International, 6 In., Pair	154.00
Landscape, Tropica, 4 X 4 In.	75.00
Man & Woman, Trent, Signed Broome, Pair	175.00
Multicolor Design, S.& S., 3 X 3 In.	20.00
Nursery Rhyme, Where Are You Going, Pretty Maid, Crane, Mosaic, 6 In.	27.50
Pegasus, Moravian, Framed	85.00
Sailing Ships, Pardee Pottery	55.00
Scenic, Claycraft, 4 X 4 In.	50.00
Sea Monster, Signed, 4 X 6 In.	10.00
Ship Design, Mercer	50.00
Ship, Moresque, 6 X 6 In.	60.00

Stove, Beaver Falls, Pa., Lady In Feathered Hat, Green, 3 In. 20.00
Tea, Souvenir, Grand Rapids, Wis., Wheelock 42.00
Weeping Willow, Bernard Leach 65.00

*Tin has been used to make household containers in America since the
seventeenth century. The first tin utensils were brought from Europe;
but by 1798, tin plate was imported and local tinsmiths made the
wares. Painted tin is called "tole" and is listed separately. Some tin
kitchen items may be found listed under Kitchen. The lithographed
tin containers used to hold food and tobacco are listed under Store,
Tin.*

TINWARE, Ashtray, Figural, Nodding Black Man Smoking Cigar, Signed Austria 35.00
Bottle, Hot Water, 1915 .... 9.00
Box, Cake, Gold Letters, Square, 10 1/2 In. 25.00
Box, Candle, Pinwheel Design, Strap Hangers, American, 5 1/2 In. 150.00
Box, Will, Coffin Shape, Dovetailed 75.00
Bucket, Child's, Lid & Bale 8.00
Chamberstick, Dated 12–3–1912 .... 25.00
Coffeepot, Marked J.P.Nowell, 18 In. 85.00
Coffeepot, Side Spout, 3 In. 45.00
Desk Set, Wood Grained, 5 Piece 55.00
Dipper, Cylindrical, Spout At Each End, Wooden Handle, 17 1/2 In. 15.00
Filler, Oil Lamp, 4 1/2 In. 39.00
Filler, Whale Oil Lamp, Curved Side Spout, Cap 65.00
Foot Warmer, Diamond & Circular, Wooden Posts & Carrying Handle 125.00
Frame, Mother & Baby Picture, Oval, 6 In. 16.00
Holder, Comb & Brush, Mirrored, Victorian 28.00
Holder, Map, Socony, Heavy Gauge 25.00
Ladle, Witch's Hat, 13 In. 19.90
Lamp, Coach, Candle, Beveled Glass, Red Lens, 17 1/2 In., Pair 55.00
Lantern, Candle, Folding, Brown Japanning, Pat. Jan. 24, 1865, 5 In. 85.00
Lantern, Candle, Pierced, Conical Top, Carrying Ring, Glass Panel 45.00
Lantern, Candle, Semicircular, 11 In. 65.00
Map Case, Civil War Period, 2 1/4 X 21 In. 49.00
Mirror, Hired Man's, Hanging, Molded Border, Round 40.00
Mirror, Shaving, Oval, Stand 12.00
Mold, Candle, 2 Tube, Tray Top, Ring, Tube 10 In. 45.00
Mold, Candle, 3 Tube, Round, Crimped 175.00
Mold, Candle, 3 Tube, Vertical Strut Brace, Manson's, 7 1/2 In. 395.00
Mold, Candle, 4 Tube 22.50
Mold, Candle, 6 Tube 60.00
Mold, Candle, 6 Tube, Arched Bracket Base, 9 1/2 In. 95.00
Mold, Candle, 9 Tube, Handle, Widely Spaced 12–In.Tubes 130.00
Mold, Candle, 12 Tube, Ear Handles, 12 In. 60.00
Mold, Candle, 24 Tube, Ear Handles, 10 In. 65.00
Mold, Candle, 36 Tube, Double Strap Handle 195.00
Mold, Candle, 48 Tube, Ear Handles, 10 1/2 In. 175.00
Mold, Candle, Single, Crimped Base, Top, & Handle, 10 1/2 In. 65.00
Pencil Case, Pedagogue, 1800s 135.00
Pitcher, Attached Funnel, 1/2 Gal. 22.00
Plate, Star Spangled Banner, Dated, 10 In. 25.00
Powder Box, Punch Design In Sliding Sleeve, 4 1/2 In. 10.00
Powder Box, Seidlitz 4.00
Rattle, Baby, Long Handle With Whistle, 5 1/2 In. 35.00
Sander, Ink, Asphaltum Finish, 19th Century 58.00
Sander, Ink, Design In Yellow Brush, C.1885 .... 215.00
Saucer, Peter Rabbit, Other Characters 110.00
Sconce, Candle, American, 19th Century, Reflector, 13 1/2 In., Pair 450.00
Sconce, Candle, Crimped Circular Crest, Tin, 13 1/2 In. 75.00
Sconce, Crimped Top Edge, Early 19th Century, 10 In. 95.00
Sconce, Ribbed Back, Crimped Semicircular Crest, 13 In. 125.00
Spice Rack, 1881, Set Of 6 Canisters 35.00
Tray, Tavern, Silhouette, 14 1/2 X 12 1/2 In. 20.00
Trumpet, Hearing, Curved End At Ear, 20 In. 95.00

Because tobacco needs special conditions of humidity and air, it has been stored in special containers since the eighteenth century. The tobacco jar is often made in fanciful shapes.

TOBACCO JAR, Allover Scenes, Boar On Lid, Blue Boar Tobacco, Silver Plate	85.00
Bearded Man With Turban, Impressed Dudson, 6 In.	95.00
Manila Bay & Dewey, Ohio ....*Color*	95.00
Russian Boy, Cossack Hat, German, Large	245.00
Ship, Artist Signed, Crown Devon	125.00
Woman's Head, With Fez, Majolica, Blonde Hair, Cigar In Mouth	100.00

The toby jug is a very special form of pitcher. It is shaped like the full figure of a man or woman. A pitcher that shows just the top half of a person is not correctly called a toby. More examples of toby jugs can be found under Royal Doulton and other factory names.

TOBY JUG, Branch Handle, Staffordshire, 6 In.	65.00
Green, Poilou, 4 1/2 In.	30.00
Man, Seated, Holds Ale Glass, Staffordshire, 8 1/2 In.	155.00
Philpot, Brown Glaze, Limoges, 6 In.	135.00
Shorter & Sons, Artist Signed, Staffordshire, 6 1/2 In.	95.00
Shorter, Staffordshire, C.1940, 5 1/2 In.	65.00
Staffordshire, Ruddy Toper In Tricorn, C.1835, 9 3/4 In.	880.00
Staffordshire, Tricorn, Holding Beaker, Bottle, Pearlware, 7 7/9in.	440.00

Tole is painted tin. It is sometimes called "japanned ware," "pontypool," or "toleware." Most nineteenth-century tole is painted with an orange-red or black background and multicolored decorations. Many recent versions of toleware are made and sold.

TOLE, see also Tinware

TOLE, Box, Bread, Lift Lid, Word Bread, 1920s	37.50
Box, Candle, Hanging, Cylindrical, Hinged Lid, Black Paint, 11 1/2 In.	45.00
Box, Deed, Decorated, 8 In.	230.00
Box, Deed, Hinged Lid, Design, Oval, 6 In.	180.00
Box, Dome Top, Brown Japanning, Yellow Swag, White Band, 4 1/4 In.	55.00
Box, Grapes, Green Foliage, Signed Peter Ompir, Red Ground, 10 3/4 In.	12.50
Box, Hinged Lid, Cylindrical, 5 1/2 X 4 3/4 In.	30.00
Box, Light Green Paint, Red & Green Striping, Floral Design, 9 3/4 In.	12.50
Candleholder, Folding, Stores 3 Candles, 5/8 X 2 X 2 3/4 In.	110.00
Canister, Chinoiserie Figure, Mounted As Lamp, 25 1/2 In., Pair	4290.00
Canister, Tea, Polychrome Design, Black Ground, 5 7/8 In.	65.00
Chamberstick, Pan, Old Black Paint, 7 1/2 In., Pair	70.00
Chandelier, 10–Sided Kerosene Font, Mirror Inserts, 3 Ft. 8 In.	1500.00
Chandelier, 9 Branches, Electrified, Round	400.00
Coal Hod, Paw Feet, Cast Handles, English, Lid, 17 1/2 X 21 1/2 In.	245.00
Coffeepot, Allover Fruit Design, 8 X 10 In.	375.00
Coffeepot, Brown Japanning, Floral Design, 8 1/2 In.	450.00
Coffeepot, Conical Form, Hinged, Red Flowers, Green Stems, 8 1/4 In.	935.00
Coffeepot, Fruit & Flower Design, Brown Japanning, 10 1/2 In.	95.00
Coffeepot, Japanning, Stylized Florals, Gooseneck Spout, 10 3/4 In.	525.00
Double Boiler, Hinged Door Opening To Kerosene Burner	50.00
Flue Cover, Little Girl In Red, Dog, Germany	35.00
Lamp, Directoire, Green Metal Shade, Scrolled Bracket, Pair	425.00
Lamp, Saucer Base, Original Green Paint & Gold Striping, 7 1/4 In.	65.00
Mug, Gold Stenciled, A Gift, Blue Paint, 2 1/4 In.	10.00
Snuffbox, Red, Sunburst	75.00
Tea Caddy, Brown Japanning, Polychrome Floral Design, 4 1/8 In.	200.00
Tea Caddy, Dark Brown, Floral Design, Oval, 4 1/4 In.	45.00
Tray, 3 Ladies Scene, Reticulated Gallery, Gilt Border, 15 X 20 In.	65.00
Tray, Bread, 7 In.	120.00
Tray, Pierced Gallery, Painted Landscape Medallion, Oval, Stand, 18 In.	2200.00
Tray, Polychrome Floral Design, Orange, Green, & Ocher, 9 X 12 1/2 In.	165.00
Wall Pocket, Painted Flowers & Leaves, Painted Black, 3 X 6 3/4 In.	40.00

Tom Mix was born in 1880 and died in 1940. He was the hero of over 100 silent movies from 1910 to 1929, and 25 sound films from 1929 to 1935. There was a Ralston Tom Mix radio show from 1933 to 1950, but the original Tom Mix was not in the show. Tom Mix comics were published from 1942 to 1953.

TOM MIX, Arrowhead, Glow In The Dark 30.00
  Badge, Dobie County 22.50
  Badge, With Silver 25.00
  Belt & Buckle, Championship 55.00
  Big Little Book, Tom Mix & His Circus On The Barbary Coast 15.00
  Big Little Kit, 1937 .... 60.00
  Bird Call, Musical 15.00
  Book, Draw & Paint, Whitman, 1935 .... 35.00
  Book, Tom Mix & The Scourge Of Paradise Valley 95.00
  Book, Western Songbook, 1935 ....37.00 To 65.00
  Bracelet, Identification 25.00
  Card, Tom Mix In Long Runs Wild, William Fox Productions 18.50
  Catalog, Premium 35.00
  Compass, Magnifier, Straight Shooter, Ralston, Plastic, 1946 .... 30.00
  Decoder, 6 Gun 45.00
  Gun, Straight Shooter, Plastic Bullet Telescope 30.00
  Gun, Wooden, No Moving Parts, 1939 .... 110.00
  Label, Cigar Box 25.00
  Neckerchief, Signed 75.00
  Newspaper, Ralston, Life Of Tom Mix, 4 Pages, Shows Premiums 38.00
  Parachute, Rocker, 1948 .... 55.00
  Periscope, Instruction Booklet, Ralston 50.00
  Poster, The Miracle Rider, Serial Movie, 26 1/2 X 41 1/4 In. 85.00
  Puzzle, Tom & Tony Jr, Original Envelope, Rexall 50.00
  Ring, Magnet 35.00
  Ring, Whistle, Sliding ....32.00 To 125.00
  Telegraph Set 48.00
  Telescope 45.00
  Television, Film 20.00
  Toy, Tony, Rocking Horse, Wood Platform 450.00
  Watch, Sun, 1935 .... 50.00

Tools of all sorts are listed here, but most are related to industry. Other tools will be found listed under Iron; Kitchen; Store; Tinware; and Wooden.

TOOL, Adze, Bowl, Handle, 3 In.Bit 35.00
  Adze, Curved Handle, Stanley 18.00
  Anvil, Artisan, Round & Square Horns, 5 1/2 In. 25.00
  Anvil, Stake, Tinsmith's 65.00
  Assay Set, J.T.Letcher, Cornwall, England, C.1880, Mahogany Case 380.00
  Auger Bit, 15/16, Winchester 10.00
  Auger, Bung, Cooper's, Tapered, Handle 10.00
  Auger, Pod, Wooden Cross Handle, 1/2 Size, 20 In. 15.00
  Ax, Broad, E.C.Simmons, Keen Kutter 115.00
  Ax, Broad, Iron, Wooden Handle, 8 X 10 1/2 In. 25.00
  Ax, Broad, Wrought Iron, Natural Curved Handle, 6 In.Blade, 22 In. 40.00
  Ax, Cooper's, Ohio Tool Co., 9 3/4 In. 50.00
  Ax, Marbles Safety, No.2, Folding, Blade Guard, Red Handles 125.00
  Ax, Surveyor's, Single Bit, Winchester 40.00
  Battery Tester, W.C.Fields, Keen Nose Lights 25.00
  Bellows, Dust, Eagle, Flowers, & Scroll, 19 In. 85.00
  Bench, Jeweler's, Foot Operated Flywheel, Mosley Lathe, Parts & Tools 550.00
  Binnacle, Copper, Oriental Compass, C.1832 .... 295.00
  Bit, Center Type, Assorted Sizes, Set Of 10 .... 20.00
  Blowtorch, Brass, 9 X 10 In. 30.00
  Book Press, Red & Black Paint, Cast Iron, 12 X 18 1/2 In. 100.00
  Box Opener & Hammer, Arm & Hammer 10.00
  Box, Saw Slot, Compartment, Painted Wood, Marked J.H.Davis 187.00

Brace Bit, Stanley, Brass Trim	143.00
Brace, Blacksmith Beam, Wrought, 12 In.	45.00
Brace, Cage Head, 2 Posts, Wrought, 14 In.	225.00
Brace, Corner & Joist Crank Operated, Goodell Tool, Pat.Dec.27, 1892	55.00
Brace, Iron, Rosewood Head, Nobels Mfg., Pat.Dec.19, 1865	32.00
Brace, Lady's, Stanley, No.1645, 12 X 4 In.	240.00
Brace, Ratchet, Iron Frame, Rose Johnson's, Pat.May 25, 1886	48.00
Brace, Scotch, Mathieson Glass, Lignum Head	75.00
Brace, Sheffield, Brass Plated, Rosewood Head	150.00
Brace, Shipwright's, Bit, 18th Century, Oak, 37 In.	445.00
Brace, Sweep Iron, J.P.Ells In Script, 14 3/4 In.	98.00
Brace, Wagon Builder's, Marked Wrot, Lignum Vitae Pad, 14 In.Sweep	40.00
Brace, Wm.Marples, Ivory Ring, Ebony	395.00
Brace, Wooden, Bit & Pad, 11 1/2 In.	250.00
Brace, Wooden, Bit, 8 In.Sweep, 20 In.Overall	275.00
Branding Iron, Sheep Marking	65.00
Broom, Birch, New Hampshire, 56 In.	150.00
Broom, Splintered Birch, 19th Century	75.00
Buttonhole Cutter, 2 Right Angle Blades, Flat Faceted Head, Iron	85.00
Calipers, Double, Wrought Iron, 23 In.	85.00
Calipers, Figural, Lady's Legs, Garters & Shoes, Brass, 5 In.	95.00
Calipers, Folding, Brass, 1 Ft.	16.00
Calipers, Log, Birch Main Leg, Brass Head, Low Jaw Mount	195.00
Carrier, Bee, Compartments, Glass Sliding Top, Wooden, 10 In.	30.00
Chain, Surveyor's, Brass Handles & Tags, Marked JTH	40.00
Chest, Lid, Storage Drawer, 3 Drawers, Brass Handles, 13 X 23 In.	78.00
Chest, Lift Top, Fitted Interior, Dovetailed, 19th Century	55.00
Chest, Pattern Maker's, 120 Tools, 4 Trays, 34 X 15 X 15 In.	475.00
Chisel, Mortise, Swan Neck Lock, Thos.Ibbotson & Co., 24 In.	45.00
Chisel, Sash Pocket, Sashmaker's	12.00
Chisel, Winchester, Wooden	17.50
Clamp, Bliss No.11, Wooden	12.00
Clamp, Estey & Co., Wooden, Opens To 8 In.	16.00
Clamp, Glue, Threaded Screws, Small	15.00
Clincher, Nail, Farrier's, Iron, 10 In.	12.00
Comb, Flax, Heckler, Norwegian, Hanging, Primitive	30.00
Compass & Calipers, English, Boxwood Scales, Brass Fittings, C.1830	435.00
Compass, Keuffel & Esser, Engineering Department, U.S.A., Leather Case	45.00
Compass, Pocket, Paper Label, Mahogany Case, 4 In.Square	40.00
Compass, Surveying, Brass Face, Signed John Beiteman	400.00
Compass, Surveying, Inclinometer & Outkeeper, A.Chandler, C.1830	950.00
Compass, Surveying, Pocket, Keuffel & Esser, C.1900, Mahogany Case	150.00
Compass, Surveying, Thos Whitney, No.438, Brass Cover, Dated 1818	895.00
Compass, Wing, Cooper's, 9 In.	12.00
Cutter, Barbed Wire, Cast Iron, A.Harrison, 1870s	32.00
Cutter, Glass, Ivory Handle, Patent 1877	85.00
Cutter, Paper, School, 1910, Maple	50.00
Damper, Furnace, Oak, Doe–Wah–Jack, Embossed, Walnut Plaque, 4 In.	65.00
Die, Blacksmith Threading, 26 In., 3 Sizes	20.00
Digger, Post Hole, Keen Kutter	22.00
Drafting Set, Ivory Handles, Rule, & Lead Container, Case, 21 Piece	150.00
Drafting Set, Steel, Ivory Rules, J.Shuttleworth, Case, 6 3/4 In.	125.00
Drill, Archimedean, Beech With Brass, 14 In.	39.00
Drill, Bow, Walnut & Brass, 10 In.	240.00
Fence Poke, Sheep, Wooden, Hand Hewn, Bent Bow With Cross, Old Patina	57.00
Flashlight, Bassett Hound, Rubber, 1949, 3 In.	5.00
Flashlight, Winchester No.6411, 5 1/2 In.	25.00
Forceps, Glass Blower's, Iron, 7 1/2 In.	45.00
Forceps, Glass Blower's, Iron, Fine Spring Steel, 15 In.	55.00
Fork, Hay, 1 Piece Of Wood, 60 In.	75.00
Fork, Hay, 1 Tine, Cast Iron	28.00
Gauge, Dovetail, Cabinet Maker's, Wooden, 2 Adjustments	65.00
Gauge, Jointer, Stanley, No.386, Original Box	15.00
Gauge, Keen Kutter, Rosewood Mortise, Brass Full Face Plate	48.00

Gauge, Marking, Stanley, No.72	10.00
Gauge, Mortise, Brass Stem, Iron Fences, 6 In.	55.00
Gauge, Mortise, M.M.Brainard, Rosewood	60.00
Gauge, Tire Pressure, Schrader–Universal, Case	12.00
Gauge, Violin Thickness, Charles Davis, Pembroke, Maine	187.00
Grinder, Wheat, Green Enameled, Early 1900	25.00
Hammer, Ball Peen, Keen Kutter	15.00
Hammer, Claw, Winchester	30.00
Hammer, Decking, Oversized, Claw, Woolford 14, 8 In.Head, 19 In.	65.00
Hammer, File Maker's, Bulbous Head, Classic Style, 5 1/2 In.	225.00
Harpoon, Adjustable Rung, Whaling	225.00
Hatchet, Brass, Open Head, Washington Silhouette, 11 1/2 In.	85.00
Hatchet, Coal, Nickle Plated, Franiville Co., Grand Rapids, 1874	35.00
Hatchet, Marble Arms & Mfg.Co., Patented 1898	110.00
Hatchet, Marbles Safety, Hunting Scene On Handle, Case	175.00
Hatchet, Stanley, Bell System, Square Wrench Opening	85.00
Hoe, Garden, Keen Kutter	22.00
Hydrometer, Sike's, 10 Brass Weights, Adjusted By Jos.Long 1897, Case	73.00
Jack, Taper, Tooled, Engraved, Iron, 9 7/8 In.	325.00
Jack, Wagon, Wooden, Primitive, 30 In.	35.00
Knife, Basket Maker's, Hickory Handle, 9 1/2 In.	45.00
Knife, Chamfer, Cooper's, Beer Barrel Type, Frog, 36 In.	200.00
Knife, Chamfer, Cooper's, Marked Taylow & Worlee, Blade 7 1/4 In.	35.00
Lace Maker, Teneriffe, Celluloid Disc, 1903	14.00
Ladder, Apple Picking, Old Blue	150.00
Ladder, Cheese, Mortised, Pinned, Chestnut, 9 X 17 In.	52.00
Ladder, Pine, Loft Type, 58 In.	25.00
Lathe Turning Set, Ashley Iles, Edinburgh, 8 Tools	75.00
Lathe, Jeweler's, Peerless	150.00
Level, Akron Eclipse, Wooden, Brass Ends, 26 In.	17.00
Level, Bench, Double Plumb, Athol Machine Co.No.35, Iron, 24 In.	55.00
Level, Boxwood, Brass Top, Inch Scale, Preston, 5/8 X 4 In.	39.00
Level, Cook, Pat.1903, Brass Ends, Benzels Corners	40.00
Level, Disston & Son, Pat.1912, Cherry On Brass Trim, 18 In.	12.00
Level, E.Preston & Sons, Ebony & Brass, 8 In.	45.00
Level, Spirit, Lacquered Brass Stand, Glass Tube, Wooden Case, English	220.00
Level, Stanley, Adjustable, Round Brass Benzels	35.00
Level, Stanley, No.3, Brass Corners	35.00
Level, Stellett Machinist, 6 In.	50.00
Level, Stratton Brothers, Pat.July 15, 1872, Mahogany, Brass, 30 In.	88.00
Level, Surveyor, Transit, Wooden Case	155.00
Level, W.Marples & Son, Rosewood & Brass, 2 Bubbles, 10 In.	55.00
Level, Winchester, 12 In.	30.00
Level, Winchester, 26 In.	85.00
Level, Winchester, Paper Label	100.00
Lever, Stanley, Dated 1890	24.00
Mathematical Set, John Field, London, Wooden Case, Late 18th Century	1900.00
Measure, Grain, Wooden, 10 In.	38.00
Micrometer Slide, English, C.1880, Ross & Co., Case, 1 X 3 In.	85.00
Micrometer, Table, M.Grossman, Glashutte, No.4618, Card Box, C.1875	280.00
Mold, Brass, For Pewter Spoons, C.1740	180.00
Mold, Brick, Wooden, Iron Reinforcement, 10 Brick, 10 3/4 X 48 In.	60.00
Molder, Crown, Reverse Ogee Iron, Birch, 5 X 14 In.	350.00
Molder, Way & Sherman, Scribe Marks On Ends	40.00
Muzzle, Ox, Oak Splint, For Garnering Grain, 11 X 12 In.	135.00
Niddy Noddy, 1/2 Skein, Short, Wooden	95.00
Niddy Noddy, Pine, Punched Design	75.00
Niddy Noddy, Wooden Pegs, Mortised, Patina, Early 19th Century, 10 In.	155.00
Paddle, Tallow, Candle Mold Tray Top, 3 1/2 X 8 1/2 In.	12.00
Padlock, Van Camps Hardware, Brass, Key	75.00
Padlock, Yale Bi–Centric, 2 Key Holes, Key	50.00
Parallel Rule, Rolling, Signed Thomas Jones, London, Ebony, 15 1/4 In.	180.00
Plane Set, Snipe Bill, Preston & Son, No.5, Box	75.00
Plane Table, Dietzgen, Surveyor	125.00

Plane, Apothecary, Reduce Compound, Prescription, 7 X 11 1/2 In. 85.00
Plane, Bailey No.27 .... 17.00
Plane, Bailey No.35, Wood Base 45.00
Plane, Bead, T.Napier, 5/8 In.Bead 58.00
Plane, Bedrock, No.605 1/2 .... 45.00
Plane, Block, Keen Kutter 35.00
Plane, Block, Wooden, 15 3/4 & 19 1/2 In., Pair 50.00
Plane, Bullnore, English, 4 In. 40.00
Plane, Cabinet Maker's, Brass Fittings, 12 Blades, Casey, Auburn, N.Y. 275.00
Plane, Cabinet Scraper, Keen Kutter, K–312 .... 150.00
Plane, Chariot, English, Gunmetal & Boxwood 195.00
Plane, Combination, Stanley No.55, 52 Cutters, 4 Boxes, Wooden Box, 1908 .... 350.00
Plane, Compass, Violin Maker's, Curved Sole, 5/8 X 2 1/2 In. 140.00
Plane, Cooper's Sun, Cherry Wood, 14 In. 110.00
Plane, Dado, A.M.Bartletts Ohio Planes, No.62 .... 20.00
Plane, Double Sash, Beech, E.W.Carpenter, Lancaster, 1830–59, 9 1/2 In. 155.00
Plane, Fiberboard, Stanley, No.193, All Blades & Attachments 150.00
Plane, Finger, Violin Maker's, 2 In. 50.00
Plane, Hinged Top, Adjusting Screw, Iron Blade, Signed P.Shea, C.1860 .... 110.00
Plane, Hollow, Toppin & Bro., No.18 .... 32.00
Plane, HSB Rev-O-Noc, 9 In. 19.00
Plane, Jo.Fuller, Birch, 9 7/16 In. 100.00
Plane, Low Angle, English, All Gunmetal 145.00
Plane, Match, Ohio Tool Co., Closed Handle Groove 20.00
Plane, Molding, Cabinet Maker's, 19th Century 15.00
Plane, Panel, English, Mahogany Infill 145.00
Plane, Pencil Sharpening, Sandusky Tool Co., 2 5/8 In. 75.00
Plane, Pistol Grip, Compass Base, S. & R.Howden, Manchester, 6 1/2 In. 55.00
Plane, Plow, Beech, Slide Arm, I.Hammond, New Haven 55.00
Plane, Plow, DeForest, Stamped W.W.Henderson, 6 Blades 75.00
Plane, Plow, Lignum Vitae, I.& E.Baldwin, New York 198.00
Plane, Plow, Ohio Tool, Mo.95 .... 90.00
Plane, Plow, Rosewood, Boxwood Arms & Nuts, J.Kellogg, Amherst 200.00
Plane, Plow, S.K.Dodge, 5 Irons 95.00
Plane, Plow, Wooden, Arrow Mammett No.121 .... 75.00
Plane, Rabbet, Keen Kutter, No.190 .... 65.00
Plane, Reversible Rocker, Union 55.00
Plane, Round, I.Cogdell, Chamfer, 1 1/2 In.Iron, 9 1/2 In. 120.00
Plane, Sash, Adjustable, J.Kellogg Amherst, Box 48.00
Plane, Sash, Molding, Pattern Maker's, 14 In. 75.00
Plane, Scotia Molding, Union Factory, H.Chapin, 7/8 In. 30.00
Plane, Side Rabbet, Marked, No.151, Pair 55.00
Plane, Smooth, Pattern Maker's, 7 Soles & Irons, Beech 60.00
Plane, Stanley, No. 25, 18 Cutters, Wooden Box, Floral Pattern 130.00
Plane, Stanley, No. 30 ....37.50 To 42.50
Plane, Stanley, No. 45, 16 Cutters, Original Wooden Box 125.00
Plane, Stanley, No.113, C.1914 .... 125.00
Plane, Sun, Cooper's, Left Hand Model, Beech 55.00
Plane, Toothing, Scroll Wedge, H.E.Frewer, Buck & Ryam Iron 34.00
Plane, Union No.26, Wooden, Iron 15.00
Plane, Wooden, E.T.Burrowes Co., 8 X 3 In. 28.00
Plane, Wooden, Scoto Works, No.3 .... 40.00
Plane, Wooden, Winchester, No.3045 .... 75.00
Plane, Wooden, Winchester, No.3205, Red Marking 55.00
Plane, Wooden, Winchester, No.3625 .... 95.00
Plane, Zenith, No.45, Original Wooden Box 150.00
Pliers, Degrees Slip Joint, Keen Kutter 20.00
Pliers, Lineman, Keen Kutter 15.00
Plumb Bob, Brass, 5 1/2 In. 8.00
Plumb Bob, Brass, Jointed At Center, 5 1/2 In. 72.00
Plumb Bob, Cylindrical, Chrome Plated, Millers Falls Tools, 1868, 4 In. 65.00
Plumb Bob, Stanley No.5, Brass Reel Upper End 95.00
Press, Splint, Basket & Chair Maker's, Crank Handle, 9 1/2 X 19 In. 170.00
Pricing Set, Monarch, Complete, All Numbers 30.00

Pricker & Cutter, Cracker, Scalloped Edge, Arched Handle, Tin, Round 85.00
Print Kit, Wooden, Rubber, Box, 80 Piece 35.00
Print Set, Sign, Wooden Box, 23 X 11 In. 23.00
Printing Press, Baltimore, No.4, Wooden Box, Litho Covered 75.00
Propeller, Airplane, Wooden, Kroehler, 32 In. 48.00
Protractor, Ruling, Brass, American, C.1800, 4 1/4 In.Radius 235.00
Pruner, Keen Kutter, 8 3/4 In. 30.00
Punch & Shears, Cleveland, 1911 .... 4.50
Quadrant, Astronomical, B.C.Phelps, 1861, Complete, American, 6 3/4 In. 2100.00
Reel, Surveyor's, American, Brass Hub, Wood Handle, C.1880 .... 195.00
Router, Beech, 4 X 12 In. 45.00
Router, Miller Falls, No.67, Extra Blades 55.00
Router, Old Woman's Tooth, Beech, A.Tomlin, 5 In. 39.00
Rug Beater, 5 Center Hearts, 1 Large Heart 29.00
Rug Beater, Heart Shape, Miniature 16.00
Rug Beater, Wire, Wooden Handle, 1910 .... 15.00
Rule, 4 Fold, Ivory, German Silver Arch Trim Impressed 83 1/2, 24 In. 195.00
Rule, Cattle Gauge Slide, J.Tree, London, Brassbound Boxwood, 8 3/4 In. 220.00
Rule, English, Conversion Of Inches To Metric, Boxwood, C.1820 .... 220.00
Rule, Folding, Stanley, Brass Lined, 24 In. 25.00
Rule, Harris & Cole Bros.Inc., Wooden, 15 In. 9.50
Rule, Hatter's, Boxwood, Brass Caliper, Tables Show Size, Head & Hat 55.00
Rule, Parallel, English, Reeves & Sons, Ltd., Brass Fittings, Rosewood 95.00
Rule, Parallel, Rosewood, Brass, 15 In. 45.00
Rule, Slide, Stanley No.12, Gunter, 24 In. 40.00
Rule, Stanley, No.62, Folding, Brass Edges 25.00
Rule, Stanley, No.87, Ivory Trim 165.00
Rule, Washington, First In War, 1732–1932, Cleaning Co., 6 In. 2.50
Ruler, Hartford Fire Insurance 40.00
Ruler, Nature's Remedy, Dallas Druggist, Wooden, 12 In. 5.50
Sash Filletster, Pattern Maker's, Wedge Arm 55.00
Sash Filletster, Wedge Arm, Brass Trim, John Moseley & Son, Box 135.00
Saw, Bow, Beech, 12 X 22 In. 45.00
Saw, Bow, Mahogany, Beech Handles, Chandler & Barber, Boston, 20 In. 50.00
Saw, Hand, Primitive, Handmade, Walnut Handle, 18 In. 17.00
Saw, Iron, Toothed Trammel, 38 In. 39.00
Scale Set, Engineer's, Stanley, Great Turnstile, Holborn, London, Case 125.00
Scale, Protractor, Ivory, Cary London, 6 In. 58.00
Scissors, Buttonhole, Tailor's, Marked Wolcott's Boston 1852 .... 25.00
Scissors, Remington, 8 In. 27.50
Scissors, Wallpaper, Murray–Black, 14 In. 25.00
Scoop, Barrel, Maple Handle, Steel 28.00
Scoop, Cranberry, Tin Bottom, Screen Top, 19 1/2 X 20 In. 105.00
Scoop, Grain, Shovel Shape, Short Hook, 15 In., 1 Piece 75.00
Scorp, Open, Hand Wrought, 1 1/4 In.Radius Cutter, 22 In. 28.00
Scraper, Buffalo Hide 125.00
Scraper, Closed Scorp, 5 1/4 In. Cutter 25.00
Scraper, Horse Sweat, Curved, Wooden, 1 Piece 28.00
Scraper, Open Scorp, 4 1/2 In. Cutter 20.00
Scraper, Rosewood & Brass, 9 1/2 In. 85.00
Scribe, Timber, Folding Race Knife, Brass Handle, Steel Blade, Marked 85.00
Scythe, Grain Cradle Sharpener, New Brunswick, C.1850 .... 110.00
Sealer Pliers, Wells Fargo Co. 125.00
Separator, Blubber, Whaling 125.00
Sharpener, Blade, Kriss Kross 12.00
Sharpener, Knife, Keen Kutter, Wooden Handle, 17 In. 14.00
Sharpener, Pencil, Baker Girl, Figural, Iron 20.00
Sharpener, Pencil, Black Face, Figural, Iron 45.00
Sharpener, Pencil, Student Lamp Shade 15.00
Sharpener, Pencil, Zeppelin Shape, Handheld, German, 3 In. 110.00
Sharpener, Scissors, Hand Held, 1858, Iron 17.00
Sharpener, Scissors, Table Top, Wooden, Manual, Uses Sandpaper 38.00
Sharpening Stone, In Wooden Frame, Hand Crank, 19 In. 25.00
Shears, Iron, Braithwait, 9 In. 13.00

Restoration of an old dollhouse should be restrained. Wash it, repair the structural problems, repaint as little as possible, and redecorate with appropriate old wallpaper fabrics and paint colors.

Tool, Spit Jack, Wall, Wrought Iron, Brass, 11 In.

Sheller, Corn, Hinged, Hand Forged Iron Teeth, Old Red	220.00
Shovel, Grain, Birch, D Handle, 18th Century, 1 Piece	150.00
Shovel, Grain, Open D Handle, Cherry, 1 Piece	195.00
Shovel, Grain, Winter Scene On Bowl, Gold On Handle, Wooden, 36 In.	155.00
Shovel, Grain, Wood, 1 Board Construction	110.00
Sickle, Barley, 18th Century, Curved Blade	35.00
Soldering Iron, Copper, Wrought Iron Twisted Handle, 22 In.	30.00
Spirit Level, Stanley, Patented 1890	20.00
Spit Jack, Wall, Wrought Iron, Brass, 11 In. ....*Illus*	800.00
Spoke Shave, Double Blade, Keen Kutter, No.97, Handles Marked	95.00
Spoke Shave, Keen Kutter, No.K95	12.00
Spoke Shave, Pattern Maker's, Double Router, Hollow Handles, Brass	40.00
Spoke Shave, Winchester, No.3250, Original Blade	95.00
Square, Adjustable, Stanley, No.30	30.00
Square, Ames Universal, 5 1/2 X 10 1/2 In.	32.00
Square, Plumb, Mahogany, Lead Bob, 29 X 21 In.	200.00
Square, T Bevel, Winchester	75.00
Stapler, Desk, Hotchkiss, No.2	15.00
Steam Engine, Wooden, Steel & Brass, Horizontal Boiler, Burner, 8 In.	125.00
Steelyard, Wrought Iron, Dated 1802, 28 In.	20.00
Steelyard, Wrought Iron, Stamped I.P.1795	55.00
Stencil, Daisy Brand, Mild Cure, Ottumwa, U.S.A., Brass, 14 X 18 In.	225.00
Stitching Palm, Sail Maker's, Leather, With Needle	25.00
Stopper, Bung Hole, For Barrel, Wooden	6.00
Stretcher, Hide, Spring Type, Steel Rods	15.00
Stretcher, Shoe, Bunion, Dated 1917	22.00
Sundial, Surveyor's, American, W.& L.E.Gurley, Case, Square, 4 In.	650.00
Sunshine Recorder, Negretti & Zambra, London, Enameled Brass, C.1925	195.00
Swift, Geometric Carved Clamps, Wooden	40.00
Swift, Pine Cone Finial, Green, Wooden	400.00
Swift, Sealing Wax Design Inlays In Clamp & Stock, Dated 1868	400.00
Swift, Umbrella, Table Mount	60.00
Tack Tray, Cobbler's, On Movable Base	15.00
Tape, Surveyor's, Champion, Steel, 100 Ft.On Reel, Handle	45.00
Telegraph Sounder, Wooden Box, L.G.Tillotson & Co., Pat.Sep.12, 1865	400.00
Trammel, Iron, Adjusts From 35 In.	20.00
Trammel, Sawtooth, Wrought Iron, Adjusts From 41 In.	45.00
Trap, Oneida, No.3, Teeth	40.00
Traveler, Wheelwright's, Iron	50.00
Vise, Cabinet Maker's, Wooden	75.00
Vise, Leather Worker's, Clamp On Block, Wooden	30.00
Wagon Jack, Pine, Copper & Iron Mount, 20 X 29 In.	40.00

Weasel, Yarn Winding 125.00
Winnower, Hickory Handles, Rosehead Nails, 46 In. 285.00
Wire Stretcher, Long Wooden Handle, 32 In. 20.00
Wrench, Adjustable, Ampco, Brass, 12 In. 89.00
Wrench, Billings 1879, Adjustable 15.00
Wrench, International Harvester 10.00
Wrench, Monkey, Keen Kutter 22.00
Wrench, Monkey, Winchester 48.00
Yarn Winder, Pine, 2 Spool, Dated 1842 .... 20.00
Yarn Winder, Primitive, Wooden Table Top, Reel, Shoe Feet, 23 X 27 In. 50.00
Yarn Winder, Primitive, Wooden, No Finish, 35 1/2 In. 55.00
Yarn Winder, Trestle Foot, Maple 110.00

Toothpick holders are sometimes called "toothpicks" by collectors. The variously shaped containers made to hold the small wooden toothpicks are often made in fanciful shapes.

TOOTHPICK, see also other categories such as Bisque; Slag; etc.
TOOTHPICK, 1939 Golden Gate Exposition, Redwood 18.00
Alabama, Clear 55.00
Atlantic City, 1906, Thumbprint, Ruby 15.00
Bead Swag, White Opalescent, Souvenir, Heisey 30.00
Bear, Silver Plate, Dated 1915 .... 35.00
Blue Pig On Boxcar 95.00
Boot, Blue 28.00
Brown Egg & Chick, Take A Pick 10.00
Button Arches, Ruby Top, 1902 .... 20.00
Camphor Glass, Button Arches, Louisberg, Minn, Scalloped 17.50
Camphor Glass, Monkey Next To Top Hat 65.00
Carnival Glass, Heron, Cattail, Fish, Blue, 3 1/2 In. 22.50
Cat & Bucket, Silver Plate, Victorian 55.00
Cat, Halloween, Occupied Japan 10.00
Charleston Expo, 1902, Button Arches, Ruby 15.00
Chick On Wishbone, Silver Plate 30.00
Clown, Spread Eagle Legs, Marked Jenning Bros., Brass 26.00
Cranberry, Threaded 35.00
Custard Glass, Central School, Alpena, Mich. 35.00
Custard Glass, Souvenir, Alcester, S.D. 30.00
Cut & Etched Birds, Bohemian Glass, Ruby 39.00
Cut Glass, Diamond & Fan, Enameled Floral, Gold Trim, 2 1/2 In. 75.00
Daisy & Button, Amber, Metal Rim 30.00
Daisy & Button, Hobbs, Vaseline Daisies 25.00
Deer, Red, Bohemian 22.00
Diamond Spearhead, Vaseline, Opalescent 25.00
Donkey, Crystal 9.50
Donkey, With Man And Tree, Silver 50.00
Dutch Child, Fishing By Wharf, Germany 25.00
Elephant Sitting, Green, Porcelain 20.00
Elephant's Head, Hanging, Amber 56.00
Empress With Leaf & Berry Etching, Clear 28.00
Enameled Violets, Marked Onset, 1 7/8 In. 200.00
Etched Floral, Scissor Cut Edge, 6 Sides, Fluted Top, Heisey 85.00
Fan, Amber 18.00
Figural, Boy & Shock Of Wheat, Silver Plate 45.00
Figural, Chick & Wishbone, Best Wishes, Silver Plate 35.00
Figural, Sailor & Barrel, Silver Plate 48.00
Francisware Swirl, Frosted 95.00
Frog, Pulling Snail, Green 75.00
Frosted Glass, Elephant, Howdah On Back 40.00
Girl, Standing, Holding Basket, Bisque, Pastel, 6 3/4 In. 125.00
Imperial, Red, Iridescent, 2 5/8 In. 12.00
Indian, Milk Glass, Painted 85.00
Loving Cup, 3 Handles, Gold Trim 15.00
Man, Sack On Shoulder, Tree Trunk, Porcelain, 3 1/2 In. 155.00
Many Daisies, 2 1/2 In. 9.50

Marble, Blue & White, Italy 8.00
Millefiori 29.00
Monkey, Darwin, Amber 75.00
Oriental Girl With Fan, Porcelain 20.00
Pink Pansy 58.00
Polish Mirror Pattern 22.00
Porcupine, Silver Plate 39.00
Ribbed Spiral, Vaseline Opal 65.00
Ruby Flash, Souvenir, Shelbia, Missouri 15.00
Saddle, Blue 28.00
Shoe, Tramp's, Amethyst 20.00
Slag Glass, Pink, Indian 18.00
Souvenir, Mt.Horeb, Wis., Custard, Gold Trim 25.00
Steuben, Handled, Footed, Signed, 1930 .... 28.00
Swan On Shell 27.00
Swan, Cobalt Blue 16.50
Top Hat, Inverted Umbrella, Brass 20.00
Trophy Style, Pink, 3 Handles, Footed, Dated 1931 .... 25.00
Truncated Cube, Clear 15.00
Vermont, Green And Gold 35.00
Vermont, Opaque Ivory 40.00
Wedding Ring, Amethyst 9.50
Woodpecker, Celluloid 10.00
Woodpecker, Metal 10.00

TORQUAY   *Torquay Terra–cotta Company was a pottery working in Hele Cross, England, from 1875 to 1909. Pieces are marked with the word "Torquay." Many types of art pottery were made in the style of the times.*

TORQUAY, Biscuit Jar, Wicker Handle, Motto, House Scene, Marked, 5 3/8 In. 85.00
Candlestick, Chamber, Motto, Many Are Called But Few Get Up, 5 In. 55.00
Coffeepot, Rooster Cover, Motto, Kindness, Marked, 6 In. 65.00
Creamer, Strach Frae The Coo 20.00
Cup & Saucer, Cottage Scenes, Incised Mark, Small 25.00
Hatpin Holder, Rooster, Motto 65.00
Pitcher, Cottage Scene, Stamped Mark, 2 In. 15.00
Pitcher, Joy Is The Mother Of All Virtues 20.00
Syrup, Cobalt Blue, Enameled Design, Squat 185.00
Vase, Daffodils, Green, 8 In. 75.00

Tortoiseshell glass was made during the 1800s and after by the Sandwich Glass Works of Massachusetts and some firms in Germany. Tortoiseshell glass is, of course, named for its resemblance to real shell from a tortoise. It has been reproduced.

TORTOISESHELL GLASS, Bowl, 7 3/4 X 3 1/2 In. 85.00
Candlestick, 19th Century, 6 In. 55.00
Pitcher, Applied Amber Handle, 8 1/2 In. 125.00
Pitcher, Water, 8 In. 275.00
Pitcher, Water, Boston & Sandwich, 8 1/2 In. 110.00
Vase, 9 In. 145.00
Vase, Bottle Shape, Ground & Polished, 12 In. 75.00
Vase, Bulbous, Flared, Crimped, 3 1/2 X 5 3/4 In. 45.00
Vase, English, C.1910, 8 In. 50.00

The shell of the tortoise has been used as inlay and to make small decorative objects since the seventeenth century. Some species of tortoise are now on the endangered species list, and objects made from these shells cannot be sold legally.

TORTOISESHELL, Box, Cover, 9 Semiprecious Stones, China, 2 3/8 X 3 3/8 In. 130.00
Cabinet, Jewelry, Mother–Of–Pearl Inlay, 23 1/2 X 23 In. 7150.00
Card Case, Lady's, Victorian 65.00
Comb, Holds Hair Back, Gold Inlay 55.00
Comb, Victorian, 7 3/4 X 6 1/4 In. 85.00
Mirror, Beveled, Miniature, 4 In. 68.00

Snuffbox, Painted Miniature, Gold, Late 18th Century, 3 In. 500.00
Snuffbox, Sterling Hinge, English, 1865, 1 1/2 X 2 1/2 In. 110.00
Tantalus, Napoleon III, Mahogany, 4 Decanters, 15 Tumblers 1500.00

 *Toys are designed to entice children; and today, they have attracted new interest among adults who are still children at heart. All types of toys are collected. Tin toys, iron toys, battery operated toys, and many others are collected by specialists. Dolls, Games, Teddy Bears, and Bicycles are listed under their own categories. Other toys may be found under company or celebrity names.*

TOY, Acrobat, Balloon, Basket, Mechanical, Somersault As Pulled, German, 1905 .... 2400.00
  Aero–Swing, Chein, Windup 185.00
  African Dancer, Pango–Pango, Windup, Tin, Japan, Original Box, 6 In. 70.00
  Airplane, Army, Wheels Fold Up, Hubley 25.00
  Airplane, Dent, Airline, Monoplane, Aluminum, 12 1/2 In. ....*Illus* 700.00
  Airplane, Ding Corrigan's Jalopy On Wing, Tin, 5 1/2 X 7 In. 65.00
  Airplane, Fighter, Battery Operated, Tin, Cockpit Opens, Lights Up, Japan 95.00
  Airplane, Friction, Aeroplane, 1920, 5 In. 15.00
  Airplane, Giro, Hubley, Cast Iron 80.00
  Airplane, Lindy, Spirit Of St.Louis 45.00
  Airplane, Monoplane, Dent, Aluminum, Question Mark, USA, 12 1/2 In. 700.00
  Airplane, Monoplane, Skywriter No.87, Katz & Co., 1934, 13 1/2 In. 175.00
  Airplane, Question Mark No.147, Katz & Co., 3 Motor, 18 In. 250.00
  Airplane, Question Mark No.247, Henry Katz & Co., Windup, 1930 .... 175.00
  Airplane, Roll Over, 1920s, Tin, Marx 65.00
  Airplane, Windup, Aeroplane, Tin, Stand, Counterweight, German, 13 X 5 In. 2250.00
  Airport No.56, Ohio Art, Boxed, 9 In. 47.50
  Ambulance, Wyandotte, Tin, 1930s 195.00
  Ambulance, Wyandotte, Windup, 7 In. 35.00
  Amos & Andy, Fresh Air Taxi, Original Box ....625.00 To 775.00
  Andy Sparkler, Squeeze Mechanism, German, 1930s 450.00
  Annie Fannie, Drink Shaker, Battery Operated, Playboy 55.00
  Aqua–Plane, Chein, Windup, 1930s 60.00
  Astronaut, Windup, Tin, Cragstan, 9 In. 250.00
  Aunt Jemima, Clockwork, Hand Painted 550.00
  B.O.Plenty & Sparkle, Tin, Windup 110.00
  Baby, Crawling, Mechanical, Irwin, Box 45.00
  Baby, Crawling, Windup, Celluloid, Sticker On Head, Box 25.00
  Baby, Crawling, Windup, Composition & Celluloid 20.00
  Baggage Truck, Buddy L, 1930s, 17 In. 110.00
  Baking Set, Parker Bros., 1920s, Box 15.00
  Baking Set, Smitty Cookie, Original Box 18.00

Don't clean badly tarnished pewter with lye unless you are aware of the physical dangers involved. The pewter won't be hurt, but you might.

Toy, Airplane, Dent, Airline, Monoplane, Aluminum, 12 1/2 I

Toy, Bedroom Set, Doll's, Painted Wood, 1870s, 8 Piece

Toy, Car & Driver, Lehmann,
Lithographed Tin,
Clockwork, 4 In.

Balloon Man, Battery Operated, Metal, 12 X 6 In.	17.50
Balloonist, Straw Basket, Tin, Painted, Clockwork, German, 15 In.	1500.00
Bambi, Steiff, Tag & Button, 5 1/2 In. ....55.00 To 65.00	
Barney Google, Washing Clothes, Mechanical, Wooden, Painted, 6 1/2 In.	70.00
Barnyard Set, English, House, 18 Lead Animals, 7 Pc. Fence, Britains Ltd.	235.00
Bartender, Cragston, Battery Operated	30.00
Battleship, Metal, Friction, 1910, 15 In.	150.00
TOY, BEAR, see also Teddy Bear	
Bear, Barney, Cragston, 4 Actions, Box	145.00
Bear, Battery Operated, Bakelite, Marx, 15 X 12 In.	145.00
Bear, Blacksmith, Battery Operated, Tin, Plush, Japan, Boxed, 6 1/2 In.	50.00
Bear, Boy & Girl, Battery Operated, Speaks, 17 In., Pair	125.00
Bear, Brummi, Battery Operated, Speaks, 17 In.	30.00
Bear, Busy Housekeeper, Battery Operated, Box	110.00
Bear, Drinking, Fur Covered, Pours From Bottle To Cup, Electric	350.00
Bear, Mechanical, Pink, Tumbler, Blue Glass Eyes, 6 In.	250.00
Bear, Pop Drinking, Battery, Alps Japan	70.00
Bear, Smoking, Battery Operated, Tin, Cloth, Japan, Box, 8 1/2 In.	25.00
Bear, Walking, Windup, Fur Covered Tin, Walks, Pauses, Turns Head, 5 In.	65.00
Beaver, Steiff, 14 1/2 In.	95.00
Bed, Doll's, 4 Poster, 10 X 7 X 6 In.	35.00
Bed, Doll's, Cast Iron, Cherub Headboard, American, 19 1/2 In.	90.00
Bed, Doll's, Complete With Linens, 26 X 28 In.	85.00
Bed, Doll's, Eastlake, Relief Design, Slats, Walnut, 28 X 16 In.	195.00
Bed, Doll's, Folding, Brass Wire, Mesh Ware Mattress, 1800s, 28 X 17 In.	75.00
Bed, Doll's, Folding, Cast Iron, 19 In.	25.00
Bed, Doll's, Tin, Early 1900s, 11 X 5 1/2 In.	22.50
Bed, Doll's, Victorian, High Back, Walnut, 12 X 24 In	165.00
Bed, Doll's, Wrought Iron, Brass Finials, 11 X 24 In.	125.00
Bedroom Set, Doll's, Painted Wood, 1870s, 8 Piece ....*Illus*	325.00
Bell Ringer, Boy Riding Dog, Cast Iron, Tin, Painted, 6 In.	600.00
Bell Ringer, Eagle, Cast Iron, Painted, 5 3/4 In.	255.00
Bell Ringer, Elephant, Tin, Painted, American, 6 1/2 In.	250.00
Bell Ringer, Horse Cart, Cast Iron, Tin, Painted, 8 In.	150.00
Bell Ringer, Poodle Dog, Cast Iron, Painted, 7 3/4 In.	475.00
Bell Ringer, Santa Claus, Windup, 5 In.	40.00
Bell Ringer, Trick Pony, Cast Iron, Painted, 7 3/4 In.	500.00
Bell Ringer, Uncle Sam, John Bull Riding, 1890s	750.00
TOY, BICYCLE, see Bicycle	
Billiard Table, Windup, Mechanical, Metal	125.00
Bird In Cage, Chirps Tune, Moves From Side To Side, Germany, 10 In.	160.00
Bird, Squeak, Papier–Mache, 6 1/4 In.	175.00

Bird, Windup, Tin Litho, Linemar 30.00
Birds In Cage, Squeak, Bellows, Papier–Mache, Wood, Wire, Straw, 8 1/2 In. 1200.00
Blimp, Graf Zeppelin, Metal Wheels, Cast Iron, 6 In. 65.00
Blimp, Sky Ranger, Vaval, Tin, 9 In. 18.00
Blocks, Alphabet & Numbers, Wooden, 1 3/4 In.Squares, Set Of 12 .... 25.00
Blocks, Alphabet, Bliss, Paper Covered, Set Of 24 .... 37.50
Blocks, Black & White Transfer, Wooden, Painted, C.1890, Set Of 15 .... 75.00
Blocks, Building, Stone, 3 Colors, Richters, Sliding Top Box 95.50
Blocks, Liberty, 1918, Original Box 30.00
Blocks, Puzzle, For Dolly & Me, C.1868, Complete, Original Box 280.00
Blocks, Puzzle, Litho, Children & Pets, Box, 20 Pieces, 6 1/2 X 8 1/2 In. 95.00
Blocks, Puzzle, Lithographed, Victorian Children, Box, Set Of 20 .... 150.00
Blocks, Puzzle, Wooden, Litho, McLoughlin's, Wooden Box 395.00
Blocks, Set, Alphabet, Litho Animals, 2 1/2 X 2 1/2 X 1/2 In. 59.00
Boat Building Set, Brittannia Rules The Waves, Wooden, English, Box 45.00
Boat, Cabin Cruiser, Windup, Ohio Art, Box 58.00
Boat, Chris Craft, Plastic, Schuco, Box 60.00
Boat, Fully Planked Hull, Model Of Gulf Coast Hurricane Victim 143.00
Boat, Queen River, Battery Operated, Metal 25.00
Boat, Speed, Mechanical, Lindstrom, No.135, Box 55.00
Boat, Tug, Battery Operated, Puffs Real Smoke, Box, Japan 45.00
Bong–A–Bell, Playskool, Wooden 16.00
Boob McNutt, Windup, Tin, Litho, Strauss, Original Box, 8 1/2 In. 500.00
Boxer, Sitting, Steiff, Sarras, Tag In Ear, 4 1/2 In. 50.00
Boxing Gloves, Tony The Tiger, Esso 10.00
Boy, On Tricycle, Celluloid & Tin 12.00
Boy, With Tin Suitcase, Celluloid, Occupied Japan 45.00
Bozo The Dog, Plush, Tin, Rollers, Remote Control, 5 X 7 In. 15.00
Broom, Original Label, Mother & Daughter Sweeping 21.00
Brutus, In Cart, Celluloid, Windup, Marx, Box 175.00
Bubbles Washing Bear, Battery, Boxed 145.00
Bucking Bronco, Windup, German, Tin, 1900s 200.00
Buffalo Bill, Lifts Rifle To Shoot, Mechanical, 1900, 9 In. 495.00
Buffalo, Iron Wheels, Steiff 650.00
Bugs Bunny & Porky Pig, Talking, Singing Jingle Bells 150.00
Building Set, Boycraft, Wooden, Boxed 28.00
Building Set, U.S.A.Capitol, 33 Presidents, Marx, 1953 .... 60.00
Building Set, Wooden, Dovetailed Box, Litho Lid, 1900s 35.00
Building, Wooden, Village Smith, Smithy, Horse, English, 10 X 4 In. 125.00
Bulldog, Pull Toy, Mechanical, Growler, Opens Fanged Mouth, Glass Eyes 795.00
Bulldog, Squeak, Stuffed, Plaster, 3 1/2 In. 270.00
Bulldozer, Battery Operated, Lunar, Box 65.00
Bulldozer, Hopper, Delta Detroit Corp., 10 In. 35.00
Bulldozer, Structo 13.00
Bureau, Doll's, 2 Shelves, Mirror, 17 X 13 In. 39.00
Bus, Arcade, Cast Iron, Blue, 5 In. 60.00
Bus, Double Decker, Interstate, With Driver, Windup, 1920s, Strauss 350.00
Bus, Double Decker, Lesney, 1920, Cast Iron 100.00
Bus, Double Decker, Queen Elizabeth II Silver Jubilee, Dinky, No.297 .... 35.00
Bus, Double Decker, With Coca–Cola Advertising, 43 In. 45.00
Bus, Greyhound Americruiser, Tin, 8 In. 14.00
Bus, Greyhound Scenic Cruiser, Gmc, 1954, Tootsietoy 13.00
Bus, Greyhound, 2 Tone, Tootsietoy, 1937 .... 25.00
Bus, Greyhound, Tootsietoy, Blue, 6 In. 28.00
Bus, Interstate, Windup, Tin, Litho, Strauss, 11 In. 400.00
Bus, Players Please On Side, English, Red, Box 16.00
Bus, Touring, Chicago World's Fair, Arcade, Cast Iron 125.00
Busy Housekeeper, Alpine 125.00
Butcher Shop, Hand Carved 525.00
Butterfly, Lithographed, Tin, Windup, 1920s, 7 1/2 In. 70.00
Butterfly, Pull Toy, Wings Flap, Tin, 9 In. ....75.00 To 85.00
Cab, Hansom, Hubley, Iron, White Horse, Blue Cab, Lady In Seat, 15 In. 90.00
Cabriolet, Kenton 425.00
Cake Set, Aluminum, Ohio Art, 28 Piece 75.00

Calliope, Royal Circus, 2 Horse, Cast Iron, Painted, Hubley, 16 In. 550.00
Camel, Walking, Windup, Tin 150.00
Canary, Singing, West Germany, Windup 65.00
Canary, Singing, Windup, West Germany, Box 65.00
Cannon, Firecracker, Admiral Dewey, Cast Iron, Kenton 175.00
Cap Bomb, Yellow Kid 50.00
Cap Gun, 1890 Scout 65.00
Cap Gun, 25 Jr., Repeating, Box 20.00
Cap Gun, 45 Automatic, Zinc, Hubley, 1940s 18.00
Cap Gun, Best, No.C19 .... 30.00
Cap Gun, Big Chief, Stevens 140.00
Cap Gun, Bigger Bang 45.00
Cap Gun, Billy The Kid 140.00
Cap Gun, Colt, Cody, 1950s 12.00
Cap Gun, Colt, Pair 120.00
Cap Gun, Cowboy 30.00
Cap Gun, Daisy, Western Type 10.00
Cap Gun, Double Barrel, 1880 .... 200.00
Cap Gun, Double Barrel, Pirate, Pair 35.00
Cap Gun, Eagle, 1890 ....25.00 To 60.00
Cap Gun, Fanner, 1950s 10.00
Cap Gun, Gold Texan 40.00
Cap Gun, Hubley, 6 In. 10.00
Cap Gun, Long Boy, Early 1900, 11 1/2 In. 18.00
Cap Gun, Model 21, Box 200.00
Cap Gun, One Shot, Marked P38, 3 1/2 In. 15.00
Cap Gun, Padlock Shape, Hubley 85.00
Cap Gun, Pal & Brave, Marked Hubley, White Metal 10.00
Cap Gun, Peacemaker, Box 25.00
Cap Gun, Pinto, Metal, 3 1/2 In. 10.00
Cap Gun, Pluck 67.50
Cap Gun, Pony Boy 10.00
Cap Gun, Presto, Kilgore, Iron 13.00
Cap Gun, Red Ranger, Wyandotte 70.00
Cap Gun, Scout, Model S6 .... 45.00
Cap Gun, Secret Compartment, Brass 25.00
Cap Gun, Special Agent 12.00
Cap Gun, Texas Jr., Holster, Pair 40.00
Cap Gun, Trooper, Hubley 12.00
Cap Gun, W In Circle 18.00
Cap Gun, Whizzer, Crank Type 50.00
Cap Gun, Wild Bill Hickok, Spurs, Jail Keys, 2 Leather Pieces 48.00
Cap Gun, Wild Bill Hickok, With Holster, Pair 150.00
Captain Video, Space Set, Boxed 45.00
Car & Driver, Lehmann, Lithographed Tin, Clockwork, 4 In. ....*Illus* 110.00
Car Set, Varianto, Schuco 95.00
Car, 1929, Model A, 4 Door, Cast Iron 30.00
Car, 1930s, Arcor Toy Co., Hard Rubber 35.00
Car, 1938 Pontiac, Arcade, Cast Iron, 6 In. 300.00
Car, Airflow, Iron, Hubley 625.00
Car, Andy Gump, Original Paint, Arcade 348, 7 In. ....325.00 To 450.00
Car, Andy Gump, Tootsietoy 195.00
Car, Austin, Racing, Box 175.00
Car, Buick Roadmaster, Dinky, Green & Yellow 65.00
Car, Buick Sportster, 1950, Marx, Tin Litho, 18 In. 45.00
Car, Cadillac, Bandi, 1961, 17 In. 95.00
Car, Chevy Cameo Pickup, Red, Tootsietoy, 4 In. 12.00
Car, Chevy Coupe, Cast Iron, Arcade, 1929, 8 In. 650.00
Car, Chevy, Deluxe Panel, Tootsietoy, Blue 10.00
Car, Convertible, Ford, 1949, Tootsietoy 20.00
Car, Convertible, Passenger Takes Picture, Box, 12 In. 35.00
Car, Convertible, Tin Litho, Red Interior, Marx, C.1930, 11 In. 110.00
Car, Corvette, 1954, Tootsietoy 25.00
Car, Crazy, Donald Duck, Tin Litho, Windup 550.00

Car, Crazy, Milton Berle, Windup, Marx, Box ....125.00 To 175.00
Car, Deusenberg, Limousine, Model, Hubley 75.00
Car, Driver Training, Advertising, Louis Marx, Box 65.00
Car, Driver Training, Magic Action, Marx 35.00
Car, Fire Chief, Marx, Windup, 7 In. 20.00
Car, Fire Chief, Pedal, Murray 125.00
Car, Fireman's, 2 Firemen In Front Seat, Battery, 10 In. 18.00
Car, Ford Fire Chief, Red, Box, 9 1/2 In. 20.00
Car, Ford Mustang, Battery Operated, Box, 16 In. 190.00
Car, Ford Mustang, Steerable Tires, White, Box 9.00
Car, Friction, 1950s, Working Windshield Wipers, Japan, 7 In. 60.00
Car, G.I.Joe, Jouncing Jeep, Unique Art, Tin 100.00
Car, Golden Arrow Racer, Kingsbury, 20 In. 235.00
Car, Hessmobil 1020, Tin, Crank, Hess, Instruction Sheet, 7 In. 425.00
Car, Jaguar, E Type, Red 10.00
Car, Jaguar, XK120, Micro, Red 40.00
Car, James Bond 007, Battery, 1925, Boxed 225.00
Car, James Bond, Gilbert, Battery Operated 175.00
Car, Kaiser, Tootsietoy, 1947, Red 28.00
Car, LaSalle Coupe, Tootsietoy, Silver & Black 100.00
Car, Lincoln Continental Mark V, Remote Control, Tin, Japan, Box, 11 In. 75.00
Car, Lincoln, 1958, Plastic, Promotional 55.00
Car, M.P., World War II, Friction 20.00
Car, Maxwell, 1911, Green, Box 18.00
Car, Mercedes, Tin, 12 In. 125.00
Car, Model A Ford, 1960s, Hubley, Pair 90.00
Car, Model A, Rumble Seat Coupe, Gold Pinstripe, Blue, Arcade, Cast Iron 250.00
Car, Model T Ford, 1920s, Cast Iron, Arcade, 6 1/4 In. 250.00
Car, Mr.Magoo, Official, Box 180.00
Car, Mustang, Plastic, Steel, Friction, Original Garage Box, 1967, 16 In. 60.00
Car, Nash, Die Cast, White Rubber Tires, Banthrico, Box, 6 1/2 In. 25.00
Car, Nelly Belle, Marx, Steel, Box 95.00
Car, Packard, 1958–63, Gray & Orange 12.00
Car, Police, Siren, Windup, 14 In. 125.00
Car, Racing, Conical Body, Pedal Power, Miniature ....*Illus* 550.00
Car, Racing, Driver, Fishtail Back, Metal Wheels, Red, Cast Metal, 5 In. 50.00
Car, Racing, Hi Speed, Mystery Action, Engine Noise, Battery Operated 60.00
Car, Racing, Hubley, Cast Iron ....35.00 To 50.00
Car, Racing, Indianapolis, Gas Motor, Propeller, Aluminum, Plastic 60.00
Car, Racing, Indy, Windup, Tin Litho, Marx 25.00
Car, Racing, Marked Wilbur Shaw Indianapolis Speedway, Metal, 9 In. 75.00
Car, Racing, No.22, Red & Gold Paint 700.00

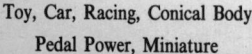

Toy, Car, Racing, Conical Body,
Pedal Power, Miniature

Toy, Truck, Dump, Buddy L, C.1932, 25 In.

Car, Racing, Offenhauser, Tootsietoy, 1947 .... 15.00
Car, Racing, Pull Toy, Star Brand Shoes, 1920s 150.00
Car, Racing, Vanwell, Early 1960s, Green, Dinky Toy 10.00
Car, Racing, Windup, Chein, 7 In. 40.00
Car, Racing, Windup, Schuco Studio 30.00
Car, Racing, Windup, Tin, Red, Marx, 13 In. 65.00
Car, Remote Control, Battery Operated, Cragstan 20.00
Car, Rolls–Royce Phantom, No.124, Dinky Toys 22.00
Car, Safe Driving School, Windup, Tin 75.00
Car, Sedan, Remote Control, Battery Operated, Cragstan 20.00
Car, Station Wagon, Studebaker, Blue, Box 16.00
Car, Studebaker, Tin, 16 In. 95.00
Car, T–Bird, Dinky Toys, Boxed 35.00
Car, Taxi, Buick, Yellow, 1959, 8 1/2 In. 25.00
Car, Tin, Coupe, Rear Spare Tire, Running Board, Painted, 18 1/2 In. 200.00
Car, Touring, Arcade, Cast Iron 175.00
Car, Touring, Driver, Tin, Litho, Fisher, 9 In. 550.00
Car, Touring, Whitanco, Made In England, Litho Tin, Driver 220.00
Car, Whoopee, Marx, Tin 175.00
Car, Yell–O Taxi, Windup, With Driver, Strauss, 1920s 475.00
Car, Yellow Cab, Cast Iron, Painted, Hubley, 7 1/2 In. 150.00
Cardinal, Squeak, 19th Century, Seated On Rock, Stenciled Leaves, 7 In. 225.00
Carnival, World War II Sailor, On Stick, U.S.Navy, Celluloid 20.00
Carousel, Tin, 4 Horse, Painted, Clockwork, German, 12 In. 1000.00
Carpet Sweeper, Bissel, Little Gem, 1940 ....24.00 To 29.00
Carriage, Doll's, Bentwood Front Wheel Supports, Wooden, Red Paint 175.00
Carriage, Doll's, Composition, Wicker, 1930, 3 In. 39.00
Carriage, Doll's, Fringed Top, Red Paint, Vermont Novelty, 36 X 29 In. 675.00
Carriage, Doll's, Hooded, 1930, Wyandotte 50.00
Carriage, Doll's, Red Leather, Collapsible 90.00
Carriage, Doll's, Westbend, 1930s, Wicker 125.00
Carriage, Doll's, Wicker, Early 1900s 175.00
Carriage, Doll's, Wicker, Porthole Windows, 1930 .... 147.00
Carriage, Pulled By 2 Horses, Driver, German 4500.00
Carrying Case, Darth Vader, Star Wars 22.00
Cart, 2 Wheel, Cast Iron, 13 In. 45.00
Cash Register, Tin, Silver Embossed, Benjamin Franklin, 7 1/2 X 6 In. 38.00
Cash Register, Tom Thumb ....10.00 To 25.00
Cat & Mouse, Windup, Made In Germany, Tin, 7 In. 70.00
Cat, As Barber, Windup, Tin, Japan, 5 In. 60.00
Cat, Black, On Red Board, Fisher Price, Battery Operated 27.50
Cat, Black, With Ball, Mechanical, Key Wind 25.00
Cat, Blue & Pink Felt Coat, 10 In. 35.00
Cat, Felix, Schoenhut 300.00
Cat, Fur, Glass Eyes, Windup, French, 1910 .... 110.00
Cat, Glass Eyes, Mohair, Windup, Key 12.00
Cat, In Basket, Steiff, Lifesize 100.00
Caterpillar, Roller, Cast Iron, Hubley, 3 1/2 In. 65.00
Chair, Doll's, Alligator Varnish, Decoupage Of Flowers On Back 110.00
Chair, Doll's, Bentwood, Pine, 16 In. 35.00
Chair, Doll's, High Back, Mirror, Candlestand, 13 X 24 In. 225.00
Chair, Doll's, High Back, Wicker, Pair 175.00
Chariot, Horse Drawn, C.1860, Tin, Hand Painted, 20 In. 1980.00
Charlie Weaver, Bartender, Battery Operated ....10.00 To 20.00
Charlie Weaver, Bartender, Battery Operated, Box 60.00
Chest, 5 Sections For Lead Soldiers, Oak, 33 X 20 X 7 In. 80.00
Chester Gump, In Cart, Pulled By Horse, Iron, 1905 .... 350.00
Chicken, Laying Egg, Wyandotte, Tin 25.00
Chicken, Windup, Tin, Chein, 3 1/2 In 12.00
Chicken, Windup, Tin, Walks & Quacks 35.00
Chimp, Long Armed, Steiff, 21 In. 100.00
Chipmunk, Steiff, 4 In. 70.00
Chipmunk, Tin Litho, Linemar 30.00
Circus Horse & Lady Rider, Schoenhut, 8 1/2 In. 125.00

Circus Horse, Musical, Pull Toy, Marx 50.00
Circus Set, Ringling, Barnum & Bailey, Lever Bros., 1948, Uncut, 35 Piece 45.00
Circus Wagon, 2 Lions, 6 Horses, Rhino, Cast Iron 850.00
Circus, Paper, Eat Holsum & Sanatara Bread, 1910, 14 Piece 38.00
City Dray, Buddy L, Steel, 1930–32, Door Open, 24 In. 500.00
Clock Kit, Meccano, Original Box 22.00
Clothes Hamper, Wicker, 11 In. 25.00
Clothesline, Wooden Pins, Dolli–Pins, 1940s 5.00
Clown Cart, With Donkey, Windup, Lehmann, Tin, 7 In. 100.00
Clown On Unicycle, Windup, Japan 35.00
Clown Organ Grinder, Dancing Plush Teddy Bear, Tin, Clockwork 1100.00
Clown, Acrobat, Balancing 30.00
Clown, Beating Black Golliwog Over Head With Mallet, Tin, Clacker 65.00
Clown, Cart & Donkey, Windup, Tin, Germany, C.1907, 7 1/2 In. 90.00
Clown, Loop The Loop, Battery Operated, Box 20.00
Clown, On Barrel, Windup, Tin, West Germany, Original Box, 8 In. 225.00
Clown, Roller Skating, Windup, Tin, Cloth, Japan, 6 In. 65.00
Clown, Roly Poly, Chimes Inside 65.00
Coal Wagon, Stanley, Metal 15.00
Coffee Grinder, Pull Out Drawer, Square, 2 1/2 X 3 1/2 In. 65.00
Coloring Set, Tom Corbett, Unused 65.00
Combat Pistol, Windup, Tin, Marx 38.00
Combine, Massey Harris Clipper, Box 225.00
Concrete Mixer, Jaeger, Doepke 150.00
Conestoga Wagon, Cast Iron Wheels, Cloth Top, Wooden, 14 In. 45.00
Conestoga Wagon, Model, Working, Wooden, Brass Trim, 13 1/2 X 17 In. 50.00
Construction Set, Spirit Of St.Louis, No.820, Metalcraft 150.00
Cookie Can, Raggedy Ann & Andy, Chein, Signed 35.00
Coon Jigger, Lehmann, Original Box 535.00
Costume, Darth Vader, Box, Size 6–12 .... 15.00
Covered Wagon, 2 Oxen, Clay, Canvas Is Tanned Skin 350.00
Cow, Bessy, Brown Velvet, Udders, Tag, Button, Bell, Collar, Steiff, 7 In. 85.00
Cow, Bessy, Steiff, Tag & Button, 7 In. 65.00
Cow, Moos, Moves, 8 X 7 In. ....*Color* 125.00
Cowboy, On Horse, Windup, Guntherman ....275.00 To 295.00
Cowboys & Indians, Crescent, 21 Piece 20.00
Cradle, Doll's, Folding, 1906, 20 In. 40.00
Cradle, Doll's, Hooded, 16 In. 95.00
Cradle, Doll's, Strombecker, 10 X 5 In. 20.00
Crane, Litho Tin, Windup, Wolverine, 14 In. 50.00
Crane, Windup, Beller, Western Germany, Tin 45.00
Crap Shooter, Cragston, Battery Operated, Box, Japan 40.00
Crayons, Bopeep, Wooden, Box Of 6 .... 7.00
Crocodile, Brown Velvet, Button, Steiff, 12 In. 65.00
Crocodile, Windup, Lehmann 550.00
Croquet Set, Little Folks Croquet, Wooden Dovetailed Box 34.00
Crow, Hopping, Linemar 75.00
Cultivator, John Deere, Rubber Tires, Metal, 6 X 9 In. 16.00
Cupboard, Glass, 1940s, Painted Blue, Pine 95.00
Dagwood The Driver, Windup, Tin, Litho, Marx, Original Box, 8 In. 500.00
Dancer & Fiddler, Clockwork, Wooden Box, Cloth Gessoed Faces, 8 3/4 In. 900.00
Dancer, Hula, Windup, Celluloid Head & Body, Tin Legs 50.00
Dancing Dan, With Microphone, Battery, Original Box 125.00
Dancing Sam, Mechanical, Japan, Box ....65.00 To 85.00
Dandy Digger, Buddy L 100.00
Dandy Jim, Clown Dancer, Strauss, 1921, Windup 285.00
Daredevil, Lehmann, Lithographed Tin, Clockwork, 7 In. ....*Illus* 90.00
Dirigible, Tin, Key Wind 55.00
Dishes, Doll's, Wooden Box, Label, 13 Piece, C.1875 .... 85.00
Distance Finder, Sgt.Preston, 1955 .... 75.00
Dog, Allie, Georgene Averill 2800.00
Dog, Celluloid, Windup, Tail Wags, Head Nods, Occupied Japan 20.00
Dog, Chasing Duck Squeak Toy, Painted Papier–Mache, 6 In. 400.00
Dog, Dachshund, Friction, Box 18.00

Dog, Fur, Glass Eyes, 8 In. 14.00
Dog, Irish Terrier, On Iron Wheels, With Button, Steiff 325.00
Dog, Mohair, Windup, Growl, Belly Button Moves, Foot Moves, Shake Off Bee 75.00
Dog, On Wooden Wheels, Steiff, Large 375.00
Dog, Plays When Crank Turns, Mattel, 1951, Tin 20.00
Dog, Rocking, With Whirling Rope, Windup, Tin, Japan, Original Box, 6 In. 25.00
Dog, Sandy, Windup, Tin, Box 345.00
Dog, St.Bernard, On Iron Wheels, Steiff 325.00
Dog, With Rider, Pull Toy, Original Paint, Tin, 9 1/2 In. 185.00
TOY, DOLL, see Doll
Dollhouse, 2–Story, Attic Window, Porch, Open Back, Labeled Schoenhut 500.00
Dollhouse, 2–Story, Glass Windows, Furnished, Litho Tin, 14 In. 360.00
Dollhouse, 2–Story, McLaughlin Bros., Victorian, Cardboard, Box, 1907–12 .... 100.00
Dollhouse, 2–Story, Porch, Glass Windows, Red & Yellow Siding, 13 In. 395.00
Dollhouse, 2–Story, Unfurnished, Litho Tin, 14 In. 385.00
Dollhouse, 2–Story, Yellow, Green Roof, Wallpaper, Litho Tin, 10 In. 350.00
Dollhouse, 4–Room, German, C.1910 .... 675.00
Dollhouse, 4–Room, WPA Stamped, 24 X 18 X 15 In. 150.00
Dollhouse, 6–Room, Shingled Roof, Furniture, Front Opens, Schoenhut 550.00
Dollhouse, Bliss, C.1900, 13 In. 475.00
Dollhouse, Bungalow, Schoenhut, 16 X 16 In. 275.00
Dollhouse, Bungalow, Side Wall Opening, Red Roof, German, 10 In. 195.00
Dollhouse, Castle, 2–Story, Opens Top & Back, Hand Crafted, 44 X 35 In. 3000.00
Dollhouse, Furniture, Bathroom Set, Pink, Renwal, 4 Piece 20.00
Dollhouse, Furniture, Bedroom, Kitchen, Living Room, Tootsietoy, 33 Pc. 200.00
Dollhouse, Furniture, Chest, Walnut, 4 X 6 X 7 In. 42.00
Dollhouse, Furniture, China Cupboard, Glass Doors, Mirror Top 97.00
Dollhouse, Furniture, Commode, Wooden, 1930s 12.00
Dollhouse, Furniture, Cupboard, Kitchen, Pressed Cardboard, O–Joy 85.00
Dollhouse, Furniture, High Chair, Wooden, 1930s 12.00
Dollhouse, Furniture, Patio Set, Tin, Floral, Table & 3 Chairs 30.00
Dollhouse, Furniture, Refrigerator, Wooden, 1930s 14.00
Dollhouse, Furniture, Stove, Green & Cream Graniteware 17.50
Dollhouse, Furniture, Table, Folding, 2 Chairs, Renwal 20.00
Dollhouse, Furniture, Vanity, 3–Way Mirror, Tootsietoy 18.00
Dollhouse, Furniture, Wicker, 4 1/2 In., 5 Piece 12.50
Dollhouse, Keystone–Boston, Painted Interior, Electrified, 1948 .... 185.00
Dollhouse, Metal, 1940s, 22 X 15 In. 34.00
Dollhouse, Ranch, Metal, Marx, Original Box, 1950s 50.00
Dollhouse, Strombecker, No.H8, 17 Pieces Of Furniture 90.00
Dollhouse, Tin Litho, 1940s, Marx, Complete, Box 45.00
Dolly Dressmaker, Battery Operated 135.00
Donkey, Braying, Pull Toy, Marked Germany, 8 X 10 In. 200.00
Donkey, Felt, Saddle, Wheels, Pewter Button, Steiff, 1898, 8 1/2 X 10 In. 595.00
Donkey, Glass Eyes, Schoenhut 65.00
Donkey, Gray, Steiff, 8 In. 40.00
Dresser, Doll's, Marked Converse, Wooden 45.00
Dresser, Doll's, Mirror & 2 Drawers, 21 In. 85.00
Dresser, Doll's, White Wood, Tole Painting, Mirror, 1911, 11 In. 75.00
Dresser, Doll's, White, 12 X 15 In. 32.00
Drum Major, No.27E, Wolverine 100.00
Drum Set, Ohio Art 16.00
Drum, Litho Of Noah's Ark & Animals, Tin, Ohio Art Co. 18.00
Drum, Wooden Sticks, Chein, Playtime Circus Design, 1930s, Tin 12.00
Drummer Bear, Windup 55.00
Drummer Boy, Bandsman Beats Bass Drum, Windup, 1930s, Marx 350.00
Drummer Boy, Tin, Windup, Chein ....55.00 To 75.00
Drying Rack, Folding, Clothes 24.00
Duck & Cart, Quack–Quack, Lehmann, Windup, Tin, 7 1/2 In. 250.00
Duck, Felt, Wheels, Pewter Button, Steiff, C.1908, 5 1/2 X 8 In. 495.00
Duck, Skiing, Linemar 100.00
Duck, Waddle, Windup, Chein 48.00
Duck, Windup, Walks & Quacks, Rabbit Fur Cover, Japan 45.00
Earth Mover, Structo, Boxed 30.00

Elephant, Battery Operated, Moves Arms, Blows Air Through Trunk, 8 In. 35.00
Elephant, On Iron Wheels, Felt, Steiff 150.00
Elephant, Plush On Tin, Windup, Glass Eyes, C.1910 .... 52.00
Elephant, Plush, Straw Filled, Iron Wheels, 10 In. 195.00
Elephant, Stuffed, On Metal Wheels, Pull Toy, 11 X 15 1/2 In. 225.00
Erector Set, Gilbert, Instructions, Metal Case, Motor, 1938 .... 175.00
Erector Set, Gilbert, No.6 1/2, Instruction Book, Copyright 1945 .... 75.00
Erector Set, Gilbert, No.7 1/2, Engineers, 1938 ....52.50 To 65.00
Erector Set, Mysto, No.00–1912, Complete, Box 150.00
Erector Set, No.10181, Builds Helicopter, Instructions 18.00
Erector Set, Rocket Launcher, No.10201, Gilbert ....70.00 To 98.00
Farm Set, Lazy Day, Tin Litho, Barn, Animals, Fence, Tractors 45.00
Farm, Paper, Carnation Milk Premiums, 1917, 5 Piece 35.00
Father Christmas, Cloth & Rabbit Fur, Plaster Hands & Face, 15 1/2 In. 550.00
Felix The Cat, Dean's Fabric, 14 In. 50.00
Felix The Cat, Jointed, Wood, 1920s, 4 In. ....95.00 To 125.00
Felix The Cat, On Scooter 300.00
Felix The Cat, Walker, Slant Board 200.00
Ferris Wheel, Mechanical, J.Chein Co., Box 135.00
Ferris Wheel, Tin, J.Chein, 16 1/2 In. 90.00
Ferris Wheel, Windup, Giant Riddle, Ohio Art, Tin 75.00
Figurine, Charlie McCarthy, Cardboard, 21 In. 30.00
Fire Engine Pump, Horse Drawn, 2 Horses, Iron 150.00
Fire Engine, Buddy L, Hook & Ladder, No.811, Box 175.00
Fire Engine, Friction, No.9161, Tin, Linemar 22.50
Fire Engine, Hook & Ladder, Buddy L, No.811 .... 175.00
Fire Engine, Rubber Tires, Chrome Ladder, Hubley 85.00
Fire Engine, Siren, Battery Operated, Box, Japan 30.00
Fire Engine, Tin, Marusan, Box, 6 In. 15.00
Fire Engine, Tin, Red Paint, 4 Men 80.00
Fire House, 6 In.Steam Engine Truck, 6 In.Hook & Ladder, Windup, 1920 .... 500.00
Fire Truck & Ladder Co., Battery Operated, Japan 20.00
Fire Truck, Beige, Early 1940s, Tootsietoy 16.00
Fire Wagon, 2 Horses, Driver, Cast Iron 97.50
Flapper, Chubby, Sitting In Fancy Chair, Celluloid, 6 In. 40.00
Food Grinder, Iron, Working 20.00
Football Player, Celluloid, Occupied Japan, 3 3/4 In. 8.00
Fort, French, Cardboard, For Toy Soldiers, Signed 250.00
Fox, Curled Up, Velvet Face, Steiff, 9 In. 75.00
Fox, Mohair, Jointed Head, Wheels, Steiff, C.1910, 6 1/2 X 9 In. 425.00
Frankie, Roller Skating Monkey, Battery, Original Box 85.00
Fred Flintstone, On Dino, Battery Operated, Linemar 125.00
Freighter, Tootsietoy 15.00
G.I.Joe & His K–9 Pups, Windup, Tin ....115.00 To 145.00
TOY, GAME, see Game
Garage, 2–Car, With Race Car, Galop, Lehmann, Windup 750.00
Garage, Service Center, Tin, Litho, Marx, 27 X 15 In. 58.00
Gas Pump, Mechanical, Cast Iron, Painted, Arcade Label, 6 1/4 In. 100.00
Gas Station, Electric, Marx 50.00
Gino, Balloon Blower, Battery Operated, Marx, Box 125.00
Girl, Bouncing Ball, Windup, Tin, 4 1/2 In. 15.00
Glider, Doll's, Folding, Wooden, Holds 2 Dolls 85.00
Godzilla, Friction, Japanese 30.00
Goggles, Groucho, On Card 35.00
Golden Goose, Lays Eggs, Pecks, Hops, 1924, Marx 30.00
Good Time Charlie, Battery, Original Box 48.00
Grandpa In Rocking Chair, Battery Operated, Japan 50.00
Grandpa, Smoking, Battery, Sun Co. 65.00
Grasshopper, Pull Toy, Hubley, Cast Iron 600.00
Great Billiard Champion, Windup, German, Box, 1910 ....350.00 To 450.00
Griddle, Bail Handle, Signed Wagner Ware, Sidney, 5 In. 22.50
Grocery Store, A & P, Fold Up, 1940s 35.00
Gun & Holster, Dragnet, Boxed 80.00
Gun & Holster, Rin Tin Tin, Cavalry, Shredded Wheat Order Form 45.00

Gun, Aircraft, Elevate, England 14.00
Gun, Atom Flash Zoomeray, Original Box 27.00
Gun, Bell Ringer, Pat.1914 .... 15.00
Gun, Cork, E–Z Ray, Tin, Unused 12.00
Gun, Dart, Tin, Wyandotte 10.00
Gun, Electronic Space, Remco, Battery Operated 15.00
Gun, Machine, World War I, Magazine Holds Wooden Bullets 47.50
Gun, Mobil Quick Fire AA, Dinky 25.00
Gun, Pistol, Big Bill, Round Hammer, Kilgore 40.00
Gun, Pistol, Big Scout, Hubley 50.00
Gun, Pistol, Stevens Peace Maker, Hubley 55.00
Gun, Ronson Repeater, Boy Scout Shooting Bear, Box 24.00
Gun, Squirt, Daisy, No.80 .... 20.00
Gun, Squirt, K, Large Bulb 20.00
Gyroscope, Hurst, Instructions, Original Box, 1940s 10.00
Ham & Sam, Black Musicians At Piano, Windup, Strauss, 1920s ....325.00 To 450.00
Hamster, Mohair, Steiff, 5 In. 50.00
Handcar, Moon Mullins & Kayo ....275.00 To 395.00
Hans & Fritz, Windup, Tin, Composition, Painted, 1944, 2 3/4 In., Pair 30.00
Happy Hooligan, Windup, Tin, Litho, Chein, 6 In. ....145.00 To 175.00
Happy Santa, Walks, Drums, Battery Operated, Box 160.00
Harold Lloyd, Face, Squeeze, Mechanism, Eyes Spark, German, 1930s 165.00
Harold Lloyd, Funny Face, Windup, Tin 425.00
Hey Hey The Chicken Snatcher, Black Man, Chicken, Dog Biting, 1920 .... 650.00
High Chair, Doll's, Convertible, 22 In. 575.00
High Chair, Doll's, Wicker, 23 In. 65.00
High Chair, Doll's, Wooden, 18 In. 35.00
High Jinks Circus Clown, Battery, Original Box 125.00
Hike–O–Meter, Wheaties 20.00
Hobbyhorse, Metal, 32 X 22 In. 175.00
Hobbyhorse, Red & Gray Paint, 43 3/4 In. 275.00
Hobbyhorse, Red Painted Frame, Laminated, Appaloosa Paint, 39 In. 500.00
Hobbyhorse, Wooden, 36 In. 100.00
Holly Chimp, Musical, Battery 35.00
Hoopy Fishing Duck, Battery, Original Box 145.00
Hooty The Owl, Art Fabric, 5 1/2 In. 42.00
Horse & Cart, Harry Porter Coal & Wood, Wooden, Wheeled Horse, 24 In. 175.00
Horse & Cart, Windup, Polychrome Transfer, German, Tin, 7 3/4 In. 12.50
Horse & Ice Truck, Yellow Truck, Silver Horse, Iron, 2 X 8 1/2 In. 95.00
Horse & Wagon, Ice, Converse, 2 Horses, 17 In. 295.00
Horse & Wagon, Wooden Horse, Tin Painted Wagon, Marked Coal 245.00
Horse On Wheels, Cloth, Leather, Iron Wheels, Steiff, 12 In. 350.00
Horse Race, Activated With Spring Lever, Adult, French 110.00
Horse Swing, Tack, Dapple Gray, Charles Henry's, 5 Ft. X 44 In. 1750.00
Horse, Mohair, Red Wooden Wheel, Saddle, Steiff, 1950s, 9 X 7 1/2 In. 135.00
Horse, On Platform & Wheels, Black, Plush 65.00
Horse, On Wheels, Metal, Original Paint, 21 X 21 In. ....*Illus* 95.00
Horse, Prancing, Hide Covered, Black & White 55.00
Horse, Pull Toy, Dapple Gray Paint, Iron Wheels On Platform, 16 1/2 In. 550.00
Horse, Pull Toy, Wood, Black Haircloth Cover, Base, Wheels, 15 X 17 In. 450.00
Horse, Pull Toy, Wooden Body, Covered In Haircloth, 27 1/2 In. 475.00
Horse, Pulling Cart Painted Red, Brown, Handmade, 21 1/2 In. 65.00
Horse, Pulling Green Tin Wagon, Cast Iron, 7 In. 49.00
Horse, Racing, Tin, Lever Action, Box, 7 1/2 X 7 1/2 In. 75.00
Horse, Running, Pull Toy, Original Paint, Tin, 5 1/2 In. 145.00
Horse, Stuffed, On Wheels, Wooden Base, Red Stripes, 13 In. 270.00
Horseless Carriage, Lehmann, Tin, Windup 350.00
Hula Dancer, Celluloid, Windup 60.00
Hutch, Doll's, Blue, 24 X 12 In. 88.00
Hutch, Doll's, Wolverine, Metal 39.00
Ice Cream Freezer, Wooden, Dana Peerless 225.00
Ice Man, Windup, Tin, Litho, Marx, 8 1/2 In. 100.00
Ice Skates, Clamp On, U.S.Club, Pair 8.50
Ice Skates, Heart Pads, Diamonds Carved In Relief, 18th Century 295.00

Ice Skates, Leather, High Button, Victorian 45.00
Ice Skates, Union Hardware Co., Extension, Leather Straps 20.00
Ice Skates, Wooden Platforms, Burl With Brass Acorn Finials 220.00
Ice Skates, Wooden, Leather Ankle Straps & Toe Supports 75.00
Ice Skates, Wooden, Wrought Iron Runner, Leather, 12 3/4 In. 25.00
Ironing Board, Little Bopeep, Tin ....12.00 To 15.00
Jack–In–The–Box, Dog, Papier–Mache, 4 1/2 In. 80.00
Jack–In–The–Box, Mattel, Tin 12.00
Jacks, Cast Iron, 7 Piece 10.00
Jazzbo Jim, Dancer On Roof, Strauss, 1921, Windup 275.00
Jazzbo Jim, Dancer, Violin Player, Unique Art, Windup, 1921 ....350.00 To 375.00
Jiggs, Windup, Tin, 4 1/2 In. 22.00
Jocco The Golfer, Golfer Spins, Hits Ball From Tee, C.1925 .... 325.00
Jockey & Horse, Windup, Celluloid On Metal 150.00
Jockey Riding Rocking Horse, Tin, Litho, Penny Toy 100.00
Joe Penner & Duck Goo–Goo, Windup, Tin, Marx, Box, 8 In. ....275.00 To 400.00
Jumping Jack, Cloth Costume, Celluloid Face, Wooden, 16 In. 15.00
Kaleidoscope, Cardboard, G.G.Bush & Co., Walnut Stand 300.00
Kangaroo, Baby In Pouch, Steiff, 11 In. 200.00
Keg, Wooden, Alphabet Scroll Printed In Blue On Cloth Tape, 3 1/4 In. 195.00
Kicker, Football, Windup, Cast Iron 125.00
Kiddie Cyclist, Teddy Lithograph, Tin, Windup, Unique Art 98.00
Kiddie Kamera, Smitty & Comic Characters 9.00
Kiddie Shoe Shine Box, Wooden, Foot Rest, 9140s 23.00
King Kong, Windup, Tin, Plastic, Cloth, Marx, 7 In. 50.00
Kitten, Striped, Jointed Head, Squat On Haunches Sleeping, Steiff, 6 In. 52.00
Kittens, On Wheels, Playing With Ball, Hand Painted, Windup, 1900 .... 375.00
Lady, Serving Tea, Battery, 8 1/2 In. 25.00
Lady, With Parasol, Windup, Tin, 6 1/2 In. 85.00
Ladybug, Friction, Tin, Lehmann, 1940s 10.00
Ladybug, Wheels, Tag & Button, Steiff, C.1950, 22 In. 375.00
Lawnmower, Tin Litho, Wooden Handle, 8 1/2 X 20 In. 10.00
Leaping Lena, Windup, Tin, Strauss 275.00
Li'l Abner Dogpatch Band, Windup, Box ....335.00 To 450.00
Lincoln Tunnel & Car Set, Windup, 6 Cars, Truck, Cop 125.00
Lion, Steiff, 10 In. 45.00
Llama, Button, Steiff, 10 In. 125.00
Llama, Tag & Button, Steiff, 6 1/2 In. 65.00
Lobster, Clockwork, German, Tin 175.00
Loveseat, Doll's, Rattan, Table, 2 Chairs, 5 1/2 In. 50.00
Maggie & Jiggs, Windup, 1924, German 1050.00
Magic Carpet, Mechanical, Clockwork, Tin, German, Propellers Rotate, 1905 .... 400.00
Magic Lantern, Tin, Painted, Wooden Base, 17 Slides 100.00
Mammy, Tin Litho, Windup, Lindstrom, 1930s 150.00
Man In The Moon, Mechanical Eye, Tin, Litho, 2 1/2 In. 90.00
Man, Shooting Pool, Windup, 1910, German, 6 In. 450.00
Man, With Banner Alms Box, Pot Metal, Mechanical Arm, 12 In. 1100.00
Manure Spreader, International, Metal, 12 In. 22.00
Meat Grinder, Arcade, Cast Iron 38.00
Melody Player, Tin, Paper Rolls, Box 80.00
Merry Makers Band, Windup, Marx, Original Box ....650.00 To 750.00
Merry-Go-Round, J.Chien 150.00
Microscope, Kit, Porter, 1954 .... 25.00
Milk Wagon, Horse & Driver, White & Red Wheels, C.1920, 6 X 12 In. 275.00
Monkey, Battery ....*Color* 35.00
Monkey, Blowing Bubbles, Battery Operated, Box, Japan ....75.00 To 88.00
Monkey, Climbing Stick, Jointed, Carved, 15 In. 195.00
Monkey, Climbing, Lehmann, Box ....225.00 To 350.00
Monkey, Drinking, Windup, Tin, Linemar, Original Box, 6 In. 90.00
Monkey, Playing Cymbals, Battery Operated ....30.00 To 35.00
Monkey, Playing Guitar, Windup, Celluloid, Japan 75.00
Monkey, Pushing Baggage Cart, Windup, Hand Painted, 1900 .... 375.00
Monkey, Riding Pump Car, Straw Stuffed, Steiff 425.00
Monkey, Weight Lifter, Battery Operated 30.00

Monkey, White Button, Steiff, 4 In. 70.00
Monkey, Yes & No, Schuco, 10 In. 115.00
Moon Rocket, Apollo, Friction, Japan, 15 In. 29.00
Motorboat, Battery, All Wood, 13 In. 60.00
Motorboat, Detachable Outboard Motor, Driver, Lindstrom, Tin, 12 1/2 In. 95.00
Motorboat, Outboard, Windup, Tin, Lindstrom, 10 1/2 In. 50.00
Motorcycle, Cop, Auburn, Rubber, Red, White Tires 28.00
Motorcycle, Delivery, Windup, Tin, Marx, Original Box, 10 In. 135.00
Motorcycle, Falls Down Then Gets Back Up, Windup, 7 In. 13.00
Motorcycle, Sparkling Soldier, Windup, Tin, Marx, Original Box, 8 1/4 In. 125.00
Motorcycle, Speed Boy Delivery, Marx 75.00
Motorcycle, White Rubber Tires, Cast Iron, Champion, 7 In. 85.00
Mouse In Bread, Surprise, Papier–Mache, 3 1/2 In. 100.00
Mouse, Drinks From Mug, Windup, German, 4 In. 67.00
Moving Van, Buddy L, 24 In. 125.00
Mr.Fox, Magician, Blows Bubbles, Battery Operated, Box 145.00
Mule, Balky, 1897, Lehmann 75.00
Mule, Leather Ears & Tail, Schoenhut, 9 X 6 In. 175.00
Musicians, Litho & Painted Tin, Gunthermann, Cloth Dressed, 8 1/2 In. 1900.00
Native On Alligator, Windup, Tin, Chein 75.00
Native With Spear & Shield, Windup, Tin, Litho, 5 1/2 In. 60.00
Noah's Ark, Tin Litho, Linemar 120.00
Noah's Ark, Wooden, Painted, 26 Carved Animals, 18 1/2 In. 140.00
Noah's Ark, Wooden, Painted, Carved Animals, 19th Century, 18 X 8 In. 275.00
Noisemaker, Lithograph, Cello Shape, Tin, Marked Germany 40.00
Nutty Mad Indian, Box, Linemar 75.00
Opera House, Wooden, 16 X 24 In. 65.00
Organ Grinder & Dancing Monkey, Germany 1000.00
Organ Grinder, Pull Toy, Grinder Plays Music, Monkey Turns, B.Hill 65.00
Ostrich Cart, Black Driver, Zulu, Lehmann, Windup, Tin, 7 1/4 In. 350.00
Paddle Ball, Raggedy Ann & Andy, Wooden 10.00
Paddy Holding Pig, Baby Rattle, Celluloid, 1920s, 8 1/2 In. 95.00
Pail, Converse, Lithograph Animals, Tin, 1915 .... 75.00
Pail, Dutch Scene, Tin, Ohio Art Co. 15.00
Pail, Jack & Jill Litho, Tin, Ohio Art, 11 In., Set Of 3 .... 19.50
Pail, Teddy Bears, Tin, Chein 23.00
Paint & Crayon Kit, Poster Paint & Watercolors, 1941, 21 X 14 In. 13.50
Paint Set, Alice In Wonderland, Tin, Litho, Box ....15.00 To 25.00
Panda, Walking, Windup, Cloth, Japan, Original Box, 5 In. 25.00
Panther, Glass Eyes, Steiff, Black, 61 In. 495.00
Paris Fisherman, F.Martin 1150.00
Parrot, Talking, Chein, 19 In. 395.00
Pastry Cart, Pierced Gallery, Rubber Rimmed Wheels, Tin, German, 4 In. 385.00
Peacock, Windup, Ebo, Marked Pao–Pao, Germany, Tin, 9 1/2 In. 35.00
Pedal Car, Austin 1750.00
Pedal Car, Cadillac, Rubber Tipped Wheels, Horn, Steelcraft, 36 In. 225.00
Pedal Car, Casey Jones No.9 .... 220.00
Pedal Car, Chain Driven, Pointed Nose, Early 1900s, Original Paint 445.00
Pedal Car, Fire Engine, 1950s 185.00
Pedal Car, Fire Engine, C.1912 .... 450.00
Pedal Car, Fire Truck, Ladder, Rubber Wheels, Black, Yellow Trim, 60 In. 350.00
Pedal Car, Flyer, Labeled Toledo, Sheet Metal & Wood, 40 In. 325.00
Pedal Car, Mustang, 1966, Ford, Box 500.00
Pedal Car, Pony Pulling Car, Legs Activated 350.00
Pedal Car, Pressed Steel, Painted, Airflow Style, Murray Co., 50 In. 225.00
Pedal Car, Rubber Tipped Wire Wheels, Sheet Metal & Wood, Blue Streak 1050.00
Pedal Car, Supersonic Jet, Murray 185.00
Pedal Car, Tractor & Cart, Victory, W.L.Products Co., All Wood 140.00
Pedal Car, Tractor, Front End Loader, Hoist In Back 400.00
Pedal Car, Tractor, International, Cast Aluminum 240.00
Pedal Car, Tractor, John Deere, 1950s 175.00
Pedal Car, Tractor, With Cart & Front End Loader 375.00
Pedal Car, Wire Wheels, Rubber Tread, Gendron Wheel Co., 42 In. 295.00
Pee Pee Puppy, Battery Operated, Expels Liquid 30.00

Phonograph, Peter Pan, Electric, Tin, 1 Record 45.00
Piano, 12 Keys, Schoenhut, 14 X 21 In. 75.00
Piano, Cupid Scene, 12 Key, Schoenhut, 12 X 14 In. 65.00
Piano, Grand, Princess Petite 20.00
Piano, Nudes & Nymphs, Schoenhut, Dated 1900, 16 In. 98.00
Piano, Player, Chein 175.00
Piano, Schoenhut, 8 1/4 In. 95.00
Piano, Schoenhut, 9 X 13 In. 55.00
Piano, With Candelabra & Iron Cabriole Legs, Schoenhut 147.00
Pick Up Sticks, Whitman Publishing, 1937 .... 8.00
Pig, Jiggling, Windup, Tin, Chein 15.00
Pig, Musical, Standing, Hide Covered, Crank Tail, 7 1/2 In. 65.00
Pig, Squeak, Papier–Mache, 5 In. 350.00
Pig, Windup, Tin Litho, Linemar 30.00
Pig, Winking, Tin, Windup, Chein 32.00
Pinball Game, Table, Red Ryder, Signed Fred Harmon 38.00
Pinball, Trik–E–Shot, Tin, Cardboard, 1930's, 13 X 24 In. 38.00
Pink Panther, Foam, England, 1964 .... 55.00
Pinocchio, Windup, Tin, Marx, 1939 .... 43.00
Pinocchio, Wooden, Jointed, 8 In. 150.00
Pip Squeak, Bird, Composition, Painted, 8 In. 185.00
Pip Squeak, Sheep, Wooly Coat, Composition, Wooden, 5 In. 185.00
Pirate, Windup, Tin, Japan, Original Box, 6 1/2 In. 55.00
Playasax, Irish Washerwoman Jig, Punched Paper Roll, 10 1/2 In. 125.00
Playland Whip, Windup, No.340, Box 250.00
Playskool Activity Set, McDonalds 32.00
Plow, Horse Drawn, Wooden, Orange & Green Repaint, 12 In. 22.50
Pony Cart, Legs Activated By Springs, Riding Toy 250.00
Pony, Riding, Wheels, Steiff, 17 In. 175.00
Pony, Wheels, Litho Sides, Bells Around Neck, C.1930 .... 49.00
Pool Player, C.1912, Kico, Tin, Windup 350.00
Porky Pig, Windup 155.00
Porky Pig, With Umbrella, Windup, Schiesinger 150.00
Powerboat, Clockwork Motor, Wood & Brass 275.00
Pretty Village, Milton Bradley, Box 95.00
Projector, Eastman Kodak, Original Box 95.00
Projector, Kodatoy, Hand Crank, 16mm., 1930 .... 35.00
Pumper, Carpenter, Iron, White Horse, Black Wagon, Red Wheels, 18 In. 800.00
Puppet, Doll, Joe Palooka 20.00
Puppet, Hand, Brown Bear, Steiff 45.00
Puppet, Hand, Mary Hartline 12.50
Purse & Doll Combination, Little Red Riding Hood 75.00
Quack–Quack, Windup, Lehmann, Tin 385.00
Quilt, Doll, 16 X 16 In. 35.00
Quilt, Doll, 18 X 24 In. 19.00
Quilt, Doll, Log Cabin Pattern, 19 1/2 X 19 1/2 In. 40.00
Rabbit, Accordion, Battery Operated, Tin, Plush, Japan, Boxed, 12 In. 160.00
Rabbit, Metal Eyes, Mohair Face, Straw Filled, 15 In. 15.00
Rabbit, Mohair, Steiff, 17 In. 225.00
Rabbit, Peter, Running, Battery Operated 88.00
Rabbit, Plush, Velvet Flop Ears & Feet, Musical, Early 20th Century 35.00
Rabbit, Pulling Tin Sled, Windup, Celluloid, Occupied Japan 30.00
Rabbit, Pulling Wagon Of Chicks, Windup, Celluloid, Occupied Japan, Box ... 55.00
Rabbit, Pulling Wagon, Tin, Chein, 11 In. 25.00
Rabbit, Seated, Battery Operated, Tin, Plush, Japan, Original Box, 6 In. 75.00
Rabbit, Standing, Mohair, Glass Eyes, 6 1/2 In. 85.00
Rabbit, Standing, Velvet, Sawdust Filled, No Eyes, 1900, 9 In. 40.00
Rabbit, Straw Stuffed, Glass Eyes, Cowboy Suit, White 50.00
Rabbit, White, Steiff, 17 In. 250.00
Railroad Station, Candlelit, C.1880, Tin 400.00
Railroad Station, Victorian, Platform, Yellow Towers, Germany, Tin, 9 In. 225.00
Ramp Walker, Black Mammy, 1940s 7.50
Ramp Walker, Red Riding Hood, 1940s 7.50
Rattle, Wood Carved, Block & Key End, Pine, 18th Century, 8 In. 57.00

Red The Iceman, Windup, Tin, Marx 385.00
Ride A Rocket, Chein, Tin 115.00
Ring, Buffalo Bill, Plastic 8.00
Ring, Captain Hawks, Sky Patrol 40.00
Ring, Captain Video, Space Gun, Early 1950s 50.00
Ring, G–Man, 1930s 7.50
Ring, Sky King TV, Instruction, Pictures, Boxed 92.50
Ring, Sky King, Electronic Television, Box 120.00
Ring–A–Ling Circus, Marx, Box 575.00
Road Grader, Nylint, Orange 18.00
Robot, Apollo 2000, Battery Operated, Tin, Japan, Original Box, 11 In. 90.00
Robot, Astro Sound, 1969 .... 35.00
Robot, Battery Operated, Marx, Box 175.00
Robot, Holding Space Gun, Tubes On Back, Windup, Japan, 7 1/2 In. 250.00
Robot, Lost In Space, Battery Operated, Box ....45.00 To 75.00
Robot, Mr Brain, Battery Operated, Remco, Boxed 52.00
Robot, Mr.Zerox, Box 70.00
Robot, Piston, Battery Operated, Marx, Box 35.00
Robot, Robby, Tin, Plastic, Japan, Battery Operated, 13 In. 400.00
Robot, Skipaks Fly In Chest, Windup, Tin, 5 1/2 In. 47.00
Robot, Video, Screen On Chest, Japan, 9 In. 135.00
Rocking Horse, 1860s, Carved 385.00
Rocking Horse, Massachusetts, Dapple Gray, Leather Seat, Painted, 31 In. 1000.00
Rocking Horse, Wood Carved, Rockers, Original Paint, 1880 .... 450.00
Roller Coaster, Playland, Windup, Cragstan, Box 75.00
Roller Coaster, Windup, 2 Car, Chein, Box 120.00
Roller Coaster, Windup, West Germany, Metal 95.00
Roller Skates, Chicago, Key, Dated 1914 .... 28.00
Rooster, Crowing, Tin, U.S.A. 30.00
Rooster, Squeak, Papier–Mache, 5 1/4 In. 175.00
Rooster, Squeak, Wooden Cage 79.00
Rooster, Steiff, 12 In. 98.00
Rubber Stamps, 9 Comic Characters, 1930s, Box 50.00
Sand Loader, Buddy L, Large 255.00
Sand Loader, Wolverine, Tin 30.00
Sand Shovel, 1930s, Tin 14.00
Sand Shovel, Big Boss, Ohio Art 5.00
Sandwich Man, Ko–Ko, Windup, Tin, Plastic, Japan, Original Box, 7 1/2 In. 40.00
Santa Claus, On Cycle, Windup, Japan, Box 35.00
Santa Claus, On Scooter, Battery Operated, Linemar ....60.00 To 75.00
Santa Claus, On Scooter, Flashing Head & Tail Lights, Battery Operated 35.00
Santa Claus, On Sleigh, Windup, Tin & Celluloid 65.00
Santa Claus, One Man Band, Battery Operated, Linemar 150.00
Santa Claus, Sleigh, Flocked Reindeer, Antlers, Papier–Mache, 11 In. 500.00
Santa Claus, Steiff, Paper Labels, 12 In. 175.00
Santa Claus, Walkie, 1930s, Box 9.00
School Slate, Child's, Wood Frame, 7 1/2 In. 12.00
Scissors, Battery Operated, Linemar 28.00
Scooter, 1940s, Original Condition 65.00
Scooter, Kick 'N Go, 3 Wheel, Chain, Honda 22.00
Scooter, Space, Battery Operated, Tin 82.00
Seal, Balancing Plastic Ball, Windup, Japan 25.00
Seal, Spinning Ball On Nose, Friction, Lehmann, Tin 20.00
Sedan, 4 Door, Turner, Steel, Blue Body, Black Top, Rubber Tires, 26 In. 900.00
Service Center, Cars, Marx 150.00
Service Station, Happy Time, Musical, Tin 85.00
Service Station, Marx, Tin, Box 27.00
Sew Master, Kaynee, Berlin, Germany, U.S.Zone 17.00
Sewing Kit, Bridal Party, 4 Dolls, Clothes, Hassenfeld Bros., 1950 .... 20.00
Sewing Machine, Crank Handle, C.1850, Cast Iron, 8 X 10 1/2 In. 150.00
Sewing Machine, Eldredgette 25.00
Sewing Machine, Electric, Little Modeste 26.00
Sewing Machine, Gateway, Tin 18.00
Sewing Machine, Hand Crank, Casige, Germany 35.00

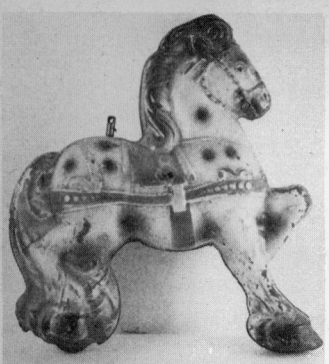

Toy, Horse, On Wheels, Metal,
Original Paint, 21 X 21 In.

Toy, Soldiers, All The Queen's Men,
British Infantry Regimental Band

Sewing Machine, Junior Miss	12.50
Sewing Machine, Little Betsy	20.00
Sewing Machine, Little Mother	22.00
Sewing Machine, Little Sister, Decals	40.00
Sewing Machine, Necchi, Little Miss Seamstress, Accessories, Box	12.00
Sewing Machine, Sew Handy, Singer, Case	35.00
Sewing Machine, Singer, Brown, Clamp, Boxed	45.00
Sewing Machine, Singer, Round Carrying Case, Black Enamel	55.00
Sewing Machine, Stitch–Well, Cast Iron	75.00
Sewing Machine, Vulvan	22.00
Sewing Machine, Wilcox & Gibbs	75.00
Shoeshine Joe, Battery Operated, Box	65.00
Shoo–Fly, Original Paint, Yellow Striping On Seat Back, 41 X 34 In.	225.00
Shooting Arcade, Batman, Boxed	35.00
Shooting Gallery, Circus, Ohio Art	30.00
Ski Jumper, Wolverine, Metal	85.00
Skier, On Slope, Flips, Wolverine	60.00
Skunk, Plush, Atomizer Between Legs, Bulb In Tail, 1930s	45.00
Sled, Child's Box, Leather Upholstery, Seat Belt	295.00
Sled, Clipper, Paris Mfg. Co., Stenciled Runners, C.1890.45 In.	225.00
Sled, Iron Runners, Wooden, Primitive, Original Brown Paint, 30 In.	185.00
Sled, Steel Frame, Oak, Red, 1920s, 48 In.	65.00
Sled, Victorian, Green & Gold, 31 In.	245.00
Sled, Winter Or Summer, Convertible Into Stroller	190.00
Sled, Wood Top, Iron Runners, Original Black, Salmon Paint, 15 3/4 In.	305.00
Sled, Wooden, Painted, Floral Design, America, 15 1/2 In.	275.00
Sleigh, Blanket Rail, Applied Carving, 19th Century, Pink & Oak, 3 Ft.	850.00
Sleigh, Child's, Wooden, Bentwood Iron Tip Rockers, Dog Painting, 30 In.	125.00
Smitty & Herby, On Motorcycle, Tootsietoy	195.00
Smitty Scooter, Boy With Oversized Cap, Windup, Tin, Marx, 8 In.	1300.00
Snoopy, The Space Traveler, Battery Operated, Box, Japan	35.00
Snowflake & Swipes, Pull, Mechanical, Tin, Nifty, Original Box, 7 1/2 In.	1000.00
Snowflake On Sparkplug, Pull Toy, Mechanical, 9 In.	1000.00
Soldier, Bengal Horse Artillery, CA1850, 8 Piece	35.00
Soldier, Coldstream Guard At Ease, Officer, Britains, 7 Piece	80.00
Soldier, Indian Army Service, Officer & Mule, No.1893, Britains, 7 Piece	125.00
Soldier, Kneeling, With Camera, Barclay B–101	18.00
Soldier, Kneeling, With Flamethrower, ML–7	58.00
Soldier, Marching, With Rifle, Jones J–32	225.00
Soldier, Montreal Rifle Rangers, CA1856, 8 Piece	30.00
Soldier, Mussolini On Horseback Saluting, Brevetto	50.00
Soldier, Nazi, Marching, Lionel, 1930s	55.00

Soldier, Parade, Overseas Cap, Manoil M–98 .... 38.00
Soldier, Scots Guards Pipers, Britains, 6 Piece 50.00
Soldier, Seated, With Phone, Jones J–22 .... 110.00
Soldier, Standing, Gas Mask & Flare Gun, Manoil M–94 .... 25.00
Soldiers, All The Queen's Men, British Infantry Regimental Band ....*Illus* 450.00
Space Blazer, Pull Toy, Fisher, No.750 .... 75.00
Space Capsule, Tin, Plastic, Battery, Cragstan, Original Box, 10 In. 85.00
Space Shuttle, Moon City, Battery Operated, Plastic, Cragston, 1969 .... 59.00
Spacecraft, USA–NASA Apollo, Battery, Tin, Plastic, Japan, Box, 9 In. 55.00
Spaceman, 6–Gun, Irwin 30.00
Spaceman, Windup, Tin, Sparks 98.00
Sparkler, Felix The Cat 125.00
Sparkplug, Horse, Schoenhut 500.00
Speedboat, Dolphin, Fleetline, Box 60.00
Speedboat, Flyer, Windup, Red Deck, Driver, Lindstrom, Tin, 14 1/2 In. 195.00
Speedy Boy Delivery, Marx 45.00
Squirrel, Perri, With Acorn, Steiff, 5 In. 75.00
Squirrel, Possy, Steiff, 6 In. 35.00
Stable, 2 Story, Groom's Apartment Above, Outside Stair, Stalls, 10 In. 245.00
Stable, 3 Stalls & Carriage House, German 475.00
Steam Engine, Model, Tin, Whistle 25.00
Steam Engine, Weeden, No.14 .... 50.00
Steam Roller, Huber, Cast Iron 80.00
Steam Shovel, Buddy L, Moline Pressed Steel Co. 150.00
Steam Shovel, Lincoln, Back Rotates, Gray, Red, 14 X 14 In. 65.00
Steam Shovel, Lincoln, Mechanical, Gray & Red 65.00
Steam Shovel, Rubber Tracks, Buddy L 49.00
Steam Shovel, Structo, 16 In. 45.00
Steam Shovel, Tonka Toys, XMB975 .... 100.00
Steam Shovel, Wyandotte 75.00
Stereo Viewer, Alley–Oop & Red Riding Hood, Electric 10.00
Stove, Cook, Cast Iron, Crescent, Coal Hod 35.00
Stove, Eagle, Nickel Plated ....100.00 To 135.00
Stove, Electric, Empire, 10 1/2 X 16 In. 25.00
Stove, Gas, Daisey, Cast Iron, 3 X 4 In. 37.50
Stove, Novelty Tin & Iron, C.1900, Complete, 8 1/2 X 6 In. 65.00
Stove, Peer Skill, Marked Rikeman & Seymour, With Utensils, C.1860 .... 365.00
Stove, Star, Cast Iron, 3 1/2 X 2 3/4 In. 45.00
Stroller, Doll's, 1940s, Tin 35.00
Stroller, Doll's, Victorian, High Back Wheels 395.00
Stroller, Doll's, Victorian, Wicker, High Wheel, Original Upholstery 495.00
Strutting Sam, Dancing Black Man, Battery Operated, Box 265.00
Submarine, Tootsietoy 12.00
Submarine, Windup, Friction, Tin 45.00
Submarine, Wolverine 69.50
Suitcase, Art Deco Design, Round 15.00
Sulky & Running Horse, Pedal 195.00
Sulky Cart, Mule & Driver, Cast Iron 225.00
Table, Doll's, Drop Leaf, Round Leaves, 13 X 14 In. 200.00
Table, Doll's, Octagonal Paneled Legs, Drawer, Cherry, 11 X 13 In. 135.00
Table, Graniteware Top, Alaphabet Around Edge 98.00
Tank, Bren Gun Carrier, Men, England 28.00
Tank, Combat, Sparking, Marx 90.00
Tank, Planet Patrol, Tin, Plastic, Windup, Japan, Original Box, 6 In. 65.00
Tank, Rollover, Windup, Marx, Box 85.00
Tank, Windup, German, Signed Gama 58.00
Target Board, Bean Bag, Wooden, Litho, Bliss, 21 X 24 In. 450.00
Tea Set, Blue Willow, Occupied Japan, 7 Piece 65.00
Tea Set, Bluebirds, 24 Piece 135.00
Tea Set, Felix The Cat Play Time, Chein Co., 7 Piece, Boxed 45.00
Tea Set, Luster, Metallic, Miniature, Marked R.O'Neill 125.00
Tea Set, Picture On Box, Ohio Art, Metal, 1939, Complete 50.00
Tea Set, Punch & Judy, Tin 125.00
Tea Set, Raggedy Ann & Andy, 1971 .... 25.00

Tea Set, Red Riding Hood, Metal 20.00
Tea Set, Royal Blue, Made In Japan, Original Box, Service For 6 .... 38.00
  TOY, TEDDY BEAR, see Teddy Bear
Teeter–Totter, Pull Toy, Iron, Alphonse & Gaston, 7 1/2 In. 270.00
Teeter–Totter, Uncle Sam, Wooden, Painted, Head Nods, 8 1/4 In. 65.00
Telephone, Lollypop, Tin 22.00
Telephone, Tin, Painted Red, Outside Bell, Wind & Ring, 3 1/2 In. 25.00
Telephone, Tootsietoy 15.00
Tidy Tim, Pushes Clean–Up Cart, Windup, 1920s, Marx 260.00
Tiger, Steiff, 72 In. 660.00
Tight Rope Dandy, Riding Bicycle, Tin, 8 In. 70.00
Tool Chest, Boy's National, Dovetailed Box 28.00
Tool Chest, Oak, Dovetailed, Mason & Parker, 4 Tools, 13 1/2 X 7 1/4 In. 38.00
Tool Set, Cast Iron, Display Card, 5 Piece ....10.00 To 15.00
Tool Set, Saw, Square, Skil Craft Corp., Chicago 55.00
Tool Set, Victorian, German, Original Card 32.00
Toonerville Trolley, Borgfeldt & Co., N.Y., Tin, Original Box, 6 1/2 In. 750.00
Top, Musical, Litho, Ohio Art Co., 7 In. 35.00
Top, Rainbow, Marx, Original Box 20.00
Top, Windup, F.Strauss, Tin, Original Paint 130.00
Tractor, Balloon Tires, Arcade, Cast Iron 45.00
Tractor, Caterpillar, Tin, 1916 .... 50.00
Tractor, Climber, Accessories, Woodhaven Metal Stamping, 1916 .... 85.00
Tractor, Climbing, Sparkling Highboy, Windup, Marx, Box 50.00
Tractor, Farm, With Driver, Auburn, Cast Iron 15.00
Tractor, Ford, Arcade, Blue, 3 1/2 In. 45.00
Tractor, Hubley Jr., 1940s, Box 40.00
Tractor, International Farmall, 1950, With Tractor Trailer, Box 600.00
Tractor, International, Metal, Rubber Tires, 8 In. 18.00
Tractor, John Deere, Cast Iron, 9 1/2 In. 20.00
Tractor, John Deere, Model D, Yellow Wheels, Metal, Green, Box 45.00
Tractor, Magic Barn, Marx, Windup, Box 60.00
Tractor, Matching Wagon, 1950s, Massey–Harris 440.00
Tractor, Steam, Mamod, Works On Kerosene 200.00
Tractor, With Driver, Fordson, Cast Iron 65.00
Tractor, With Driver, Tin Litho, 1940s 37.50
Tractor, Yipee–I–Aaay, Farmer, Windup, Tin, Original Box, 7 1/2 In. 100.00
Traffic Light, Electric, Cast Iron, Painted, A.C.Williams, 9 1/2 In. 200.00
Trailer, Horse, Wyandotte, Cab, Litho Tin Grill, Red, 22 X 8 In. 60.00
Train & Connecting Ride–On Coach Car, Keystone 295.00
Train Container, Freight, Lionel, No.205, Green Box, L Door, 4 In. 40.00
Train Set, 4 Cars, Caboose, Transformer & Track, Lionel, No.1664 .... 85.00
Train Set, New York Central, Freight, Engine, Electric, Marx, Box 150.00
Train Set, No.8042, Transformer, Track, 3 Cars 95.00
Train Station, Lionel No.138, Illuminated, Boxed 45.00
Train Station, Plasticsville, Boxed, 1950s 10.00
Train Station, Tin, Marx, 28 X 8 X 11 In. 28.00
Train, Bump 'N Go, Baltimore, Flashing Lights, Battery Operated, 12 In. 88.00
Train, Coach, Central Railroad, Tin, American, 6 1/2 In. 200.00
Train, Engine, 2 Cars, Track, American Flyer, Original Box, 1928 .... 25.00
Train, Engine, Lionel, No.726 .... 325.00
Train, Engine, No.252, 2 Passenger Cars, No.529 .... 150.00
Train, Engine, Tender, & 2 Cars, Cast Iron Wheels, Tin, Original Paint 1200.00
Train, Freight, Penna. Loco, 1939, 6 Pieces 55.00
Train, Keystone Railroad, No.6400, Riding, C.1940, 26 In. 160.00
Train, Locomotive & Tender, No.2018, Lionel 77.50
Train, Locomotive, 2 Coaches, Baggage, Transformer, Tin, Marklin 1000.00
Train, Locomotive, 3 Coaches, Gondola, Catalog, Ives O Gauge Electric 300.00
Train, Locomotive, 5 Cars, Transformer & Track, Marx 28.00
Train, Locomotive, Marklin TM800, Tender No.809 .... 75.00
Train, Locomotive, Shoofly, Tin, Wooden, American, Geo.Brown, 10 In. 350.00
Train, Locomotive, Stock, Refrigerator, Tank, Gondola, Caboose, Lionel 450.00
Train, Locomotive, Tender, Boxcar, Coach, Track, Windup, Tin, Box, Germany 90.00
Train, Locomotive, Tin, Windup, Ubilda, England, Original Box, 10 In. 70.00

Train, Locomotive, Victory, Tin, Clockwork, Stencil, American, Ives, 9 In. 1000.00
Train, Passenger, 0 Gauge, No.248, Lionel, Original Box, 1930 .... 175.00
Train, Peerless R.R., Tin, 3 Piece 660.00
Train, Riding, Steel, Marked 3000VF, Marx, 1930s 135.00
Train, Ringling Bros.Barnum & Bailey, Gilbert, American Flyer, Box 45.00
Train, Silver Mountain, Battery Operated, Japan 15.00
Train, Silver Streak Engine, Cars, Transformer, American Flyer 60.00
Train, Steam, 0 Gauge, No.565 Locomotive & 4 Cars, American Flyer 75.00
Train, Tank Transport, Mighty Antar, Dinky, Box 50.00
Train, Tin, Engine, Coal Car, Wooden Litho Freight Car, 3 Piece 225.00
Train, Windup, Cast Engine, 5 Piece, Track, Town Depot, American Flyer 125.00
Train, Windup, Engine & 3 Cars, Tracks, Hornby, Box 265.00
Train, Windup, Track, Engine, 3 Cars, Lionel 50.00
Train, With Connecting Ride On Coach, Keystone 295.00
Trolley, Carlisle, Finch, Brass, C.1905, Set Of 4 .... 6000.00
Trolley, German, Tin, 6 1/2 In. 330.00
Trolley, Headlight, Hand Pulled, Tin 55.00
Trolley, Open, City Hall Park, Lionel, 1903, 16 In. 300.00
Truck, Army, Steel, Keystone, C, 1929, 26 1/2 In. 275.00
Truck, Baggage, Buddy L, 1930s 110.00
Truck, Bell Telephone Co., Hubley, Cast Iron 100.00
Truck, Bell Telephone, Raised Lettering, C.1940s, 12 In. 35.00
Truck, Brinks Armored, Dinky 25.00
Truck, Carnation Milk, Steel 42.00
Truck, Cattle, Marx, Boxed 47.50
Truck, Cattle, Wyandotte, Cast Iron, 18 In. 50.00
Truck, Cement Mixer, Blue Circle Portland 14.00
Truck, Cement Mixer, Tonka, 1958, 14 In. 18.00
Truck, Chevy Panel, 1950, Tootsietoy, 3 In. 19.00
Truck, Cities Service Wrecker, Tin, Large 95.00
Truck, Coal, Dump, Arcade, Cast Iron, Mack Hi–Lift, 11 In. 375.00
Truck, Coal, Late 1940s, Buddy L, Cast Iron 110.00
Truck, Coal, Tin, Wooden Wheels, Marx 27.50
Truck, Coast To Coast Transport Land Mines, Windup, Tin, Walt Reach Co. 75.00
Truck, Delivery, Metal Craft, 1930 .... 110.00
Truck, Dodge, Steerable Tires, Decals On Side, 7 In. 50.00
Truck, Driver, Windup, Lehmann, Tin, 5 1/2 In. 85.00
Truck, Dump, Buddy L, C.1932, 25 In. ....*Illus* 425.00
Truck, Dump, Buddy L, Riding, 1930, 20 In. 75.00
Truck, Dump, Driver, Arcase Contractor 150.00
Truck, Dump, Ford, Hubley, 1950s, Cast Iron 25.00
Truck, Dump, Hydraulically Operated, Structo 55.00
Truck, Dump, Lever Action, Richmond Co. 65.00
Truck, Dump, Mack, Man Inside, Cast Iron 95.00
Truck, Dump, Smith, Miller, Cast Iron, 11 1/2 In. ....35.00 To 85.00
Truck, Dump, Steel, Keystone, C.1929, Crank, Black, 27 In. 130.00
Truck, Dump, Structo, 1928, 18 In. 125.00
Truck, Dump, Sturditoy, 1920s, 25 In. 175.00
Truck, Dump, Tonka Toys, XM975 .... 95.00
Truck, Emergency Auto Service, Wyandotte 55.00
Truck, Ferry's Seed, Wyandotte, 9 1/2 In. 23.00
Truck, Fire, Ladder, Rossmoyne, 33 1/2 In. 45.00
Truck, Fire, Riding, Wyandotte, 32 In. 225.00
Truck, Fire, Sit & Ride, Buddy L 200.00
Truck, Freight Carrier Trailer, Buddy L 45.00
Truck, Gasoline, Mack, Cast Iron, 5 1/2 In. 110.00
Truck, Grain, Structo, Aluminum 30.00
Truck, Heavy Duty, 6 Wheel, Canvas Top, Marx, Boxed 55.00
Truck, Heinz, Metalcraft, C.1932 .... 60.00
Truck, Hill Climber, Dated 1909, 11 In. 125.00
Truck, Hook & Ladder, Marx, Large 120.00
Truck, Hydraulic, Buddy L, Large 150.00
Truck, Ice Cream, Japan 35.00
Truck, Ice, Arcade, White Rubber Tires, 6 3/4 In. 165.00

Truck, Irish Mail, Riding ....165.00 To 250.00
Truck, Log, Strauss, Windup 85.00
Truck, Machinery Moving, Marx, Box 90.00
Truck, Merry–Go–Round, Box 80.00
Truck, Michigan Bell Telephone 35.00
Truck, Milk, Farm, Buddy L, Wooden 135.00
Truck, Mobil Gas, Litho Tin, Friction 15.00
Truck, Mobil Gasoline, Tootsietoy, Red, 9 In., 2 Piece 35.00
Truck, National Van Lines, Wyerdolle 25.00
Truck, Packard, Keystone, 1920s 295.00
Truck, Paramedic, From TV Series Emergency, Box 30.00
Truck, Parcel Post, Dayton, Sonny 250.00
Truck, Pickup, Buckeye, 12 In. 55.00
Truck, Pickup, Buddy L 400.00
Truck, Pickup, Chevron Oil, Tonka 40.00
Truck, Railway Express, Tootsietoy 75.00
Truck, RCA Service, Marx, Box 50.00
Truck, Snow Plow & Dozer, Tonka, Removable Blades 40.00
Truck, Southern Bell Telephone, Tonka Toys 200.00
Truck, Spring Front, C.1960, Yellow, Buddy L 70.00
Truck, Stake Body, Sticker On Door, Arcade, Cast Iron, 7 In. 140.00
Truck, Tank, Ford, 1949, Tootsietoy 8.00
Truck, U.S.Mail, Early 1900, Flywheel Mechanism, Tin 250.00
Truck, U.S.Mail, Keystone, Steel, Rubber Tires, Khaki Body, 26 In. 250.00
Truck, Windup, Lehmann, Tin, C.1907 .... 150.00
Truck, Wrecker, 1950s, Marx 75.00
Trunk, Doll's, 13 X 7 In. 27.50
Trunk, Doll's, 6 1/2 X 6 X 10 In. 85.00
Trunk, Doll's, Steamer, Black Metal Trim, Gray 45.00
Turtle, Riding, Steiff, 1959 .... 325.00
Typewriter, American Flyer, Simplex–A, Box 24.00
Typewriter, Berwin, Gold Color 12.00
Typewriter, Deluxe, Marx 25.00
Typewriter, Dial, Tin, Marx Jr. 18.00
Typewriter, Junior Dial, Marx, Box 20.00
Typewriter, Simplex 20.00
Typewriter, Tom Thumb, Metal 35.00
Vacuum Cleaner, Hoover, Century Of Progress 47.00
Van, Tonka Toys, XR101 .... 95.00
Van, Trojan Van, Dinky 375.00
Velocipede, Wooden, Painted, Stenciled, Cast Iron, American, 1870s, 40 In. 1000.00
Victrola, Tootsietoy 20.00
Viewmaster, Gene Autry Reel, Box 12.00
Violin, Occupied Japan, 15 In. 35.00
Wagon, 2 Horses, Red & Green, 15 In. 50.00
Wagon, Boy's, Daisy, Raised Seat & Buckboard 910.00
Wagon, Boy's, Express, Iron Spoked Wheels 235.00
Wagon, Circus, Drawn By Horse, Polar Bear Inside, Cast Iron 125.00
Wagon, Circus, Metal Wheels, Paper Litho, Tin & Wood, 7 1/2 X 8 1/2 In. 35.00
Wagon, Circus, Pulled By 4 Horses, 15 Wooden Animals On Wheels 500.00
Wagon, Circus, Pulled By 4 Horses, 8 Animals, Wooden Wheels 295.00
Wagon, Coaster, Speed Boy, Old Paint 125.00
Wagon, Covered, 2 Oxen, Clay, Tanned Skin Canvas 350.00
Wagon, Farm, 3 Horses, 11 In. 60.00
Wagon, Fire Chief, Black & Yellow, Ives, Iron, 15 1/2 In. 400.00
Wagon, Fireman, Hook & Ladder, Horses, Driver, Blue, Iron, 5 1/2 X 14 In. 260.00
Wagon, Flexible Flyer, 22 In. 41.00
Wagon, Horse Drawn, Original Paint, 6 1/2 In. 32.50
Wagon, Horse, Heavy Teaming, 2 Wooden Horses, Boston, C.1920, 34 In. 160.00
Wagon, Hy–Speed, Red, Metal Tires, 15 In. 46.00
Wagon, Iron Frame, Rubber & Metal Wheels, Gray Paint, 15 X 36 In. 85.00
Wagon, McCormick Deering, Plastic 30.00
Wagon, Seat, John Deere, Cast Iron 850.00
Wagon, Tin, Nursery Rhymes, Litho 75.00

Wagon, Wheelbarrow, Red, Tin, 17 In. 20.00
Wagon, Wooden, Green Paint, Red Paint Interior, 65 In. 800.00
Wagon, Wooden, Spoke Wheels, Removable Sides, Stenciled Design, 36 In. 450.00
Walkie–Talkie, 1930s, Instructions, Unused, Metal 45.00
Walking Gait Horse, Wooden, Wire & Rubber Wheels, 21 X 28 In. ....*Illus* 600.00
Walking Tree, Litho Tin, Plastic, Battery Operated, Marx, 14 1/2 In. 600.00
Washboard, Midget Washer, Glass 15.00
Washboard, Sanitary, Tin, Small 12.00
Washer & Dryer, Washa, Washa, Folding Clothes 150.00
Washer & Dryer, Westinghouse, Box 18.00
Washing Machine, Sunny Susie, Wringer, Buff Green 35.00
Washing Machine, Wringer, Wolverine 30.00
Watch, Pocket, Zeppelin Picture When Knob Turns, Watch Fob, 2 In.Diam. 80.00
Watch, Sun Dial, Frank Buck 65.00
Wheelbarrow, Metal, Red, Hy–Speed Rubber Tire, Wooden Handles 30.00
Wheelbarrow, Painted Revolutionary Figure With Apple, Grouse, P.Ompir 385.00
Wheelbarrow, Wooden Handles, Tin, 28 X 15 In. 75.00
Whistle, Chicken Shape, Tin, White Repaint, Germany, 3 7/8 In. 37.00
Whistle, Oscar Mayer, Wiener Shape 5.00
Whistle, Red Goose Shoes 4.50
Whistle, Sgt.Preston 24.00
Whistle, Weatherbird Rooster 15.00
Willie The Clown, Emmett Kelly, Boxed, 22 In. 250.00
Windmill, Steam, Attachment, Tin, Litho, Doll Co., Germany, 10 In. 110.00
Witch, On Broomstick, Wooden, Balance, Boxed 10.00
Wolverine, Windup, Pressed Steel, Tin, 6 Records, Zilotone, 5 In. 325.00
Woman At Sewing Machine, Windup, Tin, Polychrome Paint, 5 3/4 In. 300.00
Woodburning Set, Harry A.Ungar Inc., Manual, 1938 .... 10.00
Woodsey Owl, Advertising U.S.Forest Service, 6 In. 4.00
Woogle The Walking Horse, Plastic, Boxed 6.00
Xylophone, Minnie Mouse, Linemar 325.00
Yo–Yo, Advertising, Bush & Gerts Pianos, Tin 45.00
Yo–Yo, Mickey Mantle 20.00
Zebra, Steiff 45.00
Zeppelin, 3 Wheels, Gondola, 1930s, Metal, 27 In. 350.00
Zeppelin, Goodyear, Papier–Mache, Metal Mast, 30 In. 275.00
Zeppelin, Penny Toy, Mechanical, Propeller Rotates, German, 6 In. 210.00
Zeppelin, Pull Toy, Li'1 Giant, Tin, C.1930, 26 In. 125.00
Zeppelin, With Gondola, 3 Wheels, Metal, 1930s, 27 In. 350.00
Zylophone, 5 Discs, Ziloton 300.00

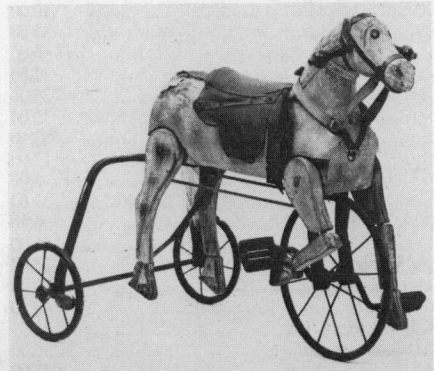

Toy, Walking Gait Horse, Wooden,

Wire & Rubber Wheels, 21 X 28 In.

Never move an object that might explode. Call the local police bomb squad. Many accidents are caused by old souvenir hand grenades and firearms.

Tramp art is a form of folk art made since the Civil War. It is usually made from chip–carved cigar boxes. Examples range from small boxes and picture frames to full–sized pieces of furniture.

TRAMP ART, Box, 8 X 9 3/4 In.	6.00
Box, Drawer, 6 1/2 X 10 X 4 In.	15.00
Box, Hinged Top, Joined Hearts, Love To Norah, 13 X 14 X 19 In.	130.00
Box, Merry Christmas & Happy New Year On Top, 6 X 6 X 4 In.	48.00
Box, Pedestal Base, Hinged Lid, 7 1/4 X 11 1/4 X 7 1/4 In.	35.00
Bureau, 2 Drawer, Lion Head Pulls, 2 Ft.	100.00
Chest, Hinged Lid, Concentric Circles, Stars, C.1930, 18 X 15 In.	990.00
Comb Case, Walnut, White Porcelain Buttons, 9 X 11 In.	45.00
Doll's Dresser	45.00
Frame, 4 X 16 X 19 In.	175.00
Frame, 8 X 10 1/2 In.	50.00
Frame, Cross Corner, Chicago, 4 1/4 X 28 1/4 In., Pair	90.00
Match Holder, Wall, Hanging	85.00
Planter, Wall	75.00
Rack, Wall, Magazine	90.00
Sewing Box, Small	35.00
Shelf, Hanging, For Sewing, 12 In.	30.00
Shelf, Wall, Double Picture	90.00
Table, Figural Log Cabin Attached To Top, 22 1/2 In.	45.00
Toy, Covered Wagon	65.00

Animal traps may be handmade. One of the most unusual is the mouse trap made so that when the mouse entered the trap, it was hit on the head with a mallet. Other traps were commercially manufactured and often are marked with the name of the manufacturer. Many traps were designed to be as humane as possible, and they would trap the live animal so it could be released in the woods.

TRAP, Bear, Hand Forged, 34 In.	225.00
Bear, Hand Forged, 46 In.	120.00
Bear, New House, C Clamp, Signed San Miguel Wool Grower's Assn.	375.00
Bear, Newhouse No.15, Jaws Open To 14 In., Primitive, 34 1/2 In.	450.00
Bear, Newhouse, No.5	250.00
Booby, To Discharge Shell, Brass & Steel, Pat.July 9, 1895, 2 3/4 In.	55.00
Cricket, 1930s, Tin Funnel	20.00
Fly, Bottle Shape, Glass	20.00
Fly, Columbia, Tin & Wire, Instructions, Round	45.00
Fly, Hanging, Tin & Wire Screen, 9 In.	22.50
Fly, Olsen & Thompson, Sur Katchem	10.00
Gopher, Fire 9 M/M Blank	85.00
Gopher, Newhouse	6.00
Gopher, Pocket, Wooden	12.50
Hand Wrought, Double Spring, 17 In.	35.00
Hand, Western Cartridge Co., Original Box	20.00
Mosquito, Minnesota	3.50
Mouse & Bug, Combination, Black Beauty	17.00
Mouse, 5 Hole, Tin	5.00
Mouse, Catchemalive, Wooden, Metal	27.00
Mouse, Fruit Jar, 1858	6.50
Mouse, Peerless	75.00
Newhouse, Oneida Community No.1, Single Spring	25.00
Newhouse, Oneida Community No.2, Double Spring	30.00
Newhouse, Oneida Community No.3, Double Spring	40.00
Partridge, Tree Hanging, Signed Oneida Kill–Um No.1, Iron	175.00
Rat, Muzzle Loading, 1862 Model, Brass	35.00
Skeet, Winchester Western, Wood & Steel	45.00
Triumph Bear, No.415–X, Teeth In Jaws, Springs	95.00
Triumph Jump, Easy–Set Square Grip, No.3	30.00
TREEN, see Wooden	

Trivets are now used to hold hot dishes. Most trivets of the late nineteenth and early twentieth centuries were made to hold hot irons. Iron or brass reproductions are being made of many of the old styles.

TRIVET, 4 Legs, Curled Handle, Wrought Iron, 10 1/2 In.	50.00
Beaver & Leaves Center, Good Luck, Cast Iron, 5 1/2 X 6 1/2 In.	75.00
Best On Earth, Iron	22.00
Brass & Wrought Iron, High Legs	175.00
Cat Head Center, Stoneware, Blue, Round, 4 1/2 In.	175.00
Chalfant, Wrought Iron	20.00
Chiseled Monogram, Heart Shape, Wrought Iron, Maine, 6 X 7 In.	1175.00
Daisy & Button, Cast Iron	8.00
Diamond With T, Cast Iron	18.00
Double Hearts, Brass	55.00
George Washington, Black Paint, Cast Iron, 9 In.	20.00
God Bless Our Home, On Horseshoe, Dated 1886	45.00
Good Luck To All Who Use This Stand, Horseshoe Shape, Iron	30.00
Groton, N.Y., Center Crown	15.00
Heart & Star, Child's, Iron, 5 In.	35.00
Heart Shape, Heart Handle, Chamfered Legs, Drake Feet, 9 In.	265.00
Heart Shape, Iron Feet, Brass, 5 3/4 In.	85.00
Heart Shape, Ram's Horns, 3 Legs, Wrought Iron, 6 In.	160.00
Hearth, Side Handle, 4 Round Standing Legs, 11 X 14 X 4 1/2 In.	195.00
Long Handle, Sliding Fork Rest, Twisted Stem, Wrought Iron, 24 In.	35.00
Ram's Horns, Queen Anne Feet, Wrought Iron, Round, 5 1/2 In.	105.00
Scrolled Design, Shaped Handle, Wrought Iron, 12 1/2 In.	75.00
Silver Overlay, Art Nouveau Floral Design	45.00
Swan Shape, Cast Iron, 4 1/2 In.	38.00
Swastika, Iron	12.50
Tree Of Life, Brass	9.00
Triangular, Iron, 6 X 12 In.	39.00

Trunks of many types were made. The nineteeth-century sea chest was often handmade of unpainted wood. Brass-fitted camphorwood chests were brought back from the Orient. Leather-covered trunks were popular from the late eighteenth to mid-nineteenth centuries. By 1895, trunks were covered with canvas or decorated sheet metal. Embossed metal coverings were used from 1870 to 1910. By 1925, trunks were covered with vulcanized fiber or undecorated metal.

TRUNK, America, 19th Century, Original Lock & Hasp, Swag Design, 29 X 14 In.	600.00
Child's, Tile Pattern, Metal, 16 In.	75.00
Document, General Gage's, 1772	4500.00
Dome Top, Bracket Base, Grain Paint, Scandinavian, 30 X 63 In.	650.00
Dome Top, New York, Wiggle Strokes, Grain Painted, 28 3/4 X 12 1/2 In	700.00
Dome Top, Original Red Paint, Iron Lock, Brass Handles, 36 X 13 In.	125.00
Dome Top, Painted Fan On Top, Stylized Flower Front, 22 1/2 X 9 In.	440.00
Hide Covered, Wrought Iron Lock, Hasp, & Handles, 24 In.	35.00
Homespun Linen Lining, Acct. Of James Reed, Iron Bound, 33 X 15 In.	45.00
Immigrant's, Jon N.Brandenbirger, Square Nails, Double Locks	1200.00
Iron Lock, Hasp, Handles, Brown Vinegar Graining, 20 1/2 X 15 3/4 In.	195.00
Leather Cover, Brass Studs, Initials W.S., Cylindrical, Wooden, 30 In.	55.00
Norwegian, Thin Stenciled Leather, Wallpaper Interior, Key, Small	125.00
Round Top, Late 1800s	500.00
Stained Pine, Hinged Dome Top, 15 X 35 X 15 In.	40.00

The Tuthill Cut Glass Company of Middletown, New York, worked from 1902 to 1923. Of special interest are the finely cut pieces of stemware and tableware.

TUTHILL, Bowl, Rex Pattern, Signed, 8 In.	1800.00
Fernery, Primrose Pattern, Signed	475.00
Plate, Primrose, 5 In.	75.00
Tumbler, Juice, Vintage Pattern, Signed, 3 3/4 In.	55.00
Vase, Candlestick Bud Shape, Fern Pattern, Signed, 16 In.	425.00
Vase, Floral, Crosshatch Band, Signed, 9 3/4 In.	210.00

Vase, Sweet Pea, Carved Tulip Design, Blank Glass, 4 3/4 In. 400.00
Vase, Trumpet, Poppy Pattern, Signed, 14 In. 1100.00

The first successful typewriter was made by Sholes and Glidden in 1874. Collectors divide typewriters into two main classifications: the index machine, which has a pointer and a dial for letter selection, and the keyboard machine, most commonly seen today.

TYPEWRITER, 1886 Hall 275.00
American Flyer, Pat.1–907–379 .... 45.00
Fox 200.00
Franklin 175.00

Uhl pottery was made in Evansville, Indiana, in 1854. The pottery moved to Huntingburg, Indiana, in 1908. Stoneware and glazed pottery were made until the mid–1940s.

UHL, Bowl, Footed 15.00
Mug 6.00
Pitcher, Blue 50.00

The first known umbrella was owned by King Louis XIII of France in 1637. The earliest umbrellas were sunshades, not designed to be used in the rain. The umbrella was embellished and redesigned many times. In 1852, the fluted steel rib style was developed and that has remained the most useful style.

UMBRELLA, Advertising, Cerosota Flour, Beach 104.50
Advertising, John & Sid Hardware, Hudson, Orange Cloth, 66 1/2 In. 30.00
Advertising, The Boston Store, Schenectady, N.Y., Cloth, 67 In. 35.00
Bird Head Handle, Celluloid, Beige 28.00
Cloisonne Handle, Gold Plated, Floral Silk, 40 1/2 In. 50.00
Horsehead Handle, Black 22.00
Parasol, Carved Handle, Brass Top, Black Cloth, Jet Beads, 23 In. 75.00
Parasol, Child's, Black Lace 32.00
Parasol, Lace, Black, Carved Handle, 1890s 30.00
Parasol, Linen, Wide Ribbon Edge 35.00
Parasol, Silk, Black Lace Cover, Lined, Ivory Handle, Fish Finial 47.50
Parasol, Silk, Black, Beaded Jet Design, 24 In. 32.50
Parasol, Victorian, Red Silk 37.00
Parasol, Victorian, Sunday Stroll, Black Silk 35.00
Wooden Handle, Cloth, Japanese, 24 In. 20.00

UNION PORCELAIN WORKS GREENPOINT N.Y.

The Union Porcelain Works was established at Greenpoint, New York, in 1848 by Charles Cartlidge. The company went through a series of ownership changes and finally closed in the early 1900s. The company made a fine quality white porcelain that was often decorated in clear, bright colors.

UNION PORCELAIN WORKS, Mug, Durance Vile 650.00
Oyster Plate, 9 1/2 In. 95.00

UNIVERSITY OF NORTH DAKOTA, see North Dakota School of Mines

Val St. Lambert Cristalleries of Belgium was founded by Messieurs Kemlin and Lelievre in 1825. The company is still in operation. All types of table glassware and decorative glassware were made. Pieces were often decorated with cut designs.

Val St Lambert

VAL ST.LAMBERT, Bottle, Cologne, Cameo Cut Flowers, Rubina, 8 In. 475.00
Candelabra, Sterling Silver & Crystal 125.00
Dish, Molded, 7 1/2 In. 25.00
Paperweight, Thistle, Frosted, Marked 25.00
Pitcher, Crystal, Signed, 8 In. 40.00
Plate, Old Masters, Rubens, Signed & Numbered 55.00
Vase, Cobalt Blue Flowers, Bronze Overlay, Signed, 12 In. 495.00

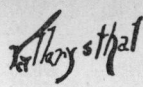

Vallerysthal Glassworks was founded in 1836 in Lorraine, France. In 1854 the firm became Klenglin et Cie. It made table and decorative glass, opaline, cameo, and art glass. A line of covered, pressed glass animal dishes was made in the nineteenth century. The firm is still working.

VALLERYSTHAL, Compote, Lacy Design, Square Top, 6 In., Pair	100.00
Dish, Cabbage Leaf, Figural, Mouse Cover	155.00
Dish, Setter Dog Cover, Blue	55.00
Figurine, Penguin, Black & White, 11 In.	35.00
Plate, Aqua, Floral, Scalloped, 7 1/2 In.	15.00
Salt, Hen, White, Covered	30.00
Vase, Figural, Frog, 9 In.	85.00

Van Briggle Pottery was made by Artus Van Briggle in Colorado Springs, Colorado, after 1901. Van Briggle had been a decorator at the Rookwood Pottery of Cincinnati, Ohio. He died in 1904. His wares usually had modeled relief decorations and a soft, dull glaze. The pottery is still working and still making some of the original designs.

VAN BRIGGLE, Ashtray, Art Deco, Figure Of Woman, 4 X 6 In.	55.00
Bookends, Bear, Standing Against Tree Trunk, Marked	198.00
Bookends, Puppy Dog, Brown & Green	100.00
Bookends, Ram, Persian Rose Glaze	70.00
Bookends, Standing Bears, Tree Trunks, Blue Green, Marked, 7 In.	198.00
Bowl, Blue Flower Panels, Buff Clay, Dated 1906, 2 X 5 3/4 In.	286.00
Bowl, Dragonfly, Shaded Blues, 8 In.	45.00
Bowl, Indian Maiden, Blue, Flower Frog, Double A Mark, 6 X 9 In.	95.00
Bowl, Kneeling Nude, Goose Flower Frog, 18 In.	200.00
Bowl, Leaaves & Flower Buds, Dated 1904, Maroon Glaze, 3 In.	250.00
Bowl, Leaf Design, 1908, Greenish Blue, 5 X 2 In.	45.00
Bowl, Persian Rose, Acorns, 6 In.	25.00
Bowl, Persian Rose, Leaf Design, 6 X 5 In.	38.00
Bowl, Persian Rose, Scalloped, Strap Handle, Marked, 2 X 8 In.	35.00
Conch Shell, Maroon, 12 In.	45.00
Conch Shell, Moonglow, 6 In.	18.00
Conch Shell, Persian Rose, 12 1/2 In.	40.00
Conch Shell, Turquoise, 9 In.	40.00
Console Set, Double Tulip Candleholders	150.00
Console Set, Oak Leaf & Acorn, Raspberry, 1926, 4 Piece	195.00
Creamer, Hopi Indian Maiden, Turquoise	45.00
Creamer, Melon Shape, Midnight Black Glaze	35.00
Dish, Brown, Footed, Anna Van Briggle, Colo. Springs, 5 In.	45.00
Dish, Mermaid On Edge, Flower Holder, Art Deco	450.00
Ewer, Persian Rose	35.00 To 45.00
Figurine, Donkey, Standing, Turquoise, 3 3/4 X 3 1/2 In.	35.00
Figurine, Elephant, Turquoise, 4 1/2 X 8 In.	75.00
Figurine, Mule, Lying Down, Turquoise, 4 X 4 1/2 In.	40.00
Figurine, Owl, Standing, Turquoise, 9 1/2 In.	85.00
Figurine, Rabbit, Turquoise, 3 In.	35.00
Flower Frog, 3 Little Frogs, Ming Blue	15.00
Flower Frog, Blue, Indian Maiden, 6 X 9 In.	125.00
Flower Frog, Reclining Woman, Blue	75.00
Lamp, 3 Handles, Footed, Turquoise, 7 1/2 In., Pair	90.00
Lamp, Cocker Spaniel, Rose Shade, Signed	195.00
Lamp, Squirrel, Original Shade, Ming Blue	125.00
Letter Holder, Swan Design, Footed, Red	45.00
Mug, Gold, Kappa Sigma Fraternity Letters, 1908–11, 4 3/4 In.	140.00
Paperweight, Elephant, Blue	75.00
Paperweight, Rabbit, Persian	95.00
Pitcher, Cobalt Blue, 7 1/4 In.	34.00
Plaque, Indian Head, Matte Brown, 5 1/2 In.	65.00
Sugar & Creamer, Child's, Turquoise, Hexagon Shape	150.00
Tumbler, Incised Bud–N–Ruth, Marked, Brown & Green, Set Of 8	50.00

Vase, 6 Leaves Around Rim, Turquoise, 8 In.	40.00
Vase, Bats Around Bottom, Dated 1916, Red & Blue, 10 3/4 In.	475.00
Vase, Blended Colors, Dated 1920, 4 In.	58.00
Vase, Blue, Cream Ground, Thistle Flowers, Marked, 7 1/2 In.	220.00
Vase, Brown, Drizzled Turquoise, Leaves, Incised 1921–22, 5 In.	50.00
Vase, Bud, Blue To Lavender, 2 Gourd Shape, 1915, 8 1/3 In.	110.00
Vase, Copper, 5 Floral Panels, Original Patina, 1908–11, 2 In.	475.00
Vase, Floral Design With Long Stems, 1915, Blue, 10 1/4 In.	275.00
Vase, Leaf & Berry Design, 1915, Mark In Center, Blue, 9 In.	250.00
Vase, Ming, Squatty, Signed, 3 In.	20.00
Vase, Mistletoe & Berry Pattern, Slate Blue, 1908–11, 2 1/2 In.	88.00
Vase, Mistletoe Design, Dated 1903, Pale Blue, 3 1/4 In.	150.00
Vase, Persian Rose, Art Nouveau, Marked, 7 3/4 In.	115.00
Vase, Persian Rose, Matte, Embossed Flowers, 8 1/2 In.	85.00
Vase, Plum, Embossed, 4 1/2 In.	35.00
Vase, Red To Green Glaze, Shape 671, 1908–11, 7 1/2 In.	395.00
Vase, Rose, Dated 1920, Blended Brown & Green, 4 In.	68.00
Vase, Rudlor, White Flowers, Green, 6 In.	50.00
Vase, Spade Shape, Leaves, Mulberry Glaze, Blue Wash, Mark, 5 In.	132.00
Vase, Tulip, Blue & Green Matte, 9 In.	55.00
Vase, Wheat Design, Blue–Green Glaze, C.1910, Marked, 15 In.	70.00
Wall Pocket, Persian Rose	85.00

Vasa Murrhina is the name of a glassware made by the Vasa Murrhina Art Glass Company of Sandwich, Massachusetts, about 1884. The glassware was transparent and was embedded with small pieces of colored glass and metallic flakes. Some of the pieces were cased. The same type of glass was made in England. Collectors often confuse Vasa Murrhina glass with aventurine, spatter, or spangle glass. There is much confusion about what actually was made by the Vasa Murrhina factory.

VASA MURRHINA, see also Spangle Glass

VASA MURRHINA, Bride's Basket, Mica Flecks, Silver Plate Frame & Feet	185.00
Ewer, Thorny Handle, Silver Spangles, Blue, 7 7/8 In.	110.00
Lamp, Fairy, Footed	250.00
Pitcher, Water, Green, Blue, White, Ruffled	185.00
Rose Bowl, Blue To White, Silver, Crimped, 5 In.	60.00
Rose Bowl, Crimped, White Lining, Mica Flakes, 4 X 3 1/4 In.	95.00
Rose Bowl, Fluted, Pink, 6 1/2 X 5 1/2 In.	85.00
Sugar Shaker, Original Lid, Pink Spatter	210.00
Toothpick, Pink Spatter, Leaf Mold	110.00
Vase, Cobalt, Mica, White Cased, Urn Shape, 5 1/2 In.	90.00
Vase, Crystal Spiral Trim, White Lining, Spangles, 8 In.	95.00
Vase, Vaseline Handles & Trim, Mica Spangles, Pink, 9 3/4 In.	95.00

Vasart is the signature used on a late type of art glass made by the Streathearn Glass Company of Scotland. Pieces are marked with an engraved signature on the bottom. Most of the glass is mottled or shaded.

VASART, Basket, Gray To Blue, Handle, Signed, Pair	25.00
Bowl, Signed, Pink & White, 5 In.	35.00

Vaseline glass is a greenish–yellow glassware resembling petroleum jelly. Some vaseline glass is still being made in old and new styles. Pressed glass of the 1870s was often made of vaseline–colored glass. The old glass was made with uranium, but the reproductions are being colored in a different way. See Pressed Glass for more information about patterns that were also made of vaseline–colored glass.

VASELINE GLASS, Bowl, Daisy & Button With Crossbar, 3 3/4 In.	90.00
Bowl, Maple Pattern, Pierced Corners, Rectangular, 10 In.	345.00
Butter, Daisy & Button, Wafer Edge, Cut Finial, Covered	65.00
Butter, Diamond & Button, Stem, Covered	65.00
Butter, Swirl, Frosted, Footed, Etched, Covered, 1/2 Lb.	150.00

Cake Plate, Pedestal, Hobnail	75.00
Candlestick, Scroll & Leaf, Pedestal, 7 X 7 In., Pair	55.00
Candy Dish, Hand Painted Flowers, Footed, Covered, 7 In.	85.00
Castor Set, Daisy & Button Pattern	375.00
Celery Dish, Pressed, 11 In.	45.00
Celery, Daisy & Button With Crossbar	40.00
Compote, Paneled, Covered, 5 X 6 1/4 In.	40.00
Compote, Twirl, Rolled Edge, U.S. Glass, 4 X 6 3/4 In.	29.00
Cruet, Daisy & Button With Crossbars, Original Stopper	135.00
Cruet, Hobnail, Original Stopper	225.00
Decanter, Grape Pattern, Sterling Silver Spigot, 15 1/2 In.	750.00
Decanter, Honeycomb, Teardop Stopper	75.00
Dish, Hen On Nest Cover, Basketweave Base, 5 1/2 X 7 In.	45.00
Dish, Sweetmeat, Silver Plate Holder, Ruby Rim, 5 7/8 In.	100.00
Ewer, Applied Flowers, Striped, Handles, 13 1/4 In, Pair	650.00
Finger Bowl, Optic Rib	45.00
Lamp, Kerosene, C.1860, Thousand Eye Base, 21 1/2 In.	1200.00
Loving Cup, 8 1/2 In.	60.00
Mug, Child's, 2 1/2 In.	15.00
Mug, Child's, Alphabet & Children	75.00
Paperweight, Mushroom Shape	50.00
Pitcher, Reed Handle, Large	38.00
Pitcher, Water, Coin Spot, Ruffled, Applied Handle	135.00
Pitcher, Water, Crystal White Overlay, Cut Back Design	125.00
Plate, Maple Leaf, 11 In.	40.00
Salt & Pepper, Foggy Bottom	40.00
Salt & Pepper, Panel & Star	23.00
Salt & Pepper, Pressed Diamond	8.00
Spooner, Stork	45.00
Sugar & Creamer, Swirl, Reverse Scroll Feet, Etched, Covered	275.00
Syrup, Spatter, Leaf Mold	285.00
Toothpick, Riverside's Ranson	39.50
Toothpick, Winsome	28.50
Town Pump	55.00
Tumble–Up, Opalescent	48.00
Vase, Etched Floral Sprays At Top, 8 In., Pair	215.00

Venetian glass has been made near Venice, Italy, from the thirteenth to the twentieth century. Thin, colored glass with applied decoration is favored, although many other types have been made.

VENETIAN GLASS, Basket, Gold Flecked Handle, Notched Rim, Purple, 7 1/2 In.	55.00
Compote, Pink Cased Bird, Enamel Design, Stem, 6 1/4 In.	165.00
Compote, Scalloped Bowl, Dragon Form Stem, Topaz, 8 In.	80.00
Decanter, Sherry, C.1875	65.00
Dish, Turquoise Over Clear, Flared, Turned Over Rim, 11 In.	28.00
Epergne, 4 Lily, Blue Ruffled Rims, Spiraled Rigaree, 16 In.	260.00
Jar, Gold Flecked Bubble Stem & Finial, Pink, Covered, 7 In.	80.00
Lemonade Set, Cobalt, Tankard, Tumbler, Lattice, Floral, 7 Pc.	140.00
Pitcher, Lavender, Clear Handle & Ruffle, 7 In.	45.00

Verlys

Verlys glass was made in France after 1931. It was made in the United States from 1935 to 1951. The glass is either blown or molded. The American glass is signed with a diamond–point-scratched name, but the French pieces are marked with a molded signature. The designs resemble those used by Lalique.

VERLYS, Ashtray, Duck	20.00
Ashtray, Horse, Rearing, Carl Schming	40.00
Ashtray, Lovebirds, Directorie Blue	85.00
Bonbon, Bouquet Pattern, Covered	185.00
Bowl, Birds & Bees, 11 1/2 In. ....85.00 To	169.00
Bowl, Orchid, 14 In.	145.00
Bowl, Pinecone, 6 3/4 In.	55.00
Bowl, Poppy, 13 1/2 In.	110.00
Bowl, Roses, 5 1/2 In.	50.00

Bowl, Waves, Frosted & Clear, 11 1/4 X 3 1/2 In.	325.00
Bowl, Wild Duck & Fish, Frosted & Clear, 13 1/2 In.	100.00
Centerpiece, Frosted Doves, Signed, Oval, 12 3/4 In.	110.00
Charger, Birds & Bees, Clear, Signed, 12 In.	169.00
Charger, Water Lilies & Pods, Frosted, Signed, 13 3/4 In.	195.00
Figurine, Pigeon, Frosted, 4 1/4 In.	285.00 To 315.00
Planter, Water Lilies, 7 X 11 In.	110.00
Vase, Clear & Frosted, Signed, 8 In.	40.00
Vase, Fish, Seahorse Handled, Embossed, Frosted, 7 In.	55.00
Vase, Maidens On 2 Sides, Frosted, Crystal, 8 1/2 X 5 In.	95.00
Vase, Mermaids & Seahorses, Signed, Amber, 11 In.	450.00

Vernon Potteries, Ltd., started in Vernon, California, in 1931. It became Vernon Kilns by 1948. The company made dinnerware and figurines until it closed in 1958. Collectors search for the brightly colored dinnerware and the pieces designed by Rockwell Kent, Walt Disney, and Don Blanding.

VERNON KILNS, Coffee Server, Homespun Pattern	15.00
Eggcup, Homespun Pattern, Pair	8.50
Figurine, Fleecing	10.00
Plate, Baker's Chocolate 175th Anniversary, 1941	22.00
Plate, Douglas MacArthur, 10 In.	16.00
Plate, Moby Dick, 9 1/2 In.	45.00
Plate, Salamina, 9 1/2 In.	95.00
Platter, Homespun Pattern, Oval	8.50
Sauce Boat, Homespun Pattern	10.00
Sugar & Creamer	10.00

Verre de soie glass was first made by Frederick Carder at the Steuben Glass Works from about 1905 to 1930. It is an iridescent glass of soft white or very, very pale green. The name means glass of silk, and it does resemble silk. Other factories have made verre de soie, and some of the English examples were made of different colors. Verre de soie is an art glass and is not related to the iridescent, pressed, white Carnival glass mistakenly called by its name.

VERRE DE SOIE, see also Steuben

VERRE DE SOIE, Goblet, Water, Steuben, 6 In.	50.00
Perfume Bottle, Jade Green Stopper, Steuben, 4 1/4 In.	150.00
Plate, 7 1/2 In.	28.00
Sherbet, Underplate, Steuben	50.00
Vase, Rainbow Iridescent, White, Bulbous, Ruffled, 7 In.	110.00
Vase, Ruffled, Narrow Neck, Flaring Base, C.1920, 4 In., Pair	45.00

Vienna Art plates are round metal serving trays produced at the turn of the century. The designs, copied from Royal Vienna porcelain plates, usually featured a portrait of a woman encircled by a wide, ornate border. Many were used as advertising or promotional items and were produced in Coshocton, Ohio, by J.F. Meeks Tuscarora Advertising Co. and H.D. Beach's Standard Advertising Co.

VIENNA ART, Plate, Anheuser Busch, Malt Nutrice, Girl, 1905	40.00
Plate, Barbee Distillery, 1905	175.00
Plate, Dr Pepper, Girl Facing Left, Dr With Period	225.00
Plate, Dr Pepper, Girl With Bottles, Dr With Period, Rectangular	160.00
Plate, Dr Pepper, Kittens, Dr With Period	150.00
Plate, Dr Pepper, Puppies, Dr With Period	160.00
Plate, Knights Of Columbus, 1905	37.50
Plate, Lady, 10 In.	47.00
Plate, Peasant Outdoor Scene, Border, Beehive Mark, 9 1/2 In.	195.00

VIENNA, see Beehive; Royal Vienna

The Villeroy & Boch Pottery of Mettlach was founded in 1841. The firm made many types of pottery, including the famous Mettlach steins. It is confusing for the collector because although Villeroy and Boch made most of its pieces in the city of Mettlach, Germany, they also had factories in other locations. There is a dating code impressed on the bottom of most pieces that makes it possible to determine the age of the piece.

VILLEROY & BOCH, see also Mettlach

VILLEROY & BOCH, Beaker, Silver Luster, Gray Ground, Cameo Design, Marked	95.00
Coffeepot, Virginia Pattern, 7 In.	115.00
Coffeepot, Virginia Pattern, Cut Sponge, 8 In.	85.00
Icon, King, Standing, Porcelain, Gold, Frame, 7 1/2 X 10 In.	181.00
Icon, Mary, Baby, Porcelain, Frame, 7 1/2 X 10 In. ....165.00 To 188.00
Pitcher, Sky Blue Cherry & Leaves, 5 In.	45.00
Plaque, Boat Scene, PUG, No.3287	44.00
Plate, Floral, 5 In.	10.00
Plate, Horse Scene, Black, White, Divided, 11 In., Set Of 6	385.00
Plate, Red & Blue Floral, 5 In., Set Of 6	36.00
Vase, Gunmetal Drip Over Green, Tan Streaks, 7 1/4 In.	22.00

VOLKMAR Corona N.Y.

Volkmar pottery was made by Charles Volkmar of New York from 1879 to about 1911. He was associated with several firms, including the Volkmar Ceramic Company, Volkmar and Cory, and Charles Volkmar and Son. Volkmar had been a painter, and his designs often look like oil paintings drawn on pottery.

VOLKMAR, Lamp, Base, 12 In.	50.00
Pitcher, Matte Blue, Green, 5 In.	35.00
Vase, Dark Green Glaze, Veining, Marked, 2 3/4 X 4 In.	242.00
Vase, Green Glaze, Rings, Cylindrical, Incised, C.1910, 8 In.	50.00

Volkstadt was a soft-paste porcelain manufactory started in 1760 by Georg Heinrich Macheleid at Volkstadt, Thuringia. Volkstadt–Rudolstadt was a porcelain factory started at Volkstadt–Rudolstadt by Beyer and Bock in 1890. Most pieces seen in shops today are from the later factory.

VOLKSTADT, Compote, 5 Cherubs Holding Fruit, 9 X 13 In.	400.00
Figurine, Butterfly	25.00
Figurine, Exotic Bird, Rococo Base, Blue, Pink, Yellow, 7 In.	65.00
Figurine, Frog, With Crown	50.00
Figurine, Maiden & Lion, 5 1/2 In.	175.00

WALLACE NUTTING photographs are listed under Print, Nutting. His reproduction furniture is listed under Furniture.

Frederich Walrath was a potter who worked in New York City, Rochester, New York, and at the Newcomb Pottery in New Orleans, Louisiana. He died in 1920. Pieces listed here are from his Rochester period.

WALRATH, Vase, Green, Blue, Matte, Foliage, 6 In.	450.00

WALT DISNEY, see Disneyana
WALTER, see A. Walter

Warwick china was made in Wheeling, West Virginia, in a pottery working from 1887 to 1951. Many pieces were made with hand-painted or decal decorations. The most familiar Warwick has a shaded brown background. The name "Warwick" is part of the mark and sometimes the word "IOGA" is also included.

WARWICK, Bowl, Floral, Flow Blue, 10 In.	70.00
Jardiniere, Floral, Red Tones	105.00
Jug, Cider, Monk ....125.00 To 150.00
Luncheon Set, Floral, 32 Piece	225.00
Mug, Monk, IOGA	75.00
Mug, Warrior, Horse, Maiden Waving, Brown, 5 In.	49.00
Pitcher, Poinsettias, Handle	95.00

Planter, Floral, IOGA 100.00
Plate, Golf, 1930s 32.00
Plate, The Broadmore, Figural, 7 In. 12.50
Platter, Blue & White, Marked, 18 X 14 In. 45.00
Server, Pancake, Roses On Ivory, Gold Trim, Ornate Finial, Marked 40.00
Syrup, Pink Roses, Dark Green To Cream, Metal Top & Collar, Marked 35.00
Tankard, Monk, IOGA 250.00
Tray, Rust Gooseberries, Brown To Cream, 9 1/4 X 6 1/2 In. 29.00
Vase, Poinsettia, Bulbous, IOGA 148.00
Vase, Young Girl, Marked, 13 In. 155.00
Wall Pocket, 11 1/2 In. 60.00

Watch fobs were worn on watch chains. They were popular during Victorian times and after. Many styles, especially advertising designs, are still made today.

WATCH FOB, Alaska Yukon Pacific Exposition, 1909 .... 75.00
American Legion, 14K Gold 195.00
Anheuser Busch ....45.00 To 75.00
Armour Co., Steer's Head 29.00
Art Nouveau, Floral, P.H.Hadley, Bellows Falls, Vt., Sterling 18.00
Atkins Saws ....45.00 To 65.00
Ax Blade, Embossed Bow, Ribbon Type, Figural 40.00
B.P.O.E., Elk's Tooth, Blue Enameled Clock, Brass 25.00
Babe Ruth, Celluloid 175.00
Babe Ruth, Picture On Front, Base Scoring On Reverse 110.00
Barker, Wheeler Co., Peoria, Art Nouveau Lady 40.00
Blatz Beer, Barrel Shape 67.50
Bull Durham, Charm, 14K Gold Plated 23.00
Bulldog Tobacco, Red Bulldog, Won't Bite, Enameled 65.00
Carwood, Buckeye Ditchers & Shovels 25.00
Case Plow Works, Hand Holding Plow 39.00
Cash Register, National, Brass 85.00
Caterpillar 12.00
Cyrus McCormick 25.00
Diamond Edge 75.00
Dr Pepper 45.00
Dr Pepper, Billiken ....48.00 To 54.00
Dr.Skiles, Denton, Texas, Sterling Silver, Doctor's Bag 25.00
Egyptian Design, Pharaoh's Head Top, Solid Silver, 3 1/4 In. ... 48.00
Elks, Head Of Elk, 2 Teeth 150.00
Elks, Strap 25.00
Embossed Farm Scene, 2 Keys, Family Seal, Sterling Silver, 12 In. 275.00
Ford Tractor ....10.00 To 17.50
GAR Delegate, Dept.Of Iowa, 1913 .... 20.00
Gohmann Bros.& Kahler Co., New Albany, Ind., Brass, Pointer Dog 35.00
Gooch's Macaroni 40.00
Green River Whiskey ....25.00 To 35.00
Heinz, Girl Holding Catsup Bottle 28.00
I.L.U. Insurance, Enameled 35.00
Insley Back Hoe 15.00
Interlocking Cement Stave Silo Co., Wichita, Silo, Cows 70.00
International Dozer 15.00
International Harvester, 2 Worlds, Equipment On Back 100.00
Iron Age Potato, Machinery 45.00
Ivory, Carved Initials 69.50
Kaiser Wilhelm & Franz Josef, Strap, 1914 .... 55.00
Kellogg Telephone 65.00
Kellogg's Toasted Corn Flakes, Enameled 85.00
Knights Of Pythias, Movable Parts, Enamel, Rubies, Diamonds .. 175.00
Knights Templar, Gold 300.00
Korns Mothers Bread, Leather, Button, Baseball Player Picture .. 30.00
Lava Soap 35.00
Lindbergh 30.00
Massachusetts Motorcycle Registration, 1912 ....75.00 To 95.00

Master Photo Finishers Of America	25.00
Mexican Border Service, 1916	50.00
Milwaukee Automobile Dealers, Show, Strap, 1916	65.00
Monogrammed Seal, Buckle, Gold Filled Mesh Band, C.1880	80.00
National Motorcycle Gypsy Tour, 1922	50.00
National Sportsman, Strap	55.00
Newark Star, Head Pin Tournament, 1915	50.00
Oakland, Porcelain, Blue & White	165.00
Oil Pull, Tractor, Brass & Porcelain	225.00
Old Reliable Coffee, Brass	34.00 To 40.00
Onyx & Carnelian, Frame, Spinning Bezel Center, 14K Gold	215.00
Ox Tobacco, Celluloid	37.00
Padlock, Hardware Co., Figural	125.00
Pan Pacific Exposition, 1915	35.00
Panhandle Old Settlers Assoc., Shape Of Texas	50.00
Peters Weatherbird Shoes, Enameled	125.00
Plymouth, Locomotive	20.00
Post Toasties	25.00
Princeton University, Brass, 1908	20.00
Red Diamond Overalls, Railroad Man	35.00
Red Goose Shoes, Enameled	75.00 To 100.00
Red Goose Shoes, Metal, Oval	100.00
Reo Car	45.00
Saddle Co., No Advertising	20.00
San Francisco Exposition, 1915	20.00
Sapolin, Enameled	25.00
Savage Rifles, Picture Of Indian With Rifle	85.00
Shapleigh Hardware	35.00
Shapleigh Hardware Co., Diamond Edge Mark Shaped	45.00
Starrett Tools	45.00
State Farm Mutual Auto Insurance Co., Car	75.00 To 100.00
Sterling Motor Truck, Milwaukee, Strap	65.00
Stewart Clipper, Strap	55.00
Swifts Premium Margarine	25.00
Turkey Coffee	60.00
Valparaiso College, 1904	15.00
Victorian, 6–Strand Braided Mesh Design, Buckle End, 14K Gold	210.00
Ward's Tip–Top Bread	45.00
Weatherbird Shoes, Enameled	95.00
Wells Shoes	35.00
Western Electric Co., Telephone	40.00
William Jennings Bryan	95.00
World's Championship Rodeo Contest, Chicago	25.00

The pocket watch was important in Victorian times because it was not until World War I that the wristwatch was used. All types of watches are collected: silver, gold, or plated. Watches are listed by company name or by style.

WATCH, Adams & Perry, No.1616, Hunting Movement, Gold Plated Case	450.00
American Waltham, Pocket, Size 18, 1899	95.00
American Watch Co., Bridge Model, Hunting Case, 21 Jewel, Yellow Gold	1350.00
American Watch Co., Pocket, Coin Silver Case, Keywind	175.00
Auburndale Lincoln, No.775, Keywind, Nickel Case	800.00
B.O.Plenty, Wristwatch, Tin, Marx, Windup	85.00
Babe Ruth, Wristwatch	125.00 To 175.00
Baum & Mercier, Lady's, 1–Carat Diamond, Gold Mesh Band	1250.00
Bracelet, Art Deco, Sapphire, 18K Gold, French, 1930s	975.00
Bucherer, Bracelet, Lady's, 18K Gold	350.00
Bugs Bunny, Wristwatch	29.00
Bulova, Lady's, 23 Jewel, 6 Diamonds, 14K White Gold	125.00
Bunn, Railroad, No.18S, 17 Jewel	210.00
Captain America, Fawcett Co., 1948	300.00
Captain Marvel, Wristwatch, Box	165.00
Caterpillar Tractor	15.00

Charlie Tuna, Wristwatch	25.00
Cinderella, In Plastic Slipper, Wristwatch	40.00
Cinderella, Wristwatch	15.00
Copenhagen, Gold	624.00
Dale Evans, Wristwatch	45.00
Dick Tracy, Wristwatch, Round, Box	125.00
Didisheim, Lapel	25.00
Dudley, Masonic, 3rd Model	2000.00
Elgin Grant, No.146001, Pocket, Gold, Open Face, 16 In.Bar Link Fob	250.00
Elgin, 15 Jewel, Hunting Case, Floral Design, Pocket	85.00
Elgin, 23 Jewel, B.W.Raymond Up & Down, Yellow Gold Filled	525.00
Elgin, Father Time, Up & Down Winding Indicator, Railroad	850.00
Elgin, Finger Bridge Veritas, 21 Jewel, Pocket	300.00
Elgin, Keywind, No.115696	350.00
Elgin, Lapel, Lady's, Art Deco, 14K Gold	150.00
Elgin, Pocket, 17 Jewel, Gold Filled Case, C.1888	135.00
Elgin, Pocket, Engraved Case, 1923	50.00
Elgin, Pocket, Size 18, 1897	95.00
Elgin, Presentation, 17 Jewel, 14K Gold, Engraved, Model 452	310.00
Elgin, Railroad, 21 Jewel, 14K White Gold, Model 478, 1926	225.00
Elgin, Railroad, Engraved Locomotive & Trains, Pocket	120.00
Elgin, Size 12, Yellow Gold Filled, 7 Jewel	95.00
Elgin, Size 16, 21 Jewel, Montgomery Dial, Gold Case	250.00
Elgin, Size 16, Father Time, Gold Case	275.00
Elgin, Size 16, Railroad, Montgomery Dial, 10K Gold Filled Case	275.00
Elgin, Veritas, 23 Jewel, Yellow Gold Filled, Pocket	275.00
Felix The Cat, Sparkler Nifty, Wristwatch, 1931	145.00
Fob, Seal Of Minnesota	12.00
French, Pocket, Gold Face, Original Chain & Key, Fusee Keywind	400.00
G.I.Joe, Wristwatch, Box	60.00
Girard–Perregaux, Pendant, Cast Bezel	275.00
Graves, Express, Open Faced Silver Fob, Chain, Vesta Case, Key, 1902	100.00
Hamilton, 23 Jewel, Model 950B, Case	400.00
Hamilton, 23 Jewel, Yellow Gold Filled	575.00
Hamilton, Model 918, 14K Solid Gold Case, Pocket	225.00
Hamilton, Model 992B, Railroad Case	165.00
Hamilton, No.19j, Pocket, Arabic Numbers, 14K White Gold, C.1935	125.00
Hamilton, No.950B, Yellow Gold Filled, Pocket	360.00
Hamilton, Railroad, 21 Jewel, 10K Yellow Gold	235.00
Hamilton, Railroad, 21 Jewel, Gold Filled Case	95.00
Hamilton, Railroad, 21 Jewel, Yellow Gold Case, Model 1909	175.00
Hamilton, Size 16, 21 Jewel, Railroad, Double Back Silver Case	250.00
Hampden, Pocket, 21 Jewel	145.00
Hampden, Pocket, Gladiator 11 Jewel, Silverode Case, C.1885	95.00
Hampden, Pocket, Locomotive On Back, No.18S	39.00
Hampden, Pocket, Railroad, 21 Jewel, Size 18	150.00
Harman, Pocket, Nurse's, Sterling Silver, 17 Jewel, Swiss, C.1910	100.00
Howard, 23 Jewel, 18K Gold, Pocket	450.00
Illinois, 23 Jewel, Sangamo Special	600.00
Illinois, 23 Jewel, Yellow Gold Filled	700.00
Illinois, Abe Lincoln, 21 Jewel, Size 18, Silver Case, Pocket	195.00
Illinois, Abe Lincoln, Pocket	75.00
Ingersoll, Nickel Over Brass, Jumbo Model	750.00
James Bond, Wristwatch, Box	125.00
Jiminy Cricket, U.S.Time Co., Wristwatch, Original Band, Price, 1948	115.00
Joe Palooka, Wristwatch, Box	200.00
Keywind, English, 18K Gold, Key & Chain, Pocket, C.1820	425.00
Lady's, 0 Size Hunter, 14K Gold	190.00
Le Coultre, Lady's, 14K Gold, Flexible Mesh 14K Gold Band, Black Face	565.00
Lester Maddox, Wristwatch, Box	15.00
Li'l Abner, Pocket	125.00
Li'l Abner, Wristwatch, Flag Waving, Box	150.00
Li'l Abner, Animated Donkey Head, Wristwatch	25.00
Longines, Man's, 20 Diamonds In Dial, 14K White Gold	200.00

Wave Crest, Box, Large

Watch, Pocket, Enameled Face,
Gold Filled Case

Lord Elgin, 23 Jewel, Railroad Movement, Blue Dial, Gold Hands	2200.00
Lucien Piccard, Lady's, 14K Gold Woven Band	350.00
Lucy, From Peanuts, Arms Are Moving Hands, Wristwatch, C.1952	15.00
Marcel Boucher, Wristwatch, Art Deco, Enameled	48.00
Marvy Marvel, Wristwatch	65.00
Movado, Black Braided Band, 14K White Gold	225.00
Movado, Lady's, Mesh Band, 14K Gold, C.1940	450.00
Patek Philippe, 18K Gold & Platinum	750.00
Pink Panther, Digital, Animated Display, Alarm Plays Theme Music	25.00
Pocket, Enameled Face, Gold Filled Case ....*Illus*	125.00
Rockford, Up & Down Indicator, Model 18S	5200.00
Rolex, Man's, Oyster, Perpetual Date Chronometer, 14K Gold Band	2500.00
Seth Thomas, Railroad, 21 Jewel, Model 260, Nickeled Silver Case	295.00
Spiro Agnew, Wristwatch, Original Box ....47.00 To 62.00
Sun Watch, Pocket, Sundial	75.00
Swiss, Enamel Design, 18 K Gold	325.00
Vanguard, Railroad, 10K Gold Filled	150.00
Verge, Georgian, Open Face, Keywind, 18K Gold, French, 1834	1500.00
Waltham, 17 Jewel, Open Face, Yellow Gold Filled, Size 12	50.00
Waltham, Lady's, Hunting Case, 7 Jewel, Yellow Gold Filled Case, 1899	195.00
Waltham, Lady's, Pocket, Size 6, Gold Filled	130.00
Waltham, No.1543, Keywind, Silver Case, Enamel Dial	650.00
Waltham, Pocket, C.1889	85.00
Waltham, Pocket, Hunting Case, Size O	89.00
Waltham, Pocket, Silver Case, 11 Jewel, C.1893	125.00
Waltham, Pocket, Silver, Rope Chain, Snake Hook For Belt, 1895	62.50
Waltham, Pocket, Stem Wind, Marked Coin Silver Case	50.00
Waltham, Premier Maximums, 18K Gold, 23 Jewel	9000.00
Waltham, Railroad King Special, Nickel Case, Screw Back	195.00
Waltham, Railroad, Pocket, Vanguard, 23 Jewel	205.00
Waltham, Size 16, 21 Jewel, 10K Gold Filled Case	275.00
Waltham, Vanguard, 23 Jewel, Railroad, Pocket	205.00
Westclox, Pocket, Ben	75.00
Winchester, Pocket	125.00
Wm.Ellery Model 1873, Pocket, 14K Gold, Size 8	225.00

Waterford–type glass resembles the famous glass made from 1783 to 1851 in the Waterford Glass Works in Ireland. It is a clear glass that was often decorated by cutting. Modern glass is being made again in Waterford, Ireland, and is marketed under the name "Waterford."

WATERFORD, Decanter, Alana Pattern, Pedestal, Loop Handle	295.00
Goblet, Water, Lismore	100.00

Vase, Bud, Signed, 7 In. 50.00

WAVE CREST
WARE

Wave Crest glass is a white glassware manufactured by the Pairpoint Manufacturing Company of New Bedford, Massachusetts, and some French factories. It was decorated by the C. F. Monroe Company of Meriden, Connecticut. The glass was painted in pastel colors and decorated with flowers. The name "Wave Crest" was used after 1898.

WAVE CREST, Biscuit Jar, Egg Crate, Enamel Design All Sides 235.00
Biscuit Jar, Opal, Floral Decor 65.00
Biscuit Jar, Square, Floral Panels, Silver Lid 295.00
Biscuit Jar, Swirl Pattern 285.00
Bottle, Perfume, Frosted Stopper 165.00
Bottle, Perfume, Lavender To Green, Enamel Floral, Marked 425.00
Box, Baby Pink, Orchid, Blue Forget–Me–Nots, Signed, 7 X 4 In. 375.00
Box, Baroque Shell, Floral, Red Banner Mark, Covered, 5 1/2 In. 550.00
Box, Beige, Pink Daisies, Blown Out Swirls, 8 X 3 3/4 In. 650.00
Box, Bishop's Hat Shape, Lined, Pink Florals, 3 X 3 In. 275.00
Box, Bittersweet Blossoms, Ormolu Trim, Hinged, 6 X 4 In. 155.00
Box, Blown Out Flowers On Hinged Lid, Lined, Signed, 4 In. 400.00
Box, Collar & Cuff, Lid Repaired, 6 1/2 X 5 1/2 In. 400.00
Box, Cream, Pink & Gold Flowers, Buds, Signed, 7 X 4 In. 350.00
Box, Double Shell Lid, Well On Each Side, Signed, Blue, 3 In. 210.00
Box, Double Shell, Pink & Blue Florals, Marked, 3 1/4 In. 350.00
Box, Floral Design, Hinged Lid, Red Banner Mark, 2 1/2 X 3 In. 150.00
Box, Glove, Sky Blue Ground, Pink Flowers, Signed, 8 X 4 In. 650.00
Box, Gold Morning Glories, Enameled Allover, Signed, 5 1/2 In. 495.00
Box, Hinged Cover, Floral Design, Red Banner, 2 1/2 X 3 In. 150.00
Box, Hinged Lid, Enameled Florals, White Ground, 7 X 4 In. 300.00
Box, Jewelry, Baroque Shell, Blue, Floral, Red Mark, 7 1/2 In. 645.00
Box, Jewelry, Baroque Shell, Pale Blue, Enameled Flowers, Marked 695.00
Box, Jewelry, Blue & White Flowers, Original Lining, 6 1/2 In. 225.00
Box, Jewelry, Hinged Lid, Swirl Pattern, Ivory Lining, 6 1/2 In. 425.00
Box, Large .... *Illus* 475.00
Box, Lid, Clear, Gold Blossoms, Samantha Howell 950.00
Box, Molded Baroque Shell, Hinged Lid, Blue, Signed, 3 1/2 In. 275.00
Box, Pin, Cupids & Flowers, Marked, 4 In. 215.00
Box, Scenic Top, Pink, Scroll Mold, 5 3/4 In. 325.00
Box, Shaded Blue Scroll, Signed, Oblong, Covered, 5 1/2 In. 285.00
Box, Shell Pattern, Enamel Flowers, Banner Mark, 3 1/2 In. 248.00
Box, Shell Top, Floral Enamel, Signed, 3 In. 220.00
Box, Shell–Like Design, Pastel Flowers, Signed, 3 X 2 1/2 In. 200.00
Box, Signed, Pink, Octagon, Covered, 3 1/2 X 3 In. 195.00
Box, Swirl Design, Floral Enamel, Blue Lined, Footed, 7 In. 595.00
Box, Swirl Pattern, Beading, Cover, Ivory Ground, 6 In. 325.00
Box, Swirl, Floral, Raised Beading, 5 1/2 In. 385.00
Box, Swirled Floral Design, Hinged, Signed, 5 X 6 In. 295.00
Box, Swirled, Flowers, Leaves, Buds, Signed, 6 1/2 In. 895.00
Box, Trinket, Open, Signed, 3 1/4 In. 55.00
Box, White, Orange, Yellow, Gray Floral Design, Signed, 2 X 3 In. 150.00
Casket, Lion's Head Footed, Brown, Red Banner Mark, 8 1/2 In. 995.00
Cookie Jar, Moon & Stars Pattern, White Beading, Blue Ground 495.00
Cookie Jar, Moon & Stars Throughout, Beading, White Ground 250.00
Cracker Jar, Apple Blossom Design, Signed C.F.M.Co. 295.00
Creamer, Yellow Daisy, Dots, Silver Collar, Handle, Helmschmied 75.00
Dish, Dresser, Gold Collar, 3 In. 90.00
Dish, Dresser, Gold Collar, Enameled Flowers, 4 1/2 In. 90.00
Dish, Dresser, Open, Gold Collar, Signed, 4 In. 98.00
Dish, Pin, Brass Collar 125.00
Dish, Swirl Design, Enameled Flowers, Brass Collar, 5 X 2 In. 105.00
Lamp, Base, Blue Flowers, Ferns, Original Burner, Chimney, 20 In. 225.00
Lamp, Oil, Electric, 23 1/2 In. 750.00
Planter, Cream Ground, Yellow & Brown Daisies, Signed 350.00
Planter, Puffy Flowers, Vines, Brass Insert, 7 In. 250.00
Salt & Pepper, Blue To White, Basket Weave Neck, Dog In Field 110.00

Salt & Pepper, Swirl, Enamel Florals, Square	155.00
Salt & Pepper, Swirled Pattern, Enamel Floral, Original Tops	165.00
Smoke Set, Ormolu Frame, Cigarette Holder, 2 Match Holders	525.00
Toothpick, Enameled Floral Design, Ormolu Base, 2 3/4 In.	285.00
Toothpick, Straight Sided, Ormolu Trim	135.00
Tray, Jewel, Floral, Handles	115.00
Vase, 2 Duck Panel, Ormolu Handles & Base, Marked, 15 3/4 In.	945.00
Vase, Cobalt Blue Enamel Design, Pink Floral, 8 3/4 In.	225.00
Vase, Ducks Flying, Signed, 15 3/4 In.	945.00
Vase, Floral Medallions, Robin Blue, Ormolu Frame, 6 3/4 In.	410.00
Vase, Floral, Cobalt Trim, Ormolu Feet, Marked, 7 1/4 In.	245.00
Vase, Irregular Enamel Design, Pink Floral, 8 3/4 In.	225.00

WEAPON, see Gun; Rifle; Sword; etc.

The earliest American weather vanes were used in seventeenth–century Boston. The direction of the wind was an indication of coming weather, important to the seafaring and farming communities. By the mid–nineteenth century, commercial weather vanes were made of metal. Today's collectors often consider weather vanes to be examples of folk art, even though they may not have been handmade.

WEATHER VANE, Arrow, Stylized Sheet Metal, 36 1/4 In.	225.00
Atlantic Salmon, New England, C.1875	375.00
Blackhawk Pattern, Gold Leaf	800.00
Bull, Standing, Verdigris, Late 19th Century, 26 In.	900.00
Butterfly & Sunflower, Iron Stem, Copper, 45 X 20 In.	6050.00
Cardinals, Copper Ball Shaft, C.1900, 55 In.	90.00
Clipper Ship, Painted Tin, American, Walnut Base ....*Illus*	375.00
Coach & 4 Horses, Cutout Silhouette, Iron, 54 1/4 In.	50.00
Cod, Copper, Full Form, Cast Zinc Head, Applied Fins, 32 In.	3700.00
Collie Dog, Original Rod, Copper, 21 X 35 In.	385.00
Cow, Copper, Painted Black & White, 33 In.	1300.00
Cow, Full–Bodied, Copper	1540.00
Cow, Full–Bodied, Mercury Glass Ball	235.00
Cow, Full–Bodied, Textured Hair Finish	2000.00
Cow, Long Horns, Copper, Molded, Silver Paint, Over Gold, 24 In.	400.00
Cushing Rooster, Original Gold Leaf, Red Painted Comb	2310.00
Directional, Copper, Cast Iron, 5 Ft.3 In.	110.00
Eagle, Copper, Spread Wings, Directionals, 1900, 3 1/2 In.	100.00
Eagle, Gilded, Copper, 27 X 25 In.	250.00
Eagle, Spread, Copper, Zinc, Sphere, Directionals, 7 Ft.	475.00
Farmer, Plow, 2 Horses, Sheet Copper, 30 1/2 In.	300.00
Fish, Gilt Copper, American, 19th Century ....*Illus*	650.00

Weather Vane, Fish, Gilt Copper,
American, 19th Century

Weather Vane, Clipper Ship, Painted Tin,
American, Walnut Base

Fish, Green & White, Polychrome, 9 X 35 In.	1100.00
Gabriel, Copper, Riveted, Double Sheet, 41 3/4 In.	1200.00
Grasshopper, Copper, Full–Bodied, Iron, 27 X 44 In.	4950.00
Horse, Copper, 3–Dimensional, Traces Of Original Paint	400.00
Horse, Double, Rider Seated On Surrey, 1930s	4985.00
Horse, Full–Bodied, Copper	2035.00
Horse, Full–Bodied, Running, Zinc Head, Copper Mane, 42 In.	935.00
Horse, Howard, Zinc	1300.00
Horse, Jumping, Spiky Mane & Tail, Sheet Metal, 21 X 33 In.	770.00
Horse, On Block Of Cherry, Full–Bodied, Copper	130.00
Horse, Prancing, Cast Zinc, Sheet Metal Tail, 33 X 25 In.	4000.00
Horse, Running, Braced Sheet Iron, 52 X 24 In.	1500.00
Horse, Running, Copper, Bullet Holes, 29 1/2 X 18 In.	650.00
Horse, Running, Copper, Green Patina, 31 1/2 In.	590.00
Horse, Running, Copper, Zinc Head, American, 19th Century, 26 In	300.00
Horse, Running, Copper, Zinc Head, Yellow Over Gilt, 29 In.	575.00
Horse, Running, Full–Bodied, Copper, Zinc, 4 Ft. 8 In.	400.00
Horse, Running, Molded Copper, 19th Century, 28 1/2 X 17 In.	450.00
Horse, Running, Mounted On Ornate Cupola, Verdigris, 66 In.	1400.00
Horse, Running, Spire & Directionals, 1860–80	1950.00
Horse, Running, Sulky, Rider, Copper, Zinc, 29 X 17 1/2 In.	1700.00
Horse, Silhouette, Sheet Metal, 22 In.	65.00
Horse, Sulky, & Rider, J.W.Fiske	6500.00
Indian, Long Headdress, Drawing Bow, Sheet Metal, 27 In.	1430.00
Indian, Silhouette, Headdress, Tomahawk, Bow, Iron, 57 In.	467.00
Man In The Moon	150.00
Model Ship, Maine	395.00
Morgan Horse, Copper, Documented	4200.00
Morgan Horse, Full–Bodied	3800.00
Peacock, Silhouette, Paddle Tail, Sheet Metal, 26 X 16 In.	990.00
Pig	45.00 To 85.00
Pig, Arrow	85.00
Pig, Copper, American, 23 1/2 X 15 1/2 X 28 In. *Illus*	4750.00
Pig, Flat	45.00
Pintail Duck, Elmer Crowell, Cape Cod	8000.00
Plow, Pulled By 2 Horses, Farmer, Copper, 30 In.	300.00
Rooster, 2–Dimensional, Gilded Copper, 19th Century	300.00
Rooster, Cast Zinc & Sheet Copper, Stand, 14 X 12 In.	4400.00
Rooster, Full–Bodied, Harvard	4400.00
Rooster, Handmade, Tin, 20th Century	85.00
Rooster, Molded, Gold Leaf, Cushing Factory, C.1883, 29 In.	2100.00
Rooster, Sheet Metal	320.00

Webb

Webb glass was made by Thomas Webb & Sons of Stourbridge, England. Many types of art and cameo glass were made by them during the Victorian era. The factory is still producing glass. Webb Burmese and Webb Peachblow are special colored glasswares of the Victorian period.

WEBB BURMESE, Lamp, Fairy, Green, Floral, Aladdin Shape, Clarke, 6 1/2 In.	695.00
Lamp, Fairy, Marked Clarke Insert, Dome Shade, 6 1/2 In.	725.00
Lamp, Fairy, Marked Ruffled Clarke Base, Signed, 5 3/4 In.	695.00
Lamp, Fairy, Porcelain Base, Original Candle, Signed	310.00
Lamp, Fairy, Pyramid, Brass Ormolu, Beveled Mirror, 8 1/4 In.	595.00
Lamp, Fairy, Ruffled Base, Clarke Insert, 19th Century, 6 In.	425.00
Lamp, Fairy, Satin Finish, Dome, Signed Clarke's Candle Cup	235.00
Rose Bowl, 8–Crimp, Leaves, Berries, Pink To Yellow, 2 1/4 In.	298.00
Rose Bowl, Red Berries, Leaves, Crimped Top, 2 1/2 X 2 3/4 In.	295.00
Toothpick, Prunus Blossoms, 2 5/8 In.	435.00
Vase, Bottle Shape, Ivy Leaves, Signed, 4 1/4 X 7 3/4 In.	850.00
Vase, Floral, Acid Finish, Crimped Top, 3 1/2 In.	320.00
Vase, Pedestal Foot, Flower Shape, Cones, Signed, 5 3/8 In.	595.00
Vase, Pinched Mouth, Spherical Shape, Enamel Floral, 2 1/2 In.	250.00
Vase, Red Tan Berries, Leaves, Pinched Top, 4 In.	285.00

Weather Vane, Pig, Copper, American, 23 1/2 X 15 1/2 X 28 In.   Webb Peachblow,
Lamp, Signed

WEBB PEACHBLOW, Dish, Shell, Matte Gold Flowers, Ruffled, 9 1/4 In.	295.00
Lamp, Fairy, Clarke Base, 19th Century, 3 3/4 In.	90.00
Lamp, Fairy, Crimped Shade, Ruffled & Fluted, 5 1/2 In.	500.00
Lamp, Signed .... *Illus*	900.00
Vase, Bottle Shape, Gold Bird, 10 1/4 In.	475.00
Vase, Butterfly, Gold & Silver Floral, Squat, 4 1/2 In.	275.00
Vase, Enameled Birds, Signed, 8 In.	275.00
Vase, Florals & Butterfly In Gold, Creamy Lining, 8 In.	495.00
Vase, Gold Encrusted Flowers & Leaves, 7 1/2 In.	895.00
Vase, Gold Floral, Rose To Pink, White Lining, 8 1/2 In.	395.00
Vase, Gold Prunus Blossoms, Leaves, Butterfly, 6 1/2 In.	325.00
Vase, Horizontal Ribbing, Narrow Neck, Bulbous, 8 1/4 In.	295.00
Vase, Raised Gold Prunus, Cream Lining, Red To Pink, 3 In.	325.00
WEBB, Berry Bowl, Underplate, Alexandrite, Crimped Rims, C.1910, 6 In.	775.00
Biscuit Jar, Opaque Flowers, Silver Plate Top, Rim, & Handle, 5 1/2 In.	1995.00
Bottle, Cologne, 3 Layers Of Glass, Amberina Over Green, 5 7/8 In.	335.00
Bottle, Cologne, Amberina Over Green, White Interior, Sterling Top	435.00
Bottle, Cologne, Blue, Floral Panels, Silver Top, Cameo, 5 In.	1395.00
Bottle, Cologne, Cameo, Pink Floral, Chartreuse, White Lining, 3 1/2 In.	795.00
Bottle, Scent, Cameo, 3 Colors, Floral, Silver Hinged Top, 2 In.	895.00
Bottle, Scent, Cameo, Reclining, Blue, Silver Hinged Top, 3 3/4 In.	595.00
Bottle, Scent, White Cameo Carved Floral, Blue Satin Ground, 3 In.	550.00
Bowl, Fishscale, Pink Shades, White, Enameled, Signed G.L.F., 7 1/2 In.	1000.00
Bowl, Intaglio Cut, Flowers, Bamboo Design, Pink, 5 3/4 In. X 3 3/4 In.	750.00
Bowl, White Opal, Pink Lining, Birds, Footed, Signed, 6 X 8 In.	485.00
Compote, Inverted Thumbprint, Pedestal, Signed, 6 X 5 In.	75.00
Cracker Barrel, Silver Plate Top & Handle, 5 X 2 3/4 In.	550.00
Egg Set, Tray, Eggcups, Spoons, Salt Dips, Napkin Rings, Silver Plate	260.00
Epergne, 3 Flower Holders, Rose Satin Glass, Mirror Base, 8 3/4 In.	1800.00
Ewer, Ribbed Design, Blue, 10 In.	380.00
Ewer, Thorn Handle, Tricornered Spout, Amber Handle, 8 1/2 In.	90.00
Inkwell, Cameo, Vaseline, Floral, Hinged Silver Top Initial, 4 1/2 In.	1500.00
Jar, Gold Washed Ormolu Mounted, Gold Outlined Leaves, 6 1/2 In.	595.00
Parfait, Leafy Swags & Flowers, Signed, 7 In.	60.00
Perfume, Floral, Blue & White, Sterling Spring Top, 3 In.	695.00
Pitcher, New England, Tankard Shape, Honeycomb Pattern,, 5 In.	325.00
Pitcher, Tankard, Fuchsia To Amber, Honeycomb, Applied Handle, 5 In.	325.00
Rose Bowl, 3–Color, Carved Flowers & Foliage, White Lining, 2 1/2 In.	995.00
Rose Jar, Squat, Domed Cover, Leaf & Fruit Design, Marked, 5 3/4 In.	1150.00
Scent Bottle, Florals & Leaves, Gold Outlining, Marked, 4 1/4 In.	650.00

Tray, Holds Napkin Ring, Spoons, 2 Eggcups, Berry Pontil 260.00
Tumbler, Juice, Alexandrite, Honeycomb, 3 5/8 In. 345.00
Vase, Allover Carving, Flowers, Arabesques, Scalloped, Marked, 7 In. 480.00
Vase, Allover Carving, Flowers, Arabesques, Squat, Marked, 4 1/4 In. 360.00
Vase, Apricot Bough & Rim, Canary Ground, Signed, 4 In. 725.00
Vase, Bands At Top & Bottom, Sculptured Leaves & Flowers, 10 1/2 In. 2250.00
Vase, Blown–Out Floral, Marked 8 In. 165.00
Vase, Blue, White Floral, Butterfly, Signed, Cameo, 7 In. 1800.00
Vase, Bluebirds, Flower, Dragonflies, Propeller Mark, 12 In., Pair 650.00
Vase, Bronze, Double Gourd, Amethyst, Fluted Rim, .12 In. 175.00
Vase, Bulbous Ovoid Body, White Cowslips, Butterflies, 8 In. 1000.00
Vase, Cameo, Blood Red, Butterflies, Roses, Flared Neck, 8 In. 1850.00
Vase, Cameo, Pink Floral, Cream, Gold Spider Web, 4 7/8 X 3 3/4 In. 395.00
Vase, Carved Flowers, Rose Satin Overlay, Butterfly On Back, 2 In. 650.00
Vase, Carved Flowers, White Bands At Top & Bottom, Citron, 2 3/4 In. 550.00
Vase, Carved Layers Of Fruits, Branches, Border, Signed, 10 1/2 In. 5500.00
Vase, Coinspot, Mother–Of–Pearl, Ruffled, Flowers, Marked, 11 1/2 In. 995.00
Vase, Coral Red, Gold Floral, White Lining, 9 X 4 1/4 In. 350.00
Vase, Elongated Neck, Bulbous Base, White Floral, Yellow, Signed, 6 In. 550.00
Vase, Enameled Birds, Floral, Dragonflies, Propeller Mark, 12 In., Pair 725.00
Vase, Enameled Gold, Daisies, Butterflies, Butterscotch To Cream, 11 In 485.00
Vase, Floral & Scrolling Carved Allover, Crimson Ground, 3 X 4 In. 795.00
Vase, Floral Design, Cranberry & White, Satin Glass, Marked, 8 In. 450.00
Vase, Gold Gilding Of Floral & Bird, Marked, Ivory, 9 3/8 In. 325.00
Vase, Jack–In–The–Pulpit, Coralene, Signed, 5 In. 195.00
Vase, Melon Form, White Enamel Blossoms & Butterfly, Marbelized, 9 In. 415.00
Vase, Mother–Of–Pearl, Signed, 10 1/2 In. 600.00
Vase, Openwork, C.1900, 7 X 8 In. 110.00
Vase, Openwork, Tooled Lattice Work Top, 8 X 6 In. 90.00
Vase, Orange Gold Shading To Base, Foil Inclusions, Bird, 9 1/2 In. 385.00
Vase, Pewter Framed, Art Nouveau Lily Pads, Green, 5 X 9 In. 115.00
Vase, Pink Morning Glory, White Overlay, Butterfly, White, 3 1/2 In. 875.00
Vase, Poppies Cut In A Band, White Top Half, Signed, Citron, 5 In. 495.00
Vase, Red, White Floral, Butterfly, Carved Border, Cameo, 9 In. 2850.00
Vase, Satin Glass, Cranberry, Signed, 8 1/2 In. 440.00
Vase, White Carved Flowers, Leaf Band, Chartreuse, 1 3/4 X 4 In. 750.00
Vase, White Satin Body, Morning Glory, Pink & White, 3 1/2 In. 875.00
Wine, Alexandrite, Baby Thumbprint, Blue To Red, To Amber, 4 1/2 In. 800.00

WEDGWOOD

Josiah Wedgwood, although considered a cripple by his brother and forbidden to work at the family business, founded one of the world's most successful potteries. The pottery was founded in England in 1759. A large variety of wares has been made, including the well-known jasperware, basalt, creamware, and even a limited amount of porcelain. The firm is still in business.

WEDGWOOD, Biscuit Barrel, Blue Jasperware, Bail Handle, Dated July 1882 .... 250.00
Biscuit Barrel, Hunt Scene All Around, Marked, Lilac, 6 1/2 In. 375.00
Biscuit Jar, Dark Blue, Classical Figures, White, Covered 285.00
Biscuit Jar, Jasperware, Classical Figures, Sage Green, 6 1/2 In. 225.00
Biscuit Jar, Jasperware, Dark Blue, Classical Figures 190.00
Biscuit Jar, Jasperware, Silver Plate Top, Rim, & Handle, 6 3/4 In. 450.00
Biscuit Jar, Lilac 250.00
Bottle, Tricolor, 10 In. 1250.00
Bowl, Basalt, Dancing Horse, Figures In Black, 10 In. 375.00
Bowl, Basalt, Embossed Stripes & Rim Design, Black, 9 1/4 X 4 In. 300.00
Bowl, Butterfly Luster, Inside & Out, Flame Red & Orange, 4 In. 175.00
Bowl, Butterfly Luster, Inside & Out, Flame Red, 4 In. 145.00
Bowl, Butterfly Luster, Octagonal, Gold Trim, Marked, 7 X 3 1/2 In. 495.00
Bowl, Dragon Luster, Fruit, Octagonal, Marked, 3 1/2 In. 375.00
Bowl, Dragon Luster, Mother–Of–Pearl, Blue, Marked, 3 1/2 In. 98.00
Bowl, Fairyland Luster, Orange & Blue, 9 1/2 In. 1100.00
Bowl, Fairyland Luster, Woodland Elves, Monogram MJ, 10 7/8 In. 1210.00
Bowl, Gold Chinese Dragons Inside & Out, Marked, 8 In. 330.00
Bowl, Hummingbird Luster, 6 1/2 In. 200.00

Bowl, Jasperware, Acanthus, Blue, 10 1/4 In. 385.00
Bowl, Jasperware, Blue, White, Classical, C.1862, Marked, 2 3/8 In. 245.00
Bowl, Jasperware, Classical Figures, Green, 8 1/2 X 3 3/4 In. 97.00
Bowl, Jasperware, Green, 8 1/2 In. 95.00
Bowl, Luster, Hummingbird, Blue, Orange Mottled, Marked, 5 In. 165.00
Bowl, Nut, Luster, Orange & Blue, Gilt Geese, Marked, 2 1/4 In. 65.00
Bowl, Raised White Figures, Dated 1942, 4 X 2 In. 65.00
Bowl, Washington & Ship, Queensware, 8 In. 55.00
Box, Blue, White Design, Heart Shape, Marked, 5 In. 35.00
Box, Covered, Jasperware, Blue, Square, 4 In. 49.00
Box, Dome Top, Scallop Edge, Green, 5 In. 35.00
Box, Jasperware, Kidney Shape, 3 In. 45.00
Box, Match, Dark Blue, 1895, 1 1/2 X 2 1/2 X 3/4 In. 85.00
Box, Match, Orchid, White, Jasperware, Mother & Child Sewing, Lid 58.00
Bulldog, Glass Eyes, Black Basalt, Marked, 2 3/4 X 2 X 5 In. 350.00
Butter Chip, Ivanhoe, Flow Blue 27.00
Cachepot, Royal Blue, Majolica, 8 1/2 X 9 In. 590.00
Calendar Tile, 1928, Plymouth Rock On Reverse 60.00
Candlestick, Green, Buff, 7 In., Pair 125.00
Candlestick, Jasperware, Blue & White, 8 In., Pair 245.00
Candlestick, Jasperware, Pillar, Sage Green, 6 3/4 In., Pair 130.00
Candlestick, Jasperware, Sage, Light Green, Buff, 7 In. 225.00
Cheese Dish, Jasperware, Blue & White, Marked, 7 1/2 X 11 In. 295.00
Chop Plate, Pearlware, Feather Edge, Floral Design, 11 1/4 In. 575.00
Clock, Jasperware, Cupid Center, Floral Rim, Green, 12 1/4 In. 550.00
Compote, Lilac, Ram's Head, Grapes, 3 1/2 X 6 In. 150.00
Creamer, Dated 1936, 4 1/8 In. 65.00
Creamer, Terra–Cotta, Enameled Flowers, 1800, Large 135.00
Cup & Saucer, Annapolis 20.00
Cup & Saucer, Ashford Gray 20.00
Cup & Saucer, Devon Sprays 35.00
Cup & Saucer, Etruria, Pink Transfer, Harvard Tercentenary, 1936 .... 25.00
Cup & Saucer, Floral, C.1820, Red Mark 375.00
Cup & Saucer, Jasperware, Green, Marked 30.00
Cup & Saucer, Jasperware, Light Blue & White, C.1862 .... 245.00
Cup & Saucer, Prince Charles, Lady Di, Marriage 22.00
Cup, 3 Handles, 2 Snakes, 1 Dragon, Signed, 2 In. 150.00
Cup, Light Green & White, 3 Handles, 5 In. 390.00
Cup, Melba, Fairyland Luster 500.00
Cup, Trophy, Light Green & White, 3 Handles, 5 In. 390.00
Cup, Yellow Luster, Stella Pattern, Louise Powell, C.1925, Marked 98.00
Dinner Set, Cornell University, Set Of 6 .... 285.00
Dish, Basalt, Basket Weave, C.1850, 4 In. 165.00
Dish, Creamware, Gold, Feather Edge, Oval, 1785, 7 1/4 X 5 3/8 In. 75.00
Dish, Vegetable, Covered, Santa Clara Pattern 38.00
Easter Egg, Jasperware 95.00
Ewer, Basalt, Basket Weave, 1850, 6 In. 145.00
Ewer, Basalt, Merman On Dolphin, Flaxman, 17 In. 700.00
Ewer, Gilded Basalt, C.1860, 15 In. 1650.00
Ewer, Gilded Basalt, Pedestal, Spout, Handle, 15 In. 1750.00
Fernery, Insert, Blue 125.00
Figurine, Bulldog, Black Basalt, Glass Eyes, 5 In. 350.00
Figurine, Cupid, Basalt, C.1840 .... 750.00
Figurine, Deer, Signed Skeaping, 7 In. 335.00
Figurine, Eros & Euphrosyne, Black Basalt, 16 1/2 In. 795.00
Figurine, Eros & Euphrosyne, Black Basalt, Marked, 16 In. 895.00
Figurine, Polar Bear, J.Skeaping, White, 7 1/4 In. 350.00
Figurine, Sphinx, Basalt 600.00
Flask, Purse, Octagon Shape, Marked, 4 In. 60.00
Flower Holder, Underplate, Dark Blue & White, Cameo, C.1850, 5 In. 190.00
Ginger Jar, Dragon Luster, Green 100.00
Gravy, Underplate, Devon Sprays 45.00
Incense Burner, Dolphin Feet, White & Light Blue 725.00
Jardiniere, Jasper Dip, C.1850, Blue, 8 1/2 In. 140.00

Jardiniere, Jasperware, Blue, C.1850, 8 1/2 In. ....155.00 To 175.00
Jug, Doric, Satyr Head, Brown, Swirl, 8 1/2 In. 200.00
Jug, Drabware, Classical Ladies On Panel, Marked, 8 In. 225.00
Paperweight, Black & White, Bicentennial, 13 Stars, Eagle 10.00
Pitcher, Bird & Fan, 6 In. 135.00
Pitcher, Deep Blue, 5 1/4 In. 88.00
Pitcher, Hunt Scene, Hound Handle, White, 5 In. 75.00
Pitcher, Jasperware, Grapes & Vines, Blue & White, 6 1/4 In. 125.00
Pitcher, Jasperware, Green, Marked, 4 1/2 In. 60.00
Pitcher, Jasperware, Hinged Metal Lid, 1875, 8 To 10 In., Set Of 3 .... 300.00
Pitcher, Jasperware, Milk, 6 1/2 In. 95.00
Pitcher, Jasperware, White, Green Design, Rope Handle, 6 In. 250.00
Pitcher, Tankard, Jasperware, Blue & White, Marked, 6 1/4 In. 145.00
Planter, Bulb, Hedgehog Form, Light Blue Glaze, 9 In. 450.00
Planter, Jasperware, Apollo & 4 Muses, 1850, Large 215.00
Planter, Jasperware, Mythical Design, Blue, 4 1/4 In. 69.00
Plaque, Blue, Green, & White, Framed, 2 1/2 In. 175.00
Plaque, Jasperware, Figures, Signed, 5 In. 155.00
Plaque, Lilac, Faun & Classical Maiden, 7 X 11 In. 400.00
Plaque, Portrait, Hamlet, Ophelia, Creamware, Dated 1879, 15 In., Pr. 1650.00
Plate, Annapolis 25.00
Plate, Battle Of Lake George, Blue 25.00
Plate, Bird & Fan, 9 In. 75.00
Plate, Boston Public Library, Blue 28.00
Plate, Brown University War Memorial 35.00
Plate, Christmas, 1984 .... 50.00
Plate, Cod Fishing, Clare Leighton, 10 1/2 In. 75.00
Plate, Communion, 14 In. 38.00
Plate, December, Flow Blue, Boy & Christmas Tree, 10 1/4 In. 125.00
Plate, December, Flow Blue, Girl & Christmas Tree 125.00
Plate, Dinner, Ashford Gray 18.00
Plate, Fairyland Luster, Blue & White Floral Border, 10 1/2 In. 1750.00
Plate, Fairyland Luster, Blue, Gold Outline, Marked, 10 3/4 In. 1695.00
Plate, Hanging, Friar Portrait, Austrian 22.00
Plate, Harvard College, 1941 .... 20.00
Plate, Historical, Boston Town House 40.00
Plate, Kings Chapel, Boston, Blue 28.00
Plate, Leaf, 8 In. 30.00
Plate, Longfellow Home, Portland 25.00
Plate, McKinley Home, Blue 32.00
Plate, Mt.Vernon, Blue 25.00
Plate, New York University, 1932 .... 25.00
Plate, Old Harvard Scene 25.00
Plate, Old North Church, Cabbage Rose Border 25.00
Plate, Oriental, 8 1/2 In. 65.00
Plate, Park Hotel & Baths, Mt.Clemens, Mich., Spirit Of 76 .... 45.00
Plate, Playing Cards, 10 In. 95.00
Plate, Portrait, President Kennedy, Light Blue & White, 4 3/8 In. 35.00
Plate, Protestant Dutch Church, Albany, 10 In. 40.00
Plate, Smith, 1932 .... 20.00
Plate, Trinity Church, Boston, Blue 27.00
Plate, University Of Pa., 1940 Bicentennial, 10 1/2 In. 18.00
Plate, Waltham Watch Factory, White Transfer, Blue, 1904, 5 1/4 In. 40.00
Plate, Wellesley, 10 1/2 In. 25.00
Plate, West Point, 1931 .... 20.00
Plate, West Point, 1933, Dark Blue, 10 1/2 In. 25.00
Plate, West Point, Dark Blue, 10 1/2 In. 20.00
Plate, Yale University, 12 Views, Set Of 12 .... 200.00
Platter, Cow, Blue & White 225.00
Platter, Pearlware, Blue Feather Edge, Rim Design, Oval, 20 3/4 In. 350.00
Platter, Seaweed & Shell, Majolica, 19 X 9 In. 200.00
Pot, Cupids, Lions & Ladies Scene, Impressed Mark, 8 1/2 In. 475.00
Salad Set, Silver, Majolica, Bowl 9 1/2 In., 3 Piece 375.00
Salt, Fairyland Luster, Blue & Orange Ground, Marked 135.00

Sauce, Underplate, Covered, Creamware, Glazed Handles, 7 In.	250.00
Spill, Black Jasperware, C.1895, Gilded, 4 In.	350.00
Sugar & Creamer, Creamware	90.00
Sugar & Creamer, Devon Sprays	42.00
Sugar, Covered, Butterfly Luster	160.00
Sugar, Covered, Jasperware	65.00
Sugar, Etruria, Creamware, Blue Flowers, Marked, 3 1/8 In.	48.00
Syrup, Dark Blue & White, C.1865, 8 In.	290.00
Tankard, Crimson, Jasper, 8 In.	475.00
Tea Caddy, Light Green & White, 7 In.	375.00
Tea Set, Jasperware, Black, Armorial, Montreal Coat Of Arms, 3 Pc.	275.00
Tea Set, Pink, Red, Blue Floral On White, Urn Mark, Gold, 11 Pc.	165.00
Tea Set, Queensware, C.1865, Lessore Studio Signature, 7 Piece	350.00
Teapot, Basalt, Silver Mounted, 1850	130.00 To 150.00
Teapot, Caneware, Foliage, Dog Knob, 1825	265.00 To 300.00
Teapot, Celadon, Classical Figures	75.00
Teapot, Jasperware, Classical Figures, Cupid In White, Blue	165.00
Teapot, Jasperware, Date Lettered 1862, Blue & White, 3 5/8 In.	450.00
Teapot, Jasperware, Sage, Light Green, Buff	125.00
Teapot, Jasperware, Wicker Covered Handle, Marked, 7 1/2 In.	650.00
Teapot, Queensware, Embossed Leaves & Fruit, Blue	40.00
Teapot, Queensware, Painted Bamboo, 1860	135.00
Teapot, Redware, Long Spout, Handle, Early 19th Century, 7 In.	290.00
Teapot, Sugar, & Creamer, White Classical Figures, Green	245.00
Tile, Calendar, 1897, Federal St.Theater	65.00
Tile, Calendar, 1898, Kings Chapel	60.00
Tile, Calendar, 1902	65.00
Tile, Calendar, 1906	65.00
Tile, Calendar, 1910	58.00
Tile, Calendar, 1916	58.00
Tile, Calendar, September, Blue, Flower Border, 8 In.	150.00
Tile, June, Wood Frame	98.00
Toothpick, 1898–1908, Dark Blue	175.00
Tray, 3 Groups Of People, Dark Blue, Signed, 6 In.	60.00
Tray, Ferrara Transfer, Mulberry, 12 1/2 In.	30.00
Trinket Set, Tray, 3 Boxes, Candlestick, Blue, White, Cherubs, 6 Pc.	220.00
Tumbler, Creamware, Hunting Scene, Silver Luster Sky, Set Of 8	150.00
Tumbler, John Peel, Silver Resist, White Polychrome	45.00
Tureen, Covered, Grindley, Blue On White, 11 In.	57.50
Tureen, Queensware, Attached Saucer, Ram's Head Handles, 7 1/4 In.	100.00
Urn, Basalt, Covered, Gilded, C.1860, 11 In.	1700.00
Urn, Basalt, Molded Cap, Double Loop Handles, 5 1/2 In., Pair	650.00
Urn, Basalt, Satyr Mask Handles, C.1800, 7 In.	115.00 To 125.00
Urn, Basalt, Warrior, 1850, 10 In.	235.00 To 250.00
Urn, Basalt, Warriors, Horses, Covered, 1850, 10 In.	300.00
Urn, Classical Maidens, 1825, Dark Blue & White, 12 In.	275.00
Urn, Covered, Jasperware, Scroll Handles, 3 Color, 8 1/2 In.	1200.00
Urn, Dark Blue & White, 2 Handles, 10 1/4 In.	375.00
Vase, 3 Section, Swan Handles, 1785, Blue & White, 10 In.	400.00
Vase, Basalt, Black, Cameo, Draped, Handles, 13 In.	160.00
Vase, Basalt, Offering To Peace, Flower, Wide Mouth, 8 In.	275.00
Vase, Basalt, Wide Mouth, Offering To Peace, 1850, 8 In.	205.00
Vase, Candlemas, 8 In.	1000.00
Vase, Cobalt, Butterflies, Gold Tracing, Flared Top, 12 In.	400.00
Vase, Covered, Pink Roses, Gold Handles, Marked, C.1900, 9 5/8 In.	398.00
Vase, Dragon Luster, Blue & Gold Iridescent, 12 In.	550.00
Vase, Dragon Luster, Blue, Design, 8 1/2 In.	350.00
Vase, Dragon Luster, Blue, Gold Designs, Marked, 9 3/4 In.	425.00
Vase, Fairyland Luster, Candlemas, 9 In.	1750.00
Vase, Fairyland Luster, Candlemas, Marked, 8 3/8 In.	1195.00
Vase, Hummingbird Luster, Blue, Gold Outlined, Marked, 5 1/8 In.	195.00
Vase, Hummingbird Luster, Trumpet, Blue, Gold, Marked, 11 3/4 In.	450.00
Vase, Jasperware, Blue, White, Medallions, Acorn Lid, 1891, 10 In.	295.00
Vase, Jasperware, Covered, Blue, White, Laurel Knop, Marked, 19 In.	1045.00

Vase, Jasperware, Gold, Black Grapes, Vines, Marked, 5 1/2 In. 295.00
Vase, Jasperware, Green, Muse Of Music & Drama, Marked, 3 3/4 In. 100.00
Vase, Jasperware, Light Blue & White, Mark CDT, 11 5/8 In. 498.00
Vase, Jasperware, Mythological Figures, Marked, Blue, 7 1/8 In. 350.00
Vase, Medallion Cupid, Horn, Light Green, Mark, 2 1/2 X 5 In. 25.00
Vase, Portland, Black Basalt Ground, Loop Handles, 10 1/4 In. 750.00
Vase, Portland, Blue Standard, White & Light Blue 1600.00
Vase, Portland, Jasperware, C.1840, 10 1/2 In. 2650.00
Vase, Portland, Light Blue & White, 3 In. 165.00
Vase, Portland, Light Blue, 7 In. 375.00
Vase, Spill, Blue, Floral, Muse Of Poetry & Drama, Marked, 4 In. 110.00
Vase, Spill, Cherubs Playing Instruments, Signed, 3 In. 60.00
Vase, Terra–Cotta, Enameled Flowers, Handle, Marked, Red, 2 In. 175.00
Vase, White Figures, Green, 4 In. 30.00
Vase, White, Leaves, Gold Trim, 2 Handles, 1880s 295.00

LOUWELSA WELLER *Weller pottery was first made in 1873 in Fultonham, Ohio. The firm moved to Zanesville, Ohio, in 1882. Art wares were first made in 1893. Hundreds of lines of pottery were made, including Louwelsa, Eocean, Dickens, and Sicardo, before the pottery closed in 1948.*

WELLER, Basket, Copra, 11 1/2 In. 195.00
Basket, Hanging, Woodcraft, Fox 185.00
Basket, Klyro, Square Handle, Brown, 7 In. 80.00
Basket, Pearl, 6 In. 90.00
Basket, Woodcraft, Acorn, 9 1/2 In. 125.00
Bowl, Atlas, Blue, 4 In. 32.00
Bowl, Bonito, 5 In. 55.00
Bowl, Bulb, Ardsley, Handles Form Cathedral Dome, 5 In. 50.00
Bowl, Claywood, Stylized Floral, Brown Interior, Small 25.00
Bowl, Console, Roma, 16 X 4 1/2 In. 85.00
Bowl, Coppertone, Figural Frog Sits On End, Fish In Relief, 10 In. 120.00
Bowl, Copra, Florals Inside & Out, Molded Handles, 9 1/2 X 3 In. 100.00
Bowl, Flemish Woodcraft, Cherries, Brown & Green Ground, 7 In. 45.00
Bowl, Flower, Green Matte, 8 1/2 In. 55.00
Bowl, Hobart, Lavender Interior, Pale Green, 9 1/2 X 3 In. 20.00
Bowl, Patra, 4 1/2 In. 40.00
Bowl, Pumila, Low, Green & Brown, 8 1/2 In. 17.50
Bowl, Turada, Turquoise & White Design, Signed M, 8 1/4 In. 110.00
Bowl, Woodcraft, Network Of Branches On Sides, Marked, 3 1/2 In. 75.00
Bowl, Woodrose, 6 1/2 In. 30.00
Box, Art Nouveau, Star Shape, Covered 60.00
Candleholder, Ardsley, 3 In., Pair 50.00
Candleholder, Lido, Blue, Double 10.00
Candlestick, Ardsley, Handles, Pair 45.00
Candlestick, Barcelona, Pair ....70.00 To 75.00
Candlestick, Figural, Black Cat, Pink Roses, High Glaze, 8 1/8 In. 125.00
Candlestick, Paragon, Gold, Pair 40.00
Clock, Fan Shape Top, Louwelsa, 7 In. 390.00
Console Set, Roma, 4 1/2 X 16 In. 85.00
Console, Silvertone, With Frog, 12 In. 100.00
Creamer, Mammy, 3 1/2 In. 40.00
Dish, Nut, Woodcraft, Squirrel 75.00
Ewer, Louwelsa, Florals, 7 In. 135.00
Feeding Dish, Zona, Duck 35.00
Feeding Set, Zona, Box, 4 Piece 200.00
Figurine, Elephant, Cactus, Green, 4 In. 65.00
Figurine, Kneeling Woman, Muskota, 6 In. 280.00
Figurine, Swan, Brighton, 4 1/2 In. 70.00
Figurine, Woodpecker, Brighton, 6 In. ....65.00 To 98.00
Flower Frog, Figural, Crab, Muskota, 8 Hole ....40.00 To 55.00
Flower Frog, Glendale 25.00
Jar, Louwelsa, Covered, 9 1/2 In. 125.00
Jardiniere, Dickens Ware, 3 Footed, Marked, 6 X 9 In. 100.00
Jardiniere, Eocean, Pink, White Mushrooms, Handles, Marked, 6 1/2 In. 150.00

Jardiniere, Etna, Rose Design, 8 1/4 X 10 1/2 In. 85.00
Jardiniere, Forest, 11 X 9 In. 150.00
Jardiniere, Forest, Pedestal, 12 1/2 X 11 In. 650.00
Jardiniere, Knifewood, Swan Design, Ivory, 5 1/2 In. 35.00
Jardiniere, Louwelsa, Floral, 10 X 8 In. 110.00
Jardiniere, Louwelsa, Slip Painted Iris, Brown Glaze, 8 1/2 In. 185.00
Jardiniere, Woodrose, 3 1/2 In. 28.50
Jug, Floretta, Brown To Gold, Handle, Double Circle Seal, 5 1/2 In. 225.00
Lamp Base, Aurelian, Floral Panel, Signed Mitchell, 1910, 14 In. 250.00
Lamp, Dickens Ware, Pansy Design, Marked 500.00
Lamp, Lamar, 13 In. 125.00
Lamp, Orris, 10 In. 75.00
Letter Holder, Dickens Ware, Clover, Signed 82.00
Match Holder, Louwelsa, Blue, Raspberry Design 96.00
Mug, Art Nouveau, Embossed, Jeweled 285.00
Mug, Claywood ....25.00 To 75.00
Mug, Creamware, Indian Brave 55.00
Mug, Etna, Thistle 75.00
Mug, Floretta, Grapes, 5 1/2 In. ....110.00 To 115.00
Mug, Louwelsa, Stem With Leaves & Cherries, 6 In. 140.00
Mug, Turada 125.00
Pitcher, Aurelian, Brown, Grape Design, Cylindrical, C.1910, 12 In. 125.00
Pitcher, Velvetone, Pink & Gold, 12 In. 58.00
Pitcher, Zona, Apples & Branch, Cream Ground, Stamp, 5 3/4 In. 70.00
Pitcher, Zona, Blue, 7 In. 85.00
Pitcher, Zona, Dancing Ducks, 3 1/2 In. 55.00
Pitcher, Zona, Strutting Duck, 8 In. 95.00
Planter, Fairfield, Bacchanalian Scene, Marked, Square, 6 In. 75.00
Planter, Ivory, Round, 7 In. 135.00
Planter, Malvern, Maroon, Green, 10 X 4 In. 45.00
Planter, Woodrose, Tub Shape, Open Tab Handles, 1 7/8 X 2 3/4 In. 50.00
Plate, Burntwood, Fish Design, Marked, 11 In. 45.00
Plate, Silvertone, 7 In. 75.00
Plate, With Flower Frog, Glendale, Gull, Cream, Brown, Blue, 15 In. 300.00
Pot, Forest, Ink Stamp, 4 1/2 In. 70.00
Sign, Dealer 325.00
Syrup, Mammy, 6 In. 300.00
Tankard, Dickens Ware, Caramel Glaze, Monk, Artist MG, 14 In. 675.00
Tankard, Dickens Ware, Majolica Top & Bottom, Cherry Art, 12 In. 450.00
Tankard, Dickens Ware, Serpents, Marked, 11 1/2 In. 550.00
Teapot, Blue, Gold Trim, 7 1/2 In. ....40.00 To 45.00
Teapot, Mammy ....395.00 To 450.00
Teapot, Pink, 6 In. 25.00
Teapot, Pumpkin, 6 In. 60.00
Teapot, Tearose, Rabbit Lid 85.00
Tobacco Jar, 2nd Dickens, Admiral, Turk, Irishman, & Chinaman, Set 2200.00
Tobacco Jar, Dickens Ware, Monk 125.00
Vase, Atlantic, Deco Top, Leafy Design On Side Panels, 10 In. 25.00
Vase, Atlas, Blue, 6 3/4 In. 40.00
Vase, Baldin, Autumn Colors, 9 3/4 In. 135.00
Vase, Baldin, Blue, 6 In. 55.00
Vase, Bedford Matte, Green, 10 In. 20.00
Vase, Bonito, Blue Daisies, 6 In. 40.00
Vase, Bud, Alvin, Tree Stump, 5 Openings, Yellow, 8 3/4 In. 30.00
Vase, Bud, Baldin, Matte Green, Red Apples, Handles, 7 In. 95.00
Vase, Bud, Lavonia 25.00
Vase, Chase, Crazing On White, Footed, 10 In. 155.00
Vase, Chengtu, 7 1/2 In. 35.00
Vase, Claywood, Tan, 8 1/2 In. 45.00
Vase, Cloudburst, Blue, Gold, Iridescent Glaze, Lassell, 12 1/2 In. 475.00
Vase, Coppertone, 6 1/2 In. 25.00
Vase, Coppertone, Artist Signed, 12 1/2 In. 125.00
Vase, Coppertone, Flower Frog With Lily Pad, 4 1/2 In. 125.00
Vase, Creamware, Cherubs In Relief, Claw Foot, 13 In. 110.00

Vase, Delsa, Yellow Flowers, White Ground, 13 In. ....52.00 To 55.00
Vase, Dickens Ware, Etched Cavalier Head, Burgess 1901, 10 1/2 In. 400.00
Vase, Dickens Ware, Portrait Of Profiled Monk, Marked, Ovoid, 14 In. 475.00
Vase, Eocean Rose, Lavender To Pink Ground, H.Pillsbury, 11 In. 295.00
Vase, Eocean, Bulbous Base, Pink Flowers, 5 In., Pair 125.00
Vase, Etna, Pansy, Bulbous, 6 In. 75.00
Vase, Etna, Pope & Rosary, 10 1/4 In. 315.00
Vase, Fan, Ardsley, 8 In. 32.00
Vase, Fleron, 8 1/2 In. 50.00
Vase, Fleron, 14 1/2 In. 48.00
Vase, Florals, Soft Corals & Greens, Signed, 18 In. 800.00
Vase, Floretta, Gray, Grapes, 7 1/2 In. 79.00
Vase, Forest, 8 1/2 In. ....42.00 To 90.00
Vase, Frosted Matte, 6 In. 65.00
Vase, Glendale, 2 Parrots On Branch, 8 1/2 In. 200.00
Vase, Glendale, 4 In. ....100.00 To 110.00
Vase, Glendale, 8 3/4 In. 295.00
Vase, Glendale, Bird Looking Over Eggs In Nest, Artist H, 6 1/2 In. 200.00
Vase, Glendale, Lovebirds On Branch, Stamp & Initial, 9 In., Pair 300.00
Vase, Hudson, Artist Signed, Floral, Bulbous, 3 1/2 In. 80.00
Vase, Hudson, Berries, Signed McLaughlin, 13 1/2 In. 275.00
Vase, Hudson, Cherry Blossom, Blue, 9 1/2 In. 150.00
Vase, Hudson, Clover & Leaves At Shoulder, Blue, 6 3/4 X 2 3/4 In. 175.00
Vase, Hudson, Floral, Signed Hester Pillsbury, 11 1/2 In. 275.00
Vase, Hudson, Gray Blue With Yellow & Green Flower, Signed DL, 6 In. 145.00
Vase, Hudson, Iris, Hester Pillsbury, 15 In. 450.00
Vase, Hudson, Perfecto, Florals In Corals & Greens, Signed, 18 In. 800.00
Vase, Hudson, Perfecto, Hand Painted, Signed, 6 In. 140.00
Vase, Hudson, Sailing Ship Scene, Gray To Pink, McLaughlin, 8 1/2 In. 1350.00
Vase, Knifewood, Daisies, Butterfly, 7 1/2 In. 75.00
Vase, Lasa, 8 3/4 In. 350.00
Vase, Lasa, Palm Tree, Gold, Red, & Silver, Signed, 5 In. 175.00
Vase, Louwelsa, Blue, Raspberry Design, 11 In. 860.00
Vase, Louwelsa, Cylindrical Shape, White Flowers, Blue, 6 3/4 In. 275.00
Vase, Louwelsa, Green To Brown, Yellow Floral, Handles, Incised, 7 In. 200.00
Vase, Louwelsa, Pillow, Floral Design, 5 1/2 In. 125.00
Vase, Louwelsa, Portrait, 12 In. 375.00
Vase, Lowelsa, Pansy, Blue, 5 In. 275.00
Vase, Malvern, 7 In. 55.00
Vase, Marbelized, Black, Gray, White, Marked, 6 1/2 In. 65.00
Vase, Marvo, Green, 7 In. 27.00
Vase, Paragon, Maroon, 7 1/2 In. 60.00
Vase, Parian, 12 In. 30.00
Vase, Pearl, 7 3/4 In. 85.00
Vase, Sicard, 15 In. 925.00
Vase, Sicard, Berries, Leaves, Blue & Green, Signed, 8 In. 390.00
Vase, Sicard, Maple Leaf Design, Triangular Shape, Signed, 7 1/2 In. 425.00
Vase, Sicard, Thistle Pattern, Marked, 7 In. 435.00
Vase, Silvertone, Calla Lilies, 11 1/2 X 6 1/2 In. 120.00
Vase, Silvertone, Flared Top, Calla Lilies, Cylindrical, 15 In. 275.00
Vase, Silvertone, Tulips, 9 1/2 In. 125.00
Vase, Silvertone, Twisted Handles, 11 3/4 In. 185.00
Vase, Turada, Pillow, 4 Feet, 6 X 6 In. 90.00
Vase, Turkis, Handle, 4 In. 15.00
Vase, Tutone, Tricorner Shape, Black, 8 In. 26.00
Vase, Voile, Green, 6 In. 22.00
Vase, Voile, Yellow & Brown, 9 In. 50.00
Vase, Wildrose, Pastel, 13 1/2 In. 65.00
Vase, Woodcraft, 4 Branches, Plums, Marked, 10 In. 68.00
Vase, Woodcraft, Embossed Tree Branches, Flowers, 10 In. 57.00
Vase, Woodcraft, Tree Trunk, Owl, & Squirrel, 18 In. 275.00
Wall Pocket, Apple Blossom 55.00
Wall Pocket, Blackberry 312.00
Wall Pocket, Blue Drapery ....30.00 To 48.00

Wall Pocket, Fairfield	50.00
Wall Pocket, Gardenia	65.00
Wall Pocket, Marvo, Green	24.00
Wall Pocket, Roma, 10 In.	40.00
Wall Pocket, Souevo, 9 In.	55.00
Wall Pocket, Squirrel	90.00
Wall Pocket, Teapot Shape, Script Mark, Turquoise, 9 In.	75.00
Wall Pocket, Tree Trunk, Petaled Flowers, Block Letters, 5 3/4 In.	58.00
Wall Pocket, Warwick, 11 1/2 In.	50.00
Wall Pocket, Woodcraft, Owl In Den, Marked, 10 1/2 In.	95.00
Wall Pocket, Woodrose, Pink, 7 In.	30.00
Window Box, Roma, Large	85.00

Thomas J. Wheatley worked with the founders of the art pottery movement in Cincinnati, Ohio, including M. Louise McLaughlin of the Rookwood Pottery. In 1880, he established his own pottery. Wheatley Pottery was purchased by the Cambridge Tile Manufacturing Company in 1927.

WHEATLEY, Vase, Applied Red & White Flowers, Leaves, 1880, Signed, 18 In.	130.00
Vase, Chrysanthemums, Mottled Ground, C.1880, Signed, 12 In.	170.00
Vase, Leaf & Bud Molded Design, Signed, Numbered, Green, 6 3/4 In.	425.00
Vase, Matte Green, Berries & Leaves In Relief, 11 1/2 X 4 In.	525.00
Vase, Matte Green, Berries & Leaves In Relief, 13 3/4 In.	412.00

Whieldon was a potter in England who worked alone and with Josiah Wedgwood in eighteenth-century England. Whieldon made many pieces in natural shapes, like cauliflowers or cabbages. The tortoiseshell glazed pieces are known as "clouded ware."

WHIELDON, Plate, Feathered Rim, Brown Sponging, Green, Amber Spots, 9 1/4 In.	175.00
Teapot, Green Glaze, Cauliflower, C.1760	1050.00

Willets Manufacturing Company of Trenton, New Jersey, worked from 1879. The company made belleek in the late 1880s and 1890s in shapes similar to those used by the Irish Belleek factory. They stopped working about 1912. Pieces were marked with a variety of marks, all including the name Willets.

WILLETS, Bowl, Hand Painted, 6 1/4 In.	175.00
Chocolate Pot, Dragon Handle, Gold Paste Floral, Cream Ground	395.00
Cup & Saucer, Heart Shape, Gold Lizard Handle	75.00
Hatpin Holder, Pink & Yellow Roses, Shaded Green	110.00
Mug, D'Arcy, Blackberry, Pair	65.00
Mug, Friendship, 3 Handles, Florals, Blue Dots, Cream Ground	325.00
Mug, Hand Painted Berries & Leaves, Coral To Cream, 4 1/2 In.	85.00
Plate, Gold Paste Spray, Scalloped Rim, Gold Brushed, 5 1/2 In.	45.00
Plate, Roses Allover, Gold Trim, 8 In.	95.00
Sugar & Creamer, Dragon Handles, Mask Spout, Floral, Pink Mark	150.00
Sugar & Creamer, Paste Gold Swags & Baskets, Pink, Pedestal	150.00
Tankard, Dragon Handle, Portrait Of Houghton's Dog, Signed, 16 In.	695.00
Tankard, Grapes, Hand Painted, Marked, 7 In.	55.00
Vase, Floral, Signed Houghton, 14 In.	425.00
Vase, Hand Painted Roses, Gold Scalloped Lip, Signed, 16 In.	195.00
Vase, Hornberg Portrait, Signed, 11 In.	60.00
Vase, Magenta Roses, Gold Rim, Shaded Green Ground, 8 1/4 In.	100.00
Vase, Portrait Of Woman, Gold Paste Work, Florals, Cream, 12 In.	795.00
Vase, Portrait, Lion, Pale Chocolate Ground, Tall	395.00
WILLOW, see Blue Willow	

Stained glass and beveled glass windows were popular additions to houses during the late nineteenth and early twentieth centuries. The old windows became popular with collectors in the 1970s; today, old and new examples are seen.

WINDOW, Leaded Glass, American Ship, Framed, 32 X 26 In.	250.00
Leaded Glass, Ruby, Cafe In White, 1900, 4 Ft. 4 In.	600.00
Leaded, Louis IV, Thorn Crown, Blue & Brown, 4 Ft.X 23 3/4 In.	880.00

Wood Carving, Religious Figure,
Blue Paint, 18 In.

Wood Carving, Lion, Lying Down, 23 X 9 1/2 In.

Stained Glass, Boy Leaning Over Balcony, 85 X 73 In.	*Color*	8000.00
Stained Glass, Central Torch, Victorian, American, 44 X 32 In.		200.00
Stained Glass, Fish Scale Design, Victorian, Amber, 59 X 15 In.		300.00
Stained Glass, Flea Circus In Ruby, Border, 1900, 5 Ft.		625.00
Stained Glass, Floral Design, 24 X 44 In.		350.00
Stained Glass, Floral Landscape, Tiffany, 50 X 36 In.		17000.00
Stained Glass, Lady & Grapes, 2 Layered, 52 X 96 In.	*Color*	7500.00
Stained Glass, Victorian, Gothic Top, American, 71 X 25 In.		275.00
Victorian, Beveled, Curved Pieces, 100 Piece, 7 X 2 Ft.		900.00

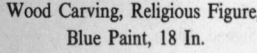 *Wood carvings and wooden pieces are listed separately in this book.*
There are also wooden pieces found in other sections, such as Kitchen.

WOOD CARVING, 19 Horses, Bamboo Root, Chinese, 19th Century	1500.00
American Officer, Sword, Gesso Wig, Painted, 14 3/4 In.	850.00
Angel & Trumpet, From Hearse, Pair	3500.00
Angels, Holding Candle, Gilt, Plinth Supported, 15 In., Pair	375.00
Bat, Fruitwood, Flared Wing, Japan, 3 In.	80.00
Bird, Long Neck, Stand, Polychrome, 28 1/2 In.	275.00
Blackamoor, Stand, Skin Breeches, Masks Base, 45 In., Pair	8800.00
Bottle, Wooden Stopper	30.00
Bust, Tribal Woman, Mahogany, Africa	75.00
Child, Seated, Long Robe, Ball In Hand, Polychrome, 15 1/2 In.	140.00
Cicada, Fruitwood, Japan, Signed, 3 1/8 In.	150.00
Crab On Shallow Lily Pad, Fruitwood, Japan, 7 In.	150.00
Dog Beside Hollow Tree Trunk, 10 In.	45.00
Door, Hearse, Black, Drapery, Columns, 53 X 23 In., Pair	250.00
Eagle On Basket, American, Burl Maple, 16 X 10 In.	3250.00
Eagle On Branch, Gessoed & Gilded, 24 In.	375.00
Eagle, Dark Finish, Glass Eyes, Primitive, 25 1/2 In.	150.00
Eagle, From Baltimore, Original Gold Gilt, Dated 1830	2250.00
Eagle, Round, 3 1/2 In.	180.00
Eagle, Spread, Oak, Carved Pedestal, 3 Paw Feet, 68 In.	1200.00
Eagle, Walnut, Standing, Leafy Mount, American, 16 X 10 In.	110.00
Eagle, Wings Spread, Black, Gold Paint, Base, 16 1/2 X 12 In.	400.00
Elephant Scene, Wautengi, C.1930, 8 X 20 In.	125.00
Figurine, Mamasan–Papasan, Japan, 19th Century, 10 In., Pair	125.00
Fish, 19 In.	40.00
Foo Dog, Teakwood, 19th Century, 17 In.	160.00
Labradorite Condor, Germany, C.Wild, 14K Gold Feet, 3 1/4 In.	225.00
Lion, Front Feet Raised, Resemble Stones, Natural, 8 3/4 In.	200.00
Lion, Lying Down, 23 X 9 1/2 In. ....*Illus*	200.00
Lotus Blossom, Seed Pod, Fruitwood, Japan, 19th Century, 17 In.	300.00

Model, Great Lakes Tanker, 7 In. 110.00
Monkey, Ebony, Africa 75.00
Moose, Wheels, Painted 742.50
Nude Stretching, S.Moselsio, Fruitwood, Base, 12 1/4 In. 350.00
Oni, Priest Carrying Umbrella, Japanese, 23 In. 385.00
Ornament, Phoenix, Gilded, 26 In. 32.50
Panel, Owl, Birds & Squirrel, In Round, Framed, 26 X 14 In. 250.00
Plaque, Crucifixion, 17th Century, 9 X 6 1/2 In. 1200.00
Rabbit, Fruitwood, Stone Eyes, Artist Signed, 1 1/2 In., Pair 600.00
Religious Figure, Blue Paint, 18 In. ....*Illus* 95.00
Shoes, Pair 32.00
Town Crier, German, 7 1/2 In. 18.00
Trout, Brown Spotted, Mounted On Driftwood 60.00
Winter Mill Scene, Florence Lake, Framed, 7 1/2 X 12 1/2 In. 20.00
Woman, Holding Rose, Stylized, 10 In. 30.00
Woman, Primitive, Old Patina, 5 3/4 In. 45.00

*Wood was used for many containers and tools used in the early home.
Small wooden pieces are called "treenware" in England, but the term
"woodenware" is more common in the United States.*

WOODEN, see also Kitchen; Store; Tool
WOODEN, Abacus, Oak, Turned Handle, 1920 .... 28.00
Ashtray, Jiggs Standing 225.00
Bed Smoother, Oak, Geometric Chipped Carving, Scandinavian, 28 In. 200.00
Bin, Grain, Pine, Large 650.00
Bin, Rice, Oriental, Figures & Animals, Gold Trim, Octagonal, C.1850 .... 785.00
Bookends, Squatting Man Smoking Pipe, Dog At Side, Teakwood 50.00
Bootjack, Pine 14.00
Bowl, American, Incised Lines On Base, Burl, 14 In. 550.00
Bowl, American, Turned Burl, Late 18th Century, 21 X 6 1/2 In. 700.00
Bowl, Ash, Burl Figure Throughout, Waxed Finish, 6 1/2 X 18 In. 350.00
Bowl, Bird's Eye, Ovoid, 24 X 14 In. 325.00
Bowl, Burled Walnut, Rimmed, 22 In. Diam. ....*Illus* 1000.00
Bowl, Butter, 14 1/2 In. 32.50
Bowl, Canted Sides, American, Burl, 18th Century, 16 X 11 In. 140.00
Bowl, Chopping, 19 X 3 1/2 In. 100.00
Bowl, Dough, 10 In. 28.00
Bowl, Dough, 1850, 29 X 18 X 8 In. 195.00
Bowl, Dough, 24 X 14 In. 75.00
Bowl, Marked Munising, 21 X 11 X 3 1/2 In. 78.00
Bowl, Oblong, 11 X 19 1/4 X 4 1/2 In. 65.00
Bowl, Original Pumpkin Paint, Large 275.00

Wooden, Bowl, Burled Walnut, Rimmed, 22 In. Diam.

Bowl, Rim End Handles, Carved Foot, Oval, Burl, 16 1/2 X 5 1/2 In. 975.00
Bowl, Rose Nail Design At Handles, Initials, 1802, 15 X 30 X 4 In. 225.00
Bowl, Scrubbed Finish, Ash Burl, 11 1/2 X 4 1/2 In. 225.00
Bowl, With Wooden Butter Scoop, 9 1/2 In. 60.00
Box, Apple Shape, Original Red & Yellow Paint, 4 1/4 In. 40.00
Box, Candle, Pine, 1 Drawer, Red Paint, 1780–1800, 14 In. 330.00
Brazier, Carved Teakwood, Etched Brass, 6 Legs, Chinese, 27 X 25 In. 650.00
Bread Board, Carved Waste Not, Round 75.00
Bucket, Hickory Bands, Bentwood Handle, Wooden Pinned, 14 X 9 In. 195.00
Bucket, Lid, Stave, Handle, Painted, E.Murdock Co., Mass.Label, 4 In. 35.00
Bucket, Lid, Wire Bale, Alligatored White Paint, 14 1/4 X 7 In. 125.00
Bucket, Stave, Metal Bands, Handle, Wire Bale, Red Paint, 4 1/2 In. 35.00
Bucket, Stove, Fitted Lid, Metal Bands, Wire Bale, Painted, 9 X 12 In. 155.00
Bucket, Sugar, 11 X 12 In. 95.00
Bucket, Sugar, Lid, Swivel Handle, Dark Paint, 9 1/2 X 7 3/4 In. 105.00
Bucket, Sugar, Original Mustard Paint 45.00
Bucket, Sugar, Stave, Lid Branded S.Hingham, Mass, 14 X 14 1/2 In. 75.00
Bucket, Sugar, Staves, Yellow Brown Graining, 9 3/4 In. 125.00
Bucket, Sugar, Vermont 85.00
Bucket, Swing Handle, Original Green Paint, Early 19th Century 360.00
Candle Safe, Match Drawer 36.00
Canister Set, Stacking, Dovetailed, Cover, 1900, 4 Piece 45.00
Canister, Covered, Sugar, Oak, Staved, Dark Green Paint, No.3, 8 In. 85.00
Carrier, Silverware, Oak, Early 1900s 20.00
Case, Silverware, Tiffany Label, Bird's–Eye Maple 100.00
Chest, Wells Fargo Express, Original Lock & Paint 1200.00
Clothes Dryer, Folding, Hanging, Tiger Maple, 7 Bars, Top Shelf 140.00
Clothespin, Handmade 5.00
Clothespin, Turned Wood, Dark Patina, 5 In. 9.00
Egg, Red, Blue, German, Set Of 10 .... 16.00
Flagon, Finial, Stave, Lid, Scroll Handle, Norway, 1768, 10 1/2 In. 150.00
Gavel, Inlaid, 2–Color Wood, Oval, 13 In. 15.00
Glove Stretcher ....5.00 To 7.50
Hat Block, Size 6 1/2 .... 20.00
Hat Rack, Folding, Walnut, Porcelain & Brass Tips 40.00
Herb Dryer, 7 Adjustable Metal Arms, Collapsible Feet 30.00
Holder, Rolling Pin, Holds 6 .... 49.00
Jar, Cover, Floral & Strawberry Design, Salmon Ground, 4 7/8 In. 450.00
Jar, Cover, Pease, 4 1/2 In. 105.00
Jar, Cover, Turned, Varnish Finish, Pease, 5 3/4 X 5 3/4 In. 130.00
Jar, Red Brown Sponge Graining, Yellow Ground, Treen, 6 3/4 In. 450.00
Jar, Treen, Turned Finial Lid, Worn Red Finish, 3 3/4 In. 70.00
Jar, Worn Varnish Finish, Pease, 3 1/2 In. 85.00
Key, Rope Bed, Hand Hewn 40.00
Knife Urn, Japanese Inlaid Lacquerware, S.Gardiner, Derby, 1767 .... 4500.00
Mold, Candle, 12 Redware Tubes, A.Wilcox, 18 X 5 1/4 X 14 1/4 In. 650.00
Mold, Candy, Bird, Nest & Dog, 2–Part, 3 1/4 X 11 3/4 In. 40.00
Mold, Cigar, Miller, Dubrul, & Peters 32.00
Mold, Cookie, Turkey, 10 X 6 In. 26.00
Mold, Maple Sugar, Initials W.H., Birch, C.1810, 1 1/2 X 4 X 8 In. 190.00
Mold, Violin Case Form, Primitive, 7 3/4 X 27 1/2 In. 15.00
Mortar & Pestle, 5 In. 65.00
Mortar & Pestle, Barrel Shape, Walnut, 19th Century, 7 X 5 3/4 In. 75.00
Mortar & Pestle, Burl, Late 18th Century, Small 100.00
Mortar & Pestle, Burlwood 140.00
Mortar & Pestle, Hardwood, 6 X 8 In. 75.00
Mortar, Burl, 6 1/4 In. 25.00
Muddler, Maple, Hand Hewn, Mushroom End, Tapered Handle, 11 In. 30.00
Noggin, Maple, 1 Piece, 7 In. 220.00
Paddle, Apple Butter, Pierced Paddle Right Angle To Handle, 43 In. 55.00
Paddle, Butter, Birch, Old Finish, 9 In. 30.00
Rack, Drying, 36 X 17 X 5 In. 45.00
Rack, Drying, Adjustable, Square To Diamond Shape, 18 1/2 In. 55.00
Sander, Pounce, For Desk, Maple, Flared Top, Incised Bands 50.00

Scoop, Burl 65.00
Sock Stretcher, 22 X 11 1/2 In., Pair 17.00
Sock Stretcher, Child's, Bird, 21 In. 29.00
Spoon, Carved, 5 1/2 In. 30.00
Spoon, Cherry, Carved Handle, Round Bowl, 18th Century 85.00
Spoon, Tasting, Fanned Coffin End Handle, C.1800, 4 1/4 In. 250.00
Spoon, Tiger Maple, 12 In. 30.00
Tankard, Pewter Trim, Ball Feet, & Lid, Norwegian, 9 1/4 In. 900.00
Tankard, Staves, Lid, Footed, Wrapped Hoops, Treen, 7 In. 350.00
Tray, Herb Cutting, Beechwood, Blade, 2 Handles, 5 3/4 X 8 1/2 In. 100.00
Tray, Knife, Pine, 2 Sections, Arched Center Handle, 4 1/2 X 9 In. 95.00
Tray, Sorting, Pine, Dovetailed, Brown Patina, 21 3/4 In. 65.00
Trencher, Birch, 1 Piece Oval, C.1800, 13 1/2 X 23 1/2 In. 140.00
Trough, Hollowed Out Of 1 Log, Drain Hole, Plug, 45 1/2 X 26 1/2 In. 200.00
Yoke, Ox, Double 127.50

Worcester porcelains were made in Worcester, England, from 1751. The firm went through many name changes and eventually, in 1862, became The Royal Worcester Porcelain Company Ltd. Collectors often refer to Dr. Wall, Barr, Flight, and other names that indicate time periods and artists at the factory. It became part of Royal Worcester Spode Ltd. in 1976.

WORCESTER, see also Royal Worcester

WORCESTER, Basket, Reticulated, Oval, Twig Handles, 6 3/4 & 7 In., Pair 2090.00
Biscuit Jar, Silver Plate Top & Handle, Marked, Beige, 6 1/2 In. 135.00
Breakfast Set, Marbelized, Fan Shape, C.1810, 5 Piece 50.00
Cottage, Figural, Outlined In Gold, C.1820, 5 In. 3400.00
Creamer, Dr.Wall, Sparrow Beak, Blue Floral, C.1760, 3 1/2 In. 50.00
Cup & Saucer, Cobalt Blue & Gold Trim, Marked, C.1793 .... 95.00
Cup & Saucer, Turquoise, Floral, Scallops, 1770–75, 5 1/8 In. 2200.00
Dish, Blind Earl, Leaf Sprays, Scalloped, C–Scrolls, 7 5/8 In. 770.00
Dish, Floral, Gilt Edge, Footed, Quatrefoil, C.1770, 12 In. 715.00
Dish, Flowers, Apple Green, C.1820, Marked, 9 In., Pair 715.00
Dish, Lettuce Leaf, Chinoiserie, 1760–65, 10 1/4 In. 495.00
Mansion House, Figural, C.1820 .... 4700.00
Mug, Cartouche Painted Birds, Blue Scale, C.1770, 5 7/8 In. 1430.00
Mug, Fruit Sprays, Blue, White, 1775–80, Marked, 5 5/8 In. 577.00
Mug, Woman Feeding Children, Inscribed Breakfast, C.1800, 5 In. 990.00
Plate, Bengal Tiger, Scalloped Rim, C.1770, Marked, 7 1/2 In. 880.00
Plate, Painted Birds, Blue Scale, C.1770, Marked, 7 1/2 In. 495.00
Teabowl & Saucer, Hop Trellis, Fluted, C.1770, 5 3/8 In. 440.00
Teabowl & Saucer, Sir Joshua Reynolds, C.1770, Marked 605.00
Teapot, Orange Brocade, Knop Cover, C.1770, 5 3/8 In. 605.00
Tray, Pen, Peasant Scene, Handles, Marked, 12 1/2 In. 935.00
Vase, Covered, Landscape, Vermicule, Chamberlain, C.1810, 19 In. 1500.00
Vase, Jewel, Ivory, 3 Feet, Grainger, Covered, 9 1/2 In. 605.00
Vase, Pitcher, White, Leaves, Gold Trim, Handles, C.1880 .... 395.00
Vase, Warwick, Cobalt Blue, 1820–25, Marked, 10 In. 550.00
Vase, Warwick, Continous Shell Border, C.1813, Marked, 7 In. 1900.00

Souvenirs of World War I and World War II are collected today. Be careful not to store anything that includes live ammunition. Your local police station will tell you how to dispose of the explosives.

WORLD WAR I, Album, Postcard, Letters, Experiences 32.50
Bayonet, Remington, 17 In. 45.00
Book, Songs & Rhymes 10.00
Box, Ammunition, Wooden, Red Paint, Iron Hinges, 13 X 8 X 4 In. 35.00
Cards, Stereo, Sepia, Tanks, Planes, Set Of 10 .... 40.00
Cigarette Case, Metal, Embossed W.R.Nicoll, 22 BTY CFA 19.00
Cigarette Lighter, Soldier's, Brass 5.45
Compass, U.S.Engineer Corps., Brass 40.00
Cover, Cushion, Paris, Fringed, Embroidered AEF, Eagle & Shield 18.00
Frame, Iron, Embossed, Design, Dated 1917 .... 35.00
Gas Mask, Canvas Bag, Instructions 25.00

Gas Mask, German, Tin Cylinder Carrying Can	15.00
Helmet, German, Camouflage	59.00
Helmet, Liner, Army	20.00
Mess Kit, German Officer, Leather Case	110.00
Periscope, Trench, Tripod	135.00
Pin, Liberty Loan, All Different, Set Of 6	20.00
Plaque, British Soldier, Brown Transfer, Bruce Baimfather	35.00
Postcard, German, Soldiers, Unused	4.50
Poster, Defeat The Kaiser & His U–Boats, 21 X 14 In.	25.00
Poster, Enlistment, I Want You, Army, 30 X 40 In	200.00
Poster, Follow The Boys, Navy Recruiting, 29 X 21 In.	40.00
Poster, Greatest Mother, Red Cross, 20 X 27 In.	20.00
Poster, I Wish I Were A Man, Christy, 1918	300.00
Poster, Loan, Air Attack Against New York, Red, White, & Blue	125.00
Poster, Save Your Child, 30 X 20 In.	25.00
Poster, Wanted Nurses, 42 X 28 In.	50.00
Rifle, Army, Training, Wooden	35.00
Saddle Bags, U.S.Army, 1917	65.00
Soldier, Japanese, Bisque, 3 1/2 In.	15.00
Spoon, Armistice, Signed Nov.11, 1918, Silver Plate	10.00
Stickpin, Uncle Sam	12.00
Textile, Embroidered, Soldier & Sailor, 20 X 17 In.	20.00
Uniform, Army	55.00
WORLD WAR II, Armband, SS, Red Ground, Beige Swastika	35.00
Badge, U.S.Zeppelin, Enameled	140.00
Banner, Nazi, DAF, Labor	69.00
Binnacle, Lifeboat, Compensator, Brass Stand & Lamp	100.00
Buckle, Belt, German	10.00
Compass, Ship, Brass	135.00
Fez, Nazi	165.00
Figurine, Plaster, Eagle, 2 Servicemen Heads & 2 Women	18.00
Flag, Japanese, Rising Sun, 13 X 19 In.	25.00
Flashlight, Navy, Box	5.00
Hat, Coast Guard, 1940s	12.00
Hat, Winter, Luftwaffe	200.00
Helmet, Camouflage, Liner	60.00
Helmet, Combat, Luftschutz, Leather Liner, Steel, Painted Black	35.00
Helmet, Flying, Leather	30.00
Helmet, German, Liner	59.00
Helmet, Japanese	65.00
Helmet, Nazi, Chicken Wire For Camouflage, Decal	85.00
Helmet, Police, Nazi, Black, 2 Decals	85.00
Instruments, Japanese Zero Aircraft	325.00
Lantern, Signal, Telescoping Legs, Candle Power, Japanese	125.00
Life Preserver, Army Air Force, Dated 1943	30.00
Life Preserver, U.S.Navy, Dated 1943	30.00
Manual, Field, Browning Machine Gun, 1940	5.50
Manual, Pictorial, World War II Aircraft	10.00
Mess Kit, Nazi, Eagle & Swastika, Steel, Dated 1942	55.00
Mug, Trench Art, Made From Shell Casings, Dated 1943–44, Italy	40.00
Navy, Uniform, Commander, Navy & Khaki, Size 36, Hat Size 7	55.00
Patches, Uniform, Japanese	25.00
Plate, Graf Zeppelin, 7 1/2 In.	65.00
Postcard, Nazi, Unused	10.00
Poster, Careless Talk Got There First, 1944, 28 X 40 In.	40.00
Poster, Hitler, Stalin, Churchill, 1943	10.00
Poster, Let's Give Him Enough, Signed Rockwell	900.00
Poster, McClelland Barclay, Color, 33 1/2 X 24 1/2 In.	24.00
Poster, Sky's The Limit, Airplane Design, 20 X 27 In.	19.00
Poster, This Is The Enemy, 22 X 28 In.	75.00
Poster, U.N., Fight For Freedom, 1942, 28 X 40 In.	30.00
Print, Mussolini & Robed Lady, Soldiers Saluting, 20 X 16 In.	25.00
Ration Book, With Stamps	8.00 To 25.00

Ration Sheet, Coupon, Fuel, 16 Stamps	10.00
Ration Token, OPA, 50 Piece	3.00
Service Banner, 1 Star	10.00
Stationery, Service Armband, Chrome Frame, C.1939, 15 X 12 In.	200.00
Tin, Collection, Hitler Youth, Marked	90.00
Uniform, Navy	75.00
Warning Kit, Official Junior Aircraft, Unused	7.00
Whistle, Ship, Figural, 4 In.	2.00

*Souvenirs of all world's fairs are collected. The first fair was the
Great Exhibition of 1851 in London. Memorabilia of fairs includes
directories, pictures, fabrics, ceramics, etc.*

WORLD'S FAIR, Ashtray, 1939, Brass	15.00
Ashtray, Century Of Progress, Chrysler, Copper, 3 X 3 In.	10.00
Atlas, 1893, Columbian Exposition	75.00
Barometer, 1939, New York, Wooden	79.00
Billfold, 1904, Brown	25.00
Book, 1893, Shepps	25.00
Book, 1933, 52 Pages, Pictures, Large	12.00
Book, 1939, New York, Official Souvenir	29.00
Book, 1939, The World Of Tomorrow, New York	15.00
Booklet, 1909, Alaska–Yukon–Pacific, 24 Illustrated Pages	9.00
Booklet, 1933, Chicago, Firestone	5.00
Booklet, 1933, Chicago, Morton Salt	5.00
Bookmark, 1898, Pictures Mrs.Grover Cleveland, Silk	25.00
Bookmark, 1939	8.00
Box, Jewelry, 1904, St.Louis, Glass, Cascade Gardens	35.00
Bracelet, 1933, Silver	35.00
Bracelet, 1939, New York	12.00
Cane, 1893, Head Of Columbus	85.00
Cane, 1934, Wooden	15.00
Cane, 1939	20.00
Cards, Playing, 1933, Unused	15.00
Cards, Playing, 1934, Chicago, Scenes Of Fair, Boxed	14.50
Compact, 1934	20.00
Creamer, 1893, Columbian, Ruby Flash	30.00
Crumber, 1933	5.00
Handkerchief, 1893, Silk	8.00
Handkerchief, 1933	12.00
Hatchet, 1893, Head Of G.Washington, Libbey Glass On Handle	70.00
Inkwell, 1904, St.Louis, Crystal, Tray	27.50
Key, 1933, Chicago, Figural, Century Of Progress	85.00
Knife, Pocket, 1933, Chicago	3.50
Lamp, Table, 1939, Milk Glass, 11 3/4 In.	45.00
Letter Opener, 1934, Chicago, Original Card	15.00
Letter Opener, St.Louis Exposition, Cupid Handle, 1904	50.00
Mandolin, 1933, New Washburn 1897	125.00
Mask, 1933, Chicago, Ed Wynn, Texaco	35.00
Match Safe, 1904, Embossed	28.00
Match Safe, 1904, St.Louis	60.00
Medallion, 1933, Bronze	15.00
Mug, 1893, Columbian, Stoneware, 4 3/4 In.	75.00
Napkin Ring, 1933, Chicago	30.00
Pennant, 1933, Chicago	15.00
Pennant, 1964–65, New York	5.00
Picture, 1904, 2 Ladies, Framed, 4 3/4 X 6 1/2 In.	23.00
Pillow, 1933, Chicago	10.00 To 26.00
Pin, Golden, 1939, Figural 39, Trylon & Perisphere	12.00
Pinback, 1904, St.Louis	28.00
Pitcher, 1939, Colonial Man, Ceramic	35.00
Pitcher, Milk, 1893, Gallery Of Fine Arts, 6 3/4 In.	110.00
Plate, 1904, Festival Hall, Glass	22.00
Plate, 1904, St.Louis, Glass, 7 1/4 In.	25.00
Plate, 1904, St.Louis, Lacy Edge	20.00

Plate, 1933, Chicago, Fair Scene, Pickard 20.00
Postcard, 1915, Panama Pacific, Set Of 4 .... 15.00
Postcard, 1939, Folder 8.00
Program, 1893 .... 6.00
Program, 1939, Billy Rose Aquacade 15.00
Program, 1939, New York 12.00
Purse, 1904, Leather 18.00
Puzzle, 1933, Chicago, Nash 22.00
Ring, 1939, New York .... 5.00 To 25.00
Rose Bowl, 1893, Amberina, World's Fair 1893 Etched 345.00
Salt & Pepper, 1934, Metal 7.50
Salt & Pepper, 1939, New York, Celluloid, Trylon & Perisphere 22.00
Salt, Columbian Expo, White, Mother-Of-Pearl, Gold Lettering 57.00
Scarf, 1939, Printed New York World's Fair, Scenes 12.00
Spoon, 1892, Chicago, Sterling Silver 18.00
Spoon, 1901 .... 10.00
Spoon, 1933 .... 4.00 To 5.00
Spoon, 1933, Silver 25.00
Spoon, 1939 .... 15.00
Spoon, 1939, Original Wooden Box, Set Of 12 .... 100.00 To 165.00
Spoon, 1964, Silver Plate, Boxed 6.50
Spoon, Drink Mixing, 1939, Glass, Box, Set Of 12 .... 22.00
Sugar & Creamer, 1893, Blue, Satin Glass, Gold Script, Libbey 500.00
Tape Measure, 1933, Sears 22.00
Teapot, 1939, Ivory 55.00
Teaspoon, 1939, New York, Administration Building 10.00
Thermometer Key, 1934, Chicago, 8 In. 7.50
Thermometer, 1933, Havoline Tower 6.00
Tie Clip, 1933, Chicago 7.00
Toothpick, 1939, Little Red Riding Hood 42.00
Tumbler, 1939, Ceramic 22.00
Tumbler, 1964, New York, Set Of 6 .... 18.00
Umbrella, 1933 .... 25.00
Vase, 1934, Century Of Progress 125.00
Viewer, 1939, 75 Views, Original Box 38.50
Watch Fob, 1933, Original Card 55.00

*Yellowware is a heavy earthenware made of a yellowish clay. It varies
in color from light yellow to orange-yellow. Many nineteenth- and
twentieth-century kitchen bowls and jugs were made of yellowware. It
was made in England and in the United States.*

YELLOWWARE, Bank, Pig, Brown Mottled 55.00
Basket, Chicken Cover, Brown 29.00
Bedpan, Open Mouthed Flying Turtle .... 50.00 To 60.00
Bowl, 2 Brown Stripes, 7 In. 18.00
Bowl, 9 1/2 In. 35.00
Bowl, Batter, 10 In.Diam. 85.00
Bowl, Blue & White Stripe, 10 1/2 In. 23.00
Bowl, Brown Stripe, 6 1/2 In. 20.00
Bowl, Brown Stripes, 4 1/4 X 2 In. 22.00
Bowl, Cobalt Glaze, 5 In. 20.00
Bowl, Cottage Scene, 7 In. 18.00
Bowl, Cottage Scene, 10 In. 35.00
Bowl, Cream Stripes, 3 X 7 In.Diam. 28.00
Bowl, Daffodil Pattern, Unglazed, Flat, 7 In. 24.00
Bowl, Early Bird Hatcheries, Advertising 28.00
Bowl, Exterior Relief, 9 In. 30.00
Bowl, Gray, 6 In. 18.00
Bowl, Gray, 8 In. 20.00
Bowl, Green Glaze, 10 In. 22.00
Bowl, Incised Pattern, 11 In. 25.00
Bowl, Mixing, Brown Bands, Impressed Weller, 12 X 5 1/2 In. 50.00
Bowl, Picket Fence, Reverse 45.00
Bowl, Stripes, 8 1/2 In. 20.00

Bowl, White Band Bordered By Brown Stripes, 7 X 3 3/8 In.	50.00
Chamber Pot, Blue Sponging, 1 5/8 In.	32.50
Crock, Butter, White & Brown Stripes, No Lid, 1/2 Gal.	42.50
Crock, Butter, White Bands	58.00
Crock, Butter, White, Brown Stripes, 1/2 Gal.	42.00
Crock, Salt, Hanging, Wall, Blue Bands	90.00
Cuspidor, Brown	29.00
Dish, Feeding, Brown Bands	75.00
Dish, Stripes, Cover, 7 In.	45.00
Flowerpot, Floral, Embossed Lion Head Handles, No Saucer	45.00
Jar, Cover, White Band, Brown Stripes, 6 X 4 1/4 In.	55.00
Mold, Pudding, Oval, 6 1/2 In.	25.00
Mug, Blue Bands	75.00
Mug, Ribbed Body, Blue Band At Top, C.1880, 1 3/4 X 2 In.	60.00
Pan, Embossed Flowers On Bottom, 10 X 3 In.	58.00
Pitcher, Blue, Spatter, Gilt, 12 In.	165.00
Pitcher, Cow, Green, 8 In.	55.00
Pitcher, Floral Design, Polychome Enameling, Luster, 7 1/4 In.	10.00
Pitcher, Rockingham Glaze, Lid, 8 3/4 In.	65.00
Plate, Westward Expansion, 11 1/4 In.	125.00
Toby Jug, Hand Molded Face, Applied Design, English, 5 3/8 In.	50.00

ZANE WARE

Zane Pottery was founded in 1921 by Adam Reed and Harry McClelland in South Zanesville, Ohio, at the old Peters and Reed Building. Zane pottery is very similar to Peters and Reed pottery, but it is usually marked. The factory was sold in 1941 to Lawton Gonder.

ZANE, Vase, Flaring Top, Landsun, 5 In.	28.00
Vase, Tan, Blue Glaze Stripes, Lansun, 10 In.	40.00
Wall Pocket, Ferrell	45.00

LA MORO

The Zanesville Art Pottery was founded in 1900 by David Schmidt in Zanesville, Ohio. The firm made faience umbrella stands, jardinieres, and pedestals. The company closed in 1962. Many pieces are marked with just the word "La Moro."

ZANESVILLE, Jardiniere, Orange & Green Spatter, 38 In.Diam.	75.00
Jug, Moonshine, Brown & White, 10 1/2 In.	15.00
Vase, Drip Brown & Blue, 9 In.	145.00
Vase, Landsun, 11 In.	80.00
Vase, Sheenware, Flared	22.00

Zsolnay pottery was made in Hungary after 1862 and was characterized by Persian, Art Nouveau, or Hungarian motifs. A series of new Zsolnay figurines with green–gold luster finish is available in many shops today. Early Zsolnay was not marked; but by 1878, the tower trademark was used.

ZSOLNAY, Boat, Ornamented & Glazed, Reticulated, Cream Ground, 13 1/2 In.	495.00
Bowl, Reticulated Gold, Persian Design, Marked, Square, 6 In.	175.00
Ewer, Green & Gold, Art Nouveau Design, Old Mark, 11 In.	230.00
Petal Jar, Pierced Allover, Enameled	225.00
Plate, Art Nouveau, 8 1/2 In.	95.00
Plate, Shell Shape, Beige, Red & Gold Flowers, Marked, 8 1/2 In.	179.00
Plate, Shell Shape, Flowers, Reticulated, Marked, 8 1/2 In.	180.00
Vase, Butterflies, Dragon In Center, 1880, 13 In.	250.00
Vase, Climbing Nude, Iridescent, 14 In.	150.00
Vase, Cobalt, Gold, Beige, Reticulated, Double Wall, 6 1/2 In.	359.00
Vase, Iridescent, 4 1/2 In.	50.00
Vase, Ornamented & Glazed, Reticulated, Cream Ground, 8 In.	495.00

OTHER KOVELS' ILLUSTRATED PRICE GUIDES

The Kovels' Illustrated Price Guide to Royal Doulton
Second Edition

Over 5,000 prices of Royal Doulton pieces, including complete listings of figurines, character jugs, limited editions, Toby jugs, dolls, as well as series ware, animals and birds, rouge flambé, and miscellaneous categories. Includes descriptions, dates of manufacture, HN listings, with a history of the Doulton factory and notes on rarities and color changes. Special section on Royal Doulton marks. Over 400 illustrations in color and black and white.

55044-X $10.95 paper

The Kovels' Illustrated Price Guide to Depression Glass and American Dinnerware
Second Edition

The most up-to-date book ever published about Depression glass and American dinnerware. Two books in one, with current prices of more than 6,000 pieces, each listed by manufacturer; with dates, descriptions, and pottery marks. Over 250 illustrations in color and black and white. Pocket-size for easy reference.

54974-3 $10.95 paper

The Kovels' Bottle Price List
Seventh Edition

Over 10,000 current prices for hundreds of types of bottles —more than any other bottle price list on the market. More than 500 illustrations in full color and black and white. Includes old and new bottles, bitters, figurals, flasks, Avons, Beams, and a host of others. Notes on styles and manufacturers, lists of bottle magazines and clubs, and an extensive bibliography. The most definitive listing of current prices available.

55426-7 $10.95 paper

MORE KOVELS' COLLECTORS' BOOKS

American Country Furniture
1780–1875

Over 700 close-up photographs identify styles, construction, woods, finishes, hardware, and other details. All the information you need to be an expert on American country furniture. Special sections on Pennsylvania, Shaker furniture, spool furniture, and furniture construction, plus an illustrated glossary of accessories and terms.

54668-X $8.95 paper
09737-0 $15.95 hardcover

Kovels' New Dictionary of Marks
Pottery and Porcelain 1850-Present

The completely new, fully illustrated *Kovels' New Dictionary of Marks* thoroughly identifies 19th- and 20th-century American, European, and Oriental marks. It makes a perfect companion to the *Dictionary of Marks: Pottery and Porcelain*, now in its fortieth printing with over 165,000 copies sold.

Each of the 3,500 entries is illustrated with a photographic reproduction of the mark, and a caption tells the name of the original manufacturer, relevant dates, material of the piece, color of the mark, country of origin, and the name of the current manufacturer. Additional information includes an index and a host of tips and guidelines to help every collector.

55914-5 $16.95 hardcover

Kovels' Know Your Antiques
Revised and Updated

The best general guide for antiques collectors in print today. Illustrated with more than 300 photographs and line drawings. Written for the novice or beginning collector, it contains information about recognizing and determining the value of virtually every type of antique. Makes identification of objects a breeze.

54501-2 $14.95 hardcover

Kovels' Know Your Collectibles

With more than 1,000 illustrations, this up-to-date guide to the latest collecting trends focuses on silver, glass, furniture, and other objects that are not old enough to be designated "antiques" but which are rapidly increasing in value and represent the collecting patterns of the future. Contains information about value, origin, availability, storage, and buying and selling.

53608-0 $16.95 hardcover

The Kovels' Collectors' Source Book

A comprehensive A to Z directory of resources for collectors, with more than 250 black-and-white photographs and line drawings. Everything you need to know to keep your collection alive, secure, and growing. Listings of clubs and publications, how-to-repair books, price guides, parts and repair services, buying by mail, auctions and auction houses, matching services, display services, booksellers, conservators, restoration sources, preservation supplies, and much more. An absolute necessity for collectors, museums, shops, clubs, organizations, and schools.

54791-0 $13.95 paper
54846-1 $24.95 hardcover

SEND ORDERS & INQUIRIES TO:
Crown Publishers, Inc.
One Park Avenue, New York, N.Y. 10016
ATT: SALES DEPT.

THE KOVELS

SALES & TITLE INFORMATION
1-800-526-4264

NAME

ADDRESS

CITY & STATE

ZIP

PLEASE SEND ME THE FOLLOWING BOOKS:

ITEM NO.	QTY.	TITLE		PRICE	TOTAL
558092	_____	Kovels' Antiques & Collectibles Price List—18th Edition	PAPER	$10.95	_____
554267	_____	The Kovels' Bottle Price List—Seventh Edition		$10.95	_____
547910	_____	The Kovels' Collectors' Source Book	PAPER	$13.95	_____
548461	_____	The Kovels' Collectors' Source Book	HARDCOVER	$24.95	_____
54668X	_____	American Country Furniture: 1780-1875	PAPER	$ 8.95	_____
097370	_____	American Country Furniture: 1780-1875	HARDCOVER	$15.95	_____
549808	_____	The Kovels' Collector's Guide to American Art Pottery	PAPER	$10.95	_____
001411	_____	Dictionary of Marks—Pottery and Porcelain	HARDCOVER	$ 8.95	_____
559145	_____	Kovels' New Dictionary of Marks	HARDCOVER	$16.95	_____
50636X	_____	A Directory of American Silver, Pewter and Silver Plate	HARDCOVER	$ 9.95	_____
549743	_____	The Kovels' Illustrated Price Guide to Depression Glass and American Dinnerware—2nd Edition	PAPER	$10.95	_____
55044X	_____	The Kovels' Illustrated Price Guide to Royal Doulton—2nd Edition	PAPER	$10.95	_____
545012	_____	Kovels' Know Your Antiques—Revised and Updated	HARDCOVER	$14.95	_____
536080	_____	Kovels' Know Your Collectibles	HARDCOVER	$16.95	_____

_____TOTAL ITEMS   Total Retail Value _____

CHECK OR MONEY ORDER ENCLOSED MADE
PAYABLE TO CROWN PUBLISHERS, INC.
One Park Avenue
New York, N.Y. 10016
or telephone 1-800-526-4264
(No cash or stamps, please)

Shipping & Handling Charge **$1.40**
for one book; 60¢ for
each additional book _____

Charge: ☐ Master Card   ☐ Visa   ☐ American Express
Account Number (include all digits)   Expires   MO   YR.

TOTAL AMOUNT DUE _____

PRICES SUBJECT TO CHANGE
WITHOUT NOTICE. If a more
recent edition of a price guide has
been published at the same price, it
will be sent instead of the old
edition.

Signature _____

Thank you for your order